MW00975530

GLOBE FEARON

LITERATURE

TEACHER'S EDITION

▪ *Silver Level* ▪

Upper Saddle River, New Jersey
www.globefearon.com

Program Reviewers

Kathy Babigian, Coordinator, Tioga Literacy Center, Fresno, California
Pat Bartholomew, M.A., Reading Specialist, Milton, Ohio
Jennifer Dilks-Mundt, English Teacher, Brant Rock, Massachusetts
Ann Fitzgerald, M.A., Education Director, Southshire Community School, North Bennington, Vermont
Pat Miller, M.A., Reading/English/Language Arts Supervisor, Prince Georges County Public Schools, Maryland
Artie P. Norton, English Teacher, Suffern, New York
Timothy Rasinski, Professor of Curriculum and Instruction, Kent State University, Kent, Ohio
Cynthia Saska, M.A., Professor of English, University of Texas, San Antonio, Texas
Margaret-Mary Sulentic, Ph.D., Assistant Professor of Literacy, Department of Curriculum and Instruction, University of Southern Mississippi, Hattiesburg, Mississippi
Dr. Helen W. Taylor, Director of Programs K-12 Curriculum and Instruction, Portsmouth City Public Schools, Virginia

Consultants

Dr. Virginia Bryg; Josephine Gemake, Ph.D.; Alfred Schifini, Ph.D.; Deborah Walker; Robert Wandberg, Ph.D.

Supervising Editor/Team Leader: Karen McCollum
Editors: Ayanna Taylor, Amy Greenberg, Theresa McCarthy
Editorial Developer: Pearson Education Development Group
Marketing Assistant: Kate Krimsky
Production Editor: Travis Bailey
Associate Production Editors: Amy Benefiel, Alia Lesser
Senior Designer: Angel Weyant
Manufacturing Buyer: Mark Cirillo
Cover and Interior Design/Production: Pearson Education Development Group
Photo Research: Pearson Education Development Group

About the Cover

3rd and Rhode Island, LeDetroit Park, Hilda Wilkinson Brown. From the Hilda Wilkinson Brown Collection. Courtesy of Lillian Thomas Burwell. This oil painting shows a simple scene of a street in Detroit. This is a reflection of Brown's ideals. She was described as a "traditional woman, an idealist in manner and mores of the then womanhood." How is Brown's painting a representation of traditional American values?

ISBN 0-130-23579-2

Printed in the United States of America
1 2 3 4 5 6 7 8 9 10   04 03 02 01 00

1-800-848-9500
www.globefearon.com

UNIT 3 *New England Speaks*

UNIT 5 *The Modern View*

Making Literature Accessible to All Students

Globe Fearon Literature is a comprehensive high school literature program that meets the needs of all students.

- *Adapted selections provide accessibility.*
- *Model lessons promote independent reading.*
- *Reading skill instruction is included with every selection.*

PURPLE LEVEL

Literature Organized by Theme

GREEN LEVEL

Literature from Around the World

STUDENT EDITION

- Skillful adaptations of the more difficult selections offer accessibility.
- Model selections guide students to become independent active readers.
- Reading skill instruction is provided with every selection.

TEACHER'S EDITION

- Teaching strategies are provided at point-of-use.
- An easy-to-follow three-step lesson plan for each selection saves time.
- Additional activities for ESL students and cooperative learning groups help teachers meet individual needs.

TEACHER'S RESOURCES

- This resource is offered in two formats: print and CD-ROM.
- Over 400 reproducibles help you to reinforce, extend, and assess understanding.
- Scoring rubrics and evaluation guides provide support for alternative assessment.
- Answer keys to all ancillaries save time.
- **CD-ROM** includes correlations to national and many state standards for reading and language arts.

ADDITIONAL ANCILLARIES

- Comprehension and Vocabulary Workbook
- Language Enrichment Workbook
- Answer Key

SILVER LEVEL
American Literature

GOLD LEVEL
British Literature

▪ *Silver Level* ▪

AMERICAN LITERATURE UNITS

Voices of Colonial America
Writers in a Growing Nation
New England Speaks
A Nation Expresses Itself
A Modern View
The Contemporary Perspective

Exciting unit openers capture students' interest.

Unit Openers explore ideas related to the unit theme and discuss how the selections relate to one another.

Timelines help to place literature in a historical context.

LITERARY HIGHLIGHTS
1844 Sarah Margaret Fuller becomes first female journalist.
1849 Hawthorne begins writing The Scarlet Letter.
1851 Melville's Moby-Dick appears.
1854 Thoreau publishes Walden.
1855 Longfellow celebrates Native American legends.
1863 President Lincoln gives the "Gettysburg Address."
1886 Emily Dickinson dies, leaving 1,775 unpublished poems.
1895 Stephen Crane publishes The Red Badge of Courage.
1840
1845
1850
1855
1860
1865
1870
1875
1880
1885
1890
1895
1848 First Women's Rights Convention held in Seneca Falls, NY.
1849 California "Gold Rush" attracts 80,000 prospectors.
1857 Supreme Court makes decision in Dred Scott case.
1865 Thirteenth Amendment abolishes slavery.
1869 Transcontinental railroad completed at Promontory, UT.
1876 Alexander Graham Bell patents the telephone.
1896 Supreme Court approves "separate but equal" racial segregation.
HISTORICAL HIGHLIGHTS
New England Speaks
The America of the 1800s was a land of great variation. Would you have preferred the wild West or the sophisticated East? If you like outdoor life, you would have enjoyed pioneering in the West. If you pre...
spend time discussing ideas, you would have been...
part of the country.
THE IMPORTAN...
In 1800...
UNIT 3
New England Speaks
We looked upon a world unknown,
On nothing we could call our own.
Around the glistening wonder bent
The blue walls of the firmament,
No cloud above, no earth below,—
A universe of sky and snow!
—John Greenleaf Whittier
Morning Light, Walter Elmer Schofield. Giraudon/Art Resource
161

Fine art fosters critical viewing skills. (**Teacher's Edition** provides **Viewing Fine Art** notes at point of use.)

An intriguing **quotation** motivates students and provides opportunities for class discussion.

Model selections guide students to become independent readers.

Focus on lessons discuss the elements of a particular genre—fiction, nonfiction, poetry, or drama—to promote student understanding.

Focus ON POETRY

What is a poem, and what does a poem do? Poetry is writing in which imaginative, colorful language is used to paint a picture in the reader's mind. It can tell a story, express feelings and thoughts, or describe things.

You can tell a poem the minute you see it; its structure is different from prose. Thoughts and feelings are captured in a more concise way. The poems you have read in this unit are made up of stanzas. **Stanzas** are divisions in poems that are made up of ... lines. The poets have chosen their words carefully to ...

things in a different way. Simile and metaphor make a connection between two unlike things that the reader might never have thought about before. On the other hand, personification and hyperbole can be used in a humorous way or for exaggeration.

Character/Speaker The voice or narrator of a poem is not necessarily the real voice of the poet. Often, poets put on a mask. They create a voice, separate from their own, to express their thoughts. The poet can write in the voice of a child, a father, a nation, or even the world.

Connotation and Denotation A reader should look closely at how poets use words. Often, writers use words that have two kinds of meanings. The connotation of a word suggests its emotional meaning—the feeling the word suggests to the reader. The ... of a word is the actual meaning of a word as given in ... "I'm nobody" Dickinson wrote:

MODEL

THE FIRST SNOW FALL

by James Russell Lowell

FOCUS ON POETRY
STUDY HINTS

Notice how Lowell uses end rhymes to link thoughts.

The snow had begun in the gloaming,
And busily all the night
Had been heaping field and highway
With a silence deep and white.

Think about the connotation of the words *ermine* and *pearl*. What feelings do they suggest to you?

5 Every pine and fir and hemlock
Wore ermine too dear for an earl,
And the poorest twig on the elm-tree
Was ridged inch deep with pearl.

The poet uses onomatopoeia. Which word is it?

From sheds new-roofed with Carrara
10 Came Chanticleer's muffled crow,
The stiff rails softened to swan's-down,
And still fluttered down the snow.

Lowell uses a simile here. What is it?

I stood and watched by the window
The noiseless work of the sky,
15 And the sudden flurries of snow-birds,
Like brown leaves whirling by.

gloaming (GLOHM ing) twilight
ermine (UR min) a weasel whose fur turns to white in the winter
Carrara (kuh RAHR uh) fine, white marble
chanticleer (CHAN tih klir) a rooster

210 ■ Unit 3

I thought of a mound in sweet Auburn[1]
Where a little headstone stood;
How the flakes were folding it gently,
20 As did robins the babes in the wood.

Create a picture in your mind of what these words are saying.

Up spoke our own little Mabel,
Saying, "Father, who makes it snow?"
And I told of the good All-father
Who cares for us here below.

Here, you find out who the speaker is. Who is it?

25 Again I looked at the snow-fall,
And thought of the leaden sky
That arched o'er our first great sorrow,
When that mound was heaped so high.

Here, the speaker shares his feelings of grief.

I remembered the gradual patience
30 That fell from that cloud like snow,
Flake by flake, healing and hiding
The scar that renewed our woe.

What simile does Lowell use here?

And again to the child I whispered,
"The snow that husheth all,
35 Darling, the merciful Father
Alone can make it fall!"

Think about the connotation of the words in this stanza.

Then, with eyes that saw not, I kissed her;
And she, kissing back, could not know
That *my* kiss was given to her sister,
Folded close under deepening snow.

Finally the speaker reveals for whom he grieves and how much he misses her.

leaden (LED un) dull, dark gray
[1]**Mt. Auburn:** a cemetery in Cambridge, Massachusetts

The First Snow Fall ■ 211

Model selections provide margin notes to help students become active readers.

Study Hints guide students as they read by pointing out important elements of the genre.

Each selection includes strategies to help students master essential skills.

*A **clear and predictable** format promotes understanding of concepts.*

The **Learn About** feature explains a key literary element of each selection.

Learn About

Sounds in Poetry

Rhythm, meter, and rhyme all add musical effects to poetry, but they are not the only devices available to poets. The use of certain letters of the alphabet affects the sound of poetry. Some letters have a soft "liquid" sound: *l*, *m*, *n*, and *r*. Other letters have a more "explosive" sound: *b*, *d*, *g*, *k*, *p*, and *t*. Poets can manipulate the use of these sounds to create soothing or exciting lines.

Repetition is part of all music, and it plays a part in the music of poetry too. For example, the repetition of initial consonant sounds, as in "They *s*at in *s*olemn *s*ilence," is called **alliteration**. The repetition of vowel sounds, as in "*I* can f*i*nd the t*i*me," is called **assonance**. The repetition of final consonant sounds, as in "fir*st* and la*st*," is called **consonance**.

As you read the following poems, ask yourself:

1. Which sound devices did Dickinson use in her poems?
2. What effect do the devices have on the poems?

WRITING CONNECTION

Write a sentence using "liquid" letters and another using "explosive" letters. Explain the effect of each sentence on you.

Reading Focus

Make Inferences An inference is a conclusion drawn from facts or evidence. You can use your own insights and knowledge of human behavior and the world around you in order to make inferences.

Reading poetry often requires the reader to infer meaning, or to think beyond the words on the page. As you read each poem, use your own knowledge and details in the poem to make inferences about the poem's meaning.

198 ■ Unit 3

In the Garden, Irving Ramsay Wiles. Christie's Images

I'm nobody

by Emily Dickinson

I'm nobody! Who are you?
Are you nobody, too?
Then there's a pair of us—don't tell!
They'd banish us, you know.

How dreary to be somebody!
How public, like a frog
To tell your name the livelong day
To an admiring bog!

dreary (DRIR ee) dull; tiresome
bog (BOG) swamp; wet ground

I'm nobody ■ 199

The **Reading Focus** provides critical reading support to increase comprehension.

Writing activities help students connect the elements of literature to their lives.

Purpose-setting questions focus students' reading.

Defined words at the bottom of the page help students build vocabulary without losing track of their reading.

Review the Selection ensures mastery of skills.

Understand the Selection contains three-tiered questions that prompt recall and higher-order thinking skills.

Write About the Selection provides process-writing opportunities.

The Think About section reviews and reinforces the literary skill taught in the lesson.

Develop Your Vocabulary reinforces students' understanding of key vocabulary.

Review the Selection

UNDERSTAND THE SELECTION

Recall

1. Where does the speaker keep the Sabbath?
2. With whom does the speaker keep the Sabbath?
3. Who is the sexton in "Some keep the Sabbath" and what does it do?

Infer

4. Explain why you think the speaker in "I'm nobody" likes being nobody.
5. In "A word is dead," why does a word come alive when it is spoken?
6. Why did Dickinson write to Higginson?
7. In your opinion, what is the theme of "The sky is low"?

Apply

8. Select your favorite Dickinson poem. Explain why it is your favorite.
9. Suppose you are a poet. Name two things you have never seen or experienced about which you might write.
10. Why might Dickinson choose to use a frog as an example of somebody?

Respond to Literature

How does Dickinson's poetry reflect Emerson's group's transcendental idea about writing?

WRITE ABOUT THE SELECTION

In the poem "I'm nobody," the speaker makes it clear that she or he prefers to be nobody. Suppose that you can either be "nobody" or "somebody." Which would you choose to be? Why? Be sure to think about the various pros and cons of your choices before you finally make up your mind.

Prewriting Write down on a piece of paper whether you want to be "nobody" or "somebody." Try to think about what each of these situations would be like and how you would feel about each. Then make a list of all the reasons you can think of for your choice.

Writing Use your list to help you write a paragraph about why you chose to be "nobody" or "somebody." Include three or more reasons why you made your choice.

Revising When you revise, make sure you have included two reasons for your choice. Then add one more reason from your list to your paragraph. Finally, reread your paragraph to make sure that your choices make sense. Revise as much as necessary to make sure that your reasons are clear.

Proofreading Read over your paragraph to check for errors. Be sure that all your sentences end with the correct punctuation marks. Check your internal punctuation as well.

THINK ABOUT SOUNDS IN POETRY

Poetry has musical qualities that prose does not have. Repetition of initial consonant letters (**alliteration**), of vowel sounds (**assonance**), and of final consonant sounds (**consonance**) help the poet to create musical effects. The use of liquid and explosive letters of the alphabet can also add to the music of poetry.

1. Which musical device is used in the first two lines of "I'm nobody"? Cite the words that produce this device.
2. Which musical device is used in the first line of "A word is dead"? Cite the words that produce this device.
3. The use of one particular letter, especially at the beginning of words, is repeated in "Some keep the Sabbath." What letter is it, and what is the name of the device it represents?
4. Does "I never saw a moor" have more liquid or more explosive sounds in the first stanza? In the second stanza?
5. Which is more important in musical devices, spelling or sound? Why?

Reading Focus

Make Inferences Choose one of Emily Dickinson's poems that you read in this selection. What inferences can you make about the poem's meaning based on your own experiences? What inferences can you make based on words or images in the poem?

DEVELOP YOUR VOCABULARY

Figurative language is the use of imagery, symbols, or other devices to create meaning beyond the dictionary meanings of the words used. For example, in the line "A narrow wind complains all day," Dickinson wrote words that do not mean exactly what they say. The wind makes a lot of noise all day; the word *complains* is used figuratively. In the line "I never saw the sea," however, Dickinson uses words with their exact dictionary meanings. The language is **literal**.

Read the sentences below. For each, indicate whether the figurative or literal meaning of the italicized word is used.

1. "How *dreary* to be somebody!"
2. "I never saw a *moor*, . . ."
3. "Nature, like us, is sometimes caught Without her *diadem*."
4. "Bell-shaped *heather* flowers were in bloom."
5. "And instead of tolling the bell for church, Our little *sexton* sings."
6. "They'd *banish* us, you know."

206 ■ Unit 3   *Review the Selection* ■ 207

Respond to Literature helps students relate the selection to their own experiences through discussion or writing.

Reading Focus questions assess students' mastery of the reading skill.

Unit Review includes literature-based activities and test-preparation strategies.

Writing activities allow students to explore key elements of literature through process writing.

Vocabulary and **grammar** reviews reinforce language skills.

UNIT 3 Review

WRITING APPLICATIONS

Write About Authors
Suppose that all the writers in the unit got together to discuss their work. What do you think they would say about their own and each other's writing? What criticisms or compliments would they offer to each other? Choose two authors from this unit and record their conversation.

Prewriting Before you begin to write, choose the two authors whose conversation you would like to think about. Then review their work. Emerson thought it was important that writers include what they believed in their writings. Examine how the work of the authors you have chosen might reflect Emerson's ideas so that you can include some interesti... icisms and co...

Write About Poetry
In this unit, you have learned some of the different elements of poetry. Now you can use what you learned to analyze a poem. Choose a poem that you enjoyed reading. Then, using a list of the elements of poetry, prepare a paper in which you discuss how understanding these elements helped you to enjoy the poem.

Prewriting Review what the elements of poetry are. Then make a list of them, being sure to include rhythm, meter, and rhyme. At the top of your list, write the name of the poem you have chosen. Then check off which elements are... poem. Y...

BUILD LANGUAGE SKILLS

Vocabulary
Onomatopoeia (AHN-uh-MAT-uh-PEE-uh) is the term used for words that imitate sounds. Some onomatopoeic words are *hiss, pop, whizz, buzz,* and *bang.* Onomatopoeia is a useful resource in the poet's—and the prose writer's—repertory of sound devices. It may be used openly, as in "Pop goes the weasel," or subtly, as in "The moan of doves in immemorial elms."
Write the following sen... underli...

Grammar, Usage, and Mechanics
When you are writing a series of three or more items in a sentence, you should use commas to separate the items.

Example: Lisa bought lace, ribbons, pins, thread, and fabric.

Some authorities permit the omission of the comma before *and* if the meaning is clear without it. Howev...

UNIT 3 Review

SPEAKING AND LISTENING

One of the easiest and most effective ways to make a piece of literature interesting is to read it aloud. As a child, you loved hearing your favorite story. As an older student, you may find a difficult piece of literature more accessible if you hear someone read it aloud. Maybe that is because when you hear something, you allow your mind to visualize the words more easily than when you have to read the words yourself.

Before you choose a selection from this unit to read aloud, acquaint yourself with the following tips. They will help you to read aloud with more confidence and feeling.

1. Be selective. Choose something that you find interesting. This is important for two reasons. First of all, if you are bored when you read it, chances are your listeners will be bored and uninterested, too. Second, it's unfulfilling to read something you don't like.
2. Read the selection to yourself and become familiar with it. Get the feel for the language. This will help you to know what expression to use when you read aloud.
3. If the selection is perfect as it is, let it be, if not, do some editing. You might want to condense some of the dialogue or the longer sections, or you might want to paraphrase certain passages.
4. Your oral reading style should fit your personality. If it's not your style to use unique voices for each character, don't do it. If it makes you uncomfortable to read dramatically, then don't do it. Be natural and the words of the selection should grab the listeners without theatrics.
5. During your reading aloud, maintain good volume and expression in your voice. Make frequent eye contact with your listeners. This will involve them and make them feel that you are reading to them individually.
6. Practice so that you feel confident in your delivery. Choose a selection or part of a selection from this unit and prepare to read it aloud. Limit your presentation to about three minutes. Review the suggestions above to help you enjoy the experience.

CRITICAL THINKING

Classifying is the act of grouping things according to some principle. For example, when you rearrange your bookshelves, you may put all the fiction books on one shelf, the biographies on another shelf, and the hobby books on a third shelf. You have classified your books by their type.

When you classify things, you put them in **categories**. A category is a group of things that have some characteristic in common. In the bookshelf example, fiction is one category, biographies another, and hobby books are the third category. The principles that determine a category are many. You may classify by size, type, color, use, shape, purpose, and so on.

To determine a category, you must be able to see similarities and differences. Noting the similarities is called **comparing**. Noting the differences is called **contrasting**.

Authors often make use of classification and categorizing in order to make comparisons and contrasts. Choose a selection from this unit that classifies or categorizes some objects, ways of life, aspects of nature, characters, or ideas. Then answer the following questions.

1. What principle determines each category? Does the author explain the classification adequately?
2. What does the category enable the author to compare or contrast?

EFFECTIVE STUDYING

Following Directions Being able to follow directions is an important skill for school and the rest of your life. Throughout life, you may need to follow directions to get from one place to another or to do something or to make something.

Many directions must be followed in a precise sequence. In such directions, you may notice words such as *first, next, then,* and *last.* These words help you keep the sequence straight.

Here are some guidelines to help you.

1. To follow oral directions
   - Listen attentively.
   - If the instructions are detailed, you may wish to take notes.
   - If there are parts you do not understand, ask questions.
   - To double check your understanding, repeat the directions.
2. To follow written directions
   - Read them carefully.
   - Make sure you understand the sequence.
   - After each step, read the direction again to be sure that you followed it correctly.
   - If pictures accompany the directions, study them carefully.

Test Preparation
Be sure to follow test directions exactly. Reread the directions for each part of the test and circle the key words before you begin to answer the questions.

240 ■ Unit 3

Unit Review ■ 241

Study skills strategies help students succeed.

Explicit instruction is given on **test-preparation** strategies.

Speaking and listening activities help students analyze literature through oral interpretation.

Critical-thinking activities increase understanding of literature.

The Teacher's Edition provides strategies at point of use.

Concise **Selection Objectives** are highlighted for quick reference.

Lesson Resources list additional program components that reinforce skills.

About the Author notes provide background information about the author of each selection.

Selection Overview

SELECTION OBJECTIVES
After completing this selection, students will be able to
- understand and identify sound devices in poetry
- write an opinion
- identify figurative and literal language in poetry
- make inferences

Lesson Resources

Works of Emily Dickinson
- Selection Synopses, Teacher's Edition, pp. T159f–T159g
- Comprehension and Vocabulary Workbook, pp. 40–41
- Language Enrichment Workbook, pp. 25–26
- Teacher's Resources Reinforcement, p. R21 Test, pp. T41–T42

More About Sounds in Poetry
Encourage students to think of sentences in which they use alliteration, assonance, and consonance. You might first want to write some examples on the chalkboard. Finally, have students write a sentence using each type or repetition on their own.

About the Author
It is somewhat difficult to understand the richness and depth of Dickinson's poetry, given the narrowness of her life. However, it is known that her family had an extensive library of almost one thousand books and that Dickinson read widely. Even so, it is believed that books were not her source of inspiration. Rather, it was probably her incredible imagination.

T198

Learn About

Sounds in Poetry

Rhythm, meter, and rhyme all add musical effects to poetry, but they are not the only devices available to poets. The use of certain letters of the alphabet affects the sound of poetry. Some letters have a soft "liquid" sound: *l*, *m*, *n*, and *r*. Other letters have a more "explosive" sound: *b*, *d*, *g*, *k*, *p*, and *t*. Poets can manipulate the use of these sounds to create soothing or exciting lines.

Repetition is part of all music, and it plays a part in the music of poetry too. For example, the repetition of initial consonant sounds, as in "They *s*at in *s*olemn *s*ilence," is called **alliteration**. The repetition of vowel sounds, as in "*I* can f*i*nd the t*i*me," is called **assonance**. The repetition of final consonant sounds, as in "fir*st* and la*st*," is called **consonance**.

As you read the following poems, ask yourself:
1. Which sound devices did Dickinson use in her poems?
2. What effect do the devices have on the poems?

Reading Focus

Make Inferences An inference is a conclusion drawn from facts or evidence. You can use your own insights and knowledge of human behavior and the world around you in order to make inferences.

Reading poetry often requires the reader to infer meaning, or to think beyond the words on the page. As you read each poem, use your own knowledge and details in the poem to make inferences about the poem's meaning.

WRITING CONNECTION

Write a sentence using "liquid" letters and another using "explosive" letters. Explain the effect of each sentence on you.

198 ■ Unit 3

Viewing Fine Art

Photography as a form of art was common in the 20th century; photographs no longer simply documented reality. Here, for example, the photographer has shot a rural scene much like a painting. The contrast of the dark tree with lighter areas and of the leaning tree with a similar arc in the woodpile; the variety of textures in wood, water; and hills; and the relationship of the myriad tiny branches to the soft hills behind—these elements all make the photograph an artistic composition. Ask: What words might you use to describe this picture? Which might you use in a poem?

Cooperative Group Activity

For the Writing Connection activity, have students work in pairs to make a list of words that have liquid and explosive sounds. Then have students use the words in sentences. Finally, have volunteers read their sentences to the class and have the class discuss how the sentences sound. Are the sentences soothing? Are the sentences exciting or explosive?

Viewing Fine Art helps teachers lead discussions about the fine art in the text and builds critical viewing skills.

Cooperative Group Activities provide alternative assessment opportunities.

Easy-to-follow three-step lesson format accompanies every selection.

In the Garden, Irving Ramsay Wiles. Christie's Images

I'm nobody

by Emily Dickinson

I'm nobody! Who are you?
Are you nobody, too?
Then there's a pair of us—don't tell!
They'd banish us, you know.

How dreary to be somebody!
How public, like a frog
To tell your name the livelong day
To an admiring bog!

dreary (DRIR ee) dull; tiresome
bog (BOG) swamp; wet ground

I'm nobody ■ 199

TEACHING PLAN

INTRODUCE

Motivation

Ask students to think about what it might be like not to leave their homes for many years. About what would they write? From where would they get their inspiration? What would they do all day? Guide students in a group discussion in which they realize that people can look inward for inspiration and ideas; that people really don't have to go very far away to find ideas about which to write. Imagination is a very powerful tool for a writer.

Purpose-Setting Question

Since Dickinson did not leave her home for many years, how might she have written in the contemporary style of the 1800s?

READ

Literary Focus: *Sounds in Poetry*

Encourage partners to read the poems to each other to better hear the sounds that Dickinson creates. Have students point out each use of alliteration, assonance, and consonance.

Reading Focus: *Make Inferences*

Ask for a volunteer to read each poem. After each poem has been read, lead a group discussion in which the class infers the meaning of the poem. Have students take notes on which inferences were made from their own knowledge verses from details in the poem.

CLOSE

Have students complete Review the Selection on pages 206–207.

ESL Activity

Have students choose something from their own cultures that may be unfamiliar to others in the class. Then have them give the object, a photograph, or a drawing of it to another student to write a poem about. They might compare their poems with "I never saw a Moor."

Develop Vocabulary Skills

Ask volunteers to use each vocabulary word in an original sentence. If students have difficulty, have them refer to how a word is used in the poems. Then ask students to replace each vocabulary word in the poems by using a word or words from the definition. Try to help them see that poets choose their words very carefully.

Viewing Fine Art

Irving Ramsay Wiles (1861–1948) painted figurative subjects and landscapes. Discuss the quiet atmosphere of this painting. Ask: What might the woman in this painting have in common with Emily Dickinson?

T199

1. **Introduce** provides ideas to motivate students and help them set a purpose for reading.

2. **Read** includes strategies to help students master the literary and reading skills in the selection.

3. **Close** references Review the Selection pages that provide opportunities for practice, application, and assessment.

ESL Activities help teachers meet the diverse needs of today's classrooms.

Activities and strategies for **building vocabulary skills** are included for each selection.

Reading comprehension and vocabulary skills are reinforced for each selection.

*The **Comprehension and Vocabulary Workbook** highlights vocabulary in each selection. Reading comprehension activities are provided to strengthen your students' understanding of each selection.*

Key vocabulary words from the selection are practiced through a variety of activities.

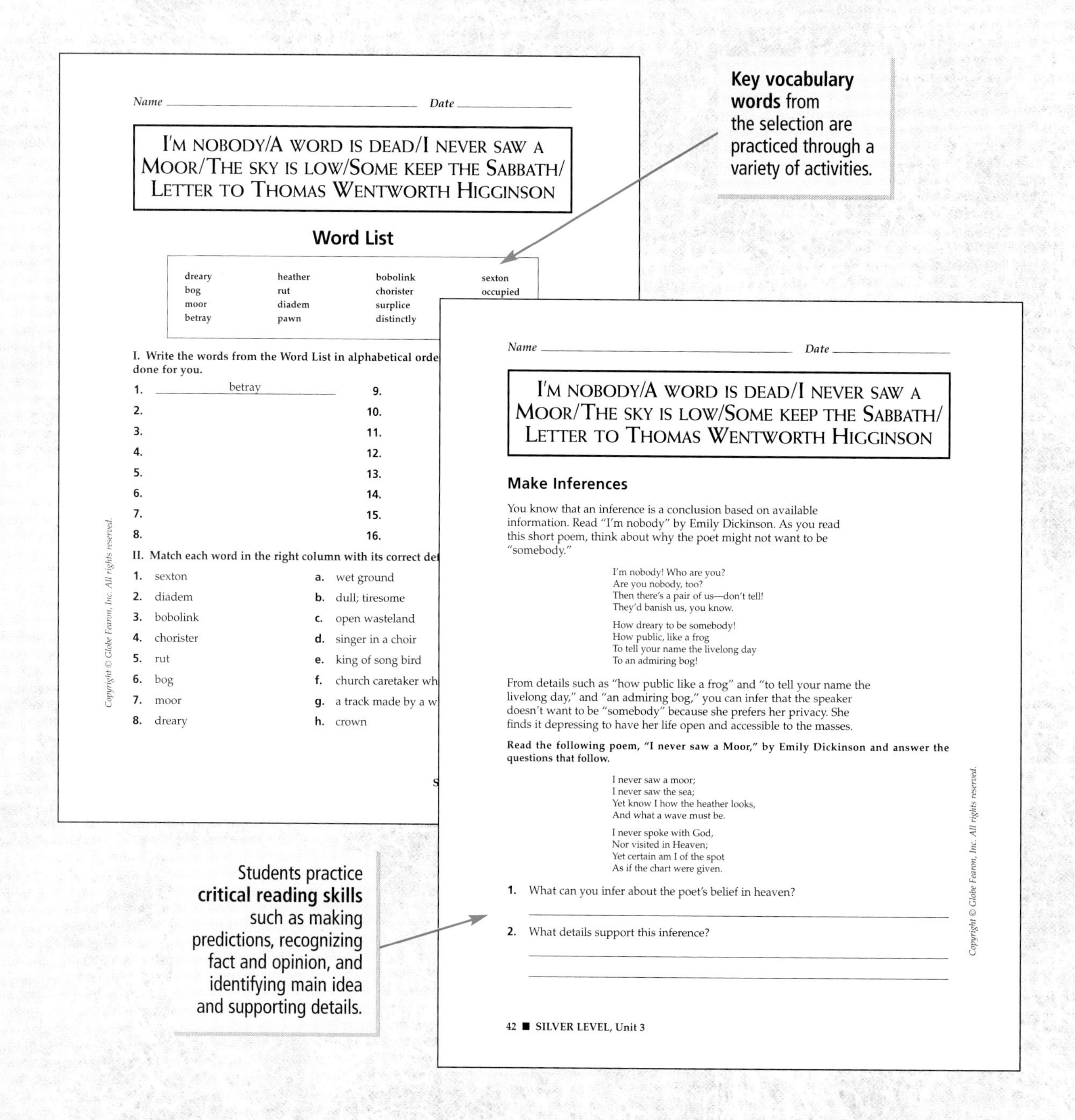

Name ______________________ Date __________

I'M NOBODY/A WORD IS DEAD/I NEVER SAW A MOOR/THE SKY IS LOW/SOME KEEP THE SABBATH/ LETTER TO THOMAS WENTWORTH HIGGINSON

Word List

dreary	heather	bobolink	sexton
bog	rut	chorister	occupied
moor	diadem	surplice	
betray	pawn	distinctly	

I. Write the words from the Word List in alphabetical orde[r] ... done for you.

1. betray
2.
3.
4.
5.
6.
7.
8.
9.
10.
11.
12.
13.
14.
15.
16.

II. Match each word in the right column with its correct de[finition] ...

1. sexton — a. wet ground
2. diadem — b. dull; tiresome
3. bobolink — c. open wasteland
4. chorister — d. singer in a choir
5. rut — e. king of song bird
6. bog — f. church caretaker wh...
7. moor — g. a track made by a w...
8. dreary — h. crown

Name ______________________ Date __________

I'M NOBODY/A WORD IS DEAD/I NEVER SAW A MOOR/THE SKY IS LOW/SOME KEEP THE SABBATH/ LETTER TO THOMAS WENTWORTH HIGGINSON

Make Inferences

You know that an inference is a conclusion based on available information. Read "I'm nobody" by Emily Dickinson. As you read this short poem, think about why the poet might not want to be "somebody."

I'm nobody! Who are you?
Are you nobody, too?
Then there's a pair of us—don't tell!
They'd banish us, you know.

How dreary to be somebody!
How public, like a frog
To tell your name the livelong day
To an admiring bog!

From details such as "how public like a frog" and "to tell your name the livelong day," and "an admiring bog," you can infer that the speaker doesn't want to be "somebody" because she prefers her privacy. She finds it depressing to have her life open and accessible to the masses.

Read the following poem, "I never saw a Moor," by Emily Dickinson and answer the questions that follow.

I never saw a moor;
I never saw the sea;
Yet know I how the heather looks,
And what a wave must be.

I never spoke with God,
Nor visited in Heaven;
Yet certain am I of the spot
As if the chart were given.

1. What can you infer about the poet's belief in heaven?
____
2. What details support this inference?
____
____

42 ■ SILVER LEVEL, Unit 3

Students practice **critical reading skills** such as making predictions, recognizing fact and opinion, and identifying main idea and supporting details.

Comprehensive support helps you manage your diverse classrooms.

*The **Language Enrichment Workbook** meets a wide range of student needs. The activities are ideal for students with limited English proficiency or for those who need extra support with language arts skills.*

Name ______________________ Date __________

I'M NOBODY/A WORD/I NEVER SAW A MOOR/
THE SKY IS LOW/SOME KEEP THE SABBATH/
LETTER TO THOMAS WENTWORTH HIGGINSON

A. Review the definitions of the figures of speech: metaphor, simile, personification, and onomatopoeia. Write them in the space below.

1. Simile:
2. Metaphor:
3. Personification:
4. Onomatopoeia:

B. Choose a *natural* event common in the area where you windstorm, forest fire, hurricane, tornado, snowstorm, tida woods or mountains or at the beach, earthquake, etc. Deve each natural event.
For instance:
Metaphor: The wind was a bulldozer, knocking down ever
Simile: A windstorm is like a giant sneezing.
Personification: The giant called Wind sneezed and blew a
Onomatopoeia: The wind whooshed away everything in it

Natural event:

1. Simile:
2. Metaphor:
3. Personification:
4. Onomatopoeia:

Activities focus on **building language skills** and on **understanding the selection.**

Name ______________________ Date __________

I'M NOBODY/A WORD/I NEVER SAW A MOOR/
THE SKY IS LOW/SOME KEEP THE SABBATH/
LETTER TO THOMAS WENTWORTH HIGGINSON

A. When Emily Dickinson talks about a "nobody" in her poem, she seems to mean a person who is not well-known. Do you agree? How would you define "nobody"? Write your definition here.

B. The opposite of "nobody" is "somebody." Using Emily Dickinson's ideas and your own, write a definition of "somebody."

C. Name three people or types of people that the American culture defines as "somebody" and briefly tell why each is considered "somebody." An example is given.

PERSON	WHY?
President of the United States	Elected by people, represents everybody

D. Name three people in your native country considered to be "somebody" and then tell why they are considered "somebody."

26 ■ SILVER LEVEL, Unit 3

The Teacher's Resources helps tailor instruction to meet individual needs.

*The **Teacher's Resources** is offered in print and CD-ROM formats. Resources include:*

- *Reinforcement worksheets for every selection*
- *Tests (customizable on CD-ROM)*
- *Writing Process worksheets*
- *Grammar, Usage, and Mechanics worksheets*
- *Literary Analysis worksheets*
- *Critical Thinking worksheets*
- *Speaking and Listening worksheets*
- *Assessment rubrics and answer keys*

The **CD-ROM** includes the reproducibles for all four levels of Globe Fearon Literature, complete answer keys, and correlations to national and many state standards.

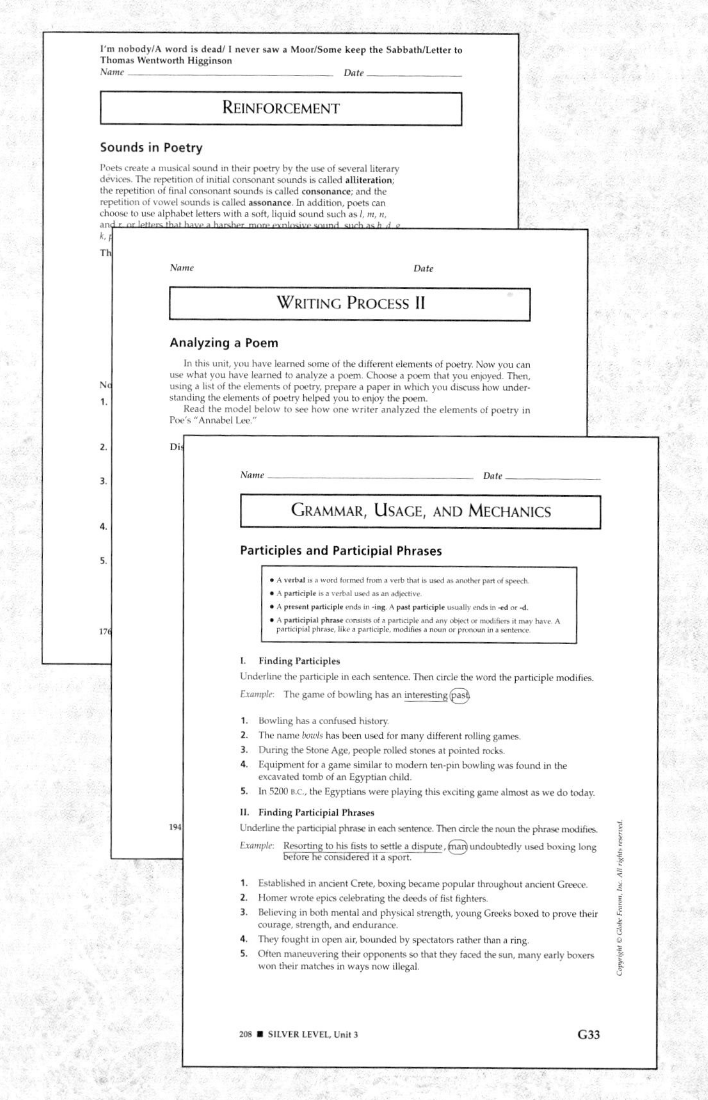

I'm nobody/A word is dead/ I never saw a Moor/Some keep the Sabbath/Letter to Thomas Wentworth Higginson

Name ______________ Date ______________

REINFORCEMENT

Sounds in Poetry

Poets create a musical sound in their poetry by the use of several literary devices. The repetition of initial consonant sounds is called **alliteration**; the repetition of final consonant sounds is called **consonance**; and the repetition of vowel sounds is called **assonance**. In addition, poets can choose to use alphabet letters with a soft, liquid sound such as *l, m, n,*

Name Date

WRITING PROCESS II

Analyzing a Poem

In this unit, you have learned some of the different elements of poetry. Now you can use what you have learned to analyze a poem. Choose a poem that you enjoyed. Then, using a list of the elements of poetry, prepare a paper in which you discuss how understanding the elements of poetry helped you to enjoy the poem.

Read the model below to see how one writer analyzed the elements of poetry in Poe's "Annabel Lee."

Name ______________ Date ______________

GRAMMAR, USAGE, AND MECHANICS

Participles and Participial Phrases

- A **verbal** is a word formed from a verb that is used as another part of speech.
- A **participle** is a verbal used as an adjective.
- A **present participle** ends in **-ing**. A **past participle** usually ends in **-ed** or **-d**.
- A **participial phrase** consists of a participle and any object or modifiers it may have. A participial phrase, like a participle, modifies a noun or pronoun in a sentence.

I. Finding Participles

Underline the participle in each sentence. Then circle the word the participle modifies.

Example: The game of bowling has an interesting past.

1. Bowling has a confused history.
2. The name *bowls* has been used for many different rolling games.
3. During the Stone Age, people rolled stones at pointed rocks.
4. Equipment for a game similar to modern ten-pin bowling was found in the excavated tomb of an Egyptian child.
5. In 5200 B.C., the Egyptians were playing this exciting game almost as we do today.

II. Finding Participial Phrases

Underline the participial phrase in each sentence. Then circle the noun the phrase modifies.

Example: Resorting to his fists to settle a dispute, man undoubtedly used boxing long before he considered it a sport.

1. Established in ancient Crete, boxing became popular throughout ancient Greece.
2. Homer wrote epics celebrating the deeds of fist fighters.
3. Believing in both mental and physical strength, young Greeks boxed to prove their courage, strength, and endurance.
4. They fought in open air, bounded by spectators rather than a ring.
5. Often maneuvering their opponents so that they faced the sun, many early boxers won their matches in ways now illegal.

208 ■ SILVER LEVEL, Unit 3 G33

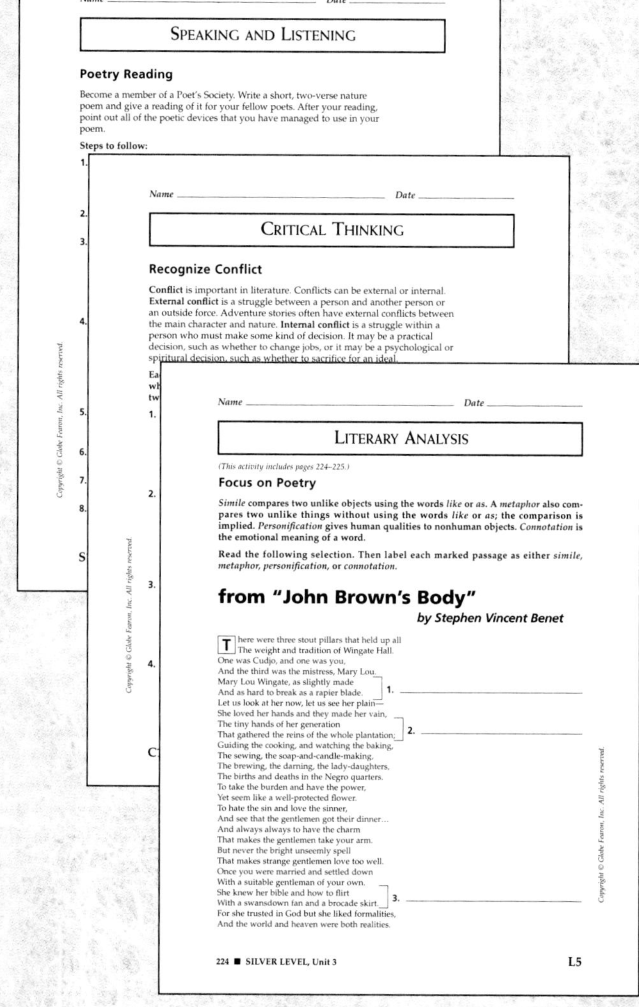

Name ______________ Date ______________

SPEAKING AND LISTENING

Poetry Reading

Become a member of a Poet's Society. Write a short, two-verse nature poem and give a reading of it for your fellow poets. After your reading, point out all of the poetic devices that you have managed to use in your poem.

Steps to follow:

Name ______________ Date ______________

CRITICAL THINKING

Recognize Conflict

Conflict is important in literature. Conflicts can be external or internal. **External conflict** is a struggle between a person and another person or an outside force. Adventure stories often have external conflicts between the main character and nature. **Internal conflict** is a struggle within a person who must make some kind of decision. It may be a practical decision, such as whether to change jobs, or it may be a psychological or spiritual decision, such as whether to sacrifice for an ideal.

Name ______________ Date ______________

LITERARY ANALYSIS

(This activity includes pages 224–225.)

Focus on Poetry

***Simile* compares two unlike objects using the words *like* or *as*. A *metaphor* also compares two unlike things without using the words *like* or *as*; the comparison is implied. *Personification* gives human qualities to nonhuman objects. *Connotation* is the emotional meaning of a word.**

Read the following selection. Then label each marked passage as either *simile, metaphor, personification,* or *connotation.*

from "John Brown's Body"

by Stephen Vincent Benet

There were three stout pillars that held up all
The weight and tradition of Wingate Hall.
One was Cudjo, and one was you,
And the third was the mistress, Mary Lou.
Mary Lou Wingate, as slightly made
And as hard to break as a rapier blade. 1. ______________
Let us look at her now, let us see her plain—
She loved her hands and they made her vain,
The tiny hands of her generation
That gathered the reins of the whole plantation; 2. ______________
Guiding the cooking, and watching the baking,
The sewing, the soap-and-candle-making,
The brewing, the darning, the lady-daughters,
The births and deaths in the Negro quarters.
To take the burden and have the power,
Yet seem like a well-protected flower.
To hate the sin and love the sinner,
And see that the gentlemen got their dinner...
And always always to have the charm
That makes the gentlemen take your arm.
But never the bright unseemly spell
That makes strange gentlemen love too well.
Once you were married and settled down
With a suitable gentleman of your own.
She knew her bible and how to flirt
With a swansdown fan and a brocade skirt. 3. ______________
For she trusted in God but she liked formalities,
And the world and heaven were both realities.

224 ■ SILVER LEVEL, Unit 3 L5

Assessment options and scoring rubrics offer maximum flexibility.

*The **Teacher's Resources** provides traditional and alternative assessment options to help teachers assess individual student needs. Included are:*

- *Selection Tests and Unit Tests in a variety of formats, customizable on CD-ROM*
- *Writing Rubrics*
- *Speaking and Listening Rubrics*
- *Peer and Self-assessment Guides*

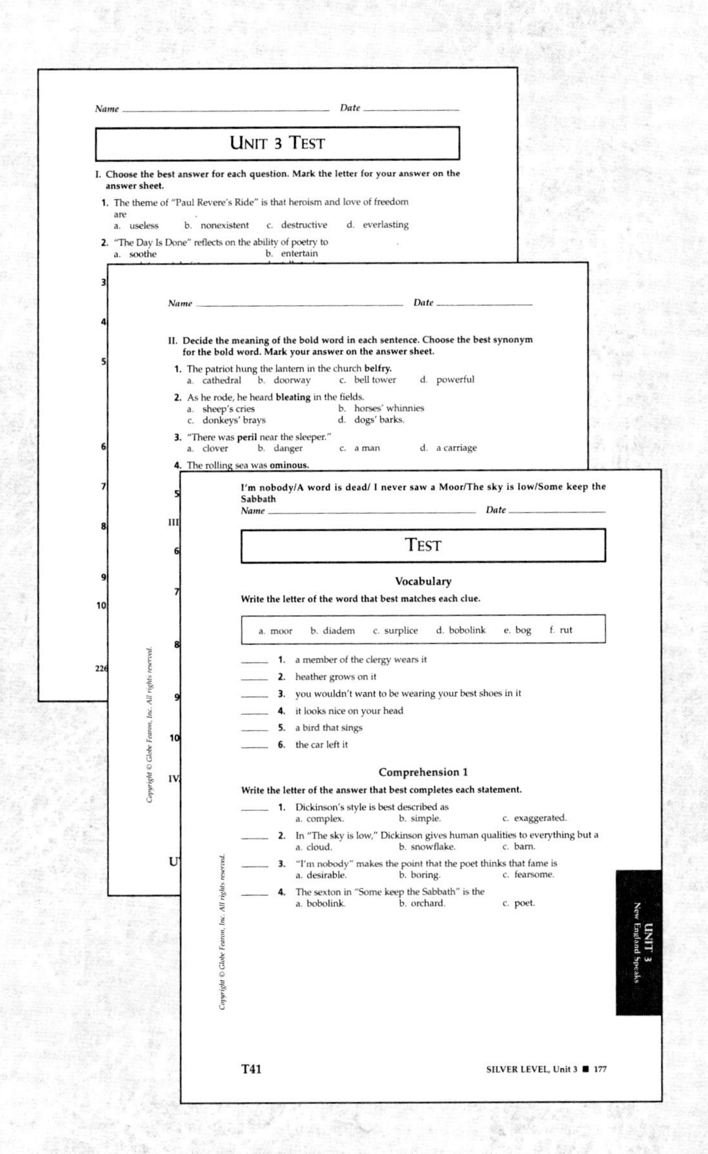

Name ______________________ Date ____________

UNIT 3 TEST

I. Choose the best answer for each question. Mark the letter for your answer on the answer sheet.

1. The theme of "Paul Revere's Ride" is that heroism and love of freedom are
   a. useless b. nonexistent c. destructive d. everlasting
2. "The Day Is Done" reflects on the ability of poetry to
   a. soothe b. entertain

Name ______________________ Date ____________

II. Decide the meaning of the bold word in each sentence. Choose the best synonym for the bold word. Mark your answer on the answer sheet.

1. The patriot hung the lantern in the church **belfry.**
   a. cathedral b. doorway c. bell tower d. powerful
2. As he rode, he heard **bleating** in the fields.
   a. sheep's cries b. horses' whinnies
   c. donkeys' brays d. dogs' barks.
3. "There was **peril** near the sleeper."
   a. clover b. danger c. a man d. a carriage
4. The rolling sea was **ominous.**

I'm nobody/A word is dead/ I never saw a Moor/The sky is low/Some keep the Sabbath

Name ______________________ Date ____________

TEST

Vocabulary

Write the letter of the word that best matches each clue.

a. moor b. diadem c. surplice d. bobolink e. bog f. rut

_____ 1. a member of the clergy wears it
_____ 2. heather grows on it
_____ 3. you wouldn't want to be wearing your best shoes in it
_____ 4. it looks nice on your head
_____ 5. a bird that sings
_____ 6. the car left it

Comprehension 1

Write the letter of the answer that best completes each statement.

_____ 1. Dickinson's style is best described as
   a. complex. b. simple. c. exaggerated.
_____ 2. In "The sky is low," Dickinson gives human qualities to everything but a
   a. cloud. b. snowflake. c. barn.
_____ 3. "I'm nobody" makes the point that the poet thinks that fame is
   a. desirable. b. boring. c. fearsome.
_____ 4. The sexton in "Some keep the Sabbath" is the
   a. bobolink. b. orchard. c. poet.

UNIT 3 New England Speaks

Copyright © Globe Fearon, Inc. All rights reserved.

T41 SILVER LEVEL, Unit 3 ■ 177

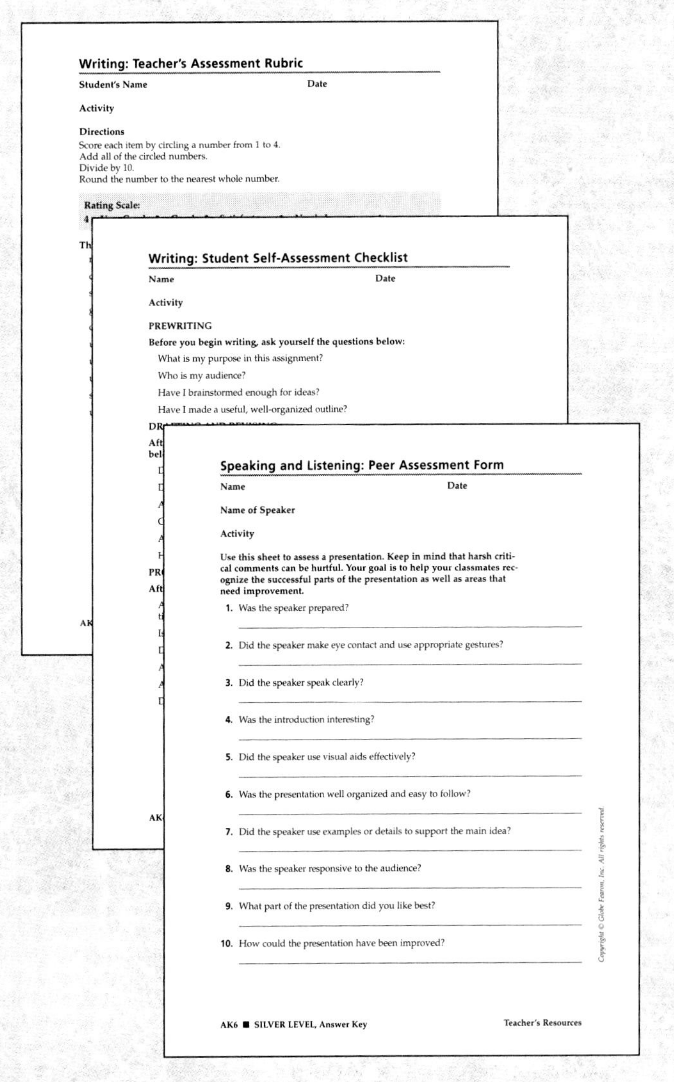

Writing: Teacher's Assessment Rubric

Student's Name Date

Activity

Directions

Score each item by circling a number from 1 to 4.
Add all of the circled numbers.
Divide by 10.
Round the number to the nearest whole number.

Rating Scale:

Writing: Student Self-Assessment Checklist

Name Date

Activity

PREWRITING

Before you begin writing, ask yourself the questions below:

What is my purpose in this assignment?
Who is my audience?
Have I brainstormed enough for ideas?
Have I made a useful, well-organized outline?

Speaking and Listening: Peer Assessment Form

Name Date

Name of Speaker

Activity

Use this sheet to assess a presentation. Keep in mind that harsh critical comments can be hurtful. Your goal is to help your classmates recognize the successful parts of the presentation as well as areas that need improvement.

1. Was the speaker prepared?
2. Did the speaker make eye contact and use appropriate gestures?
3. Did the speaker speak clearly?
4. Was the introduction interesting?
5. Did the speaker use visual aids effectively?
6. Was the presentation well organized and easy to follow?
7. Did the speaker use examples or details to support the main idea?
8. Was the speaker responsive to the audience?
9. What part of the presentation did you like best?
10. How could the presentation have been improved?

Copyright © Globe Fearon, Inc. All rights reserved.

AK6 ■ SILVER LEVEL, Answer Key Teacher's Resources

GLOBE FEARON LITERATURE

SCOPE AND SEQUENCE OF SKILLS

- READING COMPREHENSION
- LITERARY SKILLS
- VOCABULARY/WORD ATTACK
- PROCESS WRITING
- GRAMMAR, USAGE, AND MECHANICS
- CRITICAL THINKING
- SPEAKING AND LISTENING
- STUDY SKILLS
- RESEARCH SKILLS
- CRITICAL VIEWING

SCOPE AND SEQUENCE OF SKILLS	PURPLE LEVEL Units	GREEN LEVEL Units	SILVER LEVEL Units	GOLD LEVEL Units
▪ READING COMPREHENSION				
Analyze Details	1, 5	4	1, 3, 4	1, 6
Compare and Contrast	1, 6	6	1, 3, 4, 6	2, 5
Distinguish Fact From Opinion	1, 4	4	1, 4, 6	6
Draw Conclusions	1, 2	1	2, 3	3
Evaluate Writer's Purpose	1, 2	4, 6	1, 5	4, 6
Evaluate Writer's Style	3	6	5	4
Identify Cause and Effect	5, 6	1, 2, 3, 6	1, 2, 5	5
Identify Changes in Relationships	5	2, 3		
Identify Main Idea and Supporting Details	4, 5	3, 4	1, 3, 4	6
Identify Mood	2, 6	3	5	4
Identify Persuasive Techniques	1, 5	3	1, 2	
Identify Relationships Between Characters	5, 6	2, 3, 6		
Identify Sequence of Events	5	2	5, 6	5
Identify Tone	1, 3, 6	1, 3	1, 6	3, 4, 5
Interpret Character	2	1, 3, 5	4, 6	2, 3
Make Generalizations		5	1	
Make Inferences	2, 4	1, 3, 5	1, 2, 3, 4, 5, 6	3, 5
Make Judgments	1, 3			1
Paraphrase	1	2, 3	6	5
Predict Outcomes	2, 3, 4	1, 5	4	3
Recognize/Interpret Figurative Language	1, 4, 6	1, 2, 3, 4, 5	2, 3, 4, 5	1, 2, 3, 4, 5, 6
Hyperbole	1	3	1, 2, 3	6
Idioms/Dialect	1		4	3
Imagery	1	3	4, 5	1, 5, 6
Metaphors	1, 6	3, 5	3, 5, 6	2, 3, 4, 6
Personification	1	2, 3, 5	3, 6	2, 3, 6

SCOPE AND SEQUENCE OF SKILLS	PURPLE LEVEL Units	GREEN LEVEL Units	SILVER LEVEL Units	GOLD LEVEL Units
Similes	1, 6	2, 3, 5	3, 5, 6	2, 3, 4, 6
Recognize Symbolism	4	3	4, 5	2, 3, 5
Summarize Text	4	2	6	5
Use Context Clues	1, 3, 5	1, 2, 4, 6	2, 3, 5	4, 5, 6
Use Prior Knowledge	2	2		6
▪ **LITERARY SKILLS**				
Antagonist	3	4	1, 2, 5, 6	4
Author's Purpose	1, 2	3, 4, 6	1, 5, 6	4, 6
Autobiography	4	4	1, 2	6
Biography	1, 2, 3, 4, 5, 6	1, 2, 3, 4, 5, 6	1, 2, 3, 4, 5, 6	1, 2, 3, 4, 5, 6
Characterization	1, 2, 4, 5	1, 2, 3, 4, 5, 6	1, 2, 3, 4, 5, 6	1, 2, 3, 4, 5, 6
Comedy/Humor	1	1, 2, 4, 6	1, 4, 5	3, 5
Conflict	1, 2, 3, 4	1, 2, 3, 4, 6	2, 3, 4, 5	2, 3, 4, 5, 6
Connotation/Denotation	2, 3	5, 6	3, 5	1, 3
Drama	1, 2, 3	1, 3, 6	2, 5	2, 5
Epigram	6	3	1, 2, 3	3, 5
Essay			1, 3, 4	6
Fiction	1, 2, 3, 4, 5, 6	1, 2, 3, 4, 5, 6	1, 2, 3, 4, 5, 6	1, 2, 3, 4, 5, 6
Figures of Speech	1, 2, 3, 4, 5, 6	2, 3, 5	1, 2, 3, 5, 6	1, 2, 3, 4, 5, 6
Alliteration	3, 4	5	3, 5	1, 2
Hyperbole	1	3	1, 2, 3	6
Metaphors	1, 6	3, 5	3, 5, 6	2, 3, 4, 6
Onomatopoeia	3	5	2, 3, 6	5
Personification	1, 2	2, 3, 5	3, 6	3, 4, 6
Similes	1, 6	2, 3, 5	3, 5, 6	2, 3, 4, 6
Flashback	5	1	5	5
Folktales/Fables/Legends		1, 2	1, 2	1, 6
Foreshadowing	1, 2, 5	1, 2	2, 4, 5	5
Imagery	1, 2, 4, 6	2, 3	3, 4, 6	1, 2, 3, 4, 5, 6
Irony	1, 3, 5	2, 3, 6	4, 5	1, 3, 6
Journal/Diary/Letter/Almanac	1	6	1	3
Mood	2, 4	1, 3, 4, 5	1, 4, 5	1, 2, 5
Mystery/Suspense	2, 3, 4	1, 2	2, 5, 6	3, 4, 5
Nonfiction	1, 2, 3, 4, 5	1, 2, 3, 4, 5, 6	1, 2, 3, 4, 6	1, 2, 3, 5, 6
Plot Elements	2, 3, 5	1, 2, 4, 6	2, 3, 4, 5	2, 3, 4, 5, 6
Climax/Turning Point	2, 3, 5	1, 2, 4, 6	2, 3, 4, 5	2, 3, 4
Complication/Conflict	2, 3	1, 2, 4, 6	2, 3, 4, 5	2, 3, 4, 5, 6
Denouement/Conclusion/Resolution	2, 3, 5	1, 2, 4, 6	2, 3, 4	2, 4

SCOPE AND SEQUENCE OF SKILLS	PURPLE LEVEL Units	GREEN LEVEL Units	SILVER LEVEL Units	GOLD LEVEL Units
Exposition	2, 3	2, 4	1, 4	6
Falling Action/Rising Action	2, 3, 5	1, 6	4	4
Poetic Devices/Forms				
Closed Form	5, 6	3, 5	3, 4, 5, 6	2, 3, 4, 5
Open Form	1, 3, 6	3, 5	4, 5, 6	6
Repetition	4	3, 6	3, 5	5
Stanza		3	6	5
Poetry	1, 2, 3, 4, 5, 6	1, 2, 3, 4, 5, 6	1, 2, 5	1, 2, 3, 4, 5, 6
Ballad		3		1
Concrete		5		
Epic/Heroic	5	3		1
Haiku	4	3		
Lyric			2, 5	2
Narrative	2	4		1
Sonnet				2
Point of View	1, 2, 3, 4, 5, 6	1, 2, 3, 4, 5, 6	1, 2, 6	1, 2, 3, 4, 5, 6
Protagonist	3	1, 4		4
Rhyme	1, 2, 4	1, 3, 4, 5	3, 4, 5, 6	1, 2, 3, 4, 5, 6
Rhythm	3, 5, 6	3, 4, 5, 6	1, 2, 3, 5, 6	1, 2, 3, 4, 5
Satire		1		3, 4, 5, 6
Setting	2, 3, 4, 5	1, 2, 3, 4, 6	1, 4, 5, 6	1, 2, 3, 4, 5
Short Story	1, 2, 3	1, 2, 3, 4, 5, 6	2, 4, 5, 6	5, 6
Speaker	4	1, 4	1	
Style/Techniques	1, 2, 3, 4, 5, 6	1, 2, 3, 6	1, 4, 5	2
Surprise Ending	1, 2, 3, 4, 5	1, 2, 6	4, 5	
Symbols/Symbolism	2, 3, 4, 5, 6	1, 3, 4, 5, 6	1, 2, 4, 5, 6	1, 2, 3, 4, 5
Theme	1, 2, 3, 4, 5, 6	1, 2, 3, 4, 5, 6	1, 2, 3, 4, 6	1, 2, 3, 4, 5, 6
Tone/Attitude	1, 3, 4, 5, 6	1, 2, 3, 4, 5, 6	1, 4, 5, 6	1, 2, 3, 4, 5, 6
▪ VOCABULARY/WORD ATTACK				
Antonyms	6	1, 2, 5, 6	2, 3, 5, 6	5, 6
Archaic Words	1, 2	1	1	2, 3
Compound Words		3	1	6
Connotation/Denotation	2, 3	5, 6	3, 5	1, 3
Context	1, 3, 4, 5, 6	1, 2, 3, 4, 5, 6	1, 2, 3, 4, 5, 6	1, 2, 4, 5, 6
Contractions	1, 2, 4, 5	3, 4, 5	2, 4	2
Dialect	2		3	3
Dictionary Pronunciation Key	4	2, 3		4
Etymology	2, 5, 6	2, 3	1, 3, 4, 5, 6	1, 2, 3, 5

SCOPE AND SEQUENCE OF SKILLS	PURPLE LEVEL Units	GREEN LEVEL Units	SILVER LEVEL Units	GOLD LEVEL Units
Figurative Language	1, 2, 3, 4, 5, 6	1, 2, 3, 4, 5, 6	2, 3, 4, 5, 6	1, 2, 3, 4, 5, 6
Homographs		3	6	6
Homophones	1, 5, 6	1, 2, 4, 5	2, 3	1, 3, 4
Letter Sounds	1, 2, 4, 6	2, 5	3, 4, 5, 6	1, 2, 4, 5
Meanings of New Words	1, 2, 3, 4, 5, 6	1, 2, 3, 4, 5, 6	1, 2, 3, 4, 5, 6	1, 2, 3, 4, 5, 6
Multiple-Meaning Words	1, 2, 3, 4, 5	1, 2, 3, 5, 6	1, 2, 5, 6	1, 2, 3, 6
Parts of Speech	1, 2, 4, 5, 6	1, 2, 3, 4, 5, 6	1, 2, 3, 4, 5, 6	1, 2, 3, 4, 5, 6
Adjectives	1, 2, 4, 5, 6	4, 5, 6	2, 4, 5, 6	1, 3, 4, 5
Adverbs	4, 5, 6	4, 5, 6	2, 5, 6	1, 3, 4
Conjunctions	2, 6			4
Nouns	1, 2, 3, 4, 5, 6	1, 2, 3	1, 2, 4, 5, 6	1, 2, 3, 4, 5, 6
Prepositions	4			4
Pronouns	1, 3, 4, 6	1, 3, 4, 5	4, 5, 6	2, 4, 5
Verbs	1, 2, 3, 4, 5, 6	1, 2, 3, 4, 5, 6	1, 4, 5, 6	1, 2, 3, 4, 6
Phonetic Respellings	1, 2, 3, 4, 5, 6	1, 2, 3, 4, 5, 6	1, 2, 3, 4, 5, 6	1, 2, 3, 4, 5, 6
Prefixes	2, 6	2, 3, 4, 5, 6	6	4, 5
de-, dis-	2, 6	3		5
fore-		3		
il-	6			5
im-, in-, ir-, non-, un-	2, 6	2, 3, 4, 5, 6	6	4, 5
mis-			6	
pre-		5		
re-		2	6	5
Roots	1, 2, 3, 5	2, 3, 4, 5, 6	1, 2, 6	3, 4, 5
Shades of Meaning	1, 2, 4, 5	1, 2, 4, 5	3, 5, 6	1, 2, 5, 6
Slang	6	3		
Suffixes	1, 2	1, 3, 4, 5, 6	2	1, 2, 4, 5
-able	1		2	
-acy, -cy		3		
-ance, -ence	2	1, 5	2	
-ard	1			
-ation, -tion		4, 5		5
-er, -or		3	2	1
-ery				2
-ful	1		2	4
-hood		6		
-ible		5		
-ic	1			

SCOPE AND SEQUENCE OF SKILLS	PURPLE LEVEL Units	GREEN LEVEL Units	SILVER LEVEL Units	GOLD LEVEL Units
-ion		5	2	
-ish	1			4
-ity	2		2	
-less	1	4, 5, 6	2	
-ly	4	4, 5, 6	2, 5, 6	
-ment		1	2	
-ness	2	4		
-ory			2	
-tude	2			
-ward			2	
Synonyms	1, 2, 3, 4, 5, 6	1, 2, 3, 4, 5, 6	3, 5	1, 2, 5, 6
Technical/Occupational/Jargon		1, 2	5	
Word Parts	1, 2	3	1, 4, 6	6
▪ **PROCESS WRITING**				
Prewriting	1, 2, 3, 4, 5, 6	1, 2, 3, 4, 5, 6	1, 2, 3, 4, 5, 6	1, 2, 3, 4, 5, 6
Brainstorm/Freewrite	1, 2, 3, 4, 5, 6	1, 2, 3, 4, 5, 6	4, 5, 6	1, 2
List:	1, 2, 3, 4, 5, 6	1, 2, 3, 4, 5, 6	1, 2, 3, 4, 5, 6	1, 2, 3, 4, 5, 6
Actions/Events	3	1, 2	2, 3, 6	1, 3, 4, 5
Causes/Conditions/Factors	4	1, 2	4	4
Characters	3, 4, 6	5	1, 5, 6	3, 4
Descriptions	3, 6	2, 3, 5	2, 4, 5, 6	
Emotions/Thoughts	1, 3, 4, 6	1, 2, 3, 5, 6	2, 3, 6	1, 2, 4, 5
Examples/Explanations/Facts	2, 3, 4, 5, 6	2	2	1, 4
Ideas	1, 2, 3, 4, 6	2, 3, 4, 5	1, 2, 4	2, 3, 4, 5
Literary Elements	1, 4, 6	1, 2, 3, 4, 5, 6	2, 3, 5	1, 2, 3, 4, 5
Points/Reactions/Responses	2, 3, 5, 6	2, 3, 6	1, 2	
Questions/Answers/Solutions	2, 3, 5, 6	2, 5, 6	4, 5, 6	1, 2, 4, 5
Reasons	1, 3	1, 2, 3	2, 3, 4, 6	2, 5
Similarities/Differences	1, 3	5		
Words/Phrases	3	3, 5	3, 6	2
Outline	1, 2, 3, 5, 6	1, 2, 3, 4, 5, 6	1, 2, 4, 5, 6	1, 2, 3, 4
Writing	1, 2, 3, 4, 5, 6	1, 2, 3, 4, 5, 6	1, 2, 3, 4, 5, 6	1, 2, 3, 4, 5, 6
Additional Episode	1, 2, 3, 4, 5	1, 2, 3, 4, 5, 6	1, 2, 3, 4, 5	1, 2, 3, 4, 5, 6
Characterization		1, 2	2, 4, 5	
Comparisons	1, 2, 5, 6	1, 3, 4, 5	1, 2, 3, 4, 5, 6	1, 2, 3, 4, 5
Composition	1, 2, 3, 4, 5, 6	1, 2, 3, 4, 5	1, 2, 3, 4, 5, 6	1, 2, 3, 4, 5, 6
Description	1, 2, 3, 4, 5, 6	1, 2, 3, 4, 5, 6	1, 2, 3, 4, 5, 6	1, 2, 3, 4, 5, 6
Dialogue	1, 2, 5, 6	1, 2	1, 2, 3, 5, 6	1, 2, 3, 4, 6

SCOPE AND SEQUENCE OF SKILLS	PURPLE LEVEL Units	GREEN LEVEL Units	SILVER LEVEL Units	GOLD LEVEL Units
Epigram	6	3		3
Essay	3	1, 3, 4, 6	2, 5	1, 2
Explanation	2, 3, 4, 5, 6	1, 2, 3, 4, 5, 6	1, 2, 3, 4, 5, 6	1, 2, 3, 4, 5, 6
Figure of Speech		3		
Firsthand Report	2, 3, 4, 5, 6	1, 2, 3	1, 2, 3, 4, 6	2, 3, 4, 5, 6
Irony/Satire	3	1, 2	4	4
Imagery	1	3	3	4
Journal/Diary Entry	1	1, 3, 6	3	1, 3, 6
Letter	1, 2, 4	2, 3, 4, 5, 6	1, 2, 5	1
Narrative	1	1, 2	1, 2, 3, 4, 6	1, 3, 4, 5, 6
Newspaper Article	2	3, 4, 5	4, 6	1, 6
Notes	1, 2, 3, 4, 5, 6		1, 2, 3, 4	1, 3, 5, 6
Opinion	1, 2, 3, 4, 5, 6	1, 2, 3, 4, 5, 6	1, 2, 3, 4, 5, 6	1, 2, 3, 4, 5
Paragraphs	1, 2, 3, 4, 5, 6	1, 2, 3, 4, 5, 6	1, 2, 3, 4, 5, 6	1, 2, 3, 4, 5, 6
Persuasion	2, 5	1, 2, 3, 4, 5, 6	1, 2, 3, 5, 6	5
Play	3		5	
Poem	1, 2, 4, 5, 6	1, 2, 3, 4, 5, 6	3, 4, 5, 6	1, 2, 4, 5
Review	1, 4, 6	1, 2, 3, 5	1, 3	2, 4, 5, 6
Similes/Metaphors		1, 2	6	2, 3
Speech	3, 5	1, 2	1, 2	4
Story	1, 2, 5, 6	1, 2, 3, 4, 5	1, 2, 3, 4, 6	1, 3, 4, 5, 6
Summary		3	6	5
Television Report	3		1	1
Revising	1, 2, 3, 4, 5, 6	1, 2, 3, 4, 5, 6	1, 2, 3, 4, 5, 6	1, 2, 3, 4, 5, 6
Include:				
Character's Thoughts/Ideas/Feelings	3, 6	1, 2, 4	2, 6	1, 4
Description	1, 2, 5, 6	1, 3, 4	2, 6	3, 5
Details	1, 2, 3, 4, 6	1, 2, 4, 5	1, 2, 4, 5, 6	1, 2, 3, 5, 6
Dialogue	5, 6	3		2, 4
Literary Elements		3	3	
Observations	3	3	3	
Point of View		1		
Quotations	4, 5, 6	1, 5	6	3, 5
Reasons/Examples	3	4, 5	4, 6	2, 4
Topic Sentences	1, 4, 5	2		
Transition Words	4, 5	1, 4, 5		5
Maintain:				
Believability	4	1, 2, 3, 5	5	1, 2

SCOPE AND SEQUENCE OF SKILLS	PURPLE LEVEL Units	GREEN LEVEL Units	SILVER LEVEL Units	GOLD LEVEL Units
Consistency	1, 2, 3, 4, 5, 6	1, 2, 3, 4, 5, 6	1, 2, 3, 5, 6	1, 3
Clarity	1, 2, 3, 4, 6	1, 2, 3, 4, 5, 6	1, 2, 5, 6	1, 2, 3, 4, 5, 6
Order	5	2, 3, 6	5, 6	5
Proofreading	1, 2, 3, 4, 5, 6	1, 2, 3, 4, 5, 6	1, 2, 3, 4, 5, 6	1, 2, 3, 4, 5, 6
Correct:				
Capitalization/Punctuation	1, 2, 3, 4, 5, 6	1, 2, 3, 4, 5, 6	1, 2, 3, 4, 5, 6	1, 2, 3, 4, 5, 6
Grammar	1, 2, 3, 4, 6	1, 2, 3, 4	1, 2, 4, 6	1, 2, 3, 4, 5, 6
Letter/Poetry Form		2, 3		2
Paragraphing	2, 5, 6	1, 3, 4, 5, 6	4	1, 5
Spelling	1, 2, 4, 5, 6	1, 2, 3, 4, 5	1, 2, 3, 5	1, 2, 3, 4, 6
▪ **GRAMMAR, USAGE, AND MECHANICS**				
Adjectives	1, 2, 4, 5, 6	4, 5, 6	2, 4, 5, 6	1
Adverbs	4, 5, 6	4, 5, 6	2, 5, 6	1
Conjunctions	4, 5, 6	4, 5, 6	2, 5, 6	1
Nouns	1	1, 2, 3, 5, 6	5	1, 5, 6
Prepositions	4	5		3
Pronouns	2	3	1	1
Verbs	1, 3, 4	2	2	2
Punctuation	2, 4, 5, 6	1, 3, 6	1, 3, 4, 5, 6	4, 5, 6
Colon/Semicolon	4, 6	6	6	
Commas	6	3, 6	3, 4	4, 5, 6
Quotations	5, 6	1, 6	4, 5	4, 6
Word Series	2, 5, 6	6		5, 6
Sentences	1, 5	2	1, 4, 5	1, 5, 6
Syntax				3
▪ **CRITICAL THINKING**				
Analyze	1, 2, 3, 4, 5, 6	1, 2, 3, 4, 5, 6	1, 2, 3, 4, 5, 6	1, 2, 3, 4, 5, 6
Analyze Analogies		1, 6		
Analyze Details	1	1		
Analyze Syllogisms	3			
Apply	2, 3, 4	1, 2, 4, 5	1, 3, 4, 5	1, 3, 4, 6
Classify/Categorize	2		3, 5	2, 3
Compare and Contrast	1, 4, 5, 6	1, 2, 3, 4, 5, 6	1, 3, 4, 5, 6	2, 3, 5
Distinguish Fact From Opinion	1, 2, 4	4	1, 4, 6	1, 6
Draw Conclusions	1, 2, 3, 4, 5, 6	1, 2, 3, 4, 5, 6	1, 2, 3, 4, 5, 6	1, 2, 3, 4, 5, 6
Evaluate	1, 2, 3, 4	4, 5, 6	1, 2, 3, 4, 5	1, 2, 4, 6
Generalize	1, 6	2, 5	1, 4, 5	4
Infer/Interpret	1, 2, 3, 4, 5, 6	1, 2, 3	2, 3, 4, 5	1, 2, 3, 4

SCOPE AND SEQUENCE OF SKILLS	PURPLE LEVEL Units	GREEN LEVEL Units	SILVER LEVEL Units	GOLD LEVEL Units
Predict	1, 2, 3, 4	1, 2, 3	2, 5	1, 3, 4
Reason Inductively/Deductively	1, 3			
Recognize Cause and Effect	5, 6	1		1, 6
Recognize Character Conflict			2	4
Recognize Order			1, 2, 4	
Summarize	1, 2, 4	1, 2, 4	1, 5	1, 2, 5
Synthesize	4		3, 5	4
▪ **CRITICAL THINKING AND DRAMA**				
Adapt a Play for Movies/Radio/TV	2	1	2, 5	
Compare and Contrast Characters	1, 3	3, 6	2, 5	3, 4, 5
Interpret the Effect of Imagery	1			4
Make Inferences About Characters	1, 2, 3	1, 3, 6	2, 5	2, 3, 4, 5
Predict Outcomes	3	1, 3	2, 5	3, 4
Recognize Cause and Effect	1, 2, 3	1, 3, 6	2, 5	2, 3, 4
Summarize a Play				5
▪ **CRITICAL THINKING AND FICTION**				
Analyze the Effect of Setting	3, 4, 5	1, 2, 3, 4, 6	2, 4, 5, 6	1, 3, 5, 6
Analyze Sequence in a Story	1, 2, 3, 4, 5, 6	1, 2, 3, 4, 5, 6	2, 3, 4, 5, 6	1, 4
Analyze Solutions	2, 3, 5, 6	1, 2, 4	2, 4, 5, 6	6
Compare and Contrast	1, 2, 3, 4, 6	1, 2, 3, 4, 5, 6	1, 2, 3, 4, 5, 6	3, 4, 5, 6
Draw Conclusions	1, 2, 3, 4, 5, 6	1, 2, 3, 4, 5, 6	1, 2, 3, 4, 5, 6	1, 3, 4, 5
Identify Cause and Effect	1, 2, 3, 4, 5, 6		2, 3, 4, 5, 6	1, 3, 4, 5, 6
Identify Exaggeration			1	4, 6
Make Inferences About Characters	1, 2, 3, 4, 5, 6	1, 2, 3, 4, 5, 6	1, 2, 3, 4, 5, 6	1, 3, 4, 5, 6
Paraphrase	2, 3, 5		2, 6	
Recognize Relevant Details	1, 5	4	1, 3	6
Understand Plausibility	1, 2, 3, 4		1, 2, 3	
▪ **CRITICAL THINKING AND NONFICTION**				
Compare and Contrast Words	2, 3, 4	2, 3, 4, 5, 6	1, 2, 4, 6	2, 5
Evaluate Biographical/Autobiographical Subject	4	2, 4	1, 2, 6	6
Evaluate Historical Inferences	4, 5	1	1, 2	1, 3, 5, 6
Find Relevant Evidence	1, 2, 3, 4, 5	1, 2, 3, 4, 5, 6	1, 2, 3, 4, 6	2, 3, 5, 6
Infer Writer's Purpose	2, 3, 4, 5	2, 3, 6	1, 2, 4, 6	2, 5, 6
Recognize Generalizations	3, 4, 5	1, 2, 5, 6	1, 2, 4, 6	5
Recognize Persuasive Techniques	2, 3, 5	3	1, 2, 3	
Separate Details	1, 2, 3, 4, 5	1, 2, 3, 4, 5, 6	1, 2, 3, 4, 6	1, 2, 3, 5, 6
Separate Fact From Opinion	2, 3, 4	1, 2, 3, 4, 5, 6	1, 2, 6	1, 2, 5
Summarize an Essay			1, 4	

SCOPE AND SEQUENCE OF SKILLS	PURPLE LEVEL Units	GREEN LEVEL Units	SILVER LEVEL Units	GOLD LEVEL Units
Understand Sequence of Events	2, 3, 4, 5	2, 3, 4, 5, 6	1, 2, 6	2, 5
▪ **CRITICAL THINKING AND POETRY**				
Interpret Figures of Speech	1, 2 3, 6	2, 3, 5	3, 5, 6	2, 3, 4, 5, 6
Interpret Sensory Words	1		3, 5	5
Interpret Symbols	1, 2, 4, 6	3	3, 4	2, 3, 4
Make Inferences About Speaker	1, 2, 3, 4, 5, 6	1, 2, 3, 4, 5, 6	1, 2, 3, 4, 5, 6	1, 2, 3, 4, 5, 6
Make Inferences About Theme	1, 2, 3, 6	1, 2, 3, 4	1, 2, 5, 6	1, 2, 3, 4, 5, 6
Paraphrase Poetry	1, 2, 3, 4, 6	1, 3, 5, 6	2, 3, 4, 5, 6	1, 2, 3, 4, 5, 6
Recognize Assertions	1, 2, 3, 5	1, 2, 3, 4, 5, 6	1, 2, 3, 5, 6	1, 2, 3, 4, 5, 6
Understand Cause and Effect	1, 2, 3, 4, 5, 6	1, 2, 3, 4, 5, 6	1, 2, 3, 4, 5, 6	1, 2, 3, 4, 5, 6
▪ **SPEAKING AND LISTENING**				
Character Analysis and Interpretation	1, 2, 3, 5, 6	3, 4, 6	4, 5	2, 5
Create Dialogue	1, 2	1, 3	2, 3, 4, 5	3
Create Monologue	3, 5			2, 6
Debate/Panel Discussion	2, 4, 6	1, 2, 3, 4, 5, 6	3, 4, 6	1, 2, 3, 6
Dramatic Reading	6	6	3, 4	1, 2, 4, 5, 6
Fiction Analysis	2		2, 3, 5	2, 3, 4
Folktale		2		
Group Presentation		1, 2, 3, 4, 6	1	5
Interview	1, 2, 3, 4, 5, 6	2, 3, 4, 5		4
Oral Directions			1	3
Oral Interpretation	1, 2, 4, 5	1, 6	1, 2, 3	1, 4
Pantomime		5		1
Persuasive Presentation	2, 3, 4, 5	2	1, 2, 4	1, 3, 5, 6
Poetry/Song	1	2, 3, 6	2, 3, 4, 5, 6	1, 4, 5
Plot/Theme Discussion	3	4	2, 5	
Radio or Television Show	1, 4, 6	2, 3, 4, 5, 6	2, 4, 5	1, 3, 4, 5, 6
Role Play	1, 3, 4, 5, 6	6		4
Speech	4	4	1	3
▪ **STUDY SKILLS**				
Note-Taking	4	4	1	1, 4
Outline	1	4	6	6
Reading Techniques	3, 6	1, 2, 3, 6	1, 2, 4, 6	1, 2, 4, 5, 6
Preview	6	1, 6		1, 5
Identify Main Idea	3	1, 2, 3	1, 4, 6	1, 2, 4, 6
Paraphrase		3	2, 6	
Read Table of Contents	3	3		
Recognize Persuasion/Propaganda	1	3	2	

SCOPE AND SEQUENCE OF SKILLS	PURPLE LEVEL Units	GREEN LEVEL Units	SILVER LEVEL Units	GOLD LEVEL Units
Reference Books	3	6		
Study Habits	1, 2, 3, 4, 5, 6	1, 2, 3, 4, 5, 6	1, 2, 3, 4, 5, 6	1, 2, 3, 4, 5, 6
Summarize	4	3	4, 6	2, 5
Test-Taking Strategies	1, 2, 3, 4, 5, 6	1, 2, 3, 4, 5, 6	1, 2, 3, 4, 5, 6	1, 2, 3, 4, 5, 6
Essay Tests		2		
Objective Tests	5, 6	1		
▪ **RESEARCH SKILLS**				
Almanac/Atlas				6
Dictionary	3	1, 2, 3, 4, 5, 6	1, 2, 3, 4, 5, 6	1, 2, 3, 4, 5, 6
Encyclopedia			1, 5	6
Follow Directions	1, 2, 3, 4, 5, 6	1, 2, 3, 4, 5, 6	1, 2, 3, 4, 5, 6	1, 2, 3, 4, 5, 6
Glossary		2, 5	1	
Note-Taking	4	4, 6	1	
Recognize Persuasion/Propaganda		3	1	
Reference Sources	3		1	1, 6
Thesaurus				2, 5
▪ **CRITICAL VIEWING**				
Analyze and Interpret Art From Other Cultures	4, 6	1, 2, 3, 4, 5	2	6
Interpret Genre Painting		1, 3, 5	2	2, 3, 4
Interpret Impressionist Painting	1	3	4, 6	3, 4, 5, 6
Examine Landscape/Seascape	2, 4, 5	1, 2	2, 3, 4, 5, 6	2, 3, 4, 6
Examine Lithographs			1, 3, 4	
Examine Older Art Forms	6	1		1, 3
Examine Photographic, Photorealistic Art		3	3	5
Examine Portraits	5		1, 2, 5	2, 3, 4
Examine Sketches		5	4	4
Interpret Expressionistic Painting	1	2	2, 4, 6	
Interpret Modern Art	1, 2, 4, 5, 6	1, 4, 5, 6	4	5
Interpret Primitive Art			2, 3	
Interpret Realistic Art	1, 2, 3, 4, 5	5	1, 6	2
Interpret Romantic Art	2, 3		3	2, 4
Interpret Surrealistic and Mystic Art	1, 2	2, 5, 6		6

GLOBE FEARON LITERATURE PROFESSIONAL DEVELOPMENT ARTICLES

Globe Fearon understands the importance of providing quality literature instruction to students. Today's educators must do so while facing the daily challenges of meeting the diverse needs of their students. The following pages contain additional teaching suggestions to help you to tailor instruction to your students' needs. We welcome your comments and suggestions for further staff development ideas. Visit our Web site, *www.globefearon.com*, to share ideas with Globe Fearon and other educators.

Creating a Positive Environment for Diverse Learners

By Deborah Walker

The typical classroom includes students who have different ways of learning, understanding what they have just learned, and applying that understanding to other materials and situations.

ADDRESSING THE MIXED-ABILITY CLASSROOM

Teachers today, more than ever before, must accommodate a broad range of student abilities, interests, learning styles, and other special needs. The typical classroom includes students who have different ways of learning, understanding what they have just learned, and applying that understanding to other materials and situations. Students may be highly visual learners, auditory learners, tactile learners, or kinesthetic learners. To add to this complexity, a typical classroom may be comprised of students who have attained different levels of English proficiency. More special-needs students are being mainstreamed into general education classes. All of these factors combine to offer an extraordinary challenge to the educator teaching in an average classroom.

As mandated by the National Education Standards, "All students, regardless of their ability level, learning style, interests, ethnic background, or physical limitations shall have the opportunity to attain high levels of literacy." The message to educators is clear: A variety of learning approaches and activities must be employed to motivate and engage all students in the learning process. This means that teachers must recognize and respond to student diversity and then encourage all students to participate fully in the learning process.

GLOBE FEARON LITERATURE AND THE DIVERSE CLASSROOM

Globe Fearon Literature encourages and provides opportunities for students to be actively involved in the learning process. A flexible textbook, such as *Globe Fearon Literature*, combines teacher-centered instruction, oral reading, discussion opportunities, cooperative group activities, and media and technology. Following the activities in the textbook creates an ideal environment to meet the needs of diverse learners.

Additionally, to address the needs of diverse learners, a mixture of learning tasks or activities should be employed on a regular basis. With *Globe Fearon Literature*, teachers can accommodate and enable students with diverse backgrounds to be successful in a variety of learning situations, such as active inquiry, collaboration, and class interaction. Opportunities for activity-based learning should be provided as often as possible to allow all students an equal chance to succeed. Suggestions for these activities are provided in *Globe Fearon Literature*.

You can achieve a maximum degree of flexibility in the classroom by making a few adjustments to your teaching style, learning environment, and assessments. The lessons in *Globe Fearon Literature* are structured so that every student is given the opportunity to learn. By creating a student-centered environment in your classroom, your lesson plan will focus on a variety of learners—tactile, visual, kinesthetic, auditory, as well as special-needs and English-as-a-Second-language (ESL) students. Your role as teacher becomes that of facilitator, coach, and mentor to your students. You can use *Globe Fearon Literature* to enhance the knowledge of students of all abilities and help each of your students reach their individual potential.

This literature program gives you the opportunity to present a number of assignment options to your students. While all students will read the literature selection, you may assign a variety of additional in-class and homework activities to allow students to demonstrate understanding of the material. You can give students the assignments that best meets their learning styles, ability levels, or interests. For example, one student may describe in detail how a quotation from a poem relates to a piece of fine art in the Student Edition. The student may present his or her proof of understanding orally, in writing, or by using a media presentation. Another student may role-play a character in a literature selection. Class discussion will reveal whether the character is flat or round, and help to determine if the assignment was completed successfully. A group of students may work cooperatively to write a screenplay of a story.

One challenge you might have in implementing new strategies for reaching diverse learners is how to assess the outcomes in a meaningful way. Assessments are not based on the traditional percentage of correct information remembered, but on the depth of understanding of the selection that the students demonstrate. Rubrics that include the criteria that you might look for in assessing each student's performance on speaking and listening and writing activities are provided in the Answer Key section of the *Teacher's Resources*. It is useful to give students the criteria ahead of time so that everyone knows exactly what is expected of them and how the assignment will be assessed. This straightforward method helps students reflect on their preferences, explore their alternatives, organize their learning experiences, and take responsibility for their learning. It also broadens and energizes your teaching style. Reproducible rubrics and checklists for student self-assessment and peer assessment are also provided in the Answer Key section of the *Teacher's Resources*.

Promoting Comprehension Through Guided Reading Lessons

By Josephine Gemake, Ph.D.

There are many ways that students can be guided in their reading of stories, plays, essays, poems, and informational texts. Teachers' choices of methods and activities should factor in students' interests and abilities and the difficulty levels of the texts that they will read and interpret.

The scene is common in today's schools—teachers wondering how to make literature meaningful for students. Of course, there are no absolute answers. The Globe Fearon Literature program, however, offers flexible lesson formats that have been developed with today's students and teachers in mind.

The selections in the program have been carefully chosen to expose students to exemplary pieces of classic and contemporary literature. Each selection is preceded by a concise explanation of a literary element, such as tone, theme, character, setting, plot, and so on.

Reading comprehension is a key element of the Globe Fearon Literature program. A Reading Focus feature in every selection helps students become more skillful and strategic readers. Some of the comprehension techniques include making predictions, summarizing and paraphrasing texts, drawing conclusions, and identifying author's purpose.

Information about unfamiliar and difficult words is provided throughout the program. In this way, students can learn the meanings and pronunciations of words at the most relevant time—while they read.

Follow-up questions and writing activities have been designed to deepen students' understanding of the literary work they have read. Students are encouraged to discuss universal themes and how they relate to their own lives.

The Teaching Plan and point-of-use annotations in the Teacher's Edition provide activities and discussion opportunities before, during, and after reading. A description of each section of the Teaching Plan follows.

INTRODUCE

The Motivation activity and the Purpose-Setting Question help teachers guide students to activate prior knowledge and to make connections to real life. These brief activities prompt students to compare and contrast, predict, evaluate, and discuss concepts relevant to the selection they are about to read.

Teachers may also facilitate the development of new ideas by incorporating the following techniques into this section of the lesson:

- **Graphic Organizers** The use of graphic organizers—diagrams that illustrate connections among ideas—helps students to organize their thinking and to relate ideas. These organizers may be webs, maps, timelines, outlines, or idea clusters. Graphic organizers visually display associations and properties of topics. They are also used in vocabulary development to display word relationships.

- **Anticipation or Prediction Guides** To create these guides, a teacher writes statements about selections to be read on a chalkboard or reproducible. Students respond to these statements with predictions about what they think will happen. Statements are written so that thinking is stimulated at the literal, interpretive, and applied levels.
- During prereading time, strategies necessary for reading and interpreting selections are taught. Teacher modeling through "think alouds" is an important part of the procedure in skill development lessons. Think alouds enable students to watch how a teacher uses the selection objectives being taught to gain meaning from the text.

READ

In this section of the Teaching Plan, teachers are given ideas to support two key elements in the Student Edition: the Learn About feature and the Reading Focus feature. Literary skills include analysis of traditional elements of literature, such as plot, theme, character, and setting; and of literary techniques such as figurative language, foreshadowing, and flashback. Reading Focus features highlight key comprehension strategies, such as recognizing an author's purpose, identifying main idea and supporting details, summarizing and paraphrasing, and drawing conclusions.

Sidenote annotations throughout each selection provide further support for these lesson elements, as well as for critical thinking and discussion.

Teachers can also guide silent-reading comprehension using the following techniques:

- Have students read silently to find answers to questions posed by the teacher.
- Ask students to pose their own questions about events and ideas in the text and to read to find the answers.
- Have students predict, or form hypotheses, about ideas and events that will occur, and have them read to confirm or modify their predictions.

CLOSE

After reading, students complete activities in the Review the Selection section. These activities reinforce and extend ideas developed during lessons. Skills necessary for literary interpretation and appreciation are practiced, and mastery of these skills is evaluated. Vocabulary is recalled and reviewed. Reading skills and literary skills that were introduced at the beginning of a selection are reviewed and reinforced through writing. Students are also encouraged to write personal responses to each selection and to use process writing to complete an assignment.

There are many ways that students can be guided in their reading of stories, plays, essays, poems and informational texts. Teachers' choices of methods and activities should factor in students' interests and abilities and the difficulty level of the texts that they will read and interpret. The techniques described in this article will help students to develop comprehension skills and have the added advantage of being easily adapted in existing curriculum structures.

Successful Experiences in Literature for Students with Limited English Proficiency (LEP)

By Alfed Schifini, Ph.D.
Revised by Dr. Virginia Bryg

All students, including those whose primary language is one other than English, should have access to challenging material and literature. Yet not all students bring the same world knowledge and language skills to school.

Rapid demographic changes in the United States have had a direct impact on public schools. Every year, an increased number of students come to school with a primary language other than English. Students with limited English proficiency (LEP) often lack the language skills needed to benefit from instruction geared for English proficient speakers.

All students, including those whose primary language is one other than English, should have access to challenging material and literature. Yet not all students bring the same level of literacy to school. Some LEP students may never have been formally educated in their homelands. Others may have had a rich educational experience and have achieved a high level of literacy in their native language. Finally, teachers may also encounter native speakers of English who demonstrate deficiencies in literacy.

EDUCATIONAL APPROACHES

English as a Second Language

In recent years, students in U.S. schools who are totally non-English proficient have been able to gain immediate access to literature and basic subject matter through instruction in their native languages while they learn the English language. All LEP students should be provided with a rigorous program of English as a Second Language (ESL). As students' proficiency in English increases, the dependency on primary language instruction decreases. A strong ESL program provides students with the necessary foundation in English and ensures a smooth transition to instruction taught in a mainstream context.

ESL and Content Area Instruction

In addition to beginning-level ESL courses geared toward functional fluency, other ESL classes that incorporate content material, such as math, science, and social studies, have been designed for intermediate ESL speakers. These content-area ESL courses teach the terminology and key requisite concepts needed to provide a broader linguistic and experiential base for second-language learners.

Recent advances in language acquisition theory have made it clear that language is acquired by receiving meaningful input in a low-anxiety environment.

Language is more effectively learned when conscious language learning is not the focus of the lessons. It follows, therefore, that if subject matter can be made comprehensible through a variety of means, such as by demonstrations, visual aids, hands-on material and manipulation of the content, students' language development will be expanded, and requisite subject matter concepts will be acquired.

GLOBE FEARON LITERATURE PROGRAM

The Globe Fearon Literature program provides a sound approach to integrating language development and literature study. It enables students to successfully engage in experiences with literature that are appropriate to their evolving language and literacy levels. The subject matter presented in this language-sensitive fashion not only provides increased familiarity with masterworks of literature, but helps to develop the language skills necessary for academic achievement.

Globe Fearon Literature integrates language and content instruction using a variety of literary selections. Instructional strategies are designed to build on students' prior knowledge of literature. Brainstorming activities enable students to capture the broad meaning of selections before studying details. Vocabulary is acquired through interactive activities that are contextual in nature. Learning strategies such as organizing and summarizing, and a wide range of questioning techniques are included to help prepare students to meet the challenge of cognitively demanding subject matter.

SUGGESTED STRATEGIES

Teachers may consider the following strategies when working with LEP students:

- Simplify the language by using a slow but natural rate of speech, by enunciating clearly, by defining idiomatic expressions and multiple meanings before reading, and by limiting the teaching of vocabulary to those words that are key to the comprehension of the passage to be read.
- Use context clues as often as possible. Context clues give meaning to oral language as well as to written language. Common context clues include paralinguistic clues, such as gestures, facial expressions, and acting out meanings; props such as graphs, charts, real objects, bulletin board displays, maps, and timelines; and visual and word associations. Prereading discussions of visuals and other features in the text also aid in student comprehension.
- Check understanding frequently by asking for clarification and expansion of student statements. Use a variety of oral questions that are commensurate with the evolving language proficiency of the students. Provide opportunities for one-on-one interaction between students and between the teacher and students.

- Tap and focus students' prior background knowledge of the theme to be presented in the text by asking open-ended questions, such as: "Have you ever had this experience or been in this situation?" or "How would you feel if ______ happened to you?" Use real objects or visuals to stimulate prereading discussion and provide an opportunity for students to share what they already know about the topic to be read. Allow students to respond in their primary languages, if necessary, while sharing their experiences.
- Create student-centered activities by using different grouping strategies that allow students to try out their newly acquired English skills in a safe environment. By interacting with their peers, students must rephrase their thoughts and correct their own errors so that others can understand them. Pairing LEP students with English proficient students is especially effective.
- Keep in mind that language development is accelerated when students are engaged in activities that enable them to experience success. Direct error correction, especially in the initial stages of acquiring a new language, should be held to a minimum. In cognitively demanding situations, emphasis should be on what is said, rather than on form.

Block Scheduling

By Robert Wandberg, Ph.D.

Under the block scheduling format, many teachers report increased student success by using assignments and tasks that take the students deeper into the content.

DEFINING BLOCK SCHEDULING

Many literature and language arts classrooms are moving toward block scheduling as a means of delivering instruction to students. Block scheduling is frequently referred to as a 4-period schedule, a 4 X 4 schedule, or an extended-period schedule. The common threads of block scheduling are single classes that run 70 to 100 minutes rather than the more traditional classes of 45 to 55 minutes.

Block schedules offer several possible varieties. The basic format is four classes per day per term. A student in this schedule typically takes 16 classes (4 classes X 4 terms) in one school year. However, some of these classes may run for two or more terms while others may run only one term. Therefore, in reality, a student may only have 8 to 10 different classes per school year.

Some school schedules combine block and traditional schedules, where some classes, such as chemistry for example, may run for 40 minutes and other classes, such as art, for 80 minutes. Another format of the block schedule is that in which the extended length classes meet every other day. This is often called an A/B schedule. A student in the A/B schedule typically takes six, seven, or eight classes per term.

About one-third of secondary schools in United States are currently operating under some form of a block schedule.

POTENTIAL BENEFITS OF BLOCK SCHEDULING

Why do schools choose a block schedule? There are several reasons:

- to reduce the number of classes a student has during one term
- to decrease the number of classes and students a teacher has during one term
- to increase the opportunities for students to be involved in enrichment or remedial classes
- to increase the opportunities for varied instructional strategies
- to decrease student absenteeism and failure rate
- to increase interdisciplinary, cooperative teaching, and team teaching opportunities
- to increase staff development and curriculum development opportunities

Research continues to assess and evaluate teaching and learning in block schedules. Students in many block schedule schools report more positive attitudes toward school than corresponding students in traditional 7-period schedules. Indicators for this judgment include the following perceptions among students:

- higher degree of student respect and spirit within their school
- better behavior and more positive relationships among students in school
- greater respect for teachers and more positive student-teacher relationships
- a greater feeling of personal safety in school
- an increased interest and engagement in classes
- an increased level of student involvement in classroom activities
- decreased student frustrations related to homework

Teachers in block schedule schools also report more favorable attitudes about their schedule than do teachers in traditional 7-period schools. Indicators for this judgment include a belief that the block schedule

- allows teachers to do their job more effectively
- allows teachers to know their students better
- allows teachers to work equally as hard but experience less stress
- facilitates student achievement
- improves student behavior
- provides a quality educational experience for students
- provides the opportunity for more teacher collaboration
- provides feelings of respect and support from colleagues and administrators
- provides teachers the opportunity to use varied, instructionally effective strategies

Under the block scheduling format, many teachers report increased student success by using assignments and tasks that take the students deeper into the content. These assignments and tasks, developed by the teachers, are typically more student-centered and more "robust" than the assignments and tasks that they had previously used. One of the more common reasons teachers report more student success under the block system is the fact that the block schedule gives them more time for monitoring, guiding, and providing feedback to the student.

DESIGNING LESSONS FOR A BLOCK SCHEDULE

Consider the successful model of an effective block schedule lesson design as shown on page TT42. Although there are justifiable reasons to deviate from the model from time to time, such as to invite special speakers to the class or to perform student assessments, the model is recommended as a foundation for block schedule lesson structure. Listed with each step in the lesson design is the percent of total class time devoted to those activities based on an 80-minute class period.

USING GLOBE FEARON LITERATURE IN A BLOCK SCHEDULE

Here are some types of activities from *Globe Fearon Literature* that can be integrated into the extended class period. Activities such as these can be found in the Teacher's Edition and the Teacher's Resources.

1. **Poetry Reading** Students take part in a mystery poetry reading. Each student writes a four-line poem about him or herself. Another student reads each one aloud to the class, and the class guesses who wrote it.

2. **Literary Seminar** Students take part in a literary seminar. The class discusses the selections in the unit. Then students determine why the selections were placed in this unit, and compare and contrast them.

3. **Writing Screenplays** Students work in cooperative groups. Students play the role of screenwriters. Each group develops one of the unit selections into an exciting screenplay for a movie. The group then pitches its idea to the executive producers (a selected group of students or the entire class). The producers then vote on one or more screenplays to create and perform.

BLOCK SCHEDULE LESSON DESIGN

Percentage of total class time is based on an 80-minute block.

Focus and warm-up

Total time: 4–12 minutes **Teacher role:** Leader

5–15%

Focus students' attention on the lesson outcomes and learning expectations; review previous lesson(s); announcements and class management tasks.

Direct teaching

Total time: 2–20 minutes **Teacher role:** Leader

5–25%

Provide students with information, insights, and guidance necessary for successful achievement of the lesson outcomes. Methods include multi-media demonstrations, lectures, and guest speakers.

Student performance

Total time: 28–36 minutes **Teacher role:** Coach/facilitator

35–45%

Students are actively involved in learning, decision making, and creating personal meaning to the lesson outcome. Activities include student presentations, research, creations, advocacy, inventions, inquiry, analysis, assessment, evaluation, and skill development.

Closure

Total time: 4–12 minutes **Teacher role:** Coach/facilitator

15–25%

Students gather/return materials, hand in classwork and previous homework assignments, receive homework assignments, ask clarifying questions, and publish/present their work.

Review

Total time: 12–20 minutes **Teacher role:** Coach/facilitator

5–15%

Students summarize class activity and generate plans for subsequent classes, considering timelines, due dates, and future process steps. Activities include journaling, group writing, active questioning, pairing / sharing, summarizing, and planning.

ROBUST LEARNING TASK

Block schedules lend themselves to robust learning tasks. A robust learning task is a student project (assignment) that requires several classes to complete and often requires multiple integrated skills such decision-making, problem solving, inquiry, self-direction, and communication.

As teachers, we typically have and use established criteria for student performance. Similarly, we should have and use established criteria for the development and creation of robust learning tasks. Nine criteria are suggested. Tasks should be:

Authentic The task simulates a way information is handled in the world outside of school.

Teachers should ask: What do people outside of school do with this information?

Unbiased All students, regardless of culture, gender, or learning style, have an opportunity to achieve; the task does not rely on specialized knowledge or narrow interests.

Teachers should ask: Does every student have an opportunity to be successful doing this task?

Constructivist Students are actively involved in creating meaning for their learning by making decisions about the work.

Teachers should ask: Are my students doing the work and making decisions that determine the meaning for their learning?

Developmental The task is appropriate to the intellectual, physical, and psychological maturity of the students.

Teachers should ask: Is this work at the appropriate level for my students?

Embedded The task is an integral part of regular classroom work, not an add-on.

Teachers should ask: Does this task blend into my normal classroom activities?

Focused The task stays on target to assess the process/concept and topic.

Teachers should ask: Are my students demonstrating the learning called for in the standards and expectations of the course?

Generalizable The specific skills and knowledge required for the task represent the larger learning required for the content standard.

Teachers should ask: If my students do this robust task, will I be reasonably sure they have the knowledge and skills called for in the standards and expectations of the course?

High in Rigor The task represents a high learning expectation.

Teachers should ask: Does the robust task represent high expectations for student learning?

Interesting The task is engaging work for students.

Teachers should ask: Will my students be interested in doing this robust task?

How do your student assignments measure up? Consider adopting some of the strategies and criteria described here to add rigor and robustness to future assignments, especially in a block-scheduling setting. Supply students with the criteria ahead of time to ensure their awareness of the tasks on which they will be assessed.

CRITERIA FOR EVALUATING LITERATURE TEXTBOOKS

Choosing the appropriate literature textbook is a vital part of building a strong language arts program. The textbook must meet the needs of both students and teachers in addition to fulfilling the requirements of local and state curriculum guidelines. The purpose of the following survey is to assist teachers in systematically evaluating the literature materials under consideration. Study each point carefully, and then rank the various textbooks using a rating scale of 0 to 5. You may reproduce this form as needed.

RATING SCALE

5 = EXCELLENT
4 = GOOD
3 = FAIR
2 = POOR
1 = UNSATISFACTORY
0 = NOT APPLICABLE

TEXTBOOK PUBLISHER

A ____________________
B ____________________
C ____________________

STUDENT TEXT	A	B	C
1. Quality of selections			
2. Special study tips for students at the beginning of the book			
3. Balance of traditional and contemporary selections			
4. Appropriate cultural diversity and male/female representation			
5. Variety and balance of genre (fiction, poetry, nonfiction, and drama)			
6. Representation of major types of poetry			
7. Representation of major types of nonfiction			
8. Model lessons that demonstrate reading strategies			
BEFORE EVERY SELECTION			
1. Motivation for reading and purpose-setting questions			
2. Writing activity			
3. Literary skill instruction			
4. Reading skill instruction			
5. Motivating visuals			
DURING EVERY SELECTION			
1. Open layout with easy-to-read text			
2. Visuals that relate to the selection and increase comprehension			
3. Vocabulary definition			
AFTER EVERY SELECTION			
1. Open-ended questions that allow students to respond to literature			
2. Recall, inference, and application questions about the selection			
3. Writing about the selection			
4. Literary skill reinforcement			
5. Reading skill reinforcement			
6. Vocabulary reinforcement			

CONTINUED

STUDENT TEXT (CONTINUED)	A	B	C
UNIT DEVELOPMENT (INTRODUCTION AND CLOSURE ACTIVITIES)			
1. Fine Art that reflects the unit theme or literary period			
2. Opening quote or motivating introduction			
3. Appropriate historical introductions and timelines for chronologically-organized units			
4. Introduction to the unit theme for thematically-organized units			
5. Explicit instruction on effective studying and test preparation			
6. Writing process lesson			
7. Speaking and listening activities			
8. Critical-thinking activities			
9. Support for grammar, usage, and mechanics			
10. Support for test taking			

TEACHER'S EDITION	A	B	C
1. Teaching suggestions at point of use			
2. Flexible teaching opportunities			
3. Professional development articles about key trends and issues in education			
4. Suggestions for activities at various reading levels			
5. Suggestions for cooperative learning activities			
6. Selection synopses and activities			
7. Student motivation activities			
8. Block scheduling strategies			
9. Critical thinking activities			
10. Critical viewing questions and background notes about Fine Art			
11. Background information about authors			
12. ESL-appropriate activities			
13. Enrichment opportunities			
14. Comprehension checks within the selection			
15. Quizzes for each selection			
16. Answers to all review questions in Student Edition			
17. Suggestions for using technology			
18. Related materials listings			

PROGRAM COMPONENTS	A	B	C
1. Vocabulary skills reinforcement worksheets			
2. Literary skills reinforcement worksheets			
3. Reading comprehension skills reinforcement worksheets			
4. Grammar, usage, and mechanics reinforcement worksheets			
5. Critical thinking activities			
6. Writing process activities			
7. Speaking and listening activities			
8. Evaluation rubrics for alternative assessments			
9. Reading in the content areas activities			
10. Selection tests			
11. Unit tests			
12. Answer keys for all worksheets and activities Technology Components			
TECHNOLOGY COMPONENTS			
1. Answer keys to all print components			
2. Tests in a modifiable format			
3. Reinforcement and extension activities			
4. Reinforcement, writing, speaking and listening, and critical thinking worksheets			

OTHER CRITERIA	A	B	C
1. Ease of use			
2. Literature is accessible to all students			
3. Moves students from literal reading to higher level reading in a step-by-step fashion			

ADDITIONAL COMMENTS

THESE OTHER FINE GLOBE FEARON PROGRAMS HELP TEACHERS MEET THE NEEDS OF ALL STUDENTS

Globe Fearon has a strong commitment to providing high-quality reading and literature materials that motivate students. The materials on the following pages may be used as additional resources in your classroom. Visit our website,www.globefearon.com, for more information about these and other Globe Fearon products.

An array of additional Globe Fearon materials may help you to:

- Motivate students and challenge them to accelerate their learning
- Extend independent reading opportunities by providing high-interest literature at accessible reading levels
- Reinforce reading and writing skills

Enrich Your Students' Reading Experiences with High-interest Paperback Anthologies

No two students are alike in their interests or ability levels. Finding high-interest, high-quality reading materials at the appropriate reading level for each student can be a challenge.

The *Globe Reader's Collection* is a set of six anthologies of high-interest fiction, nonfiction, and drama at controlled reading levels. Providing a wide variety of themes, genres, and topics—from mythology to science fiction—this collection can extend your classroom library and enrich your students' reading experiences.

Inspire Your Students' Creativity and Critical Reading Skills

The *Stories and Plays Without Endings* series offers students the opportunity to construct appropriate endings to compelling works of fiction and drama. These books help reinforce critical reading, creative writing, and literary skills, as well as providing ideas for a variety of classroom activities, including independent writing, cooperative learning, Reader's Theater, and group discussion.

Globe Fearon Makes Classic Literature Accessible to Every Student

Literary masterpieces have influenced and inspired generations for decades. By offering three levels of many popular classics, Globe Fearon supports your efforts to make the classics available to all of your students.

■ PACEMAKER CLASSICS

For your students that are reading significantly below grade level, the *Pacemaker Classics* offer classics that have been skillfully adapted to a reading level of 3-4. These adaptations maintain the integrity and intent of the original works. *Pacemaker Classics* also contain an audio component that allows students to listen and read confidently. Comprehension is enhanced through the use of the Study Guide, which provides background information about the time periods, authors, plots, and characters, as well as teaching ideas.

■ GLOBE ADAPTED CLASSICS

Many of your students may be reading slightly below grade level. For these students Globe Fearon offers *Globe Adapted Classics*. These titles have been only slightly abridged to help students comprehend and enjoy classic pieces of literature. Reading reviews and footnotes aid in comprehension. The reading level of *Adapted Classics* varies from 5–8.

■ MASTERWORKS COLLECTION

To extend your literature instruction for students who read on level, Globe Fearon offers the *Masterworks Collection*. These softcover texts allow you to provide your students with original works for independent reading. A *Teacher's Resource Manual* offers additional teaching strategies and discussion questions to enhance comprehension.

Teach Classic Literature to Every Student in Your Class

The Pacemaker Classics and Adapted Classics series feature titles that appeal to the different interests and abilities of your students.

There are a number of ways to motivate your students to read independently and participate in cooperative group activities using these books. Here are a few suggestions.

■ SHAKESPEAREAN PLAYS

Give students the opportunity to explore the timeless themes of Shakespeare's most widely read plays.

Pacemaker Classics: Hamlet, Julius Caesar, Macbeth, A Midsummer Night's Dream, and Romeo and Juliet

Adapted Classics: Hamlet, Julius Caesar, Macbeth, Othello, and Romeo and Juliet

■ CLASSIC PLAYS

Engage students in a drama genre study, have them conduct Reader's Theater, or challenge them to write a movie screen-play based on these classic plays.

Pacemaker Classics: Antigone, Cyrano de Bergerac, A Doll's House

Adapted Classics: A Raisin in the Sun, A Doll's House, The Importance of Being Earnest (new)

■ A WORLD OF ADVENTURE

Invite students to work in small groups or pairs to create chain of events charts, to rewrite the endings, or to dramatize important scenes from these classic adventure tales.

PACEMAKER CLASSICS: The Adventures of Huckleberry Finn, The Adventures of Tom Sawyer, The Call of the Wild, The Deerslayer, Gulliver's Travels, The Last of the Mohicans, Moby Dick, Robinson Crusoe, The Sea-Wolf, 20,000 Leagues Under the Sea, The Three Musketeers, Treasure Island, Two Years Before the Mast

ADAPTED CLASSICS: The Adventures of Huckleberry Finn, The Adventures of Tom Sawyer, The Call of the Wild, Gulliver's Travels, Moby Dick, 20,000 Leagues Under the Sea, Treasure Island

■ MYSTERIOUS TALES

Mysteries provide opportunities to sharpen reasoning skills, to make and revise predictions, to rewrite story endings, and to write character sketches.

PACEMAKER CLASSICS: The Adventures of Sherlock Holmes, Dracula, Dr. Jekyll and Mr. Hyde, Tales of Edgar Allan Poe, Frankenstein, The Hound of the Baskervilles, The House of the Seven Gables, O. Henry, The Phantom of the Opera, The Turn of the Screw

ADAPTED CLASSICS: The Adventures of Sherlock Holmes, Tales of Edgar Allan Poe, Frankenstein, O. Henry, The Phantom of the Opera

GLOBE FEARON CLASSICS: Accessible Literature for All Students

THE ADVENTURES OF HUCKLEBERRY FINN
- Pacemaker Classic Reading Level 3-4 Book, Audiocassette, Study Guide
- Adapted Classic Reading Level 5-6 Book, TRM*
- Masterworks (Unabridged) Book, TRM*

THE ADVENTURES OF SHERLOCK HOLMES
- Pacemaker Classic Reading Level 3-4 Book, Study Guide
- Adapted Classic Reading Level 6-7 Book, TRM*

THE ADVENTURES OF TOM SAWYER
- Pacemaker Classic Reading Level 3-4 Book, Audiocassette, Study Guide
- Adapted Classic Reading Level 6-7 Book, TRM*

ALL QUIET ON THE WESTERN FRONT
- Pacemaker Classic Reading Level 3-4 Book, Audiocassette, Study Guide
- Adapted Classic Reading Level 5-6 Book, TRM*

ANNE FRANK: THE DIARY OF A YOUNG GIRL
- Pacemaker Classic Reading Level 3-4 Book, Audiocassette, Study Guide
- Adapted Classic Reading Level 6 Book, TRM*

ANTIGONE
- Pacemaker Classic Reading Level 3-4 Book, Audiocassette, Study Guide

AROUND THE WORLD IN 80 DAYS
- Pacemaker Classic Reading Level 3-4 Book, CD-ROM, Study Guide
- Adapted Classic Reading Level 5-6 Book, TRM*

BEOWULF
- Adapted Classic Reading Level 7-8 Book, TRM*

THE CALL OF THE WILD
- Pacemaker Classic Reading Level 3-4 Book, Audiocassette, Study Guide
- Adapted Classic Reading Level 6-7 Book, TRM*

THE CANTERBURY TALES
- Pacemaker Classic Reading Level 3-4 Book, Study Guide
- Adapted Classic Reading Level 4-5 Book, TRM*

A CHRISTMAS CAROL
- Pacemaker Classic Reading Level 3-4 Book, Audiocassette, Study Guide
- Adapted Classic Reading Level 7-8 Book, TRM*

CRIME AND PUNISHMENT
- Pacemaker Classic Reading Level 3-4 Book, Audiocassette, Study Guide

CYRANO DE BERGERAC
- Pacemaker Classic Reading Level 3-4 Book, Audiocassette, Study Guide

DAVID COPPERFIELD
- Pacemaker Classic Reading Level 3-4 Book, Audiocassette, Study Guide

THE DEERSLAYER
- Pacemaker Classic Reading Level 3-4 Book, Audiocassette, Study Guide

A DOLL'S HOUSE
- Pacemaker Classic Reading Level 3-4 Book, Audiocassette, Study Guide
- Adapted Classic Reading Level 5-6 Book, TRM*

DR. JEKYLL AND MR. HYDE
- Pacemaker Classic Reading Level 3-4 Book, Audiocassette, Study Guide

DRACULA
- Pacemaker Classic Reading Level 3-4 Book, Audiocassette, Study Guide

ETHAN FROME
- Pacemaker Classic Reading Level 3-4 Book, Audiocassette, Study Guide
- Adapted Classic Reading Level 4-5 Book, TRM*

FRANKENSTEIN
- Pacemaker Classic Reading Level 3-4 Book, Audiocassette, Study Guide
- Adapted Classic Reading Level 4-5 Book, TRM*

THE GOOD EARTH
- Pacemaker Classic Reading Level 3-4 Book, Audiocassette, Study Guide

THE GRAPES OF WRATH
- Pacemaker Classic Reading Level 3-4 Book, Audiocassette, Study Guide
- Adapted Classic Reading Level 5-6 Book, TRM*

GREAT EXPECTATIONS
- Pacemaker Classic Reading Level 3-4 Book, Audiocassette, Study Guide
- Adapted Classic Reading Level 6-7 Book, TRM*

GULLIVER'S TRAVELS
- Pacemaker Classic Reading Level 3-4 Book, Audiocassette, Study Guide
- Adapted Classic Reading Level 5-6 Book, TRM*

HAMLET
- Pacemaker Classic Reading Level 3-4 Book, Audiocassette, Study Guide
- Adapted Classic Reading Level 5-6 Book, TRM*
- Masterworks (Unabridged) Book, TRM*

HEART OF DARKNESS
- Pacemaker Classic Reading Level 3-4 Book, Audiocassette, Study Guide
- Adapted Classic Reading Level 5-6 Book, TRM*

THE HOUND OF THE BASKERVILLES
- Pacemaker Classic Reading Level 3-4 Book, Audiocassette, Study Guide

THE HOUSE OF THE SEVEN GABLES
- Pacemaker Classic Reading Level 3-4 Book, Audiocassette, Study Guide

THE HUNCHBACK OF NOTRE DAME
- Pacemaker Classic Reading Level 3-4 Book, Audiocassette, Study Guide

THE IMPORTANCE OF BEING EARNEST
- Pacemaker Classic Reading Level 3-4 Book, CD-ROM, Study Guide
- Adapted Classic Reading Level 4-5 Book, TRM*

JANE EYRE
- Pacemaker Classic Reading Level 3-4 Book, Audiocassette, Study Guide
- Adapted Classic Reading Level 4-5 Book, TRM*

JULIUS CAESAR
- Pacemaker Classic Reading Level 3-4 Book, Audiocassette, Study Guide
- Adapted Classic Reading Level 5-6 Book, TRM*
- Masterworks (Unabridged) Book, TRM*

THE JUNGLE (SINCLAIR)
- Pacemaker Classic Reading Level 3-4 Book, Audiocassette, Study Guide
- Adapted Classic Reading Level 7-8 Book, TRM*

THE JUNGLE BOOK (KIPLING)
- Pacemaker Classic Reading Level 3-4 Book, Audiocassette, Study Guide

LAST OF THE MOHICANS
- Pacemaker Classic Reading Level 3-4 Book, Audiocassette, Study Guide

*Teacher's Resource Manual

LES MISÉRABLES
- Adapted Classic Reading Level 7-8
Book, TRM*

LITTLE WOMEN
- Pacemaker Classic Reading Level 3-4
Book, Study Guide
- Adapted Classic Reading Level 5-6
Book, TRM*

LORD JIM
- Pacemaker Classic Reading Level 3-4
Book, CD–ROM, Study Guide
- Adapted Classic Reading Level 5-6
Book, TRM*

MACBETH
- Pacemaker Classic Reading Level 3-4
Book, Audiocassette, Study Guide
- Adapted Classic Reading Level 5-6
Book, TRM*
- Masterworks (Unabridged)
Book, TRM*

THE MAYOR OF CASTERBRIDGE
- Pacemaker Classic Reading Level 3-4
Book, Audiocassette, Study Guide

A MIDSUMMER NIGHT'S DREAM
- Pacemaker Classic Reading Level 3-4
Book, Audiocassette, Study Guide

MOBY DICK
- Pacemaker Classic Reading Level 3-4
Book, Audiocassette, Study Guide
- Adapted Classic Reading Level 5-6
Book, TRM*

THE MOONSTONE
- Pacemaker Classic Reading Level 3-4
Book, Audiocassette, Study Guide

MY ANTONIA
- Adapted Classic Reading Level 7-8
Book, TRM*

NARRATIVE OF THE LIFE OF FREDERICK DOUGLASS
- Pacemaker Classic Reading Level 3-4
Book, Audiocassette, Study Guide
- Adapted Classic Reading Level 5-6
Book, TRM*

O. HENRY
- Pacemaker Classic for Reading Level 3-4
Book, Study Guide
- Adapted Classic for Reading Level 7-8
Book, TRM*

O PIONEERS!
- Pacemaker Classic Reading Level 3-4
Book, Audiocassette, Study Guide

THE ODYSSEY
- Pacemaker Classic Reading Level 3-4
Book, Study Guide
- Adapted Classic Reading Level 5-6
Book, TRM*

OLIVER TWIST
- Pacemaker Classic Reading Level 3-4
Book, Audiocassette, Study Guide
- Adapted Classic Reading Level 5-6
Book, TRM*

OTHELLO
- Adapted Classic Reading Level 5-6
Book, TRM*

THE PHANTOM OF THE OPERA
- Pacemaker Classic Reading Level 3-4
Book, Audiocassette, Study Guide
- Adapted Classic Reading Level 7-8
Book, TRM*

PRIDE AND PREJUDICE
- Pacemaker Classic Reading Level 3-4
Book
- Adapted Classic Reading Level 7-8
Book, TRM*

THE PRINCE AND THE PAUPER
- Pacemaker Classic Reading Level 3-4
Book, Audiocassette, Study Guide

A RAISIN IN THE SUN
- Adapted Classic Reading Level 7-8
Book, TRM*

THE RED BADGE OF COURAGE
- Pacemaker Classic Reading Level 3-4
Book, Audiocassette, Study Guide
- Adapted Classic Reading Level 7-8
Book, TRM*
- Masterworks (Unabridged)
Book, TRM*

ROBINSON CRUSOE
- Pacemaker Classic Reading Level 3-4
Book, Audiocassette, Study Guide

ROMEO AND JULIET
- Pacemaker Classic Reading Level 3-4
Book, Audiocassette, Study Guide
- Adapted Classic Reading Level 5-6
Book, TRM*
- Masterworks (Unabridged)
Book, TRM*

THE SCARLETT LETTER
- Pacemaker Classic Reading Level 3-4
Book, Audiocassette, Study Guide
- Adapted Classic Reading Level 7-8
Book, TRM*

THE SEA-WOLF
- Pacemaker Classic Reading Level 3-4
Book, Audiocassette, Study Guide

SILAS MARNER
- Pacemaker Classic Reading Level 3-4
Book, Study Guide
- Adapted Classic Reading Level 5-6
Book, TRM*

THE STORY OF MY LIFE: HELEN KELLER
- Pacemaker Classic Reading Level 3-4
Book, CD-ROM, Study Guide
- Adapted Classic Reading Level 4-5
Book, TRM*

TALES OF EDGAR ALLAN POE
- Pacemaker Classic Reading Level 3-4
Book, Audiocassette, Study Guide
- Adapted Classic Reading Level 4-5
Book, TRM*

A TALE OF TWO CITIES
- Pacemaker Classic Reading Level 3-4
Book, Audiocassette, Study Guide
- Adapted Classic Reading Level 5-6
Book, TRM*
- Masterworks (Unabridged)
Book, TRM*

THINGS FALL APART
- Adapted Classic Reading Level 7-8
Book, TRM*

THE THREE MUSKETEERS
- Pacemaker Classic Reading Level 3-4
Book, Audiocassette, Study Guide

THE TIME MACHINE
- Pacemaker Classic Reading Level 3-4
Book, Audiocassette, Study Guide

TREASURE ISLAND
- Pacemaker Classic Reading Level 3-4
Book, Audiocassette, Study Guide
- Adapted Classic Reading Level 5-6
Book, TRM*

THE TURN OF THE SCREW
- Pacemaker Classic Reading Level 3-4
Book, Audiocassette, Study Guide

20,000 LEAGUES UNDER THE SEA
- Pacemaker Classic Reading Level 3-4
Book, Audiocassette, Study Guide
- Adapted Classic Reading Level 4-5
Book, TRM*

TWO YEARS BEFORE THE MAST
- Pacemaker Classic Reading Level 3-4
Book, Audiocassette, Study Guide

UP FROM SLAVERY
- Pacemaker Classic Reading Level 3-4
Book, CD-ROM, Study Guide
- Adapted Classic Reading Level 4-5
Book, TRM*

THE WAR OF THE WORLDS
- Pacemaker Classic for Reading Level 3-4
Book, Audiocassette, Study Guide

WUTHERING HEIGHTS
- Pacemaker Classic Reading Level 3-4
Book, Audiocassette, Study Guide
- Masterworks (Unabridged)
Book, TRM*

Other Outstanding Globe Fearon Products Provide Additional Reading Skill Support

Developing strategies for reading and comprehending literature means helping students grow as readers.

To assist those students who need additional support in developing skills and strategies for comprehension, critical thinking, and test taking, Globe Fearon can offer a range of in-depth supplemental reading materials.

- **Reading in the Content Areas:** Strategies for Reading Informational Text in Science, Math and Social Studies
- **Reading for Proficiency:** Preparation for State and Standardized Reading Tests
- **Be A Better Reader:** Comprehension, Decoding, and Study Skills

For Students Who Need Additional Instruction, Globe Fearon Offers Writing Skill Support

Extending literature means encouraging students to respond to literature or to use literature as a model for their own writing.

For students who need additional support in developing skills for persuasive or expository writing, practicing process writing, and test taking, Globe Fearon can provide a range of additional materials.

- **Writer's Toolkit:** Interactive Software to Build Writing Skills
- **Writing Across the Curriculum:** Writing in Response to Literature

- **Success in Writing:** Applications of Process Writing
- **Writing for Proficiency:** Preparation for State and Standardized Writing Tests

GLOBE FEARON

LITERATURE

▪ *Silver Level* ▪

Upper Saddle River, New Jersey
www.globefearon.com

Program Reviewers

Kathy Babigian, Coordinator, Tioga Literacy Center, Fresno, California
Pat Bartholomew, M.A., Reading Specialist, Milton, Ohio
Jennifer Dilks-Mundt, English Teacher, Brant Rock, Massachusetts
Ann Fitzgerald, M.A., Education Director, Southshire Community School, North Bennington, Vermont
Pat Miller, M.A., Reading/English/Language Arts Supervisor, Prince Georges County Public Schools, Maryland
Artie P. Norton, English Teacher, Suffern, New York
Timothy Rasinski, Professor of Curriculum and Instruction, Kent State University, Kent, Ohio
Cynthia Saska, M.A., Professor of English, University of Texas, San Antonio, Texas
Margaret-Mary Sulentic, Ph.D., Assistant Professor of Literacy, Department of Curriculum and Instruction, University of Southern Mississippi, Hattiesburg, Mississippi
Dr. Helen W. Taylor, Director of Programs K-12 Curriculum and Instruction, Portsmouth City Public Schools, Virginia

Consultants

Dr. Virginia Bryg; Josephine Gemake, Ph.D.; Alfred Schifini, Ph.D.; Deborah Walker; Robert Wandberg, Ph.D.

Supervising Editor/Team Leader: Karen McCollum
Editors: Ayanna Taylor, Amy Greenberg, Theresa McCarthy
Editorial Developer: Pearson Education Development Group
Marketing Assistant: Kate Krimsky
Production Editor: Travis Bailey
Associate Production Editors: Amy Benefiel, Alia Lesser
Senior Designer: Angel Weyant
Manufacturing Buyer: Mark Cirillo
Cover and Interior Design/Production: Pearson Education Development Group
Photo Research: Pearson Education Development Group

About the Cover

3rd and Rhode Island, LeDetroit Park, Hilda Wilkinson Brown. From the Hilda Wilkinson Brown Collection. Courtesy of Lillian Thomas Burwell. This oil painting shows a simple scene of a street in Detroit. This is a reflection of Brown's ideals. She was described as a "traditional woman, an idealist in manner and mores of the then womanhood." How is Brown's painting a representation of traditional American values?

ISBN 0-130-23578-4

Printed in the United States of America
1 2 3 4 5 6 7 8 9 10 04 03 02 01 00

1-800-848-9500
www.globefearon.com

Preview

UNIT 1 Voices of Colonial America

UNIT 2 Writers in a Growing Nation

UNIT 3 New England Speaks

UNIT 4 A Nation Expresses Itself

UNIT 5 *The Modern View*

UNIT 6 *The Contemporary Perspective*

References

How to Use This Book

Welcome to *Globe Fearon Literature*. As you read this textbook, you will learn about many new worlds. By reading literature you can experience the past and the future, and you can learn about people—how they feel and how they think.

To get the most out of this book, you will need to become an active reader. Active readers think about reading materials before they begin, during, and after they read.

TIPS FOR IMPROVING YOUR READING

Before You Read

- Think about the title of the selection. What does it tell you about the topic? What do you already know about the topic?
- Determine the genre of the selection. For example—if the selection is a poem, ask yourself, "How will this be different from reading an essay or short story?"
- Set a purpose for reading. What do you think you will learn by reading this selection?

As You Read

- Predict what you think will happen next. Then pause occasionally and ask yourself if your predictions were correct.
- Form questions about what you are reading. For example, ask yourself, "What idea is the author trying to convey?"
- When you encounter a word you are unfamiliar with, use the help that Globe Fearon Literature gives you. Difficult words are defined at the bottom of the page they appear on.

After You Read

Consider the following questions:

- Did the selection end the way you anticipated?
- What did you learn from reading this selection?
- How does this selection relate to others you have read?

THE BOOK IS ORGANIZED TO HELP YOU

Your literature book has been organized into units. Each unit is introduced with a piece of fine art and a quote. Look at these pages. What do you think this unit will be about?

The next two pages of the unit give you a preview of what to expect. These two pages will help you set the stage for reading and understanding the selections. You may want to refer back to these pages as you read through the unit.

The "Focus On" feature gives you some tips to help you understand specific genres of literature, such as fiction or poetry You will notice that each Model selection has blue notes in the margin. These are study hints to help you read actively. The notes relate back to the "Focus On" feature. The notes will help you identify key elements of the genre. Later, you can look for similar elements in other selections as you read independently.

Before each selection, you will be introduced to a reading skill, a literary skill, and a writing activity. The reading skill will help you understand what you are reading. The literary skill will call your attention to elements of literature. The writing activity will help you relate the literature to your own life.

There are review questions at the end of each selection. These questions help you think about what you have just read. They will also help you relate this selection to others that you may have read.

Globe Fearon Literature was created for you. Reading literature can be one of the most rewarding experiences you can ever have. There are new worlds to explore and exciting people to meet. It's all here. So, let's begin. . .

UNIT ACTIVITY

A Continuing Unit Project: Creating a Colonial Newspaper

Arrange students into small groups. Remind the class of the important role newspapers played in the lives of the colonists. There was no television or radio. Newspapers were the primary source of information about current events. Remind them that, during Benjamin Franklin's lifetime alone, the number of newspapers published in America grew from two to twenty-five.

Explain that each group is going to print an edition of a colonial newspaper. The material being printed will focus on information contained in this unit.

First, each group should select a name for the newspaper. Guide students in choosing an appropriate name. Remind them that the colonists had recently won their independence. They had also established a new form of government. It is quite likely that the publishers would like the word *American* to be included in the name. In this way, the paper would appeal to the patriotic instincts of readers.

Have students suggest a number of names commonly applied to newspapers. *Times*, *Gazette*, *Reporter*, *Inquirer*, and *Bulletin* are several examples you can strive to elicit with leading questions. Have each group select a different name for its newspaper. If more than one group wants to use the same name, one fair way to resolve the problem is by giving preference to the group who first suggested that name.

Students are to imagine that the year is 1799. For the purposes of this project, a few minor liberties will be taken with historical dates. Students are to assume that Washington's farewell address and Abigail Adams' letter from the White House were written within a few days of each other. Because the two works were written within this shortened time span, both will be front page news in a single edition.

The outgoing President's remarks and the incoming First Lady's views will be the stories covered. A reporter will write a news story covering Washington's address. Suggest students review articles covering current or recent presidential speeches. The groups should try to reproduce the style and organization of the modern article.

Another reporter will interview the new First Lady, Mrs. Adams. Among the items of interest to readers will be her trip from Massachusetts, her views on the new presidential residence, and her impressions of Federal City (Washington, DC).

Advise students that questions and answers can be developed from the selection. Remind them that some of Mrs. Adams' remarks were confidential, intended only for the ears of her daughter. The new First Lady, being diplomatically sensitive to the feelings of the people and her responsibilities, would not make public comments that might seem insulting or negative.

Students are also to assume that Davy Crockett is an incoming first term congressman from the frontier. One reporter will write a short human interest story about Crockett, who must have seemed outrageous and colorful to the Easterners encountering him for the first time. The story should include some direct quotes from the congressman. These can be drawn from the folk tale and the ancillary information you have given them.

Another reporter will interview Crèvecoeur, who is visiting the capital for the first time. The New York farmer and writer will express some of his views on the meaning of being American. Questions and responses can be drawn from Crèvecoeur's essay.

Patrick Henry actually died June 6, 1799. For purposes of this assignment, students are to assume that Henry's death was so recent that it is the subject of an editorial. The editor will recall Henry's famous speech in the Virginia Convention 24 years earlier. The editor will explain, for the benefit of younger readers, the effect Henry's words had in rallying public opinion in support of the revolution. Since this is an editorial, the writer is free to express personal opinions and interpretations of historical events.

Benjamin Franklin died in 1790. As the tenth anniversary of his death approaches, a commemorative edition of his writings is about to be published. It will include the autobiographical *Poor Richard's Almanack* and his shorter essays. A collection of Anne Bradstreet's poetry is also being published. These two writers will be the subjects of short book reviews appearing in the newspaper.

Lastly, the newspaper will contain a column by a reporter who has recently travelled among the Seneca tribes and wants to familiarize urban readers with the folklore of this Native American nation. This reporter will summarize for the readers a fascinating tale he heard concerning a woman chief, Godasiyo. The reporter will also explain how this work illustrates the literature and beliefs of the Seneca.

Step 1

Invite the school journalism, graphic arts, computer science, or art teacher to visit your class and discuss newspaper layouts. First, brief the teacher on the content of the proposed newspaper so that practical advice can be offered about the length and arrangement of the various articles, the use of headlines, and how many pages will be required for the paper. Allow time for students to develop proposed layouts, which the guest teacher can review, offering suggestions as needed.

Step 2

Next, take the class to the school library. Tell them to use books, encyclopedias, and the Internet to research biographical information about each of the writers and their works. They are to use this information as background in the various articles. For example, they might want to include the fact that, after his term in office, Washington retired to his farm at Mount Vernon. They might want to tell their readers how long Abigail and John Adams had been married and mention her activities while he was away from home during the Revolutionary years. They might want to include a map showing exactly where Tennessee, Crockett's home state is located. Remind them that many of the readers may not have had the benefit we today enjoy of formal instruction in geography. As a result, these readers may not have a firm understanding of where Tennessee is located.

If sufficient materials are not available at the school library, students should plan to visit the local public library as a group to do additional research. Before starting the research section of the project, you may want to devote one class period to a lesson on using the library. Explain that librarians are always willing to assist anyone having difficulty. Also be certain that students understand the difference between circulating and reference works. Understanding and planning for this difference can save valuable time when conducting research.

Closely supervise each group. Ensure that sufficient space is being allotted to each writer. Also ensure that the work is being equitably distributed among the group members and that every student is participating.

Step 3

Have students in each group write preliminary articles on paper or on a word processor. Have them use a "double-column" design to mimic actual newspapers. Distribute large-sized white poster board. Tell students to cut and arrange the articles according to the planned layout. Remind them to leave room for headlines. After arranging the articles on the poster board, they should edit as necessary so that the articles fit the format.

As students edit their articles, remind them that articles should follow the inverted pyramid style, or writing by order of importance. The article starts by answering six questions: it tells *who, what, where, whom, why*, and *how*. It then goes on to the most important detail, then the next most important detail and on down to the least important.

Collect the papers. After evaluation, display the papers around the room. You may also want to consider displaying them on a hall bulletin board or in the school library. Make arrangements beforehand with the appropriate school officials.

■ "To My Dear and Loving Husband"

by Anne Bradstreet (page 5)

SELECTION SYNOPSIS

This is an intimate love poem addressed to the poet's husband. The theme is that their love is more valuable than material possessions and the source of joy unrealized by others who have not shared such a relationship.

SELECTION ACTIVITY

Tell students to consider Bradstreet's poem as the message in a greeting card. They are going to create original art work for a front cover to accompany the verse.

Allow them to draw and color pictures, develop symbolic representations, or cut and paste magazine pictures. Distribute suitable materials for this project. Colored or plain white construction paper would be ideal. Provide crayons, markers, and magazines (for cut-and-paste art work).

If any student is having difficulty selecting a theme, suggest images associated with love or appearing in the poem itself. If your school library has books describing tips or techniques for beginning artists, collect them and bring them to class. Allow students to use them for ideas.

Collect and evaluate the students' projects. After recording the grades, return the cards to students. Praise the work of all who have shown effort.

■ "Song Concerning a Dream of the Thunderbirds"

by Teton Sioux (page 9)

SELECTION SYNOPSIS

The subject of this poem is a religious experience. The poet has become sacred through a dream in which a Native American mythological creature is revealed.

SELECTION ACTIVITY

Divide the class into small groups. On the board or overhead transparency, list several well-known mythologies. Greek, Roman, Norse, African, Native American, Chinese, and Japanese are among those you might consider. Have students copy the list into their notebooks. List enough different mythologies so that every student in each group can participate individually.

Take the class to the library. Each group should use reference materials and other works to identify from each mythology listed a creature associated with a natural phenomenon or concept. They should list the name of the creature, the phenomenon or concept with which it is associated, and a brief physical description in their notebooks. Thunder and lightning are two examples of natural phenomena you might guide the students in selecting if they are having difficulty. Earth, sky, and sea are examples of concepts that might be used in this situation.

Upon returning to the classroom, each group should construct a booklet containing its findings. For extra credit, each group, or any member of a group, may add additional details or art work to accompany the booklet. Collect the booklets and evaluate them. After grading them, display the booklets around the room.

■ "Speech in the Virginia Convention"

by Patrick Henry (page 13)

SELECTION SYNOPSIS

Patrick Henry delivered this speech at the second revolutionary convention of Virginia in 1775. This convention was held to debate the course Virginia should take in light of the deteriorating relationship between the colonists and the King's government.

Henry regarded war with England as inevitable. He begins his speech by stating his high regard for those who have already spoken in favor of compromise and continued negotiation, but slyly states that reasonable people may sometimes hold differing opinions. He then says that he considers the issue in the debate to be nothing less than a question of freedom or slavery. Henry states that hope is natural, but in time of peril it can be a dangerous illusion. He asks rhetorically if wise men engage in pretense. He then says that he would rather know the worst that can happen and prepare for it.

The orator then states that he is guided by the lamp of experience. Is there any evidence, he asks, in the colonists' experience with the British that could lead them to believe there is hope for peace? Henry answers his own question. He describes the British military presence in the colonies and states that its purpose can only be warlike. He outlines the colonists' attempt to plead their cause before the Crown and the rebuffs they have endured. He states that the colonists should deceive themselves no longer.

If they wish to remain free, he says, they must be prepared to fight. If the colonists unite, he believes they can triumph. Referring to the Battles of Lexington and Concord (in Massachusetts), he asserts that the war has already begun. Henry concludes by exhorting the Virginians to join forces with the other colonists, especially the people of Massachusetts, who are already in the field. He ends his speech with the dramatic statement, ". . .give me liberty or give me death."

SELECTION ACTIVITY

Bring a tape recorder to class. Permit each student to read the conclusion of Henry's speech (beginning with, "Gentlemen may cry 'Peace, peace. . .'") into the tape recorder. Encourage memorization, but for those students who may have difficulty or who are nervous, allow reading from the text. At the conclusion of each reading, encourage class applause. Play the tape recordings, including the applause.

Take students to the library. Guide them in identifying dramatic passages from other great American speeches. Examples might include Lincoln's Gettysburg Address, Franklin Roosevelt's first Inaugural Address, John F. Kennedy's Inaugural Address, Martin Luther King, Jr.'s "I have a dream . . . ."

Have each student copy a short passage (limit to one paragraph) from the selected speech. Upon returning to the classroom, repeat the procedure used with Henry's conclusion. Allow students to read the passage they have selected into the tape recorder. Encourage memorization, but remember to make allowances for those students who may have difficulty with retention or who may be too nervous under the circumstances. Encourage class applause. Play the tape recordings, including the applause.

■ "Farewell Address"

by George Washington (page 20)

SELECTION SYNOPSIS

George Washington delivered this speech upon announcing his decision not to seek a third term as President. Washington began by announcing his decision. He then offered advice for his fellow Americans in the years ahead.

The speaker begins with a brief introduction. He states the background and gives a general occasion for speaking. He adds a personal reason for his remarks. Washington then states his thesis (what he intends to say). He adds his theme (the need for unity if Americans are to preserve the liberty won in the Revolutionary War).

The speaker then introduces the first of three points he wishes to make, concerning ways in which to preserve that liberty. He warns against party politics and supports that point with reasons. He makes his second point: Tyrannical leaders are a threat to liberty. He suggests ways to avoid or counteract tyrannical leadership. The speaker makes his third point; he warns against foreign entanglements. He stresses the need to remain neutral toward the traditional enmities of European countries. He then reminds the nation of its obligations.

Washington concludes his speech by restating his thesis and summarizing his main points. He ends his speech by asking that he be forgiven any human failings and remembered for his good intentions and zeal to serve his country.

SELECTION ACTIVITY

Have students copy Washington's three warnings into their notebooks. Tell them to watch the evening news or read the newspaper for three consecutive nights. They are to take notes on any story that seems to be related to Washington's warnings. (Advise them that they do not have to limit their notes to stories involving only the United States.)

On the fourth day, have the class discuss their findings. List recurring themes under the proper heading on the board or overhead transparency. Under each theme list individual student comments and conclusions.

■ "Letter to Her Daughter from the New White House"

by Abigail Adams (page 27)

SELECTION SYNOPSIS

Abigail Adams wrote this letter to her daughter in Massachusetts following her arrival at the newly constructed presidential residence in Washington, DC. Adams described the rigors of the journey. She remarked upon the primitive travel conditions and explained they were lost between Baltimore and the capital. She then went on to describe the partially completed appointments in the mansion. Conditions, she says, are difficult but tolerable. She describes in detail the unfinished condition of the presidential residence. In describing the surrounding city, which was still in the first stages of development, she explains the difficulties encountered in meeting day-to-day needs. She also mentions, however, that the residents have been extremely cordial and helpful to her and the president. She concludes by stating that Mrs. Washington has sent a message inviting her to visit Mount Vernon, the Washingtons' home. She plans to make that trip as soon as circumstances allow.

SELECTION ACTIVITY

Have students research the life and career of John Adams, Abigail's husband. Tell them to include details concerning his activities prior to the Revolutionary War; his service to his country during that conflict; the missions he undertook on its behalf after independence was won; his role as Washington's Vice-President; his tenure as President; and his activities after leaving office. Each student should write at least a paragraph on Adams' major accomplishments. Students should include a second paragraph describing Adams' other activities in public life. The third and final paragraph should examine his relationship with Abigail. Two excellent sources are the *Encyclopedia Britannica* and the *Encyclopedia Americana*. Remind students to cite sources. (You could do a lesson on bibliography form here.)

When the entire class has finished this assignment, give the papers a preliminary review. Select several students to present their papers orally to the class. Collect, grade, and display students' works.

■ from *The Autobiography*

by Benjamin Franklin (page 33)

SELECTION SYNOPSIS

This selection includes three excerpts from *The Autobiography*. In the first excerpt, Franklin explains that as a teenager, he experimented with a vegetarian diet. There were a number of advantages. His food was inexpensive, so he had extra money to spend on books. His meals were light, leaving him time and a clear head to read. One day, he set sail from Boston. The ship was becalmed, and the passengers began fishing for cod, which they cooked on deck. The smell of the fish filled his nostrils, and he found an ingenious excuse for abandoning his meatless diet.

In the second excerpt, Franklin describes the events leading up to his departure from his native Boston. As a young man Franklin worked for his brother, James, who published one of the first newspapers to appear in the colonies. He was the paper boy. Soon he began writing satires and submitting them anonymously. They were popular. Franklin, after a time, revealed his authorship to his brother. The two had an argument, as James thought his younger brother was becoming conceited.

After one particular argument, Franklin set out for Philadelphia. The trip by sea and land was difficult. However, he eventually arrived in the city. The excerpt ends with Franklin, for the first time, strolling the streets of the city in which he would become famous.

In the second excerpt, Franklin describes his attempts to achieve "moral perfection." He catalogued thirteen virtues that he hoped to master and kept a written record of his progress. He found the goal more difficult than he had imagined.

As an old man, he looks back and realizes he never came close to achieving perfection. Nevertheless, he decides that even his imperfect practice of virtue has been rewarding. He thinks he is a better and happier man for the effort.

SELECTION ACTIVITY [for second excerpt, pages 35–43]

In this activity, students will illustrate and tell this story in a cartoon strip. Before you begin this activity, collect several books with pictures of colonial costumes. (A drama or history teacher in your school may be a helpful resource.) Also gather as many days' worth of cartoon strips from your local paper as possible. Bring these materials to class on the day of this project to be used by students as a guide to their cartoons.

Step 1

The day after students have read and discussed the excerpt, divide the class into small groups. Explain that each group is to assume that Franklin published this story as a cartoon in his brother's paper. Ask: "What are your favorite cartoon strips? Why?" Briefly discuss how each cartoon strip is made up of a number of frames, or single pictures, that tells a story or stories (each strip should make a point). Ask, "What would happen to the story if the frames did not appear in sequential or logical order?" Have each group cut unlined, white, 8 1/2" x 11" typing paper into four pieces (4 1/4" x 5 1/2") to be used for each frame. You might precut these with a papercutter to save time.

Step 2

Explain that each group must first decide on the main points of the story. Each of these points (or parts) will be illustrated in one frame of the cartoon. Each member of the group will be responsible for drawing at least one frame. Group members must also decide if the strip will be in black and white or in color, so that all members' art is consistent.

Provide colored markers for groups who decide on color strips. Point out that creativity and conciseness in telling the story is important. An individual's artistic talent is secondary. Remind students to refer to the resource books on period costumes. If any group or student is having difficulty with the concept of cartooning, tell them to use the cartoon strips from the local papers for ideas.

Step 3

When all students in a group have finished their frames, give the group a piece of colorful posterboard. Explain that they must paste each frame in the correct order to the posterboard. When this step is complete, students should sign and date the frames they drew. Collect, evaluate, and display the cartoons in the room for other students to enjoy.

SELECTION ACTIVITY [for entire excerpt]

This selection provides an excellent opportunity for students to write their autobiographies.

After completing and discussing this selection, explain that this is only a part of Franklin's autobiography. An autobiography usually includes important events in a person's life from birth to publication of the autobiography. Briefly review the difference between an autobiography and a biography. Ask, "Do you have to do library research when you write an autobiography? Are you expressing your opinions or the opinions of others when you write?" Explain that an autobiography gives others insights into an individual and allows others to see how certain events were important to the subject.

Step 1

Prewriting Tell students to first list all the relevant information about their birth (date, place, parents, and so forth). Next, tell them to jot down all relevant or important personal events in their lives. Finally, they should arrange these events in sequential order.

Step 2

Writing Tell students to add what they feel are important details to the events listed in Step 1. As you walk around the classroom, help any student having difficulty. Explain that while one person may think an event insignificant, another person may feel that a similar experience played an important role in shaping or changing his or her life.

Step 3

Revising Divide the class into groups of three. Have students read their autobiographies to the other members of the group. After each student has finished, group members may make suggestions to improve clarity of the work just read.

Proofreading Each student should work with a partner to proofread the final draft for any spelling, punctuation, or grammatical errors.

Collect, evaluate (include written praise as well as constructive criticism), and return to the student. This type of assignment may help you understand a student who is a discipline problem or is having difficulty in your class.

■ from *Poor Richard's Almanack*

by Benjamin Franklin (page 45)

SELECTION SYNOPSIS

This selection contains several aphorisms on varied subjects that appeared in the pages of Franklin's almanac.

SELECTION ACTIVITY

After reading and discussing this selection, tell the class that each student is to select two of these aphorisms and restate them in modern-day English. Explain they are not to use slang.

Precut 8 1/2" x 11" white typing paper in half (4 1/4" x 11") on a papercutter. As each student indicates that the assignment is finished, give them two pieces of this paper. Tell them they are to copy their interpretations of the aphorisms on these papers. Each student may decorate the ends with scrollwork or similar designs.

When all students have completed the assignment, collect the banners. Tack these onto a bulletin board devoted to Benjamin Franklin. You may want to include a copy of his picture and other relevant facts from his life. Indicate that any student who assists you with this project will receive extra credit.

■ "What Is an American?"
by Jean de Crèvecoeur (page 49)

SELECTION SYNOPSIS

The writer sets out to define an American by describing the ideas and values of those who have left Europe to settle in this new land. He begins by asserting that, unlike the homogeneous populations of Europe, many Americans marry persons of another nationality. He continues by describing them as pilgrims. They are people who have brought with them the best of what their ancestors had to offer, while leaving behind the prejudices of Europe.

In America, unlike Europe, these people will reap the benefits of their labors. This will inspire love of country. According to Crèvecoeur, Americans listen with open minds and respond accordingly.

SELECTION ACTIVITY

After reading this selection, have each student, as a homework assignment, list three admirable characteristics of Americans. As a prompt, you might tell them to think of people they admire. Which characteristics of this person, or persons, seem to illustrate what Crèvecoeur wrote? You should also advise students not to limit their thoughts to the selection. They may list other characteristics or qualities that have occurred to them, even if the writer has not mentioned these.

Collect and review the homework assignments. If any student has had difficulty, offer guidance or suggestions as needed. Return the papers to students for their review and additional work, if needed. Tell them to bring the work to class the next day.

Discuss with the class the results of their work. Encourage positive thoughts. At the same time, do not exclude criticism or disagreement so long as it is offered in a constructive, disinterested fashion. Allow ample time for a summation of the discussion. List on the board or overhead transparency positive characteristics students think people of the United States demonstrate or should exhibit.

In preparation for this project, you might want to invite a guest speaker. This speaker may be someone you know, or a relative or neighbor of a student. The guest speaker should be someone who has lived in another country and chosen to come to the United States. Ask the speaker to compare and contrast life in his or her homeland with life in the United States. Ask the speaker to explain his or her choice to come to the United States.

■ "Sunrise in His Pocket"
by Davy Crockett (page 53)

SELECTION SYNOPSIS

This is a tall tale. Virtually every statement the narrator makes is to be taken with the proverbial grain of salt. The narrator, Davy Crockett, is, in his own estimation, the strongest, smartest, fastest, and bravest person ever to walk the frontier. One winter morning, as he arose, he realized something was radically wrong. The earth had frozen on its axis and could no longer rotate. Crockett would have to correct the situation himself or humanity was doomed.

He set off on foot for "Daybreak Hill." Fortunately, he had the foresight to carry a bear along on his back. Arriving at Daybreak Hill, he assessed the situation. There was only one thing to do. Crockett pounded the bear against the ice, extracting enough grease to thaw the planet's axis and set it spinning again. He then returned home, graciously accepting the humble thanks of the sun.

SELECTION ACTIVITY

Ask students, "What do you think is the role of a book or story illustrator?"

Briefly discuss how the illustrator clarifies important parts of a story or an entire book. The illustrator tells the story through images. Tell students to think about young children's story books. Ask, "How are they different from adult books?" Guide students by pointing out that many times the story is revealed through the artwork on each page as well as by the printed words. Explain that in the nineteenth and early twentieth centuries, many "classics" contained beautiful works of art on what were called plate pages. These drawings or "plates" depicted a scene from the story. Talented artists were able to earn a steady income with these illustrations. Talk about one famous illustrator, N.C. Wyeth. His illustrations of such classics as Stevenson's *Treasure Island* are among the finest ever done. If possible, secure one of these old books and display it for students to view.

Allow students to review the story as necessary. Explain that each student is to illustrate a segment of this story. The choice is theirs. Tell them not to use cartoons but to make a collage or an original drawing. Provide crayons, colored markers, and magazines for cut-and-paste art work.

After students have completed their illustrations, tell them to write a brief synopsis of each illustrated segment. Explain that they will not be graded on their artistic talent, but will be graded on creative content and interpretation. Collect, evaluate, and display students' works in the room or on the hall bulletin board. Praise students for their effort.

■ "Godasiyo, the Woman Chief"

a Seneca legend retold by Dee Brown (page 55)

SELECTION SYNOPSIS

At the dawn of time, all Native Americans spoke the same language and lived in peace. Many lived in a village by a river. This village was governed by a wise woman chief, Godasiyo. As word spread of her wisdom, others came to the village. Soon the village spread to the other side of the river.

The tribal council house was on the south side of the river. Over a period of time, some of those living on the northern side of the river became disgruntled. A bridge was built over the river, and harmony was restored temporarily.

One day a white dog appeared in the village and was adopted by Godasiyo. The people on the northern side of the river spread rumors that the dog was really an evil spirit that should be killed. Godasiyo refused. The tribe divided into two factions. To avoid war, Godasiyo announced her intention to leave and start a new village elsewhere. Many of the people decided to go with her.

As they set out, Godasiyo rode on a platform supported on either side by a canoe. At a fork in the river, an argument arose among the people as to which branch should be taken. The tribe, including the two canoers guiding Godasiyo's platform, set off in different directions. The platform fell into the river, and Godasiyo and the white dog drowned. The people, no longer able to understand each other's speech separated into many tribes.

SELECTION ACTIVITY

In this activity, students will research and write a report on the Seneca. Ask students the following questions:

Who were the Seneca?

Of which Native American Nation were they a member?

In what part of America were the Seneca found?

Were the Seneca peace-loving?

Do the Seneca still exist today?

Tell students to use as many resources as possible to gather information and write a report on the history of the Seneca. Tell them encyclopedias are an excellent aid. They might also check the library directory for other resources, including the Internet. You might take this opportunity to teach a lesson on using the library. Include an explanation of the Dewey Decimal System. Explain that librarians are willing to assist anyone having difficulty. Remind students about the difference between circulating and reference works. This may save valuable time.

Use one class period to take the class to the school library. Walk around the library to check that all students are working on this assignment. Assist any student who is having difficulty with any phase of the assignment. Point out that students may want and/or need to do independent research at the local public library.

Collect and evaluate the reports. Select several students to read their papers to the class. Praise those who appear to have done their best, keeping in mind their abilities.

If feasible and if time allows, you could invite a Native American from any tribe to speak to the class on the tribal heritage and the outlook for that particular group today. The United States Department of Interior may be able to help you locate a person in your area.

STUDENT READING LIST

Blumberg, Rhoda. *Jefferson, Napoleon and the Louisiana Purchase*. National Geographic. 1998.

Bober, Natalie S. *Abigail Adams: Witness to a Revolution*. Simon & Schuster/Atheneum. 1955.

Dean, Ruth and Thomson, Melissa. *Life in the American Colonies*. 1999.

Ferrie, Richard. *World Turned Upside Down: George Washington and the Battle of Yorktown*. Holiday. 1999.

Uschan, Michael V. *America's Founders*. Lucent. 1999.

From Globe Fearon Educational Publisher

Adapted Classics and Masterworks Collection

The Red Badge of Courage by Stephen Crane

An American Family Series

Colony of Fear

A Matter of Pride

Two Kinds of Patriots

Multicultural Literature Collection

Plains Native American Literature

World Myths and Legends

Native American

UNIT 1 Overview

UNIT OBJECTIVES

After completing this unit, students will be able to

- understand the difference between fiction and nonfiction
- recognize the forms and elements of nonfiction
- build on knowledge of literary elements to write effectively
- use several strategies to determine word origin and meaning
- prepare an oral report
- write a description that appeals to the senses
- observe details
- take effective notes

UNIT SELECTIONS

This unit examines the style, form, and content of literature in the colonial period. During this period, the thirteen original colonies (later states) were established, the Revolutionary War was fought, and the United States was founded. The literature was primarily nonfiction.

- **"To My Dear and Loving Husband"** (p. 5) is an intimate love poem.

  LITERARY SKILL: tone

  READING SKILL: identify cause and effect

  VOCABULARY: definitions

  WRITING: love letter

- **"Song Concerning a Dream of the Thunderbirds"** (p. 9) is a Native American song.

  LITERARY SKILL: rhythm

  READING SKILL: understand the speaker's purpose

  VOCABULARY: imagery, symbolism

  WRITING: description

- **"Speech in the Virginia Convention"** (p. 13) is a passionate attempt to persuade its listeners.

  LITERARY SKILL: theme and thesis statement

  READING SKILL: recognize fact and opinion

  VOCABULARY: rhetorical questions

  WRITING: accurate reporting

- **"Farewell Address"** (p. 20) is an expository oration.

  LITERARY SKILL: elements of nonfiction

  READING SKILL: recognize support for opinions

  VOCABULARY: words used as nouns and verbs

  WRITING: organization of a speech

- **"Letter to Her Daughter from the New White House"** (p. 27) Abigail Adams describes the new and unfinished White House in a letter.

  LITERARY SKILL: description

  READING SKILL: make inferences

  VOCABULARY: change in word meanings

  WRITING: vivid description

- **from *The Autobiography* and *Poor Richard's Almanack*** (p. 33) Benjamin Franklin demonstrates the use of personal experience in writing.

  LITERARY SKILL: narration

  READING SKILL: make generalizations

  VOCABULARY: roots

  WRITING: tone and simple narrative

Voices of Colonial America

In this our western world
Be Freedom's flag unfurl'd
Through all its shores!
May no destructive blast
Our heaven of joy o'ercast,
May Freedom's fabric last
While time endures.
—Philip Freneau

The Landing of the Pilgrims, 1620. 19th century, Anonymous. The Granger Collection

Introducing the Literary Period

Organize students into groups. Have each group write a definition of freedom. Discuss the definitions, then list common elements among the definitions on the board.

Viewing Fine Art

This lithograph depicts the Pilgrims stepping ashore in Plymouth, Massachusetts, in 1620. It was made by Currier & Ives, the largest and most successful lithographic publishers of the 19th century. Lithographer Nathaniel Currier (1813–1888) founded the business in 1835. The company, Currier & Ives, was established in 1837, when bookkeeper and lithographer James Merrit Ives (1824–1895) became a partner. Currier & Ives remained in business until 1907.

Lithography is the process of printing from an image drawn on a flat stone, which is inked and wetted. The prints were drawn and reproduced in black and white. A staff of young women colored each print by hand, working from a model painting. Ask: What do the poses of the various Pilgrims indicate about their first reactions to America?

- **"What Is an American?"** (p. 49) is a short essay.
  LITERARY SKILL: point of view
  READING SKILL: compare and contrast
  VOCABULARY: word origins
  WRITING: argumentation

- **"Sunrise in His Pocket"** (p. 53) **and "Godasiyo, the Woman Chief"** (p. 55) The American oral tradition includes tall tales and legends like these excerpts.
  LITERARY SKILL: folklore
  READING SKILL: recognize main idea and supporting details
  VOCABULARY: hyperbole
  WRITING: using exaggeration for humorous effect

UNIT 1

RELATED MATERIALS

1. ***American Paradox.*** [Three videocassettes, 23 mins. each, Double Diamond Video, 1999.] Discusses importance of slavery in colonial and early America.
2. ***Liberty! The American Revolution Curriculum Package.*** [Six videos, 60 mins. each, PBS Video, 1997.] Dramatic documentary.
3. ***History Through Literature.*** [Video, 26 mins., Clearvue, 1998.] Extensive coverage connects history, English, science, and philosophy.
4. ***Benjamin Franklin 1706–1790.*** [Two audiocassettes, Caedmon/CDL.] Ed Begley reads *The Autobiography of Benjamin Franklin.*
5. ***Davy Crockett.*** [Video, 15 mins., AITECH.] Ann McGregor narrates this video from the "Stories of America Series."
6. ***George Washington.*** [Video, 15 mins., AITECH.] This video is also from the "Stories of America" and narrated by Ann McGregor.
7. The following Web sites may also be helpful. Please note that some Internet addresses change frequently. These are the latest versions:

   Lucidcafé, Benjamin Franklin at *http://www2.lucidcafe.com/lucidcafe/library/96jan/franklin.html*

   Bellingham Public Schools, Colonial American History Resources at *http://www.bham.wednet.edu/colonial.htm#Historical*

   Stonee's Lore Legends and Teachings at *http://www.ilhawaii.net/~stony/197myths.html*

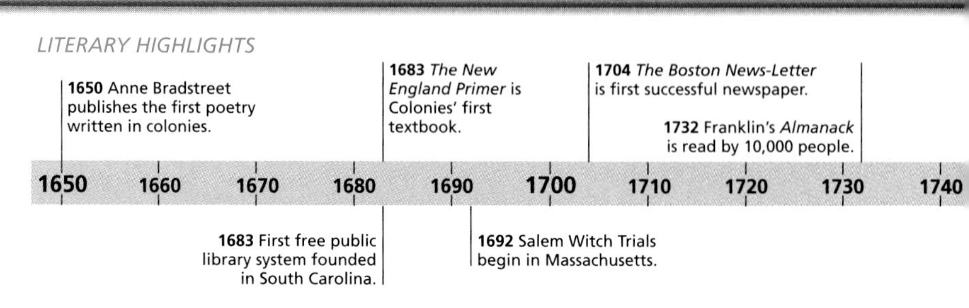
LITERARY HIGHLIGHTS
1650 Anne Bradstreet publishes the first poetry written in colonies.
1683 The New England Primer is Colonies' first textbook.
1704 The Boston News-Letter is first successful newspaper.
1732 Franklin's Almanack is read by 10,000 people.
1650 1660 1670 1680 1690 1700 1710 1720 1730 1740
1683 First free public library system founded in South Carolina.
1692 Salem Witch Trials begin in Massachusetts.
HISTORICAL HIGHLIGHTS

Voices of Colonial America

This country has gone through many drastic changes in the past two centuries. The population has grown tremendously, and modern technology has given us jet planes, automobiles, and many other advances.

In colonial America people depended on horses and on ships for transportation. The colonists built their settlements near the harbors where their ships had landed. Here they were able to receive shipments of goods they needed from Europe. Ships were the best way to move goods.

The Native Americans, who had been in America for hundreds of years before the colonists, generally did not live in the settlements. Instead they lived in the great wilderness that made up most of colonial America. Here they survived by farming, hunting, and fishing.

■ NONFICTION IN COLONIAL LITERATURE

The colonists most likely enjoyed reading for many reasons. They were probably most interested in reading in order to get information. Remember, people could not get the news on television or radio in colonial times.

Most colonial literature is nonfiction—writing that deals with facts or ideas. Like us, the colonists published newspapers. They also wrote almanacs—publications that contain a variety of practical information. In this unit, you will read a selection from *Poor Richard's Almanack*, written by Benjamin Franklin.

Since there were no telephones, colonists kept in touch by writing letters, which were delivered by men on horseback or carried by packet ships that sailed along the coast. You will read a letter from a famous letter writer, Abigail Adams.

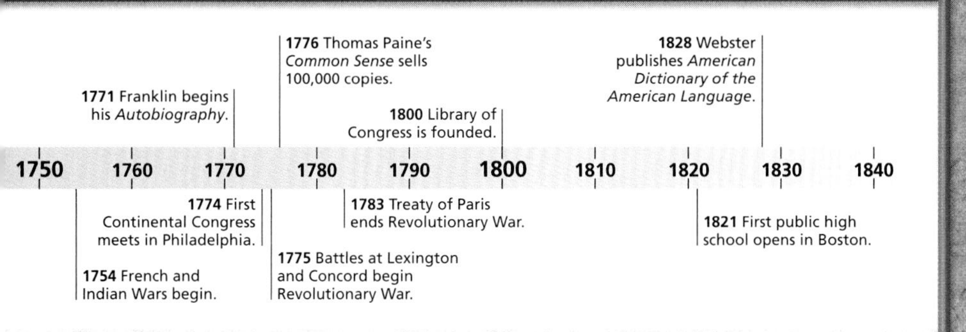
1771 Franklin begins his Autobiography.
1776 Thomas Paine's Common Sense sells 100,000 copies.
1800 Library of Congress is founded.
1828 Webster publishes American Dictionary of the American Language.
1750
1760
1770
1780
1790
1800
1810
1820
1830
1840
1774 First Continental Congress meets in Philadelphia.
1783 Treaty of Paris ends Revolutionary War.
1821 First public high school opens in Boston.
1775 Battles at Lexington and Concord begin Revolutionary War.
1754 French and Indian Wars begin.

TOPICS IN COLONIAL LITERATURE

The colonists were passionately interested in politics—after all, they witnessed the American Revolution and the founding of the United States. They liked to discuss citizens' rights. Patrick Henry's "Speech in the Virginia Convention" and George Washington's "Farewell Address" are typical of this kind of writing.

Colonists also wondered what it meant to be an American. Jean de Crèvecoeur tried to answer that question in a short essay you will read called "What Is an American?"

Biography fascinated the colonists. They enjoyed reading about people who overcame obstacles. They also believed in the importance of moral values. Benjamin Franklin's *Autobiography* deals with these subjects.

Poetry is the genre, or literary form, that the colonists often used to write about love. You will read one love poem, "To My Dear and Loving Husband," in this unit.

The colonists also enjoyed writing that offered humor through exaggeration. "Sunrise in His Pocket" is an example of a tall tale, a story that uses wild exaggeration to make people laugh.

This unit includes selections from Native American literature. "Song Concerning a Dream of the Thunderbirds" is a poem. "Godasiyo, the Woman Chief," is a legend written down by the 20th century author, Dee Brown.

As you read the selections, imagine what life was like for these colonial Americans. Ask yourself what reading might have meant to you if you had lived in colonial times.

Discussing the Literary Period

Write the following sentences on the board:

Freedom of speech does not allow a person to shout "Fire!" in a crowded theater.

Your right to extend your arm ends where my nose begins.

Ask students to agree or disagree with these sentences and explain their answers.

Ask why discussion of these sentences is appropriate for this unit.

Cooperative Group Activity

Divide the class into small groups. Have each group choose a subject about which they think there is a legitimate conflict between the rights of the individual and the rights of the community. They should then list the pros and cons for each side and debate the issue for the entire class. Examples they might consider are a debate about extending a highway through a residential area, or allowing a shopping mall to take over a strip of small businesses and part of a residential area.

Selection Overview

SELECTION OBJECTIVES

After completing this selection, students will be able to

- understand the meaning of the literary term *tone*
- recognize an author's tone
- use a consistent tone when writing a paragraph
- select and organize details in writing a paragraph
- understand the use of context and footnotes in determining the meaning of unfamiliar words
- identify cause and effect

Lesson Resources

To My Dear and Loving Husband

- Selection Synopsis, Teacher's Edition, pp. TT58–TT59
- Comprehension and Vocabulary Workbook, pp. 1–2
- Language Enrichment Workbook, p. 1
- Teacher's Resources
  Reinforcement, p. R1
  Test, pp. T1–T2

More About Tone

Writers adopt a tone that suits the feelings they want to express. "To My Dear and Loving Husband" is a love letter in poetic form addressed to the author's spouse. The tone is intimate or characterized by the sharing of deeply personal thoughts and feelings. Encourage students to suggest appropriate tones for other works that could be entitled, "To . . . ."

About the Author

Anne Bradstreet wrote her poems for her family, not for publication. Her brother-in-law had her first collection published in England in 1650, but he did not tell her until his return to America. Her descendants carefully preserved the manuscripts of her later poems, which were not published until about 200 years after her death.

Learn About

TONE

The Boating Party, Mary Cassatt. National Gallery of Art, Washington, DC/Index/Bridgeman Art Library

When you speak, your voice carries a meaning beyond the words you use. For example, if you say to someone, "I'm going shopping," your tone of voice will reflect whether you feel hope, dread, excitement, or boredom. It is not just the words you speak, but your tone of voice that reveals your feelings about the shopping trip.

Beneath the surface of their words, writers show their feelings and attitudes, too. **Tone** is the literary term used to describe a writer's feeling and attitude toward the subject matter and toward the reader. Is the writer's tone playful or serious, respectful or rude, personal or impersonal, loving or angry, light or grim—or any of many other possible attitudes?

As you read "To My Dear and Loving Husband," ask yourself:

1. What is the writer's tone?
2. How early in the poem do you recognize the tone?

READING FOCUS

Identify Cause and Effect A cause is what makes something happen. An effect is what happens as a result of an event. Each event can have many causes, and a cause can have many effects.

A writer who explores the questions "What happened?" and "Why did it happen?" must use cause and effect in his or her text. As you read Bradstreet's poem, think about the events and emotions she describes. What has caused her to feel the way she does? What are the effects of her feelings?

WRITING CONNECTION

Write a paragraph describing your favorite movie. Write a second paragraph describing a movie you did not like. Read your paragraphs and pay close attention to the tone of each one. How do the tones of your paragraphs differ?

Viewing Fine Art

Mary Cassatt (1844–1926) painted in the style of the French impressionists. She often painted touching scenes of families. Ask: What seems to be the relationship of the figures in this painting?

Cooperative Group Activity

To help students complete the Writing Connection activity, ask them to name various movies they have enjoyed. Pair students who liked the same film and have each pair collaborate on a paragraph describing the movie. Have one student from each pair read the paragraph aloud.

ESL Activity

Have students work in pairs with proficient speakers of English. Have each student take turns reading a line aloud and paraphrase its meaning. Have pairs identify which words reveal the tone of the poem.

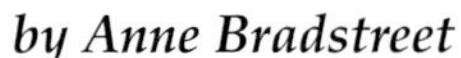

Portrait of Mr. and Mrs. Thomas Mifflin (Sarah Morris), John S. Copley. Philadelphia Museum of Art

If ever two were one, then surely we;
If ever man were loved by wife, then thee;
If ever wife was happy in a man,
Compare with me, ye women, if you can.
5 I prize thy love more than whole mines of gold,
Or all the riches that the East doth hold.
My love is such that rivers cannot quench,
Nor ought but love from thee give recompense.
Thy love is such I can no way repay,
10 The heavens reward thee manifold, I pray.
Then while we live in love let's so persever
That when we live no more we may live ever.

---

quench (KWENCH) satisfy thirst or other need
ought (AWT) anything (variation of *aught*)
recompense (REHK um pens) repayment
manifold (MAN uh fohld) in many ways
persever (pur SEV ur) continue to uphold; keep on trying
(Today the word is spelled *persevere* and pronounced *pur suh VEER.*)

TEACHING PLAN

INTRODUCE

Motivation
Ask students to describe the qualities they would value in a spouse. Examples, such as respect for the feelings of others, can be used to encourage discussion. Relate the discussion to the poem.

Purpose-Setting Question
Why do you think Anne Bradstreet's descendants carefully preserved her manuscripts?

READ

Literary Focus: *Tone*
Ask students to sum up Bradstreet's attitude toward her subject in one word. Have them give specific examples of images and phrases in the poem that support their answers.

Reading Focus: *Identify Cause and Effect*
Ask students to identify the main idea of the poem. Help them see that Bradstreet's love for her husband is an effect. Discuss what may have caused this effect.

CLOSE

Have students complete Review the Selection on pages 6–7.

Viewing Fine Art

John Singleton Copley (1738–1815) was America's foremost 18th-century painter. His many famous portraits of Paul Revere, John Adams, and other prominent colonial Americans capture both likeness and personality. Although Copley enjoyed a late success in England as a historical painter, his portraits remain his finest works. Ask: What do their expressions, clothing, and poses tell you about Governor and Mrs. Mifflin's relationship? Compare and contrast it to that of Bradstreet's relationship with her husband.

Develop Vocabulary Skills
Choose a common synonym for each vocabulary word and use it in an original sentence. Ask for volunteers to substitute the appropriate vocabulary word for the synonym in the same sentence. Then have students use the vocabulary word in an original sentence.

Mini Quiz

1. Instead of *you*, the poet refers to her husband as ________.
2. The poet challenges other ________ to compare their happiness to hers.
3. The poet prizes her husband's love more than mines of ________.
4. The poet prays the ________ will reward her husband.
5. All the riches of the ________ are less than the poet's love.

Answers
1. thee
2. women
3. gold
4. heavens
5. East

Review the Selection

UNDERSTAND THE SELECTION

Recall

1. To whom is Anne Bradstreet writing?
2. Above what does she prize her husband's love?
3. What does she pray rewards her husband?

Infer

4. How does Anne Bradstreet feel about her husband?
5. How does Bradstreet's love compare with the love of other wives?
6. How does she think her husband feels about her?
7. How long does Bradstreet want their love to last?

Apply

8. How do you think Anne Bradstreet's husband felt when he read her poem?
9. How might her husband have responded to the poem?
10. Bradstreet chose poetry to communicate her feelings. What would you write to communicate love?

Respond to Literature

Anne Bradstreet was a Puritan. Why is it surprising that this poem was written by a Puritan?

WRITE ABOUT THE SELECTION

In this selection, Anne Bradstreet chose poetry to express her feelings to her husband. He understood how she felt from the tone of her poem. Do you think she expressed herself clearly? Why or why not? What do you think his reaction was? How did he feel about her? Assume you are her husband and have decided to respond to her poem—not in poetry, but in prose.

Prewriting Compile a list of things you might say to Anne Bradstreet. Let your mind roam freely over possible responses you might make. Jot them down without thinking of how important or unimportant they may be. When you have a sizable list, consider which ones you want to use in your response. Organize your notes in the order you want to discuss them.

Writing Use your informal list to write a paragraph in the first-person ("I") point of view. Remember that you are supposed to be the husband. Make clear how you feel. Remember to keep the tone consistent.

Revising When you revise your paragraph, add details that maintain the same tone.

Proofreading Read over your paragraph. Be sure that all your sentences end with a period, question mark, or exclamation point.

UNDERSTAND THE SELECTION

Answers

1. her husband
2. mines of gold or all the riches of the East
3. the heavens
4. Answers will vary but should include the idea that she loves him passionately.
5. Answer should include the idea that she loves her husband more.
6. Answer should include the idea that she thinks he loves her.
7. forever
8. Sample answer: happy; grateful to his wife
9. Sample answer: He loved her equally.
10. Answers will vary. Some might write a letter. Others might write a poem or a song.

Respond to Literature

Unlike the stereotyped Puritans, Anne Bradstreet could express her feelings for her husband openly. Others try to show affection in other ways. Have the students organize into groups. Each group should list three indirect ways of showing affection. Examples might include teasing, making a gift, telling a mutual friend.

WRITE ABOUT THE SELECTION

Prewriting

Ask students to think about what qualities they would want to find in a person they loved. Using students' suggestions, create an outline on the board or on an overhead transparency. Answers will vary. Sample answers:

Think person is beautiful.
Love being with the person.
The person is unselfish.
The person is fun.

Have students compile their own lists. Remind students to think of themselves as Anne Bradstreet's husband.

Writing

Have students work on this section individually. Go around the class, giving help to any student who is having difficulty. Ask students if they are conveying their sentiments in a logical order.

Revising

Divide class into small groups to revise their paragraphs. Have each student read his or her own paragraph. The others may then comment on how they reacted and whether any improvements could be made.

Proofreading

Select several students' paragraphs as models for proofreading. Place the paragraphs on an overhead projector, and have the class suggest any corrections to the punctuation at the end of each sentence.

THINK ABOUT TONE

Tone is the literary term used to describe the writer's attitude toward his or her readers, toward his or her characters, and toward the subject matter of the piece. Tone contributes greatly to the effectiveness of a work. If the reader misunderstands a writer's tone, he or she will miss much of the meaning of the work.

1. Does this poem sound like a casual conversation? Explain your answer.
2. Why do you think the writer chose poetry as the genre rather than a letter?
3. What do the comparisons used in lines 5 through 10 tell the reader about the depth of the writer's emotion?
4. How does the tone contribute to the mood of the poem?
5. What effect would a touch of humor have had on the poem?

Reading Focus

Identify Cause and Effect You have paid attention to what caused the writer to feel the way she does and the effects of those causes. Name at least one cause and one effect in this poem.

DEVELOP YOUR VOCABULARY

You cannot understand the meaning of a literary work unless you understand the meanings of the words the author uses. Sometimes the **context**—the words surrounding the unfamiliar term—will suggest a meaning. When it does, you should confirm your guess by looking up the word in a dictionary.

Another place to check for the meaning of unfamiliar words is in the book itself. Sometimes, as in this book, you can find the meaning of unfamiliar words in footnotes at the bottom of the page. They also may be given at the end of a selection or in a special glossary at the end of the book.

Review the meanings of the following words from "To My Dear and Loving Husband." Write an original sentence using each word.

1. quench
2. ought
3. recompense
4. manifold
5. persevere

ESL Activity

Take the students through these steps to help them with the vocabulary.

1. Use context clues. Ask: What word or words can you substitute for *quench*?
   - **a.** A cold glass of ice water will quickly *quench* your thirst.
   - **b.** Firemen will *quench* the fire.
2. Look up *quench* in the glossary. Ask: Do any of your substitutions for *quench* appear?
3. Review the word. Ask: What is the meaning of "My love is such that rivers cannot *quench*"?
4. Use the word. Ask: What do athletes drink to *quench* their thirst during a game?

THINK ABOUT TONE

Answers

1. It does not. Answers may include the emotional, the use of *thee* and *thy*, the sentence structure, and the lack of slang.
2. Answers will vary but may suggest that poetry is an appropriate vehicle for expressing emotion.
3. Answers will vary but may suggest great depth because the comparisons are to vast ideas.
4. Answers will vary but may suggest that the loving tone adds to the seriousness and reverential mood of the poem.
5. Answers will vary but will probably suggest that humor would be inappropriate; it would have a jarring effect on the reader.

DEVELOP YOUR VOCABULARY

Sample Answers

1. The boys found it difficult to *quench* their thirst after the ten-mile hike.
2. Faith in *ought* is better than no faith at all.
3. After World War II, Germany was ordered to make payments as *recompense* for the damages done to other countries.
4. The old man felt the *manifold* rewards of having kind, successful children and grandchildren.
5. Judith was able to *persevere* through the serious, painful illness.

Reading Focus

Sample Answer

Effects of her love: she is happy, she prizes her husband's love; cause of her love: the love her husband gives her

SELECTION OVERVIEW

SELECTION OBJECTIVES

After completing this selection, students will be able to

- understand rhythm and meter
- understand the use of rising and falling syllables in creating rhythm
- understand the use of repetition in creating rhythm
- create a verbal image of a character
- use a dictionary to review word meaning
- understand the speaker's purpose

Lesson Resources

Song Concerning a Dream of the Thunderbirds

- Selection Synopsis, Teacher's Edition, p. TT59
- Comprehension and Vocabulary Workbook, pp. 3–4
- Language Enrichment Workbook, p. 2
- Teacher's Resources
  Reinforcement, p. R2
  Test, pp. T3–T4

More About Rhythm

Native Americans had an oral tradition. Their literature was not written. It was learned by memory. The natural rise and fall of syllables, as well as repetition of words and phrases, makes memorization easier.

Background Notes

The Teton Sioux believed that the Black Hills of Dakota was a holy place, and they sometimes had visions there. It was in defense of the Black Hills that the Sioux, under the religious leader Sitting Bull and the chief Crazy Horse, fought the Battle of the Little Big Horn, also known as Custer's Last Stand. Ask students if they have seen any references to this 19th-century battle on TV or in the movies.

Learn About

READING FOCUS

Understand the Speaker's Purpose

People speak and write to communicate their ideas to others. They may want to describe, to entertain, to inform, or to persuade.

Diction and tone are two elements of a text that can help you determine the speaker's purpose. Look at the speaker's diction, or word choice. Ask yourself what it tells you about the speaker's tone, or attitude, toward both the subject and the audience.

RHYTHM

Rhythm is the repetition of a pattern of sounds. It occurs in natural speech; rhythm is the "swing," or sense of movement, that the ear hears when successive syllables are stressed or unstressed.

Most poetry has very strong rhythm because the poet writes into a poem a pattern of strongly stressed syllables alternating with a pattern of unstressed syllables. Such a pattern is called **meter**. Not all poems have meter, but that does not mean that they lack rhythm. In nonmetrical poetry, rhythm is irregular and comes from the natural rise and fall of syllables. The effect is sometimes enhanced by the repetition of words or word patterns.

As you read this selection, ask yourself:

1. How does the poet use rising and falling sounds to create rhythm?
2. What two phrases does the author repeat three times? How do they affect the reader?

WRITING CONNECTION

Write down the lyrics of your favorite song. Then explain how the songwriter used rhythm to create an effect.

ESL Activity

Have students make a list of what is sacred to them and their cultures. Ask them to share this list and explain why each item is sacred.

Cooperative Group Activity

To modify the Writing Connection activity, have students identify their favorite songs. Organize students into groups based on their choices. Select a group member to record the lyrics and indicate rise and fall by notation (/\ for up, \/ for down). Each group member recites a line, suggesting accents for the recorder. Groups take turns presenting their conclusions to the class.

Develop Vocabulary Skills

Ask students to discuss the meaning of thunderbird as explained in the footnote. Then ask them for other contexts in which they may have read or heard the word.

Song Concerning a Dream of the Thunderbirds

by the Teton Sioux

Friends, behold!
Sacred I have been made.
Friends, behold!
In a sacred manner
I have been influenced
At the gathering of the clouds.
Sacred I have been made.
Friends, behold!
Sacred I have been made.

Red Thing That Touches In Marching, 1832. George Catlin.
The Granger Collection

thunderbird (THUN dur burd) in the mythology of certain North American tribes, an enormous bird supposed to produce thunder, lightning, and rain

Teaching Plan

INTRODUCE

Motivation

Obtain a photograph of Crazy Horse. In the library, research the giant sculpture of him under construction in the Black Hills. Explain that Crazy Horse often went into the Black Hills to meditate and seek guidance in leading his people.

Purpose-Setting Question

How might a people who survived by farming and hunting feel about thunder, lightning, and rain?

READ

Literary Focus: *Rhythm*

Have students read the poem to themselves to get a sense of the stressed and unstressed syllables. Then have volunteers drum out the speaking pattern on their desks.

Reading Focus: *Understand the Speaker's Purpose*

Ask students to note which words and phrases are repeated in the poem. Ask: What do these lines reveal about the speaker's purpose?

CLOSE

Have students complete Review the Selection on page 10.

Viewing Fine Art

George Catlin (1796–1872) dedicated his life to the creation of a invaluable visual record of Native American people and their lives. This watercolor sketch shows Catlin's careful attention to details of costume and hairstyle, as well as his sensitivity to the personality of the individual he painted. Ask: What is your impression of this individual's personality?

Mini Quiz

Write the following sentences on the board or overhead projector and call on students to fill in the blanks. Discuss the answers with the class.

1. The poem is a ________.
2. It concerns a ________ of the thunderbirds.
3. The poet speaks the poem directly to ________.
4. The speaker has been made ________.
5. This occurred at the gathering of the ________.

Answers

1. song
2. dream
3. friends
4. sacred
5. clouds

UNDERSTAND THE SELECTION

Answers

1. friends
2. became sacred
3. at the gathering of the clouds
4. Answers will vary. Suggested response: a religious ceremony
5. the writer and the thunderbirds
6. Answers will vary. Suggested response: Birds fly in and rain falls from the sky.
7. Answers will vary. Suggested response: It would seem logical that only a huge bird could cause the force of a storm.
8. Answers will vary. Suggested response: when there was a drought
9. Answers will vary. Suggested responses: nothing; a storm might occur.
10. Answers will vary. Suggested responses: yes, to their preschool children, and because it is part of their heritage; no, because they can read about the legend

Respond to Literature

The speaker was made sacred, a term that means "entitled to reverence or respect." Have the students identify other characteristics that they believe earn a person respect. Ask them how they would demonstrate these characteristics if they were leaders. Discuss real people who exemplify these qualities.

WRITE ABOUT THE SELECTION

Prewriting

Using the students' suggestions write two lists on the board or on an overhead transparency.

1. Characteristics
   Sample answers:
   bright, multicolored feathers
   golden eyes
   sharp talons holding lightning
2. Setting
   Sample answers:
   huge, black, billowy clouds
   glowing, red sky
   fierce wind

Review the Selection

UNDERSTAND THE SELECTION

Recall

1. To whom is the writer speaking?
2. What change did the writer undergo during the dream?
3. Where was the writer when the change took place?

Infer

4. When do you think the Sioux might sing this song?
5. Who was present at the gathering of the clouds?
6. What do you think the Sioux believe caused thunder, lightning, and rain? Why?
7. Why do you think the Sioux visualized a thunderbird as a large bird?

Apply

8. Assume you are a Sioux living in the 18th century. When might you have asked a thunderbird for help?
9. Predict what might happen after the Sioux sang this song.
10. Do you think the Sioux still tell the legend of the thunderbird? Why?

Respond to Literature

How do you think "Song Concerning a Dream of the Thunderbirds" is representative of the literature of Native Americans?

WRITE ABOUT THE SELECTION

When you read a story, you form a specific image of each character in your mind. Sometimes the writer gives a detailed description of each character. At other times, you are required to visualize the characters' appearance from context clues or information learned from another source.

In this selection, you learned that the mythical creature, the thunderbird, is huge and is supposed to cause rain and storms. This you discovered in the vocabulary definition. Still, you can envision more. For example, do you envision a large head? What is the shape of the bird's eyes, wings, claws? Describe in detail how you picture the thunderbird.

Prewriting Begin by listing at least four characteristics of your vision of the thunderbird. Include several details for each characteristic. Try to use precise and vivid words. Be sure to include some interesting adverbs to help describe how the bird moves. Describe the kind of sound it makes.

Writing Use your list to write a paragraph describing the thunderbird's appearance. In it, briefly explain the setting that surrounds the bird.

Revising Add specific details that allow others to visualize your impressions of this creature.

Proofreading Be sure each sentence begins with a capital letter.

Writing

Have students work on this section individually. Walk around the classroom, giving help to any student who is having trouble. Ask the students if they think the readers could visualize the setting from their descriptions.

Revising

Make this a cooperative group activity. Divide the class into small groups. Have each student read his or her paragraph. The others may suggest descriptive adjectives that would help them to visualize the reader's concept of the thunderbird's appearance.

Proofreading

Have each group select one member's paragraph as a model for proofreading. Put each paragraph on the overhead projector and have the class suggest improvements.

THINK ABOUT RHYTHM

Rhythm is the repetition of a pattern of sounds. Even natural speech has a rhythm of stressed and unstressed syllables. A two-syllable word with the stress on the second syllable will create a rising sound. A two-syllable word with the stress on the first syllable will create a falling sound. Words with a mixed pattern will create a rising and falling rhythm.

1. Describe the use of repetition in this poem.
2. Why do you think the song begins and ends with the same two lines?
3. What two-syllable, six-letter word accented on the second syllable does the writer repeat?
4. What two-syllable, six-letter word accented on the first syllable does the writer repeat?
5. What kind of rhythm do these accented words create?

Reading Focus

Understand the Speaker's Purpose You have studied this song to determine the speaker's purpose, or reason for the song. What is the purpose of the line "Friends, Behold!"? What is the purpose of the repetition of the word *sacred*?

DEVELOP YOUR VOCABULARY

Synonyms are words that mean the same or nearly the same. For example, you might use either *strange* or *weird* to describe something odd. Writers try to use synonyms to make their writing more interesting. Paragraphs that use the same words over and over make dull reading.

Following is a list of words you might use in writing about the meaning of the poem, "Song Concerning a Dream of the Thunderbirds." For each, write a synonym.

1. holy
2. interesting
3. invitation
4. metaphor
5. big
6. influenced

Write a short description of the poem in which you use some of your synonyms for the words in the list.

ESL Activity

Discuss Native Americans of Central America and North and South America. Have students locate areas on a map where commonly known tribes and civilizations lived, such as Aztec, Mayan, Inca, Huron, Cherokee, Sioux, Hopi, Navajo, Apache, and Mohawk.

THINK ABOUT RHYTHM

Answers

1. Repetition includes the first two lines and last two lines, the words *behold* and *sacred*, and the phrase *I have been*.
2. Answers will vary. Suggested response: The repetition "rounds out" the ideas and suggests an endless cycle of seasons and life.
3. behold
4. sacred
5. a rising and falling rhythm

DEVELOP YOUR VOCABULARY

Sample Answers

1. hallowed, blessed
2. absorbing, fulfilling
3. request, summons
4. comparison, figure of speech
5. large, massive
6. controlled, swayed

In the poem, the speaker has become blessed and has an absorbing vision to tell.

Reading Focus

Sample Answer

"Friends, Behold" asks for listeners' attention. "Sacred" is used to signal that the speaker has had a vision.

SELECTION OVERVIEW

SELECTION OBJECTIVES

After completing this selection, students will be able to

- define theme and thesis statement
- identify the theme and the thesis statement (if present) in a work
- distinguish between supporting facts and thesis
- use detail and direct quotations in summarizing a speech or essay
- recognize rhetorical questions
- recognize fact and opinion

Lesson Resources

Speech in the Virginia Convention
- Selection Synopsis, Teacher's Edition, p. TT59
- Comprehension and Vocabulary Workbook, pp. 5–6
- Language Enrichment Workbook, p. 3
- Teacher's Resources
  Reinforcement, p. R3
  Test, pp. T5–T6

More About Theme and Thesis

A fact is an actual occurrence or something that has happened. A thesis is an unproven statement that the writer believes can be supported by facts. After students have read the selection, ask them to identify two important facts that the author uses to support his thesis.

About the Author

Patrick Henry was very active in Virginia, where he served as a state representative and governor. However, he seemed reluctant to hold a federal post. He declined to be a delegate to Congress in 1778. He refused to attend the Constitutional convention in 1787. From 1794 until his death, he also refused the following offices: U.S. Senator, Secretary of State, and Chief Justice of the Supreme Court.

Learn About

Patrick Henry, after Alonzo Chappel. Archive Photos

THEME AND THESIS

Theme is the main or central idea in a literary work. It is usually a broad, abstract idea, expressed directly or indirectly.

Theme in drama, poetry, and fiction is usually expressed indirectly. It may not be apparent until after the reader has finished reading the work and thought about it. Then readers draw their own conclusions about the meaning of the work.

In nonfiction, on the other hand, theme is usually expressed directly. The reader knows it immediately because theme and the subject matter of the work are usually identical.

Writers of nonfiction not only announce their theme, they often make a statement that tells just what position they will try to prove or support. This statement is called the **thesis statement**.

As you read Patrick Henry's speech, ask yourself:

1. What is the theme, or central idea, of Henry's speech?
2. Does he make a thesis statement? If so, what is it?

READING FOCUS

Recognize Fact and Opinion Statements of fact can be proven true or false. Opinions are statements of belief. They cannot be proven true or false.

Patrick Henry tries to persuade his listeners of something. Therefore, he must give them reasons to believe what he says. As you read, look for statements of fact that his listeners can prove or disprove. Look for statements of opinion that his listeners will have to consider.

WRITING CONNECTION

Choose a newspaper editorial. Write down its theme, or central idea. Then look for the thesis statement and write it down.

Viewing Fine Art

Alonzo Chappel (1828–1887) was an illustrator of historical books and a painter of portraits, naval scenes, and landscapes. Although his spectacles, coat, and waistcoat prove that Henry is a modern man, the cape draped over his arm and knee suggests the togas of ancient Romans—members of the republic that Henry and his fellow statesmen looked to as a model for their own. Ask: How would you describe Henry's values and personality based on this portrait?

Cooperative Group Activity

Extend the Writing Connection activity by pairing students. Have each student write a one-paragraph editorial. Have each partner read the other's editorial. The students should then work together to identify the theme and thesis statement of each paragraph.

Speech in the Virginia Convention

ADAPTED

by Patrick Henry

Mr. President: No man thinks more highly than I do of the patriotism and intelligence of the worthy gentlemen who have just addressed the house. But reasonable men sometimes disagree. I intend no disrespect toward the other speakers. Still, entertaining, as I do, opinions of a character very opposite to theirs [*disagreeing with their viewpoint*], I shall speak my thoughts freely and without reserve [*openly and honestly*]. This is no time for ceremony [*empty courtesy*]. The question before the house is one of grave importance to this country. For my own part, I consider it nothing less than a question of freedom and slavery. The issue is that significant. The debate must be uncompromising. It is only in this way that we can hope to arrive at the truth and fulfill the responsibility we owe to God and our country. If I held back my opinions at such a time, for fear of giving offense [*insulting someone*], I would consider myself guilty of treason toward my country. I would be lying before God.

Mr. President: It is only natural to hope for the best in any situation. In times of peril, though, hope may be a dangerous illusion. Hope may mean that we are shutting our eyes to avoid seeing a painful truth. Hope may mean that we are listening to a siren's song until she turns us into beasts [*ignoring reality and hearing only what we want to hear*]. Is this the role that wise men should play when they are engaged in a great and difficult struggle for liberty? Do wise men pretend that all is well when their eyes and ears tell them different? For my part, whatever anguish of spirit it may cost [*no matter how painful it is to me*], I am willing to hear the whole truth: to know the worst that can happen and make plans to avert it.

I have but one lamp by which my feet are guided [*know only one way to find my path in the dark*]. That is the lamp of experience. I know only one way to predict the future. That is by the experience of the past. Judging by the past, I would like to know what the British have done to make us believe there is hope for peace. The last time we asked them to consider our rights as royal subjects, they smiled. Trust not that smile, sir, it will prove a snare to your feet [*will turn out to be a trap*].

---

grave (GRAYV) of a threatening nature; indicating great danger
significant (sig NIF uh kunt) important; momentous
siren (SY run) in Greek and Roman mythology, a sea nymph represented as part bird and part woman who lured sailors to their death by singing

TEACHING PLAN

INTRODUCE

Motivation

Bring a placard to class with the words, "If this be treason, make the most of it." Explain that today we are accustomed to seeing citizens demonstrating outside government offices. Patrick Henry would probably be a demonstrator today. Henry made speeches in the Virginia legislature. The phrase on the placard is from a speech made in 1765, asserting that the colonies had the right to govern themselves. The students are now going to read his most famous speech, made ten years later at the start of the Revolutionary War.

Purpose-Setting Question

What kind of person would say that life without liberty was meaningless?

READ

Literary Focus:
Theme and Thesis

Ask students to read the first paragraph of Henry's speech and try to identify the thesis statement. If students have difficulty, draw their attention to the sentence "I consider it nothing less than a question of freedom and slavery."

Reading Focus:
Recognize Fact and Opinion

Challenge students to go through the first paragraph of the speech, identifying each sentence as a statement of fact or opinion. Ask students to identify words and phrases (such as "For my own part") that indicate statements of opinion. Have students watch for similar phrases and words as they read the rest of the speech.

CLOSE

Have students complete Review the Selection on pages 16–17.

Develop Vocabulary Skills

Distribute a handout to the class using the vocabulary words in sentences that illustrate their meanings. Ask for volunteers to substitute a synonym for each vocabulary word. Write appropriate responses on the board.

ESL Activity

Point out the bracketed text within Henry's speech. Explain to students that these are not Henry's words, but paraphrases placed within the text to aid in students' understanding. Encourage students to use the bracketed paraphrases as needed to clarify Henry's arguments.

Reading Focus: *Recognize Fact and Opinion*

Have students go through this page of the speech, identifying statements of fact and statements of opinion. Ask them to evaluate Henry's opinions. Do they find them persuasive? Why or why not?

Literary Focus: *Theme and Thesis Statement*

Challenge students to identify the thesis statement of the entire speech. Remind them that this is the statement Henry is trying to prove to his audience, and that it must sum up all his supporting evidence. If students have difficulty, draw their attention to the sentence "Then we must fight!" in the fourth paragraph.

Do not allow yourself to be betrayed by a kiss [*deceived by a false show of friendship*]. Compare their words with their actions. Why do warlike preparations cover our waters and darken our land? Are fleets and armies necessary if peace is the British intention? Have we appeared so committed to rebellion that they must use force to win back our loyalty? Let us not deceive ourselves, sir. Fleets and armies are the implements of war and enslavement. When threats have failed, fleets and armies are the arguments to which kings resort.

I ask you, gentlemen, I ask you, sir, what means this martial array [*what is the purpose of this military buildup*]? They mean to force us into submission. Can gentlemen think of another possible motive for their actions? Has Great Britain any threatening enemy in this part of the world? No sir, she has none. These armies and navies are meant for us. They can be meant for no other. They are sent over the sea to bind and rivet those chains which the British ministry has been forging for so long.

How can we oppose them? Shall we try logic? Sir, we have been trying that for the last ten years. Have we anything new to say upon the subject? Nothing. We have discussed the subject from every possible viewpoint. Shall we resort to entreaty and supplication [*pleading and begging*]? What can we say that has not been said before? Let us not, I beseech you sir, deceive ourselves any longer.

Sir, we have done everything that could be done to avert the coming storm. We have petitioned; we have protested; we have pleaded. We have knelt before the king and asked for his justice. Our petitions have been slighted. Our protests have led to additional violence and insult. Our pleas have been ignored; and we have been spurned with contempt by the king.

Do we wish to be free? Do we mean to preserve unbroken those precious rights for which we have so long fought? Do we plan on continuing this noble struggle? Will we keep our pledge not to abandon the struggle until our liberty is won? Then we must fight! I repeat it, sir, we must fight. An appeal to arms and God Almighty is all that is left us [*our only hope*].

They tell us, sir, that we are weak. They say we cannot cope with so formidable an adversary [*so strong a foe*]. But when shall we be stronger? Will it be next week, next year? Will it be when we are completely disarmed, and when a British guard is stationed in every house? Shall we grow strong through indecision and delay? Shall we acquire the means of effective resistance lying on our backs, hugging the delusive phantom of hope [*clinging to a false hope*] until our enemies have bound us hand and foot?

---

array (uh RAY) an orderly arrangement of troops
petitioned (puh TISH und) made a formal request of someone in authority
adversary (AD vur ser ee) opponent; enemy
delusive (dih LOO siv) misleading; unreal
phantom (FAN tum) something that seems real but does not exist

Patrick Henry Speaking Against the Stamp Act in the Virginia House of Burgesses in 1765, 19th century.
The Granger Collection

Sir, we are not weak if we make a proper use of the means at our disposal. We number three million. Three million people, armed in the holy cause of liberty, in such a country as this, can defeat any force our enemy sends against us. Besides, sir, we shall not fight alone. There is a just God who presides over the destinies of nations [*rules the universe*]. He will raise up friends to fight alongside us. The battle, sir, is not won by strength alone. Battles are won by the vigilant, by the active, by the brave. Besides, we have no choice. If we were dishonorable enough to desire peace at any price, it is not too late to retire from the contest [*surrender*]. We could retreat and accept submission and slavery. The British have already forged the chains of our bondage. Their rattling can be heard on the plains of Boston. The war is inevitable. Let it come. I repeat, sir, let it come.

There is no need to extenuate the matter [*no need for further discussion*]. Gentlemen may cry "Peace, peace"—but there is no peace. The war is actually begun! The next gale that sweeps [*strong wind that blows*] from the north will bring to our ears the clash of resounding arms [*the sounds of battle*]! Our brethren are already in the field. Why stand we here idle? What is it that gentlemen wish? What would they choose? Is life so precious, or peace so sweet, as to be purchased at the price of chains and slavery? Forbid it, Almighty God! I know not what course others may take; but as for me, give me liberty or give me death!

---

inevitable (in EV ih tuh bul) certain to happen
extenuate (ik STEN yoo ayt) to lessen the seriousness of
resounding (rih ZOUND ing) loud, echoing, or prolonged sound
brethren (BRETH run) brothers; fellow members of a group

Viewing Fine Art

This historical painting was done long after the event it depicts.

In the 19th century, patriotic scenes like this one were very profitable for the artists who drew them. Other popular images of the time included the signing of the Declaration of Independence and various Revolutionary War battles. Ask: How would you describe the atmosphere in this room? Which specific details convey that atmosphere?

Critical Thinking: *Summarize*

Ask students to summarize Henry's speech in four sentences. Start them off with the following sentence. "Liberty is in danger." Follow-up sentences should include the ideas: The British armies and navies are evidence of their warlike intentions. Attempts at a peaceful solution have failed. We must fight to protect our liberty.

Mini Quiz

Write the following sentences on the board or the overhead projector and call on students to fill in the blanks. Discuss the answers with the class.

1. Henry felt that in times of peril, ________ could be a dangerous illusion.
2. The only way to predict the future, Henry thought, was to look to the ________.
3. While the British were smiling, Henry said, they were also preparing for ________.
4. Americans, he argued, were ________ million people armed in the cause of liberty.
5. With so many people poised for war, he concluded, there could be no ________.

Answers

1. hope
2. past
3. war
4. three
5. peace

UNDERSTAND THE SELECTION

Answers

1. the experience of the past
2. the colonists
3. liberty or death
4. Since his opinion is opposite to theirs; they were against revolution.
5. No. Answers may vary. Suggested response: The British actions contradict their words.
6. Henry refers to three million people.
7. with slavery
8. Answers will vary.
9. Answers will vary. Suggested response: yes, because it presented a convincing point of view.
10. Answers will vary. One possibility is as a speech, because it was more emotional.

Respond to Literature

Organize the students in groups. Explain that they are members of the Pennsylvania legislature who support Henry and those rebelling in Massachusetts. Have the groups cooperate to write a short speech which will gather support for Henry's words and the New Englanders' actions. Remind them to use writing methodology. After reviewing the finished works, you might select certain speeches and have volunteers from the appropriate groups deliver the speeches during class time.

WRITE ABOUT THE SELECTION

Prewriting

Have students observe a television reporter's delivery of the news. If possible, videotape a news broadcast. If not, tell students to watch a nightly news broadcast on the evening before the assignment. Using students' suggestions, list several of the main points of Henry's speech on the board.

Sample answers: Reasoning had failed to bring peace.

He argued that the British were prepared to attack.

The decision to fight for independence should be made quickly.

He would give his life for liberty.

Review the Selection

UNDERSTAND THE SELECTION

Recall

1. On what does Patrick Henry depend in order to predict the future?
2. Whom does Henry think the British plan to attack?
3. What does Henry say are his only alternatives?
4. What was the population of the colonies at this time?

Infer

5. What position had those who spoke before Patrick Henry taken?
6. Does Henry trust the British? Explain.
7. With what does Henry equate defeat in the coming revolution?

Apply

8. If you had been a delegate to the Virginia Convention, would you have supported Henry? Explain.
9. Do you think Patrick Henry's speech changed the minds of some delegates? Why or why not?
10. Would Henry's argument have been more effective as a letter? Explain.

Respond to Literature

Why do you think this speech was of interest to people in other colonies?

WRITE ABOUT THE SELECTION

Imagine that Patrick Henry is delivering his speech today. You are a television reporter covering the Virginia Convention. It is important that you report the main points of his speech.

Prewriting List the main points of his speech. What was the main idea of Henry's speech? What were the most important elements? Include details by quoting one or two of his lines. Add other details about the reaction that members of the Virginia Convention had.

Writing Use your list to write one or two paragraphs that will allow the viewer to understand the main ideas of Henry's speech. Always keep your audience in mind. Be sure to use words and ideas to which they can relate. In your report, use the quotations accurately to illustrate the main points. Add the details of how the audience reacted.

Revising When you revise your paragraph(s), be sure to add specific details that clarify his point of view. Try to make your report more vivid by using precise details. Check to be sure your report does not contain informal words or phrases. If you find you have used informal language, substitute more appropriate terms.

Proofreading Read over your paragraphs. Be sure you have placed quotation marks at the beginning and the end of any direct quotations you have included.

Writing

Have the students work on this section individually. Guide the students to accurate quotations in the speech. Give help to any student who is having difficulty. Ask questions about how the students think different members of the convention might have reacted. Sample answers: anger, opposition, agreement, or cheering.

Revising

Divide the class into groups of three or four. Have each student in a group read his or her report. Have the group select the member's paper that they feel is most accurate and interesting. Let students suggest revisions. After the reports are revised, have each group pretend to be news anchorpersons and deliver the report that they thought was best.

Proofreading

Select several students to write the direct quotations they used in their report on the board. Have the class suggest improvements in the use of quotation marks, where necessary.

THINK ABOUT THEME AND THESIS

Theme is the main or central idea in a literary work. It is a comment on life or on a situation in life. Nonfiction writers state their theme directly; it is the subject matter of the work. They may also make a **thesis statement**—an announcement of the position that will be proved or supported in the work.

1. What is the theme of Patrick Henry's speech?
2. Summarize Henry's thesis statement.
3. List three arguments that Henry makes in support of his thesis, or position.
4. How do you think his listeners would have reacted if he had started his speech with the paragraph beginning: "Gentlemen may cry peace, but there is no peace!"
5. What action does Henry recommend as the inevitable result of Britain's refusal to listen to the colonists' pleas and petitions?

Reading Focus

Recognize Fact and Opinion You looked carefully at Henry's speech to distinguish between fact and opinion. Name three opinions and the facts that Henry used to support each opinion.

DEVELOP YOUR VOCABULARY

Rhetoric is the art or science of using words effectively in speaking or writing. A rhetorical question is a question that does not require an answer from the listener. It is a technique used by speakers and writers in order to make a point. The author is actually making a statement. It is phrased as a question only for dramatic effect.

Patrick Henry uses this technique extensively. For example he asks, "Do wise men pretend that all is well when their eyes and ears tell them it is not?" This is a rhetorical question. The answer is so obvious that Patrick Henry does not answer it. However, he answers in detail the rhetorical question, ". . . what is the purpose of this military array?" He presents his answer as arguments to support his position.

Find three other rhetorical questions in this selection. Review the meanings of the vocabulary words from this selection. Then answer each of the three rhetorical questions in original sentences that make use of a word from the vocabulary list.

THINK ABOUT THEME AND THESIS

Answers

1. Wordings may vary, but the general idea is that liberty is in peril.
2. He says he intends to express opinions opposite to those of previous speakers. Open debate is the only way to arrive at the truth. He implies that others have argued for appeasement and that he will ask for action.
3. Answers may vary. Possible arguments are: a. It is useless to hope that there will be no struggle. b. The British troops have been sent as a threat to the colonists. c. Logic, petition, and pleas have not worked.
4. He might have frightened them. By building up to the statement slowly, he prepared them to receive his message.
5. He recommends that the colonists fight.

DEVELOP YOUR VOCABULARY

Before beginning this assignment, have several student volunteers answer the sample rhetorical questions orally. Stress the importance of using one of the vocabulary words from this selection in answering. Student answers may vary. Have students proceed with the assignment.

Sample Answers

1. Is this the role that wise men should play when they are engaged in a great and difficult struggle for liberty? No, false hope may be like listening to a *siren* sing.
2. Are fleets and armies necessary if peace is the British intention? No, there would be no military *array* if peace were their intention.
3. Shall we grow strong through indecision and delay? A quick decision is necessary to defeat the *adversary*.

Reading Focus

Sample Answer

Henry says the Americans have done everything that can be done to avert the storm. Facts to support that opinion include: the Americans have petitioned, protested, pleaded.

ESL Activity

Discuss rhetorical questions used in greeting and conversation, "How are you?" "How do you do?" "How was I supposed to know?" "Who would have thought so?" Discuss rhetorical questions that are found in other languages.

One way to classify literary works is by genre. Works that exhibit the same formal or technical characteristics belong to the same genre. Oration, autobiography, letters, and essays are examples of nonfiction genres.

The four forms of nonfiction are exposition, narration, persuasion, and description. Writers often use more than one form in a single work. Description and narration may be used to illustrate either exposition or persuasion. Exposition may be used to support persuasion.

THE FORMS OF NONFICTION

In discussing the forms of nonfiction, ask students to think of things they have read recently that would fit each of the categories: exposition, argumentation, description, or narrative. Encourage students to say why they classify each work as they do, and whether the work contains more than one form.

Have students describe the organization of a work they described above, noting what kind of information the introduction, body, and conclusion contain. Help them to understand that some newspaper articles and scientific reports give the conclusions first.

Focus ON NONFICTION

What is nonfiction? **Nonfiction** is the branch of literature that communicates information and ideas. It presents factual information. Nonfiction often offers an interpretation of the facts it presents. It can also propose opinions and theories. Nonfiction is written in prose, or ordinary language.

Forms of Nonfiction Nonfiction can be broken down into four categories, or forms. The four forms are exposition, persuasion (or argumentation), description, and narration.

Exposition is writing that explains. There are a number of writing methods used in exposition. One is definition, writing that explains the meaning of a term, such as *democracy.* Another is classification, writing that groups things or ideas according to their similarities or differences. Breaking down nonfiction into four forms involves classification. Still another method of exposition is comparison and contrast. This is writing that explains how one thing is like or unlike another thing. Writing that shows the similarities and differences between baseball and stickball is an example of comparison and contrast. A fourth type of exposition is analysis. Analysis is writing that examines the different parts of something and tells how they fit together to form a whole. Explaining the parts of a steam engine and how they work together is an example of analysis.

Persuasion (or argumentation) is writing that attempts to convince a reader or listener by showing that a statement is either true or false. While expository writing aims merely to explain, persuasion seeks to influence the reader or listener. An editorial in the newspaper urging people to vote in the next election is an example of persuasion.

Description is writing that paints word pictures of the details, qualities, or appearances of something. Specific details make the word picture come alive. The details are the result of careful observation, with attention to shapes, sizes, colors, tastes, sounds, and textures.

Narration is writing in which an event or a series of events is told. While description is concerned with how things look, narration is concerned with what happens when events occur.

Rarely will only one element of nonfiction be used in a single piece of writing. Most writing makes use of two or more.

Organization of Nonfiction Most nonfiction follows a three-part organization. There is an introduction, a body, and a conclusion.

The **introduction** may state a problem or give background or examples. In expository and persuasive writing, the author may make a **thesis statement**. This is an announcement of what is to be proved or supported in the writing. The central idea, or general topic of discussion, in exposition and persuasion is the *theme*. Writers of description use details to create a *dominant impression*. The **body** of the work is used to develop or discuss the ideas of the work. Narration is organized chronologically; that is, in the order in which events have occurred. Other kinds of writing are organized in some kind of logical order. The **conclusion** rounds out the work. It may do so by restating the thesis, by summarizing the main ideas in the body, by answering a question that was raised, or by urging the reader to future action.

Types of Nonfiction Many different kinds of literature fall into the category of nonfiction. Biography, autobiography, diaries, memoirs, journals, and letters tell about people's lives. Reports, articles, news stories, and essays deal with facts, theories, and ideas. There are many different kinds of essays. Orations, like those made by Patrick Henry and George Washington, are essays that are spoken rather than written.

Real-Life Application

Ask students to think of how they might use each of the four forms of nonfiction if they were writing their own life story, or autobiography. They might, for example, describe their house; narrate an incident; explain how their hobbies compare to those of their siblings' by classifying, defining, or analyzing the hobbies; or try to persuade readers of the value of some type of training they have had.

Selection Overview

SELECTION OBJECTIVES

After completing this selection, students will be able to

- recognize nonfiction
- understand the categories of nonfiction and recognize examples
- understand the organization of nonfiction works
- understand that oration is a spoken form of nonfiction
- write an oration using traditional organization
- recognized when the same word is being used as a noun or verb
- recognize support for opinions

Lesson Resources

Farewell Address
- Selection Synopsis, Teacher's Edition, p. TT60
- Comprehension and Vocabulary Workbook, pp. 7–8
- Language Enrichment Workbook, p. 4
- Teacher's Resources
  Reinforcement, p. R4
  Test, p. T7–T8
  Literary Analysis, pp. L1–L2

About the Author

Washington's decision not to run for a third term set a precedent that lasted for 144 years. No president ran for a third term until Franklin Roosevelt broke the tradition in 1940. He won that race and was also elected to a fourth term. After his death, a constitutional amendment prohibiting a president from serving more than two terms was passed.

The first draft of the "Farewell Address" was written by Alexander Hamilton, one of Washington's cabinet members. Washington revised that draft. To this day, presidents employ speechwriters to capture their ideas in writing.

MODEL

Farewell Address

ADAPTED

by George Washington

FOCUS ON NONFICTION STUDY HINTS

The author introduces his speech and states the background.

Friends and Fellow Citizens: My second term as President of the United States will soon expire. The time for another presidential election is drawing near. Your thoughts should be turning in that direction. It is in the public interest, therefore, that I disclose a decision I have reached. I will not be a candidate for reelection. I will not seek a third term as president.

The author gives a personal reason for speaking.

The author explains his personal reason.

For some time now, I have wished to retire from public life, but the affairs of state were unsettled. A sense of duty compelled me to stay on. I am happy to say my services are no longer needed. The Foreign and Domestic affairs of our country are now in order. I can pursue my inclination with a clear conscience.

The author tells what he intends to do in the speech. This is his thesis statement.

Here, perhaps, I should stop. But my concern for your welfare will not end with my term in office. My affection for you will only end with my death. Therefore, I will offer for your consideration some advice. These sentiments are the result of many years of experience and much observation of human nature. They are the thoughts of a parting friend, uncolored by personal or political motive.

The author begins the body of the speech.

Love of liberty is woven through every fiber of your hearts. You need no counsel from me to strengthen that attachment.

Remember, though, that the one nation you forged from thirteen colonies is the pillar on which that liberty stands. It is that

---

inclination (in kluh NAY shun) a particular disposition or bent of mind
uncolored (un KUL urd) not influenced by
counsel (KOUN sul) advice

ESL Activity

Point out the blue Study Hints in the left-hand margin of Washington's speech. Encourage students to use these study hints throughout this selection to help them follow the structure of the speech. Point out that each hint summarizes the text and also explains how it fits into the structure of a speech. Ask students to notice the elements of nonfiction, such as the opening explanation of the author's decision followed by reasons for it.

Cooperative Group Activity

Divide the class into small groups. Have each group select a speech given by a 20th-century President. Each group should look for the theme and the thesis, analyze how it is organized, and finally compare the theme to Washington's speech. Have groups present their information to the class.

George Washington, after Gilbert Stuart. The Granger Collection

TEACHING PLAN

INTRODUCE

Motivation

Bring a photograph of the Washington Monument to class. Explain that it is 555 feet high and was erected in memory of Washington. Ask the students what kind of people earn such a tribute from their countrymen and women. Ask them if they can suggest any contemporary figures who might be honored after their death and what form they think the honor might take.

Purpose-Setting Question

Kings and emperors often name cities after themselves. As it was being planned, the nation's capital was referred to as Federal City. After Washington's death, it was given its current name. Why do you think people who had fought a war for liberty would wait until after a leader's death (even a highly respected leader) to confer this honor?

READ

Literary Focus: *Nonfiction*

Point out the blue Study Hints in the left margin of the text. Have students use these hints to help them make a simple outline of this speech, writing specific headings for the introduction, the body, and the conclusion.

Reading Focus: *Recognize Support for Opinions*

Point out the thesis statement in the third paragraph of the speech, in which Washington openly states that he will share his advice—his opinions on how Americans can achieve a safe, peaceful, and happy future. As students read the speech have them find evidence Washington provides to support his opinions.

CLOSE

Have students complete Review the Selection on pages 24–25.

Develop Vocabulary Skills

Compose a paragraph using the vocabulary words at the bottom of page 22. Make copies for handouts. Leave blank spaces where the vocabulary words can be inserted. Write the vocabulary words with their meanings on the board. Ask for volunteers to suggest words to fill in the blanks on the handout.

Viewing Fine Art

Gilbert Stuart (1755–1828) was a highly skilled American artist, best known for his many portraits of George Washington. His paintings show Washington as a heroic figure. This painting is a full-length portrait, showing Washington as tall, idealized, and commanding. He dwarfs the viewer, who must look up at him. His dominating pose and the document under his hand suggest his position as a head of state. Washington was greatly beloved and Stuart's portraits of him were very popular. Ask: What does this portrait suggest about George Washington?

Reading Focus: *Recognize Support for Opinions*

Remind students that speakers often state their opinions, then give facts that support their opinions. Ask: What facts did the speaker refer to in order to support his opinion that unity was necessary for tranquility?

Literary Focus: *Nonfiction*

Ask students to look for words the author uses to persuade his audience, for example *dangerous* and *wickedness*. Discuss how such words help when trying to make a specific argument or point.

The author states the theme: the need for unity in preserving the nation's hard-won liberty.

unity of government which is the source of your real independence. The union makes possible your tranquility at home and peace abroad. Your prosperity and your liberty depend on the strength of that union.

You are all Americans. It is to America that you owe your first allegiance, not the region of your birth. That name, *America,* embraces all the common bonds you share: your manners, customs, and political beliefs. You have fought and triumphed together in a common cause. The independence and liberty you now possess result from those joint efforts and shared suffering.

The author makes his first point; he warns against party politics.

Regional loyalties are a threat to your liberty. More dangerous yet is party allegiance. Party spirit is rooted in human nature. Political parties exist to some extent under all forms of government. But it is in a democracy that they are seen in their most dangerous form.

The author supports his first point with reasons.

Parties win some elections and lose others. A party newly come to power may be tempted to take revenge for earlier defeats. You have seen how party rivalry in France has led to the execution of leaders who lost public favor. Such wickedness leads to chaos.

The author states his second point; he warns against tyrannical leaders.

The public, alarmed at the threat of lawlessness, becomes inclined to place absolute power in the hands of one strong leader who can restore order. Sooner or later, this leader raises himself above the law and becomes a tyrant. Liberty is left in ruins. Such a calamity need not happen. A wise people can prevent it by discouraging and restraining party loyalty.

The author supports his second point with ways of counteracting tyrannical government.

The framers of the Constitution wisely gave no one branch of government absolute power. The president, the congress, and the courts have separate spheres of influence. No one of the three branches can be permitted to encroach upon the powers of the others. Consolidation of power in any one branch leads to tyranny.

The need for Constitutional change may arise. Consolidation of power may seem a convenient means of effecting change. But it is the customary weapon by which free governments are destroyed. The permanent evil it sets loose outweighs the temporary

---

tranquility (tran KWIL uh tee) calmness; peacefulness
encroach (en KROHCH) to intrude upon the rights of others
consolidation (kun sol uh DAY shun) strengthening

---

ratified (RAT uh fyd) approved or confirmed

benefit that results. If change is needed, let it come through a Constitutional amendment ratified by the people.

Public morality and an educated citizenry are indispensable to the preservation of liberty. Life, reputation, and property are only safe in a land which values virtue. Only an informed public can make wise choices. Encourage, therefore, public education and the growth of educational institutions.

Be honest and generous in dealings with other nations. Strive to be at peace with all peoples but maintain a strong defense. A strong defense is the surest guarantee of peace.

The author states his third point; he warns against foreign entanglements.

Do not be drawn into European affairs. Expand trade relations but avoid permanent political alliances. The nations of Europe have warred upon each other for centuries and will continue to do so. Honor those temporary treaties signed in a time of emergency but do not extend them.

The author supports his third point with a reminder of the nation's obligations.

European quarrels are not our quarrels. We are separated by an ocean. Our destiny lies in the future. Do not be drawn into Europe's past. And in both public and private affairs, remember the maxim, "Honesty is the best policy."

I offer these thoughts as an old and true friend. I realize my words alone are no safeguard against an uncertain future. It is enough if now and then the nation remembers a friend's counsel: Discourage and restrain party allegiance. Guard against those who would use patriotism to conceal selfish interests. Avoid entanglement in European intrigues.

The author begins his conclusion. He restates his thesis and summarizes his main points.

As president, I committed no intentional errors, but I am aware of my own human frailties. Whatever mistakes I have made, I ask God to correct in the course of time. I hope my countrymen will forgive my failings, realize my good intentions, and remember my zeal to serve this land to the best of my ability.

---

ratified (RAT uh fyd) approved or confirmed

Enrichment

Note the practical effects Washington's speech had on American political traditions—the two-term limit, neutralism through much of our history, making a farewell address, and not naming a successor.

Critical Thinking: *Evaluate*

Ask the students to evaluate Washington's speech. Was it effective? Why? Why not? What was the most effective part?

Comparing Selections

Ask the students to compare and contrast tone in the speeches of Washington and Henry.

Mini Quiz

Write the following sentences on the board or overhead projector and call on students to fill in the blanks.

1. Washington wanted to retire earlier, but a sense of ________ compelled him to stay on.
2. The one nation that had been forged from thirteen colonies was, to Washington, the pillar on which the people's ________ stood.
3. Washington thought Americans should give their first allegiance to ________, not to the region of their birth.
4. Even more dangerous than regional loyalties, he thought, was ________ allegiance.
5. The new nation should expand trade, Washington said, but avoid permanent ________ alliances.

Answers

1. duty
2. liberty
3. America; the nation; the union
4. party; political party
5. political; foreign

UNDERSTAND THE SELECTION

Answers

1. He planned to retire at the end of his second term.
2. party allegiance
3. public morality and an educated citizenry
4. He was retiring from public life. No one could say his opinions were influenced by thoughts of reelection or personal gain.
5. America. He says, "It is to America that you owe your first allegiance."
6. Answers will vary. Suggested response: Only an informed public can make wise choices.
7. He thought these alliances might draw America into European wars.
8. Answers will vary. One possibility is avoid foreign entanglements.
9. Answers will vary. One possibility is that he respected their wisdom.
10. Answers will vary. One possibility is no, because he warned against the dangers of party loyalty.

Respond to Literature

Discuss the relevance of Washington's admonition today. Were his fears about tyranny, political parties, and foreign alliances justified? Are any of his fears still matters of concern to the nation?

WRITE ABOUT THE SELECTION

Prewriting

Explain that Washington's "Farewell Address" set a precedent that every American president since him has followed. Using students' suggestions, list issues that could be discussed in such a speech. Sample answers: state of the economy, foreign relations, education, and so on. Write the main parts of a speech on a board or an overhead transparency using the students' suggestions, include the type of information that should be included in each part.

Review the Selection

UNDERSTAND THE SELECTION

Recall

1. What decision did Washington disclose to his audience?
2. What did he say was more dangerous to liberty than regional loyalties?
3. What two things did he say were indispensable to liberty?

Infer

4. Why did Washington choose this time to make the remarks he did?
5. Did he owe his first loyalty to Virginia or America?
6. Why did he believe education was indispensable?
7. Why did he believe we should avoid permanent alliances with Europe?

Apply

8. Which of Washington's warnings do you think is most effectively stated?
9. What opinion do you think he held of the framers of the Constitution?
10. Do you think Washington would have approved of today's voting system?

Respond to Literature

List Washington's warnings about dangers to democracy. How do his themes reflect Washington's time?

WRITE ABOUT THE SELECTION

You have been studying the elements of nonfiction in this unit. Now it is time for you to apply that knowledge. Suppose that you are George Washington and that you are President today. You have decided not to run again and to retire to your estate at Mount Vernon. You make another "Farewell Address." What would you warn the people about today? Would any of the concerns in the original address be meaningful today?

Prewriting Decide what you will talk about in the body of your speech. Which issues will you discuss? Jot down the points that you will make in your speech. Then decide how you will introduce your speech and with what conclusions you will end.

Writing Use the information collected during the prewriting exercise to compose your speech. Some authors write the body first and then the introduction and conclusion. Write an opening and closing paragraph and at least one paragraph on an issue. If you write about two or more issues, write a brief paragraph on each.

Revising When you revise, think about adding detail. You want to have enough evidence to support your conclusion.

Proofreading Read over your essay. Be sure all your subjects and verbs agree. If the subject is singular, be sure your verb is singular. If the subject is plural, make sure your verb is plural.

Sample answers:

1. Introduction—Address the audience and give background on the issues that will be discussed.
2. Body—discuss ideas and the issue(s), point by point.
3. Conclusion—Summarize main ideas. Have students work individually on an outline of what they will include in their "Farewell Address."

Writing

Have students work individually. Walk around the classroom, giving help to those students who are having difficulty. Ask questions about how the students think certain issues affect them personally.

Revising

Assign each student a partner. After the first student reads the paper to the partner, have the partner make suggestions of details that will add evidence to support the conclusion. Then, have students reverse roles with their partners.

Proofread

Select one or two of the students' papers for proofreading on an overhead projector. Have the class check subject and verb agreement.

THINK ABOUT NONFICTION

An **oration** is a speech that is intended to inspire listeners to action. In Washington's day, oratory was a highly regarded and eagerly enjoyed mode of communication. It was especially prevalent in courtrooms, on the political stump, and at religious gatherings.

1. How many parts did George Washington's address have? Name the parts.
2. What action did George Washington hope his listeners would take?
3. Does Washington make a thesis statement in his speech? If so, what is it?
4. Summarize the three main points about which Washington cautioned his listeners.
5. Patrick Henry made a very emotional speech in defense of liberty. How would you characterize the tone of Washington's "Farewell Address"?

DEVELOP YOUR VOCABULARY

A word can sometimes be used as either a noun or a verb. For example, in the title of this selection, "Farewell Address," the word *address* is a noun meaning "speech." However, in the sentence "I will address this package to Jim J. Johnson," the word *address* is a verb meaning "to write the destination on." The meanings are clearly not the same.

The following words are also found in this selection. Each word can be used either as a noun or as a verb. If you are not certain of the meanings of each of the words, check the definitions in a dictionary.

Write a sentence using each word as a noun. Then write a sentence using each as a verb.

1. triumph
2. result
3. form
4. favor
5. counsel
6. offer
7. defeat
8. change
9. benefit
10. quarrel

THINK ABOUT NONFICTION

Answers

1. There are three parts—an introduction, a body, and a conclusion.
2. Sample answer: He hoped citizens would act upon his advice.
3. Yes, he says he "will offer for your consideration some advice."
4. Sample answer: In general, he urged his audience to avoid party politics; guard against those with selfish interests, and avoid foreign entanglements.
5. Sample answer: Washington's tone is calm and reasoned; the suggestions are offered as advice from a friend.

DEVELOP YOUR VOCABULARY

Sample Answers

1. **a.** (noun) We celebrated the football team's *triumph* with a parade.
   b. (verb) Hard work helped the colonists *triumph* over a harsh winter.
2. **a.** (noun) Joe earned a high grade as a *result* of his effective studying.
   b. (verb) The planning commission's findings will *result* in an addition to the gymnasium.
3. **a.** (noun) The *form* of a business letter is shown in your textbook.
   b. (verb) The ballerinas will *form* a circle on the stage.
4. **a.** (noun) Cheryl willingly did the *favor* for her mother.
   b. (verb) Jack's friends *favor* ice cream over pudding.
5. **a.** (noun) The townspeople appreciated the mayor's *counsel* during the recent drought.
   b. (verb) The principal will *counsel* any student who needs help.

Selection Overview

SELECTION OBJECTIVES

After completing this selection, students will be able to

- understand the use of description in nonfiction
- understand a dominant impression
- analyze the use of selected details in creating a dominant impression
- create a dominant impression in their writing
- understand that word meanings can change with time
- make inferences

Lesson Resources

Letter to Her Daughter from the New White House

- Selection Synopsis, Teacher's Edition, p. TT60
- Comprehension and Vocabulary Workbook, pp. 9–10
- Language Enrichment Workbook, p. 5
- Teacher's Resources
  Reinforcement, p. R5
  Test, p. T9–T10

More About Description

When describing, writers choose those details they consider important to the impression they want to create. Ask: If Patrick Henry had described the British presence in America, what details might he have selected? Ignored? You might start the students off with the examples: artillery as well as infantry (selected); red uniforms (ignored).

Learn About

Description

Abigail Adams, 1766, Benjamin Blyth.
The Granger Collection

Reading Focus

Make Inferences Many times you figure out how a person feels about something without being told directly. You make inferences, or use the information given to understand something not stated. As you read this selection, you will be able to make inferences about how Abigail Adams feels about living in the White House. Look for the descriptions that help you make the inferences.

Description is one of the four main forms of writing. Writers use it when they want to paint a picture in words or help the reader know what something looks, sounds, tastes, or feels like.

Details make a description come alive. Writers carefully choose the details they use in order to create a main focus for the description. This focus is called the dominant impression. The dominant impression contributes to the mood of the description and helps the reader to experience a scene or a sensation as the writer wishes. The description becomes real to the reader.

To understand a writer's dominant impression, notice not only the details selected but also the choice of words. Description is especially effective when it makes precise use of words and phrases.

As you read the selection, ask yourself:

1. On what details does Abigail Adams focus?
2. What is the dominant impression in her letter?

WRITING CONNECTION

Look at the artwork in this unit. Describe one person pictured. Create a dominant impression for your description.

About the Author

Abigail Adams became a prolific letter writer partly from necessity. During the Revolutionary War she and her husband were often separated for long periods of time. She kept him informed about family affairs by letter. While he attended to government, she had to run the family farm, requiring more letters. When they were together in France and in Washington she kept in touch with her children by letter.

She is the only woman to be both wife and mother of a president (John Quincy Adams, fifth president). She was an ardent supporter of equal educational opportunities for women and an outspoken critic of slavery.

ESL Activity

Abigail Adams's letter contains lengthy sentences made of multiple clauses which may hinder comprehension. Have students work in pairs to rewrite several long sentences as shorter sentences.

Cooperative Group Activity

Pair students to complete the Writing Connection activity. Have each student in a pair write down the dominant impression he or she wants to create and list three details that will contribute to that impression. Have the students exchange papers and offer each other suggestions for additional details.

Letter to Her Daughter from the New White House

by Abigail Adams

Washington, 21 November, 1800

My Dear Child:

I arrived here on Sunday last, and without meeting with any accident worth noticing, except losing ourselves when we left Baltimore and going eight or nine miles on the Frederick road, by which means we were obliged to go the other eight through woods, where we wandered two hours without finding a guide or the path. Fortunately, a straggling black came up with us, and we engaged him as a guide to extricate us out of our difficulty; but woods are all you see from Baltimore until you reach the *city*, which is only so in name. Here and there is a small cot, without a glass window, interspersed among the forests, through which you travel miles without seeing any human being. In the city there are buildings enough, if they were compact and finished, to accommodate Congress and those attached to it; but as they are, and scattered as they are, I see no great comfort for them. The river, which runs up to Alexandria[1], is in full view of my window, and I see the vessels as they pass and repass. The house is upon a grand and superb scale, requiring about thirty servants to attend and keep the apartments in proper order, and perform the ordinary business of the house and stables; an establishment very well proportioned to the President's salary. The lighting of the apartments, from the kitchen to parlors and chambers, is a tax indeed; and the fires we are obliged to keep to secure us from daily

---

extricate (EK strih kayt) to set free; release; disentangle
cot (KOT) cottage or small house
interspersed (in tur SPURST) scattered among other things
[1]**Alexandria:** A city in northeastern Virginia

Teaching Plan

INTRODUCE

Motivation

In the library find photos of the White House as it is today and drawings made of it during its early years. Mention that the British burned it in 1814, and it had to be rebuilt. It was at that time that the outside walls were painted white.

Purpose-Setting Question

The Adamses were the first presidential couple to occupy the White House. What experiences made Abigail especially qualified to manage a new house that had not even been completed?

READ

Literary Focus: *Description*

Have students discuss Adams's description of her journey. Ask whether she gives them a vivid impression of what it was like, and if so, which words and phrases make them feel as if they had been riding along with her.

Reading Focus: *Make Inferences*

Have students identify words and phrases in the letter that reveal Adams' attitude toward the move to the new White House. For example, after reading her description of the journey out of Baltimore to the "city," ask students what they think her attitude is toward the trip. Do they think she is glad to be moving to the new White House?

CLOSE

Have students complete Review the Selection on pages 30–31.

Develop Vocabulary Skills

Write the vocabulary words on the board. Read aloud the sentence from the selection in which each word appears. Tell the students to write their conception of what each word means. Ask for suggested meanings and write them on the board. After reading the selection, ask the students to review and refine their original definitions.

Viewing Fine Art

Benjamin Blyth had a successful career as a portraitist. He worked in oils and crayons. He advertised himself as a limner, a gilder, a miniaturist, and a portraitist.

This pastel portrait of Abigail Adams was done in 1766, a few years after the Adamses were married. Abigail was twenty-two years old when this portrait was drawn. It is the only portrait of her which shows her as a young woman. Ask: What is your impression of Abigail Adams's personality? Explain.

agues is another very cheering comfort. To assist us in this great castle, and render less attendance necessary, bells are wholly wanting, not one single one being hung through the whole house, and promises are all you can obtain. This is so great an inconvenience, that I know not what to do, or how to do. The ladies from Georgetown[2] and in the city have many of them visited me. Yesterday I returned fifteen visits—but such a place as Georgetown appears—why, our Milton is beautiful. But no comparisons—if they will put me up some bells and let me have wood enough to keep fires, I design to be pleased. I could content myself almost anywhere three months; but, surrounded with forests, can you believe that wood is not to be had because people

ague (AY gyoo) violent fever
[2]**Georgetown:** A section of Washington, DC

cannot be found to cut and cart it? Briesler entered into a contract with a man to supply him with wood. A small part, a few cords only, has he been able to get. Most of that was expended to dry the walls of the house before we came in, and yesterday the man told him it was impossible for him to procure it to be cut and carted. He has had recourse to coals; but we cannot get grates made and set. We have, indeed, come into a *new country*.

You must keep all this to yourself, and, when asked how I like it, say that I write you the situation is beautiful, which is true. The house is made habitable, but there is not a single apartment finished, and all withinside, except the plastering, had been done since Briesler came. We have not the least fence, yard, or other convenience, without, and the great unfinished audience room I make a drying-room of, to hang up the clothes in. The principal stairs are not up, and will not be this winter. Six chambers are made comfortable; two are occupied by the President and Mr. Shaw; two lower rooms, one for a common parlor, and one for a levee room. Upstairs there is the oval room, which is designed for the drawing room, and has the crimson furniture in it. It is a very handsome room now; but, when completed, it will be beautiful. If the twelve years, in which this place has been considered as the future seat of government, had been improved, as they would have been if in New England, very many of the present inconveniences would have been removed. It is a beautiful spot, capable of every improvement, and, the more I view it, the more I am delighted with it.

Since I sat down to write, I have been called down to a servant from Mount Vernon,[3] with a billet from Major Custis, and a haunch of venison, and a kind, congratulatory letter from Mrs. Lewis, upon my arrival in the city, with Mrs. Washington's love, inviting me to Mount Vernon, where, health permitting, I will go before I leave this place. . . .

Affectionately, your mother,
Abigail Adams

---

procure (proh KYUUR) to obtain or secure
recourse (REE kawrs) a turning back for aid, safety, etc.
habitable (HAB it uh bul) fit to be lived in
levee (LEV ee) a morning reception held by a person of high rank
billet (BIL it) a brief letter
[3]**Mount Vernon:** Home of George Washington, located in northern Virginia

Background Notes

Explain that the oval room Mrs. Adams mentions is today the president's office. When he speaks to the nation on television, the president usually speaks from the oval office.

Literary Focus: *Description*

Ask students to summarize the impression of the White House Abigail Adams conveys. Does it seem bleak? Uncomfortable? Stately? Ask students to defend their answers in class discussion. Have them identify details that support their impressions.

Reading Focus: *Make Inferences*

At the conclusion of the letter, ask students to discuss Adams' character. Does she seem adaptable? Patient? Optimistic? Ask what adjectives they would use to describe her and what information from the letter supports these inferences.

Critical Thinking: *Analyze*

Point out that in the next-to-last paragraph, Adams seems pleased with the White House. Ask students to point out the factors that make her "delighted with it."

Mini Quiz

Write the following sentences on the board or overhead projector and call on the students to fill in the blanks.

1. From her window, Adams had a full view of the ________.
2. Keeping the house and stables in order required the services of about ________ servants.
3. Wood for the fireplaces was hard to find because people to ________ it were scarce.
4. Adams used the audience room to ________ clothes in.
5. Adams received an invitation to visit Mrs. ________ at Mount Vernon.

Answers

1. river
2. thirty
3. cart
4. dry
5. Washington

UNDERSTAND THE SELECTION

Answers

1. Washington, DC
2. forest
3. Mount Vernon
4. President of the United States
5. fireplaces
6. Answers will vary. One possibility is that she did not want to appear ungrateful.
7. 1788
8. Answers will vary. These may include: sociable, intelligent, polite, loyal to her husband, adventurous, etc.
9. Answers will vary. Possibilities include: entertaining, overseeing the house, reading, etc.
10. Answers will vary. Possibilities include: central heating, finished rooms and stairs, surrounding fence and city, etc.

Respond to Literature

Why was the White House built near a river? Possibilities are that the colonists were dependent on rivers for travel, commerce, delivery of needed goods, and fresh water.

Why might the national capital have been located where it is? One possibility is that it is in a geographically central position between the northern and southern colonies.

WRITE ABOUT THE SELECTION

Prewriting

Have the students visualize their "dream homes" by closing their eyes for several minutes. Ask: "In what sequence do you view it?" Using the students' suggestions create an outline on the board.

Sample answers:

1. from the outside to the inside
2. from the basement to the attic
3. from room to room
4. where features are located
5. the placement of items both inside and out

Writing

Have students work on this section individually. Remind students to give their reader a tour of the house. Ask them if the reader will be able to visualize the structure when the description is completed. Go around the class, giving help to any student having difficulty.

Revising

Make this a cooperative group learning opportunity. Have each member of the group read his or her description. While a member is reading the description, have the other members of the group close their eyes and visualize the house being described. When the reader has finished, have the group members make suggestions as to how certain descriptive features might be more clearly defined. Each student might also draw a sketch and/or floorplan of the home when the written revisions are finished.

Proofreading

Have students work with a partner to determine whether any word appears to be misspelled. Check the dictionary for the spelling of any word in question.

Review the Selection

UNDERSTAND THE SELECTION

Recall

1. From what city was Abigail Adams writing?
2. What surrounded the White House?
3. What home did Mrs. Washington invite Abigail Adams to visit?

Infer

4. What elected position did Abigail Adams's husband hold?
5. How was the White House heated at that time?
6. Why did Adams ask her daughter to keep the negative comments about the White House a secret?
7. In what year did Americans begin to consider building the White House?

Apply

8. List three personal qualities you think apply to Mrs. Adams.
9. If you were in Mrs. Adams's situation, how would you spend your time?
10. How would Mrs. Adams's description of the White House differ today?

Respond to Literature

How does this selection illustrate the characteristics of colonial literature?

WRITE ABOUT THE SELECTION

In this letter, Abigail Adams described her impressions of the White House to her daughter. She painted a vivid picture of both the interior and the exterior of this famous building. As a reader, you feel as though you are being given a personal tour. If you could design your "dream house," what would it look like? Describe the appearance and the setting in which you would build it. Write about the house so that a person who has never seen it could picture it from your description.

Prewriting List the characteristics you would choose for your dream house. Include details of the interior as well as exterior features of the building. Organize your details according to room sizes, layout, placement of items, location of exterior features, building materials used, and so on.

Writing Use this list to write at least one paragraph describing the best features of your house. Select words that paint a vivid picture.

Revising When you revise your description, be sure to add specific details that illustrate the appearance of the house and its setting.

Proofreading Read over your selection. Be sure all the words are spelled correctly. If you are unsure of the spelling of a particular word, look it up in the dictionary.

THINK ABOUT DESCRIPTION

Writers use description to paint a picture for the reader. Effective writers do not list every feature of the object being described. They select those that will support their sense of what is important.

1. List five features of the White House that Mrs. Adams selected for her description.
2. What are some reactions that Mrs. Adams had to the house?
3. What was the dominant impression created in your mind by her description of these features?
4. If Mrs. Adams were describing the White House for a newspaper article, what dominant impression do you think she would try to create? Why would her description to a newspaper be different from the description written to her daughter?
5. If she were describing the White House today, how do you think her description would differ?

Reading Focus

Make Inferences How does Abigail Adams feel about being in the White House? Find three descriptions that helped you make inferences about her feelings.

DEVELOP YOUR VOCABULARY

Language is always changing. People invent new words, and others drop from current usage. New words form as the need for them arises. Sometimes old words acquire new meanings. These new meanings become part of common usage along with the original meanings of the words. At other times, the commonly used meaning of a word changes entirely. The original meaning may become lost, or **archaic**. The word may remain in the language but assume an entirely new meaning.

Using a dictionary, look for the meaning of each of the following words as they were used in Mrs. Adams's letter. Remember, these may be unusual or archaic meanings today. Then compare that meaning with the usual, or common, meaning of the words today. Write an original sentence using each word in its older meaning. Then, write an original sentence using its contemporary meaning.

1. expended
2. attend
3. design
4. audience
5. tax

ESL Activity

Have each student draw a floorplan of a typical or traditional house in his or her native country. Discuss the reasons for differences or similarities with typical American homes, such as climate or geography.

THINK ABOUT DESCRIPTION

Sample Answers

1. the size of the house, its lighting and fireplaces, the lack of bells, the plastering, the unfinished rooms, the stairs, the oval room
2. Mrs. Adams noted several inconveniences of the unfinished house: difficulties in procuring wood, the grandeur and future beauty of the rooms.
3. the makeshift nature of her life in the unfinished mansion
4. She would emphasize the beauty of the White House. It would be "politic" to emphasize positive aspects of life in the White House.
5. She would concentrate on the features of a finished and furnished house, with central heating and finished grounds.

DEVELOP YOUR VOCABULARY

Sample Answers

1. expended **a.** used up **b.** spent, as money.
2. attend **a.** look after **b.** to wait on; also, to be present.
3. design **a.** to plan to do; intend **b.** to make preliminary sketches of; plan.
4. audience **a.** an interview **b.** people assembled to hear a concert or to watch a performance.
5. tax **a.** a heavy burden or demand **b.** a compulsory payment for the support of government services.

Reading Focus

Sample Answer

She feels like she is in a "new country." She sees a full view of the river; the house is on a grand and superb scale; the more she views it, the more she is delighted with it.

SELECTION OVERVIEW

SELECTION OBJECTIVES

After completing this selection, students will be able to

- understand narration
- understand the importance of including a beginning, a middle, and an end in all forms of narration
- understand the sequence of events in simple narrative
- write a paragraph using simple narrative
- recognize roots and understand their use in forming words
- make generalizations

Lesson Resources

from *The Autobiography* and *Poor Richard's Almanack*

- Selection Synopsis, Teacher's Edition, pp. TT61–TT62
- Comprehension and Vocabulary Workbook, pp. 11–12
- Language Enrichment Workbook, p. 6
- Teacher's Resources
  - Reinforcement, p. R6
  - Test, pp. T11–T12
  - Unadapted Selection, pp. U1–U7

More About Narration

Simple narrative relates events in the order in which they happened. A great deal of nonfiction, especially biography and autobiography, use simple narration.

About the Author

Benjamin Franklin was a scientist and inventor as well as an author. Among his inventions are the Franklin stove (an efficient heating device) and the lightning rod (a safety device). Both are still used today. Ask the students if they have ever seen either invention. If so, ask them to tell where and describe their impressions.

Learn About

NARRATION

Narration is one of the four main forms of composition. It is the primary form of novels, short stories, and narrative poems, as well as of biography, autobiography, and news reports. In short, narration is the form used in fiction and nonfiction storytelling.

Stories, whether true or fictional, are about events—the birth of a new island in the Pacific, the rescue of a lost child, the appearance of Peter Rabbit in Mr. MacGregor's garden, your first birthday party. To make a good narrative, the events should have a beginning, a middle, and an end. This is part of the normal development of the plot.

The unique feature of narration is chronology. Events happen in time, and every story is told in some kind of time order. The most common time order is straightforward—from beginning to end.

As you read the next selections, ask yourself:

1. What kind of narrative writing is Franklin presenting?
2. In what order is he telling his stories?

READING FOCUS

Make Generalizations As you read, you often make generalizations, or use the information given to understand a broader idea. What generalizations can you make from Franklin's writings about his personality and about the values of the time?

WRITING CONNECTION

Write a paragraph in which you tell of an important event in your life. Give your paragraph a beginning, a middle, and an end.

ESL Activity

Have students work in pairs to read the Franklin excerpts. After reading on their own, partners can meet to discuss each one. Each partner should make sure the other can accurately summarize it. Encourage partners to discuss their impressions of Franklin's character.

from The Autobiography

ADAPTED

by Benjamin Franklin

[*This excerpt reveals events from Franklin's teen-age years.*]

When I was about 16 years old, I happened to read a book written by a man named Tryon. He recommended a vegetable diet. I decided to try it. My brother, a bachelor, did not own a home. He and his apprentices boarded in another family's house. My refusal to eat meat or fish was an inconvenience, and I was frequently chided for it.

I learned Tryon's ways of preparing some dishes, such as boiling potatoes, or rice, making hasty pudding, and a few others. Then, I made my brother a proposition. If, each week, he would give me half the money he paid for my board, I would buy my own food. He agreed instantly.

I soon discovered that I could save half what he paid me. This gave me extra money to buy books. There was another advantage to this situation. My brother and the others went from the printing house to their meals. I remained there alone.

My meals were light. Often, I ate only a biscuit, or a slice of bread, a handful of raisins or a tart from the bakery. A glass of water was my beverage. After eating, I had the rest of the time until they returned to study. I learned quickly since my mind was clear from practicing moderation in eating and drinking.

On my first voyage from Boston, the ship was becalmed off Block Island.[1] The people aboard started fishing. They hauled up

---

excerpt (ehk SURPT) a passage taken from a book; quotation
boarded (BAWRD id) had rooms and meals provided regularly for pay
chided (CHYD id) scolded
hasty pudding (HAYS tee PUUD ing) cornmeal mush
tart (TAHRT) small, filled pastry; small pie
moderation (mod uh RAY shun) avoidance of excess
becalmed (bih KAHLMD) to make motionless from lack of wind
[1]**Block Island:** an island off the coast of Rhode Island

Teaching Plan

INTRODUCE

Motivation

Point out that at the age of 16, Franklin began writing anonymous satires or humorous works ridiculing human vices or follies. Have the students discuss vices and follies they might satirize anonymously.

Purpose-Setting Question

Explain that Franklin was a diplomat who represented the colonies in France. Ask: How does Franklin's personality strike you? How do you think his personality helped him be successful as a diplomat? Representing the colonies in France?

READ

Literary Focus: *Narration*

Have students read the first paragraph of the first excerpt (pp. 33–34) and predict what will happen next. Ask how they think Franklin will tell this story. What do students think the middle and ending of the story will discuss?

Reading Focus: *Make Generalizations*

As students read, encourage them to keep a chart, using "Franklin's personality" and "American Culture" as column heads. Have students look for details that reveal aspects of Franklin's personality and aspects of American culture during his lifetime. Ask: Based on these details, what generalizations can you make about Franklin and the values of his time? Remind students to include these on their charts.

CLOSE

Have students complete Review the Selection on pages 46–47.

Develop Vocabulary Skills

Pair students. Assign each student one word from the selections. If there are more than 29 students, use selected words more than once. If fewer, exclude some selected words. Have each student write down the definition of the assigned word. Pairs should exchange definitions and write a sentence using the other student's word.

More About the Literary Period

In London in the mid-18th century newspapers, magazines, journals, and theaters were multiplying rapidly. Printers, publishers, and booksellers were often all part of one business. Franklin's expertise in writing, printing, and publishing from the early days of his *The Pennsylvania Gazette* and *Poor Richard's Almanack* made his name known to thousands of readers. By the time Franklin was sent to France to help persuade the French government to aid the colonies during the Revolution, he was a well-respected scientist, publisher, and statesman.

Viewing Fine Art

Rubens Peale (1784–1865) was one of the sons of James Wilson Peale, a prominent Philadelphia painter. Rubens and his brothers Rembrandt and Titian were all named for old master painters. Sixteen of the Peales were professional artists, three of them the first professional women painters in America.

The term *still life* is used to refer to a close-up image of objects such as a vase of flowers or a plate of fruit. Rubens Peale was a specialist in still-life painting. The influence of Dutch still-life painters is clear in the subtle gradation of light and shade and in the realism of the pieces of fruit. Why is this natural, realistically painted still-life an appropriate illustration for the selection?

Critical Thinking: *Analyze*

Ask students to read and think about the final two sentences of this excerpt. Ask: What impression does this conclusion give you of Franklin's character?

Still Life, 1857, Rubens Peale

a great many cod. Until then, I had stuck to my resolution. I had not eaten animal food. At this time, I considered catching any fish as a kind of unprovoked murder. None of them had, or ever could, do us any injury that might justify the slaughter. All of this seemed to make sense to me.

Still, I had once been a great lover of fish. Every cod that came hot from the frying pan smelled delicious. For some time, I could not decide between principle and inclination. Then I remembered something. When the fish were cut open, I had seen smaller fish taken out of their stomachs. I thought to myself, "If you eat one another, I don't see why I should not eat you." So I eagerly ate the cod, and have continued to eat with other people. Only now and then do I return to a vegetable diet. It is a convenient thing to be a reasonable creature. It enables us to find or make a reason for everything we want to do.

---

resolution (rez uh LOO shun) decision as to future action
unprovoked (un pruh VOHKT) not to stir up an action
slaughter (SLAWT ur) the killing of animals for food
principle (PRIN suh pul) a fundamental truth or rule of conduct
inclination (in kluh NAY shun) a liking or preference

[*This excerpt deals with Franklin's early career.*]

My brother began to print a newspaper, the *New England Courant*, in the year 1720 or '21. It was only the second paper to be published in America. Some of his friends tried to dissuade him, saying one newspaper was enough for America. In hindsight, their judgment seems questionable. Today, in 1771, there are at least twenty-five newspapers. No matter, my brother was determined. He composed the type[1] and printed his first edition. I was employed as the paper boy.

Some of his friends amused themselves by writing short pieces for his paper. When these gentlemen visited, I would hear them tell about the public compliments they received for their work. I decided to try my own hand.

I was still a boy and suspected that my brother would not agree to print my work. So, I disguised my handwriting and slipped an anonymous work under the printing house door. He found it in the morning. When his friends dropped by, he discussed the mysterious article with them. I listened in secret delight as they discussed its merits. Imagine my pleasure as each tried to guess the author's identity, naming only men known for their learning and imagination. Looking back, I suppose I was lucky. Being a boy, I think I overestimated their ability to judge literary merit.

At the time though I was encouraged. I submitted several more anonymous articles. Each was approved and printed. I kept my secret until I ran out of ideas. Then I revealed my identity.

---

anonymous (uh NON uh mus) written by a person whose name is withheld

[1]**composed the type:** set a piece of writing into type

Literary Focus: *Narration*

Ask students to point out details on this page that show that Franklin is looking back at events that happened a long time ago. Although he is telling about his life in chronological order, he is also commenting upon it from his present point of view.

Reading Focus: *Make Generalizations*

Tell students that Franklin began writing his autobiography in 1771 at the age of 65. The final section, completed around 1790, covered his life only until his fifty-first year. The rest of his life was covered in the many letters that he wrote. Ask: What generalizations can you make about Franklin's priorities based on these facts and what you have read thus far?

Viewing Fine Art

This painting provides interesting details about the printshop where Franklin worked. He is standing by the special compartmentalized box for storing the type. Replacing the individual letters used for a print job into the box was a necessary but tedious job. Ask students how the computer has changed the way a print shop would look today.

Discussion

Have students draw from their own experiences to discuss Franklin's relationship with his brother. Was there a rivalry between Franklin and his brother? Did Franklin's brother treat him unfairly? Is there any evidence of a sense of loyalty between the brothers toward each other?

Young Franklin as an Apprentice in James' Printshop. Corbis Bettmann

My brother's friends were impressed, but he was not pleased. He thought, probably with good reason, that I was becoming vain. This may have been one of the reasons we began to quarrel at this time.

He was my brother, but he considered himself my master. I was his apprentice in the printing trade. He expected the same services from me that he would from any other apprentice. I thought some of my assigned chores were demeaning. I expected better treatment from a brother. It did not help that my father generally took my side. My brother had a temper and often beat me. This did not improve my attitude. I longed for some means of shortening my apprenticeship. The opportunity arose in an unexpected way.

---

apprentice (uh PREN tis) a person under legal agreement to work for a specified time under a master craftsperson in return for instruction and, formerly, support

demeaning (dih MEEN ing) lowering in status or character; degrading

The members of the governing assembly took offense at an article which appeared in our paper. I have forgotten what it was about. My brother refused to identify the author. He was imprisoned for a month. I was questioned but let go with a warning. I suppose they thought it was the duty of an apprentice to keep his master's secrets.

Despite our differences, I resented my brother's confinement. I managed the paper in his absence and, on occasion, poked fun at the assembly. My brother approved of this. Others saw me in a different light. They saw me as a young genius flawed by a liking for satire and libel.

My brother was released from prison. The Assembly ordered "that James Franklin should no longer print the paper called the *New England Courant*." My brother and his friends tried to find a way around the order. Some suggested he change the name of the paper. James didn't like that idea. Someone suggested that the paper be printed under the name of Benjamin Franklin. James would still be held accountable if his apprentice was the publisher. So I was released from my apprenticeship. It was a very flimsy scheme. Still, we printed the paper under my name for several months.

Soon my brother and I had another disagreement. Since he had released me from my apprenticeship, I began looking for a new job. Under the circumstances, I suppose I was taking unfair advantage. My guilt was assuaged though when he beat me.

When he realized I was serious, James had me blackballed. No other printing house in Boston would hire me. Leaving town did not seem a bad idea at the time. I was afraid that my association with the paper would soon bring trouble. I did not want to end up in jail as James had. I decided to see New York.

My father joined my brother in opposing my plans. I secretly booked passage on a boat bound for New York and left without saying goodbye. Three days later I landed there. I was a boy of

---

satire (SA tyr) a literary work in which vices, stupidities, etc. are held up to ridicule and contempt
libel (LY bul) any written statement, not made in the public interest, tending to expose a person to public ridicule
accountable (uh KOUNT uh bul) responsible for
assuaged (uh SWAYJD) calmed
blackballed (BLAK bawld) to exclude from social life, work, etc.

Reading Focus: *Make Generalizations*

After reading this page, have students discuss the attitude of government toward newspapers in Franklin's time. Would you expect there was much freedom of press?

Literary Focus: *Narration*

Point out that the sentence "I decided to see New York" marks a transition in the story. Franklin introduces a new setting and transports the reader there in a few brief sentences. Ask students why this transition marks the end of one part of the story and the beginning of another.

Literary Focus:
Narration

Ask students to read the description of Franklin's journey by boat (beginning here and ending at the end of the next page) with attention. Have them discuss their reactions to it. Point out that Franklin describes each event as it happens. Do students think this is effective? Might they have described such a journey in some other way? If so, how?

seventeen, with a great deal of optimism and very little money.

I sought a job with old Mr. William Bradford. He had been the first printer in Pennsylvania but now published in New York. He had no openings in his firm. He suggested that I go on to Philadelphia. His son who operated a printing house there had recently lost an apprentice through death. So I set out by boat for Philadelphia.

The boat encountered foul weather, and we tried to land at Long Island. A raging surf made that impossible. So we dropped anchor and swung round towards the shore. Some curious spectators watched from the beach. We shouted to them for assistance, and they called back. But the wind was so high and the surf so loud that we could not understand each other. There were some canoes on the shore. We signaled that they should use them to bring us ashore. They either did not understand or else they thought it was a foolish idea. Soon after, they left.

Night was coming on. We had no choice but to lie at anchor until the wind died. We lay down to get some sleep. That was almost impossible. The spray from the surf washed over the boat and down upon us. We lay soaking wet all night and got very little rest.

The next day was calm and dry. We set out for Amboy. We reached port by nightfall. We had been on the water thirty hours without food.

Once on land, I realized I had a fever. I had read somewhere that cold water was a remedy for that condition. I drank large quantities of it and went to bed early. By morning the fever had left me. I set out on the next leg of my journey by foot. It was a fifty-mile walk to Burlington, New Jersey. In Burlington, I could find boats that would take me to Philadelphia.

As luck would have it, it rained hard all that day. By noon, I was thoroughly soaked and very tired. I stopped at a run down inn where I stayed the night. At this point, I began to wish I had never left home. I was a sad sight. People, seeing my condition, began to question. I could tell from their tone that they thought I was a runaway servant. I feared arrest on that suspicion.

I proceeded on my way the next morning. By evening of that day, I had gotten within eight to ten miles of Burlington. I stopped at an inn owned by a Dr. Brown. He began a conversation with me as I ate. Finding I was well read, he became very sociable and friendly. It was a chance meeting, but we struck up a friendship that lasted until the day he died.

I stayed that night in his inn. The next morning, I reached Burlington. To my dismay, the regularly scheduled boats had just left. The next scheduled departure was Tuesday. This was only Saturday.

I bought some gingerbread from an old woman and asked her advice. She invited me to stay at her house until I could get passage by water. I was sick of traveling by foot and accepted the invitation. Learning I was a printer, she suggested I stay there and start a business. I explained that I did not have the money needed to open my own shop. She was a very good hostess, and I thought I would have a pleasant stay until Tuesday, but it was not to be.

In the evening I took a walk by the river. A boat came by bound for Philadelphia. They agreed to take me on board, and I instantly agreed. As there was no wind, we rowed all the way. By midnight, some of the passengers began to argue that we must have passed the city in the dark. They would row no further. None of us knew where we were. We decided to go ashore. We rowed up a creek and landed near an old fence. It was a cold October night. We used the fence rails to build a fire and stayed where we were until daybreak.

By the light of day, one of the crew recognized the place. We were at Cooper's Creek a little north of Philadelphia. We rowed on and soon saw the outline of the city. We arrived about eight or nine o'clock Sunday morning and landed at the Market Street Wharf.

I have described my journey in some detail. I will do the same when telling of my arrival at that city. You may see the contrast between such unlikely beginnings and my current situation. I was wearing work clothes. My good clothes were being shipped from Boston. I was dirty from the trip. I had no suitcase. Dirty clothes hung from my pockets. I knew no one and nothing about the city. I was exhausted from the rowing and lack of sleep. I was very hungry.

I had only a Dutch dollar and a few coins to my name. The coins I gave to the boatman for my passage. They were reluctant

---

sociable (SOH shuh bul) enjoy the company of others

Reading Focus: *Make Generalizations*

Discuss the fact that Franklin asked advice from an old woman, and she invited him to stay at her house until he could get a boat to Philadelphia. The boat crew was willing to take Franklin along. Ask: Do these acts of generosity give students any sense of how Franklin related to strangers?

Critical Thinking: *Summarize*

Have students summarize in one paragraph Franklin's journey from Boston to Philadelphia.

Viewing Fine Art

This copy of a French portrait is one of many portraits of Franklin. Franklin is one of only two non-Presidents of the United States (the other is Alexander Hamilton) who have been honored by being portrayed on American paper currency; a portrait very similar to this one is on the $50 bill. Ask: What does this portrait reveal about Franklin's personality?

Benjamin Franklin, after J.S. Duplessis. The Granger Collection

to take money since I had rowed. I insisted, not wanting them to think I was poor.

I set out up the street, looking about as I went. Near the markethouse, I stopped at a bakery. Being from Boston, I asked for a biscuit. I was told they were not made in Philadelphia. I then asked for a threepenny loaf and got the same response. I asked for threepenny worth of any bread. The baker gave me three large puffy rolls. I was shocked at their size.

Having no room in my pockets, I set off down the street with a roll under each arm and eating the third. I went up Market Street as far as Fourth. I did not know it at the time, but I passed the home of Mr. Read, whose daughter would become my wife. I made a circle and found myself again at the Market Street Wharf near where I had landed. Being full, I gave two of the rolls to a woman and a child standing waiting for a boat.

I took a drink of water from the river. Thus refreshed, I walked again up the street. There were now many well-dressed people walking about. I followed them into a large meetinghouse and sat down. The room was quiet. Being drowsy, I fell fast asleep. Someone was kind enough to wake me when the meeting broke up. This meetinghouse, then, was the first house I entered or slept in, in Philadelphia.

[*The following excerpt relates events that occurred several years later.*]

About this time, I set a personal goal. I would attain moral perfection. I wished to be without fault. I would conquer temptation. I knew or thought I knew right from wrong. It seemed easy enough to do one and avoid the other. I soon learned such a task was easier said than done.

While concentrating on avoiding one fault, I slipped into another. Habit took over. Desire was stronger than my will. I concluded that good intentions were not enough to prevent slipping.

Bad habits must be broken. Good habits must be acquired and practiced. That was the way to reach perfection. I conceived a plan.

In books about virtue, no two writers seemed to agree on definition. Temperance, for example, some defined as moderation in

Enrichment

Ben Franklin's several-day trip would take only two to three hours today. Ask students to compare the hardships of travel in the 1700s to the hardships of travel today. Point out that sailing ships used wind as their only power source, so passengers had to pitch in and help row when the winds dies down.

Reading Focus: *Make Generalizations*

After reading this page, ask students to think about whether Franklin was very hard on himself. Ask why someone might decide to work on personal goals such as breaking bad habits and attaining moral perfection.

Literary Focus: *Narration*

As students read this section of *The Autobiography*, have them consider how it differs from the opening section. Help students see that instead of telling a connected story of events, Franklin now highlights a self-improvement procedure that he followed.

Critical Thinking: *Apply*

Have students read Franklin's first three sentences about setting a personal goal. Ask them to apply their knowledge of human nature to discuss whether or not Franklin's plan seems reasonable.

Literary Focus: *Narration*

Point out that Franklin is no longer relying on chronological order to tell his story. He has structured this portion of his narration differently. Ask students to describe this new structure. If they are having difficulty, point out that he lists reasons for taking certain actions. Help students see the cause-and-effect pattern of this narration. The structure also contains elements of a how-to manual; Franklin explains the steps he took in the process of trying to improve himself.

eating and drinking. Others thought temperance meant moderation in every pleasure and passion. I decided to write my own definitions. I chose thirteen words that identified all the virtues I thought necessary or desirable. I defined each in an aphorism.

The thirteen virtues were: Temperance, Silence, Order, Resolution, Frugality, Industry, Sincerity, Justice, Moderation, Cleanliness, Tranquility, Chastity and Humility. A few examples of the aphorisms are:

Silence: Speak only when you have something to say that may benefit yourself or others.

Industry: Waste no time; always be employed in doing something useful.

Moderation: Avoid extremes; forgive and forget insults.

Cleanliness: Tolerate no uncleanliness in body, clothes, or home.

I wanted to practice all these virtues. I thought the best way to go about it was to master one at a time. I believed that acquiring some would help me in mastering the others. I began with Temperance since a clear head makes it easier to guard against bad habits. I was anxious to gain knowledge while acquiring virtue. We learn from what we hear, not what we say. Therefore, silence would be next. I went on thus, arriving at the order shown above.

I decided to keep a record of my progress. I took a book and allotted one page to each virtue. I drew seven columns on each page, one column for every day of the week. Whenever I fell into a bad habit, I would place a black spot in the appropriate column.

I decided to practice each virtue for one week. Thus, in the first week, I practiced avoiding the least offense against Temperance. I took my chances with the others. If at the end of the week, there were no black spots in the book, I would consider Temperance to be acquired. I would then move on. I hoped that by seeing progress in my record book, I would be encouraged to continue my efforts.

I began my self improvement plan immediately. Surprisingly, I found I had more faults than I had realized. Still, I had the

---

aphorism (AF uh riz um) a short, pointed sentence expressing a truth or precept
frugality (froo GAL uh tee) careful economy; thrift
tranquility (tran KWIL uh tee) calmness, peacefulness
chastity (CHAS tuh tee) decency; modesty
humility (hyoo MIL uh tee) humbleness; the absence of pride

satisfaction of seeing myself improve. I soon needed a new record book. At first I kept diligent records. As the years went by, I became lax in my record keeping. I was too busy to take the time. Eventually, I stopped keeping records altogether. Still, I always carried my little book with me.

Order gave me the most trouble. When I was a journeyman printer, I had time to concentrate on Order. As I rose in the world, I found it became necessary to meet with business associates at their convenience. This necessity made it impossible for me to follow a preplanned schedule. I thought of giving up the attempt to acquire Order. I could live with myself if lack of Order was my only fault. This attitude was similar to that of the fox in the fable. Unable to reach some grapes, he quit trying and comforted himself with the thought that they were probably sour anyway.

The thought occurred to me that I was going to extremes by trying to be perfect. My attempts might really be a form of conceit, which is the opposite of Humility. If others found out, I might look ridiculous. Furthermore, people often hate and envy perfection in others. I convinced myself that a kind person should allow himself a few faults, if only to avoid making his own friends embarrassed by their own failings.

Now that I am old and my memory is bad, I wish I had mastered the virtue of Order. On the whole, though I never came close to achieving perfection, I think I am a better and happier man for the effort.

My descendants should know that I owe my happiness in this my seventy-ninth year to that effort. Temperance has kept me healthy. Through Industry and Frugality, I became knowledgeable and wealthy. Sincerity and Justice have gained me the respect of my countrymen. Lastly, even the imperfect practice of virtue has won me friends. I hope, therefore, that some of my descendants follow my example and reap the benefit.

---

diligent (DIL uh junt) hardworking; done with careful, steady effort
lax (LAKS) not strict or exact; careless; loose
journeyman (JUR nee mun) a worker who had satisfied his apprenticeship and thus qualified himself to work at his trade

Critical Thinking: *Analyze*

Ask students to analyze whether Franklin's reasoning about the problems of being perfect are sound logic or excuses.

Reading Focus: *Make Generalizations*

Ask students to identify what Franklin believed were his imperfections. Ask: What generalizations can you make about Franklin's self-image? Do you think he learned to accept himself?

Viewing Fine Art

This is the original title page of Benjamin Franklin's popular *Poor Richard's Almanack*, which predicted the weather for the year and contained a variety of humorous asides. The lowercase *s* was printed with a character that looked like a lowercase *f* with no crossbar, except when the *s* fell at the end of a word. The letter was still pronounced *s*. Capitalization and spelling were not standardized at this time, and end punctuation for titles and headings was normal. Today, the same information would be printed quite differently. Ask: What can you learn about the *Almanack* by studying its cover? How does the copy on the cover constitute advertising?

Poor Richard, 1733.

AN

Almanack

For the Year of Chriſt

1733,

Being the Firſt after LEAP YEAR:

And makes ſince the Creation	Years
By the Account of the Eaſtern *Greeks*	7241
By the Latin Church, when ☉ ent. ♈	6932
By the Computation of *W.W.*	5742
By the *Roman* Chronology	5682
By the *Jewiſh* Rabbies	5494

Wherein is contained

The Lunations, Eclipſes, Judgment of the Weather, Spring Tides, Planets Motions & mutual Aſpects, Sun and Moon's Riſing and Setting, Length of Days, Time of High Water, Fairs, Courts, and obſervable Days.

Fitted to the Latitude of Forty Degrees, and a Meridian of Five Hours Weſt from *London*, but may without ſenſible Error, ſerve all the adjacent Places, even from *Newfoundland* to *South-Carolina.*

By *RICHARD SAUNDERS*, Philom.

PHILADELPHIA:
Printed and ſold by *B. FRANKLIN*, at the New Printing-Office near the Market.

Poor Richard's Almanack, Title Page, First Edition, 1733. Benjamin Franklin.
The Granger Collection

from

Poor Richard's Almanack

ADAPTED

by Benjamin Franklin

[*The following aphorisms appeared in Franklin's almanac, which he began publishing in 1733.*]

1. The things which hurt, instruct.
2. Early to bed and early to rise, makes a man healthy, wealthy, and wise.
3. The sleeping fox catches no poultry.
4. Beware of little expenses; a small leak will sink a great ship.
5. Fish and visitors stink after three days.
6. A country man between two lawyers is like a fish between two cats.
7. The worst wheel of the cart makes the most noise.
8. Be slow in choosing a friend, slower in changing.
9. At the *working* man's house, hunger looks in, but dares not enter.
10. Sally laughs at everything you say. Why? Because she has fine teeth.

Literary Focus: *Aphorism*

Point out to students that an aphorism is a short statement that makes a generalization and is often witty. Aphorisms often contain a moral or a lesson.

Critical Thinking: *Apply*

Ask students to apply some of the aphorisms to their own lives, for example, lessons they may have learned from painful experiences.

Reading Focus: *Make Generalizations*

Students have been reading works by Franklin which reveal his personal concerns about how to live one's life. Ask students to make a generalization about whether Franklin drew his aphorisms from common sayings or from personal experience.

Mini Quiz

Write the following sentences on the board or overhead projector. Call on volunteers to fill in the blanks. Discuss the answers with the class.

1. In "A Vegetable Diet," the kind of fish being cooked on board ship was ________.
2. According to the *Autobiography*, Franklin's father ________ his plans to see New York.
3. At a Philadelphia bakery, Franklin bought ________.
4. The virtue that gave Franklin the most trouble was ________.
5. According to one of Franklin's aphorisms, the sleeping ________ catches no poultry.

Answers

1. cod
2. opposed
3. rolls
4. order
5. fox

UNDERSTAND THE SELECTION

Answers

1. meat and fish
2. Philadelphia
3. healthy, wealthy, and wise
4. Answers will vary but should include the concept that he could save money while on a vegetable diet.
5. Answers will vary. One possibility is that he and his brother argued, and he could not get another job in Boston.
6. He had little money and had learned that there was a position open in Philadelphia.
7. Answers will vary. One possibility is that the host tires of entertaining.
8. Answers will vary. Some would find this easy; some would find it very difficult.
9. Answers will vary. One possibility is that he and his brother would have solved their problems.
10. Answers will vary. Possibilities include: airplane, car, train, boat, and so on.

Respond to Literature

Pair students and have each pair reread each work in the selection for the purpose of finding clues to the lifestyle of the colonists. Have students copy words, phrases, and sentences that are pertinent. Then have students use their lists of words, phrases, and sentences to write a paragraph about how Franklin's works reflect the lifestyle of the colonists.

WRITE ABOUT THE SELECTION

Prewriting

Using students' suggestions, create an outline of ideas and impressions on a chalkboard or on an overhead transparency. Sample setting; friendly, warm, cozy inn: chef and assistants carefully preparing and attractively arranging food; aroma of meat is tantalizing and overwhelming. Remind students that the narrative must follow a logical and chronological sequence.

Review the Selection

UNDERSTAND THE SELECTION

Recall

1. Which foods did Franklin not eat?
2. Where did he finally settle after leaving Boston?
3. "Early to bed and early to rise makes a man" what?

Infer

4. In the first excerpt, why did Franklin have extra money to buy books?
5. Why did Franklin seek employment outside of Boston?
6. Why did Franklin leave New York City so quickly?
7. Why do you think ". . . visitors stink after three days"?

Apply

8. How difficult would it be for you to stay on a vegetable diet? Why?
9. Predict what might have happened if Franklin had stayed in Boston.
10. If you were making the trip from Boston to Philadelphia today, how would you travel?

Respond to Literature

How do you think Franklin's works reflect the lifestyle of the colonists?

WRITE ABOUT THE SELECTION

At the conclusion of the first excerpt, Franklin succumbs to the tempting aroma of fish. Suppose he had traveled by land instead of water, and that he stopped at an inn where the cook was roasting a side of fresh beef. Rewrite the conclusion to the selection. Describe in detail how the beef would tempt Franklin and cause him to go off his vegetable diet.

Prewriting Jot down your ideas of the inn, describing the activity in the kitchen and Franklin's reaction to the aroma of roasting meat. Give several reasons for Franklin's decision to eat meat. (Remember cows do not eat other cows, as fish eat other fish. Thus, you will have to invent another justification for Franklin's decision.) Put your ideas into an informal outline, showing the sequence in which you will write your paper.

Writing Use your informal outline to write a paragraph or two that will serve as a new conclusion to the selection.

Revising When you revise your paragraph, be sure the tone is consistent and similar to Franklin's tone. Check to see if you can duplicate Franklin's tongue-in-cheek ending. Try to use humor in your paragraph, as Franklin does, to make the piece more enjoyable for the reader.

Proofreading Read over your selection. Add quotation marks if you quote your own thoughts as Franklin did.

Writing

Have students work individually. Walk around the class, giving help to any student who is having difficulty. Ask the students what unique reasons they could find to justify eating the meat. Answers will vary. Sample answers: don't want to hurt the chef's feelings; innkeeper will be upset; the animal was old.

Revising

Divide students into small groups. Have each group discuss Franklin's tone in writing his story. Then each member, in turn, can read his or her paragraph. Other members may make suggestions as to how the paragraph might be revised to have a more "tongue-in-check" ending.

Proofreading

Have students work in pairs. Each partner can assist in double-checking the proper use of any quotation marks.

THINK ABOUT NARRATION

Narration is writing in which events are related in chronological order. It is used in fiction (novels and short stories), poetry (narrative poems), and nonfiction (biography, autobiography, and news stories).

1. What type of nonfiction are Franklin's stories?
2. Do you think a serious sermon on the subject of excusing one's own actions would have been more effective than the humorous ending of "A Vegetable Diet"? Explain your answer.
3. Do you think Franklin's account of his struggle with self-improvement would have been more or less effective if he had been writing of someone else's struggle? Explain your answer.
4. Explain the difference between a short story and an autobiography.
5. Why would a story in Franklin's newspaper be called a narrative?

READING FOCUS

Make Generalizations Write two generalizations about the values of Franklin's time. Then write two generalizations about Franklin's personality. Be sure to support your generalizations with details from the selection.

DEVELOP YOUR VOCABULARY

A **root** is a word or word part that is used to form other words. The addition of various prefixes or suffixes to the root word usually yields a variety of words. The root usually carries the central meaning of the word. For example, the root word *temper* is used to form the word *temperance*. *Temper* means "to regulate or mix properly." *Temperance* means "to regulate or have self-restraint in conduct, expression, or appetite." Many times you can use the root word to help you understand the meaning of a larger word. This is especially true if you know the meanings of various prefixes and suffixes.

Find the root in each of the following words. Use the root to figure out the meaning of each word. Check each meaning in a dictionary. Then write an original sentence for each word.

1. resolution
2. becalmed
3. unprovoked
4. tranquility
5. inclination
6. accountable
7. frugality
8. moderation

ESL Activity

Have students share aphorisms common in their native languages. Example, from the Japanese, "Bits of dirt make a mountain" and from the Chinese "One picture is worth a thousand words."

THINK ABOUT NARRATION

Answers

1. autobiography
2. Answers will vary. One possible answer would be no, because the sermon would have been too heavy, and the story is not meant to be didactic.
3. Answers will vary. One possible answer is that it would have been less effective because it would seem to ridicule or place blame on another person.
4. The short story is fiction; autobiography is nonfiction.
5. because it tells of events that happen in time order

DEVELOP YOUR VOCABULARY

Answers

Root word and sample answers:

1. *resolute*; My brother's *resolution* to improve his grades has made my parents happy.
2. *calm*; Our sailboat was *becalmed* in the middle of the lake.
3. *provoke*; The child was injured in an *unprovoked* attack by two dogs.
4. *tranquil*; The quiet inn brought welcome *tranquillity* to the weary travelers.
5. *incline*; Janet has an *inclination* to listen to classical music.
6. *account*; The vandals will be held *accountable* and punished for their deeds.
7. *frugal*; My mother practices *frugality* when planning the household budget.
8. *moderate*; Wanda keeps her figure by eating in *moderation*.

READING FOCUS

Sample Answer

People were hungry for information and ideas. There were 25 newspapers in the country by 1771. There was less freedom. Franklin's brother was ordered to stop publishing his newspaper.

Franklin had a sense of humor. He wrote about being surprised at having quite a few faults. He wanted to be morally perfect. He set up personal goals for improving himself.

Selection Overview

SELECTION OBJECTIVES

After completing this selection, students will be able to

- understand point of view
- recognize first-, second-, and third-person point of view
- use consistent point of view when writing a paragraph
- use a dictionary to find word etymology or history
- compare and contrast

Lesson Resources

What Is An American?

- Selection Synopsis, Teacher's Edition, p. TT63
- Comprehension and Vocabulary Workbook, pp. 13–14
- Language Enrichment Workbook, p. 7
- Teacher's Resources
  Reinforcement, p. R7
  Test, pp. T13–T14
  Unadapted Selection, p. U26

More About Point of View

After students have read the selection, point out that Crèvecoeur uses first-person point of view for effect when he refers to a particular individual ("I could show you a man . . ."). He returns to the third person when making generalizations about the qualities this man shares with other Americans. Have the students discuss the effect that the use of first person would have had on the essay, if used throughout. You might start the discussion by changing the first two sentences in the second paragraph to first person and then reading them aloud.

About the Author

Crèvecoeur's essay was part of a book he wrote entitled *Letters from an American Farmer*. The author owned a farm in New York state. Most of his writing is optimistic. A rare exception is "Description of Charles-Towne," a condemnation of slavery.

Learn About

Point of View

Essayists and storytellers choose a point of view from which to write. **Point of view** is the position from which an author writes.

In nonfiction, three points of view are used. If writers make themselves the speaker, they have used the first-person point of view. You can recognize first person by a writer's use of *I* and *me.*

If the writer addresses the reader directly, the choice is the second-person point of view. You can recognize second person by the use of the pronoun *you.*

If writers position themselves outside the material altogether, they have used the third-person point of view. You can recognize third person by a writer's use of the pronouns *he, she* or *it.*

As you read "What Is an American?" ask yourself:

1. Which point of view did Crèvecoeur use?
2. Would his essay have been as effective if he had chosen a different point of view?

Reading Focus

Compare and Contrast To compare two things, you look at what they have in common. To contrast two things, you look at ways in which they differ.

You have your own opinions about what it means to be an American. As you read, think about your own views. Compare and contrast them with those of Crèvecoeur.

WRITING CONNECTION

Write three sentences, using first-person point of view, about your participation in an after-school activity. Rewrite the sentences, using third-person point of view.

Develop Vocabulary Skills

Write the words from the bottom of page 49 and their meanings on the chalkboard. Tell students that Crèvecoeur was optimistic about America. Ask them to predict how the writer might use the vocabulary words.

ESL Activity

Ask students to share any stories they know about why their families came to the United States. Contribute any stories you know about your own family.

Cooperative Group Activity

Pair students to complete the Writing Connection activity. Have each student in a pair review the other's sentences and offer suggestions if a change is needed.

What Is an American?

ADAPTED

by Jean de Crèvecoeur

What is an American, this new man? He is a person from Europe, or the descendant of a person from Europe. I could show you a man descended from an English father and a Dutch mother. This man married a French woman. His four sons married wives from four different nations.

He is an American. He does not share the prejudices and customs of his ancestors. In America, individuals of all nations intermarry and form a new nationality. Their labors and heritage will one day cause great changes in the world. Americans are the western pilgrims. They are carrying with them the arts, sciences, vigor, and industry of all their ancestors.

People with the American spirit were scattered about in the different European countries. Here they are all part of one of the finest systems which has ever appeared.

The American, therefore, should love his country much better than the land in which either he or his ancestors were born. In America, hard work will be quickly rewarded. If he lived in Europe, his children would be hungry. In America, they are well-fed and healthy. They gladly help their father clear those fields where crops will grow. No cruel prince, rich abbot, or mighty lord will demand to share their riches.

The American is a new man. He acts from a belief in new principles. He must therefore listen to new ideas with an open mind and form new opinions. He has left behind him in Europe idleness, dependence, poverty and useless labor. In America, he will be richly rewarded for hard work. This is an American.

---

descendant (dih SEN dunt) a person who is the offspring of a certain ancestor, family, group, etc.
prejudice (PREJ uh dis) a judgment or opinion formed before the facts are known; intolerance or hatred of other races, creeds, etc.
heritage (HER ih tij) something handed down from one's ancestors, such as a characteristic, culture, or tradition
abbot (AB ut) a man who is head of a monastery

Teaching Plan

INTRODUCE

Motivation

Ask students why they think people risked the long ocean voyage to make new lives in America in Crèvecoeur's day. Ask what students think America offered immigrants.

Purpose-Setting Question

What are some of the new ideas and opinions Americans formed when they came to their new home land?

READ

Literary Focus: *Point of View*

Ask students to notice how the opening question draws their attention. Then ask them to notice how the author switches from one point of view to another. Ask if they think the author would get their attention better by using only one point of view.

Reading Focus: *Compare and Contrast*

Ask students how they would answer the question "What is an American?" today. List their answers on the board or on an overhead projector. After students have read the selection, let them compare their answers to Crèvecoeur's.

CLOSE

Have students complete Review the Selection on pages 50–51.

Mini Quiz

Write the following sentences on the board or the overhead projector and have students fill in the blanks.

1. According to Crèvecoeur, Americans do not share the ________ and customs of their ancestors.
2. The labors and heritage of the new Americans will someday cause great ________ in the world, he said.
3. Those who came to America were Europeans with the ________ spirit.
4. In America, "no cruel prince, rich abbot, or mighty lord" would take a share of a family's ________.
5. Americans form new opinions because they listen to new ________.

Answers

1. prejudices
2. changes
3. American
4. riches
5. ideas

UNDERSTAND THE SELECTION

Answers

1. Europe
2. They will bring great changes in the world.
3. hard work

Sample answers:

4. Life in Europe did not offer a common person the opportunities that could be found in America.
5. English, Dutch, or French
6. the opportunity to form a new system of government
7. In America there was more opportunity for success.
8. Any art form and science that were known at that time is acceptable.
9. They would not have been given the freedom to express their opinions or to develop new skills.
10. democracy

Respond to Literature

Organize the students into groups of four. Write the following words on the chalkboard: *ancestry*, *work habits*, *opportunities*. Have each student in a group write one sentence about a different one of the three characteristics identified. Have each group use the four sentences to write a summary of an American as he or she might have been described by Crèvecoeur.

WRITE ABOUT THE SELECTION

Prewriting

Ask questions about the characteristics students think describe an American. Using the students' suggestions, write an outline on the board or on an overhead transparency.

Sample answers:

1. People from different countries and backgrounds have intermarried.
2. Heritage is still important to many people.
3. Many cultures can influence one individual.
4. Many new opportunities are available.

Review the Selection

UNDERSTAND THE SELECTION

Recall

1. Where were the colonists from?
2. What will Americans' labors bring?
3. In America, what is quickly rewarded?

Infer

4. What is one European prejudice Americans did not share?
5. Which nations affected our arts and sciences?
6. What was the advantage of being gathered together in one country?
7. Why would the American love this new country so much?

Apply

8. If you lived in the 18th century, which arts and sciences would you have valued most?
9. Predict what would have happened to people with the "American spirit" if they had stayed in Europe.
10. Which new ideas would have appealed to you if you had lived at that time?

Respond to Literature

Do you think Crèvecoeur would have supported the American Revolution? Why or why not?

WRITE ABOUT THE SELECTION

At the time that Crèvecoeur wrote this selection, Americans were primarily of western European descent. Is this still true today? He discusses the opportunities these early immigrants had and indicates that they did not share the prejudices of their ancestors. Has this changed in any way? What are your views on what an American is today? How has the situation changed?

Prewriting Jot down all the details you can think of describing what you think an American is today. Formulate some opinions that you will want to use as main ideas. For each main idea, include details to back up the opinion it expresses. It might help you to refer to the selection for ideas.

Writing Use your notes to write two or three paragraphs that express your opinions of what an American is today. In your paper, explain your views of various nationalities and opportunities and tell whether you think prejudice plays a role in either. You might want to compare or contrast today's situation with the situation that existed in Crèvecoeur's time.

Revising When you revise your paragraph, select specific details or personal experiences that support your ideas.

Proofreading Read over your selection. Be sure you have written complete sentences that include at least one subject and verb.

Writing

Indicate that each student must decide if prejudice still exists, and if he or she feels it does, whether it affects them directly or indirectly. If the student feels that it does not, then why not? Have students work on this section individually. Assist any student who needs help. Ask questions about what priorities the students feel are important to them as Americans.

Revising

Make this a cooperative learning assignment. As each student reads his or her paper, have other members keep an open mind and respect the reader's opinion. Group members should remind the reader that personal experiences help to clarify a person's ideas.

Proofreading

Have one or two students volunteer to have their paragraphs used as models. Put the paragraphs on an overhead projector and have the class correct sentence fragments and run-on sentences.

THINK ABOUT POINT OF VIEW

Point of view is the position writers take in relation to their subject matter. Because their subject matter is often factual, or theoretical, essay writers frequently choose the third person. Some topics, however, lend themselves to the use of the first or second person.

1. Is Crèvecoeur's point of view first, second, or third person?
2. The author never states that he is an American. Would the reader be more or less likely to accept Crèvecoeur's opinions as fact if the essay began, "I am an American..."? Explain your answer.
3. Do you think Crèvecoeur is accurate in his opinions about Americans and Europeans? Explain your answer.
4. At one point in the essay, the author makes a statement about living conditions in Europe. What is Crèvecoeur's opinion of life in Europe?
5. Select one of the author's opinions. Explain why you think it is true or not true today.

READING FOCUS

Compare and Contrast You have explored your own ideas about what it means to be an American and read about Crèvecoeur's ideas. Now write a paragraph in which you compare and contrast your views with those of Crèvecoeur.

DEVELOP YOUR VOCABULARY

Etymology is the study of word origins. Every word has a history. This includes the names of the town, city, and state in which you live. Place names may reflect the ancestry of the original settlers. Dutch colonists named one of their settlements New Amsterdam after the capital of their native country, the Netherlands. When the English drove them out, the name was changed to New York. York is a city in England. This is why there are so many place names in America that include the word "new." How many can you think of?

Use a dictionary or encyclopedia to find the origin of the following place names. List each on a sheet of paper. Write your answer in an original sentence beside the name.

1. New Hampshire
2. Maine
3. Newark
4. Boston

Places may also be named for people, events, geographical features, or other characteristics. Using local sources (if necessary), find the origin of the name of your town or city and the state in which you live.

ESL Activity

Explain that 70 to 80 percent of all English words are borrowed from other languages. Latin languages and Germanic languages have both contributed a great deal to English. This is why students will often find similar-looking words (called cognates) in different languages. Encourage students to look at the derivation of any word they ever look up in a dictionary. Derivations will often help them remember the word.

THINK ABOUT POINT OF VIEW

Answers

1. third person
2. Answers will vary. One possible answer is more likely, or equally likely, because the author would have personal knowledge of his subject matter.
3. Answers will vary. One possibility would be yes, because Crèvecoeur is familiar with history in both cultures.
4. He says if one lived in Europe, one's children might go hungry, and a person in power such as a prince, an abbot, or a lord might demand a share of one's riches.
5. Answers will vary.

DEVELOP YOUR VOCABULARY

Sample Answers

1. *New Hampshire* was named for the county of Hampshire in England. It was named by Captain John Mason (1586–1635), who was granted part of the land that became New Hampshire.
2. *Maine* derived its name from the French province of Maine, north of the Loire Valley in France.
3. The city of *Newark* was named after Newark, in Nottinghamshire, England.
4. The city of *Boston* was named for Boston in Lincolnshire, England.

You may group students into small committees to research the origin of your community name. Have a representative from each group report orally on what the committee discovers.

READING FOCUS

Sample Answers

When Crèvecoeur was alive, most of the people in his area were Europeans, and he thought they were free of the prejudices of their ancestors. Today Americans are from many cultures, but we worry about prejudices a lot. Crèvecoeur thought Americans would change the world, and we know we have contributed to changing it.

SELECTION OVERVIEW

SELECTION OBJECTIVES

After completing this selection, students will be able to

- understand folklore
- distinguish between legend, myth, and the tall tale
- understand the difference between a written and an oral tradition
- use exaggeration for humorous effect
- understand the meaning of hyperbole
- recognize main idea and supporting details

Lesson Resources

Sunrise in His Pocket
Godasiyo, the Woman Chief

- Selection Synopses, Teacher's Edition, pp. TT63, TT64
- Comprehension and Vocabulary Workbook, pp. 15–16
- Language Enrichment Workbook, p. 8
- Teacher's Resources
  Reinforcement, p. R8
  Test, pp. T15–T16

More About Folklore

Myth and legend are two similar kinds of folklore. Legends usually describe the deeds of heroes and heroines. A legend often identifies a person with an historical event. A myth usually contains supernatural elements. A myth often identifies a god or a supernatural being as the cause of a natural phenomenon.

About the Author

Davy Crockett was a famous hunter, marksman, and storyteller. The people of Tennessee elected him to the state legislature and later to the U.S. Congress. In 1836, he went to help Texans in their war for independence from Mexico. Crockett was killed at the famous battle of the Alamo. "Remember the Alamo" became a rallying cry for Texan independence.

Learn About

FOLKLORE

People who have no written tradition pass their beliefs on from generation to generation as **folklore**. The materials passed on consist of myths, stories, riddles, proverbs, superstitions, ballads, songs, and customs. Among the stories told are legends and tall tales.

A **legend** is a story of the past. It often tells of an extraordinary happening. The people who tell the legend believe it. The main character may be heroic, with superhuman powers and excellent character. Legends often try to explain some mystery of human life.

A **tall tale** is a form of humor popular in early American history. It is usually set in the narrator's lifetime. For its humor, it relies on exaggeration. Its plot is deliberately outrageous and unbelievable.

As you read the next two selections, ask yourself:

1. Which selection is a legend?
2. Which selection is a tall tale?

WRITING CONNECTION

Look up the word *hero* in a dictionary. Choose a popular athlete or entertainer. Describe this person in heroic terms. Write your description so that it has the characteristics of either a tall tale or a legend.

READING FOCUS

Recognize Main Idea and Supporting Details The main idea of a story is the most important point—the statement or concept that the writer or storyteller wants you to remember. The writer provides details—descriptions, reasons, and examples—that support that main idea.

As you read "Sunrise in His Pocket" and "Godasiyo, the Woman Chief," think about the main idea of each. How can you summarize each in one sentence? What are some details that support the main idea?

Cooperative Group Activity

Pair the students to complete the Writing Connection activity. Ask each student in a pair to read the other's description and suggest details that might be added.

Sunrise in His Pocket

by Davy Crockett

I'm that same Davy Crockett that is fresh from the backwoods. I'm half horse, half alligator—and part snapping turtle, too. I can wade the Mississippi River and leap over the Ohio River. I can ride upon a streak of lightning. Thorns wouldn't dare to scratch me. I can whip my weight in wildcats—and if anyone pleases—I'll wrestle a panther, or hug a bear too close for comfort. Here is what I did on the day the sun froze.

One January morning, it was so cold the trees were too stiff to shake. The very daybreak froze solid just as it was trying to dawn. The tinder-box I used to light my fire wouldn't spark. It would no more catch fire than a raft sunk to the bottom of the sea.

Well, I decided the only way I was going to get some fire was to make it myself. I brought my knuckles together like two thunderclouds, but the sparks froze before I could collect them. So out I walked whistling "Fire in the Mountains!" as I went along in double quick time. Well, after I had walked about twenty miles I came to Daybreak Hill and discovered what was the matter.

The earth had actually frozen fast on her axis. She couldn't turn round. The sun had gotten jammed between cakes of ice under the wheels. The sun had been shining and working to get loose until he froze in his cold sweat.

---

tinderbox (TIN dur BAHKS) formerly, a metal box for holding flint for starting a fire

Teaching Plan

INTRODUCE

Motivation

Exaggeration for humorous effect is an important part of frontier literature. Here are a few examples from Crockett's political speeches:

"I've got the meanest horse, the surest rifle, the prettiest sister, and the ugliest dog in Tennessee."

"I can run faster, dive deeper, stay under longer, and come up dryer than anyone else."

"I can out-eat, out-work, out-grin, out-run, out-sneeze, out-sleep, and out-lie anything in the shape of a man or beast from Maine to Louisiana."

Purpose-Setting Question

In what ways is "Sunrise in His Pocket" typical of a tall tale?

READ

Literary Focus: *Folklore*

Ask students to pick out some examples of exaggeration in this tale, such as "I'm half horse, half alligator." Have them discuss the effect of the exaggeration.

Reading Focus: *Recognize Main Idea and Supporting Details*

The main idea of this tale is not directly stated. Encourage students to note details as they read and to put them together after reading to state the main idea of the entire selection.

CLOSE

Have students complete Review the Selection on pages 60–61.

Develop Vocabulary Skills

Write the following words on the board: *backwoods*, *wildcats*, *thunderclouds*, *cogwheel*, *daylight*, and *sunrise*. Have students suggest definitions for each word. Explain that these are compound words—each is made up of two words which appeared together so often that people eventually began writing them as one word. Have students suggest other compound words.

ESL Activity

Have students share tall tales and legends from literature. Mythological explanations can be included, such as the founding of Mexico City or the explanations for earthquakes found in various cultures.

Reading Focus: *Recognize Main Idea and Supporting Details*

Ask students to identify the main idea and supporting details of the paragraph that begins, "It was so cold. . . ."

Critical Thinking: *Generalize*

Explain that common themes run through folklore. Ask the students to make a generalization about one recurring theme in folklore based on the theme of this piece.

"C-r-e-a-t-i-o-n!" thought I. "This is the toughest form of suspension. It mustn't be endured. Something must be done or human creation is done for!"

It was so cold that my teeth and tongue were all collapsed together as tight as an oyster. But I took a fresh bear from my back. (I had picked it up along the road.) I beat the animal against the ice until the hot oil began to pour out of it on all sides. I then held the bear over the earth's axis. I squeezed the hot bear oil until I'd thawed the earth loose. Then, I poured about a ton of the hot bear oil over the sun's face.

I gave the earth's cogwheel one kick backward until I got the sun loose. I whistled, "Push along; keep moving!" In about fifteen seconds the earth gave a grunt and began to move.

The sun walked back up into the sky. It saluted me with such gratitude that it made me sneeze. Then I shouldered my bear and saluted back. As I walked home, I introduced people to the fresh daylight with a piece of sunrise in my pocket.

---

suspension (suh SPEN shun) temporary stoppage
cogwheel (KAHG hweel) a wheel with a rim notched into teeth, which mesh with those of another wheel to transmit or receive motion

GODASIYO, *the Woman Chief*

a Seneca legend retold by Dee Brown

At the beginning of time when America was new, a woman chief named Godasiyo ruled over an Indian village beside a large river in the East. In those days all the tribes spoke one language and lived in harmony and peace. Because Godasiyo was a wise and progressive chief, many people came from faraway places to live in her village, and they had no difficulty understanding one another.

At last the village grew so large that half the people lived on the north side of the river and half on the south side. They spent much time canoeing back and forth to visit, attend dances, and exchange gifts of venison, hides, furs, and dried fruits and berries. The tribal council house was on the south side, which made it necessary for those who lived on the north bank to make frequent canoe trips to consult with their chief. Some complained about this, and to make it easier for everybody to cross the rapid stream, Godasiyo ordered a bridge to be built of saplings and tree limbs carefully fastened together. This bridge brought the tribe close together again and the people praised Godasiyo for her wisdom.

Not long after this, a white dog appeared in the village, and Godasiyo claimed it for her own. Everywhere the chief went the dog followed her, and the people on the north side of the river became jealous of the animal. They spread stories that the dog was possessed by an evil spirit that would bring harm to the tribe. One day a delegation from the north bank crossed the bridge to the council house and demanded that Godasiyo kill the white dog. When she refused to do so, the delegates returned to their side of the river, and that night they destroyed the bridge.

Literary Focus: *Folklore*

Explain that many legends contain characters, animals, natural features, and events that symbolize, or stand for, concepts beyond themselves. As students read this legend, have them consider the symbolic meaning of Godasiyo, the bridge, the river, the white dog, and the quarreling people. What larger significance might each element have, beyond its literal meaning within this story?

Background Notes

"Godasiyo, the Woman Chief" is a Seneca legend. The Seneca were one of the six tribes that made up the Iroquois Nation. They lived in the northeastern United States. They called themselves Tshotinondawaga, "the people of the mountain." The Seneca fought on the English side in the Revolutionary War.

Among the Seneca, each village had a designated story teller. Story telling was a formal affair. The audience would periodically chant "he," to show they were listening. It was considered very bad luck to fall asleep during a story. At the conclusion, each member of the audience gave the story teller a small gift as a token of appreciation.

L. Knabel

From that time on people on the north bank and those on the south bank began to distrust each other. The tribe divided into two factions, one renouncing Godasiyo as their chief, the other supporting her. Bad feelings between them grew so deep that Godasiyo foresaw that the next step would surely lead to fighting and war. Hoping to avoid bloodshed, she called all members of the tribe who supported her to a meeting in the council house.

"Our people," she said, "are divided by more than a river. No longer is their goodwill and contentment among us. Not wishing to see brother fight against brother, I propose that those who recognize me as their chief follow me westward up the great river to build a new village."

Almost everyone who attended the council meeting agreed to follow Godasiyo westward. In preparation for the migration, they built many canoes of birch bark. Two young men who had been friendly rivals in canoe races volunteered to construct a special watercraft for their chief. With strong poles they fastened two large canoes together and then built a platform which extended over the canoes and the space between them. Upon this platform was a seat for Godasiyo and places to store her clothing, extra leggings, belts, robes, moccasins, mantles, caps, awls, needles, and adornments.

At last everything was ready. Godasiyo took her seat on the platform with the white dog beside her, and the two young men who had built the craft began paddling the double canoes beneath. Behind them the chief's followers and defenders launched their own canoes, which contained all their belongings. This flotilla of canoes covered the shining waters as far as anyone could see up and down the river.

After they had paddled a long distance, they came to a fork in the river. Godasiyo ordered the two young canoeists to stop in the middle of the river until the others caught up with them. In a few minutes the flotilla was divided, half of the canoes on her left, the others on her right.

The chief and the people on each side of her began to discuss the advantages and disadvantages of the two forks in the river. Some wanted to go one way, some preferred the other way. The arguments grew heated with anger. Godasiyo said that she would

---

flotilla (floh TIL uh) a fleet of boats or small ships

Literary Focus: *Folklore*

Ask students to identify the symbolism of specific events and specific items.

Reading Focus: *Identify Main Idea and Supporting Details*

Ask students to identify the main idea that motivates Godasiyo to act as she does throughout this legend. Have them identify details that support their answers.

Critical Thinking: *Evaluate*

Ask students if they think Godasiyo's decision to move West with her followers was a good one. Should she have remained in the village and tried to get the villagers to live together peacefully?

Comparing Selections

Ask students to compare the unrealistic elements of the two stories and how they fit the main idea of each story.

Literary Focus: *Foreshadowing*

Explain that foreshadowing in literature is the introduction of information that suggests to the reader a later event or outcome of the work. Ask students to identify a passage in the selection that might be considered foreshadowing to the outcome.

Reading Focus: *Identify Main Idea and Supporting Details*

Have a student read the final sentence of the legend aloud. Ask whether this might be considered the main idea of the legend. Have students give details to support their positive or negative answers to this question.

take whichever fork her people chose, but they could agree on neither. Finally those on the right turned the prows of their canoes up the right channel, while those on the left began paddling up the left channel. And so the tribe began to separate.

When this movement started, the two young men paddling the two canoes carrying Godasiyo's float disagreed as to which fork they should take, and they fell into a violent quarrel. The canoeist on the right thrust his paddle into the water and started toward the right, and at the same time the one on the left swung his canoe toward the left. Suddenly, Godasiyo's platform slipped off its supports and collapsed into the river, carrying her with it.

Hearing the loud splash, the people on both sides turned their canoes around and tried to rescue their beloved chief. But she and the white dog, the platform, and all her belongings had sunk to the bottom, and the people could see nothing but fish swimming in the clear waters.

Dismayed by this tragic happening, the people of the two divisions began to try to talk to each other, but even though they shouted words back and forth, those on the right could not understand the people on the left, and those on the left could not understand the people on the right. When Godasiyo drowned in the great river her people's language had become changed. This was how it was that the Indians were divided into many tribes spreading across America, each of them speaking a different language.

Mini Quiz

1. Crockett used a fresh ________ to get hot oil to thaw out the earth.
2. The sun saluted Crockett in such gratitude for his efforts that Crockett ________.
3. The people on the north shore of the river became jealous of Godasiyo's ________.
4. To stop the distrust between factions of the tribe, Godasiyo proposed that her followers build a new ________.
5. When Godasiyo drowned, her people's language had become ________.

Answers

1. bear
2. sneezed
3. dog
4. village
5. changed

AUTHOR BIOGRAPHY

Dee Brown (1908–   )

Dee Brown has spent a lifetime writing about the American West. His popular histories are authentic, and provide a great deal of wisdom regarding human nature.

In the area of nonfiction, he is well known for his book *Bury My Heart at Wounded Knee*. In the book, Brown uses the words of such famous Native Americans as Crazy Horse and Sitting Bull to tell the history of Native Americans between 1860 and 1890. Brown has been one of the few writers to treat westward expansion from the viewpoint of its victims—the Native American tribes.

In his most popular fictional work, *Creek Mary's Blood*, Brown tells the story of five generations of Native Americans. He wrote this story after he found an item about Creek Mary in an old book. She stormed Savannah, Georgia, with a group of male warriors to drive out the British during the Revolutionary War.

Among Brown's other works is a book about trail-driving days and the woman's role in the Old West. His first book, written in 1941, was about Davy Crockett.

Brown was born in a lumber camp in Louisiana. He grew up in Arkansas, where he first became interested in Native American history and the West.

He went to college in Arkansas and later did graduate work at George Washington University in Washington, D.C. Upon graduation, he went to work for the Department of Agriculture as a librarian. In 1948, he became a librarian at the University of Illinois. Being at the university allowed him to do extensive research on his favorite subject—the American West. Because of Brown's many years of careful research and sensitive writing, people are better able to understand the devastating effect westward expansion had on Native Americans.

MORE ABOUT THE AUTHOR

Dee Brown is best known for his books about the Indian Wars, but he has written in other areas as well. Other works include two novels, *Killdeer Mountain* and *The Way To Bright Star*; *When the Century Was Young*, a series of vignettes about his childhood in Arkansas; *Hear That Lonesome Whistle Blow*, a report on the building of railroads.

Additional Works

BY DEE BROWN

You may want to suggest these works by Dee Brown for additional reading.

The American West

Creek Mary's Blood

When the Century Was Young

Tepee Tales of the American Indians Retold for our Times

UNDERSTAND THE SELECTION

Answers

1. He used bear oil.
2. All the tribes spoke only one language.
3. They were jealous.

Sample answers:

4. She realized it was not evil.
5. She wanted to avoid war.
6. Answers will vary but should include the concept of why different Indian tribes speak different languages.
7. strong and imaginative
8. All life on earth would die.
9. They would find it humorous and laugh.
10. The Indians would still have argued.

Respond to Literature

Organize the students in groups. Have each group select one paragraph from either selection. Have them collaborate in revising that paragraph so that it exhibits the characteristics of the other selection. Have volunteers read their group's revised paragraph.

WRITE ABOUT THE SELECTION

Prewriting

Place pictures of several movie monsters on a bulletin board or have the students visualize monsters they recall from stories or movies. Using the students suggestions, create three lists on the chalkboard or on an overhead projector.

Sample answers to lists:

1. Appearance: furry, pink ball ferocious, scaly, lizard-headed slimy, green blob
2. Met while: bicycling on a country road
   walking through the graveyard at midnight
   traveling to the moon
3. Outcome: We became friends.
   I saved it from death in the swamp.
   I sent it home.

Have students proceed with their own personal three lists. Stress being creative with occurrences and conversation.

Review the Selection

UNDERSTAND THE SELECTION

Recall

1. In "Sunrise in His Pocket," what did Crockett use to thaw the earth?
2. How many languages did all the tribes speak during Godasiyo's rule?
3. Why did the tribe on the north bank want Godasiyo to kill the white dog?

Infer

4. Why did Godasiyo refuse to kill the white dog?
5. Why did Godasiyo want to move her supporters?
6. What did the legend of Godasiyo attempt to explain?
7. How did Crockett portray his character in "Sunrise in His Pocket"?

Apply

8. Predict what would happen if the sun actually did freeze.
9. Imagine Davy Crockett telling his story to a live audience. How do you think the audience would react?
10. Predict what would have happened if Godasiyo had killed the white dog.

Respond to Literature

How do heroes in tall tales reflect the spirit of their time?

WRITE ABOUT THE SELECTION

In the tale, "Sunrise in His Pocket," Davy Crockett used his imagination to exaggerate an event that did not and—realistically—could not happen. His audience loved the humor. Assume you are asked to tell a story about "The Day I Met a Creature from Outer Space." Use your imagination to exaggerate and make this experience humorous.

Prewriting Write an informal outline indicating the creature's appearance, how you met, and what occurred. Include any conversation you might have had. You might want to also include information about why the creature came to earth and whether it is friendly or dangerous.

Writing Use your informal outline to write your tall tale. In it, exaggerate various features of the creature and the events that happened during your time together. Try to make the story exciting. If possible, work in some humor.

Revising When you revise, make certain you have what appears to be a logical beginning and ending to your tale. Even though your story is not of a realistic type, it should still develop in a clear, well-organized manner.

Proofreading Read over your story. Be sure you have spelled all the words correctly. Remember, if your creature has a name, it should begin with a capital letter. The same is true for the name of the creature's home planet.

Writing

Have the students work individually. Give assistance to any student who is having difficulty. Ask questions about whether their narratives follow a chronological sequence of events as well as being outrageous.

Revising

Make this a cooperative group learning experience. Divide the class into small groups. Have each member read his or her tale. Other group members may make suggestions as to how the tale could be improved to allow for a more logical beginning and end.

Proofreading

Have the students work with partners to determine if any words have been misspelled. Check for the correct spellings in a dictionary. After the tales have been revised and proofread, have the groups put together a booklet of their tales to place on a table or bulletin board where other students can read and enjoy the stories.

THINK ABOUT FOLKLORE

Folk stories tell about many wonderful characters—talking animals, tricksters, magical beasts, supernatural helpers, ogres, numskulls, and heroes. The legend and the tall tale both tell of heroic persons. All the tales have one thing in common; they come from an oral tradition.

1. Is "Sunrise in His Pocket" a legend or a tall tale? What characteristics in the story tell you which it is?
2. Is "Godasiyo, the Woman Chief" a legend or a tall tale? What characteristics in the story tell you which it is?
3. Compare the heroic qualities of Crockett and Godasiyo.
4. The legend writer is trying to teach a history lesson. How would the use of exaggeration interfere with the writer's purpose?
5. If exaggeration were eliminated from Crockett's story, would it become believable? Why or why not?

Reading Focus

Recognize Main Idea and Supporting Details Summarize the main idea of each story in one sentence. Then provide at least three details from each story that support the main idea.

DEVELOP YOUR VOCABULARY

There are many ways of using language for humorous effect. In "Sunrise in His Pocket," Davy Crockett used exaggeration as his main tool for humor. The use of exaggeration for literary effect is called **hyperbole**. Some everyday examples of hyperbole, not necessarily humorous, are "as old as the hills" or "my feet are killing me." Neither of these expressions is meant literally, but the pictures they bring to mind are vivid. Think about what people really mean when they use these expressions.

Writers who use hyperbole for humorous effect must make it clear that they do not expect the reader to believe the exaggerations. If they do not make it clear, the statements would be taken seriously and the humor would be lost.

Look through "Sunrise in His Pocket" and choose three examples of hyperbole. List each of your choices and explain what each would mean if taken literally. Then tell why the example succeeds in being funny.

THINK ABOUT FOLKLORE

Answers

1. Tall tale; It is set in the narrator's lifetime, is full of exaggeration, is humorous, and has an outrageous plot.
2. Legend; It tells of the past, has a believable plot, relates an extraordinary event, has a heroic main character, and tries to explain a mystery.
3. Answers will vary but may suggest that both are courageous, are leaders, are wise in one way or another, are problem solvers. Differences may point out that Godasiyo is community-oriented, calm, and reasonable; Crockett is individualistic and a braggart.
4. Answers will vary but may suggest that hyperbole makes a story unbelievable; it would, therefore, lessen the credibility of a legend.
5. Answers will vary. One possible answers is no, because the events in the plot are scientifically impossible.

DEVELOP YOUR VOCABULARY

Answers

Answers will vary. Possible examples of hyperbole are Crockett's boasts that he can leap over the Ohio River or ride a streak of lightening, the assertions that the trees were too cold to shake and that daybreak froze solid, and many others. Explanations will vary.

Reading Focus

Sample Answer

Davy Crockett saved the world by unfreezing the sun. He beat a bear into giving hot oil. He poured the oil over the earth's axle and the sun's face. He kicked the earth's cogwheel loose. Because people couldn't agree, the tribes of America had to speak different languages.They couldn't decide which fork of the river to take; they argued over whether Godasiyo should be chief; they dumped Godasiyo into the river because they were fighting.

Unit Review Resources

TEACHER'S RESOURCES

- Writing Process, pp. W1–W12
- Grammar, Usage, and Mechanics, pp. G1–G12
- Speaking and Listening, pp. S1–S6
- Critical Thinking, pp. C1–C6
- Choose from Reading in the Content Areas, pp. RCA1–RCA72
- **Standardized Test Preparation**
  Unit 1 Test, pp. UT1–UT2
  Choose from Standardized Test Preparation, pp. STP1–STP31

WRITING APPLICATIONS

Write About the Literary Period

List the following names on the board: Henry, Washington, Adams, Franklin, Crèvecoeur. Beneath the name of each write an appropriate designation: governor, general, letter writer, editor, farmer. Ask the students to discuss what effect war has on people in these occupations. In appropriate columns, write selected responses.

Prewriting: Have students offer each other additional information that they know about any of these authors' lives, or additional thoughts on the effects the war might have had on them.

Writing: While students work on this section individually, give help to any student who is having difficulty. Ask questions to suggest possible responses.

Writer's Toolkit CD-ROM
Encourage students to use the Keyhole Organizer (Writing Tools, Organizing Details) as they write their draft.

Revising: Have students read their papers to partners. Tell the partners to listen for any passages that seem inconsistent with the personality of that author as expressed in the unit selection.

Proofreading: Let students exchange papers with partners for proofreading. (See suggestions in the *Teacher's Resource Book* for guidelines on peer editing and proofreading.)

Write About Genre

Explain to the students that writing about the selections will give them the opportunity to express their own ideas and to explain the relevance of the work to their own experience.

Prewriting: Have the students review the work that was done during the Focus on the Genre section.

Writer's Toolkit CD-ROM
Encourage students to complete the Notecards Activity (Writing Tools, Organizing Details) as they prewrite.

Writing: While students work on this section individually, give help to any student who is having difficulty.

Revising: Have students who have chosen different selections exchange papers and offer each other additional details for inclusion.

Cooperative Group Activity

Have students form small groups and proofread each other's papers.

UNIT 1 *Review*

WRITING APPLICATIONS

Write About the Literary Period

Most of the authors in this unit lived during the time of the Revolutionary War. Select one author. Think of the experiences that author may have had during the Revolution. Describe those experiences in a nonfiction literary work—in a speech, letter, or autobiography.

Prewriting Before you begin to write, review your author's selection, noting its tone, theme, and point of view. Freewrite your ideas. As a way to begin, ask yourself what seemed most important to that author. This may help you to determine your theme. Ask what attitude the author might have toward the war. This may help you to determine your tone. Then ask whether you want your author to be a participant or an observer. This will determine your point of view.

Writing Use your freewriting as a basis for your composition. As you begin your writing, remember to make a thesis statement. Develop the arguments for points you wish to make. If you draw a conclusion, be certain it is consistent with your thesis statement.

Revising As you revise, be sure to eliminate anything that interferes with clarity of theme, consistency of tone, or consistency of point of view.

Proofreading Make a final check of your composition. Use a dictionary to check your spelling, if necessary.

Write About Genre

You have studied the organization and types of nonfiction works. You can use your knowledge to analyze one of the nonfiction selections you have read. Choose a nonfiction work that you liked particularly well. You will analyze the work to show the impact it had on you as a reader.

Prewriting Review Focus on Nonfiction on pages 18–19. Then make notes about the beginning, body, and conclusion of the work. Name the theme of the work and look for a thesis statement. If the piece is descriptive, determine its dominant impression. If it is a narrative, try to determine its sense of movement and its meaning. Organize your notes in the way you think they should be presented.

Writing When you write, summarize the points, arguments, or events the author used to support the thesis statement, dominant impression, or sense of movement in the selection. In your conclusion, state whether you think the supporting details were adequate and what the work meant to you.

Revising Check to see if you have put your ideas in a sensible order. Transpose sentences or phrases to a better place if necessary.

Proofreading Check to see if you have used commas correctly.

BUILD LANGUAGE SKILLS

Vocabulary

A **compound word** is made up of two or more smaller words that are used as a single word. They are written in three different ways. Many compound words are combined and written together as single words. Such words are called **closed compounds**. Examples are *newspaper* and *sunrise*. Other compound verbs are written as separate words, although they have a single meaning. Such words are called **open compounds**. Examples are *hasty pudding* and *frying pan*.

A third way of writing compounds is with a hyphen between the two parts. Such words are called **hyphenated compounds**. Examples are *make-believe* and *flare-up*.

Most of the following words were used in the selections you have just read, but some of them have been written incorrectly here. Look up each compound word in a dictionary. Then write an original sentence, using the correct form of the word in your sentence.

1. back-woods
2. snappingturtle
3. thunder clouds
4. journeyman
5. meeting-house
6. know how
7. watercraft
8. day-break
9. cross-reference
10. wild cat

Grammar, Usage, and Mechanics

Abbreviations may be used for titles such as Dr., Mr., or Ms. when they are used before proper names. Notice that these abbreviations begin with a capital letter and end with a period. Abbreviations should not be used in most writing for the names of cities, states, and countries or for the months and days of the week.

Example **(incorrect):** It was a fifty-mile walk to Burlington, NJ.

Example **(correct):** It was a fifty-mile walk to Burlington, New Jersey.

Copy the following sentences. Correct unacceptable abbreviations. If abbreviations have been used correctly, write "acceptable" after the sentence.

1. His countrymen referred to him as Dr. Franklin to show their respect.
2. Abigail Adams dated her letter November 21, 1800.
3. Mr. President, I would like to address the VA Convention.
4. From Boston, Ben Franklin traveled to NY and Phila.
5. Mrs. Bradstreet wrote poetry on Saturday and attended church on Sun.

Grammar, Usage, and Mechanics

Answers

1. acceptable
2. acceptable
3. Mr. President, I would like to address the Virginia Convention.
4. From Boston, Ben Franklin traveled to New York and Philadelphia.
5. Mrs. Bradstreet wrote poetry on Saturday evening and attended church on Sunday.

More About Grammar, Usage, and Mechanics: Point out that titles such as doctor are not abbreviated unless they precede a proper name; that names of cities, states, and countries should not be abbreviated in straight text; and the months and days of the week are written out in text. Indicate that state abbreviations or postal codes are appropriate on envelope addresses and that abbreviation of dates may be used as a convenience in personal notes or diaries. Have students proceed with the text exercise.

Cooperative Group Activity

Divide students into small groups. Have each group list as many compounds as possible that include the word *school*. When finished, write the compounds on the chalkboard.

Sample answers:

1. elementary school
2. grammar school
3. middle school
4. high school
5. school-age
6. school board
7. schoolbook
8. school bus
9. school district
10. school teacher, and so on

BUILD LANGUAGE SKILLS

Vocabulary

Answers

1. backwoods
2. snapping turtle
3. thunderclouds
4. (correct)
5. meetinghouse
6. know-how
7. (correct)
8. daybreak
9. (correct)
10. wildcat

Sentences will vary.

More About Word Attack: Point out that knowing the spelling or form of a compound is critical when writing. Appropriate compound form is often essential to the meaning of a sentence. Write these examples on the board.

1. Sarah does not need to use *makeup*.
2. The couple did *make up* after their argument.

Discuss how the different written forms could alter the meaning of each sentence.

SPEAKING AND LISTENING

Motivation

Ask students if they have ever heard anyone give a review of a book, movie, or play on television. Discuss which reviews they liked best and why the students liked them.

Teaching Strategy

Guide the students through the explanation of how to give a talk, paying particular attention to the outlined steps and the practice procedures. Allow students time in class to choose their selections. Assign the practice as a homework activity.

Evaluation Criteria

Does the student's presentation clearly differentiate a beginning, middle, and end? Does the student capture the sense and meaning of the selection? Does the student speak clearly? Does the student develop each of his or her points without aimlessly bringing in unconnected ideas?

Career Connection

After reading these selections, students might consider a career as a reporter. Reporters do research, interview people, and attend meetings and public events. They use these activities as the basis for writing nonfiction articles that appear in newspapers and magazines. Reporting requires good writing and analytical skills. A high school education is a minimum requirement for small newspapers serving local communities. Larger papers and magazines usually require a college degree, although experience can sometimes be substituted. Many colleges offer majors in journalism.

UNIT 1 Review

SPEAKING AND LISTENING

Someone once said that if you want a good speech, you should make it simple and short. If you want a great speech, you should make it even simpler and shorter! Here's the secret to preparing a successful speech:

- Tell them what you're going to tell them.
- Tell them.
- Tell them what you've told them.

That sounds easy enough. The following suggestions provide specifics on how to deliver an effective speech.

1. The hardest part of any speech is the introduction. If you don't interest your audience in the first few seconds, your speech will probably fail. So, come up with a good introduction. Tell an anecdote about yourself, use a quotation, give a real-life example, or use a comparison. Make it interesting and tantalizing.
2. Don't try to say everything in the body, or main part, of your speech. Stick to one big topic. Focus your topic and organize your material. If you are giving an oral book report, tell the audience about the plot in its natural time sequence.
3. Once you've given the body of your speech, start to wrap it up. Don't drag on with extra ideas or thoughts that you don't have time to develop. Provide an interesting ending that your audience will remember. You could end with a quotation from the selection you're talking about, or simply end with a statement that gives your audience something to think about.
4. To prepare to give your speech, you'll want to follow a few simple procedures.
   - Recite the speech aloud to yourself. Use notes to help you stay on the topic.
   - Deliver the speech in front of a mirror. Notice your gestures.
   - Deliver the speech to a friend. Ask for constructive criticism and practice eye contact.
   - Practice before a small group of friends to help you get over being nervous.

Now, choose a story from this unit and give an oral report on it. Since the stories are relatively short, keep your speech to approximately three minutes. You should need only a little explanation to prepare your audience. Before you give your speech, follow the guidelines above to help you organize what you are going to say.

CRITICAL THINKING

Make Observations Observation means more than just casually looking at something. It means giving close attention to the details of whatever is under scrutiny.

An observation consists merely of sensory impressions until these impressions are put into words. The observer must note the unique qualities of whatever is being observed. An object, for example, has shape, size, color, and texture. A food also has flavor. A musical instrument makes a sound. Burning leaves create an odor. Close observation makes use of all the five senses—sight, hearing, taste, smell, and touch.

Writers are keen observers. They make readers see a scene, an object, a person, or an event as though the reader were present. They note tiny details and write them so that the images come alive. Several selections in this unit provide good examples of closely observed scenes. Choose one selection that has vivid observations and answer the following questions:

1. Consider the details in the selection. Are they specific? Why do you think the writer included them? To which of the five senses do they appeal?
2. Are any important details missing? What details would you need to get a clearer picture of the event, person, object, or scene?

EFFECTIVE STUDYING

Note Taking To study well, you must do more than just read. You will remember more if you take notes as you read and study.

Taking notes will help you to distinguish between important and unimportant ideas. Your notes will help you to remember what you read, too, because you will have to think about what to write down. Here is a guide for taking notes effectively.

1. Before reading, look at the headings in the material to be studied. They will give you clues to the organization and purpose of the material.
2. If the material you study is difficult, take notes on one section at a time.
3. In reading, separate important ideas from minor ones. Look for key words and topic sentences in specific paragraphs or passages.
4. Use your own words to record your notes except when exact quotations are needed. If you quote, use quotation marks.
5. Be brief, but avoid abbreviations that might be confusing later.

Test Preparation

You can use your notes to prepare for a test. Your notes will be a handy way to review what you have studied.

EFFECTIVE STUDYING

Teaching Strategy

Ask students to think back over their progress throughout the unit. Have them provide examples of how their own note-taking skills helped them in taking tests and completing other assignments. Have them discuss which two items on the guide they consider most helpful, and why they think as they do. Read the following sentences aloud to the class and have them write down the one-word answers.

1. Before reading, look at the ________ in the material to be studied.
2. In reading, separate ________ ideas from minor ones.
3. If the material is difficult, take notes on ________ section at a time.
4. Write notes in your own ________.
5. Avoid ________ that you may not be able to interpret later.

Answers

1. headings
2. important
3. one
4. words
5. abbreviations

CRITICAL THINKING

Sample Answers

1. Adams is specific. She mentions distance, color, size, shape, and so on. She probably included them to add interest and to paint a vivid picture for the reader. The senses to which she appeals are sight and hearing (the absence of bells for communication).
2. Adams might have described the warmth and the smell of the fires as part of their cheering comfort.

UNIT ACTIVITY

A Continuing Unit Project: Creating Advertising Brochures

Arrange students into small groups. From your own mail or from magazines, bring to class several examples of book club advertisements. Tell students that each group is going to create a "Book of the Month" advertisement brochure. Each book club will be making available to its readership all of the selections in this unit.

STEP 1

Distribute the magazines among the groups. Have each group examine different examples of this kind of advertisement. Tell them to pay particular attention to the layout. Afterward, answer any questions students may have.

You may do this phase of the project in the library if you choose, using library materials. If you choose this method, you should devote a class period to a lesson on using the library. During this lesson, stress the use of the card catalogue and the reference section of the library.

Invite the school journalism, graphic arts, or art teacher (or, if your school has a print shop, that teacher) to visit your class and speak to students about magazine layouts. First, brief the guest teacher on the content of the proposed advertisement brochure. In this way the guest teacher can be prepared to offer practical advice on copy length and arrangement of the brochure's content. Allow ample time for students to ask questions and develop proposed layouts, which the teacher can review, offering suggestions as needed.

Step 2

The advertisement brochure will include a headline. Guide students by asking them to recall sample headlines they might have seen while perusing magazines. Alternately, you might offer examples, such as EXPLORE 19th CENTURY AMERICAN LITERATURE or AMERICAN LITERATURE COMES ALIVE. Tell students to use the unit introduction as a resource in developing headlines. They may not use the title "Writers in a Growing Nation."

Have each group choose three possible headlines. From these they should choose, by popular vote, a final headline. In the event of a tie, you cast the tie-breaking vote. Be sure to praise the efforts of those whose contributions were not selected.

The brochure will also include a "featured selection." If possible, have each group select a different work as a featured selection. Have each group pick two possibilities and vote on which will be featured. The one not chosen may be given equal space as a "future featured selection."

Both current and future featured selections will be the subjects of the two paragraph promotional reviews. Tell students that these reviews should be written to arouse interest. To guide students in writing these reviews, you might use questions, such as the following, as prompts:

What have you learned about the importance of this selection in American literature?

What interesting facts do you remember about the writer and his/her place in American literature?

What literary element did you think was used most effectively or dramatically in this selection?

Why did you like this selection better than the others in the unit?

What was the central or dominating idea in each selection?

What images that lend themselves to artistic representation can you remember from each selection?

If you were reading the advertisement, what kind of information and artwork would entice you to join the book club?

Students in each group should now collaborate on writing the two reviews. Use the writing process described throughout this text.

For each of the other selections in the unit, students should design book covers that dramatically illustrate the theme or another compelling aspect of the work. The title and the writer's name must appear for each. These may be incorporated as part of the book jacket, or they may be printed neatly underneath.

In designing book jackets, students may use actual artistic representations or verbal instructions to an artist. Artwork should be encouraged; however, students should not be penalized for lack of artistic ability if verbal instructions show creativity and effort.

Provide close supervision to each group. Ensure that they are following directions. Also ensure that the work is being equitably distributed among the group members and that every student is participating.

Step 3

Distribute large-sized white poster board to each group. Tell students to cut and arrange the individual components according to the planned layout. Students should now transfer the reviews to the poster board using pencil. Remind them to leave sufficient room for the book jackets of the other works. The printers in each group should print over the pencil with ink pens or markers.

Collect the projects. After evaluating them, display students' work on the bulletin board or around the room.

If your class requires more structure, create specific questions for each selection. Some possible questions follow:

■ from *My Bondage and My Freedom*

What three character traits would you use to describe Frederick Douglass?

■ "Ain't I a Woman?"

How do you think Sojourner Truth would answer each of the rhetorical questions she asks?

■ "The Legend of Sleepy Hollow"

If you were rewriting this selection as a modern radio drama, what kind of setting would you use? Include a physical description, modern transportation, and sound effects.

■ "No More Forever"

If Chief Joseph were running for president today, what kind of issues would he stress? What position would he take on each?

■ "Annabel Lee"

Do you know anyone who has had to cope with the death of a loved one? How did they respond? How did family and friends try to help?

■ "The Tell-Tale Heart"

What emotions did you feel as you read the selection? Give specific examples from the selection that produced these emotions.

■ from *The Prairie*

With which character did you identify most closely? Why?

■ "To a Waterfowl"

Have you ever had an emotional reaction watching a pet or an animal? Explain your feelings.

■ "A Night" from *Hospital Sketches*

Do you think shared tragedy sometimes brings strangers closer to each other? Why?

■ from *My Bondage and My Freedom*

by Frederick Douglass (page 71)

SELECTION SYNOPSIS

This is an autobiographical narrative. The narrator, an escaped slave, explains how the institution of slavery victimized both the slave and the slaveholder. As a boy, he was sold to a family in Baltimore. At first, his mistress treated him more as her son's friend than a slave. She began teaching him to read. Her husband, seeing this, put an end to the lessons. The mistress, trying to justify to herself what she knew to be wrong, suppressed her natural inclinations. She became fanatical in her efforts to block his education. He, in turn, resorted to deception to acquire knowledge. She lost her humanity. The slave had to resort to deception to gain what should have been his birthright.

■ "Ain't I a Woman?"

by Sojourner Truth (page 79)

SELECTION SYNOPSIS

This is an oration or speech in which the speaker pleads eloquently for the rights of women. Using the device known as rhetoric she presents argument after argument with which the reader must agree.

SELECTION ACTIVITY

In this activity, students will have the opportunity to learn how the issues raised by Douglass and Truth are relevant to their world and lives. In preparation for the activity, hold a class discussion on equal rights. Here are the examples of the kinds of questions you might use to stimulate interest:

How would you define civil rights?

Why do you think it is important that everyone have equal opportunity? Do you think any of the issues raised by Douglass and Truth are still relevant today?

How do you think the issue of civil rights affects you personally?

What do you think are the most important civil rights laws that have been passed? You might provide several areas such as education, voting, housing, and so forth, and ask students to rank them in order of importance.

Invite a local civil rights leader or government official to speak to the class on contemporary civil rights issues. The day before, as a homework assignment, tell students to write down three questions they would like to ask the speaker. Allow enough class time for students' questions and discussion.

After the speaker has left, divide the class into groups. Have each group collaborate on listing three points from the speakers' presentation that they found particularly important or that gave them new insight into the issue of civil rights. Tell them to add original thoughts related to the list they have compiled. When the groups have finished, have a class discussion in which students from each group exchange views on the issue.

■ "The Legend of Sleepy Hollow"

by Washington Irving (page 83)

SELECTION SYNOPSIS

This is a radio dramatization of the famous ghost story. The setting is the Hudson Valley of New York State in the early 19th century. Ichabod Crane, a lanky and eccentric schoolmaster, spends much of his free time reading books on the supernatural. His position as singing master in Sleepy Hollow allows him time to court the blooming Katrina Van Tassel, to whom he gives lessons in her parents' large farmhouse. Ichabod, however, is not the only suitor for Katrina's hand; the burly boisterous Brom Van Brunt is also interested. One evening the Van Tassels throw a huge party. "Master Grasshopper" Ichabod merrily dances the shakedown with Katrina as Brom sits and broods. As the evening continues, talk centers on the headless horseman, supposedly the ghost of a Hessian soldier who had his head shot off in the Revolutionary War. Ichabod, whose absorption in witchcraft has led him to half-believe such things, quails when he hears that the headless horseman has been seen recently. Crane fears his upcoming ride home alone in the dead of the night. A frightful time ensues, with the tremulous Ichabod becoming more and more terrified. Suddenly the headless horseman appears! The mounted figure chases Ichabod, who sees it lift its detached head from the pommel and hurl it in his direction. This climax stops abruptly, and the action continues the next morning. Ichabod cannot be found and is never seen again in Sleepy Hollow. An investigating party, however, does find Ichabod's hat and a shattered pumpkin near a bridge that the schoolmaster would have had to cross. Brom, who always laughs uproariously whenever Ichabod's disappearance is mentioned, soon marries the fair Katrina.

SELECTION ACTIVITY

In this activity, students will illustrate characters from the selection. The illustration will depict the characters as students imagine each might have appeared at one particular point in the drama. Before you begin this activity, collect several books containing costumes from the period. Consult with the history teacher, the drama teacher, or librarian in your school for assistance in selecting appropriate resource materials. Bring these resource books to class on the day of the project. Allow students to use them as guides and for ideas for their illustrations.

Divide the class into groups and have each group select three characters. Then have students discuss which particular scene and moment in the drama will be illustrated. Provide guidance to each group as necessary.

Allow them to create original art, draw cartoons, or cut and paste magazine pictures to depict those characters from the drama. Point out that creativity of thought and effort are more important than an individual's artistic talent. At the same time, be certain to encourage those who have artistic talent to use this activity as an opportunity to express themselves and develop that ability.

When all groups have finished, collect and evaluate the projects. After grading, you may want to display the students' work on the bulletin board. Praise all those who made an effort.

"No More Forever"

by Chief Joseph (page 101)

SELECTION SYNOPSIS

In simple, yet eloquent language, In-mut-too-yah-lat-lat (Chief Joseph) tells the sad history of the conflict between the white man—encroaching settlers and their protective troops—and Chief Joseph's group of Nez Percé. He starts with a rather idealized picture of the life of his ancestors in the Wallowa Valley of Oregon. The first "men with white faces" were French fur traders. The French had a good relationship with the Nez Percé, as did the explorers Lewis and Clark. The trouble started when the white settlers arrived in great numbers. In some detail, the narrative surveys the broken promises, divide-and-conquer strategies, and forced evacuations used to take Nez Percé territory. Finally, against the counsel of Chief Joseph, some of his tribe resorted to arms in 1877. War broke out. Greatly outnumbered, the Nez Percé fought a series of battles as they retreated 1,300 miles over four western states before surrendering. After that, according to Chief Joseph, oral promises in the surrender agreement were broken by the United States, and the Nez Percé, virtual prisoners, were split up and sent from one reservation to another. In his appeal of 1879, Chief Joseph continues the struggle with the only weapons he has left, words that touch what he hopes is a common sense of justice.

SELECTION ACTIVITY

In this activity, students will trace and verify the historical journey of the Nez Percé tribe during their struggle to remain free. Collect history books, atlases, and encyclopedias containing information about the geography and social setting of the western United States in the late 19th century. Students may also consult the library, history teachers, and the Internet for information.

One excellent source is the *National Geographic* magazine. If this is not available in your school library, encourage students to visit the local public library as a group to conduct research, or to use the Internet.

Step 1

Say to the students: "Imagine you have a research project for your history class. You and your group must trace the journey described by Chief Joseph as he and his tribe avoided but occasionally fought battles with the army."

Allow the class time to read, review and discuss the literature. Guide them through the selection. In the beginning, point out passages that provide explicit or implicit information concerning geographical references. As you continue, provide less direct information and encourage students to take initiative in identifying information or clues. Explain that they must, using reference works, identify the geographical territory through which the tribe traveled.

Step 2

Distribute the reference works you have collected. Each group is required to draw a map of this western territory, including the states in which events occurred. After drawing and identifying the states in this section of the country, students should use a black marker to show, with dotted lines, the progression of the tribe. Explain to students the use of a legend in map making. Use examples from the *National Geographic* if available. If not, highway or other easily obtained maps are effective. As the next step, tell students to identify on their maps the approximate points where specific battles or other significant events occurred. These should be marked by a number within a circle. Have students construct a legend, which identifies events by the circled numbers.

Step 3

Have each group turn in one legible copy of the project. Evaluate the work. After grading, display in a prominent location in the room for a period of time. Then remove the papers. Make enough copies of appropriate papers for each group member. Suggest that they keep the maps at home in the event that they, at a later date, have the opportunity to visit the sites of these historical events.

"Annabel Lee"

by Edgar Allan Poe (page 117)

SELECTION SYNOPSIS

Annabel Lee is a rhythmic poem describing an obsessive reaction to the death of a loved one.

SELECTION ACTIVITY

Use the library as a resource. Obtain an audio tape of a professional actor reading the poetry of Edgar Allan Poe.

Play the tape for the class. Ask students to discuss their reactions to the printed and spoken versions of this poem. What reactions did they have that were similar? What reactions did they have that were different. List appropriate responses on the chalkboard or overhead transparency. Invite volunteers to read the poem aloud in class. Record the students' readings and play them.

■ "The Tell-Tale Heart"

by Edgar Allan Poe (page 123)

SELECTION SYNOPSIS

In this extended monologue, a deranged narrator assures us of his sanity and insists that he is really quite rational and clever as he explains how he planned and carried out the murder of an old man who had an "Evil Eye." For seven nights, the narrator cautiously entered the old man's bedroom, but he could not bring himself to commit the deed because the accursed eye was closed and therefore harmless. On the eighth night, however, the narrator found the eye open. After listening to the loud beating of the old man's heart, he smothered him with a pillow. After dismembering the body, he hid the parts under the floorboards. Then the police arrived, having been alerted by a neighbor who heard a scream. At first, the narrator tells us, he was in control and untroubled; how could the police ever solve such a perfect crime? But suddenly he heard the heart beating again—louder, louder, louder! Finally his torment was such that he was forced to scream his confession.

SELECTION ACTIVITY

Divide the class into groups and have each group adapt "The Tell-Tale Heart" as a radio drama.

Step 1

Have students use "The Legend of Sleepy Hollow" as a reference. Tell them to note the stage directions and sound effects in the radio drama.

Step 2

Tell students to identify at least ten different sound effects that can be inserted in the narrator's monologue. Some examples are the opening of the old man's bedroom door, his muffled scream, the scraping of the chair on the floor, and the progressively louder beating of the heart.

Step 3

Distribute a photocopy of the story to each group. Tell students to insert the sound effects at the appropriate places using numbered footnotes. Each group should turn in a legible copy for grading and display on the bulletin board.

■ from *The Prairie*

by James Fenimore Cooper (page 132)

SELECTION SYNOPSIS

In this excerpt, frontiersman Natty Bumppo is dying. He is visited by an army officer, Middleton, whose life Bumppo had saved a year earlier. Middleton is accompanied by his scouting party. Bumppo has been living with Pawnee Indians because he has adopted a young Pawnee chief, Hard-Heart, as his son. As Bumppo's death approaches, both Middleton and Hard-Heart are grief-stricken as they listen to Bumppo's last words.

SELECTION ACTIVITY

The Prairie is the last book in the Leatherstocking series. The narrative sequence of the books is as follows: *The Deerslayer*, *The Path Finder*, *The Last of the Mohicans*, *The Pioneers*, and *The Prairie*. The time span of the stories is from the early 1700s to 1806.

Have students do research on this eventful period in American History. Then have them write an additional episode in the life of Natty Bumppo. Have students place their characters in authentic context based on the history of the West, dates, and significant historical events.

You may want to evaluate students' work with the help of a teacher from the social studies department. If students have done valid research, perhaps they could receive dual credit for their work. This is an excellent opportunity for learning across the curriculum.

■ "To a Waterfowl"

by William Cullen Bryant (page 143)

SELECTION SYNOPSIS

This is a lyric poem. The poet, alone in the countryside, sees a single bird on its migratory flight. He finds parallels between the migration of the bird and the human experience.

SELECTION ACTIVITY

Using oil paints, watercolors, pastels, crayons, or markers, students are to create a four-panel visual representation of the bird's journey as seen through the poet's eyes. Before beginning this activity, collect books and magazines that contain colorful pictures of migratory birds such as geese, ducks, and so forth. One excellent resource is any book including the watercolors of the American ornithologist John James Audubon. Most wildlife magazines will also be an additional resource for colorful pictures. Do not assume that your students' experiences include witnessing migratory birds in flight. This is why the resource works are especially important to this assignment.

Be certain to supply an adequate supply of art materials, including crayons, colored markers, and watercolors. Decide on the size of the drawing paper and provide a supply to the class. This is an individual assignment. Consequently the time needed to complete it satisfactorily may vary depending upon the individual skills of each student. Encourage those who display artistic ability to add creative detail. Allow students to take the project home to complete.

Collect the projects and evaluate them. Remember that effort, presentation and creative interpretation should be the basis of the grade. After grading, display the students' efforts in a prominent location.

■ "A Night" from *Hospital Sketches*

by Louisa May Alcott (page 149)

SELECTION SYNOPSIS

In this autobiographical sketch, a novelist who served as a nurse in a Civil War hospital describes in matter-of-fact prose the routine horrors of a battle's aftermath. A soldier who has lost a leg in combat, delirious with pain, insists he is going to walk home. A young drummer boy, Kit, relives his combat experience in recurring nightmares. When conscious, he thinks constantly of the friend who gave his own life to save Kit's. The central drama revolves around the suffering and death of a young man fatally wounded in his first battle. This soldier, John, is at first unaware of his condition. When he learns of it, he responds stoically. The nurse, at his request, writes to his brother, who can break the news gently to John's mother. John dies bravely, shortly before his mother's reply is delivered. The nurse has the mother's letter buried with the soldier.

SELECTION ACTIVITY

Invite the school nurse or a friend, relative, or parent who is a registered nurse to speak to the class on the hospital duties of a nurse. Ask the speaker to relate these duties to war or any emergency situation. The day before the presentation, tell students to jot down three questions they had about nursing after reading the selection. Allow ample time for questions and discussion after the nurse's presentation.

STUDENT READING LIST

Erlbach, Arlene. *Worth the Risks: True Stories about Risk-takers Plus How You Can Be One*. Free Spirit. 1999

Katz, William Loren. *Black Pioneers*. Simon & Schuster. 1999

Lester, Julius. *From Slave Ship to Freedom Road*. Dial. 1998

Clinton, Catherine (ed) *I, Too, Sing America: Three Centuries of African-American Poetry*. HoughtonMifflin. 1999

From Globe Fearon Educational Publisher

Pacemaker Classics

- *The Deerslayer* by James Fenimore Cooper
- *The Last of the Mohicans* by James Fenimore Cooper
- *Tales of Edgar Allan Poe*

Adapted Classics

- *Little Women* by Louisa May Alcott
- *Narrative of the Life of Frederick Douglass*

UNIT 2
Overview

UNIT OBJECTIVES

After completing this unit, students will be able to

- understand the elements of fiction
- recognize the forms of fiction
- understand the use of narration and persuasion in nonfiction
- build on knowledge of literary elements to write effectively
- use several strategies in determining word meaning
- prepare for public speaking
- employ long-term and short-term planning in preparing for a test

UNIT SELECTIONS

This unit examines the growth of a literature that was truly American in theme, setting, and style. Several selections illustrate the optimism that existed in the years following the Revolutionary War. Some are representative of the changing mood that occurred with the coming of the Civil War and the destruction of the Native American way of life.

- **from *My Bondage and My Freedom*,** (p. 70) This excerpt is from an autobiography that discusses the author's view of slavery and those who enslaved him.
  LITERARY SKILL: autobiography
  READING SKILL: make inferences
  VOCABULARY: concrete and abstract nouns
  WRITING: description of a character
- **"Ain't I a Woman,"** (p. 79) is a powerful oration about women's rights.
  LITERARY SKILL: persuasion
  READING SKILL: understand persuasive techniques
  VOCABULARY: multiple-meaning words
  WRITING: react to persuasive writing

- **"The Legend of Sleepy Hollow,"** (p. 83) is a radio drama adapted from a ghost story with a humorous twist.
  LITERARY SKILL: plot
  READING SKILL: identify hyperbole
  VOCABULARY: onomatopoeia
  WRITING: dramatic scene
- **"No More Forever,"** (p. 101) examines westward expansion from a Native American's perspective.
  LITERARY SKILL: narration
  READING SKILL: understand sequence of events
  VOCABULARY: meaning from context
  WRITING: alternative endings
- **"Annabel Lee,"** (p. 117) is a rhythmic love poem.
  LITERARY SKILL: meter
  READING SKILL: identify cause and effect
  VOCABULARY: antonyms
  WRITING: description

Writers in a Growing Nation

There's a better day a'coming,
Will you go along with me?
There's a better day a'coming,
Go sound the jubilee!
—Pre-Civil War Spiritual

Allegory of Freedom, c. 1863, Anonymous. The Granger Collection

67

Introducing the Literary Period

Group the students. On the board or overhead projector, write: white settlers, African Americans, Native Americans. Have each group collaborate in producing a short statement explaining how each of these three communities might have defined, "a better day."

Viewing Fine Art

This oil painting is considered a primitive work of art done by an artist with little or no formal training. Ask: "How do you think the primitive artist differs from the trained artist?"

- **"The Tell-Tale Heart,"** (p. 123) is a classic short story illustrating the principle of "single effect."
  LITERARY SKILL: suspense
  READING SKILL: identify signal words
  VOCABULARY: use a glossary
  WRITING: story extension
- **from *The Prairie*,** (p. 132) is an excerpt from a novel depicting the death of an idealized American frontiersman. This is the model selection.
  LITERARY SKILL: elements of fiction
  READING SKILL: understand character
  VOCABULARY: base words and suffixes
  WRITING: eulogy
- **"To a Waterfowl,"** (p. 143) is an example of early American lyric poetry.
  LITERARY SKILL: the lyric
  READING SKILL: draw conclusions
  VOCABULARY: contractions
  WRITING: narrative
- **"A Night" from *Hospital Sketches*** (p. 149) is an autobiographical sketch describing the horrors of war and heroism in the face of death.
  LITERARY SKILL: dialogue
  READING SKILL: make inferences
  VOCABULARY: specialized vocabularies
  WRITING: letter

RELATED MATERIALS

1. ***By River, By Rail; History of Black Migration.*** [Video, 22 mins. Films for the Humanities and Science, 1998.] These personal stories deliver a real sense of the African American experience.
2. ***American Fairy Tales: from Rip Van Winkle to Rootabaga Stories.*** [Audiobook, AudioBookshelf, 1998.] This rich and varied collection was compiled by Neil Philip.
3. ***Abraham Lincoln: New Birth of Freedom.*** [Video, 60 mins. Goldhil Media, 1998.] This video provides a vivid recollection of Lincoln's era.
4. ***African-American Quilting Pt. 1: The Cloth Sings to Me.*** [Video, Filmmakers Library, 1998.] This is a beautiful mixture of African-American family life with connections to slavery.
5. ***Little Women.*** [Video, 115 mins. Columbia TriStar, 1994.] Winona Ryder stars in this faithful adaptation of the Louisa May Alcott classic.
6. The following Web sites may also be helpful. Please note that some Internet addresses change frequently. These are the latest versions:

   Frederick Douglass
   http://www.ifinet.com/~gaffa/bdpa/timeline_frederick_douglas.html

   Suffragists, University of Rochester, Department of History
   http://www.history.rochester.edu/class/suffrage/home.html

   Edgar Allan Poe, EDV Pool, University of Innsbrook, Engineering Department, Stephen Gmoser
   http://bau2.uibk.ac.at/sg/poe/poe.html

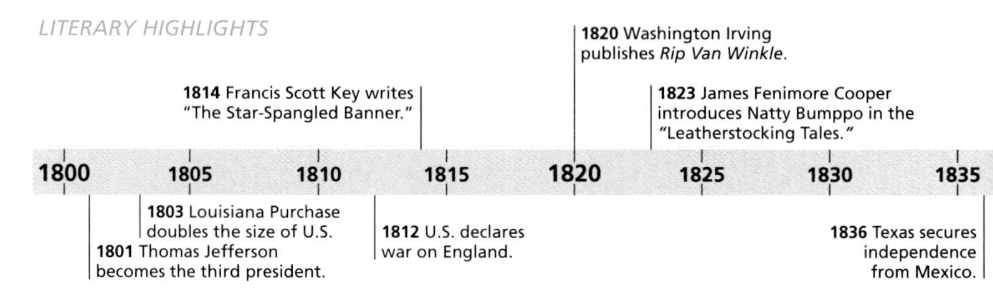
LITERARY HIGHLIGHTS
1814 Francis Scott Key writes "The Star-Spangled Banner."
1820 Washington Irving publishes Rip Van Winkle.
1823 James Fenimore Cooper introduces Natty Bumppo in the "Leatherstocking Tales."
1800
1805
1810
1815
1820
1825
1830
1835
1801 Thomas Jefferson becomes the third president.
1803 Louisiana Purchase doubles the size of U.S.
1812 U.S. declares war on England.
1836 Texas secures independence from Mexico.
HISTORICAL HIGHLIGHTS

Writers in a Growing Nation

Have you ever done something so wonderful that you felt you just had to boast about it? That is the way many Americans felt after the Revolutionary War. They had established a new nation, and they wanted to tell each other—and the rest of the world—about it.

Writers in the early 19th century liked to write about the beauties of the American scenery. They wrote optimistically about America's future.

As the Civil War approached, the mood changed. American writers became more concerned with social issues, such as slavery.

■ CHARACTERISTICS OF THE LITERATURE

In the early 19th century, many American writers turned to fiction to express their ideas.

Washington Irving wrote stories about New York's Hudson Valley. In this unit, you will read "The Legend of Sleepy Hollow," a radio adaptation of one of his most famous stories.

America's first important nature poet, William Cullen Bryant, liked to write poems about the countryside. You will enjoy the precise descriptive details and musical quality as you read his lyric poem "To a Waterfowl."

Just as American politicians were trying a new form of government, American writers were experimenting with new forms of literature. Edgar Allan Poe was highly original. If he were writing today, he would be called a horror writer. Many people give Poe credit for inventing the modern short story. In this unit, you will read his suspenseful work "The Tell-Tale Heart." You will also read "Annabel Lee," one of his poems.

James Fenimore Cooper, the first great American novelist, was as good at describing the wilderness as he was at creating characters. His greatest character is Natty Bumppo, a fictional frontiersman, whose

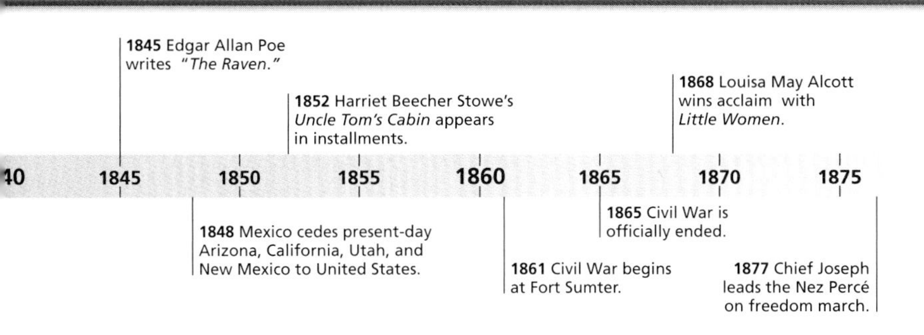
1845 Edgar Allan Poe writes "The Raven."
1852 Harriet Beecher Stowe's Uncle Tom's Cabin appears in installments.
1868 Louisa May Alcott wins acclaim with Little Women.
40
1845
1850
1855
1860
1865
1870
1875
1848 Mexico cedes present-day Arizona, California, Utah, and New Mexico to United States.
1861 Civil War begins at Fort Sumter.
1865 Civil War is officially ended.
1877 Chief Joseph leads the Nez Percé on freedom march.

life and deeds are told in five novels known as the "Leatherstocking Tales." You will meet this adventurer at the end of his life in an excerpt from *The Prairie*, the last of the tales.

■ AFRICAN AMERICAN LITERATURE

In 19th century America, the evil of slavery shamed the land. You will read selections by two freed African American slaves. In *My Bondage and My Freedom*, Frederick Douglass eloquently condemns slavery. Sojourner Truth's defiant work "Ain't I a Woman?" tells what it was like to be a woman and an enslaved person.

Growing opposition to slavery in the mid-19th century was one cause of the Civil War. In "A Night," Louisa May Alcott describes the horrors of the war as she experienced them while working in Union Army hospitals. The selection you will read is taken from her book, *Hospital Sketches*.

■ NATIVE AMERICAN LITERATURE

After the Civil War, America resumed its westward expansion. Treaties guaranteeing Native Americans rights to their land were broken. Many times Native Americans were forcibly relocated to reservations on poor lands.

Chief Joseph of the Nez Percé tribe expresses the Native Americans' point of view in "No More Forever."

In this unit, you will sample the literature of a young and growing America. As you read, ask yourself how the literature reflects the changing times.

Discussing the Literary Period

Group the students. Explain that each group is the crew of a spaceship exploring previously uncharted parts of the universe. Would they be optimistic? Have them discuss what sights they might see. Would they react with a sense of wonder? Would they want to protect what they found from environmental destruction and commercial exploitation? If they encountered alien cultures, what would they learn? What conflicts might arise? How would they resolve these conflicts?

Cooperative Group Activity

Explain that the 19th century began as a period of great optimism. Conflicts developed. Ask each group of students one of the following questions: Could the pursuit of wealth justify a society in which some groups were excluded, even enslaved, and natural resources were wantonly destroyed? Did settlement of the West entitle the pioneers to destroy a native culture? To what extent do these problems still exist in American society? What improvements have been made? What new problems do we face? Have each group write a paragraph that addresses their group's issue.

Selection Overview

SELECTION OBJECTIVES

After completing this selection, students will be able to

- understand autobiography
- understand the use of simple or chronological narrative in autobiography
- understand the elements of a well-written autobiography
- understand concrete and abstract nouns
- make inferences

Lesson Resources

from *My Bondage and My Freedom*
- Selection Synopsis, Teacher's Edition, p. T65b
- Comprehension and Vocabulary Workbook, pp. 17 –18
- Language Enrichment Workbook, p. 9
- Teacher's Resources
  Reinforcement, p. R9
  Test, pp. T17–T18
  Unadapted Selection, pp. U8–U11

More About Autobiography

A *memoir* is a nonfiction form related to autobiography. The word *memoir* means official report. Public figures, such as presidents, sometimes write memoirs after retiring from office. Memoirs usually provide personal glimpses into the background surrounding important events during a person's career. They add human perspective to history but rarely include the author's childhood or personal details as an autobiography might.

About the Author

Frederick Douglass escaped from slavery in Baltimore in 1838 at the age of twenty-one. Naval trade was crucial to Baltimore's economic growth and prosperity. As a result, sailors were less likely to be questioned closely when traveling. Douglass bought a sailor's uniform, borrowed identification from a free black sailor he knew and boarded a train to New York and freedom. One white passenger looked at him closely and apparently recognized him but said nothing to give Douglass's deception away.

Learn About

AUTOBIOGRAPHY

An **autobiography** is the true story of a person's life told by that person. Since autobiography consists of facts about a person's life, it is nonfiction.

A person's life is a story—a true story, of course. Thus, it is told in **narrative** form. That is, it tells about events as they happened, usually in chronological order. Autobiographies are usually long; most make up a whole book. Besides the facts of a person's life, the author usually writes of his or her thoughts, ideas, and inner struggles.

The point of view in an autobiography is the first person. It is the natural point of view of someone telling a personal story.

As you read this selection, ask yourself:

1. What part of his life was Douglass writing about?
2. How would his story have sounded if he had used the third-person point of view? In what way might it have been more effective? In what way might it have been less effective?

READING FOCUS

Make Inferences An inference is an understanding based on ideas or things already known. In an autobiography, you can make inferences by thinking about the significance, or importance, of events in the author's life that the author has decided to include. You may also make inferences about the author's character and values. As you read, make inferences based on the actions of the people and the events described in the autobiography.

WRITING CONNECTION

Make a list of some events or ideas that you would include in your autobiography. What point of view would you use? Would you write in chronological order?

ESL Activity

Divide the class into small groups. Discuss the fact that slavery was also practiced in other countries. Have groups discuss why oppressed people are not encouraged, or are forbidden, to learn to read. Have each group list what the ruling class has to fear.

Cooperative Group Activity

Have pairs of students make time lines of events that have happened during their lifetimes. Encourage students to use information from other sources. Have students discuss how each event has impacted their life.

from

My Bondage and My Freedom

ADAPTED

by Frederick Douglass

For seven years, I lived in Baltimore with Master Hugh's family. During this time my condition was, as weather forecasters like to say, "variable." On a positive note, I learned to read and write. On a negative note, I had to use deceit to attain this knowledge. Privately, this was humiliating to me.

My mistress, out of kindness, had begun teaching me. Her husband, Master Hugh, learned of this, forbade it. Following the letter and spirit of his orders, she stopped teaching me herself and tried to prevent my learning by other means.

In fairness to her, she did not take these steps immediately. She may have thought it unnecessary. Perhaps, she could not bring herself to shut me up in mental darkness. She needed time to harden herself to the role of slaveholder. She had to learn to ignore my humanity, to treat me as property that had no moral or intellectual worth. As I have said, my mistress, Mrs. Auld, was a kind and tender-hearted woman. When I first went to live with her, she tried her best to treat me as one human being ought to treat another.

It is easy to see that some experience is helpful in carrying out a slaveholder's duties. Nature has done almost nothing to prepare men or women to be slave or master. Only rigid training can make a person one or the other. It is hard to forget the love of freedom. It is no easier to lose respect for another's love of freedom. To her credit, Mrs. Auld was ill prepared to play the part of slaveholder. It is an unnatural position. She was more unequal to its demands than anyone I have ever met.

When she looked at me, she did not see chattel. She saw the curly-haired boy who stood by her side or sat on her lap.

---

variable (VAIR ee ih bul) likely to change
humiliating (hyoo MIL ee ayt ing) lowering of pride or dignity
tender-hearted (TEN dur hahrt id) easily moved to pity; sympathetic
chattel (CHAT ul) a movable article of personal property; owned property

Teaching Plan

INTRODUCE

Motivation

Play a song such as "The Battle Hymn of the Republic" or a 19th-century spiritual associated with the Abolitionist movement. Using the school library as a resource, discuss the Underground Railroad with the students.

Purpose-Setting Question

Why would nonfiction be an important part of literature in the years leading up to the Civil War?

READ

Literary Focus: *Autobiography*

Point out to students that autobiographies are written from a first-person point of view. This allows the author to reveal his own thoughts and feelings. Ask: How does Douglass view his mistress, Mrs. Auld?

Reading: *Make Inferences*

As students read, ask them to make inferences about each person in the narrative and the events that Douglass describes. Ask: How could these people and events have helped Douglass to become the brilliant author and orator who wrote this excerpt?

CLOSE

Have students complete Review the Selection on pages 76–77.

Develop Vocabulary Skills

Provide a handout with the vocabulary words and their definitions listed. Group the students. Have each group produce original sentences using any three of the vocabulary words. Have volunteers from each group read sentences. Ask for volunteers to suggest sentences for any words not used by the groups. Give guidance and suggestions as necessary.

Viewing Fine Art

The second quarter of the 19th century saw a growth in cities, as well as in pride and nationalism among Americans. One sign of these trends was the popularity of various American places and, in particular, cities. The print showing a bustling but attractive view of a city like Baltimore (seen here) became a sign of patriotism and boosterism in the home of residents. Prints were sold as fast as they were made; many appeared in viewbooks of major cities. The ideal print included a scene of industrial or commercial vitality, coupled with a nice forested glen in the foreground, as here, for recreation. What might a painting of your community in the second quarter of the 19th century include?

Reading Focus: *Make Inferences*

Ask: What can you infer about how Mrs. Auld felt about her husband's treatment of the slaves?

Critical Thinking: *Analyze*

Ask: What kind of personal freedom do you think Mrs. Auld had? What kind do you think she lacked?

View of Baltimore, Maryland, 1839. The Granger Collection

She saw her son Tommy's friend. I was more than property. She knew it in her heart.

I could talk and sing. I could laugh and weep. I could remember, and I could reason. I could love and hate. I was human. She, dear lady, in her mind and her heart, knew all this. How could she bring herself to treat me as a brute? Her every inclination opposed it.

The will and power of her husband said she must. He won the battle. Her noble intentions were defeated, but he did not escape the consequences.

When I entered their house, it was a happy home. She was a model of affection and concern. She was pious and upright. It was impossible to meet her without thinking, "This woman is a Christian." The sight of the least sorrow or suffering brought a tear to her eye. Innocent joy brought an immediate smile to her face. She gave bread to the hungry and clothes to the naked. She comforted every mourner within her reach.

Slavery stole those qualities from her. Domestic happiness left with them. Conscience is like a foundation. When the foundation is damaged, the building cannot be repaired. The house may collapse

---

inclination (in kluh NAY shun) a bent of mind; tendency

on the slave Monday. It will fall about master's head on Tuesday. Conscience must stand entire, or it does not stand at all. If I suffered, the family suffered.

Master Hugh had begun a chain of events. He had violated nature and conscience. He had arrested the kindness that would have enlightened my young mind. When she stopped teaching me, she had to justify her actions to herself. Having taken his side in the debate, she had to reject all her former kindness.

One needs very little knowledge of moral philosophy to see what happened. She became more violently opposed to my learning to read than her husband was. It was not enough to follow his orders. She resolved to go one step further. She became infuriated at the sight of me reading a book or a newspaper. She would rush at me in a rage and snatch the book or paper from my hands. She acted like a traitor might, if caught in the company of a dangerous spy.

Mrs. Auld was an intelligent woman. Her husband's advice and her own experience soon demonstrated to her satisfaction that education and slavery are incompatible with each other. Having convinced herself of this, she watched my every move. If I remained in a room by myself for any length of time, I was suspected of reading a book. I was at once called upon to explain my absence.

All this was entirely too late. The damage had been done. In teaching me the alphabet, in treating me with the kindness accorded another human, she had given me the inch. Nothing could prevent me from taking the yard.

I had determined that I would learn to read at any cost. I found the ways to achieve that end. The strategy I hit upon, and it was a very successful one, was to use my young white playmates as teachers.

I carried constantly a copy of Webster's spelling book in my pocket. On errands or at play, I would take my young friends aside for a lesson. I generally paid my tuition with bread which I always carried in my pocket. For a single biscuit, any of my hungry little comrades would give me a lesson more valuable than bread.

Not everyone demanded payment. There were those who took pleasure in teaching me whenever the opportunity arose. I am strongly tempted to give the names of two or three of those boys to show my affection and gratitude to them. Prudence tells me that is not a good idea. It cannot harm me, but it might embarrass them. I remember what happened to my mistress. It is an unpardonable offense to do anything, directly or indirectly to promote a slave's freedom in a slave state. It is enough to say that my warm-hearted playmates lived on Philpot Street near Durgin & Bailey's Shipyard.

---

enlightened (en LYT und) to have given the light of knowledge to
moral philosophy (MAWR ul fuh LOS uh fee) ethics; standards of conduct and moral judgment
incompatible (in kum PAT uh bul) not in agreement
prudence (PROOD uns) the quality of being cautious or discreet in conduct
warm-hearted (WAWRM hahrt id) kind, sympathetic

Reading Focus: *Make Inferences*

Ask: What can you infer about the education of enslaved people from the incidents described here?

Literary Focus: *Autobiography*

Explain that the first-person point of view in an autobiography makes the selection more personal. Ask: Do you feel that this helps you to understand Douglass's personality? Explain why you feel as you do.

Literary Focus: *Autobiography*

Ask: How is the author able to tell what others think and feel when the selection is in the first-person point of view?

Discussion

Explain that teenagers in the 19th century memorized orations and recited them at public gatherings. Large crowds would gather to listen. Have the class discuss what this reveals about the place of oration in the society of that time. Ask what topics might have been discussed (patriotism, slavery, and so forth).

Slavery was a delicate subject in Maryland. Grownups talked about it cautiously. Nevertheless, I talked about it freely with the white boys. Sitting on a curbstone or a cellar door, I would say, "I wish I could be free, as you will be when you are men. You will be free, you know, when you are twenty-one. You can go where you like, but I am a slave for life. Have I not as good a right as you to be free?"

Words like this always troubled them. It was very satisfying to me when, occasionally, the boys would bitterly condemn slavery. I could tell this was their true feeling, not the message society had taught them. Conscience is purest when it has not been compromised by the daily struggle for survival. While I was in slavery, I never met a boy who approved of the slave system. Often they would console me, wishing that somehow I would be freed. Over and over, they would say that they believed I had as much right as they did to be free. They would say that God never made anyone to be a slave. The reader can easily see that these conversations did nothing to weaken my love of liberty. They only increased my discontent at being a slave.

I read as much as I could, especially anything about the free states. By the time I was thirteen, the thought that I would be a slave for life had become intolerable. I saw no end to my bondage. I cannot tell you how much the terrible reality of my condition depressed me.

For better or worse, I had by this time made enough money to buy what was then a very popular schoolbook, the "Columbian Orator." I bought this book from Mr. Knight, on Thames Street, Fels Point, Baltimore. It cost me fifty cents. I first learned of this book from hearing some white boys discuss it. They were learning selections from it to recite at the Exhibition. The book was, indeed, fascinating. For a time, I spent every spare minute reading it.

There were many speeches about the principles of liberty in the book. Their content poured floods of light on the evil nature and character of slavery. As I read, I suddenly understood why Master Hugh was so intensely opposed to my education. I was no longer the light-hearted, happy-go-lucky boy who had arrived in Baltimore. Knowledge had opened my eyes. Before me, I saw a horrible pit and a frightful dragon waiting to pounce upon me. I saw no way to escape.

In those days, I often wished that I was a beast or a bird—anything but a slave. I cannot begin to describe my gloom and despair. I was too thoughtful to be happy. This constant thinking distressed and tormented me, but I could not get the thoughts out of my mind. Every waking moment brought a reminder.

---

curbstone (KURB stohn) stone or concrete edging of a sidewalk
compromised (KOM pruh myzd) to give up one's ideals for short-term convenient reasons
intolerable (in TOL ur uh bul) unbearable
light-hearted (LYT hahrt id) free from care

A House Slave and His Mistress at Baltimore, 1861.
The Granger Collection

There was no turning back. Liberty was the birthright of every man. Every object I saw and every sound reminded me of this. I was constantly tormented by the realization of my condition. The more beautiful my surroundings, the more desolate my condition seemed. I did not exaggerate when I say that reminders looked down from every star, smiled at me from every ray of sunlight, breathed in every wind and moved in every storm.

It may be that my changed attitude was in part responsible for the change in my mistress. I can easily believe that my downcast, discontented look was very offensive to her. Poor lady! She did not understand my problem, and I was afraid to tell her. If I could have told her the reason for my depression, it might have been better for both of us. Her abuse was useless. Blows only made the wish for liberty stronger. Nature had made us friends; slavery had made us enemies.

My interests were in direct opposition to hers, and we both had our private thoughts and plans. Her goal was to keep me ignorant. I was determined to learn despite the fact that the more I learned the more unhappy I became.

My feelings would have been the same if I had been treated kindly. I could no longer accept being a slave under any conditions. It was slavery—not its incidental abuses that I hated.

I had been cheated out of my birthright. Feeding and clothing me well could not atone for stealing my liberty from me. The smiles of my mistress could not remove the sorrow in my heart. In time, they only came to deepen my sorrow. She had changed. The reader can see that I had changed too.

She, the mistress, and I, the slave, were both victims of the same overshadowing evil—slavery. I will not censure her harshly. She cannot censure me because she knows I speak the truth. I have acted from opposition to slavery. She herself would have done the same if our circumstances had been reversed.

birthright (BURTH ryt) the rights that a person has because he/she was born in a certain family, nation, etc.
downcast (DOUN kast) sad
incidental (in suh DENT ul) casual; secondary
overshadowing (oh vur SHAD oh ing) hanging or looming over
censure (SEN shur) blame

Viewing Fine Art

This picture is an engraving made for a magazine. The art of engraving began long ago in Japan in the 8th century when artists carved into wood by hand. In Europe, the art of engraving began in the 15th century. At the time this engraving was made, machines produced thousands of them, usually for magazines. Today, there are numerous types of engraving techniques, but the basic process is the same: an illustration is carved onto a plate of metal which is then pressed into ink. The plate is then is pressed onto a surface in order to create the print. Ask: What do you think the artist was trying to show? How do you feel about the picture?

Reading Focus: *Make Inferences*

Ask: What can you infer about how Douglass views humanity from his comments about Mrs. Auld? What clues does the author give that help you infer?

Background Notes

Explain that Maryland was a "border state." Slavery was legal, but at the outset of the Civil War, Maryland remained in the Union. Place a map of the United States in 1860 on the overhead projector. Point out the location of Maryland between larger states of Pennsylvania (Union) and Virginia (Confederate). Have the students discuss how the geographic location of Maryland might have affected its inhabitants before and during the Civil War. After eliciting opinions, mention that the single bloodiest day of the battle in the Civil War took place in Antietam in Maryland.

Mini Quiz

Write the following sentences on the board or overhead projector and call on students to fill in the blanks. Discuss the answers with the class.

1. Mrs. Auld's son was named ________.
2. Douglass used ________ as payment to other boys to teach him to read.
3. Douglass never met a boy who ________ of slavery.
4. Douglass was ________ years old when he decided that being a slave for life would be intolerable.
5. Douglass's every waking moment reminded him that ________ is the birthright of every person.

Answers

1. Tommy
2. bread
3. approved
4. thirteen
5. liberty

UNDERSTAND THE SELECTION

Answers

1. Mrs. Auld, his mistress, began teaching him to read.
2. He lived in Baltimore, Maryland.
3. He found these in the *Columbian Orator*.
4. Sample answer: She had never owned a slave before and she recognized his humanity.
5. Sample answer: They realized it was wrong.
6. Sample answer: He knew knowledge would make Douglass aware that slavery was intolerable.
7. Sample answer: It robbed both of their humanity.
8. She taught him out of kindness.
9. Sample answer: In having to reject Douglass, his wife became callous toward everyone.
10. Sample answer: He might have become a house slave who never realized his potential as a human being.

Respond to Literature

The popularity of Douglass's book indicates that more people were beginning to hold anti-slavery views. A book about slavery written by a person who experienced it would help them affirm these views and perhaps persuade other people to an anti-slavery viewpoint.

WRITE ABOUT THE SELECTION

Prewriting

Explain that each student must form an opinion of Mrs. Auld and decide whether her reaction would have been positive (secretly rejoice) or negative (angry). Record the students' suggestions for both positive and negative reactions on a two column chart on a board or an overhead transparency.

Writing

Have the students work on this section individually. Walk around the classroom, giving help to any student who is having difficulty. To suggest possible ideas, ask students how they would feel in Mrs. Auld's position.

Revising

Make this a cooperative group activity. Divide class into small groups. If possible, select group members who share the same opinion. Have members take turns in reading their paragraphs to the group. When the reader has finished, others may make suggestions of adjectives or phrases that would clarify or support the opinion presented.

Proofreading

Select one or two paragraphs as models for proofreading. Place the papers on an overhead and have the class suggest corrections.

Review the Selection

UNDERSTAND THE SELECTION

Recall

1. Who began teaching Douglass?
2. Where was Douglass enslaved as a young child?
3. In what book did Douglass find writings about the principles of freedom?

Infer

4. Why did Douglass say that Mrs. Auld was ill-prepared to be a slaveholder?
5. Why did Douglass never meet a boy who approved of the slave system?
6. Why was Master Hugh so opposed to Douglass's education?
7. Why were Douglass and Mrs. Auld both victims of slavery?

Apply

8. Why did Mrs. Auld teach Douglass to read?
9. In what way did Master Hugh pay for his victory over his wife's natural kindness?
10. If Douglass had not learned to read, predict what might have happened.

Respond to Literature

What does the popularity of Douglass's writings reveal about the changing attitude toward slavery at the time?

WRITE ABOUT THE SELECTION

Frederick Douglass wrote *My Bondage and My Freedom* after he had run away and escaped slavery. In this selection, you can relate to his situation and suppose how you might have felt if you were a slave. He indicated that had the roles been reversed, Mrs. Auld would have run away from slavery, too.

Assume that Mrs. Auld, the slaveholder, has just learned of Douglass's escape. Keep in mind the type of person he has indicated that she once was and how she had changed. Does she react violently or does she secretly rejoice that he has escaped? What measures, if any, does she take to have him returned? Write a paragraph describing how you think Mrs. Auld would have reacted.

Prewriting Write an informal outline of what Mrs. Auld might have thought, said, or done. Freewrite comments she might have made.

Writing Use your informal outline to write a paragraph explaining Mrs. Auld's actions upon her discovery that Douglass was gone. In it, describe whom she might have contacted and what she might have said.

Revising When you revise your paragraph, add details that illustrate how she felt.

Proofreading Read over your selection. Be sure all your sentences end with a period, question mark, or exclamation point.

THINK ABOUT AUTOBIOGRAPHY

An **autobiography** is the history of a person's life, written by him- or herself. It is a narrative. A well-written biography tells of the inner struggles of the author, interprets the events in the light of history, and draws thoughtful conclusions about life in general.

1. Why is an autobiography written in narrative form?
2. Do you think Douglass's characterization of Mrs. Auld was accurate? Why or why not?
3. Douglass could not read Mrs. Auld's mind. On what could he judge what she might be thinking?
4. Do you agree that first-person point of view is appropriate for an autobiography? Why or why not?
5. Why do you think learning to read was so important to Douglass?

Reading Focus

Make Inferences As you read the excerpt from *My Bondage and My Freedom*, you were asked to make inferences about different aspects of the narrative. What inference did you make about how Douglass felt about Mrs. Auld? Tell which details from the autobiography helped you to make this inference.

DEVELOP YOUR VOCABULARY

Nouns can be classified in various ways. One useful distinction is between concrete and abstract nouns. **Concrete nouns** name things that exist in the physical world. The things they name can be felt, seen, heard, smelled, or tasted. Examples are *wind*, *mountain*, *horn*, *perfume*, *soup*. **Abstract nouns** name ideas, qualities, or characteristics that do not exist physically and cannot be recognized by the senses. Examples are *liberty*, *beauty*, *kindness*.

Frederick Douglass used many abstract nouns in his autobiography. List the following words from the Douglass selection. Beside each word write whether it is *concrete* or *abstract*.

1. slaveholder
2. humanity
3. freedom
4. conscience
5. newspaper
6. playmate
7. prudence
8. schoolbook
9. slavery
10. joy

THINK ABOUT AUTOBIOGRAPHY

Sample Answers

1. It deals with events and these are told in time order.
2. Yes, because he was so careful to include different responses to him.
3. Her attitude changed gradually. He had known her kindness; he knew her husband's views; he could surmise how her attitude change came about.
4. Yes, since an autobiography is one's own story told by oneself, the appropriate pronoun is *I*.
5. Reading was the key to intellectual freedom; a release from slavery, the key to physical freedom.

DEVELOP YOUR VOCABULARY

Answers

1. concrete
2. abstract
3. abstract
4. abstract
5. concrete
6. concrete
7. abstract
8. concrete
9. abstract
10. abstract

ESL Activity

Divide students into small groups, with each group having at least one English-proficient member. Have group members work together to write sentences using the words in the Develop Your Vocabulary exercise.

Reading Focus

Sample Answer

Douglass shows that he believes Mrs. Auld to be a good and kind person in her heart by his description of how she treated him as a young child. These descriptions suggest that Douglass respected her no matter how she treated him.

Selection Overview

SELECTION OBJECTIVES

After completing this selections, students will be able to

- understand persuasion and argumentation
- recognize propositions
- recognize arguments and conclusions
- understand that orations appeal to the listeners' intelligence and emotions
- write a persuasive paragraph
- understand that many words have different meanings
- understand persuasive techniques

Lesson Resources

Ain't I a Woman?

- Selection Synopsis, Teacher's Edition, p. T65b
- Comprehension and Vocabulary Workbook, pp. 19–20
- Language Enrichment Workbook, p. 10
- Teacher's Resources
  Reinforcement, p. R10
  Test, pp. T19–T20

More About Persuasion

In literature, persuasion is sometimes called argumentation. Arguments are the reasons given by the writer to demonstrate the truth or falsity of a proposition. The writer states a proposition to be proved or disproved, gives his reasons, and draws conclusions. Ask students to recall Patrick Henry or the Crèvecoeur selection of Unit 1 and identify propositions, arguments, and conclusions from either of these works.

About the Author

Sojourner Truth's given name was Isabella. In 1829, she changed her name to Sojourner (meaning "wanderer" or "traveler") Truth (because "God is Truth"). In the years that followed, she traveled across the northern states raising money to help runaway slaves.

Learn About

Sojourner Truth, 1864. The Granger Collection

Reading Focus

Understand Persuasive Techniques Writers sometimes try to persuade readers to agree with their opinions by appealing to the readers' emotions. Persuasive techniques, such as appealing to the readers' emotions, can be very effective. Think about the emotions the author is appealing to as you read.

Persuasion

Have you ever tried to persuade your parents that you need new, more expensive tennis shoes? Have you ever tried to convince a teacher that you deserve a higher grade? Did you use supporting statements or arguments to back up your appeal? Then you have used a form of discourse called **persuasion**.

The purpose of persuasion is to convince readers or listeners of the truth or falsity of a proposition. A **proposition** is a statement of what is supported or upheld. In your persuasive appeals, the propositions would have been something like: "I need new shoes" or "I should get a better grade." Then you would have given some arguments that your statements were true.

As you read this selection, ask yourself:

1. What proposition is Sojourner Truth trying to uphold?
2. Why do you think she repeats the question in the title so often? What is the purpose of repetition?

WRITING CONNECTION

Assume that you are running for the office of class president. Write a paragraph showing that you are the best person for the job. Include facts to support your propositions.

Viewing Fine Art

This portrait is of Sojourner Truth (1797–1883), remembered for her roles in the abolitionist and women's suffrage movements. Ask: What does this portrait suggest about Sojourner Truth?

Cooperative Group Activity

Pair the students. Have each pair exchange papers completed for the Writing Connection activity. Have the partners discuss whether both papers include a proposition, one or more arguments, and a conclusion.

Develop Vocabulary Skills

List the vocabulary words on the board. Summarize the definitions in one or two words beside each word. Have the students write an original sentence containing the summarized definition. Have students exchange papers and rewrite the sentences replacing each definition with a vocabulary word.

AIN'T I A WOMAN?

ADAPTED

by Sojourner Truth

Well, Children, where there is so much racket there must be something out of kilter. I think that between the Negroes of the South and the women at the North, all talking about rights, the white men will be in a fix pretty soon. But what's all this here talking about?

That man over there says that women need to be helped into carriages, and lifted over ditches, and to have the best place everywhere. Nobody ever helps me into carriages, or over mud puddles, or gives me any best place! And ain't I a woman? Look at me! Look at my arm! I have ploughed and planted. I have gathered into barns, and no man could head me! And ain't I a woman? I could work as much and eat as much as a man—when I could get it—and bear the lash as well! And ain't I a woman? I have borne 13 children, and seen them most all sold off into slavery. When I cried out with a mother's grief, none but Jesus heard! And ain't I a woman?

Then they talk about this thing in the head; what's this they call it? ["Intellect," someone whispers.] That's it, honey. What's that got to do with women's rights or Negro's rights? If my cup won't hold but a pint, and yours holds a quart, wouldn't you be mean not to let me have my little half-measure full?

Then that little man in black there, he says women can't have as much rights as men, 'cause Christ wasn't a woman! Where did your Christ come from? Where did your Christ come from? From God and a woman! Man had nothing to do with Him.

If the first woman God ever made was strong enough to turn the world upside down all alone, these women together ought to be able to turn it back, and get it right side up again! And now they is asking to do it, the men better let them.

Obliged to you for hearing me, and now old Sojourner ain't got nothing more to say.

---

kilter (KIL tur) good condition; proper order
plough (PLOU) plow; to make furrows in the earth
lash (LASH) whip

TEACHING PLAN

INTRODUCE

Motivation

Play a recording of the song, "I Am Woman." (If you cannot find it in a record store, ask a local radio station if you can borrow a copy from their library and return it after class.) Ask students afterward what they remember from the lyrics. List appropriate responses on the board. Remind the students that this selection was originally an oration. Ask the students to compare the works as they read.

Purpose-Setting Questions

On the board, write the following expression: *If I am not for myself, who will I be? If I am only for myself, who am I?* Ask students to discuss this in relation to the rights of all people.

READ

Literary Focus: *Persuasion*

Encourage students to analyze Truth's appeal. Have them list several arguments she gives for women's rights.

Reading Focus: *Understand Persuasive Techniques*

As students read, ask them to be aware of their reactions to Sojourner Truth's arguments. Do her words make them feel anger, exasperation, resentment? Discuss with students how appealing to her audience's emotions may have stirred Truth's listeners to action.

CLOSE

Have students complete Review the Selection on pages 80–81.

ESL Activity

Ask a volunteer to practice reading the speech using intonation as they think Sojourner Truth may have originally read it. Then ask the volunteer to read it aloud to the rest of the group, placing emphasis on the questions Truth asks.

Mini Quiz

1. The ________ of the South and the ________ of the North were all talking about rights.
2. When Truth cried out in grief over the sale of her children into slavery, only ________heard her.
3. "This thing in the head" that she referred to was called ________.
4. Women acting together, she thought, would turn the ________ right side up again.

Answers

1. Negroes, women
2. Jesus
3. intellect
4. world

UNDERSTAND THE SELECTION

Answers

1. She had thirteen
2. They were sold into slavery.
3. She believes women can straighten out the world.
4. She is an outspoken woman interested in women's civil rights.
5. Sample answer: "Why am I, an African American, female, former slave, not treated with the same respect and consideration as other women?"
6. Sample answer: women who are in favor of women's rights
7. Sample answer: She could do as much as or more work than any man.
8. Sample answers: angry, upset; find a way to change the situation, show anger to slaveholders
9. Sample answers: Supporters applaud and cheer. Those opposed heckle, throw things, and yell at her.
10. Sample answers: Yes, because she presented points that would be difficult to disagree with. No, perhaps because she was very emotional.

Respond to Literature

Have the class discuss whether they think Truth felt that she had suffered more or less as an African American or as a woman.

WRITE ABOUT THE SELECTION

Prewriting

Tell the students to think about the reasons that a 19th-century person might give for supporting a position on women's rights. Using the students' suggestions, list several reasons or each opinion on the board or overhead transparency.

Sample reasons:
Disagrees (Against equal rights for women)—Women are less intelligent. Women are not capable of making political decisions. Women should be satisfied with operating a household and raising children.

Agrees (in favor of equal rights for women)—Women are equally intelligent and should be equally educated. Women are capable of making political decisions. Women should be given opportunities to use their talents outside the home. Remind students that they are to write in the first-person point of view.

Writing

Have students work on this section individually. Remind them that they must decide on what their own positions might have been on women's rights given the historical context. Emphasize that their task is to show how Truth's oratory would have affected their own views. Go around the class, giving help to any student who is having difficulty.

Revising

Divide the class into small groups. Decide if student opinions show how Truth's speech changed or strengthened their views.

Proofreading

Have students check their own work. Provide help as needed.

Review the Selection

UNDERSTAND THE SELECTION

Recall

1. How many children did Sojourner Truth have?
2. What happened to her children?
3. Who does Truth believe can straighten out the world?

Infer

4. Who is Sojourner Truth?
5. What do you think Truth really means when she asks, "Ain't I a woman?"
6. What group of women does Truth represent in expressing her feelings?
7. Why does she believe she should have as many rights as men?

Apply

8. Assume a loved one is sold into slavery. How would you react?
9. Suppose you live in the nineteenth century. You hear Truth give her speech. How does the audience react?
10. Do you think Truth presented a persuasive argument? Explain.

Respond to Literature

In what way does this selection illustrate the sentiments toward African Americans and women during the nineteenth century?

WRITE ABOUT THE SELECTION

In this selection, Sojourner Truth presents a persuasive argument of human rights for African American women as well as equal rights for all women. Remember that persuasive writing presents personal viewpoints. Write an editorial to Sojourner's oration as if you were a member of the audience when she gave the speech. Which points were most important? How did she impact your own thoughts as a 19th century person?

Prewriting Decide whether you, as a 19th century person, will agree or disagree with Sojourner Truth. Jot down ideas supporting your position. Include details of why you feel this way.

Writing Use your notes to write a paragraph in the first-person point of view. Remember that you are supposed to be a person from the 19th century. In your paragraph, make certain that your opinion is clear.

Revising When you revise your paragraph, be sure to add specific points that support your opinion.

Proofreading Read over your paragraph and check your punctuation.

THINK ABOUT PERSUASION

Like Patrick Henry's and George Washington's speeches in Unit 1, Sojourner Truth's "Ain't I a Woman?" was originally an oration. An **oration** is a speech that is meant to inspire listeners to take some action. The orator appeals to the listener's intelligence but also to the listener's emotions.

1. What does Sojourner Truth accomplish by the constant repetition of her title question?
2. A rhetorical question is asked for its effect on the audience; it does not require an answer. Find at least one rhetorical question, other than the title question, in Truth's speech.
3. Does Truth's use of *ain't* and other colloquial words and phrases add to or detract from the effect of her speech? Explain your answer.
4. Which argument do you think is Truth's most effective one? Why?
5. Which aspect of Truth's speech made the stronger impression on you—her reasons or her emotional appeal? Explain your answer.

Reading Focus

Understand Persuasive Techniques
Sojourner Truth made several powerful points to appeal to the audience's emotions. Choose the point you found most compelling and explain why it made an impact on you.

DEVELOP YOUR VOCABULARY

Many words have more than one meaning. When you read these words, it is always important to understand which meaning the author intends. For example, the word *racket* can have several different meanings. In this selection, *racket* means loud, confused talk. What other meanings can it have? If a word appears to be familiar, but the meaning does not make sense in a sentence, look in a dictionary for another meaning that does make sense. By paying close attention to context clues, you will be able to figure out the correct meaning.

Following are common words that have more than one meaning. Read the list, then think of two meanings for each word. Check your meanings in a dictionary. Then, write an original sentence for each meaning of each word. Be sure that your sentences make it clear which of its meanings the word is carrying.

1. racket
2. ball
3. board
4. foot
5. band
6. ring
7. fork
8. address
9. kind
10. strike

THINK ABOUT PERSUASION

Answers

1. She drives home her point to make people think.
2. "What's that got to do with women's or Negro's rights?"
3. The words and the phrases add to the speech. By making her seem more vulnerable, her strengths stand out.
4. Answers will vary
5. Her emotional appeal because she makes listeners feel, as well as think, about equal rights.

DEVELOP YOUR VOCABULARY

Answers

Sample sentences:

1. Although the doors were closed, I still heard the *racket* out in the hallway. Bob's tennis *racket* is broken.
2. The child bounced the yellow *ball*. A fancy *ball* is being held in honor of the newly-elected president.
3. My father checked each *board* for imperfections before he nailed it in place. The passengers will *board* the train in a few minutes.
4. My entire *foot* ached after I stubbed my toe. We will need one *foot* of ribbon to complete the project.
5. The *band* played several popular tunes. The *band* of Indians traveled many miles in search of food.
6. Her engagement *ring* is beautiful. The church bell will *ring* at noon.
7. The car turned left at the *fork* in the road. Jim asked the waitress for another *fork*.
8. The principal will *address* the entire student body at today's assembly. Sam asked Jill for her home *address*.
9. My mother is *kind* to all my friends. The rose is my favorite *kind* of flower.
10. The workers at that factory decided to go on *strike*. This baseball player always seem to *strike* at the first pitch.

Reading Focus

Sample Answer

I found Truth's point that a woman was Christ's mother the most compelling. It helped me to understand her feelings about the injustices done to women and how unfounded they were.

Selection Overview

SELECTION OBJECTIVES

After reading this selection, students will be able to

- understand plot and conflict
- understand climax and denouement
- write a brief dramatic scene
- identify and use onomatopoeia in writing
- identify hyperbole

Lesson Resources

The Legend Of Sleepy Hollow

- Selection Synopsis, Teacher's Edition, p. T65c
- Comprehension and Vocabulary Workbook, pp. 21–22
- Language Enrichment Workbook, p. 11
- Teacher's Resources
  - Reinforcement, p. R11
  - Test, pp. T21–T22

More About the Literary Period

Explain that in the 18th century many colonists thought of themselves as Europeans living on a different continent. The fiction they read was usually European in setting, theme, and character. After the Revolutionary War, they began to think of themselves as Americans. Writers like Irving provided American literature. Curiously, his writing became so popular in Europe that he spent 17 years there (1815–1832). Ask the students why they think Europeans would be curious about American literature.

About the Author

The author was born in 1783 in New York City. This was the year the Treaty of Paris was signed, formally acknowledging the colonies' independence. George Washington, then commander-in-chief of the American army, was present in New York to witness the evacuation of the last British troops in America. Irving's father named the baby after the general.

Learn About

PLOT

The Legend of Sleepy Hollow, Anonymous. Corbis Bettmann

Plot is the series of events that make up the story line of a literary work. Conflict and climax are two main elements of plot.

Conflict is a clash between two opposing forces. The clash provides the dramatic action. The opposing forces may be two people—the protagonist, or main character, and an antagonist, or rival character. Sometimes the opposing forces are the main character and nature, or the main character and different impulses in his or her own mind.

The main character's attempts to resolve the conflict advance the plot toward the climax. The **climax** is the decisive turning point in the action. It is the moment when the character begins to resolve the conflict. The climax is followed by the **dénouement**, the final resolution, or outcome.

The next selection, a radio drama, is meant to be heard, not read or seen by the audience. As you read it, ask yourself:

1. Who is the protagonist in the play?
2. Why is a narrator used in the play?

READING FOCUS

Identify Hyperbole Hyperbole is an exaggerated statement often used to suggest that something is greater than it really is. An example is: "better than Mom's apple pie." Hyperbole is often found in figures of speech that compare two things, such as "my love burns brighter than the stars above."

As you read, look for instances where the author is comparing two things. Then decide if it is an exaggeration, or hyperbole. Ask yourself: Does the exaggeration make the situation humorous? Does it heighten the suspense about what will happen next?

WRITING CONNECTION

Summarize the plot of a movie you have seen recently. Name the protagonist, and explain the conflict and its resolution.

Viewing Fine Art

"The Legend of Sleepy Hollow" is a famous story written by Washington Irving. This illustration shows the main character of the story. The artist is unknown. Ask: What kind of character do you think the main character is?

Cooperative Group Activity

Group students by their responses to "What is your favorite movie?" Using the Writing Connection activity as background, have each group collaborate on one element—the conflict, for example—and produce a group description. If a group cannot produce one unified description of the element, have individuals in each group defend their positions.

THE LEGEND OF

Sleepy Hollow

a radio play based on the story by Washington Irving

CHARACTERS

ANNOUNCER
ICHABOD CRANE, *village schoolteacher*
MASTER YOST VAN HUTEN, *pupil*
KATRINA VAN TASSEL, *daughter of a wealthy Dutch farmer*
FROW VAN TASSEL, *Katrina's mother*
MYNHEER VAN TASSEL, *Katrina's father*
BROM VAN BRUNT, *young man*
HANS VAN RIPPER, *farmer*
FROW VAN RIPPER, *his wife*
FARMER VAN TIL, *neighbor*
Two Men, a Woman, several Children, a Minister

MUSIC: *"Memories." Fade in, then out slowly under voice.*

ANNOUNCER: Washington Irving's famous "Legend of Sleepy Hollow" was first read by a delighted public more than 160 years ago. But the church mentioned in the story still stands today as Irving described it, and automobiles rattle over the Headless Horseman's Bridge near Tarrytown, New York.

MUSIC: *An old tune takes us back in time.*

ANNOUNCER (*with lowered voice*): Long ago the valley called Sleepy Hollow was a place bewitched.

SOUND: *Indian war whoops. Fade and hold.*

ANNOUNCER: Some say that the old Indian chiefs held their meetings there, long before the explorer Henry Hudson discovered the spot.

---

fade in (FAYD IN) in radio, to become more distinct

TEACHING PLAN

INTRODUCE

Motivation

Discuss movies or television programs students have seen that involved ghosts. Ask them to identify the similarities among the programs. Lead them to understand that suspense is often the most common element in these types of presentations. Tell them that this play is a ghost story and that they can expect to encounter suspense as they read it.

Purpose-Setting Question

Why would Americans of Irving's day find the story of a farmer outwitting an authority figure like a teacher amusing?

READ

Literary Focus: *Plot*

Have the students read the list of characters. Explain that Ichabod is the protagonist. Tell them that Katrina is the ingenue, or innocent young woman. Ask them who will provide the exposition. Tell them that as they read they should think about an external conflict (and name the antagonist) and an internal conflict.

Reading Focus: *Identify Hyperbole*

As students read, encourage them to look for places of exaggeration and to note how this affects the mood of the selection. Does the hyperbole—exaggeration—increase the suspense? Does it add humor? Guide students to understanding the role of hyperbole in an otherwise ghostly tale.

CLOSE

Have students complete Review the Selection on pages 98–99.

Develop Vocabulary Skills

Write the terms fade in and fade out on the board with their definitions. Ask the students to suggest and define other radio, television, or film terms they have heard that provide directions to the cast and crew.

ESL Activity

Introduce students to "sound effects." Go over the script of the radio play and discuss and practice the sound effects, (war whoops, odd shrieks and laughter, wind, horse's hoofs, and so forth) so that ESL students can participate on cue in the script reading.

SOUND: *War whoops up briefly and out.*

ANNOUNCER: Some say it was a meeting place of witches . . .

SOUND: *Odd shrieks and laughter. Fade and hold.*

ANNOUNCER: . . . after they were driven out of New England . . . and you can still hear their voices in the air . . . high above the treetops.

SOUND: *Shrieks and laughter up briefly, then fade out.*

VOICES: Graymalkin! Brimstone! Meet me in the forest!

ANNOUNCER: But everyone in Sleepy Hollow agreed on one thing . . . and that was the headless ghost of a Hessian[1] soldier on horseback.

SOUND: *Wind and horse's hoofs. Fade and hold.*

ANNOUNCER: His head had been shot off by a cannonball, and he roamed the valley on windy nights.

SOUND: *Wind and hoofs up briefly. Fade slowly under and out.*

ANNOUNCER: Many worthy citizens had heard the headless horseman, and not a few of them had actually seen him with their own eyes. Of all the legends that hung about—this was the favorite legend of Sleepy Hollow.

MUSIC: *Simple country tune. Up, under, and out.*

ANNOUNCER: The schoolhouse in Sleepy Hollow was ruled over by a man named Ichabod Crane. He was tall and thin, with hands that dangled a mile out of his sleeves, and feet that might have served for shovels. He had huge ears, large glassy-green eyes, and a long nose like a bird's beak. When he walked along on a windy day, one might have taken him for a scarecrow escaped from some cornfield. But inside his own schoolroom, inside the four log walls, he ruled supreme.

SOUND: *Voices of children, up and under. Up briefly between next three speeches.*

VOICE: Sixty seconds make a minute. Sixty minutes make an hour. Twenty-four hours make a day. . . .

VOICE: The state of Connecticut is south of Massachusetts, west of Rhode Island. . . .

VOICE: The fat cat ate the rat. Run, cat, run.

SOUND: *Noise of ruler hitting desk. Children's voices fade out quickly.*

---

fade out (FAYD OUT) in radio, to become less distinct

[1]**Hessians:** German soldiers who fought for the British during the Revolutionary War

Enrichment

Make sure students understand the term *Hessian* (a German soldier hired by England to fight on their side in the American Revolutionary War). Discuss with the students why a Hessian ghost might be especially frightening to Americans only a generation or so removed from the Revolutionary War.

Reading Focus: *Identify Hyperbole*

Guide students to the announcer's description of Ichabod Crane, ". . . hands that dangled a mile out of his sleeves, and feet that might have served for shovels." What does this bit of hyperbole reveal about how others view this character? Why does the author use this technique to describe a character?

ICHABOD (*a loud comedy voice that seems to come half through the nose*)**:** Silence, children. I observe that Master Yost Van Huten is more than usually busy with his chalk and writing board. Come forward, Master Yost, and let us all admire your work.

YOST (*unhappily*)**:** Please, teacher, I don't wanna.

ICHABOD: You will bring me your writing board at once, Master Yost. Thank You. . . . Hmmm. . . . What have we here?

SOUND: *Children laughing behind their hands.*

ICHABOD (*with sound of ruler on desk*)**:** You would draw a funny picture of your teacher, would you, Master Yost? Read aloud what you have written.

YOST (*unhappily*)**:** Teacher's mad and I am glad,
And I know what'll please him . . .

ICHABOD: Go on.

YOST: A bottle of wine to make him shine,
And Katrina Van Tassel to tease him.

SOUND: *Laughter.*

ICHABOD: I have always carried in mind that wonderful rule: "Spare the rod and spoil the child:" I would not for any reason have Master Yost Van Huten spoiled. You will hold out your hand, Master Yost.

YOST: Aw, I don't wanna!

SOUND: *Ruler on child's hand and child crying out. The ruler fades, but the child continues to cry.*

ICHABOD: I am only doing my duty by your good parents, Master Yost! There! It may hurt now, my gifted young poet, but you will remember it and thank me for it in the longest day you have to live.

MUSIC: *Up to close scene, then under and out.*

ANNOUNCER: Despite his rule in the classroom and his peculiar appearance, Ichabod Crane was thought of as a man of great learning. He would quote whole pages of Cotton Mather's history of witchcraft in New England. He was the singing teacher of Sleepy Hollow, and he led the singing in church every Sunday morning.

These accomplishments put Ichabod ahead of the local country boys in winning the favors of the blooming Katrina Van Tassel, daughter of the wealthiest Dutch farmer in the neighborhood. On afternoons, when his work at the school house was over, he would walk to the Van Tassel farmhouse

Critical Thinking: *Characterization*

Have students reread the description of Ichabod Crane on this page. Ask: Using clues from what you read, how would you characterize Ichabod Crane?

Literary Focus: *Plot*

At the end of the first scene, define caricature (grotesque exaggeration of physical features for humorous effect). Ask volunteers to identify the character who is a caricature, giving specific examples. Ask other volunteers to predict this character's role in upcoming events.

(*Fading*) on the bank of the Hudson River in a green and . . .

ICHABOD: And how are you, Miss Katrina? Hmmmm! Always busy spinning, weaving, or baking your delicious little cakes, ahem—such delicious cakes!

KATRINA: It's nice of you to praise 'em, Master Crane. Won't you try some of today's baking? This honey loaf and these doughnuts. And a bit of the new cheese and a glass of father's cider.

ICHABOD (*with mouth too full, smacking lips*): Mmm! Just a bit! Just a little bit! Just a little, little bit! I'm a light eater, Miss Katrina. I take only enough to keep body and soul together!

KATRINA: But you must do more than just taste my honey loaf, Master Crane. And the coffee cake. Here, let me refill your glass, too.

ICHABOD (*speaking with difficulty through a full mouth*): Miss Katrina, your charms have made a deep impression on my heart!

KATRINA (*giggling*): Oh, Master Crane, how do you talk!

ICHABOD: (*mouth full*) Katrina, there is something I must tell you. . . . I'll thank you to pass the peach jam. . . . Something I have long been hoping. . . . Well, just a drop more cider if you insist. . . . Katrina, I love you!

KATRINA: Hist! Here comes Mother! I'll be singing!

ICHABOD: Here's my tuning fork!

SOUND: *Tuning fork sounds "A."*

KATRINA: Do-re- mi. . . . (*Sings scale. Breaks off.*)

MOTHER: (*Fade in*) Good day to you, Master Crane! I see you're giving my girl a lesson.

ICHABOD: Yes, indeed, Frow Van Tassel. Now give me an "A," Miss Katrina.

SOUND: *Tuning fork strikes "A."*

KATRINA: Ahhhh!

ICHABOD (*like a sheep*): Ahhh!

KATRINA (*up one tone*): Ohhh.

ICHABOD (*through his nose*): Ohhh! And now for the hymn for next Sunday.

BOTH: By the still stream we sat and wept,
While memory still to . . .

MOTHER (*interrupting*): Very nice, I'm sure. . . . Well, I must run along to my farm duties. Geese and ducks are foolish things, but girls can look after themselves. . . . (*Fading*) Do a good lesson, Katrina.

Literary Focus: *Plot*

Ask: What new character is introduced here? What conflict does the author describe?

ICHABOD: Miss Katrina, as I was saying . . . (*Singing scale*) do-re-me-fa-sol-la-I Love you-u-u.

KATRINA (*singing scale*)**:** Do-re-mi-fa-sol-la. This is so sudden, Master Crane!

ICHABOD: Your place forever is in my heart. . . . Just how large is this farm, Miss Katrina?

KATRINA: Three hundred acres. Ahhh!

ICHABOD (*proudly*)**:** Three hundred acres! Miss Katrina, I adore you! Tell me you'll be Missus Ichabod Crane!

KATRINA (*shyly*)**:** You must give me time to think it over. I'll give you your answer—

ICHABOD: When?

KATRINA: Next Friday week—at our. . . at my parents' big party! Do—re—mi—fa—sol—la—a—a.

MUSIC: *Up fast, then fade slowly under and out.*

ANNOUNCER: Next Friday week. . . . The days passed slowly for our impatient lover. Already, in his own mind, Ichabod saw himself master of the rich fields, the great barns, fat pigs, snowy geese, whole armies of turkeys! He knew, however, that there was someone else who wanted Katrina's hand in marriage. This was Brom Van Brunt, a husky young farmer who won all the neighborhood races and was the leader of a gang of mischief makers. Brom had bragged that he would "double the schoolteacher up and lay him on a shelf in his own schoolhouse," but Ichabod did not take his words very seriously.

To pass the time until the Van Tassels' party, Ichabod reread Cotton Mather's book on witchcraft from cover to cover. He remained at his desk in the log schoolhouse one evening so late that it was pitch-dark when he at last started homeward. As he walked along through the hollow, his teeth began to chatter, and the ordinary sounds of the night took on ghostly terrors.

MUSIC: *Notes of worry.*

SOUND: *Footsteps on gravel. Crickets. Hold under.*

ICHABOD (*to self*)**:** Ooo . . . what a spooky night. . . . J-j-just the night for the h-h-headless horseman to ride. W-w-what if I should m-m-meet him?

SOUND: *Hoot of owl.*

Critical Thinking: *Draw Conclusions*

Ask: Does Ichabod Crane want to marry Miss Katrina because he loves her or because of her inheritance?

Reading Focus: *Identify Hyperbole*

Have a volunteer read aloud the description in the announcer's speech of the riches that a marriage to Katrina Van Tassel would provide for Ichabod Crane. Ask: What hyperbole has the author used here? Why is it effective?

Literary Focus: *Plot*

Elicit from students how they think this passage sets up the action that follows. What insights does Ichabod's overly superstitious behavior give into his character?

Reading Focus: *Identify Hyperbole*

The announcer compares Crane's arms to "the flapping of great black wings." Ask: Why does the author compare Crane to a bird? Encourage students to visualize the image as they answer the question.

ICHABOD: It sounds like an owl . . . but it might be a witch. There was old Nance Dinwiddie of Salem and Bess o'Bedlam . . . she that makes cows' milk go sour and puts tar in the baby's hair. O-o-o-h.

SOUND: *Hoot of owl*

ICHABOD: Mercy on us! What a dreadful sound! Some poor homeless ghost, I make no doubt. (*Pleading*) Get back to your grave, do, that's a good ghost!

SOUND: *Hoot of owl at distance.*

ICHABOD: What a black night! Not a single star. Oooooooh! There goes one now . . . shooting across the sky. A falling star means death. Then there was that black cat I met yesterday—that's a sure sign of trouble.

SOUND: *Bullfrogs croaking.*

ICHABOD: Ahhh! Is that a bullfrog or a ghost?

SOUND: *Fade footsteps and crickets.*

MUSIC: *Up over fading sounds.*

ANNOUNCER: Finally came the evening of the big party at Mynheer Van Tassel's. Ichabod wanted to arrive in style at the home of his lady love, so he borrowed an old plow horse called Gunpowder from Hans Van Ripper, the farmer in whose home he was then staying. On this animal he made a curious sight indeed. His legs were so long that his bony knees came up to the top of the saddle, and the motion of his arms was like the flapping of great black wings. Such was the figure that arrived at Mynheer Van Tassel's farmhouse (*Fading*) to find the merrymaking in full swing.

MUSIC: *Fade in dance tune of the period.*

SOUND: *Fade in sounds of country dance and small crowd noise. Sounds and music fade down and hold.*

ICHABOD: Ah, Mynheer Van Tassel, (*Through his nose*) this is a happy event indeed!

VAN TASSEL: Evenin', Ichabod, evenin'! Fall to and help yourself to the food!

ICHABOD: What a feast! What a delightful feast! Apple and pumpkin pies . . . broiled fish and roasted chickens . . . jams made of plums and peaches from *my* own trees . . . ah, I should say *your* own trees, Mynheer Van Tassel!

MUSIC: *Dance tune ending.*

Ichabod Crane and Katrina Van Tassel, George Henry Boughton.
New York Historical Society, New York

VOICES (*calling*): Ichabod, Ichabod Crane! Show us how you dance the shakedown!

ICHABOD (*proudly*): If Miss Katrina will be my partner.

KATRINA: Yes, here I am.

MUSIC: *Fast music up, down, and hold.*

SOUND: *Clapping hands and stamping feet to time of music.*

VOICES (*together*): Go to it, Ichabod! Hooray! See the schoolmaster! *etc.*

SOUND: *All sound and music fade to distance.*

ANNOUNCER: But Brom Van Brunt, who also wanted to marry Katrina, did not feel so gay as the rest of the party.

Viewing Fine Art

George Henry Boughton (1833–1905) was an illustrator and a genre and landscape painter. Though he worked briefly in New York, he left the United States in 1861 and thereafter made his home in London. But his illustrations, like this one for "The Legend of Sleepy Hollow," were successful on both sides of the Atlantic. His most famous painting, however, is the familiar Pilgrims Going to Church which is often reproduced. Boughton had the genre artist's eye for detail and character, as can be seen in this charming illustration.

After looking at the details in the painting, what character descriptions could you add about Crane and Van Tassel to those given in the text? Why did this artist paint a scene from a fictional story?

Discussion

Discuss with the students that often our first impressions of a character may sway our future opinions about that character. Ask: When you read the dialogue from the Voices in the play, did you feel that the crowd was admiring or mocking? How do you think your opinion would have been different if you had not already formed an opinion about Crane's character?

Reading Focus: *Identify Hyperbole*

Van Brunt describes Crane in this story as "put together so loose he'll fall apart if we don't watch out." Discuss with students that we often use hyperbole in real speech and how Irving used this as a technique to make the characters seem real. Have students brainstorm other phrases to describe Crane that use hyperbole.

Critical Thinking: *Make Predictions*

Ask: How do you think Van Brunt will "fix" Ichabod Crane?

SOUND: *All sound and music up again.*

VAN BRUNT (*Over voices, viciously*)**:** You'd think it was Master Grasshopper himself clattering round the floor. He's put together so loose he'll fall apart if he don't watch out!

MAN'S VOICE (*laughing*)**:** Aha, Brom Van Brunt, they make a pretty pair dancing together, eh?

WOMAN'S VOICE (*laughing*)**:** They say the schoolmaster is counting his chickens before they're hatched.

ANOTHER'S MANS VOICE: Look at the schoolmaster eyeing her!

VAN BRUNT (*between teeth*)**:** You wait and see. I'll fix him! I'll fix him!

MUSIC: *Dance ending.*

SOUND: *Clapping and stamping out with music. Hold sound of crowd low.*

VOICES (*together*)**:** Great, Ichabod! Wonderful, Master Crane! *etc.*

VAN TASSEL (*shouting*)**:** Bring in the hot cider. Fall to, neighbors. You've got a cold ride home.

SOUND: *Glasses rattle.*

MAN (*smacking lips*)**:** Ahhhh! This is the stuff to put heart into a man! Eh, Van Til?

VAN TIL: Give me a few mugs of friend Van Tassel's hot cider, and I'll laugh at the headless horseman himself!

ICHABOD (*through his nose, unsteadily*)**:** The headless horseman! (*Lowering voice*) Has he been seen of late?

MAN: Yes, just t'other night old Brower met the horseman. "I hear you don't believe in me," says the ghost. "That I don't," says old Brower. "I think you're a lot of—" But just then the ghost caught him for such a ride as never was. Then with a clap of thunder he turned into a skeleton and flung Brower into the brook. "That'll teach you not to believe in honest ghosts," says he as he disappeared.

VOICES (*together*)**:** I hadn't heard that ! Do you mean . . . *etc.*

ICHABOD (*chattering of teeth*)**:** W-w-what a thing to happen to a body!

VAN BRUNT: Ah, that's nothing! I met the headless horseman myself t'other night coming from Tarrytown. . . .

MAN (*laughing*)**:** Coming back from the Flowing Bowl Tavern you'd see anything!

VAN BRUNT: No, I hadn't been in any tavern. I offered to race the ghost to the inn for a bowl of punch. And I'd have won the race, too, but just as we got to the bridge by the churchyard (*Pause*) he vanished into a ball of fire!

ICHABOD (*low*)**:** A ball of fire! The Sleepy Hollow bridge, you say! And tonight I have to cross it!

VAN BRUNT (*teasing him*)**:** If you get by Major André's[2] hanging tree alive, you mean, Schoolmaster. They say the goings-on around that tree, the moanings and the groanings, are terrible these nights.

VAN TIL: Well, ghosts or no ghosts, I've got to be getting home! I've got a barn full of cows to milk at daybreak.

ALL (*together*)**:** That's right. Me, too. Good-by, neighbor Van Tassel! (*Fade*) Thank you. A fine party, neighbor, *etc.*

VAN TASSEL: Good-by, friends!

FROW VAN TASSEL: And thank you all for coming!

SOUND: *Crowd noises fade out under.*

ICHABOD: I want to speak a word to your lovely daughter before I depart, Van Tassel. You—ah—give in pretty much to her wishes, I take it?

VAN TASSEL (*laughing*)**:** I love that girl even better than my pipe, Schoolmaster, and I've had just one rule bringing her up: Let her have her own way!

ICHABOD: Good! Ah! (*Calling*) Miss Katrina! Miss Katrina! May I speak with you alone?

KATRINA: (*Fade in*) Have you brought your tuning fork, Master Crane? I don't know as we would be able to talk without that! (*Giggles . . . fade out*)

MUSIC: *Up, then under and out.*

ANNOUNCER: What was said at this interview, I wouldn't pretend to say. But something must have gone very wrong, for Ichabod came forth after a while looking like a very sad scarecrow. He went into the barn, kicked poor Gunpowder awake, and set off through the hills. . . . The hour was as gloomy as himself. Driving clouds hid the stars and the moon.

MUSIC: *Notes of worry.*

SOUND: *Crickets. One horse at walk. Crack of whip. Fade crickets and horse and hold.*

---

[2]**Major John André** a British spy who was caught, tried and hanged by the patriots near Tarrytown in 1780

Literary Focus: *Suspense*

Point out to students that Van Brunt and Van Til's references to the ghost are used as an element of suspense. The suspense contrasts with the safe and happy setting of Katrina's party.

Reading Focus: *Identify Hyperbole*

Ask: What hyperbole does Crane use to describe his horse? What effect does this hyperbole cause in the reader?

Literary Focus: *Climax*

Guide students to recognize the set-up to the climax. The suspense has built to this point in the story and readers are ready to find out what will happen. Have students identify the actual climax as they read on.

ICHABOD: Get up, you crow's bait! Heaven have mercy on us! What's the matter with this animal?

SOUND: *Horse at walk. Horse stops. Crack of whip.*

ICHABOD: Giddap! Drat you, you one-eyed, knock-kneed, sway-backed nag!

SOUND: *Horse whinnies. Hoofs begin walk, hold briefly, and stop.*

ICHABOD (*in whisper*)**:** It's the hanging tree! It's the tree where they hanged André! Come, come, Gunpowder. If we're to get home before light, we've got to get by this tree somehow. I'll whistle to keep our courage up.

SOUND: *Whistling of "Yankee Doodle." Horse at walk again. Add whistling of "Yankee Doodle" in higher key and out of time with first. Then whistling stops.*

ICHABOD: Oooo . . . even the echo makes fun of me tonight!

SOUND: *Groans.*

ICHABOD: What was that?

VOICE (*ghostly*)**:** Ichabod! Ichabod Crane!

ICHABOD (*in whisper*)**:** W-w-who wants Ichabod C-c-crane?

SOUND: *Weird laughter.*

ICHABOD (*in whisper*)**:** I see it now, waiting beside the road—a man on horseback. Perhaps it's just one of the people going home from the Van Tassels' party. I'll speak to him. (*In a loud, cheerful tone*) Good evening, friend!

SOUND: *Add hoofs of second horse at walk more distant.*

ICHABOD (*afraid*)**:** W-w-who are you? Whoa, Gunpowder!

SOUND: *First horse stops. Second horse approaches.*

ICHABOD: If he's more than a human being, a hymn ought to drive him away. (*Singing through his nose in a shaky voice*) Praise God from whom all blessings flow. . . .

VOICE (*distant*)**:** Raise cod from tombs, small, large, or slow. . . .

ICHABOD: There goes that echo again, making fun of me. Oh, mercy! mercy! He's riding beside me!

SOUND: *As second horse grows louder, first horse begins walking again. Hold both low.*

ICHABOD (*in loud tone*)**:** Friend, since you don't seem any too polite tonight, I'll just take my leave of you. Giddap, Gunpowder!

SOUND: *Horse one, then horse two starts to trot.*

ICHABOD (*sadly*)**:** He's close on my heels! (*Calling*) Very well, friend, I have no mind to be polite myself, so I'll just drop behind, if you don't mind.

Mahantango Valley Farm c. 1860. Anonymous. The Granger Collection

SOUND: *Horse one, then horse two slows to walk.*

ICHABOD: He won't let me lag behind. Well, here comes the moon out from under the cloud. Now I'll get a glimpse of his face! Bless me, he hasn't any head! He's the headless horseman himself! And he's carrying his head in front of him on the saddle! Giddap, Gunpowder!

SOUND: *Horses begin to gallop. Fade into distance.*

ANNOUNCER: Away then they dashed, stones flying at every step. Ichabod's flimsy garments fluttered in the wind as he stretched his long, lean body over the horse's head in the eagerness of his flight.

SOUND: *Two horses at gallop, fade and hold.*

ICHABOD (*gasping*): There's the church bridge ahead, Gunpowder! Ghosts can't stand . . . churches! Just reach the bridge and we'll be safe!

SOUND: *Two horses galloping on dirt road, then on bridge, then on road again. A rooster crows in the distance. Hold horses low.*

Viewing Fine Art

This picture is an example of primitive, or "naive," American art. Itinerant painters and craftspersons were active throughout the country from its earliest days. Among their talents were painting signs, portraits, and walls; designing tombstones and mantels; and painting views of interiors and landscapes. A farm scene such as this one, which was made by an unknown amateur, shows the detailed precision of much folk art. Despite its odd perspective and curiously detailed distance, it has the freshness and charm that characterized much American primitive painting.

Ask: Do you think this painting is a good representation of the town of Sleepy Hollow? Why or why not?

Critical Thinking: *Infer*

Ask: Who or what do you think is chasing Ichabod Crane? Why do you think as you do?

ICHABOD: A rooster! Ghosts always vanish when they hear the first crowing! Let's see . . . if he's gone. (*Gasping*) He hasn't vanished! He's right behind me! (*Shouting*) He's going to throw his head at me! (*Screaming*) Ahhhh!

SOUND: *Horses fade quickly following scream to silence. Hold silence five seconds.*

ANNOUNCER: The next morning the old horse was found without his saddle, and with the bridle under his feet, quietly eating the grass at his master's gate. And where was Ichabod Crane? That worried Frow Van Ripper, too (*Fade*) as she said . . .

FROW VAN RIPPER: (*Fade in*) Hans Van Ripper, please to call Master Crane to breakfast. He's late for school now. And breakfast is spoiling. Hurry now!

HANS: Ja, Ja.

SOUND: *Chair scraped wood floor.*

HANS (*surprised*)**:** Why, Frow, look out the window yet. That's Gunpowder. But where is my saddle? And look at that bridle!

SOUND: *Footsteps on wood. Door opens.*

HANS (*calling*)**:** Ichabod Crane, why didn't you put Gunpowder in the barn last night? (*Short pause*) Ichabod, why don't you answer?

FROW VAN RIPPER: But, Hans, has something happened to Schoolmaster? Where is he?

MUSIC: *Up and fade out under.*

ANNOUNCER: Over at the schoolhouse the boys and girls gathered at the usual hour. As time went by and Master Crane did not appear, groups formed on the steps and in the yard. Several of the older boys strolled about the banks of the brook, while the younger ones played in the schoolyard. But still no schoolmaster! Later in the day small groups of neighbors gathered (*Fading*) to discuss the strange disappearance.

MAN 1: Ach, the poor schoolmaster. He's a strange one!

MAN 2: Wasn't he now? You should'a seen him doing the shakedown with Miss Katrina. And eat—where does he put it?

VAN TIL: Well, then, he would have to come home by the bridge and the church road. He was on Gunpowder, wasn't he, Hans?

HANS: Ja, neighbor. I lent him my horse and my best saddle to help him win Miss Katrina. (*Laughter from group*) And it looks as if we both lost! (*Laughter up and under*)

MAN 2: Let's walk down to the bridge anyhow. Maybe we can see the horse's hoofprints.

Literary Focus: *Dénouement*

Remind students that the story does not end with the climax. The dénouement includes the events that occur after the climax. Ask students what they learn in this part of the text.

MUSIC: *Up and fade out under.*

ANNOUNCER: And so the neighbors followed slowly after Ichabod's landlord, Hans Van Ripper, as he walked with bent head and searching eyes toward the Sleepy Hollow bridge. Hans noticed that the tracks of the horse's hoofs could be seen clearly in the road, and he knew that meant terrific speed. When he found his best saddle in the mud, he was speechless with anger. (*Fading*) But as the men reached the bridge . . .

MAN 1 (*excited*): Hans! There! On the bank near the water. It's Ichabod's hat!

VAN TIL: And that smashed pumpkin! Where did it come from?

HANS (*shocked*): Ichabod's hat! And so close to the water, too. We must look for his body. . . . (*Voice fading*) He must be buried in the proper way . . .

ANNOUNCER: And so the good neighbors searched the brook, but the body of the schoolmaster was not to be found. When Hans Van Ripper got home, he went to Ichabod's room. His tuning fork, his books, clothes—all were there. As he was a bachelor and had no debts, no one troubled his head any more about him. But as winter approached and the time came for stories by the fireside, the story of Ichabod's disappearance was told again and again. (*Fading*) And the legend grew until one day . . .

MUSIC: *Wedding march up and out under.*

MINISTER: Brom Van Brunt, wilt thou have this woman to be thy wedded wife . . . (*Fading to murmur, then up*) so long as ye both shall live?

VAN BRUNT: I will.

MINISTER: Katrina Van Tassel, wilt thou have this man to be. . . . (*Fading, then up*) I now pronounce that they are husband and wife.

MUSIC: *Wedding march up, fade slowly and out under.*

ANNOUNCER: At the wedding breakfast at the Van Tassel home, the conversation naturally turned to Ichabod (*Fading*) as the guests thought about the past.

SOUND: *Small crowd at breakfast. Fade and hold.*

WOMAN: Have another piece of cake, Hans.

HANS: That I will. Say, wasn't this Ichabod's favorite cake? Wonder what's become of him?

Discussion

Ask students to discuss the significance of the smashed pumpkin found by the villagers. If Ichabod's supernatural horseman was from the other world, what need would he have had for a pumpkin? Have students speculate about the reality of Ichabod's vision. Who or what might have been responsible for it?

Reading Focus: *Identify Hyperbole*

Ask: How does the announcer describe Hans Van Ripper when Hans found his saddle? Does this qualify as hyperbole? Explain your answer.

Literary Focus: *Exposition*

Discuss the role of the announcer in this selection. Ask: What important information does the announcer provide? How might this information be conveyed in other types of fiction, such as a novel or short story?

Reading Focus: *Identify Hyperbole*

Ask: Why might the author say Van Brunt laughs "fit to kill" rather than "laughs very hard"?

VAN TIL: Why, I saw Ichabod Crane in New York when I was in the city last week.

HANS (*amazed*): No . . .Van Til. You mean our Ichabod? Yi, yi, yi.

VAN TIL: You know, Hans, I've been thinking about that ride of Ichabod's. Seems to me that pumpkin we found beside his hat was more important than we thought. Whenever that story is told with Brom Van Brunt around, he always laughs fit to kill. I'm not sure about this headless horseman. (*Fade*)

SOUND: *Fade crowd noise to silence. Five seconds.*

ANNOUNCER: Although Hans Van Ripper and Farmer Van Til questioned the method of Ichabod's disappearance, a lot of people said for years that the schoolmaster had been the victim of the headless horseman. The bridge became more than ever an object of great wonder. The schoolhouse, which was never used again, was reported as haunted by Ichabod Crane's ghost. And the plowboy swore that on a still summer evening he could hear Ichabod's voice singing a sorrowful hymn among the peaceful groves of Sleepy Hollow.

MUSIC: *Up to end.*

Mini Quiz

Write the following sentences on the board or overhead projector and call on students to fill in the blanks. Discuss the answers with the class.

1. The events described took place near the present day site of ________, New York.
2. On Sundays, Ichabod led the ________ in the church.
3. As he walked through the hollow after dark, Ichabod heard ________.
4. Ichabod's horse was named ________.
5. Ichabod was later seen in ________.

Answers

1. Tarrytown
2. singing
3. crickets, owls, bullfrogs
4. Gunpowder
5. New York City

AUTHOR BIOGRAPHY

Washington Irving (1783–1859)

Washington Irving has often been called America's first great writer, a title he well deserves. Even people who have not read "Rip Van Winkle" seem to know about the character of the same name, the man who slept for twenty years. Other characters are just as famous. Irving's headless horseman, some say, still rides about Sleepy Hollow on gloomy, gray days. And what would New York City be without the Knicks, or the name "Knickerbocker"? The first Knickerbocker was one "Diedrich Knickerbocker," a name Irving invented for the author of his make-believe *History of New York*.

There is a stereotyped character known as "the typical American author" whose life goes like this. The author is born poor, struggles through early hardships, risks all to be a writer, and finally achieves success. Only the last of these is true for Irving. He was born into a comfortable business family. Instead of going to college, he traveled through Europe. At first his writing was just a hobby, and he always took a relaxed approach to his work. He defined the "happy age" of life as the time when a person can be idle and not feel guilty about it. A very social man, Irving could appreciate a well-set table and a good cigar.

Yet Irving did achieve great success. His easy, effortless style transformed all that it touched. He was equally good at humor (*Knickerbocker's History*) and horror ("The Adventure of the German Student"). In addition to many short stories, he wrote travel books, histories, and biographies. He even wrote a hit play. If Mark Twain was "the Lincoln of our literature," Irving was definitely the Washington. What is unusual about the way Washington Irving got his start as a writer?

MORE ABOUT THE AUTHOR

Imagery, characters, and visual descriptions of settings often come from the writer's own environment. Washington Irving lived in colonial America as well as Europe throughout his writing years. Where he lived affected his writing as he pulled realistic characters, events, and places—especially of colonial America—into his writing.

Additional Works
BY WASHINGTON IRVING

You may wish to suggest these works by Washington Irving for additional reading:

Diedrich Knickerbocker's History of New York, Reprint, Russell Press, 1985.

Rip Van Wrinkle and the Legend of Sleepy Hollow, Putnam Publishing Group, Two of Irving's most famous stories. (fantasy)

The Sketch-Book, Oxford University Press, 1996.

Complete Works, Richard West, 1989. (fiction and poetry)

Viewing Fine Art

The portrait shown here depicts American author Washington Irving (1783–1859) who is famous for the short stories "Rip Van Winkle" and "The Legend of Sleepy Hollow." Irving is considered to be the "first American man of letters" because he began his career shortly after America's independence from Britain. Sunnyside was where he spent his last years. Today, the home is preserved in memory of him and is visited by many tourists. The print of Sunnyside was produced by Currier & Ives, the most famous lithography company in the United States. Ask: What about this picture suggests that Irving was a very successful author?

UNDERSTAND THE SELECTION

Answers

1. the village schoolmaster
2. Katrina
3. Ichabod's hat and a smashed pumpkin
4. Sample answer: Brom Van Brunt probably was because he wanted to scare away Ichabod and marry Katrina.
5. Sample answer: No, because he was depressed after talking to her.
6. Sample answer: No, he only wanted to scare Ichabod by saying he had.
7. Sample answer: They were puzzled as to what had happened.
8. Sample answer: He bullied the children but was easily frightened by the tales of the adults.
9. Sample answer: Not many, because Brom is a bully and Ichabod is a coward, and both are opportunists. However, Brom seems intelligent, and Ichabod is educated.
10. Sample answer: He talks about the wealth of the farm. She might talk of her cooking.

Respond to Literature

Group the students. Have each group collaborate in writing a short scene extending the play. Suggestions might include Brom Van Brunt explaining to friends why he laughs when he hears "that story," teenagers encountering Ichabod's ghost in the schoolhouse, or Ichabod explaining to New Yorkers why he never vacations in the country.

WRITE ABOUT THE SELECTION

Prewriting

Using the student's suggestions, list several solutions to the mystery of Ichabod on a board or an overhead transparency.

Sample paragraphs:

Ichabod was knocked from his horse, suffered a severe blow to his head, and contracted amnesia. He wandered for months, took odd jobs, and finally became a librarian, known as John James, in a village in Vermont.

Encourage students to be creative. Remind them that the narrator tells the story when the characters do not have dialogue.

Writing

Have students work on this section individually. Walk around the class, giving assistance to any student who is having difficulty. Explain that most students will find it better to formulate an idea first and then proceed with the characters' dialogue.

Revising

Make this a cooperative group activity. Divide the class into four groups. Have each group member read his or her own play. Encourage the other members to make suggestions for better dialogue or plot.

Proofreading

Select two students' papers as models for proofreading. Place papers on the overhead projector, and have the class suggest improvements. After students have proofread, have them present final plays to the rest of the class with different volunteers reading each role. Allow time for all groups to practice and to select props if possible.

Review the Selection

UNDERSTAND THE SELECTION

Recall

1. Who was Ichabod Crane?
2. Who was the daughter of the wealthiest Dutch farmer?
3. What two items did the villagers find on the bank near the water?

Infer

4. Who was pretending to be the headless horseman? Why?
5. What answer did Katrina give Ichabod the night of the party? Explain.
6. Did Brom Van Brunt really see the headless horseman? Explain.
7. How do you think the school children reacted to Ichabod's disappearance?

Apply

8. How does Ichabod's behavior in the scenes with the school children differ from his other behavior?
9. What admirable qualities do you see in either Brom or Ichabod? Explain.
10. Suppose that Ichabod and Katrina did marry. Describe their conversations.

Respond to Literature

Each character in this story has a story of his or her own to tell. Choose a character and explain what happens to him or her after this play ends.

WRITE ABOUT THE SELECTION

At the end of the original story, Irving leaves his readers with the strong impression that Brom Van Brunt was really the one who had scared away Ichabod Crane. Still, there were others who believed the "headless horseman" had gotten him. Where had Ichabod gone? What had happened to him? Your assignment is to solve the mystery of that fateful evening.

Write one or more scenes to this play giving your solution to this mystery. Create new characters, if you wish. Write the dialogue in play form using the selection as a guide.

Prewriting Decide on an outcome for Ichabod. Write an informal outline about what happened to Ichabod and where he could be found after the story ended. In this sequel, add characters that you feel are necessary to your conclusion.

Writing Use your outline as a guide. List your characters. As you write the play, be sure each character speaks in the proper sequence to make your plot have a logical beginning, middle, and conclusion.

Revising When you revise, add details to support your solution to this mystery. Be sure each character has said exactly what you intended. Check to see that the characters do not all sound the same.

Proofreading Be sure your play is written in the correct format. Check to see that you have listed characters and have written dialogue and stage directions correctly. Check your punctuation.

THINK ABOUT PLOT

In designing the plot of a work, an author will try to keep the audience's curiosity alive and build suspense. In a carefully worked-out plot, each event serves as the cause of the next event. Cause-and-effect relationships are especially important in dramas, which have only a short time to set up the action and advance the plot.

1. What is the central conflict in the dramatization of "The Legend of Sleepy Hollow"? What questions come to mind at the beginning of the play?
2. Which character is the protagonist in the play? Which character is the antagonist? How do they relate to one another?
3. At what point in the play does the climax come?
4. What is the purpose of the announcer in this radio drama?
5. What clues do you find in the play to show that Ichabod believes the headless horseman really exists?

Reading Focus

Identify Hyperbole Choose two instances where the author used hyperbole. Write the phrases. How did Irving's use of hyperbole make the story more interesting to you?

DEVELOP YOUR VOCABULARY

Some words imitate the natural sounds they represent. For example, when you read "clanging bells," the word "clanging" imitates the sound of a bell. The formulation of words in this way is **onomatopoeia** (AHN-uh-MAT-uh-PEE-uh). Onomatopoeia can be a particularly useful tool to the radio dramatist, who must communicate the setting to the listeners through sounds. In this selection, you have seen onomatopoeia used for this purpose.

Following are phrases that were used in this selection. Choose the word in each phrase that illustrates onomatopoeia. Then, use each word to write an original sentence.

1. Indian war whoops
2. odd shrieks
3. smacking lips
4. hoot of owl
5. bullfrogs croaking
6. clapping hands
7. stamping feet
8. chattering teeth
9. crack of whip
10. horse whinnies

ESL Activity

Divide the class into small groups. Have each group discuss ghost stories from other cultures. Ask them to write short summary sentences describing the stories. Then the students should read their summaries aloud and compare these stories to "The Legend of Sleepy Hollow."

THINK ABOUT PLOT

Answers

1. The conflict is the rivalry between Ichabod and Brom Van Brunt. Will the headless horseman show himself? Is this a ghost story?
2. The protagonist is Ichabod Crane; the antagonist is Brom Van Brunt. They are in conflict.
3. The climax comes when the horseman throws his head at Ichabod.
4. The announcer tells the part of the play that isn't easily dramatized. He advances the action of the play and fills in background for a setting that cannot be seen.
5. Sample answer: his teeth chattered at ghostly sounds; his fear of nighttime; his fright when people at the party talk about the horseman; his terror when approaching the hanging tree.

DEVELOP YOUR VOCABULARY

Answers

1. whoops
2. shrieks
3. smacking
4. hoot
5. croaking
6. clapping
7. stamping
8. chattering
9. crack
10. whinnies

Sentences will vary.

Reading Focus

Sample Answer

Two choices of hyperbole are "hotter than creation" and "darker than the black hole." Both of these expressions make the story more interesting by adding drama and imagery.

Selection Overview

SELECTION OBJECTIVES

After completing this selection, students will be able to

- understand narration
- understand the use of narration in expository and persuasive writing
- understand that description may be used to support narration
- write an alternative ending to a narrative
- use context to arrive at word meaning
- understand sequence of events

Lesson Resources

No More Forever
- Selection Synopsis, Teacher's Edition, p. T65d
- Comprehension and Vocabulary Workbook, pp. 23–24
- Language Enrichment Workbook, p. 12
- Teacher's Resources
  Reinforcement, p. R12
  Test, pp. T23–T24

More About Narration

Description may be used to support narration. Chief Joseph uses description very sparingly. Advise the students to watch for adjectives and adjectival phrases that the Native Americans used to describe various regions of the western United States. Use the example "buffalo country." Ask them to provide details on what features might be found in "buffalo country" (many buffalo, good grazing, drinking water, and so forth).

Learn About

NARRATION

Narration, as you have learned, is one of the four forms of discourse. One of its purposes is to describe an event or a series of events.

Ordinarily, narration is an end in itself. Its main purpose is to interest and entertain. This is the case for short stories and novels. However, narration can also be used for other purposes. Sometimes narration is used to explain; that is, its intent is **expository**. It may also be used to present a plea for a change in attitude or to support a particular action. In this case, its purpose is **persuasive**.

The narrative itself, therefore, becomes a means to an end. Like a fable or parable in fiction, a factual narrative can also serve to illustrate a point—to teach a lesson or to seek a change in the attitudes of readers or listeners.

As you read this selection, ask yourself:

1. What is the intent of Chief Joseph's speech?
2. Is his aim well supported by his narrative?

Reading Focus

Understand Sequence of Events The sequence, or order, of events can be very important to understanding a selection. Often, an event only makes sense if you know what preceded it. As you read "No More Forever," think about the sequence of events and how they are related.

WRITING CONNECTION

Write a narrative paragraph about an injustice that you know about that was done to an individual or a group.

More About the Literary Period

In 1876, the United States celebrated its centennial, or one hundredth anniversary. Americans took pride in the accomplishments of our young land. A few years earlier the government had established Yellowstone, the first national park. A national park is an area of special scenic or historical interest protected by the government and open to the public. The flight of the few hundred Nez Percé pursued by armies carried them through Yellowstone. Discuss whether students think the treatment of the Nez Percé is consistent with American ideals and accomplishments.

ESL Activity

Have students discuss fables from other cultures. Have pairs of students choose one of those discussed. Then ask each pair to choose an Aesop fable and write a brief comparison.

Cooperative Group Activity

Pair the students. Have each partner read his or her paragraph from the Writing Connection activity to the other. Each should offer suggestions for adding explanatory details to the other partner's paragraph.

NO MORE FOREVER

by Chief Joseph
(In-mut-too-yah-lat-lat)

ADAPTED

My friends, I have been asked to show you my heart. I am glad to have a chance to do so. I want the white people to understand my people. I believe much trouble and blood would be saved if we opened our hearts more. I will tell you in my way how the Indian sees things. What I have to say will come from my heart, and I will speak with a straight tongue.

My name is In-mut-too-yah-lat-lat (Thunder Traveling over the Mountains). I am chief of a band of Nez Percé (Nose Pierced). I was born in eastern Oregon, 38 winters ago. My father (also called Joseph by white men) was chief before me. He died a few years ago. There was no stain on his hands of the blood of a white man. He left a good name on the earth. He advised me well for my people.

Our fathers gave us many laws, which they had learned from their fathers. These laws were good. They told us to treat all men as they treated us; that we should never be the first to break a bargain; that it was a disgrace to tell a lie; that it was a shame for one man to take from another his wife, or his property without paying for it. We were taught to believe that the Great Spirit sees and hears everything, and that he never forgets. Hereafter, he will give every man a spirit-home according to his deserts: if he has been a good man, he will have a good home; if he has been a bad man, he will have a bad home. This I believe, and all my people believe the same.

We did not know there were other people besides the Indian until about one hundred winters ago, when some men with white faces came to our country. They brought many things with them to trade for furs and skins. These men were French, and they called our people "Nez Percé," because some wore rings in their noses. Although very few of our people wear them now, we are still called by the same name.

The first white men of your people who came to our country were named Lewis and Clark. They also brought many things that our people had never seen.

---

deserts (dih ZURTS) reward or punishment; what is deserved

Teaching Plan

INTRODUCE

Motivation

Have students study the photograph of Chief Joseph on page 103 and discuss what kind of man he might have been. Read the "Song of Sitting Bull" to the class:

A warrior
I have been
Now
it is all over
A hard time
I have

Have students continue the discussion, thinking how the words of the song may apply.

Purpose-Setting Questions

Someone once said that history is written by the side that wins. Ask: How do you think Joseph's account will differ from those of the people who wanted to claim his lands?

READ

Literary Focus: *Narration*

Point out that the first line of this selection, "My friends, I have been asked to show you my heart" suggests that the narration will be very personal. Discuss whether personal information can be both expository and persuasive at the same time. Encourage students to read to see whether this text succeeds at one or both of these types of narration.

Reading Focus: *Understand Sequence of Events*

Because the selection is long, you may want to stop periodically and ask volunteers to summarize a section of it. List appropriate points on the board and have the class record them in their notebooks. During these discussions you may also ask students to suggest relationships between events.

CLOSE

Have students complete Review the Selection on pages 114–115.

Develop Vocabulary Skills

Provide a handout with the vocabulary words and their definitions. Have students write a short paragraph using at least three of the vocabulary words in original sentences. Ask volunteers to read paragraphs. If any words are not used by the class, ask volunteers to use those words in an original sentence. Provide suggestions as necessary.

They talked straight, and our people gave them a great feast, as a proof that their hearts were friendly. These men were very kind. They made presents to our chiefs and our people made presents to them. We had a great many horses, of which we gave them what they needed. They gave us guns and tobacco in return. All the Nez Percé made friends with Lewis and Clark, and agreed to let them pass through their country, and never to make war on white men. This promise the Nez Percé has never broken.

It has always been the pride of the Nez Percé that they were the friends of the white men. But about twenty winters ago, a number of white people came into our country and built houses and made farms. At first our people made no complaint. They thought there was room enough for all to live in peace, and they were learning many things from the white men that seemed to be good. But we soon found that the white men were growing rich very fast, and were greedy to possess everything the Indian had. My father was the first to see through the schemes of the white men. He warned his tribe to be careful about trading with them. He had suspicion of men who seemed so anxious to make money. I was a boy then, but I remember well my father's caution. He had sharper eyes than the rest of our people.

Next there came a white officer (Governor Stevens), who invited all the Nez Percé to a treaty council. He said there were a great many white people in the country, and many more would come. He wanted the land marked out so that the Indians and white men could be separated. If they were to live in peace, that was necessary, he said. The Indians should have a country set apart for them, and in that country they must stay. My father, who represented his band, refused to have anything to do with the council. He wished to be a free man. He claimed that no man owned any part of the earth, and a man could not sell what he did not own.

Governor Stevens urged my father to sign his treaty, but he refused. I will not sign your paper," he said. "You go where you please, so do I. You are not a child. I am no child. I can think for myself. No man can think for me. I have no other home than this. I will not give it up to any man. My people would have no home. Take away your paper. I will not touch it with my hand."

My father left the council. Some of the chiefs of the other bands of the Nez Percé signed the treaty. (The lands of these bands, however, were already inside the newly created reservation assigned to the Nez Percé.) Two-thirds of the Nez Percé did *not* sign. Then Governor Stevens gave them presents of blankets. My father cautioned his people to take no presents. "After a while," he said, "they will claim that you have accepted pay for your country." Since that time four bands of the Nez Percé have received annuities from the United States.

Critical Thinking: *Evaluate*

Ask: What points did Governor Stevens make to try to persuade the Nez Percé to sign the treaty? Were these points valid? Why or why not?

Reading Focus: *Understand Sequence of Events*

What happened that caused Chief Joseph's father to become wary of white men? How long before this speech did that happen?

---

annuity (un NOO uh tee) regular payment

Eight years later (1863) was the next treaty council. A chief called Lawyer, because he was a great talker, took the lead in this council. He sold nearly all the Nez Percé country. My father was not there. He said to me: "When you go into council with the white man, always remember your country. Do not give it away. I have taken no pay from the United States. I have never sold our land." In this treaty Lawyer acted without authority from our band. He had no right to sell our Wallowa River country (in Oregon). That had always belonged to my father's own people, and the other bands had never disputed our right to it. No other Indians ever claimed Wallowa.

The United States claimed they had bought all the Nez Percé country outside of Lapwai Reservation (in Idaho) from Lawyer and other chiefs. But we continued to live on this land in peace until eight years ago, when many white men began to come. We warned them against this great wrong, but they would not leave our land. The United States Government again asked for a treaty council. My father had become blind and feeble. He could no longer speak for his people. It was then that I took my father's place as chief. In this council I made my first speech to white men. I said to the agent who held the council:

"I did not want to come to this council, but I came hoping that we could save blood. The white man has no right to come here and take our country. We have never accepted any presents from the government. Neither Lawyer nor any other chief had authority to sell this land. We will defend this land as long as a drop of Indian blood warms the hearts of our men."

Chief Joseph, 1878, Cyrenius Hall. The Granger Collection

The agent said he had orders, from the Great White Chief at Washington, for us to go upon the Lapwai Reservation. If we obeyed he would help us in many ways. "You *must* move," he said. I answered him, "I will not. I do not need your help. We have plenty, and we are contented and happy if the white man will let us alone.

Viewing Fine Art

Chief Joseph was the subject of many paintings. His noble and proud bearing and the heartbreaking speech of surrender he gave made him a figure of fascination to artists. He was painted both at the site and in several portraits. The American public encouraged the government's Indian wars and simultaneously admired the Indian heroes who tried to withstand them. Art showing the nobility of the Native American was thus always popular, and many artists journeyed West to paint these vanquished (but noble) warriors. Ask: What thoughts might Chief Joseph be having as this portrait was made?

Literary Focus:
Narration

Have students find places in the narration where Chief Joseph uses persuasive language. Ask: How might his words have affected the white men with whom he was talking?

The reservation is too small for so many people with all their stock. We are free now; we can go where we please. Our fathers were born here. Here they lived, here they died, here are their graves. We will never leave them." The agent went away, and we had peace for a little while.

Soon after this my father sent for me. I saw he was dying. I took his hand in mine. He said, "My son, my body is returning to my mother earth, and my spirit is going very soon to see the Great Spirit Chief. When I am gone, think of your country. You are the chief of these people. They look to you to guide them. Always remember that your father never sold his country. You must stop your ears whenever you are asked to sign a treaty selling your home. A few years more, and white men will be all around you. They have their eyes on this land. My son, never forget my dying words. This country holds your father's body. Never sell the bones of your father and your mother." I pressed my father's hand and told him I would protect his grave with my life. My father smiled and passed away to the spirit-land.

I buried him in that beautiful valley of winding waters. I love that land more than all the rest of the world. A man who would not love his father's grave is worse than a wild animal.

For a short time we lived quietly. But this could not last. White men stole a great many horses from us, and we could not get them back. The white men told lies for each other. They drove off a great many of our cattle. Some white men branded our young cattle so they could claim them. It seemed to me that some of the white men in Wallowa were doing these things on purpose to get up a war. They knew that we were not strong enough to fight them. They forgot that years before, when the white men were few and we were strong, we could have killed them all off. But the Nez Percé wished to live at peace.

Because we did not do so, we have not been to blame. I believe that the old treaty has never been correctly reported. If we ever owned the land we own it still, for we never sold it. Suppose a white man should come to me and say, "Joseph, I like your horses, and I want to buy them." I say to him, "No, my horses suit me, I will not sell them." Then he goes to my neighbor, and says to him, "Joseph has some good horses. I want to buy them, but he refuses to sell." My neighbor answers, "Pay me the money, and I will sell you Joseph's horses." The white man returns to me, and says, "Joseph, I have bought your horses, and you must let me have them." If we sold our lands to the government, this is the way they were bought.

On account of the treaty made by the other bands of the Nez Percé, the white men claimed our lands. We were troubled greatly by white men crowding over the line. Some of these were good men, and we lived on peaceful terms with them, but they were not all good.

stock (STOK) farm animals

Critical Thinking: *Infer*

Ask: What can you infer about the white men's opinion of the Nez Percé from the author's description of their actions? Why do you think the white men felt as they did?

Reading Focus: *Understand Sequence of Events*

In this passage Chief Joseph gives a solemn oath to protect his dying father's gravesite with his life. Have students identify events that have come since his father's death.

Nearly every year the agent came over from Lapwai and ordered us on to the reservation. We always replied that we were satisfied to live in Wallowa. We were careful to refuse the presents or annuities which he offered.

Through all the years since the white men came to Wallowa we have been threatened by them. They have given us no rest. We have had a few good friends among white men, and they have always advised my people to bear these threats without fighting. Our young men were quick-tempered, and I have had great trouble in keeping them from doing rash things.

Year after year we have been threatened, but no war was made upon my people until General Howard came two years ago and told us that he was the white war-chief of all that country. He said: "I have a great many soldiers at my back. I am going to bring them up here, and then I will talk to you again. The country belongs to the government, and I intend to make you go upon the reservation."

General Howard sent out runners and called all the Indians in to a grand council. I was in that council. I said to General Howard, "I am ready to talk. I have been in a great many councils, but I am no wiser. We are all sprung from a woman, although we are unlike in many things. We cannot be made over again. You are as you were made, and as you were made you can remain. We are just as we were made, and you cannot change us. Why should children of one mother and one father quarrel—why should one try to cheat the other? I do not believe that the Great Spirit Chief gave one kind of men the right to tell another kind of men what they must do."

General Howard replied. "You deny my authority, do you? You want to dictate to me, do you?"

Then one of my chiefs—Too-hool-hool-suit—rose in the council and said to General Howard, "The Great Spirit Chief made the world as it is, and as he wanted it. He made a part of it for us to live upon. I do not see where you get authority to say that we shall not live where he placed us."

General Howard lost his temper and said, "Shut up! I don't want to hear any more of such talk. The law says you shall go upon the reservation to live, and I want you to do so."

Too-hool-hool-suit answered, "Who are you, that you ask us to talk, and then tell me I shan't talk? Are you the Great Spirit? Did you make the world? Did you make the sun? Did you make the rivers to run for us to drink? Did you make the grass to grow? Did you make all these things, that you talk to us as though we were boys? If you did, then you have the right to talk as you do."

General Howard replied, "You are an impudent fellow, and I will put you in the guardhouse."

The soldiers came forward, seized my friend, and took him to the guardhouse.

---

rash (RASH) reckless; foolhardy
impudent (IM pyoo dunt) rude; insulting

Literary Focus:
Narration

Chief Joseph uses exposition in his narration to describe what he saw happen to his people. Have students use exposition to show how the white men might have described what was happening.

Literary Focus:
Narration
Ask: What is the main point of the narration so far? Is it mostly exposition or persuasion?

My men whispered among themselves, whether they should let this thing be done. I counseled them to submit. I knew if we resisted that all the white men present, including General Howard, would be killed in a moment, and we would be blamed. While they dragged Too-hool-hool-suit to prison, I arose and said, "*I am going to talk now.* I don't care whether you arrest me or not." I turned to my people and said: "The arrest of Too-hool-hool-suit was wrong, but we will not resent the insult. We were invited to this council to express our hearts, and we have done so." Too-hool-hool-suit was prisoner for five days before he was released.

The council broke up for that day. Next day, General Howard informed me that he would give my people *thirty days* to go back home, collect all their stock, and move onto the reservation. "If you are not there in that time, I shall consider that you want to fight, and will send my soldiers to drive you on."

I said, "War can be avoided, and it ought to be avoided. I want no war. My people have always been the friends of the white man. Why are you in such a hurry? I cannot get ready to move in thirty days. Our stock is scattered, and Snake River is very high. Let us wait until fall, when the river will be low. We want time to hunt up our stock and gather supplies for winter."

General Howard replied, "If you let the time run over one day, the soldiers will be there to drive you on the reservation. And all your cattle and horses outside of the reservation at that time will fall into the hands of the white men."

I knew I had never sold my country, and that I had no land in Lapwai. But I did not want bloodshed. I did not want my people killed. I did not want anybody killed. I said in my heart that, rather than have war, I would give up my country. I would give up my father's grave. I would give up everything rather than have the blood of white men upon the hands of my people.

General Howard refused to allow me more than thirty days to move my people and their stock. I am sure that he began to prepare for war at once.

When I returned to Wallowa, I found my people very much excited. The soldiers were already in the Wallowa Valley. We held a council, and decided to move immediately, to avoid bloodshed.

Too-hool-hool-suit, who felt outraged by his imprisonment, talked for war. He made many of my young men willing to fight rather than be driven like dogs from the land where they were born. It required a strong heart to stand up against such talk, but I urged my people to be quiet, and not to begin a war.

We gathered all the stock we could find, and made an attempt to move. We left many of our horses and cattle in Wallowa, and we lost several hundred in crossing the river. All of my people succeeded in getting across in safety. Many of the Nez Percé came together in Rocky Canyon to hold a grand council.

outraged (OUT rayjd) insulted; made very angry

I went with all my people. This council lasted ten days. There was a great deal of war talk, and a great deal of excitement. There was one young brave present whose father had been killed by a white man five years before. This man's blood was bad against white men, and he left the council calling for revenge.

Again I counseled peace, and I thought the danger was past. We had not complied with General Howard's order because we could not, but we intended to do so as soon as possible. I was leaving the council to kill beef for my family, when news came that the young man whose father had been killed had gone out with several other hot-blooded young braves and killed four white men. He rode up to the council and shouted, "Why do you sit here? The war has begun already!"

I heard then that Too-hool-hool-suit had succeeded in organizing a war party. I knew that their acts would involve all my people. I saw that the war could not then be prevented. That time had passed.

I had counseled peace from the beginning. I knew that we were too weak to fight the United States. I admit that my young men did a great wrong, but I ask, who was first to blame? They had been insulted a thousand times. Their fathers and brothers had been killed. They had been told by General Howard that all the horses and cattle they had been unable to drive out of Wallowa were to fall into the hands of white men. And, added to this, they were homeless and desperate.

I would have given my own life if I could have undone the killing of white men by my people. I blame my young men and I blame the white men. I blame General Howard for not giving my people time to get their stock away from Wallowa. I do not acknowledge that he had the right to order me to leave Wallowa at any time. I deny that either my father or myself ever sold that land. It is still our land. It may never again be our home, but my father sleeps there, and I love it as I love my mother. I left there, hoping to avoid bloodshed.

I would have taken my people to the buffalo country (Montana) without fighting, if possible. I could see no other way to avoid a war. We moved over to Whitebird Creek, sixteen miles away, intending to collect our stock before leaving. But the soldiers attacked us, and the first battle was fought. We numbered in that battle sixty-six men, and the soldiers one hundred. The fight lasted but a few minutes, when the soldiers retreated before us for twelve miles. They lost thirty-three killed, and had seven wounded.

Seven days after the first battle, General Howard arrived, bringing more soldiers. It was now war in earnest. We crossed over Salmon River, hoping General Howard would follow. We were not disappointed. We got back between him and his supplies. The battle lasted all day, and was renewed next morning. We killed four and wounded seven or eight.

Five days later General Howard attacked us with 350 soldiers and settlers. We had 250 warriors. The fight lasted twenty-seven hours. We lost four killed and several wounded. General Howard's loss was twenty-nine men killed and sixty wounded.

Reading Focus:
Understand Sequence of Events

Chief Joseph asks the question, "Who was first to blame?" Have students review their notes of the events that have occurred so far to answer Chief Joseph's question with their own opinions.

Critical Thinking:
Compare and Contrast

Ask students to name similarities and differences in the ways Chief Joseph and his father dealt with the white men.

Trail of Tears, Robert Lindneux. Corbis Bettmann

The following day the soldiers charged upon us, and we retreated with our families and stock a few miles, leaving eighty lodges to fall into General Howard's hands.

Finding that we were outnumbered, we retreated to Bitterroot Valley. Here another body of soldiers and settlers came upon us and demanded our surrender. We refused. They said, "You cannot get by our fort (later called 'Fort Fizzle')." We answered, "We are going by it without fighting if you will let us, but we are going by anyhow." We then made a treaty with these settlers. We agreed not to molest anyone, and they agreed that we might pass through the Bitterroot country in peace. We bought provisions and traded stock with white men there.

We understood that there was to be no more war. We intended to go peaceably to the buffalo country, and leave the question of returning to our country to be settled afterward.

With this understanding we traveled on for four days. Thinking that the trouble was all over, we stopped and prepared tentpoles to take with us. We started again, and at the end of two days we saw three white men passing our camp. Thinking that peace had been made, we did not molest them. We could have killed or taken them prisoners, but we did not suspect them of being spies, which they were.

That night the soldiers surrounded our camp (near Big Hole, Montana). About daybreak one of my men went out to look after his horses. The soldiers saw him and

molest (muh LEST) bother; annoy

Background Notes

At an appropriate moment, mention that despite its name, bitterroot is a flowering herb known for the beauty of its flowers. The taproot, a source of starch in the diet, was highly valued by Native Americans as food. It grows in large numbers in the stony soil of the western mountains, and it is the state flower of Montana. Its botanical name *Lewsia* was given in honor of Meriwether Lewis, who collected specimens and brought them east while part of the Lewis and Clark expedition.

shot him down like a coyote. I have since learned that these soldiers were not those we had left behind. They had come upon us from another direction. The new white war-chief's name was Gibbon. He charged upon us while some of my people were still asleep. We had a hard fight. Some of my men crept around and attacked the soldiers from the rear. In this battle we lost nearly all our lodges, but we finally drove General Gibbon back. In the fight we lost fifty women and children and thirty fighting men. We remained long enough to bury our dead. The Nez Percé never make war on women and children. We could have killed a great many women and children while the war lasted, but we would feel ashamed to do so cowardly an act.

We retreated as rapidly as we could toward the buffalo country. After six days General Howard came close to us, and we went out and attacked him. We captured nearly all his horses and mules (about 250 head). We then marched on to the Yellowstone Basin (Wyoming).

On the way we captured one white man and two white women. We released them at the end of three days. They were treated kindly. The women were not insulted. Can the white soldiers tell me of one time when Indian women were taken prisoners, and held three days and then released without being insulted? Were the Nez Percé women who fell into the hands of General Howard's soldiers treated with as much respect? I deny that a Nez Percé was ever guilty of such a crime.

Nine days' march brought us to the mouth of Clark Fork of the Yellowstone. We did not know what had become of General Howard, but we supposed that he had sent for more horses and mules. He did not come up, but another new war-chief (General Sturgis) attacked us. We held him in check while we moved all our women and children and stock out of danger, leaving a few men to cover our retreat.

Several days passed, and we heard nothing of General Howard, or Gibbon, or Sturgis. We had repulsed each in turn, and began to feel secure, when another army, under General Miles, struck us (near Bearpaw, Montana). This was the fourth army, each of which outnumbered our fighting force, that we had encountered within sixty days.

We had no knowledge of General Miles's army until a short time before he made a charge upon us. He cut our camp in two, capturing nearly all of our horses. About seventy men, myself among them, were cut off. My little daughter, twelve years of age, was with me. I gave her a rope, and told her to catch a horse and join the others who were cut off from the camp. I have not seen her since, but I have learned that she is alive and well.

I thought of my wife and children, who were now surrounded by soldiers. I resolved to go to them or die. With a prayer in my mouth, I dashed unarmed through the line of soldiers. It seemed to me that there were guns on every side,

---

repulsed (rih PULST) drove back; repelled
resolved (rih ZOLVD) determined; decided

Reading Focus:
Understand Sequence of Events
Ask: What patterns do you see in the white men's actions? What patterns do you see in the Native Americans' actions?

Critical Thinking:
Analyze
Ask: Do you think that the narrator's description of the treatment of women captives is too emotional? Why do you think as you do?

Literary Focus:
Narration
Ask: What part of the narration seems most memorable? What part of this story is the saddest?

Literary Focus: *Narration*

Ask: How does Joseph's retelling of events in his narrative support his position?

Discussion

Ask students to think about Joseph's statement: "I believed General Miles, or I never would have surrendered." Ask: Do you think he should have believed him? Why or why not?

before and behind me. My clothes were cut to pieces and my horse was wounded, but I was not hurt. As I reached the door of my lodge, my wife handed me my rifle, saying: "Here's your gun. Fight!"

The soldiers kept up a continuous fire. Six of my men were killed in one spot near me. We fought at close range, not more than twenty steps apart, and drove the soldiers back, leaving their dead in our hands. We lost, the first day and night, eighteen men and three women. General Miles lost twenty-six killed and forty wounded. The following day General Miles sent a messenger into my camp under protection of a white flag. I sent my friend Yellow Bull to meet him.

Yellow Bull understood the messenger to say that General Miles did not want to kill my people unnecessarily. Yellow Bull understood this to be a demand for me to surrender and save blood. I sent him back with my answer, that I had not made up my mind, but would think about it and send word soon. A little later I walked to General Miles's tent. He met me and we shook hands. He said, "Come, let us sit down by the fire and talk this matter over." I remained with him all night. Next morning Yellow Bull came over to see if I was alive, and why I did not return.

General Miles would not let me leave the tent to see my friend alone.

Yellow Bull said to me, "They have got you in their power, and I am afraid they will never let you go again. I have an officer in our camp, and I will hold him until they let you go free."

I said, "I do not know what they mean to do with me, but if they kill me you must not kill the officer. It will do no good to avenge my death by killing him."

Yellow Bull returned to my camp. I did not make any agreement that day with General Miles. I was very anxious about my people. I knew that we were near Sitting Bull's camp in King George's land (Canada), and I thought maybe the Nez Percé who had escaped would return with assistance. No great damage was done to either party during the night.

On the following morning I returned to my camp by agreement, meeting the officer who had been held prisoner in my camp at the flag of truce. My people were divided about surrendering. We could have escaped from Bearpaw Mountain if we had left our wounded, old women, and children behind. We were unwilling to do this. We had never heard of a wounded Indian recovering while in the hands of white men.

On the evening of the fourth day, General Miles said to me in plain words, "If you will come out and give up your arms, I will spare your lives and send you to your reservation."

I could not bear to see my wounded men and women suffer any longer; we had lost enough already. General Miles had promised that we might return to our own country with what stock we had left. I thought we could start again. I believed General Miles, or *I never would have surrendered.*

On the fifth day I went to General Miles, gave up my gun, and said:

Tell General Howard that I know his heart. What he told me before I have in my heart. I am tired of fighting. Our chiefs are killed. Looking Glass is dead. Too-hool-hool-suit is dead. The old men are all dead. It is the young men who say yes or no. Ollokot is dead. It is cold and we have no blankets. The little children are freezing to death. My people, some of them, have run away to the hills, and have no blankets, no food; no one knows where they are—perhaps freezing to death. I want to have time to look for my children and see how many of them I can find. Maybe I shall find them among the dead. From where the sun now stands I will fight no more forever.

I was told we could go with General Miles to Tongue River and stay there until spring, when we would be sent back to our country. We had nothing to say about it. After our arrival at Tongue River, General Miles received orders to take us to Bismarck (North Dakota). General Miles was opposed to this order. He said, "You must not blame me. I have endeavored to keep my word, but the chief who is over me has given the order. I must obey it or resign. That would do you no good. Some other officer would carry out the order."

I believe General Miles would have kept his word if he could have done so. I do not blame him for what we have suffered since the surrender. I do not know who is to blame.

We were taken to Bismarck. Captain Johnson, who now had charge of us, received an order to take us to Fort Leavenworth (Kansas). At Leavenworth we were placed on a low river bottom, with no water except river water to drink and cook with. We had always lived in a healthy country, where the mountains were high and the water was cold and clear. Many of my people sickened and died, and we buried them in this strange land. I cannot tell how much my heart suffered for my people, while at Leavenworth.

During the hot days (July 1878) we received notice that we were to be moved farther away from our own country. We were not asked if we were willing to go. We were ordered to get into the railroad cars. Three of my people died on the way to Baxter Springs (Kansas). It was worse to die there than to die fighting in the mountains.

We were moved from Baxter Springs to the Indian Territory (Oklahoma). We had but little medicine, and we were nearly all sick. Seventy of my people have died since we moved there.

We have had a great many visitors who have talked many ways. Some of the chiefs (General Fish and Colonel Stickney) from Washington, D.C., came to see us, and selected land for us to live upon. We have not moved to that land, for it is not a good place to live.

The Commissioner Chief (E. A. Hayt) came to see us. I told him, as I told everyone, that I expected General Miles's word would be carried out. He said it could not be done. White men now lived in my country, and all the land was taken up. If I returned to Wallowa, I could not live in peace, and the government could not protect my people. This talk fell like a heavy stone upon my heart. I saw that I could not gain anything by talking to him.

Critical Thinking:
Evaluate

Mention that four years earlier, General Howard had treated the Apaches with justice. His superiors did not approve, and his military career suffered. Privately, Howard believed that the treatment of the Nez Percé was wrong. Ask the class to evaluate Howard's priorities in light of the other events described in the narration.

Reading Focus:
Understand Sequence of Events

Ask students to list the order of the moves the Nez Percé made and seasons during each location change.

Literary Focus: *Narration*

Ask: Why does Joseph explain in his narration that he doesn't understand the United States government?

Reading Focus: *Understand Sequence of Events*

State that Chief Joseph continually points out relationships between the United States government's actions and his people's actions. Have students name some of these relationships and their significance. Ask them to name one action that was followed by another. Then ask whether one action caused the other.

Then the Inspector Chief [General McNiel] came to my camp and we had a long talk. He said I ought to have a home in the mountain country north, and that he would write a letter to the Great Chief at Washington. Again the hope of seeing the mountains of Idaho and Oregon grew up in my heart.

At least I was granted permission to come to Washington, D.C., and bring my friend Yellow Bull with me. I am glad we came. I have shaken hands with a great many friends, but there are some things I want to know which no one seems able to explain. I cannot understand how the government sends a man out to fight us, as it did General Miles, and then breaks his word. Such a government has something wrong about it. I cannot understand why so many chiefs are allowed to talk so many different ways, and promise so many different things. I have seen the Great Father Chief (the President), the next Great Chief (Secretary of the Interior), and many other law chiefs (congressmen). They all say they are my friends, and that I shall have justice. But while their mouths all talk right I do not understand why nothing is done for my people. I have heard talk and talk, but nothing is done.

If the white man wants to live in peace with the Indian, he can live in peace. There need be no trouble. Treat all men alike. Give them all the same law. Give them all an even chance to live and grow. They are all brothers. The earth is the mother of all people, and all people should have equal rights upon it. You might as well expect the rivers to run backward as that any man who was born free should be contented when penned up and denied liberty.

I only ask of the government to be treated as all other men are treated. If I cannot go to my own home, let me have a home in some country were my people will not die so fast. I would like to go to Bitterroot Valley. There my people would be healthy. Where they are now they are dying. Three have died since I left my camp to come to Washington.

We only ask an even chance to live as other men live. We ask to be recognized as men. We ask that the same law shall work alike on all men. If the Indian breaks the law, punish him by the law. If the white man breaks the law, punish him also.

Let me be a free man—free to travel, free to stop, free to work, free to trade where I choose, free to choose my own teachers, free to follow the religion of my fathers, free to think and talk and act for myself—and I will obey every law, or submit to the penalty.

Whenever the white man treats the Indian as they treat each other, then we will have no more wars. We shall all be alike—brothers of one father and one mother, with one sky above us, one country around us, and one government for all. I hope that no more groans of wounded men and women will ever go to the ear of the Great Spirit Chief above, and that all people may be one people.

In-mut-too-yah-lat-lat has spoken for his people.

Mini Quiz

Write the following sentences on the board or overhead projector and call on students to fill in the blanks. Discuss the answers with the class.

1. Joseph's tribal name In-mut-too-yah-lat-lat meant ________ ________ ________ ________ ________.
2. The chief who sold nearly all the Nez Percé land in 1863 was called ________.
3. General Howard allowed the Nez Percé only ________ days to move.
4. The Nez Percé were trying to reach ________ ________ camp in Canada.
5. Joseph's wish was to be a ________ man.

Answers

1. Thunder Traveling over the Mountains
2. Lawyer
3. thirty
4. Sitting Bull's
5. free

AUTHOR BIOGRAPHY

Chief Joseph (1840–1904)

By the end of the 1870s, nearly all Native Americans in the United States had been forced onto reservations. The famous Sitting Bull had escaped to Canada. The Apache chief Geronimo was in Mexico. Then quite suddenly, in 1877, another great leader—called "Chief Joseph" by the white settlers—gained wide attention.

According to newspaper stories, Chief Joseph was the leader of the "unruly" Nez Percé (NEZ PURS) "troublemakers" in the northwestern United States. The papers claimed that rather than move onto a reservation, Joseph and his people decided to take on the U.S. Army. Retreating over a 1300-mile path through four western states, he fought off attack after attack, in each of which his force was greatly outnumbered. Moreover, all this was done while protecting hundreds of women and children and thousands of horses and cattle. Chief Joseph was not stopped until he was about 30 miles from his goal—Canada and freedom.

Once the Nez Percé War was over, however, quite a different story came out. Chief Joseph's people were not rebels but in the right: they had twice been guaranteed their homeland in the Wallowa Valley of Oregon (in 1855 and 1873). Moreover, Joseph was only one of several Nez Percé chiefs, and because he had always been a man of peace, he had lost much of his influence when the war started. In fact, during the months of the long march, Joseph's job had been to protect the women, children, and elderly, not to engage in combat. Only after the war did he emerge as *the* leader.

His hopes were never fully realized. Not until 1885 was he permitted to return to the Northwest, and then to a reservation in Washington, not to his Oregon homeland. He died on September 21, 1904.

MORE ABOUT THE AUTHOR

General Sherman admired Joseph and the Nez Percé greatly and wrote that the war was notable not only for the courage and skill displayed by the warriors but also for their kind treatment of those they warred with. They spared hundreds of lives. Joseph was a brilliant fighter but not a bloodthirsty one.

Additional Works

BY CHIEF JOSEPH

You may wish to suggest these works by Chief Joseph for additional reading:

That All People May Be One People, Send Rain to Wash the Face of the Earth, Mountain Meadow Press, 1995.

In Pursuit of the Nez Percés, Howard, Oliver O; McDonald, Duncan; Chief Joseph. Moutina Meadow Press, 1993.

UNDERSTAND THE SELECTION

Answers

1. Chief Joseph belonged to the Nez Percé tribe.
2. Chief Joseph surrendered at Bearpaw Mountain.
3. Lewis and Clark
4. Sample answer: His band had never agreed to sell its land.
5. Sample answer: Telling the truth.
6. Sample answer: The land was valuable, and white people had already settled there.
7. Sample answer: He realized his band was hopelessly outnumbered.
8. Sample answer: Yes, because negotiation was their only hope of regaining their land; No, because what the white people did was wrong.
9. Sample answer: The band would have been destroyed.
10. Sample answer: Yes, because he remained true to his principles.

Respond to Literature

The United States was founded on the belief that all men are created equal, according to the Declaration of Independence. Native Americans were not treated as equals; in many cases they were looked on as less than human. The colonists denied the principles on which the country was founded in their dealings with Native Americans. Not until the latter half of the 20th century did the U.S. government attempt to make some amends.

WRITE ABOUT THE SELECTION

Prewriting

Have students give suggestions about what might have happened to Chief Joseph's people in Canada. List several ideas on a board or an overhead transparency.

Sample responses:

1. More people died enroute, and many grew homesick later.
2. They joined forces with the Sioux, and decided to return and fight for their homelands.
3. They were welcomed to Canada, decided to stay, and developed a prosperous community.
4. Some of the group stayed in Canada; others returned, only to be captured and placed on reservations.

Writing

Have the students work on this section individually. Go around the class, giving help to any student who is having difficulty. Ask questions about how the students would want to be treated in Canada and how they would feel about living in a new land if they had been a member of Chief Joseph's group.

Revising

Have students work in small groups to revise their paragraphs. Encourage students to suggest details to improve their group members' paragraphs.

Proofreading

Have students work in pairs to read through their papers together. If any word appears to be misspelled, urge students to check in a dictionary for the correct spelling.

Review the Selection

UNDERSTAND THE SELECTION

Recall

1. To which tribe did Chief Joseph belong?
2. Where did Chief Joseph surrender?
3. Who were the first American white men that the Nez Percé ever saw?

Infer

4. Why did Chief Joseph say the government was being unfair?
5. What does Chief Joseph mean by "talking with a straight tongue"?
6. Why did the government not keep its agreement with Chief Joseph?
7. Why did Chief Joseph stop fighting?

Apply

8. If you were an Indian in Chief Joseph's band, would you have favored surrender?
9. What would have happened if Chief Joseph's band continued fighting?
10. Do you think Chief Joseph's father would have been proud of his son?

Respond to Literature

Was the treatment the Native Americans received a good example of the beliefs on which the United States was founded?

WRITE ABOUT THE SELECTION

In this selection, you have read about the plight of Chief Joseph and the Nez Percé. He had always wanted two things: peace and the land that belonged to his people. Chief Joseph surrendered believing that the United States Government had agreed to these wishes and would honor them. The government officials did not keep their word.

Before Chief Joseph surrendered, he had one other option. He could have fled into Canada. Would they have fared better or worse? Assume that he had chosen to lead his people there.

Prewriting Freewrite about what you think would have happened to Chief Joseph's group in Canada. Include details of the attitudes they might have encountered. Speculate about how they would provide food and shelter for themselves and about difficulties they might face. Then organize your notes into a brief outline.

Writing Use your outline to write a paragraph explaining what Chief Joseph's group might have experienced in Canada and how they might have been treated there.

Revising When you revise your paragraph, add details to make your ideas more vivid.

Proofreading Read over your selection and check your spelling.

THINK ABOUT NARRATION

In nonfiction, narration is concerned with personal and historical events. The intention of the narrative, however, may be **expository** (to explain) or **persuasive** (to persuade). In such writing, the narrative serves as a long example to support the point that the author wishes to make.

1. Was Chief Joseph's intention in relating the history of the Nez Percé band expository or persuasive?
2. Does Chief Joseph make a thesis statement in his speech? If so, what is it?
3. Tell where the introduction, body, and conclusion of Chief Joseph's speech occurs.
4. How did Chief Joseph establish with the reader or listener that he was honest and that he spoke to them truthfully?
5. What is the lesson that Chief Joseph's narrative best illustrates?

> ### *Reading Focus*
> **Understand the Sequence of Events** List three key events in this selection. Explain the order in which they occur and how they are related to one another.

DEVELOP YOUR VOCABULARY

Words sometimes have several meanings. If you are not sure of the meaning of a word, context clues may help. Look at the words surrounding the unfamiliar word; they may give you a hint of its meaning. Chief Joseph explains, "I am chief of a *band* of Nez Percé." The word *chief* suggests that *band* means "a group."

Read each item below. Use the context to try to figure out the meaning of each italicized word. Check your meaning in a dictionary to see that it is correct. Write an original sentence using each word.

1. The *reservation* is too small for so many people with all their stock.
2. No, my horses *suit* me, I will not sell them.
3. . . . I have had great trouble in keeping them from doing *rash* things.
4. We are all *sprung* from a woman. . . .
5. We held him in *check*, while we moved our women and children. . . .

THINK ABOUT NARRATION

Answers

1. Answers will vary. It was expository in one sense. He wanted to explain to white people "how the Indian sees things." It was persuasive in another sense. He wanted attitudes to change so that all people would be treated equally.
2. His thesis statement is in the first paragraph. He says, "I will tell you in my own way how the Indian sees things."
3. The introduction consists of the first three paragraphs. The body is the entire narrative. The conclusion begins with the paragraph in which Chief Joseph tells about coming to Washington D.C.
4. Sample answer: He says he will speak with a straight tongue; he outlines the ethical beliefs of his people; he demonstrates his friendly relations with the first white people to enter his territory.
5. Sample answer: The Nez Percé Indian wanted to live peaceably with the white people; people should keep their promises; or all people should be free and equal.

DEVELOP YOUR VOCABULARY

Answers

Sentences will vary, but word usage should correspond to the following meanings.

1. Reservations means "land that is set aside for a particular purpose."
2. Suit means "to be right for or appropriate to."
3. Rash means "reckless."
4. Sprung means "come from or arisen from some source."
5. Check means "restraint; control."

Reading Focus

Sample Answer

The Nez Percé make a promise never to make war on white men. Before he dies, In-mut-too-yah-lat-lat's father warns him to be cautious in his dealings with white men, and the white men break the promises they made to the Nez Percé. They are related because the Nez Percé promise to be peaceful with the white men but Chief Joseph's father still warns him to be cautious when dealing with white men. Eventually, the white men prove Chief Joseph's father right by breaking all promises they made with the Nez Percé.

> ### ESL Activity
> Organize the class into small groups with at least one English-proficient member in each. Have group members find additional meanings for the Develop Your Vocabulary words. Tell them to write the words and definitions as a group and check for understanding.

SELECTION OVERVIEW

SELECTION OBJECTIVES

After completing this selection, students will be able to

- understand meter
- identify two frequently used kinds of meter
- understand the use of repetition
- write a paragraph describing the setting in a fantasy
- understand antonyms
- identify cause and effect

Lesson Resources

Annabel Lee
- Selection Synopsis, Teacher's Edition, p. T65d
- Comprehension and Vocabulary Workbook, pp. 25–26
- Language Enrichment Workbook, p. 13
- Teacher's Resources
  Reinforcement, p. R13
  Test, pp. T25–T26

More About Meter

Meter is measured in feet. A foot is the name given to all the patterned groups of syllables used in poetry. The anapest is a three-syllable foot. Write on the board the opening line from "To My Dear and Loving Husband." Count the number of syllables in the line. Use notations to mark the syllables (u or l). Ask, "What is the meter, iamb, or anapest?" Explain that each line contains ten syllables in an unstressed followed by a stressed patter (five iambs). The full name given to this meter, a very common one in English, is iambic pentameter. Penta comes from pente, the Greek word for "five."

More About the Literary Period

Most American writers of Poe's period were optimistic. They used American settings in their works. Why was Poe different? Why were his settings atypical?

Learn About

METER

You have learned that all poetry has **rhythm**. It is the natural sense of movement that occurs when successive syllables are stressed or not stressed. It comes from the natural rise and fall of language.

Poets often build into their poems a strong pattern of stressed and unstressed syllables. The rhythmic pattern is so pronounced that the reader may tap a pencil to its beat. Such a pattern is called **meter**. The difference between natural rhythm and meter is that in natural rhythm, the accented syllables are random; in metrical lines of poetry, the accents come at regular intervals. Meter carries a reader along toward a planned conclusion.

The music of poetry can be enhanced by other means, too. The repetition of words and phrases and the use of rhyme add to the flow of sound.

As you read this selection, ask yourself:

1. What kind of meter can I detect in this poem?
2. Does the poet use repetition and rhyme for musical effects?

READING FOCUS

Identify Cause and Effect A cause-and-effect relationship is one in which one event (the cause) is responsible for another event (the effect). An author connects thoughts and actions by showing a cause-and-effect relationship. This helps the reader better understand the reasons why things happen. As you read this poem, note the effects, or what happens. As you reread the poem, look for the causes of each effect you noted.

WRITING CONNECTION

Write down four lines of lyrics from a favorite song. Can you detect a metrical pattern? Write a paragraph about it.

Cooperative Group Activity

Pair the students before they begin the Writing Connection activity. Have each student in a pair read the lyrics he or she has written down and the metrical pattern identified. Have both students offer suggestions as necessary to help their partner in writing the paragraph.

Annabel Lee

by Edgar Allan Poe

It was many and many a year ago,
  In a kingdom by the sea,
That a maiden there lived whom you may know
  By the name of Annabel Lee;
5 And this maiden she lived with no other thought
  Than to love and be loved by me.

I was a child and *she* was a child,
  In this kingdom by the sea,
But we loved with a love that was more than love—
10 I and my Annabel Lee;
With a love that the wingèd seraphs of heaven
  Coveted her and me.

And this was the reason that, long ago,
  In this kingdom by the sea,
15 A wind blew out of a cloud, chilling
  My beautiful Annabel Lee;
So that her high-born kinsman came
  And bore her away from me,
To shut her up in a sepulcher
20 In this kingdom by the sea.

The angels, not half so happy in heaven,
  Went envying her and me—
Yes!—that was the reason (as all men know,
  In this kingdom by the sea)
25 That the wind came out of the cloud by night,
  Chilling and killing my Annabel Lee.

---

seraph (SER uf) kind of heavenly being; winged angel
covet (KUV it) desire what belongs to another
high-born (HY bawrn) of noble birth
sepulcher (SEP ul kur) tomb; burial place

Develop Vocabulary Skills

On the board or overhead projector, write each of the vocabulary words in a sentence that illustrates its meaning. Call on volunteers to give the meaning from the context of the sentence. Have students write the appropriate responses in their notebooks and use them as reference while reading.

ESL Activity

Have students use a thesaurus to find synonyms for some of the words in the poem, such as maiden, seraphs, highborn, kinsman, demons, and dissever. Tell them to work in pairs to write sentences using the synonyms they have found.

Teaching Plan

INTRODUCE

Motivation

Use the library as a resource. Play for the students a recording of "The Raven." Explain that Poe wrote this not long before his wife's death. She was the Lenore of the poem. Have the students discuss the relationship between Poe's personal experience and the poem. Explain that "Annabel Lee" is another poem in which he expresses his grief for his dead wife.

Purpose-Setting Question

"The Raven" and "Annabel Lee" were written in the 1840s. In what way is Poe's highly personal internal struggle similar to the struggle taking shape in American society at the time? (Have students reread the Unit Introduction, if necessary.) Try to elicit the idea that America was struggling with and no longer able to ignore the reality of slavery.

READ

Literary Focus: *Meter*

Scansion is the term for the analysis of the meter in a poem. Scan is the verb form of scansion. When you have identified the pattern of stressed and unstressed syllables, you have begun scanning the poem. Scansion also includes counting the number of feet per line, counting the number of lines per stanza and analyzing the rhyme scheme.

Reading Focus: *Identify Cause and Effect*

Remind students that understanding the relationships among events helps in understanding why the events happen. Have a volunteer find and read aloud the lines that tell why Annabel Lee was taken to heaven.

CLOSE

Have students complete Review the Selection on pages 120–121.

Literary Focus:
Meter
Ask: How does the meter of this poem add to your enjoyment of it?

Reading Focus:
Identify Cause and Effect
Ask: What is the cause and effect relationship in lines 34 and 35? In lines 36 and 37?

But our love it was stronger by far than the love
    Of those who were older than we—
    Of many far wiser than we—
30 And neither the angels in heaven above
    Nor the demons down under the sea,
Can ever dissever my soul from the soul
    Of the beautiful Annabel Lee,

For the moon never beams, without bringing me dreams
35   Of the beautiful Annabel Lee;
And the stars never rise, but I feel the bright eyes
    Of the beautiful Annabel Lee;
And so, all the night-tide, I lie down by the side
Of my darling—my darling—my life and my bride,
40   In the sepulcher there by the sea,
    In her tomb by the sounding sea.

---

dissever (dih SEV ur) separate
night-tide (NYT tyd) nighttime

Mini Quiz

Write the following sentences on the board or overhead projector and call on students to fill in the blanks. Discuss the answers with the class.

1. Poe's thoughts of Annabel Lee centered on ________.
2. The killing wind blew out of a ________.
3. Her ________ bore her body away.
4. The ________ envied the love between Annabel Lee and the poet.
5. Annabel Lee's ________ cannot be dissevered from that of the poet.

Answers

1. love
2. cloud
3. kinsmen
4. angels
5. soul

AUTHOR BIOGRAPHY

Edgar Allan Poe (1809–1849)

For some authors, writing is a carefully studied skill. For others, writing is a refined art. But for a very few, writing seems the outpouring of genius that cannot be contained. Edgar Allan Poe was such an author. His life proves that true talent is a powerful force indeed.

Born in 1809, Edgar Poe never knew his father, an actor who left his family and simply disappeared. Death claimed Poe's mother, an actress, when the boy was two. But luckily, the child was taken in by John Allan, a wealthy tobacco dealer. In 1815 the Allans went to England on business, and for five years Edgar went to a private school there.

Poe's luck, however, was not to continue. He quarreled violently with John Allan. He was forced to leave the University of Virginia because of gambling debts. He joined the army for a time and then drifted here and there, unable to settle down. He got a number of jobs as an editor but lost them because of excessive drinking.

In midlife Poe was taken in by an aunt, Maria Clemm. She gave him the comfort he needed, and he began to write—and sell!—the fantastic stories that made him famous. He married Mrs. Clemm's daughter, Virginia, a girl of 13.

Troubles continued to follow the struggling author. He could not hold a job for long. His stories and poems brought in some money, but never enough for a comfortable life. He, Virginia, and Mrs. Clemm drifted into poverty. Virginia died in 1847. Two years later Poe himself was found near death in Baltimore, Maryland. He died four days later. In your opinion, what were the two worst misfortunes in Poe's unhappy life?

MORE ABOUT THE AUTHOR

In 1836 at the age of twenty-seven, Poe married a beautiful teenager, Virginia Clemm. They loved each other very much. During the first several years of their marriage, they struggled against poverty as he tried to establish a writing career. By 1842, he had achieved success and some financial security, but tragedy struck. Virginia became seriously ill with tuberculosis. She never recovered her health. Five years later (1847), she died while she was still in her twenties. Poe was crushed. He went on to write some of his most famous works, but his own health deteriorated. He died two years after her at the age of forty.

Additional Works

BY EDGAR ALLAN POE

Complete Stories and Poems, Garden City, New York, Doubleday, 1966.

Classic Poe, Commuter's Library, 1994.

Tales of Mystery and Imagination, Dearborn Trade, 1981.

Fall of the House of Usher, Demco Media, 1997.

The Raven, Abbeville Press, Inc., 1991.

Viewing Fine Art

Edgar Allan Poe (1809–1849) is known for mystery and the macabre. He lived at the cottage at Fordham, which was inspiring for him. He described the cottage in one of his stories. This portrait is a steel engraving which originally came from a watercolor painting, published in 1845. Steel engraving is a process of printing art which involves carving a drawing into a metal plate, dipping the plate into ink and pressing the plate onto the desired surface. Ask: Although engraving is a process still used, how else could you reproduce the art today with modern technology?

UNDERSTAND THE SELECTION

Answers

1. a kingdom by the sea
2. in a sepulcher by the sea
3. A chilling wind that came out of a cloud
4. Sample answer: pneumonia; other illness
5. Sample answer: She was too young
6. Sample answer: She was a highborn and deserved a grave that befitted her status.
7. No, because he states that her death was many years ago.
8. Sample answer: She would tell him to accept her death and go on with his life.
9. Sample answer: Yes, to attempt to console him.
10. Sample answer: Yes, because the husband does not seem to have a good relationship with her kinsmen.

Respond to Literature

Provide art from the 19th century that depicts daily life. Have students think about where the most important things were happening in the 19th century-expansion in the West, growth and development of cities, and the Civil War. Have students visualize what life in one of these settings would look like. Then have them write a paragraph describing the setting of Annabel Lee.

WRITE ABOUT THE SELECTION

Prewriting

Tell students to close their eyes and form a mental picture of this mysterious land and the dwelling in which Annabel Lee and the narrator live. Ask, "Where is it located?" "What are its surroundings?" "In what sequence do you envision the interior?" Allow several minutes for thought. Using the students' suggestions, create a web on the board or overhead transparency.

Samples:

1. Location (mountainside, cliff, beach, etc.)
2. surrounded by woods, huge rocks, or sand, etc.
3. View it from the outside to the inside.
4. View it room to room.
5. Imagine how it is decorated.

Writing

Have the students work on this section individually. Remind the students to give their readers a tour of the dwelling and its surrounding. Walk around the classroom, giving help to any student who is having trouble.

Revising

Make this a cooperative group activity. Divide the class into small groups. Have all members read their paragraphs. After each member has finished reading, have other group members make suggestions to improve each description. When revisions have been completed, each student could draw a sketch of the dwelling he or she has described.

Proofreading

Have students work with a partner to determine whether any word appears to be misspelled. The students should check in a dictionary for the correct spelling of any word in question.

Review the Selection

UNDERSTAND THE SELECTION

Recall

1. Where did Annabel Lee live?
2. Where did her kinsmen bury her?
3. What killed Anabell Lee?

Infer

4. What may have been the real cause of Annabel Lee's death?
5. What made Annabel Lee's death so difficult for the author?
6. Why was it necessary for her kinsmen to take her away to be buried?
7. Do you think the narrator accepted her death after a short period of time?

Apply

8. Suppose that Annabel Lee could speak from the grave. What might she say to the narrator?
9. Assume that you are one of the residents of this kingdom. Would you visit the narrator? Why or why not?
10. Do you think Annabel Lee's family opposed this marriage? Why?

Respond to Literature

Most of the literature of this period had an American setting. What about this selection is typical of the period?

WRITE ABOUT THE SELECTION

In this poem, Annabel Lee and the narrator live "in a kingdom by the sea." That kingdom is never described, but it serves to have a mysterious and fantastic quality about it. Picture the dwelling of Annabel Lee and the narrator. Is it a palace? Is it a humble house, since his social status may be lower than hers? Is it a romantic place with rich furnishings or a hovel where possessions mean nothing? Dream up the fantasy house of Annabel Lee. Think about how it is constructed, how large it is, and what kind of views it has. Think about the mood it creates as well.

Prewriting Create a web describing the surroundings in which the couple lives. Include details of the rooms and what they contain. Freewrite any conversation you can come up with between Annabel Lee and the narrator. Make some notes about how their house might affect their lives.

Writing Use your web to write a paragraph describing Annabel Lee's fantasy house.

Revising When you revise your paragraph, be sure to add details that illustrate the richness or lack of richness in the house and grounds.

Proofreading Read over your selection. Be sure to check the spelling of any unusual words you might have used.

THINK ABOUT METER

Meter refers to a pattern of stressed and unstressed syllables in poetry. It is distinguished from rhythm by its use of regularly recurring accented and unaccented syllables. Each patterned group of syllables has a name. For example, one unstressed syllable followed by one stressed syllable (as in kon-TROL) is called an **iamb**. Similarly, two unstressed syllables followed by a stressed syllable (as in kontruh-DIKT) is called an **anapest**.

1. Which meter is the basic one in "Annabel Lee"—an iamb or an anapest? Why do you say so?
2. The first two lines of the poem have been likened to the opening of a fairy tale. Do you agree? Why or why not?
3. In line 15, the meter is broken temporarily by the word *chilling*. Why do you think Poe did this?
4. What other "musical" effects did Poe use in the poem?
5. What words and phrases did Poe often repeat in the poem?

Reading Focus

Identify Cause and Effect "Annabel Lee" describes the death of someone the speaker loved deeply. What two things does the speaker say caused Annabel Lee's death?

DEVELOP YOUR VOCABULARY

An **antonym** is a word that has a meaning opposite or nearly opposite to that of another word. For example, in this selection, Poe refers to "the angels . . . in heaven" and "the demons down under the sea." *Angels* and *demons* are antonyms, or words that are opposite in meaning to each other.

Following are words used in this selection. Read the words, review the meaning of each word whose meaning is not clear to you. Some of the words are not in common use today. Check the poem to help you figure out the meanings of these words.

Select an antonym for each word. Check in a dictionary for the meaning of each antonym you have selected. Double check to be sure it has a meaning opposite to that of the original word. Then, use each antonym to write an original sentence. Be sure that your sentences include context clues to the words' meanings.

1. love
2. beautiful
3. highborn
4. shut
5. chilling
6. wise
7. dissever
8. bright

THINK ABOUT METER

Answers

1. Anapest, because it has two unstressed syllables followed by a stressed syllable.
2. Sample answer: Yes, because the lines seem to be a rewording of "Once upon a time, there was a kingdom."
3. Sample answer: The change seems to echo the chilling wind itself.
4. He used rhyme and repetition.
5. Answers may vary. Suggested response should include the words *love* and *chilling* and the phrases *In a kingdom by the sea* and with variations, *the beautiful Annabel Lee*.

DEVELOP YOUR VOCABULARY

Answers

1. love—hate, loathing
   I *hate* to be late for a meeting.
2. Beautiful—ugly
   An *ugly* beast is one of the main characters in the play.
3. highborn—lowborn
   The peasant was considered *lowborn* under the feudal system.
4. shut—open
   Tom will *open* the widows if the temperature rises above seventy degrees.
5. chilling—warming
   The weather forecaster predicts a *warming* trend in several days.
6. wise—unwise
   Jill was *unwise* not to study for the test.
7. dissever—connect
   The electricians will *connect* the new alarm system.
8. bright—dull
   Wednesday was a *dull*, dreary day.

Reading Focus

Sample Answer

The author explains that the love he shared with Annabel Lee was so deep the angels in heaven envied them. Because of this envy, the angels sent a chilling wind that caused Annabel Lee's death.

ESL Activity

Divide the class into small groups. Within the groups, have members choose words from the selection. Ask them to challenge other members to name an antonym. If the challenged members agree that there is no antonym, they should be ready to defend their answer. Have a dictionary available for them to check answers. Each group member should have an opportunity to be the challenger. Provide help to the groups as needed.

Selection Overview

SELECTION OBJECTIVES

After completing this selection, students will be able to

- understand suspense
- identify two ways in which authors build suspense
- build on knowledge of literary elements to write creatively
- determine word meaning from context
- identify signal words

Lesson Resources

The Tell-Tale Heart

- Selection Synopsis, Teacher's Edition p. T65e
- Comprehension and Vocabulary Workbook, pp. 27–28
- Language Enrichment Workbook, p. 14
- Teacher's Resources
  Reinforcement, p. R14
  Test, pp. T27–T28
  Unadapted Selection, pp. U29–U32

More About Suspense

Suspense arises from curiosity about the events in a work. What happened? What will happen? Therefore, it is an ingredient of the plot. The writer may, however, use other elements of fiction, such as description and character, to help generate or sustain suspense. In the previous unit, what two selections contained suspense? ("Godasiyo" and "The Day the Sun Froze") In this unit, which other selection relied heavily on suspense? ("The Legend of Sleepy Hollow") How did the sound effects and the announcer's narration in the selection help to create suspense? What facet of Ichabod's character helped?

About the Author

Ancient literary forms like fables and legends are in a way short stories. Many people, however, credit Poe with the invention of the modern short story. He believed that a short story would produce a "single effect." All the elements in the story should contribute to the creation of this single effect.

Poe is also credited with the invention of the modern detective story in which a master detective using logic solves what appeared to be a perfect crime. His detective, Auguste Dupin, appeared fifty years before the now more famous Sherlock Holmes.

Learn About

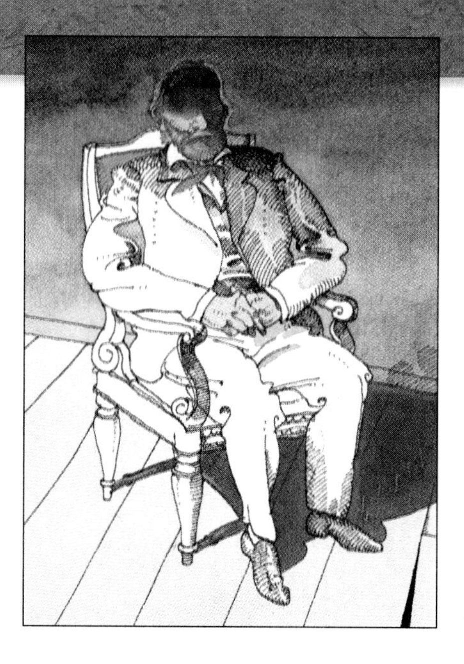

Suspense

Suspense is the growing excitement that a reader or listener feels while waiting for the climax or resolution of the events in a work of fiction. There are two kinds of suspense. In one kind, the author leaves the outcome in doubt until the very end so that the audience will wonder *who*, *what*, or *how*. In the other kind, the author lets the audience know about the outcome before the end. The big suspense is then focused on *when*.

Authors have ways of building suspense. They can create an atmosphere that contributes to it and they can **foreshadow** events, that is, they can give tantalizing hints of what may happen in the plot.

Suspense plays a part in all fiction—short stories, novels, and plays. In some works, however, it is the main ingredient.

As you read this selection, ask yourself:

1. Which of the two kinds of suspense does Poe use in this story?
2. What details besides the plot contribute to the suspense?

Reading Focus

Identify Signal Words Authors use the relationships between events to string together a story in a believable way. They often use signal words to suggest a cause-and-effect relationship or time order. As you read "The Tell-Tale Heart," look for words that signal cause and effect, such as *because*, *so*, and *since*. Also look for and words that signal a time order, such as *first*, *next*, *last*, *finally*, and *soon*.

WRITING CONNECTION

In a paragraph, describe a movie thriller you have seen recently. Explain how the suspense was achieved.

ESL Activity

Have students work in pairs to write a definition of foreshadowing. Ask them to identify foreshadowing from a previous selection. Then have pairs exchange papers for proofreading. Next, have the papers read aloud to see if the class agrees with the example.

Cooperative Group Activity

Pair the students. Have each student read his or her paragraph from the Writing Connection activity to a partner. Have the partner ask questions that may assist in improving the paragraph. Remind them to ask questions concerning *who*, *what*, *where*, *how*, and *when*.

THE TELL-TALE HEART

ADAPTED

by Edgar Allan Poe

True!—nervous—very, very dreadfully nervous I have been and am. But why *will* you say that I am mad? The disease has sharpened my senses—not destroyed—not dulled them. Above all was my sense of hearing acute. I heard all things in the heaven and in the earth. I heard many things in hell. How, then, am I mad? Listen! and observe how clearly—how calmly I can tell you the whole story.

It is impossible to say how the idea first entered my brain. But once conceived, it haunted me day and night. There was no good reason. There was no real hatred. I loved the old man. He had never wronged me. He had never given me insult. For his gold I had no desire. I think it was his eye! Yes, it was this! One of his eyes resembled that of a vulture—a pale blue eye, with a film over it. Whenever it fell upon me, my blood ran cold. And so little by little—very gradually—I made up my mind to take the life of the old man, and thus rid myself of the eye forever.

Now this is the point. You think I am mad. Madmen know nothing. But you should have seen me. You should have seen how wisely I proceeded—with what caution—with what skill—with what secrecy I went to work! I was never kinder to the old man than during the whole week before I killed him. And every night, about midnight, I turned the latch of his door and opened it—oh, so gently! And then, when I had made an opening the size of my head, I put in a dark lantern, all closed up, closed up so that no light shone out, and then I thrust in my head. Oh, you would have laughed to see how cunningly I did it! I moved my head slowly—very, very slowly, so that I might not disturb the old man's sleep. It took me an hour to move my head so far that I could see him as he lay upon his bed. Ha!—would a madman

---

acute (uh KYOOT) sharp, sensitive
conceived (kun SEEVD) thought of; imagined
cunningly (KUN ing lee) slyly

Teaching Plan

INTRODUCE

Motivation

Bring to class a tape such as *Edgar Allan Poe: Tales of Mystery and Horror*, read by Christopher Lee. Play the tape up to the phrase, "I made up my mind. . . " Stop the tape. Ask the students to predict the plot. List appropriate responses on the board.

Purpose-Setting Question

The author opens this selection with a question. How might that device entice you to read this story?

READ

Literary Focus: *Suspense*

Guide students to see that the author builds suspense from the very first line of the story. The reader immediately wonders why the main character is nervous and why he is wondering about being called mad. Ask: Which words and phrases are the most suspense-building for you? Help students see that many of them will share the same responses, suggesting that the author deliberately chose these words and phrases to build suspense.

Reading Focus: *Identify Signal Words*

The sequence of events the narrator describes in killing the old man is eerily slow. Have students note the signal words that indicate upcoming events, such as *And then* which is repeated. Ask: Why does the author repeat the same signal words over and over?

CLOSE

Have students complete Review the Selection on pages 128–129.

Develop Vocabulary Skills

Write the vocabulary words on the board or overhead projector. Have students use a dictionary to look up the definitions and write both the word and its definitions on a sheet of paper. Tell them to keep the paper handy as a reference while reading the story.

Literary Focus: *Suspense*

Explain that a symbol is something that represents itself and at the same time represents something else. Write the word *vulture* and its literal definition on the board. Ask for volunteers to identify ideas associated with the word vulture. Ask: Why do you think the narrator may have likened the old man's eye to that of a vulture? How does this intensify the suspense?

Reading Focus: *Identify Signal Words*

Have students read the passage where the old man stirs in his sleep, "For he moved on the bed suddenly, as if startled." (Second full paragraph in column one) Point out the words *as if* to indicate a cause-and-effect relationship. Have students continue reading until they get to "so I knew that he could not see the opening of the door. . . " Ask: What caused the narrator to know that the old man could not see the opening of the door?

have been so wise as this? And then, when my head was well into the room, I undid the lantern cautiously. Oh, so cautiously—cautiously (for the hinges squeaked) I undid it just so much that a single thin ray of light fell upon the vulture eye.

This I did for seven long nights—every night just at midnight—but I found the eye always closed. And so it was impossible to do the deed. For it was not the old man who vexed me, but his Evil Eye. And every morning, when the day broke, I went boldly into the room, and spoke courageously to him. I called him by name in a cheerful tone, and asked how he had passed the night. So you see he would have been a very profound old man, indeed, to suspect that every night, just at twelve, I looked in upon him while he slept.

Upon the eighth night I was more than usually cautious in opening the door. A watch's minute hand moves more quickly than did mine. Never before that night had I really *felt* just how powerful I was—just how wise. I could hardly contain my feeling of triumph. To think that there I was, opening the door, little by little. And he not even dreaming of my secret purpose or thought! I nearly chuckled at the idea—and perhaps he heard me! For he moved on the bed suddenly, as if startled. Now you may think that I drew back—but no. His room was black as pitch with the thick darkness (the shutters were fastened tight, for fear of robbers). So I knew that he could not see the opening of the door, and I kept pushing it on steadily, steadily.

I had my head in, and was about to open the lantern. All at once my thumb slipped on the tin, and the old man sprang up in the bed, crying out—"Who's there?"

I kept quite still and said nothing. For a whole hour I did not move a muscle. And in the meantime I did not hear him lie down. He was still sitting up in the bed listening—just as I have done, night after night, listening—waiting—for Death.

Then I heard a little groan, and I knew it was the groan of mortal terror. It was not a groan of pain or of grief—oh, no! It was the low stifled sound that comes from the bottom of the soul when overfilled with fear. I knew the sound well. Many a night, just at midnight, when all the world slept, it was sprung up from the bottom of my own soul, deepening, with its dreadful echo, the terrors that held me. I say I knew it well. I knew what the old man felt, and pitied him—although I chuckled at heart. I knew that he had been lying awake ever since the first slight noise, when he had turned in the bed. His fears had ever since been growing on him. He had been trying to ignore them, but could not. He had been saying to himself—"It is nothing but the wind in the chimney," or

---

vexed (VEKST) disturbed; annoyed; irritated
profound (pruh FOUND) wise; intellectually deep
pitch (PICH) a black, sticky substance formed from distilling of tar
mortal (MAWR tul) fatal; causing death
stifled (STY fuld) muffled, smothered

"It is only a mouse crossing the floor." Yes, he had been trying to comfort himself with these lies. But he had found all in vain. *All in vain.* For Death, in approaching him, had walked with his black shadow before him, and surrounded the old man. And it was that unseen shadow that made him feel, yes *feel*, the presence of my head within the room.

By then I had waited a long time, very patiently, without hearing him lie down. I decided to open a little, a very, very little crack in the lantern. So I opened it—you cannot imagine how slowly, slowly.

Suddenly a single dim ray, like the thread of a spider, shot out from the crack and fell upon the vulture eye.

It was open—wide, wide open. I grew furious as I gazed upon it. I saw it clearly, so clearly—all a dull blue, with a hideous film over it. A hideous film that chilled me to the very bones. But I could see nothing else of the old man's face or body; for I had pointed the ray as if by instinct, exactly upon the damned spot.

And now—have I not told you about my most acute senses? Now, I say, there came to my ears a low, dull, quick sound.

---

vain (VAYN) without success; useless
hideous (HID ee us) very ugly or frightening

Critical Thinking: *Analyze*

Remind students that writers include both flat and round characters in their stories. Flat characters are one dimensional, round characters are well developed. Ask: Is the old man in the story a flat or a round character? Explain.

Reading Focus:
Identify Signal Words

In his own mind, the narrator replaces the boards cleverly. Have students identify the word that signals the cause-and-effect relationship. Then have students name the cause and the effect.

Critical Thinking:
Analyze

Introduce the term *monologue*. Explain that in a monologue only one person speaks. A dialogue is verbal exchange between two or more characters. Ask the students to explain in their own words Poe's single effect. Ask why Poe does not quote the questions or the "familiar things" discussed by the police officers.

It was a sound such as a watch makes when enveloped in cotton. I knew *that* sound well too. It was the beating of the old man's heart. It increased my anger, as the beating of a drum increases a soldier's courage.

But even yet I held back, I kept still. I hardly breathed. I held the lantern motionless. I tried to see how steadily I could keep the ray upon the eye. Meantime the hellish drumbeat of the heart increased. It grew quicker and quicker, and louder and louder every instant. The old man's terror *must* have been great! It grew louder, I say, louder every moment! —do you hear me well? I have told you that I am nervous. So I am. And now at the dead hour of the night, in the dreadful silence of that old house, so strange a noise as this excited me to uncontrollable terror. Yet, for some minutes longer I held back and stood still. But the beating grew louder, louder! I thought the heart must burst. And now a new anxiety seized me —the sound would be heard by a neighbor! The old man's hour had come! With a loud yell, I threw open the lantern. I leaped toward him. He shrieked once— once only. In an instant I dragged him to the floor, and pulled the heavy mattress over him. I then smiled, to find the deed so far done. But for many minutes, the heart beat on with a stifled sound. This, however, did not worry me. It would not be heard through the wall. At length it stopped. The old man was dead. I removed the mattress and examined the corpse. Yes, he was stone, stone dead. I placed my hand upon the heart and held it there many minutes. There was no pulse. He was stone dead. His eye would trouble me no more.

If you still think me mad, you will think so no longer when I describe the wise steps I took to hide the body. The night went on, and I worked quickly, but in silence. First of all I cut up the corpse. I took off the head and the arms and the legs.

I then took up three wide boards from the floor of the room, and put all underneath. I then put the boards back so cleverly, so skillfully, that no human eye —not even *his*—could have noticed anything wrong. There was nothing to wash out—no stain of any kind, no blood-spot whatever. I had been too careful for that. A tub had caught all—ha! ha!

When I had made an end of these labors, it was four o'clock—still dark as midnight. As the bell sounded the hour, there came a knocking at the street door. I went to open it with a light heart—for what had I *now* to fear? There entered three men, who introduced themselves, with perfect courtesy, as officers of the police. A shriek, they said, had been heard by a neighbor during the night. The neighbor had been suspicious. The information had been brought to the police office. And now they (the officers) had been sent to search the house.

I smiled—for *what* had I to fear? I made the gentlemen welcome. The shriek, I said, was my own in a dream.

---

enveloped (en VEL upd) wrapped up
anxiety (ang ZY uh tee) worry

The old man, I added, was absent in the country. I took my visitors all over the house. I told them to search—search *well.* I led them, finally, to *his* bedroom. I showed them his treasures, safe, undisturbed. In the excitement of my confidence, I brought chairs into the room. I asked them *here* to rest from their work, while I myself, in the wild audacity of my perfect triumph, placed my own chair upon the very spot that lay over the corpse of the victim.

The officers were satisfied. My *manner* had convinced them. I was strangely at ease. They sat there, and after I answered their questions happily, they talked about familiar things. But, before long, I felt myself growing pale. I wished them gone. My head ached, and I imagined a ringing in my ears; but still they sat, and still they chatted. The ringing became more distinct—it continued and became ever more distinct. I talked more freely to get rid of the feeling; but the ringing went on, ever louder—until, at length, I found that the noise was *not* within my own ears.

No doubt I now grew *very* pale. But I talked more fluently, and with a louder voice. Yet the sound increased—and what could I do? It was *a low, dull, quick sound—a sound such as a watch makes when enveloped in cotton.* I gasped for breath—and yet the officers heard it not. I talked more quickly—more excitedly. But the noise steadily increased. I stood up and argued about trifles, in a high voice and with wild movements. But the noise steadily increased. Why *would* they not be gone? I paced the floor with heavy steps—but the noise steadily increased. Oh what *could* I do? I shouted—I swore! I took the chair upon which I had been sitting and pushed it loudly upon the boards, but the noise rose up over all and continued to increase. It grew louder—and louder—*louder!* And still the men chatted pleasantly, and smiled. Was it possible they heard it not? No, no! They heard! —they suspected—they *knew!* They were making a mockery of my horror!—this I thought, and this I think. But anything was better than this agony! Anything was better than this mockery! I could bear those hypocritical smiles no longer! I felt that I must scream or die! —and now—again! —listen! —louder! louder! *louder!*—

"Villains!" I shrieked. "Pretend no more. I admit the crime! Tear up the boards! —here, here!—it is the beating of his hideous heart!"

---

audacity (aw DAS uh tee) boldness; daring
fluently (FLOO unt lee) easily (of talking)
trifle (TRY ful) unimportant thing
mockery (MOK uh ree) person or thing made fun of
hypocritical (hip uh KRIT ih kul) false; not sincere

Literary Focus: *Suspense*

Ask: How does the author build the suspense here?

Critical Thinking: *Infer*

Point out that the narrator indicates that the officers suspect nothing. Ask: Why, then, did the narrator behave as he did?

Mini Quiz

Write the following sentences on the board and call on students to fill in the blanks. Discuss the answers with the class.

1. The narrator killed the old man on the ________ night that he entered his room.
2. The object that the narrator held motionless was a ________.
3. After the murder, the narrator took up ________ wide boards.
4. The police arrived at ________ o'clock in the morning.
5. The narrator told the police that the old man had gone to the ________.

Answers

1. eighth
2. lantern
3. three
4. four
5. country

UNDERSTAND THE SELECTION

Answers

1. midnight
2. the old man's clouded eye
3. A neighbor had reported a shriek.
4. Sample answer: so that the old man would not suspect his intentions
5. Sample answer: the madman's father or the landlord
6. Sample answer: a cataract
7. Sample answer: The narrator was acting strangely.
8. Sample answer: It suggests instability or overreaction on the part of someone who keeps telling the reader he is not insane
9. Answers will vary. Suggested response: What were you doing last night? How long have you lived here?
10. Sample answers: a burglar who has come to steal your valuables.

Respond to Literature

What is the single effect Poe tries to achieve in this short story? One possibility is horror. Explain that Poe was writing at a time when the scientific study of mental illness was still in its infancy. Have the class discuss whether his portrayal of mental illness is valid in light of what we know today. Guide them by mentioning the murderer's belief in his own supreme cleverness. You might also mention his need to justify to himself by thinking that there was a rational reason for the crime (the need to destroy the malevolent eye). You might also discuss conscience.

WRITE ABOUT THE SELECTION

Prewriting

Using students' suggestions, create a list on the board or an overhead transparency of the police officer's possible reactions to the sequence of events.

Sample sentences:

1. I was startled by the madman's sudden confession.
2. I attempt to control the screaming madman as he rips up the floor boards.
3. I was shocked at the discovery and reflexively struggled with and pushed the hysterical murderer to the floor.
4. I handcuffed and took the murmuring murderer to the police van.

Writing

Have students work individually. Give help to any student who is having difficulty. Ask questions about how the students would react if they had been the police officer.

Revising

Divide the class into small groups to make this a cooperative group activity. Have the members take turns reading their tales. Others can suggest improvements to make the tale more suspenseful. After all the tales have been revised and proofread, have the group make a booklet of their tales.

Proofreading

Have students work with a partner to check capitalization.

Review the Selection

UNDERSTAND THE SELECTION

Recall

1. At what hour every night did the narrator enter the old man's room?
2. What vexed the narrator?
3. Why did the policemen come?

Infer

4. Why do you think the narrator acted more kindly toward the old man for a week prior to the murder?
5. Who might the old man have been?
6. What do you think might have caused the glaze on the old man's eye that the narrator thought was evil?
7. Why did the policemen stay after the narrator answered their questions?

Apply

8. How does the expression "You protest too much," apply to the narrator's comments about his sanity?
9. What questions might the police ask the narrator?
10. Assume you are the old man. You sense something sinister. Who do you think has entered the room? Why?

Respond to Literature

Is Poe's suspenseful tale typical of the literature of this period? Explain.

WRITE ABOUT THE SELECTION

Edgar Allan Poe has been called the master of suspense. "The Tell-Tale Heart" illustrates his ability to keep a reader "on the edge of a seat." In this selection, the main character, a madman, relates his tale of horror and suspense. The madman presents the tale in a logical manner—insisting that he is not crazy.

Suppose that you are one of the policemen who has answered the neighbor's complaint. You are sitting and chatting with this madman. Suddenly he confesses to the murder and begins to rip up the floor boards looking for the "beating heart." How do you maintain your composure? What do you say? Add an episode to this tale describing the events that follow the madman's confession.

Prewriting Freewrite your ideas about what happened and how you reacted. Include details of how the madman acted.

Writing Write at least one paragraph describing the new sequence of events. Explain how you handled the situation and the madman. Remember, you are writing from the point of view of a policeman in the 19th century.

Revising When you revise your tale, add details that help keep up the element of suspense.

Proofreading Read over your selection. Be sure each of your sentences begins with a capital letter.

THINK ABOUT SUSPENSE

To achieve suspense in a story, an author may foreshadow events, create atmospheric details, add events that heighten the tension the reader feels, and use character traits that make the reader feel strongly, one way or another, about a character.

1. Who is the narrator of the story?
2. How does Poe make it clear from the outset that the narrator is insane?
3. There are two kinds of suspense, one that leaves the outcome in doubt until the end of the story and one in which the outcome is known but not when it will happen. Which type does Poe use in this story?
4. What are some details that Poe uses to build suspense in the story?
5. Why did the narrator think he heard the old man's heart beating under the floor?

Reading Focus

Identify Signal Words As you read this selection, you identified cause-and-effect relationships and the sequence of events by using signal words. Choose a series of events from the story. Write the signal words you identified. Tell why you think these words make the relationships among these events clear.

DEVELOP YOUR VOCABULARY

You will find it difficult to understand and appreciate any literary work if you do not understand the vocabulary used by the author. Sometimes you may be able to figure out the meaning of a word from **context clues**—from the words that surround the unfamiliar word. However, it is always wise to check the meaning of the unfamiliar word in a dictionary as well. At times, unfamiliar words will be defined within or following a selection. This is true in this text. Be sure to check these definitions as you read.

Review the meanings of the following words from "The Tell-Tale Heart." When you are sure you understand the words, write an original sentence for each one that shows you understand the meaning.

1. vexed
2. pitch
3. enveloped
4. audacity
5. acute
6. fluently
7. mockery
8. hypocritical
9. stifled
10. mortal

THINK ABOUT SUSPENSE

Answers

1. the murderer
2. statements such as "Why will you say that I am mad?"
3. At first the known outcome type is used since the murderer is revealed early on. After the murder, the unknown outcome predominates as the reader remains in suspense about whether the narrator will be caught.
4. Sample answer: The delay in the murder, the use of midnight and darkness for the deed; the madman's own terror, the murderer's sensitivity to sound; the victim's shriek; and so on.
5. Sample answer: A shred of conscience remained in his deranged mind, and the beating provided an excuse to confess.

DEVELOP YOUR VOCABULARY

Sample Answers

1. The old man's Evil Eye *vexed* the murderer.
2. The high *pitch* of the man's shriek awoke the neighbors.
3. A watch's ticking is muffled when it is *enveloped* in cotton.
4. The murderer showed *audacity* when he took police to the murder scene.
5. The man claimed to have an *acute* sense of hearing.
6. He spoke *fluently* as though nothing strange had occurred.
7. The police were not making a *mockery* of the man's plight.
8. The murderer thought the police were being *hypocritical* when they smiled.
9. He seemed to be *stifled* by the foul odor in the room.
10. All people are *mortal* and will die eventually.

Reading Focus

Sample Answer

An example of time order from the story is the description of how the narrator disposed of the body. He uses "First of all," and several times "I then." These words help to keep the time sequence relationships among the events clear.

Focus on Fiction

Help students understand that novels, short stories, and plays make up the category of fictional narrative. Novels are generally long and may contain many characters. The plot is usually complex, following the major characters through a series of events that may take place over a series of months or even years. These events often take place in several different settings or in one setting that changes with time.

Use examples from this book to show that a short story focuses on a few characters. The plot is often limited to a single experience that occurs within a limited span of time. The setting rarely changes.

Use "The Legend of Sleepy Hollow" to highlight that the play is a representation of a story performed live on stage by actors. The actors take the parts of the characters and speak their dialogue, or words. A full-length play is similar to a novel. Full-length plays usually contain three to five acts, or major divisions. A one-act play is similar to a short story.

ELEMENTS OF FICTION

In discussing the **setting**, ask students to think of a time and place in which they might have wanted to spend a part of their lives. Ask them to visualize the place and give details about its physical appearance, the season or period in history, and the weather and climate.

In discussing **character**, ask students to name a movie that they have recently seen. Then have them analyze the characters, listing physical features and personality traits. Have them distinguish between well-rounded and flat characters.

Continue the analysis of the movie, eliciting an outline of the **plot**. Have students name the protagonist and the antagonist and then describe the conflict, climax, and denouement.

Focus on Fiction

Fiction has several recognizable elements. Knowing them will help you to understand fictional works better. The most basic elements are setting, characters, plot, theme, and point of view.

Setting Setting is the physical place, the time, and the general background against which the action or events in a story take place. The physical place might be the great outdoors or a single room. It might be a city street or a country estate. The time might include the time of day, a particular season, or a period in history. The general background often includes a specific kind of weather or the general climate of a region.

The action of a novel, play, or short story may be set in more than one place. One part of the work may take place in one setting; another part in another setting.

Sometimes a setting can be a major force affecting events of the story. A blizzard, for example, may change the plans the characters had for going on a journey. The setting may also help the reader to understand a character better. A character who lives on a houseboat, for example, is likely to be accustomed to water and self-reliance.

Characters Characters are the inhabitants of the fictional world the author creates. Characters have physical features and personalities. The author may use physical features to shed light on a character's personality. Usually, the characters are human. Occasionally, an animal may be given a personality. Then, that animal becomes a character.

The author creates personality through the character's thoughts, words, and deeds. A character's personality may also be revealed through the opinions and attitudes expressed by other people in the story. Some characters are well-rounded and believable. A **well-rounded** character has strengths and weaknesses, as real people do. Minor characters are often **flat**, not round. They have one-dimensional personalities and may even be stereotypes.

Plot Plot is the series of events in a literary work. Conflict provides the dramatic action that advances the plot. Conflict arises when two characters important to the story struggle against one another. The main character is called the **protagonist**. His or her rival is called the **antagonist**. Conflict may also arise when one character struggles within his or her own mind about something. This kind of struggle is called **internal conflict**.

The **climax** is the decisive turning point in the action of the story. The dramatic tension, caused by the conflict, reaches its highest point at the climax. At that moment, the conflict begins to be resolved. The tension is released, and the **dénouement**, or conclusion, follows.

Theme Theme is the central or dominating idea of a literary work. In nonfiction, the theme is often stated as a topic. Theme is rarely stated in fiction. Instead, the author uses the other elements of fiction, such as plot, character, and setting, to communicate an idea or concept to the reader.

Point of View Point of view is the position from which the story is told. A fictional story may be told from the first-person or the third-person point of view.

In **first-person** point of view, the narrator is a participant in the action. He or she has a limited view of the action, and can tell the reader only what he or she sees, hears, and knows.

In **third-person** point of view, the narrator is an observer who stands outside the action. A third person narrator might be able to see, hear, and know everything that happens to all the characters or a third person narrator's point of view might be limited to the information experienced by just one character.

When the narrator can tell the innermost feelings and thoughts of only one character, the point of view is called **third-person limited**. When the third person narrator is all-knowing, the point of view is called **omniscient**. An omniscient narrator can tell the reader what the characters are thinking.

Real-Life Application

In discussing point of view, ask a student to tell a personal story. Then ask another student to tell a story about someone else. Have the audience identify the parts of speech that indicate which point of view each storyteller is using—first or third person.

SELECTION OVERVIEW

SELECTION OBJECTIVES

After completing this selection, students will be able to

- understand that fiction is narrative writing that comes from the imagination of an author
- understand that novels, short stories, and plays make up the categories of fiction
- understand the basic elements of fiction: setting, character, plot, theme, and point of view
- write a eulogy
- understand base words and suffixes
- understand character

Lesson Resources

from *The Prairie*

- Selection Synopsis, Teacher's Edition, p. T65e
- Comprehension and Vocabulary Workbook, pp. 29–30
- Language Enrichment Workbook, p. 15
- Teacher's Resources
  - Reinforcement, p. R15
  - Test, pp. T29–T30
  - Unadapted Selections, pp. U12–U15
  - Literary Analysis, pp. L4–L5

More About the Literary Period

Explain that eastern Americans were fascinated by tales of the western frontier. Cooper had a poet's gift for describing the beauty of that land. His hero, Bumppo, despises those who would destroy nature just to make money. He respects the ways of Native Americans. Ask students what they recall about "No More Forever." Would early explorers like Bumppo have approved of those who followed?

About The Author

As a teenager, Cooper joined the navy for five years. He then became a successful farmer. At the age of thirty, he wrote his first novel. His second book, *The Spy*, was a thrilling adventure story that became a popular success. It launched his career as a novelist.

The Prairie is one of five novels known collectively as *The Leatherstocking Tales*. These books chronicle the adventures of Natty Bumppo.

MODEL

from

The Prairie

by James Fenimore Cooper

FOCUS ON FICTION
STUDY HINTS

The introduction gives important background needed to understand the excerpt.

In the following excerpt, Natty Bumppo is close to death. He is visited by Duncan Uncas Middleton, an army officer whose life Bumppo had saved a year earlier, and by Middleton's scouting party. Bumppo has been living with the tribe of Hard-Heart, a young Pawnee chief, whom Bumppo had adopted as a son. As Bumppo's death approaches, the Pawnee chief and the army officer both share a deep sadness.

The author establishes the setting.

When the scouting party entered the village, its inhabitants were gathered in an open space. The Indians formed a large circle with perhaps a dozen of the principal chiefs at the center. Around them were the others arrayed, as was their custom, by age and rank. Hard-Heart waved his hand as Middleton approached. The circle parted to let him and his companions pass through. At the center, they dismounted. As their horses were led away, the strangers found themselves surrounded by a thousand grave, concerned faces.

Plot is introduced on a suspenseful note. Point of view is omniscient.

Middleton gazed about him, troubled. No song or shout had welcomed him among these people, with whom he was on the best of terms. His followers shared his apprehensions. Determination replaced anxiety in their eyes. Each man felt silently for his weapons. Yet there was no sign of hostility on the part of their hosts.

---

grave (GRAYV) serious
apprehension (ap rih HEN shun) fear, dread

ESL Activity

Have students of different cultural backgrounds discuss a favorite character from the folklore of their culture. Pair students and ask them to choose one of the characters. Have them write a short paragraph about the character and save their papers to make comparisons.

Cooperative Group Activity

Have small groups of students create a character description for the type of person who would have been an explorer in the 19th century. Then have them create a second description of an astronaut's personality characteristics in today's world. Have them look for the similarities and differences in the two descriptions.

Hard-Heart beckoned for Middleton to follow him. He led the way toward the cluster of chiefs that stood at the center. Here the visitors found the solution to the mystery.

Bumppo sat on a homemade seat. The chair, though crudely made, had been carefully designed to support his frame in an upright and comfortable posture. It was apparent at first glance that the old man was dying. His eyes were glazed, unseeing and expressionless. His skin was more sunken than before, but there all outward change ended.

The author gives details of the setting.

The author describes the character's physical appearances.

He did not suffer from any particular disease. His body had, with time, simply worn out. Life still lingered in his system. It seemed as though the spirit knew it was time to leave. Yet, it was reluctant to depart from a shell that had for so long provided honorable shelter. Middleton could almost imagine he could see the spirit fluttering about the placid lips of the old woodsman.

The conflict is revealed—Bumppo *vs.* death.

The light from the setting sun fell full upon Bumppo's solemn features. His head was bare, and his long gray hair stirred lightly in the evening breeze. His rifle lay upon his knee. The other tools of a hunter were at his side, within easy reach. The figure of a hound crouched at his feet, as if asleep. So natural was its position that Middleton had to look closely before he realized it was not alive. The Indians had, with tenderness and ingenuity, stuffed the skin of Hector, Bumppo's dead dog, and placed it there.

The character of Bumppo is slowly revealed.

Le Balafre, the old Pawnee chief, sat beside the dying trapper. His own hour of departure did not appear far off. Nearby stood other old men. They had come to watch how a just and fearless warrior would approach life's greatest journey.

Bumppo had lived a life uncorrupted by vice. The reward for his temperance was a peaceful death. His vigor had endured to the end. Decay, when it did occur, was rapid and painless.

The author sets limits on the conflict.

He had hunted with the tribe throughout the Spring and Summer. As Fall approached, his limbs suddenly became paralyzed. Soon after that, he fell into a coma. The Pawnees believed that they were going to lose, so unexpectedly, the wise friend they had come to love and respect. But, as we have already said, the soul seemed reluctant to depart. The lamp of life flickered but would not go out.

---

placid (PLAS id) quiet
ingenuity (in juh NOO uh tee) cleverness; originality
temperance (TEM pur uns) self-restraint in conduct, appetite, etc.

Develop Vocabulary Skills

Distribute a handout with the vocabulary words and definitions listed. Ask for volunteers to use each word in an original sentence. After each volunteer has read his or her sentence, call on other students to repeat the vocabulary word used and read the definition.

Teaching Plan

INTRODUCE

Motivation

Remind students that in the early 19th century, America was for the most part a beautiful, unsettled wilderness. Ask students to think about what their neighborhood would be like without the homes, businesses, schools, and so on. Suggest that they think about their transportation; about how easy it is to get from place to place. Then ask: Would you be willing to leave the security of your surroundings to explore the wilderness?

Purpose-Setting Question

If an explorer with Bumppo's values is facing a peaceful death in old age, what would he say? What pleasant memories would he think about?

READ

Literary Focus: *Elements of Fiction*

Remind students that *setting* is described on page 130. Then discuss with students how the setting of this story is integral to the story line including the complexity of the relationships among characters due to the time and place. Ask: What is the setting of this story? How does the setting affect the way you view the characters?

Reading Focus: *Understand Character*

Explain to students that the characters in this story are diverse culturally and psychologically. The description of Bumppo as a *paleface* and the differences in religious beliefs give the reader clues to cultural differences. Ask: Do these cultural differences affect how the characters feel about each other? Explain.

CLOSE

Have students complete Review the Selection on pages 140–141.

Reading Focus: *Understand Character*

Ask: How would you describe the character of Hard Heart? Does his name match his personality? Why or why not?

Literary Focus: *Plot*

Have students use clues from the plot to predict what will happen to Bumppo later in the story. Guide students to tie their answers to the central conflict, Bumppo versus Death. Ask: What do you predict the climax will be? What might be the dénouement?

The author continues the omniscient point of view.

On the day of Middleton's arrival, the old man regained consciousness. He spoke coherently. From time to time his sight returned, and he recognized those about him. It was not recovery, but a final rally before death.

Hard-Heart, leaning forward, asked sadly and politely:

Bumppo and the Pawnee speak to each other with respect.

"Does my father hear the words of his adopted son?" Hard-Heart spoke in Pawnee.

"Speak," replied the trapper in the same language. His voice was weak but the words were distinct. "I am about to depart from the Pawnee village. I shall soon be beyond the reach of your voice."

"Let the wise chief have no cares for his journey. The spirits of a hundred dead Pawnee warriors await you in the next world. They will ride at your side." In his concern for the old man, Hard-Heart had forgotten that others were waiting to speak with Bumppo.

The author hints at theme through dialogue.

"Pawnee, I die, as I have lived, a Christian," the frontiersman answered. His voice was now strong. Its force startled his listeners. "I will leave life as I came into it. Horses and arms are not needed to stand in the presence of the Great Spirit of my people. He will judge me by my deeds."

"My father will tell my young men how many enemy warriors he has defeated. He will tell what acts of valor and justice he has done so they will know how to imitate him."

"A boastful tongue is not heard in the heaven of a white-man!" Bumppo spoke solemnly. "What I have done, God has seen. What I have done well, he will remember. He will chastise me for my sins, but he will do so with mercy. No, my son, a paleface is not allowed to sing his own praises before his God."

Notice the omniscient point of view.

Hard-Heart was a little disappointed but did not want to argue. He stepped back modestly and allowed the others to approach. Middleton took Bumppo's hand in his own. He had difficulty controlling his emotions. The old man seemed lost in thought, but a joyful expression crossed his faded features at the sound of Middleton's voice.

"I hope you have not forgotten him whose life you saved."

---

coherently (koh HIR unt lee) clearly speaking
chastise (chas TYZ) punish

Sunset over the Marshes, Martin Johnson Heade. Corbis Bettmann

"I have forgotten very little that I have seen," the trapper replied in English. "I am at the end of many weary days, but there is not one of them that I would choose to forget. I remember you and your whole party. I remember your grandfather dead these many years. I am glad that you have come. Will you do a favor for an old and dying man?"

The tension relaxes as the old man finds the strength to let his last wishes be known.

"Name it," said Middleton, "and it shall be done."

"Kindness and friendship should not be forgotten. There is a settlement in the Ostego hills. It is a long journey—"

The old man's strength was fading; his breathing was labored. He spoke at short intervals. Middleton interrupted to spare him further effort.

"I know the place. Tell me what you want done."

"Take this rifle, bullet pouch, and powder horn. Send them to the person whose name is engraved on the rifle. I had the letters put there. I have long intended that he should inherit my rifle."

"He shall have it. Is there anything else I can do?"

Viewing Fine Art

Martin Johnson Heade (1819–1904) was a unique and original American artist. A specialist in still-life painting—particularly large, delicate paintings of birds and flowers—he also produced some landscapes that were extraordinarily atmospheric and often rather eerie. Heade traveled widely and was influenced by the lush colors of jungles and the more dramatic scenes of nature. His works are sometimes described as "magic realism" because they are realistic in detail but convey a strong sense of mood—often a foreboding or supernatural one. Here the combination of red and blackish-green sky makes a startling, rather frightening sunset.

Ask: How does the mood of this painting reflect the mood of what you have read so far? What words describe this painting as well as the mood of this story?

Critical Thinking: *Infer*

Ask: What can you infer are Bumppo's feelings about his life? What information helped you to make your inference?

Critical Thinking: *Evaluate*

Point out that Bumppo's understanding of the differences between his and the Pawnees' religions further demonstrates his deep understanding of both cultures. Ask: Do you think this understanding is what made it possible for Bumppo to live among the Pawnee for so long? Explain your answer.

Literary Focus: *Foreshadowing*

Remind the students that authors often give clues or hints about what will happen next in a story. This is called foreshadowing. Ask: How does Bumppo's realization that his dog was dead foreshadow his own death? What other character's death appears to be foreshadowed?

"I have few other possessions. I have given my traps to Hard-Heart. He has been a good son. Let him come closer."

Middleton explained to the Indian chief what the trapper had said. He stood back to let Hard-Heart approach.

"Pawnee," continued the old man, changing his language to suit the need. "My people have a custom. The father always leaves his son a blessing before he shuts his eyes forever. This blessing I give you. Take it for we are all children of the same God. May God look on your deeds with friendly eyes. May you never commit an act that angers him.

The old hunter shows his understanding of both cultures.

"I do not know if we shall ever meet again. There are many beliefs about an afterlife. You believe in the blessed prairies. I have faith in the sayings of my fathers. This parting may be final. Then again, we may both stand together before the face of one God.

"There is much good in both religions. Each seems suited to its own people. I go contented. Still, it is a little painful to give up the pleasures of the hunt."

Bumppo leaned forward, feeling for his dog. "Aye, Hector," he said, "we must part at last. You've been a faithful hound. Pawnee, you cannot slay the dog on my grave, as is your custom. That is not my way. If you love me, be kind to him after I have gone.

"I hear the words of my father."

"Do you hear the chief's promise, dog?" asked the trapper. Hearing no response, the old man felt for the dog's mouth. Touching its cold lips, he realized the truth. Falling back in the seat, he hung his head, as though in shock. Two young Indians took advantage of his momentary distraction. They removed the stuffed dog with the same sensitivity that had tempted them to try the deception.

The author takes pains to show the Indians' sensitivity and respect for Bumppo.

The stuffed dog is used as a symbol for the mortality of all creatures.

After a few minutes, Bumppo raised his head. "The dog is dead," he said. "A hound has his time, just as men do." He called for Middleton.

"Captain," he said, "I am glad you have come. These Indians mean well, but they do not understand our ways. Bury the dog with me."

"As you wish."

The old man retreated into his own thoughts. At times, he raised his eyes wistfully. It seemed as though he had more to say, but no words passed his lips. Noting this, Middleton asked if there was anything else he could do.

"I have no kith or kin," the trapper said. "My blood line dies with me. We Bumppos have never been chiefs. We were honest and useful in our own way. My father lies buried near the sea, but the bones of his son will whiten on the prairie."

The author gives more clues to Bumppo's character.

"Name the spot, and your remains will be buried by your father's side," said Middleton.

"No, let me sleep where I have lived, far from the din of cities. I would not like an unmarked grave, though. These redskins, fearing grave robbers, hide their dead. I paid a man in the settlements to put a tombstone on my father's grave. I paid him in beaver skins. It told passersby that a Christian lay under that ground. The words on the stone were few, but enough to tell of his manner of life, his years, his honesty."

"Would you like such a stone at your grave?"

"I! No. Hard-Heart is my only son. He knows little of white man's ways. Besides, I am already in his debt. I have been of little help to the tribe. I have no money. The rifle has some value, but I have promised it to the boy whose name is engraved on it."

"You saved my life. Many years before, you saved my grandfather's. Let me show my gratitude. A stone shall be put at the head of your grave."

The old man extended an emaciated hand and gave Middleton a squeeze of thanks.

"I thought you would be willing to do it. I was reluctant to ask since you are not my kin. Put no boastful words on the stone. My name and age, year of death, and a few words from the Bible will do. Then my name will not be altogether lost on earth. I need no more."

"It will be done," Middleton said.

Those words seemed to close the old man's accounts with this world. He drew back within himself. Middleton and Hard-Heart stood on either side of the chair. Two hours passed. Occasionally, the old man spoke, but his words were distant. He spoke of events they had not seen. The circle Middleton had ridden into

The plot is advanced through a change in Bumppo's condition.

kith (KITH) archaic meaning for friends
kin (KIN) relatives
emaciated (ih MAY see ayt id) abnormally lean

Reading Focus: *Understand Character*

Ask the students to identify the following characters and explain why each is present at the death scene: Bumppo, Middleton, principal chiefs, Hard-Heart, Hector.

Discussion

Ask the students to suggest parallels between the following pairs of characters: Bumppo/Le Balafre and Middleton/Hard-Heart.

Literary Focus: *Conflict*

Remind the students of General Howard's conflict between his private beliefs and his public actions toward the Nez Percé. Ask: How do you think Middleton would have reacted in a similar situation?

Reading Focus: *Understand Character*

Ask: Why do you think Le Balafre's speech describing Bumppo is made in the dénouement? How does this part of the story enhance the reader's understanding of Bumppo?

that morning remained unbroken. When the old man spoke, the Indians bent forward to listen. When he finished, they stood in thoughtful silence.

As the flame of life grew dimmer, his voice became hushed. His weather-beaten face often changed expression. At times, Middleton imagined he could see the workings of the old man's soul in his alternating facial expressions. Perhaps, he did. Who among the living can say? Without pretending to explain that mystery, we shall simply tell what he saw.

Notice that the narrator, using the editorial we, demonstrates his omniscience.

Another hour went by. The trapper's eyes opened and shut occasionally. When open, his eyes appeared to focus on the western horizon and the glorious colors of an American sunset. Nature and the event seemed to fill the observers with solemn awe.

The author hints at theme through setting and symbol. What does the sunset stand for?

Suddenly, the old man grasped Middleton's hand with incredible power. Supported on either side by his friend and his adopted son, Bumppo rose to his feet. Erect, he looked about him. In a voice heard throughout the surrounding throng, he pronounced one word:

"Here!"

The climax has arrived.

The sudden action and the uncommon force of his utterance took all present by surprise. Middleton and Hard-Heart, each of whom had reflexively extended a supporting hand, turned to look at their aged friend. As they did, they realized he was beyond their care. They placed the body gently in the seat. Le Balafre stood and made an announcement to the tribe. The voice of the old Indian seemed to be an echo from another world.

The dénouement begins.

"A valiant, just, and wise warrior has gone to the blessed lands of his people. When the call came, he was ready to answer. Go my children. Remember the just chief of the palefaces, and imitate his ways!"

Bumppo's character is revealed through the opinion of another.

A grave was dug beneath the shade of some noble oaks. The Pawnee keep careful watch over it. Passing travelers are shown the spot where a just white man sleeps. A stone was placed at its head with the simple inscription the trapper had requested. Middleton took only one liberty. He added, "May no wanton hand ever disturb his remains!"

---

utterance (UT ur uns) expressing by voice
reflexively (rih FLEK siv lee) an action done automatically
grave (GRAYV) burial plot
wanton (WAHN tun) mischievous, unruly

Chief Tustennuggee, 19th century. Corbis Bettmann

Viewing Fine Art

Chief Tustennuggee was a notable figure in Native American affairs. He was a Creek chief and a man of striking dignity and valor. When the Creeks were forced from their land, he spoke in favor of peaceful removal to another location in response to many promises of fair treatment from the United States government. He even went to war for the government, both as a mediator and as a soldier. Among the many artists who painted him were Charles Bird King, the portraitist for the United States Indian Museum, and John Mix Stanley, the great artist of the American West.

Ask: How do you think the artist who painted this Native American wanted to portray the subject?

Mini Quiz

Display the following sentences and call on students to fill in the blanks. Discuss the answers with the class.

1. It seemed as though Bumppo's ________ knew it was time to leave.
2. A peaceful death was Bumppo's reward for his ________.
3. The settlement to which Middleton would take Bumppo's rifle was in the ________ hills.
4. Bumppo's final word was ________.
5. The ________ keep careful watch over his grave.

Answers

1. spirit
2. temperance
3. Ostego
4. "Here!"
5. Pawnee

UNDERSTAND THE SELECTION

Answers

1. Hard-Heart, a Pawnee chief
2. Hector
3. by the sea
4. Sample answer: He was valiant, fair, and wise.
5. Sample answer: He did not want his name to be totally forgotten.
6. Sample answer: The Indians were acting strangely, and he did not know why.
7. Sample answer: He had taken good care of his body and not reacted violently towards others.
8. Sample answer: There would probably be mixed emotions—sadness for Bumppo's death and gratitude for the rifle.
9. Sample answer: Yes, because he had Bumppo's example to help him.
10. Sample answer: He talked about events that occurred during his childhood.

Respond to Literature

Answers will vary. One possibility is that he represents the passing of the optimistic age in America.

WRITE ABOUT THE SELECTION

Prewriting

Ask students, "Has anyone attended a funeral and listened to a eulogy?" (Answers will vary.) "Does anyone remember a eulogy on television or in a movie?" (Answers will vary.) If possible, secure and play a tape of an example of a eulogy. (One possibility is Senator Edward Kennedy eulogizing his brother, Robert Kennedy.)

Using students' suggestions, list several examples of Bumppo's character traits on a board or overhead transparency.

Sample list:

1. brave
2. noble
3. respected rights of others
4. generous

Review the Selection

UNDERSTAND THE SELECTION

Recall

1. Who was Bumppo's adopted son?
2. What was the name of Bumppo's dog?
3. Where was Bumppo's father buried?

Infer

4. Why did the Indians respect Bumppo?
5. Why did Bumppo want a tombstone?
6. Why was Middleton afraid when he first rode in to camp?
7. Why does the author say the reward for Bumppo's temperance was a peaceful death?

Apply

8. Suppose that you are the person whose name had been engraved on Bumppo's rifle. How would you have reacted when Middleton delivered it?
9. Suppose Hard-Heart died. Does he leave the world with as much grace as Bumppo did?
10. Suppose that you are one of the Indians present when Bumppo spoke of past events. What did he talk about?

Respond to Literature

What does Bumppo's life and death on the prairie symbolize?

WRITE ABOUT THE SELECTION

In this excerpt from *The Prairie*, Natty Bumppo asked his friend Middleton to take care of his funeral arrangements. In addition to the things Bumppo actually asked of him, Middleton probably delivered a short eulogy at Bumppo's gravesite. A **eulogy** is a speech praising a dead person. Suppose that you are Middleton and that you deliver Bumppo's eulogy. What would you say?

Prewriting Skim the story to gather data you might use in your eulogy. Organize the data as best you can and write an informal outline of the main points you would make. Tell about Bumppo's life and the example he gave to others. Include details about his personal achievements and his friendship with the Pawnees.

Writing Use your informal outline to write the eulogy. Remember to write in the first person (I) as you are supposedly Middleton. In the eulogy, include details that a friend might think important.

Revising When you revise your eulogy, be sure you have included all the points you would like people to remember about Bumppo. Add details to make the description more vivid. For each point you make, include an example from the story that illustrates your point.

Proofreading Read over your selection. Be sure each sentence is a complete thought with a subject and a predicate.

Writing

Have students work on this section individually. Remind students that they are to write in the first person. Walk around the classroom, giving help to any student who is having difficulty. To elicit possible ideas, ask questions about how students would want others to remember Bumppo if he had been their friend.

Revising

Divide students into small groups to make this a cooperative group activity. After each student reads the eulogy, have the others make suggestions of details that would improve the paragraph.

Proofreading

Select one or two of the students' essays as models. Place these on an overhead projector and have the class suggest improvements.

THINK ABOUT FICTION

Fiction is primarily narrative writing that comes from the imagination of an author. Unlike nonfiction narrative, it is not based on history or fact. Stories, told in novels, short stories, and plays, make up the category of fictional narrative. Through fiction, the reader experiences sadness, joy, humor, and other emotions common to human life and watches the resolution of lifelike conflicts and struggles.

1. Who is the protagonist in the excerpt you read? Who is the antagonist? Are they in conflict? Explain.
2. Does the setting of the excerpt contribute to your understanding of Bumppo's character?
3. What element of plot follows the climax?
4. What is an omniscient narrator able to do that narrators using other points of view cannot? Is this an advantage? Explain.
5. What do you think the theme of the excerpt is?

DEVELOP YOUR VOCABULARY

Root words are English words that have no letters or syllables added to them. **Suffixes** are word parts that can be added to base words to change their part of speech. For example, *-ful* is a commonly used suffix. Add it to *care* or *pain*, both nouns, and you have formed *careful* or *painful*, both adjectives. Here are some other suffixes and what they do:

Noun-forming suffixes: *-ance, -ion, -ity, -ment, -ness, -or, -ship*
Adjective-forming suffixes: *-able, -ful, -less*
Adverb-forming suffixes: *-ly, -ward*

Write the following words from *The Prairie*. Circle each suffix and write whether the word is a noun, an adjective, or an adverb.

1. visitor
2. comfortable
3. settlement
4. boastful
5. politely
6. kindness
7. friendship
8. modestly
9. fearless
10. outwardly
11. utterance
12. sensitively

ESL Activity

Have pairs of students work together. Ask one partner to say a word from the Vocabulary activity. The other partner gives the root word. When the partners agree on the accuracy of the response, have them write sentences using both forms of the word. If students need an additional challenge, ask them to add other suffixes to the root words, where possible, to change them to yet another part of speech.

THINK ABOUT FICTION

Answers

1. The protagonist is Natty Bumppo. The antagonist in this excerpt is death. Answers may vary. Suggested response: Yes, the conflict is between life and death.
2. Sample answer: Yes, because the woodsman was so much a part of the frontier environment that it is inconceivable that he could thrive in any other.
3. The denouement follows the climax. In it the plot is unraveled and the conclusion, or outcome, becomes known.
4. The omniscient narrator can tell what any character is thinking as well as doing. Narratives from other points of view are limited in this respect. A first-person narrator, for example, can reveal only his or her own thoughts. The omniscient point of view is an advantage because it allows the reader to learn more about all of the characters.
5. Sample answer: Despite the actuality of death, the excerpt is an affirmation of life. Bumppo's last act is to take a powerful affirmative stance, and he is concerned that his name not be lost on earth.

DEVELOP YOUR VOCABULARY

Answers

1. *-or*; noun
2. *-able*; adjective
3. *-ment*; noun
4. *-ful*; adjective
5. *-ly*; adverb
6. *-ness*; noun
7. *-ship*; noun
8. *-ly*; adverb
9. *-less*; adjective
10. *-ly*; adverb
11. *-ance*; noun
12. *-ly*; adverb

Selection Overview

Selection Objectives

After completing this selection, students will be able to

- understand the lyric
- understand how the poet uses detail, impressions, and insights to create lyrical effects
- use a lyric as a basis for writing a narrative
- understand the use of contractions in poetic meter
- draw conclusions

Lesson Resources

To a Waterfowl

- Selection Synopsis, Teacher's Edition, p. T65e
- Comprehension and Vocabulary Workbook, pp. 31–32
- Language Enrichment Workbook, p. 16
- Teacher's Resources
  Reinforcement, p. R16
  Test, pp. T31–T32

More About the Lyric

A lyre is an ancient stringed musical instrument. The earliest lyric poems were songs accompanied by the music of the lyre. Modern lyrics retain a musical quality in their language and structure.

More About the Literary Period

Remind the class that America was a young country with an exciting but uncertain future. Discuss the pioneer spirit. Talk about the migration of birds in terms of a long dangerous journey in hope of finding a safe haven. Why would Americans feel kinship with a migrating bird?

More About the Author

Bryant grew up in the beautiful countryside of western Massachusetts. He often walked in the woods, and their quiet beauty may have inspired his remark, "all the materials for poetry exist in our country." It was there, as a young man, that he wrote most of his famous poetry. At the age of thirty, he moved to New York City where studied politics and economics. He became a newspaper editor. Most of his time was from then on devoted to editorials. He strongly opposed slavery and was an early advocate of the workers' right to form labor unions.

Learn About

The Lyric

A **lyric** is a short poem usually expressing intense personal feeling. A lyric is like a still photograph as opposed to a movie. The lyric does not have a plot that is advanced through a series of events. Instead, it captures a moment in time and focuses on it very closely.

The lyric poet attempts to create a specific emotional response in the reader. The poet achieves this effect through the details, impressions, and insights that a heightened awareness makes him or her capable of expressing. The result is a vivid word picture of an experience to which the poet may give new meaning for the reader.

As you read "To a Waterfowl," ask yourself:

1. What lesson or new meaning does the author find in the migration of the bird?
2. In what way does this poem illustrate the poet's heightened awareness?

Reading Focus

Draw Conclusions Sometimes you must think beyond the words on the page to get a full meaning of the author's intent. Readers draw conclusions by using prior knowledge to arrive at a decision or judgment. As you read "To a Waterfowl," draw conclusions about what the author might think of his own life, as well as how he views birds.

Writing Connection

Select a common experience in nature, for example, leaves falling from a tree in autumn or a deer running across a green meadow. In a prose paragraph, use details, impressions, or insights to give this experience a new meaning.

ESL Activity

Ask students to identify, as the poem is read, which images emphasize loneliness, dangers, and the goal. Every poem has a speaker. Ask students to think about what is learned about the speaker of this poem.

Cooperative Group Activity

For the Writing Connection activity, have students write the words *details*, *impressions*, *insights*, leaving several lines between words. Have students brainstorm words to include in their paragraphs. Pair the students. Have each student read what he or she has written. Have the partner suggest adjectives to enhance the paragraph.

TO A WATERFOWL

by William Cullen Bryant

Whither, midst falling dew,
While glow the heavens with the last steps of day,
Far, through their rosy depths, dost thou pursue
Thy solitary way?

5 Vainly the fowler's eye
Might mark thy distant flight to do thee wrong,
As, darkly seen against the crimson sky,
Thy figure floats along.

Seek'st thou the plashy brink
10 Of weedy lake, or marge of river wide,
Or where the rocking billows rise and sink
On the chafed ocean-side?

There is a Power whose care
Teaches thy way along that pathless coast—
15 The desert and illimitable air—
Lone wandering, but not lost.

---

whither (HWI*TH* ur) to what place, point, etc.
fowler (FOUL ur) hunter of wildfowl
plashy (PLASH ee) marshy; wet
marge (MAHRJ) edge or border
chafed (CHAYFT) to have been worn away; eroded
illimitable (ih LIM ih tuh bul) endless

Develop Vocabulary Skills

Distribute a handout with the vocabulary words and their definitions. Have groups of students collaborate and use each of the words in an original sentence exploring the theme of flight. Give assistance as necessary. Ask for volunteers from each group to read two of their sentences.

Teaching Plan

INTRODUCE

Motivation

Play a tape of a nature video. Write phrases such as "lonely against the sky" and "They can because they think they can" on the chalkboard. Have students discuss why flight has always fascinated people. If necessary, introduce ideas such as the challenge, the freedom, the lure of the unknown. Relate these themes to the human journey.

Purpose-Setting Question

How do our discussions relate to Bryant's statement that "all the materials of poetry exist in our own country"?

READ

Literary Focus: *The Lyric*

Remind students that the lyric poet attempts to create an emotional response in the reader. Ask: From the subject of the poem, what emotions do you think it might elicit?

Reading Focus: *Draw Conclusions*

Guide students to understand that with poetry they must often draw conclusions in order to understand a poem or to appreciate its deeper message. Ask: What conclusion can you draw about time of day from the phrase, "with the last steps of day"? What might a "fowler" do "wrong" to a bird in flight? To what might "lone wandering, but not lost" refer?

CLOSE

Have students complete Review the Selection on pages 146–147.

Literary Focus: *Rhyme Scheme*

Explain that rhyme scheme is the arrangement of rhymes in a poem. The couplet or two-lined rhymed unit is one example of rhyme scheme. Ask where the students have seen the couplet. ("To My Dear and Loving Husband") Give an example from that poem to assist students in comprehending. Explain that another common type of scheme is the four-line stanza in which alternating lines rhyme. Lines 1 and 3 rhyme. Lines 2 and 4 rhyme. On the board, write:

a dew c
b d

Fill the blanks with the rhymes from the first stanza of "To a Waterfowl." Then write:

a c
b d

Explain that if lines 5 though 8 repeated the same rhymed sounds as lines 1 through 4, the notation would be *abab abab*. Ask students to suggest second stanza words that would fit that rhyme scheme.

Critical Thinking: *Evaluate*

Ask: How did Bryant's use of a waterfowl as the subject of this poem help to get his point across?

Reading Focus: *Draw Conclusions*

What argument does the narrator use to persuade himself that he is on the right path in life?

All day thy wings have fanned,
At that far height, the cold, thin atmosphere,
Yet stoop not, weary, to the welcome land,
20 Though the dark night is near.

And soon that toil shall end;
Soon shalt thou find a summer home, and rest,
And scream among thy fellows; reeds shall bend,
Soon, o'er thy sheltered nest.

25 Thou'rt gone, thy abyss of heaven
Hath swallowed up thy form; yet, on my heart
Deeply has sunk the lesson thou hast given,
And shall not soon depart.

He who, from zone to zone,
30 Guides through the boundless sky thy certain flight,
In the long way that I must tread alone,
Will lead my steps aright.

abyss (uh BIS) a thing too big for measurement

Mini Quiz

Write the following sentences on the board or overhead projector and call on students to fill in the blanks. Discuss the answers with the class.

1. The heavens were aglow with the last steps of ________.
2. A ________ taught the bird to find its way.
3. The birds would not land even though ________ was near.
4. At the end of the migration, the bird would ________ among its fellows.
5. Like the bird, the poet must journey through life ________.

Answers

1. day
2. power
3. night
4. scream
5. alone

UNDERSTAND THE SELECTION

Answers

1. crimson; darkly
2. alone
3. a summer home
4. in the evening
5. The bird was flying very high in the sky.
6. Sample answer: The bird was headed for its nesting place.
7. Sample answer: A goose or a duck
8. Sample answer: There is a purpose to the lives of all creatures.
9. Sample answer: He would have attempted to help it because he has deep feelings of respect for birds.
10. Sample answer: As a hunter he would see the bird as a target, but he might still have recognized its power and grace.

Respond to Literature

Group the students. Have each group compare and contrast the characters of the speaker and Bumppo. (Possibilities include: Each has a reverence for nature; both are opposed to killing animals for sport; both appear to be religious.)

WRITE ABOUT THE SELECTION

Prewriting

If your school is located near a lake, take your class to see waterfowl in their natural habitat or ask students to visit a local park, zoo, wildlife preserve, or sanctuary. Have students take notes on what they observe. If this is not possible, show pictures of waterfowl in a wildlife magazine or book to elicit possible responses from the students.

Using students' suggestions, create an outline of what the bird does and encounters and write it on the board or an overhead transparency.

Sample sentences:

1. The bird flies for eight miles before it lands on a lake, where others of its species are hiding in the reeds.
2. That evening it joins its mate and begins to make a nest.
3. The following day hunters come, and the mate is shot before it can escape.
4. This waterfowl successfully protects its nest; others are not as fortunate when predators attack.

Writing

Have students review their notes on waterfowl, and then have them work individually on their paragraphs. Go around the class, giving assistance to any student who is having difficulty.

Revising

Divide the class into small groups. Have each member read his or her adventure; others may suggest improvements in details or setting.

Proofreading

Have students work with partners to determine whether any word is misspelled. Students should check spelling in a dictionary.

Review the Selection

UNDERSTAND THE SELECTION

Recall

1. What color was the sky? How does the bird show up against it?
2. Was the bird alone or was it part of a flock?
3. What will the bird soon find?

Infer

4. At what time of day did Bryant observe the bird?
5. Why could a hunter not harm the bird?
6. Where was the bird headed?
7. What type of bird was this?

Apply

8. What lesson did Bryant learn from observing the bird?
9. Predict what might have happened if Bryant had found an injured waterfowl. Explain why.
10. Suppose that Bryant was a hunter. Do you think he would have seen the bird any differently? Compare and contrast the two viewpoints.

Respond to Literature

What characteristics do Bumppo and the speaker of this poem share?

WRITE ABOUT THE SELECTION

In this lyric poem, Bryant captured his momentary impressions of a waterfowl. Had this been a narrative poem, he would have continued to follow the bird, requiring him to write additional stanzas. Imagine that you are watching this same bird. How far does it fly? What dangers does it encounter? What is the climax of its story? Write a prose paragraph telling where you think the bird goes and what it does. The paragraph should contain a sequence of events that tell a story.

Prewriting Let your mind run free. Make a list of places the bird might go. Invent some adventures for the bird. Organize your list into an informal outline of what you envision happens to the bird. Include details of what you feel the bird might encounter. For example, it might have to escape from hunters, it might look for food, or it might have to find shelter in a storm.

Writing Use your informal outline to write a paragraph or two, telling of the bird's adventures. In your composition, briefly explain the setting where its adventure ends.

Revising When you revise, be sure to add specific details that allow others to visualize your impressions of the bird and of the setting that you chose.

Proofreading Read over your selection. Be sure all your words are spelled correctly.

THINK ABOUT LYRIC

A **lyric** is a poem that usually expresses intense personal feeling. The poet tries to create a specific emotional response in the reader. Through this response, the poet hopes the reader will share his or her intense feeling for the experience.

1. Why do you think the poet describes a "solitary" bird rather than a flock?
2. The bird is flying too high to be shot by hunters. How did you react when you read that? Why?
3. What is meant by "There is a power whose care/Teaches thy way along that pathless coast"?
4. In stanza 8, do you think the poet's "long way" refers to his journey home or his life? Why?
5. The English poet William Wordsworth said that "poetry . . . takes its origin from emotion recollected in tranquility." How does this describe the way Bryant wrote "To a Waterfowl"? Why?

Reading Focus

Draw Conclusions Tell about one conclusion that you drew about the deeper meaning of the poem. What details in the poem led you to this conclusion?

DEVELOP YOUR VOCABULARY

A poet must carefully select words to fit the meter of a poem as well as to express his or her thoughts and feelings. The **meter** is the specific pattern of stressed and unstressed syllables in each line of the poem.

Poets sometimes shorten words to keep the meter. They may make a contraction of a word or words not commonly used as contractions. A contraction is a shortened form of one or two words. Letters are removed. An apostrophe takes the place of the missing letter or letters. For example, *'twas* is a contraction of *it was*; *o'er* is the poetic contraction of *over*.

Following is a list of several contractions poets sometimes use. Study each contraction. Write the word you think the contraction represents. Check in a dictionary to be sure you are correct. (Not all the contractions will be found there, however.) Then use each contraction in an original sentence.

1. e'en
2. 'twill
3. shall't
4. 'tween
5. e'er
6. 'twixt

THINK ABOUT LYRIC

Sample Answers

1. A solitary waterfowl is an uncommon sight, and the poet saw a similarity between it and a solitary person.
2. Glad, because the bird would continue to soar.
3. The poet believes that God gave the bird its instinctual ability to find its way.
4. His life, because references to guiding the bird's flight through boundless skies are too weighty to mean merely a trip home.
5. The meaning of the poet's encounter with the solitary bird came only after it had flown out of his sight and the poet had time to think about its connection to his own life.

DEVELOP YOUR VOCABULARY

Answers

1. even
2. it will
3. shall it
4. between
5. ever
6. betwixt

Sentences will help. Give help to any student who is having difficulty.

ESL Activity

Have students work in small groups to use the contractions from the Vocabulary activity in a paragraph. Add contractions they might use every day. Where new contractions are used, ask the groups to indicate the word or words the contraction represents.

Reading Focus

Sample Answer

The speaker seems to be saying that there is a plan to life, determined by a higher power. The final stanza, in which the speaker talks of being guided by the same force as that which guides the waterfowl, led me to that conclusion.

Selection Overview

SELECTION OBJECTIVES

After completing this selection, students will be able to

- understand dialogue
- understand the use of dialogue in nonfiction or drama
- write a letter expressing feeling
- understand how specialized vocabularies develop around places and occupations
- make inferences

Lesson Resources

A Night from *Hospital Sketches*
- Selection Synopsis, Teacher's Edition, p. T65f
- Comprehension and Vocabulary Workbook, pp. 33–34
- Language Enrichment Workbook, p. 17
- Teacher's Resources
  Reinforcement, p. R17
  Test, pp. T33–T34

More About Dialogue

Dialogue helps to define the personality of each character. A kindly character may respond to a question with gentle humor. A villain may answer the same question with cruel sarcasm. Well written dialogue can also help provide or reinforce information about a character's background or education.

More About the Literary Period

Remind students that toward the middle of the 19th century, the mood in the United States changed. This mood was reflected in the literature. Mention the rise of Realism. Explain that Realism is the portrayal of people and events accurately, without attempting to idealize them.

About the Author

Louisa May Alcott's family was poor. She began writing as a teenager in the hope of helping to support her parents and three sisters. During this period, she also worked as a teacher, a maker of doll's clothing, and a domestic servant. It was only after the publication of her autobiographical *Hospital Sketches* that she was able to earn a living writing full time. She went on to write, among other works, *Little Women*, a famous novel about growing up.

Learn About

Reading Focus

Make Inferences Authors often do not explain the thoughts, feelings, and personalities of the characters in a story. Instead, the reader infers, or guesses, what the characters are like based on their words.

As you read this text, make inferences about each of these characters: the narrator, Teddy, John, and the doctor. Think about how the dialogue reveals aspects of them.

Dialogue

The written conversation of two or more people is called **dialogue.** Although it is used most often in fiction, dialogue is also used in nonfiction.

The writer of an autobiographical narrative may use dialogue to help give an easy, natural flow to the work. The people who were a part of the author's life are allowed to speak in their own words as the author remembers them. Their dialogue advances the narrative and shows events as they were.

Conversational give-and-take helps to define the personality and develop the character of each speaker. Using the direct words of people makes the writing seem more realistic.

As you read this selection, ask yourself:

1. How is dialogue used in Alcott's autobiographical narrative?
2. Does the dialogue help to make the people she worked with seem more real?

WRITING CONNECTION

Think of a conversation you recently had with a friend. Try to recall exact words. Write your conversation as accurately as you can, using each person's words in quotation marks.

ESL Activity

Explore the words *comedy* and *tragedy* by asking students to name stories or movies that fit each category.

Cooperative Group Activity

Have each student in a pair read his or her conversation from the Writing Connection activity to the partner (including quotation marks and other punctuation). Have the partners offer each other assistance as needed in using correct punctuation.

A Night *from* Hospital Sketches

by Louisa May Alcott

The hours I like best are at night, and so I was soon promoted to night nurse. I usually found the men in the most cheerful state of mind their condition allowed.

The evenings were spent in reading aloud and writing letters. I waited on and amused the men, and went with Dr. P. as he made his second daily rounds. I cared for my dozens of wounds, giving last doses of medicine and making the men cozy for the long hours to come.

I had managed to sort out the patients in the ward into three rooms. One I visited with a tray full of bandages and pins. Another I visited with books, flowers, games, and happy talk. To the third room I brought lullabies, kind words, and sometimes a helping hand in time of death.

The night I am writing about opened with a little comedy and closed with a little tragedy. I was watching beside the bed of a 12-year-old drummer boy who had come to us after a dreadful battle. A slight wound in the knee brought him there, but his mind had suffered more than his body. For days he had been reliving in his thoughts the scenes he could not forget. Then he would break out in terrible sobs which were pitiful to hear.

As I sat by him, I tried to soothe his poor brain by the constant touch of my hands over his hot forehead. In his mind he was cheering his comrades on, then counting them as they fell around him. He often grabbed my arm to drag me from the neighborhood of a bursting shell. His face burned with fever, his eyes were restless, and his head was never still. A constant stream of shouts, warnings, and broken cries poured from his lips.

It was past 11:00 and my patient was slowly wearing himself into periods of quiet. In one of these pauses, I heard a curious sound. I looked over my shoulder and saw a one-legged man hopping around the room. I recognized a soldier whose fever had taken a turn for the worse and left his mind in a state of confusion. At this point he informed me he was heading for home. When his mind was clear, the least movement produced a roar of pain. But the loss of reason seemed to have caused a change in the man and in his manner. He balanced

Teaching Plan

INTRODUCE

Motivation

Obtain a copy of *A Stillness at Appomattox* by Bruce Catton. Read to the students the account of a Civil War hospital (pp. 188–120). You may want to record it on tape beforehand, editing as you see fit. Begin with, "Most of them were simply laid on the floor." Conclude with "So they come every night." Discuss with the students the effect of such conditions on those who have been trained to save lives. After eliciting their opinions, mention that Alcott's brief stint as a nurse permanently impaired her health.

Purpose-Setting Question

Ask: In what ways do you think the Civil War contributed to the rise of Realism in literature?

READ

Literary Focus: *Dialogue*

Ask students to compare the dialogue of Bumppo and John, stressing the bravery with which each faces death. Ask: How do the death scenes of Bumppo and John, including their final speeches, compare and contrast? Which do you find more realistic?

Reading Focus: *Make Inferences*

Tell students that they will encounter dialogue from characters who lived during the Civil War. Have students infer what each of the characters thinks about the war from the dialogue. Have students keep notes on the characters' thoughts as they read.

CLOSE

Have students complete Review the Selection on pages 154–155.

Develop Vocabulary Skills

Point out the footnoted vocabulary word on page 150. Have students look up the word in the dictionary. Have a volunteer read the definitions given and identify the part of speech for each definition. Ask students to write original sentences that illustrate the different meanings of the word.

Discussion

Stop reading at the line, "As I was comforting him, a message I had been fearing came for me" (page 150, column 2). Ask students to summarize the comedy that began the night. Ask them to predict the tragedy that will end the night. Have them discuss how they would react to such a message. What kinds of things would they be prepared to say? Is a person who remains calm and unemotional on the surface in such situations necessarily unfeeling?

Reading Focus: *Make Inferences*

A doctor asks the author to tell a patient that he will surely die. Ask: What can you infer about the author from the doctor's request?

himself on one leg like a stork and refused any suggestion of mine to return to bed.

I couldn't think what to do with this creature. I was about to run for help when another wounded soldier came to the rescue. He put an end to the crisis by carrying the lively one-legged man to his bed. The one-legged soldier was worn out from his efforts and soon fell asleep.

My rescuer and I enjoyed a great laugh together, then returned to our places. Then the sound of a sob came from a bed in the corner. It was the little drummer boy. He was trying to control the sad sounds that kept breaking out.

"What is it, Teddy?" I asked, as he rubbed the tears away.

"I've got pain, ma'am, but I'm not crying for that, because I'm used to it. I dreamed Kit was here, and when I woke up he wasn't, and I couldn't help it then."

Kit was a good friend, badly hurt himself, who would not leave the drummer behind. He had wrapped him in his own blanket and carried him in his arms to the ambulance. Kit died at the door of the hospital which promised care and comfort for the drummer boy.

For ten days Teddy refused to be comforted because he had not been able to thank Kit for his protection, which may have cost him his life. This thought had been troubling him in secret. I told him that his friend probably would have died in any case, but I couldn't end his sorrow.

As I was comforting him, a message I had been fearing came for me.

"John is going, ma'am, and wants to see you, if you can come."

"I'll be there the moment this boy is asleep. Tell John so, and let me know if I am in danger of being too late."

The messenger left and while I quieted the drummer, I thought of John. He had come in a day or two after the others and was put in my "pitiful" room. He was a large man with a fine face and the most peaceful eyes I have ever seen.

When he came, I watched him for a night or two before I made friends with him. He seldom spoke and never complained. He was thoughtful and concerned while watching the suffering of others, as if he forgot his own.

One night, as I went on my rounds with Dr. P., I asked which man in the room probably suffered most. To my great surprise, the doctor glanced at John.

"Every breath he draws is like a stab, for the bullet went into his left lung and broke a rib. The poor man can find no rest because he must lie on his wounded back or else he can't breathe. It will be a long, hard struggle because of his great strength, but even this can't save him."

"You don't mean he must die, Doctor?"

"There's not the slightest hope for him, and you'd better tell him so before long. You have a way of doing such things comfortably, so I leave it to you. He won't last more than a day or two at the most."

I could have sat down on the spot and cried if I had not learned to save my tears

---

draw (DRAW) to take air into the lungs; inhale

for spare moments. Such an end seemed very hard for such a fine man. The army needed men like John who fight for freedom with both heart and hand. I could not give him up so soon. It was an easy thing for Dr. P. to say, "Tell him he must die," but a hard thing to do. I didn't have the heart to do it then, and I hoped that some change for the better might take place in spite of what Dr. P. had said.

A few minutes later I came in and saw John sitting up with no one to support him. The doctor was changing the bandage on his back.

Literary Focus:
Dialogue
Remind students that an author can choose to move a story along using dialogue. Other ways of telling the story include narration and exposition. Tell students to note the parts of the story the author tells with dialogue. Ask: What patterns do you see?

Reading Focus:
Make Inferences

Ask students to review John's dialogue. Have students infer from his dialogue why the narrator felt so warmly toward him.

Literary Focus:
Dialogue

Ask: How does the author use dialogue to reveal the thoughts and feelings of the characters?

The doctor's words made me feel sad that I had not given John those little cares and kindnesses that make the heavy hours pass earlier. He looked very lonely just then, as he sat with bent head and hands folded on his knees. I saw no sign of suffering till I looked nearer. Then I saw great tears roll down and drop upon the floor. It was a new sight there. Though I had seen many men suffer in silence or with groans of pain, none of them cried. It did not seem weak, only very moving. My heart opened wide and took him in. I gathered the bent head in my arms as freely as if he had been a little child and said, "Let me help you bear it, John."

Never on any human face have I seen so beautiful a look of thanks, surprise, and comfort, as that which he gave me.

"Thank you, ma'am," he whispered. "This is just what I wanted!"

"Then why not ask for it before?"

"I didn't like to be a trouble. You seemed so busy, and I could manage to get on alone."

"You shall not want it anymore, John."

Now I understood the sad look he sometimes gave me as I went out after a brief pause beside his bed. I had been used to stopping with those who seemed to need me more than he did. But now I knew that I brought as much comfort to him as to the others. I took the place of his mother, wife, or sister. Now while I cared for his wounds, he leaned against me, holding my hand tightly. If pain brought forth tears from him, no one saw them fall but me. I found him the manliest man of all of them, shy and brave and natural. I saw his goodness and his dreams, which had helped to make him what he was.

After that night I gave an hour of each evening that remained of his life to his comfort and pleasure. He could only speak in whispers, but what he told me added to the warmth and respect I felt for him.

Once I asked him, "Do you ever regret that you came, when you lie here suffering so much?"

"Never ma'am," he answered. "I have not helped a great deal, but I've shown I was willing to give my life, and maybe I have to. But I don't blame anybody, and if it was to do over again, I'd do it."

Then he suddenly asked: "This is my first battle. Do they think it's going to be my last?"

"I'm afraid they do, John."

It was the hardest question I ever had been called upon to answer. His clear eyes were fixed on mine, forcing a truthful answer by their own truth. He seemed a little surprised at first, as he considered the terrible fact. Then he shook his head and spoke.

"I'm not afraid, but it's difficult to believe all at once. It doesn't seem possible for such a little wound to kill me."

But John had never seen the great holes between his shoulders. He saw only the awful sights about him, and he could not believe his own wound was worse than these.

"Shall I write your mother now?" I asked, thinking that the news I had just given him might change all his plans. But I think I should have guessed his answer, knowing him as I did.

"No, ma'am, to my brother just the

same. He'll break the news to her best, and I'll add a line to her myself when you get done. I hope the answer will come in time for me to see it."

These things had happened two days earlier. Now John was dying, and the letter had not come. I had been called to many deathbeds in my life, but to none that made my heart ache as it did then. As I went in, John stretched out both hands.

"I knew you would come! I guess I'm moving on, ma'am."

He was dying so quickly that even as he spoke I saw his face grow paler. I sat down by him and wiped the drops from his forehead. I stirred the air about him with a slow wave of the fan, and waited to help him die. He stood in need of help, and I could do so little. As the doctor had said, the strong body fought against death every inch of the way. He was forced to draw each breath with pain. For hours he suffered, yet through it all, his eyes never lost their perfect calm, and his strong spirit showed in them.

Suddenly he rose up in his bed and cried out with a bitter cry that broke the silence with its terrible suffering: "For God's sake, give me air!"

It was the only cry that pain or death had squeezed from him, the only favor he had asked. None of us could grant it, for all the airs that blew were useless now. We threw up the window. The first red light of dawn was warming the sky, and we could see the rising sun. John saw it, and laid himself gently down and sighed deeply. We knew then that for him suffering was forever past. He died then, and though the heavy breaths still continued, he never spoke again. To the end he held my hand close, so close that when he was asleep at last, I could not draw it away. I felt glad that perhaps my touch had eased his hardest hour.

When they had gotten him ready for the grave, John looked to me like a hero. I felt a tender pride in my lost patient. The lovely expression on his face soon replaced the marks of pain. I longed for those who loved him best to see him as he had accepted Death.

As we stood looking at him, a letter was handed to me which had been forgotten the night before. It was John's letter, come just an hour too late for him to see it. Yet he did have it, for after I had cut some of his hair for his mother, I took off his ring to send her. Then I kissed him for her sake, and laid the letter in his hand. I felt that its place was with him. I made myself happy with the thought that even now he would have some token of the love which makes life beautiful and lives on past death.

Then I left him, glad to have known so fine a man, and carrying with me a lasting memory of him. I remembered John as he lay calmly waiting for the dawn of that long day which knows no night.

Literary Focus: *Personification*

Refer the students to the phrase "as he had accepted Death" on page 153. Ask why Death is capitalized. Assist by noting the capitalization of people's names (John, Teddy) and titles (DR. P.). Explain personification (representing a thing or an abstract idea as a person). Discuss with the class how this helps readers understand the unfamiliar or the inexplicable by presenting it in concrete terms.

Critical Thinking: *Draw Conclusions*

Ask: From what you learned about John from reading about him, what do you think his mother's letter might have said?

Mini Quiz

Write the following sentences on the board or overhead projector and call on students to fill in the blanks. Discuss the answers with the class.

1. ________ saved Teddy's life at the cost of his own.
2. John had been fatally wounded in his ________ battle.
3. John asked Alcott to write a letter to his ________.
4. At the moment of death, John cried out for ________.
5. The time of day John died was ________.

Answers

1. Kit
2. first
3. brother
4. air
5. dawn

UNDERSTAND THE SELECTION

Answers

1. a hospital during the Civil War
2. twelve
3. John
4. Kit saved Teddy's life
5. Sample answer: He saw only the small entrance wound in the front of his body.
6. Sample answer: She realized it was his last battle and that he was going to die.
7. Sample answer: He thought of others first.
8. Sample answer: I would feel sadness, compassion, and helplessness.
9. Sample answer: I might say that John gave his life for a cause he believed in.
10. Sample answer: The suffering is the same because the loss of a loved one is painful despite the reason.

Respond to Literature

Have students discuss the character of Teddy. Why do they think he acts the way he does? Are his actions and words realistic? You might mention that survivors of war and accidents in which others have been killed feel guilty. They wonder why they survived while friends or even strangers did not. Then have students discuss Dr. P's character. Do they think his attitude ("You tell him he's going to die; you're good at that sort of thing") was fair to Alcott? Did he think she could do it more sensitively than he or was he just trying to avoid an unpleasant task? Encourage diversity of opinion by noting that he could probably have avoided serving in a field hospital and Alcott does not condemn him.

Review the Selection

UNDERSTAND THE SELECTION

Recall

1. What is the setting of this selection?
2. How old is the youngest patient?
3. What patient does Alcott most admire?

Infer

4. Why did Teddy dream about Kit?
5. Why did John think his wound was not serious?
6. Why did Alcott have difficulty answering when John asked if he had been in his last battle?
7. Why did Alcott admire John so much?

Apply

8. Suppose you have to explain to John that he will die. How would you feel?
9. Suppose you were John's brother. How would you tell your mother about his death?
10. Is the suffering the same in every war?

Respond to Literature

Realism in literature is the attempt to picture things as they really are. How does this selection illustrate that trend?

WRITE ABOUT THE SELECTION

In this selection, John's mother wrote a letter to her dying son. It arrived one hour too late for John to read it. Alcott did not open it or return it; she had it buried with John. Its contents were never revealed. How do you think John's mother reacted when she learned her son was dying? Would she blame the war? What would she say to a son she would never see again? How would she comfort him?

Assume that you are that mother. You have very little time and only this letter to express your feelings to your son. Write a letter to him.

Prewriting Write an informal outline of the main points you want to include in your letter. Include details of past events you think important. You will have to assume what the relationship was between John and his mother. Think about the kind of mother such a man might have had. Also think about what John was like as a child.

Writing Use your informal outline to write your letter. In it, express your feelings for your son. As you write, keep in mind that you are writing from the perspective of a woman who is living during the time of the Civil War.

Revising When you revise your letter, be sure to include comforting thoughts.

Proofreading Read over your letter. Be sure you have used the proper punctuation for the greeting, each sentence, and the closing of the letter.

WRITE ABOUT THE SELECTION

Prewriting

Using students' suggestions, create a list of points John's mother might include in her letter. Write these on the board or an overhead transparency.

Sample points:

1. How much she loves him
2. Moments and events she remembers from his youth
3. How much she will miss him
4. Prayers for his recovery
5. Sends the love of friends and other relatives

Writing

Have each student write a letter. Remind the class to write it in the first person. Walk around the classroom, giving help to any student who is having difficulty. To elicit possible ideas, ask questions about how the students would feel and what they might want to express if a loved one was dying.

Revising

Make this a cooperative group activity. Divide the class into small groups. Have group members read their letters. After each member has finished reading, the other may make suggestions of how to add comforting thoughts.

Proofreading

Select one or two of the students' letters as models for proofreading. Put the letters on the overhead projector and have the class suggest corrections or improvements.

THINK ABOUT DIALOGUE

Dialogue is the words of real people or fictional characters. Thus, it is a conversation between two or more people. In drama, it can be the main way that the plot is developed. In nonfiction, it allows participants in a narrative to speak for themselves.

1. How does the use of dialogue in "A Night" make the people seem real?
2. Cite one example of how a speaker revealed his or her personality in dialogue.
3. Do you think Alcott understates or exaggerates the horrors of life in a wartime hospital? Explain.
4. Where is the main focus in "A Night"—on Alcott or on the men in the hospital? Explain your answer.
5. Most of the activity Alcott discusses happened in one night. Why do you think she chose to write about such a short period of time?

Reading Focus

Make Inferences As you read, you made inferences about the characters' personalities from the dialogue. What can you infer about the doctor's personality from his description of John's condition? Why do you think the author did not just report what the doctor said?

DEVELOP YOUR VOCABULARY

Sometimes a specialized vocabulary develops around a place or occupation. New words or new meanings for existing words become part of this specialized vocabulary, which is often called *jargon*. For example, if you hear the words *classroom*, *teacher*, or *schoolbus*, you immediately think of school. If you hear the words *backstage*, *cast*, or *script*, you immediately think of the theater. Can you think of other words related to the school or theater setting?

A hospital was the setting for this selection. Consequently, words commonly associated with the vocabulary of a hospital have been used. Following are words found in this selection. Review each word carefully. Look the words up in a dictionary, if necessary. Then write an original paragraph using each word at least once.

1. ambulance
2. hospital
3. medicine
4. bandage
5. rounds
6. nurse
7. doctor
8. wound

Reading Focus

Sample Answer

The doctor's dialogue indicated that he was very professional, all business, but probably compassionate. If the author had reported what the doctor said, it would have lost some of the drama. Dialogue adds interest by making the characters seem more real.

THINK ABOUT DIALOGUE

Answers

1. They speak for themselves and add naturalness to the narrative.
2. John's courage, for example, is shown in his refusal to ask for special privileges and in his calm response to the news of his own dying.
3. She understates the horrors because the war wounds are so terrible and the pain so great that no one can fully describe them.
4. The main focus is on the men. Alcott is the person who ties the lives of the men together, but her main purpose is to show the courage of the wounded men.
5. In concentrating her impressions to a short period, she could better show the many interactions that occurred in the hospital. Using a longer period of time might have overwhelmed the reader.

DEVELOP YOUR VOCABULARY

Answers

Before students write, suggest that they visualize a hospital setting. Ask if any of them have ever been a patient in, or visited a person who was a patient in, a hospital. Ask if any have seen television programs that have had hospital settings. Explain that each student should use impressions from these experiences in composing the paragraphs.

ESL Activity

Have students work in pairs to use the words from the Vocabulary activity in another setting. For example, they could use the words to describe the scene of an accident. Ask them to choose a setting and then write a short paragraph using the words in that setting.

UNIT 2 Review

WRITING APPLICATIONS

Write About Character

The characters in this unit came from different backgrounds and lived in different parts of the United States. Place any character from any selection in the setting of a different work. How would that character react? Describe that character's thoughts and words in the new setting. Include a conversation with one of the original characters from the chosen work.

Prewriting Before you begin to write, choose the character you will move. Review the setting of the selection into which you will place the character. Freewrite the character's thoughts and conversation.

Writing Introduce the work with a brief discussion of the setting. Use your freewriting as a basis for what takes place. Include physical reactions such as facial expressions, instinctive movements, and tone of voice to bring the characters to life.

Revising Be sure the setting is accurate. When describing thoughts or conversation, be sure the characters are consistent. They should not suddenly change character unless you have explained what brought about the change.

Proofreading Be certain that you have used capital letters and quotation marks correctly.

Write About Fiction

When people analyze writing, they often examine the elements of literature that apply. You have studied the elements of fiction—setting, character, plot, theme, and point of view. Choose one of the two fiction selections in this unit. Pick any three fictional elements. Decide how these elements played a role in forming your opinion of the work. You will use this information to write a critical essay.

Prewriting Write the name of the first fictional element you will discuss. List the reasons why you liked or disliked the author's use of that element. Repeat the process for the other elements you have chosen.

Writing Before you write, decide which literary elements played the most important and the least important role in forming your opinion of each work. Write about the most important element first and least important element last.

Revising Be sure that you completed each discussion of a literary element before going on to discuss the next one. If you did not write a conclusion summarizing your opinion, do so now.

Proofreading Make sure you wrote the author's name and the exact title of the selection correctly. If you used quotations, make sure they are accurate.

Writer's Toolkit CD-ROM
Encourage students to use the Pro/Con Chart (Writing Tools, Organizing Details) to complete the Prewriting activity.

Unit Review Resources

TEACHER'S RESOURCES

- Writing Process, pp. W13–W24
- Grammar, Usage, and Mechanics, pp. G13–G24
- Speaking and Listening, pp. S7–S12
- Critical Thinking, pp. C7–C12
- Choose from Reading in the Content Areas, pp. RCA1–RCA72
- **Standardized Test Preparation**
  Unit 2 Test, pp. UT3–UT4
  Choose from Standardized Test Preparation, pp. STP1–STP31

WRITING APPLICATIONS

Write About Character

Have students select one character from a selection in this unit. Then have the students choose a setting from a different selection. Pair the students. Take the class to the library. Have the students in each pair collaborate in finding more information about the setting or the character, if appropriate.

Cooperative Group Activity

Pair the students. Have them read their papers to each other. Have each partner offer suggestions for making the conversation more natural.

Writer's Toolkit CD-ROM
Encourage students to use the Descriptive Word Bin (Writing Tools, Setting) to complete the writing activity.

Write about Fiction

Have students list the elements of fiction—setting, character, plot, theme, and point of view. Let each choose the fiction selection he or she will write about. Then pair the students. Have the partners discuss details of the elements that each thinks played a role in helping them form an opinion of the work. Have the partners suggest additional details to each other.

BUILD LANGUAGE SKILLS

Vocabulary

A **homophone** is one of two or more words pronounced alike but different in meaning and spelling. When reading the printed word, you can determine which homophone an author is using from the spelling and from the context in which the word is used. When listening to spoken words, your only clue is the context.

Examples: The *council* broke up for the day, and those who had attended the meeting went home.
Again, I *counseled* peace, and my advice was heeded.

Council and *counsel* are homophones. *Council* is a noun meaning an assembly or meeting. *Counsel* can be used as a noun or a verb. It means advice or to advise.

If you had heard the example sentences spoken, you would not have had the advantage of seeing the words spelled out. However, you would have understood from the context which homophone the speaker was using. Below is a group of homophones. Write a sentence using each word in a context that provides clues to its meaning. If you do not understand the meaning of any word, look it up in the dictionary.

1. week–weak
2. earn–urn
3. coward–cowered
4. colonel–kernel
5. fowl–foul

Grammar, Usage, and Mechanics

The first word in a direct quotation or a dialogue is capitalized. A divided quotation is one in which one sentence appears in two separated parts within a single sentence. The first part of the sentence appears before a reference to the speaker. The second part appears after it. Do not capitalize the first word in the second part of a divided quotation if it is only part of a sentence.

Example: "Name it," said Middleton, "and it shall be done."

Capitalize these sentences appropriately.

1. "the dog is dead," he said.
2. General Howard replied, "you deny my authority, do you?"
3. My wife said, "here's your gun."
4. "he has come," she said, "at last."
5. "villains," I shrieked. "run."
6. "aye, Hector," he said, "we go."
7. Ichabod shouted, "he's going to throw his head at me!"
8. It was an easy thing for Dr. P. to say, "tell him he must die," but a hard thing to do.
9. I gathered the bent head in my arms . . . and said, "let me help you bear it, John."
10. "shall I write your mother now?" I asked.

Grammar, Usage, and Mechanics

Write examples on a board or overhead transparency. Point out the use of quotation marks to set off a speaker's exact words, the use of a comma to separate the quotation from other parts of the sentence, and the enclosure of the end punctuation marks.

Answers

1. "The dog is dead," he said.
2. General Howard replied, "You deny my authority, do you?"
3. My wife said, "Here's your gun."
4. "He has come," she said, "at last."
5. "Villains," I shrieked. "Run."
6. "Aye, Hector," he said, "we go."
7. Ichabod shouted, "He's going to throw his head at me!"
8. It was an easy thing for Dr. P to say, "Tell him he must die," but a hard thing to do.
9. I gathered the bent head in my arms . . . and said, "Let me help you bear it, John."
10. "Shall I write your mother?" I asked.

Cooperative Group Activity

Divide the class into small groups. Have them cooperate to write sentences for the homophones listed in the text. When all groups have completed the assignment, have each representative write the group's sentences for one set of homophones on the board. Have the class discuss the sentences and make corrections if necessary.

BUILD LANGUAGE SKILLS

Vocabulary

Sample Answers

1. A *week* is seven days./The baby is *weak* from hunger.
2. She will *earn* money by babysitting./He put the flowers in an *urn*.
3. The *coward* ran from the fight./ He *cowered* in the corner.
4. The *colonel* reviewed her troops./ The corn had many rows of *kernels*.
5. The chicken is a *fowl*./We smelled a *foul* odor.

More About Word Attack: Stress the importance of spelling all words correctly. The correct spelling of a homophone can be critical to the meaning of a written sentence.

Ask students to identify and define additional common homophones. Write their responses on a chalkboard. Possibilities are: *to*—toward, *too*—denoting excess or additional, *two*—couple.

SPEAKING AND LISTENING

Motivation

Ask students to recall talks that they particularly enjoyed. Ask how the speakers started their talks. What first captured the students' attention?

Teaching Strategy

Guide students through an explanation of how to give a talk about a work of literature. Pay special attention to the five points in the text. Allow students time in class to choose their selections. Tell students to make selections. Tell students to make sure that they have chosen a fictional work to talk about. Assign the practice as a homework activity.

Evaluation Criteria

Does the student's talk address the elements of fiction? Does the talk make the meaning of the selection clear? Was the beginning of the talk strong and interesting? Did the student deliver the talk in a positive way?

UNIT 2 Review

SPEAKING AND LISTENING

One of the goals of reading literature is to be able to talk about it with understanding and appreciation. You may want to discuss your reactions to a selection and explain why it is personally meaningful. Sometimes to discuss a selection from the point of literary analysis can be rewarding too. It can give you a deeper understanding of literature that will add to your scope of knowledge.

Your task now is to prepare a short talk about one of the fiction selections in this unit. You should center your talk around the elements of fiction: setting, characters, plot and conflict, theme, and point of view. The main purpose of your talk is to explain these elements as they relate to your selection.

To prepare your talk, review the following points:

1. Refresh your memory by reading Focus on Fiction on pp. 130–131 and understand the elements of the fiction.
2. Choose a selection that you are familiar with. Reread it and take notes on those elements that you may need to review, such as the names of characters or how the plot helps to express the theme of the story.
3. Think of a strong beginning for your talk. Try not to begin with the typical title-and-author sentence. Instead, begin in an unusual way so that your audience will be intrigued. Perhaps you will never divulge the author and title, but will ask your classmates to name them after your talk.
4. Practice your talk out loud. Stand in front of a mirror. Notice your body language. Pay attention to your posture and gestures.
5. Maintain a great attitude. Be positive. if you make a mistake in your talk, don't worry. Just go on gracefully.

Now, begin working on this assignment by choosing a selection you have enjoyed in this unit. Since you are centering this talk on the elements of the fiction, your choice will be limited. However, if your teacher doesn't object, you can go to another unit and make a selection from there. Your talk should be at least three minutes. You can share it with the whole class or with a small group as your teacher directs.

CRITICAL THINKING

Sequencing A **sequence** is a group of items organized according to a planned pattern. If you arrange the names of class members according to the grade each student made on a test, you have listed them in **numerical order**. A dictionary lists words according to their place in the alphabet, that is, in **alphabetical order**.

Literature often makes use of three other sequencing orders. Events in narratives, both fictional and nonfictional, are often written in the order in which the events occurred. That is, they are written in **chronological**, or **time order**. Descriptions are often written in **spatial order**. This means that the writer describes them according to how they are arranged physically, or according to their location, or place, in space.

In expository and persuasive writing, items are frequently arranged according to the **order of importance**. Reasons for an event or arguments in favor of a cause are given according to their importance.

Choose one selection you have recently read and ask these questions:

1. What order was used in organizing this narrative (or description or persuasive passage)?
2. Explain what other order may have worked as well or better.

EFFECTIVE STUDYING

Preparing for Tests A test measures your knowledge of certain subject material. Doing your best on a test requires both long-term and short-term planning and work. Doing well in a subject requires that follow certain guidelines

1. Long-term plan:
   - As you read, make an outline of the important points to remember.
   - Take notes in class as you listen carefully to the discussions.
   - Ask questions when you do not understand what has been discussed.
   - Always complete any assignment thoroughly and on time.
2. Short-term plan:
   - Be sure to understand exactly what material will be included in the test. If necessary, ask your teacher to clarify.
   - Briefly review the text by skimming reading selections you have read.
   - Thoroughly review all your outlines, notes, and the correct answers to your assignments.
   - On the day of the test, eat a good meal, relax, and do your best.

Test Preparation

When answering an essay test question, read the question more than once to make sure you know what is being asked. If possible, ask the teacher to clarify any words or questions you don't understand.

CRITICAL THINKING

Answers

1. chronological, or time, order for a narrative; space order for a description; logical order for a persuasive passage
2. Answers will vary.

EFFECTIVE STUDYING

Teaching Strategy

Read the following questions to the class and have students answer them. Then discuss the answers.

1. Taking a test provides a measure of ________. (*knowledge in a subject*)
2. An outline is part of a long-term study plan that helps you ________. (*note important points to remember*)
3. Ask questions to ________. (*clear up misunderstandings; get more information*)
4. Before a test you should review ________. (*your notes, outline, the text, answers to assignments*)
5. You should relax on the day of the test to ________. (*relieve stress so you can do better*)

Career Connection

After reading Alcott's "A Night" from *Hospital Sketches*, students might consider a career as part of a medical team. An important member of this team in the Emergency Medical Technician (EMT). An EMT is not a doctor or a nurse but is a paramedic who works from a specially equipped ambulance. The EMT paramedic must be, at least, a high school graduate and have passed a comprehensive first-aid and specialized equipment training program. Before EMTs are certified, they must also complete a practical training program at a hospital and learn the rudimentary principles of automobile mechanics.

Emergency Medical Technicians always work in teams. One member radios the condition of the victim to a doctor at a hospital while others comfort the victim and administer the proper emergency treatment. This treatment may include heart and lung resuscitation or the administration of oxygen or drugs. EMT teams also rescue trapped individuals.

UNIT ACTIVITY

A Continuing Unit Project: Testing Students' Knowledge And Recall

In this unit, students are going to participate in an ongoing quiz to test their recall and mastery of the material in each selection. To stimulate their interest, quizzes will be presented in a game format, "The New England Express." After reviewing the introductory material, organize students into small groups. Allow each group to select a name by which they will be collectively known during the game. Have each group choose an emblem or visual depiction (owl, lion, crown, pirate, and so forth) to represent its group during the course of the game. Each group must identify its emblem. Resolve any duplicate choices with a coin toss. Tell each group to draw two visual representations of its emblem on construction paper and to cut them out. Collect and store them in an envelope for future use.

Purchase small white boards and dry erase markers so that each small group can have one. Provide erasers or tissues for students to erase answers.

Obtain a roll of inexpensive, white shelf paper. Plot out a length that matches the length of the chalkboard in the front of the room. Affix the cardboard core to one end of the shelf paper. With the help of students interested in extra credit, plan a railway, subway, or bus line. Include a depot as a starting point, eight stations or stops, and a destination, all equidistant from each other. Let students suggest a name for the depot and the destination. Guide them in selecting appropriate names. The stations will be designated as follows:

Longfellow Lane
Thoreau Pond
Emerson Park
Hawthorne Street
Dickinson Square
Lowell Place
Melville Avenue
Whittier Way

On the day you complete each selection, unroll the paper and fasten each end to the chalkboard in the front of the room. At the end of each selection, ask the following questions (see below). Each group is to consult quietly among themselves and arrive at consensual answers. Tell each group to select a person to write their answers on their white board. When finished, another member should hold these answers up for you to see. (Be sure you have arranged the groups in such a way that one group cannot see another's answers.) If the answers are correct, another member of the group will fasten the group's emblem to the appropriate station, moving progressively through the unit. If any group does not provide the correct answers, do not advance the emblem. Tell that group to review the material. The group will be required to answer those questions and the questions for the next selection in order to advance its emblem.

Longfellow Lane

Paul Revere was alerted by signal lights hung in the belfry of the ______.

At one o'clock, Paul Revere galloped into ______; at two, he came to ______ town.

According to Longfellow, a ______ can soothe a restless feeling and banish the thoughts of day.

Thoreau Pond

______ was the stream that Thoreau went a-fishing in.

According to Thoreau, if a man does not keep pace with his companions, perhaps it is because he hears a ______.

Thoreau said, "Only that day dawns to which we are ______."

Emerson Park

Emerson believed that in good health the ______ is a drink of incredible goodness.

According to Emerson, Nature always wears the colors of the ______.

Hawthorne Street

In "David Swan," the merchant's dead son had been named ______.

The rogues were scared away from David Swan by the appearance of a ______.

Unknown to him, while David slept ______, ______, and ______ had passed right beside his path.

Dickinson Square

To Dickinson, the frog, by croaking, was telling its _______ in public.

Dickinson associates _______ with a moor and a wave with the _______.

Dickinson kept the Sabbath by _______.

Lowell Place

According to the poet, the merciful _______ made the snow-fall.

According to the poet, _______ fell from [that] cloud like snow.

Melville Avenue

The novel *Moby-Dick* begins with the words, "Call me Ishmael." The novel is written in the first person. Who was the narrator of Moby-Dick?

The twisted harpoons in Moby-Dick resembled a _______.

Ahab has two antagonists. The whale, Moby-Dick, is one; the ship's mate, _______, is the other.

Whittier Way

Since leaving Bornou land, the slave population has decreased. "Life has one, and death has two" means that two out of every _______ slaves has died.

Whittier was an American abolitionist poet. What frequently repeated line suggests the ultimate destination of the slaves?

ANSWERS TO QUIZ

Longfellow Lane
1. Old North Church
2. Lexington; Concord
3. poem

Thoreau Pond
1. Time
2. different drummer
3. awake

Emerson Park
1. air
2. spirit

Hawthorne Street
1. Henry
2. dog
3. Wealth, Love, Death

Dickinson Square
1. name
2. heather; sea
3. staying at home

Lowell Place
1. Father
2. patience

Melville Avenue
1. Ishmael
2. corkscrew
3. Starbuck

Whittier Way
1. three
2. "Where are we going, Rubee?"

For additional motivation, allow different groups to suggest ideas for a neighborhood that would surround each station. Encourage the groups to suggest not only homes, schools, theaters, and restaurants, but also cultural or educational facilities that might reflect the ideas expressed by that writer. Examples could include historical sites (Longfellow), gardens (Thoreau), woods (Emerson), and so forth. Guide students in choosing symbols that might suggest that kind of facility (spire for a church, Doric columns for a museum, book covers for a library, vines for a garden, trees for woods, and so forth). With student assistance, reproduce these symbols on the shelf paper.

If your class requires more structure, create specific questions for each selection. Some possible questions follow.

■ from "Paul Revere's Ride"

What do you think is the word that shall echo forevermore?

■ from "The Day Is Done"

How is the saying "Music has charms to soothe the savage breast" similar to the theme of this poem?

■ from *Walden*

How would you apply the idea "simplify, simplify," to your own life or the lives of people you know or have seen on television?

■ **from "Nature"**

What conclusions would you draw about your relationship to nature from your environment?

■ **"David Swan"**

What three unrealized experiences do you think may have passed by you, with the silent footsteps of the things that almost happen?

■ **"I never saw a Moor"**

Identify two things you have never seen. What one characteristic of each would you use in visualizing those things?

■ **"The First Snow-fall"**

If you were going to use a snowfall as the backdrop for a poem, what kind of experiences would you describe?

■ **from *Moby-Dick***

If you were on a ship that came upon the sole survivor of the *Pequod*, what would you think listening to his tale?

■ **"Song of Slaves in the Desert"**

If Whittier were writing today, what current American issue do you think he would choose?

Require students to illustrate their answers. Allow them to draw pictures or cartoons, to develop symbolic representations, or to cut and paste magazine pictures. After the unit has been completed, collect and evaluate the students' work.

■ **from "Paul Revere's Ride"**

by Henry Wadsworth Longfellow (page 165)

■ **from "The Day Is Done"**

by Henry Wadsworth Longfellow (page 169)

SELECTION SYNOPSES

"Paul Revere's Ride" is a narrative poem in which Longfellow recounts a famous event in American history. Paul Revere was a Boston silversmith and patriot. On April 18, 1775, he set out on horseback to warn revolutionary colonists in the towns of Lexington and Concord that British troops were approaching. His ride carried him past midnight, into the early morning hours of April 19. That morning, armed colonists clashed with British troops on the town green in Lexington, driving the king's soldiers back. The Revolutionary War had begun. The theme is that heroism and love of freedom are immortal values.

"The Day is Done" is a meditative poem. As darkness falls, the poet reflects upon the ability of poetry, particularly when read aloud, to relieve tension and soothe the mind.

SELECTION ACTIVITY

Prepare the following exercises for completion during the class period. You may distribute them to the class as a typed or printed handout. You may prefer to list each, one at a time, on the chalkboard or overhead projector.

Before distributing or listing, arrange students into small groups. To the extent possible, make each group heterogeneous. Try to include in each group at least one student who has demonstrated some comprehension of literary material beyond the literal level; at least one student, who, while showing less interpretive ability, has demonstrated enthusiasm and a willingness to work to the fullest potential; and at least one student who has difficulty with the material.

Explain that students should work together within the group to reach consensual answers. Working independently, they should answer each question one at a time. The answers should be written in pencil in their notebooks. Group members should then discuss among themselves the answer each has written, offering explanations for the choices they have made. Once a consensus has been reached, members write the group answer into the notebooks.

If you notice any group having difficulty reaching a consensus, intervene and offer guidance. Be certain you allow every student to express a view concerning the chosen answer. Do not criticize any student who has made an honest effort but has chosen an incorrect or less appropriate answer.

Guide students toward the correct or more appropriate answer using phrases such as the following: "I can understand how you might have arrived at that conclusion." "That's an interesting interpretation; it shows you have given some thought to the matter." Guide them with questions such as the following: ". . . But have you considered this fact?" "Have you thought about what the poet says here?" (pointing to a clarifying line or passage). When using information presented by other students who have chosen the correct or more appropriate answer, include information from more than one student. In this circumstance, praise all students for their efforts. Tell them that this kind of discussion is an educational experience. Tell them that if two people agree on everything they discuss, it shows that only one of them is thinking.

Exercise 1

1. The date on which Paul Revere set out on this ride was _______.
2. The British man-of-war in Boston Harbor was named the _______.
3. At midnight, Revere rode into _______ town.
4. In Concord, he heard that _______ of the flock.
5. The colonists who fought that day were not part of an organized army but local _______.

Exercise 2

(For each of these questions, be prepared to support your answer with evidence from the text.)

1. Was the poet telling his tale shortly after Revere's ride or many years later?
2. If the British had been more alert, at what point might they have intercepted Revere before he could warn the colonists?
3. Did the British troops travel by land or sea?
4. If there had been no clock in Concord, how would Revere have been able to estimate the time?
5. A siege is a battle in which one army occupies a set position around a city or other fortified place and attacks the other army, which remains behind the fortifications and fights defensively. Was the battle of Lexington a siege?

Exercise 3

Ask volunteers to state the mathematical formula for computing the rate of speed. If none can, write it for them on the chalkboard: Rate (speed) equals Distance divided by Time, or

$$R = D/T$$

Medford is five miles from Boston. Lexington is eleven miles from Boston. (If necessary, state this as Lexington is six miles from Medford.) Concord is twenty-one miles from Boston. (If necessary, state this as Concord is ten miles from Lexington.)

1. How fast was Revere's horse going between Medford and Lexington?
2. How fast was Revere's horse going between Lexington and Concord?
3. Relying on the answers to 1 and 2, do you think Longfellow was using exact timing in describing the ride? Why or why not?
4. If driving a modern automobile at 60 miles an hour, how long would it have taken Revere to travel from Medford to Lexington?
5. Driving at that same speed, how long would it have taken him to drive from Lexington to Concord?

from *Walden*

by Henry David Thoreau (page 175)

SELECTION SYNOPSIS

At the age of 27, Thoreau, a Harvard graduate and successful, innovative teacher, walked away from civilization. He went to live in a cabin in the woods near Walden Pond. He adopted this lifestyle because he "wished to live thoughtfully, to face only the bare facts of life." Thoreau spent two years in this isolated setting, learning from Nature what it had to teach. While there, he wrote a book recounting a river journey he and his now dead brother had taken several years before. He also kept a journal of his days spent in the woods. This journal became the basis for *Walden*. The book is a collection of closely related essays. Some are philosophical, exploring the meaning of life; others are practical, discussing a disciplined, economical lifestyle. Still others are vivid seasonal accounts of the natural setting and the animals that inhabit it. All are beautifully crafted, highly original, and thoughtful examples of the essayist's art.

SELECTION ACTIVITY

Divide the class into groups, and have each group discuss what kinds of seeds Thoreau may have chosen before settling in at Walden. Guide them by suggesting that they combine the practical aspects with the pleasing.

You might invite the biology teacher to speak to the class and explain the growth of plants from seeds. You might also ask that teacher to help the class choose seeds that germinate easily and help them plan a garden arrangement. Tomatoes are an example of such a vegetable. Marigolds are an example of such a flower. You might also explain that organic gardeners believe that a marigold border is a natural way to keep insects from attacking vegetable crops.

Have each group list the seeds they have selected. Collect the lists and save them for future reference. At the proper time of the year, return the lists to students. Purchase some inexpensive seed packets. Permit each group to plant and cultivate two kinds of seeds in pots in the classroom. Assign each group member, on a daily rotation, the job of caring for that group's seeds as they germinate.

from "Nature"

by Ralph Waldo Emerson (page 184)

SELECTION SYNOPSIS

This is a formal essay in which the writer examines the relationship between humans and the universe around them. He finds in nature an inner peace that results from the realization that a harmony exists between people and nature if only we take the time to look for it.

SELECTION ACTIVITY

Emerson says that he can find perfect happiness even when crossing a commons. A commons is a small city park. Encourage students to recall a visit to a city park or the local zoo. Have them review Emerson's description of crossing a commons. Tell students to draw a picture of the park or zoo as they recall it. You may want to use this as a prompt for a writing exercise. If so, use the writing process described throughout this text.

"David Swan"

by Nathaniel Hawthorne (page 189)

SELECTION SYNOPSIS

Set in early America, Hawthorne's story concerns what does not happen to a youth, named David Swan, on his journey to Boston to start clerking in an uncle's store. Feeling tired, David lies down to rest in a roadside grove. Soon, he falls asleep. A rich merchant's coach breaks down nearby, and while awaiting repair of their vehicle, the merchant and his wife enter the grove and spy the sleeping David. His open, honest face makes them consider waking him and taking him as a possible replacement for their "departed Henry." But when their servant informs them that the coach is repaired, the romantic notion of bringing David into the family business makes them feel rather ridiculous, and they depart. Then a charming young girl enters the grove to fix her garter. She and David are potentially an ideal couple, but again David sleeps and nothing happens. Finally, two thieves enter the grove. They are about to rob and perhaps kill David when a dog appears. Fearing the possible approach of the dog's owner, the two depart. David then awakes and continues his journey, unaware of all that almost happened.

SELECTION ACTIVITY

Follow the same preparations as for the exercise following "Paul Revere's Ride." Present the following exercises to the groups.

Exercise 1

Write one or two sentences that might follow each of the sentences below.

1. A young man traveling to Boston, feeling tired, stops to rest in a quiet grove.
2. A rich merchant and his wife, whose son has recently died, see him sleeping.
3. A charming young woman accidentally comes upon the sleeping figure.
4. Two criminals, seeing him, plot to steal his clothes and maybe kill him.
5. The young man awakes.

Exercise 2

Write one or two sentences that might follow each of the sentences below.

1. A poor but honest and hard-working young man takes a low-paying job, feeding and watering the horses at the Stagecoach Hill Inn, where Boston-bound travelers stop to rest.
2. He overhears a rich merchant and his wife talking. Their son, about his age, has just died. They would like to adopt a son but have no idea how to go about it. He thinks about approaching them.
3. He sees a charming young girl, the daughter of a thriving merchant. She is disillusioned by the shallowness of the young men in her social circle. He almost speaks to her, but he is too shy.
4. He hears two thieves talking. They are about to discuss plans for their next crime. As they start to leave, a dog barks at their horses, startling them. He turns to chase the dog, and they leave without seeing him.
5. The travelers continue on their respective journeys.

"I'm nobody"/"A word is dead"/"I never saw a Moor"/"The sky is low"/Some keep the Sabbath"/ "Letter to Thomas Wentworth Higginson"

by Emily Dickinson (page 199)

SELECTION SYNOPSES

Emily Dickinson's poems are short, highly original glimpses at the universal truths revealed by everyday experience.

Also included in this selection is a letter from Dickinson to the person who became her mentor.

SELECTION ACTIVITY

Arrange students in heterogeneous groups. Distribute the following handouts to each group. Have each group collaborate on reproducing a poem by Emily Dickinson. Remind them that the first letter in a poetic line is capitalized.

Title: Surgeons Must Be Very Careful
Terminal or end rhymes: careful
knife
incisions
Life
Other words: must, very, Surgeons, be
the, they, when, take, fine, their, underneath
culprit, stirs, the

If the entire class is having difficulty, provide the first word in each line. Guide students in a discussion of the theme presented in the poem.

Poem
Surgeons must be very careful
When they take the knife
Underneath their fine incisions
Lurks the culprit,—Life

"The First Snow-fall"

by James Russell Lowell (page 210)

SELECTION SYNOPSIS

The poem is a father's loving remembrance of his deceased little daughter. The falling snow reminds him of the gravesite in Mount Auburn where she is buried, and he compares the healing process following her death to the gradual accumulation of snowflakes.

SELECTION ACTIVITY

This poem, like much poetry, was inspired by strong emotions; in this case, loved mingled with grief. Have students brainstorm a list of strong emotions that might inspire a literary work. For example, students might name hate, fear, triumph, or joy.

Then have students choose one of the emotions from the list. Have each student write an original poem inspired by the emotion. Students might even try using Lowell's rhyme scheme and cadence. When students are finished, you might ask for volunteers to have a class poetry reading.

from *Moby-Dick*

by Herman Melville (page 215)

SELECTION SYNOPSIS

The novel is set in the mid-18th century. A young man, named Ishmael, has a romantic urge to become a sailor. He travels to the New England coast in hope of finding a job on a whaling ship. Staying in an inn, he shares a room with a tattooed harpooner from the South Seas, named Queequeg. Despite their cultural differences, the two become friends and decide to be shipmates.

Ishmael and Queequeg find employment on the *Pequod*, a whaling ship about to depart on a long hunt. The captain of the *Pequod* is Ahab, an experienced but mysterious figure who is viewed with a mixture of fear and awe by the local inhabitants. As Ishmael and Queequeg are about to board ship, they are accosted by a strange figure who warns them against the venture. The stranger mentions three hearses, or wooden vehicles, to convey the dead to the grave. He prophesies doom for all but one who ship out on the *Pequod*. When asked his name, he replies, "Elijah," the name of a biblical prophet who foresaw the destruction of Israel. Though shaken, the two friends are determined to embark.

On board ship, Ishmael learns the seaman's trade from the ship's officers, Starbuck, Stubb, and Flask. These three are brave and experienced whalers. Ahab remains shut up in his cabin. Although they do not see him, the crew, as they lie in their bunks below, hear Ahab pacing the deck in the dark of night. They know his step, for Ahab has lost a leg and suffered other injuries in an unsuccessful attempt to capture the legendary white whale, known to sailors as Moby-Dick.

One day, as the ship enters whaling waters, Ahab appears on deck. He announces the real purpose of the voyage as he sees it. He has spent years plotting the migration of the white whale. The *Pequod* has not sailed in search of profit to be made from whale oil. Ahab wants vengeance; he is interested only in finding and killing Moby-Dick. Starbuck is appalled. Those on board have signed a contract, pledging to return a profit to those bankers who financed the voyage. More importantly, he believes that seeking vengeance against an animal that acted only in defense of its life is blasphemy, or contempt, for the laws of nature. Ahab replies, "Speak not to me of blasphemy, man, I'd strike Heaven on the face if it insulted me."

Almost against their will, the crew is drawn into Ahab's plan by his will and his obsession for vengeance. Starbuck, believing Ahab is insane, considers mutiny. Stubb and Flask do not support him. They respect Starbuck, and distrust Ahab's judgment. However, the captain's word is law.

The *Pequod* encounters another whaling ship, the *Rachel*. The captain of that ship has seen Moby-Dick. He has lost a boat full of crewmen, including his own son, in an attempt to harpoon the white whale. He asks Ahab to interrupt his own hunt to help search for the missing crewmen (a common courtesy observed by all whalers). Ahab refuses. He wants only to know where Moby-Dick was last sighted and sails on.

Queequeg foresees his own death. He orders a coffin to be built and retreats within himself. The ship sails on. At long last, Ahab sights his enemy. He and his crew set out in small boats to harpoon the whale. In the ensuing struggle, the *Pequod* is sunk. Only Ishmael survives, clinging to the floating wooden coffin that his friend Queequeg had ordered. The *Rachel* comes by. Searching for its own lost crewmen, it finds another orphan of the sea, Ishmael.

SELECTION ACTIVITY

Group students heterogeneously. Have each group collaborate on producing two short whale songs, using rhyme:

1. This might be the song that Moby-Dick would have sung as he saw the *Pequod* approaching. Suggest the following words as end rhymes for each line of the song: danger/stranger; deep/sleep.
2. This might be the song that whales sing as they peacefully migrate. Suggest the following words as end rhymes for each line of the song: west/best; roam/home.

■ "Song of Slaves in the Desert"

by John Greenleaf Whittier (page 233)

SELECTION SYNOPSIS

The subject of this poem is the slave trade. The theme is the inhumanity of the slave trade.

SELECTION ACTIVITY

Divide the class into small groups, and take the class to the library. Have each group use encyclopedias, books, and the Internet to research the abolitionist movement in America. Using their research, have each group collaborate on writing a two-paragraph essay on the origins and efforts of the abolitionist movement. Have each group select one member to read aloud their report about the abolitionists. After each group has finished, allow the class time to comment and discuss any issue concerning this movement.

STUDENT READING LIST

Dickinson, Emily. *Complete Poems of Emily Dickinson*. Boston: Little, Brown, and Company, 1924.

Hawthorne, Nathaniel. *The Scarlet Letter*. New York: Bantam Books, 1981.

Longfellow, Henry Wadsworth. *Complete Poetical Works of Henry Wadsworth Longfellow*. Boston: Houghton Mifflin, 1920.

Lukes, Bonnie L. *Henry Wadsworth Longfellow: America's Beloved Poet*. Morgan Reynolds. 1998.

Melville, Herman. *Billy Budd*. Garden City, New York: Doubleday, 1961.

Philip, Neil (ed.) *Stockings of Buttermilk: American Folktales*. Clarion, 1999.

From Globe Fearon Educational Publisher

Adapted Classics

Moby-Dick by Herman Melville

The Scarlet Letter by Nathaniel Hawthorne

Pacemaker Classics

The House of the Seven Gables by Nathaniel Hawthorne

An American Family Series

The Journey Home

Fortune in Men's Eyes

UNIT 3 Overview

UNIT OBJECTIVES

After completing this unit, students will be able to

- understand four elements of poetry—figurative language, character/speaker, connotation and denotation, and sound devices
- read aloud to convey mood and feeling
- use effective strategies for following directions
- use knowledge of literary elements in order to write creatively and analytically
- understand and identify theme, essay, rhyme, imagery, and conflict
- use context clues to figure out word meanings
- understand and identify synonyms and antonyms
- understand and identify homophones
- identify specific and general words
- understand eponymous words
- use classifying and categorizing skills

UNIT SELECTIONS

This unit focuses on 19th-century New England literature, particularly writers from around the Boston, Massachusetts area.

- from **"Paul Revere's Ride"** (p. 165) tells about historic events that occurred in 1775 between the colonists and their British rulers. A second Longfellow poem excerpt from **"The Day Is Done"** (p. 169) completes the selection.
  LITERARY SKILL: rhyme
  READING SKILL: understand figures of speech
  VOCABULARY: words in context
  WRITING: poem extension

- from ***Walden*** by Thoreau (p. 175) and from **"Nature"** by Emerson (p. 184) present two authors' views on living with nature.
  LITERARY SKILL: essay
  READING SKILL: identify supporting details
  VOCABULARY: allusion/eponymous words
  WRITING: descriptive paragraph
- **"David Swan"** (p. 189) is a short-story fantasy.
  LITERARY SKILL: theme
  READING SKILL: draw conclusions
  VOCABULARY: synonyms
  WRITING: narrative of imaginary event
- **Works of Emily Dickinson** (p. 199) consists of five brief poems and a letter written by this popular poet.
  LITERARY SKILL: sounds in poetry
  READING SKILL: make inferences
  VOCABULARY: figurative language
  WRITING: expository paragraphs supported by reasons

New England Speaks

We looked upon a world unknown,
On nothing we could call our own.
Around the glistening wonder bent
The blue walls of the firmament,
No cloud above, no earth below,—
A universe of sky and snow!
—John Greenleaf Whittier

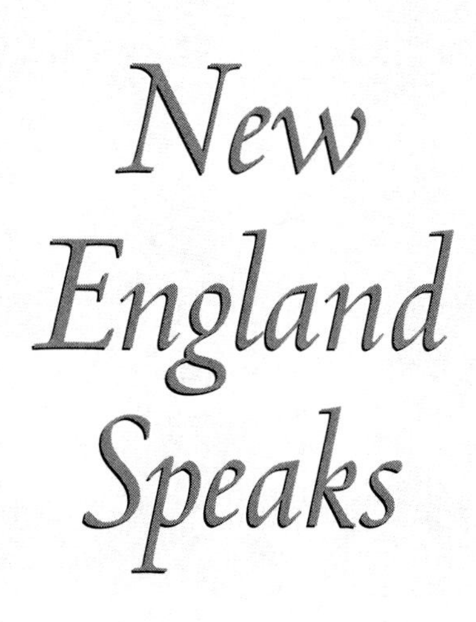

Morning Light, Walter Elmer Schofield. Giraudon/Art Resource

Introducing the Literary Period

Have a volunteer read the unit opening quotation by Whittier while students look at the painting by Schofield. Then lead a group discussion in which students tell how the opening quote and the painting might be reflective of 19th-century New England literature.

Viewing Fine Art

Walter Elmer Schofield was born in Philadelphia, Pennsylvania in 1867. He attended the Academy of Fine Arts in Philadelphia and also studied in Paris, France. His specialty was landscape painting, and *Morning Light* is very representative of landscapes that were painted in the 19th century. People were incredibly optimistic about the future of young America, and painters and other artists reflected this optimism in their sculpture, portraits, and landscapes. This painting shows a sunny view of a brook after a winter storm. Ask: How does a sunny view after a winter storm show optimism?

- **"The First Snow-fall,"** (p. 210) is the model selection. The poem is about a father's grief for a child.
  Literary Skill: elements of poetry—figurative language, character/speaker, connotation and denotation, and sound devices
  Reading Skill: paraphrase
  Vocabulary: homophones
  Writing: write a literary criticism
- from ***Moby-Dick*** (p. 215) demonstrates an epic struggle between an individual and the forces of nature. An except is provided.
  Literary Skill: conflict
  Reading Skill: visualize
  Vocabulary: antonyms
  Writing: journal entry
- **"Song of Slaves in the Desert"** (p. 233) is a moving poem in which Whittier expresses his distress over slavery.
  Literary Skill: imagery
  Reading Skill: understand contrast
  Vocabulary: general and specific words
  Writing: poetry extension

RELATED MATERIALS

1. ***Civil War Songbook*** [Songbook with historical commentary, WEM Records, 1999.] McNeil, Keith and Rusty. (eds.)
2. ***Words Like Blades: The Life and Work of Emily Dickinson*** [Video, Chip Taylor Video, 1998.] This video is an excellent tribute to an admirable woman.
3. ***Nathaniel Hawthorne*** [Video, 28 mins., Films for the Humanities and Sciences, 1998.] This video presents a journey through the themes, plots and symbolism in the author's major pieces.
4. ***Moby-Dick*** [Video, 41 mins., Films for the Humanities and Sciences, 1998.] This educational video offers an entertaining guide to the classic tale.
5. The following Web sites may also be helpful. Please note that some Internet addresses change frequently. These are the latest versions:

   Emily Dickinson, Heart's Ease Library at *http://www.hearts-ease.org/library/dickinson/index.html*

   The Home Forum, Paul Revere's Ride at *http://www.csmonitor.com/durable/1998/04/14/p8s2.htm*

   Bibliomania, Chapter V: The New England Poets at *http://www.bibliomania.com/Reference/Simonds/SHAL/pl-chap5.html#hen*

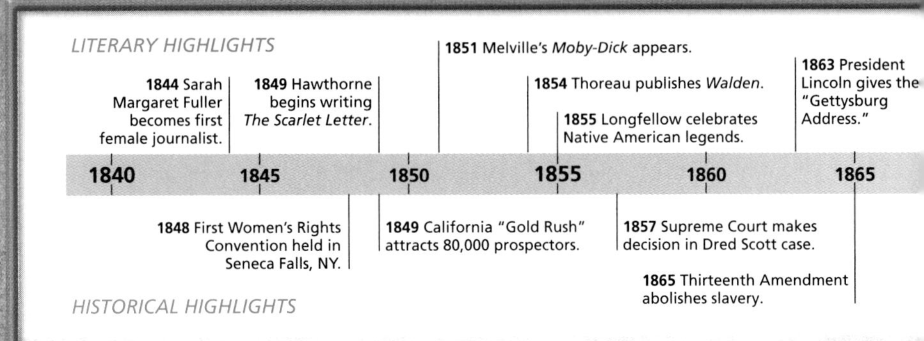
LITERARY HIGHLIGHTS
1844 Sarah Margaret Fuller becomes first female journalist.
1849 Hawthorne begins writing The Scarlet Letter.
1851 Melville's Moby-Dick appears.
1854 Thoreau publishes Walden.
1855 Longfellow celebrates Native American legends.
1863 President Lincoln gives the "Gettysburg Address."
1840
1845
1850
1855
1860
1865
1848 First Women's Rights Convention held in Seneca Falls, NY.
1849 California "Gold Rush" attracts 80,000 prospectors.
1857 Supreme Court makes decision in Dred Scott case.
1865 Thirteenth Amendment abolishes slavery.
HISTORICAL HIGHLIGHTS

New England Speaks

The America of the 1800s was a land of great variation. Would you have preferred the wild West or the sophisticated East? If you like outdoor life, you would have enjoyed pioneering in the West. If you prefer to spend time discussing ideas, you would have been happy in the eastern part of the country.

THE IMPORTANCE OF AMERICAN IDEAS

In 1800, Thomas Jefferson was elected president. Jefferson dreamed of the United States as a strong nation of individuals. This thought helped to shape America over the next hundred years. Writers no longer turned to Europe for their ideas. Instead they wanted to write about their experiences in their own country.

THE TRANSCENDENTALISTS

New England, particularly the area around Boston, was especially famous for the number of writers it produced and the influence of their ideas. One Boston group, the Transcendentalists, often met at Ralph Waldo Emerson's home. The Transcendentalists believed that people should examine their innermost feelings. Returning to nature, they thought, would help them to do this. One member of the group, Henry David Thoreau, built a humble cabin at Walden Pond near Boston, where he lived alone for over two years. His book, *Walden*, about this experience is still read all over the world.

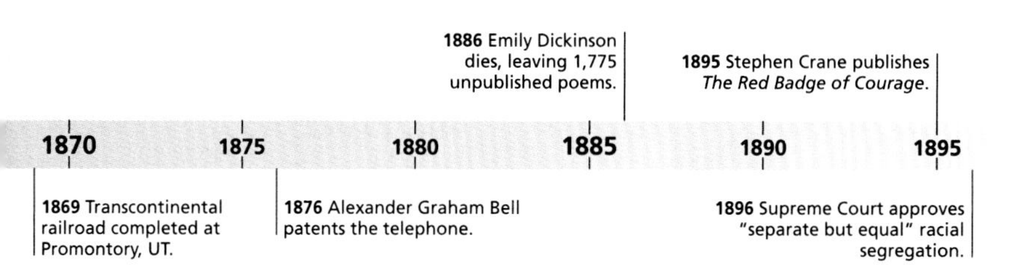
1886 Emily Dickinson dies, leaving 1,775 unpublished poems.
1895 Stephen Crane publishes The Red Badge of Courage.
1870
1875
1880
1885
1890
1895
1869 Transcontinental railroad completed at Promontory, UT.
1876 Alexander Graham Bell patents the telephone.
1896 Supreme Court approves "separate but equal" racial segregation.

The Transcendentalists influenced many writers who were not members of the group, including poet Emily Dickinson. Though only two of Dickinson's poems were published during her lifetime, today she is considered one of America's finest writers.

■ THE ABOLITIONISTS

Many 19th century writers were active in the movement to abolish slavery. Among the New England writers who protested slavery were Henry David Thoreau and the poets James Russell Lowell and John Greenleaf Whittier.

■ OTHER INFLUENCES

Some New England writers of the period did not belong to any particular group but rather based their themes on their personal experiences and interests. Nathaniel Hawthorne and Henry Wadsworth Longfellow, for example, both derived some of their inspiration from history. Herman Melville, a New Yorker, spent many years working on whaling ships. On these voyages, he gathered information for several of his books. Melville is included here because he was influenced by the Transcendentalists and because whaling is considered to be a New England topic.

The selections in this unit focus on literature from New England in the 1800s. As you read the selections, think about the ideas they contain. What thoughts and feelings do you share with the writers? Can you see how growing up in America shaped their writing?

Discussing the Literary Period

Guide students through the Period Discussion, having them pay particular attention to the influences on 19th-century New England literature. Then have them jot down where they would have enjoyed living in America in the 1800s and why. Finally, have them think about how their thoughts and feelings might have been shaped by the places they chose.

Cooperative Group Activity

Divide the class into two groups based on a part of the country they choose, either East or West. Have each group think of themselves as writers, gathering information to write books. When the groups have completed their lists, have a volunteer from each group present the group's ideas to the class. Save the lists so that students can add to them as they read the unit and have other insights about how writers gather information.

Selection Overview

UNIT OBJECTIVES

After completing these selections, students will be able to

- understand rhyme
- create a four-line stanza for a poem
- analyze rhyme in a poem
- pair words that rhyme
- understand figures of speech

Lesson Resources

from *Paul Revere's Ride*/
from *The Day Is Done*
- Selection Synopses, Teacher's Edition, p. T159d
- Comprehension and Vocabulary Workbook, pp. 35–36
- Language Enrichment Workbook, pp. 18–19
- Teacher's Resources
  Reinforcement, p. R18
  Test, pp. T35–T36

More About Rhyme

Encourage students to think about rhyming words that might create the feeling of a horse galloping down a dirt road. You might start them off with the word *flight*. Have volunteers write on the chalkboard several more words that rhyme with *flight*.

More About the Literary Period

In this selection, Henry Wadsworth Longfellow looked back to an event that had happened eighty years earlier. This event changed the course of history in the United States.

Background Notes

In the spring of 1775, the colonists had gathered together a large supply of weapons in Concord, a town near Boston. They were quite sure the British would try to capture the weapons, but they couldn't figure out which route the British could take. The British decided to go by water, and it was Dr. Joseph Warren who sent Paul Revere and William Dawes to alert the people of Concord that the British were coming.

Learn About

Rhyme

Poets use various techniques to convey their ideas and feelings. One of the devices a poet uses is repetition of sounds to create rhyme. In poetry, **rhyme** is a regular repetition of sounds.

There are two ways in which a poet can use rhyme in a poem. The kind of rhyme most frequently used is **end rhyme**. End rhymes occur when words at the end of lines rhyme with each other. *Splash* and *crash* rhyme in these lines:

Tiny waves just splash
While giant waves do crash
Upon the silent shore.

However, some writers use internal rhymes; that is, words that rhyme within a single line. In this line, *Squirrels leaping and creeping on waving branches*, the words *leaping* and *creeping* are an example of internal rhyme.

As you read the following poems, ask yourself:

1. Would the flow of the poems change if Longfellow had not used rhyme?
2. How did Longfellow's use of rhyme contribute to the pace of the poem?

Reading Focus

Understand Figures of Speech A simile is a comparison of two things using *like* or *as*. For example, "the pencil was red" might be written as "the pencil was as red as a licorice stick." A metaphor also compares but without the use of the words *like* or *as*. As you read "Paul Revere's Ride," look for these types of figures of speech. Think about how these figures of speech help create the mood, or feeling, of the poem.

WRITING CONNECTION

Make a list of six pairs of rhyming words. Then use one pair of words to write an end rhyme.

ESL Activity

Have students write down words from the list of words on the worksheet in the Language Enrichment Workbook on page 18. Mention the possibility that some words that rhyme will not be spelled the same. Also mention the possibility of homophones.

Cooperative Group Activity

For the Writing Connection activity, have students work in pairs to make a list of words that rhyme. Give each pair of students a word with which to start, or have them think of their own words.

from
Paul Revere's Ride

by Henry Wadsworth Longfellow

Listen, my children, and you shall hear
Of the midnight ride of Paul Revere,
On the eighteenth of April, in Seventy-five;
Hardly a man is now alive
5 Who remembers that famous day and year.[1]

He said to his friend, "If the British march
By land or sea from the town to-night,
Hang a lantern aloft in the belfry arch
Of the North Church tower as a signal light,—
10 One, if by land, and two, if by sea;
And I on the opposite shore will be,
Ready to ride and spread the alarm
Through every Middlesex village and farm,
For the country folk to be up and to arm."

15 Then he said, "Good night!" and with muffled oar
Silently rowed to the Charlestown shore,
Just as the moon rose over the bay,
Where swinging wide at her moorings lay
The Somerset, British man-of-war;
20 A phantom ship, with each mast and spar
Across the moon like a prison bar,
And a huge black hulk, that was magnified
By its own reflection in the tide.

---

belfry (BEL free) bell tower
moorings (MUUR ingz) ropes to fasten a ship
man-of-war (man uv WAWR) warship
spar (SPAHR) pole attached to mast
hulk (HULK) old ship
[1]**famous day and year:** Longfellow's poem was written about 80 years after the events described.

Develop Vocabulary Skills

Before students read the selection, have them look at the footnoted vocabulary words. Ask for volunteers to read each word, along with its definition. Have them use each word in an original sentence, using context words to help figure out the meaning. Write the sentences on the chalkboard. Then ask students which words would help them figure out the meaning of the word if they did not know it. Repeat this procedure with several other words from the poem, such as *muffled*, *phantom*, *gleam*, and *gloom*.

Teaching Plan

INTRODUCE

Motivation

Ask students to think about what the future of America might have been if the British had continued to rule. Encourage them to talk about how it might affect their own lives today. Ask: What would the government be like? Would the educational system be the same or different? Which sports would people play? Which musicians would people listen to?

Purpose-Setting Question

Why do you think Paul Revere volunteered to warn the people of Concord, considering the risks that were involved?

READ

Literary Focus: *Rhyme*

Read the first page of this poem aloud. Discuss the fact that this poem uses end rhyme. Ask: How does the end rhyme affect you as you listen to this poem? How does the rhyme help to show the urgency and speed with which the rider gallops?

Reading Focus: *Understand Figures of Speech*

Encourage students to sketch or visualize similes and metaphors as they read. Point out the simile in the last stanza on this page. Sketch this image on the board and have students describe how a poet might see a moon with prison bars when thinking of a moon behind a mast and spar.

CLOSE

Have students complete Review the Selection on pages 172–173.

Meanwhile, his friend, through alley and street,
25 Wanders and watches with eager ears,
Till in the silence around him he hears
The muster of men at the barrack door,
The sound of arms, and the tramp of feet,
And the measured tread of the grenadiers,
30 Marching down to their boats on the shore. . . .

On the opposite shore walked Paul Revere.
Now he patted his horse's side,
Now gazed at the landscape far and near,
Then, impetuous, stamped the earth,
35 And turned and tightened his saddle-girth;
But mostly he watched with eager search
The belfry-tower of the Old North Church,
As it rose above the graves on the hill,
Lonely and spectral and sombre and still.
40 And lo! as he looks, on the belfry's height
A glimmer, and then a gleam of light!
He springs to the saddle, the bridle he turns,
But lingers and gazes, till full on his sight
A second lamp in the belfry burns!

45 A hurry of hoofs in a village street,
A shape in the moonlight, a bulk in the dark,
And beneath, from the pebbles, in passing, a spark
Struck out by a steed flying fearless and fleet:
That was all! And yet, through the gloom and the light,
50 The fate of a nation was riding that night;
And the spark struck out by that steed, in his flight,
Kindled the land into flame with its heat. . .

It was twelve by the village clock,
When he crossed the bridge into Medford town. . . .

---

muster (MUS tur) roll call
grenadier (gren uh DIR) foot soldier
impetuous (im PECH oo us) eager; violent
girth (GURTH) strap that holds saddle on horse
spectral (SPEK trul) ghostlike
sombre (SOM bur) usually spelled somber; dark and gloomy
bulk (BULK) object; shape
fleet (FLEET) very fast

Critical Thinking: *Analyze*

Have students discuss why the British went by sea instead of land. Ask: Did they think it was faster? Did they think that they had less of a chance of being discovered?

Reading Focus: *Understand Figures of Speech*

Sometimes, an entire poem can be a metaphor. "Paul Revere's Ride" is a metaphor for the fate of the nation. Ask: What comparison is the poet making? Then ask students why Longfellow was in a good position to compare the nation's fate to Revere's ride in this poem.

Paul Revere's Ride from Boston to Lexington, 19th century. The Granger Collection

55 It was one by the village clock,
When he galloped into Lexington. . . .

It was two by the village clock,
When he came to the bridge in Concord town.
He heard the bleating of the flock,
60 And the twitter of birds among the trees,
And felt the breath of the morning breeze
Blowing over the meadows brown.
And one was safe and asleep in his bed
Who at the bridge would be first to fall,

bleating (BLEET ing) cry of sheep

Viewing Fine Art

The Romantic style in European and American fine art eventually spread as well to illustration and newspaper drawings. Here a popular 19th-century illustration portrays Paul Revere's ride in suitably romantic fashion. Note the deep-toned scene broken by the brilliantly shining moon, which just barely illuminates the hero on horseback. The cleverly designed picture with its dramatic clouds emphasizes the horse's movement by its triangular composition. The brilliantly lighted shoreline contrasts with the roof and the horse's forward motion. Before photography, pictures like this one appeared regularly in illustrated newspapers. Ask: Why is the figure on horseback looking back over his shoulder?

Literary Focus: *Rhyme*

Direct students' attention to the lines ending in ellipses that suggest missing words. Ask students to choose words that might complete the rhyme pattern for the parts of the missing stanzas. Encourage them to choose words that might also fit the context of the poem.

65 Who that day would be lying dead,
Pierced by a British musket-ball.

You know the rest. In the books you have read,
How the British Regulars[2] fired and fled,—
How the farmers gave them ball for ball,
70 From behind each fence and farm-yard wall,
Chasing the red-coats down the lane,
Then crossing the fields to emerge again
Under the trees at the turn of the road,
And only pausing to fire and load.

75 So through the night rode Paul Revere;
And so through the night went his cry of alarm
To every Middlesex village and farm, —
A cry of defiance and not of fear,
A voice in the darkness, a knock at the door,
80 And a word that shall echo forevermore!
For, borne on the night-wind of the Past,
Through all our history, to the last,
In the hour of darkness and peril and need,
The people will waken and listen to hear
85 The hurrying hoof-beats of that steed,
And the midnight message of Paul Revere.

Literary Focus:
Rhyme

Ask students if they think "Paul Revere's Ride" would be as exciting to read if Longfellow had written it as prose rather than as a rhyming poem.

---

[2]**British Regulars:** These were regular army troops.

Twilight on the Shawangunk, 1865, T. Worthington Whittredge. The Granger Collection

from THE DAY IS DONE

by Henry Wadsworth Longfellow

The day is done, and the darkness
Falls from the wings of Night,
As a feather is wafted downward
From an eagle in his flight.

5 I see the lights of the village
Gleam through the rain and the mist,
And a feeling of sadness comes o'er me
That my soul cannot resist:

A feeling of sadness and longing,
10 That is not akin to pain,
And resembles sorrow only
As the mist resembles the rain.

---

wafted (WAHFT id) blown along smoothly
akin (uh KIN) related

Viewing Fine Art

T. Worthington Whittredge (1820–1910) had been a photographer, a house and sign painter, and a portraitist before turning to the landscape work for which he is best known. After painting scenes of the eastern United States, he set off with a government exploration party to the West. The magnificent western landscape became the subject of his major works. He combined both the topographical and poetic in his landscapes, which were large, serene, and brightly lighted. "Whoever crossed the plains at that period," he wrote, "could hardly fail to be impressed with [the] vastness and silence and the appearance everywhere of an innocent, primitive existence." Ask: What images from the poem are shown in this painting?

Reading Focus: *Understand Figures of Speech*

Discuss how the poet uses figurative language in the poem. Point to the *simile* if students do not use it in their discussion of the lines, ". . . darkness/Falls from the wings of Night/As a feather is wafted downward/From an eagle in his flight." Ask students to find another simile in the poem.

Critical Thinking: *Evaluate*

Ask: How well does Longfellow create a mood of quiet and sadness?

Literary Focus: *Rhyme*

Ask: What kind of poem would you read to the poet to help him sleep? Would you choose one with a rhyming pattern? Why might this help "banish the thoughts of day"?

Critical Thinking: *Draw Conclusions*

Ask: Why does the poet prefer to have poetry read to him rather than reading it himself?

Reading Focus: *Understand Figures of Speech*

Have students find the words *care* and *cares* in the second and last stanzas on this page. Discuss the author's use of personification and why he might have chosen a feeling to take on human attributes.

Comparing Selections

Although the subjects of these poems are very different from each other, both contain many figures of speech. Find and explain a simile, a metaphor, and an example of personification in each poem.

Come, read to me some poem,
Some simple and heartfelt lay,
15 That shall soothe this restless feeling,
And banish the thoughts of day.

Such songs have power to quiet
The restless pulse of care,
And come like the benediction
20 That follows after prayer.

Then read from the treasured volume
The poem of thy choice,
And lend to the rhyme of the poet
The beauty of thy voice.

25 And the night shall be filled with music,
And the cares, that infest the day,
Shall fold their tents, like the Arabs,
And as silently steal away.

---

heartfelt (HAHRT felt) sincere; meaningful
lay (LAY) short song or story poem
benediction (ben uh DIK shun) blessing
infest (in FEST) trouble; disturb

Mini Quiz

Write the following questions on the chalkboard or overhead projector and call on students to fill in the blanks. Discuss the answers with the class.

1. The British would march either by land or by ________.
2. Paul Revere said to hang ________ lantern if the British came by land.
3. The British ship was called the ________.
4. Paul Revere waited for a message on the ________ shore.
5. His friend hung two lanterns in the belfry tower of the ________ ________ ________.

Answers

1. sea
2. one
3. Somerset
4. Charlestown
5. Old North Church

Author Biography

Henry Wadsworth Longfellow (1807–1882)

At the time of his death, and for years after, Henry Wadsworth Longfellow had no rival as America's best-loved poet. His poetry often appeared in magazines. His books were in constant demand. Schoolchildren read dozens of his poems and often had to memorize several.

Longfellow's popularity is easy to understand. He saw beauty everywhere—in an old ship against the moon in Boston Harbor, in the forests, in the fields. He was interested in the common life of the common people. He usually wrote rather simple, melodious poems that nearly everyone could understand. But most of all, he calmed the nerves of the nation. In an age when life was often hard, Longfellow told his American readers to work hard and to accept whatever fate had to offer.

Longfellow's life was mostly a comfortable one. He grew up in Maine, graduated from college at an early age, and went to Europe for further study. Afterwards, he kept two careers going at the same time—first as a poet, and second as a professor of foreign languages. He lived to see his poetry translated into 24 languages. But as he told his readers, "Into each life some rain must fall." In 1861, his wife burned to death when her dress accidentally caught fire. Longfellow's own struggle out of sorrow is reflected in some of his poems.

In his own day, what features of Longfellow's poetry do you think most appealed to his readers?

More About the Author

Henry Wadsworth Longfellow's mother read aloud to him as a young child. He enjoyed many of the classics, but the book that most influenced him was Washington Irving's *Sketch Book*.

Additional Works

by Henry Wadsworth Longfellow

The Complete Poems, Lightyear Press, 1993.

Evangeline: A Novel, Pelican Publishing Co., 1999.

Henry Wadsworth Longfellow, Grammercy, 1992.

Six Great American Poets: Poems by Poe, Dickinson, Whitman, Longfellow, Frost, and Millay, Dover Publications, 1993.

The Song of Hiawatha, Everyman Paperback Classics. Reprint Edition.

Review the Selection

UNDERSTAND THE SELECTION

Recall

1. When did Paul Revere make his ride?
2. Upon whom did he depend for information about the British troops?
3. What did the speaker in "The Day Is Done" like at the end of the day?

Infer

4. Paraphrase what Longfellow wrote about in "The Day Is Done."
5. Describe how you think the *Somerset* looked to Paul Revere as he rowed by.
6. Why do you think Longfellow wrote that "the fate of a nation was riding that night"?
7. Why do you think Longfellow wrote a poem about this night?

Apply

8. Predict what might have happened if the British had come by land.
9. What might Revere have thought while waiting for the signal?
10. Predict what you think happened to the speaker in "The Day Is Done" after hearing the poem.

Respond to Literature

How does "Paul Revere's Ride" reflect the feelings of Americans in the 1800s?

WRITE ABOUT THE SELECTION

At the conclusion of "Paul Revere's Ride," Longfellow wrote that there is "a word that shall echo forevermore!" What word was this? Remember that many colonists had fled from Europe to escape religious persecution, poverty, and oppression. What do you think freedom meant to the colonists? What does it mean to you? Suppose that you are one of those colonists who has come to America in search of freedom. Add a four-line stanza to the poem in which you write what freedom means to you.

Prewriting Jot down on a piece of paper in note form what freedom means to you. Include at least three ideas. Then, write pairs of rhyming words that relate to your ideas. Use your list to help you write the stanza.

Writing Use your notes and the list of rhyming words to write an additional stanza for "Paul Revere's Ride." Use this line to start: "Two hundred years later and no one need fear." Add four lines to this.

Revising Read your stanza several times to get a feel for the movement of the lines. Then delete or sharpen the wording of any lines that take away from the pace of the stanza.

Proofreading When writing poetry, be sure that each line begins with a capital letter and that the rhyming words are at the end of lines. Punctuate your verses as you would any prose sentence.

UNDERSTAND THE SELECTION

Answers

1. April 18, 1775, at midnight
2. a friend
3. a poem read to him or her
4. Sample answer: He wrote about sadness at the end of the day which being read to dispelled, soothing his restlessness. He then urges his companion to read.
5. Sample answer: It must have looked very large and mysterious.
6. If Paul Revere had not warned the people in time, the British might have captured the arms and eventually won the war. The colonies might have never won their independence.
7. Sample answer: Living in the 1800s, Longfellow knew the hardships and risks that colonists had faced in order to be free and so knew the value of freedom.
8. Sample answer: If the British had come by land, they might have moved faster and captured the arms.
9. Sample answer: Revere might have thought about how the British would march; how long it would take to warn the colonists; whether the colonists would be warned in time.
10. Sample answer: The speaker dozed off, daydreamed, or felt rested and relaxed.

Respond to Literature

Have students discuss why the pilgrims came to America in the first place. You might want to make a list of their reasons on the chalkboard. After the list has been completed, have students discuss how these reasons are reflected in "Paul Revere's Ride."

WRITE ABOUT THE SELECTION

Prewriting

After students have decided what "word shall echo forevermore," have them work in small groups to brainstorm what freedom means to people. Have them think about people who yearn for freedom in various parts of the world today. Do students think the reasons people want to be free now are different from the reasons people wanted freedom in 1775 or the reasons slaves wanted their freedom in the 1800s? Have them write in note form what freedom means to each of them, using the information they brainstormed.

Writing

Have students work on this section individually. Go around the class, giving help to any student who is having difficulty. Ask students how they would feel if their freedom were taken away from them.

Revising

Have students work in pairs to revise their paragraphs. Make sure they read their stanzas out loud to each other to make sure the stanzas have a good steady rhythmic pace.

THINK ABOUT RHYME

Rhyme contributed greatly to the movement and pace of the two poems you have just read. Some words that rhyme have soft sounds that can make a poem seem to move slowly. Other words have crisp sounds that produce a steady pace. In "Paul Revere's Ride," the rhymes contribute to the feeling of urgency that Longfellow has written into the poem. How will the British advance? Will it be by land or sea? Will Paul Revere warn the colonists in time?

1. What kind of rhymes did Longfellow use in "Paul Revere's Ride"?
2. What was the pace of "Paul Revere's Ride"?
3. How did the pace of "The Day Is Done" differ from that of "Paul Revere's Ride"?
4. Which of the rhyming words in the second stanza of "Paul Revere's Ride" move the poem along at a steady pace?
5. Why do these words help move the poem along at a steady pace?

Reading Focus

Understand Figures of Speech As you read "Paul Revere's Ride" and "The Day Is Done," you were asked to look for figures of speech. Choose your favorite simile or metaphor and explain how the comparison helped to create the mood of the poem.

DEVELOP YOUR VOCABULARY

Review the meanings of the vocabulary words from this selection. Context can often help you figure out the meaning of an unfamiliar word. Read this sentence: The captain gave his *heartfelt* thanks to the crew, and his warm sincerity touched them all. By the author's use of the words *warm sincerity* and *touched* you are better able to understand what *heartfelt* meant.

Read the following sentences. Use context clues to help you figure out the meaning of each italicized word. Underline the words that help you.

1. The *moorings* of the boat were not fastened tightly, and the ropes loosened.
2. The *spar* snapped in the rough winds, toppling the pole into the sea.
3. The leaves *wafted* gently through the air, moving slowly to the ground.
4. He watched the *belfry* closely, knowing at any moment he would hear the signal from the tower.
5. The *tempestuous* sea threw the boat violently in all directions.
6. The *grenadiers* moved slowly along on foot, not knowing that enemy soldiers were close behind.

THINK ABOUT RHYME

Answers

1. end rhymes
2. Sample answer: The pace moves steadily forward like the horse Revere rode.
3. Sample answer: "The Day Is Done" moves more slowly.
4. march, arch; sea, be; alarm, farm, arm
5. Sample answer: The words are short and crisp and increase the movement of the poem.

DEVELOP YOUR VOCABULARY

Sample Answers

1. ropes used to secure a boat
2. pole
3. moving slowly
4. bell tower
5. violent
6. foot soldiers

Reading Focus

Accept responses based on metaphors or similes from either of the poems.

Proofreading

Select one or two stanzas as models for proofreading. Write the stanzas on the board and have the class suggest improvements. Make sure the poems have been written in poetry form.

ESL Activity

In "Paul Revere's Ride," Henry Wadsworth Longfellow looked back to an event that had happened 80 years earlier. That event changed the course of history in the United States. Ask ESL students to share events that changed the course of history in their native countries. Challenge students to write one stanza about an event that was discussed. You may want to pair ESL students with proficient English speakers to complete the activity.

Selection Overview

SELECTION OBJECTIVES

After completing these selections, students will be able to

- understand and classify an essay
- understand eponymous words
- analyze the style of an essay
- use a dictionary to look up word histories
- write a descriptive paragraph
- identify supporting details

Lesson Resources

from *Walden*/from *Nature*
- Selection Synopses, Teacher's Edition, pp. T159e–T159f
- Comprehension and Vocabulary Workbook, pp. 37–38
- Language Enrichment Workbook, pp. 20–23
- Teacher's Resources
  Reinforcement, p. R19
  Test, pp. T37–T38
  Unadapted Selection, pp. U27–U28

More About Essays

Encourage students to think about and discuss contemporary formats in which people write essays, along with some of the topics about which people write. For example, newspapers and magazines are good formats for essays in which people write about current issues and problems.

More About the Literary Period

In these selections, Emerson and Thoreau clearly reflect the views and feelings of the Transcendentalists, the group in which both of them were heavily involved. Through nature, both of these writers were able to examine and share their innermost feelings.

About the Author

It was only after Thoreau's two-year experience at Walden Pond, where he lived in a cabin, that he was able to live the life he wanted. He wrote in the morning and spent afternoons wandering around Concord, observing birds, flowers, and animals, or rowing on the rivers and ponds, looking at the local flora and fauna. He also liked to spend time talking with Emerson, Hawthorne, and Bronson Alcott who also lived in Concord.

Learn About

Essays

Essays are nonfictional compositions. They are usually short and can be either formal or informal in style.

Formal essays are serious, very organized writings intended to inform or persuade. **Informal essays**, on the other hand, usually have a less serious purpose. They are not so rigorously organized and exhibit a more conversational style. These essays are usually meant to describe a personal experience.

There are many other classifications of essays. Sometimes essays are classified as narrative, descriptive, reflective, or editorial. These categories correspond roughly to the four types of writing: narrative, descriptive, expository, and persuasive.

As you read the following selections, ask yourself:

1. What purpose did each author have in writing the essay?
2. How would you classify each essay?

Reading Focus

Identify Supporting Details Essays are an opportunity for authors to present their own opinions on a subject. They develop their ideas through the use of details, facts, and examples. As you read the selections from *Walden* and *Nature*, look for ways in which the authors support their opinions. Jot down each opinion and how it is supported by details.

WRITING CONNECTION

Think of a prized possession that you own. Write a paragraph explaining your personal view or feeling about the object.

ESL Activity

Have a class discussion about the prevalent methods of communication in the mid-1850s and now, in both this country and other countries. How did people get their news and opinions then and now? See the worksheets on pages 20–22 in the Language Enrichment Workbook.

Cooperative Group Activity

For the Writing Connection activity, have students work in pairs to write a paragraph about a favorite possession. Be sure to have students include details about why this item is their favorite. Finally, have one volunteer from each pair read their paragraphs.

from WALDEN

ADAPTED

by Henry David Thoreau

At a certain season of our life we are accustomed to consider every spot as the possible site of a house. I have thus surveyed the country on every side within a dozen miles of where I live. In imagination I have bought all the farms in succession, for all were to be bought, and I knew their price. I walked over each farmer's land, tasted his wild apples, talked about farming with him, took his farm at his price, at any price, mortgaging it to him in my mind. I even put a higher price on it,—took everything but a deed of it. I took his word for his deed, for I dearly loved to talk. I cultivated it, and him too to some extent, I trust. Then I withdrew when I had enjoyed it long enough, leaving him to carry it on. This experience entitled me to be regarded as a sort of real-estate broker by my friends. Wherever I sat, there I might live, and the landscape radiated from me accordingly. What is a house but a *sedes*, a seat?—better if a country seat. I discovered many a site for a house not likely to be soon improved. Some might have thought it too far from the village, but to my eyes the village was too far from it. Well, there I might live, I said. And there I did live, for an hour, a summer and a winter life; saw how I could let the years run off, buffet the winter through, and see the spring come in. The future inhabitants of this region, wherever they may place their houses, may be sure that they have been anticipated. An afternoon was enough time to lay out the land into orchard, woodlot and pasture, and to decide what fine oaks or pines should be left to stand before the door, and from where each blasted tree could be seen to the best advantage; and then I let it lie, fallow perhaps, for a man is rich in proportion to the number of things which he can afford to let alone.

My imagination carried me so far that I even had the refusal of several farms—the refusal was all I wanted—but I never got my fingers burned by actual possession. The nearest that I came to actual possession was when I bought the Hollowell Place. I had begun to sort my seeds, and collected materials with which to make a wheelbarrow to carry it on or off with. But before the owner gave me a deed of it, his wife changed her mind and wished to keep it, and he offered me ten dollars to release him. Now, to speak

---

cultivated (KUL tuh vayt id) prepared and cared for the land on which plants grow
fallow (FAL oh) land that is plowed, but not seeded

TEACHING PLAN

INTRODUCE

Motivation

Find a tape that plays nature music. Have students listen quietly to the music for a few minutes and think about nature. Whether they live in urban, suburban, or rural areas, natural occurrences can be inspirational: new fallen snow, a robin picking berries, geese honking, or a sunset.

Purpose-Setting Question

What can be learned from nature?

READ

Literary Focus: *Essays*

Have students decide whether the excerpts from *Walden* and from "Nature" are formal or informal essays. Ask how the author's purpose in writing the essay might determine how formal the essay is. Then have students define the four types of writing: narrative, descriptive, expository, and persuasive. Their definitions should help them decide how each essay should be classified.

Reading Focus: *Identify Supporting Details*

Thoreau and Emerson include many details throughout these texts. Ask students to identify these details as they read and tell how they support the authors' opinions. Set up a two-column chart that students can fill out as they read. *Opinions* should head Column 1 and *Supporting Details* (or *Evidence*) should head Column 2.

CLOSE

Have students complete Review the Selection on pages 186–187.

Develop Vocabulary Skills

Before students read the selections, go over the vocabulary words footnoted in the story. Then have students work in pairs to make up sentences using each vocabulary word. Make sure students use the words correctly.

Reading Focus:
Identify Supporting Details
Ask: Why do you think Walden let the farmer keep his farm? What details can you find in the text to support your answer?

Critical Thinking:
Synthesize
Ask: How do you think Thoreau felt about landscapes?

the truth, I had but ten cents in the world, and it surpassed my arithmetic to tell, if I was that man who had ten cents, or who had a farm, or ten dollars, or all together. However, I let him keep the ten dollars and the farm too, for I had carried it far enough; or rather, to be generous. I sold him the farm for just what I gave for it. As he was not a rich man, I made him a present of ten dollars, and still had my ten cents, and seeds, and materials for a wheelbarrow left. I found thus that I had been a rich man without any damage to my poverty. But I retained the landscape, and have since annually carried off what it yielded without a wheelbarrow. With respect to landscapes:

"I am monarch of all I *survey*,
My right there is none to dispute."

I have frequently seen a poet withdraw, having enjoyed the most valuable part of a farm, while the crusty farmer supposed that he had got a few wild apples only. Why, the owner does not know it for many years when a poet has put his farm in rhyme, the most admirable kind of invisible fence, has fairly impounded it, milked it, skimmed it, and got all the cream, and left the farmer only the skimmed milk.

The real attractions of the Hollowell farm, to me, were: its complete retirement, being about two miles from the village, half a mile from the nearest neighbor, and separated from the highway by a broad field. A river bounded the farm, which the owner said protected

---

annually (AN you ul ee) occurring each year
crusty (KRUS tee) curt; rude

it by its fogs from frosts in the spring, though that was nothing to me. I was also attracted to the gray color and ruinous state of the house and barn, and the dilapidated fences, which put such an interval between me and the last occupant; the hollow and lichen-covered apple trees, gnawed by rabbits, showing what kind of neighbors I should have. But above all, the recollection I had of it from my earliest voyages up the river. The house was concealed behind a thick grove of red maples, through which I heard the house-dog bark. I was in haste to buy it, before the owner finished getting out some rocks, cutting down the hollow apple trees, and grubbing up some young birches which had sprung up in the pasture, or, in short, had made any more of his improvements. To enjoy these advantages I was ready to carry it on; like Atlas,[1] to take the world on my shoulders—I never heard what compensation he received for that—and do all those things which had no other motive or excuse but that I might pay for it and be unmolested in my possession of it. I knew all the while that it would yield the most plentiful crop of the kind I wanted if I could only afford to let it alone. But it turned out as I have said.

All that I could say, then, with respect to farming on a large scale (I have always cultivated a garden) was that I had had my seeds ready. Many think that seeds improve with age. I have no doubt that time can tell the difference between the good and the bad; and when at last I shall plant, I shall be less likely to be disappointed. But I would say to my fellows, once for all, as long as possible live free and uncommitted. It makes but little difference whether you are committed to a farm or the county jail.

Old Cato,[2] whose "Of Things Rustic" is my "Cultivator," says, and the only translation I have seen makes sheer nonsense of the passage, "When you think of getting a farm, turn it thus in your mind, not to buy greedily; nor spare your pains to look at it, and do not think it enough to go round it once. The oftener you go there the more it will please you, if it is good." I think I shall not buy greedily, but go round and round it as long as I live, and be buried in it first, that it may please me the more at last. . . .

I do not propose to write an ode to dejection, but to brag as lustily as chanticleer in the morning, standing on his roost, if only to wake my neighbors up.

When first I took up my home in the woods, that is, began to spend my nights as well as days there, which, by accident, was on Independence Day, or the fourth of July, 1845, my house was not finished for winter. It was merely a defense against the rain, without plastering or chimney. The walls were of rough weatherstained boards, with wide chinks,

---

chanticleer (CHAN tih klir) a rooster
[1]**Atlas:** from Greek mythology, a Titan who supported the heavens on his shoulders
[2]**Old Cato:** Roman statesman (234–149 B.C.)

Literary Focus: *Essays*

Ask students to summarize Thoreau's thoughts up to the day when he started to live in the woods day and night. How did these thoughts affect the descriptions of nature in this essay?

Viewing Fine Art

Self-taught or primitive artists were common all across the United States in the 19th century. In many areas of the country they were the only people to decorate homes, make portraits, design signs, or paint walls or furniture. Paul A. Siefert, who made this view of a farm in Wisconsin, came to the United States from Germany in 1867. He earned his living raising flowers, fruits, and vegetables, and later became a taxidermist and painter on glass. His watercolor paintings of Wisconsin's spacious farms and rolling hills were notable for their tiny detail, even on the most distant trees. Ask: What parts of nature are shown in this painting? Can you tell how the author feels about the relationship between people and Nature in this painting? How do you think Thoreau would feel about the scene?

Reading Focus: *Identify Supporting Details*

After students have read the passage beginning, "I went to the woods because. . . ," (the last paragraph on this page) have them point out details that support Thoreau's opinion that he needed to live this simple way of life at all costs.

Wisconsin Farm Scene, Paul Seifert. The Granger Collection

which made it cool at night. The upright white hewn posts and freshly planed door and window casings gave it a clean and airy look, especially in the morning, when its beams were saturated with dew, so that I fancied that by noon some sweet gum would exude from them. To my imagination it retained throughout the day more or less of this morning character. It reminded me of a certain house on a mountain which I had visited the year before. This was an airy and unplastered cabin. It was fit to entertain a traveling god, and where a goddess might trail her garments. The winds which passed over my home were such as sweep over ridges of mountains, bearing the broken strains, or heavenly parts only, of earthly music. The morning wind forever blows, the poem of creation is uninterrupted; but few are the ears that hear it. Olympus[3] is but the outside of the earth everywhere. . . .

I went to the woods because I wished to live thoughtfully, to face only the bare facts of life. I wanted to see if I could not learn what it had to teach, and not, when I came to die, discover that I had not lived. I did not wish to live what was not life, living is so dear. Nor did I wish to practice resignation, unless it was quite necessary. I wanted to live deep and suck out all the marrow of life, to live so sturdily and hardily as to crush all that was not life. I wanted to cut a broad path and shave close, to drive life into a corner,

[3]**Olympus:** in Greek mythology, the home of the gods

and reduce it to its lowest terms. If it proved to be mean, why then I wanted to eat the whole and genuine meanness of it, and publish its meanness to the world. If it were sublime, I wanted to know it by experience, and be able to give a true account of it in my next excursion. For most men, it appears to me, are in a strange uncertainty about it, whether it is of the Devil or of God. . . .

Still we live meanly, like ants; though the fable tells us that we were long ago changed into men. . . . It is an error upon error, and clout upon clout, and our best virtue has for its occasion a superfluous and evitable wretchedness. Our life is frittered away by detail. An honest man has hardly need to count more than his ten fingers, or in extreme cases he may add his ten toes, and lump the rest. Simplicity, simplicity, simplicity! I say, let your affairs be as two or three, and not a hundred or a thousand; instead of a million count half a dozen, and keep your accounts on your thumbnail. In the midst of this chopping sea of civilized life, such are the clouds and storms and quicksands and thousand-and-one items to be allowed for, that a man has to live, if he would not founder and go to the bottom and not make his port at all, by dead reckoning. He must be a great calculator indeed who succeeds. Simplify, simplify. Instead of three meals a day, if it be necessary eat but one. Instead of a hundred dishes, five; and reduce other things in proportion. Our life is like a German Confederacy,[4] made up of petty states, with its boundary forever changing, so that even a German cannot tell you how it is bounded at any moment. The nation itself, with all its so-called internal improvements, which, by the way, are all external and shallow, is just such an unwieldy and overgrown establishment, cluttered with furniture and tripped up by its own traps, ruined by luxury and heedless expense, by want of calculation and a worthy aim, as the million households in the land; and the only cure for it as for them is in a rigid economy, a stern and more than Spartan simplicity of life and elevation of purpose. It lives too fast. Men think that it is essential that the *Nation* have trade, and export ice, and talk through a telegraph, and ride thirty miles an hour, without a doubt, whether *they* do or not; but whether we should live like baboons or like men, is a little uncertain. If we do not get out railroad track ties and forge rails, and devote days and nights to the work, but go to tinkering upon our *lives* to improve *them*, who will build railroads? And if railroads are not built, how shall we get to heaven in season? But if we stay at home and mind our business, who will want railroads? We do not ride on the railroad; it rides upon us. . . .

Time is but the stream I go a-fishing in. I drink at it; but while I drink I see the

superfluous (suu PUR floo us) beyond what is required
dead reckoning (DED REK un ing) navigating without the assistance of stars
[4]**German confederacy:** At the time, Germany was a loose union of 38 independent states, with no common government.

Literary Focus: *Essays*

Discuss what Thoreau saw as the evils of civilized life. Then ask: What do you think Thoreau's purpose was in writing about his experiences in essay form?

Critical Thinking: *Apply*

Ask: What opinions might Thoreau have today if he were to visit our school?

sandy bottom and detect how shallow it is. Its thin current slides away, but eternity remains. I would drink deeper; fish in the sky, whose bottom is pebbly with stars. I cannot count one. I know not the first letter of the alphabet. I have always been regretting that I was not as wise as the day I was born. The intellect is a cleaver. It discerns and rifts its way into the secret of things. I do not wish to be any more busy with my hands than is necessary. My head is hands and feet. I feel all my best faculties concentrated in it. My inner feelings tell me that my head is an organ for burrowing, as some creatures use their snout and forepaws, and with it I would mine and burrow my way through these hills. I think that the richest vein is somewhere hereabouts.

I left the woods for as good a reason as I went there. Perhaps it seemed to me that I had several more lives to live, and could not spare any more time for that one. It is remarkable how easily and insensibly we fall into a particular route, and make a beaten track for ourselves. I had not lived there a week before my feet wore a path from my door to the pondside. Though it is five or six years since I trod it, it is still quite distinct. It is true, I fear that others may have fallen into it, and so helped to keep it open. The surface of the earth is soft and impressible by the feet of men; and so with the paths which the mind travels. How worn and dusty, then, must be the highways of the world, how deep the ruts of tradition and conformity! I did not wish to take a cabin passage, but rather to go before the mast and on the deck of the world, for there I could best see the moonlight amid the mountains. I do not wish to go below now.

I learned this, at least, by my experiment. If one advances confidently in the direction of his dreams, and endeavors to live the life which he has imagined, he will meet with a success unexpected in common hours. He will put some things behind and will pass an invisible boundary. New, universal, and more liberal laws will begin to establish themselves around and within him. Or the old laws will be expanded, and interpreted in his favor in a more liberal sense. He will live with the license of a higher order of beings. In proportion as he simplifies his life, the laws of the universe will appear less complex, and solitude will not be solitude, nor poverty poverty, nor weakness weakness. If you have built castles in the air, your work need not be lost; that is where they should be. Now put the foundations under them. . . .

Why should we be in such a desperate hurry to succeed, and in such desperate enterprises? If a man does not keep pace with his companions, perhaps it is because he hears a different drummer. Let him step to the music which he hears, however, measured or far away. It is not important that he should grow as soon as an apple tree or an oak. Shall he turn his

---

conformity (kun FAWR muh tee) behavior that is in agreement with current rules
common (KOM un) piece of public land

Literary Focus: *Essays*

Call attention to the passage beginning, "I left the woods for as good a reason. . . ." Have students give their own opinions of why Thoreau left the woods. Encourage them to point out parts of the text that support their opinions. Then have them compare their answers to why they think he went into the woods with their answers to why they think he left the woods.

Critical Thinking: *Apply*

Ask: What do you think you might find out about yourself if you were to spend months living in the woods alone?

spring into summer? If the condition of things which we were made for is not yet, what were any reality which we can substitute? We will not be shipwrecked on a vain reality. Shall we with pains erect a heaven of blue glass over ourselves, though when it is done we shall be sure to gaze still at the true ethereal heaven far above, as if the former were not?. . . .

However mean your life is, meet it and live it; do not shun it and call it hard names. It is not so bad as you are. It looks poorest when you are richest. The fault-finder will find faults even in paradise. Love your life, poor as it is. You may perhaps have some pleasant, thrilling, glorious hours, even in a poorhouse. The setting sun is reflected from the windows of the poorhouse as brightly as from the rich man's home. The snow melts before its door as early in the spring. I do not see but a quiet mind may live as contentedly there, and have as cheering thoughts, as in a palace. The town's poor seem to me often to live the most independent lives of any. Maybe they are simply great enough to receive without misgiving. Most think that they are above being supported by the town; but it oftener happens that they are not above supporting themselves by dishonest means, which should be more disreputable. Cultivate poverty like a garden herb, like sage. Do not trouble yourself much to get new things, whether clothes or friends. Turn the old; return to them. Things do not change; we change. Sell your clothes and keep your thoughts. God will see that you do not want society. If I were confined to a corner of an attic all my days, like a spider, the world would be just as large to me while I had my thoughts about me. The philosopher said: "From an army of three divisions one can take away its general, and put it in disorder; from the man the most abject and vulgar one cannot take away his thought." Do not seek so anxiously to

A Catskill Waterfall, Homer D. Martin.
Corbis Bettmann

Viewing Fine Art

Homer Dodge Martin (1836–1897) was an American landscape painter who specialized in scenes of the upstate region of New York. He sketched from nature and added the details and color afterwards. Martin's paintings eventually were influenced by the works of French impressionists, and he evolved a sophisticated style of subtly modulated colors and light. Some critics consider Martin to have been the artist who brought American landscape painting from the Hudson River School to the brink of impressionism. Ask: What qualities in this scene seem to illustrate what Thoreau is saying about how to live?

Literary Focus: *Essays*

Have students explain what message they get from this essay. You might have partners discuss what they have learned from the author's words, or have students write a journal entry about how the author's words have affected them.

Reading Focus: *Identify Supporting Details*

Ask: What details does Thoreau provide to convince you to accept your life as it is?

be developed, to subject yourself to many influences to be played on; it is all dissipation. Humility like darkness reveals the heavenly lights. The shadows of poverty and meanness gather around us, "and lo! creation widens to our view."[5] We are often reminded that if there were bestowed on us the wealth of Croesus[6], our aims must still be the same, and our means essentially the same. Moreover, if you are restricted in your range by poverty, if you cannot buy books and newspapers, for instance, you are but confined to the most significant and vital experiences. You are compelled to deal with the material which yields the most sugar and the most starch. It is life near the bone where it is sweetest. You are defended from being a trifler. No man loses ever on a lower level by magnanimity on a higher. Superfluous wealth can buy superfluities only. Money is not required to buy one necessary of the soul. . . .

The life in us is like the water in the river. It may rise this year higher than man has ever known it, and flood the dry uplands; even this may be the eventful year, which will drown out all our muskrats. It will not always be dry land where we dwell. I see far inland the banks which the stream anciently washed, before science began to record its freshets. Everyone has heard the story which has gone the rounds of New England. A strong and beautiful bug came out of the dry leaf of an old table of apple-tree wood. It had stood in a farmer's kitchen for sixty years, first in Connecticut, and afterward in Massachusetts. An egg had been deposited in the living tree many years earlier still, as appeared by counting the annual layers beyond it. It was heard gnawing out for several weeks, hatched perhaps by the heat of an urn. Who does not feel his faith in a resurrection and immortality strengthened by hearing of this? Who knows what beautiful and winged life, whose egg has been buried for ages under many concentric layers of woodenness in the dead dry life of society, deposited at first in the soft wood of the green and living tree, which has been gradually converted into the semblance of its well-seasoned tomb—heard perhaps gnawing out now for years by the astonished family of man, as they sat round the festive board—may unexpectedly come forth from amidst society's most trivial and handselled furniture, to enjoy its perfect summer life at last!

I do not say that the average person will realize all this; but such is the character of that morrow which mere lapse of time can never make to dawn. The light which puts out our eyes is darkness to us. Only that day dawns to which we are awake. There is more day to dawn. The sun is but a morning star.

[5]**and lo! creation widens to our view:** from the sonnet "To Night" by British poet Joseph Blanco White

[6]**Croesus:** the king of Lydia (516 B.C.) thought to be the wealthiest person of his time

Literary Focus: *Essays*

Discuss with students whether this is a formal or informal essay. Refer them to page 174 if they need information to help them form their answers. Ask: What features of this essay helped you to know whether it is formal or informal?

Reading Focus: *Identify Supporting Details*

Ask students to give examples of what Thoreau considered *meanness* in people. What can they conclude about Thoreau's view of human nature?

Critical Thinking: *Interpret*

Guide students to the end of the story of the bug. Ask: What might Thoreau consider a "perfect summer life"?

from Nature

ADAPTED

by Ralph Waldo Emerson

Comparing Selections

Have students discuss how Emerson felt about nature. Did Thoreau and Emerson agree or disagree in their thoughts?

Nature is a setting that fits equally well a funny or a sad piece. In good health, the air is a drink of incredible goodness. Crossing a bare common, in snow puddles, at twilight, under a clouded sky, without having in my thought any occurrence of special good fortune, I have enjoyed a perfect happiness. I am glad to the brink of fear. In the woods, too, a man casts off his years, as the snake sheds his skin, and at what period soever of life is always a child. In the woods is long lasting youth. Within these plantations of God, good behavior and holiness reign, a lasting festival is dressed. The guest sees not how he should tire of them in a thousand years. In the woods, we return to reason and faith. There I feel that nothing can happen to me in life—no disgrace, no accident (leaving me my eyes), which nature cannot repair. Standing on the bare ground—my head bathed by the care-free air and uplifted into infinite space—all mean self importance goes away. I become a transparent eyeball: I am nothing: I am nothing: I see all. The currents of the Universal Being circulate through me; I am part or parcel of God. The name of the nearest friend sounds then foreign and accidental: to be brothers, to be acquaintances, master or servant, is then of little importance and a disturbance. I am the lover of uncontained and immortal beauty. In the wilderness, I find something more dear than in the streets or villages. In the peaceful landscape, and especially in the distant line of the horizon, man beholds something as beautiful as his own nature.

The greatest delight which the fields and woods give is the suggestion of a mysterious relation between man and vegetable. I am not alone and unacknowledged. They nod to me, and I to them. The waving of the boughs in the storm is new to me and old. It takes me by surprise, and yet is not unknown. Its effect is like that of a higher thought or a better emotion coming over me, when I considered I was thinking justly or doing right.

Pool in the Woods, George Inness. Corbis Bettmann

Yet it is certain that the power to produce this delight does not reside in nature, but in man, or in a harmony of both. It is necessary to use these pleasures with great moderation. For nature is not always dressed in holiday attire. The same scene which yesterday breathed perfume is overspread with sadness today. Nature always wears the colors of the spirit. To a man laboring under disaster, the heat of his own fire hath sadness in it. Then there is a kind of contempt of the landscape felt by him who has just lost by death a dear friend. The sky is less grand as it shuts down over less worth in the population.

Viewing Fine Art

George Inness (1825–1894) was an American painter of romantic and idyllic scenes. His major interests were light and its effect on mood in landscape. In this painting he illuminates a dark and mysterious woodland scene with hazy moonlight. Inness sought to find in the simple beauties of nature romantic, dreamlike images. (Another picture by Inness appears on page 202.) Ask: How do you think Emerson would view this scene?

Reading Focus: *Identify Supporting Details*

Have students discuss whether or not Thoreau and Emerson would find it necessary to own a lot of material possessions. Why or why not? What details can students find in these essays to support their answers?

Literary Focus: *Essays*

What views do Thoreau and Emerson present to the reader about nature?

Mini Quiz

Write the following questions on the chalkboard or overhead projector and call on students to fill in the blanks. Discuss the answers with the class.

1. Thoreau almost bought the ________ Place.
2. Thoreau took up residence in the woods when he began to spend both his days and ________ there.
3. People might not do the same things as others because they hear the sound of a different ________.
4. Both Thoreau and Emerson turned to ________ for their ideas.
5. Emerson said that there is long-lasting ________ in the woods.

Answers

1. Hollowell
2. nights
3. drummer
4. nature
5. youth

Review the Selection

UNDERSTAND THE SELECTION

Recall

1. List two of Thoreau's examples that suggest that people live too fast.
2. When did Thoreau start living in the woods?
3. Where did Emerson find beauty?

Infer

4. Why did Thoreau live in the woods?
5. Why did Thoreau believe people should follow their dreams?
6. Briefly paraphrase how Emerson felt when he was in the woods.
7. How did nature help Emerson and Thoreau explore their feelings?

Apply

8. If you lived in the woods, would you spend a lot of time observing nature?
9. Predict what you think might happen if Thoreau had continued to live in the woods.
10. Select a line from one of the essays that you believe is a good and wise thought and tell why.

Respond to Literature

List several ways in which Thoreau's and Emerson's writings reflect the feelings of the time in which they wrote.

WRITE ABOUT THE SELECTION

Emerson and Thoreau make it very clear that nature and the wilderness were very important to them. They tell the reader that going to the country cleared their heads and made them forget their troubles. Where would you like to go to forget your troubles? Think about a special imaginary place where you would feel happy and forget your cares.

Prewriting Freewrite for a few sentences about an imaginary place where you could reflect quietly about your life. What would the place look like? How would it make you feel? How long do you think you would want to stay? You might want to jot down some extra words that describe your imaginary place.

Writing Use your ideas to write a descriptive paragraph about a wonderful place you can go when you want to forget your worries. Try to include words that consistently reflect your feelings about your special place.

Revising Reread your paragraph. When you revise, make sure you include several words that express your feelings accurately. Try to use vivid adjectives rather than settling for the first ones that come to mind.

Proofreading Read over your paragraph to check for errors. Check your punctuation and spelling, particularly the spelling of any new words you have chosen to use.

UNDERSTAND THE SELECTION

Answers

1. Examples will include: exporting ice, using a telegraph, and riding and building railroads
2. on July 4, 1845
3. in the wilderness
4. He wanted to see what nature could teach him.
5. Thoreau believed that if people followed their dreams, they would meet with success.
6. Sample answer: He felt safe and happy. All his worries left him, and he was able to absorb nature.
7. Sample answer: Nature gave them an opportunity to relax and be reflective. There was nothing in the woods to disturb them.
8. Answers will vary.
9. Sample answer: He probably would have continued to look at his innermost thoughts through the exploration of nature.
10. Sample answer: "A man is rich in proportion to the number of things which he can afford to let alone." This is good because people need to understand that material wealth isn't everything.

Respond to Literature

Divide the class into small groups and assign the name of one of the following writers: Annie Dillard, Studs Turkel, Russell Baker, Alice Walker, Jimmy Breslin, Nikki Giovanni, and James Baldwin. Ask them to find an essay or other nonfiction piece of writing by the person that reflects his or her ideas about life in the United States today.

WRITE ABOUT THE SELECTION

Prewriting

Using students' suggestions, make a list on the chalkboard of real places students like to visit to forget their troubles. Then ask students to suggest reasons why each is a good place to go to forget their troubles. Finally, have students think of their own imaginary places and jot down some details to help them write a descriptive paragraph.

Writing

Have students work on this section individually. Go around the class, giving help to any student who is having trouble.

Revising

Have students work in pairs to revise their paragraphs, making sure that each student has included several words that express their feelings.

Proofreading

Select one or two of the students' paragraphs as models for proofreading. Put the paragraphs on the overhead projector, and have the class suggest improvements.

THINK ABOUT ESSAYS

Although the Thoreau essay is an excerpt from a full-sized book, his prose and purpose follow essay style. Emerson is perhaps better known for his essays than his poetry. A very wide variety of topics and types are included in the genre of essay—so many, in fact, that critics find it difficult to categorize them all.

1. How would you classify the Thoreau excerpt—as narrative, descriptive, reflective (expository), or editorial (persuasive)? Explain.
2. Which of Thoreau's ideas did you find most thought-provoking? Why?
3. A parable is a short simple story used to point out a moral lesson. What parable did Thoreau use in his essay? What did it teach?
4. How would you classify the Emerson excerpt—as narrative, descriptive, reflective, or editorial? Explain.
5. Are the essays you have read formal or informal in style? Explain.

READING FOCUS

Identify Supporting Details Writers can make readers agree with them more readily if they provide strong support for their opinions. Thoreau and Emerson state many opinions in their essays. Choose an opinion from one of their essays and list several supporting details provided.

DEVELOP YOUR VOCABULARY

An *allusion* is a reference in speech or writing to an event, person, place, or thing that presumably is familiar to the listener or reader. Thoreau makes several allusions in his essay—to the mythological giant Atlas, to the Roman statesman Cato, and to the extremely rich king of ancient Lydia, Croesus, to name three of them.

There are a large number of English words that allude to people and places. They are called **eponymous** words. They are words derived from the name of a real or mythical person. For example, *saxophone* comes from the name of its inventor, Adolphe Sax. *Panic*, the word for a sudden, unreasoning fear, comes from the mythical god Pan, who had a reputation for frightening travelers in woodland areas.

Look up the following words in a dictionary that has word histories. Identify the meaning and place or person each word comes from.

1. cardigan
2. sandwich
3. marathon
4. quixotic
5. watt
6. cereal

DEVELOP YOUR VOCABULARY

Answers

1. a sweater that opens down the front; from the seventh Earl of Cardigan (1797–1868), an English general who wore one during the Crimean War (1854–1856)
2. two or three slices of bread with a filling of meat, cheese, or other food; from John Montagu, Earl of Sandwich (1718–1792), who ate them in order not to interrupt the play at gaming tables
3. a footrace of 26 miles, 385 yards, the distance run by a Greek runner who ran from Marathon to Athens to tell of the Greek victory over the Persians in 470 B.C.
4. visionary, impractical; from the unrealistically chivalrous main character in *Don Quixote*, by Miguel de Cervantes (1547–1616)
5. a unit of electrical power; from James Watt (1736–1819), Scottish inventor and pioneer in the development of steam engines
6. a grain used for food; from Ceres, the Roman goddess of agriculture

ESL Activity

Make sure you have dictionaries with word histories available in the classroom. Then lead a class discussion in which you discuss which word histories the students find the most interesting and why. Finally, have students look up these additional words: mausoleum, galvanize, zeppelin, silhouette, martial, jovial, meander.

THINK ABOUT ESSAYS

Answers

1. Sample answer: narrative for the most part, but the ending is persuasive. Reasons will vary.
2. Sample answer: Thoreau's insistence that one should "cultivate poverty like a garden herb, like sage."
3. He cites the story of the beautiful bug that hatched from an ancient wood. He used the story to suggest that beautiful human lives may appear from the "dry life of society . . . to enjoy its perfect summer life at last!"
4. Sample answer: It is reflective, because he aims to inform the reader of his reactions to nature. He is not trying to persuade readers into taking any particular action.
5. The style is informal. Sample answer: The essays both present personal views, draw on experience rather than knowledge, and are structured freely.

READING FOCUS

Sample Answer

Thoreau argues that the poor have all the important opportunities of the wealthy. The sun reflects as brightly through the windows of the poor as those of the rich. The poor often have more independent lives than the rich. A quiet mind may live as contentedly in a poorhouse as in a palace.

Selection Overview

SELECTION OBJECTIVES

After completing this selection, students will be able to

- understand and identify the theme of a story
- create a new event for a story
- understand and identify synonyms
- draw conclusions

Lesson Resources

David Swan
- Selection Synopsis, Teacher's Edition, p. T159f
- Comprehension and Vocabulary Workbook, pp. 39–40
- Language Enrichment Workbook, p. 24
- Teacher's Resources
  - Reinforcement, p. R20
  - Test, pp. T39–T40

More About Theme

Ask students what they think some of the great broad topics in literature are. Encourage students to discuss why writers have chosen these topics to write about over and over. Explain that the author's attitude toward these topics, as shown in this writing, is the theme. Then have students choose one of the great topics and write a paragraph about what that topic means to them.

About the Author

Because of an accident in his boyhood, Nathaniel Hawthorne was not able to participate in outdoor sports. As a result, he turned to reading, which became a lifelong passion for him. One of the subjects in which he was most interested was colonial history, and many of his literary pieces are about colonial life.

Learn About

THEME

The **theme** of a piece of literature is the message that the writer wants to convey to the reader. There are several reasons why it is important to understand the theme. First, theme helps you to understand how the writer feels about something. For example, it may be the writer's view of life. Second, theme underscores the relationship between character, events, and the outcome of the story. Finally, theme adds an extra dimension of interest to the story.

Sometimes, writers directly state the theme. However, if they do not, think about what the characters do and what happens to the characters as you read.

As you read "David Swan," ask yourself:

1. Is Hawthorne's message stated directly or indirectly?
2. What is Hawthorne's message to the reader?

READING FOCUS

Draw Conclusions When a character in a story does something, the reader can draw a conclusion about why the character acted in such a way. As you read "David Swan," think about the characters' motivation, or why they act as they do. Ask yourself: What motivates their actions? What do their actions tell about their personalities?

WRITING CONNECTION

Suppose that you are a writer. Think of a message you would like to convey to readers. Then think about a character who might be able to carry your message to the readers. Write a brief paragraph describing the character.

Cooperative Group Activity

To extend the Writing Connection activity, have students form a roundtable. Ask students who they believe are today's heroes and villains. Would they include environmentalists and polluters? Whom do they believe the transcendentalists would have seen as heroes? Why? Do they consider the character they wrote about a hero?

ESL Activity

Work with students to create a modern hero or villain. Then have them work in pairs to show how that character might convey this message: It is important not to dwell on events that might have been, could have been, or should have been. It is important to deal only with what is.

David Swan

by Nathaniel Hawthorne

We find David, at the age of 20, on the high road to the city of Boston, where an uncle was to take him behind the counter in his grocery store. Be it enough to say that he was a native of New Hampshire, born of good parents, and had received an ordinary school education. After traveling on foot from sunrise till nearly noon of a summer's day, his tiredness and the increasing heat forced him to rest. He looked ahead for a shady place where he could wait for the coming of the stagecoach. As if planted on purpose for him, there soon appeared a little tuft of maples. Then he noticed a fresh bubbling spring that seemed never to have sparkled for any traveler but David Swan. He kissed it with thirsty lips, and threw himself down on the bank. For a pillow he used some shirts and a pair of pants, tied up in a striped cotton handkerchief. The sunbeams could not reach him. The dust did not rise from the road after the heavy rain of yesterday. In short, his grassy bank suited the young man better than the softest of beds. The spring murmured sleepily beside him, and a deep sleep, perhaps hiding dreams within its depths, fell upon David Swan. But we are to relate events which he did not dream of.

While he lay sound asleep in the shade, other people were wide awake, and passed back and forth, on foot, on horseback, and in all sorts of vehicles. Some looked neither left nor right, and never knew that David was there. Some just glanced that way, without admitting the sleeper to their busy minds. Some laughed to see how soundly he slept. And several, whose hearts were full of scorn, ejected their venomous feelings on David Swan. A middle-aged widow, when no one else was near, told her-

---

tuft (TUFT) small bunch
relate (rih LAYT) tell
eject (ih JEKT) force out
venomous (VEN uh mus) poisonous; spiteful

Teaching Plan

INTRODUCE

Motivation

Ask students to think about what happens in their community while they are asleep at night. Make a list of their ideas on the chalkboard. Then elicit from students whether or not they are aware of the events and how the events influence their lives. Do they think the events might change their lives if they were aware of them? Have things passed them by because the students did not know about them?

Purpose-Setting Question

Why would Hawthorne have the main character fall asleep for most of the story?

READ

Literary Focus: *Theme*

As students read, encourage them to look for references to fortune, love, and death.

Reading Focus: *Draw Conclusions*

Ask students to make a list of the characters in the story. Have them jot down the conclusions they draw about each of them based on their actions.

CLOSE

Have students complete Review the Selection on pages 196–197.

Develop Vocabulary Skills

Ask a volunteer to read the vocabulary words footnoted in the story. As the student reads each word, write it on the chalkboard, along with its pronunciation and its definition. Then have students work in pairs to find the sentences in the story where the word is used. Have them determine which part of speech the word is. If students have difficulty, suggest that they use a dictionary to help them. Finally, have volunteers use each word in an original sentence.

self that the young fellow looked charming in his sleep. A temperance worker cursed him as an awful example of dead drunkenness by the roadside. But praise, laughter, curses, and even indifference were all one, or rather all nothing, to David Swan.

He had slept only a few minutes when a brown carriage, drawn by a handsome pair of horses, stopped nearly in front of David's resting place. A metal pin had fallen out, so that one of the wheels had slid off. The damage was slight, and brought only a moment's worry to an elderly merchant and his wife, who were returning to Boston in the carriage. While a servant started work on the wheels, the lady and gentleman sheltered themselves beneath the maple trees. There they saw the bubbling spring, and David Swan asleep beside it. The merchant stepped as lightly as he could, and his spouse tried not to rustle her silk dress.

"How soundly he sleeps!" whispered the old gentleman. "From what a depth he draws that easy breath! Such sleep as that would be worth to me more than half my income, for it would suppose good health and a mind free from troubles."

"And youth, besides," said the lady. "Even healthy and quiet old people do not sleep like this. Our slumber is no more like his than our wakefulness."

The longer they looked, the more they felt interested in the unknown youth, to whom the grassy bank and the maple shade were as a secret room. The woman suddenly perceived that a stray sunbeam fell down upon his face. She tried to push a branch to one side, so as to catch it. And having done this little act of kindness, she began to feel like a mother to him.

"Lady Luck seems to have laid him there," she whispered, "and to have brought us here to find him, after our disappointment with our cousin's son. I think I see a likeness to our departed Henry. Shall we waken him?"

"To what purpose?" said the merchant, pausing. "We know nothing about what he's really like."

"That open, honest face!" replied his wife. "This innocent sleep!"

---

temperance (TEM pur uns) belief that no one should drink alcohol
indifference (in DIF ur uns) lack of interest
spouse (SPOUS) husband or wife
perceive (pur SEEV) become aware of
departed (dih PAHRT id) dead

Literary Focus:
Plot

Ask students to identify, as they read, the three events that make up the story.

Reading Focus:
Draw Conclusions

Ask: Why does the merchant's wife want to waken David Swan? What does this tell you about her character? Why does the merchant not want to waken him? What does this tell you about his character?

Critical Thinking:
Compare

Have students compare what they know about the character traits of the merchant and the merchant's wife.

While these whispers were passing, the sleeper's breathing did not change, nor did his face show the least sign of interest. Yet Fortune was bending over him, just ready to let fall a shower of gold. The old merchant had lost his only son, and had no heir except a distant relative, with whose conduct he was dissatisfied. In such cases, people sometimes do stranger things than to act the magician and awaken this youth. He who fell asleep as a poor man would wake up to a rich life.

"Shall we not waken him?" repeated the lady, trying again.

"The coach is ready, sir," said the servant, behind.

The old couple jumped. With red faces, they hurried away. Waken the young man? Who would ever dream of doing anything so very ridiculous! The merchant threw himself back into the carriage, and filled his mind with business. Meanwhile, David Swan enjoyed his nap.

The carriage could not have gone more than a mile, when a charming young woman came along the road. Her lively step showed just how her happy heart was dancing. Perhaps it was this merry kind of motion that caused—is there any harm in saying it?—her garter to slip its knot. Knowing that the silken strap was relaxing its hold, she turned aside into the shelter of the maple trees, and there found a young man asleep by the spring!

Finding that she had stumbled into a gentleman's bedchamber, the girl blushed as red as any rose. "And for such a purpose, too!" she thought. She was about to make her escape on tiptoe—but there was peril near the sleeper. A monster of a bee had been wandering overhead—buzz, buzz, buzz—till finally it seemed to be settling on the eyelid of David Swan. The sting of a bee is sometimes deadly. The girl attacked the bee with her handkerchief, and drove it from beneath the maples. How sweet a picture! This done, with faster breath, and a deeper blush, she stole a glance at the youthful stranger for whom she had been battling with a dragon in the air.

"He is handsome!" thought she, and blushed redder yet.

How could it be that no dream of happiness should grow strong within him? How could it be that no such dream should wake him up, and allow him to see the girl? Why, at least, did no smile brighten upon his face? She had come, the maiden whose

---

peril (PER ul) danger

Literary Focus: *Theme*

Refer students to the line "Meanwhile, David Swan enjoyed his nap." Discuss how this line might lead readers to the theme of this story.

Critical Thinking: *Interpret*

Ask: What do the merchant and his wife represent? What does the young girl represent? What opportunities did the sleeping David Swan miss?

Reading Focus: *Draw Conclusions*

Discuss with students what Hawthorne reveals about the young woman by telling the reader that she brushed away a bee from David Swan. Ask: What conclusions can you draw about the young woman based on her actions?

soul, according to the old and beautiful idea, had once been separated from his own. She had come, the one that he, unknowingly, had so hoped to meet. Her, only, could he love with a perfect love. Him, only, could she receive into the depths of her heart. And now her reflection was faintly blushing in the water, by his side. Should it pass away, its happy glow would leave his life forever.

"How sound he sleeps!" murmured the girl.

She departed, but did not skip along the road so lightly as when she came.

Now, this girl's father was a thriving merchant in the neighborhood, and at the time, he happened to be looking out for just such a man as David Swan. Had David become acquainted with the daughter, he would also have become her father's clerk—and all else in natural order. So here, again, had good Fortune come near David Swan. She had stolen so near that her garments touched him lightly, and he knew nothing of the matter.

The girl was hardly out of sight when two men turned aside beneath the maple shade. Both had evil faces, set off by cloth caps which slanted down over their foreheads. Their clothing was shabby, yet had a certain smartness. These were a couple of rascals who got their living by whatever the devil sent them. Now, having no other business, they had bet the profits of their next piece of villainy on a game of cards, which they planned to play here under the trees. But, finding David asleep by the spring, one of the rogues whispered to the other:

"Hist!—Do you see that bundle under his head?"

The other villain nodded, winked, and leered.

"I'll bet you," said the first, "that there's a nice fat wallet hidden there among his shirts. And if not there, in one of his pants pockets."

"But what if he wakes up?" asked the other.

His companion pushed aside his jacket, pointed at the handle of a large knife, and nodded.

"So be it!" muttered the second villain.

They approached the unconscious David. While one pointed the dagger towards his heart, the other reached for the bundle

Critical Thinking: *Interpret*
What do the two men represent? How do they differ from the man and his wife and the young girl?

---

thriving (THRYV ing) very successful
rogue (ROHG) rascal; villain

Critical Thinking: *Apply*

Have students consider why Hawthorne chose events that included the possibilities for love, fortune, or death. Do most people search for love and fortune? How do people view death? Why do writers choose to write about these topics?

Literary Focus: *Theme*

Lead a class discussion in which students share their ideas about why the theme of this story is still interesting more than 150 years after it was written. Have students discuss how Hawthorne states his theme in the last paragraph of the story.

Reading Focus: *Draw Conclusions*

Ask: What conclusions can you draw about David Swan from his actions, or from his inaction?

under his head. Their two faces, wrinkled and ghastly with guilt and fear, bent over David. They looked horrible enough to be mistaken for fiends, should he suddenly awake. But David Swan had never worn a more tranquil face, even when asleep in his mother's arms.

"I must take away the bundle," whispered one.

"If he moves, I'll strike," muttered the other.

But, at this moment, a dog, its nose to the ground, came in beneath the trees. It looked back and forth at the two evil men, and finally at the quiet sleeper. Then it lapped at the spring.

"Ah!" said one villain. "We can't do anything now. The dog's master must be close behind."

"Let's be off," said the other.

The man with the dagger put it away, and they left the spot joking together. As for David Swan, he still slept quietly, neither conscious of the shadow of death when it hung over him, nor of the glow of renewed life when the shadow departed.

He slept, but no longer so quietly as at first. An hour's repose had taken away his tiredness. Now he moved—first the lips, without a sound—and now he talked, in an inward tone, to the vanishing ghosts of his dream. But a noise of wheels came louder and louder along the road, until it smashed through the disappearing clouds of David's sleep. He jumped up, and there was the stagecoach.

"Hello, driver!" shouted he. "Take a passenger?"

"Room on top," answered the driver.

Up climbed David, and rode away toward Boston. He never glanced back at the spring. He knew not that Wealth had thrown a golden glow upon its waters, nor that Love had sighed softly to their murmurs, nor that Death had threatened to make them red with blood. Sleeping or waking, we never hear the silent footsteps of the things that almost happen. Yet these things are always right beside our paths. It is a wonder that there should still be order enough in human life to make the future even partially known.

---

tranquil (TRANG kwul) peaceful; at rest
repose (rih POHZ) rest

Mini Quiz

Write the following questions on the chalkboard or overhead projector and call on students to fill in the blanks. Discuss the answers with the class.

1. David Swan was walking on the ________ to Boston.
2. The young woman chased away a monster of a ________.
3. The young woman's father was a ________.
4. The villains had evil ________.
5. David woke up and jumped on the ________.

Answers

1. high road
2. bee
3. merchant
4. faces
5. stagecoach

AUTHOR BIOGRAPHY

Nathaniel Hawthorne (1804–1864)

The life of the American writer Nathaniel Hawthorne is living proof that "practice makes perfect." Upon graduation from Bowdoin College in 1825, he made up his mind to be a writer. This was a courageous decision, for at the time the number of Americans who earned a living writing fiction could be counted on the fingers of one hand. Hawthorne knew what his decision would mean—practice, practice, and more practice. He returned to his mother's house in Salem, Massachusetts to write. A year passed and he was still at it. Another year went by, and then more years. After five years of effort, he had sold only one of his stories. Still more time passed. Hawthorne just wouldn't give up. Finally, after "twelve dark years" as he later called them, he published his first book, *Twice-Told Tales*.

But Hawthorne's practice paid off in perfection. Today he's recognized as one of the giants in American literature. Behind his polished sentences, the reader senses a kind, thoughtful man. Hawthorne wrote about the people of his time, of course, but first of all he wrote about ideas. What really makes a person a "criminal"? Is any person completely "good"? Which are more important to the individual, the dreams of youth or the rewards of age? Questions such as these will never die, and neither will the best of Hawthorne's stories.

What did the mature Hawthorne mean when he said there had been "twelve dark years" in his life?

MORE ABOUT THE AUTHOR

Hawthorne was born in Salem, Massachusetts, on the Fourth of July, 1804. Many of Hawthorne's works are set in New England in the 1600s. His most famous works were set in Salem and nearby Boston. His fictional works often dealt with the theme of mortality, sin, and redemption.

Additional Works

BY NATHANIEL HAWTHORNE

Hawthorne's Short Stories, Random House (Paper), 1955.

The Scarlet Letter, Bantam Classic and Loveswept, 1981.

The Hawthorne Treasury: Complete Novels and Selected Tales of Nathaniel Hawthorne, Modern Library, 1999.

UNDERSTAND THE SELECTION

Answers

1. David Swan is on his way to Boston to work for his uncle.
2. The three major events in this story are: an elderly couple stops by David Swan; a young girl stops by him; two thieves stop by to rob him.
3. Sample answer: David Swan sleeps through three events that might have changed his life. The narrator speculates on possible outcomes.
4. Some people just pass him by; some laugh; some get angry; some are indifferent.
5. Sample answer: It does not make any difference how people respond because David Swan is asleep.
6. The merchant does not want to take the risk that David Swan is not a nice person.
7. Sample answer: Love is passing her by.
8. Answers will vary. Accept all reasonable responses.
9. Answers will vary. Accept all reasonable responses.
10. Sample answer: If David Swan had known about his missed opportunities or his danger, he might have been too full of hope or fear to be at peace.

Respond to Literature

Tell students that Hawthorne liked to travel through New England unnoticed to gather information for his stories. He went to country fairs and other social meetings. Ask students how they think these travels influenced his writing.

WRITE ABOUT THE SELECTION

Prewriting

Have students make a list of events that might have happened to a young man in a grocery store in 1837. Then lead a class discussion about what David Swan might have been doing that would have prevented him from knowing about each event. Before students begin to write, encourage them to include an event in which love, fame, happiness, wealth, or sadness passes David Swan by.

Writing

Have students work on this section individually. Give help to any student who is having difficulty.

Revising

Make this a cooperative group activity. Have students work in small groups to revise their paragraphs. Remind students to make sure that the details of their events are in keeping with the way people lived in 1837.

Proofreading

Select one paragraph from each of the small groups, and put it on the overhead projector. Have the class suggest improvements.

Review the Selection

UNDERSTAND THE SELECTION

Recall

1. Where is David Swan going?
2. List three major events that occur.
3. How is this story like a fantasy?

Infer

4. How do the people who pass feel about David Swan?
5. Interpret "But praise, laughter, curses, and even indifference were all one, or rather all nothing, to David Swan."
6. Why doesn't the elderly merchant want to wake up David Swan?
7. Why are the girl's footsteps not so lively when she leaves?

Apply

8. Predict what might have happened if Swan had awakened.
9. Which event might Swan choose to wake up for? Why?
10. Explain this quote as it applies to the story: "Could we know all that *might* have happened, life would be too full of hope and fear to give us a single hour of true peace."

Respond to Literature

How does the theme of this story illustrate the writing style of the 1800s?

WRITE ABOUT THE SELECTION

At the conclusion of "David Swan," the young man wakes up and catches a stagecoach to Boston where he is to begin a new job at his uncle's grocery store. Because he had been napping, three events pass him by without his knowledge. Is it likely that more events pass him by in Boston? Why? Write a paragraph about something that happens to David Swan in Boston without his knowledge.

Prewriting Freewrite for a few minutes about an event that happens at David Swan's uncle's grocery store. Be sure to include what he was doing that prevents him from knowing about the event. Try to keep in mind that the event occurs in 1837.

Writing Use your freewriting as a basis for your paragraph. Be sure to make it clear that David Swan does not know that the event is taking place.

Revising When you revise, make sure that the details of the event are in keeping with 1837, the year the story takes place. If you have not, delete anything in the story that would not have happened in 1837.

Proofreading Read over your paragraph to check for errors. Be sure that all your sentences end with periods, question marks, or exclamation marks. Check that you have punctuated dialogue correctly and used new vocabulary words appropriately.

THINK ABOUT THEME

By understanding the theme, you can have a greater appreciation for stories you read. It also helps you to develop a clearer understanding of what a writer thinks and feels. Hawthorne introduces his own story, in which he gives the reader a clear picture of what the theme is. Then he explains that the story will illustrate this idea. In effect, he is saying to the reader: This is what I believe and now I am going to give you examples that support my idea.

1. What is the theme of "David Swan"?
2. By what means did Nathaniel Hawthorne illustrate the theme of his story?
3. What larger picture did the three events represent?
4. Did Hawthorne directly state his theme? If so, where?
5. How did the events help you understand the theme?

Reading Focus

Draw Conclusions As you read "David Swan" you drew conclusions about each character. Choose two characters and describe the conclusions you drew about each one. On which of their actions did you base your conclusions?

DEVELOP YOUR VOCABULARY

A **synonym** is a word whose meaning is similar to, or the same as, another word. For example, *indifference* means "lack of interest." Words that have similar meanings are *disinterest*, *apathy*, and *unconcern*. Knowing synonyms for many words can make your writing more interesting.

Read the sentences below. Choose a word from the list that is a synonym for each italicized word.

melodious
peril
tuft
venomous
thriving

1. The small *clump* of flowers caught his eye when he sat down by the pond.
2. Jeremy's *hostile* words hurt Kira.
3. Her antique business was *prospering* despite the business slump.
4. Because it was so cold on the mountain, the climbers were at great *risk*.
5. The parakeet imitated the *tuneful* music.

THINK ABOUT THEME

Answers

1. People are unaware of many events that almost happen. This allows them peace of mind.
2. Three events occurred while David Swan was asleep. He knew nothing about them.
3. The events represented wealth, love, and death.
4. Hawthorne stated the theme in the last paragraph.
5. Because the main character is asleep, a certain tension is created that consistently keeps the reader's attention focused on the theme.

DEVELOP YOUR VOCABULARY

Answers

1. tuft
2. venomous
3. thriving
4. peril
5. melodious

ESL Activity

Have students work with partners who are proficient English speakers to complete the vocabulary assignment. Encourage ESL students to add the synonyms to their word banks.

Reading Focus

Sample Answer

The young woman and the merchant's wife showed kindness. The young woman brushed a potentially dangerous bee away. The merchant's wife pushed a branch aside and considered whether David might be a replacement for her dead son.

Selection Overview

Selection Objectives

After completing this selection, students will be able to

- understand and identify sound devices in poetry
- write an opinion
- identify figurative and literal language in poetry
- make inferences

Lesson Resources

Works of Emily Dickinson

- Selection Synopses, Teacher's Edition, pp. T159f–T159g
- Comprehension and Vocabulary Workbook, pp. 40–41
- Language Enrichment Workbook, pp. 25–26
- Teacher's Resources
  Reinforcement, p. R21
  Test, pp. T41–T42

More About Sounds in Poetry

Encourage students to think of sentences in which they use alliteration, assonance, and consonance. You might first want to write some examples on the chalkboard. Finally, have students write a sentence using each type or repetition on their own.

About the Author

It is somewhat difficult to understand the richness and depth of Dickinson's poetry, given the narrowness of her life. However, it is known that her family had an extensive library of almost one thousand books and that Dickinson read widely. Even so, it is believed that books were not her source of inspiration. Rather, it was probably her incredible imagination.

Learn About

Sounds in Poetry

Rhythm, meter, and rhyme all add musical effects to poetry, but they are not the only devices available to poets. The use of certain letters of the alphabet affects the sound of poetry. Some letters have a soft "liquid" sound: *l*, *m*, *n*, and *r*. Other letters have a more "explosive" sound: *b*, *d*, *g*, *k*, *p*, and *t*. Poets can manipulate the use of these sounds to create soothing or exciting lines.

Repetition is part of all music, and it plays a part in the music of poetry too. For example, the repetition of initial consonant sounds, as in "They *s*at in *s*olemn *s*ilence," is called **alliteration**. The repetition of vowel sounds, as in "*I* can f*i*nd the t*i*me," is called **assonance**. The repetition of final consonant sounds, as in "fir*st* and la*st*," is called **consonance**.

As you read the following poems, ask yourself:

1. Which sound devices did Dickinson use in her poems?
2. What effect do the devices have on the poems?

Reading Focus

Make Inferences An inference is a conclusion drawn from facts or evidence. You can use your own insights and knowledge of human behavior and the world around you in order to make inferences.

Reading poetry often requires the reader to infer meaning, or to think beyond the words on the page. As you read each poem, use your own knowledge and details in the poem to make inferences about the poem's meaning.

Writing Connection

Write a sentence using "liquid" letters and another using "explosive" letters. Explain the effect of each sentence on you.

Viewing Fine Art

Photography as a form of art was common in the 20th century; photographs no longer simply documented reality. Here, for example, the photographer has shot a rural scene much like a painting. The contrast of the dark tree with lighter areas and of the leaning tree with a similar arc in the woodpile; the variety of textures in wood, water; and hills; and the relationship of the myriad tiny branches to the soft hills behind—these elements all make the photograph an artistic composition. Ask: What words might you use to describe this picture? Which might you use in a poem?

Cooperative Group Activity

For the Writing Connection activity, have students work in pairs to make a list of words that have liquid and explosive sounds. Then have students use the words in sentences. Finally, have volunteers read their sentences to the class and have the class discuss how the sentences sound. Are the sentences soothing? Are the sentences exciting or explosive?

In the Garden, Irving Ramsay Wiles. Christie's Images

I'm nobody

by Emily Dickinson

I'm nobody! Who are you?
Are you nobody, too?
Then there's a pair of us—don't tell!
They'd banish us, you know.

How dreary to be somebody!
How public, like a frog
To tell your name the livelong day
To an admiring bog!

---

dreary (DRIR ee) dull; tiresome
bog (BOG) swamp; wet ground

TEACHING PLAN

INTRODUCE

Motivation

Ask students to think about what it might be like not to leave their homes for many years. About what would they write? From where would they get their inspiration? What would they do all day? Guide students in a group discussion in which they realize that people can look inward for inspiration and ideas; that people really don't have to go very far away to find ideas about which to write. Imagination is a very powerful tool for a writer.

Purpose-Setting Question

Since Dickinson did not leave her home for many years, how might she have written in the contemporary style of the 1800s?

READ

Literary Focus: *Sounds in Poetry*

Encourage partners to read the poems to each other to better hear the sounds that Dickinson creates. Have students point out each use of alliteration, assonance, and consonance.

Reading Focus: *Make Inferences*

Ask for a volunteer to read each poem. After each poem has been read, lead a group discussion in which the class infers the meaning of the poem. Have students take notes on which inferences were made from their own knowledge verses from details in the poem.

CLOSE

Have students complete Review the Selection on pages 206–207.

ESL Activity

Have students choose something from their own cultures that may be unfamiliar to others in the class. Then have them give the object, a photograph, or a drawing of it to another student to write a poem about. They might compare their poems with "I never saw a Moor."

Develop Vocabulary Skills

Ask volunteers to use each vocabulary word in an original sentence. If students have difficulty, have them refer to how a word is used in the poems. Then ask students to replace each vocabulary word in the poems by using a word or words from the definition. Try to help them see that poets choose their words very carefully.

Viewing Fine Art

Irving Ramsay Wiles (1861–1948) painted figurative subjects and landscapes. Discuss the quiet atmosphere of this painting. Ask: What might the woman in this painting have in common with Emily Dickinson?

A word is dead

by Emily Dickinson

A word is dead
When it is said,
Some say.
I say it just
Begins to live
That day.

Literary Focus:
Sounds in Poetry

Have students count the syllables in each word of the poem, "A word is dead." Ask: How do the short words affect the reading of the poem?

Critical Thinking:
Interpret

Ask: Why does Dickinson disagree with those who think a word is dead once it is spoken?

I never saw a moor

by Emily Dickinson

I never saw a moor,
I never saw the sea;
Yet know I how the heather looks,
And what a wave must be.

I never spoke with God,
Nor visited in heaven;
Yet certain am I of the spot
As if the chart were given.

Reading Focus:
Make Inferences
Ask: What do you think the meaning of the poem is? (the power of imagination) What clues led you to infer this meaning? What leads you to infer that the poet believes in God?

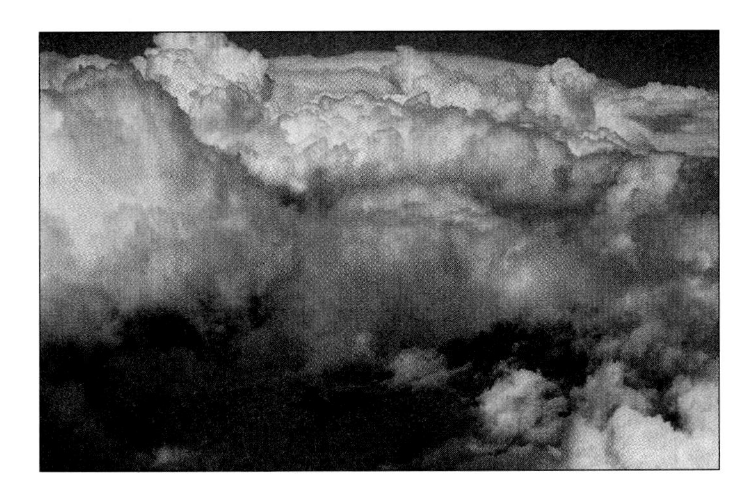

---

moor (MUUR) open wasteland
heather (HETH ur) low evergreen plant that often grows on moors

Reading Focus: *Make Inferences*

Ask: What can you infer about how the author feels about bad weather from this poem? What words in the poem support your response?

Critical Thinking: *Synthesize*

Ask students why they think that Dickinson referred to nature in so many of her poems.

Viewing Fine Art

George Inness (1825–1894) was an American landscape painter whose dreamy, romantic scenes were influenced both by the Hudson River School and impressionism. He specialized in the gentle eastern landscapes of fields and rolling hills rather than the grander scenery of the Hudson Valley or the western states. Inness tried to combine a realistic approach with luminous, light-filled images. In this scene of New Jersey, Inness took a non-dramatic view and made it into a dreamy, poetic image. (Another painting by Inness appears on page 185.) Ask: How does this painting fit the mood of Dickinson's poem?

The sky is low

by Emily Dickinson

The sky is low, the clouds are mean,
A travelling flake of snow
Across a barn or through a rut
Debates if it will go.

A narrow wind complains all day
How some one treated him;
Nature, like us, is sometimes caught
Without her diadem.

Home at Montclair, George Inness. The Granger Collection

rut (RUT) a track made by a wheeled vehicle
diadem (DY uh dem) crown (more like halo here)

Some keep the Sabbath

by Emily Dickinson

Some keep the Sabbath going to church;
I keep it staying at home,
With a bobolink for a chorister,
And an orchard for a dome.

5 Some keep the Sabbath in surplice;
I just wear my wings,
And instead of tolling the bell for church,
Our little sexton sings.

God preaches,—a noted clergyman,—
10 And the sermon is never long;
So instead of getting to heaven at last,
I'm going all along!

bobolink (BOB uh lingk) kind of song bird
chorister (KAWR ih stur) singer in a choir
surplice (SUR plis) loose-fitting garment worn by members of the clergy and choirs
sexton (SEKS tun) church caretaker who rings the bells

Comparing Selections

After students have read the poems, ask them which theme Dickinson wrote about most often.

Literary Focus: *Sounds in Poetry*

Have students listen for the sound of the letter *s* in this poem. Ask: What is the effect of this in the poem?

Reading Focus: *Make Inferences*

Ask students to infer the author's mood as expressed in the letter and to cite words or phrases to support their opinions.

Literary Focus: *Author's Purpose*

Remind students that an author has a purpose for writing, e.g., to inform, entertain, or persuade. Ask students to name the author's purpose and to give specifics to back their choices.

Background Note

Thomas Wentworth Higginson, the recipient of the letter shown here, was beginning to establish a reputation as an essayist and lecturer in the cause of reforms at the time he received his first letter from Emily Dickinson. She was responding to his "Letter to a Young Contributor," the lead article in *The Atlantic Monthly*. She knew him to be a liberal thinker who was interested in the status of women. The importance of the correspondence with Higginson, which once begun continued throughout Dickinson's life, cannot be exaggerated.

Letter to Thomas Wentworth Higginson

by Emily Dickinson

Letter to Mr. T. W. Higginson
April 15, 1862

Mr. Higginson,

Are you too deeply occupied to say if my verse is alive?

The Mind is so near itself—it cannot see, distinctly—and I have none to ask. Should you think it breathed—and had you the leisure to tell me, I should feel quick gratitude—

If I make the mistake—that you dared to tell me—would give me sincerer honor toward you—

I enclosed my name—asking you. If you please—Sir- to tell me what is true? That you will not betray me—it is needless to ask—since honor is its own pawn—

Mini Quiz

Write the following questions on the chalkboard or overhead projector and call on students to fill in the blanks. Discuss the answers with the class.

1. In "I'm nobody," the speaker thinks it would be ________ to be somebody.
2. In "A word is dead," the speaker believes that a word ________ when it is said.
3. In "I never saw a Moor," the speaker never ________ with God nor ________ heaven.
4. In "The sky is low," nature is sometimes caught without its ________.
5. In "Some keep the Sabbath," the little sexton is a ________.

Answers

1. dreary
2. begins to live
3. spoke; visited
4. diadem
5. bird

AUTHOR BIOGRAPHY

Emily Dickinson (1830–1886)

"If I read a book," wrote Emily Dickinson, "and it makes my whole body so cold no fire can ever warm me, I know that is poetry. If I feel . . . as if the top of my head were taken off, I know that is poetry. These are the only ways I know it. Is there any other way?"

"*. . . as if the top of my head were taken off . . .* "! Those are strong words, but Emily Dickinson knew what she was talking about. Today Emily Dickinson is considered one of the greatest American poets—if not *the* greatest.

Her story is a strange one. Nearly all her life was passed in a large house in Amherst, Massachusetts. As a girl she was active and fun-loving. She had a year of college. Then, in her early 20s, something happened that changed her life. It was probably a disappointing romance, but that may not be the whole story. At any rate, she started spending more and more time alone. She read a lot. She helped with family chores. She watched the wonders of nature in a private yard and garden. She stopped going to church. By and by her parents died, and her world grew smaller still. What happened outside this private world—even the Civil War—held little interest for her. She dressed only in white. She left chores outside the house to her unmarried sister, Vinnie. She refused to meet strangers. During the last ten years of her life she never went out.

Emily Dickinson died at the age of 55. Her relatives knew that poetry had been one of her interests. But she had written poetry mainly to please herself. During her lifetime, only seven of her poems had been published. Her family and a few friends had seen some others, but no one had dreamed of the surprise that came following her death. Her sister Vinnie entered her room to find drawers full of poems, trunks full of poems! In all, 1,775 were found! Most of them were arranged by year. In 1862, for instance, she had written 366 poems!

In a way, Emily Dickinson's world was small. But in another way, the world that she created was huge. Her mind stretched far, far out, beyond death—even beyond the world as we know it. Our world is richer for it.

In your opinion, what might have happened to make an active young woman slowly withdraw from society?

MORE ABOUT THE AUTHOR

Tell students that Emily Dickinson knew few of the contemporary writers of the 1800s and was little influenced by them. And yet her writing is reflective of that time period. Many of her finest poems are about nature.

Additional Works

BY EMILY DICKINSON

Collected Poems of Emily Dickinson, Outlet, 1986.

Complete Poems of Emily Dickinson, Little Brown & Co., 1976.

The Poems of Emily Dickinson, Balknap Press, September 1999.

Review the Selection

UNDERSTAND THE SELECTION

Recall

1. Where does the speaker keep the Sabbath?
2. With whom does the speaker keep the Sabbath?
3. Who is the sexton in "Some keep the Sabbath" and what does it do?

Infer

4. Explain why you think the speaker in "I'm nobody" likes being nobody.
5. In "A word is dead," why does a word come alive when it is spoken?
6. Why did Dickinson write to Higginson?
7. In your opinion, what is the theme of "The sky is low"?

Apply

8. Select your favorite Dickinson poem. Explain why it is your favorite.
9. Suppose you are a poet. Name two things you have never seen or experienced about which you might write.
10. Why might Dickinson choose to use a frog as an example of somebody?

Respond to Literature

How does Dickinson's poetry reflect Emerson's group's transcendental idea about writing?

WRITE ABOUT THE SELECTION

In the poem "I'm nobody," the speaker makes it clear that she or he prefers to be nobody. Suppose that you can either be "nobody" or "somebody." Which would you choose to be? Why? Be sure to think about the various pros and cons of your choices before you finally make up your mind.

Prewriting Write down on a piece of paper whether you want to be "nobody" or "somebody." Try to think about what each of these situations would be like and how you would feel about each. Then make a list of all the reasons you can think of for your choice.

Writing Use your list to help you write a paragraph about why you chose to be "nobody" or "somebody." Include three or more reasons why you made your choice.

Revising When you revise, make sure you have included two reasons for your choice. Then add one more reason from your list to your paragraph. Finally, reread your paragraph to make sure that your choices make sense. Revise as much as necessary to make sure that your reasons are clear.

Proofreading Read over your paragraph to check for errors. Be sure that all your sentences end with the correct punctuation marks. Check your internal punctuation as well.

UNDERSTAND THE SELECTION

Answers

1. at home
2. with nature
3. a bird that sings
4. Sample answer: If the person were well known, he or she would have to spend time with the public.
5. Sample answer: Words come alive when they are spoken because they have meaning for the listener.
6. Sample answer: She sought constructive criticism of her work.
7. Sample answer: Nature is not always nice; it can be mean and petty.
8. Answers will vary. Accept all reasonable responses.
9. Answers will vary. Accept all reasonable responses.
10. Sample answer: Dickinson chose to use a frog because it makes an ugly noise.

Respond to Literature

Have students identify the subject about which Dickinson writes that is similar to the subject other writers of that time period use. Then ask students to work in small groups to make a list of some nature topics about which they could write. Have them choose one topic that is reflective of the community in which they live. For example, students might have a river in their community; the river might reflect, or symbolize, their own changing ideas and thoughts; that is, their changing ideas can be likened to the changing current in a river.

WRITE ABOUT THE SELECTION

Prewriting

Divide the class into two groups—those who choose to be somebody and those who choose to be nobody. Have each group write a list of the pros and cons of their choices. Finally, have a volunteer read the lists.

Writing

Have students work on this section individually. If students are having difficulty, you may want to have them refer to the written lists again to help them.

Revising

Have students work in pairs to revise their work. Have them check to make sure that they have included at least two reasons for their choices. Remind them that now is the time to add one more choice.

Proofreading

Ask for volunteers to share their paragraphs with the class. Put the paragraphs on the overhead projector. Have the class suggest improvements.

THINK ABOUT SOUNDS IN POETRY

Poetry has musical qualities that prose does not have. Repetition of initial consonant letters (**alliteration**), of vowel sounds (**assonance**), and of final consonant sounds (**consonance**) help the poet to create musical effects. The use of liquid and explosive letters of the alphabet can also add to the music of poetry.

1. Which musical device is used in the first two lines of "I'm nobody"? Cite the words that produce this device.
2. Which musical device is used in the first line of "A word is dead"? Cite the words that produce this device.
3. The use of one particular letter, especially at the beginning of words, is repeated in "Some keep the Sabbath." What letter is it, and what is the name of the device it represents?
4. Does "I never saw a moor" have more liquid or more explosive sounds in the first stanza? In the second stanza?
5. Which is more important in musical devices, spelling or sound? Why?

Reading Focus

Make Inferences Choose one of Emily Dickinson's poems that you read in this selection. What inferences can you make about the poem's meaning based on your own experiences? What inferences can you make based on words or images in the poem?

DEVELOP YOUR VOCABULARY

Figurative language is the use of imagery, symbols, or other devices to create meaning beyond the dictionary meanings of the words used. For example, in the line "A narrow wind complains all day," Dickinson wrote words that do not mean exactly what they say. The wind makes a lot of noise all day; the word *complains* is used figuratively. In the line "I never saw the sea," however, Dickinson uses words with their exact dictionary meanings. The language is **literal**.

Read the sentences below. For each, indicate whether the figurative or literal meaning of the italicized word is used.

1. "How *dreary* to be somebody!"
2. "I never saw a *moor*, . . ."
3. "Nature, like us, is sometimes caught Without her *diadem*."
4. "Bell-shaped *heather* flowers were in bloom."
5. "And instead of tolling the bell for church, Our little *sexton* sings."
6. "They'd *banish* us, you know."

THINK ABOUT SOUNDS IN POETRY

Answers

1. assonance; *who*, *you*, *you*, *too*
2. consonance; *word*, *dead*
3. *S*; alliteration
4. liquid; explosive
5. sound: Sample answer: Spelling can be misleading; *though* and *rough* are spelled alike but have no other sound relationship. *Pear* and *fair* are rhyming words.

DEVELOP YOUR VOCABULARY

Answers

1. literal
2. literal
3. figurative
4. literal
5. figurative
6. literal

You may want to review what figurative and literal language is. Write the following sentences on the chalkboard:

1. The wind moans a sad song.
2. The wind is blowing hard.

Elicit from students that in the first sentence *moans* is used figuratively; in the second sentence the words are used in their dictionary meanings.

Reading Focus

Sample Answer

In "I never saw a Moor," one may infer that Emily Dickinson has a good imagination. She knows what things look like that she has never seen. She mentions heather on the moor and waves in the sea. One can also infer that she believes in God and heaven.

ESL Activity

ESL students may have difficulty with poetic form and brevity. Have these students work in pairs with proficient English speakers to paraphrase a poem into prose. Encourage students to use a dictionary to look up unfamiliar words. Then have pairs read their prose to the class.

Focus ON POETRY

Guide students through the discussion of the elements of poetry, reminding them that they have encountered these elements in the poems they have read in this unit. Then explain that they have also read both narrative and lyric poems in this unit. Remind them that a lyric poem expresses the poet's emotional response to a person, place, object, or idea; while a narrative poem tells a story about characters and events. Elicit from them which selection was a narrative poem and which selections were lyric poems.

ELEMENTS OF POETRY

In discussing the speaker of a poem, ask students to recall who they think the speaker of "Paul Revere's Ride" is? (Answers will vary. Sample answer: nation/American) Ask students to think about whom they would use to speak for them in a poem.

Have students share their thoughts about how figurative language made Dickinson's poetry more interesting to them.

Discuss how Dickinson successfully used the connotation and denotation of words in the poems.

Ask student to look back through Dickinson's poems to find out how she used sound devices to help convey her ideas. You may wish to have students jot down the words that she used and explain which sound device each is.

Focus ON POETRY

What is a poem, and what does a poem do? Poetry is writing in which imaginative, colorful language is used to paint a picture in the reader's mind. It can tell a story, express feelings and thoughts, or describe things.

You can tell a poem the minute you see it; its structure is different from prose. Thoughts and feelings are captured in a more concise way. The poems you have read in this unit are made up of stanzas. **Stanzas** are divisions in poems that are made up of two or more lines. The poets have chosen their words carefully to create rhythm and rhyme, two elements that convey thoughts and feelings and move the poem along at a steady pace.

There are a number of elements besides rhythm and rhyme that poets use to help them write poetry. These elements work together to make a poem come alive in the reader's mind. Let's look at some of these elements so that you can learn how to understand and enjoy poetry better.

Figurative Language Figurative language, such as simile, metaphor, personification, and hyperbole, is another device poets use to convey their feelings and thoughts. Figurative language paints a picture in the reader's mind that is different from that conveyed by the literal, or dictionary meaning, of individual words. It helps the reader think of something in a different way.

A **simile** compares two unlike objects using the words *like* or *as*. *She sang like a bird* is an example. A **metaphor** compares two unlike things, without using extra words to show that a comparison is being made. An example of a metaphor is: *The young dancer is a butterfly.* **Personification** gives human qualities to nonhuman objects. *The laughing brook* is an example of personification. **Hyperbole** is an exaggerated statement, such as: *That cat is as big as an elephant!* Uses of these different kinds of figurative language help to make poems more interesting and to describe things in a different way. Simile and metaphor make a connection between two unlike things that the reader might never have thought about before. On the other hand, personification and hyperbole can be used in a humorous way or for exaggeration.

Character/Speaker The voice or narrator of a poem is not necessarily the real voice of the poet. Often, poets put on a mask. They create a voice, separate from their own, to express their thoughts. The poet can write in the voice of a child, a father, a nation, or even the world.

Connotation and Denotation A reader should look closely at how poets use words. Often, writers use words that have two kinds of meanings. The connotation of a word suggests its emotional meaning—the feeling the word suggests to the reader. The denotation of a word is the actual meaning of a word as given in a dictionary. In the poem "I'm nobody" Dickinson wrote:

How dreary to be somebody!
How public, like a frog
To tell your name the livelong day
To an admiring bog!

Bog has an emotional meaning here. Dickinson did not use it to mean *swamp*, which is its dictionary meaning. She used it connotatively to imply a group of nameless, faceless people.

Sound Devices Poets also use sound devices, such as onomatopoeia and alliteration. **Onomatopoeia** is the use of words that sound like their meaning. *Splash* is an example. **Alliteration** is the repetition of initial consonant sounds in a line of poetry. *Some keep the Sabbath in surplice* is an example of alliteration. Poets use different elements because they want to share their thoughts in ways that will appeal to the imagination.

Real-Life Application

Encourage students to have a group discussion about popular music and how writers of current music might use different elements of poetry. Elicit from them if there is a rhythm to rap and other urban music. Do rap artists use sound devices to create certain feelings? Ask volunteers to recite some appropriate rap music. Finally, have students work in small groups to write a rap or similar song in which they include rhythm and sound devices. Encourage them to decide who the narrator of the song will be beforehand. The narrator will read or perform the song for the class.

SELECTION OVERVIEW

SELECTION OBJECTIVES

After completing this selection, students will be able to

- understand and identify the elements of poetry
- write a review of a poem
- identify homophones
- paraphrase

Lesson Resources

The First Snow-fall
- Selection Synopsis, Teacher's Edition, p. T159g
- Comprehension and Vocabulary Workbook, pp. 43–44
- Language Enrichment Workbook, pp. 27–28
- Teacher's Resources
  Reinforcement, p. R22
  Test, pp. T43–T44
  Literary Analysis, pp. L6–L7

More About the Literary Period

In this poem, James Russell Lowell uses nature to explore the innermost feelings of the speaker in the poem. Although Lowell was not a transcendentalist, he most certainly was aware of the writers in the group. He was also aware of contemporary issues because of the publication of his magazine. In fact, both Lowell and Thoreau were heavily involved in the abolitionist movement.

About the Author

James Russell Lowell went to Harvard University, from which he graduated with a law degree in 1840. However, he decided that he wanted to have a literary career. He founded the literary magazine, *The Pioneer*, in which he published the work of the leading writers of the day. These included Elizabeth Barrett Browning, Nathaniel Hawthorne, Edgar Allan Poe, and John Greenleaf Whittier.

MODEL

THE FIRST SNOW FALL

by James Russell Lowell

FOCUS ON POETRY STUDY HINTS

Notice how Lowell uses end rhymes to link thoughts.

The snow had begun in the gloaming,
And busily all the night
Had been heaping field and highway
With a silence deep and white.

Think about the connotation of the words *ermine* and *pearl*. What feelings do they suggest to you?

5 Every pine and fir and hemlock
Wore ermine too dear for an earl,
And the poorest twig on the elm-tree
Was ridged inch deep with pearl.

The poet uses onomatopoeia. Which word is it?

From sheds new-roofed with Carrara
10 Came Chanticleer's muffled crow,
The stiff rails softened to swan's-down,
And still fluttered down the snow.

I stood and watched by the window
The noiseless work of the sky,

Lowell uses a simile here. What is it?

15 And the sudden flurries of snow-birds,
Like brown leaves whirling by.

---

gloaming (GLOHM ing) twilight
ermine (UR min) a weasel whose fur turns to white in the winter
Carrara (kuh RAHR uh) fine, white marble
chanticleer (CHAN tih klir) a rooster

Cooperative Group Activity

Choose a natural event that would occur in the area where you live—thunderstorms for example. Have students work in pairs to think of one simile, one metaphor, and several sound devices about thunderstorms. Remind students that a poem is a colorful way to share ideas and thoughts. Have students keep their notes for a later activity.

ESL Activity

Ask students to choose two natural events—one common in the area where they live and one common in their native country—perhaps a storm or forest fire. Develop one example each of simile, metaphor, personification, and two sound devices for each event.

Develop Vocabulary Skills

Ask a volunteer to read the vocabulary words that are footnoted in the poem. As each word is read, write it on the chalkboard and pronounce it again. Repeat the definition. Ask for volunteers to orally use each word in an original sentence. If students have difficulty, have them reread the footnotes and look at how the word is used in the poem.

I thought of a mound in sweet Auburn[1]
Where a little headstone stood;
How the flakes were folding it gently,
20 As did robins the babes in the wood.

Create a picture in your mind of what these words are saying.

Up spoke our own little Mabel,
Saying, "Father, who makes it snow?"
And I told of the good All-father
Who cares for us here below.

Here, you find out who the speaker is. Who is it?

25 Again I looked at the snow-fall,
And thought of the leaden sky
That arched o'er our first great sorrow,
When that mound was heaped so high.

Here, the speaker shares his feelings of grief.

I remembered the gradual patience
30 That fell from that cloud like snow,
Flake by flake, healing and hiding
The scar that renewed our woe.

What simile does Lowell use here?

And again to the child I whispered,
"The snow that husheth all,
35 Darling, the merciful Father
Alone can make it fall!"

Think about the connotation of the words in this stanza.

Then, with eyes that saw not, I kissed her;
And she, kissing back, could not know
That *my* kiss was given to her sister,
Folded close under deepening snow.

Finally the speaker reveals for whom he grieves and how much he misses her.

---

leaden (LED un) dull, dark gray
[1]**Mt. Auburn:** a cemetery in Cambridge, Massachusetts

Mini Quiz

Write the following questions on the chalkboard or overhead projector and call on students to fill in the blanks. Discuss the answers.

1. All of the trees wore ________.
2. The twigs on the elm tree were ridged in ________.
3. The rooster sat on the white-marbled ________ of the shed.
4. The father stood by the ________, looking at the snow.
5. The child was buried in ________ cemetery.

Answers

1. ermine
2. pearl
3. roof
4. window
5. Mt. Auburn

Teaching Plan

INTRODUCE

Motivation

Find a representative painting of each of the four seasons by one of the following 19th-century artists: John Singer Sargent, Thomas Cole, Winslow Homer, or Charlotte Buell Coman. Display the pictures in the classroom. Ask students to think about an important event in their lives that excites an emotion. Ask them which picture of the seasons would best describe the event and why. Relate the discussion to "The First Snow-fall," in which Lowell uses a snowstorm to help the reader understand the feelings of the bereft father in the poem.

Purpose-Setting Question

Why would a poet use a first snow-fall to convey his feelings of grief to the reader?

READ

Literary Focus: *Elements of Poetry*

The blue side notes in this annotated lesson provide a model for students to understand the literary elements introduced in Focus on Poetry, pages 210–211. Direct students to look for words that have an emotional meaning, as well as a literal meaning, such as the word *my* in the last stanza. Ask: Why is the word *my* italicized? What is the connotation, or emotional meaning, of this word? What is the literal meaning?

Reading Focus: *Paraphrase*

Reread each stanza aloud and have students paraphrase what each stanza means. Remind students that as they paraphrase they should include all of the ideas of the author, but in their own words.

CLOSE

Have students complete Review the Selection on pages 212–213.

Review the Selection

UNDERSTAND THE SELECTION

Recall

1. When had the snow begun to fall?
2. What is the speaker watching?
3. What are the speaker's feelings, and what caused them?

Infer

4. Describe in your own words how the landscape looks outside the window.
5. How do you know the speaker has tried to hide his grief?
6. Explain in your own words what the speaker is saying in this poem.
7. Discuss why Mabel could not know what her father was thinking.

Apply

8. Select three words from the poem that describe the speaker's voice.
9. Suppose that you are the speaker in this poem. You are looking out the window at the snow. How does the snow make you feel?
10. Select the stanza from the poem that tells the reader the speaker may be recovering from his great sorrow.

Respond to Literature

How does Lowell use nature to share his feelings with the reader?

WRITE ABOUT THE SELECTION

Has James Russell Lowell written a good poem? Think about what a poem is and what it is supposed to accomplish for a few minutes. Then suppose that you are a literary critic for the school literary magazine. Your assignment is to review "The First Snow Fall." What do you feel about the poem? Does the poet successfully express his thoughts through the speaker? Is the poet's use of figurative language successful? Does it make the poem vivid in your mind? Read the poem again.

Prewriting Freewrite for a few minutes on your feelings about this poem. Look at the annotations to help you. Ask yourself: Did I enjoy reading the poem? Is it well written? Is the poet's choice of words colorful?

Writing Write a short literary criticism of "The First Snow Fall." Be sure to include terms such as *figurative language*, *speaker*, and *sound devices* in your review.

Revising When you revise, make sure you have used concrete examples from the poem in your criticism. If you haven't, go back and include them.

Proofreading Reread your criticism to check for errors. Make sure that you have spelled all the words correctly, paying particular attention to the poetry terms. Look at your sentences. Does each of them express a complete thought? If not, rewrite them.

UNDERSTAND THE SELECTION

Answers

1. at twilight
2. the snow-fall
3. The speaker is very sad because one of his daughters has died.
4. Sample answer: The landscape looked very beautiful all covered in white.
5. Sample answer: He refers to the snow as being able to "husheth all."
6. Sample answer: Even though he has grieved, patience has helped him with his grief; and things are now in God's hands.
7. Sample answer: He does not reveal his feelings; she is too young and innocent; she must see his love for her.
8. muffled, whispered, husheth
9. Sample answers: peaceful, quiet, protected, lonely, sad
10. In the eighth stanza the speaker describes how patience is helping him to recover.

Respond to Literature

Have students refer to the notes they saved from the Cooperative Group Activity at the beginning of the lesson. Ask students to add more figures of speech to their lists about the natural event they have chosen. Suggest that students think about what happens to animals and plants during the event.

WRITE ABOUT THE SELECTION

Prewriting

Bring in old newspapers and magazines in which there are book and poetry reviews. Ask students to look through them to find reviews of books and poetry. When students have compiled a number of reviews, have volunteers read several of them to the class. Then lead a class discussion in which you discuss what the writers included in their reviews to make them interesting. Suggest that students use some of the ideas to help them write their critiques. Then have students freewrite for a few minutes about what they want to include in their critiques of "The First Snow-fall."

Writing

Have students work on this section individually. If students have difficulty, let them look at the reviews the class has collected to help them. Ask them questions about how the poem made them feel, such as: Is snow soothing? Does snow make them feel sad, lonely, comforted?

Revising

Make this a cooperative group activity. Have students work in small groups to revise their reviews. Make sure that they use concrete examples from the poems in their criticisms.

Proofreading

Select one or two of the students' criticisms as models for proofreading. Put the paragraphs on the overhead projector and have the class suggest improvements.

THINK ABOUT POETRY

Various elements of poetry work together to make a poem stimulating and interesting to read. Poets work hard to choose colorful words that will express their thoughts, feelings, and ideas in an imaginative way.

In the first stanza of "The First Snow Fall," you learn the snow began at twilight. Then, through a choice of such words as *busily*, *heaping*, and *silence*, a picture begins to emerge of how the snow must have looked. Lowell's choice of words creates a quiet, rhythmic feeling, similar to a gentle snowfall.

1. Whose voice does Lowell create in this poem?
2. Which kind of figurative language does Lowell use?
3. What is being compared in the simile "And the sudden flurries of snow-birds, Like brown leaves whirling by"?
4. What is the connotation of the word "husheth" in the line "The snow that husheth all, . . ."?
5. Name the sound device that Lowell uses and give two examples of it.

DEVELOP YOUR VOCABULARY

Homophones are words that sound the same when you say them but have different meanings and spellings. For example, the words *throne* and *thrown* are homophones.

Read the following sentences. Think of a homophone for each italicized word. Then use it in an original sentence.

1. The *beech* tree my grandfather planted last year has grown a lot.
2. Samantha read her report *aloud* to the other students.
3. Christopher put a lot of hot spices in the *chili* he made last night.
4. The *herd* of wolves moved quickly through the storm to nearby caves.
5. Rosa and Luke *rowed* across Rainbow Lake to a small island where they had a picnic.
6. The best time to look for shells is when the *tide* has gone out.
7. The *weight* of the package made me think it held the books I ordered.
8. How long does Becky have to *beat* the egg whites?

THINK ABOUT POETRY

Answers

1. Lowell creates the voice of a grieving father.
2. Lowell uses simile in the poem.
3. The snow-birds are being compared to brown leaves.
4. The connotation of *husheth* is that the snow hides his grief.
5. Lowell uses onomatopoeia. Two examples are: *muffled*, *whispered*.

DEVELOP YOUR VOCABULARY

Answers

1. beach
2. allowed
3. chilly
4. heard
5. rode, road
6. tied
7. wait
8. beet

Sample sentences:

1. We spent time at the beach.
2. There was no swimming allowed.
3. The weather got chilly.
4. We heard the sirens.
5. We rode the bus on the new road.
6. The ribbon was tied in back.
7. The child had to wait a week for a new pony.
8. Her face was as red as a beet.

ESL Activity

Allow students to use a dictionary to look up the definitions of the homophones before they write their sentences. Encourage students to include these homophones in their word banks.

Selection Overview

SELECTION OBJECTIVES

After completing this selection, students will be able to

- understand and identify conflict in a story
- write a journal entry
- understand and identify antonyms
- visualize

Lesson Resources

from *Moby-Dick*
- Selection Synopsis, Teacher's Edition, pp. T159g–T159h
- Comprehension and Vocabulary Workbook, pp. 45–46
- Language Enrichment Workbook, p. 29
- Teacher's Resources
  Reinforcement, p. R23
  Test, pp. T45–T46
  Unadapted Selection, pp. U16–U25

More About Conflict

Explain to students that conflict can be both external and internal. For example, a character might be struggling against nature, while at the same time having an inner conflict about his or her own ability to survive in nature. Ask what inner struggles a person caught in a raging snowstorm might have. List their ideas on the chalkboard.

More About the Literary Period

Explain that although Melville was influenced by Emerson and the Transcendentalists, later on he did not agree with their ideas about nature. He began to point out that while nature had beauty, it also had the ability to destroy. Continue by explaining that people sometimes forget that nature gets the last word. Might Melville have encountered such a person on his own journey? Might it have influenced his writing?

Learn About

CONFLICT

Plot, as you know, consists of a conflict, an attempt to resolve the conflict, a climax (or turning point in the events), and the dénouement, the final resolution, or outcome, of the events.

The essential element in any plot, however, is the conflict. A plot cannot exist without it. The conflict is what sets off the interplay of forces that make up the events that occur.

The conflict may be of several kinds. It may be between the main character and the forces of nature, another person, or social forces, or even between opposing sides of the character's own personality.

In weaving the events of a plot, an author must arrange incidents so that they seem to grow inevitably out of the conflict. Each incident must be the cause of the next one, down to the very end.

As you read the excerpts from *Moby-Dick*, ask yourself:

1. What is the main conflict in the story?
2. Where is the turning point in the events?

READING FOCUS

Visualize One of the things that makes a story exciting is the picture that you build in your mind from the details the author provides. When an author uses imagery—words that describe the sights, tastes, smells, sounds, and feelings—in a story, you can use your mind's eye to visualize more clearly what is happening. As you read this excerpt from *Moby-Dick*, use the imagery to visualize the events.

WRITING CONNECTION

Think of a conflict that might set up a series of events that must be resolved. Describe that conflict in a paragraph.

About the Author

Melville was 22 years old when he set sail from New Bedford, Massachusetts, on board the *Acushnet* on January 3, 1841. Whaling was the leading business in the young nation because whale oil was used to light lamps until 1859, when petroleum was discovered. Melville stayed on board for 18 months until he couldn't stand the arduous conditions and difficult captain. He left the boat in the South Seas along with another young sailor.

Cooperative Group Activity

Divide the class into three groups for the Writing Connection activity. Assign each group one of the following situations: **1.** A woman is working to save endangered snow leopards; **2.** A family wants to escape from a small country in which there is religious and political persecution; **3.** Two friends are caught in a very bad hurricane at sea. Have each group make a list to arrange both internal and external conflicts that grow out of the situations that they have been assigned. Then ask a volunteer from each group to share their lists and have a class discussion.

from MOBY-DICK

ADAPTED

by Herman Melville

It was quite late in the evening when the little Moss came snugly to anchor. Queequeg and I went ashore. We didn't want to attend to any business that day, at least none but a supper and a bed. The landlord of the Spouter Inn had recommended us to his cousin Hosea Hussey of the Try Pots. He said that Hussey was the proprietor of one of the best-kept hotels in all Nantucket.[1] He had also assured us that Cousin Hosea, as he called him, was famous for his chowders. In short, he plainly hinted that we could not possibly do better than try potluck at the Try Pots. He had given us the following directions: keep a yellow warehouse on your right hand till you see a white church to the left. Then keep that on the left hand till you make a corner three points to the right. When that is done, ask the first man you meet where the place is. These crooked directions of his very much puzzled us at first, especially as, at the outset, Queequeg insisted that the yellow warehouse—our first point of departure—must be on the left side. I had understood Peter Coffin to say it was on the right. However, by walking around a little in the dark, and now and then knocking up a peaceful resident to inquire the way, we at last came to something which there was no mistaking.

Two enormous wooden pots painted black swung from the crosstrees of an old topmast and were planted in front of an old doorway. The horns of the crosstrees were sawed off on the other side, so that this old topmast looked not a little like a gallows. Perhaps I was oversensitive to such impressions at the time, but I could not help staring at this gallows with a vague misgiving. A sort of crick was in my neck as I gazed up to the two remaining horns; yes, two of them, one for Queequeg, and one for me. It's ominous, thinks I. A coffin was my innkeeper upon landing in my first whaling port. Tombstones were staring at me in the whalemen's chapel; and here a gallows! and a pair of very large black pots too! Are these last throwing out indirect hints?

I was interrupted from these thoughts

---

ominous (OM uh nus) dangerous; threatening

[1]**Nantucket:** an island, off the coast of Massachusetts, that was a huge whaling community

TEACHING PLAN

INTRODUCE

Motivation

Find a copy of the poem "Sea Fever" by John Masefield. Write the poem on the chalkboard, put it on the overhead projector, or ask volunteers to read each stanza. Then have a class discussion about why sailors are so attracted to the sea that they go back again and again despite the dangers.

Purpose-Setting Question

What might the consequences be if Captain Ahab and his crew had been successful in their attempt to kill Moby-Dick?

READ

Literary Focus: *Conflict*

Explain that in this story, the main conflict is not between the narrator and nature, but between another character, Captain Ahab, and nature. Ask: Why do you think the author chose a bystander to record this conflict?

Reading Focus: *Visualize*

Tell students to cite the examples of imagery used by Melville. They should use these examples of imagery to visualize the events in the story as they read. They can make this an ongoing activity by using a storyboard to illustrate the major events in this story.

CLOSE

Have students complete Review the Selection on pages 230–231.

Develop Your Vocabulary

Review the footnoted vocabulary words. Then have students work in pairs to look up the word origin of each vocabulary word. Tell them the word origin is usually found in brackets [ ] after the respelling and inflections (if any) in the dictionary entry. Write the following abbreviations on the chalkboard.

ME	Middle English	GK	Greek
OE	Old English	F	French
G	German	Sp	Spanish
L	Latin	On	Old Norse

Direct students to the list of abbreviations in the dictionary.

ESL Activity

Discuss and review with students various sources of words in the English language. Have students list five words in English that came from their own native language or country.

Reading Focus: *Visualize*

Ask students to visualize Mrs. Hussey and the scene described here. You might ask students to sketch her in their notebooks.

Enrichment

Explain to students that Nantucket Island and Martha's Vineyard, as well as New Bedford, Massachusetts, had huge whaling communities that were led, interestingly enough, by Quaker men. Among the people the Quakers frequently recruited for their voyages were free black men. A large number of Quakers were staunch abolitionists.

Viewing Fine Art

Nathaniel Currier (1813–1888) was a lithographer who joined up with his bookkeeper, James Ives, to form the famous firm of Currier and Ives. Currier produced numerous pictures on his own, however. Many became beloved household ornaments. Currier pictured scenes of American life of all sorts. Here he shows a dramatic whaling scene in the bright, decorative style that characterized all of his work. (Another example of Currier and Ives appears on page 1 and on page 248.) Ask: From the look of the whalers' harpoons, would you agree with Mrs. Hussey (on page 217) that the whalers should not keep the harpoons in their bedrooms? Explain.

by the sight of a freckled woman with yellow hair and a yellow gown. She was standing in the porch of the inn, under a dull red lamp swinging there. It looked much like an injured eye, and she was carrying on a brisk scolding with a man in a purple woolen shirt.

"Get along with you," she said to the man, "or I'll be combing you!"

"Come on, Queequeg," said I, "all right. There's Mrs. Hussey."

And so it turned out; Mr. Hosea Hussey was not at home, but had left a very competent Mrs. Hussey to attend to all his affairs. Upon making known our desires for supper and a bed, Mrs. Hussey, postponing further scolding for the present, ushered us into a little room, and seating us at a table spread with the leftovers of a recently concluded meal, turned round to us and said "clam or cod?"

"What's that about cods, ma'am?" said I, with much politeness.

"Clam or cod?" she repeated.

"A clam for supper? a cold clam; is *that* what you mean, Mrs. Hussey?" says I! "but that's a rather cold and clammy reception in the winter time, isn't it, Mrs. Hussey?"

But being in a great hurry to resume scolding the man in the purple shirt who was waiting for it in the entry, and seeming to hear nothing but the word "clam," Mrs. Hussey hurried towards an open door leading to the kitchen, and bawling out "clam for two," disappeared.

"Queequeg," said I, "do you think that we can make a supper for us both on one clam?"

The Whale Fishery "Laying On," 1852, Nathaniel Currier. The Granger Collection

However, a warm savory steam from the kitchen served to confuse us regarding the clam on the table. But when that smoking chowder came in, the mystery was delightfully explained. Oh, sweet friends, listen to me. It was made of small juicy clams, scarcely bigger than hazel nuts, mixed with pounded ship biscuits, and salted pork cut up into little flakes! The chowder was enriched with butter, and it was generously seasoned with pepper and salt. Our appetites had been sharpened by the frosty voyage. In particular, Queequeg seeing his favorite fishing food before him, and the chowder being surpassingly excellent, we started to eat very quickly. Then leaning back for a moment, I thought I would try a little experiment. Stepping to the kitchen door, I uttered the word "cod" with great emphasis, and resumed my seat. In a few moments the savory steam came forth again, but with a different flavor, and in good time a fine cod chowder was placed before us.

Finally, supper concluded, we received a lamp, and directions from Mrs. Hussey about how to find our beds. As Queequeg was about to precede me up the stairs, the lady reached toward him, and demanded his harpoon. She allowed no harpoon in her chambers. "Why not?" said I; "every true whaleman sleeps with his harpoon—but why not?" "Because it's dangerous," says she. "Ever since young Stiggs coming from that unfortunate voyage of his, when he was gone four years and a half, with only three barrels of oil was found dead in my first floor back, with his harpoon in his side. Ever since then I allow no boarders to take such dangerous weapons in their rooms at night. So, Mr. Queequeg" (for she had learned his name), "I will just take this here iron, and keep it for you till morning. But the chowder; clam or cod tomorrow for breakfast, men?"

"Both," says I, "and let's have a couple of smoked herring by way of variety."

When the crew signed aboard the Pequod, *the voyage was to be nothing more than a business venture. However, early in the voyage, Ahab makes clear to the crew that his purpose is to seek revenge against Moby-Dick.*

One morning shortly after breakfast, Ahab, as was his habit, climbed up the cabin gangway to the deck. There most sea captains usually walk at that hour, as country gentlemen, after the same meal, take a few turns in the garden.

Soon his steady, ivory stride was heard. To and fro he paced on his old rounds. The wood was so familiar to his step, that they were all over dented with the peculiar mark of his walk. If you looked, too, upon that ribbed and dented brow, you would also see still stranger footprints—the footprints of his one unsleeping, ever-pacing thought.

But on the occasion in question, those dents looked deeper, even as his nervous

savory (SAY vur ee) appetizing smell

Critical Thinking:
Infer
Explain that Moby-Dick is a whale, in case students do not already know that. Ask: Why might Ahab want revenge against an animal?

Literary Focus:
Conflict
Melville describes Captain Ahab's peg-legged walk. Tell students that this description sets up the reason for the conflict in this story. Have students read on to find out more about why Captain Ahab has a peg leg and how this sets up the conflict.

Literary Focus: *Conflict*

Ask: What is Ahab's single-minded thought? What kind of conflict is this?

Critical Thinking: *Analyze*

Ask: Why does Captain Ahab ask his sailors such seemingly pointless questions?

step that morning left a deeper mark. Ahab was so deep in thought that at every uniform turn that he made, now at the mainmast and now at the compass, you could almost see that thought turn in him as he turned, and pace in him as he paced. It was so completely possessing him, indeed, that it all but seemed that every move he made was based on an inner thought.

"Do you see him, Flask?" whispered Stubb; "the chick that's in him pecks the shell. It will soon be out."

The hours wore on—Ahab was now shut up within his cabin. Then later he was pacing the deck, with the same single-mindedness as before.

It drew near the close of day. Suddenly he stopped by the side of the ship on the upper deck. Inserting his bone leg into the harpoon hole there, and with one hand grasping a set of ropes, he ordered Starbuck to send everybody to the back of the boat.

"Sir!" said the mate, surprised at an order seldom or never given on shipboard except in some extraordinary case.

"Send everybody to the back," repeated Ahab. "Mastheads, there! come down!"

When the entire ship's company were assembled, the curious and fearful faces eyed him. He looked not unlike the weather horizon when a storm is coming up. Ahab rapidly glanced over the sides of the ship. Then he looked back and forth at the crew. Then acting as if not a soul were present, he continued to pace with his head bent. He was unmindful of the wondering whispering among the men. Then Stubb cautiously whispered to Flask, that Ahab must have summoned them there for the purpose of watching this ordinary event. But this did not last long. Suddenly stopping, he cried:

"What do you do when you see a whale, men?"

"Sing out for him!" was the quick answer from a score of clubbed voices.

"Good!" cried Ahab, with a wild approval in his tones. He liked the hearty reply to his unexpected question.

"And what do you next, men?"

"Lower the boats and go after him."

"And what tune is it you pull to, men?"

"A dead whale or a smashed boat!"

More and more strangely and fiercely glad and approving, grew the face of the old man at every shout. The crew began to look curiously at each other. They began to marvel at how they had become so excited at such seemingly purposeless questions.

But they were all eagerness again. Then Ahab, now with one hand reaching high up to a set of ropes, and tightly grasping it, addressed them:

"All you mastheaders have before now heard me give orders about a white whale. Look at this! Do you see this Spanish ounce of gold?"—holding up a broad bright coin to the sun—"it is a sixteen-dollar piece, men. Do you see it? Mr. Starbuck, hand me your hammer."

While the mate was getting it, Ahab, without speaking, was slowly rubbing the gold piece against the skirts of his jacket, as if to heighten its shine. Without using any words, he was humming to himself,

Whalers Capturing a Sperm Whale, 1847. The Granger Collection

producing a sound that was strangely muffled. It seemed like the mechanical humming of his mind.

Receiving the hammer from Starbuck, he advanced towards the mainmast. The hammer was uplifted in one hand, while he exhibited the gold with the other. With a high raised voice he exclaimed: "Whosoever of you kills me a white-headed whale with a wrinkled brow and a crooked jaw; whosoever of you kills that white-headed whale for me, with three holes punctured in his tail—look here, whosoever of you kills that same white whale for me, he shall have this gold ounce, my boys!"

"Huzza! huzza!" cried the seamen. Then with swinging canvas sails they cheered the act of nailing the gold to the mast.

"It's a white whale, I say," resumed Ahab, as he threw down the hammer: "a white whale. Keep your eyes peeled for him, men; look sharp for white water; if you see but a bubble, sing out."

All this while Tashtego, Daggoo, and Queequeg had looked on with even more intense interest and surprise than the rest. At the mention of the wrinkled brow and crooked jaw, they had jumped as if each was separately touched by some specific recollection.

Viewing Fine Art

Marine pictures, and whaling scenes in particular, were among the most popular of American prints. Many households in 19th-century United States had a picture of a sailing vessel or a dramatic scene of whaling hanging over their mantels. Whaling, and America's seafaring adventurers, represented many things to the new nation, including romance and independence. Small boats from New England, with only a handful of courageous men, were shown attacking the giant whales, despite pitching boats and treacherous seas. The battle to subdue nature was an on-going theme in 19th-century art, and the more dramatic the view, the better the public liked it. Ask: Think about how you have visualized whaling. How does this painting compare to the picture in your mind's eye?

Reading Focus: *Visualize*

Ask students to visualize Captain Ahab and his crew when he announces the reward for killing the whale. Contrast the seaman's reaction to the looks on Tashtego, Daggoo, and Queequeg's faces (last paragraph on page 219). Ask: What do you think the looks on these three men's faces mean? If students are using storyboards, have them include this scene.

Literary Focus: *Conflict*

Ahab replies to Starbuck by emotionally explaining why he walks with a peg leg. Discuss how his emotions further enhance the conflict of Ahab versus Moby-Dick—human against nature—in this story.

"Captain Ahab," said Tashtego, "that white whale must be the same that some call Moby-Dick."

"Moby-Dick?" shouted Ahab. "Do you know the white whale then, Tash?"

"Does he spread his tail out like a fan before he goes down?" said the Gay-Header[2] deliberately.

"And has he a curious spout, too," said Daggoo, "very bushy, and mighty quick, Captain Ahab?"

"And he has one, two, three—oh! a good many irons in his hide, too, Captain," cried Queequeg disjointedly, "all twiske-tee betwisk, like him—him—" faltering hard for a word, and screwing his hand round and round as though uncorking a bottle—"like him—him—"

"Corkscrew!" cried Ahab, "aye, Queequeg, the harpoons lie all twisted and wrenched in him. Aye, Daggoo, his spout is a big one, like a whole shock of wheat, and white as a pile of Nantucket wool after the great annual sheepshearing. Aye, Tashtego, he spreads his tail out like a fan. Death and devils! men, it is Moby-Dick you have seen—Moby-Dick—Moby-Dick!"

"Captain Ahab," said Starbuck, who, with Stubb and Flask, had been looking at the captain with increasing surprise. He at last seemed struck with a thought which somewhat explained all the wonder, "Captain Ahab, I have heard of Moby-Dick—but it was not Moby-Dick that took off your leg?"

"Who told you that?" cried Ahab; then pausing, "Aye, Starbuck; aye, my congratulations all around. It was Moby-Dick that dismasted me. It was Moby-Dick that brought me to this dead stump I stand on now. Aye, aye," he shouted with a terrific, loud, animal sob, like that of a heart-stricken moose. "Aye, aye! It was that hateful white whale that destroyed me and made me so clumsy forever and a day!" Then tossing up both arms, he shouted out: "Aye, aye! and I'll chase him round Good Hope, and round the Horn[3] before I give him up. And this is what you have shipped for men! We are going to chase that white whale on both sides of land, and over all sides of earth, till he spouts black blood and rolls fin out. What say you, men, will you join hands on it, now? I think you do look brave."

"Aye, aye!" shouted the harpooneers and seamen, running closer to the excited old man: "A sharp eye for the white whale; a sharp harpoon for Moby-Dick!"

"God bless you," he seemed to half sob and half shout. "God bless you, men. Steward! go get something to drink. But what's this long face about, Mr. Starbuck; don't you want to chase the white whale? you're not willing?"

"I am willing for his crooked jaw, and

---

[2]**Gay-Header:** Gay Head is a town on Martha's Vineyard, another island off the coast of Massachusetts that had a large whaling community.

[3]**Good Hope** and **the Horn:** two of the most dangerous sea passages in the world

for the jaws of Death too, Captain Ahab, if it fairly comes in the way of the business we follow. I came here to hunt whales, not my commander's vengeance. How many barrels will your harm yield you even if you catch it, Captain Ahab? it will not get much in our Nantucket market."

"Nantucket market! Hoot! But come closer, Starbuck. If money's to be the measurer, man, and the accountants have worked out that their great countinghouse is the globe, by surrounding it with money, then, let me tell you, that my vengeance will get a great price *here*!"

"He strikes his chest," whispered Stubb, "what's that for? He has said a lot but it doesn't mean much."

"Vengeance on a dumb animal!" cried Starbuck, "that simply doesn't make any sense! Madness! To be angry with a dumb thing, Captain Ahab, seems disrespectful."

"Listen again—a little more closely. All visible objects, man, are but as pasteboard masks. But in each event there is some unknown but still reasoning thing that puts forth its features from behind the unreasoning mask. If man will strike, strike through the mask! How can the prisoner reach outside except by breaking through the wall? To me, the white whale is that wall, shoved near to me. Sometimes I think there's nothing beyond. But it's enough. He tasks me; he heaps me; I see in him outrageous strength, with a mysterious meanness to him. That mysterious thing is chiefly what I hate. And whether I kill the white whale for money or not, I will do it because I hate him. Talk not to me of disrespect, man; I'd strike the sun if it insulted me. If the sun struck me, I'd strike back. There is ever a sort of fair play on earth because jealousy has control over all creations. But not my master, man, is even that fair play. Who's over me? Truth hath no boundaries. Don't look at me like that! You are furious. My words have enraged you. But listen, Starbuck, what is said in anger can be undone. I meant not to make you angry. Let it go. Look! Look at the crew. Don't they all agree with Ahab, in this matter of the whale? See Stubb! he laughs! See yonder Chilean! he snorts to think of it. Don't you be the only one who disagrees. You can't win, Starbuck! Deal with it. I only want you to help strike a fin; that's no wondrous accomplishment for Starbuck. You are the best lance out of all Nantucket, surely you will not hang back, when every foremasthand has clutched a whetstone. Ah! you feel uneasy. You're changing your mind. Speak, but speak!—Aye, aye! Your silence says more than words. (*Aside*) He is thinking about what I said. He's changing his mind. Starbuck now is mine. He cannot oppose me now."

"God keep me!—keep us all!" murmured Starbuck, lowly.

But in his joy at the understood

vengeance (VEN juns) causing harm to something in return for an injury or harm done
whetstone (HWET stohn) a stone used for sharpening tools

Reading Focus: *Visualize*

Ask students to visualize Starbuck's facial expressions as he listens to Ahab's emotional account. Ask: How do you think Starbuck looks when he speaks of "vengeance on a dumb animal"? Ahab then appeals to Starbuck's pride and sense of duty. Ask: What physical reaction does Starbuck make to this appeal? Do you think Ahab has changed Starbuck's mind? Explain.

Critical Thinking: *Analyze*

Have students discuss why Starbuck thinks it is disrespectful to kill Moby-Dick. Ask: Why does he refer to the whale as a dumb animal? Why is it disrespectful to be angry with a whale?

obedience of the mate, Ahab did not hear the warnings in the laughter from the hold; nor yet the warning sounds of the winds in the ropes; nor yet the hollow flap of the sails against the masts. For a moment their hearts sank in. For again Starbuck's downcast eyes lighted up with the stubbornness of life. The hidden laugh died away. The winds blew on. The sails filled out. The ship heaved and rolled as before. Ah, the warnings were everywhere. Actually, they were more predictions than warnings! Yet not so much predictions from nature, as proof of the foregoing things within the mind. With not much to hold us back, the innermost necessities in our being still drive us on.

"The cup! the cup!" cried Ahab.

Receiving the brimming pewter, and turning to the harpooneers, he ordered them to produce their weapons. Then arranging them before him with their harpoons in their hands, his three mates stood at his side with their lances. The rest of the ship's company formed a circle around the group. He stood for an instant looking directly at every man of his crew. Those wild eyes met his. They were like the bloodshot eyes of the prairie wolves when they meet the eye of their leader before he rushes on at their head in the trail of the bison. Alas, only to be caught by the hidden traps of hunters.

"Advance, mates! cross your lances full before me. Well done! Let me touch the center." He said that and then he grasped the lances at their crossed center. While so doing, he suddenly and nervously twitched them. Meanwhile he glanced intently from Starbuck to Stubb; from Stubb to Flask. It seemed as though, by some nameless, inside willpower, he wanted to shock them into having the same fiery feelings that he had within himself. The three mates quailed before his strong, mysterious presence. Stubb and Flask looked away from him. The honest eye of Starbuck fell downright.

"In vain!" cried Ahab; "but, maybe it's just as well. For if I gave you my stored, strong feelings, then I might have lost them for myself. Perhaps, too, it might have caused me to drop dead. Perhaps you don't need them. Put your lances down! And now, mates, I need to choose three men to help my brave harpooneers. Don't look down on the job. Remember that the great Pope washes the feet of beggars, using his crown for a pitcher. It is your own superiority that will make you do it. I do not order you; you make it happen to yourselves. Cut your lines and draw the poles, harpooneers!"

Silently obeying the order, the three harpooneers, now stood with the detached iron part of their harpoons, some three feet long, held, barbs up, before him.

"Do not stab me with that sharp steel! Turn them; turn them over! Don't you know the goblet end? Turn up the socket! So, so; now, advance. The irons! take them;

---

quailed (KWAYLD) lost courage; cowered

Literary Focus: *Conflict*

Starbuck's downcast eyes defy the hate Ahab feels toward the whale. Ask: What purpose does Starbuck's lack of enthusiasm serve in setting up the conflict?

Critical Thinking: *Evaluate*

Ask: Do you think Ahab is justified in going after the whale that took his leg? Explain.

hold them while I fill!" He immediately went from one officer to the other, filling the harpoon sockets with the fiery waters from the pewter.

"Now, three to three, you stand. Raise the murderous cups! Present them, you who are now part of this permanent group. Ha! Starbuck! but the deed is done! Drink, you harpooneers! drink and swear, you men that man the deathful whaleboat's bow—Death to Moby-Dick! God will hunt us all, if we do not hunt Moby-Dick to his death!" The long, barbed steel goblets were lifted; and to cries and curses against the white whale, the drinks were all at once drunk down. Starbuck paled, and turned, and shivered. Once more, and finally, the refilled pewter went the rounds among the desperate crew; when, waving his free hand to them, they all went their separate ways; and Ahab retired within his cabin.

After Moby-Dick has been sighted in the Pacific Ocean, the Pequod*'s boats follow the whale for two days. One of the boats has been sunk, and Ahab's ivory leg has been broken off. However, as the next day dawns, the chase continues.*

The morning of the third day dawned fair and fresh, and once more the solitary night man at the foremasthead was relieved by crowds of the daylight lookouts, who were on every mast and almost every pole.

"Do you see him?" cried Ahab; but the whale was not yet in sight. "Aloft there! What do you see?"

"Nothing, sir."

"Nothing! and noon at hand! The gold coin goes a-begging! See the sun! Aye, aye, it must be so. I've sailed past him. How, got the start? Aye, he's chasing *me* now; not I, *him*—that's bad. I might have known it, too. Fool! the lines—the harpoons he's towing. Aye, aye, I have run him by last night. About! about! Come down, all of you, but the regular lookouts! Make preparations to turn!"

Steering as she had done, the wind had been somewhat on the *Pequod*'s quarter. Now that the ship was being pointed in the reverse direction, she sailed hard upon the breeze as she rechurned the cream in her own white wake.

"Against the wind he now steers for the open jaw," murmured Starbuck to himself. "God keep us, but already my bones feel damp within me, and from the inside wet my flesh. I fear that I disobey my God in obeying him!"

"Stand by to help me up!" cried Ahab, advancing to the rope basket. "We should meet him soon."

"Aye, aye, sir," and straightway Starbuck helped him, and once more Ahab swung on high.

A whole hour now passed: goldbeaten out to ages. Time itself now held long breaths with sharp suspense. But at last, some three points off the weather bow,

suspense (suh SPENS) uncertainty about what will happen

Reading Focus:
Visualize

Note the change in scene from where the men are preparing to harpoon the whale to the quiet of the third day. Have students discuss the imagery that helped them visualize this shift. Have student volunteers describe their visualization of the new scene.

Ahab descried the spout again. Instantly from the three mastheads three shrieks went up as if the tongues of fire had voiced it.

"Forehead to forehead I meet you, this third time, Moby-Dick! On deck there!—turn her; turn her into the wind's eye. He's too far off to lower yet, Mr. Starbuck. The sails shake! Stand over that helmsman with a topmaul! So, so; he travels fast, and I must get down. But let me have one more good round look at the sea while I'm up here. There's time for that. An old, old sight, and yet somehow it's so young; aye, and it hasn't changed a wink since I first saw it as a boy from the sand hills of Nantucket! The same!—the same! There's a soft shower downwind. Such lovely downwinds! They must lead somewhere—to something more than common land. Downwind! the white whale goes that way; look to windward. Good-bye, goodbye, old masthead! What's this?—green: aye, tiny mosses in these warped cracks. No such green weather stains on Ahab's head! There's the difference now between man's old age and a boat's old age. But yes, old mast, we both grow old together. We are sound in our hulls, though, are we not, my ship? Yes, minus a leg, that's all. This dead wood has the better of my live flesh in every way. I can't compare with it. I've known some ships made of dead trees that outlast the lives of men made of the most vital stuff. What's that he said? he should still go before me, my pilot; and yet to be seen again? But where? Will I have eyes at the bottom of the sea? Suppose I descend those endless stairs? All night I've been sailing from him, wherever he did sink to. Good-bye, masthead—keep a good eye upon the whale while I'm gone. We'll talk tomorrow, no, tonight, when the white whale lies down there, tied by head and tail."

He gave the word. And then still gazing around him, he was steadily lowered through the blue air to the deck.

In due time the boats were lowered. While standing in his boat's stern, Ahab seemed to hold back from leaving. He waved to the mate—who held one of the tackle ropes on deck—and bade him pause.

"Starbuck!"

"Sir?"

"For the third time my soul's ship starts upon this voyage, Starbuck."

"Aye, sir, that's what you want."

"Some ships sail from their ports, and ever afterwards are missing, Starbuck!"

"Truth, sir; saddest truth."

"Some men die at ebb tide; some at low water; some at the full of the flood—and I feel now like a wave that's reached its height, Starbuck. I am old—shake hands with me, man."

Their hands met. Their eyes fastened. Starbuck spoke rapidly.

"Oh, my captain, my captain!—noble heart—go not—go not!—see, it's a brave man that knows how to weep!"

"Lower away!"—cried Ahab, tossing the mate's arm from him. "Stand by the crew!"

In an instant the boat was pulling round close under the stern.

Reading Focus: *Visualize*

Melville creates vivid images of the sea, including waves and ships, to which Captain Ahab compares himself. Ask: Why does Melville use these particular images to compare to Captain Ahab? Visualize the waves and tell how Captain Ahab is like the waves described in this section.

Discussion

Have students talk about whether they think Ahab believes he will die in this battle. Have students explain their reasoning.

Florida, John White. John R. Freeman & Co./The Fotomas Index

"The sharks! the sharks!" cried a voice from the low cabin window there; "O master, my master, come back!"

But Ahab heard nothing. His own voice was high-lifted then; and the boat leaped on.

The boats had not gone very far, when by a signal from the mastheads—a downward pointed arm, Ahab knew that the whale had sounded. He intended to be near him at the next rising. He held on his way a little sideways from the vessel. The crew maintained a profound silence, as the head-beat waves hammered and hammered against the opposing bow.

Suddenly the waters around them slowly swelled in broad circles. Then it quickly upheaved, as if sideways sliding from a submerged berg of ice, swiftly rising to the surface. A low rumbling sound was heard, a deep hum. They all held their breaths. A vast form shot lengthwise from the sea, wet with trailing ropes, harpoons, and lances. Covered in a thin drooping veil of mist, it hovered for a moment in the rainbowed air. Then it fell swamping back into the deep. Crushed thirty feet upwards, the waters flashed for an instant like heaps of fountains. Then they brokenly sank in a shower of flakes, leaving the circling surface creamed like new milk around the marble trunk of the whale.

---

sounded (SOWND ed) dove deeply downward (by a whale or fish)

Viewing Fine Art

John White, a friend of Sir Walter Raleigh, first arrived in the New World in about 1585. His maps of the coastline of Virginia, Carolina, and Florida are among the first of the United States. They are notable not only for their accurate details of rivers and shoals, but for their lovely delicacy of design and water-coloring. Map making in that time was considered a form of art as well as a science; the pictorial images of sea monsters, sailing ships, and the flying fish add to the sense of the unknown felt by these first intrepid explorers. Ask: What comments do you think Captain Ahab would make upon looking at this detailed and colorful map?

Literary Focus: *Conflict*

The climax begins with the appearance of Moby-Dick. Have students predict how the conflict in this story will be settled. Ask: Do you think the human or Nature will win in the end? Encourage students to support their opinions.

Literary Focus: *Conflict*

Moby-Dick's condition adds to the drama. Ask: If Moby-Dick represents Nature, how might agitating him affect the outcome of the conflict? Does it matter that Ahab is also clearly angered in this conflict?

Critical Thinking: *Analyze*

Ask: Why does Ahab care more about killing the whale than staying alive?

"Give way!" cried Ahab to the oarsmen. The boats darted forward to the attack. Maddened by yesterday's fresh irons that rotted in him, Moby-Dick seemed absolutely sure of what he was doing. The wide layers of welded tendons overspreading his broad white forehead looked knitted together beneath the transparent skin. Head on, he came churning his tail among the boats. And once more he beat them apart. The irons and lances spilled out from the two mates' boats. And one side of their boat was caved in at the bow. But Ahab's boat was left almost without a scar.

Daggoo and Queequeg were stopping the trained planks. The whale swam out from them, turned, and showed one entire flank as he shot by them again. At that moment a quick cry went up. Lashed round and round to the fish's back; bound up in the turns upon turns in which, during the past night, the whale had reeled the lines around him, the half-torn body of a sailor was seen. His clothes were torn to shreds; his swollen eyes turned full upon old Ahab.

The harpoon dropped from his hand.

"You have fooled me!"—drawing in a long lean breath—"Aye, this, *this* then is the hearse that you promised. Away, mates, to the ship! Those boats are useless now. Repair them if you can in time, and return to me. If not, Ahab is sure enough to die—Down, men! If anything jumps from this boat I stand in, I shall harpoon it. You are not other men, but my arms and my legs; and so obey me—Where's the whale? gone down again?"

But he looked too near the boat. As if bent upon escaping with the corpse he bore, Moby-Dick was now again steadily swimming forward. He had almost passed the ship—which thus far had been sailing in the opposite direction to him. He seemed swimming with his utmost speed. He was now only intent upon pursuing his own straight path in the sea.

"Oh! Ahab," cried Starbuck, "not too late is it, even now, the third day, to stop. See! Moby-Dick is not after you. It is you, you, who is madly after him!"

Setting sail to the rising wind, the only boat was swiftly going downwind. And at last when Ahab was sliding by the vessel, close enough to distinguish Starbuck's face as he leaned over the rail, he hailed him to turn the vessel about. Then he asked him to follow, not too swiftly, but at a good distance behind. Glancing upwards he saw Tashtego, Queequeg, and Daggoo, eagerly mounting to the three mastheads. The oarsmen were rocking in the two wooden boats which had just been lifted to the side. They were busily at work repairing them. One after the other, through the portholes, as he sped, he also caught flying glimpses of Stubb and Flask, busying themselves on deck among bundles of new irons and lances. As he saw all this; as he heard the hammers in the broken boats; far other hammers seemed driving a nail into his heart. But he rallied. And now he noticed that the vane or flag was gone from the main masthead, he shouted to Tashtego, who had just gained that perch, to descend again for another flag, and a hammer and nails, and so nail it to the mast.

Whether exhausted by the three days' running chase, and the resistance to his swimming because of the knotted ropes around him, or whether it was some inactive dishonesty and malice in him: whichever was true, the White Whale's way now began to lessen. The boat was rapidly nearing him once more. The whale's last start, however, had not been so long a one as before. And still as Ahab glided over the waves the unpitying sharks accompanied him; and so stubbornly stuck to the boat; and so continually bit at the plying oars, that the blades became jagged and crunched. They left small splinters in the sea, at almost every dip.

"Heed them not! those teeth but give new rowlocks to your oars. Pull on! 'tis the better rest, the sharks' jaw than the yielding water."

"But at every bite, sir, the thin blades grow smaller and smaller!"

"They will last long enough! pull on!—But who can tell"—he muttered—"whether these sharks swim to feast on the whale or on Ahab?—But pull on! Aye, all alive, now—we near him. The helm! take the helm! let me pass"—and so saying, two of the oarsmen helped him forward to the bows of the still flying boat.

As the boat was cast to one side, it landed next to the White Whale's body. The White Whale seemed strangely oblivious of the boat's advance. Sometimes whales act that way. Ahab was fairly within the smoky mountain mist, which, thrown off from the whale's spout, curled round his great mountainous hump. He was very close to him; when, with body arched back, and both arms lifted high, he darted his fierce iron and his far fiercer curse into the hated whale. As both steel and curse sank to the socket, as if sucked into a swamp, Moby-Dick twisted and turned. He rolled the top part of his body against the bow. And, without putting a hole in the boat, he suddenly turned it over. If it had not been for the upper part of the side of the boat to which he then clung, Ahab would once more have been tossed into the sea. As it was, three of the oarsmen had no idea that Ahab had attacked the whale. They were therefore unprepared for its attack and were flung out of the boat. Two of them clutched the side of it and hurled themselves bodily inboard again. The third man helplessly dropped behind the boat but he was still afloat and swimming.

Almost at the same moment, with amazing speed, the White Whale swam through the rolling sea. But when Ahab cried out to the steersman to take new turns with the line, and hold it so; and commanded the crew to turn round on their seats, and tow the boat up to the mark; the moment the undependable line felt that double strain and tug, it snapped in the empty air!

---

malice (MAL is) desire to see others harmed

Reading Focus: *Visualize*

The battle between human and beast is fully described on these pages. Have students use the descriptions of the events, as well as the emotional undercurrents, to visualize the scene. Encourage students to use what they know about human nature as they visualize how the seamen and Captain Ahab look throughout this ordeal. If students are using storyboards, have them represent the actions here.

Critical Thinking: *Analyze*
What details tell you of the damage done to the ship? Do you think the ship and its crew will survive?

"What breaks in me? My strength cracks!—it's whole again; oars! oars! Row towards him!"

Hearing the tremendous rush of the sea-crashing boat, the whale wheeled around to present his blank forehead. In that turn, he caught sight of the nearing black hull of the ship. He may have believed it was the source of all his trouble. He also may have thought it was a noble enemy. Whatever, all of a sudden, he bore down upon its advancing bow, clamping his jaws amid fiery showers of foam.

Ahab staggered; his hand struck his forehead. "I grow blind; hands! stretch out before me that I may yet find my way. Isn't it night?"

"The whale! The ship!" cried the fearful oarsmen.

"Oars! oars! Row the boat. It may be too late for Ahab to make his mark this one last time! I see: the ship! the ship! Go on, my men! will you not save my ship?"

But as the oarsmen violently forced their boat through the sledge-hammering seas, two planks burst through the bow of the boat. In an instant almost, the temporarily weakened boat lay nearly level with the waves. Its half-wading, splashing crew, tried hard to stop the gap and bail out the pouring water. But it didn't work.

From the ship's bows, nearly all the seamen now hung inactive. They still held hammers, bits of plank, lances, and harpoons in their hands, just as if they had come from their various employments. All their spellbound eyes looked at the whale. On either side of him was a huge semicircle of foam as he rushed toward them. Punishment, swift vengeance, everlasting harm were in his whole being. In spite of all that living man could do, his forehead hit the ship's right bow. The men and wood reeled. Some fell flat upon their faces. Like dislodged trucks, the heads of the harpooneers aloft shook on their bull-like necks. Through the hole, they heard the water pour, as a mountain stream pours down a narrow gorge.

"The ship! The hearse!—the second hearse!" cried Ahab from the boat; "its wood could only be American!"

Diving beneath the settling ship, the whale ran quivering along its keel. Then turning under water, he swiftly shot to the surface again. Then he stopped within a few yards of Ahab's coat, where, for a time, he lay quiet.

"I turn my body from the sun. Where are you, Tashtego? Let me hear your hammer. Oh! my wonderful boat, masts that did not surrender, the uncracked keel, and only god-bullied hull. The firm deck, and proud steering gear, and Polepointed bow—death-glorious ship! Must you then sink, and without me? Am I cut off from the last fond pride of meanest shipwrecked captains? Oh, lonely death

---

quivering (KWIV ur ing) trembling; slight vibrating motion
keel (KEEL) a piece of wood that runs along the center line from front of the boat to the back

on lonely life! Oh, now I feel my most incredible greatness lies in my most incredible grief. This is the greatest moment of my life and now that it has reached its peak there is nothing left for me but death. Towards you I roll, you all-destroying but unconquering whale; to the last I fight with you. From the bottom of my heart I stab at you; for hate's sake I spit my last breath at you. Sink all coffins and all hearses to one common pool! Since neither can be mine, let me then tow to pieces, you damned whale! *Thus*, I give up the spear!"

The harpoon was darted; the stricken whale flew forward; with igniting speed the line ran through the groove;—ran afoul. Ahab stooped to clear it. He did clear it. But the flying turn caught him round the neck, and voicelessly he was shot out of the boat. Not even the crew knew he was gone. In the next instant, the whale broke the rope, knocked down an oarsman, and striking the sea, disappeared in its depths.

For an instant, the dazed boat's crew stood still. Then they turned. "The ship? Great God, where is the ship?" Soon they saw her. She was a fading phantom, as in a mirage. Only the uppermost masts were out of the water; however, the loyal harpooneers still maintained their sinking lookouts on the sea. And now, circles grabbed hold of the lone boat itself. All its crew, and each floating oar, and every lance pole, and spinning, living and not living thing, all round and round in one circle, carried the smallest chip of the *Pequod* out of sight.

Now small birds flew screaming over the yet yawning gulf; a sullen white surf beat against its steep sides; then all collapsed, and the great shroud of the sea rolled on as it rolled five thousand years ago.

---

phantom (FAN tum) an unreal mental image
sullen (SUL un) sulky and brooding; moody
shroud (SHROWD) something that hides or protects

Literary Focus: *Theme*

Ask students to discuss what the theme of this story is. You might want to begin the discussion by asking them if they recognize good and evil forces in the selection. Who is good? Who is evil? Do they see nature as predatory, that is, able to destroy humankind for its own profit? If so, what would Nature profit from destroying humans?

Reading Focus: *Visualize*

Have students visualize Ahab before he thrusts the harpoon one last time at Moby-Dick. Ask: What was the condition of the *Pequod* and the whaling boats at this time? Why did Ahab attack the whale against all odds? Describe what happened to the ship, the whaling boats, and the crew after Ahab's final action.

Mini Quiz

Write the following questions on the chalkboard or overhead projector and call on students to fill in the blanks. Discuss the answers with the class.

1. Mrs. Hussey ran the Try Pots Inn on ________ Island.
2. The name of the whaling boat was the ________.
3. The only crew member to speak out against Ahab was ________.
4. Moby-Dick had taken off Ahab's ________.
5. Moby-Dick was sighted in the ________ Ocean.

Answers

1. Nantucket
2. *Pequod*
3. Starbuck
4. leg
5. Pacific

Review the Selection

UNDERSTAND THE SELECTION

Recall

1. Why did Ahab seek revenge?
2. What did Ahab offer the men if they killed Moby-Dick?
3. Where did Ahab say he would go to search for Moby-Dick?

Infer

4. Why did Starbuck protest Ahab's intention to kill Moby-Dick?
5. Give a brief description of Ahab telling what kind of man he was.
6. What might the fight between Ahab and Moby-Dick really represent?
7. Read the last paragraph of *Moby-Dick* again. Then use your own words to tell what Melville meant.

Apply

8. How might Ahab have felt upon first seeing Moby-Dick?
9. Suppose that you are Moby-Dick. Describe your feelings about human beings.
10. Select an important event from *Moby-Dick* and tell why it made the story more interesting.

Respond to Literature

Explain how Emerson's influence on Melville is reflected in *Moby-Dick*.

WRITE ABOUT THE SELECTION

Herman Melville spent a lot of time on whaling ships where he gathered information for several books, including *Moby-Dick*. It is possible that he kept a journal to record his thoughts and observations about whaling and the sea. Imagine it is 1838, and you are on a whaling ship. How do you feel about the ocean? How do you feel about hunting whales? What is the weather like? What is life like aboard a whaling ship? Write a journal entry.

Prewriting Freewrite for a few minutes to explore what you want to include in your journal entry. Describe what the ocean looked like, how it smelled, and what sea life you saw. You might want to include a whale sighting or a whale hunt. Try to capture the excitement and the danger of your situation.

Writing Write a journal entry about a day at sea on a whaling boat. Include your thoughts and recollections of the day.

Revising When you revise, make sure that you have included several observations about sea life. If you have not, be sure to include them during your revision. Conversely, if you have included any passages that do not relate to ocean life, eliminate these when you revise.

Proofreading Reread your journal entry to check for errors. Be sure all your sentences end with periods, question marks, or exclamation points.

UNDERSTAND THE SELECTION

Answers

1. Ahab sought revenge because the whale had caused him to lose his leg.
2. He offered them an ounce of gold.
3. He said that he would go anywhere, even to Good Hope and the Horn.
4. He was not interested in vengeance. Vengeance could not be sold.
5. Sample answer: He was an intense, brooding man, full of malice and anger.
6. Sample answer: the battle between human beings and nature
7. Sample answer: The sea is part of nature, and nature remains unchanged no matter how many human beings try to conquer it.
8. Sample answer: I am happy because I will have vengeance.
9. Sample answer: Human beings are cruel and foolish.
10. Answers will vary. Accept all reasonable answers.

Respond to Literature

Emerson believed that writers should use nature to reflect their ideas, thoughts, and feelings. Melville used nature to explore his feelings about human beings.

Remind students Melville gathered information while he was whaling. Assign three groups one of the following: **1.** Find out where and why the whaling industry began and when it ended; **2.** Find paintings, photographs, poetry, and journals of whaling voyages; **3.** Find out how whale products were used. Have groups present their findings to the class.

WRITE ABOUT THE SELECTION

Prewriting

Have students use the information they gathered about whaling to help them write a journal entry. You may want to have a class discussion to encourage students to think about what life might have been like on a whaling boat. How would life on a boat be affected by bad weather? What would it be like to be away from home for many months at a time, even a year? What would they miss the most?

Writing

Have students work on this section individually. Give help to any student who is having difficulty.

Revising

Make this a cooperative group activity. Have students work in small groups to revise their journal entries. Remind them to make sure they have included several observations about life at sea.

Proofreading

Select one or two journal entries to use as models for proofreading. Put the paragraphs on the overhead projector and have the class make suggestions for improvements.

THINK ABOUT CONFLICT

One type of conflict in literature is the struggle that results from the interaction between characters representing opposite forces in a plot. The main character is called the **protagonist**; the rival character is called the **antagonist**. The protagonist and the antagonist struggle against each other. Each should be motivated to resolve the conflict. If the characters lack purpose or other motivation, the plot will seem amateurish to the reader or listener. If the characters are well-motivated, the plot will be more satisfying.

1. Who is the protagonist in the excerpts? Who is the antagonist? Describe the main conflict between them.
2. At what point does the climax, or the turning point, of the story come?
3. In the madness of the pursuit, one character was the voice of reason. Whose voice was that?
4. Why did Ahab not heed the warnings of the voice of reason? What was driving him?
5. What was the resolution of the story?

Reading Focus

Visualize As you read this excerpt from *Moby-Dick*, you were able to visualize certain scenes from the story. What scene in this story remains most vivid to you? Give some examples of the imagery that helped you visualize this scene.

DEVELOP YOUR VOCABULARY

An **antonym** is a word that has a meaning opposite, or almost opposite, to that of another word. For example, *enormous* means "huge" or "very big." Words that mean the opposite are *tiny* and *little*.

Read the sentences below. Choose a word from the list that is an antonym for each italicized word. Then write a sentence using the word.

malice	effortless
vague	vengeance
ominous	calm

1. The weather was *favorable* for an afternoon sail.
2. No *mercy* was shown to the defendant when his sentence was given.
3. Your *kindness* during this difficult time is greatly appreciated.
4. Lucy gave a *specific* description of the house so they wouldn't miss it.
5. The first day of rehearsal is always *chaotic*!
6. The sailors' work was *arduous*; it lasted from morning until night.

THINK ABOUT CONFLICT

Answers

1. Captain Ahab; the white whale; The main conflict is between Ahab, who has an obsessive hatred of the whale, and the whale, maddened by harpoon wounds, who seeks self-preservation.
2. The turning point comes when the *Pequod*'s men come face to face with the white whale and begin the actual struggle with it.
3. Starbuck's
4. His obsession with the whale allowed him to dismiss the warnings.
5. Ahab was killed, and the whale swam away.

DEVELOP YOUR VOCABULARY

Answers

1. ominous
2. vengeance
3. malice
4. vague
5. calm
6. effortless

Sample sentences:

1. The thunder sounded ominous.
2. The man was seeking vengeance.
3. There was no malice meant by the remark.
4. The professor's answer was vague.
5. The seas became calm.
6. Our attempts at peace were futile.

Reading Focus

Sample Answer

The scene where Moby-Dick attacks the ship is very vivid. At first the "sea-crashing boat" seems strong, but the whale sees it as an "enemy" and rams the ship in a "semicircle of foam." The men "reeled," and the water poured in "as a mountain stream." Some of the crew "fell flat upon their faces."

Selection Overview

SELECTION OBJECTIVES

After completing this selection, students will be able to

- understand and interpret imagery
- create phrases that evoke imagery
- create a new stanza for a poem
- identify specific and general words
- understand contrast

Lesson Resources

Song of Slaves in the Desert

- Selection Synopsis, Teacher's Edition, p. T159h
- Comprehension and Vocabulary Workbook, pp. 47–48
- Language Enrichment Workbook, pp. 30–31
- Teacher's Resources
  Reinforcement, p. R24
  Test, pp. T47–T48

More About Imagery

Encourage students to suggest words that create powerful images to describe a desert. You might begin by writing this image on the chalkboard: scorching sun. Then have volunteers write several more images on the chalkboard.

More About the Literary Period

Many writers in New England spent years of their lives devoted to the abolition of slavery in the United States. Why do you think the written word was a powerful tool to use to fight slavery?

About the Author

John Greenleaf Whittier was one of many New Englanders staunchly opposed to slavery. He worked in the antislavery movement for 30 years. He spoke out against slavery in his poetry and newspaper articles, along with another well-known journalist, William Lloyd Garrison. At the same time, Frederick Douglass and Sojourner Truth, who were freed slaves, spoke out against slavery as well.

Learn About

IMAGERY

People learn about the world through their senses—sight, hearing, smell, taste, and touch. The poet is especially sensitive to sense impressions. To express an experience of a place, for example, the poet will depend greatly on sense impressions. These, added to thought and emotion, bring the scene alive for the reader.

Sense impression translated into words is called **imagery**. The poet will generally choose specific words rather than general ones to make the strongest statement. A *white-petaled daisy*, for example, is more specific than a *flower*. The more specific the poet is, the more vivid the imagery in the poem will be. The poet looks for fresh ways of expressing sense impressions, of course.

As you read the poem, ask yourself:

1. What sense impression did Whittier express in the poem?
2. Which sense did he call upon most for his imagery?

Reading Focus

Understand Contrast To contrast is to look at differences. Seeing how one situation differs from another often provides important information. As you read "Song of Slaves in the Desert," think about how the lives of the people who have been captured will differ in quality from their lives in Africa. Look for places in the poem that contrast these two ways of life.

WRITING CONNECTION

Write *sight*, *sound*, *smell*, *taste*, *touch* on a piece of paper. Under each heading, write several phrases that create an image for that word. For example, *sound*: crashing, pounding waves.

Cooperative Group Activity

Write the name of your community on the chalkboard. For the Writing Connection activity, divide the class into five groups and assign them one of the following senses: sight, sound, smell, taste, touch. Then have each group write three phrases that identify their community through sight, sound, smell, taste, or touch. When each group has completed the assignment, have a volunteer from each group read their phrases to the class.

ESL Activity

Ask students who remember or have visited their native country, what sights, sounds, smells, and tastes they associate with it. Then have them contrast each one with something they associate with the United States. Invite volunteers to share their responses with the class.

Song of Slaves in the Desert

by John Greenleaf Whittier

Where are we going? where are we going,
Where are we going, Rubee?
Lord of peoples, lord of lands,
Look across these shining sands,
5 Through the furnace of the noon,
Through the white light of the moon.
Strong the Ghiblee wind is blowing,
Strange and large the world is growing!
Speak and tell us where we are going,
10 Where are we going, Rubee?

Bornou land was rich and good,
Wells of water, fields of food,
Dourra fields, and bloom of bean,
And the palm-tree cool and green:
15 Bornou land we see no longer,
Here we thirst and here we hunger,
Here the Moor-man smites in anger:
Where are we going, Rubee?

When we went from Bornou land,
20 We were like the leaves and sand,
We were many, we are few;
Life has one, and death has two:
Whitened bones our path are showing,
Thou All-seeing, thou All-knowing!

Ghiblee (GIB lee) night wind that makes an eerie sound
Bornou land (BAWR noo) reference to homeland in Africa
Dourra (DUUR uh) (usually spelled durra) a kind of grain grown in Northern Africa
smites (SMYTS) inflicts a heavy blow; kills by striking
Moor (MUUR) referring to the African slave traders

Develop Vocabulary Skills

Ask volunteers to read the vocabulary words and the definitions that are footnoted in the story. Remind students that words often change; they may no longer be commonly used in the English language or may have changed spellings. For example, *dourra* is a kind of grain grown in North Africa; its present-day spelling is *durra*.

Teaching Plan

INTRODUCE

Motivation

Ask students to think about what it must have been like to be captured and taken from one's homeland. Find the poem, "The Slave Auction" by Frances E. W. Harper. Before reading the poem, tell students that Harper was born free in Baltimore, Maryland. She was a widely celebrated poet who was also very active in the antislavery movement. Encourage students to think about how they feel as you read the poem.

Purpose-Setting Question

Why would writers from New England continue to speak out against slavery when every Northern state had already abolished slavery years before?

READ

Literary Focus: *Imagery*

Remind students that imagery includes references to sights, sounds, smells, tastes, and the feeling of touch. Have students make a chart and look for references to each of the senses (sight, smell, taste, touch, and sound) as they read. Discuss how the imagery in this poem brings the reader into the sensory world of these captured people.

Reading Focus: *Understand Contrast*

Ask students to look for ways that Whittier contrasts the life the African people had in their homeland with the unknown land they are traveling toward. Ask: What does the contrast reveal about how the poet feels about these people's homeland and their journey?

CLOSE

Have students complete Review the Selection on pages 236–237.

Literary Focus: *Imagery*

Ask: Which elements of poetry did Whittier use in "Song of Slaves in the Desert"?

Critical Thinking: *Analyze*

Even though Whittier had never been to Africa and was not a former slave, he was able to relate to the feelings of the captured African people. Why do you think Whittier was able to do this?

Reading Focus: *Understand Contrast*

Whittier contrasts humans with the divine. Discuss the stanza beginning "We are weak, but Thou art strong." Discuss how each line contrasts the enslaved people and their captors to a god.

25 Hear us, tell us, where are we going,
Where are we going, Rubee?

Moons of marches from our eyes
Bornou land behind us lies;
Stranger round us day by day
30 Bends the desert circle gray;
Wild the waves of sand are flowing,
Hot the winds above them blowing,—
Lord of all things! where are we going?
Where are we going, Rubee?

35 We are weak, but Thou art strong;
Short our lives, but Thine is long;
We are blind, but Thou hast eyes;
We are fools, but Thou art wise!
Thou, our morrow's pathway knowing
40 Through the strange world round us growing,
Hear us, tell us where are we going,
Where are we going, Rubee?

African Slave Trade, The Granger Collection

Viewing Fine Art

In the days before photography was invented, illustrated newspapers provided the American public with pictures. These portrayals of "current events" became a prime form of propaganda against slavery. The strongly abolitionist sentiments of many artists, like the one who made this picture, were clearly seen, and did much to mobilize sentiment against the horrors of the slave trade. The weeping Africans, violently gesturing trader, and departing boats conveyed the situation better than words could. The artist as social critic was an important force in 19th-century America; and though as "pure" art his works may not have been exceptional, as catalysts for change they were very important. Ask: What emotions was the artist portraying? What is the cause of these emotions? Note the light and dark areas of the painting. What might these elements signify?

Mini Quiz

Write the following questions on the chalkboard or overhead projector and call on students to fill in the blanks. Discuss the answers with the class.

1. Bornou land was in ______.
2. The ______ is a nightwind that makes an eerie noise.
3. As the slaves traveled across the desert, they were ______ and ______.
4. As they traveled from their homeland, many slaves ______ along the way.
5. For every person on the journey, ______ have died.

Answers

1. Africa
2. Ghiblee
3. hungry; thirsty
4. died
5. two

Review the Selection

UNDERSTAND THE SELECTION

Recall

1. About whom is this poem written?
2. Where did the Africans live?
3. Identify the speaker of the poem.

Infer

4. Explain the line, "Where are we going, . . . ?"
5. In your own words describe what "Bornou land" was like.
6. Interpret this line: "Here the Moor-man smites in anger."
7. Which line did Whittier use to describe the passage of time?

Apply

8. Which line best describes what the song of the slaves was?
9. Suppose that you could answer the speaker in this poem. How would you respond?
10. The speaker states several times that the world is getting larger and growing. What does he or she mean by these words?

Respond to Literature

How does the "Song of Slaves in the Desert" reflect how writers of the 1800s were writing?

WRITE ABOUT THE SELECTION

John Greenleaf Whittier vividly described his feelings about slavery in "Song of Slaves in the Desert." In this poem, he made it very clear that he opposed slavery. Think about the question that the speaker repeats over and over again. "Where are we going? Where are we going? Where are we going, Rubee?" Write another stanza for this poem in which you answer that question. Describe what the speaker encounters after arriving at his or her destination.

Prewriting Before you start, reread the poem. Think about how Whittier used imagery. Then jot down some words or phrases you might want to use in the stanza you write. Visualize how it might look, feel, and sound to arrive in a new land.

Writing Use your notes to help you write a stanza in which you answer the question, "Where are we going?" Be sure to include several examples of imagery. You might want to compare the place from which the speaker came to the new place in which he or she arrives.

Revising When you revise, make sure that you have included two examples of imagery. If you have not, be sure to include them in your revision.

Proofreading Read over your paragraph to check for errors. Be sure each line of your poem begins with a capital letter.

UNDERSTAND THE SELECTION

Answers

1. people captured in Africa to be enslaved in the United States
2. Bornou
3. The speaker is those Africans who have been taken from their homeland to become enslaved.
4. Sample answer: When the Africans were taken from their land, they had no idea where they were being taken; therefore, they repeatedly asked among themselves, "Where are we going?"
5. Sample answer: The land was rich and fertile; there was plenty of water; the trees made it cool.
6. Sample answer: The slave traders whipped and beat the slaves.
7. Whittier used the line, "Moons of marches from our eyes."
8. Sample answer: "Where are we going?"
9. Answers will vary. Accept all reasonable answers.
10. Sample answer: The slaves travel farther away from home each day; they see parts of the world they did not know existed.

Respond to Literature

Encourage students to look in their local libraries for other poems, essays, speeches, songs, or spirituals that reflect how writers have felt about slavery, and how writers addressed it. When groups have completed their assignments, work together with them to present a poetry/prose reading for other members of the school.

WRITE ABOUT THE SELECTION

Prewriting

Using the information that students have gathered for their Respond to Literature assignment, encourage them to discuss what happened to the slaves when they arrived in America. Make a list of their responses on the chalkboard. Have students use the list to write another stanza that answers the question: "Where are we going?"

Writing

Have students work in pairs to write a stanza. Encourage them to use as much imagery as they can, but remind them that, at the least, they must include two examples.

Revising

Have pairs switch papers with another pair of students to revise their stanzas.

Proofreading

Ask several volunteers to share their work with the class. Put the stanzas on the overhead projector and have the class suggest improvements, paying particular attention to the structure of the stanza.

THINK ABOUT IMAGERY

Imagery is the translation into words of sense impressions gained through sight, hearing, smell, taste, and touch, or feeling. No poem can be judged by its imagery alone, but imagery can vastly enhance the impact of the poem on the reader.

1. What senses does Whittier call on to tell how hot the march across the desert was?
2. What specific images do the African people in this poem have of their native Bornou land?
3. What specific images do they have of their desert environment?
4. What does Whittier mean when he says the Africans "were like the leaves and sand"? Why does he use the past tense?
5. The captured people repeatedly ask "Where are we going, Rubee?" To whom do you think the name *Rubee* refers? Explain your answer.

READING FOCUS

Understand Contrast What contrast does the poem make between the people's fate in an unknown land and their lives in Africa? Provide lines from the poem that illustrate the contrast.

DEVELOP YOUR VOCABULARY

Images that use specific words are more vivid than those that use general words. Specific words, however, can differ in their meaning. The most specific words in a language are those that refer to one-of-a-kind people, animals, places, or things: Michael Jackson, Lassie, Mount St. Helens, the *Mona Lisa*. It is not always necessary to be quite so specific as these, however. Somewhat more general terms would be *singer*, *dog*, *volcano*, and *painting*. Least specific of all would be *man*, *animal*, *mountain*, and *artwork*.

Rearrange these lists in order from most specific to most general.

1. shoe, footwear, cross-trainers, sneaker
2. publication, *Time*, periodical, magazine
3. male, Michael J. Fox, actor, TV star
4. literature, poetry, poem, "Song of Slaves in the Desert"
5. drum, percussion instrument, musical instrument, snare drum

ESL Activity

Have students read one stanza at a time and summarize each stanza in one sentence. Examples are:

1. Slaves are being driven across the desert.
2. He describes the land from which the slaves were taken.
3. There were many people when they started out, but now a number have died; they want to know where they are going.
4. They have traveled for a long time; their surroundings become more unfamiliar every day.
5. The speaker asks again where they are going.

THINK ABOUT IMAGERY

Answers

1. sight, feeling
2. rich, good land; water wells; fields of food, including dourra and beans; cool green palm trees
3. furnace-hot days; strong hot winds, shining sands; waves of sand; thirst and hunger; death and whitening bones
4. He means that there were many Africans at the beginning of the march; he uses the past tense because they are dying in great numbers.
5. Sample answer: Rubee refers to God or to whatever deity the Africans worshiped before they were captured by slavedrivers.

DEVELOP YOUR VOCABULARY

Answers

1. cross-trainers, sneaker, shoe, footwear
2. *Time*, magazine, periodical, publication
3. Michael J. Fox, TV star, actor, male
4. "Song of Slaves in the Desert," poem, poetry, literature
5. snare drum, drum, percussion instrument, musical instrument

READING FOCUS

Sample Answer

The people's lives in Bornou land were good. The land was "rich and good" with "wells of water, fields of food." They had plenty to eat from the "Dourra fields, and bloom of bean," and they were sheltered by "the palm tree, cool and green." But their journey makes them fear their fate, because "Here we thirst, and here we hunger." Many of them have already died, and "Whitened bones our path are showing." Everything becomes "Stranger round us day by day."

UNIT 3 Review

Unit Review Resources

TEACHER'S RESOURCES

- Writing Process, pp. W25–W36
- Grammar, Usage, and Mechanics, pp. G25–G36
- Speaking and Listening, pp. S13–S18
- Critical Thinking, pp. C13–C18
- Choose from Reading in the Content Areas, pp. RCA1–RCA72
- **Standardized Test Preparation**
  Unit 3 Test, pp. UT5–UT6
  Choose from Standardized Test Preparation, pp. STP1–STP31

WRITING APPLICATIONS

Write About Authors

Suppose that all the writers in the unit got together to discuss their work. What do you think they would say about their own and each other's writing? What criticisms or compliments would they offer to each other? Choose two authors from this unit and record their conversation.

Prewriting Before you begin to write, choose the two authors whose conversation you would like to think about. Then review their work. Emerson thought it was important that writers include what they believed in their writings. Examine how the work of the authors you have chosen might reflect Emerson's ideas so that you can include some interesting criticisms and compliments in the conversation. Jot down notes to help you write your conversation.

Writing Use your notes as a basis for your conversation. Be sure to include in the dialogue criticisms and compliments that each writer might have made about the other's work. When you write the dialogue be sure to set off the speaker's name with a colon (:) as in a drama.

Revising As you revise, be sure that you have included both criticisms and compliments. If you have not, be sure to include them in your revision.

Proofreading Reread your dialogue to check for errors in spelling and punctuation. Be sure you have put a colon (:) after each speaker's name.

Write About Poetry

In this unit, you have learned some of the different elements of poetry. Now you can use what you learned to analyze a poem. Choose a poem that you enjoyed reading. Then, using a list of the elements of poetry, prepare a paper in which you discuss how understanding these elements helped you to enjoy the poem.

Prewriting Review what the elements of poetry are. Then make a list of them, being sure to include rhythm, meter, and rhyme. At the top of your list, write the name of the poem you have chosen. Then check off which elements are used in the poem. You might also want to jot down specific kinds of figurative language that were used or how the poet used sound devices and imagery.

Writing Using your list and notes, write an analysis in which you tell how the elements of poetry increased your appreciation of the poem. Be sure to include specific examples.

Revising When you revise, make sure that you have made a reference to at least four different elements of poetry that increased your appreciation of the poem.

Proofreading Check your paper for errors in punctuation. Make sure that you have spelled all the words correctly.

WRITING APPLICATIONS

Write About Authors

Cooperative Group Activity

Prewriting: Divide the class into groups. Have each student choose which writer he or she would like to be. Then tell students to have a conversation, assuming the role of the writer. Encourage them to include criticisms and compliments about the other writers' works. Finally, have students choose two writers for whom they would like to write a conversation.

Writing: Have students work on this section individually. Offer help to any student who is having difficulty.

Revising: Have students work in pairs, reading their conversations to partners. Encourage partners to listen for criticisms and compliments. If they have not included both, make sure they include them in their revisions.

Writer's Toolkit CD-ROM

Proofreading: Have students exchange papers with partners for proofreading. Encourage students to use the Self-Evaluation Checklist (Writing Tools, Revising/Editing) to complete the **proofreading** activity.

Write About Poetry

Prewriting: Review the Focus on Poetry section, along with other lessons on sounds, rhyme, and imagery. Have students make a chart on the chalkboard listing the elements of poetry. Lead a group discussion in which students analyze and criticize a poem from this unit.

Writing: While students work on this section individually, go around the class offering help to any student who is having difficulty. Remind students that they may refer to the lessons in their text or to the chart on the chalkboard.

Cooperative Group Activity

Revising: Have students work in pairs, each reading his or her analysis to a partner. Have the partner listen to make sure the other student has included references to four different elements of poetry.

Proofreading: Have students exchange papers with partners for proofreading. Make sure they pay particular attention to punctuation and the spelling of poetry terms.

BUILD LANGUAGE SKILLS

Vocabulary

Onomatopoeia (AHN-uh-MAT-uh-PEE-uh) is the term used for words that imitate sounds. Some onomatopoeic words are *hiss*, *pop*, *whizz*, *buzz*, and *bang*. Onomatopoeia is a useful resource in the poet's—and the prose writer's—repertory of sound devices. It may be used openly, as in "Pop goes the weasel," or subtly, as in "The moan of doves in immemorial elms."

Write the following sentences. Then underline the onomatopoeic word in each one.

1. The chains in the back of the trunk clanked as we drove over the rough road.
2. The sleigh bells jingled merrily as the horse pulled us through the newly fallen snow.
3. A green snake slithered unnoticed through the tall grass.
4. Drops of water plopped into the puddles of water the rain had created.
5. High above us a skein of geese honked as they flew south.
6. A tiny locomotive chugged up the steep mountainside.
7. The ignition turned over, sputtered, and then died.
8. A whole sack of flour fell to the floor with a dull thud.

Grammar, Usage, and Mechanics

When you are writing a series of three or more items in a sentence, you should use commas to separate the items.

Example: Lisa bought lace, ribbons, pins, thread, and fabric.

Some authorities permit the omission of the comma before *and* if the meaning is clear without it. However this can sometimes lead to uncertainty of meaning.

Example: Alex bought Redbook, Sports Illustrated and Travel and Leisure.

If the comma is omitted before *and*, a reader might assume that *Travel and Leisure* is two magazines. A comma before *and* makes it clear that *Travel and Leisure* is a single magazine.

If you always put a comma before *and*, you will not have to stop and think whether the meaning is clear.

Add commas where they are needed in the following sentences.

1. Jack brought climbing boots walking boots sneakers and loafers with him.
2. Lee read Travels with Charley Twenty Thousand Leagues Under the Sea and Crime and Punishment last summer.
3. Larry subscribes to National Geographic Visions and Field and Stream.
4. Chris sent books magazines records tapes and newspapers to her brother in Ecuador.

Grammar, Usage, and Mechanics

Answers

Point out that although some authorities allow the omission of a comma before the *and* if the sentence would not be confusing, a writer will always be clear if he or she uses it. Then have students add commas to the sentences in the book. Placement of commas should be as follows:

1. Jack bought climbing boots, walking boots, sneakers, and loafers with him.
2. Lee read *Travels with Charley, Twenty Thousand Leagues Under the Sea*, and *Crime and Punishment* last summer.
3. Larry subscribes to *National Geographic*, *Visions*, and *Field and Stream*.
4. Chris sent books, magazines, records, tapes, and newspapers to her brother in Ecuador.

Cooperative Group Activity

Have students work in pairs to add commas to the sentences in the student text. When they have completed that task, ask volunteers to state why they did, or did not, put commas in certain places in the sentences.

BUILD LANGUAGE SKILLS

Vocabulary

Answers

1. clanked
2. jingled
3. slithered
4. plopped
5. honked
6. chugged
7. sputtered
8. thud

More About Word Attack: Point out to students that *onomatopoeia* is often used by poets and writers to help the reader hear the sound of something, such as that of an animal or bird. Write this example from "Paul Revere's Ride" on the chalkboard:

He heard the bleating of the flock,
And the twitter of the birds among the trees,

Elicit from students that bleating and twitter are both *onomatopoeic* words.

Cooperative Group Activity

Divide the class into small groups. Have them work together to figure out the onomatopoeic word in each sentence in the student text.

SPEAKING AND LISTENING

Motivation

Ask students to name some poems they have enjoyed hearing read aloud. Discuss why they enjoyed hearing them read aloud and what characteristics of voice or expression made the poem more interesting.

Teaching Strategy

Guide students through the tips about how to read a selection aloud. Allow students time in class to choose their selection. Tell them to make sure the selection they choose will be interesting to read aloud. Assign the practice as a homework activity.

Evaluation Criteria

Did the students' oral interpretations clearly express the mood and tone of the selection? Did students make eye contact? Did they express themselves well? After students have completed their oral readings, be sure to compliment them on some aspect of their reading before you make suggestions for improvements. You may want to use the following evaluation code to guide you:

NI Needs Improvement
A Adequate
G Good
O Outstanding

UNIT 3 Review

SPEAKING AND LISTENING

One of the easiest and most effective ways to make a piece of literature interesting is to read it aloud. As a child, you loved hearing your favorite story. As an older student, you may find a difficult piece of literature more accessible if you hear someone read it aloud. Maybe that is because when you hear something, you allow your mind to visualize the words more easily than when you have to read the words yourself.

Before you choose a selection from this unit to read aloud, acquaint yourself with the following tips. They will help you to read aloud with more confidence and feeling.

1. Be selective. Choose something that you find interesting. This is important for two reasons. First of all, if you are bored when you read it, chances are your listeners will be bored and uninterested, too. Second, it's unfulfilling to read something you don't like.
2. Read the selection to yourself and become familiar with it. Get the feel for the language. This will help you to know what expression to use when you read aloud.
3. If the selection is perfect as it is, let it be, if not, do some editing. You might want to condense some of the dialogue or the longer sections, or you might want to paraphrase certain passages.
4. Your oral reading style should fit your personality. If it's not your style to use unique voices for each character, don't do it. If it makes you uncomfortable to read dramatically, then don't do it. Be natural and the words of the selection should grab the listeners without theatrics.
5. During your reading aloud, maintain good volume and expression in your voice. Make frequent eye contact with your listeners. This will involve them and make them feel that you are reading to them individually.
6. Practice so that you feel confident in your delivery. Choose a selection or part of a selection from this unit and prepare to read it aloud. Limit your presentation to about three minutes. Review the suggestions above to help you enjoy the experience.

Career Connection

After reading Thoreau and Emerson's works, students may be interested in careers that would allow them to experience nature on a regular basis. There are many careers in this field, from working in a greenhouse or nursery to biological research. One career that requires sensitivity to nature is landscape design. Landscape designers work with people and businesses to provide a natural design for the outside of buildings and homes. Landscape designers have at least a two-year technical degree. They can also be highly specialized through extensive experiences or a college degree.

CRITICAL THINKING

Classifying is the act of grouping things according to some principle. For example, when you rearrange your bookshelves, you may put all the fiction books on one shelf, the biographies on another shelf, and the hobby books on a third shelf. You have classified your books by their type.

When you classify things, you put them in **categories**. A category is a group of things that have some characteristic in common. In the bookshelf example, fiction is one category, biographies another, and hobby books are the third category. The principles that determine a category are many. You may classify by size, type, color, use, shape, purpose, and so on.

To determine a category, you must be able to see similarities and differences. Noting the similarities is called **comparing**. Noting the differences is called **contrasting**.

Authors often make use of classification and categorizing in order to make comparisons and contrasts. Choose a selection from this unit that classifies or categorizes some objects, ways of life, aspects of nature, characters, or ideas. Then answer the following questions.

1. What principle determines each category? Does the author explain the classification adequately?
2. What does the category enable the author to compare or contrast?

EFFECTIVE STUDYING

Following Directions Being able to follow directions is an important skill for school and the rest of your life. Throughout life, you may need to follow directions to get from one place to another or to do something or to make something.

Many directions must be followed in a precise sequence. In such directions, you may notice words such as *first*, *next*, *then*, and *last*. These words help you keep the sequence straight.

Here are some guidelines to help you.

1. To follow oral directions
   - Listen attentively.
   - If the instructions are detailed, you may wish to take notes.
   - If there are parts you do not understand, ask questions.
   - To double check your understanding, repeat the directions.
2. To follow written directions
   - Read them carefully.
   - Make sure you understand the sequence.
   - After each step, read the direction again to be sure that you followed it correctly.
   - If pictures accompany the directions, study them carefully.

Test Preparation

Be sure to follow test directions exactly. Reread the directions for each part of the test and circle the key words before you begin to answer the questions.

EFFECTIVE STUDYING

Teaching Strategy

Guide students through the student text, offering further suggestions as to when listening to directions can be helpful. Then write the following questions on the chalkboard or overhead projector and call on students to fill in the blanks. Discuss the answers with the class.

1. To follow oral directions, it is best to ________ attentively.
2. Take ________ if the directions are detailed.
3. Ask ________ if there is something you do not understand.
4. Written directions must be ________ carefully.
5. If there are pictures, look at them ________.
6. If there are steps, read the directions ________ to make sure you understand them.

Answers

1. listen
2. notes
3. questions
4. read
5. carefully
6. again

CRITICAL THINKING

Sample Answers

1. Thoreau categorizes people on the basis of wealth. He explains that material things are not important.
2. Answers will vary. Some answers might include the following: independence vs. dependence on things, enjoyment of the beauty of nature, peace of mind, honesty vs. dishonesty.

UNIT ACTIVITY

A Continuing Unit Project: Illustrated Reading Logs

A log is a useful learning tool that can focus students' attention on the material at hand and allow them the opportunity to explore their own ideas and opinions. In addition, the log entries can serve as prewriting activities or as notes for studying in preparation for testing.

Have students produce illustrated reading logs as they read this unit. After they have read a selection, ask students to write their responses in an expressive style. Make sure they understand they are writing about their thoughts and feelings, not merely repeating facts from the literature. Encourage students to jot down any thoughts or questions about the content, as well as the relationship between the selection and the historical period in which it was written (ways in which the selection illustrates the thinking, the social setting, the burning issues, and so forth of the times). Also encourage students to relate the themes to their own experiences. Allow five to ten minutes for each entry. Students need write no more than half a page for each entry.

In preparation, review the annotated selection from the previous unit. Guide students in the use of certain annotations as prompts for their own thoughts. Do not permit simple rephrasing of the annotations. Ask questions that will trigger original thoughts and encourage students to take the ideas expressed in the annotations one step further.

Here are some general questions you can ask the class:

Have you read any other stories in which the conflict was between the protagonist and death?

If not, have you seen any movies or television shows exploring this conflict?

Are there any similarities between the two?

Are there differences between the two?

Which did you like better?

Have you had any personal experiences in which this conflict arose?

How did the person react?

How did you feel?

Why do you think the Pawnee respected Bumppo so much?

Do you admire him? Why or why not?

Have you had any personal experiences with someone from another culture?

In what ways was your experience similar to Bumppo's?

In what ways was your experience different?

What did you learn from this experience?

Now have the class read the other selections. Tell students they will be annotating each selection they read. The annotations should include both observations on the literary aspects of each work and personal observations. Here is a general question you can ask the class.

What did you learn today?

Poetry of Walt Whitman

What kind of rhyme scheme does Whitman use?

How would you feel about the assassination of a president?

Have you heard adults discuss any of the political assassinations of the 1960s? What did they say?

"The Gift of the Magi"

How would you summarize the plot of this story?

Why do you think O. Henry calls his characters the wisest of all?

Do you agree with him?

"The Revolt of Mother"

How would you describe mother's character?

Do you admire her? Why? Why not?

"How to Tell a Story"

Write down your favorite joke as you remember it. In light of Twain's advice on how to tell a story, how would you rewrite it?

In retelling it, what devices would you use? Where would you use them?

"To Build a Fire"

What was the theme of this story?

How do you feel about this story?

■ "America the Beautiful"

Find, and illustrate with a passage, two examples of figurative language from this poem.

Do you share the poet's feelings about America? Why? Why not?

■ Poetry of Sara Teasdale

What is a couplet?

Are any of these poems written in couplets? Explain your answer.

Have you ever wished upon a star? What was your wish?

What aspect of life would you barter for?

(The last two questions can be answered in the third person, as a short story or poem. That way, a student's wish can remain a secret.)

■ "Richard Cory"

Why is this poem ironic?

Did you identify with the narrator or Richard Cory?

Do you think we can ever really understand what another person is thinking? Why? Why not?

Require students to illustrate the entries. Allow them to draw pictures or cartoons, develop symbolic representations, or cut and paste magazine pictures. In addition, students will create a cover and a table of contents.

Logs may be read aloud or by another student. Questions, opinions, and comments should be shared with the class as a whole or in small groups.

After the unit has been completed, collect and evaluate the illustrated reading logs.

■ Poetry of Walt Whitman

(page 247)

SELECTION SYNOPSES

■ "I Hear America Singing"

The subject of this poem is the various occupations of the American people. The theme suggests America as a melting pot; from the rich diversity of its people with their different experiences emerges a strong melodious song, or cultural harmony.

■ "O Captain! My Captain!"

The subject of this poem is the death by assassination of President Abraham Lincoln just days after the Civil War had ended. The theme is the unfairness of Lincoln's death just as the terrible conflict he had sought to avoid came to an end and the union he sought to preserve was saved. The poet also suggests that Lincoln's death had stolen much of the joy from what should have been a time of celebration.

■ "When I Heard the Learn'd Astronomer"

The subject of this poem is the poet's dissimilar reactions to a lecture on astronomy and a walk under the stars.

The theme is that the romance and the wonder of the stars can be appreciated during a solitary walk at night in a way that scientific facts and figures can never duplicate.

SELECTION ACTIVITIES

Depending on the time available and the abilities of your students, you should decide on the approach you will take in using the following activities.

■ "I Hear America Singing"

Find a recording of the Woody Guthrie folk song, "This Land Is Your Land, This Land Is My Land." Play it in class. Distribute a handout, or print the lyrics on the chalkboard or overhead transparency to facilitate understanding and retention. Discuss the thematic similarities between this song and the poem.

Tell students that they are about to do a research activity. You may want to do a lesson explaining certain requirements of research: preplanning (selection and organization of their material), use of source works, the importance of footnotes, a bibliography, and crediting writers whose works have provided information.

Collect and bring to class books and articles that identify and discuss prominent American folksingers. One good magazine reference is *Rolling Stone*. Another good source is the music department at the local library. You may also want to consult one of the music teachers at your school.

First, students should select several folksingers. You may want to guide them by briefly discussing several. Aim for cultural diversity. Examples include Buffie Saint Marie. You might want to expand the list and include rock stars, some of whose work has folk overtones or themes. Examples include Bruce Springsteen, Billy Joel, Dionne Warwick, Simon and Garfunkel, and Bob Dylan.

Once students have selected singers, tell them to visit the music department of their local or school library to conduct research. They are to select songs with lyrics they find interesting. They should play the songs at the library or in their homes, if the records or tapes circulate. They should also use encyclopedias, books, and magazines to research the life of the artist each has chosen.

First, have students write biographies of the singers. Next, have students explain their choices of song and singer. Tell them they must interpret the song lyrics and explain the theme. Ask students to include one or two sentences on what the chosen song means to them and how it relates to their experiences.

■ "O Captain! My Captain"

Tell students they are going to write a report on the assassination of President Abraham Lincoln. The report is to be at least three paragraphs in length. For background and reference materials, they should visit the school library. They may also want to consult with one or more of the social studies teachers. One good reference source is *The Day Lincoln Was Shot* by Jim Bishop. Another is Carl Sandburg's biography of Lincoln. Explain to students that this is a multivolume work. To save time, they should consult the index to locate the section on the President's death. A third source is Bruce Catton's history of the Civil War. Again, this is a multivolume work. Tell the class that any student who includes and cites a source work written in 1865 will receive extra credit.

In preparation for writing the report, review the writing process. You may also want to guide the class with the following questions:

Who was the assassin?

What was his motive?

Where did the assassination take place?

When did the assassination occur?

Students should not limit their answers to the dates. They should also discuss the historical context in which the Civil War had just ended.

How did the assassination happen?

What were the events leading up to and immediately preceding the assassination?

Where was Lincoln buried?

How was his body transported to the gravesite?

What was the reaction of the American people?

What were some of the immediate and long-term effects of Lincoln's death on American history?

To be certain that students are on the right track, you may want to collect and review notes or first drafts. Offer suggestions as necessary. After you have collected and graded the reports, display them on the bulletin board without displaying grades.

■ "When I Heard the Learn'd Astronomer"

After students have read the poem, tell them that they have just gained insights into Whitman's preference to studying the stars. They are going to prepare oral reports to be delivered in class. In these reports, they will describe personal experiences from which they gained new insights or perspectives.

To guide students in preparing and delivering the report you may want to make the following suggestions. First, each student should select a topic. Next, students should jot down as many ideas as possible on 3 × 5 index cards. After reviewing the cards, students should organize their notes in sequential order. Tell them that the night before delivering the reports, they should practice in front of a mirror or before a family member to gain experience and confidence. You may want to refer to the Speaking and Listening Skills sections found throughout this text for additional information.

■ "The Gift of the Magi"

by O. Henry (page 255)

SELECTION SYNOPSIS

Della Young, a young married woman, has only $1.87 (in the year 1905) to buy her husband Jim a Christmas present. She sells her long hair, her prized possession, for $20.00, with which she buys a platinum chain for Jim's prized possession, a gold watch. Then she returns to their apartment, puts her hair in short curls, and waits for Jim to arrive. He is shocked to see Della, for it turns out that he is carrying a set of fancy combs purchased for her to wear in her long hair. When Della presents him with the chain, she learns that he has sold his watch to buy the combs. The writer concludes that it is the spirit of giving that is important and states that the sacrifices of Jim and Della rival the gifts given long ago by the Magi to the Christ Child.

SELECTION ACTIVITY

Identify a home for the elderly in the area of the school. Visit that home after school, or call the director by telephone. Gather the names of the residents.

Divide the class into small groups. Determine group size by the number of residents in the home. Explain to students that they will use one class period to make greeting cards for the residents of the home. These greeting cards should contain friendly, optimistic messages.

Encourage students to use original verse. If this proves too difficult for any of the groups, guide them in selecting appropriate verses from the text or a poetry anthology.

Each card can be made from construction paper or other materials available through the school. Have samples of greeting cards displayed as models. Students in each group should cut the paper to the size of an unfolded greeting card and fold it in half. The selected verse should be printed neatly and legibly on the inside of the card. If the students have the artistic ability, encourage them to draw scrollwork or other designs in the corners as a border. Have students design an appropriate cover for each card. They may decorate them with crayon, markers, or pictures from magazines. Encourage individual artistic creativity wherever possible.

Each member of the group should sign the card. The verse should be preceded by the name of the recipient. Have the class visit the home and deliver the cards to the residents. Encourage conversation between students and the elderly. If this is not possible, place all the cards in a large manila envelope, and mail or deliver them to the director of the home for distribution.

■ "The Revolt of Mother"

by Mary E. Wilkins Freeman (page 267)

SELECTION SYNOPSIS

The setting for this story is rural New England, near the end of the 19th century. Sarah Penn, the perfect farm wife, learns that her husband, Adoniram, is having a new barn built to house the additional cattle he plans on buying. Sarah and Adoniram Penn have been married 40 years. They have two children: a son, Sammy, and a daughter, Nanny. Nanny is engaged to be married.

The Penns had very little in the way of material possessions when they first married. They bought the farm on which they live and moved into the tiny dwelling that stood on the land. Adoniram promised Sarah that one day she would live in a grand house. Over the years, they have worked hard and the farm has prospered. Adoniram has at every opportunity improved the buildings in which the livestock and the farm equipment are kept. This make good business sense. The grand house has never materialized. Sarah has kept her own counsel and never complained. However, by now, she has had enough. She confronts her husband about his plans. He is embarrassed and does not want to discuss the subject, not even when Sarah reminds him that Nanny's wedding celebration should take place in better surroundings.

The new barn, a magnificent structure, is built, and the livestock will soon arrive. Adoniram receives a letter from his brother-in-law, Hiram. Hiram has learned that a horse, the kind of work horse Adoniram has always wanted, is for sale. Adoniram leaves immediately for Hiram's farm in neighboring Vermont.

While he gone, Sarah has an inspiration. With her children's help, she moves the household furniture and appliances into the new barn. When the recently bought cattle arrive, she puts three in empty stalls in the old barn. The fourth she installs in the old house.

The neighbors soon learn of the strange events at the Penn farm. Sarah is living in the barn and, according to rumor, four cows are residing in the house. Convinced she has gone mad, they anxiously await Adoniram's return. In the meantime, they persuade the local minister to visit her. Sarah tells the minister that she asked God's guidance before making her decision, and she has no intention of backing down.

On the day Adoniram arrives home, a crowd of neighbors has gathered at the boundary of his property. They greet him as he passes and wait for the fireworks to start.

Arriving at the house, Adoniram is confused. The door is locked (to keep the cow from escaping). Their door was seldom locked. He sees no sign of his wife or children. (Of course, he is not expecting to find them in the barn.)

He leads the horse to the barn. Opening the door, he finds his family and their household possessions inside. His favorite dinner is ready on the stove. The kitchen table is set.

Sarah explains that, by adding a few walls and windows and making other renovations here and there, the barn can be converted into the house of her dreams, a home that would be a proud setting for Nanny's wedding celebration. Adoniram washes up and sits down to dinner. His wife and children wait for his reaction. After the meal, he looks up with tears in his eyes. He tells Sarah, "I'll—put up the—partitions, an'—everything you—want . . . I hadn't no idee you was so set on't as all this comes to."

SELECTION ACTIVITY

Collect magazines such as *Better Homes and Gardens* and *House Beautiful*. From the library, obtain how-to books on decorating and construction. One excellent source is the *Sunset Series*. Divide the class into small groups. Have each group sketch or trace their concept of a well-constructed barn.

Consult with and invite the home economics teacher who is most familiar with interior decorating to speak to the class on inexpensive and creative ways to improve any home. If possible, invite an architect or independent contractor to discuss the most cost-effective ways to convert or renovate a building. Have these resource people or the mathematics teacher discuss the development of floor plans.

Explain that each group is to convert its selected barn into a beautiful home, using a minimum amount of money and maximum amounts of creativity and hard work. First, each group should develop a floor plan for this dwelling. Next, each group is to decorate at least three rooms in the home, illustrating each with cut-and-paste magazine pictures or, preferably, original artwork. Finally, each group should indicate what the exterior structure will resemble when finished. Again, encourage original artwork or allow cut-and-paste magazine pictures.

When students have finished, collect the completed plans and write comments praising each for as many aspects of the project as are justified. Make enough copies of each for all the students in the groups. Return a copy of the work, to which they have contributed, to each student. Tell them to take the copies home and keep them for future reference.

Have different members of each group write a "thank you" note to each of the resource persons who have spoken to the class. If possible, send a copy of each group's project to each resource person.

■ "How to Tell a Story"

by Mark Twain (page 289)

SELECTION SYNOPSIS

This selection is essentially a short treatise on humor that contains two excellent examples of amusing stories. Twain first distinguishes what he calls the "comic" story, a short sequence of happenings that leads to a punch line and "explosion after explosion of horse-laughter." Twain tells the story of "The Wounded Soldier" as an example. The humorist then explains how the same story can be related in what he calls the "humorous" fashion. The humorous tale goes on and on, contains many unexpected turns and amusing surprises, and depends for its effect more on the manner of the narrator than on the matter of the story itself. "An Encounter With an Interviewer" is the hilarious example. Here Twain, playing his imagined self, insists on misinterpreting or giving illogical answers to a series of questions from a young journalist.

SELECTION ACTIVITY

Explain that stand-up comics are usually given a set period of time in which to perform their acts. They cannot finish too quickly or extend their performances without upsetting the rest of the show. As Twain explained in his article, timing is critical to humor.

Tell students that when Woody Allen, the famous filmmaker, was a young comic, he frequently told the same joke approximately halfway through his act. He would take out a pocket watch and hold it up for the audience to see. He would then say, "This is a family heirloom. My grandfather sold it to me on his deathbed." The humor was in the incongruity. Grandparents do not sell prized family possessions to their heirs. Furthermore, dying people have no need of money.

The audience would laugh, but they never understood the reason Allen told this joke when he did. He wanted to check the time. By knowing how much time he had left to perform, he would go faster or slower to finish his act on time.

Divide the class into groups of three. Provide a handout, on which the tale of the wounded soldier is printed as Twain wrote it, to each group. Tell students to annotate the story, deciding on the physical gestures, facial expressions, and pauses that might accompany the tale when told.

Bring a tape recorder to class. Using a lottery system, select which students from each group will play the soldier, his wounded comrade, and the officer. Allow each group to perform a skit based on the tale in front of the class, incorporating gestures, expressions, and pauses. Record and play the results for the class.

■ "To Build a Fire"

by Jack London (page 299)

SELECTION SYNOPSIS

One morning, a man is traveling on foot through the frozen Yukon with a big husky. His destination is a camp where he plans to rejoin his companions at about six o'clock. It is cold—75 degrees below zero! It is so cold that numbness deadens any feeling in his extremities. When he stops for lunch, he builds a fire, warms his limbs, and proceeds. Soon, he accidentally falls through a thin sheet of ice covering a spring and wets his feet. Knowing that wet feet will freeze, he has no other choice but to stop and build another fire. Unfortunately he builds the fire under a snow-covered spruce tree. An avalanche of snow puts the fire out, and the man must start again. His heroic efforts to build a fire are recorded in minute detail. Finally, when the fire is laid, his freezing fingers cannot handle the matches upon which his life depends. In desperation, he attempts to kill the dog for the warmth of its body, but he cannot accomplish this task, either. Finally, he tries to run on completely numb feet, but he lacks the strength. He falls and slips off to sleep, quietly meeting death as the dog continues the journey alone.

SELECTION ACTIVITY

Tell students to write the same story from a different point of view. This time, the dog will be the protagonist, and the story will be told from its point of view.

Use the writing process that has been explained throughout the text. In the prewriting phase, students should identify six incidents that trigger reactions in the dog. Guide them in selecting the following six incidents:

The man stops for lunch and builds a fire.

The man slips through the ice, wetting his feet.

Snow from the spruce tree puts out his second fire.

His fingers are too cold to rebuild the fire.

He tries unsuccessfully to kill the dog.

As the man dies, the dog continues the journey alone.

Students should imagine the dog's instinctive reaction to each of the six events. Each student should freewrite the dog's reactions.

Writing Students should write the story, briefly outlining the man's activities, and describe in greater detail the dog's reactions and growing apprehension as it senses changes in the man.

Revising Students should rewrite the story, adding detail and precision.

■ "America the Beautiful"

by Katherine Lee Bates (page 317)

SELECTION SYNOPSIS

This is a patriotic hymn celebrating the past and future of America through images evoking its natural beauty and the heroism of its people.

■ Poetry of Sara Teasdale

(page 323)

SELECTION SYNOPSIS

This selection includes four short poems from the works of Sara Teasdale. The subjects and themes are varied. Each poem illustrates the poet's striking use of language and her perception of the truths underlying human experience.

■ "Richard Cory"

by Edwin Arlington Robinson (page 331)

SELECTION SYNOPSIS

This is an ironic poem that suggests the truth in the following expression: "You can never understand another person until you have walked a mile in his shoes."

SELECTION ACTIVITY

Arrange students into small groups. Have each group select one poem from the selections above. Distribute to each group a handout on which the poem that group has selected is printed. Margins should be wide enough to permit handwritten annotations.

Each group should participate in annotating the selected poem. First, have students review the annotations for the selections in the previous units. Then have students in each group write at least three annotations for the selected poem. One annotation should identify a mechanical aspect of poetry. Rhyme and meter are examples. The second annotation should define and identify an example of figurative language. Simile, metaphor, and personification are examples. The third annotation should address theme, identifying a line, phrase, or stanza that suggests the central or dominating idea in the chosen poem. Collect and evaluate each group's annotations.

STUDENT READING LIST

Paulsen, Gary. *Soldier's Heart*. New York: Delacorte, 1998.

Carbone, Elisa. *Stealing Freedom*. New York: Knopf, 1998.

Wiener, Gary (ed). *Readings on Walt Whitman*. San Diego, CA: Greenhaven, 1999.

Johnson, Angela. *Other Side: Shorter Poems*. New York: Orchard Books, 1998.

Boreth. Craig. *Hemingway Cookbook*. Chicago: Chicago Review Press, 1998.

From Globe Fearon Educational Publisher

Experiencing Poetry
Adapted Classics
Huckleberry Finn
Tom Sawyer
Selected Stories by O. Henry *Reader*

UNIT 4
Overview

UNIT OBJECTIVES

After completing this unit, students will be able to

- understand the basic elements of fiction
- read poetry aloud
- write cause-and-effect exposition, an interpretation of an analogy, an epilogue, a newspaper article, a new story ending, and poem stanzas
- think critically about the relationships of parts to the whole in literature
- write a summary
- understand Latin and Greek word origins, idioms, dialect, and syllabification

UNIT SELECTIONS

The period covered in this unit is 1855–1915. The two main features of this period were changes in technology (the Industrial Revolution) and the issue of the abolition of slavery (the Civil War). The most popular forms of literature during this time were fiction and poetry.

- **"I Hear America Singing"/ "O Captain! My Captain!"/ "When I Heard the Learn'd Astronomer"** (p. 247) These poems demonstrate the democratization of literature during the period.

  LITERARY SKILL: symbolism

  READING SKILL: compare and contrast

  VOCABULARY: Latin/Greek word origins

  WRITING: cause and effect

- **"The Gift of the Magi"** (p. 255) This realistic short story has a surprise ending.

  LITERARY SKILL: character

  READING SKILL: understand imagery

  VOCABULARY: idioms

  WRITING: analogy

- **"The Revolt of Mother"** (p. 267) This short story, which is the model selection, reflects the agrarian economy of the period.

  LITERARY SKILL: elements of fiction

  READING SKILL: interpret character

  VOCABULARY: dialect

  WRITING: epilogue

- **"How to Tell a Story"** (p. 289) illustrates two ways to make listeners laugh.

  LITERARY SKILL: exposition

  READING SKILL: compare and contrast

  VOCABULARY: syllabification

  WRITING: newspaper article

- **"To Build a Fire"** (p. 299) describes a life-and-death struggle in the frozen north.

  LITERARY SKILL: setting

  READING SKILL: predict outcomes

  VOCABULARY: Inuit words

  WRITING: new story ending

UNIT 4
A Nation Expresses Itself
Dark hills at evening in the west,
Where sunset hovers like a sound
Of golden horns that sang to rest
Old bones of warriors under ground.
—Edwin Arlington Robinson
243

A Rest on the Ride, Albert Bierstadt. Three Lions/Superstock

Introducing the Literary Period

Have someone read the Edwin Arlington Robinson quotation aloud. Ask the students to name actual locations they have traveled to, read about, or seen pictures of that the quotation evokes. Discuss the mental pictures and emotions the quotation brings to mind. Have students compare and contrast their own reactions with the reactions people might have had to this quotation between 1855 and 1915.

Viewing Fine Art

Albert Bierstadt was born in Germany and studied in various European countries. He achieved fame as a painter of American landscapes. He first saw the Rocky Mountains in 1858, when he traveled west as part of a team of government surveyors.

Bierstadt sketched any scenery that impressed him. Later, in his studio, he developed his sketches into paintings, many of which were quite large. They were very popular in both Europe and the United States during the 1860s and 1870s. Perhaps his most famous painting was a ten-foot-high landscape of the Rockies, which was exhibited at New York City's Metropolitan Museum of Art in 1863. Ask: What impression do you have of this landscape? Is it a place you would like to visit?

- **"America the Beautiful"** (p. 317) is a patriotic song.
  LITERARY SKILL: rhyme
  READING SKILL: support an opinion
  VOCABULARY: vivid adjectives
  WRITING: additional stanza

- **Poetry of Sara Teasdale** (p. 323) These poems describe a range of human emotions.
  LITERARY SKILL: rhyme scheme
  READING SKILL: recognize figures of speech
  VOCABULARY: words used as both nouns and verbs
  WRITING: additional stanza

- **"Richard Cory"** (p. 331) This brief poem tells of the sudden suicide of a man everyone envied.
  LITERARY SKILL: irony
  READING SKILL: make inferences from connotations
  VOCABULARY: vivid verbs
  WRITING: additional stanza

UNIT 4

RELATED MATERIALS

1. **Soldier's Heart** [by Gary Paulsen, audiobook, Recorded Books, 1998.]
2. **Forgotten Fourteen** [video, 28 mins., Jackson Associates, 1998.] The video tells about a victorious Civil War regiment composed of former slaves.
3. **Freedom on My Mind** [video, 110 mins., California Newsreel] This video presents the trials and tribulations of African Americans.
4. **Harriet Tubman: Conductor on the Underground Railroad** [audiotape, Recorded Books, 1999.]
5. **O. Henry: A Celebration** [audiotape, 330 mins., Baker & Taylor] On this tape, 26 readers share O. Henry's biography and 17 of his best-loved stories.
6. **The Great Ray Charles** [Atlantic Records] "America the Beautiful"
7. **Walt Whitman** [Britannica Learning Materials]
8. **The World of Mark Twain** [film, 31 min., op. cit., Guidance Associates]
9. **The Revolt of Mother** [film, 60 min., University of Illinois Film Center] The film presents a dramatization of Freeman's short story.
10. The following Web sites may also be helpful. Please note that some Internet addresses change frequently. These are the latest versions:

    America the Beautiful,
    Virtually Falmouth,
    Fuzzylu Multimedia
    http://www.fuzzylu.com/falmouth/bates/america.html

    Mark Twain in His Times,
    The Electronic Text Center,
    University of Virginia
    http://etext.virginia.edu/railton/ind ex2.html

    American Memory,
    Library of Congress,
    Walt Whitman Collection
    http://lcweb2.loc.gov/wwhome.html

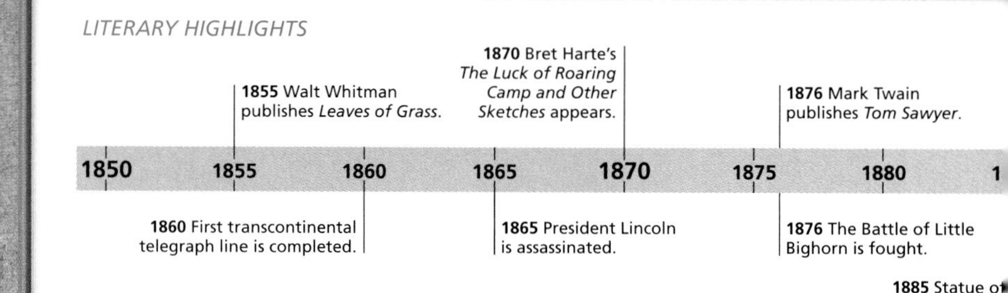

LITERARY HIGHLIGHTS
1855 Walt Whitman publishes Leaves of Grass.
1870 Bret Harte's The Luck of Roaring Camp and Other Sketches appears.
1876 Mark Twain publishes Tom Sawyer.
1850
1855
1860
1865
1870
1875
1880
1860 First transcontinental telegraph line is completed.
1865 President Lincoln is assassinated.
1876 The Battle of Little Bighorn is fought.
1885 Statue of Liberty is dedicated
HISTORICAL HIGHLIGHTS

A Nation Expresses Itself

Before 1855, America consisted of farms and small towns. Between 1855 and 1915, however, there were many changes. The nation became industrialized. Goods that used to be made mainly at home—everything from clothes to furniture—could now be produced in greater quantity and at lower cost in factories. Large cities grew up around the factories. Many Americans and immigrants moved to a city during this period.

This was an age of great inventions. It was the invention of new machinery that made it possible for goods to be mass produced. Beginning in the mid-nineteenth century, you could have sent a telegram. After 1876, you could have made a telephone call. You could have taken a train across the continent in 1869, bought a car around the turn of the century, or even—if you were daring enough—flown in an airplane after 1903.

■ ABOLITION AND THE CIVIL WAR

The most important change in America was the abolition of slavery. This long-overdue measure finally became law with the Emancipation Proclamation of 1863.

Unfortunately, it took a Civil War to bring it about. Eleven Southern states seceded from the Union, many people were killed, and at the war's end a great President was assassinated. Although the Civil War ended with a Union victory in 1865, many years passed before the bitter feelings between North and South were healed.

■ LITERATURE: FICTION AND POETRY

During this time, people turned more and more to reading for pleasure. The most popular kinds of reading material between 1855 and 1915 were fiction and poetry.

Walt Whitman was called the People's Poet. He loved to write about America and the lives of everyday Americans. You will read three of his poems. "I Hear America Singing" tells of ordinary people enjoying their

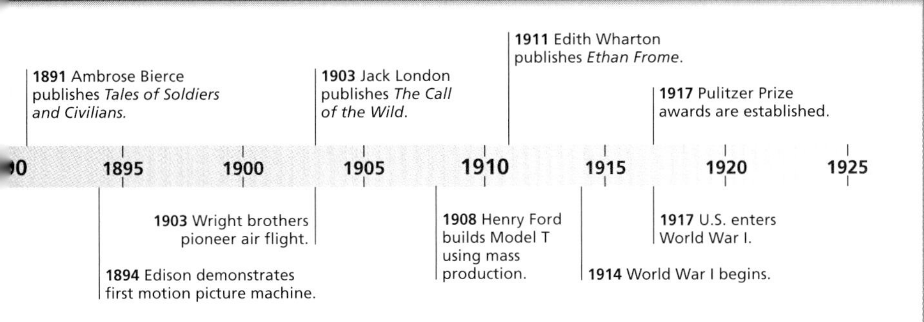
1891 Ambrose Bierce publishes *Tales of Soldiers and Civilians.*
1903 Jack London publishes *The Call of the Wild.*
1911 Edith Wharton publishes *Ethan Frome.*
1917 Pulitzer Prize awards are established.
1895
1900
1905
1910
1915
1920
1925
1903 Wright brothers pioneer air flight.
1894 Edison demonstrates first motion picture machine.
1908 Henry Ford builds Model T using mass production.
1917 U.S. enters World War I.
1914 World War I begins.

work, their country, and their lives in general. "When I Heard the Learn'd Astronomer" is about a student's reaction to a lecture about the stars. "O Captain! My Captain!" is a tribute to President Lincoln.

O. Henry, whose real name was William Sydney Porter, began writing short stories while serving time in prison for embezzlement. When you read "The Gift of the Magi," keep in mind that O. Henry's stories are known for their surprise endings.

Mark Twain's real name was Samuel Langhorne Clemens. He took his pen name from a term he learned while working on a steamboat. It refers to measuring the depth of the water. Twain became famous for creating such characters as Tom Sawyer and Huckleberry Finn. You will learn how he did this when you read his nonfiction article, "How to Tell a Story."

If you like adventure stories, you are sure to enjoy Jack London's "To Build a Fire," which is set in the Yukon of northern Canada during the Gold Rush. London was the first American author to become a millionaire, but he lost his money and died at the age of forty.

In 1922 Edwin Arlington Robinson received the first Pulitzer Prize for poetry. His poems have been described as short stories in verse. Like O. Henry, Robinson liked surprise endings, as you will see in "Richard Cory."

This period saw the emergence of more women writers. Three are highlighted in this unit. All were poets, but Mary E. Wilkins Freeman also wrote novels and short stories such as "The Revolt of Mother."

Sara Teasdale's first book of poems was published before she was twenty-five. Although her poetry generally stresses hope, she led a sad and lonely life. Do you think you can tell her true feelings from her poetry?

You have probably heard the first verse of "America the Beautiful" many times. However, Katharine Lee Bates wrote more than one stanza.

As you read these selections, try to notice differences from writings of earlier eras. Think about the differences you see.

Discussing the Literary Period

Guide students through the opening section of the discussion of the period 1855–1915 in America. Discuss each of the questions raised in the section. For example: If students think they would have been tired of writing letters, what alternatives would have been available? Why? (A possible answer is sending a telegram—the first transcontinental telegraph became operational in 1861. Another possible answer is making a telephone call—the telephone was invented in 1876.)

Other discussion questions about the period include:

- slavery—How did it happen? Why was it wrong? Are there remnants of it in today's world?
- quality of life before the advances in communications and transportation in this period—What was it like? How have things changed? Would they have enjoyed living then?
- gold-seeking in the Yukon—Would students have liked to be part of the "gold rush"? Do they understand the hardships and failures that were encountered?
- reading for pleasure—Do they do it? How often? Why/why not?
- poetry—Do they read it? Like it? Enjoy it more or less than prose?

Cooperative Group Activity

Divide the class into odd-numbered groups of five or more. Have each group discuss the topics and questions suggested in the "Discussing the Literary Period" note. Have each group attempt to reach a consensus on its answers. Each group can submit majority and minority reports on those issues for which no consensus has been achieved.

Selection Overview

SELECTION OBJECTIVES

After completing these selections, students will able to

- understand the meaning and significance of symbolism in poetry
- describe the meaning of symbols related to America
- identify changes in the life of the times as expressed through poetry
- write about cause and effect
- use a dictionary to understand Greek and Latin word origins
- compare and contrast

Lesson Resources

I Hear America Singing
O Captain! My Captain!
When I Heard the Learn'd Astronomer

- Selection Synopses, Teacher's Edition, p. T241c
- Comprehension and Vocabulary Workbook, pp. 49–50
- Language Enrichment Workbook, pp. 32–34
- Teacher's Resources
  Reinforcement, p. R25
  Test, pp. T49–T50

More About Symbolism

Symbols are normally tangible things that students can easily visualize and relate to. They usually represent abstract concepts that may not be so easily grasped.

Ask the students to identify symbols in each of the poems. Have them suggest symbols they encounter in everyday life, and have a volunteer list their ideas on the board. Discuss how symbols evoke reactions in their audience and what reactions are evoked.

More About the Literary Period

The poem "O Captain! My Captain!" is one of many literary pieces that have immortalized Abraham Lincoln. The story of Lincoln's boyhood is well-known: he educated himself, reading by the light of a fire in a log cabin. This humble beginning was parlayed into the presidency—one of the most noteworthy in our nation's history. In many ways, Lincoln was the epitome of the "American Dream."

If Lincoln could, through hard work, become President, why can't you? America is still the land of opportunity. Appreciate it. Rejoice in it. Sing about it. Most importantly, make the most of it. This was Walt Whitman's message.

Cooperative Group Activity

With students in small groups, extend the Writing Connection activity by asking each group to think of:

1. a national symbol (the flag, bald eagle)
2. a state symbol (Texas: the Lone Star State)
3. a school symbol (school colors or mascot)
4. something that symbolizes their group

Have students list the reasons their group chose the symbols it did. Have one student read the symbols and the group's reasons for selecting them.

Learn About

SYMBOLISM

A **symbol** is something that represents, or stands for, something else. You will recognize some symbols from ordinary life: the scales of justice, the dove of peace, the donkey and elephant of the Democratic and Republican parties, the Stars and Stripes for the United States of America, the "*V* for Victory" sign. The meaning of all of these symbols is commonly agreed upon, but it is not always simple. The image behind a symbol may be a blend of many ideas and attitudes.

In literature, authors may not depend upon commonly agreed-upon symbols. Instead, they may devise their own from the context or substance of what they write about. The reader must make the connection between the literal image and the idea or the quality it stands for.

As you read these poems, ask yourself:

1. What symbol or symbols does Whitman use in each poem?
2. Why did he choose that symbol?

Reading Focus

Compare and Contrast You compare things by looking at what they have in common, and you contrast them by looking at their differences. Three poems by the same person may have many things in common, but their differences can surprise you and teach you something about the poet. As you read the poems of Walt Whitman, think about their similarities and differences. How do you know that they were all written by the same person? What qualities tell you this?

WRITING CONNECTION

There are many symbols associated with the United States. Think of two such symbols and describe what they mean to you and why you associate them with this country.

I HEAR AMERICA SINGING

by Walt Whitman

I hear America singing, the varied carols I hear,
Those of mechanics, each one singing his as it should be blithe and strong,
The carpenter singing his as he measures his plank or beam,
The mason singing his as he makes ready for work, or leaves off work,
5 The boatman singing what belongs to him in his boat, the deck-hand singing on the steamboat deck,
The shoemaker singing as he sits on his bench, the hatter singing as he stands,
The wood-cutter's song, the plowboy's on his way in the morning, or at noon intermission or at sundown,
The delicious singing of the mother, or of the young wife at work, or of the girl sewing or washing,
Each singing what belongs to him or her and to none else,
10 The day what belongs to the day—at night the party of young fellows, robust, friendly,
Singing with open mouths their strong melodious songs.

---

blithe (BLY*TH*) happy; cheerful
mason (MAY sun) stone worker
hatter (HAT ur) hat maker
robust (roh BUST) strong; healthy

TEACHING PLAN

INTRODUCE

Motivation

"When I Heard the Learn'd Astronomer" concerns intellectual curiosity. "I Hear America Singing" speaks of pride and fulfillment from work well done. Talk about the concepts of learning and work. How do the students relate their education to their future? Do they look forward to productive working lives? How will what they learn in school facilitate their adult lives? To what do they aspire?

Purpose-Setting Question

What common, symbolic threads tie these three poems together?

READ

Literary Focus: *Symbolism*

Ask: What do you think each person in the poem stands for (the mechanic, the carpenter, and so on)? What larger meaning do these characters have beyond their identities as individuals? For what do they seem to be symbols?

Reading Focus: *Compare and Contrast*

Have students compare and contrast the lives of all the people mentioned in the poem. Ask: How are their lives alike and how are they different? What are some of the similarities and differences in how Whitman chooses to write about these people? Does Whitman seem to admire any of these characters more than another? Why do you think so?

CLOSE

Have students complete Review the Selection on pages 252–253.

Develop Vocabulary Skills

Review the footnoted vocabulary words and their definitions. Use each word in a complete sentence yourself, then have at least one student do the same, aloud. Make sure that each student uses at least one of the words in a sentence.

ESL Activity

Hold a group discussion on a country's symbols, specifically on flags, colors, mascots, and famous people who exemplify that country. Have students fill in these categories from their own homelands. Talk about differing national meanings and gestures.

Viewing Fine Art

William Trost Richards (1833–1905) specialized in marine paintings, though he also painted a number of landscapes and portraits. Richards's paintings of the ocean and breaking waves came after years of study of the sea; he was anxious to paint the dramatic power of wave formations as they broke along the shore. Ask: How would you describe the mood created by contrasting elements of shape, color, and so forth in this painting?

Literary Focus: *Symbolism*

Ask: What do you think the "fearful trip" is a symbol of? Remind them that Lincoln was assassinated almost immediately after the Civil War ended.

Critical Thinking: *Analyze*

Ask: What is the effect of the poem's rhyme scheme and meter on its subject matter? Think about how you would have reacted to reading a prose statement about Lincoln's death. In what ways is this poetic statement effective?

The League Long Breakers Thundering on the Reef, William Trost Richards. The Brooklyn Museum

O CAPTAIN! MY CAPTAIN!

by Walt Whitman

O Captain! my Captain! our fearful trip is done,
The ship has weather'd every rack, the prize we
sought is won,
The port is near, the bells I hear, the people
all exulting,
While follow eyes the steady keel, the vessel grim
and daring;
5 But O heart! heart! heart!
O the bleeding drops of red,
Where on the deck my Captain lies,
Fallen cold and dead.

weather (WE*TH* ur) last through; endure
rack (RAK) hardship; torture
exulting (ig ZULT ing) rejoicing; showing joy
keel (KEEL) "backbone" of a ship

O Captain! my Captain! rise up and hear the bells;
10 Rise up—for you the flag is flung—for you the bugle trills,
For you bouquets and ribbon'd wreaths—for you the shores a-crowding
For you they call, the swaying mass, their eager faces turning;
Here Captain! dear father!
This arm beneath your head!
15 It is some dream that on the deck,
You've fallen cold and dead.

My Captain does not answer, his lips are pale and still,
My father does not feel my arm, he has no pulse nor will,
The ship is anchor'd safe and sound, its voyage closed and done,
20 From fearful trip the victor ship comes in with object won;
Exult O shores, and ring O bells!
But I with mournful tread,
Walk the deck my Captain lies,
Fallen cold and dead.

Reading Focus:
Compare and Contrast

Remind students that this poem is about President Lincoln and that Whitman is describing his feelings about Lincoln's assassination. Ask students to compare and contrast their own feelings about the death of a historical figure, a prominent person, or someone they know with Whitman's expressions of grief for "the Captain." Ask whether students can identify with the feelings Whitman expresses.

---

trill (TRIL) play music with a quivering sound
will (WIL) wishes; desires
object (OB jekt) purpose; goal
tread (TRED) step; walk

Comparing Selections

Ask the students if they can discuss any common threads of symbolism among the three poems or between any two. (Expand on previous explanation of symbols.)

Literary Focus: *Rhyme*

Discuss the rhyme schemes in these three poems. Since two of them have no end rhymes, why do they qualify as poetry? You could briefly discuss rhythm and meter.

Reading Focus: *Compare and Contrast*

Ask: What two experiences does Whitman compare and contrast in this poem? Compare and contrast similar experiences of your own. Brainstorm differences and similarities between reading about something such as astronomy and experiencing it directly.

WHEN I HEARD THE LEARN'D ASTRONOMER

by Walt Whitman

When I heard the learn'd astronomer,
When the proofs, the figures, were ranged in
  columns before me,
When I was shown the charts and diagrams, to
  add, divide, and measure them,
When I sitting heard the astronomer where he
  lectured with much applause in the lecture-
  room,
How soon unaccountable I became tired and sick,
Till rising and gliding out I wandered off by
  myself,
In the mystical moist night-air, and from time to
  time,
Looked up in perfect silence at the stars.

---

ranged (RAYNJD) set forth; arranged
unaccountable (un uh KOWN tuh bul) for no apparent reason
mystical (MIS tih kul) mysterious; having a hidden meaning

Mini Quiz

Write the following questions on the board or overhead projector and call on students to fill in the blanks. Discuss the answers with the class.

1. When Whitman hears America singing, he hears "varied ________."
2. The captain's fearful ________ is done.
3. The captain lies on the ________; he has fallen ________ and ________.
4. The young student had heard an ________ giving a ________.
5. After leaving the lecture, the student looked up at the ________ in perfect ________.

Answers

1. carols
2. trip
3. deck; cold; dead
4. astronomer; lecture
5. stars; silence

AUTHOR BIOGRAPHY

Walt Whitman (1819–1892)

"Wake up, America!" Walt Whitman's poetry seems to shout. "Wake up and look around. Wake up and listen. Wake up to a new life in a world that is wonder-full."

If any American deserves the title "People's Poet," it is Walt Whitman. He thought of himself as the poet of democracy. Everything inspired Whitman. Everything had meaning for him. His aim was to tell Americans about themselves in a way that would make them, too, feel fully alive.

Whitman was born into a farm family on Long Island, near New York City. At the age of eleven, he dropped out of school and went to work for a lawyer. In the years that followed, he worked as a carpenter, teacher, and newspaper writer and editor. These different trades and his travels around the United States gave him firsthand knowledge of the people he was later to celebrate in his poetry.

In 1850 Whitman suddenly quit a job as an editor and went back to live with his mother and father. Once a well-known figure in newspaper and political circles, he simply dropped out of sight. Then followed the five "dark years" in his life. Apparently he worked now and then as a carpenter, but most of the time he must have written poetry. In 1855 the "dark years" came to an end. In that year he gave the world *Leaves of Grass*, which, with its original poetic style, became perhaps the most important single collection of poems by an American poet. *Leaves of Grass* marks a turning point in American poetry, for it touches on all aspects of life, including subjects not previously found in verse. In 1856 an expanded edition appeared, after which Whitman continued to work on the volume, adding and dropping poems throughout most of his life.

Whitman was over 40 when the Civil War began, but he insisted on doing his part. He spent the war years nursing and comforting injured soldiers. By the end of the war, many wounded soldiers had met the big friendly man who usually dressed in a shabby wide-brimmed hat and an open shirt and jacket. The war service, however, affected Whitman's own health. In 1873, he suffered a stroke which made him an invalid for the last years of his life.

Why is Walt Whitman suited to the title "People's Poet"?

MORE ABOUT THE AUTHOR

Walt Whitman had eight brothers and sisters. He was the second oldest. His younger brother, George, fought in the Civil War on the side of the Union. During the war, George was wounded, and Walt went to Virginia to take care of him. After this, Walt began visiting hospitals for wounded soldiers on both sides. He read to them, helped nurse them, and raised money for their treatment. Eventually, Walt himself became an invalid for the last 18 years of his life.

For the last 19 years of his life, Walt lived in a house in Camden, New Jersey, where distinguished writers from all over the world came to visit him.

Additional Works

BY WALT WHITMAN

Complete Poetry and Collected Prose. Ed. by Justin Kaplan. Library of America.

Whitman's Notebooks. The Library of Congress's American Memory Collection. http://lcweb2.loc.gov/ammem/wwhome.html

UNDERSTAND THE SELECTION

Answers

1. Students should name four of the following: mechanic, carpenter, mason, boatman, deckhand, shoemaker, hatter, woodcutter, plowboy, mother, wife, seamstress, washmaid.
2. The Captain is dead.
3. "When I Heard the Learn'd Astronomer" contrasts the difference between the dry study of the stars and the wonder of the actual universe.
4. Sample answer: All are manual labor; nine of the occupations are "blue collar" trades, or wage-earning occupations. The other four are domestic.
5. Sample answer: The Captain symbolizes President Abraham Lincoln.
6. Sample answer: the "ship of state," the Union, North and South, our unified country and its government
7. Sample answer: The speaker is a person who would rather daydream or experience nature than listen to a lecture.
8. Sample answer: While Whitman may hear actual singing, he is really speaking of their inner feelings of joy and pride. "His" America is made up of many different workers who are fulfilled in their work.
9. Sample answer: The poem was meant to comfort and cheer people. The "Captain" may be dead, but the "ship" is "anchored safe and sound, its voyage closed and done."
10. Sample answer: The speaker learned that he could discover the stars within himself.

Review the Selection

UNDERSTAND THE SELECTION

Recall

1. Name four occupations Whitman mentions in "I Hear America Singing."
2. What is wrong with the Captain in "O Captain! My Captain!"?
3. What is "When I Heard the Learn'd Astronomer" about?

Infer

4. Identify a common element among the occupations mentioned in "I Hear America Singing."
5. In "O Captain! My Captain!," whom does the Captain symbolize?
6. What does the ship symbolize?
7. Describe the speaker in "When I Heard the Learn'd Astronomer."

Apply

8. In "I Hear America Singing," what does Whitman really hear?
9. Was "O Captain! My Captain!" written to sadden or cheer people?
10. What did the speaker learn from the "learn'd astronomer"? Explain.

Respond to Literature

Many changes in American life took place during this period. Identify a change implied in any of the poems.

WRITE ABOUT THE SELECTION

"O Captain! My Captain!" is full of symbolism. The two main symbols are the Captain and the ship. Reread the poem. You have already thought about who and what these symbols represent. What do you suppose was the cause of the Captain's death? What do you think will be the effect of his death upon the ship?

Prewriting Cause and effect are important elements of any logical thought process. For every effect, there must be a cause. Think about the Captain's death, in terms of its cause and its effect upon the fate of his ship. To help do this, make a chart with two columns. Write the headings *Cause* and *Effect* at the tops of the columns. In the first column, write down your ideas about possible causes. In the second column, write down what you think would be the effect resulting from each cause.

Writing Using your chart, write a paragraph about the cause and effects of the Captain's death. Be specific about who the Captain stands for and what the ship represents.

Revising In your discussion of effects, include additional symbolism to show how one effect can also become the cause of another effect.

Proofreading Review your paragraph to make sure that all sentences are complete sentences, with subject and verb.

Respond to Literature

Divide the class into five or more groups. Have each group discuss the changes in American life during this period. Have each group then vote on one. Record on the board the majority choice of each group. Have the class discuss what it considers the most important change.

There are several possible responses: for example, the Industrial Revolution; the end of the Civil War and reunification of the North and South; the increasing emphasis on scientific thinking.

WRITE ABOUT THE SELECTION

Prewriting

Make two columns on the board, headed (a) *Cause—Captain's Death*; (b) *Effect—upon ship*. Have two students at the board, one for each column. Ask the class for ideas—first about cause, then about effect. These are to be recorded on the board.

Writing

Based on the ideas on the board, have each student individually write a paragraph illustrating one cause and effect of the Captain's death and the symbolism involved in the Captain and ship. Go around the class, giving help to any student who is having difficulty.

THINK ABOUT SYMBOLISM

A **symbol** is something that represents, or stands for, something else. It does not always stand for an actual object, organization, or other concrete thing, however. It can also represent something intangible, such as an emotion or an idea.

1. In "I Hear America Singing," what do you think the various trades symbolize? Why do the tradespeople sing?
2. In "O Captain! My Captain!" Whitman uses the image of the ship symbolically. What does the ship symbolize?
3. What "fearful trip" has the Captain, who was Abraham Lincoln, been through?
4. In the same poem, what would you say was the "prize" that was sought and won?
5. What did the actual stars in "When I Heard the Learn'd Astronomer" symbolize and why was their meaning so important?

DEVELOP YOUR VOCABULARY

English has been enriched by borrowing words from other languages such as Latin and Greek. Latin words entered English at several times in history. In ancient times, settlers from Roman-occupied areas brought Latin words with them wherever they traveled. Later, Roman missionaries brought words as well as religion to Britain. In the eleventh century, the French conquered England. Both Latin and Greek words entered English through French. The last great period of borrowing from Latin and Greek came in the sixteenth century. Interest in classical learning flourished, and English writers used many Latin and Greek words in their writing.

The following words all came from Latin or Greek. Look up each word in a dictionary that gives word histories and write whether the word is of Latin or Greek origin.

1. astronomer
2. port
3. mechanic
4. mystical
5. star
6. lecture

READING FOCUS

Compare and Contrast As you read the poetry of Walt Whitman, you probably noticed that the poems are similar in some ways but different in others. In what ways are the poems alike? What are some important differences?

THINK ABOUT SYMBOLISM

Answers

1. Answers will vary. Sample answer: The trades symbolize the diversity of the American people, and the tradespeople sing because they are free.
2. Sample answer: the ship of state
3. The trip symbolizes the divisive and devastating Civil War, which the country had just been through.
4. Sample answer: most likely, the reunification of the North and South
5. Sample answer: The real stars symbolized the wonder of the universe, in contrast to the lecture, which had been dry and uninspiring.

DEVELOP YOUR VOCABULARY

Answers

1. Greek
2. Latin
3. Greek
4. Greek
5. Latin
6. Latin

READING FOCUS

Sample Answer

Similarities: All three poems have a first-person speaker who appears as a character in the poem. All three discuss the speaker's emotions. Differences: "O Captain! My Captain!" has many short lines of verse; the other two have long lines. "Oh Captain! My Captain!" uses end rhymes; the other two do not. Each poem expresses a different emotion.

Revising

Make this a cooperative group activity. Have students work in small groups to revise their paragraphs.

Proofreading

Select one or two of the students' paragraphs as models for proofreading. Put the paragraphs on the overhead projector and have the class suggest improvements.

ESL Activity

Review the Latin and Greek words listed above. They are words related to learning and science. Have students make a list of words from their cultures which are now used in English in these ways.

Selection Overview

SELECTION OBJECTIVES

After completing this selection, students will be able to

- evaluate types of characters
- describe characters in terms of physical appearance and personality
- understand analogies
- write an explanation of an analogy
- understand idioms
- use a dictionary to look up the meaning of an idiom
- understand imagery

Lesson Resources

The Gift of the Magi

- Selection Synopsis, Teacher's Edition, p. T241d
- Comprehension and Vocabulary Workbook, pp. 51–52
- Language Enrichment Workbook, pp. 35–37
- Teacher's Resources
  Reinforcement, p. R26
  Test, pp. T51–T52

More About Character

Characters may be flat or round; also, static or dynamic. Often, flat characters are also static, and round are dynamic. This does not necessarily have to be the case.

Ask the students to think about the characters in other selections they have read and identify those who they feel are round/dynamic and flat/static. Then, have them give reasons for the characters they've chosen in each category.

Background Note

The rapid growth of cities was an important characteristic of this period in American history. Many people moved to cities with the hope of better jobs and more money, but working conditions were often poor and money scarce. In "The Gift of the Magi," the Youngs' living conditions show some of the difficulties people in cities faced.

Learn About

CHARACTER

A character is a person in a narrative. In fiction, characters are made-up people. They may be patterned after real persons, or they may be figments of the author's imagination.

Authors determine when and how much to tell readers about the characters. They may give a great deal of detail about a character right away, or they may let the reader determine what the character is like through his or her words and actions as the story progresses. They may give a detailed physical description of a character, or they may let the reader create his or her own mental image. A character's personality traits, value system, or frame of mind may be well-defined from the beginning of the story or may be left to the reader to figure out as the plot unfolds.

As you read "The Gift of the Magi," ask yourself:

1. What do the characters look like?
2. What type of people are they?

Reading Focus

Understand Imagery Imagery is language that appeals to your senses. Writers use imagery to try to make readers see sights, hear sounds, feel textures, smell scents, and taste flavors. Writers use only words to make you sense these things. As you read "The Gift of the Magi," look for images that make the settings and characters come alive for you. Note places in the text that make you see, hear, feel, smell, or taste something specific.

WRITING CONNECTION

If you were to write a short, fictional story, describe two characters that you would include. Give details of their physical appearance and personality.

ESL Activity

Discuss O. Henry with the class. See worksheet in the Language Enrichment Workbook, page 37, on the differences in gift-giving customs between different cultures. On what occasions do other cultures give gifts? Could the situation in "Magi" have happened in another culture?

Cooperative Group Activity

For the Writing Connection activity, divide the class into groups of three (or a larger number, depending on class size). Have each group work together to describe the two characters that they would include in a short story. The description should include physical appearance as well as personality.

After the characters have been described, each group member should describe the characters as flat/round or static/dynamic. Students should give reasons for their answers. Then have the groups discuss the choices and reasons.

THE GIFT OF THE MAGI

ADAPTED

by O. Henry

One dollar and eighty-seven cents. That was all. And sixty cents of it was in pennies. Pennies saved one and two at a time by bulldozing the grocer and the butcher until her cheeks burned with embarrassment. Three times Della counted it. One dollar and eighty-seven cents.[1] And the next day would be Christmas.

There was clearly nothing to do but flop down on the shabby little couch and howl. So Della did it. Which instigates the reflection that life is made up of three stages—sobs, sniffles, and smiles, with sniffles in the lead.

While the woman of the home is gradually coming down from the first stage to the second, take a look at the house. A furnished apartment at eight dollars per week. It did not exactly look like a *poor*house but it certainly brought that word to mind. Nothing worked exactly as it should. In the lobby below was a letter box into which no letter would go, and an electric button from which no mortal finger could tease a ring. And fixed to the box was a card with the name Mr. James Dillingham Young.

The "Dillingham" had been flung to the breeze during a former period of prosperity, when its owner was being paid thirty dollars per week. Now, when the income had shrunk to twenty dollars, the letters of Dillingham looked blurred, as though they were thinking seriously of contracting to a modest and unassuming little D. But whenever Mr. James Dillingham Young

---

Magi (MAY jy) the three wise men who, according to the biblical story, made the journey to Bethlehem to present gifts to the Christ child
bulldozing (BUL dohz ing) bullying; threatening
instigate (IN stuh gayt) bring about; stir up
reflection (rih FLEK shun) serious thought
contracting (kun TRAKT ing) growing smaller
unassuming (un uh SOOM ing) modest; quiet
[1]**One dollar and eighty-seven cents:** This story first appeared in 1905, when a dollar could buy much more than it can now. Think of all sums mentioned as multiplied by ten.

Teaching Plan

INTRODUCE

Motivation

In the early part of the 20th century, people tended to be less materialistic and more content with simpler values and things. Ask the students to think about their most recent exchange of gifts. What type of presents did they want? What type did they give? How important was the monetary value of these gifts? Did they derive more pleasure from giving or receiving? Then explain that, in the story, the two main characters are willing to sacrifice things of great value to themselves for the sake of the other's happiness.

Purpose-Setting Question

Would you sacrifice something that meant alot to you in order to make someone happy? What would you sacrifice?

READ

Literary Focus: *Character*

Ask students to notice how the characters feel about each other as they read. Suggest that they relate the characters' feelings for each other to their actions.

Reading Focus: *Understand Imagery*

Explain that both the title and the main idea of this story are images relating to the significance of gifts. Ask for possible meanings for the title. Remind students to be alert to images throughout.

CLOSE

Have students complete Review the Selection on pages 262–263.

Develop Vocabulary Skills

Write the vocabulary words on the board and have the students look them up in a dictionary, writing down the definitions.

Reading Focus:
Understand Imagery
Ask students to discuss O. Henry's description of Della's hair. Ask: How do these images strengthen your understanding of why Della takes such pride in her hair?

came home and reached his apartment above, he was called Jim and greatly hugged by Mrs. James Dillingham Young, already introduced to you as Della. Which is all very good.

Della finished her cry and powdered her cheeks. She stood by the window and looked out dully at a gray cat walking a gray fence in a gray backyard. Tomorrow would be Christmas Day, and she had only one dollar and eighty-seven cents with which to buy Jim a present. She had been saving every penny she could for months, with this result. Twenty dollars a week doesn't go far. Expenses had been greater than she had planned. They always are. Only one dollar and eighty-seven cents to buy a present for Jim. Her Jim. Many a happy hour she had spent planning for something nice for him. Something fine and rare and sterling—something just a little bit near to showing him the honor of being Mrs. James Dillingham Young.

There was a tall wall mirror between the windows of the room. Perhaps you have seen a wall mirror in an eight-dollar apartment. A very thin and very agile woman may, by seeing her reflection in a number of rapid steps, get a fairly good idea of her looks. Della, being slender, had mastered the art.

Suddenly she whirled from the window and stood before the glass. Her eyes were shining brightly, but her face lost its color within twenty seconds. Rapidly she pulled down her hair and let it fall to its full length.

Now, the James Dillingham Youngs owned just two things in which they both took a mighty pride. One was Jim's gold watch that had been his father's and his grandfather's. The other was Della's hair. Had the Queen of Sheba[2] lived in the apartment across the air shaft, Della would have let her hair hang out the window to dry some day just to make fun of her Majesty's jewels and gifts. Had King Solomon been the janitor, with all his treasures piled up in the basement, Jim would have pulled out his watch every time he passed, just to see him pull at his beard with envy.

So now Della's beautiful hair fell about her, rippling and shining like a cascade of brown waters. It reached below her knees and made almost a garment for her. And then she did it up again nervously and quickly. Once she faltered for a minute and stood still while a tear or two splashed on the worn red carpet.

On went her old brown jacket. On went her old brown hat. With a whirl of skirts and with the brilliant sparkle still in her eyes, she fluttered out the door and down the stairs to the street.

Where she stopped, the sign read: "Madame Sofronie. Wigs and Hair Goods of All Kinds." One flight up Della ran, and collected herself, panting. Madame was a

---

agile (AJ ul) nimble; well-coordinated
cascade (kas KAYD) waterfall
[2]**Queen of Sheba:** According to the Bible, the Queen of Sheba traveled from ancient Ethiopia to Israel to visit King Solomon. Amazed by the King's wisdom, she gave him much gold and other valuable gifts. (I Kings 10:1–13.)

large woman, chilly and much too white.

"Will you buy my hair?" asked Della.

"I buy hair," said Madame. "Take your hat off, and let's have a sight at the looks of it."

Down rippled the brown cascade.

"Twenty dollars," said Madame, lifting the hair with a practiced hand.

"Give it to me quick," said Della.

Oh, and the next two hours tripped by on rosy wings. Forget the hashed metaphor. Della was ransacking the stores for Jim's present.

She found it at last. It surely had been made for Jim and no one else. There was no other like it in any of the stores, and she had turned all of them inside out. It was a platinum watch chain, simple in design, free of silly and cheap decoration. It was even worthy of The Watch. As soon as she saw it, she knew it must be Jim's. It was like him. Quietness and value—the description applied to both. Twenty-one dollars they took from her for it, and she hurried home with the eighty-seven cents. With that chain on his watch, Jim might be properly anxious about the time in any company. Grand as the watch was, he sometimes looked at it on the sly because of the old leather strap that he used in place of a chain.

When Della reached home, her wild delight gave way a little to good common sense. She got out her hair curlers and lighted the gas stove. Then she went to work repairing the damage made by generosity added to love. Which is always a tremendous task, dear friends—a mammoth task.

Within forty minutes her head was covered with tiny, close-lying curls that made her look wonderfully like a playful schoolboy. She studied her reflection in the mirror long and carefully.

"If Jim doesn't kill me," she said to herself, "before he takes a second look at me, he'll say I look like a Coney Island chorus girl.[3] But what could I do? Oh, what could I do with a dollar and eighty-seven cents?"

At seven o'clock the coffee was made, and the frying pan was on the back of the stove, hot and ready to cook the chops.

Jim was never late. Della held the chain in her hand and sat on the corner of the table near the front door. Then she heard his step on the stair away down on the first flight, and she turned white for just a moment. She had a habit of saying little silent prayers about the simplest everyday things, and now she whispered: "Please, God, make him think I am still pretty."

The door opened, and Jim stepped in and closed it. He looked thin and very serious. Poor fellow—he was only twenty-two. He needed a new overcoat and he was without gloves.

Jim stopped inside the door. He froze suddenly, his eyes fixed upon Della.

---

trip (TRIP) run gracefully and lightly
hashed (HASHT) jumbled; all mixed up
metaphor (MET uh fur) figure of speech that makes a comparison
ransacking (RAN sak ing) searching furiously
[3]**Coney Island chorus girl:** A night-club dancer at Coney Island, once a busy amusement center on the edge of New York City.

Enrichment

This story takes place before synthetic materials were invented. At that time all wigs and hairpieces had to be fabricated from real human hair.

Literary Focus: *Character*

Ask: How would you characterize Madame Sofronie? What are your reactions to her?

Critical Thinking: *Evaluate*

Ask students to evaluate Della's sale of her hair. Ask: Do you think she did the right thing? What might you have done in her place?

Critical Thinking: *Evaluate*

Point out that Della has spent more on Jim's present than Jim earns in a week. Remind students that the Youngs' doorbell and letterbox need repairs. Add that saving $1.87 took Della several months. Ask: How would you evaluate Della's decision to spend so much on Jim's present? Would you have done the same thing? Why or why not?

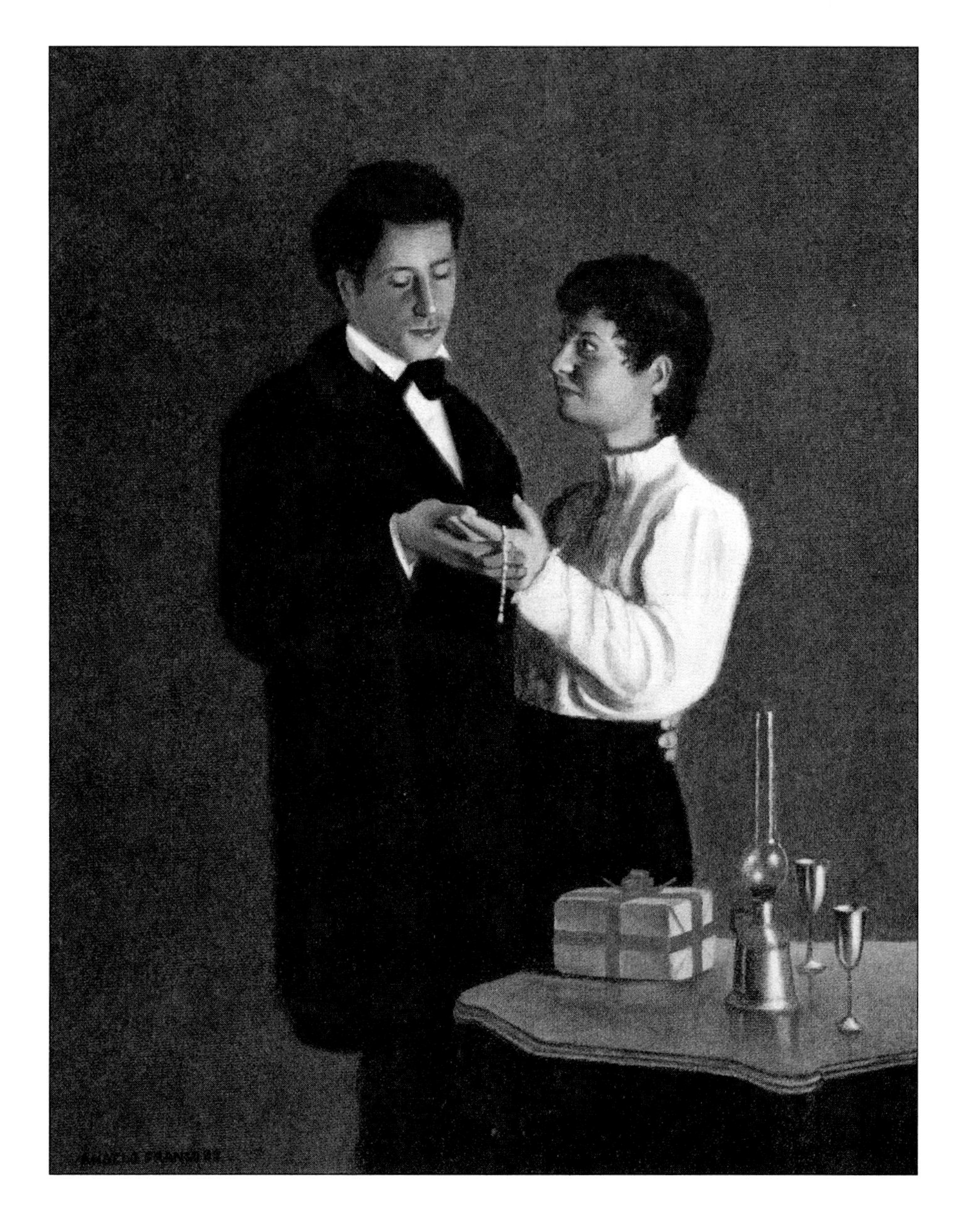

There was an expression in them that she could not read, and it terrified her. It was not anger, nor disappointment, nor surprise, nor horror, nor any of the feelings she had been prepared for. He simply stood staring at her fixedly with that strange expression on his face.

Della wriggled off the table and went for him.

"Jim, darling!" she cried. "Don't look at me that way. I had my hair cut off and sold it, sure! But I did it because I couldn't live through Christmas without giving you a present. It'll grow out again. You won't mind, will you? I just had to do it. My hair grows awfully fast. Say "Merry Christmas," Jim, and let's be happy. You don't know what a nice—what a beautiful, nice gift I've got for you."

"You've cut off your hair?" he asked laboriously, with effort, as if he had not really noticed that fact yet, even after the hardest mental work.

"Cut it off and sold it," said Della. "Don't you like me just as well, anyhow? I'm *me* without my hair, aren't I?"

Jim looked about the room curiously.

"You say your hair is gone?" he said, speaking almost like an idiot.

"You needn't look for it," said Della. "It's sold, I tell you—sold and gone, too. It's Christmas Eve, Jim. Be good to me, because the hair went for you. Maybe the hairs of my head were numbered," she went on with a sudden serious sweetness, "but nobody could ever count my love for you. Shall I put the chops on, Jim?"

Out of his trance Jim seemed quickly to wake. He took Della in his arms. For ten seconds let us examine with discreet curiosity some unimportant object in the other direction. Eight dollars a week or a million a year—what is the difference? A mathematician would give you the wrong answer. The Magi brought valuable gifts, but this was not among them. That mysterious sentence will be illuminated later on.

Jim drew a package from his overcoat pocket and threw it on the table.

"Don't make any mistake, Dell," he said, "about me. I don't think there's anything in the way of a haircut or a shampoo that could make me like my girl any less. But if you'll unwrap that package, you may see why you had me going when I first walked in."

Nimble white fingers tore at the string and paper. And then an ecstatic scream of joy. And then—alas!—a rapid change to wild tears and heavy sobs.

For there lay The Combs—the set of combs, side and back, that Della had worshipped for long in a Broadway window. Beautiful combs, pure tortoiseshell with jeweled rims—just the shade to wear in the beautiful vanished hair. They were expensive combs, she knew. She had wanted them more than anything in the world, without the smallest hope of ever owning them. And now they were hers! But the waves of hair that should have held the combs were gone.

---

laboriously (luh BAWR ee us lee) with much labor and care
discreet (dih SKREET) wisely careful
illuminate (ih LOO muh nayt) make clear
nimble (NIM bul) quick and accurate; agile

Literary Focus: *Character*

Ask: What are your reactions to Jim? What kind of person does he seem to be? Encourage students to turn back to the opening pages of the story, looking for information about Jim, as they consider this question.

Reading Focus: *Understand Imagery*

Ask students to give their reactions to Della's figure of speech "Maybe the hairs of my head were numbered, but nobody could ever count my love for you." Ask: How does this imagery relate to Della's character? What does it say about her?

Discussion

At the end of the story, Della opens the gift from Jim and her initial joy turns to tears. Ask: Can you anticipate the reason for this?

Reading Focus: *Understand Imagery*

Ask: What do the combs and the watch chain symbolize? Point out the story's title and the parallel O. Henry draws between this exchange of gifts and the gifts the Magi gave to the baby Jesus. Have students discuss how both sets of gifts are images relating to the significance of gifts.

Literary Focus: *Character*

Have students discuss O. Henry's judgment about his characters in the story's final paragraph. Ask: Do you agree with him? Why or why not?

Critical Thinking: *Analyze*

Ask: Does the monetary value of the gifts matter? Explain.

Suddenly she hugged them to her throat, and before long she was able to look up with dim eyes and a smile. "My hair grows so fast, Jim," she said.

And then Della leaped up like a little singed cat and cried, "Oh, oh!"

Jim had not yet seen his beautiful present. She held it out to him eagerly upon her opened hand. The platinum seemed to flash with a reflection of her bright and ardent spirit.

"Isn't it something, Jim? I hunted all over town to find it. You'll have to look at the time a hundred times a day now. Give me your watch, I want to see how the chain looks on it."

Instead of obeying, Jim tumbled down on the couch and put his hands under the back of his head and smiled.

"Dell," said he, "let's put our Christmas presents away and keep them awhile. They're too nice to use just now. I sold the watch to get the money to buy your combs. And now, suppose you put the chops on."

The Magi, as you know, were wise men—wonderfully wise men—who brought gifts to the Babe in the manger. They invented the art of giving Christmas presents. Being wise, they no doubt gave wise gifts. And here I have lamely told you the sad little story of two foolish children who most unwisely sacrificed for each other the greatest treasures of their house. But in a last word to the wise of these days, let it be said that of all who gave gifts these two were the wisest. Of all who give and receive gifts, such as they are wisest. Everywhere they are wisest. They are the Magi.

---

ardent (AHR dunt) very eager; passionate

Mini Quiz

Write the following questions on the board or overhead projector and call on students to fill in the blanks. Discuss the answers with the class.

1. The story takes place on ________.
2. The two most important things that Jim and Della own are his ________ and her ________ .
3. Della's gift to Jim cost ________ dollars.
4. After selling her hair and buying her gift, Della had ________ cents left.
5. Della thought that the qualities of ________ and ________ applied to both Jim and the watch chain.

Answers

1. Christmas Eve
2. watch; hair
3. twenty-one
4. eighty-seven
5. quietness; value

Author Biography

O. Henry (1862–1910)

William Sydney Porter, or "O. Henry," was born in Greensboro, North Carolina. As a young man, he worked in Texas on a ranch, in a bank, and on a newspaper. Charged with stealing money from the bank, he fled to Central America. But news of his wife's illness brought him back, and he faced the bank robbery charges.

He practiced writing short stories while in prison. After his release, he moved to New York City and wrote a story a week for popular magazines. He made a lot of money but died before he was 50.

Today O. Henry is remembered as the master of the surprise ending. Among his best-known stories are "The Last Leaf," "The Furnished Room," and "The Gift of the Magi."

More About the Author

O. Henry spent the last nine years of his life in New York City. Although many of his stories are set in different parts of the United States and in Central and South America, he is best known for stories about the lives of everyday New Yorkers. The characters in his stories were usually plain, simple people, but the plots often contained examples of irony and coincidence, coupled with a surprise ending. "The Gift of the Magi" is one of the best illustrations of this. He wrote so much and so often that several collections of his stories were not published until after his death.

Additional Works

by O. Henry

The Gift of the Magi and Other Short Stories. Dover Publications, 1992.

Tales of O. Henry. Barnes and Noble Books, 1993.

The Best Short Stories of O. Henry. Random House, 1994.

UNDERSTAND THE SELECTION

Answers

1. Della has $1.87.
2. She receives $20.
3. She buys her husband a platinum watch chain that is "simple in design, free of silly and cheap decoration."
4. Sample answer: He thinks it sounds more respectable.
5. Sample answer: She is happy and excited. The time "tripped by on rosy wings."
6. Sample answer: Jim's gold watch is his most valued possession, and she wants him to be able to show it off.
7. Sample answer: They are unselfish in their love for each other.
8. Sample answer: She is ashamed. She is embarrassed to have to "bulldoze the grocer and the butcher."
9. Some adjectives could be: loving, caring, giving, sacrificing, generous, honored, proud.
10. Sample answer: The reader is allowed to share Della's thoughts and emotions, but not Jim's. Therefore the reader's mental picture of Della is more detailed.

Respond to Literature

Review the discussion of the period at the beginning of the unit for relevant clues. Conduct a general class discussion on material values—then versus now. Answers will vary, but you should mention that people seemed to place more value in simple objects and simpler things.

WRITE ABOUT THE SELECTION

Prewriting

Conduct a class discussion about the meaning of analogy. Divide the class into relatively large groups, for "brainstorming" purposes. Each group appoints one member to record ideas under the Magi column, another to record those under Della and Jim.

Review the Selection

UNDERSTAND THE SELECTION

Recall

1. How much money does Della have at the beginning of the story?
2. How much does she receive for selling her hair?
3. What gift does she buy for her husband?

Infer

4. Why does Jim use his middle name on his card?
5. How does Della feel while shopping for Jim's present?
6. Why does she buy the particular present that she does?
7. Why are these two "the wisest"?

Apply

8. How do you think Della feels about her poverty? Why do you think so?
9. What adjectives would you use to describe Della's feeling toward Jim?
10. Is your mental picture of one character clearer than the other? If so, explain why.

Respond to Literature

How do you think "The Gift of the Magi" reflects the material values of the early 1900s?

WRITE ABOUT THE SELECTION

An **analogy** compares two different things that share one element. This comparison can be between two concrete objects or between two abstract thoughts. Sometimes the easiest or clearest way to explain something unfamiliar is through an analogy with something that is familiar.

In this selection, although "the Magi" are part of the title, they are not mentioned until the end of the story. The plot does not involve them directly. The author uses them to draw an analogy. What is this analogy? How does it clarify the meaning of the story?

Prewriting To help understand the analogy, try "brainstorming." Use two lists. Under the heading *magi*, write ideas about the meaning of the Magi's gifts in the New Testament story of the Christ child. In a second list, under the heading *Della and Jim*, write ideas about the meaning of their gifts to each other.

Writing Compare the ideas in the two lists. Identify similarities between them. Then write a paragraph explaining the analogy upon which the title of the story is based.

Revising Rewrite the paragraph to include at least one example of the four types of sentences: declarative, interrogative, imperative, and exclamatory.

Proofreading Check the punctuation mark at the end of each sentence.

Writing

Have students work on the section individually. Go around the class, giving help to any student who is having difficulty. Ask questions to help students focus on the analogy in the title.

Revising

Make this a cooperative group activity. Have students work in small groups to revise their paragraphs, making sure each has included at least one example of the four types of sentences.

Proofreading

Select one or two paragraphs as models for proofreading. Put the paragraphs on the overhead projector and have students check for correct punctuation marks at the end of each sentence.

THINK ABOUT CHARACTER

Authors sometimes discuss the characteristics and traits of a character directly. In addition, they often give indirect clues from which the reader can surmise or guess other traits of the individual. Readers can watch for things the characters say, descriptions of what they think, and their actions.

1. How does O. Henry define Jim and Della's characters?
2. What indirect clues about their personalities can you find in the story?
3. Do you think that one character appreciates his or her Christmas present more than the other? Why?
4. What is your mental picture of Madame Sofronie?
5. What would you say the future holds for Della and Jim's marriage?

Reading Focus

Understand Imagery As you read "The Gift of the Magi," you looked for imagery in the story. What are some images that helped the story come alive for you? To which of your five senses did these images appeal?

DEVELOP YOUR VOCABULARY

An **idiom** is an expression that has a meaning that is often different from the literal meaning of the words that form it. *With a high hand*, for example, has nothing to do with the location of a hand; it means "in a dictatorial manner."

Idioms are listed in your dictionary after the definitions of the entry word that is the main word in the phrase. Look up the italicized idioms in these quotations from "The Gift of the Magi." Then write an original sentence, using the idiom as it is used here.

1. ". . . life is *made up* of three stages, sobs, sniffles, and smiles."
2. "While the woman . . . is gradually *coming down* from the first stage to the second . . ."
3. "Della would have let her hair hang out the window . . . just *to make fun of* her Majesty's jewels and gifts."
4. "And then she *did* it *up* again . . ."
5. ". . . *before long* she was able to look up with . . . a smile."

Reading Focus

Sample Answer

The description of Della's long hair appeals to both sight (its length and color, its ripple and shine) and touch (its weight and the way it warms her like a garment).

ESL Activity

Ask each student to bring to class an idiom in his or her native language. Ask the student to explain the meaning of the idiom and use it in a sentence.

THINK ABOUT CHARACTER

Answers

1. He defines them by their physical appearances, their actions, and their emotions.
2. Sample answers: Jim, despite a 33% cut in pay, appears to be diligent, hard-working, conscientious, and kind. Della seems to be emotional and easily worried but also determined and resourceful.
3. Sample answer: Each character appreciated his or her present equally, since each understood the sacrifice made by the other to obtain it.
4. Madame Sofronie is mentioned only briefly. Answers may vary. Sample answer: somewhat unpleasant; very abrupt
5. Sample answer: The future looks bright for Della and Jim, who are obviously deeply in love with each other and willing to make sacrifices to make the other happy.

DEVELOP YOUR VOCABULARY

Answers

1. composed
2. calming herself
3. to mock, ridicule
4. to arrange the hair so that is off the neck and shoulders
5. soon

Sample sentences:

1. People say that success is made up of 90% perspiration and 10% inspiration.
2. Miss America is just now coming down from the excitement of the pageant.
3. The boys flexed their biceps just to make fun of skinny little Jeffrey.
4. Shelly combed out her long hair and then did it up again into a ponytail.
5. Carl turned off the TV, and before long his homework was finished.

Focus ON FICTION

Discuss with students what makes fiction uniquely fiction. Compare a short story with a news story or news feature; a feature film with a documentary. Ask for students' ideas about what the two have in common and what makes each form unique.

ELEMENTS OF FICTION

Refer students to the section on fiction in Unit 2 (pages 130–131). Review **point of view** with the students, then ask students to describe the point of view in several selections. Discuss what points of view could be expressed in the examples above (i.e., feature film versus documentary). Have students give the reasons why they identify a particular point of view in each selection.

Ask individual students to describe how a particular selection would be changed if it were told from a different point of view.

Have students describe the **settings** of "The Gift of the Magi," citing specific examples from the story. Discuss whether setting is always important, asking students to compare the settings of other selections in the unit and their relative importance to the stories or poems.

Have students list what types of things make up the setting of a story; also, how to tell the point of view of a story. Ask them to write down what setting elements they find in "The Revolt of Mother" and how they determined its point of view. Discuss the various answers.

Focus ON FICTION

Fiction is any literary work that portrays imaginary characters and events. The basis of all fiction is the imagination of the author. Fiction is meant primarily to be entertaining. It may also be used for such purposes as teaching, influencing, or inspiring.

A work of fiction can take many forms. Chief among these are novels, short stories, plays, and poems. Several literary elements are associated with these various forms of fiction: setting, character, plot, theme, tone, imagery, and symbolism.

Setting The setting of a story is the time and place in which it happens. The time may be the hour of the day, the season, the year, or a period in history. The place may include the general geographical location and environment as well as weather, scenery, terrain, sounds, and smells. It can also include specific places and objects such as buildings, furniture, clothing, windows, and animals. The clearer and more well-defined the setting, the more real and believable the story becomes.

Character A character is a person in a story. There is often a great deal to find out about characters, particularly main characters. For example, values and frame of mind are two features to look for. Characters can be **flat**, one-dimensional stereotypes. These are usually secondary figures. Main characters should be **round**—individuals with personalities you get to know.

Plot The plot consists of the events that happen in a story. It serves as a framework that establishes a relationship between episodes. Plot brings order by showing a few selected characters and incidents and uniting them into a whole. It organizes a story into a beginning, a middle, and an ending.

Sometimes, an author will give clues about what is going to happen in the plot. This is known as **foreshadowing**. Incidents build, through **rising action**, to a **climax**, or turning point. This may happen at the end of the story, or the climax may be followed by **falling action** and the **resolution** of the conflict.

The plot always centers on a **conflict**. This meeting of opposing forces may be internal (within the character) or external (between characters or between a character and some other force, such as nature). In the case of conflict between two characters, the main character is the **protagonist**; the other is the **antagonist**.

Theme The theme is the meaning or message of a story. It is some central idea about life that the author is attempting to communicate. The theme may be stated clearly at any point in the story, or the author might leave it for the reader to determine.

Tone Tone is the author's attitude toward either the subject matter or the reader. It may take many forms—serious or humorous, formal or informal, or direct or symbolic.

Imagery and Figurative Language Imagery refers to the collection of images in a work of literature. Images are sensory in nature, meaning that they are designed to appeal to one of the five senses. Figures of speech, or figurative language, include simile and metaphor. **Similes** state a direct comparison between two unlike objects. They are often introduced with *like* or *as*. For example, *The house was like an empty cavern.* **Metaphors** suggest a comparison, giving one object the qualities of another. For example, *The house was an empty cavern.*

Symbolism Symbolism is the use of one thing to represent another. Usually, the symbol is concrete and stands for some abstract idea, feeling, or quality.

The following is an annotated version of "The Revolt of Mother." **Annotated** means that notes have been added at various points in the story. The purpose of these annotations is to help you see and understand the function and interrelationships of literary elements in a work of fiction.

As you read, ask yourself:

1. How closely connected are the elements of character and plot? Is the concept of conflict involved with both of these?
2. What is the theme? What clues are given about the theme?

Real-Life Application

Divide the class into two groups. Ask the students to debate whether "The Revolt of Mother" would make a good movie or documentary. Discuss whether the characters are believable or how they could be made to be believable; where the story might be set; whom they would cast as the main characters and why; and what theme would be expressed.

Selection Overview

SELECTION OBJECTIVES

After completing this selection, students will be able to:

- appreciate the importance of setting to a story
- identify and understand the interrelationship between such fictional elements as setting, character, plot, and theme
- identify the theme of a story
- identify and understand sub-elements of fiction, such as protagonist and antagonist, the nature of conflict, and the climax and resolution
- write an epilogue
- recognize and understand the usage of dialect
- interpret character

Lesson Resources

The Revolt of Mother
- Selection Synopsis, Teacher's Edition, p. T241e
- Comprehension and Vocabulary Workbook, pp. 53–54
- Language Enrichment Workbook, pp. 38–40
- Teacher's Resources
  Reinforcement, p. R27
  Test, pp. T53–T54
  Literary Analysis, pp. L8–L11

Cooperative Group Activity

Divide the class into two groups. Ask each group to brainstorm and list words and phrases for common objects and actions that might not be understood or might be phrased differently in another part of the country. List equivalents, if they are known. (For example, a carbonated beverage is known as soda, pop, or tonic in different parts of the country.) Ask each group to write and perform a short dialogue using words and phrases peculiar to their own region.

Homestead of Ellsworth Ball, detail, Sallie Cover. Private Collection

266 ■ Unit 4

About the Author

Mary E. Wilkins Freeman (1852–1930) was born in eastern Massachusetts and spent her early years there and in Vermont. She wrote realistically about New Englanders' constant struggle with their sometimes harsh environment and their determination to triumph over it. "The Revolt of Mother" is an especially good example of this theme.

Viewing Fine Art

This painting of the Ball homestead in Nebraska was done by neighbor Sallie Cover in the 1880s. The painting is of the Folk Art genre. Folk artists are self taught and focus on how things appear to them rather than how they actually appear. Usually the work lacks three dimensionality. Ask: How does the painting show that Cover enjoyed the rural way of life?

THE REVOLT OF MOTHER

ADAPTED

by Mary E. Wilkins Freeman

"Father!"

"What is it?"

"What are them men diggin' over in the field for?"

There was a sudden dropping and enlarging of the lower part of the old man's face, as if some heavy weight had settled therein; he shut his mouth tight, and went on harnessing the great bay mare. He hustled the collar on to her neck with a jerk.

"Father!"

The old man slapped the saddle on the mare's back.

"Look here, Father, I want to know what them men are diggin' over in the field for, an' I'm goin' to know."

"I wish you'd go into the house, Mother, an' tend to your own affairs," the old man said then. He ran his words together, and his speech was almost as inarticulate as a growl.

But the woman understood; it was her most native tongue. "I ain't goin' into the house till you tell me what them men are doin' over there in the field," said she.

Then she stood waiting. She was a small woman, short and straight-waisted like a child in her brown cotton gown. Her forehead was mild and benevolent between the smooth curves of gray hair; there were meek downward lines about her nose and mouth; but her eyes, fixed upon the old man, looked as if the meekness had been the result of her own will, never of the will of another.

They were in the barn, standing before the wide-open doors. The spring air, full of the smell of growing grass and unseen blossoms,

FOCUS ON FICTION STUDY HINTS

This is the first glimpse of the antagonist.

This is the first glimpse of the protagonist. It also foreshadows the conflict to come.

You are given a physical description of one character.

TEACHING PLAN

INTRODUCE

Motivation

Ask what the status of rural women was in this period. Did they have any way of asserting themselves? What limits were imposed on women's freedom?

Purpose-Setting Question

What could cause a mother to "revolt"?

READ

Literary Focus:
Elements of Fiction

Ask: What clue does the title offer about the importance of character to this story? Point out that students will also notice the impact of setting.

Reading Focus:
Interpret Character

Tell students that they can understand story characters by examining the characters' words and actions, by the author's description of characters, and by the way in which story characters interact. Suggest to students that as they read they note some of their opinions about the main characters based on these criteria.

CLOSE

Have students complete Review the Selection on pages 286–287.

Develop Vocabulary Skills

Review the footnoted vocabulary words and their definitions. Find each word in context and ask students to rephrase each sentence incorporating the definition rather than the given word.

ESL Activity

Discuss with the class dialect, colloquial jargon, slang, etc. Recognize definitions and types. Have groups discuss dialects and styles of language in their native countries.

Background Notes

During this period most authors wrote realistic stories including local color. Local color is the use of real places, the dialect of a particular area, and actual events. For example, "The Gift of the Magi" is a local-color story that takes place in New York City. "The Revolt of Mother" depicts rural life in Massachusetts in the late 19th century.

A good description of part of the setting is provided here.

came in their faces. The deep yard in front was littered with farm wagons and piles of wood; on the edges, close to the fence and the house, the grass was a vivid green, and there were some dandelions.

How is imagery used to describe the way Mother is standing?

The old man glanced doggedly at his wife as he tightened the last buckles on the harness. She looked as immovable to him as one of the rocks in his pasture land, bound to the earth with generations of blackberry vines. He slapped the reins over the horse, and started forth from the barn.

"Father!" said she.

The old man pulled up. "What is it?"

"I want to know what them men are diggin' over there in that field for."

"They're diggin' a cellar, I s'pose, if you've got to know."

"A cellar for what?"

"A barn."

"A barn? You ain't goin' to build a barn over there where we was goin' to have a house, Father?"

The old man said not another word. He hurried the horse into the farm wagon and clattered out of the yard, jouncing as sturdily on his seat as a boy.

The woman stood a moment looking after him, then she went out of the barn across a corner of the yard to the house. The house, standing at right angles with the great barn and a long reach of sheds and outbuildings, was infinitesimal compared with them. It was scarcely as commodious for people as the little boxes under the barn eaves were for doves.

Imagery is used to describe the girl's face.

A pretty girl's face, pink and delicate as a flower, was looking out of one of the house windows. She was watching three men who were digging over in the field which bounded the yard near the road line. She turned quietly when the woman entered.

"What are they diggin' for, Mother?" said she. "Did he tell you?"

"They're diggin' for—a cellar for a new barn."

"Oh, Mother, he ain't going to build another barn?"

Reading Focus:
Interpret Character

Point out that this is the fourth time the woman has asked her husband what is being built. Ask: What does this suggest about both her character and his?

Literary Focus:
Conflict

Ask: What do the contrasting descriptions of the house and the other farm buildings suggest about the main conflict of the story?

---

doggedly (DAWG id lee) persistently; stubbornly
infinitesimal (in fin ih TES uh mul) too small to be measured
commodious (kuh MOH dee us) spacious; roomy

"That's what he says."

A boy stood before the kitchen glass combing his hair. He combed slowly and painstakingly, arranging his brown hair in a smooth hillock over his forehead. He did not seem to pay any attention to the conversation.

"Sammy, did you know Father was going to build a new barn?" asked the girl.

The boy combed assiduously.

"Sammy!"

He turned, and showed a face like his father's under his smooth crest of hair. "Yes, I s'pose I did," he said, reluctantly.

"How long have you known it?" asked his mother.

"Bout three months, I guess."

"Why didn't you tell of it?"

"Didn't think 'twould do no good."

"I don't see what Father wants another barn for," said the girl, in her sweet, slow voice. She turned again to the window and stared out at the digging men in the field. Her tender, sweet face was full of a gentle distress. Her forehead was as bald and innocent as a baby's, with the light hair strained from it in a row of curl papers. She was quite large, but her soft curves did not look as if they covered muscles.

Her mother looked sternly at the boy. "Is he goin' to buy more cows?" said she.

How does the plot begin to develop?

The boy did not reply; he was tying his shoes.

"Sammy, I want you to tell me if he's goin' to buy more cows."

"I s'pose he is."

"How many?"

"Four, I guess."

His mother said nothing more. She went into the pantry, and there was a clatter of dishes. The boy got his cap from a nail behind the door, took an old arithmetic book from the shelf, and started for school. He was lightly built, but clumsy. He went out of the yard with a curious spring in his hips that made his loose home-made jacket tilt up in the rear.

The girl went to the sink and began to wash the dishes that were piled up there. Her mother came promptly out of the pantry

---

hillock (HIL uk) a small hill; mound

Critical Thinking: *Infer*

Why do you think the father kept the new barn a secret from his wife?

and shoved her aside. "You wipe 'em," said she. "I'll wash. There's a good many this mornin'."

The mother plunged her hands vigorously into the water; the girl wiped the plates slowly and dreamily. "Mother," said she, "don't you think it's too bad Father's going to build that new barn, much as we need a decent house to live in?"

This shows the author's attitude toward the two main characters.

Her mother scrubbed a dish fiercely. "You ain't found out yet, we're womenfolks, Nanny Penn," said she. "You ain't seen enough of menfolks yet to. One of these days you'll find it out, and then you'll know that we know only what menfolks think we do, so far as any use of it goes, an' how we'd ought to reckon menfolks in with Providence, an' not complain of what they do any more than we do of the weather."

Discussion

Ask: What is Sarah Penn's attitude toward men? What does she mean when she compares men's actions to Providence or the weather?

"I don't care; I don't believe George is anything like that, anyhow," said Nanny. Her delicate face flushed pink; her lips pouted softly, as if she were going to cry.

"You wait an' see. I guess George Eastman ain't no better than other men. You hadn't ought to judge Father, though. He can't help it, 'cause he don't look at things jest the way we do. An' we've been pretty comfortable here, after all. The roof don't leak —ain't never but once—that's one thing. Father's kept it shingled right up."

"I do wish we had a parlor."

"I guess it won't hurt George Eastman any to come to see you in a nice clean kitchen. I guess a good many girls don't have as good a place as this. Nobody's ever heard me complain."

"I ain't complained either, Mother."

"Well, I don't think you'd better, a good father an' a good home as you've got. S'pose your father made you go out an' work for your livin'? Lots of girls have to that ain't no better able to than you be."

Reading Focus: *Interpret Character*

Point out that, although Sarah disagrees with her husband, she doesn't let her daughter criticize him. Ask: What does this suggest about her character?

Can you find any theme clues here?

Sarah Penn washed the frying pan with a conclusive air. She scrubbed the outside of it as faithfully as the inside. She was a masterly keeper of her box of a house. Her one living room never seemed to have in it any of the dust which the friction of life with inanimate matter produces. She swept, and there seemed to be no dirt to go before the broom; she cleaned, and one could see no difference. She was like an artist so perfect that he has

inanimate (in AN uh mit) not living or moving

apparently no art. Today she got out a mixing bowl and a board, and rolled some pies, and there was no more flour upon her than upon her daughter who was doing finer work. Nanny was to be married in the fall, and she was sewing on some white cambric and embroidery. She sewed industriously while her mother cooked; her soft milk-white hands and wrists showed whiter than her delicate work

"We must have the stove moved out in the shed before long," said Mrs. Penn. "Talk about not havin' things, it's been a real blessin' to be able to put a stove up in that shed in hot weather. Father did one good thing when he fixed that stove pipe out there."

The literary elements of setting and character are interwoven here.

Sarah Penn's face as she rolled her pies had that expression of meek vigor which might have characterized one of the New Testament saints. She was making mince pies. Her husband, Adoniram Penn, liked them better than any other kind. She baked twice a week. Adoniram often liked a piece of pie between meals. She hurried this morning. It had been later than usual when she began, and she wanted to have a pie baked for dinner. However deep a resentment she might be forced to hold against her husband, she would never fail in sedulous attention to his wants.

Nobility of character manifests itself at loopholes when it is not provided with large doors, Sarah Penn's showed itself today in flaky dishes of pastry. She made the pies faithfully, while across the table she could see, when she glanced up from her work, the sight that rankled in her patient and steadfast soul—the digging of the cellar of the new barn in the place where Adoniram forty years ago had promised her their new house should stand.

What is the author's attitude toward Sarah?

The pies were done for dinner. Adoniram and Sammy were home a few minutes after twelve o'clock. The dinner was eaten with serious haste. There was never much conversation at the table in the Penn family. Adoniram asked a blessing, and they ate promptly, then rose up and went about their work.

Sammy went back to school, taking soft sly lopes out of the yard like a rabbit. He wanted a game of marbles before school, and feared his father would give him chores to do. Adoniram hastened to the door and called after him, but he was out of sight.

---

cambric (KAM brik) very fine, thin linen or cotton
sedulous (SEJ uh lus) hard-working; diligent; persistent

Critical Thinking: *Analyze*

Have students analyze the phrase "meek vigor." If necessary, students should look up both words in a dictionary. Point out that these two words are an unusual pairing since they are somewhat opposite in meaning. Ask: What does the phrase suggest about Sarah?

Literary Focus: *Character*

Point out the sentence beginning "Nobility of character manifests itself. . .," and ask students to explain what it means. Emphasize that this kind of direct statement is one way a writer can reveal character to a reader.

"I don't see what you let him go for, Mother," said he. "I wanted him to help me unload that wood."

Adoniram went to work out in the yard unloading wood from the wagon. Sarah put away the dinner dishes, while Nanny took down her curl papers and changed her dress. She was going down to the store to buy some more embroidery and thread.

When Nanny was gone, Mrs. Penn went to the door. "Father!" she called.

"Well, what is it!"

"I want to see you jest a minute, Father."

"I can't leave this wood nohow. I've got to git it unloaded and go for a load of gravel afore two o'clock. Sammy had ought to helped me. You hadn't ought to let him go to school so early."

"I want to see you jest a minute."

"I tell ye I can't, nohow, Mother."

Reading Focus: *Interpret Character*
Point out that once again, Sarah has repeated a demand until Adoniram gives in. Ask: What does this tell about his character?

Imagery is used to describe Sarah's movements.

"Father, you come here." Sarah Penn stood in the door like a queen; she held her head as if it bore a crown; there was the patience which makes authority in her voice. Adoniram went.

Mrs. Penn led the way into the kitchen, and pointed to a chair. "Sit down, Father," said she; "I've got somethin' I want to say to you."

He sat down heavily; his face was quite stolid, but he looked at her with restive eyes. "Well, what is it, Mother?"

"I want to know what you're buildin' that new barn for, Father?"

"I ain't got nothin' to say about it."

"It can't be you think you need another barn?"

"I tell ye I ain't got nothin' to say about it, Mother; an' I ain't goin' to say nothin'."

"Be you goin' to buy more cows?"

Adoniram did not reply; he shut his mouth tight.

"I know you be, as well as I want to. Now, Father, look here"—Sarah Penn had not sat down; she stood before her husband in the humble fashion of a Scripture woman—"I'm goin' to talk real plain to you; I never have sence I married you, but I'm goin' to now. I ain't never complained, an' I ain't goin' to complain now, but I'm goin' to talk plain. You see this room here, Father; you look at it well. You see there ain't no carpet on the floor, an' you see the paper is all dirty and droppin' off the walls. We ain't had no new paper on it for ten year, an' then I put it on myself, an' it didn't cost but nine cents a roll. You see this room, Father; it's all the one I've had to work in an' eat in an' sit in sence we was married. There ain't another woman in the whole town whose husband ain't got half the means you have but what's got better. It's all the room Nanny's got to have her company in; an' there ain't one of her mates but what's got better, an' their fathers not so able as hers is. It's all the room she'll have to be married in. What would you have thought, Father, if we had had our weddin' in a room no better than this? I was married in my mother's parlor, with a carpet on the floor, an' stuffed furniture, an' a mahogany card table. An' this is all the room my daughter will have to be married in. Look here, Father!"

Sarah Penn went across the room as though it were a tragic stage. She flung open a door and disclosed a tiny bedroom only large enough for a bed and bureau, with a path between. "There, Father," said she, "there's all the room I've had to sleep in

---

stolid (STOL id) expressing little emotion

Critical Thinking: *Infer*

Ask: What do you think are Adoniram's reasons for refusing to explain himself to Sarah? What might make him refuse to discuss his decision?

Literary Focus: *Plot*

Ask: Do you think Nanny's upcoming wedding is going to force Mrs. Penn into action? Predict what might happen.

Literary Focus: *Setting*

Sarah gives a detailed description of her house. Ask: How does this description affect your opinion of Sarah's desire for a new house? What is your opinion of Adoniram's decision to build a new barn instead?

in forty year. All my children were born there—the two that died an' the two that's livin'. I was sick with a fever, there."

She stepped to another door and opened it. It led into the small, ill-lighted pantry. "Here," said she, "is all the buttery I've got—every place I've got for my dishes, to set up my victuals in, an' to keep my milk pans in. Father, I've been takin' care of the milk of six cows in this place, an' now you're goin' to build a new barn, an' keep more cows, an' give me more to do in it."

She threw open another door. A narrow, crooked flight of stairs wound upward from it. "There, Father," said she, "I want you to look at the stairs that go up to them two unfinished chambers that are all the places our son and daughter have had to sleep in all their lives. There ain't a prettier girl in town nor a more ladylike one than Nanny, an' that's the place she has to sleep in. It ain't so good as your horse's stall; it ain't so warm an' tight."

Setting, character, and plot all come together here. This illustrates the interrelationship among these elements.

Sarah Penn went back and stood before her husband. "Now, Father," said she, "I want to know if you think you're doin' right and accordin' to what you profess. Here, where we was married forty year ago, you promised me faithful that we should have a new house built in that lot over in the field before the year was out. You said you had money enough, an' you wouldn't ask me to live in no such place as this. It is forty year now, an' you've been makin' more money an' I've been savin' of it for you ever sence, an' you ain't built no house yet. You've built sheds an' cow houses an' one new barn, an' now you're goin' to build another. Father, I want to know if you think it's right. You're lodgin' your dumb beasts better than you are your own flesh and blood. I want to know if you think it's right."

"I ain't got nothin' to say."

"You can't say nothin' without ownin' it ain't right, Father. An' there's another thing—I ain't complained; I've got along forty year an' I s'pose I should forty more, if it wa'n't for that—if we don't have another house. Nanny she can't live with us after she's married. She'll have to go somewhere else to live away from us, an' it don't seem as if I could have it so, noways, Father. She wa'n't ever strong. She's got considerable color, but there wa'n't never any backbone to her. I've always took the heft of everything off her,

---

pantry (PAN tree) a small room or closet off the kitchen, where cooking ingredients and utensils, china, etc., are kept

an' she ain't fit to keep house an' do everything herself. Think of her doin' all the washin' and ironin' and bakin' with them soft white hands and arms, an' sweepin'. I can't have it so, noways, Father."

Mrs. Penn's face was burning; her mild eyes gleamed. She had pleaded her little cause like a Webster; she had ranged from severity to pathos; but her opponent employed that obstinate silence which makes eloquence futile with mocking echoes. Adoniram arose clumsily.

"Father, ain't you got nothin' to say?" said Mrs. Penn.

"I've got to go off after that load of gravel. I can't stan' talkin' all day."

"Father, won't you think it over an' have a house built there instead of a barn?"

"I ain't got nothin' to say."

Adoniram shuffled out. Mrs. Penn went into her bedroom. When she came out, her eyes were red. She had a roll of unbleached cotton cloth. She spread it out on the kitchen table, and began cutting out some shirts for her husband. The men over in the field had a team to help them this afternoon; she could hear their halloos. She had a scanty pattern for the shirts; she had to plan and piece the sleeves.

Nanny came home with her embroidery and sat down with her needlework. She had taken down her curl papers, and there was a soft roll of fair hair like an aureole over her forehead; her face was as delicately fine and clear as porcelain. Suddenly she looked up and the tender red flamed over her face and neck. "Mother," said she.

How is imagery used to describe Nanny's face?

"What say?"

"I've been thinking—I don't see how we're goin' to have any wedding in this room. I'd be ashamed to have his folks come if we didn't have anybody else."

"Mebbe we can have some new paper before then; I can put it on. I guess you won't have no call to be ashamed of your belongin's."

---

pathos (PAY thos) an element in experience evoking pity
obstinate (OB stuh nut) stubborn
halloos (huh LOOZ) shouts; yells; calls
aureole (AWR ee ohl) a halo
porcelain (PAWR suh lin) china

Critical Thinking: *Evaluate*

Ask students to evaluate the case Sarah has made for a new house. Ask: Are her points well taken and her desire for a new house reasonable? Explain.

Reading Focus: *Interpret Character*

What does Adoniram's refusal to discuss the conflict suggest about his character?

Here is another example of foreshadowing. You are given a plot clue about what will happen later. Do you have any ideas?

"We might have the wedding in the new barn," said Nanny, with gentle pettishness. "Why, Mother, what makes you look so?"

Mrs. Penn had started and was staring at her with a curious expression. She turned again to her work, and spread out a pattern carefully on the cloth. "Nothin'," said she.

Presently Adoniram clattered out of the yard in his two-wheeled dump cart, standing as proudly upright as a Roman charioteer. Mrs. Penn opened the door and stood there a minute looking out; the halloos of the men sounded louder.

It seemed to her all through the spring months that she heard nothing but the halloos and the noises of saws and hammers. The new barn grew fast. It was a fine edifice for this little village. Men came on pleasant Sundays, in their meeting suits and clean shirt bosoms, and stood around it admiringly. Mrs. Penn did not speak of it and Adoniram did not mention it to her, although sometimes upon a return from inspecting it, he bore himself with injured dignity.

Does this give you a clue to the theme?

"It's a strange thing how your mother feels about the new barn," he said, confidentially, to Sammy one day.

Sammy only grunted after an odd fashion for a boy; he had learned it from his father.

The plot is about to take an unexpected twist.

The barn was all completed ready for use by the third week in July. Adoniram had planned to move his stock in on Wednesday; on Tuesday he received a letter which changed his plans. He came in with it early in the morning. "Sammy's been to the post office," said he, "an' I've got a letter from Hiram." Hiram was Mrs. Penn's brother who lived in Vermont.

"Well," said Mrs. Penn, "what does he say about the folks?"

The new plot event is revealed. What plot question does this raise?

"I guess they're all right. He says he thinks if I come up country right off there's a chance to buy jest the kind of a horse I want." He stared reflectively out of the window at the new barn.

Mrs. Penn was making pies. She went on clapping the rolling pin into the crust, although she was very pale, and her heart beat loudly.

"I dun' know but what I'd better go," said Adoniram. "I hate to go off jest now, right in the midst of hayin', but the ten-acre lot's cut,

---

edifice (ED uh fis) a large structure

Literary Focus: *Plot*

Point out the two important elements of this section in the story: Sarah is in some way excited because Adoniram is leaving town. Remind students of Nanny's suggestion that "we might have the wedding in the new barn." Ask: What do you think will happen once Adoniram has left for Vermont?

an' I guess Rufus an' the others can git along without me three or four days. I can't get a horse round here to suit me, nohow, an' I've got to have another for all that wood haulin' in the fall. I told Hiram to watch out an' if he got wind of a good horse to let me know. I guess I'd better go."

"I'll get out your clean shirt an' collar," said Mrs. Penn calmly.

She laid out Adoniram's Sunday suit and his clean clothes on the bed in the little bedroom. She got his shaving water and razor ready. At last she buttoned on his collar and fastened his black cravat.

Adoniram never wore his collar and cravat except on extra occasions. He held his head high, with a rasped dignity. When he was all ready, with coat and hat brushed, and a lunch of pie and cheese in a paper bag, he hesitated on the threshold of the door. He looked at his wife and his manner was defiantly apologetic. "*If* them cows come today Sammy can drive them into the new barn," said he, "an' when they bring the hay up they can pitch it in there."

"Well," replied Mrs. Penn.

Adoniram set his shaven face ahead and started. When he had cleared the doorstep, he turned and looked back with a kind of nervous solemnity. "I shall be back by Saturday if nothin' happens," said he.

"Do be careful, Father," returned his wife.

She stood in the door with Nanny at her elbow and watched him out of sight. Her eyes had a strange, doubtful expression in them; her peaceful forehead was contracted. Nanny sat sewing. Her wedding day was drawing nearer and she was getting pale and thin with her steady sewing. Her mother kept glancing at her.

"Have you got that pain in your side this mornin'?" she asked.

"A little."

Mrs. Penn's face as she worked, changed; her perplexed forehead smoothed; her eyes were steady, her lips firmly set. She formed a maxim for herself, although incoherently with her

A new plot question: What does Sarah have in mind?

cravat (kruh VAT) a necktie; scarf
maxim (MAK sim) a statement of a general truth
incoherently (in koh HIR unt lee) not logically; disjointedly

Critical Thinking: *Analyze*

Point out the phrase "defiantly apologetic." Ask students to describe feelings that might make them both defiant and apologetic at the same time. Ask: What must Adoniram be feeling?

Reading Focus: *Interpret Character*

Ask: What do you think Adoniram feels about having refused to give Sarah the new house he had always promised her? Which details in the story support your answers?

Reading Focus:
Interpret Character

Explain that Sarah did nothing to bring about Hiram's letter; she tells herself that it happened by "a providence," or lucky act of fate. She feels justified in going ahead with her plan for this reason. As students read further and see what she does, ask what her self-justification suggests about her character.

Literary Focus:
Theme

Point out that this is independent confirmation that the new barn was not needed. Ask: How does this fact relate to the story's theme?

unlettered thoughts. "Unsolicited opportunities are the guideposts of the Lord to the new roads of Life," she repeated in effect, and she made up her mind to her course of action.

"S'posin' I *had* wrote to Hiram," she muttered once, when she was in the pantry. "S'posin' I had wrote and asked him if he knew of any horse? But I didn't, an' Father's goin' wa'n't any of my doin'. It looks like a providence." Her mother's voice rang out quite loud at the last.

"What you talkin' about, Mother?" called Nanny.

"Nothin'."

Mrs. Penn hurried her baking; at eleven o'clock it was all done. The load of hay from the west field came slowly down the cart track and drew up at the new barn. Mrs. Penn ran out. "Stop!" she screamed, "stop!"

The men stopped and looked; Sammy upreared from the top of the load and stared at his mother.

"Stop!" she cried out again. "Don't you put the hay in that barn; put it in the old one."

This is a brief description of a stereotyped, secondary character. Would this character be considered round or flat?

"Why, he said to put it in here," returned one of the haymakers wonderingly. He was a young man, a neighbor's son, whom Adoniram hired by the year to work on the farm.

"Don't you put the hay in the new barn; there's room enough in the old one, ain't there?" said Mrs. Penn.

"Room enough," returned the hired man, in his thick, rustic tones. "Didn't need the new barn, nohow, as far as room's concerned. Well, I s'pose he changed his mind." He took hold of the horses' bridles.

Mrs. Penn went back to the house. Soon the kitchen windows were darkened and a fragrance like warm honey came into the room.

Nanny laid down her work. "I thought Father wanted them to put the hay into the new barn?" she said, wonderingly.

"It's all right," replied her mother.

Sammy slid down from the load of hay and came in to see if dinner was ready.

"I ain't goin' to get a regular dinner today, as long as Father's

---

rustic (RUS tik) of or living in the country, rural; simple, plain; rough, awkward

Homestead of Ellsworth Ball, detail, Sallie Cover. Private Collection

gone," said his mother. "I've let the fire go out. You can have some bread an' milk an' pie. I thought we could get along." She set out some bowls of milk, some bread and a pie on the kitchen table. "You'd better eat your dinner now," said she. "You might jest as well get through with it. I want you to help me afterward."

Nanny and Sammy stared at each other. There was something strange in their mother's manner. Mrs. Penn did not eat anything herself. She went into the pantry and they heard her moving dishes while they ate. Presently she came out with a pile of plates. She got the clothes basket out of the shed and packed them in it. Nanny and Sammy watched. She brought out cups and saucers and put them in with the plates.

"What you goin' to do, Mother," inquired Nanny, in a timid voice. A sense of something unusual made her tremble, as if it were a ghost. Sammy rolled his eyes over his pie.

Viewing Fine Art

See note on page T266. Ask: What do you learn about rural life from this painting?

Critical Thinking: *Analyze*

Ask the students to analyze Sarah's state of mind and motivation. Ask: Were her attitude and subsequent behavior justified? Why or why not?

"You'll see what I'm goin' to do," replied Mrs. Penn. "If you're through, Nanny, I want you to go upstairs and pack your things; an' I want you, Sammy, to help me take down the bed in the bedroom."

"Oh, Mother, what for?" gasped Nanny.

"You'll see."

Some imagery that may be unfamiliar is explained.

During the next few hours a feat was performed by this simple pious New England mother which was equal in its way to Wolfe's storming of the Heights of Abraham. It took no more genius and audacity of bravery for Wolfe to cheer his wondering soldiers up those steep precipices, under the sleeping eyes of the enemy, than for Sarah Penn, at the head of her children, to move all their little household goods into the new barn while her husband was away.

Nanny and Sammy followed their mother's instructions without a murmur; indeed, they were overawed. There is a certain uncanny and super-human quality about all such purely original undertakings as their mother's was to them. Nanny went back and forth with her light loads and Sammy tugged with sober energy.

Do you think this is the climax of the plot?

At five o'clock in the afternoon the little house in which the Penns had lived for forty years had emptied itself into the new barn.

Every builder builds somewhat for unknown purposes, and is in a measure a prophet. The architect of Adoniram Penn's barn, while he designed it for the comfort of four-footed animals, had planned better than he knew for the comfort of humans. Sarah Penn saw at a glance its possibilities. Those great box stalls, with quilts hung before them, would make better bedrooms than the one she had occupied for forty years, and there was a tight carriage room. The harness room, with its chimney and shelves, would make a kitchen of her dreams. The great middle space would make a parlor, by-and-by, fit for a palace. Upstairs there was as much room as down, With partitions and windows, what a house there would be! Sarah looked at the row of stanchions before the allotted space for cows, and reflected she would have a front entry there.

Literary Focus:
Setting

Have students contrast this description of the new barn with Sarah's description of the old house on pages 273–274. Ask: How does the setting help readers understand both character and plot?

---

precipices (PRES uh pis iz) steep cliffs; vertical or hanging rock faces
stanchions (STAN chunz) upright bars, beams or posts used as support

At six o'clock the stove was up in the harness room, the kettle was boiling, and the table set for tea. It looked almost as homelike as the abandoned house across the yard had ever done. The young hired man milked, and Sarah directed him calmly to bring the milk to the new barn. He came gasping, dropping little blots of foam from the brimming pails on the grass. Before the next morning he had spread the story of Adoniram Penn's wife moving into the new barn all over the little village. Men assembled in the store and talked it over; women with shawls over their heads scuttled into each other's houses before their work was done. Any deviation from the ordinary course of life in this quiet town was enough to stop all progress in it. Everybody paused to look at the staid, independent figure on the side track. There was a difference of opinion with regard to her. Some held her to be insane; some, of a lawless and rebellious spirit.

Friday the minister went to see her. It was in the forenoon, and she was at the barn door shelling peas for dinner. She looked up and returned his salutation with dignity; then she went on with her work. She did not invite him in. The saintly expression of her face remained fixed, but there was an angry flush over it.

The minister stood awkwardly before her, and talked. She handled the peas as if they were bullets. At last she looked up and her eyes showed a spirit that her meek front had covered for a lifetime.

"There ain't no use talkin', Mr. Hersey," said she. "I've thought it all over and over, an' I believe I'm doin' what's right. I've made it the subject of prayer, and it's betwixt me an' the Lord an' Adoniram. There ain't no call for nobody else to worry about it."

Could this be another theme clue?

"Well, of course, if you have brought it to the Lord in prayer, and feel satisfied that you are doing right, Mrs. Penn," said the minister helplessly. His thin, gray-bearded face was pathetic. He was a sickly man; his youthful confidence had cooled; he had to scourge himself up to some of his pastoral duties, and then he was prostrated by the smart.

"I think it's right jest as much as I think it was right for our forefathers to come over from the old country 'cause they didn't have what belonged to 'em," said Mrs. Penn. She arose.

---

scourge (SKURJ) to whip; to chastise, punish
prostrated (PROS trayt id) laid low; completely overcome

Critical Thinking: *Evaluate*

Ask students to evaluate the town's reaction to Sarah's actions. Ask: Why are people so shocked and horrified at what she has done? Point out that in a small New England town, everyone would know what everyone else's houses looked like; neighbors would have known that the Penn's house was shabby and too small.

Reading Focus: *Interpret Character*

Ask: Why does Sarah react as she does to the minister's visit?

Literary Focus: *Conflict*

Point out that the meeting between Sarah and the minister is an example of external conflict. Ask: What is the source of the conflict? How does Sarah get the best of it?

Critical Thinking: *Analyze*

Ask: Why does Sarah take the trouble to prepare Adoniram's favorite supper?

Symbolism is used here. Plymouth Rock symbolizes the start of a new life in a new environment for the Penn family, just as it did for the Pilgrims.

The barn threshold might have been Plymouth Rock from her bearing. "I don't doubt you mean well, Mr. Hersey," said she, "but there are things people hadn't ought to interfere with. I've been a member of the church for over forty year. I've got my own mind an' my own feet, an' I'm goin' to think my own thoughts an' go my own ways, an' nobody but the Lord is goin' to dictate to me unless I've a mind to have him. Won't you come in an' set down? How is Mis' Hersey?"

"She is well, I thank you," replied the minister. He added some more perplexed, apologetic remarks; then he retreated.

He could expound the intricacies of every character study in the Scriptures; he was competent to grasp the Pilgrim Fathers and all historical innovators; but Sarah Penn was beyond him. He could deal with primal cases, but parallel ones worsted him. But, after all, although it was aside from his province, he wondered more how Adoniram Penn would deal with his wife than how the Lord would. Everybody shared the wonder. When Adoniram's four new cows arrived, Sarah ordered three put in the old barn, the other in the house where the cooking stove had stood. That added to the excitement. It was whispered that all four cows were domiciled in the house.

Toward sunset on Saturday, when Adoniram was expected home, there was a knot of men in the road near the new barn. The hired man had milked, but he still hung around the premises. There were brown bread and baked beans and a custard pie; it was the supper that Adoniram loved on a Saturday night. She had on a clean calico and she bore herself imperturbably. Nanny and Sammy kept close at her heels. Their eyes were large, and Nanny was full of nervous tremors. Still there was to them more pleasant excitement than anything else. An inborn confidence in their mother over their father asserted itself.

Is this rising action leading to the climax, or is it falling action headed toward resolution?

Sammy looked out of the harness-room window. "There he is," he announced, in an awed whisper. He and Nanny peeped around the casing. Mrs. Penn kept on about her work. The children

---

intricacies (IN trih kuh seez) complexities; complications
innovators (IN uh vayt urz) makers of changes; introducers of new methods
imperturbably (im pur TUR buh blee) in a manner that cannot be excited; impassively

watched Adoniram leave the new horse standing in the drive while he went to the house-door. It was fastened. Then he went around to the shed. That door was seldom locked, even when the family was away. The thought of how her father would be confronted by the cow flashed upon Nanny. There was a hysterical sob in her throat. Adoniram emerged from the shed and stood looking about in a dazed fashion. His lips moved; he was saying something, but they could not hear what it was. The hired man was peeping around a corner of the old barn but nobody saw him.

Adoniram took the new horse by the bridle and led him across the yard to the new barn. Nanny and Sammy slunk close to their mother. The barn doors rolled back and there stood Adoniram, with the long mild face of the great Canadian farm horse looking over his shoulder.

Nanny kept behind her mother, but Sammy stepped suddenly forward and stood in front of her.

Adoniram stared at the group, "What on airth you all down here for?" said he. "What's the matter over to the house?"

"We've come here to live, Father," said Sammy. His shrill voice quavered out bravely.

"What—" Adoniram sniffed—"what is it smells like cookin'?" said he. He stepped forward and looked in the open door of the harness room. Then he turned to his wife. His old bristling face was pale and frightened, "What on airth does this mean, Mother?"

Do you think this is a plot clue, a theme clue, or both?

"You come in here, Father," said Sarah. She led the way into the harness room and shut the door. "Now, Father," said she, "you needn't be scared. I ain't crazy. There ain't nothin' to be upset over. But we've come here to live an' we're goin' to live here. We've got jest as good a right here as new horses and cows. The house wa'n't fit for us to live in any longer, an' I made up my mind I wa'n't goin' to stay there. I've done my duty by you forty year an' I'm goin' to do it now, but I'm goin' to live here. You've got to put in some windows an' partitions, an' you'll have to buy some furniture."

"Why, Mother!" the old man gasped.

"You'd better take your coat off an' get washed—there's the wash basin—an' then we'll have supper."

"Why, Mother!"

Reading Focus: *Interpret Character*

Remind students that in the beginning of the story, Sammy conspired with his father to keep the new barn a secret from his mother. Here, however, at the story's climax, he bands together with his mother and sister against Adoniram. Ask: What does this tell you about Sammy? Why do you think he "changed sides"? How might the personalities of Adoniram and Sarah have affected Sammy?

Viewing Fine Art

The last great era of figurative painting in the United States took place from the late 1920s to the 1940s. Realists who devoted themselves to picturing the people and life of a certain area of the country were known as "regionalists." Among them were artists who portrayed the Midwest, and others who painted city dwellers and urban slums. Georges Schreiber (1904–1977) was a Belgian-American Regionalist who captured the windswept, lonely aura of an Arkansas farm in his work. Ask: How does this painting help you understand Sarah Penn's attitudes and her actions?

From Arkansas, 1943, Georges Schreiber

Sammy went past the window, leading the new horse to the old barn. The old man saw him and shook his head speechlessly. He tried to take off his coat, but his arms seemed to lack the power. His wife helped him. She poured some water into the tin basin and put in a piece of soap. She got the comb and brush and smoothed his thin grey hair after he had washed. Then she put the beans, hot bread and tea on the table. Sammy came in and the family drew up. Adoniram sat looking dazedly at his plate and they waited.

"Ain't you goin' to ask a blessin', Father?" said Sarah.

And the old man bent his head and mumbled.

All through the meal he stopped eating at intervals and stared furtively at his wife, but he ate well. The home food tasted good to him and his old frame was too sturdily healthy to be affected by his mind. But after supper he went out and sat down on the step of the smaller door at the right of the barn, through which he had meant his Jerseys to pass in stately file, but which Sarah designed for her front house-door, and he leaned his head on his hands.

After the supper dishes were cleared away and the milk pans washed, Sarah went out to him. The twilight was deepening. There was a clear green glow in the sky. Before them stretched the smooth level of field; in the distance was a cluster of haystacks like the huts of a village; the air was very calm and sweet. The landscape might have been an ideal one of peace.

Sarah bent over and touched her husband on one of his thin, sinewy shoulders. "Father!"

The old man's shoulders heaved; he was weeping.

"Why, don't do so, Father," said Sarah.

"I'll—put up the—partitions, an'—everything you—want, Mother."

Sarah put her apron up to her face; she was overcome by her own triumph.

Adoniram was like a fortress whose walls had no active resistance, and went down the instant the right besieging tools were used. "Why, Mother," he said hoarsely, "I hadn't no idee you was so set on't it as all this comes to."

The last plot question is answered. The conflict has been resolved. Do you think this is the climax, the resolution, or both?

Finally, the theme is made clear. Imagery is added to enhance the meaning.

---

besieging (bih SEEJ ing) hemming in with armed forces; closing in; overwhelming

Literary Focus: *Plot*

Ask: What is the final resolution of the conflict?

Reading Focus: *Interpret Character*

Ask: Why do you think Adoniram "had no idea" what a determined person Sarah was? What does his ignorance of her true personality suggest about both his own character and hers?

Critical Thinking: *Apply*

Ask: What effect do you think Mother's revolt will have on the family hereafter?

Mini Quiz

Write the following questions on the board or overhead projector and call on students to fill in the blanks. Discuss the answers with the class

1. As the story opens, Mother questions Father about why men are ________ in the field.
2. Sammy, the son, upon being questioned by his mother, tells her that his father has gone off to buy ________.
3. Nanny, the daughter, was looking forward to ________ in the fall.
4. Adoniram took a trip to ________ to buy ________ from someone who lived near Sarah's ________.
5. ________ ________ is used to symbolize what Sarah's new home meant to her.

Answers

1. digging
2. cows
3. marriage
4. Vermont; a horse; brother Hiram
5. Plymouth Rock

UNDERSTAND THE SELECTION

Answers

1. spring
2. They were digging a cellar for a new barn.
3. 40 years
4. Sample answer: He has become obsessed with his work and no longer notices how the family lives.
5. Sample answer: She thinks men see things differently from women and that women have to accept this as they accept the weather.
6. Answers will vary, but the upcoming wedding should be mentioned. Sarah does not want the next generation to live as poorly as she has.
7. Sample answer: At first she is worried that he will make her change her mind. Once she has spoken her mind, she realizes that she is right and has nothing to fear from the minister.
8. Sample answers: Too small overall; no parlor; no carpet; dirty, old wallpaper in kitchen; tiny downstairs bedroom; small, ill-lit pantry; two unfinished children's bedrooms
9. She was very neat and clean. Answers will vary. Sample answers: She scrubbed the frying pan inside and out; the living room was never dusty; she swept regularly; she could make pies without getting flour on herself.
10. Sample answers: The new cows and hay would have been put into the new barn; the family would not have moved in.

Review the Selection

UNDERSTAND THE SELECTION

Recall

1. In which season is the story set?
2. Why were the men digging?
3. How long had Sarah and Adoniram been married?

Infer

4. Why do you think Adoniram has never built a new house?
5. Discuss Sarah's attitude toward men.
6. Why do you think Sarah finally decides to act?
7. Why does Sarah not invite the minister in at first, and why does she later ask him in to sit down?

Apply

8. Give three examples to show why the old house was inadequate.
9. Select two setting descriptions that illustrate the type of housekeeper Sarah was.
10. What would have and have not happened if Adoniram did not receive the letter from Hiram when he did?

Respond to Literature

Do you think the lifestyle of the Penn family was unusual for that period in American history? Explain.

WRITE ABOUT THE SELECTION

An **epilogue** is writing added to the end of other writing. The dictionary defines *epilogue* as "a closing section added to a novel, play, etc., providing further comment, interpretation, or information."

At the end of "The Revolt of Mother," the new barn had become a new house. Suppose that you dropped by to visit the Penn family one year after the story ended. Write an epilogue to the story based on your observations.

Prewriting Think about the changes in character and setting you would observe. Write down ideas about what might have happened to the members of the Penn family and to their farm in the year since. Include ideas about Adoniram's feelings and state of mind, both at the end of the story and one year later.

Writing Bring these ideas together and write an epilogue to the story. Describe the changes, in terms of character and setting, that have taken place during the year since the story ended. Be sure to include sufficient details.

Revising Make the reader's mental picture clearer and more vivid by adding visual imagery to your description.

Proofreading Where a noun is described by more than one adjective, make sure the adjectives are separated by commas. Check that there is no comma between adjectives separated by *and*.

Respond to Literature

Discuss the nature of our country's agrarian economy during this period. Point out that the Penns' lifestyle was very common. Everyone had to work very hard to keep the farm and home running.

Ask students how they would feel about living and working on a farm. If any students already do, have them share their experiences. Have two volunteers go to the board—one to list *Advantages*, the other to list *Disadvantages* as they are brought up by the class. At the end, tally the entries under each heading to see which outnumbers the other.

WRITE ABOUT THE SELECTION

Prewriting

Have the students brainstorm their ideas of the changes. Write down their ideas on the board or an overhead transparency. List them under two headings: *Setting* and *Character*.

Writing

Have students work on this section individually. Go around the class, giving help to any student having difficulty. Question possible changes in characters' feelings and environment.

Revising

Make this a cooperative group activity. Have students work in small groups to revise their epilogues.

THINK ABOUT FICTION

It is the imagination of the author, rather than factual data, which forms the basis of any fictional work. This is not to say that fiction cannot include such things as historical events or the personal experiences of real people—including the author. These types of things can be woven into the story. However, the heart and soul of fictional literature remains the author's imagination.

1. Which element of setting—time or place—would you consider dominant in the story? Why?
2. Interpret the author's tone. What is her attitude toward the protagonist and antagonist?
3. Describe the type of conflict involved in the plot. Was there more than one type? Explain your answer.
4. What do you consider the climax or turning point of the plot? Is the resolution found in the climax or elsewhere? Explain your answer.
5. State in your own words what you consider to be the theme of the story.

DEVELOP YOUR VOCABULARY

A **dialect** is the form, or variety, of a spoken language used by members of a region, a community, or a social group. Each dialect has pronunciations, grammatical features, and vocabulary that are peculiar to it and different from those of other dialects.

In "The Revolt of Mother," the characters speak in dialect. The author shows that certain speech sounds are omitted by using an apostrophe in their place. She spells some words in the phonetic patterns used by the characters.

Rewrite each of these sentences from the story in standard English.

1. "You hadn't ought to judge Father, though."
2. "I ain't got nothin' to say about it, Mother; an' I ain't goin' to say nothin'."
3. "We ain't had no new paper on it for ten year."
4. "S'posin' I had wrote to Hiram."
5. "There ain't no call for nobody else to worry about it."

THINK ABOUT FICTION

Answers

1. Place. The story revolves around a farm, barn, and house. The season of the year is somewhat important, but the actual year is not.
2. Answers will vary. Basically, more sympathetic toward and admiring of the former; harsh and critical toward the latter
3. Primarily external—between two characters; however, there were suggestions of inner conflict within these two as well.
4. The turning point comes when Sarah sees Adoniram's absence as a providence, allowing her freedom to act. The resolution comes at the end.
5. Sample answer: The theme, the dominating idea of the work, is that women as well as men have worth, value, and the right to be heard.

DEVELOP YOUR VOCABULARY

Sample Answers

1. You shouldn't judge Father, though.
2. I haven't anything to say about it, Mother; and I am not going to say anything.
3. We haven't had any new paper on it for ten years.
4. Suppose that I had written to Hiram.
5. There is no reason for anyone else to worry about it.

Have the class find other quotes written in dialect throughout the story. Ask one student to write the sentences in dialect on one side of the board. Have another student write a revised, proper sentence next to each, as suggested by the class.

Proofreading

Select one or two of the students' epilogues as models for proofreading. Put the paragraphs on the overhead projector and have the class suggest improvements.

ESL Activity

Work with the students to develop epilogues or alternate endings of this story. Group discussions: What part did fate play in the outcome? What if women had had more rights and freedoms at the time? Work toward writing an epilogue.

Selection Overview

Selection Objectives

After completing this selection, students should be able to

- understand the nature and purpose of exposition
- use exposition to define an object
- take notes during an interview
- write a newspaper article based on interview notes
- divide polysyllabic words into single syllables
- compare and contrast

Lesson Resources

How to Tell a Story
- Selection Synopsis, Teacher's Edition, p. T241f
- Comprehension and Vocabulary Workbook, pp. 55–56
- Language Enrichment Workbook, pp. 41–42
- Teacher's Resources
  Reinforcement, p. R28
  Test, pp. T55–T56

More About Exposition

It has been noted that exposition may be used to define, compare and contrast, classify, and analyze. Any or all of these may be used in a single work. Ask the students to write down methods Twain uses in his essay.

Although exposition is primarily used in nonfiction, it may be used in conjunction with other types of writing. The examples Twain uses, for instance, are narrative. Exposition is the principal form of writing in the textbooks used in other courses students are presently studying.

ESL Activity

Work with students to come up with a definition of exposition and various factors related to it. See the Language Enrichment Workbook, pages 41–42.

Learn About

Samuel L. Clemens (Mark Twain) and His Memories, 1880. The Granger Collection

Reading Focus

Compare and Contrast You have learned that comparing means finding similarities and contrasting means finding differences. By highlighting the common and unique qualities of different stories, you can learn more about each.

In "How to Tell a Story," Mark Twain states that there are three different kinds of stories. As you read, pay attention to how he compares and contrasts the three. Think about why he finds one kind of story much funnier than the other two.

Exposition

Exposition, along with narration, description, and persuasion, is one of the four forms of discourse. The purpose of exposition is to explain. It is the kind of writing done, for example, to interpret facts and opinions, to explain the nature of freedom, to outline the structure of a government, or to account for events in history. In short, it is the kind of writing in which an author gives information about a subject.

Authors have several ways of explaining a subject. They may **define** it—tell what it is and demonstrate its purpose. They may **compare and contrast** it with something else—show its likenesses and differences. They may **classify** it—put it in its type or class. They may **analyze** it—focus on its elements and their significance.

As you read this selection, ask yourself:

1. Which way or ways of explaining does Twain use in this work?
2. Which form of discourse did Twain use in the examples he gives?

Writing Connection

Choose an object, such as a favorite possession, and write a paragraph defining its nature and use.

Viewing Fine Art

In both America and Europe, 19th-century newspapers were illustrated with caricatures—drawings that exaggerated their subjects for purposes of humor, satire, or political or social commentary. Cartoons by such artists as Thomas Nast (U.S.) and Honoré Daumier (France) were so clever that they often swayed public opinion. Purely humorous drawings like this one of Twain have all but died out since the invention of photography. Ask: What impression of Twain does this drawing give?

Cooperative Group Activity

For the Writing Connection activity, group students into threes or fours according to similar interests. In groups students will choose their favorite possessions. Have groups brainstorm elements that might be discussed—use, shape, color, weight, size, and so on. Then have students write their paragraphs individually.

Old Barn in Field of Asters, Henry Poor. Corbis Bettmann

HOW TO TELL A STORY

ADAPTED

by Mark Twain

I do not claim that I can tell a story as it ought to be told. I only claim to know how a story ought to be told, for I have been almost daily in the company of the most expert storytellers for many years.

There are several kinds of stories, but only one difficult kind—the humorous. I will talk mainly about that one. The humorous story is American; the comic story is English; the witty story is French. The humorous story depends for its effect upon the *manner* of the telling; the comic story and the witty story upon the *matter*.

The humorous story may be spun out to great length, and may wander around as much as it pleases, and arrive nowhere in particular; but the comic and witty stories must be brief and end with a point. The humorous story bubbles gently along; the others burst.

The humorous story is strictly a work of art—high and delicate art—and only an artist can tell it. But no art is necessary in telling the comic and the witty story; anybody can do it. The art of telling a humorous story—understand, I mean by word of mouth, not print—was created in America, and has remained at home.

TEACHING PLAN

INTRODUCE

Motivation

Use a tape recording of Mark Twain talking about his life and how different events affected his writings. You could also use a tape of Twain reading something that he had written or telling a story.

Impress upon the class that Twain is considered probably the foremost humorist of his time and that he was, in his time, a nationally-known celebrity.

Purpose-Setting Question

Would you rather be considered humorous, comic, or witty? What are the differences?

READ

Literary Focus: *Exposition*

Students might expect an exposition to be dry and humorless. Suggest that as they read they look for ways in which Twain inserts humor into this exposition.

Reading Focus: *Compare and Contrast*

Point out that Twain defines humorous, comic, and witty stories by comparing and contrasting them. Have students use his comparisons and contrasts to write brief definitions of each kind of story.

CLOSE

Have students complete Review the Selection on pages 296–297.

Develop Vocabulary Skills

Write the vocabulary words in one or two columns on the board. Select a volunteer for each word, who will: (1) look it up in a dictionary; (2) write it in syllable form on the board, next to the whole word; (3) write a brief definition.

Viewing Fine Art

Henry Varnum Poor (1888–1970) painted in a gentle style, favoring dreamy pastoral scenes like the one shown here. His emphasis on calm and quietude is evident in this picture. Poor was also a potter; he used clay from his native Hudson Valley to make his ceramics. Poor continued to paint representational art like this painting after the advent of abstract art. Ask: What is your impression of this place?

Reading Focus:
Compare and Contrast

Ask the students to decide as they read whether either story would be funnier or more amusing if told (properly) rather than read.

The humorous story is told gravely. The teller does his best to conceal the fact that he even dimly suspects that there is anything funny about it. But the teller of the comic story tells you beforehand that it is one of the funniest things he has ever heard, then tells it with eager delight, and is the first person to laugh when he gets through. Sometimes, if he has had good success, he is so glad and happy that he will repeat the "nub" of it and glance around from face to face, collecting applause, and then repeat it again. It is a pathetic thing to see.

Very often, of course, the rambling humorous story also finishes with a nub, point, snapper, or whatever you like to call it. Then the listener must be alert, for in many cases, the teller will divert attention from that nub by dropping it in a carefully casual and indifferent way, as though he does not even know it is a nub.

But the teller of the comic story does not slur the nub; be shouts it at you—every time. And when he prints it, in England, France, Germany, and Italy, he *italicizes* it, puts some whooping exclamation points after it, and sometimes explains it in a parenthesis. All of which is very depressing, and makes one want to renounce joking and lead a better life.

Let me set down an instance of the comic method, using a story which has been popular all over the world for twelve or fifteen hundred years. The teller tells it in this way:

The Wounded Soldier

In a certain battle a soldier whose leg had been shot off appealed to another soldier who was hurrying by to carry him to the rear, informing him at the same time of the loss which he had sustained. The generous son of Mars,[1] shouldering the unfortunate, proceeded to carry out his desire. The bullets and cannonballs were flying in all directions, and presently one of the latter took the wounded man's head off—without, however, his deliverer being aware of it. In no long time he was hailed by an officer, who said:

"Where are you going with that carcass?"

"To the rear, sir—he's lost his leg!"

"His leg, really?" responded the astonished officer; "you mean his head, you fool."

At that the soldier relieved himself of his burden, and stood looking down upon it in great perplexity. At length he said:

"It is true, sir, just as you have said." Then after a pause he added, "*But he told me* IT WAS HIS LEG! ! ! !"

---

pathetic (puh THET ik) pitiful
divert (dih VURT) turn aside
indifferent (in DIF ur unt) not caring
slur (SLUR) make unclear; pass over carelessly
renounce (rih NOUNS) rejected; abandon with disgust
sustained (suh STAYND) experienced; suffered
carcass (KAHR kus) dead body, usually of an animal
perplexity (pur PLEK sih tee) confusion; uncertainty
[1]**Mars:** In ancient Roman mythology, Mars was the god of war.

Here the narrator bursts into explosion after explosion of horse-laughter, repeating that nub from time to time through his gaspings and shriekings and suffocatings.

It takes only a minute and a half to tell that in its comic story form, and isn't worth the telling after all. Put into the humorous story form, it takes ten minutes, and is about the funniest thing I have ever listened to—as James Whitcomb Riley[2] tells it.

He tells it in the character of a dull-witted old farmer who has just heard it for the first time, thinks it is unspeakably funny, and is trying to repeat it to a neighbor. But he can't remember it, so he gets all mixed up and wanders helplessly round and round, putting in tedious details that don't belong in the tale and only retard it; taking them out and putting in others that are just as useless; making minor mistakes now and then and stopping to correct them and explain how he came to make them; remembering things which he forgot to put in their proper place and going back to put them in there; stopping his narrative a good while in order to try to recall the name of the soldier that was hurt, and finally remembering that the soldier's name was not mentioned, and remarking thoughtfully that the name is of no real importance, anyway—better, of course, if one knew it, but not essential, after all—and so on, and so on, and so on.

To string incongruities and absurdities together in a wandering and sometimes purposeless way, and seem innocently unaware that they are absurdities, is the basis of the American art, if my position is correct. Another feature is the slurring of the point. A third is the dropping of a studied remark apparently without knowing it, as if one were thinking aloud. The fourth and last is the pause.

The pause is a very important feature in any kind of story, and a frequently recurring feature, too. It is a dainty thing, and delicate, and also uncertain and treacherous; for it must be exactly the right length—no more and no less—or it fails of its purpose and makes trouble.

On the platform I used to tell a story about a man who came to interview me once to get a sketch of my life. I consulted with a friend—a practical man—before he came, to know how I should treat him.

"Whenever you give the interviewer a fact," he said, "give him another fact that will contradict it. Then he'll go away with a jumble that he can't use at all. Be gentle, be sweet, smile like an idiot—just be natural." That's what my friend told me to do, and I did it:

An Encounter with an Interviewer

The nervous, dapper young man took the chair I offered him, and said he was connected with the *Daily Thunderstorm*, and added:

---

tedious (TEE dee us) boring; tiresome
incongruity (in kon GROO ih tee) something not fitting or not in harmony
absurdity (ab SUR duh tee) something absurd or ridiculous
recurring (rih KUR ing) occurring again and again
dapper (DAP ur) neat, trim
[2]**James Whitcomb Riley:** (1849–1916) a popular poet and speaker at the time

Discussion

After reading each story, ask the class if they thought it was funny or amusing. Ask why or why not.

Literary Focus: *Exposition*

Point out that the first paragraph in the right column is entirely expository. Ask: What necessary features of a well-told humorous story does Twain list?

Reading Focus: *Compare and Contrast*

Have students compare and contrast the personalities of Twain and the reporter to this point in the interview. Ask: Which character is the more clever of the two? Why do you think so?

"Hoping it's no harm, I've come to interview you."

"Come to what?"

"*Interview* you."

"Ah! I see. Yes—yes. Um! Yes—yes."

I was not feeling bright that morning. Indeed, my powers seemed a bit under a cloud. However, I went to the bookcase, and when I had been looking six or seven minutes, I said:

"How do you spell it?"

"Spell what?"

"Interview."

"Oh, my goodness! What do you want to spell it for?"

"I don't want just to spell it; I want to spell it to see what it means."

"In, *in*, ter, *ter*, *in*ter—"

"Then you spell it with an *I*?"

"Why, certainly!"

"Oh, that is what took me so long."

"Why, my *dear* sir, what did *you* propose to spell it with?"

"Well, I—I—hardly know. I had the Unabridged, and I was looking around in the back end, among the pictures. But it's a very old edition."

"Why, my friend, they wouldn't have a *picture* of it in even the latest e— My dear sir, I beg your pardon, I mean no harm in the world, but you do not look as—as—intelligent as I had expected you would. No harm—I mean no harm at all."

"Oh, don't mention it! It has often been said, and by people who would not flatter me, that I am quite remarkable in that way. Yes—yes; they always speak of it with pleasure."

"I can easily imagine it. But about this interview. You know it is the custom, now, to interview any man who has become famous."

"Indeed, I had not heard of it before. It must be very interesting. What do you do it with?"

"Ah, well—well—well—it *ought* to be done with a club in some cases. But usually the interviewer asks questions and the interviewed answers them. It is all the rage now. Will you let me ask you certain questions to bring out the salient points of your public and private history?"

"Oh, with pleasure—with pleasure. I have a very bad memory, but I hope you will not mind that. That is to say, it is an irregular memory—very irregular. Sometimes it goes in a gallop, and then again it will be as much as a week passing a given point. This is a great grief to me."

"Oh, it is no matter, so you will try to do the best you can."

"I will. I will put my whole mind on it."

"Thanks. Are you ready to begin?"

"Ready."

Q. How old are you?

A. Nineteen, in June.

Q. Indeed, I would have taken you to be thirty-five or -six. Where were you born?

A. In Missouri.

Q. When did you begin to write?

A. In 1836.

Q. Why, how could that be, if you are only nineteen now?

A. I don't know. It does seem curious, somehow.

---

salient (SAY lee unt) important; remarkable

Q. It does, indeed. Whom do you consider the most remarkable man you ever met?

A. Aaron Burr.[3]

Q. But you never could have met Aaron Burr, if you are only nineteen years—

A. Now, if you know more about me than I do, what do you ask me for?

Q. Well, it was only a suggestion; nothing more. How did you happen to meet Burr?

A. Well, I happened to be at his funeral one day, and he asked me to make less noise, and—

Q. But, good heavens! If you were at his funeral, he must have been dead, and if he was dead how could he care whether you made a noise or not?

A. I don't know. He was always a particular kind of man that way.

Q. Still, I don't understand it at all. You say he spoke to you, and that he was dead.

A. I didn't say he was dead.

Q. But wasn't he dead?

A. Well, some said he was, some said he wasn't.

Q. What did you think?

A. Oh, it was none of my business! It wasn't any of my funeral.

Q. Did you—However, we can never get this matter straight. Let me ask about something else. What was the date of your birth?

A. Monday. October 31, 1693.

Q. What! Impossible! That would make you a hundred and eighty years old. How do you account for that?

A. I don't account for it at all.

Q. But you said at first you were only nineteen, and now you make yourself out to be one hundred and eighty. It is an awful discrepancy.

A. Why, have you noticed that? (Shaking hands.) Many a time it has seemed to me like a discrepancy, but somehow I couldn't make up my mind. How quick you notice a thing!

Q. Thank you for the compliment, as far as it goes. Had you, or have you, any brothers or sisters?

A. Eh! I—I—I think so—yes—but I don't remember.

Q. Well, that is the most extraordinary statement I ever heard!

A. Why, what makes you think that?

Q. How could I think otherwise? Why, look here! Who is this a picture of on the wall? Isn't that a brother of yours?

A. Oh, yes, yes, yes! Now you remind me of it; that *was* a brother of mine, That's William—*Bill* we called him. Poor old Bill!

Q. Why? Is he dead, then?

A. Ah! Well, I suppose so. We never could tell. There was a great mystery about it.

Q. That is sad, very sad. He disappeared, then?

A. Well, yes, in a sort of general way. We buried him.

---

discrepancy (dih SKREP un see) difference; variation

[3]**Aaron Burr:** U.S. Vice President 1801–1805, died in 1836, the year after Twain was born.

Enrichment

Point out to students that Mark Twain's response to the interviewer is a put-on. By maintaining this pose, Twain exasperates the reporter. Thus Mark Twain creates an absurd and comic scenario.

Literary Focus: *Exposition*

Ask students to point out some of the obvious absurdities in Twain's replies, such as his claim to have met Aaron Burr. Ask: Does this approach fit your idea of exposition? Explain.

Critical Thinking: *Infer*

Ask students to infer why Twain reacts as he does to the reporter. Ask them to point out clues in the story that suggest why Twain would not simply give factual answers to the reporter's questions.

Literary Focus: *Character*

Ask students to describe the character of Twain and that of the reporter. Ask: Why does each character act as he does in this interview?

Critical Thinking: *Evaluate*

Ask students to evaluate each of Twain's stories in terms of his definition of what is funny as well as their own definitions. Ask: Do you find the "comic" story more amusing than the "humorous" one? Explain.

Reading Focus: *Compare and Contrast*

Ask students to compare and contrast the two stories Twain has told. Ask: Which one did you find funnier? Why?

Q. *Buried* him! *Buried* him, without knowing whether he was dead or not?

A. Oh, no! Not that. He was dead enough.

Q. Well, I confess that I can't understand this. If you buried him, and you knew he was dead—

A. No! no! We only thought he was.

Q. Oh, I see! He came to life again?

A. I bet he didn't.

Q. Well, I never heard anything like this. *Somebody* was dead, *Somebody* was buried. Now, where was the mystery?

A. Ah! That's just it! That's it exactly. You see, we were twins—defunct and I—and we got mixed in the bathtub when we were only two weeks old, and one of us was drowned. But we didn't know which. Some think it was Bill. Some think it was me.

Q. Well, that *is* remarkable. What do *you* think?

A. Goodness knows! I would give whole worlds to know. This solemn, this awful mystery has cast a gloom over my whole life. But I will tell you a secret now, which I never have revealed to any creature before. One of us had a peculiar mark—a large mole on the back of his left hand; that was *me. That child was the one that was drowned!*

Q. Very well, then, I don't see that there is any mystery about it, after all.

A. You don't? Well, *I* do. Anyway, I don't see how they could ever have been such a blundering lot as to go and bury the wrong child. But, 'sh!—don't mention it where the family can hear of it. Heaven knows they have heartbreaking troubles enough without adding this.

Q. Well, I believe I have got material enough for the present, and I am very much obliged to you for the pains you have taken. But I was a good deal interested in that account of Aaron Burr's funeral. Would you mind telling me what it was that made you think Burr was such a remarkable man?

A. Oh! It was a mere trifle! Not one man in fifty would have noticed it at all. When the sermon was over, and the procession all ready to start for the cemetery, and the body all arranged nice in the hearse, he said he wanted to take a last look at the scenery, and so he *got up and rode with the driver.*

Then the young man reverently withdrew. He was very pleasant company, and I was sorry to see him go.

---

defunct (dih FUNGKT) dead person
hearse (HURS) carriage for taking the dead to the grave

Mini Quiz

Write the following questions on the board or overhead projector and call on students to fill in the blanks. Discuss the answers with the class.

1. Twain mentions three kinds of stories: ________, ________, and ________.
2. The humorous story depends on the ________ in which it is told.
3. Twain says that telling a humorous story is an ________ that began in ________.
4. "The Wounded Soldier" is an example of a ________ story.
5. "An Encounter With an Interviewer" is an example of a ________ story.

Answers

1. humorous; witty; comic
2. manner
3. art; America
4. comic
5. humorous

Author Biography

Mark Twain (1835–1910)

"The difference between the right word and the almost right word," wrote Mark Twain, "is the difference between lightning and the lightning bug." Finding that *just-right* word was Mark Twain's specialty.

America's favorite humorist was born Samuel Langhorne Clemens in 1835. He grew up in Hannibal, Missouri, on the west bank of the Mississippi River. His father died when he was 12, and "Sam'l" quit school to go to work for a printer. That was the first of his four careers. In the late 1850s he became a steamboat pilot, and in the 1860s he turned to newspaper work. Sketches and stories written for newspapers soon made him known across the country.

While working on his famous book *The Adventures of Tom Sawyer*, he often wrote fifty pages a day. After that book, he went on to write such classics as *Life on the Mississippi* and *The Adventures of Huckleberry Finn*.

Twain had many friends and was a concerned family man. He traveled often to many parts of the world. He made, lost, and then remade a fortune in business. But the shock of his wife's death in 1904 left him a troubled man, and his last years were not happy ones. His birth in 1835 had coincided with the appearance of Halley's comet. Knowing that the comet's next visit was due in 1910, Twain told his friends that he would "go out with it," too.

Twain was right about his death. This self-educated genius, this "Lincoln of our literature," died peacefully on the night of April 21, 1910.

More About the Author

During the course of his life, Mark Twain became involved in several money-making ventures. Unfortunately, most of them failed. After one particularly disastrous investment, in a type of printing machine that did not work, Twain was left penniless. In order to make some money, he went on a worldwide lecture tour. Mark loved to talk and to tell humorous stories. Many people said that his speaking style was much like that of President Lincoln. For this reason, he has been called "the Lincoln of literature."

Ask the students if they have ever read any of Twain's famous books about Tom Sawyer and Huckleberry Finn. How relevant do they think these stories are to today's world?

Additional Works

By Mark Twain

The 1,000,000 Bank-Note and Other New Stories. New York: Oxford, 1996.

The Adventures of Tom Sawyer. New York: Viking, 1987. This book is based on Twain's childhood in Hannibal, Missouri.

The Adventures of Huckleberry Finn. New York: Penguin, 2000. Generally considered Twain's greatest work, the book is a sequel to *Tom Sawyer*.

Review the Selection

UNDERSTAND THE SELECTION

Recall

1. What three types of stories does Mark Twain talk about?
2. Which of these is most difficult?
3. What country does he say is associated with this most difficult type?

Infer

4. Whom does Mark Twain respect more, a storyteller or a story writer?
5. How does he feel about comic stories?
6. How does Twain feel about America as compared to other countries?
7. Why does Twain say that he is sorry to see the young man go?

Apply

8. Do you agree that this kind of story is more difficult to tell and therefore superior to the other kinds? Why?
9. How does Twain use pauses in "An Encounter with an Interviewer"?
10. What type of story is "An Encounter with an Interviewer"? Explain.

Respond to Literature

Do you think writers today are more concerned with storytelling than they were in Twain's time? Why?

WRITE ABOUT THE SELECTION

As an example of humorous story telling, Mark Twain writes about an interview he once had with a newspaper reporter. During the interview, Twain deliberately tried to confuse the interviewer by contradicting himself and making statements that were absurd or that made no sense.

Put yourself in the interviewer's position. Would you have realized what Twain was doing, or would you have thought he was crazy? How would you have written up the answers in a newspaper article?

Prewriting When conducting an interview, note taking is very important. Assume you are the reporter in the story. Reread the interview and jot down notes from Twain's answers as you go along. Be sure to include some direct quotes. When you are finished, organize your notes in outline form, using dots or "bullets" in front of main ideas, and dashes for details that relate to each main idea.

Writing On the basis of your notes, write a newspaper article reporting the results of your interview. Also include your perception of Twain and his responses. Decide on a particular tone to use in the article. State, at the end, what tone you have used.

Revising Rewrite the article to the extent necessary to change the tone. Specify at the end what the new tone is.

Proofreading Check for proper use of quotation marks and capitalization.

UNDERSTAND THE SELECTION

Answers

1. humorous, comic, witty
2. humorous
3. America
4. Sample answer: Twain respects storytellers because they use the humorous form. He makes sarcastic remarks about those who write stories.
5. Answers will vary but should suggest that he hates them or that they depress him.
6. Sample answer: He likes America much better. He associates America with humorous stories, which he likes, and European countries with comic and witty stories, which he dislikes.
7. Sample answer: He is being humorous here. He actually does not like the interviewer but has enjoyed confusing him.
8. Answers will vary. Responses should refer to Twain's reasons.
9. Sample answer: Twain, the author, uses pauses to draw the story out. Twain, the character, uses pauses to confuse the interviewer.
10. Humorous: it's longer, it rambles; there's no punch line; and the manner of telling it can make a big difference.

Respond to Literature

Discuss the changes in humorous entertainment that have come about from television and movies—for example, situation comedies ("sitcoms") on TV or comic movies.

Does the class think that Mark Twain would be successful today as a stand-up comedian telling humorous stories?

WRITE ABOUT THE SELECTION

Prewriting

Divide the class into pairs for role-playing purposes. One member of each pair will be Twain, the other the interviewer. Have them, pair by pair, act out the interview for the class, using the text of Twain's story as the basis. Allow the Twain-player to ad lib as he or she sees fit. The interviewer will have to take notes as Twain responds to the questions. Then have students reverse roles so that each partner has an opportunity to take notes.

Writing

Have students work on this section individually. Go around the class, giving help to any student who is having difficulty. To suggest possible ideas, ask students what a newspaper article contains. Remind them that they must include answers to the questions *who*, *what*, *where*, *when*, and *why*.

Revising

Make this a cooperative group activity. Have students work in groups to revise their paragraphs.

Proofreading

Select one or two other students' interviews as models for proofreading. Put the interviews on the overhead projector and have the class suggest improvements.

THINK ABOUT EXPOSITION

Defining, comparing and contrasting, classifying, and analyzing are techniques used in expository writing. **Exposition** is the form of discourse used to explain or inform. Expository works often begin with a **thesis statement**, a statement of what the author intends to explain in the work. Expository essays usually have a beginning, a middle, and an end.

1. Does Twain make a thesis statement? If so, what is it?
2. Which of the techniques of exposition do you see in Twain's essay? Support your ideas with examples.
3. What form of discourse other than exposition does Twain use?
4. For what purpose does he use this other form of discourse?
5. Does Twain's essay have a recognizable beginning, middle, and end?

Reading Focus

Compare and Contrast Look at Twain's comparison and contrast of the three types of stories: comic, witty, and humorous. According to Twain, how are these three types of stories similar? How are they different?

DEVELOP YOUR VOCABULARY

A dictionary gives not only the correct spelling and definition of a word, but also shows how the word is divided into syllables. Consult a dictionary to review the meaning of the following words from the story. Also, rewrite each word in syllable form. Then identify the five words that contain four or more syllables. Show that you understand the meaning of these five words by using each of them in a short paragraph with a humorous tone.

1. pathetic
2. divert
3. indifferent
4. slur
5. renounce
6. sustained
7. carcass
8. perplexity
9. tedious
10. incongruity
11. absurdity
12. recurring
13. dapper
14. salient
15. discrepancy
16. defunct
17. hearse

THINK ABOUT EXPOSITION

Answers

1. Yes; he says he knows how a story should be told and implies that that is what he will tell in his essay.
2. Answers may vary. However, all four types can be found. Classification: He notes three kinds of stories. Comparison and Contrast: He discusses likenesses and differences between humorous stories and comic and witty stories. Analysis: He takes "The Wounded Soldier" apart and shows how it works. Definition: He demonstrates the four bases of the American art.
3. narration
4. for the examples
5. It has a beginning and a middle; the second example serves also as the ending.

DEVELOP YOUR VOCABULARY

Answers

(Asterisks indicate words of four or more syllables.)

1. pa • the • tic
2. di • vert
3. in • diff • er • ent*
4. slur
5. re • nounce
6. sus • tained
7. car • cass
8. per • plex • i • ty*
9. te • di • ous
10. in • con • gru • i • ty*
11. ab • surd • i • ty*
12. re • cur • ing
13. dap • per
14. sa • li • ent
15. dis • crep • an • cy*
16. de • funct
17. hearse

Divide the class into groups for the purpose of writing the short humorous paragraphs.

ESL Activity

Discuss with students the differences in humor; comic wit; absurdity; incongruity; entertainment; funny, silly, jokes; punch lines; surprise endings; irony; etc. Have groups discuss humor in various cultures and come up with some differences in their own cultures.

Reading Focus

Sample Answer

The three types of stories are similar in that each has a point. They differ in that the humorous story depends for its effect on the manner of telling, whereas the comic and witty stories depend on the matter. The humorous story can be longer than the witty or comic story.

SELECTION OVERVIEW

SELECTION OBJECTIVES

After completing this selection, students should be able to

- understand the importance of setting to a story
- describe the time and place of a setting
- evaluate the dominance of time versus place in a setting
- write a new ending to a story, based on setting changes
- use a dictionary to determine word origins
- predict outcomes

Lesson Resources

To Build a Fire

- Selection Synopsis, Teacher's Edition, p. T241g
- Comprehension and Vocabulary Workbook, pp. 57–58
- Language Enrichment Workbook, pp. 43–44
- Teacher's Resources
  Reinforcement, p. R29
  Test, pp. T57–T58

More About Setting

Many times setting is employed as the dominant literary element in a work of fiction, so as to describe local environment, customs, and mannerisms of a specific region. In such instances, place becomes the more important feature, although the time period could well affect the story also.

Ask the students to think of a story that they are familiar with (other than those in this unit), in which the place of a setting is the crucial element. Have them write down a description of the place and the reasons why it is so important to the story.

More About the Literary Period

The period of the late 1800s was one of expansion, both in the United States and Canada. This expansion was not only technological and economic, but geographic as well. For example, the states of Idaho, Montana, North Dakota, South Dakota, Utah, Washington, and Wyoming were admitted to the Union between 1889 and 1896. Also, the Yukon became an established territory of Canada on June 13, 1898.

Discuss with the class whether they would have liked to participate in the Gold Rush and what they think it would have been like, given the weather conditions.

Cooperative Group Activity

Divide the class into pairs for the Writing Connection activity. Have each pair discuss experiences they have had recently that they might write about. Have them describe the setting—time and place—to each other. Then ask each student to decide which possible topic to write about. Allow time in class for students to write their descriptions.

Learn About

READING FOCUS

Predict Outcomes To predict means to make an educated guess about what will happen next. When you read a story, you can use details, foreshadowing, and various clues to predict the story's outcome or ending. As you read "To Build a Fire," think about the importance of the title. Pay attention to the role of the fire in the story, to the man's character, and to the dog's concerns. Try to use these clues to predict the outcome of the story.

SETTING

Setting refers to where and when a story takes place, as well as to the general background of the action. Authors often describe the setting in detail. The more important the place of the action is to the plot, the more important it is for the author to describe it.

The location of a story may be very specific—a particular room in a particular house, a dungeon in a castle, or a shack in the woods. Behind the specific location there is always some general location—mountains, the desert, the seashore, a region, a city, or a country. The time of a story may specify day or night, a season of the year, or an historical era. Sometimes the location is the more important element in the setting; at other times, the time period is dominant.

As you read the story, ask yourself:

1. How important is the setting to this story?
2. Is time or place the more important element in the story?

WRITING CONNECTION

Think back to an enjoyable experience you have had recently. In four or five lines, describe the setting—time and place—of this experience.

To Build a Fire

ADAPTED

by Jack London

Day had broken cold and gray, exceedingly cold and gray, when the man turned aside from the main Yukon trail and climbed the high earth-bank. Ahead of him, a dim and little-traveled trail led eastward through the fat spruce timberland. It was a steep bank, and he paused for breath at the top, excusing the act to himself by looking at his watch. It was nine o'clock. There was no sun nor hint of sun, though there was not a cloud in the sky. It was a clear day, and yet there seemed to be a subtle gloom over the face of things that made the day dark, and that was due to the absence of sun. This fact did not worry the man. He was used to the lack of sun. It had been days since he had seen the sun, and he knew that a few more days must pass before that cheerful orb would just peep above the hills and dip immediately from view.

The man flung a look back along the way he had come. The Yukon River lay a mile wide and hidden under three feet of ice. On top of this ice were as many feet of snow. It was all pure white, rolling in gentle undulations where the piles of ice had formed. North and south, as far as his eye could see, it was unbroken white, except for a small dark line that curved and twisted out of sight. This dark hairline was the trail—the main trail that led south five hundred miles to the Chilcoot Pass, Dyea, and salt water, and that led north seventy miles to Dawson, and still on to the north to St. Michael, on Bering Sea, a thousand miles and half a thousand more.

But all this—the mysterious, far-reaching hairline trail, the absence of sun, the tremendous cold, and the strangeness of it all—made no impression on the man.

---

subtle (SUT ul) faint and mysterious
orb (AWRB) round object
undulation (un juh LAY shun) wavy form or outline
hairline (HAIR lyn) very thin line

Teaching Plan

INTRODUCE

Motivation

Use a map or a globe to show the location of the Yukon in relation to the western United States and Alaska. Show pictures of the Gold Rush and the Yukon Territory in the 1890s. Discuss things such as temperature levels, wind strength, and amount of snowfall in that area during the winter, using sources such as an encyclopedia or the *National Geographic* magazine. Relate the information to the importance of setting to this story.

Purpose-Setting Question

What would be the motivation for someone to set out alone, on foot, to travel such a relatively long distance in such cold?

READ

Literary Focus: *Setting*

Have students describe the setting after they have read the story's opening paragraph. Ask them questions about time of day, season, weather, temperature, what the area looks like, and so on. Have students keep this time and place in mind as they continue reading.

Reading Focus: *Predict Outcomes*

Have students read the title and try to predict what role a fire might play in the story. Encourage students to look for other clues in the story and try to predict the outcome as they read.

CLOSE

Have students complete Review the Selection on pages 314–315.

Develop Vocabulary Skills

Many of the vocabulary words are root words to which suffixes have been added. Write these on the board. Have volunteers isolate the root words and guess the meaning of the longer words, based on the root words. Familiarize students with the other vocabulary words in the story. Have students use each word in an original sentence, orally.

ESL Activity

Discuss with the class how settings (Canadian-Alaskan frontier) and time (Gold Rush days) affects the story's course and actions of its character. Other factors in the result include such things as fate, religion, and economic status of the characters. Have groups discuss what a change in setting to another locale would do to the story. To move it to the native country of the students, what could be done to adapt the story?

Reading Focus: *Predict Outcomes*

Ask students to predict the effect the man's lack of imagination may have on him. As students read further, point out that he is alone (except for the dog) in a bitterly cold place.

Critical Thinking: *Analyze*

Ask the students to question the main character's purpose for being in this setting. (Their answer should be tied in with the Gold Rush.)

It was not because he was long used to it. He was a newcomer in the land, a *chechaquo*. This was his first winter. The trouble with him was that he was without imagination. He was quick and alert in the things of life, but only in the things, and not in their meanings. Fifty degrees below zero meant eighty-odd degrees of frost. Such fact impressed him as being cold and uncomfortable, and that was all. It did not lead him to meditate about his frailty as a creature of temperature. Neither did he think about the weakness of all people, able only to live within certain narrow limits of heat and cold. From there on it did not lead him to thoughts of immortality and man's place in the universe. Fifty degrees below zero stood for a bit of frost that hurt and that must be guarded against by the use of mittens, earflaps, warm boots, and thick socks. Fifty degrees below zero was to him just exactly fifty degrees below zero. That there should be anything more to it than that was a thought that never entered his head.

As he turned to go on, he spat speculatively. There was a sharp little explosion that startled him. He spat again. And again, in the air, before it could fall to the snow, the spittle popped. He knew that at fifty below spittle exploded on the snow, but this spittle had popped in the air. Undoubtedly it was colder than fifty below. How much colder he did not know. But the temperature did not matter. He was bound for the old claim on the left fork of Henderson Creek, where the men were already. They had come over mountains from the Indian Creek country, while he had come the other way. He had wanted to take a look at the possibilities of getting out logs in the spring from the islands in the Yukon. He would be in camp by six o'clock. That was a bit after dark, it was true, but the men would be there, a fire would be going, and a hot supper would be ready. As for lunch, he pressed his hand against the bundle under his jacket. It was also under his shirt, wrapped up in a handkerchief and lying against the naked skin. It was the only way to keep the biscuits from freezing. He smiled to himself as he thought of those biscuits, each cut open and sopped in bacon grease, and each enclosing a generous slice of fried bacon.

He plunged in among the big spruce trees. The trail was faint. A foot of snow had fallen since the last sled had passed, and he was glad he was without a sled, traveling light. In fact, he carried nothing but the lunch wrapped in the handkerchief. He was surprised, however, at the cold. It certainly was cold, he told himself. He rubbed his numb nose and cheekbones with his mittened hand. He was a warm-whiskered man, but the hair on his face

---

meditate (MED uh tayt) think deeply; ponder
immortality (im aw TAL ih tee) unending life
speculatively (SPEK yuh tiv lee) thinking about possibilities
spittle (SPIT ul) saliva; what one spits

did not protect the high cheekbones and the eager nose from the frosty air.

At the man's heels trotted a dog, a big husky. It was almost a wolf-dog, gray-coated and without any real difference from its brother, the wild wolf. The animal was saddened by the tremendous cold. It knew that this was no time for traveling. Its instinct told it a truer tale than was told to the man by the man's judgment. In truth, it was not just colder than fifty below zero. It was colder than sixty below, than seventy below. It was seventy-five below zero. Since the freezing point is thirty-two above zero, it meant that there were one hundred and seven degrees of frost. The dog did not know anything about thermometers. Possibly in its brain there was no sharp awareness of a condition of very cold such as was in the man's brain. But the beast had its instinct. It experienced a vague apprehension about the cold that made it sneak along at the man's heels. It questioned every movement of the man, as if expecting him to go into camp or to find shelter somewhere and build a fire. The dog had learned fire. Now it wanted fire, or else to dig under the snow and curl up away from the air.

The frozen moisture of the dog's breath had settled on its fur in a fine powder of frost, and its muzzle and eyelashes were whitened by its snowy breath. The man's red beard and mustache were likewise frosted, but more solidly. The ice on his face increased with every warm, moist breath he took. Also, the man was chewing tobacco, and the ice made his lips so stiff that he was unable to clear his chin when he spat out the juice. The result was that an icy brown beard was increasing its length on his chin. If he fell down it would shatter like glass into small pieces. But he did not mind it, really. It was the penalty all tobacco-chewers paid in that country. And he had been out before in two cold snaps. They had not been so cold as this, he knew. But by the thermometer at Sixty Mile he knew they had been fifty below and fifty-five.

He held on through the woods for several miles, crossed a wide flat place, and dropped down a bank to the frozen bed of a small stream. This was Henderson Creek, and he knew he was ten miles from the fork. He looked at his watch. It was ten o'clock. He was making four miles an hour, and he calculated that he would arrive at the fork at half-past twelve. He decided to celebrate that event by eating his lunch there.

The dog dropped behind again at his heels, with its tail drooping, as the man swung along the creekbed. The furrow of the old sled trail was plainly visible, but a dozen inches of snow covered the marks of the last runners. In a month no man had come up or down that silent creek. The man held steadily on. He was not much given to thinking, and just then he

Literary Focus: *Setting*
Here London gives his readers the exact temperature. Ask: What effect does this new detail about the setting have on you? How would you feel about traveling alone on foot in such weather?

---

apprehension (ap rih HEN shun) worry; fear of a coming event
muzzle (MUZ ul) mouth and nose of an animal

Trapper in the Wilderness, Sydney Laurence. The Shelburne Museum, Shelburne, VT

had nothing to think about. He knew that he would eat lunch at the fork and that at six o'clock he would be in camp with the men. There was nobody to talk to; and, had there been, speech would have been impossible because of the ice on his mouth. So he continued monotonously to chew tobacco and to increase the length of his brown beard.

Once in a while the thought reiterated itself that it was very cold and that he had never experienced such cold. As he walked along he rubbed his cheekbones and nose with the back of his mittened hand. He did this automatically, now and again changing hands. But rub as he would, the instant he stopped his cheekbones went numb, and the following instant the end of his nose went numb. He was sure to frost his cheeks; he knew that. He wished he had made a nose strap of the sort Bud wore in cold snaps. Such

reiterate (ree IT uh rayt) repeat tiresomely

Reading Focus: *Predict Outcomes*

Remind students of the title of the story. Ask: What do you think may happen to make the man stop and build a fire?

Viewing Fine Art

Sydney Laurence (1865–1940) was an American Realist painter who studied at the National Academy in Paris and led an extremely adventurous life. The scene in this painting is in the wilderness of Alaska, which he traveled to in 1906 to search for gold. While in Alaska, he took a four-month trip with a dog sled and a team of dogs. He also built a cabin there with material from his dog sled. He returned to his cabin many times and painted frequently while there. Supposedly, as a young boy, he ran away to sea, became the first mate of a ship, and saved the captain's life when the ship capsized. As an adult, he was a war correspondent and traveled extensively to China and Africa. American Realists were known for their landscapes and their concern with detail and accuracy. Ask: How does this painting help you to visualize the setting of the story?

a strap passed across the cheeks, as well, and saved them. But it didn't matter much, after all. What were frosted cheeks? A bit painful, that was all. They were never serious.

Empty as the man's mind was of thoughts, he was keenly observant. He noticed the changes in the creek, the curves and bends and logjams, and always he sharply noted where he placed his feet. Once, coming around a bend, he shied quickly, like a startled horse, curved away from the place where he had been walking, and took several steps back along the trail. The creek, he knew, was frozen clear to the bottom—but he knew also that there were springs that bubbled out from the hillsides and ran along under the snow and on top of the ice of the creek. He knew that the coldest snaps never froze these springs, and he knew likewise their danger. They were traps. They hid pools of water under the snow that might be three inches deep, or three feet. Sometimes a skin of ice half an inch thick covered them, and in turn was covered by the snow. So when one broke through he kept on breaking through, sometimes wetting himself to the waist.

That was why he had shied in such panic. He had felt the softness under his feet and heard the crack of a snow-hidden ice-skin. And to get his feet wet in such a temperature meant trouble and danger. At the very least it meant delay, for he would be forced to stop and build a fire. Then he would have to bare his feet while he dried his socks and boots. He stood and studied the creek bed and its banks and decided that the flow of water seemed to come from the right. He reflected awhile, rubbing his nose and cheeks. Then he moved to the left, walking carefully and testing each step. Once clear of the danger, he took a fresh chew of tobacco and swung along at his four-mile gait.

In the next two hours he came upon several similar traps. Usually the snow above the hidden pools had a sunken, solid appearance that advertised the danger. Once again, however, he had a close call, and another time, suspecting danger, he made the dog go on in front. The dog did not want to go. It hung back until the man shoved it forward, and then it went quickly across the white, unbroken surface. Suddenly it broke through, floundered to one side, and got away to safety. It had wet its feet and legs, and almost immediately the water turned to ice. It made quick efforts to lick the ice off its legs, then dropped down in the snow and began to bite out the ice that had formed between the toes. This was a matter of instinct. To permit the ice to remain would mean sore feet. It did not know this. It just obeyed the mysterious orders that came from somewhere deep inside it. But the man knew, having made a judgment on the subject, and he removed the mitten from his right hand

---

shied (SHYD) drew back
reflect (rih FLEKT) think
gait (GAYT) manner of walking or running

Literary Focus: *Theme*

Again the author reiterates that the man's mind is empty of all thoughts. This becomes a recurrent theme. Ask: As the story develops, does this theme foreshadow the character's actions?

Critical Thinking: *Evaluate*

Have students evaluate the man's persistence in traveling in light of the dog's uneasiness. Ask: Has the man taken enough precautions to protect himself?

Literary Focus:
Setting

Ask students to discuss the weather conditions and the man's mental state at this point. Ask: What might happen to a man who is forgetful in a dangerous setting like the one he is in?

and helped tear out the ice pieces. He did not uncover his fingers more than a minute, and was astonished at the swift numbness that hit them. It certainly was cold. He pulled on the mitten hastily, and beat the hand savagely across his chest.

At twelve o'clock the day was at its brightest. Yet the sun was too far south on its winter journey to appear in the sky. The man walked under a clear sky at noon and cast no shadow. At half-past twelve, to the minute, he arrived at the fork of the creek. He was pleased at the speed he had made. If he kept it up, he would certainly be with the men by six. He unbuttoned his jacket and shirt and drew forth his lunch. The action took no more than a quarter of a minute, yet in that brief time the numbness laid hold of the exposed fingers. He did not put the mitten on right away, but instead struck the fingers a dozen sharp smashes against his leg. Then he sat down on a snow-covered log to eat. The sting that followed the striking of his fingers against his leg stopped so quickly that he was startled. He had had no chance to take a bite of biscuit. He struck the fingers again and returned them to the mitten, baring the other hand for the purpose of eating. He tried to take a mouthful, but the ice on his face prevented it. He had forgotten to build a fire and thaw out. He chuckled at his foolishness, and as he chuckled he noted the numbness creeping into the bare fingers. Also, he noted that the stinging which had first come to his toes when he sat down was already passing away. He wondered whether the toes were warm or numb. He moved them inside the boots and decided that they were numb.

He pulled the mitten on hurriedly and stood up. He was a bit frightened. He stamped up and down until the stinging returned into the feet. It certainly was cold, was his thought. That man from Sulphur Creek had spoken the truth when telling how cold it sometimes got in this country. And he had laughed at him at the time! That showed one must not be too sure of things. There was no mistake about it—it was cold. He walked up and down, stamping his feet and swinging his arms, until he felt the returning warmth. Then he got out matches and proceeded to make a fire. From the bushes where high water of the spring had left a supply of twigs, he got his firewood. Working carefully from a small beginning, he soon had a roaring fire. He thawed the ice from his face, and in the protection of the fire he ate his biscuits. For the moment the cold was defeated. The dog took satisfaction in the fire, too, stretching out close enough for warmth and far enough away to escape being burned.

When the man had finished, he filled his pipe and took his comfortable time over a smoke. Then he pulled on his mittens. He settled the ear-flaps of his cap about his ears, and took the creek trail up the left fork. The dog was disappointed. It didn't want to leave the fire. This man did not know cold. Possibly all the man's ancestors had known nothing of cold, of real cold, of cold one hundred and seven degrees below the freezing point. But the dog knew. All its ancestors had known, and the knowledge had come down to it.

It knew that it was not good to walk abroad in such fearful cold. This was the time to lie snug in a hole in the snow and wait for better weather. There was no great intimacy between the dog and the man. The one was the slave of the other. The only caresses it ever received were the caresses of the whip. So the dog made no effort to communicate its apprehension to the man. It was not concerned about the safety of the man. It was for its own sake that it wanted to stay by the fire. But the man whistled, and spoke to it with the sound of a whip, and the dog swung in at the man's heel and followed after.

The man took a chew of tobacco and proceeded to start a new amber beard. Also, his moist breath quickly covered with white his mustache and eyebrows. There did not seem to be so many dangerous springs on the left fork of the Henderson, and for half an hour the man saw no signs of any. And then it happened. At a place where there were no signs, where the snow was soft and unbroken, the man broke through. It was not deep. He wet himself halfway to the knees before he floundered out.

He was angry, and cursed his luck aloud. He had hoped to get into camp with the men at six o'clock. This would delay him an hour, for he would have to build a fire and dry out his socks and boots. This was imperative at that low temperature—he knew that much. He turned aside to the bank, which he climbed. On top, tangled in the bushes around the trunks of several small spruce trees, was some dry firewood. There were sticks and twigs, but also larger branches and fine, dry, last-year's grasses. He threw down several large pieces on top of the snow. This served for a foundation and prevented the young flame from drowning itself in the snow it otherwise would melt. The flame he got by touching a match to a small piece of birch bark that he took from his pocket. This burned even more easily than paper. Placing it on the foundation, he fed the young flame with dry grass and with the tiniest dry twigs. He worked slowly and carefully, keenly aware of his danger. Gradually, as the flame grew stronger, he increased the size of the twigs with which he fed it. He squatted in the snow, pulling the twigs out from the brush and feeding them directly to the flame. He knew there must be no failure. When it is seventy-five below zero, a man must not fail in his first attempt to build a fire—that is, if his feet are wet. If his feet are dry, and he fails, things are different. He can run along the trail for half a mile and regain his circulation. But the circulation of wet and freezing feet cannot be regained by running when it is seventy-five below. No matter how fast he runs, the wet feet will freeze harder and harder.

All this the man knew. The old-timer on Sulphur Creek had told him about it

---

intimacy (IN tuh muh see) very close friendship, even love
imperative (im PER uh tiv) really necessary; essential

Critical Thinking: *Evaluate*

Ask: Which character knows better about weather conditions, the dog or the man? Explain your answers, using evidence from the story.

Reading Focus: *Predict Outcomes*

Ask students to predict what will happen, now that the man has had the accident he was afraid of. Remind them to consider not only the temperature but also what they know of the man's character.

Critical Thinking: *Evaluate*

Ask: How would you evaluate the man's response to the old-timer's warning? Think about times you have ignored the advice of more experienced people and what the results were.

in the fall, and now he was glad for the advice. Already all feeling had gone out of his feet. To build the fire he had been forced to remove his mittens, and the fingers had quickly gone numb. His walking speed of four miles an hour had kept his heart pumping blood to the surface of his body and to all the extremities. But the instant he stopped, the action of the pump slowed down. The cold of space had settled down on the unprotected tip of the planet. And he, being on that unprotected tip, received the full force of the blow. The blood of his body drew back before it. The blood was alive, like the dog, and like the dog it wanted to hide away and cover itself up from the fearful cold. So long as he walked four miles an hour, he pumped that blood to the surface. But now it ebbed away and sank down into the recesses of his body. The extremities were the first to feel its absence. His wet feet froze faster, and his bare fingers numbed faster, though they had not yet begun to freeze. Nose and cheeks were already freezing, while the skin of all his body chilled as it lost its blood.

But he was safe. Toes and nose and cheeks would be only touched by the frost, for the fire was now beginning to burn with strength. He was feeding it with twigs the size of his finger. In another minute he would be able to feed it with branches the size of his wrist. Then he could remove his wet boots and socks. While they dried, he could keep his naked feet warm by the fire, rubbing them at first, of course, with snow. The fire was a success. He was safe. He remembered the advice of the old-timer on Sulphur Creek, and smiled. The old-timer had been very serious in laying down the law that no man must travel alone in the Klondike[1] after fifty below. Well, here he was. He had had the accident. He was alone, and he had saved himself. Those old-timers were rather too fearful, some of them, he thought. All a man had to do was to keep his head, and he was all right. Any man who was a man could travel alone. But it was surprising, the speed with which his cheeks and nose were freezing. And he had not thought his fingers could go lifeless in so short a time. Lifeless they were, for he could hardly make them move together to grip a twig, and they seemed far from his body and from him. When he touched a twig, he had to look and see whether or not he had hold of it. The wires were pretty well down between him and his finger-ends.

All of which counted for little. There was the fire, snapping and growing and promising life with every dancing flame. He started to untie his boots. They were coated with ice. The thick German socks were like sheaths of iron halfway to the knees. The boot laces were like rods of

---

extremities (ik STREM ih teez) hands and feet; parts farthest away
ebb (EB) flow back or away
recess (rih SES) interior place
sheath (SHEETH) protective covering
[1]**The Klondike:** an area in northern Canada, next to Alaska.

steel all twisted and knotted as by some conflagration. For a moment he tugged with his numb fingers. Then, realizing the folly of his effort, he drew his knife.

But before he could cut the strings, it happened. It was his own fault or, rather, his mistake. He should not have built the fire under the spruce tree. He should have built it in the open. But it had been easier to pull the twigs from the brush and drop them directly on the fire. The tree under which he had done this carried a lot of snow on its branches. No wind had blown for weeks, and each branch was fully loaded. Now he had a growing fire, and he had been moving about under the tree. The heat and motion were not much, so far as he was concerned, but they were enough to bring about the disaster. High up in the tree one branch dumped its load of snow. This fell on the boughs beneath, making them dump their snow. This continued, spreading out over the whole tree. It grew like an avalanche, and it descended without warning upon the man and the fire. The fire was blotted out! Where it had burned was a mantle of fresh and disordered snow.

The man was shocked. It was as though he had just heard his own sentence of death. For a moment he sat and stared at the spot where the fire had been. Then he grew very calm. Perhaps the old-timer on Sulphur Creek was right. If he had only had a companion he would have been in no danger now. The other person could have built the fire. Well, it was up to him to build the fire over again, and this second time there must be no failure. Even if he succeeded, he would most likely lose some toes. His feet must be badly frozen by now, and there would be some time before the second fire was ready.

Such were his thoughts, but he did not sit and think them. He was busy all the time they were passing through his mind. He made a new foundation for a fire, this time in the open, where no treacherous tree could blot it out. Next, he gathered dry grasses and tiny twigs. He could not bring his fingers together to pull them out, but he was able to gather them by the handful. In this way he got many rotten twigs and bits of green moss that he didn't want, but it was the best he could do. He worked methodically, even collecting an armful of the larger branches to be used later when the fire gathered strength. And all the while the dog sat and watched him. There was a certain wishful look in its eyes, for it looked upon him to build a fire, and the fire was slow in coming.

When all was ready, the man reached in his pocket for a second piece of birch bark. He knew the bark was there. Though he could not feel it with his fingers, he could hear its crisp sound as he reached for it. Try as he would, be could not get hold of it. And all the time, in his mind, was the knowledge that each instant his feet were freezing. This

---

conflagration (kon fluh GRAY shun) huge fire
mantle (MAN tul) something that covers
methodically (muh THOD ik lee) orderly; systematically

Reading Focus: *Predict Outcomes*

After the snow fell from the tree, extinguishing the fire, the author says of the man: "It was as though he had just heard his own sentence of death." Ask the class what will happen to the man after this.

Literary Focus: *Setting*

Point out that the man has ignored certain aspects of the setting, such as the temperature and the nearness of the spruce tree, with its dangerous load of snow. As students read on to the end of the story, have them discuss how London links character and setting to bring about the ending of his story.

Critical Thinking: *Evaluate*

As students read these two pages, have them evaluate the steps the man takes to save himself from freezing. Ask: What you would do in such a situation?

Literary Focus: *Setting*

Read the sentence "He put his whole soul into getting the matches" aloud. Ask: How does this statement make the setting especially clear?

thought might have put him in a panic, but he fought against it and kept calm. He pulled on his mittens with his teeth. He swung his arms back and forth, beating his hands with all his might against his sides. He did this sitting down, and he stood up to do it. All the while the dog sat in the snow, its tail curled around warmly over its feet, and its sharp wolfears pricked forward eagerly as it watched the man. And the man, as he beat his feet and waved his arms and hands, felt a great wave of envy. He knew that the dog was warm and safe in its natural covering.

After a time he was aware of the first far-away signals of feeling in his beaten fingers. The faint tingle grew stronger till it grew into a stinging ache that was excruciating, but the man greeted it with satisfaction. He stripped the mitten from his right hand and brought forth the birch bark. The bare fingers were quickly going numb again. Next he pulled out his bunch of matches. But the tremendous cold had already driven the life out of his fingers. In his effort to separate one match from the others, the whole bunch fell in the snow. He tried to pick it out of the snow, but failed, The dead fingers could neither touch nor grasp. He was very careful. He drove the thought of his freezing feet, and nose, and cheeks, out of his mind. He put his whole soul into getting the matches. He watched his hands, using the sense of vision in place of that of touch. When he saw his fingers on each side of the bunch, he closed them. That is, he tried to close them, for the wires were down, and the fingers did not obey. He pulled the mitten on the right hand, and beat it fiercely against his knee. Then, with both mittened hands, he scooped the bunch of matches, along with much snow, into his lap. Yet he was no better off.

After some trouble he managed to get the bunch between the heels of his mittened hands. In this way he carried it to his mouth. The ice snapped and broke when by a tremendous effort he opened his mouth. He drew the lower jaw in, and curled the upper lip out of the way. Then he scraped the bunch with his upper teeth in order to separate a match, He succeeded in getting one, which he dropped on his lap. He was no better off. He could not pick it up. Then he devised a way. He picked it up in his teeth and scratched it on his leg. Twenty times he scratched before he succeeded in lighting it. As it flamed he held it with his teeth to the birch bark. But the burning fumes went up his nostrils and into his lungs, causing him to cough spasmodically. The match fell into the snow and went out.

The old-timer on Sulphur Creek was right, he thought in the sad moment that followed. After fifty below, a man should travel with a partner. He beat his hands, but failed to regain any feeling. Suddenly he bared both hands, removing the mittens with his teeth. He caught the whole bunch of matches between the heels of his hands. His arm muscles

---

excruciating (ik SKROO shee ayt ing) very painful
spasmodically (spaz MOD ik lee) in sudden bursts

were not frozen, and he could press the hand-heels tightly against the matches. Then he scratched the bunch along his leg. It roared into flame, seventy matches at once! There was no wind to blow them out. He kept his head to one side to escape the fumes and held the blazing bunch to the birch bark. As he so held it, he became aware of feeling in his hand. His flesh was burning. He could smell it. Deep down below the surface he could feel it. The feeling turned into pain that grew and grew. And still he endured it, holding the flame of the matches clumsily to the bark that would not light easily because his own burning hands were in the way.

At last, when he could endure no more, he jerked his hands apart. The blazing matches fell sizzling into the snow, but the birch bark was on fire. He began laying dry grasses and the tiniest twigs on the flame. He could not pick and choose, for he had to lift the fuel between the heels of his hands. Small pieces of rotten wood and green moss clung to the twigs, and he bit these off as well as he could with his teeth. He cherished the flame carefully and awkwardly.

It meant life to him. The lack of blood on the surface of his body now made him begin to shiver, and he grew more awkward. A large piece of green moss fell directly on the little fire. He tried to poke it out with his fingers, but his shivering body made him poke too far, and he disturbed the center of the little fire. The burning grasses and tiny twigs separated

and scattered. He tried to poke them together again, but in spite of the effort, his shivering got away with him, and the twigs were hopelessly scattered. Each twig gave a puff of smoke and went out. The fire had failed. He had failed. As he looked apathetically about him, his eyes chanced on the dog. The animal was sitting across the ruins of the fire from him, in the snow, slightly lifting one front foot and then the other.

The sight of the dog put a wild idea into his head. He remembered the tale of

---

apathetically (ap uh THET ik lee) with little or no feeling

Reading Focus: *Predict Outcomes*

Ask students to predict whether this fire will remain lit or whether it too will go out. Have students point to details in the story that support their predictions.

Critical Thinking: *Analyze*

Out of desperation, the man considers killing the dog, so that he could "bury his hands in the warm body until the numbness went out of them. Then he could build another fire." Ask: What do you think of this idea? Do you think it is justifiable in this situation?

Literary Focus: *Theme*

Point out the phrase "It was a matter of life and death, with the chances against him." Ask: Was this sentence true at the beginning of the story, given the cold temperature and the man's decision to travel alone in it? Use this sentence to formulate a statement of the story's overall theme.

Reading Focus: *Predict Outcomes*

Have students predict whether the man will reach the camp. Have them give reasons for their predictions.

the man, caught in a blizzard, who killed a steer and crawled inside the dead body, and so was saved. He would kill the dog now. He would bury his hands in the warm body until the numbness went out of them. Then he could build another fire. He spoke to the dog, calling it to him. But in his voice was a strange note of fear that frightened the animal, who had never known the man to speak in such a way before. Something was the matter. The dog felt the danger. It knew not what danger, but somewhere, somehow, in its brain there rose a distrust of the man. It flattened its ears down at the sound of the man's voice. It would not come to the man. He got on his hands and knees and crawled toward the dog. This unusual posture again made the dog suspicious, and the animal sidled away.

The man sat up in the snow for a moment and struggled for calmness. Then he pulled on his mittens, by using his teeth, and got to his feet. He glanced down, in order to make sure that he was really standing up, for the absence of feeling in his feet left him separated from the earth. His standing up in itself started to drive the webs of suspicion from the dog's mind. And when he spoke an order with the sound of a whip in his voice, the dog obeyed once again and came to him. As it came within reaching distance, the man lost his control. His arms flashed out to the dog. Then he discovered that his hands could not grasp, that there was neither bend nor feeling in the fingers. He had forgotten for the moment that they were frozen and that they were freezing more and more. All this happened quickly. But before the animal could get away, he had its body in his arms. He sat down in the snow, and in this way held the dog, while it snarled and whined and struggled.

But it was all he could do, hold its body in his arms and sit there. He realized that he could not kill the dog. There was no way to do it. With his helpless hands he could neither draw nor hold his knife. Nor could he choke the animal. He let it go, and it plunged wildly away, with tail between legs, and still snarling. It stopped forty feet away and looked at him curiously, with ears sharply forward. The man looked down at his hands in order to locate them, and found them hanging on the ends of his arms. It struck him as curious that one should have to use his eyes in order to find out where his hands were. He began swinging his arms back and forth, beating the mittened hands against his sides. He did this for five minutes, very hard. His heart pumped enough blood up to the surface to put a stop to his shivering. But no feeling returned to the hands. They hung like weights on the ends of his arms.

A certain dull fear of death came to him now. This fear quickly became poignant as he realized that it was no longer a matter of just freezing his fingers and toes. It was no longer a matter of losing his hands and feet. No, it was a matter of life and death, with the chances against him. This threw

---

sidle (SYD ul) move sideways; edge along slyly
poignant (POIN yunt) sharp; keenly felt

him into a panic, and he turned and ran up the creek bed along the old, dim trail. The dog joined in behind and kept up with him. He ran blindly, without any real purpose in mind, filled with a fear such as he had never known in his life. Slowly, as he plowed and floundered through the snow, he began to see things again. The banks of the creek. The old logjams. The sky. The running made him feel better. He did not shiver. Maybe, if he ran on, his feet would thaw out. Anyway, if he ran far enough, he would reach camp and the men. Without doubt he would lose some fingers and toes and some of his face. But the men would take care of him, and save the rest of him when he got there. And at the same time there was another thought in his mind that said he would never get to the camp. It was too many miles away. The freezing had too great a start on him, and he would soon be stiff and dead. This second thought he tried to keep in the background. Sometimes it pushed itself forward and demanded to be heard, but he forced it back and tried to think of other things.

It struck him as curious that he could run at all. His feet were so frozen that he could not feel them when they struck the earth and took the weight of his body. He seemed to himself to glide along above the surface. He seemed to have no connection with the earth. Somewhere he had once seen a winged Mercury,[2] and he wondered if Mercury felt as he felt when skimming over the earth.

His idea of running until he reached camp had one thing wrong with it: he lacked the endurance. Several times he stumbled, and finally he fell. When he tried to rise, he failed. He must sit and rest, he decided. The next time he would try only to walk and keep on going. As he sat and regained his breath, he noted that he was feeling quite warm and comfortable. He was not shivering, and it even seemed that a warm glow had come to his chest. And yet, when he touched his nose or cheeks, there was no feeling. Running would not thaw them out. Nor would it thaw out his hands and feet. Then the thought came to him that the frozen portions of his body must be growing larger. He tried to keep this thought down, to forget it, to think of something else. He was aware of the panicky feeling that it caused, and he was afraid of the panic. But the thought came again, and kept on coming, until he had a vision of his body totally frozen. This was too much. He made another wild run along the trail. Once he slowed down to a walk, but the thought of the freezing made him run again. And all the time the dog ran with him, at his heels. When he fell down a second time, it curled its tail over its front feet and sat facing him, curiously eager. The warmth and safety of the animal angered him, and he cursed it till it flattened down its ears appeasingly. This

appeasingly (uh PEEZ ing lee) in a manner to please or obey

[2]**Mercury:** the ancient Roman god who served as messenger of the gods and is often pictured with wings on his heels

Critical Thinking: *Analyze*

Ask: Do you think the outcome of the story to this point might have been different if the relationship between the dog and man had been a loving one? Why do you think as you do?

Reading Focus: *Predict Outcomes*

Ask students to predict the ending of the story at this point. Ask: What do you think will happen to the man? Why? Ask students to point to specific details in the story that foreshadow the ending they predict.

Literary Focus: *Conflict*

One element common to both character and plot is the notion of conflict. Conflict does not have to be between two characters. What type of conflict is found in the story?

time the shivering came more quickly upon the man. He was losing in his battle with the frost. It was creeping into his body from all sides. The thought of it drove him on, but he ran no more than a hundred feet, when he staggered and fell. It was his last panic. When he had recovered his breath and control, he sat up and thought about meeting death with dignity. However, the idea did not come to him in such terms. His idea of it was that he had been making a fool of himself. He had been running around like a chicken with its head cut off—such was the simile that occurred to him. Well, he was bound to freeze anyway, and he might as well take it with dignity. With this new-found peace of mind came the first drowsiness. A good idea, he thought, to sleep off to death. It was like taking an anesthetic. Freezing was not so bad as people thought. There were lots worse ways to die.

He pictured the men finding his body next day. Suddenly he found himself with them, coming along the trail and looking for himself. And, still with them, he came around a turn in the trail and found himself lying in the snow. He did not belong with himself anymore, for even then he was out of himself, standing with the men and looking at himself in the snow. It certainly was cold, was his thought. When he got back to the States he could tell the folks what real cold was. He drifted on from this to a vision of the old-timer on Sulphur Creek. He could see him quite clearly, warm and comfortable, and smoking a pipe.

"You were right, old hoss. You were right," the man mumbled to the old-timer of Sulphur Creek.

Then the man drowsed off into what seemed to him the most comfortable and satisfying sleep he had ever known. The dog sat facing him and waiting. The brief day drew to a close in a long, slow twilight. There were no signs of a fire to be made, and besides, never in the dog's experience had it known a man to sit like that in the snow and make no fire. As the twilight drew on, its need for the fire mastered it. It lifted its feet up and down. It whined softly, then flattened its ears down, expecting to be scolded by the man. But the man remained silent. Later, the dog whined loudly. And still later it crept close to the man and caught the scent of death. This made the animal bristle and back away. A little longer it delayed, howling under the stars that leaped and danced and shone brightly in the cold sky. Then it turned and trotted up the trail in the direction of the camp it knew, where were the other men, men with food and fire.

---

anesthetic (an is THET ik) substance that lessens pain

Mini Quiz

Write the following questions on the board or overhead projector and call on students to fill in the blanks. Discuss the answers with the class.

1. The setting of the story is the ________.
2. The man knew that the temperature had to be more than ________ degrees below zero.
3. The man was accompanied by a ________.
4. When the man tried to eat, the ________ on his face prevented it.
5. When the man called to the dog to kill him, the dog sensed ________ and would not come.

Answers

1. Yukon
2. fifty
3. husky (dog)
4. ice
5. danger

AUTHOR BIOGRAPHY

Jack London (1876–1916)

Jack London was born in San Francisco. He grew up there and in nearby Oakland. At fifteen he was a high-school dropout, a married man, and known as the "Prince of the Oyster Pirates." He worked in a canning factory and tramped around the United States. At seventeen he sailed the Pacific as a crew member on a sealing ship. At twenty-one he joined the gold rush in the Yukon, a region of northern Canada and the setting of "To Build a Fire." Like the characters in his stories and novels, London seemed always in motion.

However, London found the time to read a good deal. When he was about twenty, he decided to be a writer, and he thought a college education would be necessary. For three months he studied for hours every day to pass the entrance exams for the University of California. He succeeded—but then found college too slow for him. For the second time in his life he became a dropout.

London wrote about 150 short stories, selling his first one in 1899. In 1903, *The Call of the Wild*, a novel about a dog, made him famous. From then until his death, he averaged four books a year. He also served as a war reporter in the Far East and Mexico. He was the first American author to earn more than a million dollars from his writing, but he spent it quickly and finally suffered financial disaster while still a young man.

The brief biography you have just read gives several details about London's life before the age of twenty-one. In your opinion, in what way might these experiences have enriched his fiction?

MORE ABOUT THE AUTHOR

Although Jack London lived only 40 years, those years were filled with adventure. He tended to go overboard over a project; eventually, however, he lost interest. When he went to the Yukon in 1896, after the Gold Rush had begun, he packed eight thousand pounds of supplies, including many books. London returned home about a year later without ever having mined an ounce of gold. However, the Yukon formed the setting for many of his stories, including "To Build a Fire."

Later in his life, London sailed from California to Hawaii. He built a castle-like house in California that burned down before it was finished. By 1913, many considered London the highest paid, best-known writer in the world. However, his ventures cost him his fortune.

Additional Works

BY JACK LONDON

You may wish to suggest these works by Jack London for additional reading:

The Call of the Wild. New York: Dover, 1991. This recent edition of the 1903 masterpiece tells the story of the heroism of the dog Buck.

White Fang. New York: Dover, 1991. Another of London's popular novels tells the adventures and hardships of a dog-wolf.

Five Great Short Stories. New York: Dover, 1992. These short stories relate more exciting adventures.

UNDERSTAND THE SELECTION

Answers

1. in the Yukon
2. biscuits and fried bacon
3. to a camp where the other men were waiting for him
4. Sample answer: He is unable to imagine that something might go wrong and so is unprepared.
5. Sample answer: The dog knows things from instinct and experience. Since the man is doing things that the dog knows are wrong, the dog assumes it is because he has no similar instinct or experience.
6. They were necessary to start a fire. Birch bark burns very easily.
7. There was no bond of affection or loyalty between them. The man was insensitive toward the dog. The dog was obedient from training, not love.
8. Answers will vary but should include some of the following: how surprising the cold is, the dog's instinct, the dog's apprehension, the old-timer's warning.
9. He would not have traveled alone in weather that cold and probably would have gotten to the camp safely.
10. Sample answers: Yes, because one would be safe with reasonable care. No, because the cold was too intense.

Respond to Literature

For what reasons other than looking for gold might the man have gone to the Yukon? Have students list jobs that might have been needed in the gold fields. (Sample answers: cook, clothing supplier, salesman for digging tools, assayer, banker, food suppliers, construction workers, dog sledders) Ask students which job they might have liked best if they had gone to the gold fields. Remind them that very few prospectors actually found gold.

Review the Selection

UNDERSTAND THE SELECTION

Recall

1. Where is "To Build a Fire" set?
2. What does the man eat for lunch?
3. Where is the man heading?

Infer

4. London writes that "he was without imagination." Why is this a problem?
5. Why does the dog think that "the man's ancestors had known nothing of cold"?
6. Explain the importance of the pieces of birch bark in the man's pocket.
7. Describe the relationship between the man and the dog.

Apply

8. How does London foreshadow the tragedy at the end of the story?
9. Predict what might have happened if the man had taken the advice of the old-timer from Sulphur Creek.
10. Would you have attempted what this man did? Why or why not?

Respond to Literature

Do you think the Gold Rush was the reason the man placed himself in this setting? Explain.

WRITE ABOUT THE SELECTION

Were you surprised at the ending or did you expect it? There are several other possible endings that the story could have if some of the elements of the story were changed: for example, the setting. What might have happened if there were no underground springs hidden beneath the snow? What might have happened if the temperature were only 50 degrees below zero, instead of 75 below? A change in the setting could affect the outcome of the story.

Think of some changes to the setting and some different endings to the story that may have resulted from these changes. Then write a new ending.

Prewriting Think about these changes and list them. Think about different endings that would result from these changes.

Writing Write a new ending to the story. Explain how the changes in the setting have contributed to this.

Revising Make one more change to the setting that reinforces the new ending. Does the new ending reflect the changes you have made in the setting?

Proofreading Read your revised paragraph over. Make sure that all your sentences are complete. Remember, complete sentences include a subject (a person, place, or thing) and a predicate that shows an action or a state of being.

WRITE ABOUT THE SELECTION

Prewriting

Separate the class into groups. Have each group discuss setting changes and results, and then write them down in a cause-and-effect outline.

Writing

Have students work on this section individually. Go around the class, giving help to any student who is having difficulty. To aid students, ask them questions about possible results from various circumstances.

Revising

Make this a cooperative group activity. Have students work in small groups to revise their story endings.

Proofreading

Select one or two of the students' story endings as models for proofreading.

THINK ABOUT SETTING

Setting deals primarily with place and time. It also includes everything in the environment, such as objects that are important to the story.

1. How important is the setting to this story?
2. Which aspect of setting—time or place—is dominant in this story? Explain why.
3. Pick three sentences from the story that describe the different elements of nature that contribute to the setting. Explain their significance to the plot.
4. Do you consider the dog to be part of the setting or a character? Why?
5. The author does not give the man's name or any details of his background. Does this work? Explain.

> ***Reading Focus***
>
> **Predict Outcomes** As you read "To Build a Fire," you made predictions about the outcome of the story. Did you predict the outcome of the story correctly? If so, identify the clues in the story that helped you make your prediction. If not, identify the clues that suggested the ending you predicted.

DEVELOP YOUR VOCABULARY

The Inuit people of the far north, where "To Build a Fire" takes place, have contributed several words to English. *Inuit* is the preferred term for the people we used to call Eskimos. These people live near the Arctic Circle, where it is very cold. They have learned over generations how to keep warm in such a frozen climate.

Look in a dictionary that has word histories for the meaning of each of the following words. Then use each word in a sentence of your own. Tell how each object named might or might not have helped save the life of the main character of "To Build a Fire."

1. anorak
2. husky
3. igloo
4. malamute
5. mukluk
6. umiak

THINK ABOUT SETTING

Answers

1. It is the primary focus.
2. Place is dominant; the story revolves around it.
3. Answers will vary, but should focus on such things as temperature, snow, ice, water, and fire. These are all central to the plot of the story.
4. Sample answer: The dog is a character. He is important because of the contrast between his response to the setting and the man's response to it.
5. Answers will vary. Students should recognize that such details are not important to the story. The man symbolizes humanity; he is not important as an individual.

DEVELOP YOUR VOCABULARY

Answers

1. anorak—a heavy jacket with a hood, worn in the cold North
2. husky—a hardy dog used for pulling sleds in the Arctic
3. igloo—an Eskimo (Inuit) house or hut, usually dome-shaped and built of blocks of packed snow
4. malamute—any of a breed of large, strong dogs developed as a sled dog by the Alaskan Eskimo (Inuit)
5. mukluk—an Eskimo (Inuit) boot made of sealskin or reindeer skin
6. umiak—a large open boat made of skins stretched over a wooden frame

Sentences will vary.

> **ESL Activity**
>
> Go over the Inuit words listed above. They are words dealing with getting shelter from the cold weather. What are words from other cultures which serve the same function—and have we taken words from them in the same way?

Reading Focus

Sample Answer

Students who predicted the ending correctly should point to such hints as the man's lack of imagination, the dog's concerns, the fact that the man doesn't know how cold it is, the danger of the underground springs, and the man's forgetfulness of crucial facts about the setting. Students who predicted a different ending should point to the man's caution about the underground springs, his common sense about walking at a certain pace, his skill in building the first fire, and the nearness of the camp. Students should realize that London does an outstanding job of foreshadowing the man's death.

Selection Overview

SELECTION OBJECTIVES

After completing this selection, students should be able to:

- understand the concept of rhyme
- write two lines that rhyme
- identify imagery in a poem
- write a stanza of a poem
- use strong, vivid adjectives to describe
- support an opinion

Lesson Resources

America the Beautiful
- Selection Synopsis, Teacher's Edition, p. T241g
- Comprehension and Vocabulary Workbook, pp. 59–60
- Language Enrichment Workbook, p. 45
- Teacher's Resources
  Reinforcement, p. R30
  Test, pp. T59–T60

More About Rhyme

Rhymes can be classified by the number of syllables that sound alike and by the position of the accented syllables. **Masculine rhymes** are based on the last syllable of each word. One syllable words thus also fall into this category. *Fun* and *run* are masculine, or singular, rhymes, as are polysyllabic words, such as *intent* and *repent*. **Feminine rhymes** contain two consecutive syllables that rhyme, the second being unaccented. For example, *walking* and *talking*. This is also known as **double rhyme**. **Triple rhyme** denotes the same sound in three consecutive syllables, the first of which is accented—for example, *scenery* and *machinery*.

Ask the student to review the three Whitman poems and identify the types of rhymes in each.

More About the Literary Period

Late in this period, poetry became more available to the general public with the founding of *Poetry, A Magazine of Verse* in 1912. Until this time most poetry by lesser-known poets was published in magazines and newspapers. Poets who had been experimenting with new forms, ideas, and subject matter attained a much wider audience. Modern poets owe a great debt to poets of the 19th century.

Learn About

Rhyme

Rhyme is the recurrence of the same or similar sounds at regular intervals in one or more lines of poetry. The sameness in rhyme is based on the sounds of the vowel and the consonant that follows it. For example, *fit* and *sit* have the same vowel sound followed by the same consonant sound. Only the consonant before the vowel is different. This kind of rhyme is called **perfect rhyme**.

The rhyme must also involve the accented syllable. For example, two words ending in *-ing* do not necessarily rhyme because the *-ing* syllable does not have the emphasis, or accent. Thus, *saying* and *playing* rhyme, but *looking* and *seeing* do not.

Most rhymes are **end rhymes**; that is, the words with the same sounds are at the end of the lines. However, poems may also have **internal rhymes**—two rhyming words within the same line.

As you read the selection, ask yourself:

1. Which are the rhyming words in the poem?
2. Does the author use end rhymes, internal rhymes, or both?

Reading Focus

Support an Opinion It is important to support an opinion. Giving reasons for an opinion makes the opinion more convincing. As you read this poem, look for how the writer supports her opinion that America is beautiful.

WRITING CONNECTION

Write two lines that have end rhymes. Write two lines that have internal rhymes.

ESL Activity

Have groups develop lists of adjectives that could be used to describe the newer states of the union—Hawaii, Alaska, Arizona, and New Mexico.

Cooperative Group Activity

For the Writing Connection activity, divide the class into groups of three. Have each group write down pairs of rhyming words they might use in their two-line verses. Have students discuss ideas they might write about in their pairs. Then have students work individually on their poems.

Mount Katahdin, Maine, 1853, Frederick Edwin Church. The Granger Collection

AMERICA THE BEAUTIFUL

by Katherine Lee Bates

O beautiful for spacious skies,
For amber waves of grain,
For purple mountain majesties
Above the fruited plain!

TEACHING PLAN

INTRODUCE

Motivation

Show pictures of slides of some scenes pictured in the poem, such as the Rocky Mountains or the Grand Canyon.

Play a recording of the song. It would be interesting to contrast two versions—a traditional rendition, preferably one containing all four stanzas, and then the somewhat unorthodox arrangement by Ray Charles.

Purpose-Setting Question

When you hear the word *America* what do you picture in your mind?

READ

Literary Focus: *Rhyme*

Point out that "skies" and "majesties" look as though they should rhyme, since they end with the same combinations of letters. However, they are not pronounced alike; they do not rhyme. Explain that because English is a difficult language in which to write rhymes, poets often use this kind of visual rhyme. Have students watch for another example as they continue reading the poem.

Reading Focus: *Support an Opinion*

The title of the poem suggests what the writer thinks about America. Ask: What is the writer's opinion about America? What details in the poem support that opinion?

CLOSE

Have students complete Review the Selection on pages 320–321.

Develop Vocabulary Skills

Review the definitions of the two footnoted vocabulary words. Then have the students select three adjectives or participles from the poem and explain how each is used to enhance the imagery.

About the Author

"America the Beautiful" was first published on the Fourth of July, 1895, in a magazine called *The Congregationalist.* Bates is said to have gotten the inspiration for the words to this poem from the top of Pike's Peak in Colorado and sights of some exhibitions at the Chicago World's Fair in 1893.

Viewing Fine Art

Frederick Church (1826–1900) was a major figure in American landscape painting. His landscapes are noted for their brilliant light, mountainous wilds, and many-colored skies. Ask: What is your impression of this landscape? How do you think Church wanted you to feel?

Viewing Fine Art

Emil Nolde (1867–1956) was a German expressionist painter whose deep colors and emotionally powerful canvases help define the style. Nolde used vigorous brushwork and a free sense of design in paintings that were almost religious in their exaltation and intensity. Here he depicts a wheat field in typically dramatic fashion. Compare Nolde's painting to wheat fields painted by George Inness (page 202) and Grant Wood (page 479). Ask: What part of "America the Beautiful" could this painting illustrate?

Literary Focus: *Imagery*

Ask the class for different examples of imagery found in the poem and what these images suggest to them. (For example, "amber waves of grain," "purple majesties," etc.)

Wheatfield Watercolor, Emil Nolde. Corbis Bettmann

5 America! America!
God shed His grace on thee
And crown thy good with brotherhood
From sea to shining sea!

O beautiful for pilgrim feet,
10 Whose stern, impassioned stress
A thoroughfare for freedom beat
Across the wilderness!
America! America!
God mend thine every flaw,
15 Confirm thy soul in self-control,
Thy liberty in law!

O beautiful for heroes proved
In liberating strife,
Who more than self their country loved,
20 And mercy more than life!
America! America!
May God thy gold refine,
Till all success be nobleness
And every gain divine!

25 O beautiful for patriot dream
That sees beyond the years
Thine alabaster cities gleam
Undimmed by human tears!
America! America!
30 God shed His grace on thee
And crown thy good with brotherhood
From sea to shining sea!

impassioned (im PASH und) determined; filled with passionate feeling
thoroughfare (THUR oh fair) passage; way through

Reading Focus: *Support an Opinion*

Ask: How does Bates support her claim that America is beautiful for its heroes?

Critical Thinking: *Evaluate*

Ask students to evaluate the speaker's attitude toward the United States. Ask: Do you think the poem accurately describes the U.S. and its history? If not, what do you think the poem should mention that it does not?

Enrichment

For several decades, there have been those who believe that "America the Beautiful" should be this country's national anthem. Ask the class to discuss their preference—the present anthem, "America the Beautiful," or some other song. (You may want to take a vote to determine the class's favorite.)

Mini Quiz

Write the following questions on the board or overhead projector and call on students to fill in the blanks. Discuss the answers with the class.

1. "O beautiful for ________ skies"
2. "O beautiful for ________ feet"
3. "O beautiful for heroes ________"
4. "O beautiful for ________ dream"
5. The words "________ ________" are repeated in each stanza, as is the word ________.

Answers

1. spacious
2. pilgrim
3. proved
4. patriot
5. America! America!; God

UNDERSTAND THE SELECTION

Answers

1. There are four stanzas.
2. Three colors are mentioned: amber, purple, and alabaster. Gold in not used as a color, but as the metal itself.
3. The second half of the first stanza is repeated in the second half of the last stanza.
4. Sample answer: "Fruited plain" could refer to the grain-producing plains of the Midwest or to other vegetable and fruit-growing areas of the country.
5. Answers will vary, but should refer in some way to obeying laws.
6. "From sea to shining sea" refers to the Atlantic and Pacific Oceans.
7. Answers will vary but should mention wars fought for freedom: specifically, the Revolutionary War and the Civil War.
8. Answers will vary. Responses should mention how people use it.
9. Sample answer: Stanzas are the paragraphs of poetry. They are distinctly defined segments of form and substance, as are paragraphs in prose.
10. Two rhyming schemes are used throughout the four stanzas: (a) end rhymes in the first and third lines, the second and fourth lines, and the sixth and eighth lines; (b) internal rhymes within the seventh line.

Respond to Literature

Write on the board or overhead transparency the specific examples of America today as they are suggested. Discuss these examples with the class. You could ask the students to transfer one or more of their mental pictures to paper by drawing a picture, as best they can. You may want to make the pictures more vivid, and the exercise more interesting, by providing some colored markers.

Review the Selection

UNDERSTAND THE SELECTION

Recall

1. How many stanzas are there all together in "America the Beautiful"?
2. What colors are mentioned?
3. Is any part of the poem repeated? If so, which part?

Infer

4. What does "fruited plain" mean?
5. To what do you think "Confirm thy soul in self-control" refers?
6. To what does the reference "from sea to shining sea" refer?
7. What is "liberating strife"?

Apply

8. Would you say that "America the Beautiful" is a poem or a song—or both? Explain.
9. Do you see any relationship between stanzas in poetry and paragraphs in prose? Explain.
10. What kind of rhyming scheme can you notice? Is more than one pattern used? Explain.

Respond to Literature

Does the imagery in this poem apply to America today in the same way as when Katherine Lee Bates wrote it? Explain.

WRITE ABOUT THE SELECTION

There are many great things in America to be seen and experienced. When you think about our country, what other images come to your mind? Write another stanza to "America the Beautiful."

Prewriting One good way to organize descriptive thoughts and details is the "cluster" method. Start by writing the name of your subject, in this case "America, " in the middle of a page and draw a circle around it. Next, think of at least four things in and about America. Write these down around the subject word; circle them and draw a line between each of these and "America." Finally, think of at least two descriptive terms for each of these things. Write these down around the word they describe; circle them and draw lines between each and the term being described. You will now have a cluster of at least eight adjectives connected to four nouns, connected to the subject.

Writing Using the nouns and adjectives from your cluster, write a description of America. Put this in the form of an additional stanza to "America the Beautiful."

Revising Enhance your imagery by adding one more adjective to each description you have used. Are your adjectives and details concrete? Do they appeal to the reader's senses?

Proofreading Make sure you have used commas to separate adjectives used in a series to describe the same noun.

WRITE ABOUT THE SELECTION

Prewriting

Since students are being told to organize their thoughts by using the "cluster" method, arrange them in clusters themselves. Each group can prepare its own cluster diagram. Then have them share their ideas with the class.

Writing

Have students work on this section individually. Go around the class, giving help to any student who is having difficulty. To suggest new images, refer students to the class discussion or ask questions to elicit new adjectives.

Revising

Make this a cooperative group activity. Have students work in small groups to revise their stanzas.

Proofreading

Select one or two of the students' stanzas as models for proofreading. Put the stanzas on the overhead projector and have the class suggest improvements.

THINK ABOUT RHYME

Rhyme adds greatly to the beauty of much poetry, but have you thought about why this is so? One reason is that rhyme has a musical quality; the repetition of sounds has an echo-like quality that is pleasing to the ear. Rhyme also has a rhythmic function; it is a kind of "time-beater" since the rhyming words note the end of a **verse**, or line of poetry. It also helps to delineate divisions of the poem.

1. Which words in the first four lines of each stanza rhyme?
2. What are rhymes of this kind called?
3. What end rhymes are there in the second four lines of each stanza?
4. Are there any other rhymes in the second four lines of each stanza? If so, what are they called?
5. Are there imperfect rhymes in the poem? If so, what are they?

READING FOCUS

Support an Opinion How did Katherine Lee Bates support her opinion that America is beautiful in these areas?

- its physical beauty
- its history in becoming a country
- its struggles

DEVELOP YOUR VOCABULARY

Adjectives are words that describe. They are used to limit, or modify, the meaning of nouns. In her poem, Bates uses strong, vivid adjectives to create images for the reader. Some of these are *spacious*, *amber*, *purple*, *fruited*, *impassioned*, *liberating*, and *alabaster*. Notice that her choices include not only adjectives but participles used as adjectives.

Read the following sentences. Then change the italicized weak adjective in each for a more vivid one. You can use two or more adjectives for the italicized one, if you wish.

1. An *awful* rain fell all day.
2. The doorbell made a *funny* noise.
3. I had a *great* time at the picnic.
4. The day of our hike was *nice*.
5. We moved the *old* bed up to the attic.

THINK ABOUT RHYME

Answers

1. the first and third; the second and fourth
2. end rhymes
3. The second and fourth lines rhyme.
4. There are rhyming words within the third line; internal rhymes.
5. Yes; skies-majesties, proved-loved

DEVELOP YOUR VOCABULARY

Sample Answers

1. driving, pounding, sleeting, pouring
2. strange, odd, peculiar, curious, bizarre
3. delightful, splendid, unforgettable, stupendous, superb
4. sunny, clear, bright, cloudless
5. antique, broken-down, time-worn, old-fashioned

READING FOCUS

Sample Answer

beauty: spacious skies, beautiful scenes of crops and mountains; history: pilgrims carrying on through hardships; struggles: heroes working for liberty with plans of peace

ESL Activity

Have students write a one-stanza poem describing a great thing to see or experience in their native countries or cultures. Have them read their poems aloud to the class.

Selection Overview

SELECTION OBJECTIVES

After completing these selections, students should be able to

- understand the concept of a rhyme scheme
- identify and notate a rhyme scheme
- write a stanza of a poem
- identify words that can be used as nouns and verbs and distinguish their usage
- recognize figures of speech

Lesson Resources

Poetry of Sarah Teasdale
- Selection Synopsis, Teacher's Edition, p. T241g
- Comprehension and Vocabulary Workbook, pp. 61–62
- Language Enrichment Workbook, pp. 47–48
- Teacher's Resources
  - Reinforcement, p. R31
  - Test, pp. T61–T62

More About Rhyme Scheme

One well-known rhyme scheme is the Spenserian. This nine-line pattern is: a-b-a-b-b-c-b-c-c. This shows that the nine lines are composed of three rhyming sounds. One sound (a) is rhymed in two words; another (c) in three; and the other (b) in four.

Have the class compare this rhyme scheme with the eight-line pattern of "America the Beautiful." What is the rhyme scheme and how does it differ from the Spenserian one? Does every line rhyme with another? Are there any imperfect end rhymes?

After each student has written down his or her own answers, have a volunteer write these on the board, calling on students at random and recording the consensus responses.

Learn About

RHYME SCHEME

Rhymes usually occur in the same places throughout a poem. This regularity is known as the **rhyme pattern** or **rhyme scheme**. You can detect a rhyme scheme by assigning letters to designate the words at the end of the lines. The same letter is used for words having the same sounds. Thus, a simple rhyme scheme would be *abcb*. This pattern shows that the words at the end of lines two and four rhyme, but that the words at the end of lines one and three do not.

There are many different kinds of rhyme schemes. They depend on the number of lines per stanza and on which lines rhyme. It is not necessary that every line rhyme with some other line.

As you read the poems by Teasdale, ask yourself:

1. Which are the rhyming words in each poem?
2. What is the rhyme scheme of each poem?

READING FOCUS

Recognize Figures of Speech A figure of speech is an imaginative statement rather than a statement of fact. Instead of saying "The sun was setting," a writer might say "The red sun was pasted in the sky like a wafer." The statement is not literally true; it is an imaginative way to make the reader see the sunset.

Look for figures of speech in Teasdale's poems. Examine the suggested meaning of the words in each figure of speech to help determine the picture the poet is trying to create.

WRITING CONNECTION

Think of a four-line stanza of a poem that you know. If you can't think of a poem, think of a song or nursery rhyme. Write it down. Then, using the form shown above, write the rhyme scheme.

About the Author

Sara Teasdale was a prolific poet. She wrote numerous poems, enough to fill six published volumes. Much of her poetry concerns the themes of hope, beauty, and love, in contrast to her own sad, lonely, and sickly life. She was married, but not to the man she really loved. She divorced, but her real love committed suicide. Her health began to fail, but some considered her a neurotic hypochondriac. Suffering from despair and disillusionment about love and life, Sara eventually took her own life, at age 48.

Cooperative Group Activity

Divide the class into pairs for the Writing Connection activity. Have each pair make a list of songs or nursery rhymes that they know. Let students help each other in writing the rhyme scheme of one or more items on the list. Have someone from each pair read the lines and the rhyme scheme. Ask the class to judge whether each rhyme scheme is correct.

BARTER

by Sara Teasdale

Life has loveliness to sell,
    All beautiful and splendid things,
Blue waves whitened on a cliff,
    Soaring fire that sways and sings,
5 And children's faces looking up
Holding wonder like a cup.

Life has loveliness to sell,
    Music like a curve of gold,
Scent of pine trees in the rain,
10 Eyes that love you, arms that hold,
And for your spirit's still delight,
Holy thoughts that star the night.

Spend all you have for loveliness,
    Buy it and never count the cost;
15 For one white singing hour of peace
    Count many a year of strife well lost,
And for a breath of ecstasy
Give all you have been, or could be.

---

barter (BAHRT ur) trade; exchanging one thing for another
soaring (SAWR ing) rising or gliding high into the air
wonder (WUN dur) feeling of surprise, admiration, awe, caused by something strange, unexpected, or incredible
star (STAHR) to mark or set with stars, as a decoration
strife (STRYF) troublesome conflict; quarreling
ecstasy (EK stuh see) a feeling of overpowering joy; great delight

TEACHING PLAN

INTRODUCE

Motivation

Get a copy of one or more of Sara Teasdale's books of poetry. Read a few selected poems to the class, other than the ones in this unit, and call upon a few students with expressive voices to read some others aloud. Pick pieces that are positive and optimistic in nature, reflecting the poet's love and appreciation of beauty and nature.

Purpose-Setting Question

Is it possible to discern a relationship between the theme of a poem and its rhyme scheme; that is, can a simple, basic rhyme scheme be used to reinforce or underline a simple, basic theme?

READ

Literary Focus: *Rhyme Scheme*

Make the students aware of the rhyme schemes in each poem. Challenge them to write out each poem's rhyme scheme. Students can compare and contrast the rhyme schemes of the four poems at the end.

Reading Focus: *Recognize Figures of Speech*

Help students recognize the opening line of the poem as a figure of speech. Ask: Can life literally "sell" anything? Explain that this kind of figure of speech is called personification. Have students watch for further figures of speech as they read the poems.

CLOSE

Have students complete Review the Selection on pages 328–329.

ESL Activity

Go over rhyme schemes of poems in this unit; blank verse for Whitman, rhyming patterns for "America the Beautiful," Teasdale's poems, and "Richard Cory." Review rhythm and rhyme.

Develop Vocabulary Skills

Familiarize students with the vocabulary words footnoted in the poems. Use each vocabulary word in an original sentence and ask for volunteers to give other original sentences orally.

Viewing Fine Art

Abstract painters have frequently painted various elements from nature, in this case Northern Lights. Abstract art is not representational. This painting by Sydney Lawrence is not intended to reproduce the experience a person would have looking at the actual Northern Lights, or at a photograph of them. An abstract painting concentrates on color, shape, form, and design. It comments on its subject on a philosophical rather than literal level, trying to reveal something about it that a person would not normally see for himself or herself. Ask: What does this painting have in common with the star in Teasdale's poem?

Literary Focus: *Symbolism*

Ask: What do you think the star symbolizes? Point out that it is a falling star, visible only for a moment. If any student has ever seen a star fall, have the student describe his or her feelings at that sight.

The Northern Lights, Sydney Laurence. Shelburne Museum, Shelburne, VT

THE FALLING STAR

by Sara Teasdale

I saw a star slide down the sky,
Blinding the north as it went by,
Too burning and too quick to hold,
Too lovely to be bought or sold,
Good only to make wishes on
And then forever to be gone.

THE LONG HILL

by Sara Teasdale

I must have passed the crest a while ago
  And now I am going down—
Strange to have crossed the crest and not to know,
  But the brambles were always catching the hem of my gown.

5 All the morning I thought how proud I should be
  To stand there straight as a queen,
Wrapped in the wind and the sun with the world under me—
  But the air was dull, there was little I could have seen.

It was nearly level along the beaten track
10 And the brambles caught in my gown—
But it's no use now to think of turning back,
  The rest of the way will be only going down.

Southwest Wind, Childe Hassam. Corbis Bettmann

crest (KREST) the top of anything; summit; ridge
brambles (BRAM bulz) prickly shrubs

Viewing Fine Art

Childe Hassam (1859–1935) has often been called "America's Monet" because his impressionistic paintings reminded critics of those of the great French artist. A native of Massachusetts, Hassam began his career as an illustrator. He discovered the world of impressionist painting on a trip to Paris. He adopted its style and techniques and had a successful career after returning to the United States. Ask: Do you think Teasdale might have found this scene familiar? Explain.

Reading Focus: *Recognize Figures of Speech*

Ask: What do you think the phrase "wrapped in the wind" means? Point out that a person cannot literally wrap himself or herself in air. Have students paraphrase the figure of speech and think about why Teasdale used it instead of a more literal expression such as "blown by the wind."

Critical Thinking: *Analyze*

Have students analyze the effect of the poem's uneven line length and rhythm. Have students speak the stanzas aloud and try to find the beat of the poem. Ask: Why do you think Teasdale chose to use an unsteady beat and such a variety of line length?

Reading Focus: *Recognize Figures of Speech*

Ask: What are your reactions to the figure of speech "bright April/Shakes out her rain-drenched hair."? Challenge students to write their own figures of speech about a rainy April day.

Literary Focus: *Rhyme Scheme*

Ask: What is the rhyme scheme of this poem? Why do you think Teasdale chose to rhyme lines 3 and 7? Consider the effect of the repetition of the word *hearted*.

Critical Thinking: *Generalize*

Ask students to generalize about these four poems. (They all deal with timeless notions: beauty, love, life, aging, death, etc.)

Comparing Selections

Ask: In what ways are the poems in this section alike? In what ways are they different? Consider all aspects of poetry in your answers. For example, does more than one poem express the same mood? Does more than one poem have the same rhyme scheme? to what effect?

I SHALL NOT CARE

by Sara Teasdale

When I am dead and over me bright April
    Shakes out her rain-drenched hair,
Tho' you should lean above me broken-hearted,
    I shall not care,

I shall have peace, as leafy trees are peaceful
    When rain bends down the bough,
And I shall be more silent and cold-hearted
    Than you are now.

A Summer Night, 1890, Winslow Homer. The Granger Collection

---

drenched (DRENCHT) soaked; wet all over
bough (BOU) a large branch of a tree

Mini Quiz

Write the following questions on the board or overhead projector and call on students to fill in the blanks. Discuss the answers with the class.

1. "________ has loveliness to ________."
2. "I saw a ________ slide down the sky."
3. "I must have passed the ________ a while ago."
4. "And I shall be more ________ and cold-hearted than you are now."
5. "Spend all you have for ________."

Answers

1. Life; sell
2. star
3. crest
4. silent
5. loveliness

Author Biography

Sara Teasdale (1884–1933)

Readers of the hopeful poems of Sara Teasdale are tempted to see her as the happiest of human beings. Such readers forget to separate the *speaker* in a poem from the *poet*. Her life was often a troubled one. As she herself put it in a poem called "The Long Hill," after one has achieved a certain height in life, "The rest of the way will be only going down."

Born in St. Louis, Missouri, Sara Teasdale won early success as a poet. She published her first poems as a girl and her first book before she was twenty-five. For years she was in and out of love with a well-known poet named Vachel Lindsay. But she could not bring herself to accept the second-place role of a famous man's wife in the America of the time. Finally, Lindsay married someone else, and Teasdale rushed into a bad marriage with a businessman named Filsinger. In 1929 she divorced Filsinger and turned again to Lindsay. But it was too late. Lindsay killed himself in 1931, leaving her a lonely, disappointed woman. In 1933 Teasdale, too, committed suicide.

These sad facts help to make the point, once again, that the speaker in a poem is not to be confused with the poet. We can safely say, however, that Sara Teasdale must have known moments of great beauty. Perhaps she valued these moments all the more because of the numerous disappointments and tragedies in her life.

How did Sara Teasdale's life differ from the kind of life suggested by many of her poems?

More About the Author

Sara Teasdale is considered one of the finest lyric poets of her time. Besides the several volumes of poetry, she also published an anthology of poetry for young people. As time went on, her poetry increasingly spoke of suffering and loss.

Additional Works
by Sara Teasdale

You may wish to suggest these works by Sara Teasdale for additional reading.

The Collected Poems. Buccaneer Books, 1996. A recent publication of her poems.

Helen of Troy and Other Poems. MesaView, 1999. A collection of Teasdale's poems.

UNDERSTAND THE SELECTION

Answers

1. loveliness
2. It is too lovely.
3. the crest of a hill
4. Answers will vary. Sample answer: "Barter." It speaks of the loveliness and beauty of life.
5. Sample answer: It could be, literally, a comet. Also, it could symbolize fleeting, unrealized hopes or dreams.
6. Sample answer: The hill could be the author's life. The crest is the high point of that life; it represents achievement, fulfillment, happiness, or simply age.
7. Sample answer: *You* could be a husband or other loved one who has not returned the speaker's love. It could also refer to fate, or life overall, which has not been kind.
8. Answers will vary, but should include any three of these: waves on a cliff; fire; children's faces; music; scent of pine trees in the rain; eyes; arms; thoughts; peace; breath of ecstasy. Experiences/reminiscences will vary.
9. Answers will vary. If positive: "too lovely," "good to make wishes on." If negative: "too burning . . . quick," "good only to make wishes on," "forever . . . gone."
10. Sample answer: old age and death

Respond to Literature

Discuss the nature of the topics of the poems. Have four volunteers list them on the board, appropriately, under each of the four poem titles. Then have the class consider these topics.

Review the Selection

UNDERSTAND THE SELECTION

Recall

1. Which word in each stanza summarizes the theme of "Barter"?
2. In "The Falling Star," why can't you buy or sell a falling star?
3. In "The Long Hill," what has the speaker "passed" and "crossed"?

Infer

4. Of these four poems, which is the most positive or optimistic? Why?
5. What could "The Falling Star" symbolize?
6. What do the "hill" and the "crest" represent in "The Long Hill"?
7. In "I Shall Not Care," explain who "you" might be.

Apply

8. Select three things described in "Barter." Of what experiences does each remind you?
9. Is the mood of "The Falling Star" positive or negative? Explain.
10. Predict what the speaker is heading toward at the end of "The Long Hill."

Respond to Literature

By reading Teasdale's poems, could you tell when they were written? Explain.

WRITE ABOUT THE SELECTION

The last line of "The Long Hill" speaks of "the rest of the way . . . only going down." What do you think "the rest of the way" refers to? What does "only going down" mean? Think about what the hill represents and the kind of journey the speaker is making. Consider what might happen to the speaker from this point onward, Add a fourth stanza to "The Long Hill."

Prewriting Write down different ideas about what lies ahead for the speaker. Think about what kinds of things might happen and how the speaker might react.

Writing Transform these ideas into a fourth stanza of the poem. Make the new stanza four lines long, and try to match the rhythm of the rest of the poem. Do not be concerned about rhyme at this stage. Try to continue the thought process set forth in the poem, and bring the plot to an ultimate conclusion.

Revising Keeping the same thought content, revise the new stanza to follow either the rhyme scheme that has been established or a new pattern. At least two of the lines should rhyme. Using the "a-b . . ." method, indicate at the end what rhyme scheme you have used.

Proofreading Make sure that at least two of the four lines end in "perfect" rhymes. Check that the rhyme scheme is accurate and that your stanza has the right sound by reading it aloud.

WRITE ABOUT THE SELECTION

Prewriting

Divide the class into groups of four. Have each group write down its ideas. Have students discuss the possibilities. Write down their ideas on the board or an overhead projector.

Writing

Have students work on this section individually. Go around the class, giving help to any student who is having difficulty. To suggest possible outcomes, refer students to the ideas on display. Emphasize that the stanza should contain an ultimate conclusion to the poem.

Revising

Make this a cooperative group activity. Reconvene the original groups of four and have students make suggestions to each other about how to make the poems rhyme.

Proofreading

Select one or two of the students' stanzas as models for proofreading. Put the stanzas on the overhead projector and have the class suggest improvements. Have them verify that at least two of the four lines are perfect rhymes. Extra credit or some sort of prize or special recognition could be given to any student that manages to rhyme all four lines, a-a-a-a or a-b-a-b.

THINK ABOUT RHYME SCHEME

Once a rhyme scheme has been established in the first stanza, it is usually followed in all subsequent stanzas. The pattern of the rhymes helps to give a certain form to each stanza and to the poem as a whole.

1. What is the rhyme scheme of "Barter"? What do you notice about the first and third lines of each stanza?
2. What is the rhyme scheme in "The Falling Star"?
3. What is the rhyme scheme of "The Long Hill"?
4. What is the rhyme scheme in "I Shall Not Care"? Does the poem contain internal rhymes as well as end rhymes?
5. Find three instances in these poems in which the rhyming words have different numbers of syllables.

READING FOCUS

Recognize Figures of Speech Choose one figure of speech from any of the four poems in this selection. Paraphrase it as a plain statement of fact and compare the two versions. Why do you think Teasdale chose to use the figure of speech rather than the literal statement? What does it contribute to the poem that the literal statement does not?

DEVELOP YOUR VOCABULARY

A noun names a person, a place, or a thing. A verb names an action or a state of being. Some words can be used as both nouns and verbs. Their part of speech depends on how they are used in a sentence. For example: Joe and Emma have to *look* for the book, You should have seen the *look* on his face. In these sentences, *look* is used first as a verb, then as a noun. The way in which any word is classified as a part of speech depends on the way it is used in a sentence.

Review the meaning of the following words in a dictionary. State which way each is used in the context of the poem. Then write two sentences for each of the words, using the word as a noun in one sentence and as a verb in the other. At the end of each sentence, tell how the word has been used.

1. barter
2. waves
3. wonder
4. star
5. cost
6. crest

THINK ABOUT RHYME SCHEME

Answers

1. a-b-c-b-d-d; The first and third lines are the only lines in each stanza that do not rhyme with any other lines.
2. a-a-b-b-c-c
3. a-b-a-b
4. a-b-c-b; No, the poem contains only end rhymes.
5. "Barter": *delight, night*; *ecstasy, be*; "The Long Hill": *ago, know*

DEVELOP YOUR VOCABULARY

Answers

1. barter—noun
2. waves—noun
3. wonder—noun
4. star—verb
5. cost—noun
6. crest—noun

Sample sentences:

1. The exchange of a dictionary for a magazine was a poor *barter*. —noun
   The boy tried to *barter* his baseball cards for an autographed ball.—verb
2. The *waves* crashed loudly on the rocky shore. —noun
   The politician *waves* to his supporters crowded in the gym.—verb
3. The child's eyes were filled with *wonder* at the beautiful sight.—noun
   Do you *wonder* about the fate of the dinosaurs?—verb
4. The sky was so cloudy there was not a *star* in sight.—noun
   She will *star* in the school play. —verb
5. The *cost* of a new car has become very great.—noun
   The video *cost* more than his monthly baby-sitting income.—verb
6. The hikers were exhausted when they reached the *crest* of the hill. —noun
   The tide will *crest* at 6:00 P.M.—verb

ESL Activity

Ask each student to bring to class a poem in his or her native language. Ask the student to compare the poem with the poems in this selection with regard to form, imagery, rhyme scheme, theme, or any other poetic elements. Have students read the poems aloud.

READING FOCUS

Sample Answer

Figure of speech: "Life has loveliness to sell."

Literal statement: Life has many lovely things.

Teasdale liked the idea of life as a big department store that a person can go into, admiring some things in passing and buying others to take home and treasure. The literal statement doesn't offer this idea of life as a store.

Selection Overview

SELECTION OBJECTIVES

After completing this selection, students should be able to

- grasp the concept of irony
- understand "irony of situation"
- write an ironic statement
- write a stanza to a poem
- select and use vivid verbs
- make inferences from connotations

Lesson Resources

Richard Cory
- Selection Synopsis, Teacher's Edition, p. T241g
- Comprehension and Vocabulary Workbook, pp. 63–64
- Language Enrichment Workbook, pp. 49–50
- Teacher's Resources
  Reinforcement, p. R32
  Test, pp. T63–T64

More About Irony

Irony of situation differs from verbal irony in that it involves happenings or events, as opposed to words. However, the two may be, and often are, combined.

Ask the students if they can detect either form of irony in "Richard Cory." Which type and why?

About the Author

Although Edwin Arlington Robinson began writing poetry at the age of 11, he was practically unknown until he was 50. Then, for the last ten to fifteen years of his life, he, along with Robert Frost, had the reputation of being one of the greatest poets in the United States.

Unfortunately, neither this acclaim nor much else in life seemed to give him particular enjoyment. He had few friends and was never married. His obituary said, in part, that "poetry played the part of wife, children, job, and recreation."

It has also been said of Robinson that he was "obsessed by failure and in love with death." He died of natural causes at age 65.

Learn About

IRONY

Irony occurs when the intent or tone of the words used is exactly opposite of what the actual meaning of the words say. For example, if someone asks you if you mind having a flu shot, you may reply, "I can hardly wait!" Are you really eager to have the shot, or are you dreading it? Your words say you are eager, but your tone of voice expresses a feeling that is the opposite of eager. This example explains one kind of irony.

Another kind is called **irony of situation.** This term refers to events that turn out to be the opposite of what you expect or consider appropriate. Suppose, for example, that someone taunts you for some misfortune. If that person, without knowing it, is at that moment suffering the same misfortune, that is irony of situation.

As you read the poem, ask yourself:

1. Which type of irony does the poem tell about?
2. Does the author offer any comment about the events?

Reading Focus

Make Inferences From Connotations

Connotations suggest connections beyond a word's literal meaning. For example, you might describe a man's profile as "carved from flint." The phrase suggests a quality of hardness and harshness that the word *strong* does not convey. As you read "Richard Cory," think about the connotations of each word used to describe him. What inferences can you make about Richard Cory from these connotations?

WRITING CONNECTION

Assume that a friend has just broken a favorite possession of yours. Write what you would say that would show a contrast between what your words are and what you mean.

Enrichment

Have students research the life of the "working poor" in this period to tell how they lived, what they ate, how much schooling they had, the types of jobs available to them, and how much child labor there was.

ESL Activity

Encourage students to use the footnotes to help them understand the poem's sophisticated vocabulary. Have them try reading it aloud to appreciate the sound of the words. Challenge them to think about the relationship between sound and meaning.

Cooperative Group Activity

To extend the Writing Connection activity, divide the class into small groups. Ask the groups to select one member's completed assignment to analyze. Have them cooperate in writing a paragraph that tells how they decided it was irony and how well they think it was conveyed.

RICHARD CORY

by Edwin Arlington Robinson

Whenever Richard Cory went down town,
We people on the pavement looked at him:
He was a gentleman from sole to crown,
Clean favored, and imperially slim.

5 And he was always quietly arrayed,
And he was always human when he talked;
But still he fluttered pulses when he said,
"Good-morning," and he glittered when he walked.

And he was rich—yes, richer than a king—
10 And admirably schooled in every grace:
In fine, we thought that he was everything
To make us wish that we were in his place.

So on we worked, and waited for the light,
And went without the meat, and cursed the bread;
15 And Richard Cory, one calm summer night,
Went home and put a bullet through his head.

---

favored (FAY vurd) featured
imperially (im PIR ee ul ee) supremely
arrayed (uh RAYD) dressed
admirably (AD mur uh blee) excellently
fine (FYN) summary; conclusion

TEACHING PLAN

INTRODUCE

Motivation
Play the song "Richard Cory" by Simon and Garfunkel for the class. Note the differences between the lyrics of the song and the words of the original poem. Discuss whether such elements as character, setting, plot, and theme are basically the same in the two.

Purpose-Setting Question
What conditions make it possible to convey irony of situation in a single, final line of a poem, as in "Richard Cory"?

READ

Literary Focus: *Irony*
Ask: Why is the ending of the poem ironic? Compare and contrast this irony to the irony of "The Gift of the Magi."

Reading Focus: *Make Inferences from Connotations*
Ask: What are some of the connotations of words like *crown*, *imperially*, *arrayed*, *glittered*, and *king*? What do the connotations of these words suggest to you about Richard Cory? You might tell students that King Richard I of England was called "Richard Coeur de Lion" (French for "Lion-hearted"), and point out the similarity between "Coeur" and "Cory."

CLOSE

Have students complete Review the Selection on pages 332–333.

Critical Thinking: *Analyze*
Have students analyze their reactions to the ending of the poem. Ask: Were you surprised or confused? Do you feel dislike or approval?

Develop Vocabulary Skills
Before reviewing the definitions of the vocabulary words, ask the students to try to figure out their meanings, based upon the context in which they are used. Then have students demonstrate their understanding by writing down a synonym for each word.

Mini Quiz

Write the following questions on the board or overhead projector and call on students to fill in the blanks. Discuss the answers with the class.

1. The main character in the poem is called ________ ________.
2. He is described as a ________.
3. When he walked, he ________.
4. The narrator and others ________ the bread.
5. The main character ends up by ________ himself.

Answers
1. Richard Cory
2. gentleman
3. glittered
4. cursed
5. shooting

UNDERSTAND THE SELECTION

Answers

1. He was "imperially slim" or very thin.
2. "Good morning"
3. summer
4. He probably traveled in an open car, since (a) he was quite wealthy; (b) the people looked at him from "on the pavement." The poem states that he "glittered" when he walked.
5. Answers will vary, but should imply "from head to toe."
6. Sample answer: He was very attractive.
7. Sample answer: because they had no meat
8. Answers will vary, but should imply that he probably would have been quite pleasant and civil. He would not have been snobbish or conceited, since "he was always human when he talked" and was a gentleman.
9. Answers could include: rich/wealthy, well-mannered, gracious, well-dressed, well-educated, polite, gentlemanly, nice, pleasant, happy on the outside but sad on the inside, etc.
10. Sample answer: Despite having material goods, his life lacked purpose.

Respond to Literature

Have students look up and briefly describe the nature and hierarchy of British royalty; that is, let them state the relative position of a duke, earl, or lord to a prince or queen. Write these titles on the board and illustrate them by a chart. At the end, poll the class to determine which title they would assign to Richard Cory.

Review the Selection

UNDERSTAND THE SELECTION

Recall

1. What type of physical build did Richard Cory have?
2. What are the only words he is quoted as saying in the poem?
3. In what season did he kill himself?

Infer

4. How do you think Richard Cory traveled about? Explain why you have this impression.
5. Paraphrase the expression "from sole to crown."
6. Why do you think he "fluttered pulses" when he spoke to people?
7. Why do you think people "cursed the bread"?

Apply

8. How do you think Cory would have treated you if you met? Why?
9. Select three adjectives to describe this man.
10. Why do you think Richard Cory killed himself?

Respond to Literature

Suppose that Richard Cory had lived in a country that had royalty. What do you think his position would have been?

WRITE ABOUT THE SELECTION

"Richard Cory" not only has a surprise ending, but a shocking and violent one. The last line stands out in stark contrast to everything that has preceded it. It changes the meaning and impact of the poem.

The image we are given of this man through the first fifteen lines of the poem gives us no reason to suspect the outcome or climax.

Have you ever heard the saying "All that glitters is not gold"? Think about its meaning as it applies to the poem. Write a fifth stanza to "Richard Cory" that uses the idea of that saying. Expand on the idea and explain it as best you can.

Prewriting Think about how this saying can be applied to the plot of the poem. Jot down your thoughts in note form.

Writing Arrange your notes and write a fifth stanza to the poem. This will be the resolution—following the climax—of the plot. In this resolution stanza, describe how the saying relates to the climax. Write four lines. Have at least two of them end in rhyming words.

Revising Follow the same rhyming scheme by having the last words of the first and third lines rhyme as well as those of the second and fourth lines.

Proofreading Check your stanza for spelling errors. Also make sure that you followed the *abab* rhyme scheme.

WRITE ABOUT THE SELECTION

Prewriting

Have the class, individually, write notes on their thoughts about the saying.

Writing

Have students work on this section individually. Go around the class, giving help to any student who is having difficulty. To suggest possible responses, ask questions to focus students' thoughts on the meaning of "All that glitters is not gold" and its connection with the poem.

Revising

Make this a cooperative group activity. Divide the class into groups of three. Have the group review each group member's poem and revise it to conform to the a-b-a-b scheme.

Proofreading

Select one or two of the students' poems as models for proofreading. Put the poems on the overhead projector and have the class suggest improvements.

THINK ABOUT IRONY

Irony is a common form of expression in literature—as in life. It is an effective way of contrasting the literal meaning of words with the opposite meaning behind those words. Irony of situation refers to events that are contrary to what the reader or characters in the literary work expect or believe to be appropriate.

1. Which sort of irony does Robinson use in his poem?
2. What characteristics of Richard Cory made him someone with whom people would like to change places?
3. Does the author have any comments to make about the ending of the poem? If so, what is his message?
4. What does Robinson mean when he says that Richard Cory "glittered when he walked"?
5. Does the poem suggest to you any general lessons about life? If so, what are they?

Reading Focus

Make Inferences From Connotations List some of the words and phrases used to describe Richard Cory. Identify what these words and phrases connote beyond their literal definitions. Then explain what you infer about Cory from the language used to describe him.

DEVELOP YOUR VOCABULARY

Robinson creates some memorable images in "Richard Cory." Note particularly his choice of verbs. Cory wasn't merely *dressed*; he was *arrayed*. He didn't *make pulses skip a beat*; he *fluttered pulses*. Other people didn't *complain* about their lot; they *cursed* the bread.

Verbs are important in writing. Since they carry the action, strong, vivid verbs can make your writing lively.

Choose the most vivid verbs from the list in parentheses:

1. The thief (*walked*, *slunk*, *crept*, *went*) away in the night.
2. Alfonso (*tiptoed*, *moved*, *walked*) across the library.
3. My brother (*devoured*, *gobbled*, *ate*) the snacks eagerly.
4. The fire (*flamed*, *burned*, *blazed*) hotly in the fireplace.
5. The child (*pleaded*, *asked*, *requested*) not to be punished.

THINK ABOUT IRONY

Answers

1. irony of situation
2. Sample answers: his wealth, his human demeanor, his gentlemanly behavior, and his grace and bearing
3. He does not comment; he merely relates the incident.
4. Sample answers: Cory was such an object of envy that all eyes turned toward him, and his bearing and manner gave him an aura of success. He may also have worn an expensive watch or cufflinks that literally reflected sunlight.
5. Sample answers: One really never knows what another person's life is like; Richard Cory must have had many inner problems that were not apparent to others; one's own lot in life may be better than another's whose life seems so full of advantages.

DEVELOP YOUR VOCABULARY

Answers

1. slunk
2. tiptoed
3. gobbled
4. blazed
5. pleaded

Have each student write a reason for the verb choice he or she makes.

ESL Activity

Discuss the use of vivid verbs such as hurled, flashed, and zoomed. Have students describe the images these words evoke. Then have students relate the images to the life of Richard Cory.

Reading Focus

Answer

Students should list the following: *gentleman*, *crown*, *imperially slim*, *arrayed*, *glittered*, and *richer than a king*. Students should identify the connotations of aristocracy and royalty suggested by these words. They should infer that Cory was handsome, graceful, dignified, courteous, pleasant, and charismatic. They might also infer that he seemed a little detached or remote, as royalty is from its subjects.

Unit Review Resources

TEACHER'S RESOURCES

- Writing Process, pp. W37–W48
- Grammar, Usage, and Mechanics, pp. G37–G48
- Speaking and Listening, pp. S19–S24
- Critical Thinking, pp. C19–C24
- Choose from Reading in the Content Areas, pp. RCA1–RCA72
- **Standardized Test Preparation**
  Unit 4 Test, pp. UT7–UT8
  Choose from Standardized Test Preparation, pp. STP1–STP31

WRITING APPLICATIONS

Write About Character

Identifying and focusing on the qualities of three characters will help students compare and contrast how each character reflects city or country life in the period.

Prewriting: Encourage students to choose three main characters. Have students focus on qualities such as courage, greed, bravery, steadiness, or selfishness. Ask individual students to describe the settings in which the characters find themselves. Ask: Do the characters reflect city or country life? How?

Writer's Toolkit CD-ROM Encourage students to use the Character Trait Word Bin (Writing Tools, Gathering Details) to complete the Prewriting activity.

Writing: To help a student think about individual qualities, suggest a single quality one character may exhibit.

Revising: Pair students who have chosen one or more of the same characters. Have them discuss and compare their work and then revise.

Proofreading: Have the same pairs of students exchange papers for proofreading. See the Teacher's Resource Binder for guidelines on peer editing and proofreading.

UNIT 4 Review

WRITING APPLICATIONS

Write About Character

The Civil War brought about a change in the American economy. America switched from a predominantly agricultural economy to a manufacturing one. The literature of the age, however, reflected both city and country life.

Select three characters from the selections in this unit. Discuss how each of them reflects life in the city or country, whichever is appropriate during this period.

Prewriting Select the three characters. With each name as the heading, make a list of words and phrases that describe their qualities (as opposed to physical characteristics). Make a list for each character, circling the qualities the three have in common, and checking off the ones they do not share with the others.

Writing Using your lists of descriptions, write a paragraph comparing the similarities of these three characters. Explain how they are alike, despite the different settings in which they are found. Include at least two descriptive words or phrases from the text for each one.

Revising Check to see that you have accurately described the characters. Change vague adjectives and verbs to vivid ones.

Proofreading Since you have used quotes from the text, check that your usage of commas, quotation marks, and capitalization is correct.

Write About Elements in Fiction

In the section entitled "Focus on Fiction," six literary skills were discussed. Choose any of the selections in this unit, except the annotated one, and write a critical analysis of its four basic elements: setting, character, plot, and theme.

Prewriting Organize the facts about these elements by making a three-column chart. First, list the "5 Ws": *who*, *what*, *when*, *where*, *why*. Next to each of these, write which of the four literary elements is associated with it. Then, in the third column, write down the appropriate information you have chosen.

Writing Use your "5 Ws" chart to relate each element to the selection. Include the following points in your analysis:

Setting—What is the time and place?

Character—Identify the protagonist and antagonist. Are they *round* or *flat*?

Plot—What is the nature of the conflict? What is the climax?

Theme—What is the meaning, or message? Why do you think this?

Revising Expand the "5 Ws" by analyzing the climax. Tell at what point it occurs and whether it is followed by falling action leading to a resolution.

Proofreading Read over your analysis. Make sure that all sentences are complete and that your page is divided properly into paragraphs.

Write About Elements in Fiction

Prewriting: Write a sample chart on the board so that students have a clear idea of the prewriting exercise.

Writing: Students should work on this section individually. Give help to any student who is having difficulty.

Writer's Toolkit CD-ROM Encourage students to use the Story Map (Writing Tools, Gathering Details) to complete the Writing activity.

Revising: Discuss the meaning of the terms *falling and rising action*, *climax*. Then have students follow the directions in this section.

Proofreading: Have students proofread their papers independently before calling on volunteers to read their work aloud.

Cooperative Group Activity

Have students complete the proofreading exercise, exchange papers to double-check their work, and write a few constructive criticisms or opinions about each other's work.

BUILD LANGUAGE SKILLS

Vocabulary

A **contraction** is a shortened form of one or two words. Two words may be combined by replacing one or more letters with an apostrophe.

Examples: you're = you are
that's = that is
I'd = I had
how's = how is
he'll = he will
isn't = is not
won't = will not

In the annotated story in this unit, it was noted that the language used by the characters was a dialect. A dialect was used to provide regional, social, and character clues.

The following words from passages in the story are contractions. Copy the list. Next to each, write the word or words that the contraction stands for and indicate whether it is standard English or colloquial.

1. s'pose
2. you've
3. didn't
4. 'twould
5. I'll
6. there's
7. you'll
8. we'd
9. hadn't
10. can't
11. 'cause
12. don't
13. an'
14. we've
15. I'm
16. ain't
17. what's
18. it's
19. she'll
20. I've

Grammar, Usage, and Mechanics

When you are writing or quoting, you should know when to use capital letters. If the sentence contains a direct quotation, capitalize the first word of the quotation. Do not capitalize the first word of an indirect quotation.

Examples: All at once, I heard Chuck say, "The circus is in town."
All at once, I heard Chuck say that the circus is in town.

In writing lines of poetry, capitalize the first word of each line, unless the poet does not follow this procedure.

Example:
I measure every grief I meet
With analytic eyes,
I wonder if it weighs like mine
Or has an easier size.
—Emily Dickinson

Capitalize these sentences and quotations correctly.

1. "nevertheless, i will go," Andy said.
2. soon Lois said that the mail had come.
3. my friend said, "this book is good."
4. there was water in the pool.

Grammar, Usage, and Mechanics

Answers

1. "Nevertheless, I will go," Andy said.
2. Soon Lois said that the mail had come.
3. My friend said, "This book is good."
4. There was water in the pool.

Write these sentences on the board:

1. "The road is long," said John.
2. Jerry asked, "What's your name?"
3. Finally, Eleanor said that she would help.

Point out the use of capital letters in the examples. Have students note the placement of quotation marks and punctuation in sentences 1 and 2 and the absence of quotation marks in sentence 3.

Cooperative Group Activity

Pair the students and have them work together on the text samples. Then have the pairs construct ten examples of their own. Have each pair exchange their examples with another pair for connecting.

BUILD LANGUAGE SKILLS

Vocabulary

Answers

1. suppose*
2. you have
3. did not
4. it would*
5. I will
6. there is
7. you will
8. we had
9. had not
10. cannot
11. because*
12. do not
13. and*
14. we have
15. I am
16. are not*, is not*, am not*
17. what is
18. it is
19. she will
20. I have

Starred items are colloquial.

More About Word Attack: Remind students that a contraction is one word that stands for two. To help students place the apostrophe correctly, explain how it takes the place of the letters that are dropped.

For example:
is not—replace *o* with apostrophe = *isn't*
he will—replace *wi* with apostrophe = *he'll*

Write a list of contractions on the board. Ask students to tell which letters have been replaced by an apostrophe.

SPEAKING AND LISTENING

Discuss with students the idea that poems are meant to be read aloud so that the listener can hear or experience the rhythm, alliteration, rhyme, tone, emphasis, etc., that the poem may contain.

Teaching Strategy

To demonstrate effective reading, choose a short poem or a limerick and read it to the class, first, in a monotone; then, in a normally expressive reading. Review the seven-step instruction with the class. Have the students select poems they will read aloud. Students are to complete steps two and three, reading the poem three times and deciding on the mood of the poem before practicing it aloud. Ensure that students have not selected poems that are too long to be read as part of a class. Assign the practice activities (steps four, five, and six) as homework.

Evaluation Criteria

Do the students offer expressive readings of their poems? Is the mood accurately conveyed? Are their readings effective renderings of the poems? How well have the students followed the guidelines? Are all the words in the poem pronounced correctly? Grade performance on a 1–10 scale.

UNIT 4 Review

SPEAKING AND LISTENING

In an earlier lesson you were asked to read aloud. In that lesson, it was suggested that you choose something to read aloud that you especially liked. In this lesson that is also one of the suggestions. However, since this time you will be asked to read a poem aloud, there are additional ideas that will make the experience an enjoyable one for you and for your audience.

1. Start with the basics—select a poem that you *like*!
2. Read the poem at least three times: the first time to get acquainted with it, the second time to identify any words that may be difficult, and the third time to grasp the meaning of the poem.
3. Decide what the mood of the poem is. This is important because you want your voice to convey the feeling of the poem. Decide if the poem has different moods. If so, you will want to adapt your voice to fit those moods.
4. Practice reading the poem aloud until your voice perfectly reflects the mood(s) of the poem. You want to find the right voice; so ask someone to listen to you while you read. Ask for their suggestions on how you might improve your reading.
5. If possible, tape-record yourself reading the poem. Listen to your voice as you say the words of the poem. Pay attention to the pauses you make. Ask yourself if your voice sounds natural and whether or not the emotion of the poem is coming through.
6. Once you have prepared your poem for reading aloud, practice it several times. You don't need to memorize it, but you want to be thoroughly familiar with it.
7. When you present your poem to your class, be sure you can see your audience and that you maintain some eye contact. This will involve your listener and it will help you pay attention to your body language.

Now, look back at the poems in this unit and choose one of them to present orally. With your teacher's permission, you may select a poem from another source if you prefer. At any rate, follow the guidelines above to help you prepare for reading a poem aloud, The important thing is to choose a poem whose meaning is special to you. Select a poem you really like and share it.

Career Connection

After reading "How to Tell A Story," students might be interested in a career as a newspaper reporter. A career as a reporter usually requires a college education, though some newspapers may offer part-time work and an opportunity to advance, based on experience rather than a degree.

People who are interested in becoming reporters must have a good command of grammar and spelling, a knack for writing, an ability to handle deadline pressure, and the ability to type and take accurate notes. They must like communicating with a wide variety of people.

CRITICAL THINKING

Part-Whole Relationships A **whole** is all of something. A whole is made up of **parts**. Look at a piano, for example. It is made up of keys, pedals, strings, hammers, felts, and a wooden case. It takes all of these parts working together to make up the whole that is a piano.

Understanding the relationship of part to whole is the key to understanding anything—a poem, an idea, a jet engine, a way of doing something, an organization, a clock mechanism, a football team, the plot of a story, a car, the recipe for a cake, a family, an insect, or a flower.

Literature often deals with part-whole relationships. Consider Walt Whitman's "I Hear America Singing," for example. In this poem, Whitman lists the songs of various American workers. Each song, as he sees it, is a part that contributes to the whole of America—to the varied carols he hears.

To understand a piece of literature, you must see how all the parts work together as a whole. Choose any selection in this unit. List as many of the elements that contribute to it as you can. Then answer the following questions.

1. Which are major elements of the whole and which are minor elements?
2. If any element were changed, how would the other elements be affected? Would the nature of the work change?

EFFECTIVE STUDYING

Summarizing You will often need to prepare a summary of your work. A **summary** is a brief digest of the main ideas in a lecture, a performance, or a piece of writing. Do not confuse summarizing with rewording; a summary condenses the ideas, it does not simply restate them.

Here is how to write a summary:

1. Before writing:
   - Read the material carefully.
   - Look for the main idea or ideas.
   - Topic sentences and key words in the material may be of help.
2. Writing:
   - Write down the main idea or ideas in your own words, but be exact.
   - Be brief; remember, you are trying "to make a long story short."
   - Omit unimportant ideas.
   - Combine ideas when doing so will make the summary shorter or clearer.
3. After writing:
   - Review your summary to be sure that all the necessary information has been included.
   - Clarify any ideas that have not been expressed clearly.

Test Preparation

Summarizing your class notes is a good way to prepare for a test. You might also summarize a piece of writing to answer an essay question.

EFFECTIVE STUDYING

Teaching Strategy

Call on individual students to define *summary* and give their ideas on how to summarize. Introduce discussion questions such as:

- Why are summaries useful?
- Who uses summaries?
- What does a good summary contain? What does it leave out?

As an exercise, ask students to summarize a movie they have seen or a book they have read recently.

Use these exercises for review.

1. A summary is a brief ________.
2. Before writing a summary, first carefully ________ the material.
3. The summary focuses on the main ________ of the material.
4. ________ ideas should be omitted.
5. The summary should be written in your own ________.

Answers

1. digest
2. read
3. idea or ideas
4. Unimportant
5. words

CRITICAL THINKING

Sample Answers

For "Gift of the Magi":

1. *Major elements*: the personalities of the two characters, setting (economic, especially), the point of view (third person/omniscient narrator)
   Minor elements: secondary characters, geographic setting, tone
2. The nature of the work would change. The omniscient narrator allows the reader to see inside the characters' heads; he can make their motivations clear, provide some objectivity. This story would not be so effective if told from either Della's or Jim's point of view. This story hinges on the economic situation that forces Della to sell her hair and Jim his watch. These actions are also a result of the type of characters they are—caring and self-sacrificing.

UNIT ACTIVITY

A Continuing Unit Project: Producing Illustrated Reading Logs

A log is a useful learning tool that can focus the students' attention on the material at hand and allow them the opportunity to explore their own ideas and opinions. In addition, the log entries can serve as prewriting activities or as notes for studying in preparation for testing.

Have students produce illustrated reading logs as they read this unit. The logs will have two distinct kinds of entries. The first will be oriented toward literary elements. Students will apply previously learned knowledge by identifying at least two literary elements that are present in the selection. They will list the elements, followed by the definition or one important fact about the element. They will then apply this knowledge to the selection just read, citing a line, stanza, or passage that illustrates the writer's use of that element.

When identifying the line, stanza, or passage, they should enclose it within quotation marks and copy it exactly. If it is too long to copy with ease, allow them to substitute ellipses (. . .) for the writer's words at strategic points. For example, they might have summarized a passage from Patrick Henry's speech at the Virginia Convention as follows: "Gentlemen may cry 'Peace, peace'—but there is not peace. . . as for me, give me liberty or give me death!" If you allow students to use this technique, be certain they record enough actual language to retain the sense of the passage. This is important for later reference and review. They need to have recorded enough information so that the log will be a meaningful study prompt and permit them to locate the passage in the full work.

The second kind of entry will be reader-oriented. These entries should include students' personal reactions and thoughts about the selection. After they have read a selection, ask students to write their responses in an expressive style. Make sure they understand they are writing about their thoughts and feelings, not merely repeating facts from the literature. Encourage students to jot down any thoughts or questions about the content and the relationship between the selection and the historical period in which it was written (ways in which the selection illustrates the thinking, the social setting, important issues, and so forth of the times). Also encourage students to relate the themes to their own experiences. Allow five to ten minutes for each entry. Students need write no more than half a page for each entry.

In preparation, review the elements of nonfiction, fiction, and poetry, discussed in previous units. You may want to distribute a handout with these three headings—nonfiction, fiction, poetry—listed at the top and the elements for each heading listed in a column down the left side of the page. Another way of presenting this prompt material is to write the headings on separate sections of the board, listing the appropriate elements beneath each. As a third possibility, you might write the genres and list the appropriate elements beneath each on separate overhead transparencies showing each one, in turn after the completion of a relevant selection.

Have students use these lists as prompts for their entries on literary elements. Because of the diverse nature of the material, it should be possible for students to identify a number of different literary elements. Encourage students to cite as many as possible and to avoid unnecessary repetition of any one element. At the same time, caution them against trying to force an inappropriate element into a selection just for the sake of identifying it in the unit.

Guide students in the use of certain annotations or definitions from the previous units as prompts for their own thoughts. Do not permit simple rephrasing of the definitions or annotations. Ask questions that will trigger original thoughts and encourage students to take the ideas expressed in the annotations one step further.

Here are some general questions you can ask the class to stimulate thought about the literary elements:

What are the elements of nonfiction?

How would you define narration?

Have you read any selections in previous units that illustrate the use of exposition in literature? Explain your answer by referring to a particular part of the work.

How would you define description?

Have you read any selections in previous units that illustrate the use of description in literature? Explain your answer by referring to a particular part of that work.

How would you define exposition and persuasion?

Have you read any selections in previous units in which these literary elements played an important role? If so, identify the selection and discuss briefly the use of one of these literary elements in that selection. If not, identify another selection and discuss how the use of that literary element might have contributed to the effectiveness of the other selection.

What are the elements of fiction?

How would you define setting?

Have you read any selections in previous units that illustrate the use of setting in literature? Explain your answer by referring to a particular part of that work.

How would you define plot?

Have you read any selections in previous units that illustrate the use of plot in literature? Explain your answer by referring to specific details from that work.

How would you define character, theme, and point of view?

Have you read any selections in previous units that illustrate the use of these elements in literature? Explain your answers by referring to particular parts of those works. If not, identify another selection and explain how the use of one of these elements might have contributed to that work. Refer to specific parts of that selection in your explanation.

Have you seen any movies or television shows illustrating any of these literary elements? If so, identify the show and explain your answers. Use the same technique for the elements of poetry.

Here are some general questions you can ask the class to stimulate thinking about the personal-response entries in their logs.

What did you learn today?

What questions do you have about what you read?

Did anything confuse you?

What is the point of the selection?

What connection to your life can you make from today's selection?

Did you recognize any characteristics of the writer or characters in the work that reminded you of people you have met?

Did you recognize any events that were parallel or similar to events you have experienced or witnessed?

Did the setting seem familiar to you? If so, did the writer do a good job in describing the setting? If the setting was not familiar to you, did the writer create a vivid picture that allowed you to see the place in your mind?

What about this unfamiliar setting confirmed ideas you already had?

What about this unfamiliar setting surprised you or gave you new insights?

What do you think of the selection?

If you did not use a selection's Response to Literature question for a cooperative group activity, you might consider using it as a writing prompt for the reading logs.

■ "A Day's Wait"

Why do you think the boy refused to let anyone enter his room? In a similar circumstance, would you have acted this way?

■ "Lament"

■ "Afternoon on a Hill"

Do you think "Afternoon on a Hill" describes an experience that really happened to the poet?

■ "home"

How did you feel about any one character in this story?

■ "Dream Variations"

■ "Theme for English B"

■ from *Montage of a Dream Deferred*

Which one of these poems was your favorite? How is it like music?

■ "Fog"

Do you think the fog as described by the poet is something to be feared? Why? Why not?

■ "The Pasture"

■ "The Road Not Taken"

■ "Stopping by Woods on a Snowy Evening"

Which of these poems was your favorite? Have you considered memorizing the one you liked the most? Would you like to read it aloud in private? Would you like to read it aloud in class?

■ **"Lily Daw and the Three Ladies"**

Did you identify with the character of Lily Daw in this story? Why? Why not?

■ ***The Still Alarm***

How would you react in an emergency?

■ ***Invasion from Mars***

Were you surprised by the ending to this selection? Why? Why not?

■ **"Futility"**

Do you think that anything created by people is as beautiful as nature? Explain your answer.

Require students to illustrate the log entries. Some of the literary elements will lend themselves more readily to illustration than others. Do not be overly concerned about the relationship between the elements and the illustrations. Personal expression, content retention, and understanding are more important to this aspect of the work.

Allow students to draw pictures or cartoons, develop symbolic representations, or cut and paste magazine pictures. Encourage original artwork but explain to the class that creative thought, attention to detail, and effort are what you are seeking. Have students create a cover and a table of contents for the log.

Logs may be read aloud or by another student. Questions, opinions, and comments should be shared with the class as a whole or in small groups. After the unit has been completed, collect and evaluate the illustrated reading logs. Be certain that you find something to praise in each student's log, provided, of course, that honest effort is reflected in the work.

■ **"A Day's Wait"**

by Ernest Hemingway (page 343)

SELECTION SYNOPSIS

According to Carlos Baker, Hemingway's biographer, this story is based on a true event. Schatz, the writer's son (by his first wife Hadley), has recently left France to join his father (and second wife) in the United States. One morning, Schatz feels ill, and Hemingway sends for the doctor, who diagnoses influenza and leaves certain capsules. In the boy's presence, the doctor reports his temperature as "one hundred and two." During the day, the boy acts strangely stoical and refuses to be interested in any diversion. Hemingway goes out for some hunting and returns to find that his son has refused to let anyone into the room. His temperature is taken again, and suddenly the boy wants to know what time he is going to die. Asked why he thinks he will die, he says that in France he heard that one can't live long with a fever of 44 degrees. Seeing the reason for the boy's odd behavior, Hemingway explains the difference in measurements (Fahrenheit vs. Celsius).

SELECTION ACTIVITY

Review briefly with the class Schatz's fear that he was dying because the doctor said he had a temperature of 102 degrees (Fahrenheit). He thought this because in France he had heard that a person could not survive very long with a temperature above 44 degrees (Celsius or Centigrade).

Briefly discuss the fact that in this country, we traditionally have measured body temperature using the Fahrenheit scale. Most other countries in the world use the Celsius or Centigrade method of measurement, based on a scale of 0 to 100 degrees.

Write on the board or the overhead transparency the following examples drawn from each of the two temperature scales:

Freezing point of water:	0 degrees C
	32 degrees F
Boiling point of water:	100 degrees C
	212 degrees F

Ask students if they have learned about these different scales in a science or mathematics class. Answers will vary.

Write on the board or the overhead transparency the following information. To convert temperature in degrees Celsius, or Centigrade, to degrees Fahrenheit, use the following formula. Multiply the Celsius, or Centigrade, temperature by the fraction nine/fifths ($9/5$). Then add 32.

To clarify and check student comprehension, write on the board or overhead transparency:

$100 \times 9/5 = 900/5 = 180$ degrees

$180 + 32 = 212$ degrees

100 degrees C = 212 degrees F

During this exercise, do not write the answers. Ask for volunteers to do the mathematics involved.

Write on the board or overhead transparency the following information. To convert temperature in degrees Fahrenheit to degrees Celsius, or Centigrade, use the following formula. Subtract 32 and then multiply by five/ninths ($5/9$).

To clarify and check student comprehension, write on the board or an overhead transparency:

32 − 32 = 0 degrees

0 × $\frac{5}{9}$ = 0 degrees

32 degrees Fahrenheit = 0 degrees Celsius, or Centigrade

During this exercise, do not write the answers. Ask for volunteers to do the mathematics involved. You may have to remind students that 0 multiplied by any number equals 0.

You may want to use additional examples of your own. Finally, refer to the story. Have students convert the boy's Fahrenheit temperature of 102 degrees to Celsius. Have them determine what 44 degrees Celsius would be on the Fahrenheit scale.

■ "Lament"

by Edna St. Vincent Millay (page 351)

SELECTION SYNOPSIS

The subject of this poem is a man's death. The narrator (apparently the deceased man's widow) tells her two children about his death at the breakfast table. Her tone is understated and matter of fact, although it is obvious she is struggling to control her emotions. She advises them that life must go on, even if we do not understand why such terrible things happen.

■ "Afternoon on a Hill"

by Edna St. Vincent Millay (page 352)

SELECTION SYNOPSIS

The subject of this poem is an imagined time spent on a hill. The tone is ecstatic as the poet suggests a perfect day, appreciating the small wonders of nature.

SELECTION ACTIVITY

Arrange students into heterogeneous groups. Distribute the following handout to each group. Have students in each group use the lists to try to reproduce the lines as Millay wrote them in "Renascence."

First word of each line:

The
No
Above
No

Last (rhyming) words in each line:

side
wide
sky
high

Other words in each line (not in order):

line 1—out, stands, either, world, on
line 2—heart, the, wider, than, is
line 3—stretched, world, is, the, the
line 4—higher, soul, is, the, than

Answers from "Renascence"

The world stands out on either side
No wider than the heart is wide;
Above the world is stretched the sky,—
No higher than the soul is high.

Provide assistance as needed. Guide students in a discussion of a theme suggested by these lines. You may want to have students create original artwork or cut and paste pictures from magazines to accompany the verse. If so, display them around the room. Occasionally, if students are having difficulty or seem sad, remind them of these lines from Millay.

■ "home"

by Gwendolyn Brooks (page 357)

SELECTION SYNOPSIS

A mother and her two daughters sit talking quietly on the porch of their home. They have lived there 14 years, but they are on the verge of losing the house unless the father can obtain a loan extension from the Home Owners' Loan. The three talk as they wait for him to return with the loan officer's answer.

They are not optimistic about his chances. They try to put on a brave front and cheerfully talk about living in new surroundings. Beneath the masks, however, is a tremendous sadness, which occasionally bursts free.

They see the father returning home. As he approaches, they can determine nothing from his appearance. He passes them and enters the house, followed by the mother. The daughters wait anxiously. The mother reappears and announces that the loan was approved. She plans a "homeowners" party.

SELECTION ACTIVITY

Here are some sentences from "home." Write these sentences on the board or an overhead transparency.

1. "We'll be moving into a nice flat somewhere."
2. "Those flats, as the girls and Mama knew well, were burdens on wages twice the size of Papa's."
3. ". . . I've been getting tireder and tireder of doing that firing." [of the furnace]
4. "Sometimes the weather was just right for that." [building a fire in the fireplace]
5. "It's just going to kill Papa!"
6. ". . .if you want to know the truth, this is a relief. . ." [losing the house]
7. "It's all over. Everything is all right."

Exercise A

Group students heterogeneously. Have each group decide which of the sentences above describes the true feelings of the characters. Students should write that sentence and the words *true feelings* beside that sentence in their notebooks. They should write the other sentences followed by the word *pretense* in their notebooks.

Exercise B

Have each group collaborate on writing two statements Papa might have made upon his return home if he had not gotten the loan. One sentence should be an expression of his true feelings. The other should be a pretense so that his family does not think he is upset over losing the house.

Exercise C

Have each group collaborate on writing two sentences. One should describe Papa's feelings as he approached the house. The second should be what they think he might have said to Mama inside the house.

For B and C above, use the writing process described elsewhere in this text. Collect and evaluate students' work. After evaluating, display the papers on the bulletin board.

■ "Dream Variations"

■ "Theme for English B"

■ from *Montage of a Dream Deferred*

by Langston Hughes (pages 363–368)

SELECTION SYNOPSES

Included are samples from the collected works of this poet. The theme of Hughes's poetry is the conflict which African Americans experienced in the 1920s. In "Dream Variations" and "Theme for English B," the poet relates his personal thoughts and struggles. The excerpt from *Montage of a Dream Deferred* is a poetry sampler of Hughes's impressions of the lifestyles and dashed hopes of African Americans during this era.

SELECTION ACTIVITY

The day before this activity, tell students to read and review the Hughes's collection of poetry for homework. Explain that they should first read each poem silently to themselves; then, they should read each aloud several times to capture the mood and rhythm they think Hughes intended for the poems. Point out that his language is direct and uncomplicated. His rhythm is similar to the music associated with jazz and the soulful sounds of "blues." If possible, students may want to listen to similar music on a local radio station or CDs to hear these rhythms before reading aloud.

The day of the activity, bring a tape recorder to class. Select several students to read each poem aloud as they have interpreted it. Make certain that each student participates in the activity. After all the poems have been taped, play the students' readings. Encourage students to make comments, and guide them by offering constructive criticism.

Ask the class, "What was your favorite poem from this collection?" Select several students to respond with explanations. Point out that Hughes wrote these poems, challenging racial inequality, in the 1920s. Ask: "Do you think these poems reflect the African Americans' experience today?" Answers will vary.

Briefly explain that in art a montage is a picture made up of a number of smaller, separate pictures. Ask the class, "Do you think *montage* is a good word to describe Hughes's book of poetry? Why?" Answers may vary. Ask, "What do you think the phrase 'dream deferred' means?" Guide students in understanding that Hughes was describing the often-postponed hope of African American people to live in a society that treats all people as equals. He used "deferred" because prejudice and preferential treatment existed at that time.

Have the class select a name for the taped project that they have just completed. Using students' suggestions, list titles on the board or overhead projector. When you have written at least three suggestions, have the class vote. Tell students that they are welcome to listen to the tape again, when they have a free period.

■ "Fog"

by Carl Sandburg (page 373)

SELECTION SYNOPSIS

The poet compares fog to a cat.

SELECTION ACTIVITY

Have students compare other natural phenomena to animals.

■ "The Pasture"

■ "The Road Not Taken"

■ "Stopping By Woods on a Snowy Evening"

by Robert Frost (pages 377–380)

SELECTION SYNOPSES

These are three meditative poems with various themes. In each, the setting is rural United States, although the landscape of "The Road Not Taken" is allegorical.

SELECTION ACTIVITY

Discuss the imagery in these three poems. Have each student select one image from any of the three poems and draw a visual representation of that image. Encourage original artwork from those students who have the ability. Permit others to cut and paste pictures from magazines. Praise the efforts of all who have tried to do their best.

■ "Lily Daw and the Three Ladies"

by Eudora Welty (page 385)

SELECTION SYNOPSIS

Three ladies in a small southern town receive a letter they have been expecting. The Ellisville Institute for the Feeble Minded, at Ellisville, has agreed, at their request, to admit Lily Daw. Lily is an orphan who has been supported since childhood by the people of the town. The ladies have decided that it is best for all concerned if Lily, now an adult, were to be institutionalized.

Lily refuses. The night before, she met a man from a traveling tent show. The tent show has left town. Nevertheless, Lily insists that she plans to marry the man. The ladies are aghast. Using small gifts as bribes, they convince her to go to the institute.

As the train is about to leave, Lily's suitor arrives. The ladies change their plans for Lily and arrange a quick wedding. As the train pulls away, the townspeople, who have gathered, begin to cheer.

SELECTION ACTIVITY

Guide students in a discussion of motivation in fictional characters. The focus of the discussion should be on Lily, the three ladies, and the suitor. Here are some questions to use as prompts for students' thoughts:

Why do you think Lily agreed to marry the xylophone player?

Why do you think she agreed to go to Ellisville?

Do you think she is mature enough to get married?

Why do you think the ladies wanted Lily to go to Ellisville?

What does their willingness to let her marry a man she hardly knows tell you about their real motivation?

Why do you think the xylophone player wants to marry Lily?

Do you think this is a good basis for a lasting relationship?

■ *The Still Alarm*

by George S. Kaufman (page 397)

SELECTION SYNOPSIS

As the play opens, Ed and Bob, two old friends, are saying goodbye after a reunion in Bob's hotel room. All seems natural—and rather pointless—until a bellboy enters and casually announces that the hotel is on fire.

The audience soon realizes that the characters are responding to the emergency in a most unusual way. They are remaining calm and polite, talking of trivia, even as the fire reaches the floor beneath. They meet the situation with a sense of bemused wonder, not with the expected, wild alarm. Idle talk of moving to a better hotel is interrupted by the arrival of two firefighters who seem equally unconcerned. As the play ends, one of the firefighters leans out of the window to light a cigar from the flames, while the other plays "Keep the Home Fires Burning" on the violin. Lights slowly dim to red.

SELECTION ACTIVITY

Pair off students and have each pair decide upon a joke appropriate to use at school that both have heard and think is funny. The joke should involve a conversation between two people. Have each pair collaborate on writing the joke as dialogue. They should include directions, appropriate facial expressions, and physical gestures.

Review what students have written for appropriateness to a classroom situation. Offer guidance as needed. Do not collect the papers at this point.

Videotape each pair willing to perform the skit. Encourage applause from the class. Replay the results.

Collect and evaluate the written work. After evaluating, display students' papers on a bulletin board.

Invasion from Mars

by Howard Koch (page 408)

SELECTION SYNOPSIS

This is a radio adaptation of H. G. Wells's novel *War of the Worlds*.

As the play opens, a narrator provides exposition, explaining that for years Earth has been watched by alien beings living on Mars. An announcer gives an uneventful weather report and returns the broadcast to the regularly scheduled program of live music.

After a brief musical interlude, another announcer interrupts with a special bulletin. Astronomers have witnessed a series of explosions on the planet Mars. The station again returns to its regular programming. Seconds later, the music is again interrupted. Strange atmospheric activity and a shock wave resembling an earthquake, have been reported in New Jersey.

A reporter on the scene in New Jersey describes for the audience a "meteorite" that has crashed into the earth. The "meteorite" turns out to be a Martian spaceship. As state police arrive, aliens emerge from the spaceship. The Martians attack, and the reporter's broadcast is interrupted in midsentence.

The network announcer in New York tells the audience that transmission from New Jersey has been lost. He then reads a report stating that over 40 people have been killed. Soon after, a representative of the New Jersey governor announces that martial law has been declared in the state. The radio continues to broadcast scattered reports as they are sent and to interview scientists.

Contact is re-established, and a military officer describes the carnage. The network announcer interrupts to announce that thousands of soldiers have been killed in a battle with the Martians, who now control large areas of the state.

The situation in New Jersey worsens, and panic spreads into neighboring states. Reports start arriving of similar landings throughout the country. The network announcer tells the audience that the Martians are in the streets of New York. They can be seen from the studio. "This is the end."

A scientist, near the site of the original landing reads the notes he is writing. He fears he is the last person alive on Earth. As he goes on recording his experiences, he tells of a meeting with another man. This stranger plans to hide below ground and organize a resistance band. Eventually, he hopes to take over the world, killing the Martians with their own weapons and enslaving any humans who remain alive. The scientist then enters a strangely empty and quiet New York City, only to find that the Martians have died.

Where modern weapons failed, nature conquered. The Martians were killed by a common bacteria not present on Mars. Consequently, their bodies had not developed a resistance to this bacteria as part of their immune systems. Life on Earth returns to normal. The scientist, however, fears that humanity has won only a temporary reprieve from whatever malevolent forces exist in space.

SELECTION ACTIVITY

Reproduce on a handout, the board, or an overhead transparency several features from the drama that can be enhanced by the use of sound effects. Discuss with the class the kinds of sound effects that would be appropriate. Have volunteers record these sounds on tape.

Read the play in class. Divide each of the parts into segments, and assign different students to each of the major parts, so that all have the opportunity to participate in this activity.

Remind students that this was written over 60 years ago. The cast was all male, reflecting the times. Today, many women are employed in the media and the sciences in professional positions and, to a lesser extent, in the military. In assigning parts, be certain to use gender-neutral patterns of assignment.

■ "Futility"

by Mary S. Hawling (page 439)

SELECTION SYNOPSIS

In this poem, Hawling describes the frustration inherent in the creative process. She concludes by comparing her struggle to create something beautiful with the effortlessness of the beauty that a bird creates when it flies "across the sky."

SELECTION ACTIVITY

Have students draw a picture of one of the natural events described in the poem. Use students' drawings as springboards for discussion on the subject of the effort of creativity. Lead students to compare, for example, the effortless beauty of actual windblown trees and the time it takes a person to either paint such a scene or describe it in words. Display students' artwork in the classroom.

STUDENT READING LIST

Abdul-Jabbar, Kareem and Steinberg, Alan. *Black Profiles in Courage: A Legacy of African-American Achievement.* Morrow, 1996.

Bloom, Harold (ed). *Eudora Welty.* Chelsea House, 1999.

DeFusco, Andrea (ed). *Readings on Robert Frost.* Greenhaven, 1999.

Oliver, Charles. *E. Hemingway A–Z.* Fanfile, 1999.

Parks, Rosa and Haskins, Jim. *Rosa Parks: My Story.* Dial, 1992.

Wukovitz, John F. *Anne Frank.* Lucent, 1998.

From Globe Fearon Educational Publisher

Multicultural Literature Collection
- *African American Literature*
- *African American Poetry*
- *Experiencing Poetry*

Adapted Classics
- *The War of the Worlds* by H. G. Wells

Science Fiction Fastbacks
- *The Champion*
- *Eden's Daughter*

Freedom Fighters
- *Malcolm X*

Flights of Fantasy Scenes
- *Eddie's Magic Radio*
- *A Haunting Melody*

UNIT 5
Overview

UNIT OBJECTIVES

After completing this unit, students will be able to

- understand the elements of drama
- make inferences about character, setting, conflict, theme, and author's purpose
- understand and evaluate alliteration, rhythm, rhyme, symbolism, and imagery
- distinguish between denotation and connotation, and simile and metaphor
- use context clues
- evaluate figurative expressions
- understand and identify synonyms and antonyms
- improvise story dialogue

UNIT SELECTIONS

"The Modern View" introduces students to poetry, short stories, and drama selections from the remarkably productive first half of the 20th century.

- **"A Day's Wait"** (p. 343) explores the meaning of courage.

  Literary Skill: character

  Reading Skill: identify imagery

  Vocabulary: synonyms

  Writing: an opinion essay

- **"Lament" and "Afternoon on a Hill"** (p. 351) reflect the new social concerns about women's subjects and themes.

  Literary Skill: lyric poetry

  Reading Skill: evaluate the writer's purpose

  Vocabulary: figurative language

  Writing: a brief lyric poem

- **"home"** (p. 357) focuses on the role of the family in coping with life's crises.

  Literary Skill: setting

  Reading Skill: recognize implied themes

  Vocabulary: context

  Writing: a descriptive passage

- **Poems by Langston Hughes** (p. 363) illustrate the importance of equality for all U.S. citizens.

  Literary Skill: conflict

  Reading Skill: evaluate the poet's style

  Vocabulary: similes and metaphors

  Writing: a persuasive essay

- **"Fog"** (p. 373) reflects the modern poetic technique of free verse.

  Literary Skill: mood

  Reading Skill: recognize figurative language

  Vocabulary: denotation and connotation

  Writing: a brief poem or comparison

- **Three poems by Robert Frost** (p. 377) dramatize the new role of nature in modern poetry in the United States.

  Literary Skill: symbolism

  Reading Skill: make inferences

  Vocabulary: word histories

  Writing: a brief symbolic poem

- **"Lily Daw and the Three Ladies"** (p. 385) shows why regional literature has a nationwide appeal.

  Literary Skill: character

  Reading Skill: interpret dialogue

UNIT 5

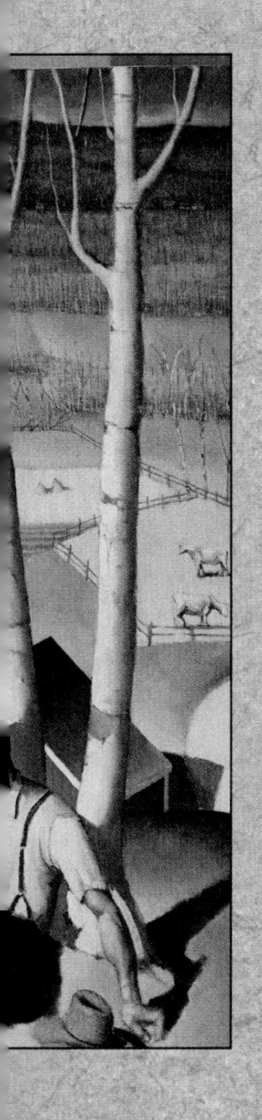

The Modern View

When all our hopes are sown on stony ground,
And we have yielded up the thought of gain,
Long after our last songs have lost their sound
We may come back, we may come back again.
—Arna Bontemps

Janitor's Holiday, Paul Sample. The Metropolitan Museum of Art, Arthur Hoppock Hearn Fund

339

Introducing the Literary Period

Have students suppose that they are teaching the opening quotation. Ask them to write four questions about it that they would like to ask the class. Have them pay attention to the figurative expressions, as well as to the tone of the quotation. After the writing session, call on students to read their questions. Discuss with them the ideas that the quotation expresses, the frustrations produced by misfortune and the optimism that helps people persevere in the face of difficulty.

Viewing Fine Art

Paul Sample belonged to the American Scene group of painters. Like other artists in this group, such as Grant Wood and Thomas Hart Benton, he focused on regional concerns and placed a great emphasis on American values in his work. Ask: What values do you see portrayed in this painting?

VOCABULARY: adverbs and adjectives
WRITING: an evaluation essay

- ***The Still Alarm*** (p. 397) is a popular depression-era comedy play.
  LITERARY SKILL: humor
  READING SKILL: understand cause and effect
  VOCABULARY: words used as nouns and verbs
  WRITING: a humorous scene
- ***Invasion from Mars*** (p. 408) the model selection, illustrates the power that radio broadcasts once had over the imagination of listeners.
  LITERARY SKILL: elements of drama—character, setting, plot, symbolism, allegory, and theme
  READING SKILL: understand sequence of events
  VOCABULARY: jargon
  WRITING: a short radio drama
- **"Futility"** (p. 439) summarizes the emotion that many U.S. citizens of this period must have shared about the prospects for world peace.
  LITERARY SKILL: tone
  READING SKILL: evaluate the poet's purpose
  VOCABULARY: antonyms
  WRITING: a personal letter

UNIT 5

RELATED MATERIALS

1. ***Ernest Hemingway: Grace Under Pressure*** [Video, 55 mins., Films for the Humanities.] This overview of Hemingway's personal life and writing career is narrated by Anthony Burgess.
2. ***Edna St. Vincent Millay*** [Audiocassette, "Poetic Heritage Series" from Summer Stream Press.] On this audiotape, the poet reads excerpts from her work.
3. ***Gwendolyn Brooks*** [Video, 30 mins., Indiana Audiovisual Center.] The poet discusses her poetry and the Chicago settings that inspired it.
4. ***The Poetry of Langston Hughes*** [Audiocassette, Caedmon.] Langston Hughes reads "Dream Variations," "Montage," and other poems.
5. ***Robert Frost in Recital*** [Audiocassette,Caedmon.] Robert Frost reads "The Road Not Taken" and other poems.
6. ***A Conversation With Eudora Welty*** [Video, 30 mins., NETCHE Nebraska Education TV Council for Higher Education.] The writer discusses why she is drawn to, and writes about, the South.
7. ***Audiodrama 101*** [Audiotape, Lend-a-Hand Society, 1998.] This is an "onstage" production designed to introduce students to well-known writers.
8. ***Robert Frost: New England in Autumn*** [Video, 30 mins., Monterey Home Video, 1997.] Here is a dramatized sampling of Frost's most famous poems.
9. The following Web sites may also be helpful. Please note that some Internet addresses change frequently. These are the latest versions:

   The ultimate UFOlogists Home Page at *http://ourworld.compuserve.com/homepages/AndyPage/*

   Poet Heroes, Langston Hughes by Jeff Trussell at *http://myhero.com/poets/hughes.asp*

   Robert Frost, The Legacy of an American at *http://hometown.aol.com/lastampede/homepage.htm*

LITERARY HIGHLIGHTS

1913 Robert Frost's first volume of poetry, *A Boy's Will*, appears.

1916 Carl Sandburg publishes *Chicago Poems*.

1918 Willa Cather's novel, *My Antonia*, is published.

1926 Langston Hughes's first poetry is published.

1910 1915 1920 1925

1918 World War I armistice is signed.

1920 Nineteenth Amendment gives women the right to vote.

1927 Charles Lindbergh flies nonstop from New York to Paris.

HISTORICAL HIGHLIGHTS

The Modern View

You probably know people who lived in America between 1915 and 1946. Have you ever asked them what their lives were like during those years? In those three decades, Americans went through two world wars, a period of great prosperity, and a period of terrible economic hardship.

WORLD WAR I AND THE 1920s

In 1914, World War I erupted and spread quickly across Europe. Three years later the United States was swept into the conflict. Americans' struggles and sacrifices at home, in factories, and on distant battlefields helped to win the war in 1918. After World War I, many people wanted a better life. They dedicated themselves to making money and having fun. The decade became known as the Roaring Twenties.

THE LOST GENERATION

What is your feeling about this new attitude in the United States in the 1920s? Some U.S. writers were impatient with it. They believed that the war had forever altered their lives. They felt alienated, or cut off, from a country whose values they no longer shared. These writers became known as the Lost Generation. Some of them chose to leave the United States and live in Europe.

POETRY IN THE 1920s

In the 1920s, some American poets became dissatisfied with traditional poetry. Robert Frost and Carl Sandburg developed new kinds of poetry using repetition and colloquial, or everyday, speech. They stopped using nature as a kind of romantic inspiration. Nature, they believed, was simply a powerful force, neither good nor bad. They helped to create modern poetry.

1929 William Faulkner publishes *The Sound and the Fury.*

1932 Pearl Buck receives Pulitzer Prize for *The Good Earth.*

1939 John Steinbeck's *The Grapes of Wrath* appears.

1940 Richard Wright publishes *Native Son.*

1945 Gwendolyn Brooks's first book of poems is published.

1930 | 1935 | 1940 | 1945

1929 Stock market crash begins world-wide depression.

1939 Germany invades Poland; World War II begins.

1941 Japan's attack on Pearl Harbor brings U.S. into World War II.

1945 Two atomic bombs dropped on Japan end war.

SOCIAL CHANGE

In the 1920s, a group of African American writers decided to use literature as a peaceful instrument of social change. Many joined a New York City movement that became known as the Harlem Renaissance. In an explosion of creativity, African American writers and poets like Langston Hughes transferred the sounds and rhythms of music, especially jazz, to their own work. Their writing not only protested social injustice and racial discrimination; it also expressed pride in African American achievements and culture.

In 1920, women were finally recognized as United States citizens and given the right to vote. The growing awareness of women's rights produced important new literature by women writers, including Gwendolyn Brooks in Chicago; Eudora Welty in the South; and Edna St. Vincent Millay in New York City. Yet each of these writers was able to generalize her experiences and express essential truths about all people.

DEPRESSION AND WAR

On October 29, 1929, the stock market crashed, triggering the Great Depression. For the next 12 years, millions of Americans lived in poverty. Popular entertainment provided some relief. People flocked to movie theaters to witness the "talking picture."

By 1930, one out of three American homes had a radio. In 1937 millions of Americans heard President Roosevelt denounce the dictators in Europe and Japan. The threat of another world war was growing, and people were anxious. Listening to a realistic radio drama, *The War of the Worlds*, in 1938, thousands of people thought Martians had landed.

Unfortunately, Americans did not have to wait very long for real war to break out. In 1941, the United States was propelled into World War II, which lasted until 1945 and cost millions of lives.

As you read the selections, ask how they relate to your own life.

Discussing the Literary Period

Guide students through the opening paragraph of the period discussion. Tell them to take notes as they read, comparing the events presented in this section with ones they have experienced in their own lives.

Read through the rest of the section with students and allow time for discussion of each question. You might bring to class the work of photographers such as Dorothea Lange and Margaret Bourke-White, who chronicled the emotional effect of this period on the lives of many U.S. citizens. At the end, ask students to develop additional questions they would like to have answered about the historical, political, social, and literary events of this period.

Cooperative Group Activity

Divide the class into small groups. Have the members of each group synthesize the notes they took as they read the section. The members should come to a consensus about what to include on a group list, comparing the events written about in this section with events students have experienced in their own lives. Then have the groups compare lists. Save the lists to compare with new information students discover as they read the selections in class.

Selection Overview

Selection Objectives

After completing this selection, students will be able to

- understand character
- analyze a person's character traits
- write an opinion essay
- infer character traits through dialogue, action, and author's comments
- use context clues to choose synonyms
- identify imagery

Lesson Resources

A Day's Wait

- Selection Synopsis, Teacher's Edition, p. T337c
- Comprehension and Vocabulary Workbook, pp. 65–66
- Language Enrichment Workbook, pp. 51–52
- Teacher's Resources
  Reinforcement, p. R33
  Test, pp. T65–T66

More About Character

Have students brainstorm a list of round characters they have encountered in the preceding unit. Create a chalkboard chart, captioned with the terms *description*, *dialogue*, *actions*, and *commentary*. Using their suggestions, fill in the chart with story details about how the author(s) developed one or two of these characters.

About the Author

Ernest Hemingway spent a lifetime wrestling with the idea of courage. Prevented by an eye injury from joining the U.S. Army in World War I, he served in the Ambulance Corps in France and Italy and was severely wounded while rescuing an injured soldier. This experience prompted him to focus on the physical and psychological elements of courage. Discuss with students what a writer who has experienced war first-hand might write about.

Learn About

Reading Focus

Identify Imagery Imagery consists of words that describe what you might feel, hear, see, taste, or smell if you were in the scene. Writers use imagery to make the readers feel as though they are experiencing the story or poem first-hand. Look for imagery as you read the story.

Character

A **character** in literature is the representation in words of a person, or in some instances, an animal. Writers reveal the traits, or personality, of a character through description, dialogue, actions, and commentary. Often, writers present direct information about a character. This may include a description of a character's physical appearance. The words a character uses may clearly tell what he or she is thinking and feeling.

Writers also present less obvious, indirect information, called **character clues**. You can look closely at what a character does, says, feels, and thinks, and how other characters talk about and act toward that character, to make intelligent guesses about that character's personality.

As you read "A Day's Wait," ask yourself:

1. What kind of character is Schatz?
2. What actions does he take that reveal his character?

Writing Connection

Write a paragraph that reveals a strong character trait of a person you know well. Be sure to include enough specific information to help your reader decide what this person is really like.

More About the Literary Period

Influenza, or the common flu, was a poorly understood, dangerous illness during Hemingway's lifetime. Between 1918 and 1920, a global influenza epidemic killed many, including 550,000 Americans. Hemingway's contemporary readers understood fully the threat of death in this short story.

ESL Activity

Write the following adjectives on the chalkboard: brave, kind, resolute, patient, terrified, courageous. Have students write them on index cards. As they read the story, have them decide whether the adjective describes the father or the son. Discuss their reasoning.

Cooperative Group Activity

Pair students and have them create "character questionnaires," listing questions that will help them examine the personality of a character. Using the groups' suggestions, create a consensus questionnaire on the chalkboard. Have students refer to it as they write their character descriptions for the Writing Connection activity.

A DAY'S WAIT

by Ernest Hemingway

He came into the room to shut the windows while we were still in bed and I saw he looked ill. He was shivering, his face was white, and he walked slowly as though it ached to move.

"What's the matter, Schatz?"

"I've got a headache."

"You better go back to bed."

"No. I'm all right."

"You go to bed. I'll see you when I'm dressed."

But when I came downstairs he was dressed, sitting by the fire, looking a very sick and miserable boy of nine years. When I put my hand on his forehead I knew he had a fever.

"You go up to bed," I said, "you're sick."

"I'm all right," he said.

When the doctor came he took the boy's temperature.

"What is it?" I asked him.

"One hundred and two."

Downstairs, the doctor left three different medicines in different colored capsules with instructions for giving them. One was to bring down the fever, another a purgative, the third to overcome an acid condition. The germs of influenza can only exist in an acid condition, he explained. He seemed to know all about influenza and said there was nothing to worry about if the fever did not go above one hundred and four degrees. This was a light epidemic of flu and there was no danger if you avoided pneumonia.

Back in the room I wrote the boy's temperature down and made a note of the time to give the various capsules.

---

purgative (PUR guh tiv) strong laxative
influenza (in floo EN zuh) disease usually called "flu"

TEACHING PLAN

INTRODUCE

Motivation

Discuss with students whether it is better to face personal obstacles alone or share these experiences with a friend. Relate the discussion to Schatz's afternoon ordeal.

Purpose-Setting Question

Which is worse, physical pain or the emotional turmoil that often accompanies it?

READ

Literary Focus: *Character*

Ask students to make a list of words that describe each of the characters in this story as they read.

Reading Focus: *Identify Imagery*

Tell students that the author has provided imagery, words that draw the reader in by appealing to the senses of sight, sound, smell, taste, and touch. Ask students which words help them readily visualize the scenes. Encourage students to make word webs with the five senses as center ovals. Then have them include images in the story that relate to each sense on the appropriate word web.

CLOSE

Have students complete Review the Selection on pages 348–349.

Develop Vocabulary Skills

Write the footnoted vocabulary words on the chalkboard, supplying definitions if necessary. Use each word in an original sentence and call on students to do the same.

Critical Thinking: *Make Connections*

Have students think about the early 1900s and the types of diseases that routinely killed people. Ask: How likely is it that Schatz would have reacted the same way to the flu today?

Reading Focus: *Identify Imagery*

Discuss the use of imagery in "varnished with ice." Ask: What do you visualize when you read this description? How does it make you feel about the scene?

"Do you want me to read to you?"

"All right. If you want to," said the boy. His face was very white and there were dark areas under his eyes. He lay still in the bed and seemed very detached from what was going on.

I read aloud from Howard Pyle's *Book of Pirates*; but I could see he was not following what I was reading.

"How do you feel, Schatz?" I asked him.

"Just the same, so far," he said.

I sat at the foot of the bed and read to myself while I waited for it to be time to give another capsule. It would have been natural for him to go to sleep, but when I looked up he was looking at the foot of the bed, looking very strangely.

"Why don't you try to go to sleep? I'll wake you up for the medicine."

"I'd rather stay awake."

After a while he said to me, "You don't have to stay in here with me, Papa, if it bothers you."

"It doesn't bother me."

"No, I mean you don't have to stay if it's going to bother you."

I thought perhaps he was a little lightheaded and after giving him the prescribed capsules at eleven o'clock I went out for a while.

It was a bright, cold day, the ground covered with a sleet that had frozen so that it seemed as if all the bare trees, the bushes, the cut brush and all the grass and the bare ground had been varnished with ice. I took the young Irish setter for a little walk up the road and along a frozen creek, but it was difficult to stand or walk on the glassy surface and the red dog slipped and slithered and I fell twice, hard, once dropping my gun and having it slide away over the ice.

We flushed a covey of quail under a high clay bank with overhanging brush and I killed two as they went out of sight over the top of the bank. Some of the covey lit in trees, but most of them scattered into brush piles and it was necessary to jump on the ice-coated mounds of brush several times before they would flush. Coming out while you were poised unsteadily on the icy, springy

---

slither (SLI*TH* ur) slip and slide
flush (FLUSH) drive birds or animals from hiding place
covey (KUV ee) flock of birds

Adirondacks, Winslow Homer. Corbis Bettmann

brush they made difficult shooting and I killed two, missed five, and started back pleased to have found a covey close to the house and happy there were so many left to find on another day.

At the house they said the boy had refused to let anyone come into the room.

"You can't come in," he said. "You mustn't get what I have."

I went up to him and found him in exactly the position I had left him, white-faced, but with the tops of his cheeks flushed by the fever, staring still, as he had stared, at the foot of the bed.

I took his temperature.

"What is it?"

"Something like a hundred," I said. It was one hundred and two and four tenths.

"It was a hundred and two," he said.

Viewing Fine Art

Winslow Homer (1836–1910) created some of his finest works in the Adirondacks mountain region of New York State. Homer was fascinated with nature, its light, and man's relationship to it. He saw the human being as interdependent with nature, as its adversary, and as the user of its bounty. Many of his paintings show the sea's challenge to mankind, or, as here, man as an intruder into the wonder of unspoiled natural beauty. Homer's exceptional ability with watercolors (seen here) allowed him to capture the sense of silence, of flickering light, and of dense shadow in the forest. (Another painting by Winslow Homer appears on page 326.) Ask: What mood does Homer create in this painting? How does it relate to the story?

Literary Focus:
Character

Ask: Why does the father not tell the boy the exact temperature? How does the boy know what it is?

Literary Focus: *Character*

Encourage students to evaluate the father's personality. Have them suggest what they know about him. Ask: Is he a good father? Are any of his actions surprising? Have students point out specific passages that support their evaluations.

Critical Thinking: *Infer*

Explain that Schatz could have spared himself an afternoon of anguish simply by sharing his feelings with his father. Encourage students to suggest why Schatz keeps his innermost feelings to himself.

"Who said so?"

"The doctor."

"Your temperature is all right," I said. "It's nothing to worry about."

"I don't worry," he said, "but I can't keep from thinking."

"Don't think," I said. "Just take it easy."

"I'm taking it easy," he said and looked straight ahead. He was evidently holding tight onto himself about something.

"Take this with water."

"Do you think it will do any good?"

"Of course it will."

I sat down and opened the *Pirate* book and commenced to read, but I could see he was not following, so I stopped.

"About what time do you think I'm going to die?" he asked.

"What?"

"About how long will it be before I die?"

"You aren't going to die. What's the matter with you?"

"Oh, yes, I am. I heard him say a hundred and two."

"People don't die with a fever of one hundred and two. That's a silly way to talk."

"I know they do. At school in France the boys told me you can't live with forty-four degrees. I've got a hundred and two."

He had been waiting to die all day, ever since nine o'clock in the morning.

"You poor Schatz," I said. "Poor old Schatz. It's like miles and kilometers. You aren't going to die. That's a different thermometer. On that thermometer thirty-seven is normal. On this kind it's ninety-eight."

"Are you sure?"

"Absolutely," I said. "It's like miles and kilometers. You know, like how many kilometers we make when we do seventy miles in the car?"

"Oh," he said.

But his gaze at the foot of the bed relaxed slowly. The hold over himself relaxed too, finally, and the next day it was very slack and he cried very easily at little things that were of no importance.

---

commence (kuh MENS) begin

Reading Focus: *Identify Imagery*

Ask: How had Schatz changed by the end of the story? How did the author's description help you to visualize this change?

Mini Quiz

Write the following questions on the chalkboard or read them aloud. Call on students to fill in the blanks.

1. Schatz is ________ years old.
2. Schatz was in no danger as long as his fever stayed below ________.
3. Schatz's father went outside to hunt ________.
4. "A Day's Wait" takes place during the season of ________.
5. Schatz's father compared ________ to miles to explain Schatz's correct temperature.

Answers

1. nine
2. 104°
3. quail
4. winter
5. kilometers

AUTHOR BIOGRAPHY

Ernest Hemingway (1899–1961)

Quick! List three facts about a famous living American writer.

Could you do it? Maybe. But if you'd lived during the time of Ernest Hemingway, you probably could have done it easily. Wherever he went and whatever he did, Hemingway was always big news. His name was often in the headlines:

HEMINGWAY BREAKS NOSE IN BOXING RING
PLANE CRASH KILLS HEMINGWAY IN AFRICA
GOOD NEWS: HEMINGWAY ALIVE!
HEMINGWAY MARRIES FOR FOURTH TIME
HEMINGWAY YACHT IN U-BOAT CHASE
GUN ACCIDENT INJURES HEMINGWAY

A bear of a man, Hemingway photographed well. All America knew what he looked like. He seemed always in action: skiing in Switzerland, hunting in Africa, fishing from his private yacht, risking his life as a reporter on distant war fronts. Yet, somehow during his active life, he took the time to write the stories and novels that won him the highest honor a writer can earn, the Nobel Prize.

"All you have to do is, write one true sentence," Hemingway discovered when he was starting out. "Write the truest sentence you know." That one sentence, he found, would lead to another, to a paragraph, to a story. He disliked fancy writing; he wanted it pure and simple, lifelike and honest. Do you think any other author of our century has had a greater influence upon modern American writers than Ernest Hemingway?

How did Hemingway differ from the stereotype you may have in mind of a "famous author"?

MORE ABOUT THE AUTHOR

Unlike other expatriate writers who returned to the mainstream of American literary life, Hemingway elected to remain on the boundaries of society, living in places like Key West, Florida, the island of Bimini, and in Cuba. He used this separation to critically examine society and to perfect his prose style, uninterrupted by everyday distractions.

Additional Works

BY ERNEST HEMINGWAY

True at First Light, Simon & Schuster Trade, 1999.

The Sun Also Rises, Warner Books, Incorporated, 1995.

The Collected Poems of Ernest Hemingway, Folcroft Library Editions, 1989.

A Farewell to Arms, International Book Centre, Incorporated, 1985.

UNDERSTAND THE SELECTION

Answers

1. 9:00 a.m. until late afternoon
2. the foot of his bed
3. one hundred two and four-tenths
4. Schatz tells his father to leave the room if he is bothered by the boy's condition.
5. Schatz wants to spare his father the anguish of seeing his son die.
6. when he relaxes his gaze at the foot of his bed
7. Sample answer: Schatz knows he will not die; he relaxes and behaves like an ordinary sick child.
8. Sample answer: thoughts about trying to be strong and brave, fears about death and missing my family
9. Sample answer: He would not have been so scared; the story would then be about a normal illness, not about a moment of crisis.
10. Answers will vary. Titles should reflect information or imagery from the story.

Respond to Literature

Have students identify the major international conflicts of the period. Discuss with them Hemingway's role as an ambulance driver in World War I and as a frontline journalist in both the Spanish Civil War and World War II. Ask them what role a writer's real-life experiences play in his or her choice of fictional subjects and themes.

WRITE ABOUT THE SELECTION

Prewriting

Write these phrases on the board, asking students what character traits they reveal.

Setting: A basketball game.

1. A player deliberately pushes or trips an opposing player.
2. A player slams down the ball after the referee's call.
3. A player extends a hand to a fallen, opposing player.
4. A player congratulates an opposing player after a fine play.
5. A player remains in the game, even when hurt.
6. A player shakes his or her opponent's hand after the game.

Writing

Have students work on their paragraphs individually. Circulate around the class, offering help to any student who is having difficulty.

Revising

Make this a cooperative group activity. Have students work in small groups, exchanging papers and making suggestions for improvement.

Proofreading

Review common proofreading marks with the class. Then select one or two of the students' paragraphs as models for proofreading. Put the paragraphs on the overhead projector and have the class suggest improvements.

Review the Selection

UNDERSTAND THE SELECTION

Recall

1. Between what times of day does "A Day's Wait" take place?
2. At what object in his room does Schatz constantly gaze?
3. What is Schatz's temperature the second time it is taken?

Infer

4. What is the first clue that Schatz is worried about more than his fever?
5. Why does Schatz suggest to his father that he may leave the room?
6. How does the reader know when Schatz has stopped worrying?
7. Why does Schatz cry very easily the next day?

Apply

8. If you were Schatz, what thoughts would run through your mind?
9. What might have happened if Schatz had heard what the doctor really said?
10. Choose two other appropriate titles for "A Day's Wait."

Respond to Literature

What events in the early twentieth century might have prompted Hemingway to write this story of courage?

WRITE ABOUT THE SELECTION

"A Day's Wait" is about a boy's courage in the face of what he thinks is overwhelming danger. The author implies that a person's true character is revealed only when he or she is facing ultimate peril. This would still hold true if the danger were only in the person's mind. Do you agree with this idea? Are there other circumstances in which a person's true character can be revealed? Think of other circumstances in which someone's true character is revealed and write a short paragraph that explains your views.

Prewriting Freewrite an informal list of situations, such as an argument, a sports competition, or a date, in which people are apt to reveal their true characters. The incident could be something ordinary that happens every day. Then, freewrite specific character traits that may surface in the particular situation you choose to write about.

Writing Use your freewriting lists to write a paragraph that explains one situation, other than danger, in which a person's true character is revealed.

Revising Reread your paragraph and decide whether any specific information can be added to make your explanation clearer to a reader. Have you made clear the reasons behind people's actions?

Proofreading Read over your paragraph and check for errors.

THINK ABOUT CHARACTER

A **character** is a person or animal in a story, poem, or drama. Readers infer what a character's words, actions, feelings, and thoughts really show about his or her personality. Readers may also learn about a character through the things other characters say about him or her.

1. What kind of a person is Schatz?
2. Writers usually describe a character's physical appearance. Yet, in the story, Hemingway only describes Schatz's face, and then, briefly. What other character clues help you to determine what Schatz is really like?
3. Select three of Schatz's statements and explain how each contributes to your understanding of his character. Explain what each statement revealed about him.
4. Understanding a character's personality allows you to predict how he or she may react to other events. When he is older, how might Schatz react to a physically dangerous fire or storm? Explain your answer.

Reading Focus

Identify Imagery As you read, you were able to identify words that described sights, sounds, smells, tastes, and feelings of touch. Choose an example of imagery from the story that particularly appealed to you. Explain why you chose it.

DEVELOP YOUR VOCABULARY

A **synonym** is a word that has the same or nearly the same meaning as another word. For instance, Schatz is described as being *detached*—not really involved with what is going on in his room. The author might have used the words *distracted* or *preoccupied* as synonyms for *detached*.

Read the sentences below and choose the best synonym for the *italicized* word.

1. He could fall and *slither* across the frozen pond.
   - **a.** pause
   - **b.** glide
   - **c.** relax
   - **d.** listen
   - **e.** stumble
2. Hunters often use dogs to *flush* their prey from hiding places.
   - **a.** dislodge
   - **b.** smell
   - **c.** force
   - **d.** recover
   - **e.** convince
3. We were startled by a *covey* of pigeons . . .
   - **a.** handful
   - **b.** group
   - **c.** feather
   - **d.** line
   - **e.** regiment
4. Each time that his father *commenced* reading, Schatz would turn away.
   - **a.** halted
   - **b.** interrupted
   - **c.** started
   - **d.** paused
   - **e.** ended

THINK ABOUT CHARACTER

Answers

1. Sample answer: Schatz is courageous, honest, and inquisitive.
2. Students should mention what Schatz says and what comments the author makes about him.
3. Answers will vary.
4. Answers will vary. Most students will say Schatz will be courageous and, if others are present, sensitive to their feelings and needs.

DEVELOP YOUR VOCABULARY

Answers

1. (b) glide
2. (a) dislodge
3. (b) group
4. (c) started

You might want to write these additional story words on the chalkboard and have students suggest synonyms for each: *miserable*: sad, wretched; *various*: different; *scattered*: separated, dispersed; *absolutely*: completely, without question.

Reading Focus

Sample Answer

On page 344, the description the author gives of the outdoor scene and how he describes the way "the red dog slipped and slithered," helps me to see the wintery scene and to feel the cold.

ESL Activity

Have students work in pairs to write descriptive sentences. Give each pair of students these words: *grass*, *leaves*, *ice*, *lettuce*, and *heat*. Ask them to write sentences including each word, adding descriptive language to elicit a sensory response.

SELECTION OVERVIEW

SELECTION OBJECTIVES

After completing these selections, students will be able to

- understand the structure and content of lyric poetry
- use alliteration to write advertising jingles
- analyze two lyric poems
- write a lyric poem
- understand how consonants determine rhythm
- understand figurative language
- evaluate the writer's purpose

Lesson Resources

Lament/Afternoon on a Hill

- Selection Synopses, Teacher's Edition, pp. T337d
- Comprehension and Vocabulary Workbook, pp. 67–68
- Language Enrichment Workbook, pp. 53–54
- Teacher's Resources
  Reinforcement, p. R34
  Test, pp. T67–T68

More About Lyric Poetry

Explain to students that lyric poems were originally sung to the accompaniment of a small harp, or lyre. Point out that lyric poems now depend on the beauty and rhythm of language to achieve musical or song-like effects. Using students' suggestions, create a class list of topics and themes that are suitable for this poetic form. Save this list for use with the Write About the Selection activity.

About the Author

Throughout her life, Edna St. Vincent Millay sought to combine the elements of poetry, music, and drama. In addition to her thriving poetry career—she published more than eleven volumes of verse—she performed as a professional actress with the *Provincetown Players* in Massachusetts and wrote popular magazine sketches under the pseudonym Nancy Boyd. Angered by the rise of foreign dictatorships during the 1930s, she devoted herself to democratic causes by writing numerous radio plays and speeches in support of the democratic side during the Spanish Civil War.

Learn About

LYRIC POETRY

Of the many types of poetry written, the lyric is perhaps the most varied in structure, subject matter, and mood. Some characteristics that **lyric poems** have in common, however, are these: they are brief and imaginative; they have "melody;" they express the personal, emotional feelings and thoughts of a single speaker.

Lyric poems make use of many poetic techniques to achieve their musical quality. Two such techniques are repetition and alliteration. **Repetition**, using the same or similar words over again, may occur at regular or irregular places in the poem. Alliteration is also a device of repetition. In **alliteration**, it is the initial consonant (or sometimes vowel) sounds of nearby words that are repeated, as in "*Bend* the *bow*; let the *bolt burst* the *bubble* apart."

As you read the poems, ask yourself:

1. What unified emotional impression does each poem make?
2. What poetic devices are used in each poem?

READING FOCUS

Evaluate the Writer's Purpose Evaluating the writer's purpose means figuring out why the author wrote something. This will give you insight into the deeper meanings of the work. Also, as a reader you can evaluate whether you agree or disagree with the author's attitude toward the subject. As you read each of these poems, decide what the poet's purpose is and whether you agree with it.

WRITING CONNECTION

Using alliteration, write a four-line stanza in which at least two words in each line begin with the same sound.

ESL Activity

Ask students to explain whether it is customary in their own cultures to talk about those who have died. As appropriate, invite students to share any rituals common to death in their cultures. Be sensitive to those who have recently lost a loved one.

Cooperative Group Activity

Tell students that advertising jingles and slogans use alliteration to capture consumer interest. Pair students and have them use alliteration to write a four-line jingle for an object in the classroom as they complete the Writing Connection activity. Have one student in each pair read the stanza, and ask the class to choose the most effective jingle.

Lament

by Edna St. Vincent Millay

Listen, children:
Your father is dead.
From his old coats
I'll make you little jackets;
5 I'll make you little trousers
From his old pants.
There'll be in his pockets
Things he used to put there,
Keys and pennies
10 Covered with tobacco;
Dan shall have the pennies
To save in his bank;
Anne shall have the keys
To make a pretty noise with.
15 Life must go on,
And the dead be forgotten;
Life must go on,
Though good men die;
Anne, eat your breakfast;
20 Dan, take your medicine;
Life must go on;
I forget just why.

My Family, Leopold Seyffert. The Brooklyn Museum

Teaching Plan

INTRODUCE

Motivation

Write these opening lines from one of Edna St. Vincent Millay's sonnets on the chalkboard or on an overhead transparency.

"'I will put Chaos into fourteen lines
And keep him there;
And let him thence escape
If he be lucky."

Discuss what the poet is saying through these lines.

Purpose-Setting Question

Ask: Are some topics best addressed by male or female writers and poets?

READ

Literary Focus: *Lyric Poetry*

Have students read through "Lament." Ask: What kind of mother is the speaker? Cite references in the poem to support your opinion.

Reading Focus: *Evaluate the Writer's Purpose*

Ask: How do you think the author views the speakers of "Lament" and "Afternoon on a Hill?" What makes you think this?

CLOSE

Have students complete Review the Selection on pages 354–355.

Develop Vocabulary Skills

Have students read through "Afternoon on a Hill" to find words with more than one meaning, that can be used as other parts of speech, and that have different pronunciations. Have students use the words in sentences. Provide assistance as needed.

Viewing Fine Art

Leopold Seyffert (1887–1956) was an American portrait painter. The peak of his career was from 1913–1926. He is best known for portraits of important people in art and industry. In his lifetime, he painted over 400 of them. Portrait painting is difficult because the subjects are people, called *sitters*, who must sit still for a long time. It is said that Leopold Seyffert's friendly and humorous personality made the sitter's job comfortable and even fun. Ask: If you were a portrait painter, what would you do to make the sitter feel at ease?

Critical Thinking: *Infer*

Tell students that every poem has a speaker. They should read "Lament" to identify the speaker. How does she feel about the children? about the father? What does she tell us about herself in the last two lines? In the poem "Afternoon on a Hill," at what two locations does the speaker feel at home?

Literary Focus: *Lyric Poetry*

Ask: Why is this poem considered a lyric?

Reading Focus: *Evaluate the Writer's Purpose*

Ask: What is the poet's purpose for writing this poem?

Discussion

Ask students if a poet must directly experience the thoughts and emotions that he or she writes about. Elicit the idea that although a lyric poem expresses personal feelings and thoughts, it need not be autobiographical. In "Lament," Edna St. Vincent Millay vividly conveys the emotions of a grieving wife, even though she herself never felt them. Point out that a great poet uses imagination to communicate emotions and thoughts that he or she has not experienced.

Comparing Selections

Ask: How are these poems different in tone? in form?

Afternoon on a Hill

by Edna St. Vincent Millay

I will be the gladdest thing
    Under the sun!
I will touch a hundred flowers
    And not pick one.
5 I will look at cliffs and clouds
    With quiet eyes,
Watch the wind bow down the grass,
    And the grass rise.
10 And when lights begin to show
    Up from the town,
I will mark which must be mine,
    And then start down!

Mini Quiz

Write the following questions on the chalkboard or read them aloud. Call on students to fill in the blanks.

1. There are ________ characters in "Lament."
2. The little girl's name is ________.
3. The speaker will make little ________ and ________ from the father's old clothing.
4. The speaker of "Afternoon" will look at ________ and ________ with "quiet eyes."
5. The speaker will leave the hill when she sees ________ from the ________.

Answers

1. three
2. Anne
3. jackets; trousers
4. cliffs; clouds
5. lights; town

AUTHOR BIOGRAPHY

Edna St. Vincent Millay (1892–1950)

Edna St. Vincent Millay was a writer who wanted to tell the truth about life and love from a woman's point of view. In the 1920s, Millay became a symbol of life, love, and a newfound freedom. She would start a poem:

> What lips my lips have kissed, and
> where, and why,
> I have forgotten . . .

In the 1920s, this was scandalous, but for many people delightfully so. Curious poetry lovers flocked to her poetry readings across the country. There they found a small, attractive young woman with golden red hair, a sensitive voice, and a dignified manner. They also found that Millay's reputation as a symbol of bright, adventurous youth was only part of the picture. Most of her best poems did not concern love at all, and she often spoke of sorrow, hardship, and loss. It is upon this reputation that her fame rests.

Hardship and loss were hardly strangers to the young poet. Her early life on the coast of Maine had been generally happy but far from easy. Her parents were divorced when she was a young girl, and for years her mother supported the family on what she could earn as a nurse. Although Millay was an active, prize-winning student in high school, there was no money for college. Accepting this loss as a fact of life, she continued to work at her poetry. A long poem called "Renascence," written when she was nineteen, brought her early fame. Then came college, success, years of travel, and a good marriage. Much of her later work reveals an inner anguish caused by what she saw as human injustice and stupidity. Her greatest regret was that even a perfect poem can do little to remake an imperfect world.

Why do you think Millay's poems were so shocking in the 1920s?

MORE ABOUT THE AUTHOR

To many of her contemporaries, Edna St. Vincent Millay symbolized the liberated woman of the 1920s. Her poetry challenged prevailing male chauvinism, proving that women could write as openly and as effectively about love as could men.

Additional Works

BY EDNA ST. VINCENT MILLAY

Letters, Greenwood Publishing Group, Incorporated, 1973.

Collected Lyrics, HarperCollins Publishers, Incorporated, 1969.

UNDERSTAND THE SELECTION

Answers

1. A woman talks with her children about the death of their father.
2. keys, pennies, tobacco
3. sun, flowers, cliffs, clouds, wind, grass
4. They are young: Dan is old enough to have a piggy bank; Anne is still fascinated by the sound of jingling keys.
5. Sample answer: She has not; she cannot explain, even to herself, why life must go on.
6. Sample answer: The future tense shows anticipation or longing for this experience.
7. Sample answer: The person is carefully observing the scene while trying not to disturb it.
8. Sample answer: She is a strong, caring mother, who bolsters her children even as she questions the future.
9. Sample answer: The joy of participating in nature without having to take from it.
10. Answers will vary but should refer to the poem and the woman's children.

Respond to Literature

Ask students in what year women were given the right to vote in the United States (1920). Encourage them to suggest what this says about women's traditional, and emerging, roles in society. Elicit the idea that women were supposed to contain their feelings and just fulfill their roles as mothers and wives. Point out that "Lament" deals with a novel subject for poetry of that time: the inner feelings of a woman.

WRITE ABOUT THE SELECTION

Prewriting

Use the class list you developed in the "More About Lyric Poetry" section to help students brainstorm events for their poems.

Review the Selection

UNDERSTAND THE SELECTION

Recall

1. What is the subject of "Lament"?
2. What items does the wife retrieve from her husband's pockets?
3. Identify the elements of nature mentioned in "Afternoon on a Hill."

Infer

4. How old do you think the two children in "Lament" are? Why?
5. Has the speaker in "Lament" accepted her husband's death? Explain.
6. Why is "Afternoon on a Hill" written in the future tense?
7. In "Afternoon on a Hill," what do you think "quiet eyes" means?

Apply

8. How would you characterize the mother in "Lament"?
9. On one level, "Afternoon on a Hill" is about someone thinking about spending an afternoon on a hill. What is another meaning of the poem?
10. Why will the speaker in "Lament" remember that life must go on?

Respond to Literature

How does the subject matter of "Lament" reflect the changing roles of women in U.S. society during the 1920s?

WRITE ABOUT THE SELECTION

From reading "Afternoon on a Hill," you have seen that a poem need not be about an extraordinary event or experience. What makes an ordinary event come alive however, is the arrangement of vivid, descriptive words. Almost any event or experience can be made significant through the use of interpretation and creativity. Write a short poem about an incident in your own life this week, that at first seemed unimportant or insignificant.

Prewriting Brainstorm an event you experienced this week. It could be one of the following: a small act of kindness; the joy of watching a sports team win; or perhaps discovering a new side to a friend's personality. Then decide what rhythm or flow you think will best communicate the experience in a poem.

Writing Now, write a short poem that shows the true importance of something that happened to you this week. In it, try to have the poem's rhythm match the rhythm of the event. Use Millay's poems as models if you wish.

Revising When you revise your poem, read it out loud to determine if the way the words flow contributes to how you feel about the event. Your words should capture the mood of the event.

Proofreading Read your poem and check for errors. Use the correct line format for poetry.

Writing

Have students work on their poems individually. Go around the class, giving help to any student who is having difficulty.

Revising

Make this a cooperative group activity. Have students work in small groups to revise their poems. Then call on volunteers to share their poems with the class. Ask students if they learned something special from a poem.

Proofreading

Select one or two of the students' poems as models for proofreading. Put the poems on the overhead projector and have the class suggest improvements. Tell students that poets often intentionally break rules of grammar and punctuation. Allow them to leave unchanged any student's "intentional" errors.

THINK ABOUT LYRIC POETRY

Lyric poems may have any of a number of rhythmic patterns and may be either rhymed or unrhymed. Sometimes rhythms can be varied by the kinds of consonants the poet chooses. For instance, consonants like *l*, *m*, *n*, and *r* can be drawn out to produce a smooth rhythm when spoken aloud. Consonants like *b*, *d*, *k*, *p*, and *t*, however, create a quickened or staccato rhythm.

1. What rhythmic devices can you find in the first poem you read, "Lament"?
2. What rhythmic devices do you find in the second poem "Afternoon on a Hill"?
3. How does the repetition of the sentence "Life must go on" in "Lament" contribute to the meaning of the poem?
4. Explain the sequence of events in "Afternoon on a Hill."
5. Who is the speaker in each poem?

Reading Focus

Evaluate the Writer's Purpose What do you think the poet's purpose is in "Lament"? What is the poet's purpose in writing "Afternoon on a Hill"? Provide details from each poem to support your responses.

DEVELOP YOUR VOCABULARY

Figurative language is a way of putting words and phrases together to create a meaning that is different from the dictionary meaning of the individual words. For instance, in "The reader *jumped* to the wrong conclusion," the word *jump* is used figuratively to suggest that the reader assumed something too quickly.

Words or phrases that mean exactly what they say are called **literal language**. In "The track runner *jumped* the hurdles successfully," the words mean exactly, or literally, what they say.

For each pair of sentences below, determine which sentence uses figurative and which sentence uses literal language.

1. The substitute teacher *saddled* us with too much homework.
2. The cowboy *saddled* his spotted pony and began his journey.
3. The pianist *struck the right notes.*
4. The politician *struck the right notes* in her reelection speech.

THINK ABOUT LYRIC POETRY

Answers

1. repetition of words, phrases, and lines; varied meter; some rhyme; consonants that create a quickened pace, especially in the middle of the poem
2. regular rhyme scheme, regular meter, alliteration of *cl*, *w*, and *m* words
3. Sample answer: The mother is trying to convince herself that, indeed, life must go on.
4. The speaker imagines herself observing nature and daydreaming on a hill. She will return to the town, or reality, when evening comes.
5. Sample answer: The grieving mother in "Lament," the poet herself in "Afternoon on a Hill."

DEVELOP YOUR VOCABULARY

Sample Answers

1. Figurative
2. Literal
3. Literal
4. Figurative

Reading Focus

Sample Answer

The poet's purpose for writing "Lament" is to express that life must go on after a loved one dies, however difficult that may be. This is supported by the mother's concern for her children's daily needs, such as breakfast and medicine. The poet's purpose for "Afternoon on a Hill" may be to express that life is wondrous and the speaker feels grateful to be a part of it all. This is shown through the language and punctuation in the poem.

ESL Activity

To help students complete the Develop Your Vocabulary activity, have them try to visualize or draw what is happening in each sentence. Explain that the sentences for which they can draw a concrete picture use literal language. The others use figurative language.

Selection Overview

Selection Objectives

After completing this selection, students will be able to

- understand setting
- use vivid details to describe a setting
- write a descriptive passage
- analyze the effect of setting on the mood of a story
- use context to determine word meaning
- recognize implied themes

Lesson Resources

home

- Selection Synopsis, Teacher's Edition, p. T337d
- Comprehension and Vocabulary Workbook, pp. 69–70
- Language Enrichment Workbook, pp. 55–56
- Teacher's Resources
  Reinforcement, p. R35
  Test, pp. T69–T70

More About Setting

To help students fully understand setting, you might pose questions about "A Day's Wait," such as: Where and when did it take place? How did the setting affect the characters and action of the story? How did it contribute to the mood? Outline a chart on the chalkboard, captioned with: *where*, *when*, *effect on characters*, *effect on events*, and *effect on mood*. Then, have small groups of students choose a selection they have read in a preceding unit and fill in their own "setting charts." Encourage them to share and discuss their answers.

Learn About

Setting

Setting is the time and place in which fiction, such as a short story, poem, or play, occurs. You can think of setting as the total environment, or the created world, in which a work of literature happens.

To determine setting, look for word clues that tell *where* and *when* the story takes place. For example, look for specific words and phrases that describe the location and scenery of the story. To understand the *when* of a story—its time frame—read for details that show the historical time period, season of year, and time of day. Remember, too, that story settings can change over time.

Setting is crucial because it can affect people and events in a story. Setting can force a character to act or feel in certain ways. For example, you would expect a person who is caught in a terrible snowstorm to behave differently than one who is relaxing on a warm, sunny beach.

As you read "home" ask yourself:

1. What is the setting of the story?
2. How does the setting affect the character's behavior?

Reading Focus

Recognize Implied Theme A theme is the message that a story is written to convey. An implied theme is one that you must infer from the work as a whole. As you read "home," think about the larger message the author may be sending.

Writing Connection

Writers use details to help the reader visualize a setting. Write a brief description of a favorite place and include vivid and specific details.

About the Author

Gwendolyn Brooks was born in Topeka, Kansas, but grew up, and continues to live, in Chicago, Illinois. Much of her poetry and prose focuses on the everyday experiences of urban African Americans. Her writing is characterized by a strong sense of rhythm and the use of colloquial speech. A writer of great compassion, Gwendolyn Brooks has achieved both critical and popular success. For her second book of poems, *Annie Allen*, she became the first African American to win the Pulitzer Prize for poetry.

More About the Literary Period

The promise of secure, high paying jobs in defense plants during World War I drew thousands of African Americans to northern cities, like New York, Newark, St. Louis, and Chicago. Unfortunately, racial segregation compelled them to settle and live in urban ghettos.

Cooperative Group Activity

To complete the Writing Connection activity, develop a class consensus of a favorite place. Have pairs of students write a vivid sentence about an aspect of the setting: location, scenery, historical time period, etc. Combine the sentences in a single descriptive passage.

home

ADAPTED

by Gwendolyn Brooks

What had been wanted was this always, this always to last, the talking softly on this porch, with the snake plant in the jardiniere in the southwest corner, and the obstinate slip from Aunt Eppie's magnificent Michigan fern at the left side of the friendly door. Mama, Maud Martha, and Helen rocked slowly in their rocking chairs, and looked at the late afternoon light on the lawn, and at the emphatic iron of the fence and at the poplar tree. These things might soon be theirs no longer. Those shafts and pools of light, the tree, the graceful iron, might soon be viewed possessively by different eyes.

Papa was to have gone that noon, during his lunch hour, to the office of the Home Owners' Loan. If he had not succeeded in getting another extension, they would be leaving this house in which they had lived for more than 14 years. There was little hope. The Home Owners' Loan was hard. They sat, making their plans.

"We'll be moving into a nice flat somewhere," said Mama. "Somewhere on South Park, or Michigan, or in Washington Park Court." Those flats, as the girls and Mama knew well, were burdens on wages twice the size of Papa's. This was not mentioned now.

"They're much prettier than this old house," said Helen. "I have friends that wouldn't come down this far for anything, unless they were in a taxi."

Yesterday, Maud Martha would have attacked her. Tomorrow she might. Today she said nothing. She merely gazed at a little hopping robin in the tree, her tree, and tried to keep her eyes dry.

---

jardiniere (jahr duh NIR) a decorative flower pot or stand
obstinate (OB stuh nut) stubborn
emphatic (em FAT ik) very striking; definite
flat (FLAT) an apartment with rooms on one floor

Teaching Plan

INTRODUCE

Motivation

To help students appreciate the historical background of "home," you might read excerpts from Stud Terkel's *Hard Times: An Oral History of the Great Depression*. Encourage students to imagine the hardships and strains placed on a family living during this time.

Purpose-Setting Question

How can a family help its individual members during periods of crisis?

READ

Literary Focus: ***Setting***

As students read, encourage them to list words and phrases that describe the setting. Then have them decide which of the phrases are probably most accurate.

Reading Focus: ***Recognize Implied Theme***

Point out to students that they may need to read all, or most of, the story before deciding upon the implied theme. Ask: What clues can you use to discover the implied theme?

CLOSE

Have students complete Review the Selection on pages 360–361.

Develop Vocabulary Skills

Call on a volunteer to read the footnoted vocabulary words and their definitions. Suggest a synonym for each word, then have pairs of students compete to see which pair can list the most synonyms for each word.

ESL Activity

Read the first paragraph to the students. Discuss it so that students can visualize this scene. Ask students to read the last two lines carefully to find out why this moment is so precious to the characters in the story. Draw a diagram of this scene.

Discussion

Ask students from what point of view, or perspective, the story is told. You might ask them: Who is telling the story? Do you learn the thoughts and feelings of different characters or of just one character? Elicit that "home" is narrated in the third-person point of view. An omniscient narrator enters the minds of the characters at different times to let the reader experience feelings and thoughts of the characters. A first-person narrator tells the story from that one character's voice.

Literary Focus: *Setting*

Ask: Why do people change their minds about how they feel about the setting?

"Well, I do know," said Mama, turning her hands over and over, "that I've been getting tireder and tireder of doing that firing. From October to April, there's firing to be done."

"But lately we've been helping, Harry and I," said Maud Martha. "And sometimes in March and April and in October, and even in November, we could build a little fire in the fireplace. Sometimes the weather was just right for that."

She knew, from the way they looked at her, that this had been a mistake. They did not want to cry.

But she felt that the little line of white, somewhat ridged with smoked purple, and all that cream-shot saffron, would never drift across any western sky except that in back of this house. The rain would drum with as sweet a dullness nowhere but here. The birds on South Park were mechanical birds, no better than the poor caught canaries in those "rich" women's sun parlors.

"It's just going to kill Papa!" burst out Maud Martha. "He loves this house! He *lives* for this house!"

"He lives for us," said Helen. "It's us he loves. He wouldn't want the house, except for us."

"And he'll have us," added Mama, "wherever."

"You know," Helen sighed, "if you want to know the truth, this is a relief. If this hadn't come up, we would have gone on, just dragged on, hanging out here forever."

"It might," allowed Mama, "be an act of God. God may just have reached down, and picked up the reins."

"Yes," Maud Martha cracked in, "that's what you always say —that God knows best."

Her mother looked at her quickly, decided the statement was not suspect, looked away.

Helen saw Papa coming. "There's Papa," said Helen.

They could not tell a thing from the way Papa was walking. It was that same dear little staccato walk, one shoulder down, then the other, then repeat, and repeat. They watched his progress. He passed the Kennedy's, he passed the vacant lot, he passed Mrs. Blakesmore's. They wanted to hurl themselves over the fence, into the street, and shake the truth out of his collar. He opened his gate—

---

firing (FYR ing) to light a fire in a boiler
saffron (SAF run) bright, orange-yellow color
staccato (stuh KAHT oh) short, distinct movement

Oil Sketch for *American Gothic*, Grant Wood. Rinard Collection, Estate of Grant Wood/Licensed by VAGA, New York, NY

the gate—and still his stride and face told them nothing.

"Hello," he said.

Mama got up and followed him through the front door. The girls knew better than to go in too.

Presently Mama's head emerged. Her eyes were lamps turned on.

"It's all right," she exclaimed. "He got it. It's all over. Everything is all right."

The door slammed shut. Mama's footsteps hurried away.

"I haven't given a party since I was eleven. I'd like some of my friends to just casually see that we're homeowners."

---

presently (PREZ unt lee) in a little while

Viewing Fine Art

Grant Wood (1892–1942) was an American painter who pictured scenes of the farm belt of the Midwest. Although his famous painting "American Gothic" satirized the people of those farms, Wood was greatly admired as a champion of the "American way of life." The old farmhouse seen here seems to represent Midwestern America itself; Wood was known as a "regionalist" because he captured the essence of the region. In the painting seen on page 479, a more characteristic painting by Wood can be seen. Ask: How does this house resemble the house in the story? How does it differ?

Reading Focus: *Recognize Implied Theme*

Refer students to the line "Her eyes were lamps turned on. 'It's all right,' she exclaimed. 'He got it. It's all over. Everything is all right.'" Discuss how these lines might lead readers to the implied theme of this story.

Mini Quiz

Write the following questions on the chalkboard or read them aloud. Call on students to fill in the blanks.

1. This story takes place on a ________ of a house.
2. An ________ fence surrounds the yard of the house.
3. Maud Martha's husband's name is ________.
4. The family has lived in the same ________ for more than ________ years.
5. The family could tell ________ from Papa's ________ walk.

Answers

1. porch
2. iron
3. Harry
4. house; fourteen
5. nothing; staccato

Review the Selection

UNDERSTAND THE SELECTION

Recall

1. Where does "home" take place?
2. For whom are the women waiting?
3. Would it cost the family the same, more, or less money to live in a flat?

Infer

4. Do you think the family could move into a nice flat? Why?
5. Do you think Helen is stating her real feelings about moving away?
6. Why does Maud Martha fear that her comment about "a little fire in the fireplace" will make the others cry?
7. Why does Helen decide to give a party at the conclusion of the story?

Apply

8. Defend or refute: "Characters always believe they have complete control over their lives."
9. Contrast Mama's attitude about leaving with Maud Martha's. Would you expect a mother to act this way?
10. Brooks tries to show people coping with disappointment. Is she successful? Explain.

Respond to Literature

How does "home" reflect the experience of many American families?

WRITE ABOUT THE SELECTION

Suppose that Papa's homeowners' loan extension has not been approved, and the family has to move into an apartment. How would the characters feel about their new home? Would they adjust in time? Which character would have the most difficult time? How would they get along with the neighbors? Write a brief passage that describes one aspect of their new neighborhood or apartment.

Prewriting Write an informal outline describing what this new location might look like. Think about the scenery, the outside of the building, and the neighborhood as well as the apartment's individual rooms. include the time of day or particular season in your outline.

Writing Use your informal outline to write a passage that describes one aspect of the family's new home. In it, create a mood appropriate to the way the family members might really feel. Try to make the characters' reactions consistent with their personalities and their attitudes.

Revising When you revise your passage, consider whether the descriptive words or phrases you used reflect the mood or atmosphere of the setting.

Proofreading Read over your passage to check for errors. Be sure that all your sentences end with periods, question marks, or exclamation marks. Check your internal punctuation as well. Review the correct use of commas.

UNDERSTAND THE SELECTION

Answers

1. on the family's porch
2. Papa
3. more
4. Sample answer: No, they would not be able to afford a nice flat.
5. Sample answer: No, she is deliberately looking on the bright side of things to avoid sadness about leaving her home.
6. Sample answer: It will make them think of losing the comfort and sense of family that this shared ritual symbolizes.
7. Sample answer: She wants to share and celebrate her joy at being able to stay in her house.
8. Sample Answer: No one in "home" has much control over their present problem; each is pessimistic about the future.
9. Sample answer: Maud Martha is more forthright about her sadness. Mama assumes a parental role, acting with a positive outlook.
10. Answers will vary. Most students will say that she is successful. Students should use examples from the story.

Respond to Literature

Have students suggest what life might have been like during the Depression. Point out that many families lost their savings when banks failed and they couldn't purchase food, pay medical expenses, or make rent or mortgage payments. Many families experienced the threat of losing their homes.

WRITE ABOUT THE SELECTION

Prewriting

Using students' suggestions, create a sample outline on the chalkboard or an overhead transparency.

Sample outline:

I. Interior of a new apartment
   A. Small and cramped
   B. No room for family's furniture
   C. Torn wallpaper
   D. Flaking paint
II. Winter, evening

Writing

Have students work on this section individually. Offer help to those who are having difficulty.

Revising

Make this a cooperative group activity. Have pairs of students exchange passages and suggest revisions. Have them focus on varying sentence length.

Proofreading

Choose several passages and display them on an overhead projector. Ask students to suggest spelling and other improvements.

THINK ABOUT SETTING

Setting often contributes to a particular mood or atmosphere in a story, poem, or play. A large, comfortable front porch establishes one set of feelings, while a small, cramped apartment creates quite different feelings. Characters in a story are usually influenced by the setting.

1. Describe the setting that Gwendolyn Brooks created in "home."
2. What time of day does "home" take place?
3. How does the setting contribute to the mood or atmosphere of "home"?
4. Find two descriptions of the setting of "home" that you feel are especially powerful or vivid. What words does the author use to help you picture the setting?
5. The setting of "home" is perhaps the dominant element in the story. Should setting always be this important? Explain.

READING FOCUS

Recognize Implied Theme What was the implied theme in "home"? What clues in the story helped you to determine this?

DEVELOP YOUR VOCABULARY

You can often figure out the meaning of an unfamiliar word by looking closely at its **context**, that is, the words that surround it. For example, you may be unfamiliar with the meaning of *recluse* in "The old *recluse* lived alone, cut off from the rest of the world." By examining the words surrounding *recluse*, you should be able to guess that it means, "someone who lives alone, away from others."

Use context clues to determine the meaning of the italicized words below. Then, use all the italicized words in original sentences.

1. The *obstinate* teenager refused her parents' repeated requests to clean her room.
2. The grasshopper made short *staccato* hops across the corn field.
3. Her responsibility was *firing* the cold, unlit stove . . .
4. The vocabulary test would begin *presently*; I had about five minutes.

ESL Activity

Organize students into small groups, having each retell "home" from either Mama's, Maud Martha's, or Helen's point of view. Ask the class to make suggestions for improvements.

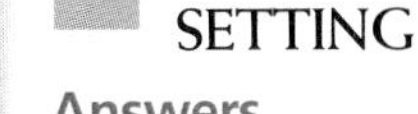

THINK ABOUT SETTING

Answers

1. The setting is a friendly front porch of a cherished family home, complete with attractive plants and rocking chairs. A poplar tree stands in the front yard; an iron fence separates the house from the outside world.
2. late afternoon
3. Sample answer: The setting creates a warm, loving feeling about the family's home.
4. Answers will vary.
5. Sample answer: Because setting affects characters and events, its importance should be similar to the purpose it serves in the particular story.

DEVELOP YOUR VOCABULARY

Answers

1. unyielding, stubborn
2. abrupt, distinct
3. applying fire to, igniting
4. soon

Sentences will vary.

READING FOCUS

Sample Answer

The implied theme is that our homes mean so much to us that we can't face how horrible it would feel if we were to lose them. This is inferred through the characters' attitudes toward the possibility of losing their home.

SELECTION OVERVIEW

SELECTION OBJECTIVES

After completing these selections, students will be able to

- understand and identify external and internal conflicts
- write creatively about conflict
- write a persuasive essay
- understand and identify similes and metaphors
- evaluate the poet's style

Lesson Resources

Dream Variations/Theme for English B/from Montage of a Dream Deferred

- Selection Synopses, Teacher's Edition, p. T337e
- Comprehension and Vocabulary Workbook, pp. 71–72
- Language Enrichment Workbook, p. 57
- Teacher's Resources
  - Reinforcement, p. R36
  - Test, pp. T71–T72

More About Conflict

Explain to students that poems and stories may contain more than one conflict and more than one theme. Often, the main character's struggle with nature or with other people is complicated by a struggle within himself or herself. Point out how the grieving wife in the poem "Lament" struggled to deal both with her children's needs and with her own grief. You might explain that just as in real life, a conflict in literature may have no definite resolution.

More About the Literary Period

During the 1920s Harlem, in New York City, was the artistic capital for African American writers, poets, and dramatists. Of their many important achievements, two stand out in importance: gaining a new respect for African American creative expression and introducing themes of racial equality into the mainstream of literature in the United States.

Learn About

Self Portrait, Marvin Gray Johnson. National Museum of American Art

CONFLICT

In literature, **conflict** is the struggle that occurs between opposite forces in a plot. As you know, there are two types of conflict. The first, **external conflict**, involves a person's struggle against an outside force, such as another person, nature, or even the society in which he or she lives.

Internal conflict, as you may suspect, involves an emotional or psychological struggle within a person's mind. In this type of conflict, an individual is divided by two opposing ideas or feelings.

It may help you to think of conflict as a battle, the fighting of which produces a certain tension. This tension excites our interest. We read further to see who wins a particular struggle and how the tension is released.

As you read the following poems by Langston Hughes, ask yourself:

1. What external and internal conflicts occur in the poems?
2. How, if ever, are these conflicts resolved?

READING FOCUS

Evaluate the Poet's Style A poet's style is how the poet conveys a message. Does the poet use a particular poetry form, such as lyric or free verse? Does the poet use a particular type of speech—formal or informal? The style a poet chooses often greatly affects the meaning of his or her work. As you read these poems, look for a common style that would define the poetry of Langston Hughes.

WRITING CONNECTION

Write a short paragraph, or a four-line stanza, about an important conflict in your own life. Describe whether the struggle is external, internal, or both.

Viewing Fine Art

Marvin Gray Johnson (1896–1934) was, in the 1920s, part of the earliest group of African American artists to exhibit together. Johnson, who is noted for his paintings based on African American religious themes and spirituals, also made some striking portraits, including the self-portrait seen here. Like many of his colleagues, he was searching for a way to express his African heritage. Here he placed two African masks in the background of his portrait. Ask: Why do you think the artist chose to use masks in the background?

Cooperative Group Activity

Have students work on the Writing Connection activity individually. Then divide students into small groups, having them exchange papers and offer responsible criticism. Using each group's suggestions, create a class list of conflicts. Have students explain how each of these conflicts might be resolved.

DREAM VARIATIONS

by Langston Hughes

To fling my arms wide
In some place of the sun,
To whirl and to dance
Till the white day is done.
5 Then rest at cool evening
Beneath a tall tree
While night comes on gently,
  Dark like me—
That is my dream!

10 To fling my arms wide
In the face of the sun,
Dance! Whirl! Whirl!
Till the quick day is done,
Rest at pale evening . . .
15 A tall, slim tree . . .
Night coming tenderly
  Black like me.

The Dress She Wore Was Blue, John Henry series by Palmer Hayden. Museum of African American Art, Palmer C. Hayden Collection

TEACHING PLAN

INTRODUCE

Motivation

Play a jazz recording to familiarize students with the musical elements that Langston Hughes transferred to his poetry. You might highlight the "scat" singing of Ella Fitzgerald or Sarah Vaughn, or the virtuoso techniques of pianist Thomas "Fats" Waller or trumpet player Louis Armstrong.

Purpose-Setting Question

Is literature an effective weapon for effecting social change?

READ

Literary Focus: *Conflict*

Have students compare and contrast the two stanzas in "Dream Variations." Ask: Which words and phrases are directly repeated? Which have been slightly altered? What is the main difference between these two dreams?

Reading Focus: *Evaluate the Poet's Style*

Ask students to read to consider how Langston Hughes's style compares with the style of the other lyric poems they have read in this unit and previous units.

CLOSE

Have students complete Review the Selection on pages 370–371.

ESL Activity

Have groups of students organize a chart on which they list examples of ways people experience racial discrimination in the United States or in other countries: in housing, education, jobs and economic opportunities, social situations, and life in general.

Develop Vocabulary Skills

Familiarize students with the vocabulary words footnoted in the story. Use each word in a context sentence, then call upon students to do the same. You might want to pinpoint geographical locations (including New Orleans) on a map.

Viewing Fine Art

Palmer Hayden (1890–1973) was one of the best known African American artists. He studied art in Paris and by 1931 had introduced African American subject matter to a European audience. Hayden received numerous awards and honors for his paintings. Many were based on folklore, including a series on John Henry, the legendary steelworker. This is one painting from that series. Hayden's style was deliberately naive, in keeping with the folkloric subjects of his work. (See Viewing Fine Art note on page 367.) Ask: What is naive about this artwork?

Reading Focus:
Evaluate the Poet's Style

Ask: How well do you think the poem answers the assignment "Theme for English B"?

THEME FOR ENGLISH B

by Langston Hughes

The instructor said,

Go home and write
a page tonight.
And let that page come out of you—
5 *Then, it will be true.*

I wonder if it's that simple?

I am twenty-two, colored, born in Winston-Salem.[1]
I went to school there, then Durham,[2] then here
to this college on the hill above Harlem.[3]
10 I am the only colored student in my class.
The steps from the hill lead down into Harlem,
through a park, then I cross St. Nicholas,
Eighth Avenue, Seventh, and I come to the Y,
the Harlem Branch Y, where I take the elevator
15 up to my room, sit down, and write this page:

It's not easy to know what is true for you or me
at twenty-two, my age. But I guess I'm what
I feel and see and hear, Harlem, I hear you:
hear you, hear me—we two—you, me talk on this page.
20 (I hear New York, too.) Me—who?
Well, I like to eat, sleep, drink, and be in love.
I like to work, read, learn, and understand life.
I like a pipe for a Christmas present,
or records—Bessie,[4] bop, or Bach.

---

[1]**Winston Salem:** city in North Carolina
[2]**Durham:** city in North Carolina
[3]**Harlem:** a section of New York City that mostly lies between the East and Hudson Rivers and north of Central Park
[4]**Bessie Smith:** a famous jazz singer

25 I guess being colored doesn't make me *not* like
the same things other folks like who are other races.
So will my page be colored that I write?
Being me, it will not be white.
But it will be
30 a part of you, instructor.
You are white—
yet a part of me, as I am a part of you.
That's American.
Sometimes perhaps you don't want to be a part of me.
35 Nor do I often want to be a part of you.
But we are, that's true!
As I learn from you,
I guess you learn from me—
although you're older—and white—
40 and somewhat more free.

This is my page for English B.

Literary Focus:
Conflict
Ask: What conflict does the author pose in his poem "Theme for English B"?

Critical Thinking:
Synthesize
Call on volunteers to paraphrase "Dream Variations" and "Theme for English B." Have students suggest what is lost through each "translation." Encourage them to discuss the essential differences between poetry and prose.

Background Notes

American jazz is a mixture of African and West Indian musical rhythms and religious spirituals that developed in New Orleans at the turn of the century. Originally, jazz musicians could not read music; they played entirely by ear. Accordingly, they considered the composition of jazz to be less important than the actual execution of the music. Their tradition of improvisation and experimentation strongly influenced the poetry of Langston Hughes.

Literary Focus: *Conflict*

Ask: What forces is the poet struggling with in this montage of poems?

Critical Thinking: *Infer*

Ask: Do you think the narrator of the poem is happy? Explain your answer.

from Montage of a Dream Deferred

ADAPTED

by Langston Hughes

Dream Boogie

Good morning, daddy![1]
Ain't you heard
The boogie-woogie rumble
Of a dream deferred?

5 Listen closely:
You'll hear their feet
Beating out and beating out a—

You think
It's a happy beat?

10 Listen to it closely:
ain't you heard
something underneath
like a—

What did I say?

15 Sure,
I'm happy!
Take it away!

Hey, pop!
Re-bop!
20 *Mop!*

Y-e-a-h!

---

montage (mon TAHZH) picture made up of a number of separate pictures
deferred (dih FURD) put off
[1]**daddy:** here slang for "friend" or "brother"

Midsummer Night in Harlem, Palmer Hayden.
Museum of African American Art

Warning

Daddy,
don't let your dog
curb you!

Tell Me

Why should it be *my* loneliness,
Why should it be *my* song,
Why should it be *my* dream
deferred
overlong?

Request

Gimme $25.00
and the change.
I'm going
where the morning
and the evening
won't bother me.

Argument

White is right,
Yellow mellow,
Black, get back!

Do you believe that, Jack?

5 Sure do!

Then you're a dope
for which there ain't no hope.
Black is fine!
And, God knows,
10 *It's mine!*

Reading Focus:
Evaluate the Poet's Style
Ask students to describe pictures in their minds created by the language in this poetic montage.

Viewing Fine Art

Palmer Hayden's (1890–1973) scenes in Harlem were among the first to picture African American urban life. (See also page 363.) Hayden received some criticism from other African American artists for his portrayals of Harlem, because of his perceptions and rather naive style. Here he attempts to include many aspects of life on a hot summer night in the city: the churchgoers, the children on the stoops, the chatting neighbors, the joyriders, the elderly—Hayden presents a panoramic view. Ask: How does this painting represent Langston Hughes's montage?

Background Notes

The "blues" are melancholy ballads about lost fortunes and, more commonly, lost love. Sadness and loss are common subjects in blues songs, which are characterized by a simple structure and frequent repetition of lines.

Literary Focus: *Conflict*

Remind students of the meaning of external and internal conflict. Ask: Are the poet's conflicts more external or internal? Explain.

Reading Focus: *Evaluate the Poet's Style*

Have students point out the examples of slang in these poems and suggest their meaning. Encourage them to discuss when the use of slang is appropriate and when it is not.

Comparing Selections

Have students compare the conflicts in each of the Hughes poems.

Blues at Dawn

I don't dare start thinking in the morning.
I don't dare start thinking in the morning.
If I thought thoughts in bed,
Them thoughts would bust my head—
5 So I don't dare start thinking in the morning.

I don't dare remember in the morning.
Don't dare remember in the morning.
If I recall the day before,
I wouldn't get up no more—
10 So I don't dare remember in the morning.

Harlem

What happens to a dream deferred?

Does it dry up
like a raisin in the sun?
Or fester like a sore—
5 And then run?
Does it stink like rotten meat?
Or crust and sugar over—
like a syrupy sweet?

Maybe it just sags
10 like a heavy load.

Or does it explode?

Island

Between two rivers,
North of the park,
Like darker rivers
The streets are dark.

5 Black and white,
Gold and brown—
Chocolate-custard
Pie of a town.

Dream within a dream
10 *Our dream deferred.*

Good morning, daddy!

Ain't you heard?

Mini Quiz

Write the following questions on the chalkboard or read them aloud. Call on students to fill in the blanks.

1. The speaker of "Theme for English B" is ________ years old.
2. He realizes that both he and his instructor can ________ from each other.
3. Many of these poems are about ________ ________.
4. ________ lies "Between two rivers, North of the park."
5. The poet asked whether a "dream deferred" festered like a ________.

Answers

1. twenty-two
2. learn
3. racial equality
4. Harlem
5. sore

AUTHOR BIOGRAPHY

Langston Hughes (1902–1967)

Who are you, Langston Hughes? What do you stand for? Let's let the poet himself tell us:

> I play it cool
> And dig all jive.
> That's the reason
> I stay alive.
>
> My motto,
> As I live and learn,
>   is:
> *Dig and Be Dug*
> *In Return.*

The American people have "dug" the poetry of Langston Hughes for over seventy years. His language is direct and uncomplicated. He catches the rhythms of jazz and the soulful sounds of the blues. In his own words, he gives us the "music of a community."

Langston Hughes was born in Joplin, Missouri, in 1902. After high school he traveled, worked at odd jobs, and polished his writing in his spare time. His first book, *The Weary Blues*, came out in 1926. Soon after graduating from Lincoln University, in Pennsylvania in 1929, he settled down in the Harlem section of New York City. In addition to poetry, Hughes wrote stories, novels, plays, articles for magazines and newspapers, and even an autobiography. During his life his name appeared on the covers of about thirty books.

The short poem on the left is entitled "Motto." What do the last two lines mean? How is that meaning related to Langston Hughes's life and career?

MORE ABOUT THE AUTHOR

Langston Hughes knew that he was an African American poet in a white poet's world. While he sought to express the African American experience, using unconventional imagery and diction, he feared that his poetry would be judged only by traditional standards of literary excellence.

Additional Works
BY LANGSTON HUGHES

The Dream Keeper, Alfred A. Knopf Incorporated, 1986.

Jazz, Franklin Watts Incorporated, 1982.

Short Stories, Hill & Wang, Incorporated, 1997.

UNDERSTAND THE SELECTION

Answers

1. at the Harlem branch of the "Y"
2. Answers may include: the title, "Dream Boogie," boogie-woogie, "a happy beat," and "Blues at Dawn," or some of the sounds or rhythms of the poems
3. a dream deferred
4. Sample answer: equality
5. Sample answer: It warns against allowing your possessions to control you.
6. Sample answer: He is trying to show all the elements or aspects of the same theme.
7. Sample answer: He wants to be acknowledged for whom and what he really is.
8. Sample answer: He is an excellent student, observant and questioning, and he has a sense of humor.
9. Sample answer: He might have become a musician since music plays a vital role in his poetry.
10. Sample answer: The instructor will give the page an "A" because, although it is unconventional, it fulfills the assignment by expressing a certain truth about the writer.

Respond to Literature

Write the names of these prominent African American civil rights leaders on the board and have students discuss their roles: W.E.B. Dubois (writer, co-founder of the NAACP), and Marcus Garvey (leader who urged African Americans to return to Africa, start businesses, and so on). Elicit the idea that Langston Hughes's calls for racial equality and African American pride, or awareness, paralleled the rise of the civil rights movement beginning in the 1920s.

WRITE ABOUT THE SELECTION

Prewriting

Using students' suggestions, create a sample web on the chalkboard or on an overhead transparency.

Review the Selection

UNDERSTAND THE SELECTION

Recall

1. In "Theme for English B," where does the speaker live?
2. Identify three musical elements in *Montage*.
3. In "Harlem," what is compared to "a raisin in the sun" and "rotten meat"?

Infer

4. What is the "dream deferred"?
5. "Warning," is an example of figurative language. Explain what it means.
6. Why does the poet call his poem a "montage"? Explain.
7. In "Dream Variations," what is the speaker's real hope?

Apply

8. How would you characterize the speaker in "Theme for English B"?
9. What might Hughes have done if he hadn't become a poet?
10. In "Theme for English B," how might the instructor grade the poet's theme?

Respond to Literature

How are the themes of Hughes's poems consistent with developments in America during the early 20th century?

WRITE ABOUT THE SELECTION

In the 1920s, Langston Hughes wrote poems that challenged racial inequality in the United States. If he were living today, would the poet find these same conditions? What has changed? What has remained the same? Write a brief, persuasive paragraph that explains whether or not Langston Hughes would encounter similar societal conflicts today.

Prewriting Make a web to organize your thoughts. Note your central opinion in the middle of the diagram. Next, list the main reasons that support your opinion. Then, note important details about each reason.

Writing Use your web to write a brief, persuasive paragraph. In it, explain whether Langston Hughes would find in our society the same conflicts that existed during his lifetime. Remember to list your reasons in the order of their importance. Discuss similarities and differences between conditions in the 1920s and those today.

Revising When you revise your paragraph, check to see if you have used convincing words and phrases that emphasize your views. Reread your last sentence to make sure it leaves the reader with a vivid impression.

Proofreading Read over your paragraph to check for errors. Be sure that you have used persuasive words accurately, and that you have spelled them correctly.

Writing

Have students work on this section individually. Help any student who is having difficulty. To suggest possible responses, ask questions about what current social conditions Langston Hughes might praise or condemn.

Revising

Make this a cooperative group activity. Have students work in small groups to revise their paragraphs.

Proofreading

Select one or two of the students' paragraphs as models for proofreading. Put the paragraphs on the overhead projector and have the class suggest improvements.

THINK ABOUT CONFLICT

External conflict always involves a struggle between a person and an opposing force, such as another person, nature, or society. **Internal conflict**, however, concerns a struggle within a person's own mind. Conflict is not only an element in a plot, it can also become the theme—the central, or dominating, idea in an author's work.

1. What external or internal conflict does the speaker of "Blues at Dawn" experience?
2. What opposing thoughts or feelings does the speaker of "Theme for English B" reveal?
3. In "Argument," part of the speaker's ordeal involves an external or outside force. What is that force?
4. How is the tension that is expressed throughout "Dream Boogie," finally released?
5. A conflict is resolved when one side wins the "battle." Does "Montage" seem to end with any resolution? What gives you the feeling that the conflict will continue?

READING FOCUS

Evaluate the Poet's Style How would you describe Langston Hughes's style? How does his style of writing affect the meaning of the poems?

DEVELOP YOUR VOCABULARY

A **simile** is a direct comparison in which one thing is said to be similar to, or like, something else. The words *like* or *as* are used in a simile. In "He's as skinny as a rail," a person is compared to a rail to show how thin he is.

A **metaphor** is a comparison in which one thing is said to *be* something else. A metaphor often uses the words *is, are, was,* or *were*. In "A blanket of snow covered our village," snow is compared to a blanket to create a visual picture of the spreading snow.

Read the sentences below and tell which contain a simile and which contain a metaphor. What is being compared?

1. The professional wrestler's body was as solid as a rock.
2. Their escape plan was a shining jewel, perfect in every way.
3. The tears from her eyes fell like tiny raindrops.
4. Pace yourself, for life is a long and winding road.
5. Always courageous, the comic book hero had nerves of steel.

ESL Activity

Ask students to determine which of the poems in this collection can speak for other groups of people in the United States or in other parts of the world.

THINK ABOUT CONFLICT

Answers

1. Sample answer: internal: The speaker cannot help thinking about the harsh aspects of his life, yet he knows that this only produces pain.
2. Sample answer: One part of the speaker feels obligated to think and feel based solely on his skin color; another part knows that these same thoughts and emotions are cherished by all people.
3. Answers will vary. One possibility is society's racial prejudices.
4. Sample answer: It is released through an emotionally explosive jazz stanza.
5. The conflict, racial prejudice, is not resolved. By ending with the line with which it begins, the poem suggests that a cycle is repeating.

DEVELOP YOUR VOCABULARY

Answers

1. simile; compares the wrestler's body to rock
2. metaphor; compares an escape plan to a shining jewel
3. simile; compares tears to tiny raindrops
4. metaphor; compares life to a long and winding road
5. metaphor; compares nerves to steel

READING FOCUS

Sample Answer

Hughes uses an informal style with language patterns that reflect his culture. There is also an emphasis on musical phrases. The style affects the meaning by providing a context for his ideas; we know that he is talking about Harlem and the African American experience by the style of his writing.

Selection Overview

SELECTION OBJECTIVES

After completing this selection, students will be able to

- understand and identify the literary devices that suggest mood
- use vivid language to create mood
- write a short comparison poem
- understand denotation and connotation
- recognize figurative language

Lesson Resources

Fog

- Selection Synopsis, Teacher's Edition, p. T337f
- Comprehension and Vocabulary Workbook, pp. 73–74
- Language Enrichment Workbook, p. 58
- Teacher's Resources
  Reinforcement, p. R37
  Test, pp. T73–T74

More About Mood

Choose a poem from this unit that students have read and have a volunteer write it on the board. Using students' suggestions, circle the descriptive words or phrases, actions, and images that suggest the mood of the poem. You might point out the poetic devices, such as alliteration and repetition, used to create this mood.

About the Author

Carl Sandburg was not a regional writer. Rather, he celebrated the enormous diversity of the U.S. experience. The titles of his four most famous volumes reflect his broad interests: *Chicago Poems, Cornhuskers, Smoke and Steel, Slabs of the Sunburnt West.* Sandburg felt as confident writing about immigrants and factory workers as he did exploring the colorful landscapes of the country. Encourage students to discuss which popular, contemporary writers share Sandburg's wide scope of interest.

Learn About

Mood

Whether reading a letter from a friend or listening to a favorite song, you are constantly responding to feelings suggested by words and phrases.

Works of literature, too, summon emotional responses. The feelings that a poem, play, or short story conveys are called its **mood**. The mood may be peaceful, gloomy, joyous, or mysterious. In other words, mood is the total atmosphere that a writer creates through his or her imaginative use of language.

Mood is suggested through setting, imagery, action, and the words of characters. For example, an autumn afternoon setting may establish an atmosphere of serenity. Conversely, startled deer, fleeing from a thunderstorm, can suggest a mood of uncertainty and fear.

When reading, look at how the descriptive words create a mood.

As you read "Fog," ask yourself:

1. What mood, or feeling, does this poem give you?
2. What sensory details contribute to this mood?

Reading Focus

Recognize Figurative Language Figurative language is often used to compare things in literature and poetry. The comparison can be a metaphor in which one thing stands for something else. For example, "The star was a beacon." Read "Fog" to discover what metaphor Sandburg uses for fog.

WRITING CONNECTION

Write a four-sentence passage that describes the room in which you are sitting. Using sensory details, suggest the mood of the room.

More About the Literary Period

Carl Sandburg awakened many Americans to the delights of poetry. During the twenties and thirties he toured the country, reading his innovative, free-verse poetry, giving lectures, and playing folk ballads on the guitar. Sandburg was also a journalist, serving as a writer and editor on the *Chicago Daily News*.

ESL Activity

Pair students and assign each pair a topic (snow, hail, clouds, lightning). Have each pair briefly describe its topic. Then read "Fog" aloud and have students compare their descriptions to Sandburg's description of fog.

Cooperative Group Activity

Write the following words on the chalkboard: *tense*, *cheerful*, *solemn*, *monotonous*, *exciting*. To complete the Writing Connection activity, have pairs of students choose mood words and write descriptions of the classroom that suggest the specific mood. Have a member of each pair read their passage.

FOG

by Carl Sandburg

The fog comes
on little cat feet.

It sits looking
over harbor and city
on silent haunches
and then moves on.

Savannah Nocturne, Eliot Clark

TEACHING PLAN

INTRODUCE

Motivation

Encourage students to suggest which aspects of poetry they find confusing or difficult to understand. Relate the discussion to Sandburg's poems, which have been acclaimed for their directness of language, startling imagery, and relative verbal simplicity.

Purpose-Setting Question

What techniques do poets use to portray common objects in surprising new ways?

READ

Literary Focus: *Mood*

Ask: What words describe the mood in this poem? You may use words outside of the poem.

Reading Focus: *Recognize Figurative Language*

Review the meaning of metaphor. Then ask: Can you consider this entire poem a metaphor? Why or why not?

Critical Thinking: *Analyze*

Ask: Do you think this poem is one to be read strictly for enjoyment or does it have a deeper meaning? Explain your answer.

CLOSE

Have students complete Review the Selection on pages 374–375.

Mini Quiz

Write the following questions on the chalkboard or read them aloud. Call on students to fill in the blanks.

1. The ________ comes.
2. It comes on little ________ feet.
3. It looks over ________ and ________.
4. It sits on ________ haunches.
5. Later it ________.

Answers

1. fog
2. cat
3. harbor, city
4. silent
5. moves

Viewing Fine Art

Eliot Clark (1883–1980) was an American artist who was born in New York. He was committed to art throughout his life; he worked as not only a painter but also as an art teacher and lecturer. He wrote several books about art. *Savannah Nocturne* is painted in the impressionist style. Impressionists are known for applying small daubs of paint, to create dazzling, bright impressions of nature. They are more interested in capturing the mood of what they see rather than what is actually there. Ask students how the mood of this painting relates to the poem.

UNDERSTAND THE SELECTION

Answers

1. fog
2. He compares the fog to a cat.
3. a harbor and its adjacent city
4. Sample answer: the sense of sight
5. Sample answer: Like a stray cat, the fog is an uninvited guest.
6. It makes no sound.
7. Sample answer: The phrases suggest a certain tide or flow, the fog comes, moves on, and comes again.
8. Sample answer: The "cat" metaphor is complete, concrete, and thus, effective.
9. Sample answer: an animal that is quick, soundless, and perhaps sneaky
10. Sample answer: A poem is an ideal way to create an immediate picture in a reader's mind.

Respond to Literature

Choose several other poems from the unit and create a chalkboard chart. Caption it with *Length*, *Rhythm*, *Rhyme*, *Imagery*, *Figurative Language*, and *Setting*. Using students' suggestions, fill in the chart and discuss each new element. Elicit the idea that "Fog" is short, has a distinct rhythm, uses imagery and figurative language, and does not rhyme. Like Langston Hughes's poems, but unlike Edna St. Vincent Millay's, it takes place in a city.

WRITE ABOUT THE SELECTION

Prewriting

Using students' suggestions, create a sample list on the chalkboard. Sample list: *earthquake*: *destructive, terrifying, smashing, tearing, shattering noises, senseless, random*; *elephant*: *powerful, surprisingly swift*

Review the Selection

UNDERSTAND THE SELECTION

Recall

1. What is the poem's subject?
2. To what object does the poet compare this subject?
3. What is the setting of the poem?

Infer

4. To which sense does the poem most appeal?
5. Is the fog an invited guest?
6. What do you know about the sound of fog from this poem?
7. What do the phrases "comes on" and "moves on" suggest about the fog's visits?

Apply

8. The poet compares the fog to just one thing throughout the poem. Is this effective? Explain.
9. To what other animal might you compare fog? Explain.
10. Why do you think Sandburg chose to write a *poem* about fog, instead of a short story or nonfiction article?

Respond to Literature

Compare "Fog" to other poems you have read in this unit. What elements does it have in common with them? What elements differ?

WRITE ABOUT THE SELECTION

Many students consider "Fog" one of their favorite poems. Perhaps this is because comparison between an element of nature and an animal is a visually appealing way of thinking about these two subjects. Write a six-line poem in which you compare a natural event, such as a winter snowstorm, an earthquake, or a cooling summer rain, to an animal. Make sure that you can think of similarities between the event and the animal.

Prewriting After choosing the subjects you want to compare, make a list of the character traits of the animal and a list of vivid details about the natural event. Decide how you will show similarities between the two.

Writing Use your informal outline to write a six-line poem that compares the natural event to the animal. In it, try to match the characteristics of the animal with those of the natural event. Think carefully about the characteristics of each as you write.

Revising When you revise your poem, be sure that the details you use are consistent with the physical qualities of both the natural event and the animal.

Proofreading Read over your poem to check for errors. Make sure you use a consistent method of capitalizing and punctuating the poem. Remember to start a new line of text for each new line of the poem.

Writing

Have students write their six-line poems individually. Walk around the class, helping any students who have difficulty.

Revising

Make this a cooperative group activity. Have students work in small groups to revise their poems. They might share them with the class.

Proofreading

Select one or two of the students' poems as models for proofreading. Put the poems on the overhead projector and have the class suggest improvements.

THINK ABOUT MOOD

Mood is the feeling that a work of literature expresses to the reader. Mood is created through the author's choice of sensory words, setting details, actions, and words that characters speak. It also results from an author's use of such techniques as meter, rhyme (or no rhyme), alliteration, repetition, imagery, and symbolism. In short, mood is created by combinations and variations in the poetic and literary devices available to the writer.

1. Describe the mood of "Fog."
2. What descriptive words or phrases does the poet use to create this feeling?
3. What other words might you use to add to this particular mood?
4. The poet purposely selects certain traits of a cat and leaves out others. How would the mood of the poem change if the poet had compared the fog to a kitten? Would the poem be as successful?
5. The poet uses alliteration in the poem. What two sounds does he particularly repeat?

READING FOCUS

Recognize Figurative Language What metaphor is used for fog in this poem? Why do you think the poet uses this metaphor?

DEVELOP YOUR VOCABULARY

The **denotation** of a word is its usual meaning, or "dictionary definition." The **connotation** of a word is the feeling or thought that the word suggests. For instance, *beckon*, *invite*, and *summon* have similar denotations, or definitions, but their connotations are different. The word *beckon*, is somehow more mysterious or tantalizing than the more conventional word *invite*.

For each sentence below, choose the word with the more vivid connotation and explain your reasoning.

1. The stallion (*jumped*, *bounded*) over the wooden fence in one easy motion.
2. The (*musty*, *stale*) odor of the attic reminded me of a damp shoe.
3. A few crumbling bricks were all that was left of the (*old*, *ancient*) Greek temple.
4. Which soldier dared to follow the enemy down the dark (*cavity*, *hole*)?
5. This particular robbery case (*confused*, *baffled*) the detective.
6. The (*hungry*, *famished*) hikers frantically searched for something to eat.

THINK ABOUT MOOD

Answers

1. Sample answer: quiet, mysterious, observant
2. "little cat feet," "It sits looking," "silent haunches," "then moves on"
3. Answers will vary.
4. Sample answer: The mood would be more playful and perhaps inappropriate.
5. *k* as in *comes*, *cat*, and *looking*; *s* as in *sits*, *city*, *silent*, and the similar sounds in *haunches*.

DEVELOP YOUR VOCABULARY

Sample Answers

1. bounded
2. musty
3. ancient
4. cavity
5. baffled
6. famished

Answers and reasons will vary.

READING FOCUS

Sample Answer

The author compares the fog to a cat. He may have watched the fog roll in unannounced and have had the same experience with a cat creeping quietly into a room.

ESL Activity

Have pairs of students write sentences about weather conditions. Then have partners underline a word that could be more vivid in their partner's sentences. The original writer replaces the underlined words with more vivid vocabulary. Encourage the use of a thesaurus.

SELECTION OVERVIEW

SELECTION OBJECTIVES

After completing these selections, students will be able to

- understand common symbols
- identify and evaluate literary symbolism
- discuss the rise of modern poetry
- write a short, revelatory poem
- determine word origins
- make inferences

Lesson Resources

The Pasture/The Road Not Taken/Stopping by Woods on a Snowy Evening

- Selection Synopses, Teacher's Edition, p. T337f
- Comprehension and Vocabulary Workbook, pp. 75–76
- Language Enrichment Workbook, p. 59
- Teacher's Resources
  Reinforcement, p. R38
  Test, pp. T75–T76

More About Symbolism

Tell students that a symbol is something that suggests a broader meaning. It often produces powerful associations of ideas and feelings in a reader or viewer. To familiarize students with the frequency of symbols in daily life, draw these common ones on the chalkboard or on an overhead transparency. Have students tell the thoughts and ideas they associate with each, adding new symbols if possible.

symbol for peace
symbol for stopping
symbol for money
symbol for no smoking

More About the Literary Period

Robert Frost is one of the first modern American poets. He used traditional conventions like rhymed couplets, sonnets, and blank verse to address modern themes. Frost also employed the diction and rhythm of common New England speech to create provocative, dramatic narratives.

Learn About

READING FOCUS

Make Inferences Making inferences means making logical guesses about information not stated directly in a story or poem. You can do this by paying attention to clues the author provides, or by applying your own knowledge and experiences. You can make inferences to connect ideas, to figure out a mystery, or to predict what might happen next. As you read these poems, make inferences about the situations presented.

SYMBOLISM

A **symbol** is something that stands for, or represents, something else. In literature, a symbol is a person, place, object, or event that represents a particular idea or concept. For example, the Statue of Liberty is more than just a large object that stands in New York City's harbor. For people all over the world, the Statue of Liberty represents (or symbolizes) the freedom and justice that is found in the United States.

Writers use symbols to convey a deeper meaning than could be expressed by the **literal**, or exact meaning, of the words. If, for instance, the Statue of Liberty were mentioned several times in a poem about immigrants journeying to the United States, you might conclude that the poem was about freedom and justice.

As you read the following poems by Robert Frost, ask yourself:

1. What symbols does the poet use in his poems?
2. What ideas or concepts do these symbols represent?

WRITING CONNECTION

Many sports teams use animals or objects in their names. Think of the Chicago Bears and the Oakland Raiders. What is the name of your school's sports team? Explain briefly the idea symbolized by that name.

ESL Activity

Have groups of students devise a flag for their school, using symbols that can be understood by all people in the world.

Cooperative Group Activity

To complete the Writing Connection activity, divide the class into small groups. Have each group brainstorm the full names of six professional sports teams, explaining the symbolism of each name. Choose a volunteer to record the groups' responses on the chalkboard. Call on students to relate the meaning of these names to the name of their school's sports team.

The Pasture

by Robert Frost

I'm going out to clean the pasture spring;
I'll only stop to rake the leaves away
(And wait to watch the water clear, I may):
I shan't be gone long.—You come too.

I'm going out to fetch the little calf
That's standing by the mother. It's so young
It totters when she licks it with her tongue.
I shan't be gone long.—You come too.

Evening Glow, The Old Red Cow, Albert Pinkham Ryder.
The Brooklyn Museum

---

fetch (FECH) get and bring back

Teaching Plan

INTRODUCE

Motivation

To dramatize Robert Frost's innovate approach to poetry, recite a 19th-century rhyming poem, then play a recording of Frost reading one of his own poems. Discuss with students the differences in rhythm, rhyme, and most importantly, subject matter.

Purpose-Setting Question

What does Robert Frost's poetry reveal about his attitude toward life?

READ

Literary Focus: *Symbolism*

The symbols in these poems can be found in individual words or in the poem as a whole, called an allegory. Ask: Which poems have individual words or phrases as symbols? Which seem allegorical?

Reading Focus: *Make Inferences*

Have students think about the commentary the author makes in these poems and ask themselves why he does this. For example, they might ask themselves: Why does the speaker ask someone to come with him twice in "The Pasture"?

CLOSE

Have students complete Review the Selection on pages 382–383.

Develop Vocabulary Skills

Read the footnoted vocabulary words and supply a definition for each. Call on students to create original sentences for each word. Point out that Robert Frost frequently used simple words to make his poems more accessible.

Viewing Fine Art

Albert Pinkham Ryder (1847–1917) was one of American's mystical artists, who, like their counterparts in Europe, pictured romantic, emotional, or literary subjects. But Ryder also painted landscapes with farm animals. He turned even these prosaic subjects into soft and haunting paintings. The simplicity of his composition allowed the artist to focus on the evening glow of light, the textures of the field, and the solid blackness of the cow. Ask: What symbolism might there be in this painting?

The Road Not Taken

by Robert Frost

Two roads diverged in a yellow wood,
And sorry I could not travel both
And be one traveler, long I stood
And looked down one as far as I could
5 To where it bent in the undergrowth;

Then took the other, as just as fair,
And having perhaps the better claim,
Because it was grassy and wanted wear;
Though as for that, the passing there
10 Had worn them really about the same,

And both that morning equally lay
In leaves no step had trodden black.
Oh, I kept the first for another day!
Yet knowing how way leads on to way,
15 I doubted if I should ever come back.

I shall be telling this with a sigh
Somewhere ages and ages hence:
Two roads diverged in a wood, and I—
I took the one less traveled by,
20 And that has made all the difference.

diverge (dih VURJ) spread apart

Critical Thinking: *Contrast*

Ask students to list all of the differences between the two roads in "The Road Not Taken."

Literary Focus: *Symbolism*

Ask: What do the roads in this poem symbolize? Does the poem as a whole (allegory) symbolize something?

Reading Focus: *Make Inferences*

Ask: What do you infer from the lines "Yet knowing how way leads on to way, I doubted if I should ever come back"?

Landscape, Ernest Lawson. The Brooklyn Museum

Viewing Fine Art

Ernest Lawson (1873–1939) was a landscape artist whose impressionistic style was characterized by a heavy use of paint and decorative, jewel-like colors. Though he studied in France, where he absorbed impressionist teachings, Lawson returned to the New York area to paint in a style that was more rugged and individualistic than that of the other American impressionists. Here, in a Lawson landscape, is a turn-of-the-century style that would soon be displaced in the art world by scenes of urban bustle (the Ashcan School) and the first tremors of abstract art. Ask: How do you think Frost would feel about this road in the wood?

Discussion

Have students discuss the frequent use of repetition and alliteration in the poems. You might ask them: What words or phrases are repeated? Which words begin with the same sounds? Discuss with them how these literary devices contribute to the rhythm of each poem.

Viewing Fine Art

Although new styles of painting, such as social realism and abstraction, swept through the art world in the United States in the 1920s and 1930s, painters like John F. Carlson (1875–1945) continued to paint in more traditional styles. Delicate, impressionistic landscape pictures seemed old-fashioned in the 20th century world of fast-paced new ideas, but groups of artists steeped in traditional art values ignored the new trends. Here Carlson pictures a quiet forest scene, far from both the bustling cities of the era and the changing styles of art. Ask: How does the painting illustrate the poem? How do its images differ?

Literary Focus: *Symbolism*

Remind students that nature is a recurring subject in Robert Frost's poetry. Point out that both "Road" and "Woods" are set in woods or a forest. Have students suggest the thoughts, ideas, and feelings they associate with woods or forests and what these places symbolize.

Reading Focus: *Make Inferences*

Tell students that paraphrasing the individual lines in a poem can help them to understand it better. Chose one of the poems in this selection and call on students to rephrase each line. Discuss why they must use more words than the poet did to explain his meaning.

Critical Thinking: *Infer*

Ask: What is the author's message in each poem? What led you to infer this?

Comparing Selections

These poems have similar settings. Have pupils discuss other similarities they see. Then have them cite any differences.

Woodland Repose, John F. Carlson. Toledo Museum of Art

Stopping by Woods on a Snowy Evening

by Robert Frost

Whose woods these are I think I know.
His house is in the village though;
He will not see me stopping here
To watch his woods fill up with snow.

5 My little horse must think it queer
To stop without a farmhouse near
Between the woods and frozen lake
The darkest evening of the year.

He gives his harness bells a shake
10 To ask if there is some mistake.
The only other sound's the sweep
Of easy wind and downy flake.

The woods are lovely, dark and deep.
But I have promises to keep,
15 And miles to go before I sleep,
And miles to go before I sleep.

Mini Quiz

1. In "The Pasture," the spring is clogged with ________.
2. In "The Road Not Taken," the speaker has to choose between ________.
3. In "The Road Not Taken," leaves turn ________ when walked upon.
4. The woods in "Stopping by Woods on a Snowy Evening" belong to a man who lives in the ________.
5. In "Stopping by Woods on a Snowy Evening," the speaker hears the sounds of ________ and the sweep of the ________, and________.

Answers

1. leaves
2. two roads
3. black
4. village
5. harness bells, easy wind, downy flake

Author Biography

Robert Frost (1874–1963)

One day in 1909 the State Superintendent of Schools in New Hampshire dropped into a small high school. His inspection included an English classroom—and a happy surprise. "A class of boys and girls were listening open-mouthed to the teacher," he wrote later. "Slumped down behind a desk at the front of the room was a young man who was talking to the students as he might talk to a group of friends around his own fireside." The inspector had discovered "the best teacher in New Hampshire."

Inspector Charles Silver couldn't have known, of course, that he had also discovered a talented young poet named Robert Frost. His visit was to mark a turning point in Frost's life. Up to that time, Frost had thought of himself as a failure. He had failed at college, dropping out after two years. He had failed as a chicken farmer. And most important to him, he had failed to get many of his poems printed.

Then the turning point arrived. With Silver's help, Frost found a job teaching in a New Hampshire school. He still wanted to write, however, and in 1912, he sold his farm and moved his family to England, an attempt to "get away from it all." In 1913, his first book of poems was accepted by a London publisher. At the age of 39, Frost was finally on his way. He decided to return to the United States after the beginning of WW I.

Before long, Robert Frost was able to live the life he wanted. He bought a small farm in New Hampshire. He taught and traveled a little. He published book after book and collected prize after prize. His hair slowly turned gray with age, and white with wisdom. "America's beloved poet" lived to be nearly 90.

Frost is often called a "nature poet," but he never liked the term. "I guess I'm just not a nature poet," he once said. "I have only written two poems without a human being in them." He might have added that his real subject was *human* nature.

More About the Author

In 1899 Robert Frost left Harvard University to live on a small farm, purchased by his grandfather in Derry, New Hampshire. For ten hard years, Frost labored to support his wife and four children, while experimenting with poetry. During this formative period, Frost came to view rural New England, and nature in general, in a dramatic, new way that he would reveal in *North of Boston*, a book of poems. Discuss with students what someone might learn about life, working with nature so closely (patience, courage, strength, acceptance).

Additional Works

by Robert Frost

Collected Poems, HarperCollins Publishers, Incorporated, 1956.

Early Poems, Viking Penguin, 1998.

North of Boston Poems, W. Clement Stone, PMA Communications, Incorporated, 1977.

Mountain Interval: And New Hampshire Poems, NAL, 1999.

Poems, Everyman's Library, 1997.

The Road Not Taken & Other Poems, HarperCollins Publishers, Incorporated, 1988.

Robert Frost Selected Poems, Random House Value Publishing, Incorporated, 1997.

UNDERSTAND THE SELECTION

Answers

1. rake leaves from a pasture spring, fetch a little calf
2. in a forest
3. A man, or woman, halts a horse-drawn sleigh in the dark woods to watch a snowfall.
4. autumn
5. Sample answer: It has been used less than the other. The speaker wants to experience something less common.
6. Sample answer: No, he "must think it queer," and "gives his harness bells a shake," to show his concern.
7. Sample answer: The speaker feels serene and thoughtful.
8. Sample answer: He was inviting his listeners to explore nature with him through his poems.
9. Sample answer: The last line suggests that the speaker is content with his original choice and would probably make it again.
10. Answers will vary but should refer to the line "I have promises to keep."

Respond to Literature

Discuss with students the thoughts and feelings they associate with a warm spring day and with a winter blizzard. Elicit the idea that nature is an ever-changing force, sometimes friendly, sometimes deadly. Point out that Robert Frost, like other "modern" poets, does not romanticize nature; for them, it is an unyielding force to be understood and experienced.

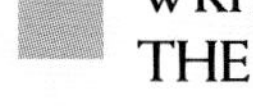

WRITE ABOUT THE SELECTION

Prewriting

Using students' suggestions, create a sample chart.

Sample situation: You encounter an injured person.

Choices:

1. stay and offer comfort
2. ignore the situation
3. leave to summon help

Decision: stayed and offered comfort

Result: became good friends

Review the Selection

UNDERSTAND THE SELECTION

Recall

1. In "The Pasture" what two actions does the speaker plan to accomplish?
2. Where does "The Road Not Taken" take place?
3. What happens in "Stopping by Woods on a Snowy Evening"?

Infer

4. In which season does "The Road Not Taken" take place?
5. Why do you think the speaker in "The Road Not Taken" chooses the road that he or she does?
6. Do you think the horse in "Stopping by Woods on a Snowy Evening" shares the speaker's thoughts?
7. What does the speaker of "Stopping by Woods" feel?

Apply

8. Why might Frost have often begun his poetry readings with "The Pasture"?
9. Would the speaker of "The Road Not Taken" now choose the other road?
10. Where do you think the speaker in "Stopping by Woods" is going?

Respond to Literature

How does the poet's use of nature reflect one aspect of modern poetry?

WRITE ABOUT THE SELECTION

The speaker of "The Road Not Taken" seems to feel that his or her choice of the proper road in life has produced favorable results. Have you made difficult choices in life, too? How have these decisions worked out? Write a two-stanza poem about a difficult choice you have made, and describe the results.

Prewriting Create a cause-and-effect chart. In it, list an important situation you once faced in your life. Then, draw arrows from this situation, linking the choices available to you at the time, the decision you eventually made, and the results of that specific decision.

Writing Use your informal cause-and-effect chart to write a two-stanza poem that describes the particularly difficult choice you made, and the effects of that choice on your life today. You may choose to follow one of Robert Frost's rhyme schemes.

Revising When you revise your poem, make sure you have described the original situation, your decision, and the effects of that decision. Read closely to see whether any symbols you used clearly represent your ideas or feelings about that important decision.

Proofreading When you proofread your poem, you may find it necessary to change the order of certain words or letters. Use this proofreading mark [N] to make those changes. This is called transposing (tr.).

Writing

Make this an individual writing assignment. Help students if necessary.

Revising

Make this a cooperative group activity. Have pairs of students exchange poems for revision. Then ask them to share their poems with the class.

Proofreading

Select one or two of the students' poems as models for proofreading. Put the poems on the overhead projector and have the class suggest improvements.

THINK ABOUT SYMBOLISM

Writers use symbols to deepen and enrich the meaning of a work of literature. Symbols may or may not be simple, however. The image behind the symbol may consist of many ideas and attitudes. You might find it helpful to think of a **symbol** as something visible used to represent something invisible, such as an idea, concept, or hidden truth.

1. What symbols does the poet use in "The Road Not Taken"?
2. What do you think the two roads in "The Road Not Taken" represent? Explain your thinking.
3. In "Stopping by Woods on a Snowy Evening," what is the literal meaning of the word *miles*?
4. What idea or concept is conveyed by the poet's use of the word *miles*?
5. In the work of Robert Frost and many other poets water is a symbol of truth. Explain how this symbol contributes to your understanding of "The Pasture."

READING FOCUS

Make Inferences What inferences did you make about the farm and the two woods described in these poems? What personal experiences did you draw from to make these inferences?

DEVELOP YOUR VOCABULARY

The development of the English language falls into three historical periods. The oldest, the Old English (or Anglo-Saxon) period, began around A.D. 440, when northern European tribes invaded the British Isles. The blending of their languages produced what we now call Old English.

Over the centuries, Old English gave way to Middle English and then to Modern English. Many changes occurred. In addition, English acquired hundreds of thousands of words from other languages.

Robert Frost's poetic vocabulary is made up almost exclusively of words that trace back to Old English. Look up the following words in a dictionary that has word histories. Which words do not come from Old English. From what languages do they come?

1. rake
2. watch
3. tongue
4. pasture
5. yellow
6. both
7. morning
8. black
9. doubt
10. sigh
11. hence
12. house
13. stop
14. snow
15. farm
16. wind

THINK ABOUT SYMBOLISM

Answers

1. two roads
2. Sample answer: They may represent paths in life, or choices people are forced to make.
3. a measured unit of distance
4. Sample answer: *Miles* probably symbolizes a great distance yet to travel in life.
5. Sample answer: The poet invites the reader to discover certain truths about the relationship between people and nature that poetry can help make "clear."

DEVELOP YOUR VOCABULARY

Sample Answers

4. *Pasture* comes from Old French.
9. *Doubt* comes from Old French.
15. *Farm* comes from Latin.

All others derive from Old English.

You might have students brainstorm a list of words that they use in ordinary speech, then use a dictionary to determine their histories, or origins.

READING FOCUS

Sample Answer

The farm and the two woods suggested a sense of solitude and peace. Having visited rural areas, I was able to picture how they may have looked and how they are conducive to quiet reflection.

ESL Activity

You might have students brainstorm a list of words that they use in ordinary speech. Then have them use a dictionary to determine their histories, or origins.

Selection Overview

SELECTION OBJECTIVES

After completing this selection, students will be able to

- understand and identify flat and round characters
- use vivid words to describe character
- write an opinion essay
- form adverbs from adjectives
- interpret dialogue

Lesson Resources

Lily Daw and the Three Ladies
- Selection Synopsis, Teacher's Edition, p. T337f
- Comprehension and Vocabulary Workbook, pp. 77–78
- Language Enrichment Workbook, p. 60
- Teacher's Resources
  Reinforcement, p. R39
  Test, pp. T77–T78

More About Character

Explain to students that in adventure, suspense, and mystery fiction, action-filled plots take precedence over characterization. Short story writers like Eudora Welty, however, usually emphasize character development. They know that most people are not what they appear to be. Therefore, they place their characters in crucial situations that test their attitudes and reveal their true personalities.

About the Author

Eudora Welty was born in Jackson, Mississippi, in 1909. After graduation from the University of Wisconsin and a brief advertising course at the Columbia University Business School, she returned to the South during the height of the Depression. Welty traveled across Mississippi for the W.P.A. (Works Progress Administration), interviewing people and photographing them. Many of the interesting characters from her fiction are composite portraits of the people she met during this "journey."

Learn About

CHARACTER

Summer at Campobello, New Brunswick, detail, Edward W.D. Hamilton. Museum of Fine Arts, Boston

You know from previous selections that writers create characters through description, dialogue, action, and the comments made about them by other characters in the story.

In literature, a character can be either flat or round. A **flat character** shows you only one side of his or her personality and is therefore not very true to life. A flat character usually represents a single idea or attitude. Many fairy tale characters are flat since they have only one of their personality traits exposed. An example would be a wicked stepmother.

A **round character** is someone you come to know from the inside out. A round character has many sides and is much more complex and lifelike. He or she is capable of responding to certain problems and situations in ways that may surprise you.

As you read "Lily Daw and the Three Ladies," ask yourself:

1. Which characters are uncomplicated, or flat?
2. Which characters do or say things that surprise you?

Reading Focus

Interpret Dialogue Dialogue is the words that characters speak in a story. As in real life, what the characters say may not be what they really feel or believe. You must use the context and tone of their words to interpret their real meanings. As you read this story, think about what the ladies mean when they speak, rather than concentrating on the actual words they say.

WRITING CONNECTION

Write a description of your favorite person. Include those specific qualities that make him or her a special, unique human being.

More About the Literary Period

Although she was deeply affected by the economic hardships and misery caused by the Depression, Eudora Welty was captivated by those things that remained constant during this period of turmoil—namely, the unchanging, tragicomic aspects of human nature.

ESL Activity

Have students make a list that will include each character in the story. Students may write or draw to remind themselves of each character's personality.

Cooperative Group Activity

Develop a class list of favorite people, including family, sports, and entertainment figures. Then divide the class into small groups, asking each to select a person to write about. Tell students to focus on that person's appearance, outlook on life, and unique habits. Have students share their work with the class.

LILY DAW AND THE THREE LADIES

ADAPTED

by Eudora Welty

Mrs. Watts and Mrs. Carson were both in the post office in Victory when the letter came from the Ellisville Institute for the Feeble-minded of Mississippi. Aimee Slocum, with her hand still full of mail, ran out in front and handed it straight to Mrs. Watts and they all three read it together. Mrs. Watts held it taut between her pink hands and Mrs. Carson underscored each line slowly with her thimbled finger. Everybody else in the post office wondered what was up now.

"What will Lily say," beamed Mrs. Carson at last, "when we tell her we're sending her to Ellisville!"

"She'll be tickled to death," said Mrs. Watts, and added in a gutteral voice to a deaf lady, "Lily Daw's getting in at Ellisville!"

"Don't you-all dare go off and tell Lily without me!" called Aimee Slocum, trotting back to finish putting up the mail.

"Do you suppose they'll look after her down there?" Mrs. Carson began to carry on a conversation with a group of Baptist ladies waiting in the post office. She was the Baptist preacher's wife.

"I've always heard it was lovely down there, but crowded," said one.

"Lily lets people walk over her so," said another.

"Last night at the tent show—" said another, and then popped her hand over her mouth.

"Don't mind me; I know there are such things in the world," said Mrs. Carson, looking down and fingering the tape-measure which hung over her bosom.

"Oh, Mrs. Carson. Well, anyway, last night at the tent show, why, the man was just before making Lily buy a ticket to get in."

"A ticket!"

"Till my husband went up and explained she wasn't bright, and so did everybody else."

---

feeble-minded (FEE buhl MIN dihd) an out-of-date expression for a person with a weak or slow mind
taut (TAWT) stretched tightly
underscored (UN dur skawrd) underlined
thimbled (THIM buld) wearing a small, protective cap used in sewing
gutteral (GUT ur ul) harsh or growling sound

TEACHING PLAN

INTRODUCE

Motivation

Discuss with students this quotation by Eudora Welty: "Like a good many other writers, I am myself touched off by place, the place where I am and the place I know." Relate the discussion to the particularly "southern" characters students will meet in the selection.

Purpose-Setting Question

Why do some people enjoy taking advantage of others?

READ

Literary Focus: *Character*

Have students create a character chart. Ask them to classify each story character as flat or round and list one or two strong personality traits for each. Have students add characters to the chart as they are introduced. Have them save their lists for later use.

Reading Focus: *Interpret Dialogue*

After reading, have students reread just the dialogue. Ask: What can you tell about each character from what each one says?

CLOSE

Have students complete Review the Selection on pages 394–395.

Develop Vocabulary Skills

Use the footnoted vocabulary words in context sentences on the chalkboard. Then have students do the same on paper. Since slang plays a key role in the selection, you might ask them to suggest contemporary substitutes for these words.

Discussion

Point out the author's use of foreshadowing in the first paragraph of the story. Ask: Does the author make effective use of this device? Discuss students' opinions. Then encourage students to look for other examples of foreshadowing in the story.

Viewing Fine Art

Edward W.D. Hamilton was a popular painter of genteel scenes at the turn of the century. His pretty scene here of a summer house in Campobello with its climbing rose bushes, view of the sea, and lounging (but elegant) ladies captured a time and place sweetly. And the artist at the same time incorporated a few architectural and formal elements (note the shadows and the various vertical accents) into his work. Changing trends in art, and society, soon left the market for paintings like this behind, a part of a nostalgic past. Ask: What might people from the early 20th century have liked about this painting?

Summer at Campobello, New Brunswick, Edward W.D. Hamilton. Museum of Fine Arts, Boston

The ladies all clicked their tongues.

"Oh, it was a very nice show," said the lady who had gone. "And Lily acted very nice. She was a perfect lady—she just set in her seat and stared."

"Oh, she can be, she can be," said Mrs. Carson, shaking her head and turning her eyes up.

"Yes'm, she kept her eyes on what's that thing makes all the commotion? The xylophone," said the lady. "Didn't turn her head to the right or left the whole

commotion (kuh MOH shun) noisy confusion

time. Sat in front of me."

"The point is, what did she do after the show?" asked Mrs. Watts practically. "Lily has gotten so she is very mature for her age."

"Oh, Hermine!" protested Mrs. Carson, looking at her wildly for a moment.

"And that's how come we are sending her to Ellisville," finished Mrs. Watts.

"I'm ready, you-all," said Aimee Slocum, running out with white powder all over her face. "Mail's up."

"Well, of course, I do hope it's for the best," said several of the other ladies. They did not go at once to take their mail out of their boxes; they felt a little left out.

The three women stood at the foot of the water tank.

"To find Lily is a different thing," said Aimee Slocum. "Where in the wide world do you suppose she'd be?"

"I don't see a sign of her either on this side of the street or on the other side," said Mrs. Carson as they walked along.

Ed Newton was stringing Redbird school tablets on the wire across the store.

"If you're looking for Lily, she come in here an' tole me she was goin' to git married, while ago," he said.

"Ed Newton!" cried the ladies, clutching one another. Mrs. Watts began to fan herself at once with the letter from Ellisville. She wore widow's black and the least thing made her hot.

"Why, she's not, she's going to Ellisville, Ed," said Mrs. Carson gently. "Mrs. Watts and I and Aimee Slocum are sending her, out of our own pockets. Besides, the boys of Victory are on their honor—Lily's not going to get married, that's just an idea she's got in her head."

"More power to you, ladies," said Ed Newton, spanking himself with a tablet.

They saw Estelle Mabers sitting on the rail of the bridge over the railroad track, slowly drinking a Ne-Hi orange drink. "Have you seen Lily?" they asked her.

"I'm supposed to be out here watching for her now," said the Mabers girl, as though she weren't there yet. "For Jewel. Jewel says Lily come in the store while ago and took a two-ninety-eight hat and wore it off. Jewel wants to swap her something else for it."

"Oh, Estelle, Lily says she's going to get married!" cried Aimee Slocum.

"Well, I declare," said Estelle; she never understood anything.

Loralee Adkins came riding by in her Willys-Knight[1], blowing the horn to find out what they were talking about.

Aimee ran waving out into the street and yelled: "Loralee, you got to ride us up to Lily Daw's. She's up yonder fixing to git married!"

"Well, that just shows you right now," said Mrs. Watts, groaning as she was helped into the back seat. "What we've got to do is persuade Lily it will be nicer to go to Ellisville."

"Just to think." While they rode around the corner Mrs. Carson was going

---

tablet (TAB lit) pad of writing paper
[1]**Willys-Knight:** type of car made in this period

Reading Focus: *Interpret Dialogue*

Assign students the roles of the characters in this story and one student the role of narrator. Have the class read aloud through page 387 as story theater.

Literary Focus: *Character*

Ask: Which character has the author avoided directly introducing at this point in the story? Why?

Critical Thinking: *Infer*

Point out the author's frequent use of figurative language. Ask: How does comparing Mrs. Carson's voice to "soft noises in the henhouse at twilight" contribute to your understanding of her character?

Literary Focus: *Character*

Ask: What do you learn about Lily from Lily? What do you learn about her from the other characters?

on in her sad voice, like soft noises in the henhouse at twilight. "We buried Lily's poor defenseless mother. We gave Lily all her food and kindling and every stitch she had on. Sent her to Sunday school to learn the Lord's teachings, had her baptized a Baptist. And when her old father commenced beating her and tried to cut her head off with the butcher-knife, why, we took her away from him and gave her a place to stay."

The paintless frame house was three stories high in places and had red and green stained-glass windows in front and gingerbread around the porch. It leaned steeply to one side and the front steps were gone. The car drew up under the cedar tree.

"Now Lily's almost grown up," Mrs. Carson continued; "in fact, she's grown," she concluded, getting out.

"Talking about getting married," said Mrs. Watts disgustedly. "Thanks, Loralee, you run on home."

They climbed over the dusty zinnias onto the porch and walked through the open door without knocking.

Lily was there, in the empty dark center hall, kneeling on the floor beside a small open trunk. ("There certainly is always a funny smell in this house. I say it every time I come," said Aimee Slocum.)

When Lily saw them she put a zinnia in her mouth.

"Hello, Lily," said Mrs. Carson reproachfully.

"Hello," said Lily, and gave a suck on the zinnia stem that sounded exactly like a jay-bird. She was wearing a petticoat for a dress, one of the things Mrs. Carson kept after her about. Her milky-yellow hair streamed freely down from under a new hat. You could see the wavy scar on her throat if you knew it was there.

Mrs. Carson and Mrs. Watts, the two fattest, sat in the double rocker. Aimee Slocum sat on the wire chair donated from the drugstore that burned.

"Well, what are you doing, Lily?" asked Mrs. Watts.

Lily smiled.

The trunk was old and lined with yellow and brown paper with an asterisk pattern showing in darker circles and rings. The ladies indicated mutely that they did not know where in the world it had come from. It was empty except for two bars of soap and a green washcloth, which Lily was trying to arrange in the bottom.

"Go on and tell us what you're doing, Lily," said Aimee Slocum.

"Packing, silly," said Lily.

"Where are you going?"

"Going to get married, and I bet you wish you was me now," said Lily. But shyness overcame her suddenly and she popped the zinnia back in her mouth.

"Talk to me, dear," said Mrs. Carson.

---

kindling (KIND ling) small pieces of dry firewood
stitch (STICH) slang for clothing
reproachfully (rih PROHCH fuh lee) scolding; blaming
petticoat (PET ee koht) type of woman's underskirt
asterisk (AS tur isk) star-shaped sign or symbol
mutely (MYOOT lee) silently

"Tell old Mrs. Carson why you want to get married."

"No," said Lily, after a moment's hesitation.

"Well, we've thought of something that will be so much nicer," said Mrs. Carson. "You can go to Ellisville."

"Won't that be lovely?" said Mrs. Watts. "Why, yes."

"It's a lovely place," said Aimee Slocum uncertainly.

"You've got bumps on your face," said Lily.

"Aimee, dear, you stay out of this if you don't mind," said Mrs. Carson anxiously. "I don't know what it is coming over Lily when you come around her."

Lily stared at Aimee Slocum meditatively.

"There—wouldn't you like to go to Ellisville now?" asked Mrs. Carson.

"No'm," said Lily.

"Why not?" All the ladies looked down at her in impressive astonishment.

"'Cause I'm goin' to git married," said Lily.

"Well, and who are you going to marry, dear?" said Mrs. Watts. She knew how to pin people down and make them deny what they'd already said.

Lily bit her lip and began to smile. She reached into the trunk and held up both cakes of soap and wagged them.

"Tell us," said Mrs. Watts, "who you're going to marry, now?"

"A man last night."

There was a gasp from each lady. The possible reality of a lover descended suddenly like a summer hail over their heads. Mrs. Watts stood up.

"One of those show fellows! A musician!" she cried.

Lily looked up in admiration.

"Did he—did he do anything to you?" It was still only Mrs. Watts who could take charge.

"Oh, yes'm," said Lily. She patted the cakes of soap fastidiously with the tips of her small fingers and tucked them in with the washcloth.

"What?" demanded Aimee Slocum, tottering before her scream.

"Don't ask her what," said Mrs. Carson. "Tell me, Lily, are you the same as you were?"

"He had a red coat, too," said Lily graciously. "He took little sticks and went ping-pong! ding-dong!"

"Oh, I think I'm going to faint," said Aimee Slocum.

"The xylophone!" cried Mrs. Watts. "The xylophone player they talked about! Why, the coward, he ought to be run out of town on a rail."

"Oh, he is out of town by now," cried Aimee. "Don't you know—the sign in the cafe—Victory on the ninth and Como on the tenth? He's in Como! Como!"

"Then we'll bring him back!" cried Mrs. Watts. "He can't get away from me!"

"Hush," said Mrs. Carson. I don't think it's any use following that line of

---

meditatively (MED uh tayt iv lee) thinking quietly
reality (ree AL uh tee) truth; fact
fastidiously (fa STID ee us lee) very sensitive; dainty

Critical Thinking: *Predict*

Have students summarize the immediate conflict in the story. Then have them predict how this conflict will be resolved and whether or not Lily will get married. Tell students to check their predictions at the end of the story.

Reading Focus: *Interpret Dialogue*

Ask: Why does Mrs. Watts call the xylophone player a coward?

Reading Focus: *Interpret Dialogue*

Have pairs of students read aloud from a passage they found particularly interesting. Ask them to practice reading aloud with their partners. Then have them alternate reading aloud to the class. Ask students to decide whether or not each pair captured the correct tone of the passage. Then ask: How does the tone of the dialogue contribute to your understanding of the character's meaning?

Literary Focus: *Character*

Have students discuss the strategy that the three ladies use to convince Lily to go to Ellisville. Elicit the idea that their strategy progresses from bribery to trickery to outright lying. Ask: Are the ladies try to help Lily or are they simply trying to get rid of her? Explain your answer.

Discussion

Ask students why they think the ladies in Victory are anxious to get Lily off their hands.

reasoning at all. It's better in the long run for him to be gone out of our lives for good and all. That kind of a man. He wanted Lily's body alone. He wouldn't make the poor little thing happy, even if we was to force him to marry her like he ought, at the point of a gun."

"Still," began Aimee.

"Shut up," said Mrs. Watts. "Mrs. Carson, you're right, I suppose."

"This is my hope chest[2], see?" said Lily. "You haven't looked at it. I've already got soap and a washrag. And I have my hat—on. What are you-all going to give me?"

"Lily," said Mrs. Watts, starting over, "we'll give you lots of gorgeous things if you'll only go to Ellisville instead of getting married."

"What will you give me?" asked Lily.

"I'll give you a pair of hem-stitched pillowcases," said Mrs. Carson.

"I'll give you a big caramel cake," said Mrs. Watts.

"I'll give you a souvenir from Jackson, a little toy bank," said Aimee Slocum. "Now will you go?"

"No'm," said Lily.

"I'll give you a pretty little Bible with your name on it in real gold," said Mrs. Carson.

"What if I was to give you a pink crepe-de-chine brassiere with adjustable shoulder straps?" asked Mrs. Watts grimly.

"Oh, Hermine."

"Well, she needs it," said Mrs. Watts. "Unless she'll wear dresses in Ellisville."

"I wish *I* could go to Ellisville!" said Aimee Slocum luringly.

"What will they have for me down there?" asked Lily softly.

"Oh! Lots of things. You'll weave baskets, I expect . . ." Mrs. Carson looked vaguely at the others.

"Oh, yes, they'll let you make all sorts of baskets," said Mrs. Watts; then her voiced too trailed off.

"No'm, I'd rather git married," said Lily.

"Lily Daw! Now that's just plain stubbornness!" cried Mrs. Watts. "You almost said you'd go and then took it back."

"We've all asked God, Lily," said Mrs. Carson finally, "and God seemed to tell us—Mr. Carson too—that the place where you ought to be, so as to be happy, was Ellisville."

"We've really just got to get her there—now!" screamed Aimee Slocum suddenly. "Suppose—! She can't stay here! *You know—you* know!"

"Oh, no, no, no," said Mrs. Carson hurriedly. "We mustn't think that."

"Could I take my hope chest—for Ellisville?" asked Lily shyly, looking at them sidewise.

"Why, yes," said Mrs. Carson blankly.

"If I could just take my hope chest!"

"All the time it was just her hope chest!" cried Aimee Slocum.

---

[2]**hope chest:** box in which a woman collects linen and clothing before being married

luringly (LUUR ing lee) to tempt or attract

Lady in a Black Hat, J. Alden Weir. The Brooklyn Museum

"It's settled!" Mrs. Watts struck her palms together.

"Praise the fathers," murmured Mrs. Carson.

"O.K.—Toots!" said Lily, her eyes gleaming with the triumph of a quotation.

The ladies were backing away to the door. "I think I'd better stay," said Mrs. Carson, stopping in her tracks. "Where—where could she have learned that terrible expression?"

"Pack her things," said Mrs. Watts. "Make the 12:35."

In the station the train was puffing. Nearly everyone in Victory was hanging around waiting for it to leave. The Victory Civic Band was scattered through the crowd. Ed Newton gave false signals to start on his bass horn. Everybody wanted to see Lily all dressed up, but Mrs. Carson and Mrs. Watts had sneaked her into the train from the other side of the tracks. The two ladies were going to travel as far as Jackson to help Lily change trains.

Lily sat between them with her hair combed and pinned up into a figure-eight knot under a small blue hat without flowers. She wore a thin made-over black dress from Mrs. Watts's last summer's mourning. Pink straps glowed through. She had a purse and a Bible and a cake in a tin box, all in her lap.

Aimee Slocum had been getting the outgoing mail stamped and bundled. She stood in the aisle of the coach now, tears shaking from her eyes. "Good-bye, Lily," she said. She was the one who felt things.

"Good-bye, silly," said Lily.

"Oh, dear, I hope they get our telegram to meet her in Ellisville!" Aimee cried suddenly, as she thought how far away it was. "And it was so hard to get it all in ten words, too."

"Get off, Aimee," said Mrs. Watts, all settled and waving her dressy fan from the funeral parlor. "I declare I'm so hot, as soon as we get a few miles out of town I'm going to slip my corset down."

"Oh, Lily, be good down there, weave baskets and do anything else they tell you—it's all because they love you." Aimee drew her mouth down and backed down the aisle.

Lily laughed. She pointed across Mrs. Carson out the window toward a man who had stepped off the train and stood

Viewing Fine Art

J. Alden Weir (1852–1896) was an American artist who was active as a founder and organizer of "The Ten" (a group of American impressionists) and as a portraitist and landscape artist. Weir studied in Paris, and he brought home some of the impressionists' ideas. Despite their influence, his work had more to do with structure and careful draftsmanship than the hazy light and thick paint of the impressionists. Weir's portraits were generally painted against a dark background, giving the face and features a bright and charming simplicity. Ask: Which of the women in this story would you think most resembles the "Lady in a Black Hat"? Why?

Literary Focus: *Character*

Ask: Which of the characters in this story would you choose as a friend? Have students explain their answers, making specific references to the text.

Discussion

Have students visualize the events that take place when Lily recognizes the xylophone player from the train window. Encourage them to picture how Lily, Mrs. Carson, and Mrs. Watts felt. Ask students to discuss and compare their "mental pictures" with a partner.

there in the dust. He was a stranger and wore a cap. "Look," she said, laughing softly through her fingers.

"Don't look," said Mrs. Carson, very distinctly, as if to impress these two column words out of all she had ever spoken upon Lily's soft little brain. "Just don't look at anything till you get to Ellisville."

Outside, Aimee Slocum was crying and almost ran into the stranger. He wore a cap and was short and seemed to have on perfume.

"Could you tell me, lady," he said, "where a little lady lives in this burg[3] name of Miss Lily Daw?" He lifted his cap; he had red hair.

"What do you want to know for?" asked Aimee.

"Talk louder," said the stranger. He almost whispered, himself.

"She's gone away—she's gone to Ellisville!"

"Gone?"

"Gone to Ellisville!"

"Well, I like that!" breathed the man.

"What business did you have with the lady?" cried Aimee suddenly.

"We was only going to get married, that's all," said the man. He laid the cap back on his hair and gave an agitated pat to the plaid-covered button.

Aimee Slocum started to scream in front of all those people. She almost pointed to the long black box she saw lying on the ground at the man's feet. Then she jumped back in fright. "The xylophone! The xylophone!" she cried, looking back and forth from the man to the hissing train. The bell began to ring hollowly and the man was talking.

"Did you say Ellisville—that in the state of Mississippi?" He was writing in a red notebook entitled *Permanent Facts & Data*. "I don't hear well."

Aimee nodded her head up and down.

Under "Ellis-Ville Miss" he was drawing a line; now he was flicking it with two little marks. "Maybe she didn't say she would. Maybe she said she wouldn't." He suddenly laughed very loudly, after the way he had whispered. Aimee cringed. "Women!—Well, if we play anywheres near Ellisville, Miss., in the future, I may look her up, and I may not," he said.

The bass horn sounded the true signal for the band to begin.

"Wait!" Aimee Slocum did scream. "Wait, Mister! I can get her for you!"

Then there she was back on the train screaming in Mrs. Carson's and Mrs. Watts's faces. "The xylophone player! He meant it! He wants to marry her! There he is!"

"Nonsense," murmured Mrs. Watts, peering over the others to look where Aimee pointed. "If he's there I don't see him. Where is he? You're looking at One-Eye Beasley."

"That little man with the cap—no, with the red hair! Hurry—the train—"

"Is that really him?" Mrs. Carson asked Mrs. Watts in wonder. "Mercy! He's small, isn't he?"

"Never saw him before in my life," cried Mrs. Watts.

[3]**burg:** slang for small town

The Coming Train, Edward Lamson Henry. Toledo Museum of Art

"Come on!" cried Aimee Slocum. Her nerves were all unstrung.

"All right. Hold your horses, girl," said Mrs. Watts. "Come on," she cried thickly to Mrs. Carson.

"Where are we going now?" asked Lily as they struggled down the aisle.

"We're taking you to get married," said Mrs. Watts. "Mrs. Carson, you'd better call up your husband from the station."

"But I don't want to git married," said Lily, beginning to whimper. "I'm going to Ellisville."

"Hush, and we'll all have some ice cream cones later," whispered Mrs. Carson.

Just as they appeared on the steps of the train the band went into the "Independence March."

The xylophone player was still there. He came up and said, "Hello, Toots. What's up—tricks?" and kissed Lily with a smack, after which she hung her head.

"So you're the young man we've heard so much about," said Mrs. Watts. Her smile was brilliant. "Here's your little Lily."

"What say?" asked the xylophone player.

"My husband happens to be the Baptist preacher of Victory," said Mrs. Carson, in a louder voice. "Isn't that lucky? I can get him here in five minutes."

They were in a circle around the xylophone player, all going into the white waiting-room.

"Oh, I feel just like crying, at a time like this," said Aimee Slocum. She looked back and saw the train moving slowly away, going under the bridge at Main Street. Then it disappeared around the curve.

"And whom have we the pleasure of addressing?" Mrs. Watts was shouting.

The band went on playing. Some of the people thought Lily was on the train, and some swore she wasn't. Everybody cheered, though, and a straw hat was thrown into the telephone wires.

Viewing Fine Art

The painter of this nostalgic landscape, Edward Lamson Henry (1841–1919), was an American painter who is all but forgotten today. In his time, like many other sensitive and conservative artists, he sought to capture the vanishing past of American life—its small towns and simple pleasures. Henry painted dryly naturalistic works that were often more illustration than original artwork, but his historical paintings were quite popular in a nation that craved familiar and nostalgic scenes. Ask: What dialogue might you hear among the characters who are waiting on the depot platform?

Reading Focus: *Interpret Dialogue*

Ask: Why does Mrs. Carson say, "Hush, and we'll all have some ice cream cones later" to Lily?

Critical Thinking: *Apply*

Tell students to use what they have learned about the story's characters to explain whether or not they were surprised by the ending of the story.

Mini Quiz

Write the following questions on the chalkboard or read them aloud. Call on students to fill in the blanks.

1. Mrs. Carson is the wife of the ________.
2. Lily and the ________ player met at the ________ ________.
3. Mrs. Watt's first name is ________.
4. Lily keeps her prized possessions in a ________ ________.
5. Lily is forced to choose between getting ________ and going to ________.

Answers

1. Baptist preacher
2. xylophone; tent show
3. Hermine
4. hope chest (or old trunk)
5. married; Ellisville

UNDERSTAND THE SELECTION

Answers

1. Victory
2. They buried Lily's mother, gave her food, firewood, and clothing, sent her to religious school, and saved her from her father's violent attacks.
3. to the Ellisville Institute for the Feeble-Minded
4. Aimee Slocum; postmistress
5. Sample answer: Mrs. Watts; "it was still only Mrs. Watts who could take charge."
6. Answers will vary.
7. Sample answer: They probably don't want to give Lily time to change her mind.
8. Sample answers: "going to get married," and "I bet you wish you was me now" or her rational answers to their demands that she go to Ellisville
9. Answers will vary. Students may say that they were acting in their own, not Lily's best interests.
10. Sample answer: You would probably be surprised to learn that you were actually getting married.

Respond to Literature

Discuss with students the effect of World War I on the growth of the women's movement. Mention that women's work in factories, with the Red Cross, and selling government bonds helped to focus attention on their importance in U.S. society. This new awareness prompted the adoption of the Nineteenth Amendment, and opened the fields of law, medicine, engineering, and journalism to women. Emphasize that in literature, it was no longer considered inappropriate for writers to focus on female themes and characterizations.

WRITE ABOUT THE SELECTION

Prewriting

Have students use their "character charts" suggested on page T385 for this assignment. Ask them to brainstorm ingredients for a successful marriage.

Review the Selection

UNDERSTAND THE SELECTION

Recall

1. Where does the story take place?
2. How have the three ladies helped Lily Daw in the past?
3. Where do they want to send her?

Infer

4. Who, among the three ladies, is employed? What is her job?
5. Who is the leader? Explain.
6. Would Lily have been happy at Ellisville? Explain.
7. Why are the three ladies so anxious to get Lily Daw on the first train?

Apply

8. Select a passage that shows Lily is not as "feeble-minded" as the ladies want to believe.
9. Were the three ladies acting in Lily's best interest when they decided not to send her to Ellisville?
10. If you were the xylophone player, would you be surprised by the end of the story?

Respond to Literature

Discuss which changes in U.S. society during the 1920s and 1930s gave Eudora Welty the opportunity to explore women's characters.

WRITE ABOUT THE SELECTION

At the conclusion of the story, Lily Daw is taken from the train against her will to be married to a man she doesn't really know. Based on your understanding of Lily's character, and the character of the xylophone player, write two paragraphs that explain whether you think Lily's marriage is a good idea. Include reasons to support your opinions.

Prewriting Write an informal list of each character's qualities, or personality traits. It may help to reread those sections of the story, including dialogue and comments, that vividly illustrate both Lily's and the xylophone player's characters.

Writing Use your lists to write two paragraphs that express your opinion of Lily's upcoming marriage. In it, use specific examples from the story to support your opinion.

Revising When you revise your work, make sure the first sentence of each paragraph begins with a clear, convincing statement. Check to see if you have included enough comments and dialogue from the story to support this statement. Finally, make sure your final paragraph closes with a sentence that reinforces your original opinion.

Proofreading Find and correct punctuation errors in your two paragraphs. Where necessary, add commas, quotation marks, and periods. Check your spelling to be sure it is correct.

Writing

Have students work on their paragraphs individually. Offer help to those having difficulty.

Revising

Make this a cooperative group activity. Have small groups of students exchange papers to make revising suggestions. You might have the class discuss the pros and cons of Lily's marriage.

Proofreading

Select one or two of the students' essays as models for proofreading. Put the essays on the overhead projector and have the class suggest improvements.

THINK ABOUT CHARACTER

Although flat characters are usually less complex and lifelike than round characters, they still serve an important purpose. Often, writers create a variety of simple, or flat, characters to give you a vivid impression about the different kinds of people who live in a particular place.

1. What kind of characters are Ed Newton, Estelle Mabers, and Loralee Adkins? How do you know?
2. Briefly characterize Aimee Slocum.
3. What does their last-minute decision to make Lily marry the xylophone player reveal about the three ladies?
4. Describe what the author thinks about Mrs. Carson in the sentence, "Mrs. Carson was going on in her sad voice, like soft noises in the henhouse at twilight."
5. What does Lily Daw do or say in the story that surprises you?

READING FOCUS

Interpret Dialogue In the story, whose dialogue was the easiest to interpret? Why do you think this is so?

DEVELOP YOUR VOCABULARY

Adjectives are words that modify nouns and pronouns. For instance, *talented* writer, *several* typewriters, *plastic* cup. **Adverbs** are words that modify adjectives, verbs, and other adverbs. For instance, spoke *loudly*, *reasonably* correct, ran *quickly*.

You can often form adverbs from adjectives by adding the suffix *-ly* to the adjective. For instance, "The children's problem was most *unfortunate*." "*Unfortunately*, the children's problem was never solved."

Copy the adjectives below on a separate sheet of paper and write an original sentence for each. Then add *-ly* to each adjective and write a sentence that shows your understanding of the newly formed adverb.

1. mute
2. fastidious
3. anxious
4. eager
5. hesitant
6. dangerous
7. serious
8. bright

THINK ABOUT CHARACTER

Answers

1. Their personalities are composed of few elements. They are flat characters because they have only one side of their personalities developed.
2. Sample answer: She is a simple-minded yet sensitive woman, prone to excitable outbursts.
3. Sample answer: They are really selfish, insensitive, and perhaps even cruel.
4. Sample answer: The author does not think very highly of her; she is compared to clucking hens.
5. Answers will vary. Students may say her preference for marriage over going to Ellisville or her sudden objection to getting married.

DEVELOP YOUR VOCABULARY

Answers

1. mutely
2. fastidiously
3. anxiously
4. eagerly
5. hesitantly
6. dangerously
7. seriously
8. brightly

Sentences will vary.

ESL Activity

Have pairs of students look for adverbs in sentences in the selection. Then have them each rewrite five of the sentences, replacing the adverbs with ones from the vocabulary lesson. Ask how the meaning of the sentence changes.

READING FOCUS

Sample Answer

Lily's dialogue was the easiest to interpret because she spoke honestly, without a hidden agenda.

Selection Overview

Selection Objectives

After completing this selection, students will be able to

- understand and identify the elements of humor
- evaluate humorous statements, actions, or events
- add a humorous scene to the selection
- understand dramatic irony
- understand words used as nouns and verbs
- understand cause and effect

Lesson Resources

The Still Alarm

- Selection Synopsis, Teacher's Edition, p. T337f
- Comprehension and Vocabulary Workbook, pp. 79–80
- Language Enrichment Workbook, p. 61
- Teacher's Resources
  Reinforcement, p. R40
  Test, pp. T79–T80

More About Humor

Explain to students that humor has a serious side. It can focus on the shortcomings of people. Humor exposes what is pompous, ridiculous, and absurd. Direct students' attention to the preceding selection, "Lily Daw and the Three Ladies." Have students choose passages that show a character's shortcomings.

More About the Literary Period

Discuss the idea that plays and movies provided many Americans with comic relief from the stark reality of the depression years. Point out that movie stars such as James Stewart, Cary Grant, W.C. Fields, and Claudette Colbert began their careers in Depression-era comedies. Ask students to suggest present-day comic stars and explain why they are so popular.

Learn About

Humor

In literature, humor is any writing that produces an amused response. As you explore humor, you will develop the ability to distinguish between the different techniques that writers use to make you laugh.

Much of what we find funny, or humorous, comes from the comic reactions of characters to a particular problem or situation. When a character makes sharp, clever remarks about a situation, we may laugh at his wit. When someone behaves in a way that is entirely unexpected, or "out of character," we often find that person's actions amusing.

Humor often comes from the difference between what you think will happen in a situation, and what actually occurs. An example of this **irony of situation**, is when a tragic or seemingly dangerous event turns out to be quite funny.

As you read *The Still Alarm*, ask yourself:

1. Which dialogue or actions in the play are humorous?
2. What makes them humorous?

Reading Focus

Understand Cause and Effect In many works of literature an author first creates an event—the cause. Then the author shows a logical effect to demonstrate that the events are related. However, sometimes the effect is unexpected, and that makes the story or play funny. Look for unexpected effects as you read *The Still Alarm*. Think about how these unexpected events add humor to the play.

Writing Connection

Think about the last time you laughed, and write a brief paragraph that explains what made you think the statement, action, or event to which you reacted was funny.

About the Author

George Simon Kaufman (1889–1961) was one of the most productive and innovate dramatists of the 20th century. He wrote more than forty plays and musical comedies, of which *You Can't Take It with You* (1936), and *The Man Who Came to Dinner* (1939) are the most famous. Kaufman was also an accomplished stage director and screen writer.

ESL Activity

Have a volunteer draw a diagram of the stage on the chalkboard, using suggestions from the class and the directions at the beginning of the play. Make sure that students are familiar with the setting of the play before they begin to read it.

Cooperative Group Activity

Pair students and have them help each other to complete the Writing Connection assignment. Ask a member of each pair first to relate the anecdote or incident as it happened and then to read his or her explanatory paragraph. Ask the class to decide if it really expresses what is funny about the anecdote.

THE STILL ALARM

by George S. Kaufman

(Vital Note: It is important that the entire play be acted calmly and politely, in the manner of an English drawing-room[1] comedy. No actor ever raises his voice; every line must be read as though it were an invitation to a cup of tea. If this direction is disregarded, the play has no point at all.)

The scene is a hotel bedroom. Two windows are in the rear wall with a bed between them. A telephone stand is at one end of the bed and a dresser is near the other. In the right wall is a door leading to the hall with a chair nearby. In the left wall is a door to another room; near it is a small table and two chairs. ED *and* BOB *are on the stage.* ED *is getting into his overcoat as the curtain rises. Both are at the hall door.*

ED: Well, Bob, it's certainly been nice to see you again.
BOB: It was nice to see *you*.
ED: You come to town so seldom, I hardly ever get the chance to—
BOB: Well, you know how it is. A business trip is always more or less of a bore.
ED: Next time you've got to come out to the house.
BOB: I want to come out. I just had to stick around the hotel this trip.
ED: Oh, I understand. Well, give my best to Edith.
BOB (*remembering something*): Oh, I say, Ed. Wait a minute.
ED: What's the matter?
BOB: I knew I wanted to show you something. (*Crosses to table. Gets roll of blueprints from drawer.*) Did you know I'm going to build?

[1]**drawing room:** formal living room or parlor. A "drawing room comedy" is a humorous play acted out in a dignified, serious manner.

TEACHING PLAN

INTRODUCE

Motivation

You might play recordings of stand-up comedians or comic duos, such as Bill Cosby or Abbott and Costello. Discuss with students the differences between spontaneous verbal humor, like wit and sarcasm, and the careful preparations involved in creating and performing a comic routine or a humorous play.

Purpose-Setting Question

If *The Still Alarm* were performed today, would modern audiences find it humorous?

READ

Literary Focus: *Humor*

Direct students to the "Vital Note" at the beginning of the play. Have students think about this note as they read. Ask: Why does the play have no point at all if the actors don't read the script with a calm, unhurried tone?

Reading Focus: *Understand Cause and Effect*

Kaufman continuously sets up situations that should result in a particular way, but don't. As students read, have them note how the unexpected reactions of the characters create humor.

CLOSE

Have students complete Review the Selection on pages 404–405.

Develop Vocabulary Skills

Familiarize students with the vocabulary words footnoted in the story. Use each vocabulary word in an original sentence and ask students to suggest several antonyms for words that have antonyms.

Literary Focus: *Humor*

Explain to students that comic presentation depends on a number of elements, timing being one of the most important. Point out that speaking a line a split second sooner or later than intended can make the different between laughter and boredom. Have groups of students work together to act out a "scene" from the play. Tell them to pay close attention to the timing and "delivery" of their lines.

ED (*follows to table*)**:** A house?

BOB: You bet it's a house! (*Knock on hall door.*) Come in! (*Spreads plans.*) I just got these yesterday.

ED (*sits*)**:** Well, that's fine! (*The knock is repeated—louder. Both men now give full attention to the door.*)

BOB: Come! Come in!

BELLBOY (*enters*)**:** Mr. Barclay?

BOB: Well?

BELLBOY: I've a message from the clerk, sir. For Mr. Barclay personally.

BOB (*crosses to* BOY)**:** I'm Mr. Barclay. What is the message?

BELLBOY: The hotel is on fire, sir.

BOB: What's that?

BELLBOY: The hotel is on fire.

ED: This hotel?

BELLBOY: Yes, sir.

BOB: Well—is it bad?

BELLBOY: It looks pretty bad, sir.

ED: You mean it's going to burn down?

BELLBOY: We think so—yes, sir.

BOB (*a low whistle of surprise*)**:** Well! We'd better leave.

BELLBOY: Yes, sir.

BOB: Going to burn down, huh?

BELLBOY: Yes, sir. If you'll step to the window you'll see. (BOB *goes to a window.*)

BOB: Yes, that is pretty bad. H'm (*to* ED). I say, you really ought to see this—

ED (*crosses to window, peers out*)**:** It's reached the floor right underneath.

BELLBOY: Yes, sir. The lower part of the hotel is about gone, sir.

BOB (*still looking out—looks up*)**:** Still all right up above, though. (*Turns to* BOY.) Have they notified the Fire Department?

BELLBOY: I wouldn't know, sir. I'm only the bellboy.

BOB: Well, that's the thing to do, obviously—(*Nods head to each one as if the previous line was a bright idea.*)—notify the Fire Department. Just call them up, give them the name of the hotel—

ED: Wait a minute. I can do better than that for you. (*To the* BOY.) Ring through to the Chief, and tell him that Ed Jamison told you to telephone him. (*To* BOB.) We went to school together, you know.

BOB: That's fine. (*To the* BOY) Now, get that right. Tell the Chief that Mr. Jamison said to ring him.

ED: *Ed* Jamison.

BOB: Yes, *Ed* Jamison.

BELLBOY: Yes, sir. (*Turns to go.*)

BOB: Oh! Boy! (*Pulls out handful of change; picks out a coin.*) Here you are.

BELLBOY: Thank you, sir. (*Exit* BELLBOY.)

(ED *sits at table, lights cigarette, and throws match on floor, then steps on it. There is a moment's pause.*)

BOB: Well! (*Crosses and looks out window.*) Say, we'll have to get out of here pretty soon.

Reading Focus: *Understand Cause and Effect*

Ask: What effect would you expect when Ed Jamison tells the bellboy to call the Chief of Police? What actually happens?

Critical Thinking: *Evaluate*

Ask: Is the author succeeding in being humorous? What might happen if the actors were not following the "vital note" in the stage directions?

Critical Thinking: *Analyze*

Have students discuss specific changes they would make to transform this play from a comedy into a serious drama. Point out that a drama often focuses on a painful or serious issue while a comedy depicts that which is amusing. Using students' suggestions, create a study chart of statements, actions, and events from the play that are humorous. Then have students explain how these comic elements could be made tragic.

Literary Focus: *Humor*

Ask: Why is it funny when Ed says, "Maybe there's been some kind of accident"?

ED (*going to window*): How is it—no better?

BOB: Worse, if anything. It'll be up here in a few moments.

ED: What floor *is* this?

BOB: Eleventh.

ED: Eleven. We couldn't jump, then.

BOB: Oh, no. You never could jump. (*Comes away from window to dresser.*) Well, I've got to get my things together. (*Pulls out suitcase.*)

ED (*smoothing out the plans*): Who made these for you?

BOB: A fellow here—Rawlins. (*Turns a shirt in his hand.*) I ought to call one of the other hotels for a room.

ED: Oh, you can get in.

BOB: They're pretty crowded. (*Feels something on the sole of his foot; inspects it.*) Say, the floor's getting hot.

ED: I know it. It's getting stuffy in the room, too. Phew! (*He looks around, then goes to the phone.*) Hello. Ice water in eleven eighteen. (*Crosses to table.*)

BOB (*at bed*): That's the stuff. (*Packs.*) You know, if I move to another hotel I'll never get my mail. Everybody thinks I'm stopping here.

ED (*studying the plans*): Say, this isn't bad.

BOB (*eagerly*): Do you like it? (*Remembers his plight.*) Suppose I go to another hotel and there's a fire there, too!

ED: You've got to take *some* chance.

BOB: I know, but here I'm sure. (*Phone rings.*) Oh, answer that, will you, Ed? (*To dresser and back.*)

ED (*crosses to phone*): Sure. (*At phone.*) Hello— Oh, that's good. Fine. What? Oh! Well, wait a minute. (*To* BOB.) The firemen are downstairs and some of them want to come up to this room.

BOB: Tell them, of course.

ED (*at phone*): All right. Come right up. (*Hangs up, crosses, and sits at table.*) Now we'll get some action.

BOB (*looks out of window*): Say, there's an awful crowd of people on the street.

ED (*absently, as he pores over the plans*): Maybe there's been some kind of accident.

---

plight (PLYT) bad condition or problem
absently (AB sunt lee) with attention elsewhere
pore over (PAWR OH vur) study carefully

BOB (*peering out, suitcase in hand*): No. More likely they heard about the fire. (*A knock at the door.*) Come in.

BELLBOY (*enters*): I beg pardon, Mr. Barclay, the firemen have arrived.

BOB: Show them in. (*Crosses to door.*)

(*The door opens. In the doorway appear two* FIREMAN *in full regalia. The* FIRST FIREMAN *carries a hose and rubber coat; the* SECOND *has a violin case.*)

FIRST FIREMAN (*very apologetically*): Mr. Barclay.

BOB: I'm Mr. Barclay.

FIRST FIREMAN: We're the firemen, Mr. Barclay. (*They remove their hats.*)

BOB: How de do?

ED: How de do?

BOB: A great pleasure, I assure you. Really must apologize for the condition of this room, but—

FIRST FIREMAN: Oh, that's all right. I know how it is at home.

BOB: May I present a friend of mine, Mr. Ed Jamison—

FIRST FIREMAN: How are you?

ED: How are you, boys? (SECOND FIREMAN *nods.*) I know your Chief.

FIRST FIREMAN: Oh, is that so? He knows the Chief—dear old Chiefie. (SECOND FIREMAN *giggles.*)

BOB (*embarrassed*): Well, I guess you boys want to get to work, don't you?

FIRST FIREMAN: Well, if you don't mind. We would like to spray around a little bit.

BOB: May I help you?

FIRST FIREMAN: Yes, if you please. (BOB *helps him into his rubber coat. At the same time the* SECOND FIREMAN, *without a word, lays the violin case on the bed, opens it, takes out the violin, and begins tuning it.*)

BOB (*watching him*): I don't think I understand.

FIRST FIREMAN: Well, you see, Sid doesn't get much chance to practice at home. Sometimes, at a fire, while we're waiting for a wall to fall or something, why, a fireman doesn't really have anything to do, and personally I like to see him improve himself symphonically. I hope you don't resent it. You're not antisymphonic?

---

regalia (rih GAYL yuh) signs of royalty, such as special dress (here used ironically)
antisymphonic (an tih sim FON ik) against music

Reading Focus: *Understand Cause and Effect*

Ask: What causes the firemen to arrive? What effect would you expect from their entrance under normal conditions? What effect occurs in this play?

Critical Thinking: *Evaluate*

Ask: Using the information you have learned so far, what do you think the author's purpose is? How well do you think the author has achieved this purpose? Why do you think as you do?

Literary Focus: *Humor*

Look back to *Learn about Humor* on page 396. Why is it funny that Ed and Bob are not concerned about the danger from the fire?

BOB: Of course not—(BOB *and* ED *nod understandingly; the* SECOND FIREMAN *is now waxing the bow.*)

FIRST FIREMAN: Well, if you'll excuse me—(*To window. Turns with decision toward the window. You feel that he is about to get down to business.*)

BOB: Charming personalities.

ED (*follows over to the window*)**:** How is the fire?

FIRST FIREMAN (*feels the wall*)**:** It's pretty bad right now. This wall will go pretty soon now, but it'll fall out that way, so it's all right. (*Peers out.*) That next room is the place to fight it from. (*Crosses to door in left wall.* BOB *shows ties as* ED *crosses.*)

ED (*sees ties*)**:** Oh! Aren't those gorgeous!

FIRST FIREMAN (*to* BOB)**:** Have you the key for this room?

BOB: Why, no. I've nothing to do with that room. I've just got this one. (*Folding a shirt as he talks.*)

ED: Oh, it's very comfortable.

FIRST FIREMAN: That's too bad. I had something up my sleeve, if I could have gotten in there. Oh, well, may I use your phone?

BOB: Please do. (*To* ED) Do you think you might hold this? (*Indicates the hose.*)

ED: How?

FIRST FIREMAN: Just crawl under it. (*As he does that.*) Thanks. (*At phone.*) Hello. Let me have the clerk, please. (*To* SECOND FIREMAN.) Give us that little thing you played the night the Equitable Building burned down. (*Back to phone.*) Are you there? This is one of the firemen. Oh, *you* know. I'm in room—ah—(*Looks at* BOB.)

BOB: Eleven-eighteen.

FIRST FIREMAN: Eleven-eighteen, and I want to get into the next room—Oh, goody. Will you send someone up with the key? There's no one in there? Oh, super-goody! Right away. (*Hangs up.*)

BOB: That's fine. (*To* FIREMEN.) Won't you sit down?

FIRST FIREMAN: Thanks.

ED: Have a cigar?

FIRST FIREMAN (*takes it*)**:** Much obliged.

BOB: A light?

FIRST FIREMAN: If you please.

ED (*failing to find a match*)**:** Bob, have you a match?

BOB (*crosses to table*)**:** I thought there were some here. (*Hands in pockets.*)

FIRST FIREMAN: Oh, never mind. (*He goes to a window, leans out, and emerges with cigar lighted.* BOB *crosses to dresser, slams drawer. The* SECOND FIREMAN *taps violin with bow.*)

FIRST FIREMAN: Mr. Barclay, I think he's ready now.

BOB: Pardon me.

(*They all sit. The* SECOND FIREMAN *takes center of stage, with all the manner of a concert violinist. He goes into "Keep the Home Fires Burning."* BOB, ED, *and* FIRST FIREMAN *wipe brow as lights dim to red on closing eight bars.*)

---

emerge (ih MURJ) come out into view

Reading Focus: *Understand Cause and Effect*

Ask: What overall effect does the fire have on the characters in this play?

Discussion

Discuss with students the content of a modern comedy of manners. Ask: What modern attitudes or manners might be ridiculed? What place might serve as a setting? Who might the characters be?

Mini Quiz

Write the following questions on the chalkboard or read them aloud. Call on students to fill in the blanks.

1. The play takes place in a ________ ________.
2. Ed ________ and Bob ________ are the main characters in this play.
3. Bob is extremely proud of the ________ for his house.
4. Ed orders ________ ________ from room service to quench his thirst.
5. The fireman who plays the violin is called ________.

Answers

1. hotel room
2. Jamison; Barclay
3. blueprints
4. ice water
5. Sid

Review the Selection

UNDERSTAND THE SELECTION

Recall

1. On which floor of the hotel does the play take place?
2. What instrument does the Second Fireman play?
3. What song is played at the end?

Infer

4. How do you know that Bob is from out of town?
5. What is the name of Bob's wife? How do you know?
6. How does the First Fireman light his cigar?
7. Why is Ed's reaction to the crowd in the street so unusual?

Apply

8. Compare and contrast the behavior of the firemen in *The Still Alarm* to the actions of real firefighters.
9. If you were in the hotel, what would you do?
10. Discuss why the blueprints for Bob's new house make an excellent subject for conversation in this play.

Respond to Literature

Explain why an American audience in the 1930s might be entertained by *The Still Alarm*.

WRITE ABOUT THE SELECTION

Much of what is humorous about *The Still Alarm* comes from the way each character calmly ignores the danger of the fire, even as the hotel is literally burning down. Add an episode, or scene, to the play that shows Bob trying to reserve a room in another hotel.

Prewriting Write a list of questions that will help you imagine the kind of conversation that Bob might have with the hotel manager, and how Ed might react to it. Think about the tone of voice Bob might use, the reasons he might tell for wanting to move to another hotel, and the pointless comments that Ed would probably make.

Writing Use your list of questions to add a short, humorous scene to the play. In it, write dialogue that shows Bob attempting to reserve a room at a hotel across town. When you write the dialogue for Bob and Ed, have them speak the way they do in the play.

Revising When you revise your scene, read it aloud to see whether you have captured the proper mood. Check to see that your stage directions describe the emotions and gestures of each character in an accurate way.

Proofreading Reread your scene and correct any punctuation errors. Make sure that your written script resembles the format of *The Still Alarm*.

UNDERSTAND THE SELECTION

Answers

1. the eleventh floor
2. the violin
3. "Keep the Home Fires Burning"
4. Bob mentions that he is in town on a business trip; Ed comments that Bob seldom comes to town.
5. Edith; Ed says, "Well, give my best to Edith."
6. He uses the flames from the hotel fire.
7. Sample answer: Contrary to readers' expectations, Ed doesn't make the logical connection between the hotel fire and the curious spectators in the street.
8. Sample answer: Real firefighters do not have time to be as civil and courteous as the ones in the play; real firefighters don't request room keys—they break down doors; real firefighters don't play musical instruments during emergencies.
9. Sample answer: act as crazily as the other characters and listen to the violin concert; leave
10. Sample answer: The conversation is ironic, Bob speaks about creating a building, while the very one he is in is burning down.

Respond to Literature

Discuss with students whether comedy is as important as "serious" literature. Elicit the idea that comedy often reveals essential truths about human behavior and removes the sting from painful experiences. Point out that Depression-era audiences were desperately poor, so it was entertaining to see people behaving nonchalantly about an entire hotel burning down.

WRITE ABOUT THE SELECTION

Prewriting

Using students' suggestions, write a list of questions on the chalkboard or on an overhead projector.

Writing

Make this a cooperative group activity. Tell students that George S. Kaufman wrote most of his plays with a collaborator. Have pairs of students work on this section. Walk around the class, helping those pairs having difficulty.

Revising

Have each pair read their scene to the class. You might have students comment on the funniest scenes.

Proofreading

Display several scripts on an overhead projector and have the class suggest improvements in format.

THINK ABOUT HUMOR

Sometimes an author will share with you an important secret that the characters in the play, poem, or short story don't know. This technique, called **dramatic irony**, can help you appreciate the humorous aspects of a problem or situation that the characters do not even know is funny.

1. How do Bob and Ed react when they first learn of the fire?
2. What do you know that the two characters fail to understand?
3. Playing a violin during a fire is an allusion, or reference, to a famous historical event. The Roman Emperor Nero was said to have played the violin while he watched Rome burn. How does this allusion contribute to the humor of the play?
4. Why is it essential that *The Still Alarm* be acted in a dignified, serious manner?

READING FOCUS

Understand Cause and Effect Identify a cause and effect relationship in the play. Is it humorous? Explain why or why not.

DEVELOP YOUR VOCABULARY

Nouns are words that name people, places, objects, or ideas. In the sentence, "The committee met secretly," *committee* is the noun. **Verbs** are words that express action or a state of being. In the sentence, "He sprinted for the bus," *sprinted* is the verb.

Read each of the sentences below and decide whether the italicized word is used as a noun or a verb. You may consult a dictionary to learn how each word is used in the sentence.

1. The batter slammed the *pitch* against the outfield wall.
   Pitch in and we'll finish the job today.
2. This inflatable bag will *cushion* the stuntwoman's fall.
   I sat down on the soft *cushion*.
3. Our new quarterback just may *spark* this team to victory.
   We need a small *spark* to light this fire.
4. A small *shudder* passed through him.
   I *shudder* to think of the hard work ahead.

THINK ABOUT HUMOR

Answers

1. Sample answer: They don't appear very concerned.
2. Sample answer: The reader knows how serious and dangerous the fire is.
3. Sample answer: Like the unconcerned emperor, the characters in this play are merely amused, not frightened, by the fire.
4. Sample answer: Since the humor of the play stems from the characters' failure to recognize their peril, they must remain unruffled and dignified.

DEVELOP YOUR VOCABULARY

Answers

1. Noun; verb
2. Verb; noun
3. Verb; noun
4. Noun; verb

READING FOCUS

Sample Answer

The fire causes the floor to get hot (page 400); Ed calls room service for ice water. This is humorous because one would expect the room occupants to panic, rather than to calmly call for ice water.

ESL Activity

Have pairs of students think of other sentences using the italicized words in the "Develop Your Vocabulary" activity. The first student chooses one definition and makes a statement. Each partner must choose the other definition for their sentences.

Focus on Drama

Guide students through a discussion of the elements of drama. Use the following questions to remind them that they have encountered many of these elements in the short stories and poems they have read in this unit.

ELEMENTS OF DRAMA

In discussing **character**, ask students which people they know who they would describe as round characters and which are flat characters. Suggest that they think about the differences between friends and acquaintances and between immediate family members and distant relatives.

Ask students to compare **setting** in the poems of Langston Hughes and Robert Frost. Have them discuss whether each poet's choice of locale is appropriate to his purpose.

Ask students to think about the name of the town in the story, "Lily Daw and the Three Ladies." Have them explain what "Victory" **symbolizes**.

Have students explain what types of **conflict** Schatz experiences in "A Day's Wait." Elicit the idea that he has an external conflict with an outside force (disease) as well as an internal conflict (how to act bravely in the face of approaching death).

Discuss the **theme** of "home." Elicit the idea that families are an important "life support" system in times of upheaval and fear.

You might have students develop additional questions, then work in small groups to determine and discuss their answers.

Focus on Drama

A drama, or play, is a work of literature intended to be spoken or acted out. While drama shares many elements (or essential parts) with poetry, fiction, and nonfiction, it also has qualities which make it unique. Studying how the elements of drama work together can help you better understand a particular play.

Character In literature a character is the representation of a person or animal. A playwright—the author—creates action and personalities through the dialogue spoken between characters. These characters reveal themselves by the way they speak.

Sometimes a character will speak directly to the audience. During this **soliloquy**, the character tells us directly about his or her hopes, fears, dreams, and intentions.

In a play, many of the minor, or less important characters, are flat, and the major, or main, characters are round. **Flat characters** show only one side, or aspect, of their personality, and usually represent a single idea or attitude. **Round characters** are more complete human beings whose reactions to certain problems and events may surprise you.

Setting Setting is the time and place in which a play, poem, or story occurs. Stage plays are usually limited to three or four **sets**, or locations, while radio, television, and movie plays can take place in an unlimited number of settings.

To determine the *when* of a setting, you should look for clues that tell the historical time period, time of day, season of year, or passage of time. The *where* of a play is its location, scenery, even natural events, such as the weather.

While reading a play, you should pay attention to the **stage directions**. These are instructions that tell how characters should talk and move, and help you visualize the setting.

Plot In literature, plot is the sequence of related events that make up a story. In drama, plot is established through connected **scenes**, or incidents, that usually take place in one location, and focus on a single conversation or event.

Plot begins with exposition, which gives you the background information you need to understand the action. Exposition is followed by complication. As the plot becomes more complicated, you approach the climax, or turning point, of the play. After the climax, you know how the drama will end. In the final part of the play, called the resolution, the conflict is resolved.

The plot of a drama may be moved along by a narrator, or announcer. You may think of this character as a storyteller who provides you with information not spoken by the characters.

Plot does not have to flow in chronological order. Sometimes, a writer will use **foreshadowing** to give you hints about events that are going to happen. Writers also use **flashbacks** to go back in time and tell you about something important that happened.

Conflict To figure out the plot, you should think about the *conflicts* that the characters experience. **External conflict** is a struggle with an outside force, such as another person, nature, or society. **Internal conflict** is the emotional or psychological battle that takes place within a character.

Symbolism and Allegory Often, a writer may use a person, place, object, or event that represents, or **symbolizes** a special idea, concept, or hidden truth. When an entire play or story is symbolic, we call it an **allegory**. Allegories are often used for explaining moral principles.

Theme The central message, or main point, of a play, poem, or story is called its theme. Understanding the relationship between characters, events, and their outcomes, helps you figure out the basic idea about human experience, or theme.

As you read *Invasion from Mars*, ask yourself:

1. What characters are introduced?
2. When does the play take place? How many different settings are described?
3. What are the conflicts? How is the main conflict resolved?
4. Does the play have a theme? What is it?

Real-Life Application

Discuss with students the fact that the titles of popular songs, movies, and plays often give broad hints about their themes. Have students work in small groups to brainstorm two examples from each category—songs, movies, and plays—and discuss the relationship of each title to the theme. Encourage each group to share their thoughts with the class.

Selection Overview

SELECTION OBJECTIVES

After completing this selection, students will be able to

- understand and identify the elements of drama
- understand the difference between stage plays and radio plays
- write a brief radio drama
- understand jargon
- understand sequence of events

Lesson Resources

Invasion from Mars
- Selection Synopsis, Teacher's Edition, p. T337g
- Comprehension and Vocabulary Workbook, pp. 81–82
- Language Enrichment Workbook, pp. 62–63
- Teacher's Resources
  Reinforcement, p. R41
  Test, pp. T81–T82
  Literary Analysis, pp. L12–L13

More About the Literary Period

In 1935, Italy invaded Ethiopia; in 1936, civil war broke out in Spain and Hitler invaded the Rhineland; in September 1938, he seized parts of Czechoslovakia. By October 31, 1938, the date of this radio broadcast, many Americans were anxious about the threat of another world war. *Invasion from Mars* capitalized on these concerns and fears.

Background Notes

Mercury Theatre on the Air was a series of weekly radio programs produced by Orson Welles and the famous American director-actor, John Houseman. The programs featured dramatizations of classic novels and short stories, as well as of contemporary plays. *War of the Worlds*, the seventeenth show of this series, was intended to be a simple Halloween prank.

MODEL

Invasion from Mars

ADAPTED *by Howard Koch*

CHARACTERS

THREE ANNOUNCERS
ORSON WELLES
CARL PHILLIPS, *radio commentator*
PROFESSOR RICHARD PIERSON, *astronomer*
A POLICEMAN
MR. WILMUTH, *a farmer*
BRIGADIER GENERAL MONTGOMERY SMITH
HARRY McDONALD
CAPTAIN LANSING
SECRETARY OF THE INTERIOR
SOLDIERS OF THE 22ND FIELD ARTILLERY: *An officer, a gunner, and an observer*
LIEUTENANT VOGHT, *commander of an Army bomber plane*
FIVE RADIO OPERATORS
A STRANGER

COLUMBIA BROADCASTING SYSTEM
ORSON WELLES AND MERCURY THEATRE
ON THE AIR
SUNDAY, OCTOBER 30, 1938
8:00 TO 9:00 P.M.

ANNOUNCER: The Columbia Broadcasting System and its associated stations present Orson Welles and the Mercury Theatre on the Air in a radio play by Howard Koch suggested by the H. G. Wells novel *The War of the Worlds.* (*Mercury Theatre Musical Theme*)

ANNOUNCER: Ladies and gentlemen: the director of the Mercury Theatre and star of these broadcasts, Orson Welles . . .

ORSON WELLES: We know now that in the early years of the twentieth century this world was being watched closely by

FOCUS ON DRAMA STUDY HINTS

Notice the foreshadowing here. What event are you being prepared for?

Cooperative Group Activity

Divide the class into small groups. Assign each member the role of set designer, lighting designer, costumer, or make-up person. Have students read the play, taking notes about how they would fulfill their specific tasks if this play was performed before a live audience. At the end of the selection, students will discuss their creative choices with their group, then present their "design" ideas to the class.

intelligences greater than man's and yet as mortal as his own. We know now that as human beings busied themselves about their various concerns they were examined, perhaps almost as narrowly as a man with a microscope might scrutinize the transient creatures that swarm and multiply in a drop of water. With infinite contentment people went to and fro over the earth about their little affairs, serene in the assurance of their rule over this small spinning fragment of solar driftwood which by chance or design man has inherited out of the dark mystery of Time and Space. Yet across an immense ethereal gulf, minds that are to our minds as ours are to the beasts in the jungle, intellects vast, cool and unsympathetic, regarded this earth with envious eyes and slowly and surely drew their plans against us. In the thirty-eighth year of the twentieth century came the great disappointment.

It was near the end of October. Business was better. The war was over. More men were back at work. Sales were picking up. On this particular evening, October 30, the Crossley service[1] estimated that thirty-two million people were listening in on radios.

ANNOUNCER: . . . for the next twenty-four hours not much change in temperature. A slight atmospheric disturbance of undetermined origin is reported over Nova Scotia,[2] causing a low pressure area to move down rather rapidly over the northeastern states, bringing a forecast of rain, accompanied by winds of light gale force. Maximum temperature 66; minimum 48. This weather report comes to you from the Government Weather Bureau.

. . . We now take you to the Meridian Room in the Hotel Park Plaza in downtown New York, where you will be entertained by the music of Ramon Raquello and his orchestra.

(Spanish theme song . . . fades.)

---

mortal (MAWR tul) subject to death
transient (TRAN shunt) not permanent; passing quickly
ethereal (ih THIR EE uhl) of the upper regions of space
[1]**Crossley service:** a service that estimated the size of radio audiences as the Nielsen rating service estimates the size of television audiences today
[2]**Nova Scotia:** a southeastern province of Canada

TEACHING PLAN

INTRODUCE

Motivation

Ask students to discuss what they might do if they heard that extraterrestrial beings had landed in New Jersey.

Purpose-Setting Question

If we had the chance to communicate with extraterrestrial beings, what would you tell them about Earth?

READ

Literary Focus: *Drama*

The blue side notes in this annotated lesson provide a model for students to understand the literary elements introduced in Focus on Drama, pages 406-407. Use the annotation questions as starting points for class discussion and critical thinking exercises. The questions can also be used to check students' comprehension and recall.

Reading Focus: *Understand Sequence of Events*

Have students jot down each new scene in the order in which it occurs to help them follow the sequence of events of the play.

CLOSE

Have students complete Review the Selection on pages 436–437.

Develop Vocabulary Skills

You might choose to teach the footnoted vocabulary words by treating them in three sections: scientific terms, geographical locations, and plain vocabulary. Supply definitions for these words and use them in context sentences. You might bring to class illustrations of the scientific instruments.

ESL Activity

Provide a radio broadcast for students to listen to and discuss. If possible, provide a radio drama from the past—often available on audiocassette from local libraries. Discuss how students must infer what is happening from the dialogue and the narrator's words.

Literary Focus: *Setting*

Review the settings of Announcer 3, Announcer 2, Carl Phillips and Professor Pierson, gas eruptions, and earthquake-like shock. Have students record the change of settings.

Background Notes

The years between 1925 and 1950 were known as "The Golden Age of Broadcasting." Millions of American families listened nightly to their favorite comedians (Fred Allen, Jack Benny, Bob Hope), soap operas (*The Guiding Light*, *One Man's Family*), and radio dramas (*Buck Rogers in the Twenty-fifth Century*, *The Green Hornet*, *The Shadow*).

Note the new setting. Observe how frequently the setting begins to change.

ANNOUNCER THREE: Good evening, ladies and gentlemen. From the Meridian Room in the Park Plaza in New York City, we bring you the music of Ramon Raquello and his orchestra. With a touch of the Spanish, Ramon Raquello leads off with "La Cumparsita."

(*Piece starts playing.*)

Here is the first hint of the problem, or conflict.

ANNOUNCER TWO: Ladies and gentlemen, we interrupt our program of dance music to bring you a special bulletin from the Intercontinental Radio News. At twenty minutes before eight, central time, Professor Farrell of the Mount Jennings Observatory, Chicago, Illinois, reports observing several explosions of flaming gas, occurring at regular intervals on the planet Mars.

The spectroscope indicates the gas to be hydrogen and moving toward the earth with enormous speed. Professor Pierson of the observatory at Princeton[3] confirms Farrell's observation, and describes the phenomenon as (quote) like a jet of blue flame shot from a gun (unquote). We now return you to the music of Ramon Raquello, playing for you in the Meridian Room of the Park Plaza Hotel, situated in downtown New York.

(*Music plays for a few moments until piece ends . . . sound of applause*)

Now a tune that never loses favor, the ever-popular "Stardust." Ramon Raquello and his orchestra . . .

(*Music*)

ANNOUNCER TWO: Ladies and gentlemen, following on the news given in our bulletin a moment ago, the Government Meteorological Bureau has requested the large observatories of the country to keep an astronomical watch on any further disturbances occurring on the planet Mars. Due to the unusual nature of this occurrence, we have arranged an interview with the noted astronomer, Professor Pierson, who will give us his

---

spectroscope (SPEK truh skohp) a scientific instrument used to identify substances

phenomenon (fih NOM uh non) a fact or event that can be described in a scientific way

[3]**Princeton:** a university in New Jersey

views on this event. In a few moments we will take you to the Princeton Observatory at Princeton, New Jersey. We return you until then to the music of Ramon Raquello and his orchestra.

(*music . . .*)

ANNOUNCER TWO: We are ready now to take you to the Princeton Observatory at Princeton where Carl Phillips, our commentator, will interview Professor Richard Pierson, famous astronomer. We take you now to Princeton, New Jersey.

The main character or protagonist, is introduced.

(*Echo chamber*)

PHILLIPS: Good evening, ladies and gentlemen. This is Carl Phillips, speaking to you from the observatory at Princeton. I am standing in a large semi-circular room, pitch black except for an oblong split in the ceiling. Through this opening I can see a sprinkling of stars that cast a kind of frosty glow over the complex mechanism of the huge telescope. The ticking sound you hear is the vibration of the clockwork. Professor Pierson stands directly above me on a small platform, peering through the giant lens. I ask you to be patient, ladies and gentlemen, during any delay that may arise during our interview. Beside his ceaseless watch of the heavens, Professor Pierson may be interrupted by telephone or other communications. During this period he is in constant touch with the astronomical centers of the world . . . Professor, may I begin our questions?

PIERSON: At any time, Mr. Phillips.

PHILLIPS: Professor, would you please tell our radio audience exactly what you see as you observe the planet Mars through your telescope?

PIERSON: Nothing unusual at the moment, Mr. Phillips. A red disk swimming in a blue sea. Transverse stripes across the disk. Quite distinct now because Mars happens to be at the point nearest the earth . . . in opposition, as we call it.

Why is this information important to the plot development?

PHILLIPS: In your opinion, what do these transverse stripes signify, Professor Pierson?

PIERSON: Not canals, I can assure you, Mr. Phillips, although

---

oblong (OB lawng) rectangle shaped
transverse (trans VURS) crossing from side to side

Reading Focus: *Understand Sequence of Events*

Have students summarize what has happened, in chronological order, up to this point in the play.

Critical Thinking: *Analyze*

Tell students to use what they have learned about imagery to identify it in Phillips's speech. Ask: What senses does the imagery appeal to? How effective is it?

Background Notes

Inform students that theater professionals, specializing in scenery, lighting, costumes, and make-up, are hired by the director of a play. Their job is to interpret the playwright's written directions and translate them into colorful, dramatic stage effects. Point out that in radio dramas these "interpreters" are absent. The listening audience depends entirely on the writer's imagination to supply these elements. He or she, therefore, must strike a delicate balance between narration, description, and dialogue.

Literary Focus:
Character

Ask: How do you think Phillips is reading his lines? Does he sound excited? Is he calm? Read his lines aloud as you think he should interpret them.

Critical Thinking:
Analyze

Ask: What conversations do you think people at home, listening on their radios, are having at this point?

Here, the plot begins to build. Does Professor Pierson see any relationship between the disturbances on Mars and these earthquake shocks?

that's the popular conjecture of those who imagine Mars to be inhabited. From a scientific viewpoint the stripes are merely the result of the planet's atmospheric conditions.

PHILLIPS: Then you're quite convinced as a scientist that living intelligence as we know it does not exist on Mars?

PIERSON: I should say the chances against it are a thousand to one.

PHILLIPS: And yet how do you account for these gas eruptions occurring on the surface of the planet at regular intervals?

PIERSON: Mr. Phillips, I cannot account for it.

PHILLIPS: By the way, Professor, for the benefit of our listeners, how far is Mars from the earth?

PIERSON: Approximately forty million miles.

PHILLIPS: Well, that seems a safe enough distance.

PHILLIPS: Just a moment, ladies and gentlemen, someone has just handed Professor Pierson a message. While he reads it, let me remind you that we are speaking to you from the observatory in Princeton, New Jersey, where we are interviewing the world-famous astronomer, Professor Pierson . . . One moment, please. Professor Pierson has passed me a message which he has just received . . . Professor, may I read the message to the listening audience?

PIERSON: Certainly, Mr. Phillips.

PHILLIPS: Ladies and gentlemen, I shall read you a wire addressed to Professor Pierson from Dr. Gray of the National History Museum, New York. "9:15 P.M. Eastern Standard Time. Seismograph registered shock of almost earthquake intensity occurring within a radius of twenty miles of Princeton. Please investigate. Signed, Lloyd Gray, Chief of Astronomical Division." . . . Professor Pierson, could this occurrence possibly have something to do with the disturbances observed on the planet Mars?

PIERSON: Hardly, Mr. Phillips. This is probably a meteorite of unusual size and its arrival at this particular time is merely a

---

conjecture (kun JEK chur) an opinion formed without facts but based on pertinent knowledge or experience; guess
seismograph (SYZ muh graf) an instrument that records the intensity and duration of earthquakes
intensity (in TEN suh tee) strength; force
meteorite (MEET ee uh ryt) part of a heavenly body that passes through the atmosphere and falls to the earth's surface as a piece of matter

coincidence. However, we shall conduct a search, as soon as daylight permits.

PHILLIPS: Thank you, Professor. Ladies and gentlemen, for the past ten minutes we've been speaking to you from the observatory at Princeton, bringing you a special interview with Professor Pierson, noted astronomer. This is Carl Phillips speaking. We now return you to our New York studio.

(*Fade in piano playing*)

ANNOUNCER TWO: Ladies and gentlemen, here is the latest bulletin from the Intercontinental Radio News. Montreal, Canada: Professor Morse of McGill University reports observing a total of three explosions on the planet Mars, between the hours of 7:45 P.M. and 9:20 P.M., Eastern Standard Time. This confirms earlier reports received from American observatories. Now, nearer home, comes a special announcement from Trenton,[4] New Jersey. It is reported that at 8:50 P.M. a huge, flaming object, believed to be a meteorite, fell on a farm in the neighborhood of Grovers Mill, New Jersey, twenty-two miles from Trenton. The flash in the sky was visible for several hundred miles and the noise of the impact was heard as far north as Elizabeth.

We have sent a special mobile unit to the scene, and will have our commentator, Mr. Phillips, give you a word description as soon as he can reach there from Princeton. In the meantime, we take you to the Hotel Martinet in Brooklyn, where Bobby Millette and his orchestra are offering a program of dance music.

Note how the change of setting adds a certain reality, or truth, to the broadcast.

(*Swing band for twenty seconds . . . then cut*)

ANNOUNCER TWO: We take you now to Grovers Mill, New Jersey. (*Crowd noises . . . police sirens*)

PHILLIPS: Ladies and gentlemen, this is Carl Phillips again, at the Wilmuth farm, Grovers Mill, New Jersey. Professor Pierson and myself made the eleven miles from Princeton in ten minutes. Well, I . . . I hardly know where to begin, to paint for you a word picture of the strange scene before my eyes, like

[4]**Trenton:** the capital of New Jersey

Reading Focus: *Understand Sequence of Events*

Have students make a time line of the events that have occurred to this point in the play. Have them refer to the time line on pages 340–341 if they need a model.

Discussion

Ask students to think about how events are covered in the media today. Have them discuss how coverage might be different today from how it is portrayed in the play.

Notice the descriptive words that help you visualize this new setting.

something out of a modern *Arabian Nights*.[5] Well, I just got here. I haven't had a chance to look around yet. I guess that's it. Yes, I guess that's the . . . thing, directly in front of me, half buried in a vast pit. Must have struck with terrific force. The ground is covered with splinters of a tree it must have struck on its way down. What I can see of the . . . object itself doesn't look very much like a meteor, at least not the meteors I've seen. It looks more like a huge cylinder. It has a diameter of . . . what would you say, Professor Pierson?

PIERSON (*off*)**:** About thirty yards.

PHILLIPS: About thirty yards . . . The metal on the sheath is . . . well, I've never seen anything like it. The color is sort of yellowish-white. Curious spectators now are pressing close to the object in spite of the efforts of the police to keep them back. They're getting in front of my line of vision. Would you mind standing on one side, please?

POLICEMAN: One side, there, one side.

PHILLIPS: While the policemen are pushing the crowd back, here's Mr. Wilmuth, owner of the farm here. He may have

---

sheath (SHEETH) a case or covering

[5]***Arabian Nights:*** a collection of tales from Arabia, India, and Persia.

some interesting facts to add . . . . Mr. Wilmuth, would you please tell the radio audience as much as you remember of this rather unusual visitor that dropped in your backyard? Step closer, please. Ladies and gentlemen, this is Mr. Wilmuth.

WILMUTH: I was listenin' to the radio.

PHILLIPS: Closer and louder, please.

WILMUTH: Pardon me!

PHILLIPS: Louder, please, and closer.

WILMUTH: Yes, sir—while I was listening to the radio and kinda drowsin', that Professor fellow was talkin' about Mars, so I was half dozin' and half . . .

Notice that Mr. Wilmuth says he was listening to the radio program. Why does the writer have him make this remark?

PHILLIPS: Yes, Mr. Wilmuth. Then what happened?

WILMUTH: As I was sayin', I was listenin' to the radio kinda halfways . . .

PHILLIPS: Yes, Mr. Wilmuth, and then you saw something?

WILMUTH: Not first off. I heard something.

PHILLIPS: And what did you hear?

WILMUTH: A hissing sound. Like this: sssssss . . . kinda like a Fourt'-of-July rocket.

PHILLIPS: Then what?

Reading Focus:
Understand Sequence of Events

Have students retell what Wilmuth saw and heard in the chronological order he suggests.

Literary Focus:
Setting

Ask: How does "on the scene" reporting make this seem more realistic? Is radio the only way you could make this seem real to people?

Critical Thinking:
Evaluate

Ask: Does Wilmuth appear to be a reliable eyewitness? Why or why not?

Literary Focus: *Character*

Point out that there are many characters in this radio play. Students have already encountered seven of them. Have students make an ongoing chart, classifying each character according to his or her style of speaking and by at least two strong personality traits.

Critical Thinking: *Classify*

Have students classify Announcer 2, Announcer 3, Phillips, Pierson, and Wilmuth according to their jobs and how much of the actual object they see. Tell them to predict what happens after the humming sound is heard.

Enrichment

Point out that the character of Carl Phillips had real-life counterparts during the 1930s. Radio commentators, such as Lowell Thomas, Edward R. Murrow, and Walter Winchell achieved celebrity status as the first "anchormen." Have students suggest present-day television journalists—male and female—who have reached a similar level.

Tell briefly whether Mr. Wilmuth is a flat or round character.

WILMUTH: Turned my head out the window and would have swore I was asleep and dreamin'.

PHILLIPS: Yes?

WILMUTH: I seen a kinda greenish streak and then zingo! Somethin' smacked the ground. Knocked me clear out of my chair!

PHILLIPS: Well, were you frightened, Mr. Wilmuth?

WILMUTH: Well, I—I ain't quite sure. I reckon I—I was kinda riled.

PHILLIPS: Thank you, Mr. Wilmuth. Thank you.

WILMUTH: Want me to tell you some more?

PHILLIPS: No . . . That's quite all right, that's plenty.

PHILLIPS: Ladies and gentlemen, you've just heard Mr. Wilmuth, owner of the farm where this thing has fallen. I wish I could convey the atmosphere . . . the background of this . . . fantastic scene. Hundreds of cars are parked in a field in back of us. Police are trying to rope off the roadway leading into the farm. But it's no use. They're breaking right through. Their headlights throw an enormous spot on the pit where the object's half buried. Some of the more daring souls are venturing near the edge. Their silhouettes stand out against the metal sheen.

Here Mr. Phillips helps you picture the setting in your mind.

(*Faint humming sound*)

One man wants to touch the thing . . . he's having an argument with a policeman. The policeman wins . . . Now, ladies and gentlemen, there's something I haven't mentioned in all this excitement, but it's becoming more distinct. Perhaps you've caught it already on your radio. Listen: (*Long pause*) . . . Do you hear it? It is a curious humming sound that seems to come from inside the object. I'll move the microphone nearer. Here. (*Pause*) Now we're not more than twenty-five feet away. Can you hear it now? Oh, Professor Pierson!

To what sense does Mr. Phillips' description appeal?

PIERSON: Yes, Mr. Phillips?

PHILLIPS: Can you tell us the meaning of that scraping noise inside the thing?

PIERSON: Possibly the unequal cooling of its surface.

PHILLIPS: Do you still think it's a meteor, Professor?

---

riled (RYLD) irritated; angered

silhouettes (sil oo ETS) dark shapes, or outlines, seen against a light background

PIERSON: I don't know what to think. The metal casing is definitely extraterrestrial . . . not found on this earth. Friction with the earth's atmosphere usually tears holes in a meteor. This thing is smooth and, as you can see, shaped like a cylinder.

How has Professor Pierson's attitude changed?

PHILLIPS: Just a minute! Something's happening! Ladies and gentlemen, this is terrific! This end of the thing is beginning to flake off! The top is beginning to rotate like a screw! The thing must be hollow!

Here the plot begins to build faster.

VOICES: She's a movin'!
Look, the darn thing's unscrewing!
Keep back, there! Keep back, I tell you!
Maybe there's men in it trying to escape!
It's red hot, they'll burn to a cinder!
Keep back there. Keep those idiots back!

What feelings do the shouting background voices convey?

(*Suddenly the clanking sound of a huge piece of falling metal*)

VOICES: She's off! The top's loose!
Look out there! Stand back!

PHILLIPS: Ladies and gentlemen, this is the most terrifying thing I have ever witnessed . . . Wait a minute! *Someone's crawling out of the hollow top*. Someone or . . . something. I can see peering out of that black hole two glowing disks . . . are they eyes? It might be a face. It might be . . .

(*Shout of awe from the crowd*)

PHILLIPS: Good heavens, something's wriggling out of the shadow like a gray snake. Now it's another one, and another. They look like tentacles to me. There, I can see the thing's body. It's large as a bear and it glistens like wet leather. But that face. It . . . it's indescribable. I can hardly force myself to keep looking at it. The eyes are black and gleam like a serpent. The mouth is V-shaped with saliva dripping from its rimless lips that seem to quiver and pulsate. The monster or whatever it is can hardly move. It seems weighed down by . . . possibly gravity or something. The thing's raising up. The crowd falls back. They've seen enough. This is the most extraordinary experience. I can't find words . . . I'm pulling this

Here, an alien character is introduced. What do Mr. Phillips's sensory words suggest about the visitor?

---

friction (FRIK shun) resistance
pulsate (PUL sayt) throb in a regular rhythm

Reading Focus: *Understand Sequence of Events*

Have students update their time lines.

Discussion

At the point at which the tentacled creature emerges, stop to discuss how communication could be established with it.

Critical Thinking: *Compare*

Have students explain how realistic this part of the play is. Ask them which parts are believable and which are not. Ask them if Carl Phillips's reactions to the emerging Martians are believable. Compare his descriptions to a contemporary television journalist's on-the-scene account of a battle or a natural disaster.

Literary Focus: *Plot*

The conflict is set up by this point in the play. Ask: What kind and amount of destruction do you think the "humped shape" will wield? How far do you think the authors will take this spoof?

microphone with me as I talk. I'll have to stop the description until I've taken a new position. Hold on, will you please, I'll be back in a minute.

(*Fade into piano*)

ANNOUNCER TWO: We are bringing you an eyewitness account of what's happening on the Wilmuth farm, Grovers Mill, New Jersey. (*More piano*) We now return you to Carl Phillips at Grovers Mill.

PHILLIPS: Ladies and gentlemen (Am I on?). Ladies and gentlemen, here I am, in back of a stone wall that adjoins Mr. Wilmuth's garden. From here I get a sweep of the whole scene. I'll give you every detail as long as I can talk. As long as I can see. More state police have arrived. They're drawing up a cordon in front of the pit, about thirty of them. No need to push the crowd back now. They're willing to keep their distance. The captain is speaking with someone. We can't quite see who. Oh yes, I believe it's Professor Pierson. Yes, it is. Now they've parted. The professor moves around one side, studying the object, while the captain and two policemen advance with something in their hands. I can see it now. It's a white handkerchief tied to a pole . . . a flag of truce. If those creatures know what that means . . . what anything means! . . . *Wait!* Something's happening!

Notice the continuing use of foreshadowing.

Would you expect visitors from another planet to understand our symbol for peace?

(*Hissing sound followed by a humming that increases in intensity.*)

A humped shape is rising out of the pit. I can make out a small beam of light against a mirror. What's that? There's a jet of flame springing from that mirror, and it leaps right at the advancing men. It strikes them head on! Good Lord, they're turning into flame!

(*Screams and unearthly shrieks*)

Now the whole field's caught fire. (*Explosion*) The woods . . . the barns . . . the gas tanks of automobiles . . . it's spreading everywhere. It's coming this way. About twenty yards to my right . . .

Is the conflict external or internal?

---

cordon (KAWR dun) a line or circle of police stationed around an area to guard it

(*Crash of microphone . . . then dead silence*)

ANNOUNCER TWO: Ladies and gentlemen, due to circumstances beyond our control, we are unable to continue the broadcast from Grovers Mill. Evidently there's some difficulty with our field transmission. However, we will return to that point at the earliest opportunity. In the meantime, we have a late bulletin from San Diego, California. Professor Indellkoffer, speaking at a dinner of the California Astronomical Society, expressed the opinion that the explosions on Mars are undoubtedly nothing more than severe volcanic disturbances on

What do the explosions on the surface of Mars really represent?

Literary Focus: *Plot*

Make a plot diagram to show the events thus far. Include the characters, setting, rising action, and conflicts. Provide space for climax and dénouement to complete the diagram as you continue reading.

Reading Focus: *Understand Sequence of Events*

Have students use stage directions to help them order the rising events.

Critical Thinking: *Predict*

Have students explain the difference between the weapons used by the Martians and those used by the "Earthlings." Ask them to predict what the Martians will do next and how the "Earthlings" will respond. Have students recheck their answers at the end of the radio drama.

the surface of the planet. We continue now with our piano interlude.

(*Piano . . . then cut*)

Ladies and gentlemen, I have just been handed a message that came in from Grovers Mill by telephone. Just a moment. At least forty people, including six state troopers lie dead in a field east of the village of Grovers Mill, their bodies burned and twisted beyond all possible recognition. The next voice you hear will be that of Brigadier General Montgomery Smith, commander of the state militia at Trenton, New Jersey.

SMITH: I have been requested by the governor of New Jersey to place the counties of Mercer and Middlesex as far west as Princeton, and east to Jamesburg, under martial law. No one will be permitted to enter this area except by special pass issued by state or military authorities. Four companies of state militia are proceeding from Trenton to Grovers Mill, and will aid in the evacuation of homes within the range of military operations. Thank you.

Notice how the tension *appears* to be resolved. Do you think the Martians will decide to seek peace?

ANNOUNCER: You have just been listening to General Montgomery Smith, commanding the state militia at Trenton. In the meantime, further details of the disaster at Grovers Mill are coming in. The strange creatures, after making their deadly assault, crawled back in their pit and made no attempt to prevent the efforts of the firemen to recover the bodies and extinguish the fire. Combined fire departments of Mercer County are fighting the flames which threaten the entire countryside.

We have been unable to establish any contact with our mobile unit at Grovers Mill, but we hope to be able to return you there at the earliest possible moment. In the meantime we take you—uh, just one moment please.

(*Long pause*)

Notice that the Announcer has lowered his voice. Why does he do this?

(*Whisper*) Ladies and gentlemen, I have just been informed that we have finally established communication with an

---

interlude (IN tur lood) musical performance between the acts of a play
martial law (MAHR shul LAW) temporary rule by the military authorities
militia (muh LISH uh) an army of citizens rather than professional soldiers, called out in time of emergency

eyewitness of the tragedy. Professor Pierson has been located at a farmhouse near Grovers Mill where he has established an emergency observation post. As a scientist, he will give you his explanation of these terrible events. The next voice you hear will be that of Professor Pierson, brought to you by direct wire. Professor Pierson.

PIERSON: Of the creatures in the rocket cylinder at Grovers Mill, I can give you no reliable information—either as to their nature, their origin, or their purposes here on earth. Of their destructive instrument I might venture some conjectural explanation. For want of a better term, I shall refer to the mysterious weapon as a heat ray. It's all too evident that these creatures have scientific knowledge far in advance of our own. It is my guess that in some way they are able to generate an intense heat in a chamber of practically absolute nonconductivity. This intense heat they project in a parallel beam against any object they choose, by means of a polished parabolic mirror of unknown composition, much as the mirror of a lighthouse projects a beam of light. That is my conjecture of the origin of the heat ray . . .

How do the words that Professor Pierson uses make him sound like a scientist?

ANNOUNCER TWO: Thank you, Professor Pierson. Ladies and gentlemen, here is a bulletin from Trenton. It is a brief statement informing us that the burnt body of Carl Phillips has been identified in a Trenton hospital. Now here's another bulletin from Washington, D.C.

Office of the director of the National Red Cross reports ten units of Red Cross emergency workers have been assigned to the headquarters of the state militia stationed outside of Grovers Mill, New Jersey. Here's a bulletin from state police, Princeton Junction: The fires at Grovers Mill and vicinity are now under control. Scouts report all quiet in the pit, and no sign of life appearing from the mouth of the cylinder . . . And now, ladies and gentlemen, we have a special statement from Mr. Harry McDonald, vice-president in charge of operations.

McDONALD: We have received a request from the militia at Trenton

---

eyewitness (EYE wit nis) person who actually saw something happen
nonconductivity (non kon duk TIV uh tee) the ability to contain and not transmit heat
parabolic (par uh BOL ik) bowl shaped

Literary Focus: *Plot*

Choose a volunteer to read Professor Pierson's analysis of the Martians' capabilities. Have students point out the use of foreshadowing and explain what the passage suggests about the fate of the people living in New Jersey and, for that matter, all over the world.

Reading Focus: *Understand Sequence of Events*

Have students name the authorities who play a role in this play in the order in which they appear. Ask: How does the number and type of authorities, and the order in which they appear, build the suspense?

Background Notes

Although manned space flight was little more than a dream to most scientists, rocket research during this period was progressing rapidly. In 1926, Robert H. Goddard, the father of American rocketeering, launched the world's first liquid-propellant rocket. By 1930 the American Interplanetary Society was experimenting with high-altitude rockets and publicizing the idea of space flight. Five years after this broadcast, German scientists developed and launched their destructive V-2 rocket, the first projectile to leave and reenter the Earth's atmosphere.

to place at their use our entire broadcasting facilities. In view of the seriousness of the situation, and believing that radio has a definite responsibility to serve in the public interest at all times, we are turning over our facilities to the state militia at Trenton.

ANNOUNCER: We take you now to the field headquarters of the state militia near Grovers Mill, New Jersey.

Do you think the conflict has been resolved?

CAPTAIN: This is Captain Lansing of the signal corps,[6] attached to the state militia now engaged in military operations in the vicinity of Grovers Mill. Situation arising from the reported presence of certain individuals of unidentified nature is now under complete control.

What do the Captain's words suggest about his abilities as a commander?

The cylindrical object which lies in a pit directly below our position is surrounded on all sides by eight battalions of infantry, without heavy fieldpieces, but adequately armed with rifles and machine guns. All cause for alarm, if such cause ever existed, is now entirely unjustified. The things, whatever they are, do not even venture to poke their heads above the pit. I can see their hiding place plainly in the glare of the searchlights here. With all their reported resources, these creatures can scarcely stand up against heavy machine-gun fire. Anyway, it's an interesting outing for the troops. I can make out their khaki uniforms, crossing back and forth in front of the lights. It looks almost like a real war. There appears to be some slight smoke in the woods bordering the Millstone River. Probably fire started by campers. Well, we ought to see some action soon. One of the companies is deploying on the left side. A quick thrust and it will all be over. Now wait a minute! I see something on top of the cylinder. No, it's nothing but a shadow. Now the troops are on the edge of the Wilmuth farm. Seven thousand armed men closing in on an old metal tube. Wait, that wasn't a shadow! It's something moving . . . solid metal . . . kind of a shieldlike affair rising up out of the cylinder . . . It's going higher and higher. Why, it's standing on legs . . . actually rearing up on a sort of metal framework. Now it's reaching above the trees and the searchlights are on it! Hold on!

---

fieldpieces (FEELD pees iz) mobile artillery
deploying (dih PLOI ing) spreading out
[6]**signal corps:** the part of the army in charge of communications

ANNOUNCER: Ladies and gentlemen, I have a grave announcement to make. Incredible as it may seem, both the observations of science and the evidence of our eyes lead to the inescapable assumption that those strange beings who landed in the Jersey farmlands tonight are the vanguard of an invading army from the planet Mars. The battle which took place tonight at Grovers Mill has ended in one of the most startling defeats ever suffered by an army in modern times; seven thousand men armed with rifles and machine guns set against a single fighting machine of the invaders from Mars. One hundred and twenty known survivors. The rest are scattered over the battle area from Grovers Mill to Plainsboro crushed and trampled to death under the metal feet of the monster, or burned to cinders by its heat ray. The monster is now in control of the middle section of New Jersey and has effectively cut the state through its center. Communication lines are down from Pennsylvania to the Atlantic Ocean. Railroad tracks are torn and service from New York to Philadelphia discontinued except routing some of the trains through Allentown and Phoenixville.[7] Highways to the north, south, and west are clogged with frantic human traffic. Police and army reserves are unable to control the mad rush. By morning the fugitives will have swelled Philadelphia, Camden and Trenton, it is estimated, to twice their normal population.

At this time, martial law prevails throughout New Jersey and eastern Pennsylvania. We take you now to Washington for a special broadcast on the National Emergency . . . the Secretary of the Interior . . .

SECRETARY: Citizens of the nation: I shall not try to conceal the gravity of the situation that confronts the country, nor the concern of your government in protecting the lives and property of its people. However, I wish to impress upon you—private citizens and public officials, all of you—the urgent need of calm and resourceful action. Fortunately, this powerful enemy is still confined to a comparatively small area, and we

Note the outcome of the battle between the Martians and the army. Predict what the Martians will do next.

Describe the reactions of people in New Jersey and Pennsylvania.

What is the Secretary of Interior really feeling? Is he optimistic?

Reading Focus: *Understand Sequence of Events*

Use a map of the East Coast to show where the main incident occurred and where people fled. Ask: If this were a true story, where would people go next?

Literary Focus: *Symbolism*

Ask: What do you think the aliens symbolize to people in the United States?

Critical Thinking: *Evaluate*

Ask: Do you think the authors went too far to scare the public? Should they have impersonated the Secretary of the Interior?

---

assumption (uh SUMP shun) idea accepted as true without proof
vanguard (VAN gahrd) the part of an army that goes ahead of the main body in an advance
[7]**Allentown and Phoenixville:** cities in eastern Pennsylvania

Critical Thinking: *Analyze*

Call on students to identify the destructive effects of the Martian invasion.

Literary Focus: *Character*

Ask: Do you think that Professor Pierson is dead? Explain why you think as you do.

may place our faith in the military forces to keep them there. In the meantime, placing our faith in God, we must continue the performance of our duties each and every one of us, so that we may confront this destructive enemy with a nation united, courageous, and consecrated to the preservation of human supremacy on this earth. I thank you.

ANNOUNCER: You have just heard the Secretary of the Interior speaking from Washington. Bulletins too numerous to read are piling up in the studio here. We are informed that the central portion of New Jersey is blacked out from radio communication due to the effect of the heat ray upon power lines and electrical equipment. Here is a special bulletin from New York. Cables received from English, French, German scientific organizations offering assistance. Astronomers report continued gas outbursts at regular intervals on planet Mars. Majority voice opinion that enemy will be reinforced by additional rocket machines. Attempts made to locate Professor Pierson of Princeton, who has observed Martians at close range. It is feared he was lost in recent battle. Langham Field, Virginia: Scouting planes report three Martian machines visible above treetops, moving north toward Somerville with population fleeing ahead of them. Heat ray not in use; although advancing at express-train speed, invaders pick their way carefully. They seem to be making conscious effort to avoid destruction of cities and countryside. However, they stop to destroy power lines, bridges, and railroad tracks. Their apparent objective is to crush resistance, paralyze communication, and disorganize human society.

How do you know that so far, the Martians have only landed in the United States?

Here is a bulletin from Basking Ridge, New Jersey: Raccoon hunters have stumbled on a second cylinder similar to the first lying in the great swamp twenty miles south of Morristown. U.S. army fieldpieces are proceeding from Newark to blow up second invading unit before cylinder can be opened and the fighting machine rigged. They are taking up position in the foothills of Watchung Mountains.[8] Another bulletin from Langham Field, Virginia: Scouting planes report enemy machines, now three in number, increasing speed northward

Notice the increasing number of bulletins. How do they contribute to the growing tension in the drama?

---

consecrated (KON sih krayt id) dedicated

[8]**Watchung Mountains:** a range of low mountains in New Jersey

kicking over houses and trees in their evident haste to unite with their allies south of Morristown. Machines also sighted by telephone operator east of Middlesex within ten miles of Plainfield. Here's a bulletin from Winston Field, Long Island. Fleet of army bombers carrying heavy explosives flying north in pursuit of enemy. Scouting planes act as guides. They keep speeding enemy in sight. Just a moment please. Ladies and gentlemen, we've run special wires to the artillery line in adjacent villages to give you direct reports in the zone of the advancing enemy. First we take you to the battery of the 22nd Field Artillery, located in the Watchung Mountains.

Is this new development a genuine cause for hope?

OFFICER: Range, thirty-two meters.
GUNNER: Thirty-two meters.
OFFICER: Projection, thirty-nine degrees.
GUNNER: Thirty-nine degrees.
OFFICER: Fire! (*Boom of heavy gun . . . pause*)
OBSERVER: One hundred and forty yards to the right, sir.
OFFICER: Shift range . . . thirty-one meters.
GUNNER: Thirty-one meters.
OFFICER: Projection . . . thirty-seven degrees.
GUNNER: Thirty-seven degrees.
OFFICER: Fire! (*Boom of heavy gun . . . pause*)
OBSERVER: A hit, sir! We got the tripod of one of them. They've stopped. The others are trying to repair it.
OFFICER: Quick, get the range! Shift thirty meters.
GUNNER: Thirty meters.
OFFICER: Projection . . . twenty-seven degrees.
GUNNER: Twenty-seven degrees.
OFFICER: Fire! (*Boom of heavy gun . . . pause*)
OBSERVER: Can't see the shell land, sir. They're letting off a smoke.
OFFICER: What is it?
OBSERVER: A black smoke, sir. Moving this way. Lying close to the ground. It's moving fast.
OFFICER: Put on gas masks. (*Pause*) Get ready to fire. Shift to twenty-four meters.
GUNNER: Twenty-four meters.

Describe the conflict in this scene.

---

adjacent (uh JAY sunt) near or next to
tripod (TRY pod) three legged support

Discussion

Have pairs of students reread this section of the drama to the class. Ask students to discuss which performances best capture the "heat of the battle," and why they think as they do.

Reading Focus: *Understand Sequence of Events*

Have students order the events from the end of the announcement of the Secretary of the Interior to the bottom of page 425.

What happens to the soldiers?

OFFICER: Fire! (*Boom*)

GUNNER: Still can't see, sir. The smoke's coming nearer.

OFFICER: Get the range. (*Coughs*)

OBSERVER: Twenty-three meters. (*Coughs*)

OFFICER: Twenty-three meters. (*Coughs*)

GUNNER: Twenty-three meters. (*Coughs*)

OBSERVER: Projection, twenty-two degrees. (*Coughing*)

OFFICER: Twenty-two degrees. (*Fade in coughing*)

(*Fading in . . . sound of airplane motor*)

Where are the Martians now heading?

Notice the rising level of tension in the Commander's voice. What does his final action tell about the Commander's character?

COMMANDER: Army bombing plane, V-8-43, off Bayonne, New Jersey, Lieutenant Voght, commanding eight bombers. Reporting to Commander Fairfax, Langham Field . . . This is Voght, reporting to Commander Fairfax, Langham Field . . . Enemy tripod machines now in sight. Reinforced by three machines from the Morristown cylinder . . . six altogether. One machine partially crippled. Believed hit by shell from army gun in Watchung Mountains. Guns now appear silent. A heavy black fog hanging close to the earth . . . of extreme density, nature unknown. No sign of heat ray. Enemy now turns east, crossing Passaic River into the Jersey marshes. Another straddles the Pulaski Skyway.[9] Evident objective is New York City. They're pushing down a high tension power station. The machines are close together now, and we're ready to attack. Planes circling, ready to strike. A thousand yards and we'll be over the first—eight hundred yards . . . six hundred . . . four hundred . . . two hundred . . . There they go! The giant arm raised . . . Green flash! They're spraying us with flame! Two thousand feet. Engines are giving out. No chance to release bombs. Only one thing left . . . drop on them, plane and all. We're diving on the first one. Now the engine's gone! Eight . . .

OPERATOR ONE: This is Bayonne, New Jersey, calling Langham Field . . .

This is Bayonne, New Jersey, calling Langham Field. Come in, please . . . Come in, please. . .

OPERATOR TWO: This is Langham Field . . . go ahead . . .

OPERATOR ONE: Eight army bombers in battle with enemy tripod

---

density (DEN suh tee) thickness

[9]**Pulaski Skyway:** an elevated highway in eastern New Jersey

Reading Focus: *Understand Sequence of Events*

Provide a map of the East Coast for students to retell the events in order while pointing to the location each occurred.

Critical Thinking: *Analyze*

Ask: What makes this battle seem real? What might give it away as being fiction?

machines over Jersey marshlands. Engines disabled by heat ray. All crashed. One enemy machine destroyed. Enemy now discharging heavy black smoke in direction of—

OPERATOR THREE: This is Newark, New Jersey . . .

This is Newark, New Jersey . . .

Warning! Poisonous black smoke pouring in from Jersey marshes. Reaches South Street. Gas masks useless. Urge population to move into open spaces . . . automobiles use Routes 7, 23, 24 . . . Avoid congested areas. Smoke now spreading over Raymond Boulevard . . .

How powerful is the Martian's poison gas?

OPERATOR FOUR: 2X2L . . . calling CQ . . .

2X2L . . . calling CQ . . . 2X2L . . . calling 8X3R . . .

Come in, please . . .

OPERATOR FIVE: This is 8X3R . . . coming back at 2X2L.

OPERATOR FOUR: How's reception? How's reception? K, please. Where are you, 8X3R?

What's the matter? Where are you?

(*Bells ringing over city gradually diminishing*)

ANNOUNCER: I'm speaking from the roof of Broadcasting Building, New York City. The bells you hear are ringing to warn the people to evacuate the city as the Martians approach. Estimated in last two hours three million people have moved out along the roads to the north. Hutchison River Parkway still kept open for motor traffic. Avoid bridges to Long Island . . . hopelessly jammed. All communication with Jersey shore closed ten minutes ago. No more defenses. Our army wiped out . . . artillery, air force, everything wiped out. This may be the last broadcast. We'll stay here to the end . . . People are holding service below us . . . in the church.

(*Voices singing hymn*)

Now I look down the harbor. All manner of boats, overloaded with fleeing population, pulling out from docks.

(*Sound of boat whistles*)

Streets are all jammed. Noise in crowds is like New Year's Eve in the city. Wait a minute . . . Enemy now in sight above

---

congested (kun JEST id) clogged, overcrowded

Literary Focus: *Setting*

Ask students to visualize the scene that is being described by the Announcer. Have them explain their "mental pictures," pointing out specific words and phrases that contribute to their impressions.

Critical Thinking: *Apply*

Note the interruption by the original announcer. Ask: What do you think listeners' reactions were to this information? Did they believe it?

What words or phrases help you determine the size of the Martian machines?

the Palisades.[10] Five great machines. First one is crossing river. I can see it from here, wading the Hudson like a man wading through a brook . . . A bulletin's handed me . . . Martian cylinders are falling all over the country. One outside Buffalo, one in Chicago, St. Louis . . . seem to be timed and spaced . . . Now the first machine reaches the shore. He stands watching, looking over the city. His steel, cowlish head is even with the skyscrapers. He waits for the others. They rise like a line of new towers on the city's west side . . . Now they're lifting their metal hands. This is the end now. Smoke comes out . . . black smoke, drifting over the city. People in the streets see it now. They're running toward the East River . . . thousands of them, dropping in like rats. Now the smoke's spreading faster.

Notice the comparison of people to rats. What attitude does this comparison suggest?

It's reached Times Square. People trying to run away from it, but it's no use. They're falling like flies. Now the smoke's crossing Sixth Avenue . . . Fifth Avenue . . . one hundred yards away . . . it's fifty feet . . .

OPERATOR FOUR: 2X2L calling CQ . . .
2X2L calling CQ . . .
2X2L calling CQ . . . New York.
Isn't there anyone on the air?
Isn't there anyone . . .
2X2L—

Notice that the original announcer interrupts the radio drama to tell the audience something important.

ANNOUNCER: You are listening to a CBS presentation of Orson Welles and the Mercury Theatre on the Air in a original dramatization of *The War of the Worlds* by H. G. Wells. The performance will continue after a brief intermission.
This is the Columbia . . . Broadcasting System.

(*Music*)

Explain the meaning of the figurative expression, "small island of daylight."

PIERSON: As I set down these notes on paper, I'm consumed by the thought that I may be the last living man on earth. I have been hiding in this empty house near Grovers Mill—a small island of daylight cut off by the black smoke from the rest of the world. All that happened before the arrival of these monstrous creatures in the world now seems part of another life

---

cowlish (KOUL ish) hood shaped
[10]**Palisades:** the line of steep cliffs in northeastern New Jersey and southeastern New York on the west shore of the Hudson River

. . . a life that has no relation to the present, furtive existence of the lonely derelict who pencils these words on the back of some astronomical notes bearing the signature of Richard Pierson. I look down, at my blackened hands, my torn shoes, my tattered clothes, and I try to connect them with a professor who lives at Princeton, and who on the night of October 30, glimpsed through his telescope an orange splash of light on a distant planet. My wife, my fellow professors, my students, my books, my observatory, my . . . my world . . . where are they? Did they ever exist? Am I Richard Pierson? What day is it? Do days exist without calendars? Does time pass when there are no human hands left to wind the clocks? . . . In writing down my daily life I tell myself I shall preserve human history between the dark covers of this little book that was meant to record the movements of the stars . . . But to write I must live, and to live I must eat . . . I find moldy bread in the kitchen, and an orange not too spoiled to swallow. I keep watch at the window. From time to time I catch sight of a Martian above the black smoke.

Notice the plot development. Can Professor Pierson believe what has happened to him?

What does Professor Pierson seem to be questioning?

The smoke still holds the house in its black coil . . . But at length there is a hissing sound and suddenly I see a Martian mounted on his machine, spraying the air with a jet of steam, as if to clear away the smoke. I watch in a corner as his huge metal legs nearly brush against the house. Exhausted by terror, I fall asleep . . . It's morning. Sun streams in the window. The black cloud of gas has lifted, and the scorched meadows to the north look as though a black snowstorm has passed over them. I venture from the house. I make my way to a road. No traffic. Here and there a wrecked car, baggage overturned, a blackened skeleton. I push on north. For some reason I feel safer trailing these monsters than running away from them. And I keep a careful watch. I have seen the Martians feed. Should one of their machines appear over the top of trees, I am ready to fling myself flat on the earth. I come to a chestnut tree. October, chestnuts are ripe. I fill my pockets. I must keep alive. Two days I wander in a vague northerly direction through a barren world. Finally I notice a living creature . . . a small red squirrel in a beech tree. I stare at him, and wonder. He stares back at me.

Imagine what it might be like to think you were the last person on Earth. How would you feel?

furtive (FUR tiv) sneaky secretive

Reading Focus:
Understand Sequence of Events

Have students note all references to time in Professor Pierson's account.

Literary Focus:
Setting

Ask: What mood or atmosphere is suggested by Professor Pierson's observations?

Reading Focus: *Understand Sequence of Events*

Ask: What conflicts have been presented so far, and in what order?

Literary Focus: *Character*

Compare and contrast the characters of the Stranger and Pierson. Ask: Why do you think the author decided to include an evil character other than the aliens?

I believe at that moment the animal and I shared the same emotion . . . the joy of finding another living being . . . I push on north. I find dead cows in a brackish field. Beyond, the charred ruins of a dairy. The silo remains standing guard over the wasteland like a lighthouse deserted by the sea. Astride the silo perches a weathervane. The arrow points north.

Notice Professor Pierson's use of flashback. What might this suggest about the outcome of his story?

Next day I came to a city vaguely familiar in its contours, yet its buildings strangely dwarfed and leveled off, as if a giant had sliced off its highest towers with a capricious sweep of his hand. I reached the outskirts. I found Newark, undemolished, but humbled by some whim of the advancing Martians. Presently, with an odd feeling of being watched, I caught sight of something crouching in a doorway. I made a step toward it, and it rose up and became a man—a man, armed with a large knife.

Here, a new conflict begins to develop.

STRANGER: Stop . . . Where did you come from?

PIERSON: I come from . . . many places. A long time ago from Princeton.

STRANGER: Princeton, huh? That's near Grovers Mill!

PIERSON: Yes.

What do his comments suggest about the Stranger's character?

STRANGER: Grovers Mill . . . (*Laughs as at a great joke*) There's no food here. This is my country . . . all this end of town down to the river. There's only food for me . . . Which way are you going?

PIERSON: I don't know. I guess I'm looking for—for people.

STRANGER: (*nervously*) What was that? Did you hear something just then?

PIERSON: Only a bird (*marvels*) . . . A live bird!

STRANGER: You get to know that birds have shadows these days . . . Say, we're in the open here. Let's crawl into this doorway and talk.

PIERSON: Have you seen any Martians?

STRANGER: They've gone over to New York. At night the sky is alive with their lights. Just as if people were still living in it. By daylight you can't see them. Five days ago a couple of them carried something big across the flats from the airport. I believe they're learning how to fly.

---

brackish (BRAK ish) salty and marshy
capricious (kuh PRISH us) without apparent reason

PIERSON: Fly!

STRANGER: Yeah, fly.

PIERSON: Then it's all over with humanity. Stranger, there's still you and I. Two of us left.

STRANGER: They got themselves in solid; they wrecked the greatest country in the world. Those green stars, they're probably falling somewhere every night. They've only lost one machine. There isn't anything to do. We're done. We're licked.

If you were listening to this radio drama in 1938, would this statement have caused you to jump up and look outside your windows?

PIERSON: Where were you? You're in a uniform.

STRANGER: What's left of it. I was in the militia—National Guard . . . That's good! Wasn't any war any more than there is between men and ants.

Does the Stranger feel the participants in the war were evenly matched?

PIERSON: And we're edible ants. I found that out . . . What will they do to us?

STRANGER: I've thought it all out. Right now we're caught as we're wanted. The Martian only has to go a few miles to get a crowd on the run. But they won't keep doing that. They'll begin catching us systematic like—keeping the best and storing us in cages and things. They haven't begun on us yet!

PIERSON: Not begun!

STRANGER: Not begun. All that's happened so far is because we don't have sense enough to keep quiet . . . bothering them with guns and such stuff and losing our heads and rushing off in crowds. Now instead of our rushing around blind we've got to fix ourselves up according to the way things are now. Cities, nations, civilization, progress . . . done.

PIERSON: But if that's so, what is there to live for?

STRANGER: There won't be any more concerts for a million years or so, and no nice little dinners at restaurants. If it's amusement you're after, I guess the game's up.

PIERSON: And what is there left?

STRANGER: Life . . . that's what! I want to live. And so do you! We're not going to be exterminated. And I don't mean to be caught, either, and tamed, and fattened like an ox.

PIERSON: What are you going to do?

STRANGER: I'm going on . . . right under their feet. I gotta plan. We humans as humans are finished. We don't know enough. We gotta learn plenty before we've got a chance. And we've got to live and keep free while we learn. I've thought it all out, see.

Does the Stranger see the Martian invasion the same way as Professor Pierson?

Discussion

Ask students to contrast the attitudes of the Stranger and Pierson.

PIERSON: Tell me the rest.

What does the Stranger think about the way that most people used to live?

STRANGER: Well, it isn't all of us that are made for wild beasts, and that's what it's got to be. That's why I watched you. All these little office workers that used to live in these houses—they'd be no good. They haven't any stuff to 'em. They just used to run off to work. I've seen hundreds of 'em, running wild to catch their commuters' train in the morning for fear that they'd get canned if they didn't; running back at night afraid they won't be in time for dinner. Lives insured and a little invested in case of accidents. And on Sundays, worried about the hereafter. The Martians will be a blessing for those guys. Nice roomy cages, good food, no worries. After a week or so chasing about the fields on empty stomachs they'll come and be glad to be caught.

PIERSON: You've thought it all out, haven't you?

What is the Stranger's view of human beings?

STRANGER: You bet I have! And that isn't all. These Martians will make pets of some of them, train 'em to do tricks. Who knows? Get sentimental over the pet boy who grew up and had to be killed. And some, maybe, they'll train to hunt us.

PIERSON: No, that's impossible. No human being . . .

STRANGER: Yes, they will. There's people who'll do it gladly. If one of them ever comes after me . . .

Do Professor Pierson and the Stranger seek the same human qualities in each other?

PIERSON: In the meantime, you and I and others like us . . . where are we to live when the Martians own the Earth?

STRANGER: I've got it all figured out. We'll live underground. I've been thinking about the sewers. Under New York are miles and miles of 'em. The main ones are big enough for anybody. Then there's cellars, vaults, underground storerooms, railway tunnels, subways. You begin to see, eh? And we'll get a bunch of strong people together. No weak ones, that garbage, out.

PIERSON: And you meant me to go?

STRANGER: Well, I gave you a chance, didn't I?

PIERSON: We won't quarrel about that. Go on.

STRANGER: And we've got to make safe places for us to stay in, see, and get all the books we can—science books. That's where people like you come in, see? We'll raid the museums, we'll even spy on the Martians. It may not be so much we have to learn before—just imagine this: four or five of their own fighting machines suddenly start off—heat rays right and left

Critical Thinking: *Analyze*

Ask: What dilemma does Professor Pierson face? How does this confrontation add to the suspense, or tension, of the drama?

and not a Martian in 'em. Not a Martian in 'em. But humans—humans who have learned the way how. It may even be in our time. Gee! Imagine having one of them lovely things with its heat ray wide and free! We'd turn it on Martians, we'd turn it on people. We'd bring everybody down to their knees.

What is the Stranger's goal?

PIERSON: That's your plan?

STRANGER: You and me and a few more of us we'd own the world.

PIERSON: I see.

STRANGER: Say, what's the matter? Where are you going?

PIERSON: Not to your world . . . Good-bye, stranger . . .

What does "world" mean in this phrase?

PIERSON: After parting with the artilleryman, I came at last to the Holland Tunnel.[11] I entered that silent tube anxious to know the fate of the great city on the other side of the Hudson. Cautiously I came out of the tunnel and made my way up Canal Street.

I reached Fourteenth Street, and there again were black powder and several bodies, and an evil ominous smell from the gratings of the cellars of some of the houses. I wandered up through the Thirties and Forties;[12] I stood alone on Times Square.[13] I caught sight of a lean dog running down Seventh Avenue with a piece of dark brown meat in his jaws, and a pack of starving mongrels at his heels. He made a wide circle around me, as though he feared I might prove a fresh competitor. I walked up Broadway in the direction of that strange powder—past silent shop windows, displaying their quiet wares to empty sidewalks—past the Capitol Theater, silent, dark—past a shooting gallery, where a row of empty guns faced a halted line of wooden ducks. Near Columbus Circle I noticed models of 1939 motorcars in the showrooms facing empty streets. From over the top of the General Motors Building, I watched a flock of black birds circling in the sky. I hurried on. Suddenly I caught sight of the hood of a Martian machine, standing somewhere in Central Park, gleaming in the late afternoon sun. An insane idea! I rushed recklessly across

What sensory words does the author use to help you visualize the remains of New York City?

Note the foreshadowing; when do birds usually "circle in the sky"?

ominous (OM uh nus) threatening; sinister

[11]**Holland Tunnel:** a tunnel under the Hudson River between New York and New Jersey

[12]**Thirties and Forties:** numbered streets across Manhattan

[13]**Times Square:** the center of the theater district in New York City

Reading Focus: *Understand Sequence of Events*

Have students retell the events that occurred from the time Pierson met the Stranger to when he said good-bye.

Literary Focus: *Setting*

Ask: Why do you think the author uses so many setting changes?

Reading Focus:
Understand Sequence of Events
Ask: Why were the birds chosen to come into the scene after the aliens were destroyed?

Critical Thinking:
Draw Conclusions
What is ironic about the way the Martians died?

Columbus Circle and into the Park. I climbed a small hill above the pond at Sixtieth Street. From there I could see, standing in a silent row along the mall, nineteen of those great metal Titans, their cowls empty, their steel arms hanging limp by their sides. I looked in vain for the monsters that inhabit those machines.

What conflict is finally resolved in this climax?

Suddenly, my eyes were attracted to the immense flock of black birds that hovered directly below me. They circled to the ground, and there before my eyes, stark and silent, lay the Martians, with the hungry birds pecking and tearing brown shreds of flesh from their dead bodies. Later when their bodies were examined in laboratories, it was found that they were killed by the putrefactive and disease bacteria against which their systems were unprepared . . . slain, after all man's defenses had failed, by the humblest thing that God in His wisdom put upon this earth.

Before the cylinder fell there was a general belief that through all the deep of space no life existed beyond the petty

---

Titans (TYT unz) giants
putrefactive (pyoo truh FAK tiv) rotting; decomposing

surface of our tiny planet. Now we see further. Dim and wonderful is the vision I have pictured in my mind of life spreading slowly from this little seedbed of the solar system throughout the inanimate vastness of space. But that is a remote dream. It may be that the destruction of the Martians is only a reprieve. To them, and not to us, is the future ordained perhaps.

Here, the author gives you a hint about the theme of the radio drama.

Strange it now seems to sit in my peaceful study at Princeton writing down this last chapter of the record begun at a deserted farm in Grovers Mill. Strange to see from my window the university spires dim and blue through an April haze. Strange to watch children playing in the streets. Strange to see young people strolling on the green, where the new spring grass heals the last black scars of a bruised earth. Strange to watch the sightseers enter the museum where the disassembled parts of a Martian machine are kept on public view. Strange when I recall the time when I first saw it, bright and clean-cut, hard and silent, under the dawn of that last great day.

Notice that the action has shifted to the present time.

(*Music*)

This is Orson Welles, ladies and gentlemen, out of character to assure you that *The War of the Worlds* has no further significance than as the holiday offering it was intended to be. The Mercury Theatre's own radio version of dressing up in a sheet and jumping out of a bush and saying Boo! Starting now, we couldn't soap all your windows and steal all your garden gates, by tomorrow night . . . so we did the next best thing. We destroyed the world before your very ears, and utterly ruined the Columbia Broadcasting System. You will be relieved, I hope, to learn that we didn't mean it, and that both institutions are still open for business. So good-bye everybody, and remember, please, for the next day or so, the terrible lesson you learned tonight. That grinning, glowing, globular invader of your living room is an inhabitant of the pumpkin patch, and if your doorbell rings and nobody's there, that was no Martian . . . it's Hallowe'en.

To what event does the narrator compare the radio drama, "Invasion from Mars"?

Who is this invader?

---

inanimate (in AN uh mit) without life
reprieve (rih PREEV) postponement
globular (GLOB yuh lur) rounded

Background Notes

The radio broadcast had two important effects. The near nationwide panic that it caused compelled the Federal government to take steps to prevent this kind of radio show from ever being repeated. Also, its popularity catapulted Orson Welles into the public spotlight. He was hired to write, direct, and star in his own Hollywood movies, of which "Citizen Kane" (1941) is considered by many critics to be the finest American film ever produced.

Literary Focus: *Drama*

Ask students if a stage presentation of this drama might be more effective than its current format for radio broadcasting. Why do they think as they do?

Mini Quiz

Write the following sentences on the chalkboard. Call on students to fill in the blanks and explain their reasoning.

1. According to Orson Welles ________ million people listened to this radio broadcast.
2. The Martians used a ________ ________ to attack the curious onlookers at Wilmuth Farm.
3. The Secretary of the ________ tried to calm the nation's fears about the Martian threat.
4. Professor Pierson resisted the ________ offer to take control of the ________.
5. Professor Pierson's first clue that the Martians were ________ was a flock of black birds.

Answers

1. thirty-two
2. heat ray
3. Interior
4. Stranger's, world
5. dead

Review the Selection

UNDERSTAND THE SELECTION

Recall

1. Where do the Martians first land?
2. Where does Pierson work?
3. Identify the Martians' primary objective.

Infer

4. Describe the reactions of most New Yorkers to the Martian invasion.
5. Why is the Martians' final defeat ironic? Explain your answer.
6. Why does the original announcer interrupt the radio play?
7. Why do you think Professor Pierson decides not to join the Stranger?

Apply

8. Briefly characterize the Martians. Support your answer with specific words and phrases from the play.
9. Compare and contrast the play with a real emergency broadcast.
10. Imagine you were listening to the radio in New Jersey on the night of October 30, 1938. How would you have responded?

Respond to Literature

What technological changes in the United States during the 1930s gave *Invasion from Mars* such a large audience?

WRITE ABOUT THE SELECTION

When Howard Koch was thinking about the setting for his drama, he opened a map, closed his eyes, and dropped his pencil directly on a town called Grovers Mill. Then he began to develop characters, think about dialogue, and create conflicts that would make his audience sit at the edge of their seats.

Imagine you have just encountered an army of aliens marching on your town or city. Write a short radio drama in which you try to tell a friend, a member of your family, or a teacher, about the very real danger they face.

Prewriting Make an informal list of the elements of drama that you will include in your scene. Include details of setting, dialogue that reveals both your own and your listener's character, and of course, a conflict (perhaps this person refuses to believe your story).

Writing Use your informal list to write a brief radio drama in which you attempt to convince someone you know, of an alien invasion. In it, include as many elements of drama as you can.

Revising When you revise your scene, reread it to discover if listeners can understand it without having to see it.

Proofreading When you proofread your scene, check to see if the commas, periods, and exclamation points are properly placed.

UNDERSTAND THE SELECTION

Answers

1. Grovers Mill
2. at the Princeton Observatory
3. They seek to "crush resistance, paralyze communication, and disorganize human society."
4. Sample answer: They panicked, creating traffic jams on the highways leading from the city.
5. Sample answer: The most powerful creatures in the universe were defeated by the smallest creatures, bacteria.
6. Sample answer: He wants to assure the listening audience that the events described were part of a play, not actual events.
7. Sample answer: Unlike the Stranger, Professor Pierson has no desire to control human beings and take over the world.
8. Sample answer: They are destructive creatures who are subject to human diseases.
9. Sample answer: Announcers in both situations describe events in detail, conduct interviews, and give traffic reports. The play, however, compresses time and shows some personal things that a real broadcast would not.
10. Answers will vary. Responses should include references to the script.

Respond to Literature

Discuss with students the major source of family entertainment today (television). Point out that previous to the dominance of television, radio played a similar role in U.S. culture. Following the first commercial radio broadcast in 1920, millions of Americans gathered nightly around their radios, listening to their favorite programs, much as we watch television shows today.

WRITE ABOUT THE SELECTION

Prewriting

Using students' suggestions, create an informal list of several elements on the chalkboard.

Sample Element of Drama: Warm, summer night.

Wind starts whipping tree branches.

Streetlights begin exploding.

Blinding light pierces the darkness.

Writing

Have students work on this section individually. Ask questions about how he or she would feel in this situation. Help any student who is having difficulty.

Revising

Have students read their scenes, asking if the class can visualize the events. Have students make revisions based upon class suggestions.

Proofreading

Make this a cooperative group activity. Have students work in small groups to proofread their scenes.

THINK ABOUT DRAMA

Once a drama is written, the finished **script** is performed by actors, who make the printed words come alive.

The **characters** include the people, animals, or even Martians in a drama. Their personalities are revealed by actions and **dialogue**. Characters are often affected by their **setting**, the time and place in which their stories take place. The sequence of actions, events, and conflicts that characters experience is called the **plot**. The principal, or main, message of a play is called its **theme**.

1. Describe in detail two settings from *Invasion from Mars*.
2. Reread the dialogue on pages 411 through 413. What kind of man is Professor Pierson?
3. What is the central conflict?
4. What kind of conflict does Pierson face? What choice does he make?
5. What is the theme of the drama?

DEVELOP YOUR VOCABULARY

Jargon refers to the particular words and phrases, or special language, used by a group of people who share the same job, profession, hobby, or interest. When musicians talk about playing a *gig*, or hiring *roadies*, for example, they are using jargon to talk about their next concert or performance, and the people who handle their musical equipment when they are touring on the road.

Jargon is usually understood by people who are part of the group. Those outside the group however, may be unfamiliar with the unusual words and terms.

Use a dictionary or encyclopedia to determine the meaning of each of the following "space" jargon words, and write original sentences using six of them. If you choose, you may suggest additional space jargon words.

1. booster
2. G-suit
3. pitch
4. dry run
5. Mach
6. touchdown
7. glitch
8. LEM

THINK ABOUT DRAMA

Answers

1. Answers will vary. Students should especially use words that appeal to their senses of sight, smell, hearing, and vision.
2. Sample answer: He is a brave, compassionate human being who believes in civilization and is committed to scientific investigation.
3. the survival of the United States versus the supremacy of the Martians
4. Sample answer: An internal conflict; he turns down the Stranger's suggestion that they join forces and take over the world.
5. Sample answer: We are not alone in the universe.

DEVELOP YOUR VOCABULARY

Answers

1. *booster*: early stage of a multistage rocket
2. *G-suit*: anti-gravity pressure suit
3. *pitch*: the downward or upward movement of a capsule or space shuttle
4. *dry run*: test or practice space flight
5. *Mach*: unit of extremely high speed
6. *touchdown*: landing, as performed by the space shuttle
7. *glitch*: computer failure or error
8. *LEM*: Lunar Excursion Module

Sentences will vary.

ESL Activity

Have small groups brainstorm more jargon words and phrases associated with space. Have a recorder make a list of the words and phrases. Then have students take turns saying a sentence using one of the words or phrases in context.

Selection Overview

SELECTION OBJECTIVES

After completing this selection, students will be able to

- understand and evaluate tone in literature
- identify conversational tone
- write a personal letter that expresses admiration
- understand and identify antonyms
- evaluate the poet's purpose

Lesson Resources

Futility
- Selection Synopsis, Teacher's Edition, p. T337g
- Comprehension and Vocabulary Workbook, pp. 83–84
- Language Enrichment Workbook, p. 64
- Teacher's Resources
  Reinforcement, p. R42
  Test, pp. T83–T84

More About Tone

Inform students that in conversation, tone can be suggested by pitch, stress, and volume. In literature, however, tone cannot be suggested by voice. A writer indicates tone by the words he or she selects, their arrangements, and the specific context in which they are found. Write the following expressions on the board and have students discuss the different tone that each suggests: "Good Afternoon." "Afternoon." "Beautiful afternoon, isn't it?" "My, it's a fine afternoon."

Background Notes

American poetry suffered a decline after the death of Walt Whitman in 1892. Harriet Monroe paved the way for a revival when she founded *Poetry: A Magazine of Verse*. It became the rallying point for some of the greatest poets of the 1900s. It gave poets an audience and provided a vehicle for experimentation.

Learn About

TONE

In literature, **tone** is a writer's emotional attitude toward his or her subject. Tone is expressed through a writer's choice of words and details, and the way that he or she describes characters and events.

You may find it helpful to think of tone as a writer's way of "speaking." If, for example, a writer feels pleasantly amused or happy about a particular subject, he or she might "speak" with descriptive words, such as *gleeful*, *delighted*, or *thrilled*.

As you read, pay close attention to the words and phrases that a writer uses to reveal his or her particular attitude. Ask yourself whether these words suggest a tone of anger, sadness, joy, amazement, or some other emotion.

As you read "Futility," ask yourself:

1. What is the tone, or author's attitude, in this poem?
2. What words or phrases help you to determine this attitude?

READING FOCUS

Evaluate the Poet's Purpose Knowing the writer's purpose, or reason for writing a piece, helps the reader know how to react to it. Think about the poet's purpose as you read "Futility."

WRITING CONNECTION

On a piece of paper, write the words "Nice outfit." Say the words out loud. What attitude do they suggest? Now, write the various meanings you might achieve if you pronounced this phrase in different tones of voice.

More About the Literary Period

Although World War II ended in 1945, Americans in 1946 were alarmed at the developing "Cold War" between the United States and Russia. Many people were concerned that the growing international hostility between these two superpowers would engulf the world in another, far more damaging conflict.

Develop Vocabulary Skills

Familiarize students with the footnoted vocabulary words. Use each word in an original sentence, then call on volunteers to do the same. You might ask students to create original sentences, using the words *surging* and *effortless*, too.

Cooperative Group Activity

Have students work in pairs to complete the Writing Connection activity. Tell them to include examples of sarcasm and irony, as well as of a serious attitude. Have a member of each pair pronounce their phrase variations, and ask students to explain their meaning. You might have them brainstorm additional phrases and work on these.

FUTILITY

by Mary S. Hawling

I try to capture rhythm with
The make-shift words that limit me:
The wind has more success than I
By simply bending down a tree.

5 I seek for color, and must be
Content with some cold, distant name:
Yet swiftly, as the night walks near,
The sky is surging bronze and flame.

I struggle for a single line
10 To measure an emotion by:
A wild bird, effortless, takes wing
And writes a poem across the sky.

---

futility (fyoo TIL ih tee) lack of success; uselessness
make-shift or **makeshift** (MAYK shift) substitute; temporary

TEACHING PLAN

INTRODUCE

Motivation

Discuss with students the strategies they develop to achieve an important goal. Point out that the more a person "invests" in reaching that goal, the more he or she is aggravated when the results don't quite turn out as planned. Relate the discussion to Mary S. Hawling's frustration about writing the best poem that she possibly can.

Purpose-Setting Question

In life and in literature, do we always mean what we say or write?

READ

Literary Focus: *Tone*

Ask: What does the poet think of writing poetry?

Reading Focus: *Evaluate the Poet's Purpose*

Have students note what the poet seeks, struggles for, and tries to capture in this poem.

CLOSE

Have students complete Review the Selection on pages 440–441.

ESL Activity

Organize students into small groups. Have each group identify the elements of poetry mentioned in the poem. Ask them to suggest additional comparisons between these poetic elements and nature.

Mini Quiz

Write the following questions on the chalkboard or read them aloud. Call on students to fill in the blanks.

1. The poet tries to capture ________ with makeshift words.
2. The ________ bends down a tree.
3. The sky surges ________ and ________.
4. A line will measure an ________.
5. A ________ writes a poem across the sky.

Answers

1. rhythm
2. wind
3. bronze, flame
4. emotion
5. bird

Review the Selection

UNDERSTAND THE SELECTION

Recall

1. What has more success than the speaker at capturing rhythm?
2. According to the speaker, what colors light the night sky?
3. To what does the speaker compare a wild bird?

Infer

4. Do you think the speaker of the poem finds writing difficult? Explain.
5. Explain the meaning of *name* in "Content with some cold distant name."
6. What do the last two lines of the poem mean to you?
7. What do you think the speaker is saying about writing a poem?

Apply

8. Compare and contrast the poet's efforts with the efforts of nature.
9. Do you think the author is successful in communicating beauty?
10. Choose two new titles for the poem.

Respond to Literature

Do you think "Futility" is an appropriate choice to conclude this unit? What events in the early 20th century might be characterized as futile?

WRITE ABOUT THE SELECTION

Have you ever tried to communicate a special feeling about a person, idea, or event, but were unable to find the proper combination of words and phrases that expressed your attitude? Mary S. Hawling expresses that situation in her poem, "Futility." Write a brief letter to a friend in which you explain exactly why you admire a particular person.

Prewriting Think of a person you know well, or have read about. What qualities about him or her do you find admirable? What is special about the person? Make an informal list of descriptive words that might convey this specific attitude.

Writing Use your informal list to write a brief letter to a friend. In it, express your admiration about an acquaintance or historical figure.

Revising When you revise your letter, imagine you are the person to whom it is addressed. Think whether you could determine the writer's tone of admiration. Then, make sure that you have included enough specific details and descriptive words that consistently express a tone of admiration.

Proofreading Read over your completed letter to check for spelling errors. If you are unsure about the correct spelling of a particular word, consult the dictionary. Spelling mistakes can distract your reader and make it hard for him or her to understand what you are trying to say.

UNDERSTAND THE SELECTION

Answers

1. the wind
2. bronze, other flame colors, such as red, orange, and yellow
3. The effort to write one line of poetry that expresses emotion.
4. Sample answer: Yes; she uses words such as "try to capture," "struggle," and "must be content."
5. Sample answer: *Name* refers to a word that fails to illustrate an object or an idea adequately because it is only a word, not the object itself.
6. Sample answer: Nature is more beautiful than any poem.
7. Sample answer: Writing a poem is a constant struggle between the writer's poetic techniques, such as sensory words, rhyme, and imagery, and the subject matter itself.
8. Sample answer: While a poet fights to create a poem, a thing of beauty, nature accomplishes its goals simply, swiftly, and effortlessly.
9. Sample answer: The poet is very successful; she makes the movement, color, and emotions come alive.
10. Answers will vary; they should refer to the poem's content.

Respond to Literature

Have students identify the wars and economic disasters that plagued the early 20th century (two world wars, the Spanish Civil War, the Great Depression). Encourage them to discuss the meaning of *futility*. Elicit the idea that the title of this poem may express a general feeling of unease or disappointment with these destructive, historical events.

WRITE ABOUT THE SELECTION

Prewriting

Have students brainstorm a list of people that they admire. Using their suggestions, create a chalkboard chart of descriptive words and phrases that reflect admiration for, or about, these figures.

Writing

Have students write their letters individually. Go around the class, offering help to students who have difficulty.

Revising

Make this a cooperative group activity. Divide the class into small groups. Collect all the letters from each group and distribute them to another group. Have groups offer suggestions for revising the letters they receive.

Proofreading

Choose several letters and use them as models for proofreading. Display them on an overhead transparency and call on students to suggest improvements in spelling, punctuation, and grammar.

THINK ABOUT TONE

When we talk about the sarcastic tone of a cutting remark or the friendly tone of a personal letter, we mean the specific attitude that is expressed by the speaker or writer. Another way to understand a writer's **tone**, is to think of it as his or her tone of voice. Just as you speak harshly when you are angry, an angry writer will use descriptive words that convey that feeling. A writer who is trying to convey a sympathetic tone will use words that express sympathy.

1. Does the title of the poem suggest that it will have a certain tone?
2. Does your reading of the poem support the view?
3. What word details help you to determine the tone of the poem?
4. What words would you use to change this tone?
5. The author says that writing a poem is an exercise in futility. Do you agree with her attitude? Explain the reasons for your opinion.

Reading Focus

Evaluate the Poet's Purpose What do you think the poet's purpose was in writing "Futility"? Why do you think she expressed these thoughts in a poem? How did you react, knowing her purpose?

DEVELOP YOUR VOCABULARY

Antonyms are words that have opposite, or nearly opposite, meanings. For example, *reprimand* means "to scold harshly." An antonym for *reprimand* is *praise*. Understanding antonyms helps you to figure out contrasting ideas or statements.

Read each sentence below and choose the correct antonym for each italicized word. You may consult a dictionary.

1. The teacher *deferred* our test until next week.
   a. postponed **c.** rushed
   b. delayed **d.** moved
2. Preparing for the debate had put him in a *pensive* mood.
   a. thoughtful **c.** tired
   b. silly **d.** cultured
3. The *tumult* from the cheering crowd drowned out the announcer's voice.
   a. disturbance **c.** silence
   b. uproar **d.** screaming
4. Lost in a pleasant *reverie*, she didn't hear the doorbell ring.
   a. distraction **c.** daydream
   b. concentration **d.** diversion

ESL Activity

Have students return to the "Develop Your Vocabulary" activity on this page to name a synonym for each of the italicized words. Have students use a dictionary or a thesaurus.

THINK ABOUT TONE

Answers

1. The title suggests a tone of disappointment or unhappiness.
2. Answers will vary. Some students may agree; others may say that because the poem successfully captures the essence of nature, it does not express futility.
3. Answers will vary. Students should point to the phrases "make-shift words," "cold, distant name," "struggle." They should notice, too, the beautiful imagery of nature.
4. Answers will vary. One possibility is substituting positive, hopeful words for the ones chosen in the preceding answer.
5. Answers will vary. Many students will disagree with the statement.

DEVELOP YOUR VOCABULARY

Answers

1. (c) rushed
2. (b) silly
3. (c) silence
4. (b) concentration

You might select other vocabulary words from the selection and have students suggest antonyms for each.

Reading Focus

Sample Answer

The author is expressing her frustration with trying to write a perfect poem, especially when nature, which she is trying to write about, is so perfect on its own. She may have written these thoughts out of frustration with the process and to help others understand how difficult it is to write a good poem. Students may say they reacted by recognizing how difficult it is to write a poem.

Unit Review Resources

TEACHER'S RESOURCES

- Writing Process, pp. W49–W60
- Grammar, Usage, and Mechanics, pp. G49–G60
- Speaking and Listening, pp. S26–S30
- Critical Thinking, pp. C25–C30
- Choose from Reading in the Content Areas, pp. RCA1–RCA72
- **Standardized Test Preparation**
  Unit 5 Test, pp. U9–U10
  Choose from Standardized Test Preparation, pp. STP1–STP31

WRITING APPLICATIONS

Write About Conflict

Use the unit time line to review with students the social changes that took place in the United States during the first half of the 20th century. Then have the students brainstorm contemporary social changes (expanding civil rights to women, renew interest in preserving the environment). Point out that these developments have long been important themes in U.S. history and literature.

Prewriting: Choose a selection that focuses on the role of women in society or on nature and discuss with students the relevance of its theme to our present society. Have a volunteer record the major points of the discussion on the chalkboard. Reinforce the idea that the impact of good literature doesn't diminish with age.

Writing: Have students write their essays individually. Help any student who is having difficulty. Tell all students to include sufficient facts and details to make their arguments accurate and persuasive.

Revising: Let students exchange essays with partners for revising. Have them determine whether or not the transition between the two paragraphs is logical and appropriate.

UNIT 5 Review

WRITING APPLICATIONS

Write About Conflict

If there is a single element that links the different selections in this unit, it is the conflict between tradition and social change. Do you think the changes that are expressed in these stories, poems, and dramas are limited only to their specific time period? Or, do some have a more timeless meaning? Choose one selection in this unit and explain whether it would have the same impact if it had been written today.

Prewriting Before you begin to write your essay, think of a selection in this unit that you feel has a timeless message, or theme. Ask yourself whether the events, situations, or conflicts in it, have any significance for the social changes happening in the United States today. Then freewrite your response.

Writing Use your freewriting to write a two-paragraph essay that explains which selection might have a large impact on a modern audience.

Revising When you revise your essay, make sure that you have included specific details from the selection to support your argument.

Proofreading If you have used compound sentences in your essay, make sure that a comma separates the two distinct thoughts in that sentence. Be alert for errors in capitalization. Remember that proper names and story titles are always capitalized.

Write About Literary Elements

One of a writer's chief responsibilities is to make you, the reader, familiar with the unfamiliar. Think about the literary elements—character, dialogue, setting, plot, symbolism, and theme—that you have studied in this unit. Choose one selection and write a paragraph that explains which elements helped you feel "at home" in the writer's created world.

Prewriting Before you begin to write, review your responses to the questions in the "Think About . . ." sections in this unit. Then, make an informal list of the literary elements that appeared in your chosen selection, and think about how the author successfully combined these elements in the story, poem, or drama.

Writing Use your informal list to write a brief essay that describes which combination of literary elements effectively drew you into the writer's imaginary world. In it, make specific references to descriptions, dialogue, events, and situations.

Revising When you revise your essay, check to see if the sentences vary in length. Mixing long and short sentences can help you capture and maintain your reader's interest.

Proofreading When you proofread your essay, make sure that you have used quotation marks to indicate an author's exact words. Check to see that all commas, and periods have been placed inside quotation marks.

Write About Literary Elements

Explain to students that they are literary critics writing book reviews. Here is their opportunity to launch the career of a poet, short story writer, or dramatist.

Prewriting: Guide students through the "Think About . . ." sections. Choose one selection to use as an example.

Writing: While students work on this section individually, offer help to any student who is having difficulty.

Revising: Have students suggest strategies for revision (combining sentences, varying sentence word order and length, supporting topic sentences with details.) Then ask students to revise their own work independently.

Writer's Toolkit CD-ROM

Encourage students to use the Sentence Length Checker (Writing Tools, Revising/Editing) to complete the Revising activity.

Proofreading: Organize students into small groups and have them proofread each other's paragraphs.

BUILD LANGUAGE SKILLS

Vocabulary

Context often provides clues that help you figure out the meaning of an unfamiliar word. You can also use context clues to determine the proper meaning of a word that has several definitions.

For example, *house* can mean: a dwelling; a royal family; a building where animals are kept; or a legislative assembly. In the sentence, "We saw the lizards in the zoo's reptile *house*," only the third meaning of *house* fits the context.

Read each sentence below and choose the meaning that best fits the context.

1. Besides being a true artist, Hemingway was a great historical *figure*.
   a. outline or shape
   b. illustration or diagram
   c. special person
2. The news reporter traveled to every *corner* of our state to cover the story.
   a. secret place
   b. particular region
   c. awkward position
3. Taking math and history will help me achieve a *broad* education.
   a. long
   b. varied
   c. easy to understand
4. The first draft of the escape plan was *rough*, but we could always revise it.
   a. not level
   b. violent or stormy
   c. unfinished

Grammar, Usage, and Mechanics

A well-written sentence should contain enough words to achieve your intended effect. Too few words might not provide your reader with enough information and too many words can distract your reader.

Repetition is a common cause of unclear sentences. Often, you can make a sentence more concise by eliminating repeated words and redundant phrases, different groups of words that mean exactly the same thing.

Read the sentences below. Underline the repeated words or redundant phrases. Then make each sentence more concise.

1. We toured the old ancient war museum.
2. Our principal gave a long speech that was lengthy and put us to sleep.
3. At first his initial look didn't reveal anything unusual about the setting.
4. Robert Frost became the most famous and well-known poet in America.
5. The homework the teacher gave was the tenth assignment she had given this week.
6. She saw some prehistoric tools that had been used before history was written.
7. They had played a practical joke on Sam deliberately on purpose.

Grammar, Usage, and Mechanics

Sample Answers

1. We toured the old war museum.
2. Our principal gave a lengthy speech that put us to sleep.
3. His initial look didn't reveal anything unusual about the setting.
4. Robert Frost became the most famous poet in America.
5. This was the tenth homework assignment our teacher had given us this week.
6. She saw some prehistoric tools.
7. They have played a practical joke on Sam deliberately.

Write these sentences on the chalkboard:

1. We agreed to talk about the plan and discuss it at our next meeting.
2. Gwendolyn Brooks was praised equally for her compassion and kindness, and for her beautiful poetry.

Point out that repetition can ruin the meaning, flow, and impact of a sentence. Ask students which words are repeated needlessly in these sentences. (1. "talk about," "discuss"; 2. "compassion," "kindness"), and have them revise each one. ("We agreed to discuss the plan at our next meeting." "Gwendolyn Brooks was praised equally for her compassion and her beautiful poetry.")

BUILD LANGUAGE SKILLS

Vocabulary

Answers

1. (c) special person
2. (b) particular region
3. (b) varied
4. (c) unfinished

More About Word Attack: Explain to students that by paying close attention to the context in which a word is found, they can often figure out its appropriate definition. Write this example from *Invasion from Mars* on the chalkboard.

"Due to the unusual nature of this occurrence, we have arranged an interview with the noted astronomer. . ."

Point out that nature can mean 1) all things in the universe; 2) surroundings that are not artificial; 3) a simple way of life; 4) the special qualities that make a thing what it is. Explain that only the fourth meaning of nature makes proper sense in the context of this sentence.

SPEAKING AND LISTENING

Motivation

Discuss with students situations in which improvisation can be a handy, if not critical, skill (comic routines, impromptu speeches, press conferences, teaching).

Teaching Strategy

Guide students through the explanation of improvised dialogue, outlining each of the five steps on the chalkboard. You might have students improvise dialogue from a favorite movie or short story. Give students time to organize into small groups and choose their selections. Have students work on their improvisations in class or assign the exercise as a homework activity.

Evaluation Criteria

Create a class list for evaluating the performances, and have students "grade" each improvisation. Possible evaluation questions may include: Does the essential idea of the scene come through? Does the improvisation reflect the correct sequence of the selection? Is each character's personality "true" to the selection?

UNIT 5 Review

SPEAKING AND LISTENING

Improvised dialogue is a kind of reader's theatre. It is a form of oral presentation that has an emphasis on devising and reading dialogue rather than on memorizing lines that are already written. Improvised dialogue is less structured than a scripted play or the dialogue in a story because it is composed and performed without much preparation. It can be used to tell a folk tale, to play a scene from a story, to convey the message of a poem, or to show the relationship between characters. In short, improvised dialogue has a wide range of uses. In fact, there is no limit to its possibilities as long as you use your imagination.

There are a few guidelines that you should be familiar with if you are to be successful. Read these before you try your hand at improvised dialogue.

1. Since improvised dialogue is an activity that gives little time for preparation, it is important that each participant be familiar with the material used for the dialogue. It should be understood by all those involved.
2. Once the selection has been read and discussed, choose the cast of characters. The participants should decide how the scene they will improvise will be set up. One way to arrange the characters is to have them sit in a row in order of their appearance. Then they can move in and out of the scene as needed.
3. Practice and replay the scene. Since this is improvised—using more or less spur-of-the-moment dialogue—your words may change, but the idea of the scene will remain the same. Practicing and replaying the scene will work out the rough spots.
4. Cooperation is a key to successful improvised dialogue. Each character will have to listen and be attentive to catch their own cues.

Now that you have some basic guidelines, choose a selection from this unit and try your hand at improvised dialogue. Devise dialogue where none previously existed and replay the scene before an audience. Limit your dialogue to about three minutes. Remember, you need a pretty good idea of the sequence of the events and the characters, so get to know them.

Career Connection

After reading *Invasion from Mars*, students might be interested in a career in broadcast radio or sound production. Technical schools that teach these skills require their students to have a high school education. Career possibilities for this kind of work abound in the radio, television, and film industries. Electronics technicians troubleshoot and repair broken studio equipment. Sound engineers record and edit audiotapes and mix sound effects. People who want to work in this field should enjoy solving problems and must like working long hours under the pressure of a deadline.

CRITICAL THINKING

Make Inferences An **inference** is a conclusion drawn from known facts or evidence. Look at this example:

If the motor is broken, the machine will not run. The motor is broken.

What can you infer, or conclude, from these statements of fact? The logical conclusion, or inference, is that the machine will not run.

Authors often make the reader supply inferences about a character or an event. They may choose not to state certain information. Using information that *is* supplied, the reader may infer the missing information. The evidence to support the inference may come from the expressions and gestures of characters, action and details in the plot, sensory words, descriptions, and dialogue.

Choose a selection and study it to discover what new inferences you can make about character, setting, conflict, theme, or the author's purpose. As you study, answer the following questions:

1. What evidence is available on which to base an inference? Explain.
2. What evidence is missing? Do I know of similar people or situations like the one in the literary work?

EFFECTIVE STUDYING

Read Effectively Not everything you read deserves the same amount of attention. If you read something for fun, you probably find the reading easy. You are using **rapid reading** skills for such material.

Some things, like looking over a page to find a specific piece of information—a telephone number, a particular date, a statistic—requires a kind of reading called **skimming**. For skimming, you merely run your eyes down the page, stopping when you find the information you want.

Careful reading is needed when you want to remember details. Careful reading is used for reading textbooks or for taking tests.

Critical reading is reading in which you need to stop to examine and weigh ideas, understand them, and form opinions about them.

Here are some guidelines for reading effectively:

- Pace your reading according to the purpose for which you are reading.
- Try to increase the number of words your eyes focus on at any given time.
- Read a lot to increase your vocabulary.

Test Preparation

In a test situation, read the directions carefully to be sure you understand them. If the test requires that you respond to a reading selection, use your critical reading skills.

EFFECTIVE STUDYING

Teaching Strategy

Read the following questions to the class and call on students to answer them. Encourage students to explain their answers.

1. Careful reading helps when you are reading ________ or ________ for tests.
2. Use rapid reading skills when you are reading for ________.
3. Skimming helps you find ________ ________, particular ________, and ________.
4. Always ________ your reading to your specific purpose.
5. Reading a lot helps to increase your ________.

Answers

1. textbooks, studying
2. fun
3. telephone numbers, dates, statistics
4. pace or match
5. vocabulary

CRITICAL THINKING

Answers

Sample answers for inferring the theme of "Lily Daw and the Three Ladies":

1. The story provides abundant evidence about the characters, their motivations, and actions.
2. Lily's full feelings and the xylophone player's full personality are missing evidence. Students may name people who are mentally challenged or people who try to control others' lives.

UNIT ACTIVITY

A Continuing Unit Project: Publishing a Literary Magazine

Divide the class into three heterogeneous groups. Explain to students that each group is going to "publish" a literary magazine. Tell them that a literary magazine may contain short works of literature, reviews or critiques of works published elsewhere, and opinion pieces and letters to the editor from readers. Background or biographical articles about writers are another possibility. Interviews with writers might also appear within its covers.

For motivational reinforcement, explain to students that this project will give them the opportunity to express their own ideas and opinions. It will also allow them to explain the relevance of the literature they are studying to their own experiences.

Students will use the unit introduction as a source work to develop a theme statement for the magazine. They should identify in the unit introduction short statements that describe developments in U.S. life and history, which influenced the literature written during this period.

Call on volunteers and list their ideas on the board. You can guide students by asking leading questions. Examples of such questions follow:

What were the major issues concerning rights that arose during this period?

What two groups found educational and employment opportunities opened to them that were previously denied?

What effect did the emergence of individuals from these groups have on American literature?

What kinds of themes appeared in the works of writers during this period?

On the board or an overhead transparency, write the following phrase, "The publishers and editors of this magazine intend to ______."

Guide students by suggesting ideas for a three-sentence theme statement for each of their magazines. Here are some examples of ideas they might include:

Publish the works of new, exciting young writers.

Publish multicultural works.

Publish the works of male and female writers.

Publish the works of writers with fresh insights into current issues.

When each group has decided upon a theme statement for their magazine, write these statements on the board or an overhead transparency. Have students copy the statements into their notebooks and keep them for future reference.

After completing each selection, review with students the elements of literature that apply.

Guide students in deciding how they will incorporate each selection into the literary magazines by discussing the following with the class:

Have students decide if this selection is appropriate for inclusion in their literary magazines.

Ask if they think it would be a good subject of a literary review.

Ask if they think it could be the focus of an opinion piece or letter to the editor.

Ask if the writer appears to be an appropriate choice for a biographical sketch.

Ask if the writer appears to be an interesting person to interview for their magazines.

Encourage constructive discussion among the members of each group. Caution them that, at this point, it is too early to make a final decision. They should list three tentative options. Tell them to keep the list for future reference. They should also keep relevant comments, which have been made by group members, for future reference.

After you have completed the unit, have students collect and review the options and comments they have made during the unit. Invite your journalism, graphic arts, or art teacher (or, if your school has a print shop, that teacher) to visit your class and discuss magazine layouts.

First, brief the guest teacher on the project and the contents of the proposed magazine. This way practical advice can be offered to students on the length of copy and arrangement of various magazine articles, the use of headings, and how many words should be allotted to each kind of entry or article.

Allow ample time for students' questions and to develop sample layouts, which the guest teacher can review. This will allow the guest speaker an opportunity to offer specific suggestions to each group.

Next, take the class to the school library. Tell them to use books, encyclopedias, and the Internet to research biographical information about each of the writers and their other works. They should also check to see if the library has any examples of literary magazines. You should precheck to see if these are available.

If sufficient research materials are not available in the school library, students, in their groups, should plan to visit the local public library to do additional research. You should provide examples of actual literary magazines to the class and circulate them among the groups as additional guidance.

Before starting the research section of the project, you may want to devote one class to a lesson on using the library, including the on-line card catalogue. Explain that librarians are always willing to assist anyone having difficulty. Also be certain students understand the difference between circulating and reference works. Understanding and planning for this circumstance can save valuable time when conducting research.

Now have each group decide, based on the results of their research, the contents of their magazines. Remind each group to include as least one literary work from the unit. For obvious reasons, it must be short; therefore, it will almost certainly be a poem. In addition, each group must include at least one literary review, opinion piece or letter to the editor, one biographical sketch, and one interview with a writer.

To the extent possible, encourage each group to include original works by group members. These pieces should appear under a heading entitled, "New Writers Showing Promise." When the actual magazine has been completed, have students in each group design artwork for inclusion with some of the entries.

As a final step, have students design covers for the magazines. Encourage original artwork from students who have the ability. Also permit cutting and pasting from magazines. The emphasis should be on effort. Remind students to include a page with the theme statement they had previously written. On this page, each group should also list the names of contributing editors, interviewers, researchers, writers, and artists. Repeat names as necessary to insure full credit for the work performed. Each group should also prepare a table of contents.

Provide close supervision for each group. Ensure that a number of writers from the unit will be included in some way. Also ensure that the work is being equitably distributed among the group members, and all are participating. When all the groups have completed their magazines, display these in a glass-encased bulletin board in the hallway of the school or in the school library. Make arrangements with the appropriate school officials beforehand.

■ "The Secret"

by Denise Levertov (page 451)

SELECTION SYNOPSIS

The subject of this poem is gaining new insights from poetry. The theme suggests that one of the joys of poetry is that repeated readings can bring fresh insights and new discoveries.

SELECTION ACTIVITY

Pair students to collaborate on writing a biography of the poet. They should use the school library and, if necessary, the local public library for information. You may want to devote one class to a lesson on using the reference department in a library. Invite the school librarian to visit the class or, preferably, prearrange a trip to the library for hands-on experience.

Each biography should be at least three paragraphs in length. It should include personal information about the poet. Each biography should also contain a list of other significant poems or collections of poems by the poet. Collections should be listed by title, publisher, city, and year in which it first appeared.

Have students do the actual writing in class. Use the writing process described throughout this text. Provide help as needed to any pair having difficulty.

■ "Snow"

by Dorothy Aldis (page 455)

SELECTION SYNOPSIS

This is a short, lyrical description of snow, in vivid, visual terms.

■ "Umbilical"

by Eve Merriam (page 456)

SELECTION SYNOPSIS

This is a humorous poem that compares a person's attachment to a transistor radio to the umbilical cord by which infants are bound to their mothers.

■ "Cumulus Clouds"

by Sheryl Nelms (page 457)

SELECTION SYNOPSIS

This is an extended metaphor describing the clouds in figurative language.

SELECTION ACTIVITY

Divide the class into groups of three. Have students in each group select one of the poems to be read aloud. Have the groups practice quietly. Partners should offer each other suggestions for word emphasis and rhythmic reading.

Bring a tape recorder to class. Ask for volunteers to read the poem they have rehearsed aloud in class. Record and play the results. Encourage as many students as possible to participate. Advise students that they should try to memorize the poem beforehand; however, allow them to hold the text while reading to avoid loss of memory from nervousness. Encourage applause from class members and record the applause for playback.

■ "Two Kinds" from *The Joy Luck Club*

by Amy Tan (page 461)

SELECTION SYNOPSIS

This selection is from Amy Tan's first novel *The Joy Luck Club*, which examines the relationships between four Chinese-born women and their American-born daughters. In this excerpt, a Chinese mother who believes that in the United States anything is possible has high hopes for her daughter. Thinking that she can make her child into a prodigy, she gives her daughter various tests. The daughter repeatedly fails the tests and becomes frustrated and angry. The mother then exchanges house cleaning for piano lessons with Mr. Chong, a neighbor. The daughter is a poor pupil, and when she has to perform at a talent show, she embarrasses herself and her mother. When the mother insists that her daughter continue lessons, the daughter rebels and says some very harsh things to her mother. After that, the lessons are never mentioned again. The daughter feels that she continues to disappoint her mother but is happy at being her own person. When the daughter becomes an adult, her mother offers her the piano as a gift. The daughter sees the gift as a sign of forgiveness.

SELECTION ACTIVITY

If possible, invite a relative born in another country to visit the class. Ask the guest to talk about his or her experiences with United States culture, in particular, the similarities and differences between the guest's native culture and the new culture. Also ask the visitor to address the possible issue of tensions between the younger generation and an older one resulting from cultural differences.

After the arrangements for the visitor have been made, announce the visit to the class. If the visitor agrees to answer questions, tell students to prepare some beforehand. Tell students they will be expected to take notes and write a paragraph or two about the guest's speech. In the paragraphs, students should compare and contrast the visitor's experiences with those of the story characters. If a guest is not available to visit the class, have students interview immigrants that they know (relatives, neighbors).

■ "The World Is Not a Pleasant Place to Be"

by Nikki Giovanni (page 473)

SELECTION SYNOPSIS

The subject of this poem is love, or affection. The poet suggests that life is a pleasant experience only if a person loves and is loved in return.

SELECTION ACTIVITY

Have each student privately choose someone who has made life more pleasant for the student. It may be a relative, a friend, or a teacher. Tell students that each will compose an original verse and cover design for a greeting card. This card may be sent to the person if the student so chooses. If the student does not choose to do so, respect these wishes. Also, indicate that the student never has to mention the name of the recipient.

Distribute suitable materials for this project. Colored or white construction paper would be ideal for this project. Provide crayons, markers, and magazines (for cut-and-paste art).

If any student is having difficulty, give assistance or guidance as needed. If your school library has a rhyming dictionary, you may want to bring it to class for students' use. Provide samples of poetry anthologies from which they might find inspiration. One excellent example is Globe Fearon's *Experiencing Poetry* by Eileen Thompson.

Collect and evaluate the students' projects. After recording the grades, return the cards to their authors for distribution or retention as they desire. Praise the work of all who have shown effort.

"Journey"

by Joyce Carol Oates (page 477)

SELECTION SYNOPSIS

This essay is an example of unusual use of point of view. The writer delivers a monologue, using the pronoun *you*. The *you* of the work may be the reader, or the speaker addressing herself as though she were a different individual.

A motorist sets out early in the morning on a journey by car. The trip begins high in the mountains, and she can see her destination in the distance. She has brought along a traveler's map.

After several hours on a major highway, she grows tired of the monotony. Seeing a smaller road that appears to run parallel, she turns into it. This road leads her deep into a forest, and she loses sight of her destination.

By mid-afternoon, she has tired of this road. Seeing an even smaller road, she turns onto it. The road is rough and unpaved. The surrounding countryside is uninhabited. The road soon narrows to a twisting dirt lane in which grass in growing. At times she can go no faster than five miles an hour and realizes she will not reach the city before dark.

Late in the afternoon, she decides to park her car and continue on foot. By evening, she is tired and wonders whether she has made a mistake. Finding herself at the edge of a forest as night approaches, she resists the thought that she is lost. She knows where her car is parked, the travel map is on the seat. She concludes that if the day were to begin all over again, she would stay on the highway.

SELECTION ACTIVITY

Pair students to collaborate on rewriting this essay as a journal entry. Use the writing process described throughout this text.

Provide students with the following guidance before they begin the project.

They should date the journal in the upper left-hand margin.

On the board or an overhead transparency write the following; early morning, late morning, early afternoon, late afternoon, and evening. Tell students that, for the journal, they are to translate these approximations given by Oates into exact times (for example, early morning equals 6:00 A.M.). Remind students that A.M. is used for the hours between 12 midnight and 11:59 in the morning; P.M. is used for the hours between 12 noon and 11:59 at night. Tell them to be certain they do not confuse these terms in their journals.

Tell students to select three important facts provided by Oates concerning her trip, during each of the five periods listed. For example, in the early morning:

1. She started out high in the mountains.
2. She could see her destination.
3. She was traveling on a major highway.

from *Black Boy*

by Richard Wright (page 485)

SELECTION SYNOPSIS

This dramatic episode in Wright's early life is often anthologized under the title "Hunger." Wright was a small boy at the time, living with his mother and brother in a shabby Memphis, Tennessee, apartment. The hunger that occasionally makes him dizzy and listless also increases his bitterness against his father, who has recently left the family.

Finally, his mother secures employment as a cook. The boys must take on more responsibility, and Richard is told that he will have to do the food shopping. On his first trip to the store, he is mauled and robbed by a gang of boys. When his mother comes home, she gives him more money and sends him out again. The same thing happens, and he returns in tears. Instead of offering comfort, his mother gives him still more money and a stick. She orders him to fight and promises to beat him if he returns without the groceries. Nearly crazed with fear, he starts out. When the gang closes in, he goes into motion, cracking skulls in an eruption of frenzy. The boys run off, and Wright makes the rest of the trip unmolested, proud of his new status.

SELECTION ACTIVITY

Have students work in pairs to write a biography of Richard Wright. They should use the school library and, if possible, the Internet for information. You may want to devote one class to a lesson on using the library, in particular the reference department. Invite the school librarian to visit the class and speak, or prearrange with the librarian a visit to the library for hands-on experience.

Each biography should include personal information about the author, such as birth date (and date of death if applicable), education and employment experience, awards if any, and so forth. It should also contain a list of major works by Mr. Wright. These should include the title, publisher, city and year in which each first appeared.

Have students do the actual writing in class. Use the writing process described throughout this text. Provide help as needed to any pair having difficulty.

Collect and evaluate the biographies. After returning them, encourage students to read their work in front of the class. Have students discuss and comment on the writer and his career.

■ "Little Things Are Big"

by Jesús Colón (page 497)

SELECTION SYNOPSIS

Jesús Colón relates a haunting incident in "Little Things Are Big." A black Puerto Rican and a recent arrival on the mainland, Colón is riding the subway late at night. A young white woman gets on, carrying a baby and a suitcase, while caring for two small children at the same time. She prepares to get off at Atlantic Avenue, which is also Colón's destination. A white man stands up and helps her out of the car. As the train pulls away, Colón realizes that he and the woman are the only adults on the platform. He sincerely wants to help her down the long flight of stairs, but he realizes that she might be prejudiced. She might even scream if he walked in her direction. He hesitates a moment, then bolts away and runs down the stairs. Later he feels ashamed and resolves to offer assistance in any similar situation in the future.

SELECTION ACTIVITY

Tell students they are going to write a shorter version of this same story. This time Jesús Colón decides to help the woman.

Use the writing process that has been explained throughout this text. Explain that students should think of themselves as this woman, who is traveling with her young children. She must constantly be aware of any strange circumstances in order to protect her children. Tell them to infer why she is traveling at this hour and her destination.

Prewriting Have students jot down the woman's thoughts from the time she enters the train until she sees Jesús Colón come to help her. Using students' suggestions, list several ideas on the board or overhead transparency. To elicit responses, ask, "Do you think this woman feels Colón might help her? Does she feel hopeful? Does she fear for the safety of her children?"

Writing As students write, walk around the classroom. Give assistance to any student having difficulty. Tell them to imagine how they would feel under similar circumstances and suggest possible responses.

Revising Remind students to include the woman's positive reaction after Colón helps her. Tell them to think about her possible responses to him.

Proofreading Have students work with a partner to determine if there are any errors in spelling, punctuation, and grammar.

Collect and evaluate the papers. Select several students to read their stories to the class. Students should discuss ways to overcome prejudice and racism.

"Where Have You Gone"

by Mari Evans (page 503)

SELECTION SYNOPSIS

This is a poem about a person whose lover has left. The theme suggested in the surprise conclusion is that people sometimes love in the words of Shakespeare, "not wisely but too well."

SELECTION ACTIVITY

Have the class discuss why people sometimes love people who do not appear to merit the affection. If possible, obtain recordings of songs that examine this theme and play them in class.

If records or tapes are not available, you might start the discussion by telling the class that a famous French writer, Albert Camus, once suggested that friendships usually end, not because we no longer find the friend interesting or amusing, but because we suspect the friend no longer finds us interesting or amusing. Ask students what they think this says about human needs.

"Everyday Use"

by Alice Walker (page 507)

SELECTION SYNOPSIS

On a hot day, a widow sits on her porch. She is awaiting a visit from one of her two daughters. The other daughter is inside the tiny, modest home. As she waits, the mother thinks about the past.

The daughter still at home, Maggie, was badly burned twelve years before when the family's previous home burned down. Good natured and shy, Maggie will soon marry a local man. Together, they will struggle to get by in the years ahead. Maggie has always accepted the fact that she is neither bright nor pretty.

Dee, the other daughter, is attractive and intelligent. Aggressive and well-educated, Dee had always adopted a superior attitude toward her family. She is now returning home for a brief visit with her husband, whom they have never met.

Dee and her husband arrive. Both have adopted African names and dress. After dinner, Dee begins selecting artifacts made by her ancestors. Ignoring the practical functions each serve, she will display them as decorations. When Dee insists on taking her grandmother's quilts (promised to Maggie), the mother has had enough. Maggie will have these and put them to everyday use as their grandmother had intended. Dee leaves, commenting pretentiously that her mother and her sister do not understand their heritage. After she goes, Maggie and mother sit happily on the porch until bedtime.

from *The Woman Warrior*

by Maxine Hong Kingston (page 521)

SELECTION SYNOPSIS

Brave Orchid is an elderly Asian woman, who immigrated to America as a young woman. She is at the San Francisco airport, awaiting the arrival of her sister, whom she has not seen in 30 years. Her two Asian-American children and her sister's only daughter have accompanied her. Her children have wandered off into the airport shops. Her niece waits with her.

Brave Orchid's children return to tell her the plane has arrived. The four peer anxiously at the passengers. Each time a younger woman approaches, Brave Orchid is convinced that it must be her sister. The niece, who had visited her mother five years earlier, gently disagrees. As a thin old woman appears, the niece shouts, "Mother!" The two sisters are shocked at how old the other now looks, and they chide each other. Age and many years of separation notwithstanding, as they leave the airport, the relationship they shared as girls begins to surface.

SELECTION ACTIVITY

Have students compare and contrast the personalities and relationships between the two pairs of sisters in these two stories. Here are some questions you can use as prompts.

In conversation, which of the two seems to show more consideration and concern for her sister, Brave Orchid or Dee? Support your choice with examples from the stories.

Which of the two do you think shows more genuine feeling for her sister, Brave Orchid or Dee? Support your choice with examples from the stories.

■ **"This Is Just to Say"**
by William Carlos Williams (page 531)

■ **"The Term"**
by William Carlos Williams (page 531)

SELECTION SYNOPSES

In the first poem, Williams describes the taste of plums he has just eaten. He regrets that because he has eaten them, someone else cannot enjoy the same taste. In the second poem, Williams describes seeing a sheet of paper, about the size and shape of a man, being run over by a car. The paper rises up, being picked up by the wind. The difference between a man and the man-shaped paper is the paper's continued existence.

SELECTION ACTIVITY

In this activity, students will research facts about the life of William Carlos Williams and read at least four of his other poems. You may wish to gather books to have in the classroom about the poet and his poems. As an alternative, you may wish to prepare a short biography on Williams and separate copies that include about ten of his poems.

Step 1

Say to students: William Carlos Williams was a pediatrician, who lived in New Jersey, and was also a poet. He felt a poem should see something "with great intensity of perception." As you read about his life and read at least four of his poems, think about whether the poems describe one thing with intensity.

Give students time to read about Williams and to read a few of his poems. Some poems worth considering are "The Yachts," "On Gay Wallpaper," and "To a Poor Old Woman."

Step 2

Have students write one or two sentences about each of the poems they have read. You might wish to have students read a few of these poems aloud in class. Then have students read their sentences about the poem.

Step 3

Display typed versions of the poems on a bulletin board entitled "More From William Carlos Williams." Near the display, have books available that include Williams' poems for those interested in reading more.

STUDENT READING LIST

Anaya, Rudolfo. *My Land Sings*. Morrow, 1999.
Chambers, Veronica. *Mama's Girl*. Putnam/Riverhead.
Feelings, Tom. *The Middle Passage*. Dial, 1999.
Peck, Richard. *Amanda Miranda*. Dial, 1999.
Salinger, Jerome David. *Catcher in the Rye*. Little, 1951.
Second Sight: *Stories for a New Millennium*. Putnam/Philomel, 1999.
Sinott, Susan. *Lorraine Hansberry: Award-winning Playwright and Civil Rights Activist*. Conain Press, 1999.
Tan, Amy. *The Joy Luck Club*. Putnam, 1989.
Walker, Alice. *The Color Purple*. Harcourt Brace, 1982.

From Globe Fearon Educational Publisher

Experiencing Poetry
Adapted Classics
- *A Raisin in the Sun* by Lorraine Hansberry

African American Biographies
- *Actor Denzel Washington*
- *Astronaut Mae Jemison*

Chinese American Literature
- "*My Mother's English*," by Amy Tan

Uptown, Downtown Series
- *Looking for Trouble*
- *Wheels of Danger*

Sportellers
- *Catch the Sun*
- *Strike Two*

UNIT 6 Overview

UNIT OBJECTIVES

After completing this unit, students will be able to

- understand the four basic elements of autobiography: narrative style, point of view, purpose, and introspection
- write an autobiographical narrative
- use a dictionary to determine word origins
- use colons and semicolons properly
- prepare and conduct a reader's debate
- organize thoughts and notes in an outline

UNIT SELECTIONS

This unit covers the period since 1946, the contemporary period.

- **"The Secret"** (p. 451) Two young girls discover the "secret of life" in a line of poetry.

  LITERARY SKILL: poetic form

  READING SKILL: summarize text

  VOCABULARY: synonyms

  WRITING: conversation

- **"Snow"/"Umbilical"/"Cumulus Clouds"** (p. 455) are three short poems that present different ways of viewing the world.

  LITERARY SKILL: figurative language

  READING SKILL: paraphrase poetry

  VOCABULARY: new meanings for existing words

  WRITING: description of a scene

- **"Two Kinds"** from ***The Joy Luck Club*** (p. 461) is the story of the uneasy relationship between a Chinese-born mother and her American-born daughter.

  LITERARY SKILL: characters' motive

  READING SKILL: use word identification

  VOCABULARY: suffixes

  WRITING: an article

- **"The World Is Not a Pleasant Place to Be"** (p. 473) is a poem about loving and being loved.

  LITERARY SKILL: tone

  READING SKILL: understand levels of meaning

  VOCABULARY: homophones

  WRITING: a persuasive paragraph

- **"Journey"** (p. 477) relates a tale of imagination and fantasy.

  LITERARY SKILL: point of view

  READING SKILL: make inferences

  VOCABULARY: antonyms

  WRITING: descriptive paragraph

- from ***Black Boy*** (p. 485) tells about an inner-city youth who learns to defend himself.

  LITERARY SKILL: purpose

  READING SKILL: understand meaning through context

  VOCABULARY: word origins

  WRITING: paraphrase and summarize a story

- **"Little Things Are Big"** (p. 497) is the model selection, and focuses on the detrimental effects of racism.

  LITERARY SKILL: elements of autobiography: narrative style, point of view, purpose, and introspection

  READING SKILL: recognize facts and opinions

  VOCABULARY: word families

  WRITING: retell a story from a different point of view

- **"Where Have You Gone"** (p. 503) describes feelings toward a loved one who has left.

  LITERARY SKILL: free verse

UNIT 6

The Contemporary Perspective

Wish for nothing larger
Than your own small heart
Or greater than a star.
—Alice Walker

Christina's World, Andrew Wyeth, 1948. Tempera on gessoed panel, 32¼" × 47¾" (81.9 × 121.3 cm). Collection, The Museum of Modern Art, New York. Purchase. Photograph ©2000 The Museum of Modern Art, New York

447

READING SKILL: interpret character

VOCABULARY: words used as nouns and verbs

WRITING: a persuasive paragraph

- **"Everyday Use"** (p. 507) explores different ways of viewing a common heritage.

  LITERARY SKILL: theme

  READING SKILL: compare and contrast

  VOCABULARY: adverbs, adjectives

  WRITING: descriptive paragraph

- from ***The Woman Warrior*** (p. 521) focuses on pride in heritage and the clash between two cultures.

  LITERARY SKILL: character

  READING SKILL: understand sequence of events

  VOCABULARY: base words and prefixes

  WRITING: a newspaper interview/character sketch

- **"This Is Just to Say"/ "The Term"** (p. 531) are two short insightful poems about everyday experiences.

  LITERARY SKILL: open form

  READING SKILL: compare and contrast

  VOCABULARY: antonyms

  WRITING: a short poem

Introducing the Literary Period

Invite a panel of four or five guest speakers who were adults by 1946 to visit your class. Tell students ahead of time that they will be meeting some "time travelers" from 1946, and encourage them to prepare questions about the time period. Try to include guests of both sexes and several ethnic groups. Ask each to prepare brief remarks on how society has changed since 1946 and what impact this has had on him or her. Allow time for students to ask their questions.

Viewing Fine Art

Andrew Wyeth, now in his eighties, is probably the most popular painter of his time. His works are detailed and realistic, with a photographic quality about them. He is noted for painting uncrowded rural scenes, which serve as reminders of early life in the United States.

The settings he uses most are Maine and his native Chester County, Pennsylvania. The people in his paintings are usually family members, friends, or neighbors. The subject of "Christina's World" is a Wyeth neighbor in Maine (Christina Olson) who was stricken with poliomyelitis. One day in 1948, Wyeth observed her picking berries in a field. She paused momentarily and looked up at her house. It is this dramatic, haunting scene Wyeth captured in the painting.

Ask: What does the distance between Christina and her house suggest about Christina's world?

RELATED MATERIALS

1. ***Spoken Arts Treasury of 100 Modern American Poets Reading Their Poems—volume XV*** [Spoken Arts, Dept. R86, Box 289, New Rochelle, NY 10802, SA1054.] This volume includes Denise Levertov.
2. ***Favorite American Poems*** [Caedmon Records] These poems are read by Ed Begley.
3. ***Beyond the Blues: American Negro Poetry*** [Argo Records/ Spoken Word Division] These poems are read by Brock Peters, Vinette Carroll, Gordon Heath, and Cleo Laine.
4. ***Critical Companions to Popular Contemporary Writers*** [CD-ROM, Greenwood Electronic Media, 1999.]
5. ***Martin Luther King: The Man and the Dream*** [videocassette, A&E Video, 1998.]
6. ***Rosa Parks: Path to Freedom*** [Filmmakers Library, 1996.]
7. ***Native Son*** by Richard Wright. [audiobook, 2 hrs., Harper Audio, 1998.] Abridged version read by James Earl Jones.
8. ***December Stillness*** [4 audiocassettes, 4:45 hrs., Recorded Books, 1999.] Julie Dretzen tells Mary Downing Hahn's tender and realistic story of a father's war experiences in Vietnam.
9. ***Choosing Sides: I remember Vietnam the War at home*** [2 videocassettes, 48 mins. ea., A&E, 1997.] Presents first-person recollections of POWs, health personnel, soldiers, and peace activists.
10. ***National Museum of Women in the Arts Collections*** [CD-ROM, SRA/McGraw-Hill, 1999.] This CD-ROM includes an extensive cross-section of female artists.
11. ***Writing Women's Lives*** [videocassette, 60 mins., Films for the Humanities and Sciences, 1995.] This is a thought-provoking discussion of how eight female authors became famous writers.
12. ***Fury for the Sound: Women at Clayoquot*** [videocassette, 52 mins., Bullfrog Films, 1997.] Because they protested to save the environment in British Columbia, women are imprisoned and abused.
13. The following Web sites may also be helpful. Please note that some Internet addresses change frequently. These are the latest versions:

    PBS, Richard Wright, Black Boy *http://www.pbs.org/rwbb/rwtoc.html*

    A response to Maxine Hong Kingston's Woman Warrior *http://sterling.holycross.edu/departments/english/mwong/fyp/sinton/wom_warrior.html*

    The Academy of American Poets, William Carlos Williams *http://www.poets.org/LIT/POET/Wcwilfst.htm*

LITERARY HIGHLIGHTS

1949 Arthur Miller's play, *Death of a Salesman*, wins acclaim.

1952 Ernest Hemingway's *The Old Man and the Sea* appears.

1959 Lorraine Hansberry's *A Raisin in the Sun* is produced.

1962 Rachel Carson's *Silent Spring* is published.

1967 Joyce Carol Oates publishes *A Garden of Earthly Delights*.

1950 1955 1960 1965 1970

1950 President Truman orders U.S. troops to Korea.

1954 Supreme Court bans segregation in public schools.

1955 Martin Luther King, Jr., leads a boycott of buses in Montgomery, Alabama.

1963 President Kennedy is assassinated.

1967 Thurgood Marshall is first African-American Supreme Court Justice.

1969 Two American astronauts are first to walk on the moon.

HISTORICAL HIGHLIGHTS

The Contemporary Perspective

At the beginning of this book, you supposed that you were a visitor from colonial America. Now think about being a time traveler from fifty years ago. Think of the changes you would see in the United States today.

Are you surprised at how much time people spend watching TV? Fifty years ago, television was a new medium. Do you wonder at all the tasks computers perform? Fifty years ago, computers were just beginning to come into use. Are you amazed by the space program? In your time, space exploration was only an idea.

Now think about the opportunities available to people in this country. They may surprise you, too.

CIVIL RIGHTS MOVEMENTS

How would you feel if you were not allowed to sit at a lunch counter or go to a school of your choice because of your race? Martin Luther King, Jr., and other great African American leaders led civil rights workers in peaceful protests against these and other injustices. Their efforts were responsible for such laws as the Civil Rights Act of 1964, which banned discrimination in education, employment, voting, and public facilities.

During this time too, women demanded equal rights. The women's rights movement has succeeded in making more types of jobs available to women and in reducing other discrimination against women.

These and similar movements have helped make people in the United States aware of the need to respect all people's rights.

NEW VOICES IN LITERATURE

Fifty years ago, you might not have had the chance to read some of the selections in this book. The writers may have been ignored because of their race or their gender, or both. Today, all have a chance to be

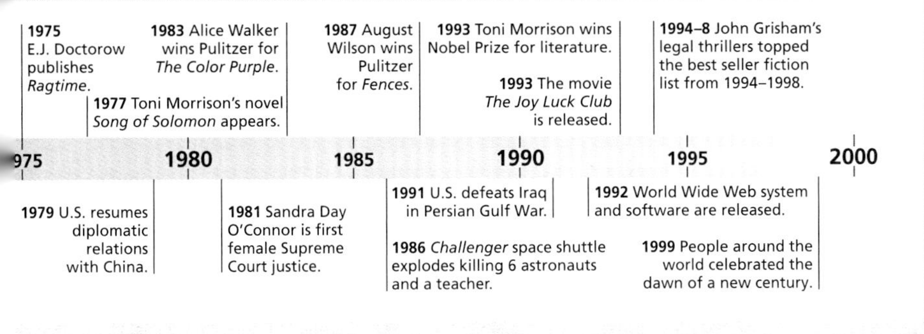
1975 E.J. Doctorow publishes Ragtime.
1983 Alice Walker wins Pulitzer for The Color Purple.
1977 Toni Morrison's novel Song of Solomon appears.
1987 August Wilson wins Pulitzer for Fences.
1993 Toni Morrison wins Nobel Prize for literature.
1993 The movie The Joy Luck Club is released.
1994–8 John Grisham's legal thrillers topped the best seller fiction list from 1994–1998.
975
1980
1985
1990
1995
2000
1979 U.S. resumes diplomatic relations with China.
1981 Sandra Day O'Connor is first female Supreme Court justice.
1991 U.S. defeats Iraq in Persian Gulf War.
1992 World Wide Web system and software are released.
1986 Challenger space shuttle explodes killing 6 astronauts and a teacher.
1999 People around the world celebrated the dawn of a new century.

heard. In this unit, you will read the works of a variety of writers—men and women, African American, white, and Hispanic. They tell about their values and opinions. Readers learn their points of view.

Characters in literature often search for a meaning to their lives, just as real people do. Has your reading ever helped you discover something you have always wondered about? In "The Secret," two young girls discover the secret of life in a single line of a poem.

Do you always agree with your friends? Today we know that it is all right to see things differently. The second selection in this unit consists of three poems that present unusual ways of looking at the world.

The characters in "Two Kinds" and "The World Is Not a Pleasant Place to Be" illustrate a common need: to love and be loved. They realize that people depend on others for many things. What things do you depend on from your family and friends?

It is a common experience to make a decision that turns out differently than expected. If this has ever happened to you, you will enjoy the story "Journey." It describes a choice and its results.

Two aspects of the terrible impact of racism are shown in *Black Boy* and "Little Things Are Big." In the first, a poor young boy learns to survive in a tough world. In the second, a young man personally experiences the effects of racism. How do these stories help you to understand how racism affects people?

What aspects of your heritage are you especially proud of? "Everyday Use" and *The Woman Warrior*, celebrate two different cultures.

The final selections, "This Is Just to Say" and "The Term," describe everyday experiences in new ways.

Literature today reflects a variety of ideas. What values and ideas are important to you? Which can you find in these selections?

Discussing the Literary Period

Review The Contemporary Perspective with students. Allow time for class discussion of each question posed in the student text.

Ask the class what they think life would have been like as a member of a minority group (racial, ethnic, gender, religious) before the days of the civil rights and equal rights movements, and subsequent legislation aimed at correcting inequalities. Discuss the beneficial effects of the Civil Rights Act of 1964 and the equal rights movement. Ask students to what extent, and in what forms, discrimination and prejudice still exist in contemporary America. Ask how these forces are reflected in literature, films, music, and television. Have students give examples.

Cooperative Group Activity

Divide the class into groups of four or five students. Direct each group to develop a short skit, depicting a scene from everyday life in the United States for presentation to the class. Have them act out the scene in two ways: first, showing what could happen to a member of a minority group in such a setting before the passage of the Civil Rights Act of 1964 and similar legislation, and second, what it is like today. Discuss with the class what differences there might be. Sample settings could include: a bus, a lunch counter, a water fountain, a courtroom, a department store, a movie theater, a school bus, an employment interview, etc. Make sure each group utilizes a different setting. Once each group has prepared its skit, have them present it to the class. This activity could be spread over several days to allow students time for research and development of a representative scene with appropriate dialogue.

Selection Overview

SELECTION OBJECTIVES

After completing this selection, students will be able to

- identify and define a stanza
- rewrite a poem in sentence form
- write a fictional conversation based on a poem
- discuss poetic form
- understand and utilize synonyms
- summarize text

Lesson Resources

The Secret

- Selection Synopsis, Teacher's Edition, p. T445c
- Comprehension and Vocabulary Workbook, pp. 85–86
- Language Enrichment Workbook, pp. 65–66
- Teacher's Resources
  Reinforcement, p. R43
  Test, pp. T85–T86

More About Form

Form takes on various meanings in relation to poetry. *Stanza form* refers to the organization of verses within the poem. *Verse form* refers to the organization of rhythm elements (feet and meter) within a line. Also, there is the *form of images* (the interrelationships among them) and the *form of ideas* (the organization or structure of thought).

Have students review the other poems in this unit. Ask them to identify the stanza form (number and length of stanzas) and the verse form (number of accented syllables and feet per line). Are images interrelated? Are thoughts organized by stanza? Is there more than one thought per stanza? Is one idea carried over from one stanza to another?

Learn About

POETIC FORM

A poem can be written in many different ways. A poem can read like a speech or like someone talking to you. How a poem affects you as you read it depends partly on its form, the way the poem is organized. Nothing about a poem is accidental; its words and the way they are organized are carefully considered.

There are different ways a poem can be organized; one basic way is by stanza. A **stanza** is simply two or more lines of poetry grouped together. A stanza may consist of one thought, action, image, or emotion, or more than one. Stanzas can be arranged by the passage of time, by subject, or as part of a series, one leading to the next. A stanza may have meaning by itself; some stanzas must be read together to have meaning.

As you read "The Secret," ask yourself:

1. How does one stanza lead to another?
2. How could the poem be organized differently?

READING FOCUS

Summarize Text When you summarize text, you condense it to its most important points. Even a short poem can be summarized in a sentence or two that express the main idea or ideas of the poem. After you read the next selection, reread it and try writing a summary of its meaning. Notice how doing this improves your understanding of the main idea.

WRITING CONNECTION

The form of a poem can make its meaning clearer or more difficult. Rewrite the poem in sentence form to see if the effect is different.

About the Author

Although the poet, Denise Levertov (1923–1997), was born in Essex, England, she became a U.S. citizen in 1955 after she married an American. Levertov claims a romantic ancestry: Welsh mysticism on her mother's side and Russian Hassidic influences from her father's. In 1965, she initiated the Writers' and Artists' Protest Against the War in Vietnam.

Develop Vocabulary Skills

This selection contains no footnoted vocabulary words. Discuss with students the everyday language that the poet uses in this selection. Great literature does not necessarily have to be written using "literary language," and in this case, the poet seems to be speaking as she would in ordinary conversation.

Cooperative Group Activity

Pair students for the Writing Connection activity. Have them work together to rewrite the poem in sentence form. Ask each pair if they think this makes the meaning clearer or more difficult to understand. Why is this? Do both students agree? Tally the answers, by group, to see if there is a class consensus, or at least a majority opinion.

THE SECRET

by Denise Levertov

Two girls discover
the secret of life
in a sudden line of
poetry.

5 I who don't know the
secret wrote
the line. They
told me

(through a third person)
10 they had found it
but not what it was
not even

what line it was. No doubt
by now, more than a week
15 later, they have forgotten
the secret,

the line, the name of
the poem. I love them
for finding what
20 I can't find,

and for loving me
for the line I wrote,
and for forgetting it
so that

25 a thousand times, till death
finds them, they may
discover it again, in other
lines

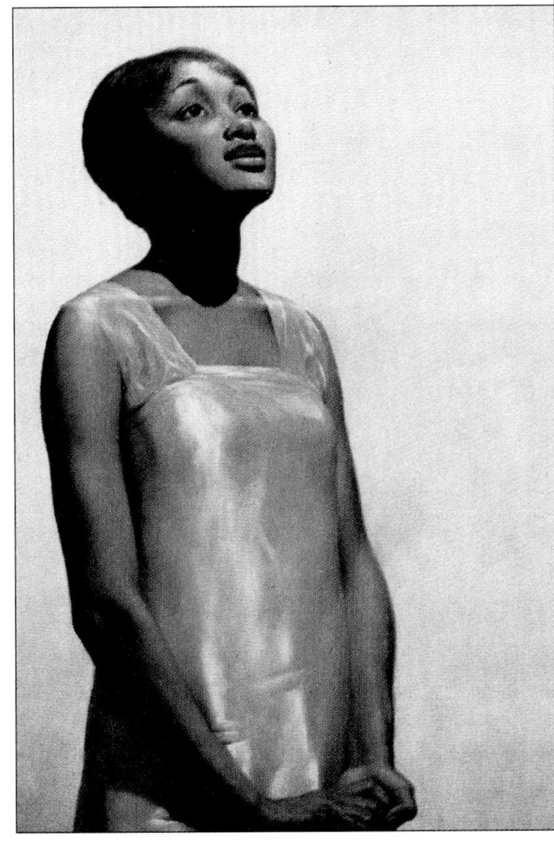

Ruby Green Singing, James Chapin.
Norton Museum of Art, West Palm Beach, FL.
Bequest of R.H. Norton

in other
30 happenings. And for
wanting to know it,
for

assuming there is
such a secret, yes,
35 for that
most of all.

TEACHING PLAN

INTRODUCE

Motivation

Poetry and other forms of literature often contain, as in this poem, "the secret of life," whether in one line or as a whole. Discuss with the class works they have read that really "spoke" to them. Ask volunteers to describe a poem, story, or work of art that they read or saw and identified with. Ask what it was in the works that had personal meaning to them.

Purpose-Setting Question

What is the real purpose of poems, novels, stories, and so forth? To merely entertain the reader? As personal expression for the writer? To communicate with others?

READ

Literary Focus: *Poetic Form*

This poem is an example of free verse. Discuss with students how free verse differs from other forms of poetry.

Reading Focus: *Summarize Text*

Work with students to define the poet's message in the poem. It might be helpful to have students read the poem aloud, sentence by sentence rather than line by line. Clarify the meaning of each sentence before moving on to the next.

CLOSE

Have students complete Review the Selection on pages 452–453.

Mini Quiz

Write the sentences on the board. Call on students to fill in the blanks and discuss the answers.

1. ________ wrote this poem.
2. Two ________ discover something in a poem.
3. They find the ________ of life.
4. They read the poem a ________ ago.
5. They may discover the secret again in other ________ or other ________ .

Answers

1. Denise Levertov
2. girls
3. secret
4. week
5. lines; happenings

Viewing Fine Art

James Chapin (b. 1887) was an American painter who, in a rather conservative style, painted pictures of American workers, such as farm hands and railroad laborers, and a series devoted to boxers. This portrait is one of several he made of African Americans. Ask: What type of song do you do you think Ruby Green is singing? What makes you think that?

UNDERSTAND THE SELECTION

Answers

1. in a line of poetry
2. for assuming there is such a secret to be found
3. They told someone, who told the poet.
4. by reading a poem
5. They can discover it again somewhere else.
6. Sample answer: In other poetry, other people, other events
7. Sample answer: The line of poetry "suddenly" becomes clear to them; its secret is a sudden and accidental discovery.
8. Sample answer: One would know by the change it would make in one's life. The discovery of a more important secret might make one forget.
9. Sample answers: nature, science, and art
10. Sample answer: "A Discovery"

Respond to Literature

One possible answer to the question is that the search can give meaning and direction to people's lives. Conduct a free-ranging class discussion on where to look for the "meaning of life": in nature, books, television shows, a church, other people, etc.

WRITE ABOUT THE SELECTION

Prewriting

Students are to work on this section individually. To start them off, suggest a question yourself per the directions. Then have students think up five questions of their own.

Writing

Students are to work on this section individually. Go around the room, offering help to anyone having difficulty.

Review the Selection

UNDERSTAND THE SELECTION

Recall

1. Where is the secret of "The Secret" discovered?
2. Why does the poet love the two girls "most of all"?
3. Explain how the poet knew the girls discovered the secret.

Infer

4. How did the two girls discover the secret?
5. The girls forgot the secret—why isn't that important?
6. Name several other places the secret might be found.
7. Why is the line of poetry described as sudden?

Apply

8. Imagine you discovered the secret of life. What do you think it is? How would you know when you found it? What might make you forget it?
9. Where would you look for the secret of life?
10. Write another title for the poem.

Respond to Literature

This poem says that the secret of life is ours to discover. Why is it important that we do?

WRITE ABOUT THE SELECTION

In "The Secret," the poet describes her own reaction to the girls' discovery. Think about what happens from the two girls' point of view. They read a poem, discover a secret, tell someone about it, and then forget both the poem and the secret. Write a conversation you might have with the girls in which you remind them of and question them about the poem and their discovery.

Prewriting Outline a list of five questions you would like to ask the two girls and what you think their answers would be. Think about how you would try to find out about the secret.

Writing Use your informal outline to write a conversation between yourself and the girls, based on the questions you've thought up.

Revising When you revise what you wrote, make sure the questions are specific. If necessary, reword the questions to make them clearer.

Proofreading Read over your conversation to check for errors. Periods and commas are always placed inside quotation marks. Exclamation points, question marks, and dashes are placed inside quotation marks when they are part of the quotation and outside quotation marks if they are not part of the quotation. Check your writing to see if the quotation marks are placed correctly.

Revising

Make this a cooperative group activity. Divide the class into pairs of students, who will work on this section together. Have the students evaluate each other's questions in terms of specificity, making suggestions that would improve each other's writing.

Proofreading

Select one or two of the students' conversations as models for proofreading. Put the conversations on the overhead projector and have the class suggest improvements.

THINK ABOUT POETIC FORM

The division of a poem into stanzas is only one aspect of poetic form. Each aspect, or element, of the poem except the **substance**—what the poem is about—contributes to the form. Rhythms fall into forms, as do meters. Rhyme scheme, if there is one, is a matter of form. So are length of line, length of poem, each individual image, and the relationship of one image to another. In short, **form** concerns the pattern, or structure, that is used to give expression to what the author wishes to say—to the content, or substance, of the poem.

1. Describe the form of the stanzas in "The Secret."
2. Where is the most important thought of the poem located?
3. Does each stanza contain a single thought or emotion?
4. What is the poet explaining in lines 21 to 35?
5. How would the effect of the poem be changed if the lines were grouped into one long stanza?

> ***Reading Focus***
> **Summarize Text** After you read "The Secret," you summarized it. In one sentence, state the main idea. How did summarizing the poem help you understand its meaning?

DEVELOP YOUR VOCABULARY

What do the words *foreign* and *alien* have in common? They are **synonyms**, meaning that they share the same, or almost the same, meaning.

In daily usage, however, synonyms can carry meanings that are quite different. Consider the noun *speech*, meaning "a talk or address given in public." Synonyms for *speech* include *address*, *oration*, *lecture*, *talk*, and *sermon*. Each of these synonyms means more than the general definition of *speech*. You would expect to hear a lecture in a classroom or a speech at a political meeting, but not in a church, where a sermon might be expected instead.

1. Which of the following are synonyms for *happening*?
   a. schedule　**b.** occurrence　**c.** location　**d.** event
2. Which of the following words are synonyms for *beautiful*?
   a. pretty　**b.** lovely　**c.** wealthy　**d.** abundant

THINK ABOUT POETIC FORM

Answers

1. The poem is made up of four-line stanzas.
2. at the end
3. No, some contain more.
4. her reaction to what happened
5. Sample answer: The poem would be more difficult to understand.

DEVELOP YOUR VOCABULARY

Answers

1. b. occurrence; d. event
2. a. pretty; b. lovely

Reading Focus

Sample Answer

Life holds meaning and secrets for us to discover. Writing the summary helped me understand the poem because I had to look at the poem carefully to separate the main idea from many extra details.

ESL Activity

Have students work in pairs with proficient speakers of English to complete the vocabulary assignment. Encourage students to define all the words and include them in their word banks.

Selection Overview

SELECTION OBJECTIVES

After completing these selections, students will be able to

- define figurative language
- recognize and understand four types of figurative language: personification, onomatopoeia, simile, and metaphor
- use a figure of speech in writing
- write a descriptive paragraph
- use words in other contexts
- paraphrase poetry

Lesson Resources

Snow/Umbilical/Cumulus Clouds

- Selection Synopses, Teacher's Edition, pp. T445c–T445d
- Comprehension and Vocabulary Workbook, pp. 87–88
- Language Enrichment Workbook, p. 67
- Teacher's Resources
  Reinforcement, p. R44
  Test, pp. T87–T88

More About Figurative Language

Review the four types of figures of speech mentioned in the text: personification, onomatopoeia, simile, and metaphor. Inform the class that there are other figures of speech as well, such as hyperbole. Hyperbole is deliberate exaggeration, used to increase the dramatic or humorous effect of a statement. The statement is not meant to be taken literally. For example, a person might be referred to as being "as strong as an ox"; a story is "as old as time," a youngster is "as fresh as a daisy." Point out that while all of these examples involved simile, as seen from the use of *as*, this is not essential to hyperbole. Ask students if they can think of any examples of hyperbole in any of the poems or stories in this unit. Give them some more examples and ask them to think up some of their own.

Learn About

Reading Focus

Paraphrase Poetry When you paraphrase, you restate the speaker's experiences and feelings in your own words. Restating the lines or stanzas of a poem will help you to clarify their meanings. As you read the next three poems, practice paraphrasing the lines of each one.

Figurative Language

Figurative language is language that departs from the original, exact, or literal meaning of words in order to achieve a fresh way of expressing an idea or image. Some types of figurative language are listed below.

Personification is a figure of speech in which inanimate things or abstract ideas are given human qualities or sensibilities.

Onomatopoeia is the use of words whose sounds suggest their meaning. Some examples are *buzz*, *jingle*, *bang*, and *pop*.

Simile is a figure of speech in which one thing is specifically likened to a dissimilar thing; the words *like* or *as* are used in the comparison.

Metaphor is a figure of speech in which two dissimilar things are likened to each other directly, as if one were the other.

As you read the poems, ask yourself:

1. What figures of speech are used in the poems?
2. What fresh impressions do you get from reading the poems?

WRITING CONNECTION

Write four sentences, using a different figure of speech in each.

ESL Activity

Have students complete the Language Enrichment Workbook worksheet, page 67, on personification, onomatopoeia, simile, metaphor, and hyperbole. Ask: Why are these figures of speech used? Do they help people to imagine things?

Cooperative Group Activity

Divide the class into groups of four students for the Writing Connection activity. Each member will be assigned one of the four figures of speech to use in a sentence. They will then pass their papers to the group member on their left, who will write another sentence using their assigned figure of speech. Continue passing the papers until each group member has written one sentence for each of the four types of figures of speech. Have the group collectively review all the sentences for correct usage of each figure of speech. Circulate among the groups to answer questions and make random progress checks. The finished work can be displayed around the classroom for students to compare.

SNOW

by Dorothy Aldis

The fenceposts wear marshmallow hats
On a snowy day;
Bushes in their night gowns
Are kneeling down to pray—
And all the trees have silver skirts
And want to dance away.

December Snow, C.E. Burchfield. Kennedy Galleries, Inc.

TEACHING PLAN

INTRODUCE

Motivation

Ask students to think of common, everyday expressions such as "as big as a house," "dog-tired," "dumber than a post." Explain that these are similes and a metaphor, and that the use of simile and metaphor is not restricted to literature. They are in our everyday speech, although we may not consciously recognize them.

Purpose-Setting Question

Why do writers use simile and metaphor? Why don't they just describe things as they are?

READ

Literary Focus:
Figurative Language

Review the figures of speech introduced in the *Learn About* section on page 454. Tell students to look for these figures of speech as they read the poems.

Reading Focus:
Paraphrase Poetry

Work with the class to paraphrase each of the poems. Allow students to work in pairs or small groups. Have students read their work to each other. After students have paraphrased the poems, have them state the meaning of each one.

CLOSE

Have students complete Review the Selection on pages 458–459.

About the Authors

Dorothy K. Aldis (1896–1966) was born in Chicago, Illinois. A poet and writer of novels, children's verse, and books for youth, her verses have been reprinted hundreds of times in anthologies, collections, and magazines.

Eve Merriam (1916–1995) was born in Philadelphia, Pennsylvania. She lived and worked most of her life in New York City. She was a writer and a producer for radio. She taught creative writing at the university level and composed song lyrics, juvenile biographies, and history books, as well as poetry.

Viewing Fine Art

Charles Burchfield (1893–1967) was an American regionalist painter, whose canvasses pictured small-town homes and streets. Ask: What do you learn about the small town in the United States from this painting?

Discussion

After reading "Umbilical," discuss with the class the meaning of the word *umbilical* as it is used in the poem. Ask for volunteers to suggest the things they could not live without.

Literary Focus: *Figurative Language*

Remind students that onomatopoeia is a kind of figure of speech in which the sound of a word suggests its meaning. Ask them to read the last line of the poem aloud. Discuss the repetition as a kind of onomatopoeia and ask how the word *sOWnd* should be read.

Still Life Radio Tube, Stuart Davis.
The Bettmann Archive

UMBILICAL

by Eve Merriam

You can take away my mother,
you can take away my sister,
but don't take away
my little transistor.

5 I can do without sunshine,
I can do without Spring,
but I can't do without
my ear to that thing.

I can live without water,
10 in a hole in the ground,
but I can't live without
that sound that sound that sound that sOWnd.

---

transistor (tran ZIS tur) here, it means a transistor radio
umbilical (um BIL ih kul) here, necessary for life; from "umbilical cord," which keeps an unborn baby alive

Develop Vocabulary Skills

Review the vocabulary words with the class. Ask for volunteers to use each word in an original sentence.

Viewing Fine Art

Stuart Davis (1894–1964) was an early abstractionist who first exhibited with the pioneers of modern art at the Armory Show in New York in 1913. Davis developed his own style of abstraction, which included many recognizable forms and symbols, like numbers, letters, matchbook covers, and (as seen above) radio tubes. By combining these familiar images in hard-edged, bright-colored compositions, Davis mirrored the United States' machine-oriented culture and widespread advertising. Ask students how many different objects and patterns they can find in the painting.

Cloud World, Dixon. Arizona West Galleries

Cumulus Clouds

by Sheryl Nelms

a gallon of
rich
country cream

hand-whipped
5 into stiff
peaks

flung
from the beater

into dollops
10 across a blue oilcloth

---

cumulus (KYOO myuh lus) a type of rounded, fluffy cloud
dollops (DOL ups) mounds
oilcloth (OIL klawth) waterproofed cloth

Reading Focus: *Paraphrase Poetry*

Ask for volunteers to share examples of the paraphrases they wrote for each of these poems.

Comparing Selections

In each poem, figurative language is used to help the reader visualize an image. Ask: For which poem was it easiest for you to visualize the image? Why?

Critical Thinking: *Analyze*

Call on volunteers to analyze each of the three poems in terms of these questions: To whom is the speaker speaking? What is the message of each poem? How can each poem be characterized? What can we know, or infer, about each poet from her poem?

Viewing Fine Art

In this painting a contemporary artist explores both distance and spatial relationships. The flattening out of the landscape, and the patterning of the cloud formations make this painting simultaneously a surface design and evocation of the vast Southwestern landscape. Like "op" art (or art of optical illusions) the blue between the clouds can be seen as jutting forward or as receding behind the clouds. Ask: How does this painting show the vastness of the landscape?

Mini Quiz

Write the following sentences on the board and call on students to fill in the blanks. Discuss the answers with the class.

1. The ________ wear marshmallow hats.
2. ________ wear nightgowns.
3. The poet can't live without that ________.
4. The clouds described are ________.
5. The country cream is ________.

Answers

1. fenceposts
2. Bushes
3. sound
4. cumulus
5. rich

Review the Selection

UNDERSTAND THE SELECTION

Recall

1. What is described in "Snow"?
2. How is the sky described in "Cumulus Clouds"?
3. What is most important to the person in "Umbilical"?

Infer

4. What general image does Dorothy Aldis use for snow?
5. What color are the clouds?
6. Why are the bushes described as kneeling?
7. Why do you think the last word in "Umbilical" is spelled "sOWnd"?

Apply

8. Imagine a snow-covered field. What is an everyday household object to which you could compare it?
9. Write another title for "Umbilical." Be sure it expresses the poem's meaning.
10. Why do you think the speaker of "Umbilical" says "you can take away my mother" and "sister"?

Respond to Literature

We live in a high-tech society; what does the poem "Umbilical" say about the effect of technology in our lives?

WRITE ABOUT THE SELECTION

To which of your five senses does the imagery in "Cumulus Clouds" appeal? Write a paragraph that describes a day like the one in "Cumulus Clouds." The paragraph should appeal to all five senses.

Prewriting Think about the rest of the scene in the poem—the place, the time of day, the season, the weather—and how it would appeal to each of your five senses. Make a chart with each sense used as a heading. On the left hand side, write down several elements of the setting. Next to the element, under the appropriate heading, write a word which describes the element as it relates to one of the five senses.

Writing Using the words in your chart, write a paragraph-long description of the entire scene as you imagine it.

Revising Try to include as many adjectives in your description as you can to make the scene more vivid. For example, instead of saying "a tree," revise your writing to tell what kind of tree it is.

Proofreading Read over your description to check for errors. Be sure that your adjectives modify nouns and that your adverbs modify verbs, adjectives or other adverbs.

UNDERSTAND THE SELECTION

Answers

1. fenceposts, bushes, trees
2. as a blue oilcloth
3. the transistor
4. clothing
5. The clouds are white.
6. They are bent over from the weight of the snow.
7. Sample answer: The poet is mimicking the sound of someone singing a pop tune, the type of music to which the speaker is probably listening. It may be loud enough to hurt the listener's ears.
8. Sample answer: a blanket
9. Sample answer: "My Radio"
10. Sample answer: to let you know how important the transistor is to him or her

Respond to Literature

Divide the class into groups of four or five students, depending on class size. Ask each group to come up with a list of five effects of technology on our lives which are positive, and five effects of technology which are negative. Set a time limit for this activity.

Have the groups read their lists to the rest of the class. After each, discuss the validity of the point made.

WRITE ABOUT THE SELECTION

Prewriting

Students are to work on this section individually. You may wish to draw a chart showing the five senses on the board so that the class has an example to follow to better understand the directions.

Writing

Students are to write their descriptive paragraph independently, using the charts they have drawn up. Go around the class helping any students having difficulty.

Revising

Make this a cooperative group activity. Divide the class into pairs of students and have them read each other's paragraphs. Ask them to write (in pencil) suggested additional adjectives in the appropriate places in each other's work. Ask those who suggested additional adjectives to explain their suggestions and how the writing might be improved.

Proofreading

Have students return each other's papers. Select one or two of the students' paragraphs as models for proofreading. Put the paragraphs on the overhead projector and have the class suggest improvements

ESL Activity

Work with small groups to complete the prewriting phase. Have students describe the present day rather than one they remember. Help them find and list appropriate words for their sensory descriptions.

THINK ABOUT FIGURES OF SPEECH

Figures of speech help to clarify and illustrate ideas. They make writing more vivid and give life to inanimate objects. They aid readers in making new associations. A figure of speech is sometimes so essential to a poem that to remove it would destroy the poem.

1. When Aldis says that fenceposts wear hats she is using what figure of speech? Name two other examples of this figure of speech in her poem.
2. The title "Umbilical" is an example of which figure of speech? What comparison is implied in the title?
3. Why does the poet spell the last *sound* in "Umbilical" as *sOWnd*?
4. The entire third poem is an extended metaphor for what two things?
5. Are there any similes in the three poems? If so, where are they?

Reading Focus

Paraphrase Poetry You have paraphrased the poems you just read. In your own words, state how paraphrasing helped to clarify the poems' meanings for you.

DEVELOP YOUR VOCABULARY

There are many ways in which the vocabulary of English has expanded. One way is by the addition of new words to the language. Another is by adding new meanings to existing words. Many words have gained new meanings by way of **metaphor**. The process is simple: a word used in one context is applied, by its similarity, to an object in another context. This is how names of parts of the body came to be applied to so many other things. Examples are the *arms* and *legs* of a chair, the *hands* and *face* of a clock, or the *eye* of a potato.

In the following sentences, all of the items *except one* are correct. Which item in each sentence is the incorrect one?

1. *Saws*, *rakes*, *gears*, and *rivers* have teeth.
2. A *drum*, *beet*, *hammer*, and a *pin* have a head.
3. A *bottle*, *violin*, *bale of hay*, and a *person* have a neck.
4. A *laundry bag*, *bed*, *book page*, and a *hill* have a foot.

THINK ABOUT FIGURES OF SPEECH

Answers

1. personification, suggested responses: bushes that wear nightgowns, trees that have skirts, and trees that want to dance
2. metaphor; the poet likens her linkage to the radio to the linkage of a dependent child on his or her mother
3. Sample answer: It is onomatopoeic for the sound of a radio or of a pop singer on the radio, and it also represents the volume of sound as painful to the ear.
4. clouds and sky
5. No, there are none.

DEVELOP YOUR VOCABULARY

Answers

1. rivers
2. beet
3. bale of hay
4. laundry bag

Reading Focus

Sample Answer

Rewording the poems made it necessary to look at the meaning of each word carefully and think about how the poet intended it to be used. This helped to focus on the meaning of the poems.

Selection Overview

SELECTION OBJECTIVES

After completing this selection, students will be able to

- define *motive* and give examples of it from the story
- write a paragraph to explain a personal motive
- interview a subject and write a newspaper article based on the interview
- use quotation marks correctly
- analyze how suffixes change word meanings
- use word identification

Lesson Resources

Two Kinds
- Selection Synopsis, Teacher's Edition, T445d
- Comprehension and Vocabulary Workbook, pp. 89–90
- Language Enrichment Workbook, p. 68
- Teacher's Resources
  Reinforcement, p. R45
  Tests, pp. T89–T90

More About Motive

Tell students that most people are interested to know what makes other people behave as they do. Bring in a newspaper or magazine article that describes a situation in which a person has reacted in an unusual way. Ask students to speculate on the reason or reasons for the behavior. Discuss with students whether the reasons were internal or were the result of outside physical forces.

About the Author

Amy Tan (1952–), is a contemporary U.S. writer whose novels often describe the tension between mothers and daughters. "Two Kinds" is taken from Tan's first novel *The Joy Luck Club* (1989) which won The National Book Award. In 1993 the novel was made into a major motion picture. Tan's work has been translated into twenty languages.

Learn About

READING FOCUS

Use Word Identification What do you do when you encounter a word you do not understand? A dictionary may not always be close at hand. Therefore, it is helpful to know how to figure out word meanings. To do this, break the word down into prefixes, suffixes, roots, and other words with which you are familiar. As you encounter unfamiliar words, ask yourself:

1. Which parts of this word look familiar?
2. What are the meanings of the recognizable word parts?
3. What can I infer is the meaning of the whole word?

CHARACTERS' MOTIVES

A **motive** is an emotion or reason that causes a character to behave in a certain way. A motive may also cause an action to occur. There may even be more than one motive behind a character's actions.

The motive may come about as a result of outside forces. It may be a deep impulse within a person.

An author does not always clearly state characters' motive. Often you must read between the lines to identify it.

As you read this selection, ask yourself:

1. Why is the character behaving as she does?
2. Are the causes of her behavior internal or external?

WRITING CONNECTION

Write a short paragraph describing how you behaved in a specific social situation. What external or internal motives caused your behavior?

ESL Activity

Some students may have difficulty getting started with the Writing Connection activity. If so, pair students and ask them to brainstorm some experiences. Next, have them compose a topic sentence. Then ask partners to work individually. When their paragraphs are complete, ask partners to check each other's work and make suggestions for improvement.

Cooperative Group Activity

Before students begin their paragraphs, tell them they will share their writing with classmates. After students have completed the Writing Connection activity, divide the class into small groups. Have each group member share his or her paragraph with the group. Ask groups to discuss the similarities and differences in their motives.

TWO KINDS

from The Joy Luck Club

by Amy Tan

My mother believed you could be anything you wanted to be in America. You could open a restaurant. You could work for the government and get good retirement. You could buy a house with almost no money down. You could become rich. You could become instantly famous.

"Of course you can be prodigy, too," my mother told me when I was nine. "You can be best anything. What does Auntie Lindo know? Her daughter, she is only best tricky."

America was where all my mother's hopes lay. She had come here in 1949 after losing everything in China: her mother and father, her family home, her first husband, and two daughters, twin baby girls. But she never looked back with regret. There were so many ways for things to get better.

We didn't immediately pick the right kind of prodigy. At first my mother thought I could be a Chinese Shirley Temple. We'd watch Shirley's old movies on TV as though they were training films. My mother would poke my arm and say, "*Ni kan*" — You watch. And I would see Shirley tapping her feet, or singing a sailor song, or pursing her lips into a very round O while saying, "Oh my goodness."

"*Ni kan*," said my mother as Shirley's eyes flooded with tears. "You already know how. Don't need talent for crying!"

Soon after my mother got this idea about Shirley Temple, she took me to a beauty training school in the Mission district and put me in the hands of a student who could barely hold the scissors without shaking. Instead of getting big fat curls, I emerged with an uneven mass of crinkly black fuzz. My mother dragged me off to the bathroom and tried to wet down my hair.

"You look like Negro Chinese," she lamented, as if I had done this on purpose.

The instructor of the beauty training school had to lop off these soggy clumps to make my hair even again. "Peter Pan is very popular these days," the instructor assured my mother. I now had hair the length of a boy's, with straight-across bangs that hung at a slant two inches above my eyebrows. I liked the haircut and it made me actually look forward to my future fame.

In fact, in the beginning, I was just as excited as my mother, maybe even more so.

---

prodigy (PRAHD uh jee) a child remarkably bright in some way

Teaching Plan

INTRODUCE

Motivation

Point out that the mother in "Two Kinds" was born in China. Then ask a volunteer to read the first three paragraphs of the story. Ask: Do you think people who are born in the United States have the same expectations of this country as people who are foreign-born? Do you think immigrants expect too much of the United States? Have students explain their responses.

Purpose-Setting Question

Is it possible for someone to expect too much of another person?

READ

Literary Focus: *Characters' Motives*

To help students better understand the characters' motives in "Two Kinds," have them make a graphic organizer labeled *cause* and *effect*. As they read, suggest they answer each question in the *Learn About* section on page 460 for each character in the story. Answers to question one belong in the *cause* column and the description of the character's reaction belongs in the *effect* column.

Reading Focus: *Use Word Identification*

Have students list unfamiliar words in their journals as they read. Suggest students work with partners to break the words into parts using a three-column chart labeled: *prefix*, *root*, *suffix*. Have them try to infer meaning of the longer word by looking at the different parts. Encourage students to check their definitions with the dictionary. To model the exercise, write the word *unspeakable* on the board. Have students break the word into parts, define each part, and define the word.

CLOSE

Have students complete Review the Selection on pages 470-471.

Develop Vocabulary Skills

Review the footnoted vocabulary words, their pronunciations, and their definitions. Use each word in a complete sentence and indicate the part of speech. Then challenge students to use other forms of the words in original sentences.

Reading Focus:
Use Word Identification
Have students find a word whose meaning they do not understand. Help them break the word into word parts and fill out their charts. Then have them try to infer the meaning of the longer word by looking at their charts. Remind students that they can check their definitions with the dictionary.

I pictured this prodigy part of me as many different images, trying each one on for size. I was a dainty ballerina girl standing by the curtains waiting to hear the right music that would send me floating on my tiptoes. I was like the Christ child lifted out of the straw manger, crying with holy indignity. I was Cinderella stepping from her pumpkin carriage with sparkly cartoon music filling the air.

In all of my imaginings, I was filled with a sense that I would soon become *perfect*. My mother and father would adore me. I would be beyond reproach. I would never feel the need to sulk for anything.

But sometimes the prodigy in me became impatient. If you don't hurry up and get me out here, I'm disappearing for good," it warned. "And then you'll always be nothing."

Every night after dinner, my mother and I would sit at the Formica kitchen table. She would present new tests, taking her examples from stories of amazing children she had read in *Ripley's Believe It or Not*, or *Good Housekeeping*, *Reader's Digest*, and a dozen other magazines she kept in a pile in our bathroom. My mother got these magazines from people whose houses she cleaned. And since she cleaned many houses each week, we had a great assortment. She would look through them all, searching for stories about remarkable children.

The first night she brought out a story about a three-year-old boy who knew the capitals of all the states and even most of the European countries. A teacher was quoted as saying the little boy could also pronounce the names of the foreign cities correctly.

"What's the capital of Finland?" my mother asked me, looking at the magazine story.

All I knew was the capital of California, because Sacramento was the name of the street we lived on in Chinatown. "Nairobi!" I guessed, saying the most foreign word I could think of. She checked to see if that was possibly one way to pronounce "Helsinki" before showing me the answer.

The tests got harder—multiplying numbers in my head, finding the queen of hearts in a deck of cards, trying to stand on my head without using my hands, predicting the daily temperatures in Los Angeles, New York, and London.

One night I had to look at a page from the Bible for three minutes and then report everything I could remember. "Now Jehoshaphat had riches and honor in abundance and . . . that's all I remember, Ma," I said.

And after seeing my mother's disappointed face once again, something inside of me began to die. I hated the tests, the raised hopes and failed expectations. Before going to bed that night, I looked in the mirror above the bathroom sink and when I saw only my face staring back—and that it would always be this ordinary face—I began to cry. Such a sad, ugly girl! I made high-pitched noises like a crazed animal, trying to scratch out the face in the mirror.

Formica (for MY kuh) trade name for heat-resistant plastic

And then I saw what seemed to be the prodigy side of me—because I had never seen that face before. I looked at my reflection, blinking so I could see more clearly. The girl staring back at me was angry, powerful. This girl and I were the same. I had new thoughts, willful thoughts, or rather thoughts filled with lots of won'ts. I won't let her change me, I promised myself. I won't be what I'm not.

So now on nights when my mother presented her tests, I performed listlessly, my head propped on one arm. I pretended to be bored. And I was. I got so bored I started counting bellows of the foghorns out on the bay while my mother drilled me in other areas. The sound was comforting and reminded me of the cow jumping over the moon. And the next day, I played a game with myself, seeing if my mother would give up on me before eight bellows. After a while I usually counted only one, maybe two bellows at most. At last she was beginning to give up hope.

Two or three months had gone by without any mention of my being a prodigy again. And then one day my mother was watching *The Ed Sullivan Show* on TV. The TV was old and the sound kept shorting out. Every time my mother got halfway up from the sofa to adjust the set, the sound would go back on and Ed would be talking. As soon as she sat down, Ed would go silent again. She got up, the TV broke into loud piano music. She sat down. Silence. Up and down, back and forth, quiet and loud. It was like a stiff embraceless dance between her and the TV set. Finally she stood by the set with her hand on the sound dial.

She seemed entranced by the music, a little frenzied piano piece with this mesmerizing quality, sort of quick passages and then teasing lilting ones before it returned to the quick playful parts.

"*Ni kan*," my mother said, calling me over with hurried hand gestures, "Look here."

I could see why my mother was fascinated by the music. It was being pounded out by a little Chinese girl, about nine years old, with a Peter Pan haircut. The girl had the sauciness of Shirley Temple. She was proudly modest like a proper Chinese child. And she also did this fancy sweep of a curtsy, so that the fluffy skirt of her white dress cascaded slowly to the floor like the petals of a large carnation.

In spite of these warning signs, I wasn't worried. Our family had no piano and we couldn't afford to buy one, let alone reams of sheet music and piano lessons. So I could be generous in my comments when my mother bad-mouthed the little girl on TV.

"Play note right, but doesn't sound good! No singing sound," complained my mother.

"What are you picking on her for?" I said carelessly. "She's pretty good. Maybe she's not the best, but she's trying hard." I knew almost immediately I would be sorry I said that.

---

bellows (BEHL ohz) roars; loud noises
mesmerizing (MEHZ muh ry zing) hypotizing; casting a spell
sauciness (SAH see nuhs) state of being bold or rude
cascaded (kas KAY dihd) flowed down like a small waterfall

Critical Thinking: *Analyze*

Ask: Why do you think the narrator's attitude toward herself changes?

Literary Focus: *Characters' Motives*

Ask: What was the narrator's motive for performing badly on her mother's tests?

Literary Focus: *Characters' Motives*

Ask: What dialogue on this page states the mother's motive for making her daughter take piano lessons? What is the cause of her behavior?

Discussion

Ask: What generalization does the narrator make about Mr. Chong? How did you identify this generalization? Are most generalizations untrue? Explain.

"Just like you," she said. "Not the best. Because you not trying." She gave a little huff as she let go of the sound dial and sat down on the sofa.

The little Chinese girl sat down also to play an encore of "Anitra's Dance" by Grieg. I remember the song, because later on I had to learn how to play it.

Three days after watching *The Ed Sullivan Show,* my mother told me what my schedule would be for piano lessons and piano practice. She had talked to Mr. Chong, who lived on the first floor of our apartment building. Mr. Chong was a retired piano teacher and my mother had traded housecleaning services for weekly lessons and a piano for me to practice on every day, two hours a day, from four to six.

When my mother told me this, I felt as though I had been sent to hell. I whined and then kicked my foot a little when I couldn't stand it anymore.

"Why don't you like me the way I am? I'm *not* a genius! I can't play the piano. And even if I could, I wouldn't go on TV if you paid me a million dollars!" I cried.

My mother slapped me. "Who ask you be genius?" she shouted. "Only ask you be your best. For your sake. You think I want you be genius? Hnnh! What for! Who ask you!"

"So ungrateful," I heard her mutter in Chinese. "If she had as much talent as she has temper, she would be famous now."

Mr. Chong, whom I secretly nicknamed Old Chong, was very strange, always tapping his fingers to the silent music of an invisible orchestra. He looked ancient in my eyes. He had lost most of his hair on top of his head and he wore thick glasses and had eyes that always looked tired and sleepy. But he must have been younger than I thought, since he lived with his mother and was not yet married.

I met Old Lady Chong once and that was enough. She had this peculiar smell like a baby that had done something in its pants. And her fingers felt like a dead person's, like an old peach I once found in the back of the refrigerator; the skin just slid off the meat when I picked it up.

I soon found out why Old Chong had retired from teaching piano. He was deaf. "Like Beethoven!" he shouted to me. "We're both listening only in our head!" And he would start to conduct his frantic silent sonatas.

Our lessons went like this. He would open the book and point to the different things, explaining their purpose: "Key! Treble! Bass! No sharps or flats! So this is C major! Listen now and play after me!"

And then he would play the C scale a few times, a simple chord, and then, as if inspired by an old, unreachable itch, he gradually added more notes and running trills and a pounding bass until the music was really something quite grand.

I would play after him, the simple scale, the simple chord, and then I played some nonsense that sounded like a cat running up and down on top of garbage cans.

---

sonatas (suh NAH tuhs) compositions for one or two musical instruments

Old Chong smiled and applauded and then said, "Very good! But now you must learn to keep time!"

So that's how I discovered that Old Chong's eyes were too slow to keep up with the wrong notes I was playing. He went through the motions in half-time. To help me keep rhythm, he stood behind me, pushing down on my right shoulder for every beat. He balanced pennies on top of my wrists so I would keep them still as I slowly played scales and arpeggios. He had me curve my hand around an apple and keep that shape when playing chords. He marched stiffly to show me how to make each finger dance up and down, staccato like an obedient little soldier.

He taught me all of these things, and that was how I also learned I could be lazy and get away with mistakes, lots of mistakes. If I hit the wrong notes because I hadn't practiced enough, I never corrected myself. I just kept playing in rhythm. And Old Chong kept conducting his own private reverie.

So maybe I never really gave myself a fair chance. I did pick up the basics pretty quickly, and I might have become a good pianist at that young age. But I was so determined not to try, not to be anybody different that I learned to play only the most ear-splitting preludes, the most discordant hymns.

Over the next year, I practiced like this, dutifully in my own way. And then one day I heard my mother and her friend Lindo Jong both talking in a loud bragging tone of voice so others could hear. It was after church, and I was leaning against the brick wall wearing a dress with stiff white petticoats. Auntie Lindo's daughter, Waverly, who was about my age, was standing farther down the wall about five feet away. We had grown up together and shared all the closeness of two sisters squabbling over crayons and dolls. In other words, for the most part, we hated each other. I thought she was snotty. Waverly Jong had gained a certain amount of fame as "Chinatown's little Chinese Chess Champion."

"She bring home too many trophy," lamented Auntie Lindo that Sunday. "All day she play chess. All day I have no time do nothing but dust off her winnings." She threw a scolding look at Waverly, who pretended not to see her.

"You lucky you don't have this problem," said Aunt Lindo with a sigh to my mother.

And my mother squared her shoulders and bragged: "Our problem worser than yours. If we ask Jing-mei wash dish, she hear nothing but music. It's like you can't stop this natural talent."

And right then, I was determined to put a stop to her foolish pride.

A few weeks later, Old Chong and my mother conspired to have me play in a talent show which would be held in the

---

arpeggios (ahr PEHJ ee ohz) notes in a chord played in quick succession
staccato (stuh KAHT oh) music played with distinct breaks between notes
reverie (REHV uh ree) dreamy thoughts of pleasant things
petticoats (PEHT ee kohts) lace or ruffles on the bottom of a skirt
spinet (SPIHN it) small piano

Reading Focus: *Use Word Identification*

Point out the word *discordant*. Ask volunteers to name and define the word parts as they list them on their charts. Then ask several students to use the word in an original sentence.

Literary Focus: *Characters' Motives*

The narrator states that she intends to put a stop to her mother's foolish pride. Ask: How can you interpret this statement as foreshadowing? How can it reveal a motive for future behavior?

Critical Thinking: *Infer*

Ask: What is significant about the title of the piece the narrator is to play at the talent show?

Background Notes

The Joy Luck Club referred to in the story was a group of four Chinese mothers with American-born daughters. They met on a regular basis to socialize, play games, and reminisce about the past.

church hall. By then, my parents had saved up enough to buy me a secondhand piano, a black Wurlitzer spinet with a scarred bench. It was the showpiece of our living room.

For the talent show, I was to play a piece called "Pleading Child" from Schumann's *Scenes from Childhood*. It was a simple, moody piece that sounded more difficult than it was. I was supposed to memorize the whole thing, playing the repeat parts twice to make the piece sound longer. But I dawdled over it, playing a few bars and then cheating, looking up to see what notes followed. I never really listened to what I was playing. I daydreamed about being somewhere else, about being someone else.

The part I liked to practice best was the fancy curtsy: right foot out, touch the rose on the carpet with a pointed foot, sweep to the side, left leg bends, look up and smile.

My parents invited all the couples from the Joy Luck Club to witness my debut. Auntie Lindo and Uncle Tin were there. Waverly and her two older brothers had also come. The first two rows were filled with children both younger and older than I was. The littlest ones got to go first. They recited simple nursery rhymes, squawked out tunes on miniature violins, twirled Hula Hoops, pranced in pink ballet tutus, and when they bowed or curtsied, the audience would sigh in unison, "Awww," and then clap enthusiastically.

When my turn came, I was very confident. I remember my childish excitement. It was as if I knew, without a doubt, that the prodigy side of me really did exist. I had no fear whatsoever, no nervousness. I remember thinking to myself, This is it! This is it! I looked out over the audience, at my mother's blank face, my father's yawn, Auntie Lindo's stiff-lipped smile, Waverly's sulky expression. I had on a white dress layered with sheets of lace, and a pink bow in my Peter Pan haircut. As I sat down I envisioned people jumping to their feet and Ed Sullivan rushing up to introduce me to everyone on TV.

And I started to play. It was so beautiful. I was so caught up in how lovely I looked at first I didn't worry how I would sound. So it was a surprise to me when I hit the first wrong note and I realized something didn't sound quite right. And then I hit another and another followed that. A chill started at the top of my head and began to trickle down. Yet I couldn't stop playing, as though my hands were bewitched. I kept thinking my fingers would adjust themselves back, like a train switching to the right track. I played this strange jumble through two repeats, the sour notes staying with me all the way to the end.

When I stood up, I discovered my legs were shaking. Maybe I had just been nervous and the audience, like Old Chong, had seen me go through the right motions and had not heard anything wrong at all. I swept my foot out, went down on my knee, looked up and smiled. The room was quiet, except for Old Chong, who was beaming and shouting,

---

Joy Luck Club (JOY LUK KLUB) a group of women who met to play games and tell stories

"Bravo! Bravo! Well done!" But then I saw my mother's face, her stricken face. The audience clapped weakly, and as I walked back to my chair, with my whole face quivering as I tried not to cry, I heard a little boy whisper loudly to his mother, "That was awful," and the mother whispered back, "Well, she certainly tried."

And now I realized how many people were in the audience, the whole world it seemed. I was aware of eyes burning into my back. I felt the shame of my mother and father as they sat stiffly throughout the rest of the show.

We could have escaped during intermission. Pride and some strange sense of honor must have anchored my parents to their chairs. And so we watched it all: the eighteen-year-old boy with a fake mustache who did a magic show and juggled flaming hoops while riding a unicycle. The breasted girl with white makeup who sang from *Madama Butterfly* and got honorable mention. And the eleven-year-old boy who won first prize playing a tricky violin song that sounded like a busy bee.

After the show, the Hsus, the Jongs, and the St. Clairs from the Joy Luck Club came up to my mother and father.

"Lots of talented kids," Auntie Lindo said vaguely, smiling broadly.

"That was somethin' else," said my father, and I wondered if he was referring to me in a humorous way, or whether he even remembered what I had done.

Waverly looked at me and shrugged her shoulders. "You aren't a genius like me," she said matter-of-factly. And if I hadn't felt so bad, I would have pulled her braids and punched her stomach.

But my mother's expression was what devastated me: a quiet, blank look that said she had lost everything. I felt the same way, and it seemed as if everybody were now coming up, like gawkers at the scene of an accident, to see what parts were actually missing. When we got on the bus to go home, my father was humming the busy-bee tune and my mother was silent. I kept thinking she wanted to wait until we got home before shouting at me. But when my father unlocked the door to our apartment, my mother walked in and then went to the back, into the bedroom. No accusations. No blame. And in a way, I felt disappointed, I had been waiting for her to start shouting, so I could shout back and cry and blame her for all my misery.

I assumed the talent-show fiasco meant I never had to play the piano again. But two days later, after school, my mother came out of the kitchen and saw me watching TV.

"Four clock," she reminded me as if it were any other day. I was stunned, as though she were asking me to go through the talent-show torture again. I wedged myself more tightly in front of the TV.

"Turn off TV," she called from the kitchen five minutes later.

I didn't budge. And then I decided. I didn't have to do what my mother said

---

accusations (AK yoo ZAY shuhnz) charges of wrongdoing
fiasco (fee AS koh) a humiliating failure

Critical Thinking:
Draw Conclusions
Ask: Do you think the narrator had a realistic attitude toward her performance? What story clues helped you reach your conclusion?

Reading Focus:
Use Word Identification
Ask students to figure out the meaning of *accusation*. Ask them: What does *accuse* mean? What is the function of the *-tion* suffix?

Literary Focus:
Characters' Motives
Ask: What motive does the narrator state for wanting her mother to scold her? Why is it more comfortable to blame someone else, rather than yourself, for your problems?

Literary Focus: *Characters' Motives*

Ask: What factors may have driven the mother to want great things from her daughter? Were these expectations realistic? Were they fair? Explain.

Discussion

In some cultures, absolute obedience is expected and given. Ask: Why would this fact cause conflict between the narrator and her mother?

anymore. I wasn't her slave. This wasn't China. I had listened to her before and look what happened. She was the stupid one.

She came out of the kitchen and stood in the arched entryway of the living room. "Four clock," she said once again, louder.

"I'm not going to play anymore," I said nonchalantly. "Why should I? I'm not a genius."

She walked over and stood in front of the TV. I saw her chest was heaving up and down in an angry way.

"No!" I said, and I now felt stronger, as if my true self had finally emerged. So this was what had been inside me all along.

"No! I won't!" I screamed.

She yanked me by the arm, pulled me off the floor, snapped off the TV. She was frighteningly strong, half pulling, half carrying me toward the piano as I kicked the throw rugs under my feet. She lifted me up onto the hard bench. I was sobbing now, looking at her bitterly. Her chest was heaving even more and her mouth was open, smiling crazily as if she were pleased I was crying.

"You want me to be someone that I'm not!" I sobbed. "I'll never be the kind of daughter you want me to be!"

"Only two kinds of daughters," she shouted in Chinese. "Those who are obedient and those who follow their own mind! Only one kind of daughter can live in this house. Obedient daughter!"

"Then I wish I wasn't your daughter. I wish you weren't my mother," I shouted. As I said these things I got scared. It felt like worms and toads and slimy things crawling out of my chest, but it also felt good, as if this awful side of me had surfaced, at last.

"Too late change this," said my mother shrilly.

And I could sense her anger rising to its breaking point. I wanted to see it spill over. And that's when I remembered the babies she had lost in China, the ones we never talked about. "Then I wish I'd never been born!" I shouted. "I wish I were dead! Like them."

It was as if I had said the magic words. Alakazam!—and her face went blank, her mouth closed, her arms went slack, and she backed out of the room, stunned, as if she were blowing away like a small brown leaf, thin, brittle, lifeless.

It was not the only disappointment my mother felt in me. In the years that followed, I failed her so many times, each time asserting my own will, my right to fall short of expectations. I didn't get straight A's. I didn't become class president. I didn't get into Stanford. I dropped out of college.

For unlike my mother, I did not believe I could be anything I wanted to be. I could only be me.

And for all those years, we never talked about the disaster at the recital or my terrible accusations afterward at the piano bench. All that remained unchecked, like a betrayal that was now unspeakable. So I never found a way to ask her why she had hoped for something so large that failure was inevitable.

And even worse, I never asked her what frightened me the most: Why had she given up hope?

For after our struggle at the piano, she never mentioned my playing again. The lessons stopped. The lid to the piano was closed, shutting out the dust, my misery, and her dreams.

So she surprised me. A few years ago, she offered to give me the piano, for my thirtieth birthday. I had not played in all those years. I saw the offer as a sign of forgiveness, a tremendous burden removed.

"Are you sure?" I asked shyly. "I mean, won't you and Dad miss it?"

"No, this is your piano," she said firmly. "Always your piano. You only one can play."

"Well, I probably can't play anymore," I said. "It's been years."

"You pick up fast," said my mother, as if she knew this was certain. "You have a natural talent. You could be genius if you want to."

"No I couldn't."

"You just not trying," said my mother. And she was neither angry nor sad. She said it as to announce a fact that could never be disproved. "Take it," she said.

But I didn't at first. It was enough that she offered it to me. And after that, every time I saw it in my parents' living room, standing in front of the bay windows, it made me feel proud, as if it were a shiny trophy I had won back.

Last week I sent a tuner over to my parents' apartment and had the piano reconditioned, for purely sentimental reasons. My mother had died a few months before and I had been getting things in order for my father, a little bit at a time. I put the jewelry in special silk pouches. The sweaters she had knitted in yellow, pink, bright orange—all the colors I hated—I put those in moth-proof boxes. I found some old Chinese silk dresses, the kind with little slits up the sides. I rubbed the old silk against my skin, then wrapped them in tissue and decided to take them home with me.

After I had the piano tuned, I opened the lid and touched the keys. It sounded even richer than I remembered. Really, it was a very good piano. Inside the bench were the same exercise notes with handwritten scales, the same secondhand music books with their covers held together with yellow tape.

I opened up the Schumann book to the dark little piece I had played at the recital. It was on the left-hand side of the page, "Pleading Child." It looked more difficult than I remembered. I played a few bars, surprised at how easily the notes came back to me.

And for the first time, or so it seemed, I noticed the piece on the right-hand side. It was called "Perfectly Contented." I tried to play this one as well. It had a lighter melody but the same flowing rhythm and turned out to be quite easy. "Pleading Child" was shorter but slower; "Perfectly Contented" was longer, but faster. And after I played them both a few times, I realized they were two halves of the same song.

---

disproved (dis PROOVD) shown to be incorrect or false

Critical Thinking: *Analyze*

Ask: Why do you think the mother no longer insisted on piano lessons for her daughter?

Mini Quiz

Write these sentences on the board or overhead transparency. Then call on students to fill in the blanks. Discuss the answers with the class.

1. The mother wanted her daughter to become a ________.
2. The piano teacher's name was ________.
3. The narrator performed at a ________ ________.
4. The mother said that daughters are of two kinds: those who follow their own minds and those who are ________.
5. The mother offered her daughter the ________ for her 30th birthday.

Answers

1. prodigy
2. Mr. Chong
3. talent show
4. obedient
5. piano

UNDERSTAND THE SELECTION

Answers

1. She cleans Mr. Chong's house in exchange for lessons and access to a piano.
2. Old Chong
3. Sample answer: She is ashamed and quiet.
4. Sample answer: She feels that people can become whatever they want if they do their best.
5. Sample answer: She resents him. She gives him an unflattering nickname and takes advantage of his disabilities.
6. Sample answer: She thinks that she had the kind of daughter who follows her own mind.
7. Sample answer: He probably isn't. The narrator indicates he probably doesn't remember her performance.
8. Answers will depend on personal experience and personality.
9. Sample answer: Some common conflicts are disagreements about curfews, grades, and choice of friends.
10. Sample answer: A good mother should have unselfish love for her children and want the best for them. A good daughter should be truthful and loving.

Respond to Literature

Ask students to list things causing tension between the mother and daughter. They may include: differences in culture mother grew up in, different interests, individual personalities, age difference.

Review the Selection

UNDERSTAND THE SELECTION

Recall

1. How did the mother pay for her daughter's piano lessons?
2. What did the narrator call her piano teacher?
3. Describe the mother's reaction to her daughter's performance.

Infer

4. How are the mother's hopes for her daughter a reflection of her attitude toward the United States?
5. What is the narrator's attitude toward Mr. Chong? How do you know?
6. In the mother's opinion, what kind of daughter is the narrator?
7. Was the father involved in his daughter's life? Explain.

Apply

8. When someone has high expectations for you, are you motivated to do your best or to give up?
9. What are some common conflicts that arise between young people and their parents or guardians?
10. What are two qualities of a good mother? A good daughter?

Respond to Literature

What causes tension between the mother and daughter in "Two Kinds"?

WRITE ABOUT THE SELECTION

The mother in "Two Kinds" has lived in China and the United States. She is an eyewitness to the differences—cultural, physical, and economic—between these countries.

For this assignment you are to be a newspaper reporter assigned to interview the mother for a story. Newspaper stories usually include information that answers these questions: *Who? What? Where? When? Why? How?* Write a brief newspaper article about an interview with the mother.

Prewriting Think of as many questions as you can that you would like to ask the mother. Be sure that you address the six questions mentioned above. Choose the ten most important questions and number them. Then, answer them as you think the mother would.

Writing In a brief article, write an account of your interview with the mother, based on the ten questions. Use prewriting questions, and write what you think the mother's answers would be.

Revising One way to make your interview subject seem more like a real person is to tell your reader what the subject looks like and how she acts. Add a description of the mother to your article.

Proofreading Read over your article to check for errors. Remember that quotation marks enclose direct quotations. Indirect quotations do not require quotation marks.

WRITE ABOUT THE SELECTION

Prewriting

Make this a cooperative group activity. Have the class as a whole brainstorm questions that could be asked. Encourage students to say whatever they are thinking without worrying about being correct, incorrect, or off-target. Have two volunteers write the suggestions on the board as the rest of the class says them. The suggestions can be used as a basis for this section.

Writing

Have students work on this section individually. They should synthesize their prewriting material into an article and use quotes.

Revising

Have students work on this section with partners. They may be allowed to refer to the story for details.

Proofreading

Have pairs exchange articles and check each other's work. They should circle incorrect punctuation with a pencil and write the corrections for the writers to see.

THINK ABOUT MOTIVE

Writers reveal characters' motives as a means of creating round, more complete characters. Identifying and analyzing these motives help the reader gain insight into the character's personality.

1. What are the mother's motives for wanting her daughter to be a prodigy?
2. What do these motives reveal about the mother's personality?
3. What is the narrator's motive for refusing to master the piano?
4. What does her refusal to play the piano reveal about her personality?
5. Is the daughter driven by outside forces, or does a deeper impulse explain her behavior? Explain.

> *READING FOCUS*
> **Use Word Identification** Choose two words from the selection that were unfamiliar to you. List and define the word parts. Then define the complete word. Next, use each word in a sentence about the story.

DEVELOP YOUR VOCABULARY

A suffix is a word part added to the end of a base word to make a new word. By adding a suffix to a root, or base, word, you can change the meaning. For example, the word *care* means "to feel an interest or worry." When you add the suffix *–less* to the root word to make *careless*, the meaning is the opposite, or "done without care." More than one suffix can be added to the same word, such as *care*, *careless*, *carelessly*.

The words below came from the story. Identify and define each root word within the longer word. Then identify the suffix or suffixes and meaning of the longer word. Use the longer word in an original sentence.

Suffixes	Meaning
-ful	full of
-ly	in a certain way
-ness	the condition that is

1. carelessly
2. enthusiastically
3. nervousness
4. frighteningly
5. instantly
6. powerful

READING FOCUS

Sample Answer

Expectation: expect (to look forward to); *-ation* (noun-forming suffix); Expectation means something expected. *Memorize*: memor(y) (something kept in mind); *-ize* (make); Memorize means to commit to memory. The daughter had a difficult time meeting her mother's *expectations*. The daughter was supposed to *memorize* her piano piece for the talent show.

> **ESL Activity**
> You may want to pair students to complete the Vocabulary activity. Have partners work together to find the recognizable parts of the words. Ask them to guess at meanings and then check them in the dictionary.

THINK ABOUT MOTIVE

Answers

1. She wants the best for her daughter, but she also wants her daughter to make her proud. She is motivated to live by the values of her Chinese culture.
2. She is an authoritarian but loving parent. She still values the Chinese customs and ideals.
3. She is motivated by her need to find her own way. She does not want her mother dictating what she should put her best work into.
4. She is independent and obstinate. She doesn't want to be managed.
5. The daughter is driven by outside forces, mainly the desire to please her mother. However, she has a deeper impulse of needing to be her own person.

DEVELOP YOUR VOCABULARY

Answers

1. *carelessly*—root: *care*; "to feel an interest or worry"; suffixes: *-less*, *-ly*; "to do something without worry." She performed her work *carelessly*, as if she didn't care.
2. *enthusiastically*—root: *enthuse*; "to show a strong liking"; suffixes: *-ic*, *-al*, *-ly*; "a strong liking or interest." The fans shouted *enthusiastically*.
3. *nervousness*—root: *nerve*; "fibers within the brain and spinal cord; suffixes: *-ous*, *-ness*; "restless and easily annoyed or frustrated"; The suspect displayed no *nervousness*.
4. *frighteningly*—root: *fright*; "sudden fear"; suffixes: *-en*, *-ing*, *-ly*; "to cause sudden fear"; The car came *frighteningly* close.
5. *instantly*—root: *instant*; "soon to happen"; suffix: *-ly*; "to cause to happen soon"; Realizing his mistake, the driver *instantly* moved back to his side of the road.
6. *powerful*—root: *power*; "ability to do, act, produce"; suffix: *-ful*; "having much power"; The batter had a very *powerful* swing.

Selection Overview

SELECTION OBJECTIVES

After completing this selection, students will be able to

- define tone, recognize its purpose, and give examples of it
- write two paragraphs with different tones
- write a persuasive paragraph
- write from a consistent, first-person point of view
- define and identify homophones
- understand levels of meaning

Lesson Resources

The World Is Not a Pleasant Place to Be

- Selection Synopsis, Teacher's Edition, p. T445d
- Comprehension and Vocabulary Workbook, pp. 91–92
- Language Enrichment Workbook, pp. 69–70
- Teacher's Resources
  Reinforcement, p. R46
  Test, pp. T91–T92

More About Tone

The term *tone* is sometimes confused with the *mood* of a work of literature. Tone centers on the author's emotional attitude toward the subject matter; mood refers to the specific language the author uses to call up the readers' emotional responses. Tone may be formal or sarcastic, playful, ironic, etc.

Various poetic techniques can be used to create a mood or set a tone. Among these are meter, rhyme, imagery, and symbolism. Ask the class how these things contribute to the tone of this poem.

About the Author

Nikki Giovanni, born in 1943 in Knoxville, Tennessee, is a poet, writer, and lecturer who has traveled around the world and enjoys reading her poetry to any type of audience. She has been given more than twenty awards for her humanitarianism, service to others, and contributions to arts and letters.

Giovanni established herself in the 1960s as one of the premier figures in the black literary renaissance. She writes poetry, nonfiction, and essays. She has been a professor of creative writing at various universities, and has recently served as director of the Warm Hearth Writer's Workshop.

Learn About

Tone

No matter what its subject is, every work of literature carries with it its own, individual **tone**. Tone can be defined as the author's attitude toward the subject of his or her work. Tone is also defined as the author's attitude toward the audience reading his or her work.

As you read a poem ask yourself how the poet feels about his or her subject. Tone can be any number of different attitudes toward the subject of the work: formal, serious, informal, playful, intimate, sarcastic or doubtful, to name a few. A subject important to the writer may be treated solemnly or seriously. The writer will treat the subject seriously if he or she wants you to take it seriously.

As you read the poem, ask yourself:

1. How does the poet feel about her subject?
2. How does the poet want the reader to feel about the subject?

Reading Focus

Understand Levels of Meaning Many writers—and especially poets—write on more than one level of meaning. You can take their words literally, but there is also a deeper meaning. For example, the story of the three little pigs can be enjoyed just as it is told, but may also be taken as a lesson about the results of acting foolishly. In the poem on the next page, the first three stanzas have two levels of meaning. After reading the poem a few times, write down the deeper meaning that you find.

WRITING CONNECTION

Writers use tone to reveal their attitude toward a subject. Think of an activity you like and one that you do not like. Write a paragraph about each, telling your reader why you like or do not like the activity. Compare the tone of each paragraph with that of the other.

Cooperative Group Activity

Have students write, individually, both paragraphs for the Writing Connection activity. Have them describe on a separate sheet of paper what they consider to be the tone of each paragraph. Then, have pairs of students exchange papers. After reading the paragraphs, each student should write down his or her perceptions of the author's tone. Then the partners can compare notes to see how well the authors communicated their attitude toward the subject matter.

Develop Vocabulary Skills

There are no footnoted vocabulary words in this selection. Introduce the concept of homophones and how to find them in a dictionary by looking up alternate spellings.

The World Is Not a Pleasant Place to Be

by Nikki Giovanni

the world is not a pleasant place
to be without
someone to hold and be held by

a river would stop
5 its flow if only
a stream were there
to receive it

an ocean would never laugh
if clouds weren't there
10 to kiss her tears

the world is not
a pleasant place to be without
someone

Honeymooners, William H. Johnson. The Aaron Douglas Collection of The Amistad Research Center, Tulane University

Mini Quiz

Write the following sentences on the board or overhead projector and call on students to fill in the blanks. Discuss the answers with the class.

1. The poem was written by ________ ________ .
2. The poet says oceans can ________ .
3. Clouds kiss the ocean's ________ .
4. Everyone needs someone to ________ .
5. Without someone, the ________ is not a ________ place to be.

Answers

1. Nikki Giovanni
2. laugh
3. tears
4. hold
5. world; pleasant

Teaching Plan

INTRODUCE

Motivation

Ask students to think about what things are most important to them: possessions, family, friends, pets, hobbies, television, education, etc. Which of these could they do without if they had to? Which of these could they not live without?

Purpose-Setting Question

Would the world be unpleasant for a person who had no one in their life? Explain.

READ

Literary Focus: *Tone*

Do you think the poet is serious about the subject in this poem? How does that affect the tone?

Reading Focus: *Understand Levels of Meaning*

Help students understand that, in the first stanza, the literal meaning is only subtly different from the deeper meaning. In the second and third stanzas, there are two distinct levels of meaning. Have students restate the meanings on both levels. Elicit that all four stanzas actually have the same deeper meaning.

CLOSE

Have students complete Review the Selection on pages 474–475.

Viewing Fine Art

William H. Johnson (1901–1970) was an African American artist who spent much of his career as an expatriate in Europe. He returned to Harlem in 1938 and devoted himself to a more direct, less academic style. He turned to this style in order to better express the "spirit and flavor" of African American life. Have students find elements that appear childlike and more direct.

UNDERSTAND THE SELECTION

Answers

1. twice
2. someone to hold and be held by
3. a river, a stream, an ocean, a cloud
4. Sample answer: to talk
5. Sample answer: sad
6. Sample answer: A statement; The poet is stating a strong feeling about life.
7. Sample answer: rainfall
8. Sample answer: love for and from another person
9. They are all some form of water.
10. Sample answer: the sun shining on flowers

Respond to Literature

The answers to this question will vary, but should make reference to technology, the environment, or other uncertainties of the late 20th century. Discuss with the class the things that are specific to their time that did not exist one hundred years ago (or that people were not aware of), such as: air and water pollution; nuclear weapons; "miracle drugs" such as penicillin; space travel; the concept of equal rights for all despite differences in race, color, creed, etc.; the population explosion.

WRITE ABOUT THE SELECTION

Prewriting

Students are to work on this section individually. As an example, create two lists, per the directions, on the chalkboard for students to get an idea of what they are supposed to do. Have them come up with an original idea for their own writing.

Writing

Students are to work on this section individually as well. Go around the room, offering assistance to any student who is having difficulty.

Review the Selection

UNDERSTAND THE SELECTION

Recall

1. How often is the title repeated?
2. What do we need to make the world a pleasant place?
3. What elements of nature are mentioned in the poem?

Infer

4. Why do you think the river in this poem would stop by a stream?
5. How do you think the ocean feels?
6. Would you describe this poem as a question? an answer? a statement?
7. What natural event could be represented by the image of a cloud kissing the ocean's tears?

Apply

8. How else could you define "someone to hold and be held by"?
9. What do the images of nature all have in common?
10. What other moment in nature can illustrate the theme of this poem?

Respond to Literature

In this poem, Giovanni describes a need that all people share. What must people have in order to survive? What is most important to you? Explain.

WRITE ABOUT THE SELECTION

"The World Is Not a Pleasant Place to Be" is a poem which considers a single idea—the need for love that all human beings share. It is this feeling which makes the world, according to the poet, a pleasant place to live. Think of something in your life which makes your world pleasant. Can you think of a concrete example to illustrate it? Write a paragraph to persuade people that your concept is important.

Prewriting Think of a simple concept whose presence in your life is important. The concept could be something such as "freedom," "nature," or "art," for example. Make two lists—the first a list of key words which define the concept; the second, a list of reasons that explain why you think the concept is important.

Writing Write a persuasive paragraph to convince the reader of the concept's importance. First, define the concept, using the key words in your first list. Then present your argument by writing about the reasons in your second list.

Revising To make sure the reader understands the importance of the concept in your life, add to your paragraph an actual example that illustrates it.

Proofreading Read over your paragraph to check for errors. When you write about your life, or something that happened to you, you should write from the first-person point of view.

Revising

Based on their paragraphs, students are to come up with an example from their own lives and add it to their writing.

Proofreading

Make this a Cooperative Group Activity. Pair students and have them exchange papers with their partners to check for a consistent, first-person point of view. Errors should be circled in pencil by the proofreader and corrected by the writer.

THINK ABOUT TONE

Tone may be described as a common ground between the author and the reader, reached when both understand what the author is trying to create. If the reader misunderstands a writer's tone, he or she will miss a great deal of the meaning of the work.

1. The poem "The World Is Not a Pleasant Place to Be" gives two examples illustrating its main idea. Where are they?
2. How did you feel after you read the poem?
3. What emotions are expressed in the poem?
4. Characterize the tone of the poem.
5. What does the image of "to kiss her tears" suggest to you?

READING FOCUS

Understand Levels of Meaning As you read "The World Is Not a Pleasant Place to Be," you thought about the levels of meaning in the poem. What deeper meaning beyond the literal did you find in the first three stanzas? Write down the literal meaning and the deeper meaning of each stanza.

DEVELOP YOUR VOCABULARY

Homophones are words that sound alike but are different in spelling, meaning, and origin. Read this sentence, for example: The Smiths' party was a *boar, accept* for *there* food. The writer has incorrectly used homophones for the three italicized words in the sentence. Corrected, the sentence would read: The Smiths' party was a *bore, except* for *their* food.

Using a homophone in place of the correct word in a sentence can confuse the reader and make nonsense of your writing. If you are not sure of which homophone to use, check in a dictionary.

Look at the poem to find a homophone for each of these words.

1. floe
2. wood
3. knot
4. plaice
5. bee
6. two
7. buy
8. tiers

THINK ABOUT TONE

Answers

1. in the second and third stanzas
2. Sample answers: sad, moved, intrigued
3. Sample answers: love, happiness, need, unhappiness
4. Sample answers: serious, sad, intimate
5. Sample answer: an act of comfort

DEVELOP YOUR VOCABULARY

Answers

1. floe—flow
2. wood—would
3. knot—not
4. plaice—place
5. bee—be
6. two—to, too
7. buy—by
8. tiers—tears

READING FOCUS

Sample Answer

First stanza: Everyone needs someone to hold and be held by./Everyone needs to love and be loved. Second stanza: A river would stop its flow if a stream were there to receive it./ Everyone needs someone to hold them. Third stanza: An ocean wouldn't laugh without clouds to kiss her tears./To be happy, everyone needs someone to love them.

ESL Activity

Have students complete the worksheets on pages 69–70 of the Language Enrichment Workbook to give them more practice using homophones.

Selection Overview

SELECTION OBJECTIVES

After completing this selection, students will be able to

- define and identify point of view, including first- and second-person and both omniscient and limited third-person types
- write an outline
- write a descriptive paragraph
- use compound adjectives correctly
- define and utilize antonyms
- make inferences

Lesson Resources

Journey
- Selection Synopsis, Teacher's Edition, p. T445e
- Comprehension and Vocabulary Workbook, pp. 93–94
- Language Enrichment Workbook, pp. 71–72
- Teacher's Resources
  Reinforcement, p. R47
  Test, pp. T93–T94

More About Point of View

Review the three most widely-used points of view: first-person narrator, third-person limited, and third-person omniscient. What are the main distinctions among them? Also, discuss the seldom-employed second-person point of view, in which this story is told. Ask the students why, in their estimation, this point of view is so rarely employed. Have they encountered this before? If so, do they remember the title or substance of the story? Ask them to describe it to the class.

Temporarily turn the focus from fiction to nonfiction, specifically, to autobiography (which is exhibited in the two selections following this one). After briefly defining autobiography, ask the class which point of view is appropriate to this form of writing. Can more than one point of view be used? Which? Why?

Learn About

Nichols Canyon Road, David Hockney. Art Resource

Reading Focus

Make Inferences When you make an inference, you come to your own conclusion based on information you have received. For example, a detective who knows that a criminal is heading to the airport with a bag of stolen money infers that the crook is about to leave town. Active readers are like detectives. They use information from the text to infer something that is not directly stated. As you read the next selection, ask yourself questions that begin with *Why* or *How*. Then, use clues in the selection to infer the answers.

Point of View

Point of view refers to the vantage point from which an author views the events of a fictional story. Sometimes an author takes the position of an all-knowing observer who can describe the events and thoughts of all characters in the story. This point of view, called the **omniscient point of view**, is written in the third person. An author may write in the third person but present the story as seen by only one character. This is called the **limited point of view.**

At other times a single character tells the story as he or she experienced it. Such a character may be the main character, a minor one, or a mere bystander. In any case, the character, called a **first-person narrator**, tells the story in the first person.

It is very rare that any story is told in the second person. Second-person point of view means the author places you, the reader, as the character experiencing the events.

As you read the story, ask yourself:

1. Who is telling the story?
2. In what person is the story told?

WRITING CONNECTION

Write a paragraph in the first person, telling a brief story. Rewrite the paragraph, using the third person. Compare the two.

Viewing Fine Art

David Hockney (b. 1937) is one of England's best-known artists. With dashing color and free use of modern styles, Hockney has become a popular figure in the modern art world. Among his accomplishments are stage sets, costumes, and illustrations. His paintings are particularly well-liked, perhaps because they combine pop art and abstract expressionism with a pictorial quality. Here, the landscape of his adopted home in California is shown in brilliant color. Have students note the childlike quality of the painting. Ask: How does the childlike style relate to the topic of "Point of View?"

Cooperative Group Activity

Group the class into pairs for the Writing Connection activity. Instruct each student to independently write a paragraph in the first person. Next, have the partners exchange paragraphs and rewrite their partner's paragraph in the third person. Then have the pairs compare both sets of paragraphs.

JOURNEY

by Joyce Carol Oates

You begin your journey on so high an elevation that your destination is already in sight—a city that you have visited many times and that, moreover, is indicated on a traveler's map you have carefully folded up to take along with you. You are a lover of maps, and you have already committed this map to memory, but you bring it with you just the same.

The highway down from the mountains is broad and handsome, constructed after many years of ingenious blasting and leveling and paving. Engineers from all over the country aided in the construction of this famous highway. Its cost is so excessive that many rumors have circulated about it—you take no interest in such things, sensing that you will never learn the true cost anyway, and that this will make no difference to your journey.

After several hours on this excellent highway, where the sun shines ceaselessly and where there is a moderate amount of traffic, cars like your own at a safe distance from you, as if to assure you that there are other people in the world, you become sleepy from the monotony and wonder if perhaps there is another, less

---

elevation (el uh VAY shun) a high place
ingenious (in JEEN yus) clever, resourceful
excessive (ik SES iv) going beyond what's right or usual
moderate (MOD ur it) within reasonable limits; not excessive
monotony (muh NOT un ee) tiresome sameness

TEACHING PLAN

INTRODUCE

Motivation

Make a game of group storytelling with the class as a whole. Select one student to start the story of a journey. For example: "One sunny day I got onto my bike with an apple in my pocket and rode up the street to . . . " The next student will continue the story until the entire class has contributed. Encourage students to add as much detail and description as possible; allow them to take the story wherever they want it to go, no matter how fantastic it gets.

Purpose-Setting Question

Why does the author tell the story from the second-person point of view? How much would the story be changed if it were told from a different point of view?

READ

Literary Focus: *Point of View*

After the class has read the first few paragraphs of this selection, stop them and ask them how this story differs in point of view and style of narration from others they have read. As they continue, ask for additional examples that illustrate second-person point of view.

Reading Focus: *Make Inferences*

Encourage students to think of their own questions about the events in this story. Then guide them to infer answers by using their own knowledge and information from the story. Model questioning techniques for students by asking questions such as: Why would someone bring a map if it isn't needed? Why would someone leave a good road for a rougher one? Is this story really about roads, or something else?

CLOSE

Have students complete Review the Selection on pages 482–483.

Develop Vocabulary Skills

Call on volunteers to write the vocabulary words on the chalkboard in syllable form. Ask others to define them in their own words, without checking the footnoted definitions first. Call on others to correct any definitions offered that may be incorrect.

About the Author

Joyce Carol Oates, the American novelist and short story writer, was born in 1938. Her lengthy novels portray extremes of human passion and violence and are predominantly naturalistic. There are suggestions of the neo-Gothic in her writing, some of which depends heavily on fantasy and the surrealistic, as in this selection.

ESL Activity

Have students hold a group discussion and do the Language Enrichment worksheet on the metaphorical characteristics of the story, which is really about freedom of choice in life. What freedom of choice is there in students' native cultures?

Critical Thinking: *Synthesis*

Tell students that the entire story can be taken symbolically as well as literally. Ask them to keep this in mind as they continue reading, and challenge them to be able, by the end of the story, to state what the journey symbolizes.

Reading Focus: *Make Inferences*

Point out the paragraph beginning: "By mid-afternoon . . ." Ask: What are the good qualities of the new road described in this paragraph? What are its bad qualities? What can you infer about whether the narrator likes the road?

Literary Focus: *Point of View*

Ask: What pronoun is consistently used in this selection? How does that help you identify the point of view?

perfect road parallel to this. You discover on the map a smaller road, not exactly parallel to the highway and not as direct, but one that leads to the same city.

You turn onto this road, which winds among foothills and forests and goes through several small villages. You sense by the attitude of the villagers that traffic on this road is infrequent but nothing to draw special attention. At some curves the road shrinks, but you are fortunate enough to meet no oncoming traffic.

The road leads deep into a forest, always descending in small cramped turns. Your turning from left to right and from right to left, in a slow hypnotic passage, makes it impossible for you to look out at the forest. You discover that for some time you have not been able to see the city you are headed for, though you know it is still somewhere ahead of you.

By mid-afternoon you are tired of this road, though it has served you well, and you come upon a smaller, unpaved road that evidently leads to your city, though in a convoluted way. After only a moment's pause you turn onto this road, and immediately your automobile registers the change—the chassis bounces, something begins to vibrate, something begins to rattle. This noise is disturbing, but after a while you forget about it in your interest in the beautiful countryside. Here the trees are enormous. There are no villages or houses. For a while the dirt road runs alongside a small river, dangerously close to the river's steep bank, and you begin to feel apprehension. It is necessary for you to drive very slowly. At times your speedometer registers less than five miles an hour. You will not get to the city before dark.

The road narrows until it is hardly more than a lane. Grass has begun to grow in its center. As the river twists and turns, so does the road twist and turn, curving around hills that consist of enormous boulders, bare of all trees and plants, covered only in patches by a dull, brown lichen that is unfamiliar to you. Along one stretch, rocks of varying sizes have fallen down onto the road, so that you are forced to drive around them with great caution.

---

hypnotic (hip NOT ik) causing sleep
convoluted (KON vuh loot id) twisting; indirect
chassis (CHAS ee) a car's frame
apprehension (ap rih HEN shun) fear; dread
lichen (LY kun) a mosslike plant which grows on rocks and trees

Stone City, Iowa, Grant Wood. Joslyn Art Museum, Omaha, Nebraska. Estate of Grant Wood/Licensed by VAGA, New York, NY

Navigating these blind turns, you tap your horn to give warning in case someone should be approaching. But it is all unnecessary, since you come upon no other travelers.

Late in the afternoon, your foot numb from its constant pressure on the accelerator, your body jolted by the constant bumps and vibrations of the car, you decide to make the rest of your journey on foot, since you must be close to your destination by now.

A faint path leads through a tumble of rocks and bushes and trees, and you follow it enthusiastically. You descend a hill, slipping a little, so that a small rockslide is released; but you are able to keep your balance. At the back of your head is the precise location of your parked car, and behind that the curving dirt road,

---

navigating (NAV uh gayt ing) steering
enthusiastically (en thoo zee AS tik lee) eagerly

Viewing Fine Art

Grant Wood (1892–1942) was an American painter who combined qualities of primitive painting with much more sophisticated ideas. He was also a chronicler of life in the Midwestern farm belt. In his famous work seen here, he combined a flat and exceptionally clear delineated style with a complicated study of distance and space. The careful arrangement of the ornamented hills in light and shade shows the painting to be much more than just a decorative depiction of a bountiful harvest. Ask: What elements of this painting are especially appropriate for Oates's story?

Critical Thinking:
Predict
Ask: What is going to happen next? Will "you" reach the city?

Critical Thinking: *Summarize*

After students have read the story, call on several to summarize it.

Reading Focus: *Make Inferences*

Ask students what questions they have about the story. Ask other students to volunteer answers to their classmates' questions and to explain how they made these inferences.

Literary Focus: *Point of View*

Call on students to name the elements of setting in the story and the descriptive details that enhance the story's setting. Ask: Did the second-person point of view change how you visualized the setting?

and behind that the other road, and then the magnificent highway itself: you understand that it would be no difficult feat to make your way back to any of these roads, should you decide that going by foot is unwise. But the path, though overgrown, is through a lovely forest, and then through a meadow in which yellow flowers are blooming, and you feel no inclination to turn back.

By evening you are still in the wilderness and you wonder if perhaps you have made a mistake. You are exhausted, your body aches, your eyes are seared by the need to stare so intently at everything around you. Now that the sun has nearly set, it is getting cold; evenings here in the mountains are always chilly.

You find yourself standing at the edge of a forest, staring ahead into the dark. Is that a field ahead, or a forest of small trees? Your path has long since given way to wild grass. Clouds obscure the moon, which should give you some light by which to make your way, and you wonder if you dare continue without this light.

Suddenly you remember the map you left back in the car, but you remember it as a blank sheet of paper.

You resist telling yourself you are lost. In fact, though you are exhausted and it is almost night, you are not lost. You have begun to shiver, but it is only with cold, not with fear. You are really satisfied with yourself. You are not lost. Though you can remember your map only as a blank sheet of paper, which can tell you nothing, you are not really lost.

If you had the day to begin again, on that highway which was so wide and clear, you would not have varied your journey in any way: in this is your triumph.

---

feat (FEET) accomplishment
inclination (in kluh NAY shun) preference
seared (SIRD) scorched; burned
obscure (ub SKYOOR) darken; dim; hide from sight

Mini Quiz

Write the following sentences on the board and call on students to fill in the blanks. Discuss the answers with the class.

1. The destination of the journey is a ________.
2. The journey begins at a ________ elevation.
3. The journey is taken, at first, in a ________.
4. The dirt road runs along a ________.
5. The journey ends at ________.

Answers

1. city
2. high
3. car
4. river
5. nightfall

AUTHOR BIOGRAPHY

Joyce Carol Oates (1938–)

"If you are a writer, you locate yourself behind a wall of silence, and no matter what you are doing, driving a car or walking or doing housework, which I love, you can still be writing, because you have that space."

This remark by Joyce Carol Oates may explain why she is one of the most productive and versatile writers today. To her, writing is mostly daydreaming. When the idea is all set in her mind, she just sits down and writes it.

Oates has been creating fictional worlds all her life, which began in Lockport, New York, and continued in a rural area of Erie County. She submitted her first novel to a publisher at the age of fifteen. It was rejected for being too depressing, but this slight did not stop her. She entered Syracuse University in 1956, and she wrote a novel each semester. She went on to become co-winner of the *Mademoiselle* college fiction award in 1959 for her short story "In the Old World." In addition to writing, upon graduation in 1960, she was elected to the Phi Beta Kappa honor society and was valedictorian of her class.

Joyce Carol Oates does not spend all of her time writing. In addition to her one to four volumes a year, she involves herself in a parallel career in teaching. From 1962 to 1967, she taught at the University of Detroit and from 1967 to 1978 at the University of Windsor in Ontario. In 1978, she joined the faculty of Princeton University. Her books have won many awards, and her talent seems to continue to grow. She has earned a reputation as one of America's finest and best-known writers.

Oates says that she locates herself behind a "wall of silence" to write her stories. Why do you suppose that such a "wall of silence" is necessary for a writer?

MORE ABOUT THE AUTHOR

From the time of her childhood, Joyce Carol Oates felt compelled to put her thoughts into story form. Even before she learned to write, she had such a desire to tell stories that she drew books of picture tales. Today, in addition to short stories and novels, she has written literary criticism, poetry, and plays. She has even won a lifetime achievement award for her writing in the horror genre. Much of her fiction and poetry involves bloody or brutal imagery and is written with a dark tone.

Additional Works

BY JOYCE CAROL OATES

You may wish to suggest these works by Joyce Carol Oates for additional reading:

Because It Is Bitter, and Because It Is My Heart, Dutton, 1990.

Upon the Sweeping Flood and Other Stories, New York: Vanguard, 1966.

Where Are You Going, Where Have You Been?: Selected Early Stories, Ontario Review Press, 1993.

UNDERSTAND THE SELECTION

Answers

1. not much; a moderate amount
2. the city
3. at nightfall
4. Sample answer: It cost so much to build.
5. Sample answer: The broad highway has become boring.
6. Sample answer: You've spent the whole day traveling.
7. Sample answer: After all, a journey was accomplished, and the path taken was beautiful and unique.
8. Sample answer: You would have reached the city after a short time, but it would have been a boring trip.
9. Sample answer: You might have found a quick, simple way to the city with it.
10. Sample answer: life or life goals

Respond to Literature

Answers to this question will vary, but responses should make reference to American society. Discuss with the class why individual choice is important, yet why a free society/democracy depends on citizens to voluntarily follow certain rules of behavior, whether self-imposed or imposed by governments. For example: politeness, consideration (self-imposed); obeying laws (government-imposed).

WRITE ABOUT THE SELECTION

Prewriting

Make this a cooperative group activity involving the class as a whole. Select one student to stand at the chalkboard and draw a map of the journey in the story. Have the rest of the class direct the student as to how the map should look. Use that map as a basis for students to write, individually, their outline of a journey. They may first draw their own map of this journey to help them visualize the sequence of events.

Review the Selection

UNDERSTAND THE SELECTION

Recall

1. How much traffic is on the highway?
2. What is the destination?
3. When does the journey end?

Infer

4. Why do you think the broad highway is famous?
5. Why do you think you turn off onto a smaller road?
6. Why do you think your destination must be close as you start walking on the path?
7. Why does the day end in triumph?

Apply

8. Predict what might have happened if you had not turned off the broad highway.
9. What might have happened if you had not left the map in the car?
10. What do you think this journey represents?

Respond to Literature

Think about the freedom you have to make important decisions in your life. Different people choose different roads to follow. Why do you think it is important that choices and the freedom to choose are available to everyone?

WRITE ABOUT THE SELECTION

"Journey" ends in the forest, with night falling and you on foot. You have made a number of choices during the day. What would have happened if you had not decided to drive down smaller and smaller roads? How long would it take to reach the city? What would you do there? Write a paragraph that describes an alternate journey in which you made other choices and followed other roads.

Prewriting Write an informal outline of the sequence of events that would occur if you had stayed on the main highway. Use your imagination to create a different set of circumstances and a different ending.

Writing Use your informal outline to write a five-sentence paragraph describing the alternate journey. Be sure to include a description of how you feel during this journey.

Revising When you revise your paragraph, add specific details about the weather, the scenery, and the highway to create your own setting. The language you use should create a vivid mental image in your readers' minds.

Proofreading Read over your paragraph to check for errors. If you use compound adjectives, use a hyphen between them. For example: the tree-lined highway, the sun-splashed beach, the cloud-flecked sky. Check to see that you have used commas correctly as well.

Writing

Students are to work on this section individually. Go around the room and assist any student who is having difficulty.

Revising

Students are to revise their own work, adding descriptive details to present a clearer picture of what they are writing about.

Proofreading

Select one or two of the students' paragraphs as models for proofreading. Put the paragraphs on the overhead projector and have the class suggest improvements.

THINK ABOUT POINT OF VIEW

Point of view is very important in fiction because it governs how the writer tells the story. If, for example, the first-person narrator tells the story, only his or her thoughts can be recorded, and only actions that he or she views can be told.

1. The grammatical person used in this story is unusual. Who is it?
2. Some people would think that "you" in the story is not really "the person being spoken to" but a substitute for "I." Do you agree? Why or why not?
3. How did the author's use of *you* make you feel as you read the story?
4. Do you think "you" should have been more concerned about "your" plight as the way became more and more difficult? Why or why not?
5. Do you think the end of the strange journey was indeed a triumph for "you"?

READING FOCUS

Make Inferences Write a few of the *Why* and *How* questions you asked yourself as you read "Journey." For each question, state the inferences you made and provide details from the story that helped you make it.

DEVELOP YOUR VOCABULARY

An **antonym** is a word whose meaning is the opposite of that of another word. *Happy* and *sad* are common examples.

Words are sometimes antonyms in one context but not in another. The adjectives *fast* and *slow* are usually antonyms. In the sentence "The carrots are *fast* in the ground," however, *fast* means "firmly fixed." The opposite of *fast* in this sentence is not *slow*, but *loose*.

The *italicized* words below are from "Journey." Choose the word that is the better antonym in the context given.

1. an *excessive* explanation:
   a. moderate **b.** insufficient
2. *ingenious* blasting:
   a. stupid **b.** unskillful
3. *convoluted* roadway:
   a. straight **b.** simple
4. follow the path *enthusiastically*:
   a. unwillingly **b.** soberly

THINK ABOUT POINT OF VIEW

Answers

1. second person—*you*, the person spoken to
2. Sample answer: It would make no sense to tell "you" a story that happened to "you," and only "I," the narrator, would know so many details of thought and action.
3. Sample answer: As a reader I felt immediately involved in the story.
4. Sample answer: Yes, because of the nearness of the river, the darkness, the need to go by foot, and the lack of a map.
5. Sample answer: No, because the storyteller really was lost and can no longer see the city. Yes, because she came through the journey despite its oddness and knows she will find the city eventually.

DEVELOP YOUR VOCABULARY

Answers

1. (b) insufficient
2. (b) unskillful
3. (a) straight
4. (a) unwillingly

ESL Activity

Pair students with proficient English-speaking students. Have students use a thesaurus to find two antonyms of the following words from "Journey": *obscure*, *perfect*, *elevation*. Encourage students to sketch an image for each word and its corresponding antonym.

READING FOCUS

Sample Answer

Question: Why do "you" decide to leave the first two roads? Answer: Things that are too easy get boring—"you become sleepy." Question: Why does the author talk repeatedly about the importance of viewing the scenery? Answer: She thinks that the experience is more important than reaching her goal—"the path, though overgrown, is through a lovely forest, . . ."

Selection Overview

Selection Objectives

After completing this selection, students will be able to

- define *autobiography*
- discuss the purpose of autobiography
- write a paraphrase of a story
- capitalize proper nouns correctly
- research the histories and meanings of words taken from Greek and Latin
- understand meaning through context

Lesson Resources

from *Black Boy*
- Selection Synopsis, Teacher's Edition, pp. T445e–T445f
- Comprehension and Vocabulary Workbook, pp. 95–96
- Language Enrichment Workbook, pp. 73–74
- Teacher's Resources Reinforcement, p. R48 Test, pp. T95–T96

More About Purpose

Review the four general purposes of writing: to inform, to describe, to entertain or amuse, or to persuade. Ask students what types of literary works would reflect each kind of author's purpose. Ask for specific examples of each. For example: documentaries are written to inform. Travelogues are written to describe. Mystery novels and comic strips are written to entertain and amuse. Political literature is written to persuade.

Is it possible for an author to have more than one purpose in writing a particular work? For example, satire is written to persuade or inform, as well as to amuse. Ask for other examples.

Discuss the various purposes for writing an autobiography. When reading an autobiography, how important is it to realize and understand the writer's purpose?

Learn About

Slum Child, Margaret Burroughs. Collection of the artist

Reading Focus

Understand Meaning Through Context

When you come upon an unfamiliar word as you read, you might be able to figure out what the word means by looking at the rest of the sentence or the paragraph it is in. As you read the excerpt from *Black Boy*, jot down each unfamiliar word. Then write what you think it means, based on the context of the sentence or sentences around it.

Purpose

Authors write to inform, to describe, to entertain or amuse, or to persuade. Any one or more of these may serve as an author's reason for giving readers a unified impression of his or her character, personality, and thoughts.

Autobiography can be defined as a narrative of an author's life written by him- or herself. What might motivate a person to write his or her own life story? Perhaps the author was a part of historical events or movements that would make his or her life inherently interesting.

An author may know, too, that his or her life experience and philosophy are so special that it may help or inspire others. The mere process of exploring one's own personality may result in insights that the author knows will interest the reader.

As you read the incident from Wright's boyhood, ask yourself:

1. Why did Wright tell the incident?
2. What did he want to accomplish by telling it?

Writing Connection

Write a short paragraph telling of an incident from your life. Then write another telling why you chose that incident.

Viewing Fine Art

Margaret Burroughs is an African American artist who pictures life in urban areas. Here she shows a child in front of the tenements of the city. How does the theme of the painting relate to the theme of *Black Boy*?

Cooperative Group Activity

For the Writing Connection activity, instruct the students to write both paragraphs independently on separate sheets of paper. The second one should give one of the four purposes listed in the text.

Then group the class into small groups of three or four students. Have each group's members exchange their first paragraphs only. Upon reading each of the other members' paragraphs, direct students to write a guess as to the writer's purpose, or purposes, for choosing that particular incident. Have each student compare these written reactions with his or her own purpose(s). How evident were their purposes to the others?

from BLACK BOY

by Richard Wright

Hunger stole upon me so slowly that at first I was not aware of what hunger really meant. Hunger had always been more or less at my elbow when I played, but now I began to wake up at night to find hunger standing at my bedside, staring at me gauntly. The hunger I had known before this had been no grim, hostile stranger; it had been a normal hunger that had made me beg constantly for bread, and when I ate a crust or two I was satisfied. But this new hunger baffled me, scared me, made me angry and insistent. Whenever I begged for food now my mother would pour me a cup of tea which would still the clamor in my stomach for a moment or two; but a little later I would feel hunger nudging my ribs, twisting my empty guts until they ached. I would grow dizzy and my vision would dim. I became less active in my play, and for the first time in my life I had to pause and think of what was happening to me.

"Mama, I'm hungry," I complained one afternoon.

"Jump up and catch a kungry," she said, trying to make me laugh and forget.

"What's a *kungry*?"

"It's what little boys eat when they get hungry," she said.

"What does it taste like?"

---

gauntly (GAWNT lee) in the manner of a thin bony person
grim (GRIM) very serious
still (STIL) make calm and quiet
clamor (KLAM ur) noise; excitement

TEACHING PLAN

INTRODUCE

Motivation

Wright's biographical work describes African American culture and family life in America at a time when segregation and racial prejudice were the norm. Obtain a video that discusses this issue and show it to the class. Students may not realize the living conditions which African Americans were forced to endure at that time. Discuss this with the class.

Purpose-Setting Question

The lives of the students in the class may be very different from or share similarities with the life of the young Richard Wright. What elements of his autobiography do they relate to? Do they have anything in common with the young boy in the story?

READ

Literary Focus: *Purpose*

Remind students that this excerpt is autobiographical and nonfiction. Show students on the board that the word *autobiography* comes from Latin and Greek root words *auto*, for *self*; *bios*, for *life*; and *graph*, for *writing*, thus giving the word its literal meaning of *self-life-writing*. Direct students to consider Wright's purpose(s) as they read.

Reading Focus: *Understand Meaning Through Context*

Direct students to try to guess the meaning of an unknown word based on its context before checking footnoted words at the bottom of the page. They can then use the book definition to confirm the guess. Model this skill with the word *kungry* near the end of the page.

CLOSE

Have students complete Review the Selection on pages 492–493.

Develop Vocabulary Skills

Assign a word from the footnoted lists to each student or to a pair of students; have them look the word up in the dictionary. Then have them "act out" the word in class. Have the rest of the class try to guess the word.

About the Author

From harsh beginnings, Richard Wright made himself into the premier voice of African Americans in the 1940s and 1950s with the publication of his autobiographical *Black Boy*. He fled to Europe to escape American racism and died in Paris in 1960. The second volume of his autobiography, *American Hunger*, was published in 1977, though he had written it in 1940.

ESL Activity

Invite students to bring to class any autobiographies they may have of well-known people from their culture or previous country. Allow them to share these with the class and tell a few important things about the person.

Literary Focus: *Purpose*

Ask: What is Wright's purpose in using dialogue to tell his story rather than just relating that he was constantly hungry? What impression does the dialogue make on the reader?

Reading Focus: *Understand Meaning Through Context*

Ask students the meaning of *bewilderment*. Have them identify context clues in the paragraph.

Critical Thinking: *Interpret*

Ask: What does Wright mean when he says that he thought of his father "with a deep biological bitterness"?

"I don't know."

"Then why do you tell me to catch one?"

"Because you said that you were hungry," she said, smiling.

I sensed that she was teasing me and it made me angry.

"But I'm hungry. I want to eat."

"You'll have to wait."

"But I want to eat now."

"But there's nothing to eat," she told me.

"Why?"

"Just because there's none," she explained.

"But I want to eat," I said, beginning to cry.

"You'll just have to wait," she said again.

"But why?"

"For God to send some food."

"When is He going to send it?"

"I don't know."

"But I'm hungry!"

She was ironing and she paused and looked at me with tears in her eyes.

"Where's your father?" she asked me.

I stared in bewilderment. Yes, it was true that my father had not come home to sleep for many days now and I could make as much noise as I wanted. Though I had not known why he was absent, I had been glad that he was not there to shout his restrictions at me. But it had never occurred to me that his absence would mean that there would be no food.

"I don't know," I said.

"Who brings food into the house?" my mother asked me.

"Papa," I said. "He always brought food."

"Well, your father isn't here now," she said.

"Where is he?"

"I don't know," she said.

"But I'm hungry," I whimpered, stomping my feet.

"You'll have to wait until I get a job and buy food," she said.

As the days slid past the image of my father became associated with my pangs of hunger, and whenever I felt hunger I thought of him with a deep biological bitterness.

---

image (IM ij) mental picture
pangs (PANGZ) sharp pains

Martial Memory, Philip Guston. Eliza McMillan Fund, The Saint Louis Art Museum

Viewing Fine Art

Philip Guston (b. 1913) is a U.S. painter who became a well-known abstract expressionist. Before turning to abstract painting, however, he worked in a more realistic style. Here, for example, in a painting made in 1941, he uses a collection of familiar symbols and flat shapes to show a memory of small boys preparing for battle on a city street with make-believe weapons. Ask students if they think such a scene might occur today. If so, what might be different? What might be the same?

My mother finally went to work as a cook and left me and my brother alone in the flat each day with a loaf of bread and a pot of tea. When she returned at evening she would be tired and dispirited and would cry a lot. Sometimes, when she was in despair, she would call us to her and talk to us for hours, telling us that we now had no father, that our lives would be different from those of other children, that we must learn as soon as possible to take care of ourselves, to dress ourselves, to prepare our own food; that we must take upon ourselves the responsibility of the flat while she worked. Half frightened, we would promise solemnly. We did not understand what had happened between our father and our mother and the most that these long talks did to us was to make us feel a vague dread. Whenever we asked why father had left, she would tell us that we were too young to know.

One evening my mother told me that thereafter I would have to do the shopping for food. She took me to the corner store to show me the way. I was proud; I felt like a grownup. The next afternoon I looped the basket over my arm and went down the pavement toward the store. When I reached the corner, a gang of boys grabbed me, knocked me down, snatched the basket, took the money, and sent me running home in panic. That evening I told my mother what had happened, but she made no comment; she sat down at once, wrote another note, gave me more money, and sent me out to the grocery again. I crept down the steps and saw the same gang of boys playing down the street. I ran back into the house.

"What's the matter?" my mother asked.

"It's those same boys," I said. "They'll beat me."

"You've got to get over that," she said. "Now, go on."

"I'm scared," I said.

"Go on and don't pay any attention to them," she said.

I went out of the door and walked briskly down the sidewalk, praying that the gang would not molest me. But when I came abreast of them someone shouted.

"There he is!"

They came toward me and I broke into a wild run toward home. They overtook me and flung me to the pavement. I yelled,

---

flat (FLAT) apartment
dispirited (dih SPIR it id) discouraged; low in spirits
molest (muh LEST) bother, annoy

Background Notes

Explain to the class that supermarkets and convenience stores did not exist in the time Wright is describing. Groceries were bought from a small neighborhood store; if you were poor, you would buy as much food each day as you could afford.

pleaded, kicked, but they wrenched the money out of my hand. They yanked me to my feet, gave me a few slaps, and sent me home sobbing. My mother met me at the door.

"They b-beat m-me," I gasped. "They t-t-took the m-money."

I started up the steps, seeking the shelter of the house.

"Don't you come in here," my mother warned me.

I froze in my tracks and stared at her.

"But they're coming after me," I said.

"You just stay right where you are," she said in a deadly tone. "I'm going to teach you this night to stand up and fight for yourself."

She went into the house and I waited, terrified, wondering what she was about. Presently she returned with more money and another note; she also had a long heavy stick.

"Take this money, this note, and this stick," she said. "Go to the store and buy those groceries. If those boys bother you, then fight."

I was baffled. My mother was telling me to fight, a thing that she had never done before.

"But I'm scared," I said.

"Don't you come into this house until you've gotten those groceries," she said.

"They'll beat me; they'll beat me," I said.

"Then stay in the streets; don't come back here!"

I ran up the steps and tried to force my way past her into the house. A stinging slap came on my jaw. I stood on the sidewalk, crying.

"Please, let me wait until tomorrow," I begged.

"No," she said. "Go now! If you come back into this house without those groceries, I'll whip you!"

She slammed the door and I heard the key turn in the lock. I shook with fright. I was alone upon the dark, hostile streets and gangs were after me. I had the choice of being beaten at home or away from home. I clutched the stick, crying, trying to reason. If I were beaten at home, there was absolutely nothing that I could do about it; but if I were beaten in the streets, I had a chance to fight and defend myself. I walked slowly down the sidewalk, coming closer to the gang of boys, holding the stick tightly. I was so full of fear that I could scarcely breathe. I was almost upon them now.

---

wrench (RENCH) twist

Reading Focus:
Understand Meaning Through Context
Ask students to define the word *baffled* in line 17 of this page, using the context of the short paragraph. Ask them to think of a synonym that would also work in the sentence.

Literary Focus:
Purpose
Ask: Why does the author build suspense on this page? Does the use of dialogue increase or decrease the suspense?

Critical Thinking:
Predict
Ask: What do you think will happen next? Will Richard be robbed and beaten again?

"There he is again!" the cry went up.

They surrounded me quickly and began to grab for my hand.

"I'll kill you!" I threatened.

They closed in. In blind fear I let the stick fly, feeling it crack against a boy's skull. I swung again, lamming another skull, then another. Realizing that they would retaliate if I let up for but a second, I fought to lay them low, to knock them cold, to kill them so that they could not strike back at me. I flayed with tears in my eyes, teeth clenched, stark fear making me throw every ounce of my strength behind each blow. I hit again and again, dropping the money and the grocery list. The boys scattered, yelling, nursing their heads, staring at me in utter disbelief. They had never seen such frenzy. I stood panting, egging them on, taunting them to come on and fight. When they refused, I ran after them and they tore out for their homes, screaming. The parents of the boys rushed into the streets and threatened me, and for the first time in my life I shouted at grownups, telling them that I would give them the same if they bothered me. I finally found my grocery list and the money and went to the store. On my way back I kept my stick poised for instant use, but there was not a single boy in sight. That night I won the right to the streets of Memphis.

---

lamming (LAM ing) striking
retaliate (rih TAL ee ayt) strike back
stark (STAHRK) complete; downright
utter (UT ur) complete
frenzy (FREN zee) madness; rage
egging (EG ing) urging
taunting (TAWNT ing) daring; teasing
poised (POIZD) set and ready

Critical Thinking: *Evaluate*

Ask students to evaluate the mother's actions. Ask: Did she do the right thing in forcing her son to return to the grocery store and face the gang of boys? What would have happened if she had not?

Literary Focus: *Purpose*

Point out to students that Wright describes the action of the fight with active verbs and fast-moving, powerful sentences. Have students find examples on this page of words and phrases related to violence. Ask why they think Wright chose to describe the incident in this way.

Reading Focus: *Understand Meaning Through Context*

Have students cover the definitions at the bottom of the page with a hand or small piece of paper. Then read aloud each word in the list and have students locate the word and look for context clues to its meaning. Have students share their ideas and support their answers.

Mini Quiz

Write the following sentences on the board or overhead projector and call on students to fill in the blanks. Discuss the answers with the class.

1. When the boy was hungry, his mother would pour him a cup of ________.
2. He thinks of his father with ________.
3. His mother got a job as a ________.
4. The boy first went alone to the store in the ________.
5. The third time, he carried a ________.

Answers

1. tea
2. bitterness
3. cook
4. afternoon
5. stick

AUTHOR BIOGRAPHY

Richard Wright (1908–1960)

If the previous selection appeals to you, you might try looking for the book in a library. It is from *Black Boy*, the first volume of Richard Wright's autobiography, published in 1945. The book is powerful. The life Wright led as a child was a tough one, indeed.

Wright was born on a farm near Natchez, Mississippi, in 1908. His family moved here and there, at last settling in Memphis, Tennessee. When his parents separated, his mother had to work long hours to support the family. Wright hung out on the streets and in vacant lots. He learned to amuse the customers in bars by drinking liquor. "I was a drunkard in my sixth year," he tells us, "before I had begun school." Then his mother became very ill, and he spent some time in an orphanage. He quit school after the ninth grade and worked at several low-paying jobs. Always interested in books, he read more and more. He learned that life *could* be different. He began to believe that maybe he *did* have a chance at a happier life, after all. *Black Boy* ends as he leaves the South in 1927, to start a new life in Chicago.

But sadly, there was prejudice in the North, too. Wright still found that he was thought of as an African American first, a person second. After the success of *Black Boy* in 1945, he decided to move to Europe. He spent his last years in France and died in Paris in 1960. The second volume of his autobiography, *American Hunger*, written in the 1940s, was published in 1977.

Richard Wright had an interest that gave his life a turn for the better. What was this interest? How did it help him?

MORE ABOUT THE AUTHOR

Richard Wright grew up in a brutal, cruel world, where even his own adult family members assaulted him physically and psychologically, withheld affection from him, squelched his gifts and talents, and tried to force him to submit to the bleak existence of an African American man in the South of that time. The books he read were the key elements in his self-education and his self-deliverance from a nightmarish life. Through his own writing, he was able to better understand himself, to speak out, and to inspire others to fight against racism.

Additional Works

BY RICHARD WRIGHT

You may wish to suggest these works by Richard Wright for additional reading:

Black Boy: A Record of Childhood and Youth, Harper, 1945, reprinted 1969.

Native Son, Harper, 1940, published with restored text, 1991.

Uncle Tom's Children: Four Novellas, Harper, 1938. Expanded edition published as *Uncle Tom's Children: Five Long Stories*, 1938, reprinted, 1965.

Review the Selection

UNDERSTAND THE SELECTION

Recall

1. In what way does hunger affect the boy physically?
2. What does his mother give him to defend himself with?
3. Where does the boy live?

Infer

4. What does the absence of the father mean for the family?
5. Why does the boy's mother keep sending him to the store?
6. What is the turning point in the story?
7. Why does the boy shout at the grownups, too?

Apply

8. Do you think the boy's mother did the right thing? Why do you think so?
9. Predict what might happen the next time the boy goes to the store.
10. Describe what kind of person the boy will be after his experience on the street.

Respond to Literature

Describe something that happened to you which you considered to be a turning point in your life.

WRITE ABOUT THE SELECTION

If you were asked to tell what happened in *Black Boy* in a few sentences, how would you do it? You could paraphrase the story, or retell it in a condensed, or shorter, form. This would include the most important events, characters, and their reactions. A lot happens in *Black Boy* that you will want to include, but remember to focus on the crisis, which is the most important part. Ask yourself what specific things lead up to the crisis. Write a paragraph that paraphrases the story.

Prewriting Make a list of the events in the story as they happen, from beginning to end. Choose the ones you think are most important to include in your paragraph.

Writing Using your list of events, write a paragraph that paraphrases the story in your own words. Write it as if you were telling a friend what happened in the story.

Revising Reread your paraphrase to see if the events you wrote about follow each other logically. Does one event lead naturally to the next? If necessary, insert an event which helps your audience to make sense of the story.

Proofreading Read over your paragraph to check for errors. Remember that proper nouns are capitalized. Make sure you have capitalized proper nouns such as the characters' names and the name of the city where the story takes place.

UNDERSTAND THE SELECTION

Answers

1. It makes his stomach ache, makes him dizzy, dims his vision, and makes him less active.
2. a long, heavy stick
3. Memphis
4. There is no money for food; his mother must work to support the family.
5. to teach him to defend himself
6. the fight with the gang of boys
7. Sample answer: He is not afraid of them; he is feeling triumphant.
8. Answers will vary. Suggested responses should draw on evidence from the story, particularly details about the options available to the family.
9. Sample answer: The gang of boys will leave him alone.
10. Sample answer: stronger, more sure of himself, not afraid of anyone

Respond to Literature

The answers to this question will vary. Responses should include some description of how the moments described altered the students' character. Ask for suggestions of real life characters who faced similar moments in their lives; describe how they responded. Discuss these with the class.

WRITE ABOUT THE SELECTION

Prewriting

When students have completed their lists, have them rank the items listed in order of importance. Ask for volunteers to name the most important thing they have listed, then the least. Discuss these with the class.

Writing

Students are to work on this section individually and paraphrase the story in their own words. If any students are having difficulty, review their lists with them and make suggestions.

Revising

Make this a cooperative learning opportunity. Have students work in small groups to revise their paragraphs.

Proofreading

Select one or two of the students' paragraphs as models for proofreading. Put the paragraphs on the overhead projector and have the class suggest improvements.

ESL Activity

Discuss with students any ways in which they had to prove themselves or gain acceptance when they first came to this country or first found themselves in a predominantly English-speaking situation.

THINK ABOUT PURPOSE

People are innately curious about other people's lives. When these lives have impacted history, autobiographies may reveal new insights into events. The author may interpret facts and demonstrate his or her character or habit of mind.

1. What is Wright's purpose(s) in telling this incident—to inform, describe, entertain, or persuade?
2. What do you think the incident relayed in this excerpt represented to Wright?
3. What did Wright want to accomplish by telling this incident?
4. Why do you think Wright did not try to use the incident to "teach" readers how to raise children?
5. The incident is from Wright's autobiography. Why do you think he chose to write his life story?

READING FOCUS

Understand Meaning Through Context

As you read the excerpt from *Black Boy,* you guessed the meaning of unfamiliar words by looking for clues in the text. Choose four words that can be understood by looking at context. Then write the phrase or sentence that helped you understand each word.

DEVELOP YOUR VOCABULARY

At one point in the autobiographical incident, Wright admits that the gang of boys sent him "running home in panic." The word *panic* has an interesting history. It comes from Pan, Greek god of the fields, forests, flocks, and shepherds, who frightened people as they were traveling through the woods. An unreasonable fear is still called a *panic*.

The English language contains a number of words whose roots can be traced back to characters from Greek and Roman mythology. Look up the following words in a dictionary that has word histories. Give the meaning and origin of each word.

1. narcissus
2. martial
3. titan
4. jovial
5. atlas
6. Saturday
7. volcano
8. museum
9. tantalize
10. cereal

DEVELOP YOUR VOCABULARY

Answers

1. *narcissus*: a flower—from Narcissus, a beautiful youth who loved his own reflection and changed into a flower.
2. *martial*: of war—from Mars, Roman god of war
3. *titan*: a person of great size or power—from Titan, giant deity in Greek myth
4. *jovial*: full of good humor—from Jove, the Roman god Jupiter
5. *atlas*: a book of maps—from Atlas, a Titan forced to support the heavens on his shoulders; he was often shown on the title page of early map books.
6. *Saturday*: a day of the week—from Saturn, Roman god of agriculture
7. *volcano*: a vent in the earth's crust that erupts sporadically—from Vulcan, Roman god of fire and metalworking
8. *museum*: a place for exhibiting artistic, historical, or scientific objects—from the Muses, Greek goddesses of arts, literature, and science
9. *tantalize*: to tease—from Tantalus, a Greek mythological king who was doomed to have food or drink recede whenever he reached for either
10. *cereal*: grains—from Ceres, Roman goddess of agriculture

READING FOCUS

Sample Answer

retaliate; "Realizing that they would retaliate if I let up for but a second, I fought to lay them low, to knock them cold, to kill them so that they could not strike back at me."

THINK ABOUT PURPOSE

Sample Answers

1. Wright wanted to describe his childhood and perhaps inform readers of the poverty of his time.
2. how his life changed
3. to relate a growth experience, and to state the importance of "winning the streets of Memphis"
4. He may have understood that he and his mother did what they had to and he did not feel it was right to judge her actions or his own.
5. His experience as an African American offered important insights into the larger background of race relations in the United States.

Focus on Nonfiction

Point out to students that sometimes an autobiography is disguised as fiction, as in a short story or a novel. Ask the class if they consider the excerpt from *Black Boy* to be strictly autobiographical, meaning autobiography under the guise of fiction rather than straight fiction. Ask: Why do students think this? Ask the same question about "Little Things Are Big" after the selection is read.

Based on what they have read, what do the students consider to be Richard Wright's purpose in writing *Black Boy*? After they have read the selection, ask why students think Jesús Colón recounted the experience described in "Little Things Are Big"?

Do students consider Wright to be introspective in that selection? If so, to what degree? Can students say the same for Colón? Ask the class for the basis of their opinions and have them cite examples from the text.

ELEMENTS OF NONFICTION

Review the elements of autobiography:

- narrative style—a story about the events in an author's life
- point of view—always the first-person, since the writer is also the main character
- purpose—the reason why the author chose to write his or her life story
- introspection—the writer's observations and self-analysis

Discuss introspection as it relates to purpose at greater length with the class: While an autobiography is by its very nature subjective, the element of introspection is essential if the author is to avoid a merely self-serving dissertation. An introspective autobiographer should be capable of examining his or her own thoughts, feelings, motives, and reactions in a thorough, honest, and thoughtful manner. This gives the reader a more accurate and complete picture of the author.

Focus on Nonfiction

To understand what an autobiography is, look at the word itself. It breaks down into three parts: *auto-*, *bio-* and *-graphy*. The dictionary will tell you that *auto-* means "self," *bio-* means "life," and *-graphy* means "a process, a manner or a method of writing."

When the three parts are combined, you can see that *autobiography* means "a self-written life story," or the story of a person's life written by himself or herself.

An autobiography can take one of several forms. There is the autobiography itself, a written story. There is also the journal, the diary, letters, and memoirs. These are all autobiographical works.

The first three, journals, diaries, and letters, are not usually intended for publication by the writer. They may serve the writer as a basis or as sources for the autobiography. Memoirs focus on the writer's involvement in public events and relationships with notable people.

Four elements are important in an autobiography. They are narrative style, point of view, purpose, and introspection. It is important to remember that autobiography, like all nonfiction, is based on fact. It consists of real events that happened to real people.

Narrative Style An autobiography is written in narrative style, that is, it tells a story. The narrative consists of events in the writer's life. A writer will organize the narrative in one of several ways. The most obvious—and the most common—is chronological. **Chronological** means "in time order." A chronological narrative is one that describes the events in the order in which they occurred.

Another method is to begin the autobiography with an event that the writer sees as most important in his or her life. The rest of the autobiography is then organized around this primary event.

Point of View In literature, point of view means the position from which the work is presented. In autobiography, since the writer is also the main character, the point of view is always first-person. The clues that tell the reader that the story is written from a first-person point of view are the words *I*, *me*, *my*, and *mine*.

The first-person point of view allows the reader to see the world through the eyes of the author. The reader gains a new perspective on events and other people. It seems as if the reader is inside the writer's mind, listening to his or her internal dialogue—the debate with self.

Purpose When you read an autobiography, consider the purpose of the writer. Was it to inform, describe, entertain, or persuade? More specifically, was it to glorify the writer? Was the purpose to make a point or proclaim a message? Was it to moralize about aspects of life? Was the purpose to satisfy the reader's curiosity about a personality?

An autobiography may be written for one of these purposes or a combination of them. There is always a reason why a writer decides to write his or her autobiography.

Introspection Introspection is an important element of autobiography. Introspection is the observation and analysis of oneself. An introspective person is one who closely and thoughtfully examines his or her own feelings, thoughts, and reactions.

Introspection can help the writer to analyze the role of self in a given situation. It thus adds another dimension to autobiography. It gives the reader a more complete portrait of the writer. It may also give the reader a chance to find something in common with his or her own life—something that every person shares. Reading an autobiography may tell the reader how different people are from each other, and in some ways, how much alike.

As you read "Little Things Are Big," examine the story to identify the elements of autobiography. Ask yourself these questions:

1. What form of autobiography is this story?
2. What is the point of view of the writer?
3. What do you think Colón's purpose was in writing this story?

Real-Life Application

Ask students how many of them have ever read an autobiography. Have each student write a list of ten people, alive or dead, whom they admire. Direct them to include as least one person in each of the following fields: literature, history, politics, sports, music, movies, and television. The remaining three fields can be at their discretion.

As a homework assignment, students are to go to the library and research to see who, if anyone, on their lists has written an autobiography. If none has, the students will have to choose someone else. If two or more have, students should pick one. Have them check the book out of the library, read it, and submit a brief book report (suggested length: one to two pages). The book report should: (1) give a concise summary of the writer's life; (2) analyze the book in terms of the four elements of autobiography; (3) discuss if and how the book has altered the student's opinion or image of the subject.

Selection Overview

SELECTION OBJECTIVES

After completing this selection, students will be able to

- understand and define autobiography and its several forms: the written story, the journal, the diary, memoirs, and letters
- discuss the four elements of autobiography: narrative style, point of view, purpose, and introspection
- retell a story from a different point of view
- write in the first-person point of view
- research and understand Latin and Greek word parts
- recognize facts and opinions

Lesson Resources

Little Things Are Big

- Selection Synopsis, Teacher's Edition, p. T445f
- Comprehension and Vocabulary Workbook, pp. 97–98
- Language Enrichment Workbook, p. 75
- Teacher's Resources
  - Reinforcement, p. R49
  - Test, pp. T97–T98
  - Literary Analysis, pp. L14–L15

Cooperative Group Activity

After reading, divide the class into small groups. Have each group decide a different ending to the story. Have students in each group take the roles of the characters in the story and act out their new endings for the rest of the class. Take a vote on which ending was the most realistic, the funniest, the most unrealistic, the most serious, etc.

MODEL

Little Things Are BIG

ADAPTED

by Jesús Colón

Focus on Nonfiction STUDY HINTS

The title gives you a clue to the story's theme, or message.

It was very late at night on the eve of Memorial Day. She came into the subway at the 34th Street station. I am still trying to remember how she managed to push herself in, with a baby on her right arm, a valise in her left hand, and two children, a boy and a girl about three and five years old, trailing after her. She was a nice-looking white lady in her early twenties.

At Nevins Street, Brooklyn, we saw her preparing to get off at the next station, Atlantic Avenue, which happened to be the place where I too had to get off. Just as it had been a problem for her to get on the subway, it was going to be a problem for her to get off. She had two small children to take care of, a baby on her right arm and a medium-sized valise in her left hand.

And there I was, also preparing to get off at Atlantic Avenue, with no bundles to take care of—not even the usual book under my arm, without which I feel that I am not completely dressed.

As the train was entering the Atlantic Avenue station, some white man stood up from his seat and helped her out of the car, placing the children on the long, deserted platform. There were only two adult persons on the long platform sometime after midnight on the eve of Memorial Day.

---

valise (vuh LEES) small suitcase

Teaching Plan

INTRODUCE

Motivation

Autobiography is the story of one person's life in which readers may find parallels with their own lives, inspiration, or a sense of fellowship. Find another interesting autobiography (a popular music, film or television, or sports personality) and read excerpts from it to the class. Encourage students to discuss similar autobiographies they may have read.

Purpose-Setting Question

In what ways is this selection relevant to the students and their lives? Does reading this help them to understand that appearance does not necessarily define another human being?

READ

Literary Focus: *Elements of Autobiography*

The blue side notes in this annotated lesson provide a model for students to understand the literary elements introduced in Focus on Nonfiction, pages 494–495.

Point out that this story is an excellent example of introspection. Ask students what insight we get into the thoughts of the author when, in the first two paragraphs, he repeats the description of the woman with the baby, the valise, and the two small children.

Reading Focus: *Recognize Facts and Opinions*

Define *fact* and *opinion* for students. Then, have students look at the last sentence of each paragraph on this page, and discuss which express an opinion and which express a fact. Have students look for other sentences in the story that express an opinion. Ask: Why do you think an autobiographical account may contain fewer facts than opinions?

CLOSE

Have students complete Review the Selection on pages 500–501.

Develop Vocabulary Skills

Use the vocabulary words in sentences—some correctly, some incorrectly. Call on individual students to say whether the word in each sentence has been used correctly. Then have a student use the word correctly in an original sentence.

Background Notes

Jesús Colón is a writer who was born in Puerto Rico and emigrated to New York City, as have nearly two million of his fellow Puerto Ricans. Although Puerto Rico is a self-governing commonwealth of the United States, many of its citizens would like Puerto Rico to become America's 51st state. Puerto Ricans are U.S. citizens and can vote in national primary elections, although not national general elections. Puerto Rico has one representative in Congress, and a resident commissioner, who has a voice but no vote, except in committee.

Manufacturing, agriculture, and tourism are three of Puerto Rico's main industries. The island is three-fourths mountainous and its capital is San Juan.

Literary Focus: *Setting*

When the class has finished reading the story, call on volunteers to describe the setting and tell how it affects the narrator, the woman, and the events of the story.

I could see the steep, long concrete stairs going down to the Long Island Railroad or into the street. Should I offer my help as the American white man had done at the subway door, placing the two children outside the subway car? Should I take care of the girl and the boy? Should I take them by their hands until they reached the end of the steep, long concrete stairs of the Atlantic Avenue station?

You begin to get an idea of what kind of person the narrator is.

Courtesy is a characteristic of the Puerto Rican. And here I was—a Puerto Rican. Hours past midnight, valise, two white children, and a white lady with a baby on her arm badly needing somebody to help her until she got down the long concrete stairs.

Introspection: The narrator describes his feelings, observations and an analysis of his reactions.

But how could I, a black and a Puerto Rican, approach this white lady? I knew she very likely might be prejudiced against blacks and everybody with foreign accents. And we were in a deserted subway station, very late at night.

What would she say? What would be the first reaction of this white American woman, perhaps coming from a small town, with a valise, two children and baby on her right arm? Would she say, "Yes, of course, you may help me?" Or would she think that I was just trying to get too familiar? Or would she think worse than that perhaps? What would I do if she let out a scream as I went toward her to offer my help?

Was I misjudging her? So many slanders are written every day in the newspapers against the blacks and Puerto Ricans. I hesitated for a long, long minute. The ancestral manners that the most illiterate Puerto Rican passes on from father to son were struggling inside me. Here was I, way past midnight, face to face with a situation that could very well explode into an outburst of prejudice.

It was a long minute. I passed on by her as if I saw nothing. As if I didn't care about her need. Like a rude animal walking on two legs, I just moved on. I half ran down the long subway platform, leaving the children and the valise and her with the baby on her arm. I took the steps of the long concrete stairs in twos until I reached the street. The cold air slapped my warm face.

---

characteristic (kar ak tuh RIS tik) special quality
slander (SLAN dur) lie; harmful statement
ancestral (an SES trul) coming from an ancestor
illiterate (ih LIT ur it) unable to read

This is what racism and prejudice and artificial divisions can do to people and to a nation!

Colón states his message, which the story illustrates. Notice how he emphasizes it.

Perhaps the lady was not prejudiced after all. Or not prejudiced enough to scream at the coming of a black man toward her in a lonely subway station a few hours past midnight.

If you were not prejudiced, I failed you, dear lady. I know that there is a chance in a million that you will read these lines. I am willing to take that millionth chance. If you were not that prejudiced, I failed you, lady, I failed you, children. I failed myself to myself.

I buried my courtesy early on Memorial Day morning. But here is a promise that I make to myself here and now: If I am ever faced with a situation like that again, I am going to offer my help regardless of how the offer is going to be received.

Then I will have my courtesy with me again.

Here is the story's resolution. Colón describes prejudice's effect on him and his reaction. In doing so he tells you a great deal about the kind of person he is and what he thinks is right.

---

racism (RAY siz um) racial prejudice

Critical Thinking: *Generalize*

Ask students to generalize about the events of the story: What really happened? What is the conflict?

Reading Focus: *Recognize Facts and Opinions*

Have students identify the facts and opinions on this page. Discuss how the lines between the two become blurred when events are presented through one person's perspective.

Mini Quiz

Write the following sentences on the board and call on students to fill in the blanks. Discuss the answers with the class.

1. The story takes place in a ________ station.
2. The narrator was carrying ________.
3. There were ________ adult persons present.
4. ________ is characteristic of the Puerto Rican.
5. The time was a few hours past ________.

Answers

1. subway
2. nothing
3. two
4. Courtesy
5. midnight

UNDERSTAND THE SELECTION

Answers

1. the night before Memorial Day
2. Atlantic Avenue
3. three
4. Sample answer: He was raised to be courteous.
5. Sample answer: Some white people are prejudiced against black or Puerto Rican people. This woman is white; he is black and Puerto Rican.
6. Sample answer: The narrator has experienced the effects of prejudice; he was afraid of her reaction.
7. Sample answers: ashamed, indecisive, unsure, upset
8. Sample answer: She accepts help, turns him down, or gets frightened.
9. Sample answer: No, because he would like to help the woman
10. Answers will vary. Responses should refer to the information in the story. He would have approached her with his natural courtesy.

Respond to Literature

Sample Answer

His awareness makes him decide not to help the woman because he fears his offer might be misinterpreted; he knows his race is a factor.

WRITE ABOUT THE SELECTION

Prewriting

Make this a cooperative group activity. Group students into small groups and have them brainstorm ideas per the directions for prewriting. One person in each group should write down all the ideas; students can choose among them and come up with more of their own to list on their charts.

Review the Selection

UNDERSTAND THE SELECTION

Recall

1. When does the story take place?
2. Which is the narrator's subway stop?
3. How many children did the woman have with her?

Infer

4. Why do you think that the narrator feels he should help the woman?
5. Why might the woman be afraid of the narrator?
6. Why did the narrator decide not to help the woman?
7. Explain how the narrator felt after he passed the woman.

Apply

8. Predict what might have happened if the narrator had offered to help the woman.
9. Is the narrator prejudiced? Explain.
10. What is your opinion of the narrator's decision? If he had decided to help the woman, how could he have approached her?

Respond to Literature

How does the narrator's awareness of prejudice in the United States affect his actions? Is this a positive or negative effect?

WRITE ABOUT THE SELECTION

You have learned about elements of autobiography in this unit. One of those elements is point of view. Autobiography is written from the **first-person point of view**. This is because the person in the story, the "main character," is also the person telling the story.

There is another person in "Little Things Are Big" who is important—the woman with three young children. Suppose this story is part of *her* autobiography; suppose that she is telling you about the incident. She would likely see it in a different way. Retell this story in one paragraph from the woman's point of view.

Prewriting Make a chart that lists who you think the woman is; what you think she sees; and how you think she reacts. In each category, list key words or ideas which you can expand into a story.

Writing Using your chart, write a one-paragraph story that describes the events of "Little Things Are Big" from the woman's point of view.

Revising Read the story again to remind yourself of the sequence of events. Add details or explanations to your paragraph which make the reasons for her reactions understandable to the reader.

Proofreading Check your paragraph to make sure you have written consistently in the first person. Remember that the first-person point of view is indicated by the words *I*, *me*, *my*, and *mine*.

Writing

Students are to work on this section individually. Give help to any student who is having problems.

Revising

Students are to work on this section individually as well. Details can be details of setting, character or plot, whichever is most useful.

Proofreading

Select one or two of the students' stories as models for proofreading. Put the stories on the overhead projector and have the class suggest improvements.

THINK ABOUT AUTOBIOGRAPHY

Autobiography is a true story in which the narrator/writer is the main character. Events in the life story of the writer are told from his or her point of view. The narrator also describes his or her emotions, reactions, and thoughts.

1. Describe Colón's instinctive reaction when he sees the woman and her children.
2. Colón says he usually has a book under his arm. What does this tell you about him?
3. List several ways the narrator describes himself.
4. What reactions does the incident cause in the narrator?
5. What lesson does Colón tell you he has learned?

DEVELOP YOUR VOCABULARY

Colón asks if he *misjudged* the woman in the subway. Perhaps, he mused, she was not *prejudiced* after all. Both *italicized* words in the preceding two sentences contain the Latin word part *jus* or *juris*, meaning "law." Some Latin and Greek word parts are at the core of whole families of English words. *Jus* and *juris* are the core part of a word family that includes all the words below.

Look up the meaning of each word in the list below. Do they all have something to do with law today? Think about their meanings. Then use each word in a sentence of your own.

1. just
2. injury
3. jurisdiction
4. jurisprudence
5. adjust
6. jury
7. justice
8. perjury
9. judge
10. jurist

THINK ABOUT AUTOBIOGRAPHY

Answers

1. He wants to assist them.
2. Sample answers: He is a student; he likes to read.
3. as an adult, a Puerto Rican, a rude animal
4. anger about prejudice, feelings of failure
5. Sample answers: "Little things are big"; it is up to the individual to combat prejudice; prejudice is a formidable force in America; by giving in to it, he failed himself, the woman, and his ancestral tradition of courtesy; a person must be true to him or herself.

DEVELOP YOUR VOCABULARY

Answers

1. *just*—right or fair
2. *injury*—harm or damage, physical or legal
3. *jurisdiction*—the administration of justice
4. *jurisprudence*—the philosophy of law
5. *adjust*—to change or make suitable
6. *jury*—a group of people sworn to decide a law case
7. *justice*—the quality of being right; fairness
8. *perjury*—the willful telling of a lie while under oath to tell the truth in a court of law
9. *judge*—a public official with authority to hear and decide cases in a court of law
10. *jurist*—an expert in law; a judge

All words have some connection with law and justice today. Sentences will vary.

ESL Activity

Have students hold a group discussion and do the worksheet from the Language Enrichment Workbook, page 75, on different forms of nonfiction and on how being afraid to speak English can affect a non-English speaker's behavior.

Selection Overview

SELECTION OBJECTIVES

After completing this selection, students will be able to

- understand and define free verse
- write a conversation and convert it to poetic units
- write a persuasive paragraph
- identify words used as both noun and verb and use them correctly in a sentence
- interpret character

Lesson Resources

Where Have You Gone

- Selection Synopsis, Teacher's Edition, p. T445g
- Comprehension and Vocabulary Workbook, pp. 99–100
- Language Enrichment Workbook, p. 76
- Teacher's Resources
  Reinforcement, p. R50
  Test, pp. T99–T100

More About Free Verse

Free verse is focused on irregular rhythmic cadences and repetitions of phrases, images, and syntax patterns. Conventional meter is not employed. Rhyme is ordinarily not involved, but it may be loosely used.

Discuss with the class the concept of poetic rhythm, in terms of irregular cadence. Cadence is measured movement. It is a subtle quality, dependent upon word accents and voice emphasis. While cadence is measured movement, it is not as structured as formal, metrical movement. It is generally found woven loosely into large units of syllables.

In free verse, the cadence is irregular. Ask students to give examples of both regular and irregular cadences. Can they perceive an irregular cadence in this poem?

Have they encountered free verse elsewhere in this unit? What are their impressions and opinions of free verse versus traditional rhymed, metrical verse? Which do they suppose is more difficult to write and why?

Learn About

FREE VERSE

Poetry that does not depend on rhyme or a regular meter is known as **free verse**. For its effectiveness, free verse depends on a variety of natural rhythms and the repetition of images and phrases.

In conversation, people naturally emphasize or accent certain words. Their tone varies, their voices rise at the end of a question or fall at the end of a statement. Unlike other types of poetry, free verse is characterized by these natural rhythms. The rhythmical unit to note is the stanza, not the foot or line.

Certain words or whole lines of free verse are repeated for emphasis. A line may not be repeated word for word, but may be varied to enrich the emotion it expresses.

As you read "Where Have You Gone," ask yourself:

1. What does the poet repeat?
2. Does reading the poem aloud help you to understand it better?

READING FOCUS

Interpret Character All good writers give clues about the personalities of their characters. Active readers use these clues to form an impression of each character. As you read the next selection, think about the two characters: the speaker and the one being spoken of. What clues can you find to help you understand their personalities?

WRITING CONNECTION

Some verse can be read as if one person is talking to another. Write a short conversation with one person asking questions, and the other person answering. Then try casting the conversation in poetic units.

About the Author

Mari Evans was born in Toledo, Ohio, in 1923. She has been an instructor in African American literature and a writer-in-residence at Indiana and Purdue Universities.

In 1970, she won the first annual poetry award of the Black Academy of Arts and Letters for her collection of poems "I Am A Black Woman." She produces, writes, and directs the television program "The Black Experience." Her poems have been reprinted in over two hundred anthologies and textbooks. She also writes juvenile books, plays and contributes to periodicals.

Cooperative Group Activity

Group the class into pairs for the Writing Connection activity. One partner will provide questions, the other will give answers. Together, they will rewrite the conversation as free verse.

ESL Activity

Have students do the worksheet on free verse, page 76 of the Language Enrichment Workbook. Have students test and identify some rhythms and repetitive phrases.

WHERE HAVE YOU GONE

by Mari Evans

Alta, Aaron Douglas. Collection of Fisk University Art Museum

Where have you gone

with your confident
walk with
your crooked smile

why did you leave (5)
me
when you took your
laughter
and departed

are you aware that (10)
with you
went the sun
all light
and what few stars
there were? (15)

where have you gone
with your confident
walk your
crooked smile the
rent money (20)
in one pocket and
my heart
in another. . .

TEACHING PLAN

INTRODUCE

Motivation

Try to obtain a videocassette or soundtrack that features the poetry of Mari Evans to play for the class. If work by Evans can't be found, play a recording of poetry written by other African American poets.

Purpose-Setting Question

Free verse reads, and sounds, very much like someone talking to you in ordinary conversation. Ask: Is free verse easier to write than other forms of poetry? Is it easier for a poet to express him- or herself in free verse? Is free verse easier to read and understand?

READ

Literary Focus: *Free Verse*

Call on students to identify and describe the imagery in the poem. Are there similes, metaphors, or other figures of speech?

Reading Focus: *Interpret Character*

Have students ask themselves these questions while reading the poem: Who is the speaker? What are the speaker's emotions? Who is being addressed? What kind of person is the person being addressed?

CLOSE

Have students complete Review the Selection on pages 504–505.

Viewing Fine Art

Aaron Douglas (1899–1979) was an African American artist. Perhaps the best known of Harlem's painters, he worked both in a semi-abstract style and in the realistic portrait technique seen here. Ask: What adjectives would you use to describe the effect of the young woman in the painting? Do you think these also apply to the speaker in the poem?

Develop Vocabulary Skills

There are no vocabulary words footnoted in the selection. Give the class an example of a word that can be used as both noun and verb; ask each student for an example of such a word and to use it in an original sentence. Discuss how the meaning of such a word can be determined from its context.

Mini Quiz

1. The speaker has lost her ________ ________ and her ________.
2. The person addressed has a ________ walk.
3. The person addressed took his ________ .
4. When that person left, so did the ________, all ________ and ________.
5. The person's smile is ________.

Answers

1. rent money; heart
2. confident
3. laughter
4. sun; light; stars
5. crooked

UNDERSTAND THE SELECTION

Answers

1. "your" laughter
2. as having a confident walk, a crooked smile
3. the rent money, the speaker's heart
4. Sample answers: husband, lover, boyfriend
5. Sample answer: night and day; the speaker's entire world
6. She loves and misses him.
7. Sample answers: a con man; a thoughtless, selfish person
8. Answers will vary. Responses should refer to the character of both the speaker and "you."
9. Sample answer: No, because she is aware that he has taken the rent money
10. Sample answers: happy, loving, angry about the rent money

Respond to Literature

Answers to this question will vary. Responses should relate love, loss or longing to specific examples from the students' own lives. Would this poem be as effective if expressed in declarative sentences rather than a series of questions?

WRITE ABOUT THE SELECTION

Prewriting

Students are to work on this section individually; discuss the questions in the introductory part of this activity with students who are having trouble formulating an opinion.

Writing

Students are to work on this section individually as well. If any students have trouble with this section, suggest an opening sentence for their paragraph such as "You will like this poem because . . ." or "I thought this poem was . . ."

Revising

Make this a cooperative group activity. Have each student exchange his or her paper with a neighbor, who will read it, sum up the writer's opinion, and discuss with the writer whether or not the statement was clearly stated. Those whose statements are not clear enough can then revise their work with suggestions from those who read their paper.

Proofreading

Select one or two of the students' paragraphs as models for proofreading. Put the paragraphs on the overhead projector and have the class suggest improvements.

Review the Selection

UNDERSTAND THE SELECTION

Recall

1. In the second stanza, what does the speaker say has been taken?
2. How is "you" described?
3. What was in the pockets of the "you" in the poem?

Infer

4. To whom is the speaker speaking?
5. What does "the sun," "all light," and "what few stars there were" imply?
6. How does the speaker feel about "you" in the poem?
7. What kind of person do you think "you" is?

Apply

8. Do you think that the speaker of the poem knew that "you" was going to leave? Why do you think so?
9. Do you think that the speaker is "blindly" in love with "you"? Why do you think so?
10. Predict how the speaker might feel if "you" returned.

Respond to Literature

What emotions does the speaker express in "Where Have You Gone"? What situations in your life have made you feel the same way?

WRITE ABOUT THE SELECTION

The speaker in "Where Have You Gone" uses a series of questions to carry her message and to express the way she feels about what has happened. Why do you think the "you" in the poem left? Do you think the speaker is more deeply affected than "you"? What is your opinion of the poem itself?

Prewriting Decide how you feel about the poem, and make a list of reasons to support your opinion. Arrange your list by putting the most important reasons first, the next most important second, and so forth. Use quotes from the poem to illustrate or back up your opinions. This will help lend weight to your viewpoint.

Writing Write a short paragraph to persuade your audience to share your opinion of the poem. Begin the paragraph by stating your opinion. Then build your case using the reasons in your list in the order that you listed them.

Revising Read your paragraph. Ask yourself if the statement of your opinion would be clear to someone reading it for the first time. Do all your reasons support your opinion? If you find one that doesn't, leave that sentence out.

Proofreading Read over your paragraph to check for errors. Remember that commas are used after introductory phrases and to separate adjectives that come before a noun.

THINK ABOUT FREE VERSE

Rhymes are not required in free verse. In this poem phrases are repeated in varying ways to create a poem. The poem is organized into stanzas and expresses an emotion, an opinion, or an idea. Because it is not bound by strict rules of rhyme or meter, free verse often reads like the natural rhythms of speech.

1. What is the main emotion expressed by the poem?
2. List the verbs in the poem that suggest that feeling.
3. The title of the poem is in the form of a question. Keeping that in mind, describe the content of the poem itself.
4. List all of the lines or phrases that literally, or with variations, are repetitions of the poem's title.
5. Why is "the/ rent money/ in one pocket and my heart/ in another" such a startling comparison?

Reading Focus

Interpret Character As you read "Where Have You Gone" you looked for clues about the personalities of the speaker and the one being spoken to. What did you decide? Write a paragraph telling what you think each character is like, and tell what clues make you think so.

DEVELOP YOUR VOCABULARY

"I always *vote* in the election; I know my *vote* makes a difference."

The *italicized* words in the sentence look like the same word, but they are different from each other. How do they differ? The first time the word *vote* is used, it is used as a verb. The second time *vote* is used, it is used as a noun. **Nouns** are words that name a person, place, idea, or object. **Verbs** are words that express an action or a state of being.

Look at the italicized words in the following sentences and write down whether they are nouns or verbs.

1. Let's go for a *walk*.
2. Did you *label* the package?
3. The explorers hope to *land* safely in a friendly country.
4. We saw a *play* performed at the theater.
5. Shall I *paint* the ceiling white?

THINK ABOUT FREE VERSE

Answers

1. Sample answer: loss
2. *gone*, *leave*, *took*, *departed*, *went*
3. It is a series of questions aimed at one person.
4. Where have you gone? Why did you leave? Where have you gone?
5. Sample answers: The rent money is tangible, something real. The poet's heart is an abstraction, an image.

DEVELOP YOUR VOCABULARY

Answers

1. noun
2. verb
3. verb
4. noun
5. verb

ESL Activity

Have students work in pairs to use each italicized word in the vocabulary activity in two original sentences. Each word should be used as a noun and as a verb.

Reading Focus

Sample Answer

I think the speaker is a sad, lonely young woman because she says the other person left and took the laughter from her. I also think she is depressed because she says he took the sun, light, and stars. I think she is in financial trouble, because he took her rent money.

I think the other person is a man who has a sense of humor because he smiles and laughs, and he is fun to be around because he was the light in her life. He is also cruel because he not only walked out on her, but he also took her rent money.

Learn About

Reading Focus

Compare and Contrast When you compare two things, you look at how they are the same. When you contrast, you look at differences. One way to do this is to use a simple graphic organizer, with one column to note things that are the same and one column for differences. The next selection describes two sisters. Divide your paper in half. Write *Same* at the top of one half and *Different* at the top of the other. As you read about the two sisters, jot down your observations about how they are the same and how they are different.

Theme

The central idea of a literary work is called the **theme**. In nonfiction, the general topic of discussion is the theme. The writer takes a position on the topic and proves or supports that position.

The fiction writer, the poet and the dramatist have a variety of ways to express the theme of a work. It may be expressed through the character, through the action and events, or through the images the author uses. The theme is not the "moral of the story," however. It is a truth about life. It presents no rule to live by, but makes a statement about the way people behave. Sometimes the theme is not specified. Readers may have to draw their own conclusions about what it is.

As you read "Everyday Use" ask yourself:

1. What is the theme of "Everyday Use"?
2. Is the theme made clear in the story? If so, how?

Writing Connection

Write a five-sentence paragraph about a fictional person whose actions demonstrate or express some particular attitude toward patriotism.

Selection Overview

Selection Objectives

After completing this selection, students will be able to

- define and discuss theme in fiction and nonfiction
- write a paragraph on a certain theme
- write a paragraph describing the setting of a story
- describe what an adverb is
- distinguish adverbs from adjectives
- compare and contrast

Lesson Resources

Everyday Use

- Selection Synopsis, Teacher's Edition, p. T445g
- Comprehension and Vocabulary Workbook, pp. 101–102
- Language Enrichment Workbook, pp. 77–78
- Teacher's Resources
  - Reinforcement, p. R51
  - Test, pp. T101–T102

More About Theme

In works of fiction, the theme is an abstraction made tangible. This is accomplished by representing the abstract notion as a person, image, or action. Since a theme is often implied, a certain amount of awareness or mental acuity is required to recognize what statement the author is making.

Discuss with the class the recognition of theme in short stories as opposed to poetry. Do the students feel that it is generally easier to spot the theme in one genre versus the other? Why? Is theme more evident when represented through characters, actions, or events, rather than through images? If so, why?

More About the Literary Period

Discussions and descriptions of African American culture, including the family, history, heritage, myths, and way of life, by African American writers have been introduced to the general reading public only within about the last fifty years. Why has this happened only recently? Does this mean the earlier, accepted notions of "American literature" were wrong since African American writers were excluded?

Cooperative Group Activity

Divide the class into groups. Have each student read his or her paragraph from the Writing Connection activity to the group. Instruct the listening students to confer and reach a consensus as to what attitude the character is exhibiting. Is it the same attitude that the writer intended to communicate?

ESL Activity

Have students complete the worksheet on themes from the Language Enrichment Workbook, pages 77–78. What are themes? How does an author present theme?

Everyday Use

by Alice Walker

I will wait for her in the yard that Maggie and I made so clean and wavy yesterday afternoon. A yard like this is more comfortable than most people know. It is not just a yard. It is like an extended living room. When the hard clay is swept clean as a floor and the fine sand around the edges lined with tiny, irregular grooves, anyone can come and sit and look up into the elm tree and wait for the breezes that never come inside the house.

Maggie will be nervous until after her sister goes: she will stand hopelessly in corners, homely and ashamed of the burn scars down her arms and legs, eying her sister with a mixture of envy and awe. She thinks her sister has held life always in the palm of one hand, that "no" is a word the world never learned to say to her.

You've no doubt seen those TV shows where the child who has "made it" is confronted, as a surprise, by her own mother and father, tottering in weakly from backstage. (A pleasant surprise, of course: What would they do if parent and child came on the show only to curse out and insult each other?) On TV mother and child embrace and smile into each other's faces. Sometimes the mother and father weep, the child wraps them in her arms and leans across the table to tell how she would not have made it without their help. I have seen these programs.

Sometimes I dream a dream in which Dee and I are suddenly brought together on a TV program of this sort. Out of a dark and soft-seated limousine I am ushered into a bright room filled with many people. There I meet a smiling, gray, sporty man like Johnny Carson who shakes my hand and tells me what a fine girl I have. Then we are on the stage and Dee is embracing me with tears in her eyes. She pins on my dress a large orchid, even though she has told me once that she thinks orchids are tacky flowers.

---

awe (AW) wonderment; admiration
confronted (kun FRUNT id) set face to face
tacky (TAK ee) too showy; not fashionable

Teaching Plan

INTRODUCE

Motivation

Ask how many of the students have read the book or seen the movie, *The Color Purple*. Ask those who have read or seen it to describe it to the rest of the class, discussing its plot, characters, and setting, and giving their opinion of it as a story.

Purpose-Setting Question

Are there cultural differences in this story that identify its author as an African American writer? Is her theme universal or applicable only to African American society?

READ

Literary Focus: ***Theme***

Discuss the possible meaning of the title. Tell students that the title gives an important clue to the theme, or message, of the story. Ask them to watch for the author's message as they read.

Reading Focus: ***Compare and Contrast***

Students will easily be able to find ways in which the sisters are different. Ask students to record these differences. You might also have them find and jot down the similarities between Maggie and her mother, although there are fewer similarities.

CLOSE

Have students complete Review the Selection on pages 518–519.

Develop Vocabulary Skills

Read the list of vocabulary words to the class. Ask for volunteers to define the words they know and to use them in original sentences from which, by context, the meanings of the words can be deduced.

About the Author

Alice Walker, born in Georgia in 1944, is recognized as one of the United States' leading writers. She has won the Pulitzer Prize and the National Book Award. She writes novels, poems, short stories, and works of nonfiction.

Her novel, *The Color Purple*, was made into a hugely successful film; other works include a book of essays, *In Search of Our Mothers' Gardens*, and a biography of her "spirit helper" and artistic role model, *Langston Hughes: American Poet*.

In real life I am a large, big-boned woman with rough, man-working hands. In the winter I wear flannel nightgowns to bed and overalls during the day. I can kill and clean a hog as mercilessly as a man. My fat keeps me hot in zero weather. I can work outside all day, breaking ice to get water for washing; I can eat pork liver cooked over the open fire minutes after it comes steaming from the hog. One winter I knocked a bull calf straight in the brain between the eyes with a sledge hammer and had the meat hung up to chill before nightfall. But of course all this does not show on television. I am the way my daughter would want me to be: a hundred pounds lighter, my skin like an uncooked barley pancake. My hair glistens in the hot bright lights. Johnny Carson has much to do to keep up with my quick and witty tongue.

But that is a mistake. I know even before I wake up. Who ever knew a Johnson with a quick tongue? Who can even imagine me looking a strange white man in the eye? It seems to me I have talked to them always with one foot raised in flight, with my head turned in whichever way is farthest from them. Dee, though. She would always look anyone in the eye. Hesitation was no part of her nature.

"How do I look, Mama?" Maggie says, showing just enough of her thin body enveloped in pink skirt and red blouse for me to know she's there, almost hidden by the door.

"Come out into the yard," I say.

Have you ever seen a lame animal, perhaps a dog run over by some careless person rich enough to own a car, sidle up to someone who is ignorant enough to be kind to him? That is the way my Maggie walks. She has been like this, chin on chest, eyes on ground, feet in shuffle, ever since the fire that burned the other house to the ground.

Dee is lighter than Maggie, with nicer hair and a fuller figure. She's a woman now, though sometimes I forget. How long ago was it that the other house burned? Ten, twelve years? Sometimes I can still hear the flames and feel Maggie's arms sticking to me, her hair smoking and her dress falling off her in little black papery flakes. Her eyes seemed stretched open, blazed open by the flames reflected in them. And Dee. I see her standing off under the sweet gum tree she used to dig gum out of; a look of concentration on her face as she watched the last dingy gray board of the house fall in toward the red-hot brick chimney. Why don't you do a dance around the ashes? I'd wanted to ask her. She had hated the house that much.

I used to think she hated Maggie, too. But that was before we raised the money, the church and me, to send her to Augusta to school. She used to read to us without pity; forcing words, lies, other folks' habits, whole lives upon us two, sitting trapped and ignorant underneath her voice. She washed us in a river of make-believe, burned us with a lot of knowledge we didn't necessarily need to know.

---

sidle (SYD ul) move sideways; edge along slyly

Literary Focus: *Theme*

Read aloud to students the first long paragraph on this page. Have them close their eyes and try to picture the character. Discuss the ways the author uses description to make the mother seem so real. Ask students if the mother reminds them of anyone they know and how her personality might reflect the theme.

Background Notes

Explain to students that Johnny Carson was a popular late night talk show host on the "The Tonight Show."

Reading Focus: *Compare and Contrast*

Ask students to contrast the real Mama to the one her daughter, Dee, wants her to be. Discuss which version of Mama the students find most interesting.

Critical Thinking: *Infer*

Ask: Why does Maggie walk the way she does? Do you think that Dee had a happy childhood? Why or why not?

Family, Charles H. Alston. Whitney Museum of American Art

Viewing Fine Art

Charles H. Alston (b. 1907) is an African American artist whose works have combined a semi-abstract style with black subject matter. Like his colleagues in various African American art movements, Alston seeks a way to express his heritage within a framework of contemporary painting. In this picture the family is simplified into large rectangular shapes that intersect and form part of an overall design. Ask: In what ways is the painting appropriate to the story? Consider mood, characters, and setting.

Reading Focus:
Compare and Contrast

Discuss the similarities and differences of Mama, Maggie, and Dee as described on this page.

Critical Thinking:
Interpret

Ask: What does Mama mean when she says, "I used to love to milk till I was hooked in the side in '49"?

Pressed us to her with the serious way she read, to shove us away at just the moment, like dimwits, we seemed about to understand.

Dee wanted nice things. A yellow organdy dress to wear to her graduation from high school; black pumps to match a green suit she'd made from an old suit somebody gave me. She was determined to stare down any disaster in her efforts. Her eyelids would not flicker for minutes at a time. Often I fought off the temptation to shake her. At sixteen she had a style of her own: and knew what style was.

I never had an education myself. After second grade the school was closed down. Don't ask me why: in 1927 colored asked fewer questions than they do now. Sometimes Maggie reads to me. She stumbles along good-naturedly but can't see well. She knows she is not bright. Like good looks and money, quickness passed her by. She will marry John Thomas (who has mossy teeth in an earnest face) and then I'll be free to sit here and I guess just sing church songs to myself. Although I never was a good singer. Never could carry a tune. I was always better at a man's job. I used to love to milk till I was hooked in the side in '49. Cows are soothing and slow and don't bother you, unless you try to milk them the wrong way.

I have deliberately turned my back on the house. It is three rooms, just like the one that burned, except the roof is tin; they don't make shingle roofs anymore. There are no real windows, just some holes cut in the sides, like the portholes in a ship, but not round and not square, with rawhide holding the shutters up on the outside. This house is in a pasture, too, like the other one. No doubt when Dee sees it she will want to tear it down. She wrote me once that no matter where we "choose" to live, she will manage to come see us. But she will never bring her friends. Maggie and I thought about this and Maggie asked me, "Mama, when did Dee ever *have* any friends?"

She had a few. Furtive boys in pink shirts hanging about on washday after school. Nervous girls who never laughed. Impressed with her, they worshiped the well-turned phrase, the cute shape, the scalding humor that erupted like bubbles in lye. She read to them.

When she was courting Jimmy T she didn't have much time to pay to us, but turned all her faultfinding power on him. He *flew* to marry a cheap city girl from a family of ignorant flashy people. She hardly had time to recompose herself.

When she comes I will meet—but there they are!

Maggie attempts to make a dash for the house, in her shuffling way, but I stay her with my hand. "Come back here," I say. And she stops and tries to dig a well in the sand with her toe.

---

organdy (AWR gun dee) kind of thin crisp cotton cloth
pumps (PUMPS) kind of low cut shoes for women
furtive (FUR tiv) sly; shifty
recompose (ree kum POHZ) pulls oneself together; become calm again

It is hard to see them clearly through the strong sun. But even the first glimpse of leg out of the car tells me it is Dee. Her feet were always neat-looking, as if God himself had shaped them with a certain style. From the other side of the car comes a short, stocky man. Hair is all over his head a foot long and hanging from his chin like a kinky mule tail. I hear Maggie suck in her breath. "Uhnnnh," is what it sounds like. Like when you see the wriggling end of a snake just in front of your foot on the road. "Uhnnnh."

Dee next. A dress down to the ground, in this hot weather. A dress so loud it hurts my eyes. There are yellows and oranges enough to throw back the light of the sun. I feel my whole face warming from the heat waves it throws out. Earrings gold, too, and hanging down to her shoulders. Bracelets dangling and making noises when she moves her arm up to shake the folds of the dress out of her armpits. The dress is loose and flows, and as she walks closer, I like it. I hear Maggie go "Uhnnnh" again. It is her sister's hair. It stands straight up like the wool on a sheep. It is black as night and around the edges are two long pigtails that rope about like small lizards disappearing behind her ears.

"Wa-su-zo-Tean-o!" she says, coming on in that gliding way the dress makes her move. The short stocky fellow with the hair to his navel is all grinning and he follows up with "Asalamalakim, my mother and sister!" He moves to hug Maggie but she falls back, right up against the back of my chair. I feel her trembling there and when I look up I see the perspiration falling off her chin.

"Don't get up," says Dee. Since I am stout it takes something of a push. You can see me trying to move a second or two before I make it. She turns, showing white heels through her sandals, and goes back to the car. Out she peeks next with a Polaroid. She stoops down quickly and lines up picture after picture of me sitting there in front of the house with Maggie cowering behind me. She never takes a shot without making sure the house is included. When a cow comes nibbling around the edge of the yard she snaps it and me and Maggie *and* the house. Then she puts the Polaroid in the back seat of the car, and comes up and kisses me on the forehead.

Meanwhile Asalamalakim is going through motions with Maggie's hand. Maggie's hand is as limp as a fish, and probably as cold, despite the sweat, and she keeps trying to pull it back. It looks like Asalamalakim wants to shake hands but wants to do it fancy. Or maybe he don't know how people shake hands. Anyhow, he soon gives up on Maggie.

"Well," I say. "Dee."

"No, Mama," she says. "Not 'Dee,' Wangero Leewanika Kemanjo!"

"What happened to 'Dee'?" I wanted to know.

"She's dead," Wangero said. "I couldn't bear it any longer, being named after the people who oppress me."

---

cowering (KOU ur ing) crouching in fear

Background Notes

Describe to students the 1960s when black consciousness, black power, black pride, and so on, came into being and when black Americans began to celebrate their African heritage by adopting traditional African names, clothing, and hairstyles as an expression of pride in their heritage. Show photographs from this period and read from the writings of Malcolm X, Eldridge Cleaver, James Baldwin, etc.

Discussion

Discuss with the class how the effects of the 1960s (as described above) still reverberate in the United States today and ask them to describe how their lives are affected.

Literary Focus: *Theme*

Ask: How does Dee's name change contribute to the theme?

Reading Focus:
Compare and Contrast

Have students look at the illustration on this page. Ask: Is this more likely to be Mama's house or Dee's house? Have students use story details to support their answers. Ask them the question again after they have read page 513.

"You know as well as me you was named after your aunt Dicie," I said. Dicie is my sister. She named Dee. We called her "Big Dee" after Dee was born.

"But who was *she* named after?" asked Wangero.

"I guess after Grandma Dee," I said.

"And who was she named after?" asked Wangero.

"Her mother," I said, and saw Wangero was getting tired. "That's about as far back as I can trace it," I said. Though, in fact, I probably could have carried it back beyond the Civil War through the branches.

"Well," said Asalamalakim, "there you are."

"Uhnnnh," I heard Maggie say.

"There I was not," I said, "before 'Dicie' cropped up in our family, so why should I try to trace it that far back?"

He just stood there grinning, looking down on me like somebody inspecting a Model A car. Every once in a while he and Wangero sent eye signals over my head.

"How do you pronounce this name?" I asked.

"You don't have to call me by it if you don't want to," said Wangero.

"Why shouldn't I?" I asked. "If that's what you want us to call you, we'll call you."

"I know it might sound awkward at first," said Wangero.

"I'll get used to it," I said. "Ream it out again."

---

ream (REEM) enlarge; open up (here used figuratively)

Well, soon we got the name out of the way. Asalamalakim had a name twice as long and three times as hard. After I tripped over it two or three times he told me to just call him Hakim-a-barber. I wanted to ask him was he a barber, but I didn't really think he was, so I didn't ask.

"You must belong to those beef-cattle peoples down the road," I said. They said "Asalamalakim" when they met you, too, but they didn't shake hands. Always too busy: feeding the cattle, fixing the fences, putting up salt-lick shelters, throwing down hay. When the white folks poisoned some of the herd the men stayed up all night with rifles in their hands. I walked a mile and a half just to see the sight.

Hakim-a-barber said, "I accept some of their doctrines, but farming and raising cattle is not my style." (They didn't tell me, and I didn't ask, whether Wangero (Dee) had really gone and married him.)

We sat down to eat and right away he said he didn't eat collards and pork was unclean. Wangero, though, went on through the chitlins and corn bread, the greens and everything else. She talked a blue streak over the sweet potatoes. Everything delighted her. Even the fact that we still used the benches her daddy made for the table when we couldn't afford to buy chairs.

"Oh, Mama!" she cried. Then turned to Hakim-a-barber. "I never knew how lovely these benches are. You can feel the rump prints," she said, running her hands underneath her and along the bench. Then she gave a sigh and her hand closed over Grandma Dee's butter dish. "That's it!" she said. "I knew there was something I wanted to ask you if I could have." She jumped up from the table and went over in the corner where the churn stood, the milk in it clabber by now. She looked at the churn and looked at it.

"This churn top is what I need," she said. "Didn't Uncle Buddy whittle it out of a tree you all used to have?"

"Yes," I said.

"Uh huh," she said happily. "And I want the dasher, too."

"Uncle Buddy whittle that, too?" asked the barber.

Dee (Wangero) looked up at me.

"Aunt Dee's first husband whittled the dash," said Maggie so low you almost couldn't hear her. "His name was Henry, but they called him Stash."

"Maggie's brain is like an elephant's," Wangero said, laughing. "I can use the churn top as a centerpiece for the alcove table," she said, sliding a plate over the churn, "and I'll think of something artistic to do with the dasher."

When she finished wrapping the dasher the handle stuck out. I took it for a

---

doctrine (DOK trin) belief, theory
collards (KOL urdz) kind of green vegetable
chitlins (CHIT linz) hog intestines used as food
clabber (KLAB ur) sour, thick milk
dasher (DASH ur) plunger with paddles for stirring
alcove (AL kohv) opening off a room

Critical Thinking: *Infer*

Ask: Why did Mama walk a mile and a half just to see the men sitting up all night with rifles? Why was this a special sight?

Reading Focus: *Compare and Contrast*

Ask students to contrast Dee's and Mama's feelings about the quilts and their purpose. Ask if there are any similarities about how Dee and Mama view the quilts.

Literary Focus: *Theme*

Point out to students the phrase "everyday use" about two-thirds of the way down the second column. Elicit that the phrase is also in the story title, and is probably related to the theme of the story. Have students reread the paragraph with the phrase and comment on what the conflict and the theme might be.

moment in my hands. You didn't even have to look close to see where hands pushing the dasher up and down to make butter had left a kind of sink in the wood. In fact, there were a lot of small sinks; you could see where thumbs and fingers had sunk into the wood. It was beautiful light yellow wood, from a tree that grew in the yard where Big Dee and Stash had lived.

After dinner Dee (Wangero) went to the trunk at the foot of my bed and started rifling through it. Maggie hung back in the kitchen over the dishpan. Out came Wangero with two quilts. They had been pieced by Grandma Dee and then Big Dee and me had hung them on the quilt frames on the front porch and quilted them. One was in the Lone Star pattern. The other was Walk Around the Mountain. In both of them were scraps of dresses Grandma Dee had worn fifty and more years ago. Bits and pieces of Grandpa Jarrell's Paisley shirts. And one teeny faded blue piece, about the size of a penny matchbox, that was from Great Grandpa Ezra's uniform that he wore in the Civil War.

"Mama," Wangero said sweet as a bird. "Can I have these old quilts?"

I heard something fall in the kitchen, and a minute later the kitchen door slammed.

"Why don't you take one or two of the others?" I asked. "These old things was just done by me and Big Dee from some tops your grandma pieced before she died."

"No," said Wangero. "I don't want those. They are stitched around the borders by machine."

"That'll make them last better," I said.

"That's not the point," said Wangero. "These are all pieces of dresses Grandma used to wear. She did all this stitching by hand. Imagine!" She held the quilts securely in her arms, stroking them.

"Some of the pieces, like those lavender ones, come from old clothes her mother handed down to her," I said, moving up to touch the quilts. Dee (Wangero) moved back just enough so that I couldn't reach the quilts. They already belonged to her.

"Imagine!" she breathed again, clutching them closely to her bosom.

"The truth is," I said, "I promised to give them quilts to Maggie, for when she marries John Thomas."

She gasped like a bee had stung her.

"Maggie can't appreciate these quilts!" she said. "She'd probably be backward enough to put them to everyday use."

"I reckon she would," I said. "God knows I been saving 'em for long enough with nobody using 'em. I hope she will!" I didn't want to bring up how I had offered Dee (Wangero) a quilt when she went away to college. Then she had told me they were old-fashioned, out of style.

"But they're *priceless*!" she was saying now, furiously; for she has a temper. "Maggie would put them on the bed and in five years they'd be in rags. Less than that!"

"She can always make some more," I said. "Maggie knows how to quilt."

---

rifling (RY fling) searching; going through hurriedly

Critical Thinking: *Draw Conclusions*

Have students use what they have learned about the three main characters to answer these questions: Who might the woman in this illustration be? Could she be Mama? Why or why not? Could she be Maggie? Why or why not? Could she be Dee? Why or why not? Encourage students to revisit descriptions of the characters and their manner of dress. Students should conclude that the illustration does not fit any of the characters exactly. Ask which character it most closely fits.

Literary Focus: *Theme*

Call on individual students to describe the setting, plot, tone, and characters of the story. Call on others to identify figurative language if it is used. Discuss how each relates to the theme.

Dee (Wangero) looked at me with hatred. "You just will not understand. The point is these quilts, *these* quilts!"

"Well," I said, stumped. "What would *you* do with them?"

"Hang them," she said. As if that was the only thing you could do with quilts.

Maggie by now was standing in the door. I could almost hear the sound her feet made as they scraped over each other.

"She can have them, Mama," she said, like somebody used to never winning anything, or having anything reserved for her. "I can 'member Grandma Dee without the quilts."

I looked at her hard. She had filled her bottom lip with checkerberry snuff and it gave her face a kind of dopey, hangdog look. It was Grandma Dee and Big Dee who taught her how to quilt herself. She stood there with her scarred hands hidden in the folds of her skirt. She looked at her sister with something like fear but she wasn't mad at her. This was Maggie's portion. This was the way she knew God to work.

When I looked at her like that something hit me in the top of my head and ran down to the soles of my feet. Just like when I'm in church and the spirit of God touches me and I get happy and shout. I did something I never had done before: hugged Maggie to me, then dragged her on into the room, snatched the quilts out of Miss Wangero's hands and dumped them into Maggie's lap. Maggie just sat there on my bed with her mouth open.

"Take one or two of the others," I said to Dee.

But she turned without a word and went out to Hakim-a-barber.

"You just don't understand," she said, as Maggie and I came out to the car.

"What don't I understand?" I wanted to know.

"Your heritage," she said. And then she turned to Maggie, kissed her, and said, "You ought to try to make something of yourself, too, Maggie. It's really a new day for us. But from the way you and Mama still live you'd never know it."

She put on some sunglasses that hid everything above the tip of her nose and her chin.

Maggie smiled; maybe at the sunglasses. But a real smile, not scared. After we watched the car dust settle I asked Maggie to bring me a dip of snuff. And then the two of us sat there just enjoying, until it was time to go in the house and go to bed.

---

checkerberry (CHEK ur ber ee) kind of small red berry (wintergreen)

Reading Focus: *Compare and Contrast*

After students have finished the story, ask them if Dee is the only one who understands heritage. Discuss. Ask students to compare and contrast what heritage means to Mama, Maggie, and Dee.

Mini Quiz

Write these sentences on the board and call on students to fill in the blanks. Discuss the answers with the class.

1. The narrator has ________ daughters.
2. She lives in a small house with ________ .
3. Dee has a ________ complexion than Maggie.
4. Her mother and the ________ raised money for Dee to attend school.
5. At 16, Dee had a ________ of her own.

Answers

1. two
2. Maggie
3. lighter
4. church
5. style

AUTHOR BIOGRAPHY

Alice Walker (1944–)

Alice Walker, winner of both the Pulitzer Prize and the National Book Award, became a writer at age eight. Her story is an interesting one.

One day in Georgia in 1952, an eight-year-old Alice was shot accidentally in the right eye with a BB gun by one of her brothers. The family had little money, and the best medical attention was not available. She went blind in that eye. The pain ceased after a few days, but the scar tissue remained.

Ironically, the loss of an eye enabled the girl to "see." She soon found herself writing down thoughts and impressions in a notebook, and she discovered that the writing made her feel better. She also started to read a great deal.

Writing and reading helped erase the mental scars, but the scarred eye remained until Alice was 14, when an operation removed the disfigurement. Other changes followed fast. By graduation time she was not only class valedictorian but also voted "Most Popular." Her partial blindness, as well as her ability, qualified her for a special scholarship for the handicapped to Spelman College. She later transferred to Sarah Lawrence College, graduating in 1965.

Walker continued to write in notebooks at Sarah Lawrence and soon found herself writing poetry at a furious pace. She showed the poems to one of her teachers, the poet Muriel Rukeyser. With Rukeyser's help and encouragement, the poems became Alice Walker's first book, *Once* (1968).

Author of poems, novels, short stories, and works of nonfiction, Alice Walker is recognized today as one of America's leading writers. Her most famous work is probably *The Color Purple,* which also became a well-known film. Of general interest are a book of essays, *In Search of Our Mothers' Gardens*, and a biography of her "spirit helper," *Langston Hughes: American Poet.*

MORE ABOUT THE AUTHOR

Alice Walker was born in 1944 in Eatonton, Georgia, and grew up in that rural agricultural community, where most African Americans worked as tenant farmers. Much of her work recalls and is enriched by this Southern background. In addition, she was very active in the Civil Rights Movement, and is particularly a champion of women's sexual, political, and racial equality. She has been criticized for her sometimes unflattering portraits of African American men, but is admired for her sensitive style and the lyrical quality of her writing.

Additional Works

BY ALICE WALKER

You may wish to suggest these works by Alice Walker for additional reading:

The Color Purple (novel), Harcourt Brace Jovanovich, 1982.

In Love and Trouble: Stories of Black Women, Harcourt Brace Jovanovich, 1973.

To Hell With Dying (juvenile), illustrations by Catherine Deeter, Harcourt Brace Jovanovich, 1988.

Possessing the Secret of Joy (novel), Harcourt Brace Jovanovich, 1992.

UNDERSTAND THE SELECTION

Answers

1. Maggie and Dee are the narrator's daughters.
2. in a three-room house in the country
3. Wangero Leewanika Kemanjo
4. She has done hard, outdoor "man's work" chores all her life.
5. She didn't want to be named after her "oppressors."
6. Sample answers: her dress; her hair; her speech
7. Sample answer: the family's heritage
8. Sample answer: It makes one dislike her attitude and greediness. She wants things from the house for display purposes but does not show true respect for her family and background.
9. Sample answers: compassion; wisdom; generosity; strength; honesty
10. Sample answers: a new generation of black women, coming of age in the modern world

Respond to Literature

Answers to this question will vary. Sample answers: pride in being black and of African origin, appreciation of African American culture; Mama and Maggie value the quilts because of who made them and how they can be used.

Have students further respond to these literature questions: Of the three women in the story, which is the most sympathetic character? Which one is most like the author?

WRITE ABOUT THE SELECTION

Prewriting

Students are to work on this section individually. Review the elements of setting before the class begins this section.

Writing

Make this a cooperative group activity. Divide the class into groups of four or five, each member with his or her list of five setting details in hand. Have each group collaborate on a drawing based on the story: it may be a drawing of the characters or the house, but should be inspired by the setting and include some of the details the students have thought up. The drawings can then be displayed around the classroom for the groups to compare. Then have students write their descriptions individually.

Revising

Students are to work on this section individually; remind them to incorporate impressions of all five senses into their descriptions.

Proofreading

Select one or two of the students' descriptions as models for proofreading. Put the description on the overhead projector and have the class suggest improvements.

Review the Selection

UNDERSTAND THE SELECTION

Recall

1. How are the three women in the story related to each other?
2. Where does the narrator live?
3. What is Dee's "new" name?

Infer

4. Why does the narrator describe her hands as "rough, man-working hands"?
5. Why did Dee change her name?
6. Name three other details that tell you that Dee has changed.
7. What do the quilts symbolize?

Apply

8. How does the story make you feel about Dee and why?
9. Name two qualities in the mother that you admire.
10. What do you think Dee represents as compared to her sister and her mother?

Respond to Literature

The women in the story share a heritage, but they value objects from that heritage for different reasons. Why does Dee value the objects? Why do Maggie and her mother value them?

WRITE ABOUT THE SELECTION

The setting of a story can affect your reaction to it. Visualize the mother and Maggie in "Everyday Use" living in a luxurious, ten-room apartment in New York City. Think about them living in an igloo in Alaska. Would the story seem real to you in either of those settings? Write a paragraph that describes the story's setting.

Prewriting Find the details in the story which describe the setting. Then think up five more details which can help to illustrate the setting. List all ten.

Writing In your own words, write a one-paragraph description of the story's setting which creates a vivid picture in the reader's mind. Start outside the house; describe the yard and the appearance of the house. End with a description of the rooms in the house.

Revising To help your readers get a complete picture of the setting, use all five senses: sight, hearing, touch, taste, and smell. Add details which will make the reader feel the setting, as well as see it.

Proofreading Read over your paragraph to check for errors. The possessive form of a noun is shown by using an apostrophe. An apostrophe and an *s* form the possessive of singular nouns. For plural nouns that end in *s* add only an apostrophe. Make sure you have spelled possessive forms correctly.

THINK ABOUT THEME

The **theme** of a work is its main, or central, idea. If you are stating the theme of a work, the wording should point out some general truth, or idea, about life. Some people confuse the theme of a literary work with a "lesson about life." Fables, like those of Aesop, always end with a **moral**, a lesson about how to conduct one's behavior. The theme statement observes a truth but makes no rules to imply it, leaving the reader to discover it by thought.

1. What is the theme of "Everyday Use"?
2. Why did Dee rename herself?
3. Why did the mother snatch the quilts away from Dee and give them to Maggie?
4. Do you think that Walker is making a moral statement about heritage? If so, what is it?

READING FOCUS

Compare and Contrast As you read "Everyday Use," you compared and contrasted aspects of the two sisters. Write one paragraph that describes their similarities and another paragraph that describes their differences.

DEVELOP YOUR VOCABULARY

Adverbs are words that modify verbs, adjectives, and other adverbs. To *modify* means "to limit or restrict in meaning." Many adverbs end in *-ly*; these adverbs usually tell *how*. **Adjectives** are words that modify nouns or pronouns. Descriptive adjectives tell *what kind*. Some of these adjectives also end in *-ly*.

Look at this sentence from "Everyday Use": "she will stand hopelessly in corners, homely and ashamed. . . ." *Hopelessly* modifies the verb *stand* and is an adverb. *Homely* modifies the pronoun *she* and is an adjective.

Tell whether the *italicized* word is an adjective or an adverb.

1. "She held the quilts *securely* in her arms. . . ."
2. "I can kill and clean a hog as *mercilessly* as a man."
3. "I never knew how *lovely* these benches are."
4. "She stumbles along *good-naturedly* but can't see well."

THINK ABOUT THEME

Sample Answers

1. There are many ways to understand one's heritage; heritage is an important part of one's identity; there are deep as well as superficial ways of appreciating one's heritage.
2. Dee was adopting many outward ways of displaying her heritage because it was fashionable to do so.
3. She realized that Maggie had been denied more than Dee and that Maggie's appreciation of the quilts was deeper than Dee's.
4. Yes, live your heritage; integrate it into your daily life; make it for "everyday use"; do not make a merely superficial display of it.

DEVELOP YOUR VOCABULARY

Answers

1. adverb
2. adverb
3. adjective
4. adverb

ESL Activity

Have students work in pairs with proficient English speakers to complete the vocabulary exercise. Have them role-play each sentence to determine the meaning of each italicized word.

READING FOCUS

Sample Answer

Maggie and Dee have the same mother and were raised together in a little country house. They both value their ancestry, although for different reasons.

The sisters differ in many ways. Physically, they have different skin color, hair, and body shapes. Their goals in life, their values, and their level of education also differ.

SELECTION OVERVIEW

SELECTION OBJECTIVES

After completing this selection, students will be able to

- define and discuss characters in fiction and nonfiction
- write a description of a real person
- conduct a newspaper-type interview
- understand and identify base words and prefixes, and use prefixes to make new words
- understand sequence of events

Lesson Resources

from *The Woman Warrior*

- Selection Synopsis, Teacher's Edition, p. T445g
- Comprehension and Vocabulary Workbook, pp. 103–104
- Language Enrichment Workbook, p. 79
- Teacher's Resources
  Reinforcement, p. R52
  Test, pp. T103–T104

More About Character

In both fiction and nonfiction, when an author presents a character with a fully-rounded personality, that character is said to be *round* as opposed to *flat*. Round characters are complex and three-dimensional. Most major characters in fiction are round. Flat characters are usually of minor importance.

A character who is somehow changed by the events of a story is considered *dynamic*. On the other hand, characters who exhibit little or no change throughout a story are termed *static*.

Ask students to give examples from selections in this unit of round/dynamic characters. Note whether the work is fiction, poetry, or nonfiction. What conclusions or generalizations can be drawn from this discussion?

Learn About

CHARACTER

In literature, a character is simply a person in a story. In fiction, characters are imaginary people who spring from the mind of the writer. In nonfiction, the writer describes a real person.

There are three basic methods of revealing character in writing. In the first, the writer provides a clear and comprehensive description of the person. In the second, the writer shows the person in action. The personality is defined by what the individual does. In the third method, the writer tells the person's thoughts, emotions, and reactions to events. The third method, of course, is impossible for the nonfiction writer unless he or she learns about the inner life of the individual from interviews or close personal relationships. Even then, the writer must use his or her imagination.

As you read this personal recollection, ask yourself:

1. How does the writer show the personality of the main character?
2. Is the main character believable?

READING FOCUS

Understand Sequence of Events Story events are usually told in chronological, or time, order. The author describes the first happening, then the second, and so on. Sometimes, signal words such as *first*, *next*, or *finally* are used to indicate time order; sometimes there are no signal words, and you rely on story context. As you read the next selection, pay attention to the sequence of events. Jot down any signal words you notice.

WRITING CONNECTION

Write a short paragraph describing someone you know. Provide a clear and complete description of the person.

ESL Activity

Have students hold a group discussion on the roles of men and women in their cultures. Encourage the class to discuss in a respectful manner the similarities and differences among the various culture groups represented.

Cooperative Group Activity

Divide the class into groups of four or five students for the Writing Connection activity. Instruct each student to write a descriptive paragraph about one of the other group members. Each student will then read his or her paragraph to the group, who will then attempt to deduce which group member is being described. After the identity of each character is revealed, direct the group to discuss how clear and comprehensive the description was. In other words, would this character be considered round? Is the character dynamic or static?

from THE WOMAN WARRIOR

by Maxine Hong Kingston

When she was about sixty-eight years old, Brave Orchid took a day off to wait at San Francisco International Airport for the plane that was bringing her sister to the United States. She had not seen Moon Orchid for thirty years. She had begun this waiting at home, getting up a half-hour before Moon Orchid's plane took off in Hong Kong. Brave Orchid would add her will power to the forces that keep an airplane up. Her head hurt with the concentration. The plane had to be light, so no matter how tired she felt, she dared not rest her spirit on a wing but continuously and gently pushed up on the plane's belly. She had already been waiting at the airport for nine hours. She was wakeful.

Next to Brave Orchid sat Moon Orchid's only daughter, who was helping her aunt wait. Brave Orchid had made two of her own children come too because they could drive, but they had been lured away by the magazine racks and the gift shops and coffee shops. Her American children could not sit for very long. They did not understand sitting; they had wandering feet. She hoped they would get back from the pay t.v.'s or the pay toilets or wherever they were spending their money before the plane arrived. If they did not come back soon, she would go look for them. If her son thought he could hide in the men's room, he was wrong.

"Are you all right, Aunt?" asked her niece.

"No, this chair hurts me. Help me pull some chairs together so I can put my feet up."

She unbundled a blanket and spread it out to make a bed for herself. On the floor she had two shopping bags full of canned peaches, real peaches, beans

Develop Vocabulary Skills

Review the vocabulary words with the class; call on volunteers to suggest synonyms for each of the words. Discuss the answers with the class.

About the Author

Maxine (Ting Ting) Hong Kingston was born in Stockton, California, in 1940; both her parents had emigrated from China. Her father Tom was a scholar, manager of a gambling house, and laundry worker; her mother Ying Lan was a practitioner of medicine and midwifery, a field hand, and a laundry worker. Much of Kingston's work is based on the myth and history she learned as a child. Her stories are in many cases attempts to merge aspects of her Chinese heritage and U.S. culture.

Named a Living Treasure of Hawaii in 1980, Kingston is a professor of English at the University of Hawaii. She won the National Book Critics Circle award for general nonfiction in 1976 for *The Woman Warrior: Memoirs of a Girlhood Among Ghosts.*

Teaching Plan

INTRODUCE

Motivation

Give a short history of the massive immigration of Chinese people to the United States during the late 1800s and early 1900s; tell how those emigres were treated, and describe the limited opportunities they found in the United States as they attempted to become U.S. citizens and still retain their own culture.

Purpose-Setting Question

How do we define ourselves, our identity? By the place we were born? By our ancestors? By our immediate family? By our lives at present? By the place where we live? By a combination of any or all of these things?

READ

Literary Focus: *Character*

Direct students to enjoy and get to know Brave Orchid as they read the story. Remind them that a lot can be learned about a character from noticing what the person thinks, says, and does. As they read, have students jot down their impressions of Brave Orchid. Ask them to decide by the end of the story whether Brave Orchid is a flat or round character, and dynamic or static.

Reading Focus: *Understand Sequence of Events*

Tell students before they begin reading that the chronological order of events in the story is sometimes interrupted by the main character's thoughts. Have students make a timeline to help them keep track of the sequence of events.

CLOSE

Have students complete Review the Selection on pages 528–529.

Literary Focus: *Character*

Direct students' attention to the long paragraph in the first column. Read the paragraph aloud as students read along silently. Ask students what they can tell about Brave Orchid from this description of her thoughts. List their conclusions.

Critical Thinking: *Interpret*

Ask: Why does Brave Orchid call the soldiers "Army and Navy Ghosts"?

Reading Focus: *Understand Sequence of Events*

Ask: What phrase in the second-to-last paragraph signals time order? What word in the last paragraph is also a signal word?

wrapped in taro leaves, cookies, Thermos bottles, enough food for everybody, though only her niece would eat with her. Her bad boy and bad girl were probably sneaking hamburgers, wasting their money. She would scold them.

Many soldiers and sailors sat about, oddly calm, like little boys in cowboy uniforms. (She thought "cowboy" was what you would call a Boy Scout.) They should have been crying hysterically on their way to Vietnam. "If I see one that looks Chinese," she thought, "I'll go over and give him some advice." She sat up suddenly; she had forgotten about her own son, who was even now in Vietnam. Carefully she split her attention, beaming half of it to the ocean, into the water to keep him afloat. He was on a ship. He was in Vietnamese waters. She was sure of it. He and the other children were lying to her. They had said he was in Japan, and then they said he was in the Philippines. But when she sent him her help, she could feel that he was on a ship in Da Nang. Also she had seen the children hide the envelopes that his letters came in.

"Do you think my son is in Vietnam?" she asked her niece, who was dutifully eating.

"No. Didn't your children say he was in the Philippines?"

"Have you ever seen any of his letters with Philippine stamps on them?"

"Oh, yes. Your children showed me one."

"I wouldn't put it past them to send the letters to some Filipino they know. He puts Manila postmarks on them to fool me."

"Yes, I can imagine them doing that. But don't worry. Your son can take care of himself. All your children can take care of themselves."

"Not him. He's not like other people. Not normal at all. He sticks erasers in his ears, and the erasers are still attached to the pencil stubs. The captain will say, 'Abandon ship,' or, 'Watch out for bombs,' and he won't hear. He doesn't listen to orders. I told him to flee to Canada, but he wouldn't go."

She closed her eyes. After a short while, plane and ship under control, she looked again at the children in uniforms. Some of the blond ones looked like baby chicks, their crew cuts like the downy yellow on baby chicks. You had to feel sorry for them even though they were Army and Navy Ghosts.

Suddenly her son and daughter came running. "Come, Mother. The plane's landed early. She's here already." They hurried, folding up their mother's encampment. She was glad her children were not useless. They must have known what this trip to San Francisco was about then. "It's a good thing I made you come early," she said.

---

taro (TAHR oh) kind of tropical plant used for food
Filipino (fil uh PEE noh) native of the Philippines
downy (DOU nee) soft; fluffy
encampment (en KAMP munt) camp and equipment

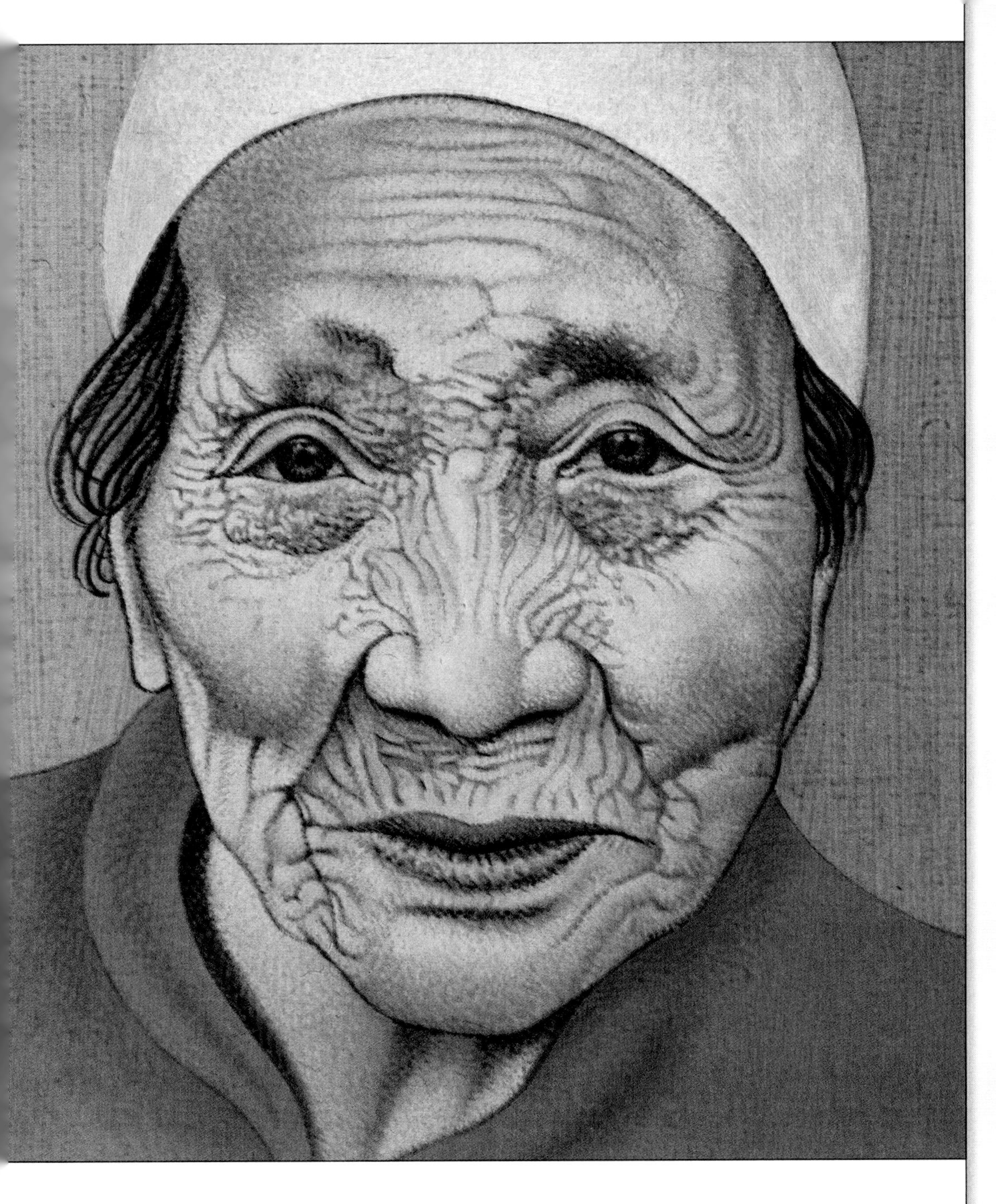

Critical Thinking: ***Analyze***

Ask students to identify the point of view of the narrator, and tell if the viewpoint is limited or omniscient.

Critical Thinking: ***Draw Conclusions***

After reading this page, ask students if they have enough evidence now to conclude what Brave Orchid means when she refers to "ghosts."

Brave Orchid pushed to the front of the crowd. She had to be in front. The passengers were separated from the people waiting for them by glass doors and walls. Immigration Ghosts were stamping papers. The travellers crowded along some conveyor belts to have their luggage searched. Brave Orchid did not see her sister anywhere. She stood watching for four hours. Her children left and came back. "Why don't you sit down?" they asked.

"The chairs are too far away," she said.

"Why don't you sit on the floor then?"

No, she would stand, as her sister was probably standing in a line she could not see from here. Her American children had no feelings and no memory.

To while away time, she and her niece talked about the Chinese passengers. These new immigrants had it easy. On Ellis Island[1] the people were thin after forty days at sea and had no fancy luggage.

"That one looks like her," Brave Orchid would say.

"No, that's not her."

Ellis Island had been made out of wood and iron. Here everything was new plastic, a ghost trick to lure immigrants into feeling safe and spilling their secrets. Then the Alien Office could send them right back. Otherwise, why did they lock her out, not letting her help her sister answer questions and spell her name? At Ellis Island when the ghost asked Brave Orchid what year her husband had cut off his pigtail, a Chinese who was crouching on the floor motioned her not to talk. "I don't know," she had said. If it weren't for that Chinese man, she might not be here today, or her husband either. She hoped some Chinese, a janitor or a clerk, would look out for Moon Orchid. Luggage conveyors fooled immigrants into thinking the Gold Mountain was going to be easy.

Brave Orchid felt her heart jump—Moon Orchid. "There she is," she shouted. But her niece saw it was not her mother at all. And it shocked her to discover the woman her aunt was pointing out. This was a young woman, younger than herself, no older than Moon Orchid the day the sisters parted. "Moon Orchid will have changed a little, of course," Brave Orchid was saying. "She will have learned to wear western clothes." The woman wore a navy blue suit with a bunch of dark cherries at the shoulder.

"No, Aunt," said the niece. "That's not my mother."

"Perhaps not. It's been so many years. Yes, it is your mother. It must be. Let her come closer, and we can tell. Do you think she's too far away for me to tell, or is it my eyes getting bad?"

"It's too many years gone by," said the niece.

---

conveyor (belt) (kun VAY ur) endless moving belt or platform for carrying objects short distances

[1]**Ellis Island:** an island in New York harbor that served for years as an immigration examination center.

alien (AY lee un *or* AYL yun) non-citizen; foreigner

Brave Orchid turned suddenly—another Moon Orchid, this one a neat little woman with a bun. She was laughing at something the person ahead of her in line said. Moon Orchid was just like that, laughing at nothing. "I would be able to tell the difference if one of them would only come closer," Brave Orchid said with tears, which she did not wipe. Two children met the woman with the cherries, and she shook their hands. The other woman was met by a young man. They looked at each other gladly, then walked away side by side.

Up close neither one of those women looked like Moon Orchid at all. "Don't worry, Aunt," said the niece, "I'll know her."

"I'll know her too. I knew her before you did."

The niece said nothing, although she had seen her mother only five years ago. Her aunt liked having the last word.

Finally Brave Orchid's children quit wandering and drooped on a railing. Who knew what they were thinking? At last the niece called out, "I see her! I see her! Mother! Mother!" Whenever the doors parted, she shouted, probably embarrassing the American cousins, but she didn't care. She called out, "Mama! Mama!" until the crack in the sliding doors became too small to let in her voice. "Mama!" What a strange word in an adult voice. Many people turned to see what adult was calling, "Mama!" like a child. Brave Orchid saw an old, old woman jerk her head up, her little eyes blinking confusedly, a woman whose nerves leapt toward the sound anytime she heard "Mama!" Then she relaxed to her own business again. She was a tiny, tiny lady, very thin, with little fluttering hands, and her hair was in a gray knot. She was dressed in a gray wool suit; she wore pearls around her neck and in her earlobes. Moon Orchid *would* travel with her jewels showing. Brave Orchid momentarily saw, like a larger, younger outline around this old woman, the sister she had been waiting for. The familiar dim halo faded, leaving the woman so old, so gray. So old. Brave Orchid pressed against the glass. That old lady? Yes, that old lady facing the ghost who stamped her papers without questioning her was her sister. Then, without noticing her family, Moon Orchid walked smiling over to the Suitcase Inspector Ghost, who took her boxes apart, pulling out puffs of tissue. From where she was, Brave Orchid could not see what her sister had chosen to carry across the ocean. She wished her sister would look her way. Brave Orchid thought that if *she* were entering a new country, she would be at the windows. Instead Moon Orchid hovered over the unwrapping, surprised at each reappearance as if she were opening presents after a birthday party.

"Mama!" Moon Orchid's daughter kept calling. Brave Orchid said to her children, "Why don't you call your aunt too?

hover (HUV ur) stay nearby; linger about

Literary Focus: *Character*

Have students describe Moon Orchid. Ask: Are Moon Orchid and Brave Orchid round or flat characters? Cite evidence for your answer.

Reading Focus: *Understand Sequence of Events*

Ask students to find the word and the phrases that signal time order in the last paragraph of the first column on this page.

Critical Thinking: *Analyze*

Ask these questions of the class after they have completed the story: What are ghosts? Why does Brave Orchid call them ghosts? Does Brave Orchid have mystical powers? Discuss the answers with the class.

Literary Focus: *Character*

Ask the class to evaluate the character of Brave Orchid. Call on students for one-word descriptions of the kind of person this character is.

Discussion

Ask students to describe, in their own words: the narrator of the story; to name the point of view from which the story is told; to give details of the setting; to specify the writer's tone; to explain the theme of the work.

Reading Focus: *Understand Sequence of Events*

Have students restate the events in the order in which they occurred from the time the sisters meet until the end of the story. Encourage them to use time-order signal words.

Maybe she'll hear us if all of you call out together." But her children slunk away. Maybe that shame-face they so often wore was American politeness.

"Mama!" Moon Orchid's daughter called again, and this time her mother looked right at her. She left her bundles in a heap and came running. "Hey!" the Customs Ghost yelled at her. She went back to clear up her mess, talking inaudibly to her daughter all the while. Her daughter pointed toward Brave Orchid. And at last Moon Orchid looked at her—two old women with faces like mirrors.

Their hands reached out as if to touch the other's face, then returned to their own, the fingers checking the grooves in the forehead and along the sides of the mouth. Moon Orchid, who never understood the gravity of things, started smiling and laughing, pointing at Brave Orchid. Finally Moon Orchid gathered up her stuff, strings hanging and papers loose, and met her sister at the door, where they shook hands, oblivious to blocking the way.

"You're an old woman," said Brave Orchid.

"Aiaa. *You're* an old woman."

"But you are really old. Surely, you can't say that about me. I'm not old the way you're old."

"But *you* really are old. You're one year older than I am."

"Your hair is white and your face all wrinkled."

"You're so skinny."

"You're so fat."

"Fat women are more beautiful than skinny women."

The children pulled them out of the doorway. One of Brave Orchid's children brought the car from the parking lot, and the other heaved the luggage into the trunk. They put the two old ladies and the niece in the back seat. All the way home—across the Bay Bridge, over the Diablo hills, across the San Joaquin River to the valley, the valley moon so white at dusk—all the way home, the two sisters exclaimed every time they turned to look at each other, "Aiaa! How old!"

Brave Orchid forgot that she got sick in cars, that all vehicles but palanquins made her dizzy. "You're so old," she kept saying. "How did you get so old?"

Brave Orchid had tears in her eyes. But Moon Orchid said, "You look older than I. You *are* older than I," and again she'd laugh. "You're wearing an old mask to tease me." It surprised Brave Orchid that after thirty years she could still get annoyed at her sister's silliness.

---

slunk (SLUNK) moved in a fearful or embarrassed way
inaudibly (in AW duh blee) not being heard
gravity (GRAV ih tee) dignity; seriousness
oblivious (uh BLIV ee us) unaware; unmindful
palanquin (pal un KEEN) carriage on poles that is carried on people's shoulders

Mini Quiz

Write the following sentences on the board or overhead projector and call on students to fill in the blanks. Discuss the answers with the class.

1. Brave Orchid's ________ stays with her in the airport.
2. Brave Orchid thinks her son is in ________.
3. Moon Orchid is Brave Orchid's ________.
4. When Brave Orchid came to the United States, the trip took ________ days.
5. Brave Orchid refers to the United States as the ________ ________.

Answers

1. niece
2. Vietnam
3. sister
4. forty
5. Gold Mountain

Review the Selection

UNDERSTAND THE SELECTION

Recall

1. How old is Brave Orchid?
2. When had she last seen her sister?
3. How many children does Moon Orchid have?

Infer

4. Why is Brave Orchid worried about her son?
5. Why does Brave Orchid bring food to the airport?
6. Who are the people Brave Orchid calls "ghosts"?
7. Explain how Brave Orchid feels when she first sees her sister.

Apply

8. Suppose you are meeting a family member you haven't seen for many years. What emotions might you feel?
9. Do you think the sisters are very similar or very different? Why do you think so?
10. How would you characterize Brave Orchid?

Respond to Literature

Does Brave Orchid feel more Chinese than American? What examples of her Chinese identity are found in the story?

WRITE ABOUT THE SELECTION

Characters in nonfiction are real people, but unless they are well known, the writer cannot assume that the reader knows them. The writer must supply details about the characters.

Suppose you are a newspaper reporter, and you have been assigned to interview the two sisters who have been reunited after thirty years. Write an interview with Brave Orchid and Moon Orchid.

Prewriting Write down two lists of five questions each. The first is a list of questions to ask Brave Orchid. The second is a list of questions to ask Moon Orchid.

Writing Write the interview using a question-and-answer format. Based on your list, write out the questions, addressing them to one or the other of the sisters. Then write the replies as you think the characters would answer.

Revising With a few adverbs, you can make this interview even more interesting. Insert adverbs to show the sisters' reactions to your questions. For example, does Brave Orchid reply calmly, seriously, excitedly, or angrily?

Proofreading Read over your interview to check for errors. Quotation marks are used to set off conversation. They are placed after the punctuation of a direct quotation, whether the punctuation is a comma, a question mark or an exclamation point. Be sure all of your quotation marks are in the right place.

UNDERSTAND THE SELECTION

Answers

1. sixty-eight
2. thirty years ago
3. one, a daughter
4. He is in the military in the Vietnam War.
5. She went there many hours before the plane was due.
6. Caucasians, or non-Asians
7. Sample answer: surprise that her sister has aged
8. Sample answer: excitement, anticipation, nervousness
9. Sample answer: similar because the author describes "two old women with faces like mirrors" and because they act the same way on the ride home
10. Sample answer: more Chinese than American; self-centered; conservative; unwilling to accept change

Respond to Literature

Answers will vary. A suggested response is: Yes; her name, her belief in willpower and spirit(s), her mistrust of "ghosts," her identifying her children as "American."

Other respond-to-literature questions: Does Brave Orchid's niece feel more Chinese than American? Why does she stay with her aunt rather than go off with her "American" cousins? How will Moon Orchid react to them; that is, will she see her sister and daughter as "Americanized"?

WRITE ABOUT THE SELECTION

Prewriting

Discuss the reporter's "five W's" with the class: *who*, *what*, *when*, *where*, *why*. Discuss the small details that can make a character sketch reveal a personality: gestures and movements, facial expressions, clothing, manner of speaking, etc. Then have the students do the prewriting section.

Writing

Students are to work on this section individually. Offer assistance to any student who is having difficulty.

Revising

Students are to work on this section individually as well. Ask the class to suggest adverbs that will make the actions of characters more vivid. For contrast, ask them to suggest adverbs that would be inappropriate to describe a person's actions.

Proofreading

Make this a cooperative group activity. Divide the class into pairs of students and have them check each other's work. Proofreaders should circle incorrect punctuation with a pencil and write out the correct punctuation for the writer to see.

ESL Activity

Have students conduct a group interview with a person who has come here from another country. Have students prepare questions ahead of time and write the results as a newspaper article.

THINK ABOUT CHARACTER

In fiction, the characters are imaginary, created in the writer's mind. In nonfiction the people described are real. Both fiction and nonfiction writers strive to present fully rounded depictions of personalities. They may include extensive physical description, a many-sided view of personality traits, and the individual's actions, opinions, beliefs, ideas, and thoughts.

1. Who is the most memorable character in the selection? Explain why.
2. What clues are you given about the character of Moon Orchid?
3. Are Brave Orchid's children well-rounded characters? Explain.
4. What does Brave Orchid's decision to arrive early at the airport tell you about her?
5. What does the emotion expressed in the final sentence tell you about Brave Orchid?

Reading Focus

Understand Sequence of Events List the signal words and phrases that helped you understand the sequence of events. Use some of these words in a brief summary of the story's events.

DEVELOP YOUR VOCABULARY

Base words are English words that have no letters or syllables added to them. Prefixes are word parts that can be added to base words to change their meaning. For example, *un-* is a commonly used prefix. Add it to *smiling* or *wrap*, and you have formed *unsmiling* and *unwrap*, both of which mean the opposite of the original word. Here are some common prefixes and their meanings:

mis-: wrong, badly, incorrectly
un-: not, the opposite of
re-: back or again

Write the following words from the selection. Then add one or more prefixes from the list and tell the meaning of each new word.

1. spell
2. new
3. sure
4. faded
5. wrinkled
6. take
7. turned
8. known
9. easy
10. discover
11. understood
12. safe

THINK ABOUT CHARACTER

Answers

1. Sample answer: Brave Orchid, since she is the one the author knows best
2. She is Brave Orchid's sister. She is small and thin. She laughs easily. She is silly.
3. No, they are described only briefly.
4. Sample answers: She is concerned and anxious about her sister. She is determined. She is patient.
5. She considers herself to be, and probably is, a serious person.

DEVELOP YOUR VOCABULARY

Answers

1. spell: misspell (spell wrongly); respell (spell again)
2. new: renew (make new again)
3. sure: unsure (not sure)
4. faded: unfaded (not faded)
5. wrinkled: unwrinkled (not wrinkled)
6. take: mistake (take wrongly; make an error); retake (take again)
7. turned: unturned (the opposite of turned); returned (turned again, came back)
8. known: unknown (not known)
9. easy: uneasy (not at ease; uncomfortable)
10. discover: rediscover (discover again)
11. understood: misunderstood (understood wrongly)
12. safe: unsafe (not safe)

Reading Focus

Sample Answer

Signal words and phrases: *already, suddenly, after a short while, for four hours, then, finally, at last, this time, all the while, all the way.* Brave Orchid waits for a long time at the airport for the sister she has not seen in 30 years. Finally Moon Orchid, who has come all the way from Hong Kong, arrives. The years have changed how they look to each other, but their feelings have stayed the same.

SELECTION OVERVIEW

SELECTION OBJECTIVES

After completing these selections, students will be able to

- understand open poetic form
- use vivid words to write a poem in open poetic form
- evaluate why people act in certain ways
- create a poetic response to a poem
- analyze open poetic form
- use antonyms
- compare and contrast

Lesson Resources

This Is Just to Say/The Term

- Selection Synopses, Teacher's Edition, p. T445h
- Comprehension and Vocabulary Workbook, pp. 105–106
- Language Enrichment Workbook, p. 80
- Teacher's Resources
  Reinforcement, p. R53
  Test, pp. T105–T106

About the Author

William Carlos Williams was born on September 17, 1883, in Rutherford, New Jersey. His English father and Puerto Rican mother provided him with a rich background in literature and art. For more than forty years, he worked as a doctor, writing and publishing his poems on the side. He said that his role as a doctor allowed him "to follow the poor defeated body into those gulfs and grottos . . . , to be present at deaths and births, at the tormented battles between daughter and diabolic mother." Being a doctor also freed him from any financial or political pressure. However, it meant that he would have to work much harder since he was trying to perform two jobs simultaneously.

Learn About

READING FOCUS

Compare and Contrast When you compare, you see how things are alike; when you contrast, you look at their differences. The two poems on the next page are by the same author, William Carlos Williams. After you have read both poems several times, look for ways in which the poems are alike and ways in which they are different. Think about their form, the main idea of each, the use of figurative language, and their tone.

OPEN FORM

Form is the structure of a poem. One frequently used form is open form. **Open form** means that the poem is written in one long, continuous structure with no stanzas.

Open form is often called **free verse** because it does not have meter, rhyme, or stanzas. It does, however, have some pattern of organization. Open form, or free verse, uses the length of the line and the way words and phrases are grouped to tie ideas together and emphasize them. The white spaces that are left between lines and words also add emphasis. Sometimes the white spaces are placed between lines at regular intervals, such as every four lines. These white spaces may make the poem look as if it has stanzas.

Open form makes it possible for a poet to express thoughts in new ways.

As you read "This Is Just to Say" and "The Term," ask yourself:

1. What is the form of "This Is Just to Say"?
2. What is the form of "The Term"?

WRITING CONNECTION

Open form allows a poet freedom. Use open form to write a four-line poem about something familiar, such as an apple.

Develop Vocabulary Skills

Familiarize students with the vocabulary word footnoted in the poem. Ask them to look up the word *rumpled* in a dictionary. Then ask for volunteers to use the vocabulary word in an original sentence.

ESL Activity

Have students bring in an object from their life and write a four-line, open form poem about it. Pair students with native English speakers and have partners read their poems aloud to each other. Then have students discuss the objects they brought in with their partners.

Cooperative Group Activity

For the Writing Connection activity, choose an object with which all students would be very familiar. Have students work in small groups to write group four-line poems. Have a member from each group read the group's poem. Have the class evaluate whether each poem captures the essence of the object and compare the strengths and weaknesses of each poem.

This Is Just to Say

by William Carlos Williams

I have eaten
the plums
that were in
the icebox

5 and which
you were probably
saving
for breakfast

Forgive me
10 they were delicious
so sweet
and so cold

The Term

by William Carlos Williams

A rumpled sheet
of brown paper
about the length

and apparent bulk
5 of a man was
rolling with the

wind slowly over
and over in
the street as

10 a car drove down
upon it and
crushed it to

the ground. Unlike
a man it rose
15 again rolling

with the wind over
and over to be as
it was before.

---

rumpled (RUM puld) wrinkled

Teaching Plan

INTRODUCE

Motivation

Ask students to think about a time they took something that belonged to someone else. Encourage them to talk about the way they felt and the ways they could have compensated for the thing they took.

Purpose-Setting Question

Why would a poet compare a piece of paper to a man?

READ

Literary Focus:
Open Form

Point out to students that open form is managed differently in the two poems. Have them analyze and comment on how Williams uses phrasing and white spaces in the poems. Discuss how each form affects the meaning.

Reading Focus:
Compare and Contrast

As students read the two poems, have them show the similarities and differences in a Venn diagram.

CLOSE

Have students complete Review the Selection on pages 532–533.

Mini Quiz

Write the following sentences on the board or overhead projector and call on students to fill in the blanks. Discuss the answers.

1. The poet found the plums in the ________.
2. The poet thought the plums were being saved for ________.
3. The poet saw a ________ sheet of ________ paper rolling with the wind.
4. After the car drove over the paper, it returned to its ________ shape.
5. At the end of the poem, the paper is again ________ with the ________.

Answers

1. icebox
2. breakfast
3. rumpled; brown
4. original
5. rolling; wind

UNDERSTAND THE SELECTION

Answers

1. plums from the icebox
2. the length and bulk of a man
3. It was crushed to the ground.
4. They were delicious, sweet and cold.
5. He is writing a note to ask forgiveness for taking the plums.
6. It has the same size; it can be crushed by a car.
7. A man would not return to his original shape after being crushed by a car.
8. Sample answer: A plum would more likely be a fruit purchased as a special treat.
9. Answers will vary. Most students might say it would show the fragility of a man as compared to a piece of paper.
10. Answers will vary. Paper might be compared to a blank wall or, if rumpled, to a tumbleweed; and man to a robot or a tree or another living form.

Respond to Literature

Have students identify the reasons people take things they should not take. Make a list of the reasons and have students rate them in terms of which are most forgivable. Determine in what order the poet's reasons should come. Then have students discuss the things they have said to explain their taking something. Compare these to the poet's mode of explanation. Ask them which ways of saying you are sorry would be most effective and why.

WRITE ABOUT THE SELECTION

Prewriting

Using students' suggestions, write on the board notes about what might be said to the poet.

Sample. I was unhappy when I found the plums missing as I had bought them as a special treat for my lunch the next day. I had been looking forward to eating them but have forgiven the poet since his poem-note was so lovely.

Writing

Have students work on this section individually. Go around the class, giving help to any student who is having difficulty.

Revising

Make this a cooperative learning opportunity. Pair students to revise their poems.

Proofreading

Select one or two of the students' poems as models for proofreading. Put the poems on the overhead projector and have the class suggest improvements.

ESL Activity

Have students of like cultures meet in a group. Ask them to describe or explain ways of saying they are sorry that are acceptable in their cultures. Compare various responses and cultures.

Review the Selection

UNDERSTAND THE SELECTION

Recall

1. In "This Is Just to Say," what did the speaker eat?
2. In "The Term," how big was the brown paper?
3. What happened to the paper when the car drove over it?

Infer

4. Why did the speaker eat the plums?
5. Why did the poet write the poem?
6. What are two ways that the paper is like a man?
7. How is the paper unlike a man?

Apply

8. Why do you think the poet chose plums rather than apples, bananas, or oranges?
9. Why do you think the poet compared the paper to a man?
10. What would you compare a piece of paper to? A man to?

Respond to Literature

Why do people, like the speaker in "This Is Just to Say," take things they should not take? How would you explain taking something that you should not have?

WRITE ABOUT THE SELECTION

Imagine that you have just received the poem "This is Just to Say." It is your plums that the poet has just eaten. How do you feel about the poet eating your fruit? Has the poem made you forgive the poet for eating them? Write a response to the poet, telling him how you feel. Your response should be in the form of a poem that is at least four lines in length.

Prewriting Write notes about what you will say to the poet. include details about what you had planned to use the plums for, how you felt when you found the plums missing, and what effect his poem had on you. Decide if the mood of your poem will be serious or amusing.

Writing Use your notes to write your poem, telling the poet how you felt about his taking your plums. Make sure your poem clearly indicates whether you forgive the poet or are unhappy with his actions. Choose words that will create the exact mood you want to convey.

Revising When you revise, add any details that will intensify the mood of your poem. Eliminate any boring phrases. Substitute interesting words for ordinary ones.

Proofreading Reread your poem to check for errors. You may not want to use any punctuation. However, be sure that you have capitalized the first word in each line.

THINK ABOUT POETIC FORM

Form refers to the shape, or pattern, of a poem. **Open form**, or free verse, does not have meter, rhyme, or stanzas. Using open form allows a poet greater freedom in presenting his or her ideas and emotions.

1. "This Is Just to Say" is written in open form. In what ways can this poem be called free verse?
2. Why are there spaces between every four lines?
3. What does the speaker tell about in the first four lines? In the next four? In the last four?
4. What is the form in "The Term"?
5. How many sentences are there in the poem?
6. Why are there open spaces every three lines?

> ### READING FOCUS
> **Compare and Contrast** As you read "This Is Just to Say" and "The Term," you compared and contrasted the poems. What is one way in which the poems are similar? What is one way in which they are different? Consider the form, the main idea, the use of figurative language, and the tone of each poem.

DEVELOP YOUR VOCABULARY

An **antonym** is a word that has the opposite or nearly the opposite meaning of another word. For example, *out* is an antonym for *in* because it has the opposite meaning.

1. Write antonyms for the following words.
   a. sweet
   b. cold
   c. rumpled
   d. man
   e. slowly
   f. over
   g. down
   h. to
2. Reread the two poems to find antonyms for the following words.
   a. like
   b. blame
   c. fell
   d. after
   e. tasteless
   f. wasting
   g. unseen
   h. without
3. Write an original sentence for each of the words that are antonyms for the words in question 2.

ESL Activity

Ask students to work independently on numbers 1 and 2. For number 3, allow group work. Have students write original sentences.

THINK ABOUT POETIC FORM

Answers

1. The poem has no rhyme, no stanzas, and no set rhythm.
2. The spaces are used to add emphasis and to separate ideas.
3. In the first four he tells what he did; in the second four he says that he knows he shouldn't have done it; and in the last four he tells why he did it.
4. The form is open, or free, verse.
5. There are two sentences.
6. The open spaces add emphasis and separate ideas. The lines roll just as the paper rolls.

DEVELOP YOUR VOCABULARY

Sample Answers

1. (a) sour (b) hot (c) smooth (d) woman (e) quickly (f) under (g) up (h) (away) from
2. (a) unlike (b) forgive (c) rose (d) before (e) delicious (f) saving (g) apparent (h) with
3. (a) My sister is *unlike* me in many ways.
   (b) *Forgive* me for eating the plums.
   (c) The boxer *rose* from his knees to face his opponent again.
   (d) He had looked just as fierce *before* he was knocked down.
   (e) Plums are certainly *delicious*.
   (f) I was *saving* my money to buy a compact disc player.
   (g) The cat was the *apparent* size of a large raccoon.
   (h) Will you go *with* me to the store?

READING FOCUS

Sample Answer

The poems are alike in that they are both written in open form, or free verse. Differences include the main ideas of the poems and the use of figurative language. "This Is Just to Say" is an apology and does not use figurative language. "The Term" uses the metaphor of a sheet of paper to describe the resilience of a man.

UNIT 6 Review

WRITING APPLICATIONS

Write About the Literary Period

"American" is often used as an umbrella term that applies to every citizen in this country. Yet many different kinds of people live under that umbrella. They represent different ethnic groups, different cultures, different heritages. The selections in this unit include works by American writers of various backgrounds.

Identify three distinct cultures described in the selections in this unit. What values are important to the characters within those selections?

Prewriting Make a chart with three headings across the top. Each heading should list the name of one selection you have chosen. Under each heading, list key words or phrases that identify the values you have discovered.

Writing Write a paragraph comparing and contrasting the differences and similarities in values found in the stories you have chosen.

Revising Illustrate your points by quoting from the selections. Choose sentences or descriptions that support your opinions.

Proofreading Capitalize all important words in the title of a book, poem, or short story. Underline the title of a book in your writing or italicize it if using a computer. Put quotation marks around the title of a poem or short story. Check your work to see if you have punctuated the titles correctly.

Write About Genre

In reading about autobiography, you have learned that it is a unique form of nonfiction. You have read about four important elements of autobiography—point of view, purpose, introspection and narrative.

Think of a memorable event in your life. How did it affect you? What did you learn from it? When and where did it happen? Write about this event as if it were a chapter in your autobiography.

Prewriting Make a chronological list—from beginning to end—of what happened during this event in your life. Make another list of words you would use to describe yourself. Make a third list of key words that describe how you felt and what you thought about the event.

Writing Based on your chronological list, write a narrative of the event. Use your other two lists to tell more about yourself and describe your thoughts and reactions during the event.

Revising Add vivid adjectives and adverbs to emphasize your reactions and to make your feelings clear.

Proofreading Make sure the verbs in your sentences agree with their subjects. Singular subjects take singular verbs; plural subjects take plural verbs. Check the verb in each sentence to make sure each verb agrees with the subject and not another word in the sentence.

Unit Review Resources

TEACHER'S RESOURCES

- Writing Process, pp. W61–W72
- Grammar, Usage, and Mechanics, pp. G61–G72
- Speaking and Listening, pp. S31–S36
- Critical Thinking, pp. C31–C36
- Choose from Reading in the Content Areas, pp. RCA1–RCA72
- **Standardized Test Preparation**
  Unit 6 Test, pp. UT11–UT12
  Choose from Standardized Test Preparation, pp. STP1–STP31

WRITING APPLICATIONS

Write About the Literary Period

Discuss the ideal of a "melting pot" type of assimilation, coupled with an equally strong emphasis on pride in heritage and retention of cultural distinctions and identity. Ask the students if they feel part-American and part something else. Does it make a difference to them or to other students?

Prewriting: Illustrate the chart on the chalkboard. Tell students to write down the cultures involved, as well as the titles of the selections.

Writing: Group the class by the selections chosen. Have the group members collaborate on comparing and contrasting.

Revising: Direct the students to independently find illustrative quotations.

Proofreading: Have students exchange papers for proofreading purposes.

Write About Genre

To aid the students in organizing their thoughts, have them write the following words down the left side of a sheet of paper, skipping about five lines between each: *event*; *effect*; *lesson*; *when*; *where*.

Give them time to think of an event and jot down notes. While the students are doing this, do the same yourself. Write your responses on the board.

Prewriting: Review the meaning of a chronological list. Illustrate the three lists on the chalkboard, next to your responses to the above, by filling in each list with words and phrases pertinent to your own experience. Have students do the same, independently.

Writer's Toolkit CD-ROM

Encourage students to use the timeline (Writing Tools, Organizing Details) to complete the Prewriting activity.

Writing: This is also an individual exercise. Make yourself available to answer questions and render assistance.

Revising: Pair the students and have them exchange papers and critique the vividness and clarity of their partner's narrative.

BUILD LANGUAGE SKILLS

Vocabulary

Writers in this unit have represented various ethnic cultures. These same cultures—and many others—have contributed words to the English language.

English owes part of its richness to the thousands of words it has borrowed from other languages. The greatest number of borrowings are from Latin and French, but the German, Dutch, Scandinavian, and Greek languages are the sources of many others. The Near East, the Far East, Africa, Australia, Oceania, and our Native Americans have all contributed words to English. A common reason for borrowing is the use of a native name for an unfamiliar thing.

Look up each of the following words in a dictionary and write down the language or place from which the word originally came.

1. okra
2. shampoo
3. hurricane
4. coach
5. cockroach
6. chocolate
7. algebra
8. chipmunk
9. tea
10. boomerang
11. broccoli
12. geyser
13. bog
14. ceramic
15. morgue
16. kimono
17. yogurt
18. ukulele
19. amok
20. yacht
21. jaguar
22. pajamas
23. kindergarten
24. bayou
25. walrus
26. llama

Grammar, Usage, and Mechanics

The colon (:) is used before an extended quotation, explanation, or example.

Example: "Maggie will be nervous until after her sister goes: she will stand hopelessly in corners, homely and ashamed of the burn scars down her arms and legs, eying her sister with a mixture of envy and awe."

One use of the semicolon (;) is to separate related clauses of a sentence.

Example: "They did not understand sitting; they had wandering feet."

Read these sentences, which are taken from selections in this unit. Add a colon or semicolon in the blank space.

1. I was proud ______ I felt like a grownup.
2. "Then stay in the streets ______ don't come back here!"
3. I am the way my daughter would want me to be ______ a hundred pounds lighter, my skin like an uncooked barley pancake.
4. His words stopped ______ somehow, he couldn't get the right ones to come out.
5. Always too busy ______ feeding the cattle, fixing the fences, putting up salt lick shelters, throwing down hay.

Grammar, Usage, and Mechanics

Answers

1. ; 2. ; 3. : 4. ; 5. :

Cooperative Group Activity

Divide the class into five groups. Have them answer the examples in the text. Then assign each group one of the five previous units in the book to research additional examples of sentences containing colons and semicolons. The group may choose to divide the selections among themselves. Conduct a contest to see which group finds the most examples in a specified amount of time.

BUILD LANGUAGE SKILLS

Vocabulary

Answers

1. okra—West African
2. shampoo—Hindi (India)
3. hurricane—Taino (West Indies)
4. coach—Hungarian
5. cockroach—Spanish
6. chocolate—Nahuatl [Aztec] (Mexico)
7. algebra—Arabian
8. chipmunk—Algonquian (North America)
9. tea—Chinese
10. boomerang—Australia
11. broccoli—Italian
12. geyser—Old Norse (Iceland and Scandinavia)
13. bog—Gaelic and Irish (Scotland and Ireland)
14. ceramic—Greek
15. morgue—French
16. kimono—Japanese
17. yogurt—Turkish
18. ukulele—Hawaiian
19. amok—Malay (Malay Peninsula; Malay Archipelago)
20. yacht—Dutch
21. jaguar—Tupi (South America)
22. pajamas—Persian
23. kindergarten—German
24. bayou—Choctaw (N. America)
25. walrus—Danish
26. llama—Quechua (S. America)

More About Word Attack: Demonstrate to the class how to use a dictionary to find word origins. Show where in the definition these are found. Review the abbreviations used—you could list all or some of these on the chalkboard.

SPEAKING AND LISTENING

Motivation

Ask students if they have taken part in or witnessed a formal debate, either live or on television. By way of reference, you could mention the tradition of televised Presidential debates, begun in 1960, and their effect on the elections. Ask students who have participated in or observed a debate to comment on their impressions of the experience.

Teaching Strategy

Be prepared to moderate the class organizational discussion, as well as the debate itself. You may wish to consult a debating manual or *Robert's Rules of Order* before beginning this exercise. Part of Step #4 may be a homework assignment, but the others will have to be done in class.

Evaluation Criteria

Depending on the organization of the debate(s), either the nondebating audience (in the case of a single panel) or the other debating "societies" (in the case of groups) will evaluate and declare a winning side. For evaluation purposes, you may wish to refer to a debate manual or suggest criteria such as the following:

- clarity and conciseness of presentation
- thought content
- compelling argumentation
- persuasiveness of overall case

In any event, the evaluators should each be given a sheet with the criteria listed and rating system explained, for uniform evaluation purposes. Use either a numbered (1–5) or lettered (A–E) rating scale.

UNIT 6 Review

SPEAKING AND LISTENING

Reader's debate is a chance for everyone in class to act as a critic and to discuss the pros and cons of a selection. There are several ways to organize a debate. One way is to have half the class defend and the other half criticize a selection. Another way is to select a panel to debate while other class members listen. A third way is to divide the class into groups and have group debates. Whichever method you choose, you will find that talking about literature, having the chance to listen to other opinions, and hearing different points of view will give you a better understanding of the selection.

Before you take part in a reader's debate, read the suggestions. They will give you ideas on how to prepare and conduct a reader's debate.

1. As a class, decide how you will organize your debate. Use one of the methods suggested, or come up with another that suits you.
2. Discuss the length of time for the debate. Both sides—the defending and the criticizing—should have equal time for their arguments. Decide if one side will present its entire argument first or if the discussion will go back and forth between sides.
3. Examine the selection you have chosen. Discuss the focus of the debate. There are endless possibilities here. You can concentrate on the plot of the story, the characters, the ending, the author's style, the use of literary devices, illustrations, or the title itself. Brainstorm for a minute or two and you'll come up with numerous options.
4. Give each side time to contemplate their argument. Whether you are defending or criticizing the selection, have definite arguments to make. Be sure to substantiate your views. Using facts, as well as opinions, is advisable.
5. Be courteous during the debate. Your purpose is to listen and learn from others' opinions. Comments should be made concerning the selection, not pointed toward other debators.

To begin your reader's debate choose a selection from this unit. It can be anything you have read, fiction or nonfiction. After you have made your choice, reread the steps above and begin to organize so that you can enjoy the successful experience of a reader's debate.

Career Connection

Computerization is now the dominant trend in information processing. This has opened up new fields with great opportunities.

There are two- and four-year college programs, which offer training in programming and other technical aspects of working with computers. However, for some careers in technology, a high school diploma may be all that is required. Programmers, processing technicians, data entry clerks, analysts, media specialists, and Internet specialists, among others, all have a place in the computerized world of today.

CRITICAL THINKING

Compare and Contrast To **compare** means "to show likenesses." To **contrast** means "to show differences." You will use these processes every time you make a choice. Suppose, for example, that you want to decide between two pairs of jeans. You would compare or contrast their style, price, workmanship, and so on. Noting the similarities and differences would give you a basis for deciding.

You can also compare and contrast people, actions, theories, and issues. The purpose is to find which is better, more useful, or more interesting.

Literature often invites readers to make comparisons or contrasts between types of selections or literary elements. Choose two stories, poems, autobiographical excerpts, or characters to compare and contrast. Then answer the following questions.

1. What common ground do the two items share? Are the items to be compared enough alike to make a comparison possible? Are they different enough to make a contrast useful?
2. Why is making a comparison or contrast helpful? What elements or aspects of the two items will it be useful to compare or contrast?

EFFECTIVE STUDYING

Outlining To study well or to write a paper well, you will need to organize your notes or ideas. One way to get your thoughts in order is to put them in an outline.

An **outline** is a summary of a topic; it lists the most important points and subpoints in the order in which you will present them in a paper or will want to recall them for study. The numbering and form of an outline follows fixed rules.

1. Write an outline this way:

   Title
   I. Main point
   - **A.** Subpoint
   - **B.** Subpoint
     - **1.** Detail
     - **2.** Detail
       - **a.** Subdetail
       - **b.** Subdetail

   II. Main point
2. Follow these rules:
   - If you subdivide a Main point, have at least two subpoints beneath it. You cannot subdivide any topic into fewer than two points.
   - Outlines may be written in sentences or in phrases. Do not mix types.

Test Preparation

When taking an essay test, you might first want to organize your thoughts by creating an outline. Although this takes some time, it will help you write a clearer essay more quickly.

EFFECTIVE STUDYING

Teaching Strategy

Copy the sample outline in the text onto the board. Use the Period Discussion at the beginning of this unit. Give the class a few minutes to review it. Then have the students discuss what the writer's outline for this section would have looked like. Write their ideas and suggestions on the chalkboard, next to the sample outline. Have them begin by listing the main points. Then fill in subpoints, details, etc., under each main point. While writing this outline on the board, call the students' attention to the rules in the text for capitalization, indenting, periods, subpoints, and consistency. Have the students compare this outline with the completed narrative.

CRITICAL THINKING

Sample Answers

(1) "The World Is Not A Pleasant Place To Be" and (2) "Where Have You Gone"

1. Common ground: short; written in free verse; written by contemporary, African American, women poets
   Similarities—use of repetition; negative emotions; tone: serious, intimate, sad
   Differences—In the first, emotions can be interpreted as positive or negative; in the second, the poet expresses negative emotions only.
2. Purpose: find similarities and differences in two examples of contemporary free verse poetry. Elements to compare/contrast: verse form; length; tone; emotions expressed; imagery; rhyme.

Glossary

PRONUNCIATION KEY

Accent is the force or stress given to some words or syllables in speech. In this book, accent is indicated by the use of uppercase letters. One syllable words are always shown as accented. Thus, the pronunciation of *hand* is (HAND). In words of more than one syllable, the accented syllable is printed in uppercase letters. The other syllable or syllables are printed in lowercase letters. Thus, the pronunciation of *handbag* is (HAND bag).

Letter(s) in text words	*Letter(s) used in respelling*	*Sample words*	*Phonetic respelling*
a	**a**	bandit	(BAN dit)
a	**ay**	makeup	(MAYK up)
a	**air**	daring	(DAIR ing)
a	**ah**	dart	(DAHRT)
a	**uh**	about	(uh BOUT)
a	**aw**	ball	(BAWL)
e	**e**	denim	(DEN im)
e	**eh**	ingest	(in JEHST)
e	**ih**	delight	(dih LYT)
e	**u**	darken	(DAHR kun)
e	**ee**	he	(HEE)
i	**i**	mitten	(MIT un)
i	**ih**	gravity	(GRAV ih tee)
i	**y**	idle	(YD ul)
i	**eye**	idea	(eye DEE uh)
i	**ee**	medium	(MEE dee um)
i	**uh**	possible	(POS uh bul)
o	**o**	bottle	(BOT ul)
o	**u**	gallon	(GAL un)
o	**oh**	open	(OH pun)
o	**aw**	horn	(HAWRN)
oo	**oo**	move	(MOOV)
oo	**uu**	football	(FUUT bawl)
oo	**oo**	pool	(POOL)
oi	**oi**	point	(POINT)
ou	**ou**	output	(OUT put)
u	**u**	upshot	(UP shot)
u	**uh**	support	(suh PAWRT)
u	**oo**	ruler	(ROO lur)
y	**i**	rhythm	(RITH um)
y	**ee**	lazy	(LAY zee)
y	**y**	thyme	(TYM)

A

abbot (AB but) a man who is head of a monastery *p. 49*

absently (AB sunt lee) with attention elsewhere *p. 400*

absurdity (ab SUR duh tee) something absurd or ridiculous *p. 291*

abyss (uh BIS) a thing too big for measurement *p. 144*

accountable (uh KOUNT uh bul) responsible for *p. 37*

accusations (AK yoo ZAY shunz) charges of wrongdoing *p. 468*

acute (uh KYOOT) sharp, sensitive *p. 123*

adjacent (uh JAY sunt) near or next to *p. 425*

admirably (AD mur uh blee) excellently *p. 331*

adversary (AD vur ser ee) opponent; enemy *p. 14*

agile (AJ ul) nimble; well-coordinated *p. 256*

ague (AY gyoo) violent fever *p. 28*

akin (uh KIN) related *p. 169*

alcove (AL kohv) opening off a room *p. 513*

alien (AY lee un or AYL yun) non-citizen; foreigner *p. 524*

ancestral (an SES trul) coming from an ancestor *p. 498*

anesthetic (an is THET ik) substance that lessens pain *p. 311*
annually (AN you ul ee) occurring each year *p. 176*
annuity (un NOO uh tee) regular payment *p. 102*
anonymous (uh NON uh mus) written by a person whose name is withheld *p. 35*
antisymphonic (an tih sim FON ik) against music *p. 401*
anxiety (ang ZY uh tee) worry *p. 126*
apathetically (ap uh THET ik lee) with little or no feeling *p. 309*
aphorism (AF uh riz um) a short, pointed sentence expressing a truth or precept *p. 42*
appeasingly (uh PEEZ ing lee) in a manner to please or obey *p. 311*
apprehension (ap rih HEN shun) worry; fear of a coming event; dread *pp. 132, 301, 478*
apprentice (uh PREN tis) a person under legal agreement to work for a specified time under a master craftsperson in return for instruction and, formerly, support *p. 36*
ardent (AHR dunt) very eager; passionate *p. 260*
arpeggios (ahr PEHJ ee ohz) notes in a chord played in quick succession *p. 465*
array (uh RAY) an orderly arrangement of troops *p. 14*
arrayed (uh RAYD) dressed *p. 331*
assuaged (uh SWAYJD) calmed *p. 37*
assumption (uh SUMP shun) idea accepted as true without proof *p. 423*
asterisk (AS tuh risk) star-shaped sign or symbol *p. 388*
audacity (aw DAS uh tee) boldness; daring *p. 127*
aureole (AWR ee ohl) a halo *p. 275*
awe (AW) wonderment; admiration *p. 507*

B

barter (BAHRT ur) trade; exchanging one thing for another *p. 323*
becalmed (bih KAHLMD) to make motionless from lack of wind *p. 33*
belfry (BEL free) bell tower *p. 165*
bellows (BEHL ohz) roars; loud noises *p. 462*
benediction (ben uh DIK shun) blessing *p. 170*
besieging (bih SEEJ ing) hemming in with armed forces; closing in; overwhelming *p. 285*
billet (BIL it) a brief letter *p. 29*
birthright (BURTH ryt) the rights that a person has because he/she was born in a certain family, nation, etc. *p. 75*
blackballed (BLAK bawld) to exclude from social life, work, etc. *p. 37*
bleating (BLEET ing) cry of sheep *p. 167*
blithe (BLYTH) happy; cheerful *p. 247*
boarded (BAWRD id) had rooms and meals provided regularly for pay *p. 33*
bobolink (BOB uh lingk) kind of song bird *p. 203*
bog (BOG) swamp; wet ground *p. 199*
Bornou land (BAWR noo) reference to homeland in Africa *p. 233*
bough (BOU) a large branch of a tree *p. 326*
brackish (BRAK ish) salty and marshy *p. 430*
brambles (BRAM bulz) prickly shrubs *p. 325*
brethren (BRETH run) brothers; fellow members of a group *p. 15*
bulk (BULK) object; shape *p. 166*
bulldozing (BUL dohz ing) bullying; threatening *p. 255*
burden (BURD uhn) heavy load *p. 469*

C

cambric (KAM brik) very fine, thin linen or cotton *p. 271*
capricious (kuh PRISH us) without apparent reason *p. 430*
carcass (KAHR kus) dead body, usually of an animal *p. 290*
Carrara (kuh RAHR uh) fine, white marble *p. 210*
cascade (kas KAYD) waterfall *p. 256*
cascaded (kas KAY dihd) flowed down like a small waterfall *p. 463*
censure (SEN shur) blame *p. 75*
chafed (CHAYFT) to have been worn away; eroded *p. 143*
chanticleer (CHAN tih klir) a rooster *pp. 177, 210*
characteristic (kar ak tuh RIS tik) special quality *p. 498*
chassis (CHAS ee) a car's frame *p. 478*
chastise (chas TYZ) punish *p. 134*
chastity (CHAS tuh tee) decency; modesty *p. 42*
chattel (CHAT ul) a moveable article of personal property; owned property *p. 71*
checkerberry (CHEK ur ber ee) kind of small red berry (wintergreen) *p. 516*
chided (CHYD id) scolded *p. 33*
chitlins (CHIT linz) hog intestines used as food *p. 513*
chorister (KAWR ih stur) singer in a choir *p. 203*
clabber (KLAB ur) sour, thick milk *p. 513*
clamor (KLAM ur) noise; excitement *p. 485*
cogwheel (KAHG hweel) a wheel with a rim notched into teeth, which mesh with those of another wheel to transmit or receive motion *p. 54*
coherently (koh HIR unt lee) clearly speaking *p. 134*

collards (KOL urdz) kind of green vegetable *p. 513*
commence (kuh MENS) begin *p. 346*
commodious (kuh MOH dee us) spacious; roomy *p. 268*
common (KOM un) piece of public land *p. 180*
commotion (kuh MOH shun) noisy confusion *p. 386*
compromised (KOM pruh myzd) to give up one's ideals for short-term convenient reasons *p. 74*
conceived (kun SEEVD) thought of; imagined *p. 123*
conflagration (kon fluh GRAY shun) huge fire *p. 307*
conformity (kun FAWR muh tee) behavior that is in agreement with current rules *p. 180*
confronted (kun FRUNT id) set face to face *p. 507*
congested (kun JEST id) clogged, overcrowded *p. 427*
conjecture (kun JEK chur) an opinion formed without facts but based on pertinent knowledge or experience; guess *p. 412*
consecrated (KON sih krayt id) dedicated *p. 424*
consolidation (kun sol uh DAY shun) strengthening *p. 22*
contracting (kun TRAKT ing) growing smaller *p. 255*
conveyor belt (kun VAY ur BEHLT) endless moving belt or platform for carrying objects short distances *p. 524*
convoluted (KON vuh loot id) twisting; indirect *p. 478*
cordon (KAWR dun) a line or circle of police stationed around an area to guard it *p. 418*
cot (KOT) cottage or small house *p. 27*
counsel (KOUN sul) advice *p. 20*
covet (KUV it) desire what belongs to another *p. 117*
covey (KUV ee) flock of birds *p. 344*
cowering (KOU ur ing) crouching in fear *p. 511*
cowlish (KOUL ish) hood shaped *p. 428*
cravat (kruh VAT) a necktie; scarf *p. 277*
crest (KREST) the top of anything; summit; ridge *p. 325*
crusty (KRUS tee) curt; rude *p. 176*
cultivated (KUL tuh vayt id) prepared and cared for the land on which plants grow *p. 175*
cumulus (KYOO myuh lus) a type of rounded, fluffy cloud *p. 457*
cunningly (KUN ing lee) slyly *p. 123*
curbstone (KURB stohn) stone or concrete edging of a sidewalk *p. 74*

D

dapper (DAP ur) neat, trim *p. 291*
dasher (DASH ur) plunger with paddles for stirring *p. 513*
dead reckoning (DED REK un ing) navigating without the assistance of stars *p. 179*
deferred (dih FURD) put off *p. 366*
defunct (dih FUNGKT) dead person *p. 294*
delusive (dih LOO siv) misleading; unreal *p. 14*
demeaning (dih MEEN ing) lowering in status or character; degrading *p. 36*
density (DEN suh tee) thickness *p. 426*
departed (dih PAHRT id) dead *p. 190*
deploying (dih PLOI ing) spreading out *p. 422*
descendant (dih SEN dunt) a person who is the offspring of a certain ancestor, family, group, etc. *p. 49*
deserts (dih ZURTS) reward or punishment; what is deserved *p. 101*
diadem (DY uh dem) crown (more like halo here) *p. 202*
diligent (DIL uh junt) hardworking; done with careful, steady effort *p. 43*
discreet (dih SKREET) wisely careful *p. 259*
discrepancy (dih SKREP un see) difference; variation *p. 293*
dispirited (dih SPIR it id) discouraged; low in spirits *p. 488*
disproved (dis PROOVD) shown to be incorrect or false *p. 469*
dissever (dih SEV ur) separate *p. 118*
diverge (dih VURJ) spread apart *p. 378*
divert (dih VURT) turn aside *p. 290*
doctrine (DOK trin) belief, theory *p. 513*
doggedly (DAWG id lee) persistently; stubbornly *p. 268*
dollops (DOL ups) mounds *p. 457*
Dourra (DUUR uh) (usually spelled durra) a kind of grain grown in Northern Africa *p. 233*
downcast (DOUN kast) sad *p. 75*
downy (DOU nee) soft; fluffy *p. 522*
draw (DRAW) to take air into the lungs; inhale *p. 150*
dreary (DRIR ee) dull; tiresome *p. 199*
drenched (DRENCHT) soaked; wet all over *p. 326*

E

ebb (EB) flow back or away *p. 306*
ecstasy (EK stuh see) a feeling of overpowering joy; great delight *p. 323*
edifice (ED uh fis) a large structure *p. 276*
egging (EG ing) urging *p. 490*

eject (ih JEKT) force out *p. 189*
elevation (el uh VAY shun) a high place p. *477*
emaciated (ih MAY see ayt id) abnormally lean *p. 137*
emerge (ih MURJ) come out into view *p. 403*
emphatic (em FAT ik) very striking; definite *p. 357*
encampment (en KAMP munt) camp and equipment *p. 522*
encroach (en KROHCH) to intrude upon the rights of others *p. 22*
enlightened (en LYT und) to have given the lights of knowledge to *p. 73*
enthusiastically (en thoo zee AS tik lee) eagerly *p. 479*
enveloped (en VEL upd) wrapped up *p. 126*
ermine (UR min) a weasel whose fur turns to white in the winter *p. 210*
ethereal (ih THIR ee ul) of the upper regions of space *p. 409*
excerpt (ehk SURPT) a passage taken from a book; quotation *p. 33*
excessive (ik SES iv) going beyond what's right or usual *p. 477*
excruciating (ik SKROO shee ayt ing) very painful *p. 308*
extenuate (ik STEN yoo ayt) to lessen the seriousness of *p. 15*
extremities (ik STREM ih teez) hands and feet; parts farthest away *p. 306*
extricate (EK strih kayt) to set free; release; disentangle *p. 27*
exulting (ig ZULT ing) rejoicing; showing joy *p. 248*
eyewitness (EYE wit nis) person who actually saw something happen *p. 421*

F

fade in (FAYD IN) in radio, to become more distinct *p. 83*
fade out (FAYD OUT) in radio, to become less distinct *p. 84*
fallow (FAL oh) land that is plowed, but not seeded *p. 175*
fastidiously (fa STID ee us lee) very sensitive; dainty *p. 389*
favored (FAY vurd) featured *p. 331*
feat (FEET) accomplishment *p. 480*
feeble-minded (FEE buhl MIN dihd) an out-of-date expression for a person with a weak or slow mind *p. 385*
fetch (FECH) get and bring back *p. 377*
fiasco (fee AS koh) a humiliating failure *p. 468*
fieldpieces (FEELD pees iz) mobile artillery *p. 422*
Filipino (fil uh PEE noh) native of the Philippines *p. 522*
fine (FYN) summary; conclusion *p. 331*
firing (FYR ing) to light a fire in a boiler *p. 358*
flat (FLAT) an apartment with rooms on one floor *pp. 357, 488*
fleet (FLEET) very fast *p. 166*
flotilla (floh TIL uh) a fleet of boats or small ships *p. 57*
fluently (FLOO unt lee) easily (of talking) *p. 127*
flush (FLUSH) drive birds or animals from hiding place *p. 344*
Formica (for MY kuh) trade name for a heat-resistant plastic *p. 461*
fowler (FOUL ur) hunter of wildfowl *p. 143*
frenzy (FREN zee) madness; rage *p. 490*
friction (FRIK shun) resistance *p. 417*
frugality (froo GAL uh tee) careful economy; thrift *p. 42*
furtive (FUR tiv) sly; shifty; sneaky, secretive *pp. 429, 510*
futility (fyoo TIL uh tee) lack of success; uselessness *p. 439*

G

gait (GAYT) manner of walking or running *p. 303*
gauntly (GAWNT lee) in the manner of a thin bony person *p. 485*
Ghiblee (GIB lee) night wind that makes an eerie sound *p. 233*
girth (GURTH) strap that holds saddle on horse *p. 166*
gloaming (GLOHM ing) twilight *p. 210*
globular (GLOB yuh lur) rounded *p. 435*
grave (GRAYV) of a threatening nature; indicating great danger; serious *pp. 13, 132*
grave (GRAYV) burial plot *p. 138*
gravity (GRAV ih tee) dignity; seriousness *p. 526*
grenadier (gren uh DIR) foot soldier *p. 166*
grim (GRIM) very serious *p. 485*
guttural (GUT ur ul) harsh or growling sound *p. 385*

H

habitable (HAB it uh bul) fit to be lived in *p. 29*
hairline (HAIR lyn) very fine line *p. 299*
halloos (huh LOOZ) shouts; yells; calls *p. 275*
hashed (HASHT) jumbled; all mixed up *p. 257*
hasty pudding (HAY stee PUUD ing) cornmeal mush *p. 33*
hatter (HAT ur) hat maker *p. 247*

hearse (HURS) carriage for taking the dead to the grave *p. 294*
heartfelt (HAHRT felt) sincere; meaningful *p. 170*
heather (HETH ur) low evergreen plant that often grows on moors *p. 201*
heritage (HER ih tij) something handed down from one's ancestors, such as a characteristic, culture, or tradition *p. 49*
hideous (HID ee us) very ugly or frightening *p. 125*
highborn (HY bawrn) of noble birth *p. 117*
hillock (HIL uk) a small hill; mound *p. 269*
hover (HUV ur) stay nearby; linger about *p. 525*
Hula Hoops (HOO lah HOOPS) plastic hoops twirled around the body by rotating the hips *p. 466*
hulk (HULK) old ship *p. 165*
humiliating (hyoo MIL ee ayt ing) lowering of pride or dignity *p. 71*
humility (hyoo MIL uh tee) humbleness; the absence of pride *p. 42*
hypnotic (hip NOT ik) causing sleep *p. 478*
hypocritical (hip uh KRIT ih kul) false; not sincere *p. 127*

I

illimitable (ih LIM ih tuh bul) endless *p. 143*
illiterate (ih LIT ur it) unable to read *p. 498*
illuminate (ih LOO muh nayt) make clear *p. 259*
image (IM ij) mental picture *p. 486*
immortality (im awr TAL ih tee) unending life *p. 300*
impassioned (im PASH und) determined; filled with passionate feeling *p. 319*
imperative (im PER uh tiv) really necessary; essential *p. 305*
imperially (im PIR ee ul ee) supremely *p. 331*
imperturbably (im pur TUR buh blee) in a manner that cannot be excited; impassively *p. 282*
impetuous (im PECH oo us) eager; violent *p. 166*
impudent (IM pyoo dunt) rude; insulting *p. 105*
inanimate (in AN uh mit) not animated; dull; spiritless; without life *pp. 270, 435*
inaudibly (in AWD uh blee) not being heard *p. 526*
incidental (in suh DENT ul) casual; secondary *p. 75*
inclination (in kluh NAY shun) a particular disposition or bent of mind; tendency; a liking or preference *pp. 20, 34, 72, 480*
incoherently (in koh HIR unt lee) not logically; disjointedly *p. 277*
incompatible (in kum PAT uh bul) not in agreement *p. 73*
incongruity (in kon GROO ih tee) something not fitting or in harmony *p. 291*
indifference (in DIF ur uns) lack of interest *p. 189*
indifferent (in DIF ur unt) not caring *p. 290*
inevitable (in EV ih tuh bul) certain to happen *p. 15*
infest (in FEST) trouble; disturb *p. 170*
infinitesimal (in fin ih TES uh mul) too small to be measured *p. 268*
influenza (in floo EN zuh) disease usually called "flu" *p. 343*
ingenious (in JEEN yus) clever, resourceful *p. 477*
ingenuity (in juh NOO uh tee) cleverness; originality *p. 133*
innovators (IN uh vayt urz) makers of changes; introducers of new methods *p. 282*
instigate (IN stuh gayt) bring about; stir up *p. 255*
intensity (in TEN suh tee) strength; force *p. 412*
interlude (IN tur lood) musical performance between the acts of a play *p. 420*
interspersed (in tur SPURST) scattered among other things *p. 27*
intimacy (IN tuh muh see) very close friendship, even love *p. 305*
intolerable (in TOL ur uh bul) unbearable *p. 74*
intricacies (IN trih kuh seez) complexities; complications *p. 282*

J

jardiniere (jahr duh NIR) a decorative flower pot or stand *p. 357*
journeyman (JUR nee mun) a worker who had satisfied his apprenticeship and thus qualified himself to work at his trade *p. 43*

K

keel (KEEL) a piece of wood that runs along the center line from the front of the boat to the back; "backbone" of a ship *pp. 228, 248*
kilter (KIL tur) good condition; proper order *p. 79*
kin (KIN) relatives *p. 137*
kindling (KIND ling) small pieces of dry firewood *p. 388*
kith (KITH) archaic meaning for friends *p. 137*

L

laboriously (luh BAWR ee us lee) with much labor and care *p. 259*
lamming (LAM ing) striking *p. 490*
lash (LASH) whip *p. 79*
lax (LAKS) not strict or exact; careless; loose *p. 43*
lay (LAY) short song or story poem *p. 170*

leaden (LED un) dull, dark gray *p. 211*
levee (LEV ee) a morning reception held by a person of high rank *p. 29*
libel (LY bul) any written statement, not made in the public interest, tending to expose a person to public ridicule *p. 37*
lichen (LY kun) a mosslike plant which grows on rocks and trees *p. 478*
light-hearted (LYT hahrt id) free from care *p. 74*
luringly (LUUR ing lee) to tempt or attract *p. 390*

M

Magi (MAY jy) the three wise men who, according to the biblical story, made the journey to Bethlehem to present gifts to the Christ child *p. 255*
make-shift (MAYK shift) substitute; temporary *p. 439*
malice (MAL is) desire to see others harmed *p. 227*
manifold (MAN uh fohld) in many ways *p. 5*
man-of-war (man uv WAWR) warship *p. 165*
mantle (MAN tul) something that covers *p. 307*
marge (MAHRJ) edge or border *p. 143*
martial law (MAHR shul LAW) temporary rule by the military authorities *p. 420*
mason (MAY sun) stone worker *p. 247*
maxim (MAK sim) a statement of general truth *p. 277*
meditate (MED uh tayt) think deeply; ponder *p. 300*
meditatively (MED uh tayt iv lee) thinking quietly *p. 389*
mesmerizing (MEHZ muh ry zing) hypnotizing; casting a spell *p. 463*
metaphor (MET uh fur) figure of speech that makes a comparison *p. 257*
meteorite (MEET ee uh ryt) part of a heavenly body that passes through the atmosphere and falls to the earth's surface as a piece of matter *p. 412*
methodically (muh THOD ik lee) orderly; systematically *p. 307*
militia (muh LISH uh) an army of citizens rather than professional soldiers, called out in time of emergency *p. 420*
mockery (MOK uh ree) person or thing made fun of *p. 127*
moderate (MOD ur it) within reasonable limits; not excessive *p. 477*
moderation (mod uh RAY shun) avoidance of excess *p. 33*
molest (muh LEST) bother, annoy *pp. 108, 488*
monotony (muh NOT un ee) tiresome sameness *p. 477*
montage (mon TAHZH) picture made up of a number of separate pictures *p. 366*
moor (MUUR) open wasteland *p. 201*
Moor (MUUR) referring to the African slave traders *p. 233*
moorings (MUUR ingz) ropes to fasten a ship *p. 165*
moral philosophy (MAWR ul fuh LOS uh fee) ethics; standards of conduct and moral judgment *p. 73*
mortal (MAWR tul) fatal; causing death; subject to death *pp. 124, 409*
muster (MUS tur) roll call *p. 166*
mutely (MYOOT lee) silently *p. 388*
muzzle (MUZ ul) mouth and nose of an animal *p. 301*
mystical (MIS tih kul) mysterious; having a hidden meaning *p. 250*

N

navigating (NAV uh gayt ing) steering *p. 479*
night-tide (NYT tyd) nighttime *p. 118*
nimble (NIM bul) quick and accurate; agile *p. 259*
nonconductivity (non kun duk TIV uh tee) the ability to contain and not transmit heat *p. 421*

O

object (OB jekt) purpose; goal *p. 249*
oblivious (uh BLIV ee us) unaware; unmindful *p. 526*
oblong (OB lawng) rectangle shaped *p. 411*
obscure (ub SKYOOR) darken; dim; hide from sight *p. 480*
obstinate (OB stuh nut) stubborn *pp. 275, 357*
oilcloth (OIL klawth) waterproofed cloth *p. 457*
ominous (OM uh nus) dangerous; threatening; sinister *pp. 215, 433*
orb (AWRB) round object *p. 299*
organdy (AWR gun dee) kind of thin crisp cotton cloth *p. 510*
ought (AWT) anything (variation of *aught*) *p. 5*
outraged (OUT rayjd) insulted; made very angry *p. 106*
overshadowing (oh vur SHAD oh ing) hanging or looming over *p. 75*

P

palanquin (pal un KEEN) carriage on poles that is carried on people's shoulders *p. 526*

pangs (PANGZ) sharp pains *p. 486*
pantry (PAN tree) a small room or closet off the kitchen, where cooking ingredients and utensils, china, etc., are kept *p. 274*
parabolic (par uh BOL ik) bowl shaped *p. 421*
pathetic (puh THET ik) pitiful *p. 290*
pathos (PAY thos) an element in experience evoking pity *p. 275*
perceive (pur SEEV) become aware of *p. 190*
peril (PER ul) danger *p. 192*
persever (pur SEV ur) continue to uphold; keep on trying (Today the word is spelled *persevere* and pronounced *pur suh VEER.*) *p. 5*
petitioned (puh TISH und) made a formal request of someone in authority *p. 14*
petticoat (PET ee koht) type of woman's skirt *p. 388*
petticoats (PEHT ee kohts) lace or ruffles on the bottom of a skirt *p. 465*
phantom (FAN tum) something that seems real to the eye but does not exist; an unreal mental image *pp. 14, 229*
phenomenon (fih NOM uh non) a fact or event that can be described in a scientific way *p. 410*
pitch (PICH) a black sticky substance formed from distilling of tar *p. 124*
placid (PLAS id) quiet *p. 133*
plashy (PLASH ee) marshy; wet *p. 143*
plight (PLYT) bad condition or problem *p. 400*
plough (PLOU) plow; to make furrows in the earth *p. 79*
poignant (POIN yunt) sharp; keenly felt *p. 310*
poised (POIZD) set and ready *p. 490*
porcelain (PAWR suh lin) china *p. 275*
pore over (PAWR OH vur) study carefully *p. 400*
precipices (PRES uh pis iz) steep cliffs; vertical or overhanging rock faces *p. 280*
prejudice (PREJ uh dis) a judgment or opinion formed before the facts are known; intolerance or hatred of other races, creeds, etc. *p. 49*
presently (PREZ unt lee) in a little while *p. 359*
principle (PRIN suh pul) a fundamental rule of conduct *p. 34*
procure (proh KYUUR) to obtain or secure *p. 29*
prodigy (PRAHD uh jee) a child remarkably bright in some way *p. 461*
profound (pruh FOUND) wise; intellectually deep *p. 124*
prostrated (PROS trayt id) laid low; completely overcome *p. 281*
prudence (PROOD uns) the quality of being cautious or discreet in conduct *p. 73*
pulsate (PUL sayt) throb in a regular rhythm *p. 417*
pumps (PUMPS) kind of low cut shoes for women *p. 510*
purgative (PUR guh tiv) strong laxative *p. 343*
putrefactive (pyoo truh FAK tiv) rotting; decomposing *p. 434*

Q

quailed (KWAYLD) to lose courage; cower *p. 222*
quench (KWENCH) satisfy thirst or other need *p. 5*
quivering (KWIV ur ing) trembling; slight vibrating motion *p. 228*

R

racism (RAY siz um) racial prejudice *p. 499*
rack (RAK) hardship; torture *p. 248*
ranged (RAYNJD) set forth; arranged *p. 250*
ransacking (RAN sak ing) searching furiously *p. 257*
rash (RASH) reckless; foolhardy *p. 105*
ratified (RAT uh fyd) approved or confirmed *p. 23*
reality (ree AL uh tee) truth; fact *p. 389*
ream (REEM) enlarge; open up (here used figuratively) *p. 512*
recess (rih SES) interior place *p. 306*
recompense (REK um pens) repayment *p. 5*
recompose (ree kum POHZ) pull oneself together; become calm again *p. 510*
recourse (REE kawrs) a turning back for aid, safety, etc. *p. 29*
recurring (rih KUR ing) occurring again and again *p. 291*
reflect (rih FLEKT) think *p. 303*
reflection (rih FLEK shun) serious thought *p. 255*
reflexively (rih FLEK siv lee) an action done automatically *p. 138*
regalia (rih GAYL yuh) signs of royalty, such as special dress (here used ironically) *p. 401*
reiterate (ree IT uh rayt) repeat tiresomely *p. 302*
relate (rih LAYT) tell *p. 189*
renounce (rih NOUNS) reject; abandon with disgust *p. 290*
repose (rih POHZ) rest *p. 194*
reprieve (rih PREEV) postponement *p. 435*
reproachfully (rih PROHCH fuh lee) scolding; blaming *p. 388*
repulsed (rih PULST) drove back; repelled *p. 109*
resolution (rez uh LOO shun) decision as to future action *p. 34*
resolved (rih ZOLVD) determined; decided *p. 109*
resounding (rih ZOUND ing) loud, echoing, or prolonged sound *p. 15*

retaliate (rih TAL ee ayt) strike back *p. 490*
reverie (REHV uh ree) dreamy thoughts of pleasant things *p. 465*
rifling (RY fling) searching; going through hurriedly *p. 514*
riled (RYLD) irritated; angered *p. 416*
robust (roh BUST) strong; healthy *p. 247*
rogue (ROHG) rascal; villain *p. 193*
rumpled (RUM puld) wrinkled *p. 531*
rustic (RUS tik) of or living in the country, rural; simple, plain; rough, awkward *p. 278*
rut (RUT) a track made by a wheeled vehicle *p. 202*

S

saffron (SAF run) bright, orange-yellow color *p. 358*
salient (SAY lee unt) important; remarkable *p. 292*
satire (SA tyr) a literary work in which vices, stupidities, etc. are held up to ridicule and contempt *p. 37*
sauciness (SAH see nuhs) state of being bold or rude *p. 463*
savory (SAY vur ee) appetizing smell *p. 217*
scourge (SKURJ) to whip; to chastise, punish *p. 281*
seared (SIRD) scorched; burned *p. 480*
sedulous (SEJ uh lus) hard-working; diligent; persistent p. 271
seismograph (SYZ muyh graf) an instrument that records the intensity and duration of earthquakes *p. 412*
sepulcher (SEP ul kur) tomb; burial place *p. 117*
seraph (SER uf) kind of heavenly being; winged angel *p. 117*
sexton (SEKS tun) caretaker who rings the bells *p. 203*
sheath (SHEETH) protective covering or case *pp. 306, 414*
shied (SHYD) drew back *p. 303*
shroud (SHROWD) something that hides or protects *p. 229*
sidle (SYD ul) move sideways; edge along slyly *pp. 309, 508*
significant (sig NIF uh kunt) important; momentous *p. 13*
silhouettes (sil oo ETS) dark shapes, or outlines, seen against a light background *p. 416*
siren (SY run) in Greek and Roman mythology, a sea nymph represented as part bird and part woman who lured sailors to their death by singing *p. 13*
slander (SLAN dur) lie; harmful statement *p. 498*
slaughter (SLAWT ur) the killing of animals for food *p. 34*
slither SLITH ur) slip and slide *p. 344*
slunk (SLUNK) moved in a fearful or embarrassed way *p. 526*
slur (SLUR) make unclear; pass over carelessly *p. 290*
smites (SMYTS) inflicts a heavy blow; kills by striking *p. 233*
soaring (SAWR ing) rising or gliding high into the air *p. 323*
sociable (SOH shuh bul) enjoy the company of others *p. 39*
sombre (SOM bur) usually spelled somber; dark and gloomy *p. 166*
sonatas (suh NAH tuhs) compositions for one or two musical instruments *p. 464*
sounded (SOWND ed) dove deeply downward (by a whale or fish) *p. 225*
spar (SPAHR) pole attached to mast *p. 165*
spasmodically (spaz MOD ik lee) in sudden bursts *p. 308*
spectral (SPEK trul) ghostlike *p. 166*
spectroscope (SPEK truh skohp) a scientific instrument used to identify substances *p. 410*
speculatively (SPEK yuh luh tiv lee) thinking about possibilities *p. 300*
spinet (SPIHN it) small piano *p. 465*
spittle (SPIT ul) saliva; what one spits *p. 300*
spouse (SPOUS) husband or wife *p. 190*
staccato (stuh KAHT oh) short, distinct movement; music played with distinct breaks between notes *pp. 358, 465*
stanchions (STAN chunz) upright bars, beams or posts used as support *p. 280*
star (STAHR) to mark or set with stars, as a decoration *p. 323*
stark (STAHRK) complete, downright *p. 490*
stifled (STY fuld) muffled, smothered *p. 124*
still (STIL) make calm and quiet *p. 485*
stitch (STICH) slang for clothing *p. 388*
stock (STOK) farm animals *p. 104*
stolid (STOL id) expressing little motion *p. 273*
strife (STRYF) troublesome conflict; quarreling *p. 323*
subtle (SUT ul) faint and mysterious *p. 299*
sullen (SUL un) sulky and brooding; moody *p. 229*
superfluous (suu PUR floo us) beyond what is required *p. 179*
surplice (SUR plis) loose-fitting garment worn by members of the clergy and choirs *p. 203*

suspense (suh SPENS) uncertainty about what will happen *p. 223*

suspension (suh SPEN shun) temporary stoppage *p. 54*

sustained (suh STAYND) experienced; suffered *p. 290*

T

tablet (TAB lit) pad of writing paper *p. 387*

tacky (TAK ee) too showy; not fashionable *p. 507*

taro (TAHR oh) kind of tropical plant used for food *p. 522*

tart (TAHRT) small, filled pastry; small pie *p. 33*

taunting (TAWNT ing) daring; teasing *p. 490*

taut (TAWT) stretched tightly *p. 385*

tedious (TEE dee us) boring; tiresome *p. 291*

temperance (TEM pur uns) self-restraint in conduct, appetite, etc. *p. 133*

temperance (TEM pur uns) belief that no one should drink alcohol *p. 190*

tender-hearted (TEN dur hahrt id) easily moved to pity; sympathetic *p. 71*

thimbled (THIM buld) wearing a small, protective cap used in sewing *p. 385*

thoroughfare (THUR oh fair) passage; way through p. *319*

thriving (THRYV ing) very successful *p. 193*

thunderbird (THUN dur burd) in the mythology of certain North American Indians, an enormous bird supposed to produce thunder, lightning, and rain *p. 9*

tinderbox (TIN dur BAHKS) formerly, a metal box for holding flint for starting a fire *p. 53*

Titans (TYT unz) giants *p. 434*

tranquil (TRANG kwul) peaceful; at rest *p. 194*

tranquility (tran KWIL uh tee) calmness, peacefulness *pp. 22, 42*

transient (TRAN shunt) not permanent; passing quickly *p. 409*

transistor (tran ZIS tur) here, it means a transistor radio *p. 456*

transverse (trans VURS) crossing from side to side *p. 411*

tread (TRED) step; walk *p. 249*

trifle (TRY ful) unimportant thing *p. 127*

trill (TRIL) play music with a quivering sound *p. 249*

trip (TRIP) run gracefully and lightly *p. 257*

tripod (TRY pod) three-legged support *p. 425*

tuft (TUFT) small bunch *p. 189*

tutus (TOO TOOZ) skirts worn by ballerinas *p. 466*

U

umbilical (um BIL ih kul) here, necessary for life; from "umbilical cord," which keeps an unborn baby alive *p. 456*

unaccountable (un uh KOUNT uh bul) for no apparent reason *p. 250*

unassuming (un uh SOOM ing) modest; quiet *p. 255*

uncolored (un KUL urd) not influenced by *p. 20*

underscored (UN dur skawrd) underlined *p. 385*

undulation (un juh LAY shun) wavy form or outline *p. 299*

unprovoked (un pruh VOHKT) not to stir up an action *p. 34*

utter (UT ur) complete *p. 490*

utterance (UT ur uns) expressing by voice *p. 138*

V

vain (VAYN) without success; useless *p. 125*

valise (vuh LEES) small suitcase *p. 497*

vanguard (VAN gahrd) the part of an army that goes ahead of the main body in an advance *p. 423*

variable (VAIR ee ih bul) likely to change *p. 71*

vengeance (VEN juns) causing harm to something in return for an injury or harm done *p. 221*

venomous (VEN uh mus) poisonous; spiteful *p. 189*

vexed (VEKST) disturbed; annoyed; irritated *p. 124*

W

wafted (WAHFT id) blown along smoothly *p. 169*

wanton (WAHN tun) mischievous, unruly *p. 138*

warm-hearted (WAWRM hahrt id) kind, sympathetic *p. 73*

weather (WETH ur) last through; endure *p. 248*

whetstone (HWET stohn) a stone used for sharpening tools *p. 221*

whither (HWITH ur) to what place, point, etc. *p. 143*

will (WIL) wishes; desires *p. 249*

wonder (WUN dur) feeling of surprise, admiration, awe, caused by something strange, unexpected, or incredible *p. 323*

wrench (RENCH) twist *p. 489*

Index of Titles and Authors

Index of Skills

Index of Fine Art

ACKNOWLEDGMENTS

Unit 1: "Godasiyo, the Woman Chief" from *Teepee Tales of the American Indian*. Retold by Dee Brown. **Unit 3:** All Dickinson poetry reprinted by permission of the publishers and the Trustees of Amherst College from *The Poems of Emily Dickinson*, Ralph W. Franklin, ed., Cambridge, Mass: The Belknap Press of Harvard University Press. Copyright © 1998 by the President and Fellows of Harvard College. Copyright © 1951, 1955, 1979 by the President and Fellows of Harvard College. "From Walden" from *The Writings of Henry David Thoreau, Walden*. Edited by: J. Lyndon Shanley. Copyright © 1971 renewed 1973 reprinted by permission of Princeton University Press. "from Nature" from *The Collected Works of Ralph Waldo Emerson*. Arranged by Alfred R. Ferguson. Harvard University Press. **Unit 4:** "I Shall Not Care." Reprinted with the permission of Scribner, a Division of Simon & Schuster from *The Collected Poems of Sara Teasdale*. Copyright © 1937 by Macmillan Publishing Company; copyright renewed © 1965 by Morgan Guaranty Trust Company of New York. "The Falling Star." Reprinted with the permission of Scribner, a Division of Simon & Schuster from *The Collected Poems of Sara Teasdale*. Copyright © 1937 by Macmillan Publishing Company; copyright renewed © 1965 by Morgan Guaranty Trust Company of New York. "The Long Hill." Reprinted with the permission of Scribner, a Division of Simon & Schuster from *The Collected Poems of Sara Teasdale*. Copyright © 1937 by Macmillan Publishing Company; copyright renewed © 1965 by Morgan Guaranty Trust Company of New York. "The Revolt of Mother" from *The Revolt of Mother & Other Stories* by Mary Wilkins. The Feminist Press. **Unit 5:** "Afternoon on a Hill" by Edna St. Vincent Millay. From *Collected Poems*, HarperCollins. Copyright © 1917, 1945 by Edna St. Vincent Millay. All rights reserved. Reprinted by permission of Elizabeth Barnett, literary executor. "Lament" by Edna St. Vincent Millay. From *Collected Poems*, HarperCollins. Copyright © 1921, 1948 by Edna St. Vincent Millay. All rights reserved. Reprinted by permission of Elizabeth Barnett, literary executor. "home" from *The World of Gwendolyn Brooks* by Gwendolyn Brooks. Copyright © 1971 by Gwendolyn Brooks Blakely. "Lily Daw & The Three Ladies" from *Selected Stories of Eudora Welty* by Eudora Welty. Copyright © 1936, 1937, 1938, 1939, 1941, 1943 by Eudora Welty. Harcourt, Inc. in the United States, Canada, and Open. Russell Volkening for British rights. "Fog" from *Carl Sandburg Selected Poems* Edited by: George Hendrick and Willene Hendricks. Copyright © 1996 by Maurice C. Greenbaum & Philip G. Carson as Trustees for the Carl Sandburg Farney Trust. "The Pasture" from *The Poetry of Robert Frost* edited by Edward Connery Lathem. Copyright © 1951 by Robert Frost, copyright 1923, 1939, 1967, 1969 by Henry Holt and Co. Reprinted by permission of Henry Holt and Company, LLC. "The Road Not Taken" from *The Poetry of Robert Frost* edited by Edward Connery Lathem. Copyright © 1951 by Robert Frost, copyright 1923, 1939, 1967, 1969 by Henry Holt and Co. Reprinted by permission of Henry Holt and Company, LLC. "Stopping by Woods on a Snowy Evening" from *The Poetry of Robert Frost* edited by Edward Connery Lathem. Copyright © 1951 by Robert Frost, copyright 1923, 1939 © 1967, 1969 by Henry, Holt and Co. Reprinted by permission of Henry Holt and Company, LLC. "Invasion From Mars" from *The Panic Broadcast* by Howard Koch. Copyright © 1940 by Hadley Cantril, © renewed 1967 by Howard Koch. "Theme for English B" from *Collected Poems* by Langston Hughes. Copyright © 1994 by the Estate of Langston Hughes. Reprinted by permission of Alfred A. Knopf, a Division of Random House Inc. "Harlem" from *Collected Poems* by Langston Hughes. Copyright © 1994 by the Estate of Langston Hughes. Reprinted by permission of Alfred A. Knopf, a Division of Random House Inc. "Dream Variations" from *Collected Poems* by Langston Hughes.

Copyright © 1994 by the Estate of Langston Hughes. Reprinted by permission of Alfred A. Knopf, a Division of Random House Inc. "Montage of a Dream Deferred" from *Collected Poems* by Langston Hughes. Copyright © 1994 by the Estate of Langston Hughes. Reprinted by permission of Alfred A. Knopf, a Division of Random House Inc. "Island" from *Collected Poems* by Langston Hughes. Copyright © 1994 by the Estate of Langston Hughes. Reprinted by permission of Alfred A. Knopf, a Division of Random House Inc. "Blues at Dawn" from *Collected Poems* by Langston Hughes. Copyright © 1994 by the Estate of Langston Hughes. Reprinted by permission of Alfred A. Knopf, a Division of Random House Inc. "The Still Alarm" by George S. Kaufman. Copyright © 1925 by George S. Kaufman. Copyright 1930 by Brady & Wimn Productions Corp. Copyright © 1952 & 1957 by George S. Kaufman. "A Day's Wait" from *Winner Take Nothing* by Ernest Hemingway. Copyright © 1933 Charles Scribner's Sons; renewal copyright © 1961 Mary Hemingway. Copyright 1930 Charles Scribner's Sons; renewal copyright © 1958. Copyright 1932, 1933 Charles Scribner's Sons; renewal copyright © 1960 Ernest Hemingway, © 1961 Mary Hemingway. Copyright © 1932 Ernest Hemingway; renewal copyright © 1960. Copyright 1933 Charles Scribner's Sons; renewal copyright © 1961 Ernest Hemingway. Copyright © 1933 Charles Scribner's Sons; renewal copyright © 1961 Mary Hemingway. Copyright 1933 Ernest Hemingway, renewal copyright ©1961. Used by permission of the Ernest Hemingway Foreign Rights Trust for the world outside of the U.S. and Canada. Simon & Schuster US and Canada. **Unit 6:** "Where Have You Gone" from *I Am a Black Woman*, published by Wm. Morrow & Co., 1970, by permission of the author. "Everyday Use" from *In Love & Trouble: Stories of Black Women*, © 1973 by Alice Walker. Published by Harcourt Brace, Inc. "Journey" from *The Poisoned Kiss and Other Stories from the Portuguese*. Copyright © 1975 by Joyce Carol Oates. Reprinted by permission of John Hawkins & Associates, Inc. Excerpt from "Little Things are Big." *A Puerto Rican in New York and Other Sketches*. by Jesus Colon. Mainstream Publishing. "Umbilical" from *Finding a Poem* by Eve Merriam. Copyright © 1970 Eve Merriam. Copyright renewed 1998 by Dee Michel and Guy Michel. Used by permission of Marian Reiner. "The Secret" by Denise Levertov, from *Poems 1960–1967*, copyright 1964 by Denise Levertov. Reprinted by permission of New Directions Publishing Corp. "This Is Just to Say" and "The Term" by William Carlos Williams, from *Collected Poems: 1909–1939*, Volume I. Copyright © 1938 by New Directions Publishing Corp. Reprinted by permission of New Directions Publishing Company. "Two Kinds" from *The Joy Luck Club* by Amy Tan. Copyright © 1989 by Amy Tan. Published by Ballantine Books. Excerpt from *Black Boy* by Richard Wright. Copyright © 1937, 1942, 1944, 1945 by Richard Wright. Copyright renewed 1973 by Ellen Wright. Reprinted by permission in the United States, Canada and the Philippines by HarperCollins. John Hawkins rest of World. "The World is Not a Pleasant Place To Be" from *My House* by Nikki Giovanni. Copyright © 1972 by Nikki Giovanni. Reprinted by permission of HarperCollins Publishers, Inc/William Morrow. "Woman Warrior" from *Memories of a Girlhood Among Ghosts* by Maxine Hong Kingston. Published by Random House. "Snow" from *Everything and Anything* by Dorothy Aldis. Published by G.P. Putnam's Sons. "Cumulus Clouds" by Sheryl Nelms from *Modern Maturity Magazine*, 8–9/1985.

Note: Every effort has been made to locate the copyright owner of material reprinted in this book. Omissions brought to our attention will be corrected in subsequent editions.

Art Credits

Illustrations

Unit 1: p. 32: Amanda Wilson; p. 45: Jeni Bassett; p. 49: Richard Martin; p. 56: Lonnie Knabel; **Unit 2:** p. 118: Ron De Felice; pp. 122, 125: Joe Ciardello; p. 151: Lisa Young; **Unit 3:** pp. 174, 176, 182: Den Schofield; p. 203: Donna Day; p. 204: Guy Porfirio; **Unit 4:** p. 246: John Labbe; pp. 254, 258, 260: Angelo Franco; pp. 266, 272, 279: Eva Auchincloss; p. 309: Bradford Brown; p. 330: Anthony Carnabuci; **Unit 5:** p. 372: Ruth Lozner/K. Hayes; p. 376: Laura Hartman-Maetro; pp. 414–415, 419, 434: Paul Casale/Melissa Turk and the Artist Network; **Unit 6:** p. 450: Edgar Blakeney; p. 454: Gary Underhill; pp. 461, 464, 466: Guy Porfirio; p. 472: Eva Auchincloss; p. 496: William Ramos; p. 506: Cindy Spencer; pp. 520, 523, 527: Kye Carbone; p. 530: Marlies Merk-Najaka.

Photographs

Unit 1: p. 8: Stone; p. 12: Archive Photos; p. 28: Vanessa Vick/Photo Researchers Inc.; p. 48: Dale Boyer/Photo Researchers Inc.; p. 52: Westlight; p. 59: Courtesy of Dee Brown; **Unit 2:** p. 97: The Granger Collection; p. 113: Corbis Bettmann; p. 119: The Granger Collection; **Unit 3:** p. 164: The Granger Collection; p. 171: Corbis Bettmann; p. 188: Gavriel Jecon/Stone; p. 191: John Chard/Stone; p. 195: The Granger Collection; p. 198: The Granger Collection; p. 201: Palmer Kane/The Stock Market; p. 205: J. Sommer Collection/Archive Photos; p. 232: The Stock Market; **Unit 4:** p. 251: The Granger Collection; p. 261: The Granger Collection; p. 272: Randy Masser/International Stock; p. 295: Library of Congress/The Bridgeman Art Library; p. 298: Chip Porter/Alaska Stock Images; p. 313: Corbis Bettmann; p. 316: Rafael Macia/Photo Researchers, Inc.; p. 322: Willard Clay; p. 327: Corbis Bettmann; **Unit 5:** p. 342: Corbis Bettmann; p. 347: Corbis Bettmann; p. 350: Corbis Bettmann; p. 352: Lowell Georgia/Photo Researchers Inc.; p. 353: The Granger Collection; p. 365: Courtesy of the Library of Congress; p. 369: The Granger Collection; p. 381: E.O. Hoppé/Corbis; p. 399: Corbis Bettmann; **Unit 6:** p. 460: Wayne Hoy/The Picture Cube, Inc.; p. 481: Bernard Gotfryd/Archive Photos; p. 491: Corbis Bettmann; p. 517: Renato Rotolo/Corbis.

Note: Every effort has been made to locate the copyright owner of material reprinted in this book. Omissions brought to our attention will be corrected in subsequent editions.